Fifth Edition
Marriages *and* Families

DIVERSITY AND CHANGE

Mary Ann Schwartz

Northeastern Illinois University

BarBara Marliene Scott

Northeastern Illinois University

PEARSON

Prentice
Hall

Upper Saddle River, New Jersey 07458

Library of Congress Cataloging-in-Publication Data

Schwartz, Mary Ann.
   Marriages and families : diversity and change / Mary Ann Schwartz, BarBara
Marliene Scott.—5th ed.
      p. cm.
   Includes bibliographical references and index.
   ISBN 0-13-228769-2
   1. Marriage—United States.   2. Family—United States.   I. Scott, BarBara Marliene.
II. Title.
   HQ536.S39 2006
   306.80973—dc22

                                                                         2006031312

Editorial Director: Leah Jewell
Executive Editor: Jennifer Gilliland
VP, Director of Production and Manufacturing: Barbara Kittle
Director of Marketing: Brandy Dawson
Executive Marketing Manager: Marissa Feliberty
Prepress and Manufacturing Manager: Nick Sklitsis
Prepress and Manufacturing Buyer: Brian Mackey
Full-Service Project Management: Peggy Hood and Sarvesh Mehrotra, TechBooks/GTS
Production Liaison: Cheryl Keenan
Editorial Assistant: Lee Peterson
Marketing Assistant: Irene Fraga
Creative Design Director: Leslie Osher
Art Director, Interior Design and Cover: Kathryn Foot
Director, Image Resource Center: Melinda Lee Patelli
Manager, Rights and Permissions: Zina Arabia
Manager, Visual Research: Beth Brenzel
Manager, Cover Visual Research and Permissions: Karen Sanatar
Photo Researcher: Kathy Ringrose
Image Permissions Coordinator: Nancy Seise
Director, Media and Assessment: Shannon Gattens
Cover Art: Adam Crowley, Getty Images, Gary Buss, Getty Images, Getty Images, Inc.

This book was set in 11/12 Janson by TechBooks/GTS and was printed and bound
by Von Hoffmann. The cover was printed by Phoenix Color Corp.

For permission to use copyrighted material, grateful acknowledgment is made to the copyright
holders listed on page 599, which is considered an extension of this copyright page.

Pearson Education LTD.   Pearson Education North Asia Ltd
Pearson Education Singapore, Pte. Ltd   Pearson Educación de Mexico, S.A. de C.V
Pearson Education, Canada, Ltd   Pearson Education Malaysia, Pte. Ltd
Pearson Education–Japan   Pearson Education, Upper Saddle River, New Jersey
Person Education Australia PTY, Limited

10 9 8 7 6 5 4 3 2
ISBN: 0-13-228769-2

The twenty-first century began in the midst
of much violence—ethnic and religious conflicts,
terrorist attacks, and ongoing civil wars.
Today, millions of families continue to suffer
the loss of loved ones, destruction of
their homes, and unimaginable deprivations.
We dedicated the fourth edition
to these families. We continue to recognize
these families and we again dedicate
the fifth edition to their courageous struggles
to rebuild their lives.

Brief Contents

Contents

Chapter 4

THE MANY FACES OF LOVE   91

Chapter 5

DATING, COUPLING, AND MATE SELECTION   125

Chapter 9

REPRODUCTION AND PARENTING 285

Chapter 10

EVOLVING WORK
AND FAMILY STRUCTURES 329

Chapter 14

MARRIAGES AND FAMILIES IN LATER LIFE   459

Chapter 15

MARRIAGES AND FAMILIES
IN THE TWENTY-FIRST CENTURY:
U.S. AND WORLD TRENDS   487

Boxes

STRENGTHENING MARRIAGES AND FAMILIES

IN OTHER PLACES

DEBATING SOCIAL ISSUES

WRITING YOUR OWN SCRIPT

APPLYING THE SOCIOLOGICAL IMAGINATION

FAMILY PROFILE

Preface

In this fifth edition of *Marriages and Families: Diversity and Change*, there is a conscious effort to present a continuity of major issues, concerns, and themes on contemporary marriages, families, and intimate relationships. Our initial resolve when writing the first edition of this textbook has not changed, and it informs this fifth edition as well. The subtitle of this book, *Diversity and Change*, continues to be the major thematic framework that runs through all 15 chapters and is informed by the scholarship of a wide variety of scholars, most notably scholars of color and feminist scholars in sociology and from across a number of other academic disciplines. The emphasis on diversity helps students to understand that there are many different forms of intimate relationships beyond the traditional heterosexual, two-parent, white, middle-class family and the legally sanctioned heterosexual marriage. As we show throughout this textbook, marriages and families more generally include single-parent families, headed by women or men; lesbian or gay families with or without children and with or without a live-in partner; adoptive and foster families; biracial and multiracial families; cohabiting couples involving heterosexual or homosexual partners; and blended families that emerge following divorce, remarriage, or simply when people bring to a new relationship children from a previous intimate relationship. In this context, we treat marriages and families as social constructs whose meanings have changed over time and from place to place.

Consistent with this position, we continue to give high priority to framing our discussions of marriages and families in historical context. Most, if not all, aspects of our lives are shaped by larger historical circumstances. To be born during a particular historical period is to experience intimacy, marriage, family life, childbearing and child rearing, family decision making, household labor, and marital and family satisfaction (to name a few) in particular ways that are germane to the time, place, and social structure within which we find ourselves. For example, the economic growth and prosperity of the 1950s, a period during which the nuclear family was idealized, encouraged or made possible this particular family structure. During this period, both women and men married at early ages, had children within a relatively short interval from the wedding, and generally stayed married until the death of one spouse. For many families, a husband's income was sufficient to support the family. Thus, wives and mothers typically remained at home fulfilling domestic and child-care roles. Although economic conditions have changed, now often requiring multiple wage earners, this 1950s "idealized" image continues to dominate popular discourse on marriages and families. In the 1990s and into the beginning of the twenty-first century, however, most children have been growing up either in single-parent families or in remarried families and/or in families where both parents worked outside the home. Framing our discussion of marriages and families in

historical context not only provides students with knowledge about marriages and families in earlier periods of U.S. history but also enables them to understand and interpret the changes that are occurring around them in marriages and families today.

Our objectives in this fifth edition are simple yet significant:

- to help students recognize and understand the dynamic nature of marriages, families, and intimate relationships;
- to enable students to recognize, confront, and dispel prominent myths about marriages, families, and intimate relationships;
- to help students see the interactive relationships of race, class, gender, and sexual orientation;
- to encourage an informed openness in student attitudes that will empower them to make informed choices and decisions in their own marriage, family, and intimate relationships;
- to enable students to see how marriages, families, and intimate relationships around the world are increasingly affected by global events, particularly trade imbalances, armed conflicts, and acts of terrorism; and
- to provide students with a comprehensive introduction to a number of key issues facing marriages and families in the twenty-first century.

In this age of rapid communication and technological changes, not only does the evening news bring into our homes stories about marriages and families in distant places, but, more importantly, the news also calls attention to how political and economic decisions, both national and international, affect families in the United States as well as those in other countries of the world. For example, decisions of multinational corporations to relocate from one country to another in pursuit of lower labor costs and less regulation impact families in both countries. On the one hand, family budgets and patterns of living are often seriously disrupted when a family member loses a job because a business moves offshore. On the other hand, family patterns are also affected when members must work for subsistence-level wages, often in an unhealthy environment. In this example, the experiences of these families are globally interdependent.

In addition, issues of violence and the massive abuse of human beings both nationally and internationally crowd our psyches. In the United States, racism, hate crimes, street violence, the escalation of violence in schools, and threats of terrorist attacks are indeed very troubling issues faced by all families. Elsewhere, the violence and atrocities related to political, cultural, religious, and ethnic conflicts in Afghanistan, Iraq, Israel, Lebanon, and the Sudan have had devastating consequences for millions of families. These global incidents are not unrelated to life in the United States. In turn, both human and financial resources must be reallocated from domestic agendas to help meet humanitarian commitments around the world. By examining the process of globalization and its consequences or, as C. Wright Mills (1959) suggested, by grasping history and biography and the connections between the two, students should be better able to understand their personal life experiences and prepare themselves for meeting the challenges of living in a global society.

Rapid changes in the racial and ethnic composition of the U.S. population, due to immigration and differential fertility rates, have focused our nation's attention on diversity. Although some dimensions of this issue are new, a historical review quickly shows that throughout U.S. history marriages and families have taken many diverse forms. A focus on structured relationships such as race, class, gender, and sexual orientation allows us to see how marriages and families are experienced differently by different categories of people. In this fifth edition, we continue to make a special effort to treat this diversity in an integrative manner. Thus, we have no separate chapters on class or families of color. Instead, when marriage and family experiences are differentiated by race, class, or gender, these differences are integrated into the discussion of specific experiences. Two examples will illustrate this point. First, although the vast majority of all Americans will eventually marry, the marriage rate is lower for some groups than others. White females are more likely to marry than African American females, who are confronted with an increasing shortage of African American males of comparable age and education. Second, although both women and men suffer from the dissolution of their marriages through divorce or death, gender also differentiates those experiences in important ways. The most striking difference is an economic one: the standard of living declines for women and children but it is stable or improves for men.

It is not always easy to discuss diversity, partly because our thinking about diversity is itself diverse. One of the first issues we face in discussing diversity is language—what are the appropriate designations to use in reference to different groups at this point in time? Names are often controversial and reflect a power struggle over who has the right or authority to name. Not surprisingly, those in positions of power historically have assumed that right and authority. As the "named" groups themselves become more powerful and vocal, however, they often challenge the naming process and insist on designations they believe more clearly express their sense of their own identity. For example, as a result of pressure from people with mixed ancestry, the U.S. Census Bureau gave official recognition to a biracial or multiracial category on its year 2000 census forms. However, even this is not without problems. The multiracial category has yielded significant changes in the number of reported members in various racial and ethnic groups of color. This fact has political and economic significance in terms of the distribution of governmental resources and services.

Although there is no unanimity on these matters even among members of the same group, some terms have emerged as the preferred ones. Thus, for example, Latina/o is preferred to Hispanic, Native American is preferred to American Indian, lesbian and gay are preferred to homosexual, and African American is preferred to black. Throughout this text we try to be consistent in using the preferred terms. When we make specific comparisons by race, however, we use the terms *black* and *white* for ease of presentation. In addition, we have consciously avoided using the term *minority group* to refer to racial and ethnic groups in our society. Instead, we use the term *people of color*. Although this term is not problem-free, it avoids an implicit assumption in the term *minority* that groups so designated are not part of the dominant culture in terms of shared values and aspirations.

NEW AND EXPANDED FEATURES

Marriages and Families: Diversity and Change continues to be distinguished from other textbooks in a number of important ways, including the new and expanded features of the fifth edition.

In the News

The In the News chapter opener has been a popular feature in past editions of this textbook. In this edition, we continue the trend of beginning each chapter with the In the News feature. These chapter openers continue to be true stories of people caught up in the web of marriage and family relationships or issues that are either directly or indirectly related to marriage, family, and intimacy. Following each In the News feature is a series of questions under the heading "What would you do?" This feature helps students to see the relevance of many political, economic, and cultural issues of the day to ordinary people's lives and invites them to reflect on the topics covered in that chapter in light of their own value expectations and experiences.

Strengthening Marriages and Families Features

As in previous editions of this textbook, this box appears in several key chapters and continues to use a question-and-answer format with family therapist Joan Zientek. The purpose of this box is to introduce students to the concept of family therapy and show them how such therapy can help family members confront some of the many issues and problems that today's families might encounter. For example, in Chapter 8 Joan Zientek describes how couples can improve communication and resolve conflicts, and in Chapter 15 she provides guidance to parents on how to talk to their children about terrorism.

Internet Resources: Applying the Sociological Imagination Box

This new box combines two features from the fourth edition, the Searching the Internet and the Applying the Sociological Imagination boxes. These new boxes immediately take a student to a Website(s) where they can find up-to-date data on relevant topics discussed in the chapter. Each box contains questions to help students develop a sociological perspective in analyzing aspects of marriages and families. The questions are designed to help students see the relationship between personal behavior and how society is organized and structured. For example, in Chapter 2 students can learn at a glance from statistics presented about the characteristics of the welfare population, helping to dispel many of the myths about this population. In Chapter 9 students are directed to Websites that provide historical data about Father's Day as well as factual information about today's fathers. In addition, at the end of some of these chapters students are provided with thought-provoking questions or suggestions for projects that test their ability to use the sociological imagination while using resources found via the Internet.

Family Profiles Features

This popular feature, first introduced in the second edition, continues to provide photos and profiles of real people, including what these families view as major challenges in their current stage in their family life cycle and the philosophy that guides their behavior in their marriage and family relationships. These family profiles allow students to read about and understand how diverse individuals and families navigate their everyday lives as members of marriages, families, domestic partnerships, and/or other intimate relationships. For example, in Chapter 8, the Schroeder family is profiled, providing students with a glance of how members of this family view their lives and experiences as an interracial family. And, the profile of the Parkinson family in Chapter 9 shows us how a parental leave helped a new father bond with his infant son. These family profiles serve as a good basis for students to examine their own attitudes and values regarding where they are in their family's life cycle.

In Other Places Features

Students remain interested in learning about diverse forms of marriages and families. Therefore, this box continues to offer students insights into the diverse structures and functions of marriages and families, both global and local. For example, in Chapter 11, they can learn about global responses to violence and sexual assault against women. And in Chapter 14, students can see how more liberal divorce laws and changing social and economic conditions have contributed to an increase in divorce and remarriage in countries like Korea and China. Each In Other Places box includes a series of questions under the heading "What do you think?" These questions require students to reflect on cultural similarities and differences. It also helps students understand that culture is relative.

Debating Social Issues Features

In recent years considerable controversy has surrounded numerous policy issues regarding marriages and families. Students often hear media stories designed to grab headlines rather than inform the public about the different perspective people have on these difficult and often emotionally laden issues such as abortion (Chapter 9) and immigration (Chapter 15). Thus, we have restructured the Social Policy Issues box that was in the fourth edition into a Debating Social Issues box. We have included one in every chapter to help students understand the pro and con arguments that surround a given policy issue and then use the related questions to help them clarify their own views on the subject.

Writing Your Own Script Features

These exercises again can be found at the end of each chapter. Students and instructors have told us that this focused approach makes it easy for students to reflect on their own life choices and in writing their own marital or relationship scripts. In this way, students are encouraged to think sociologically about their personal decision making in light of the relevant research presented in that chapter.

New and Expanded Themes

One of the criticisms students sometimes make about marriage and family courses and their related textbooks is that they are pessimistic in tone and content. They use as examples the high divorce rate, individual and family violence, poverty, inequality, and sexual problems. Students realize these patterns of behavior are real and must be addressed, but they also want to know more about how to strengthen marriages and families. Therefore, in addition to our featured Strengthening Marriages and Family box, we have added a section at the end of each chapter, Supporting Marriages and Families, that discusses various initiatives being carried out or proposed to help individuals, couples, and families in their relationships and, where appropriate, suggests areas in which resources and support for families are still needed.

In addition, we have enriched each chapter by incorporating hundreds of new research studies. We have also included new photos, examples, tables, and figures to illustrate contemporary marriage and family concepts, events, trends, and themes.

- Changing immigration patterns have resulted in greater racial, ethnic, and racial diversity among families in the United States and throughout the world (Chapters 1 and 15).
- Just as families are changing, so, too, is the discipline of sociology. Although in the past women and people of color were involved in research and theorizing about marriages and families, their contributions were largely ignored. But today women and people of color are gaining much deserved recognition as researchers and theorists (Chapter 2).
- Generally, when we think of changes in gender roles, we think of change in a linear pattern moving toward greater equality. However, although women's rights in Northern Kenya are gaining strength, women in Afghanistan and Iraq are seeing their rights erode (Chapter 3).
- Most often when we think about love, we think about people who love each other as being close in age. But an increasing number of people are falling in love and establishing intimate relationships with people much older or younger than themselves (Chapter 4).
- Although interracial dating has become more acceptable to Americans in recent years, there is a generation gap in terms of acceptance. For example, the generations born before 1913 are the least accepting and generation Y (born since 1977) are the most accepting (Chapter 5).

- For most American teens oral sex is not "really" sex; real sex, they believe, is vaginal intercourse. This perspective puts young people in jeopardy of contracting sexually transmitted diseases, including HIV/AIDS. The incidence of AIDS is increasing dramatically around the globe (Chapter 6).

- Despite great controversy, Massachusetts became the first and, to date, only state to allow same-sex marriage. The lifestyles of the unmarried population continue to take many diverse forms (Chapter 7).

- Although some people think of premarital agreements as cold, unromantic, and businesslike, an increasing number of couples are making them part of their marriage preparation. Additionally, because conflict is now recognized as a normal part of intimate relationships, many couples are participating in marriage preparation classes that teach conflict resolution skills (Chapter 8).

- Polls show that an increasing number of fathers desire to spend more time and develop a closer relationship with their children. New research documents the importance of fathers in the lives of children, indicating that when fathers provide strong emotional, financial, and other support, their children are likely to be healthier physically and psychologically (Chapter 9).

- Despite the economic prosperity of the 1990s, the income gap between wealthy and poor families widened considerably. Recently, media headlines proclaimed a "mommy exit" from the work force, but is it true and, if so, what does it mean? (Chapter 10).

- Violence within families continues to be a major problem in the United States and in many other countries. The most vulnerable family members are children 3 years and younger and the elderly. Contemporary judicial and legislative approaches to domestic violence are sometimes more punitive toward the victim than the perpetrator (Chapter 11).

- Although the overall divorce rate has decreased slightly over the past several years, the rate remains high and varies among different groups and in different geographic regions. Several states are trying to reverse this trend by instituting covenant marriages (Chapter 12).

- Greater numbers of children are living in stepfamilies. Although no precise figures exist on the number of children being raised in lesbian and gay stepfamilies, the increasing use of reproductive technology (Chapter 9) and changes in adoption laws (Chapter 15) suggest that more children will live in lesbian and gay stepfamilies in the future (Chapter 13).

- People are living longer. Expectations are there will be over a million centenarians in the United States by 2050. Contrary to popular stereotypes, the majority of older people maintain their independence and enjoy an active social life (Chapter 14).

- As globalization expands, so, too, does the inequality that accompanies it, leaving many children and families behind. Rising inequality can result in an increase in racial bias, xenophobia, isolationist tendencies, and religious intolerance. In this process, individuals and societies who are among the most disadvantaged sometimes respond with violence and acts of terrorism (Chapter 15).

PEDAGOGY: READER INVOLVEMENT

Marriages and Families: Diversity and Change is intended as a text that challenges students to become involved in a direct way by examining their personal belief systems as well as societal views of the many forms that marriages and families have taken in the past and are taking in the present. Based on over 45 years of combined teaching experiences, we have found that a course on the sociology of marriages and families almost always invokes concern and interest among students regarding how the general principles and descriptions of marriages and families in a given textbook apply to and are similar to or different from their own personal experiences. Thus, throughout the process of revising this book, we continued to use an innovative, sensitive, and inclusive approach to writing about marriages and families. We use a sociological and feminist–womanist perspective, encouraging the application of the sociological imagination to everyday life. In this context, we focus on the link between social structure and our personal experiences of marriages, families, and intimate relationships. That is, we examine how cultural values, historical context, economic and political changes, and structured relationships of race, class, gender, sexual orientation, and age interact and affect individuals and groups as they create, sustain, and change their various intimate relationships. There are many benefits to using a sociological approach to study marriages and families. Most importantly, such an approach enables us to understand the constraints and opportunities that affect our lives and those of other people, thereby positioning us to make more discriminating and successful decisions and to exercise greater control over our lives.

The positive response of students as well as instructors to the pedagogical strategies included in the first four editions encouraged us to continue them in this edition. It has been gratifying to hear how these strategies have facilitated students' involvement in understanding marriages and families and empowered them to make more informed lifestyle decisions.

Key Terms

The important terms and concepts that help us to understand and analyze marriages and families are boldfaced and defined in the text. The key terms are also listed at the end of each chapter and defined in the glossary at the end of the book as a way of facilitating the study and review process.

Chapter Questions

Throughout this edition, students will find a shaded question mark that asks them to apply the material in the chapter to their own experiences and to critically evaluate aspects of interpersonal relationships.

End-of-Chapter Study Aids

At the end of each chapter, students will find a summary of the chapter's main points, a list of key terms, and a set of questions for study and discussion. The chapter summary and key terms are designed to facilitate a quick review of the material in the text. The study questions are to help students stretch their understanding of marriages and families beyond the contents of this textbook. Finally, we provide suggestions for additional resources. These resources include traditional sociological materials as well as relevant literary works pertaining to a topic or general theme of the chapter. The use of literature is intended to enrich the study of sociology and provide yet another springboard from which students can develop a more in-depth understanding of various sociological concepts. New to this edition are suggested popular films and documentaries that add a visual dimension to a subject that can provide insights into people's feelings and experiences. In addition, we include a number of Internet sites whereby students can explore and do independent research on marriage and family issues. Given the fluidity of many Websites, we have listed only those that have proven to be relatively stable over time, that are well documented, and that are updated as needed.

Appendixes

The appendices included at the back of the book supplement the text's sociological discussion of key aspects of relationships by providing technical information on sexual dysfunctions and sexually transmitted diseases (Appendix A), human anatomy and reproduction (Appendix B), abortion techniques (Appendix C), and methods of birth control (Appendix D).

SUPPLEMENTS

Instructors and students who use our textbook have access to a number of materials especially designed to complement the classroom lectures and activities and enhance the student's learning experiences.

For the Instructor

Instructor's Resource Manual with Tests   This essential instructor tool includes detailed chapter outlines, learning objectives, teaching suggestions, discussion questions, and class exercises. Also included is a test bank that contains over 1600 questions in multiple-choice, true–false, and essay formats. All multiple-choice and true–false questions are page referenced to the text.

TestGEN-EQ   This computerized software allows instructors to create their own personalized exams, to edit any or all test questions, and to add new questions. Other special features of this program, which is available on a dual-platform CD-ROM, include random generation of an item set, creation of alternate versions of the same test, scrambling question sequence, and test preview before printing.

ABCNEWS */Prentice Hall Video Library for Marriages and the Family*   Selected video segments from award-winning ABC News programs such as *Nightline*, *ABCWorld News Tonight*, and *20/20* accompany topics featured in the text. An instructor's guide is also available. Please contact your Prentice Hall representative for more details.

PowerPoint Slides   These slides combine graphics and text in a colorful format to help you convey sociological princi-ples in a new and exciting way. For easy access and download, these slides are available at http://www.prenhall.com.

On-line Learning Solutions   Prentice Hall is committed to providing our leading content to the growing number of courses being delivered over the Internet by developing relationships with the leading course management platforms. Please contact your local Prentice Hall representative.

For the Student

Study Guide   Created for the students, this manual offers chapter-by-chapter outlines, learning objectives, and a chapter review that includes key points and self-test questions keyed to the text.

Companion Website™   In tandem with the text, students can now take full advantage of the World Wide Web to enrich their study of material found in the text. This resource correlates the text with related material available on the Internet. Features of the Website include chapter objectives, study questions, Census updates, as well as links to interesting material and information from other sites on the Web that can reinforce and enhance the content of each chapter. Address: www.prenhall.com/Schwartz

Research Navigator™ can help students complete research assignments efficiently and with confidence by providing three exclusive databases of high-quality scholarly and popular articles accessed by easy-to-use search engines.

- EBSCO's ContentSelect™ Academic Journal Database, organized by subject, contains 50–100 of the leading academic journals for sociology. Instructors and students can search the online journals by keyword, topic, or multiple topics. Articles include abstract and citation information and can be cut, pasted, e-mailed, or saved for later use.
- *The New York Times* Search-by-Subject Archive provides articles specific to sociology and is searchable by keyword or multiple keywords. Instructors and students can view full-text articles from the world's leading journalists writing for *The New York Times*.
- Link Library offers editorially selected "*Best of the Web*" sites for sociology. Link libraries are continually scanned and kept up to date, providing the most relevant and accurate links for research assignments.

Gain access to Research Navigator™ by using the access code found in the front of the brief guide called *The Prentice Hall Guide to Research Navigator™*. The access code for Research Navigator™ is included with every guide and can be packaged with the text. Please contact your Prentice Hall representative to order.

ACKNOWLEDGMENTS

Although we continue to refer to this book as ours, we recognize that such an endeavor can never singularly be attributed to the authors. As with any such project, its success required the assistance of many people from many different parts of our lives. Our interaction with students both within and outside the classroom continues to have a significant impact on our thinking and writing about marriages and families, and that impact is quite visible in this fifth edition. Our decisions to retain and, in some cases, update, certain pedagogical aids, such as the boxed features and the examples used in the text, were made in response to student questions, reactions, and discussions. Student feedback was also instrumental in the development of the applied exercises, which we have found to be most effective in teaching about marriage and family issues and concerns.

We would especially like to thank the skilled librarians at Northeastern Illinois University, particularly Richard Higginbotham and Patrice Stearley, for their invaluable assistance in helping us track down the latest data on marriages and families. We also wish to acknowledge the skilled professionals at Prentice Hall—the editors, artists, designers, and researchers who saw this edition through the process, from its inception through the many stages of development and production. We owe a particular debt of gratitude to Chris DeJohn, Jennifer Gilliand, and Nancy Roberts whose support, patience, and perseverance was a major factor in our completing this project. We are grateful to Valle Hansen, Editorial Assistant/Sociology, for her helpful suggestions and to Kathy Ringrose for her dedicated photo research. Special thanks go to Peggy Hood and Sarvesh Mehrotra for their excellent skill in preparing this book for production. Our thanks also go to permission editors and all others whose tasks were so essential to the production of this book.

The timely, thoughtful, and extensive reactions, suggestions, and critical reviews of the previous editions of this textbook were greatly appreciated and, in each case, they have helped us avoid major mistakes and weaknesses while enhancing our ability to draw upon the strengths of the book. We are also grateful to the reviewers of this edition:

Preston Dyer	Baylor University
Jane Hellinghausen	Odessa College
Judy Rommel	University of Wisconsin
Rosemary Barr	Eastern New Mexico University
Gordon Knight	Green Mountain College
Donna Crossman	The Ohio State University
Ralph Peters	Floyd College
Ralph LaRossa	Georgia State University
Wade Luquet	Gwynned-Mercy College
Doug Dowell	Heartland Community College
Eunice Beatty	University of Kentucky

We are especially appreciative of the strong support we received from our colleagues in the Sociology Department at Northeastern Illinois University. In this regard, we especially thank the Sociology Department administrative assistant, Arlene Benzinger, whose diligent efforts assisted us in numerous ways.

We again wish to acknowledge and thank our marriages and families (nuclear, extended, blended, and fictive) for continuing to love, understand, and support us as we undertook, for yet another time, the demands and responsibilities involved in researching, writing, and revising this fifth edition. As in the past, when our time, attention, and behavior were dedicated to this endeavor, often at the expense of our time, attention, and activities with them, they remained steadfast in their support and encouragement. Now that we have finished this edition, they are as proud as we are and rightfully so, for this book, too, is as much theirs as ours. Its completion is due in large part to their understanding and the sacrifices they made to facilitate our ability to revise this book. We thank our parents, Helen and Charles Schwartz and Lillian Johnson, for their love and continuing support throughout our lives. As always, our partners, Richard and Roger, gave us their unconditional support and contributed to partnerships that were significantly critical to our meeting the various demands and deadlines that revising this book engendered. In addition, we continue to acknowledge our children, Jason, Roger Jr., Dionne, and Angella, granddaughters Courtney and Mariah, and grandson Roger III (Trey) for their unwavering love, patience, and understanding when our work forced us to miss family gatherings and events. We thank them all, especially for providing us with continuing opportunities for the exploration and understanding of marriage and family life.

Last, but certainly not least, we wish to acknowledge and thank each other. As with the previous editions, this book has been a joint effort in every sense of the word. Time has not diminished our appreciation of each other's skills, perspective, humor, and experiences, and our collaborative effort continues to deepen our appreciation and respect for one another. We continue to learn from one another about diversity and the differential impact of race on various intimate relationships. In the process, we continue to learn more about a particular type of intimate relationship, one based upon love, respect, commitment, understanding, tolerance, and compassion: namely, friendship.

Keeping in Touch

Just as we appreciate all of the comments, suggestions, and ideas that we received on the first four editions of this textbook, we would like to hear your reactions, suggestions, questions, and comments on this new edition. We invite you to share your reactions and constructive advice with us. You can contact us at: m-schwartz@neiu.edu or b-scott1@neiu.edu.

Mary Ann Schwartz
BarBara Marliene Scott

About the Authors

Dr. Mary Ann Schwartz has been married for 30 years. She earned her bachelor of arts degree in sociology and history from Alverno College in Milwaukee, Wisconsin, her master's degree in sociology from the Illinois Institute of Technology in Chicago, and her doctorate in sociology from Northwestern University in Evanston, Illinois. She is Professor Emerita of Sociology and Women's Studies and former chair of the Sociology Department at Northeastern Illinois University, where she cofounded and was actively involved in the Women's Studies Program. She also served as a faculty consultant to the Network for the Dissemination of Curriculum Infusion, an organization that presents workshops nationally on how to integrate substance abuse prevention strategies into the college curriculum.

Throughout her educational experiences, Professor Schwartz has been concerned with improving the academic climate for women, improving student access to higher education, and improving the quality of undergraduate education. As a union activist, Professor Schwartz worked to win collective bargaining for higher education faculty in Illinois. She served as union president at Northeastern and spent over eight years as the legislative director for the University Professionals of Illinois, where she lobbied for bills of interest to higher education faculty and students. She edited the union's newsletter, *Universities 21*, which is devoted to sharing ideas on academic issues. She continues to be active in the labor movement and serves as an officer in the retiree's chapter.

Professor Schwartz's research continues to focus on marriages and families, socialization, nonmarital lifestyles, work, aging, and the structured relationships of race, class, and gender. Although she found teaching all courses thought provoking and enjoyable, her favorites were Marriages and Families; Women, Men, and Social Change;

Sociology of Aging; and Introductory Sociology. In her teaching she employed interactive learning strategies and encouraged students to apply sociological insights in their everyday lives. Seeing students make connections between their individual lives and the larger social forces that influence them remains one of the most rewarding and exciting aspects of her teaching career.

Dr. BarBara M. Scott has been married for over 41 years and is the proud mother of two sons and proud grandmother of three grandchildren: two granddaughters and one grandson. As a wife and mother of two small children, she returned to school, earning a bachelor of arts degree in sociology and two different master's degrees: a master of arts degree in sociology and a master of philosophy from Roosevelt University in Chicago, and later a doctorate in sociology from Northwestern University in Evanston, Illinois. Dr. Scott is a professor of sociology, African and African American studies, and women's studies, and coordinator of the African and African American Studies Program at Northeastern Illinois University. She has served as president of the Association of Black Sociologists, a national organization. Dr. Scott is also a former chair of the Sociology, Criminal Justice, Social Work, and Women's Studies departments at Northeastern Illinois University. She is a strong advocate for curriculum transformation and the integration of race, class, gender, and sexual orientation into the college curriculum, as well as a social activist who has been in the forefront of organizing among national and international women of color, both within and outside academia.

Professor Scott has received meritorious recognition for her work and has served for over 30 years as an educational and human resource consultant. She has coordinated the Women's Studies Program, is a founding member of the university's Black Women's Caucus, and is the faculty sponsor for the undergraduate chapter of the Alpha Kappa Alpha Sorority on her campus. Her research and teaching interests include marriages and families, particularly African American families; the structured relationships of race, class, gender, and sexual orientation; institutionalized racism and inequality; cultural images and the social construction of knowledge in the mass media; and Africana (aka Black) women's studies. She finds teaching challenging and invigorating; among her favorite courses are Marriages and Families, Sociology of Black Women, Sociology of Racism, and Introductory Sociology. She is an enthusiastic advocate of *applying sociology* to the everyday worlds in which we live and routinely engages her students in field research in the communities in which they live and work. After years of teaching, she still gets excited about the varied insights that sociology offers into both the most simple and the most complex questions and issues of human social life.

IN THE NEWS

London, England

On April 9, 2005, 56-year-old Charles, the prince of Wales and heir to the throne of England, and 57-year-old Camilla Parker Bowles, friends for over 30 years and lovers for much of that time, married in a simple civil ceremony in the Guildhall in Windsor, a town west of London. Noticeably absent from the civil ceremony was Charles's mother, Queen Elizabeth of England. After their marriage, the royal couple drove a short way up the hill to Windsor Castle, which towers over the town. There some 800 guests, including Charles's parents, Prime Minister Tony Blair, members of royal families from around the world, relatives, Camilla's former husband, and friends joined them for the blessing of their marriage, presided over by the archbishop of Canterbury, the Most Reverend Rowan Williams. In an unusual departure from similar religious services, the couple said they were very sorry for their past mistakes and heartily repented their sins. This departure was necessitated by the history of their ongoing relationship over the years and the fact that they were both divorced. As the future king, Charles would be the head of the Church of England, and many clergy and laity alike still disapprove of remarriage by divorced people, especially in cases where their relationship was instrumental in the dissolution of an existing marriage. Recent polls suggest that the public remained somewhat divided, with 40 percent in favor of the marriage, 36 percent opposing the marriage, and 24 percent indifferent. However, the majority of the public were opposed to the idea of Queen Camilla (cited in Hundley, 2005). That the church and government gave official sanction to this relationship may make Charles more fortunate than one of his ancestors, King Edward VIII, who in 1936 had to renounce the throne to marry the woman he loved, Wallis Simpson, a twice-divorced American.

Charles and Camilla first met at a polo match in 1970 and Camilla is said to have asked him, "My great-grandmother was your great-great grandfather's mistress, so how about it?" They dated until Charles went abroad with the navy. It was rumored that Charles's parents disapproved of his relationship with a commoner. In 1973, Camilla married Andrew Parker Bowles, a long-time suitor; the couple had two children. Prince Charles remained friends with the Bowles and was godfather to their son. In 1981, supposedly at the recommendation of Camilla, Charles married the young Lady Diana Spencer in a televised storybook wedding. She became the popular princess of Wales and the couple had two children together. However, the marriage soon floundered; Diana contended that "there were three people in the marriage, so it was quite crowded." Charles and Diana separated in 1991, and a few months later the tape of a 1989 telephone conversation between Charles and Camilla in which he says "I love you" was made public. In a later interview Charles admitted to adultery during his marriage but did not name Parker Bowles. In 1995, Camilla and her husband divorced and thereafter she became Charles's semiofficial companion. The following year Charles and Diana's divorce was granted. Charles's relationship with Camilla was unpopular with the public and became even more so after Diana was killed in a Parisian car crash in 1997. Camilla retreated into the background until 1999, when Charles introduced her to Prince William and Prince Harry, his sons by Diana. A year later Charles brought her home to meet his parents. From then on she frequently appeared by his side at official events and she eventually moved into his renovated Clarence House to live with him. In February of 2005, Charles publicly announced his engagement to Camilla.

Sources: Sarah Lyall, 2005, "Charles and Camilla, Married at Last, and With Hardly a Hitch," *New York Times* (April 10): 1, 8; Sarah Lyall, 2005, "Charles Calls End to the Affair: He'll Happily Wed His Camilla," *New York Times* (February 11): 1, 10.

The family, and marriage as a process that can generate it, exists in some form in all societies. Families are created by human beings in an attempt to meet certain basic individual and social needs, such as survival and growth. Marriage and family are among the oldest human social institutions. An institution consists of patterns of ideas, beliefs, values, and behavior that are built around the basic needs of individuals and society and that tend to persist over time. **Institutions** represent the organized aspects of human social existence that are established and reinforced over time by the various norms and values of a particular group or society. The family as an institution organizes, directs, and executes the essential tasks of living for its members. Although, historically, marriage and family have been considered the most important institutions in human society, humans have created many other important institutions, for example, education, government, the economy, religion, and law. Throughout this textbook, we will examine how these other institutions affect marriages and families.

Families encompass cultural patterns as well as social structure. For example, as the case of Prince Charles and Camilla illustrates, the cultural recognition of mating is intimately bound up with familial and societal norms and customs about who are appropriate mates. As we discuss in detail in Chapter 5, two of the most common ways in which families regulate who their members can mate with is through rules of *exogamy* (the requirement that marriage must occur outside a group) and *endogamy* (the requirement that marriage occur within a group). Clearly, Charles's initial relationship with Camilla and Edward VIII's marriage to Wallis Simpson years earlier were deemed unacceptable to their families and, especially in the King's case, to the entire country. In some societies, for example, among the various ethnic groups in Karachi, marital endogamy is so important that an infraction of the rule is not only considered a violation of group customs but also cause for violent retribution. Kanwar Ahson and Riffat Afridie, members of different ethnic groups, married over her father's objection. The news of their marriage set off ethnic rioting in Karachi, which left two people dead and eight others injured. Later Kanwar was severely wounded in a shooting and he and his wife were forced into hiding to avoid further violence. Riffat's father and brother were suspected of doing the shooting because they believed their family and group's "honor" were violated by the marriage (Associated Press, 1998). Similarly, a 23-year-old Jordanian, Rania Arafat, was shot by her younger brother for refusing to marry the cousin to whom she had been promised by her family (Perkins, 2000). According to the Human Rights Commission of Pakistan, more than 1100 women are deliberately killed each year for violating cultural traditions. Many experts believe the reported number of such honor killings is only a fraction of the actual killings that take place. Although both political and religious leaders have spoken out against this practice, it remains rampant in a number of Middle Eastern communities where the perpetrators, mostly male family members, generally go unpunished. Opponents of attempts to outlaw honor killings argue that without such controls on women, families would disintegrate.

CONTEMPORARY DEFINITIONS OF MARRIAGES AND FAMILIES

Because all of us belong to some sort of family and have observed marriages (including our parents—and perhaps our own), we probably think we know exactly what the terms *marriage* and *family* mean. Although marriage and family go hand in hand, they are not one and the same. You might ask, then, exactly what are they? Take a few minutes to jot down your perceptions, definitions, and ideas about each of these institutions. How did you define them? Not surprisingly, many of your definitions and images of marriages and families are probably tied to ideas about a "traditional" family that consists of a husband, wife, and their children, an image often portrayed in both popular and academic literature and transmitted throughout American popular culture. This family pattern is an institution of the past, if indeed it ever really existed at all. To be sure, it is far from typical today. Many people reading this textbook, for example, come from single-parent families or families that include a stepparent and stepsiblings or half-siblings. Some of you perhaps moved between your parents' separate households as you were growing up or lived under the guardianship of a grandmother, a great-grandmother, or some other relative. And still others grew up in families where their parents were of different races or of the same sex. Therefore, more accurate definitions of marriages and families must take into account the many different forms of marriages and families that have existed historically and still exist today, both in the United States and in other countries and cultures.

What Is Marriage?

Marriage has been defined in the United States as a legal contract between a woman and a man who are at or above a specified age and who are not already legally married to someone else. Although some people still regard this definition as adequate, increasing numbers of scholars and laypersons alike consider it too narrow. By focusing on heterosexuality and the legal aspect of marriage alone, it excludes a variety of relationships, such as some heterosexual and homosexual cohabitive relationships that function in much the same way as legally sanctioned marriages, albeit without the same legal protection. Thus, in this book we utilize a more encompassing and reality-based definition of **marriage** as a union between people (whether widely or legally recognized or not) that unites partners sexually, socially, and economically; that is relatively consistent over time; and that accords each member certain agreed-upon rights.

Types of Marriages   Marriages across cultures generally have been either monogamous or polygamous. **Monogamy** involves one person married to another person of the other sex. Although, legally, monogamy refers to heterosexual relationships, any couple can be monogamous if they are committed exclusively to each other sexually and otherwise during the course of the relationship. Monogamy is the legally recognized marital structure in the United States. However, approximately one-half of all marriages in this country end in divorce, and the vast majority of divorced people remarry. Thus, the U.S. marriage pattern is more accurately classified as **serial monogamy**. Individuals may marry as many times as they like as long as each prior marriage was ended by death or divorce.

In some societies, polygamy is the accepted marriage structure. **Polygamy** is a broad category that generally refers to one person of one sex married to several people of the other sex. It can take one of two forms: **polygyny,** in which one male has two or more wives; and **polyandry,** in which one female has two or more husbands. Even though the practice of polyandry is rare, polygyny is legally practiced in many parts of the world such as the Middle East, South America, Asia, and in parts of Africa. In Saudi Arabia, for instance, there are wealthy men who have as many as 11 wives and 50 or more children (Dickey and McGinn, 2001). Some anthropologists have estimated that three-fourths of the world's societies prefer some type of polygamy, although they say most people within these societies lack the resources to afford more than one spouse (Nanda, 1994).

Many Americans tend to view polygamy as an exotic relationship that occurs in societies far remote from the United States. However, although both forms of polygamy are illegal in the United States, some religious and parareligious groups here routinely practice polygyny. Despite the illegality of polygamy, it thrives in states such as Utah and Arizona, where an estimated 50,000 to 60,000 residents are part of families with more than one wife. For example, among a polygamous Mormon sect in Colorado City, Arizona, a typical household consists of a husband and three or more wives (Tanner and Tanner, 2001). One man in Salt Lake City is believed to have fathered as many as 200 children by several wives. The Church of Jesus Christ of Latter-day Saints renounced polygamy over 100 years ago and excommunicates its practitioners, but Mormons participating in plural marriages defend polygamy as a fulfillment of their religion as prescribed by their ancestors (Janofsky, 2001). Although this form of marriage is illegal, few of its practitioners are ever prosecuted. One of the few exceptions occurred in 2001, when a polygamist was prosecuted for the first time in 50 years, and then convicted on polygamy charges 2002. Some observers believe this happened only because the polygynist, a man with 5 wives and 29 children, brought public attention to himself and the thousands of people living in plural families by going on national television talk shows and openly discussing his own and others' plural marriages. For years now, the practice of polygamy by some in these communities, and the Church of Jesus Christ of Latter-day Saints more generally, has raised serious issues concerning the physical abuse of children; child sexual molestation and abuse by some religious high priests, bishops, and others in the polygamous community, felony rape; and statutory rape (some of the plural brides become wives as young as age 13) (Janofsky, 2003).

As we indicated, polyandry is rare, but it can be found in the Himalayan areas of South Asia, in parts of Africa, China, Sri Lanka, northern India, Oceania, the Suruí of northwestern Brazil, and among some Native Americans. Anthropologists have recorded two forms of polyandry: *fraternal polyandry,* in which a group of brothers share a wife, and *nonfraternal polyandry,* in which a woman's husbands are not related. Fraternal polyandry is common in the mountainous areas of Nepal and Tibet. For example, among the Tibetan Nyinba, brothers live together throughout their lives in large patrilineal households where they share a common estate, common domestic responsibilities, and a common wife with whom each maintains a sexual relationship. Generally, when a child is born into these marriages, the child is acknowledged by and develops a special relationship with one of the possible fathers, even if biological paternity cannot be determined. This type of polyandry can be understood, in part, as a response to a shortage of women due to a lower survival rate in comparison to men. It also has important economic implications. Because brothers share a wife, their joint estate remains intact from generation to generation and is not subject to the fragmentary and inefficient divisions that might occur if each belonged to a separate conjugal unit. According to some anthropologists, polyandry most often occurs in societies in which women hold relatively high social status. However, it does not reflect the same stratification pattern as polygyny because a woman's social position and prestige are not determined by the number of husbands she can amass (Stone, 1997). Today, in Tibet (once considered the world's most polyandrous society), under the political control of the People's Republic of China, polyandry has been outlawed, making it difficult to document its occurrence. In other areas of the world, due to widespread Westernization as a result of colonialism and imperialism, many traditional societies have been drastically altered or destroyed, so the practice of polyandry in the past may not be accurately known (Wikipedia, 2005).

A third form of marriage is **cenogamy,** or **group marriage,** in which all of the women and men in a group are simultaneously married to one another. Like polygamy, this form of marriage is also illegal in the United States. In the mid-1800s, however, the Oneida Community, a communal group living in New York, practiced cenogamy until they were forced to disband.

What Is a Family?

What is a family? This question is not to be taken lightly. Clearly, over the last decade questions and issues relating to family, marriage, and intimacy have become highly publicized, causing many of us to question what family, family values, marriage, and intimacy are and how these terms relate to our lives. Social definitions of what constitutes a family have varied historically. It is worth noting, for example, according to family historian Stephanie Coontz (1992), the word *family* originally meant a band of slaves. Even after the word came to apply to people affiliated by blood and marriage, for many centuries the notion of family referred to authority relations rather than love relations. The sentimentalization of family life and female nurturing was historically and functionally linked to the emergence of competitive individualism and formal egalitarianism for men. As the stories of Prince Charles and Camilla Parker Bowles, Kanwar and Riffat, and of honor killings suggest, social definitions of families raise important public policy issues. These issues are related to issues of power and control and the ability of individuals and institutions to exert their will over others. An important question in this regard is, Who defines or who has the right to define family? Power gives one the leverage not only to define but also to set public policy based on a particular set of beliefs, in turn impacting the ways in which various individuals are treated. One thing that seems clear from the opening vignette is that static images and definitions of families from the past do not provide us with an accurate picture of families today.

Like marriage, family has been defined historically in rigid and restrictive language. For example, the U.S. Census Bureau defines a family as two or more persons (one of whom is the householder) living together and related by blood, marriage, or adoption. As with the popular definition of marriage, this definition of family is limiting in that it does not take into account the considerable diversity found in families. Thus, we define **family** as any relatively stable group of people bound by ties of blood, marriage, adoption; or by any sexually expressive relationship; or who simply live together, and who are committed to and provide each other with economic and emotional support. According to this more inclusive definition, a family can be any group of people who simply define themselves as family based on feelings of love, respect, commitment, and responsibility to and identification with one another. This concept of family has a subjective element in that it takes into account people's feelings of belonging to a particular group. Thus, communes as well as cohabiting individuals either of the same or other sex, who identify themselves as a family, meet these criteria and can be considered families. Most Americans, it seems, agree with this broader definition. Recent research, for example, finds that while Americans continue to place a high value on family life, they do so today with a vastly expanded concept of family beyond the traditional nuclear form.

Types of Families   As with marriages, several types of families are worth noting. The **family of orientation** is the family into which a person is born and raised. This includes, for example, you, your parents, and any siblings you may have. In contrast, when we marry, or have an intimate relationship with someone, or have children, we create what sociologists call the **family of procreation.** Some of us were born into a **nuclear family,** consisting of a mother, father, and siblings. Others were born into an **extended,** or **multigenerational, family,** consisting of one or both of our parents, our siblings, if any, and other relatives, including grandparents. In both urban and rural areas of the United States, a form of the traditional extended family is often evident. That is, in many neighborhoods, especially those with ethnic or poor and working-class groups, a variety of relatives live, not necessarily in the same household but in very close proximity to one another (upstairs, next door, down the block, around the corner), interact on a frequent basis, and provide emotional and economic support for one another. Some sociologists have labeled this family form the **modified extended family.**

As you read this book, you will discover that the family mosaic in the United States is not limited to nuclear and extended families. As our definition implies, there is a wide variety of families, and thus a wide variety of terms to identify them. For example, *voluntarily child-free families* consist of couples who make a conscious decision not to have children. *Single-parent families* (resulting either from divorce, unmarried parenthood, or death of a parent) consist of one parent and her or his children. Sometimes these families are specifically described as female- or male-headed families. In either case, legal marriage is not a criterion for family status, as the parent may or may not have been legally married.

Reconstituted, blended, or *stepfamilies* are formed when a widowed or divorced person remarries, creating a new family that includes the children of one or both spouses. Over the last several decades, *racially and ethnically mixed families* have become an ever-growing part of the American national landscape. Depending on who is doing the estimating, mixed or multiracial families make up somewhere between 1 and 5 percent of the U.S. population. There are more than 4.5 million married and unmarried couples in the United States who are mixed racially or ethnically. And, according to recent Census data, 2.8 million children under age 18 and nearly 7 million Americans of all ages identify as more than one race. In addition, one in six adopted children is of a different race from their parents (Fields, 2004; Wiltenburg and Paulson, 2003). *Lesbian* and *gay families* are composed of individuals of the same sex who live together and identify themselves as a family; these relationships may or may not include natural-born or adopted children. Between 1 and 5 million children in the United States live in families in which at least one parent is lesbian or gay. One-third of lesbian households and one-fifth of gay male households, for example, have children (Patterson, 2002; U.S. Census Bureau of Household and Family Statistics, 2000).

An increasing number of people living in the United States, especially children, live in foster families. For example, an estimated 523 million children currently live in foster care, one-fourth of whom (23 percent) live in foster family homes with relatives (The AFCARS Report, 2005). A *foster family* consists of one or two parents and one or more children who have been taken away from their biological families (parents) and become wards of the state. Foster parents typically raise these children as their own. Other contemporary forms of the family include two families living in the same household, and what some social scientists call the "*surrogate,* or *chosen, family*"—set of "roommates" or group of people either of different or the same sex who choose to share the same household and who define themselves as a family. Traditionally, families in the United States have had a patriarchal structure. A **patriarchal family** is a family in which the male (husband or father) is the head of the family and exercises authority and decision-making power over his wife and children.

Race, Class, and Gender

Race, class, and gender are three of the most important social categories of experience for individuals and families in the United States, primarily because these categories also represent significant, comprehensive, and structured systems of oppression for some individuals and groups and privilege for others. Historically, some families in the United States have experienced social, political, and economic inequalities vis-à-vis other families, principally as a consequence of their race, ethnicity, ancestry, social class, sex or gender, or other characteristics defined as inferior.

At a very elementary level, we can say that family experiences are shaped by the choices that individual members make. However, the options that families have available to them and thus the choices they make are either limited or expanded by the ways in which race, class, and gender are organized. To fully understand families and how they function, then, we must examine the influence of race, class, and gender on family resources and processes and explore how these factors have shaped and continue to shape the experiences of families throughout the world.

Race, class, and gender are interrelated or interactive categories of social experience that affect all aspects of human life, shaping all social institutions and systems of meaning, including the institutions of marriage and family, as well as family values. By "interrelated," we mean that there are complex interconnections among race, class, and gender such that families are not separately affected because of the racial composition of their members, to which is added the influence of their economic situation, after which comes the impact of the gender of their members. In other words, race, class, and gender are not independent variables that can be tacked onto each other or separated at will. They are concrete social relations that are interconnected with one another, and their various intersections produce specific effects. Thus, any concrete analysis of marriages and families must take this into account. As sociologists Margaret Andersen and Patricia Hill Collins (1992) have observed, race, class, and gender are part of the total fabric of experience for *all* families. Although these categories are different aspects of social structure, individual families experience them simultaneously. The meaning of the concepts of race, class, and gender as interrelated or interactive categories of experience refers not only to the simultaneity of oppression or privilege but also to the multiplicative relationships among these experiences (for example, see King, 1990).

Understanding race, class, and gender in this way also allows us to see the interrelationship of other important categories of social experiences, such as ethnicity, sexual orientation, age, religion, geographic location, historical context, and physical and mental abilities. Later in this chapter we will see that many of these categories of experience have been interwoven in family form and functioning throughout U.S. history.

The growing visibility of multiracial families calls attention to the diversity of American families. It also makes it even more critical that policies relating to marriages and families address the intersections of race, class, and gender on family functioning.

FAMILY FUNCTIONS AND THE DEBATE OVER FAMILY VALUES

Historians and the lay public alike have often discussed families in terms of the vital social functions they serve for individuals and the society at large. These functions have included regulation of sexual behavior, reproduction, social placement, socialization, economic cooperation, and the provision of care, protection, and intimacy for family members.

Social Functions of Families

Regulation of Sexual Behavior   Every society is concerned about the sexual behavior of its members. In most societies, sexual behavior is regulated and enforced within the context of families. Although the **norms**—cultural guidelines or rules of conduct that direct people to behave in particular ways—governing sexual behavior vary among societies, no known society allows its members to have sexual relations with whomever they please. For example, all societies prohibit sexual relations between blood or close relatives; this is

known as the incest taboo. Forcing people to have sexual relations outside the family unit promotes alliances between families, reinforces their social independence, and prevents or minimizes sexual jealousies and conflicts within families. The set of relatives subject to the taboo varies across societies, however. Whereas in most societies parents and siblings are subject to the incest taboo, in ancient Egyptian and Hawaiian societies, siblings in the royal families were permitted to mate with and marry each other; in some cases, father–daughter marriages were also permitted. This system preserved the purity of royalty, enabled the royal family to maintain its power and property, and prevented the splintering of its estate through inheritance.

Moreover, in most contemporary societies sexual relations are linked with marriage. Even in those societies where it is not, their members' sexual behavior is nonetheless regulated so that it reinforces the social order. For example, among the Masai (a polygynous pastoral group in Africa), where men dominate in the family, young wives of older men are allowed to take lovers discreetly from the unmarried warrior class. If the wife becomes pregnant from such a relationship, family stability is not disrupted. The children from these unions simply belong to the husband and further increase his wealth and prestige.

Reproduction   To perpetuate itself, a society must produce new members to replace those who die or move away. In most societies, families are given the primary responsibility for reproducing the species. The reproductive function of families is considered to be so important that many societies employ a variety of practices to motivate married couples to have children. For example, in the United States, couples typically receive tax exemptions and other tax breaks for each child they produce. Couples who cannot or consciously choose not to have children are penalized by tax laws and are sometimes stigmatized by society's members. In addition, sexual intercourse that occurs outside marriage or that will not produce children, such as lesbian or gay sexual relations, is highly stigmatized and discouraged.

In contrast, in some societies concern with reproduction translates primarily into a concern with population control. Families are motivated to keep society manageable through population control. In this context, in 1952, India became the first country in the world to launch a national family planning campaign in response to population growth. Most developing nations soon followed suit. For example, viewing runaway population growth as a serious impediment to economic prosperity, Kenya developed a national family planning campaign in the late 1960s to limit population growth. The country's official population policy calls for matching population size with available resources, but it leaves the actual decision on family size up to individual families. In contrast, China's *one-child policy*—perhaps the best-known family planning and population control policy in the world—stipulates that urban couples should have only *one child* and families that violate the policy where it is most strictly enforced face mandatory abortions and severe financial penalties, while single-child couples throughout the country receive a number of benefits such as free medical care, better child care, preferential housing, and work and cash bonuses (NOVA, 2004) (see In Other Places box).

Social Placement   When new members are born into society, they must be placed within the social structure with a minimum of confusion and in a way that preserves order and stability. The **social structure** of society refers to the recurrent, patterned ways that people relate to one another. It consists of an intricate web of social **statuses,** a position in a group or society, and **roles,** a set of behaviors associated with a particular status. Members of society must be placed within these statuses and motivated to play the appropriate roles. One of the ways in which families function is to assign social status to individuals on the basis of their membership within that particular family. The status placement function of families occurs at a number of levels. On one level, families confer statuses that orient members to a variety of interpersonal relationships involving parents, siblings, and a variety of relatives. In addition, simply by being born into or raised in a particular family we automatically inherit membership in, and the status of, certain basic groups, including racial, ethnic, religious, class, and nationality. Social status influences almost every aspect of our lives. It influences the way we see the world as well as how the world sees us. Much of what we consider as our unique values and preferences are really the results of our assignment to certain statuses through our families. As you will learn in later chapters, statuses such as race and class impact families differentially depending on where families fall within these status hierarchies. Lower- and working-class families as well as certain racial and ethnic families, for example, face greater risks of experiencing poverty, welfare dependency, low academic achievement, being the victims of crime, being victimized by unscrupulous businesspeople, violence, and higher infant as well as adult mortality rates.

Socialization   Human babies are born with no knowledge of the norms, values, and role expectations of their society. However, they soon learn what their society considers appropriate ways of acting, thinking, and feeling. Children's social development, as well as the continuation of society, depends on the **socialization** process, a lifetime of social interaction through which people learn those elements of culture that are essential for effective participation in social life. Today, as in the past, families are the primary transmitters of culture to each new generation of the young. Through the socialization process, children learn the language of their culture and the accumulated knowledge, attitudes, beliefs, and values not only of the larger culture but also of their family group and the social and interpersonal skills necessary to function effectively in society. Many people in our society believe that because parents are more likely than others to be deeply committed to their own offspring, they are thus the best or most appropriate socializing agents. Compulsory education, however, has placed a significant amount of the socialization function in the hands of the state and schools. In addition, the increasing need for mothers to work outside the home has placed part of this function in the hands of child-care workers; and the mass media, especially television, have become important agents of socialization.

Economic Cooperation   Children have physical and economic needs as well as social needs. They must be fed, clothed, and sheltered. Providing for these needs is the basic economic function of families. Families are responsible for the physical and economic well-being not only of their children but of all members of their family. In the past, families consumed primarily the goods that they produced. Although this is no longer true, families are still productive economic units; however, the value of what they produce is less recognized today. The goods and services produced by families today are delivered primarily by women (for example, child care and housework). Because men have moved outside the home to work and receive wages and women's work within the family is unpaid, the productive and essential nature of families achieved through the work that women (and some stay-at-home husbands) do has been overlooked, downplayed, and often trivialized. Nevertheless, in every society and every household, women provide critical economic support to their families, whether in agriculture or by earning income in the informal or formal labor market. When all of women's work, paid and unpaid, is taken into account, their economic contribution is generally greater than that of men. The changing structures of families notwithstanding, they continue to divide essential tasks among their members and cooperate economically to meet each one's physical, social, and economic needs. Each member's economic fate is tied to that of the family as a whole.

IN OTHER PLACES

CHINA'S FERTILITY POLICY

Over a quarter of a century ago, China embarked on a bold new fertility policy in an effort to slow its population growth and to encourage economic development. This policy, popularly known as the one-child policy, was controversial from its very beginning both inside and outside of China. Proponents argued that such a policy was necessary to prevent uncontrolled population growth that threatened to further deplete natural resources, harm the environment, and impoverish an ever-increasing percentage of Chinese society. Opponents feared that enforcement of such an unprecedented policy would lead to human rights violations, especially for women who could be coerced into having abortions and/or face sterilization. They also worried that limiting a couple's reproduction to only one child would change China's traditional family structure, create gender imbalances due to the ongoing preferences for sons, and as a consequence, increase the number of elderly citizens who would lack traditional family support. When the Central Committee of the Chinese Party announced the new policy, it indicated it would be temporary, that once the goals were accomplished, in about 30 years, a new policy

could be adopted (Feng, 2005). However, the initial implementation of the policy met with strong resistance, especially in rural areas where children were economic assets to their farming parents. Thus, from about 1984 on, policymakers adjusted the one-child nationwide policy to accommodate a variety of circumstances. For example, some rural areas were exempted from the policy; other provinces allowed couples who themselves were only children to have two children. Urban residents whose first child was physically handicapped and remarried couples who did not each have a child from their previous

marriages as well as ethnic minorities were also exempted.

As the initial 30-year target approaches, scholars and policymakers are debating the wisdom, necessity, and consequences of this fertility policy. Although there is widespread agreement that over the past 25 years China's fertility rate has dropped to a level below replacement, resulting in a population of about 1.3 billion rather than the anticipated 1.6 billion, and that its economic growth has increased the per capita standard of living of its citizens by more than fourfold, there is no consensus as to whether the one-child policy was

---

Care, Protection, and Intimacy During infancy and early childhood, humans cannot take care of themselves and thus are totally dependent on their caretakers. A large amount of sociological and psychological research indicates that, in addition to the necessities of life, human infants also need warmth and affection. Furthermore, even as adults, humans need intimacy and often need other human beings for care and protection during periods of illness, disability, or other dependencies. Ideally, families function to provide an intimate atmosphere and an economic unit in which these needs can be met. As the center of emotional life, families can provide the love, caring, and emotional support that we need to lead happy, healthy, and secure lives that cannot easily be obtained outside the family context. For many of us, our families will be our most important source of comfort and emotional support throughout life.

Any given family may or may not perform any or all of these functions. The family as an institution is so diverse that not all families fulfill all of these functions; those who do, do not always fulfill them well. That we live in a time

of transition and change is unquestionable. Thus, many of the activities previously identified by social scientists as family functions have been taken over by or are shared with other societal institutions, such as schools, religious organizations, mass media, and government agencies. The socialization of children and stabilization for adult family members, however, remain one of the primary functions of families.

Contrasting Views of Families

Some people see the loss of family function as a contributing factor to a variety of social ills that beset modern families. A proponent of this point of view, social scientist Christopher Lasch (1977, 1978) contends that the encroachment of outside institutions, especially the state, has left modern families with too few functions to perform. Even the socialization function, which had been a primary function of families, has been largely taken over by an educational system that increasingly communicates a set of values and behaviors that may conflict with the realities of some

necessary to achieve these results. Dissenters point out that China's fertility levels were already declining rapidly in the 1970s before the onset of the one-child policy. They also argue that changes in China's economic system, such as the breakup of collective farming and a greater emphasis on education and improving people's job skills, contributed more to achieving economic gains than that particular fertility policy. Similarly, there is general agreement that China faces numerous challenges in the coming decades, stemming primarily from a sex ratio that is seriously out of balance. Worldwide the norm seems to be about 105 to 107 boys born for every 100 girls. In 2000, the ratio in China was 119.2, up from 108.5 in 1982 (Feng, 2005). However, in some areas, like Hainan Island, the ratio was skewed even more dramatically, 130 boys to 100 girls. In many elementary school classrooms there are three times as many boys as girls (Lev, 2005). Some social scientists fear that this demographic trend will lead to a situation where over the next two decades some 40 million Chinese males will be unable to find brides. Lacking the stability that family life traditionally provides, they predict that many of these unmarried men will engage in violent activities such as trafficking in women and social rebellion. Political scientists Valerie Hudson and Andrea den Boer (2004) point out that in in northern China of the 1850s, after decades of starvation conditions caused by floods and droughts in which families turned to female infanticide to save resources, up to 25 percent of adult males were unable to marry. A good portion of these men formed criminal gangs that combined into small armies controlling an extensive amount of territory, taking the ruling Qing dynasty years to quell. However, not all social scientists accept a causal relationship between an imbalanced sex ratio and male violence, citing a variety of possible alternative explanatory variables for male violence such as economic status, cultural norms, and type of governmental controls.

In a similar vein, not all population experts believe that the one-child policy can adequately explain the imbalance in China's sex ratio. They point to China's age-old preference for boys and the new technology that allows parents to know the sex of their unborn child. Armed with this knowledge, parents who desire a son may abort a female fetus, abandon a female infant, put her up for adoption, or neglect to report the birth to the authorities. This latter possibility is suggested by the fact that the 2000 census revealed more surviving individuals ages 10–14 in 2000 than those counted at ages 0–4 in the 1990 census with a more balanced sex ratio among the same birth cohorts as time passed (Shuzhou and Fubin, 2003). Similar behavior is also found in India, a country that does not have a one-child policy. Nevertheless, demographic trends in China have spurred officials to again readjust its birth control policy, emphasizing education and population services over enforcement, particularly in promoting the value of girls and limiting prenatal screening.

What do you think? Should governments develop policies regarding reproduction? If so, what techniques should governments use to enforce their policies? If not, what mechanisms could societies use to control their population size? Should there be a relatively equal number of females and males in any given society? If so, what means should a society take to ensure a balanced sex ratio? If not, how should societies and families cope with more females than males, or vice versa? How would you react if the U.S. government established a one- or two-child policy?

families. Thus, the function of modern families has been reduced to a small number of specialized functions, such as affection and companionship. Lasch, along with a number of other people, including a long line of politicians and the religious right, believes families are in grave danger today, perhaps even in a state of crisis and moral decay. Many of these people consider the family to be seriously flawed and its breakdown the major source of most societal ills (illegitimacy, divorce, declining educational standards, drug addiction, delinquency, violence, HIV/AIDS). Others view the family as the foundation of society. Although some people view the family with nostalgia and confusion, others see it as foundational but undergoing massive changes that are connected to other transformations that society is living through.

These contrasting views of the family, and many gradations of them, are as prevalent today as they were in the 1990s when sparked by the so-called conservative revolution. Today marriages and families continue to be in a state of transformation and to be political issues. Some political conservatives, for example, want to put fathers back at the head of families as the breadwinners and protectors of women and children. Some liberals (among them some feminists), on the other hand, have long argued that the patriarchal family is the major source of women's oppression and inequality.

Some people have seen evidence of the decline and moral decay of families in terms of a number of contemporary patterns of marriage and family life today: the transformation of women's roles both inside the home and in the world at large, the increasing number of children and families that are beset by serious stresses and troubles, the high divorce rates, lower marriage and birth rates, the increase in single-parent families, the high rate of welfare dependency, sexual permissiveness, the increasing number of public disclosures of incest and sexual and mental abuse of children, the increasing number of unmarried couples living together openly, unmarried mothers keeping their babies, and the legalization of abortion and gay marriage. In addition, a number of individual events that occurred during the closing decade of the twentieth century gave credence to those who view the traditional family as under siege or in decline. For example, survey data during the

DEBATING SOCIAL ISSUES

EXPLORING THE DEBATE OVER GAY MARRIAGE

The issue of same-sex marriage, almost unimaginable in the United States a few decades ago, has become so potent that it is a major issue in public and popular discourse, debate, and legal actions across the country and is one of the most significant civil and human rights issues of contemporary U.S. history. Marriage is a critical issue because it touches simultaneously on questions of love and sex, religion and politics, access to legal and economic benefits, and the role of government in our personal lives. There are literally hundreds of rights, benefits, and protections that accompany civil marriage in the United States. Because they are so automatic, most heterosexuals take these rights for granted. However, lesbian and gay couples do not enjoy this same civil rights (GLSEN, 2003).

The national debate surrounding the rights of same-sex couples to marry intensified in 2004 after the state of Massachusetts became the first and thus far the only state in the country to legalize same-sex marriage. Since that time more than 6000 lesbian and gay couples have wed in that state. Moreover, for short intervals of time in 2004, same-sex couples in San Francisco, and in various towns in New Mexico and New York, were able to obtain marriage licenses, although none were able to register their marriages. In a national backlash, 18 states have passed constitutional amendments to ban gay marriage and the president of the United

States remains one of the most powerful and most visible opponents of same-sex marriage. Some observers of the controversy over same-sex marriage say that the issue contributed to polarizing the country during the 2004 presidential election, ultimately helping to reelect George W. Bush (Badkhen, 2005).

There is a range of complex issues reflected in the marriage debate, some normative, some moral, and others legal. However, in less complicated and complex terms, among those who oppose same-sex marriage, some of the major arguments include the following: most religions of the world consider homosexuality unaccept-

---

1990s indicated that young people in America were becoming sexually active at younger and younger ages; one in four sixth graders in New Haven, Connecticut, was sexually active; a Virginia woman made national news after castrating her husband, who she claimed had repeatedly raped and abused her over the course of their married life (that same year close to 4 million women were battered by a husband or lover); several cities passed domestic partnership laws giving lesbian and gay cohabiting couples some of the same legal rights previously reserved for married couples; and scientists at George Washington University successfully cloned human embryos, raising the possibility that in the near future, couples can have identical twins of different ages (Newman, 1995).

Added to events such as these, recent events such as the legalization of same-sex marriage in Massachusetts in 2004 and civil unions in Connecticut in 2005 (essentially the same as same-sex marriage) have caused many people, from social scientists to public officials to ordinary people, to take the position that the tradition of human family life is being replaced by an alien and destructive set of relationships that is tearing at the very heart of U.S. society (see Debating Social Issues box). Critics of the modern family, such as political conservatives and other "traditionalists," attribute this so-called family breakdown to a general decline in family values, which, in turn, is often associated with feminism, the sexual revolution, lesbian and gay liberation, generous

able and sinful; same-sex marriage would weaken the definition and respect for the institution of marriage; same-sex marriage would further weaken the traditional family values essential to society; and the legalization of same-sex marriage would provide a slippery slope that would ultimately destroy the whole idea of marriage (Messerli, 2005). Some opponents of same-sex marriage believe it to be an oxymoron, an ideological invention designed to force societal acceptance of homosexuality. Most opponents of same-sex marriage share the viewpoint of President Bush, that marriage is an institution between one woman and one man only. One of the most common arguments against legalizing same-sex marriage is that it would subvert the stability and integrity of heterosexual marriages and families; it would further weaken the traditional family values essential to society. Some opponents fear that legalizing same-sex marriage will somehow influence young people to try out same-sex relationships. This is perhaps most evident in the bans that many schools and libraries have instituted with regard to books and materials that depict same-sex relationships. The opposition to same-sex marriages at the state level is reflected in the fact that through the end of 2004, 37 states had passed "defense of marriage" legislation that banned same-sex marriage and several other states had similar legislation pending; and at this writing four states had marriage laws that specifically prohibit same-sex marriage. Essentially, then, in 88 percent of the country, the law sanctions heterosexual marriage and denies same-sex couples the same legal and civil right. And some opponents,

including President George W. Bush, favor a U.S. constitutional amendment that would define marriage as being between a man and a woman, thus barring same-sex marriages (Scott and Schwartz, 2006; GLSEN, 2005).

On the other side of the debate, those who support same-sex marriage argue that marriage is a civil right and the denial of marriage as an option for lesbians and gays not only violates their civil rights but also their religious freedom. Marriage, they say, is a secular activity and should not be governed by religious ideology. Lesbian and gay couples ought to be allowed the option of civil marriage, which does not entail any religious ceremonies and ought to be acceptable to those who object to same-sex marriages on the grounds of their religious beliefs. In fact, they argue, many religious views are outdated and should be modified to reflect the changes in society. Legalizing same-sex marriage would provide lesbians and gays with the fundamental American freedom of having the right to choose whether and whom to marry. Proponents argue further that same-sex marriage does not threaten the institution of marriage—an institution that has been in a state of flux for centuries: for example, it was only after the Civil War that African Americans were allowed to marry in all areas of the United States; it was only after a U.S. Supreme Court decision in 1967 that mixed-race couples could marry anywhere in the United States; but, until recently, same-sex couples could not marry anywhere in the world. Rather than weakening marriages and families, proponents of same-sex mar-

riage argue that expanding the definition of marriage will strengthen it, not destroy it. Giving lesbians and gays the same rights to marry as heterosexuals would reinforce the commitment of many same-sex couples to live within long-term, committed relationships and encourage other who might not otherwise do so; it would encourage people to have strong family values, discourage high-risk sexual lifestyles, and encourage monogamy. In a cultural and social climate where HIV/AIDS is a pandemic that disproportionately impacts gay men, encouraging monogamy and long-term commitment is a rational public health policy (Scott and Schwartz, 2006).

Same-sex marriage is not a new concept, nor is it an issue unique to the United States. Since 1989, a number of countries have legalized same-sex unions, including Denmark, Germany, Holland, Belgium and Ontario, a province of Canada. So, should the United States follow suit? Should same-sex marriage be legalized across the country?

What do you think? On which side of the debate do you fall? Try explaining your position using sociological insights, concepts, and theoretical paradigms (see Chapter 2). Why, do you think, it is important to lesbians and gays that they have a legal right to marry? Is it a fundamental civil right or a special privilege? Explain your answer. In your opinion, would same-sex marriage require a redefinition of marriage? If so, how might we redefine marriage?

welfare policies, and the increasing demands for social and political rights (Stacey, 1996).

The issue of "family values" has long polarized Americans. Protracted public discourse about family values continues to polarize Americans, constituting, what some have labeled an ideological fault line, which determines what newspapers people read, what television programs they watch, what circles they socialize in, what jokes they tell, what political party they vote for, and even what church they attend. The issue of family values shapes public discourse and debate on a variety of other social issues such as same-sex marriage, sex and violence on television, abortion, the ideal of the traditional family as heterosexual consisting of two parents, the role of

women in society, the role of women within marriages and families, the place of motherhood, what constitutes pornography, sex education and prayer in schools, censorship, the place of religion in politics, and whether society should be allowed to impose structures that protect "traditional values" (Supporting Family Values, 2005). Although staunch political and religious conservatives carried the profamily campaign in the 1980s, academicians, most of them also political conservatives, became the chief profamily spokespersons in the 1990s. Grounding their claims in social science, they declared that the primary source of family decline over the past three decades has been cultural, and they called for a restoration of the supremacy of the nuclear family. The religious right, conservative politicians, and other conservatives carry the banner today and have broadened the debate to include *traditional values and moral values.*

On the other side of these debates are those who are equally concerned about the problems of modern families but who view current events and trends in marriage and family life as indicative of the redefinition of marriages and families in the context of the massive transformation that took place worldwide over the last several decades. They concede that marriages and families may perform fewer direct functions for individual members than they did in the past and that there are serious problems associated with marriage and family life today. They argue, however, that marriage and family life are still extremely important to most people in the United States. They cite census data indicating that the United States has perhaps the highest marriage rate in the industrial world. For example, although women and men are postponing marriage until later ages than in the past, they are still marrying in high numbers. In 2003, for instance, the majority of women and men had been married by the time they were 30–34 years of age (72 percent), and among women and men 65 years old and over, 96 percent had been married (Fields, 2003). Although people may delay marriage, almost everyone (90 percent) marries at least once and almost all who do marry either have or want to have children. And although the United States has one of the highest divorce rates in the world, the overwhelming majority of divorced people remarry. This point of view suggests that marriage and family life in the United States today is a complex mixture of both continuity and change (see, for example, Skolnick and Skolnick, 1999).

Furthermore, those who take this point of view cite survey results reporting that most people in the United States hold the family in high regard and report high levels of satisfaction with their own family life. They refute the idealized version of families of the past and give us instead a picture of a traditional family that was often rigid and oppressive. They remind us that members of traditional families were often expected to fit into roles based on a clear division of labor along age and gender lines. Frequently, this resulted in a very restrictive life, especially for women and children. They also question the premise that family values and traditional family structure are one and the same and that both are synonymous with stability. What, they ask, are family values? What have they been historically? Are they fundamentally different today than in the past? Who is to say which family values are correct? Rather than debate something called "family values" they say, the focus should be on *valuing families.*

How does the polarization of the discourse on family values into a two-sided debate affect our understanding of what is happening to families today? Is there only one accurate image of the family? Were families of yesterday really the way we perceive them to be? Were the "good old days" really that good for all marriages and families? Why is valuing families, regardless of the form they take, considered to be antifamily by some groups? Explain.

DEBUNKING MYTHS ABOUT MARRIAGES AND FAMILIES

Take another few minutes to think about the "traditional family." Again, if you are like most people, your vision of the traditional family is similar to or the same as your more general view of families. Therefore, you probably describe the traditional family in terms of some combination of the following traits:

- Members loved and respected one another and worked together for the good of the family.
- Grandparents were an integral and respected part of the family.
- Mothers stayed home and were happy, nurturant, and always available to their children.
- Fathers worked and brought home the paycheck.
- Children were seen and not heard, were mischievous but not "bad," and were responsible and learned a work ethic.

These images of past family life are still widely held and have a powerful influence on people's perceptions and evaluations of today's families. The problem, however, is that these are mostly mythical images of the past based on many different kinds of marriages and families that never coexisted in the same time and place. A leading authority on U.S. family history, Stephanie Coontz (1992), argues in her book *The Way We Never Were* that much of today's political and social debate about family values and the "real" family is based on an idealized vision of a past that never actually existed.[1] Coontz further argues that this idealized and selective set of remembrances of families of yesteryear in turn determines much of our contemporary view of traditional family life. A look at some statistics and facts from our historical past supports her argument.

- We bemoan the increasingly violent nature of families (and rightfully so). As you will see in Chapter 11, however, the United States has a long and brutal history of child and woman abuse. Therefore, we cannot blame domestic violence on recent changes in family life or on the disappearance of family values and morals.
- We think that contemporary high school dropout rates are shockingly high. As late as the 1940s, however, less than one-half of all young people entering high school managed to finish, producing a dropout rate that was much higher than today's.
- Violence in all aspects of society is high today, but before the Civil War, New York City was already considered the most dangerous place in the world to live. As a matter of fact, the United States has had the highest homicide rates in the industrial world for almost 150 years. And among all the relationships between murderers and their victims, the family relationship is most common.

---

[1]The rest of our discussion concerning the myths and realities of family life, past and present, owes much to the work of Coontz. She has written profusely on the social origins and history of U.S. families from the 1600s forward. She has also lectured extensively in Europe and the United States on family history and sociology. She places contemporary family crises in the context of history and exposes many of the myths that surround and cloud contemporary discussions and debates about family values and the way U.S. families actually were.

STRENGTHENING MARRIAGES AND FAMILIES
Talks with Family Therapist Joan Zientek

INTRODUCING FAMILY THERAPY

In various chapters throughout this textbook we will call on Joan Zientek, a marital and family therapist, to answer questions about how families cope with major problems and what they can do to strengthen family relationships. Ms. Zientek is a graduate of the Family Institute, Institute of Psychiatry of Northwestern Memorial Hospital Medical School. She has been in private practice for over 20 years. In addition, she presents seminars on various family and human relations topics to school faculties, parent groups, and service organizations. In addition, she serves as a consultant to many school districts. Ms. Zientek developed and conducts a program entitled *FOCUS ON E.Q.: A Social Skills Training Program for Kids* and is the author of *Mrs. Ruby's Life Lessons for Kids*, a storybook and workbook on emotional intelligence.

What Is Family Therapy? Family therapy is a systems approach to helping families function more effectively. It views the family as a web of interlocking relationships within which every member is intimately linked in a powerful way with every other person in the family. Family therapy starts with the assumption that an individual's problems are an overt manifestation of a larger, less obvious family systems problem. Thus, problems are seen as existing between people, rather than solely within them. Unlike psychoanalysis, which delves into the origin of problems, family therapy focuses on the circular interaction between and among individuals that keeps the problem going. The desired outcome is change rather than insight.

Who Can Benefit from Family Therapy? All individuals and families experience problems from time to time and, for the most part, many of these can be resolved without therapy. However, when a couple marries,

the intensity of that bond, its reminiscent impact of each person's family of origin experiences, along with the demands of negotiating life as a dyad, often cause latent unresolved issues from childhood to emerge. These are acted out in the marriage relationship and can be disruptive and confusing to the couple. Also, as families move from one life stage to another, from the birth of children to the retirement years, some individuals and families may need special support to make the required adaptations in family patterns and relationships. At other times, situational difficulties may be caused by divorce, remarriage, illness, death, unemployment, or relocation. The family therapist also works with individuals and subsystems of the family, treating problems that stem from emotional and biochemical issues, such as depression, attention deficit disorder, or addictions. Nonetheless, the family therapist always maintains a systems framework, knowing that changes any individual(s) make influence and are influenced by the system in which they live.

Do Myths about Family Life Have Any Relationship to How Families Function? They can. Family relationships are often portrayed in the sitcoms of the 1950s and in the love songs that have endured over time as smooth, effortless, and a haven of emotional support. Today many of us still want to believe the myth that an ideal family life truly does exist. However, those dreams can be shattered in an instant by news of the high divorce rate, the escalation of suicide among teens, of children being killed by the hands of their parents, and by the economic struggles of a good portion of our country. At the same time, we live in a culture of high expectations, prosperity, and a cultural mandate to have it all: monetary success, a wonderful family, and above all, great sex. The myth that the perfect life is possible for all leads to feelings of dissatisfaction that become intolerable when the standards are sky high. According to Joshua Coleman (2003), author of *Imperfect Harmony*, "There is an enormous amount of pressure on marriage to live up to an unrealistic ideal."

- Although alcohol and drug abuse are at alarmingly high rates today, they were widespread well before modern rearrangements of gender roles and family life. In 1820, for example, alcohol consumption was three times higher than today. There was also a major epidemic of opium and cocaine addiction in the late nineteenth century. Over time, these and other problems led to the emergence of a new field called *family therapy* that is designed to help families cope with and resolve problems (see the Strengthening Marriages and Families box).

As these facts demonstrate, our memory of past family life is often clouded by myths. A **myth** is a false, fictitious, imaginary, or exaggerated belief about someone or something. Myths are generally assumed true and often provide the justification or rationale for social behaviors, beliefs, and institutions. In fact, most myths do contain some elements of truth. As we will see, however, different myths contain different degrees of truth.

Some family myths have a positive effect in the sense that they often bond individual family members together in familial solidarity. When they create unrealistic expectations about what families can or should be and do, however, myths can be dangerous. Many of the myths that most Americans hold today about traditional families or families of the past are white middle-class myths. This is true because the mass media, controlled primarily by white middle-class men, tend to project a primarily white middle-class experience as a universal trend or fact. Such myths, then, distort the diverse experiences of other familial groups in this country, both presently and in the past, and they do not even describe most white middle-class families accurately. We now take a closer look at four of the most popular myths and stereotypes about the family that are directly applicable to current debates about family life and gender roles: (1) the universal nuclear family, (2) the self-reliant traditional family, (3) the naturalness of different spheres for wives and husbands, and (4) the unstable African American family.

Myth 1: The Universal Nuclear Family

Although some form of marriage and family is found in all human societies, the idea that there is a universal, or single, marriage and family pattern blinds us to the historical reality and legitimacy of diverse marriage and family arrangements. The reality is that marriages and families vary in organization, membership, life cycles, emotional environments, ideologies, social and kinship networks, and economic and other functions. Although it is certainly true that a woman and man (egg and sperm) must unite to produce a child, social kinship ties or living arrangements do not automatically flow from such biological unions. For example, some cultures have weddings and cultural notions about monogamy and permanence, but other cultures lack one or more of these characteristics. In some cultures, mating and childbirth occur outside legal marriage and sometimes without couples living together. In other cultures, wives, husbands, and children live in separate residences.

During the 1950s, the idea of the nuclear family was idealized as millions of Americans came to accept a media version of the American family as a middle-class institution consisting of a wise father who worked outside the home; a mother whose major responsibility was to take care of her husband, children, and home; and children who were well behaved and obedient. This image, depicted in a number of 1950s family sitcoms, such as *Leave It to Beaver*, *Father Knows Best*, *The Donna Reed Show*, and *The Adventures of Ozzie and Harriet*, is said to represent the epitome of traditional family structure and values. Many critics of today's families see the movement away from this model as evidence of the decline in the viability of the family, as well as a source of many family problems.

It is true that, compared with today, the 1950s were characterized by younger ages at marriage, higher birth rates, and lower divorce and premarital pregnancy rates. To present the 1950s as representing "typical" or "normal" family patterns, however, is misleading. Indeed, the divorce rates have increased since the 1950s, but this trend started in the nineteenth century, with more marital breakups in each succeeding generation. Today's trends of low marriage, high divorce, and low fertility are actually consistent with long-term historical trends in marriage and family life. Recent changes in marriage and family life are considered deviant only because the marriage rates for the postwar generation represented an all-time high for the United States. This generation married young, moved to the suburbs, and had three or more children. The fact is that this pattern was deviant in that it departed significantly from earlier twentieth-century trends in marriage and family life. According to some, if the 1940s and 1950s had not happened, marriage and family life today would appear normal (Skolnick and Skolnick, 1999). Although some people worry that young people today are delaying marriage to unusually late ages, Figure 1.1 shows that the median age at first marriage in 2003, 25.3 for women and 27.1 for men, the highest levels since these data were first recorded in 1890, more closely approximates the 1890 average than it does the 1950s' average of 20.3 for women and 22.8 for men. The earlier age at marriage in the 1950s was a reaction to the hardships and sacrifices brought about by the depression and World War II. Thus, marriage and family life became synonymous with the "good life." Furthermore, images of the good life were now broadcast into living rooms across the country via the powerful new medium of television. Even then, however, there were signs that all was not well. Public opinion polls taken during the 1950s suggested that approximately 20 percent of all couples considered themselves unhappy in marriage, and another 20 percent reported only "medium happiness" (quoted in Mintz and Kellogg, 1988:194).

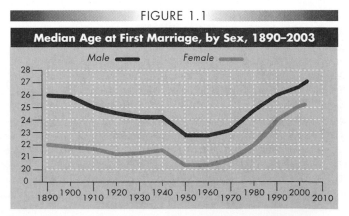

FIGURE 1.1

Median Age at First Marriage, by Sex, 1890–2003

Source: Adapted from Arlene F. Saluter, 1995, "Marital Status and Living Arrangements: March 1994," U.S. Census Bureau, *Current Population Reports*, Series P-20-484 (Washington, DC: U.S. Government Printing Office); A3, Table A-2; and Jason, Fields, 2003, "America's Families and Living Arrangements: 2003," U.S. Census Bureau, *Current Population Reports*, P20-553. (Washington, DC: U.S. Government Printing Office).

Connected to the myth of the idealized nuclear family is the myth that families have been essentially the same over the centuries until recently, when they began to disintegrate. The fact is that families have never been static, they have always changed: When the world around them changes, families change in response. The idea of the traditional family of old is itself relative. According to John Gillis (1999), we are in the habit of updating our notion of the traditional family so that the location of the "good old days" of the family constantly changes. For example, the Victorians saw the traditional family as rooted in a time period prior to industrialization and urbanization; for those who came of age during World War I, the traditional family was associated with the Victorians themselves. Although there is growing acceptance of diverse family forms, many people today still think of the 1950s and 1960s as the epitome of traditional marriage and family life.

Myth 2: The Self-Reliant Traditional Family

The myth of the self-reliant family assumes that families in the past were held together by hard work, family loyalty, and a fierce determination not to be beholden to anyone, especially the state. It is popularly believed that such families never asked for handouts; rather, they stood on their own feet even in times of crisis. Unlike some families today, who are welfare dependent or rely upon some other form of state subsidy, families of yesteryear did not accept or expect "charity." Any help they may have received came from other family members.

This tendency to overestimate the self-reliance of earlier families ignores the fact that external support for families has been the rule, and not the exception, in U.S. family history. Although public assistance has become less local and more impersonal over the past two centuries, U.S. families have always depended to some degree on other institutions. For example, colonial families made extensive use of the collective work of others, such as African American slaves and Native Americans, whose husbandry and collective land use provided for the abundant game and plant life colonial families consumed to survive. Early families were also dependent on a large network of neighbors, churches, courts, government officials, and legislative bodies for their sustenance. For example, the elderly, ill, and orphaned dependents were often taken care of by people who were not family members, and public officials often gave money to facilitate such care. Immigrant, African American, and native-born white workers could not have survived in the past without sharing and receiving assistance beyond family networks. Moreover, middle-class as well as working-class families were dependent on fraternal and mutual aid organizations to assist them in times of need.

Today, no less than in the past, families need help at one time or another. The changing economy, high unemployment and underemployment rates, and recessions have led to increasing rates of poverty. Poor and working-class families have little access to major societal resources and thus often need some sort of assistance in order to survive. It is not always so easy for middle-class families either. According to some observers, a middle-class lifestyle is becoming increasingly out of reach for middle-class families, many of whose middle-class status depends entirely on one or more wage earners. Because of recessions, unemployment, the outsourcing of jobs, and increasing medical costs, many among these families need assistance at some time.

Myth 3: The Naturalness of Different Spheres for Wives and Husbands

This myth dates to the mid-nineteenth century, when economic changes led to the development of separate spheres for women and men. Prior to this, men shared in child rearing. They were expected to be at least as involved in child rearing as mothers. Fatherhood meant much more than simply inseminating. It was understood as a well-defined set of domestic skills, including provisioning, hospitality, and child rearing (Gillis, 1999). With industrialization, wives and mothers became the caregivers and moral guardians of the family, while husbands and fathers provided economic support and protection and represented their families to the outside world. Thereafter, this arrangement was viewed as natural, and alternative forms were believed destructive to family harmony. Thus, today's family problems are seen as stemming from a self-defeating attempt to equalize women's and men's roles in the family. It is assumed that the move away from a traditional gendered division of labor to a more egalitarian ideal denies women's and men's differing needs and abilities and thus destabilizes family relations. Those who hold to this myth advocate a return to traditional gender roles in the family and a clear and firm boundary between the family and the outside world. As we shall see later on, however, the notions of separate spheres and ideal family form are far from natural and have not always existed.

Myth 4: The Unstable African American Family

Although many critics of today's families believe the collapse of the family affects all racial and ethnic groups, they frequently single out African American families as the least stable and functional. According to sociologist Ronald Taylor (1998), myths and misconceptions about the nature and quality of African American family life are pervasive and deeply entrenched in American popular thought. Although there are far fewer systematic studies of black families than of white families, African American families have been the subject of far more sweeping generalizations and myths. The most pervasive myth, the myth of the collapse of the African American family, is fueled by racist stereotypes and media exaggerations and distortions that overlook the diversity of African American family life. No more is there one black family type than there is one white family type.

Nonetheless, this myth draws on some very real trends that affect a segment of the African American community. In the 1960s, social historian Andrew Billingsley (1968) called attention to the division of the African American community along class lines and demonstrated the importance of social class in any analysis of African American families. According to Billingsley, three distinct classes were visible in the African American community: (1) a small upper class that stresses family and is politically conservative; (2) a middle class concerned with family, respectability, and individual and family achievement; and (3) a lower class made up of stable working-class families and both stable and multiproblem poor families. It is generally from the multiproblem poor families within the lower class (which some contemporary sociologists refer to as an "underclass") that stereotypes and generalizations are made about all African American families.

This segment of African American families experiences a pattern of chronic and persistent poverty. Some of the most visible manifestations of this pattern are high levels of unemployment, welfare dependency, low marriage rates, high rates of teenage pregnancy, mother-focused families composed of a mother and her dependent children, an increasing number of crack-addicted babies, and an escalating level of violence. For example, although nonmarital childbearing is no longer unusual among most groups in the United States, for African Americans in general it has become majority behavior. In 2003, 68 percent of African American babies were born to unmarried mothers (Sailer, 2003), a trend especially evident among lower-income and less-educated African Americans. In addition, there has been a major increase in the number of African American one-parent families. Although these trends have occurred among white families as well, their impact on black families has been much more substantial, resulting in increasingly different marital and family experiences for these two groups (Taylor, 1998).

Based on middle-class standards, these trends seem to support the myth of an unstable, disorganized family structure in one segment of the African American community. And, indeed, among some individuals and families, long-term and concentrated poverty and despair, racism, social contempt, police brutality, and political and governmental neglect have taken their toll and are often manifested in the behaviors just described. To generalize these behaviors to the entire African American community, however, is inaccurate and misleading. Moreover, to attribute these behaviors, when they do occur, to a deteriorating, immoral family lifestyle and a lack of middle-class family values ignores historical, social, and political factors, such as a history of servitude, legal discrimination, enforced segregation and exclusion, **institutional racism**—the systematic discrimination against a racial group by the institutions within society—and structural shifts in the economy and related trends that have created new and deeper disparities in the structure and quality of family life between blacks and whites in this society. In addition, such claims serve to perpetuate the myth that one particular family arrangement is a workable model for all families in modern society.

As it happens, most of the common knowledge whites and others have about the nature of African American families is not true. Many of the current "facts" they cite are half-truths that seriously impede responsible discussion of the dilemmas facing African American families today. Without much doubt, not only the black underclass but also many black families across class differ from the white middle-class ideal primarily because their circumstances are and have been different. Nevertheless, these differences have often been exaggerated, and where they occur among African American families they frequently have been sources of strength rather than weakness. According to Coontz, many of the variations found in African American families have produced healthy individuals with a strong group conscious-

ness that has helped them cope with widespread racism, violence, and poverty and often to rise above these limitations. (These variations are examined in later chapters of this text.) This view is supported, in part, by statistics that show an increasing number of African Americans are graduating from high school, attending college, and experiencing some advances in economic and material well-being. Many sociologists today take the position that there is no one family type; African American families, like other families, should be viewed as unique and essential subcultural family forms and not simply as deviant departures from white middle-class family forms. Assuredly, the lack of adequate resources, access to stable employment, quality education, racism, discrimination, and inequalities are the problems impacting these families—not some mysterious self-perpetuating pathology in the African American family.

This discussion of mythical versus real families underscores the fact that not all families are the same; there is not now and never has been a single model of the family. Families and their experiences are indeed different; however, difference does not connote better or worse. The experiences of a poor family are certainly not the same as those of a rich family; the experiences of a young family with young children are little like those of either a child-free family or an older family whose children have "left the nest." Even within families the experiences of older members are different from those of younger members, and the experiences of females and males are different. Certainly the experiences of Latina/o, Native American, Asian American, and African families are not the same as those of white families, regardless of class. Nor are lesbian and gay family experiences the same as heterosexual family experiences. Families are products of their historical context, and at any given historical period families occupy different territories and have varied experiences, given the differential influence of the society's race, class, and gender systems.

FAMILIES IN EARLY AMERICA

When the first English and Dutch settlers arrived on the eastern seaboard of North America in the early seventeenth century, there were already between 1 and 2 million people living here, composing more than 240 distinct groups, each with its own history, culture, family, and patterns of **kinship**—people who are related by blood, marriage, or adoption, or who consider one another family (Mintz and Kellogg, 1988). By the end of that century, a variety of immigrants, primarily from Scotland, Ireland, Germany, and France, had arrived in North America. In addition, large numbers of Africans were forcibly brought to the colonies and sold into slavery. Thus, from the very beginning, the United States was economically, racially, ethnically, religiously, and familially diverse. Consequently, any attempt to describe families of the past must take this diversity into account. One chapter in a textbook cannot possibly convey how all these different groups struggled to adapt to a new and often hostile environment and at the same time to create and maintain a stable family structure. Thus, our depiction of family life in the seventeenth and eighteenth centuries is limited to three groups: white colonial families, African

American families, and Native American families. A great deal of African American family history was connected with slavery. Because slavery ended only after the Civil War, our discussion of African American families contains references to the nineteenth century as well.

Colonial Families

Our knowledge of family life among the first immigrants to this country comes primarily from three sources: (1) surviving physical objects, such as furniture, tools, and utensils; (2) personal diaries, letters, sermons, literary works, and wills, which contain references to the relationships that existed among different family and community members; and (3) census data and other public records. Given that these materials represent only fragmentary remains of that period, our understanding of family life in colonial America is somewhat impressionistic. We do know, however, that there was considerable variation in family organization among the colonists, reflecting the differences in cultural backgrounds that they brought with them, as well as differences in the local conditions they encountered in the areas in which they settled. Limitations of space prevent a full discussion of this diversity; hence, our discussion focuses primarily on family life in the northern colonies and incorporates some examples from the other colonies.

Household Composition   A popular belief about colonial America is that most people lived in extended families. Research, however, shows that the opposite was true. Early colonial families, with few exceptions, were nuclear families, consisting of wife, husband, and children (Greven, 1970; Laslett, 1971). Immediately after marriage, the couple was expected to establish their own household. About the only exception to this pattern was when elderly parents were unable to care for themselves and, out of necessity, had to live with their adult children. Nevertheless, colonial families differed in at least three major respects from the modern nuclear family. First, nonkin, such as orphans, apprentices, hired laborers, unmarried individuals, and children from other families, could and often did join colonial households. These "servants," as they were referred to, lived and worked as regular members of the household. Additionally, at times local authorities would place criminals and poor people with families. These people were to provide service to the household in return for care and rehabilitation.

Second, the family formed the basic economic unit of colonial society. Women, men, and children combined their labor to meet the subsistence needs of the family. Until approximately the middle of the eighteenth century, relatively little was produced to sell. Calling this pattern the "family-based economy," social historians Louise Tilly and Joan Scott (1978:12) observed, "Production and family life were inseparably intertwined, and the household was the center around which resources, labor, and consumption were balanced."[2] Hence, as the basic economic unit of life,

the family was synonymous with whoever lived and worked within the household, rather than being strictly defined by blood and marital ties.

Finally, unlike today, the functions of the colonial family and the larger community were deeply intertwined. In his book *A Little Commonwealth*, historian John Demos (1970:183–84) describes how the family in Plymouth colony functioned as a business, a school, a vocational institute, a church, a house of corrections, and at times a hospital, an orphanage, and a poorhouse. Although the family was involved in these tasks, public authorities determined how the tasks were to be met. Social life was highly regulated. Individuals were told where to live, how to dress, what strangers to take in and for how long. Unlike today, there was little privacy within or among households. Sexual matters, for example, were discussed openly. Because much of daily living took place in common rooms, children were not sheltered from knowledge of sexual matters. Public documents from that period show that neighbors often reported violations of sexual norms and that punishment for such violations was carried out in public. For example, a woman could be flogged if she refused to name the father of a child born out of wedlock. If marriage followed a premarital pregnancy, however, little concern was expressed. This was not uncommon, as evidenced by the fact that in seventeenth-century Maryland, one-third of the immigrant women whose marriages are recorded were pregnant before the ceremonies (cited in Coontz, 1988:89).

Marital Roles   The colonial family was a patriarchy. Fathers were regarded as the head of the family, and they exercised authority over wives, children, and servants. Men represented their households in the public sphere and held positions of leadership in the community. However, not all fathers were in this position. Those without property themselves came under the rule of the propertied class. The ownership of property gave men considerable power in their families, and their decisions to distribute property to their offspring had a profound effect on their children's choice of careers and on when and who their children married. This practice often kept children economically dependent on their parents for much of their adult lives.

Legally, a father had the right to determine who could court his daughters, and it was up to him to give consent to a child's marriage or withhold it. His decision was based largely on whether the marriage would maintain or enhance the economic and political status of the family. Although romantic love may have existed between courting couples, marriage was viewed first and foremost as an economic arrangement, with the assumption that affection would develop after marriage (Mintz and Kellogg, 1988). Evidence of this attitude and its subsequent change comes from an examination of divorce records. It was only after 1770 that divorce records named loss of affection as a reason for terminating the marriage.

Under these patriarchal arrangements, wives were expected to be submissive and obedient to their husbands. Although unmarried women had the right to own property, enter into contracts, and represent themselves in court, after marriage the English concept of *coverture* was evoked, whereby the wife's legal identity was subsumed in that of

---

[2]This pattern was not unique to Europe and colonial America. The family-based economy can still be found in rural areas around the world, especially in developing countries.

her husband, giving him the authority to make decisions for her. This doctrine was often ignored in practice, however. Records show that some colonial women, especially widows, entered into contracts and operated stores; ran taverns; and worked as millers, tanners, blacksmiths, silversmiths, shoemakers, and printers—occupations usually held by men.

Although both wives and husbands contributed their skills and resources to the household, the actual division of labor was based on sex. For the most part, husbands did the planting, harvesting, bookkeeping, and supervisory tasks. Wives were responsible for cooking, sewing, milking, cleaning, and gardening. In addition, they produced many products for home consumption and traded surplus goods with other families. A wife sometimes served as a "deputy husband," assuming her husband's responsibilities when he was away on business or military duty. Thus, women often performed traditional male tasks. Men, however, only infrequently reciprocated by performing women's domestic chores (Riley, 1987:13). Today, our culture views child rearing as predominantly women's work. Yet, according to historian Carl Degler (1980), child rearing in the colonial period was mainly the task of fathers, who were responsible for transmitting religious values and for instilling discipline in their offspring. As we shall see, economic changes in the nineteenth century caused a major shift in family roles.

Childhood   The social experiences of colonial children differed in several major ways from those of children today. First, survival to adulthood was less likely. Death rates among children were higher than among other age groups. In the more prosperous and healthier communities in seventeenth-century New England, one out of ten children died in infancy; in other communities, the rate was one out of three (Mintz and Kellogg, 1988:14). Initial interpretations of these high death rates suggested that parents protected themselves emotionally by developing an indifference toward young children. Historical documents belie this viewpoint, however, revealing the immense sorrow parents experienced at the death of a child.

Second, child rearing did not occupy the same place it does today. For example, well-to-do families often employed wet nurses to breast-feed and care for infants so that mothers could concentrate their attention on household duties. Children were not viewed as "innocent beings"; rather, they were seen as possessing original sin and stubborn willfulness. Thus, child-rearing practices were designed to break down a child's willful nature. Religious instruction, threats, and even physical beatings were frequently used to discipline wayward children. There were even "stubborn child" laws in early New England that prescribed the death penalty for persistent disobedience to parents. Although there is no record that such sanctions were ever invoked, their very existence symbolized society's concern for domestic tranquility (Powers, 1966).

Third, childhood itself was quite short. Around the age of 6 or 7, both girls and boys assumed productive roles. Girls were taught domestic skills, such as sewing, spinning, and caring for domestic animals. Like their mothers, they also assisted their fathers in the fields or in the shops. Young boys worked small looms, weeded fields, and were taught a craft. Finally, around the age of 14, many colonial children from all social classes were "put out" to other families to learn a trade, to work as servants, or to receive the proper discipline their natural parents could not be expected to deliver (Mintz and Kellogg, 1988).

There was, however, at least one aspect of colonial childhood similar to today. Many children in colonial families spent part of their life in a single-parent family. For example, parental death rates in late seventeenth-century Virginia were so high that most children were reared by just one parent, and more than one-third lost both parents (Darrett and Rutman, 1979:153). Thus, many colonial children, like millions of children today, lived part of their lives in stepfamilies, a topic we discuss in detail in Chapter 13.

Thus far, the family patterns we have been discussing applied primarily to the white settlers. People of color had very different experiences. In the process of adapting to their environment, they created some distinct patterns of family life.

African American Families under Slavery

Andrew Billingsley (1968) points out three important elements that distinguish the experience of African Americans from that of other groups in the United States.

1. Unlike most of their colonial contemporaries, African Americans came to America from Africa and not from Europe.
2. They were uprooted from their cultural and family moorings and brought to the United States as slaves.
3. From the beginning, and continuing even today, they were systematically excluded from participation in the major institutions of U.S. society.

Numerous writings have traced the problems of modern African American families to the experience of slavery. Clearly, slavery had a devastating effect on families. The day-to-day stresses of living as a slave and many specific practices of slaveholders undermined the authority and stability of many of these families. Slaveholders often prohibited legal marriages among slaves, sold family members away from one another, and sexually exploited African American women. Nonetheless, a growing body of research shows that many slaves established strong marital and family arrangements that endured for long periods of time, even under conditions of separation. Family arrangements followed fairly distinct patterns, beginning with courtship and often marriage, followed by childbearing and child rearing.

Slave Marriages   Although southern laws prohibited slaves from contracting legal marriages, some slaveholders granted permission for their slaves to marry, and a few even provided separate living quarters or household goods for the new couple. For many slaves, the solemnity of the occasion was marked by a religious ceremony at which either a black or white minister officiated. Between 1841 and 1860, half of the marriages in South Carolina's Episcopal churches were between slaves (Blassingame, 1979:166). Other marriage rituals were used as well, the most common of which involved the couple's jumping over a broomstick. A former Alabama slave, Penny Anderson, described the ceremony this way: "After supper dey puts de broom on de floor and de couple takes de hands and steps over de broom, den dey am out to bed" (quoted in Gutman, 1976:275). These rituals, however, did not guarantee that a couple could live together. Slave spouses often had different owners and lived on different plantations; thus, they could see each other only when their masters permitted visits or when, risking severe punishment, they went off on their own.

Although many slave marriages were stable, slave couples lived under the constant fear of forced separation. The reality of these fears was expressed in some of the vows these couples took, "Until death or distance do you part" (quoted in Finkelman, 1989: xii). This fear became a reality for many slave couples, as evidenced by numerous accounts of ex-slaves who referred to earlier marriages terminated by sale to new owners. Some slaves, however, fought back against this separation. Historian Eugene Genovese (1974) found considerable evidence that when couples were separated by their masters, they often ran away in an attempt to be together. Furthermore, one of the first things African Americans did after the Civil War was to seek out lost relatives on other plantations and to legalize marriages made unofficially under slavery.

According to Genovese, slave communities exhibited a high degree of sexual equality. This pattern has been linked to the slaves' African heritage and to the similar work roles they had on the plantations, where women worked alongside men in the fields and in the master's house. Although slave parents did not have legal authority over their own children, there is considerable evidence to show that both women and men had ongoing involvement with their families and that both sexes participated in child rearing.

Childhood Despite the abuses of slavery, African Americans succeeded in forming and maintaining families. Nineteenth-century census data show that both before and after slavery, most African Americans lived in two-parent households. According to plantation records examined by social historian Herbert Gutman (1976), slave women frequently bore their first child in their late teens. Because of harsh living conditions, more than one-third of the babies born to slave women died before the age of 10, a rate double that for white infants (Mintz and Kellogg, 1988:72, 73). As soon as they were able, slave children worked in the barnyards or in the master's house and soon followed their parents into the fields. Between the ages of 7 and 10, children had to leave their parents' cabin and move into quarters occupied by other unmarried youth.

Slave parents had to overcome many obstacles to hold their families together. Many succeeded in asserting some small measure of independence by securing additional food for their families by hunting small game and cultivating small gardens. Like other parents, they instructed their children in religious and cultural beliefs and trained them in various crafts. They also developed networks of extended kin that helped family members survive the material privations and harsh treatment under slavery and the chaotic economic conditions that followed them into freedom after the Civil War.

TABLE 1.1

Naming Practices among the Stirling Plantation Slaves, West Feliciana Parish, Louisiana, 1808–1865

Date of Birth	Name of Newborn	Name of Parents	Relation of Newborn to Person with Same Name
1808	Leven	Big Judy–Leven	Father
1833	Julius	Dolly–Sidney	Father's father
1836	Ginny	Clarice–John	Mother's mother
1837	Hannah	Liddy–Luke	Mother's sister
1839	Barika	Nelly	Mother's husband (stepfather)
1846	Antoinette	Henrietta	Mother's sister's son (dead)
1846	Hester	Harriet–Sam	Father's sister
1853	Monday	Sophy–Sampson	Father's brother
1865	Duncan	Antoinette–Primus	Dead sibling

Source: Adapted from Herbert G. Gutman, 1976, "The Black Family," *Slavery and Freedom, 1750–1925* (New York: Vintage Books): 119–21.

Extended Kinship Patterns According to Gutman (1976), strong kinship feelings among slaves are evident from the naming practices of slave families. Table 1.1 shows that slave parents frequently named their children after fathers, grandparents, recently deceased relatives, and other kin. Gutman believed this kin network was especially important in helping slaves adapt to family breakup. When children were sold to neighboring plantations, any blood relative living there took over parental functions. In the absence of such relatives, strangers assumed these responsibilities. Slave children were taught to call all adult slaves "aunt" and "uncle" and younger slaves "sister" and "brother," practices that created a sense of mutual obligation and responsibility among the broader slave population. Later, these naming practices enabled scholars to trace descendants of slave families.

Free African American Families

Prior to the Civil War, there were approximately 250,000 free African Americans in the United States. About 150,000 lived in the South, and the remaining 100,000 lived in the North (Mintz and Kellogg, 1988). Many slaves freed themselves by running away; others were freed by slaveholders after the American Revolution. A few managed to buy their own freedom. Freedom, however, did not mean full integration into the larger society. In many communities, both in the North and South, free African Americans were not allowed to vote, hold public meetings, purchase liquor, marry whites, or attend white churches and schools. Although some men were able to earn a livelihood as carpenters, shoemakers, tailors, and millwrights, most lived in conditions of extreme poverty (Berlin, 1974).

Most free African American families were structured around two-parent households. Nevertheless, as today, inadequate family income, high levels of unemployment, illness, and early death put considerable strain on these families. One study found, for example, that in Philadelphia during the nineteenth century, between one-fourth and one-third of the city's African Americans lived in female-headed households, a figure two to three times higher than that for other groups in the city. This differential is explained by two factors. First, slaveholders tended to free women rather than men. Employment opportunities were better for women than men in urban areas, as whites sought black women to be domestic servants, cooks, nurses, and seamstresses. Many fathers remained slaves and could not migrate with their families. Consequently, free African American women outnumbered men in urban areas. Second, then as now, life expectancy was lower for African Americans, especially for men, leaving many women widowed by their 40s. When property holdings are held constant, however, the higher incidence of one-parent families among African Americans largely disappears, revealing the significant impact of economic factors on family stability (Mintz and Kellogg, 1988:78–79).

SLAVERY'S HIDDEN LEGACY: RACIAL MIXING

Rumors about a sexual liaison between Thomas Jefferson, the third president of the United States, and his young slave, Sally Hemings, circulated during his lifetime but were not responded to by Jefferson. Hemings, who was born in 1772 or 1773, was the illegitimate half-sister of Jefferson's wife Martha—the offspring of a relationship between Martha's father, John Wayles, and a slave, Elizabeth Hemings. For almost two centuries, most white historians debunked the notion of Jefferson's fathering a child with a slave, citing his negative views on racial mixing and his moral stature. As a result of their own cultural biases, some of these historians ignored corroborating evidence and discredited the strong oral tradition attesting to the relationship that was passed down through Hemings's descendants. However, recent DNA tests performed on the descendants of the families of Thomas Jefferson and Sally Hemings have illuminated a hidden legacy of slavery—the common biological heritage of many whites and African Americans. These test results, reported in the prestigious journal *Nature* (1998), offer compelling new evidence that Jefferson fathered at least one of Hemings's children, her last son, known as Eston Hemings Jefferson. Eston, who was said to have borne a striking resemblance to Thomas Jefferson, was freed by Jefferson in his will and moved first to Ohio, where he worked as a professional musician, and then to Madison, Wisconsin, where he lived his life as a member of the white community. Three other surviving Hemings children were allowed to leave the plantation, and at least two of them, like Eston, are believed to have blended into white society, leaving behind numerous descendants who even today are unlikely to suspect that their ancestry is either African or presidential (Murray and Duffy, 1998).

In an effort to deepen conversations about race, Pennsylvania State University Sociology Professor Samuel Richards gave his students the opportunity to take a DNA test to determine their genetic ancestry. Many of the students who volunteered to take the test were surprised by the results. A 20-year-old light-skinned student who always thought of himself as black was surprised to see results showing him to be 52 percent African and 48 percent European. He then recalled a great-grandfather who was so fair, he could pass as white. Another student, a 21-year-old public relations major, always thought of herself as half black and half white because her mother is Irish–Lithuanian and her father West Indian. She said, "Some people think it's funny that I consider myself Irish and celebrate St. Patrick's Day because no matter how you cut it, when you look at me you don't think, there goes a white girl." Yet she was surprised at her test results that showed her to be 58 percent European and 42 percent African American (Daly, 2005). As Professor Richards's students discussed their test results, they found

Descendants of third president Thomas Jefferson and descendants of his slave, Sally Hemings, pose for a group shot at his plantation in 1999 for the first time in 170 years during the Monticello Association's annual meeting in Charlottesville, Virginia.

that their family experiences mirrored that of many other Americans. As more historians trace African American and white families across time, the more likely we are to discover common biological roots. For example, Edward Ball (1998/1999), a white man remembering the childhood stories his father told him of his rice planter ancestors in South Carolina, set out in search of his family history. Through his painstaking research of family and community records across the country, he was able to track down many descendants of Ball slaves and coax them into telling the oral traditions of their families, which revealed much about the lives of blacks and whites of earlier generations. After the publication of his *Slaves in the Family*, he was contacted by other Ball slave descendants and discovered that he, too, shared common ancestry with them.

What the DNA tests cannot answer, and what is frequently missing from narratives of biological mixing, is the nature of the intimate relationship between the races. It was certainly true that slaveholders legally could, and frequently did, sexually assault and rape their slaves. Even many years after slavery was abolished white men could easily take advantage of black women. In 2003, Essie Mae Washington-Williams, a 78-year-old retired school teacher, revealed that she was the daughter of the late U.S. Senator Strom Thurmond of South Carolina. In 1925, the year she was born, her mother, Carrie Butler, was a 16-year-old maid in the Thurmond family home where the then 22-year-old Thurmond lived with his parents. An aunt took Essie Mae to live in Pennsylvania when she was 6 months old. She did not meet Thurmond until returning to South Carolina for a funeral in 1941 when she was 16. Thurmond, the longest-serving senator in U.S. history, ran for president in 1948 on the ticket of the States Rights Party that believed strongly in racial segregation and opposed civil rights legislation. Although he never acknowledged his daughter in his lifetime, he did meet with her on a number of occasions and provided her with some financial support. Although we know that the Butler–Thurmond relationship was one that involved unequal power, we do not know whether it involved any emotional intimacy. However, evidence in the Jefferson–Hemings case points more in the direction of a caring and loving relationship than an openly abusive or exploitive one. That members of different racial and ethnic groups can and do have happy and successful marital relationships can be seen by examining current interracial marriages, a subject we will discuss in more detail in Chapter 8.

Native American Families

A review of the literature on family life among early Native American peoples reveals that no one description adequately covers all Native American families. Prior to European settlement of North America, Native American peoples were widely dispersed geographically. As a result, each group developed an economic system, a style of housing, and a kinship system that fit the demands of its particular environment. Even those groups living in the same region of the country were likely to develop different organizational patterns (Mintz and Kellogg, 1988). For example, there were

Although education and economic development have provided a middle-class lifestyle for some Native Americans, many others continue to experience high levels of poverty and unemployment.

two basic language groups among the Woodland groups living in the Northeast: the Algonquin and the Iroquois. The social and economic unit of the Algonquins was a dome-shaped structure called a *wigwam*, usually occupied by one or two families. In contrast, the basic social unit of the Iroquois was the *longhouse*, a large, rectangular structure containing about ten families.

Among groups living in the Southeast, social life centered around the extended family. After marriage, the new husband went to live in his wife's family's household. For many tribes living in what is now California, however, that pattern was reversed, and the wife moved in with her husband's family after marriage. The basic economic unit for the Eskimos who inhabited the Arctic regions was either a family composed simply of wife, husband, and children or a household containing two such families.

Rules of Marriage and Descent Native American women married early, many between the ages of 12 and 15. Men were usually several years older than women when they married. There was considerable variation in mate selection among different groups. Some permitted free choice, whereas others practiced arranged marriages. The rules of marriage also varied from one group to another. Although most Native American peoples practiced monogamy, some were polygamous. Unhappy marriages were easily dissolved in some groups, with either spouse able to divorce the other. Among some peoples, special practices governed widowhood. In the *sororate*, a widower married a sister of his deceased wife; in the *levirate*, a widow married one of her dead husband's brothers.

Rules of descent also varied among Native American societies. Some societies, like that of the Cheyenne, were **patrilineal**, whereby kinship or family lineage (descent) and inheritance come through the father and his blood relatives. Others, like that of the Pueblos, were **matrilineal**, whereby kinship or family lineage (descent) and inheritance come through the mother and her blood relatives.

Historical records indicate that Native American families were generally small. Infant and child mortality were high. Additionally, mothers nursed their children for two or more years and refrained from sexual intercourse until the child was weaned. In contrast to early European families, Native American parents rarely used physical punishment to discipline their children. Instead, they relied on praise, ridicule, and public rewards to instill desired behavior. Among some groups, child care was in the hands of mothers; among others, fathers and maternal uncles played a more significant role. From early on, children worked alongside their parents and other adults to learn the skills that would be required of them as adults.

Consequences of European Contact One of the first consequences of contact with Europeans was a sharp increase in mortality rates. Native Americans lacked immunity to the diseases carried by white settlers. Consequently, thousands died from influenza, measles, smallpox, and typhoid fever. And although some of the early contact between the two groups was friendly and characterized by mutual exchanges of goods and services, the clash of cultural differences soon dominated intergroup contacts. Europeans found it difficult to understand and even harder to appreciate the diverse patterns of family life that existed among Native Americans. Ethnocentrism, the belief that one's culture is superior to others, led the Europeans to denigrate the lifestyles of Native Americans and to treat them as subhuman. This inability and unwillingness to accept Native American culture as valid, combined with the introduction of firearms and alcohol and the ever-increasing competition for land, led to violent clashes between the two groups. In the end, many Native Americans were displaced from their homelands and forced onto reservations, where many of their cultural values and practices were systematically undermined. Other Native Americans "disappeared" into the larger population, publicly not acknowledging their ancestry. This changed somewhat in 1990, when large numbers of young adult Native Americans living in large cities suddenly appeared in the census count. This development has been attributed to the popularity of movies like *Dances with Wolves* that portrayed Native Americans in a positive light, as well as the ongoing struggle of many tribes to revitalize their culture and build a strong economic base for their members.

FAMILIES IN THE NINETEENTH CENTURY

Major changes occurred in the United States at the beginning of the nineteenth century, radically transforming family life. New technology brought about the creation of the factory system, which required a concentrated supply of labor away from the home. Wage labor took the place of working private family farms or shops as the main means of earning a living. The patriarchal preindustrial household no longer functioned as a unit of economic production. Consequently, it grew smaller in size as apprentices and other live-in laborers gradually left to find work in the new factories. Over time the nuclear family of only parents and children became

the new family form, a form that has lasted well into the twentieth century. Work and family became separated, leading to the development of a division of family labor that divided the sexes and the generations from each other in new and far-reaching ways. These changes did not affect all families in the same way, however. There were significant variations across race and class.

Emergence of the Good Provider Role

In the opening stages of industrialization, women and children worked in the factories. After that period, however, men became the predominant workers in the factories, mines, and businesses of the nation. According to sociologist Jessie Bernard (1984), a specialized male role known as the *good provider* emerged around 1830. The essence of this role was that a man's major contribution to his family is economic, that is, as primary (and often sole) wage earner. Masculinity became identified with being a successful breadwinner (Demos, 1974). To be a success in the breadwinning role men had to concentrate their energies on work, and other roles, such as husband, father, and community member, became less important. Consequently, husbands and fathers were often emotionally as well as physically distant from their families. More and more, a man's status and therefore that of his family, depended on his occupation. A man's success was measured by whether he could afford to keep his wife and children out of the labor force.

The Cult of Domesticity

The movement of production out of the household affected the roles of women, too. Although from the beginning of U.S. history women were encouraged to think of themselves primarily in a domestic role, as industrialization advanced this ideology became even more prevalent. Now women were expected to stay at home, have children, and be the moral guardians of the family. This *cult of domesticity*, or as historian Barbara Welter (1978) called it, the "cult of true womanhood," was the counterpart to the good provider role. If men were to spend long hours working away from home, then women would offer men emotional support, provide for their daily needs, raise the children, and, in short, create for men a "haven in a heartless world" (Lasch, 1977). Aspects of this domestic role were oppressive and limiting for women, who by and large were excluded from most institutional life outside the family.

Changing Views of Childhood

The economic transformation that took place in the early nineteenth century altered not only marital roles but also children's roles. Childhood came to be seen as a distinct period, a time of innocence and play without much responsibility. Children no longer had to begin productive work at an early age. Instead, they became economic dependents. During this time, children's birthdays became occasions to celebrate, and the first specialty toy stores for children were opened. For the first time, books written especially for children were published, and other books were targeted for mothers to give them guidance about child rearing.

The Impact of Class and Ethnicity

The family lifestyle just described applied primarily to white middle- and upper-class families, in which the father made a "family wage" that enabled him to support his entire family. In contrast, large numbers of African American, immigrant, and native-born white working-class men found it impossible to support their families on their income alone. Thus, the working-class family did not embrace the ideal of privacy and separate spheres of a nuclear unit to the same degree that the middle class did. Working-class family boundaries were more fluid. Between 1850 and 1880, the number of extended families among the urban, industrial, immigrant working class increased (Coontz, 1988:306).

Additionally, working-class family life, both for blacks and whites, did not develop in isolation from the community. Alleys, stoops, gangways, and streets functioned as common areas where adults could socialize, exchange information, and observe their children at play. Contrary to many stereotypes of working-class families, there was no simple or rigid gender differentiation in these activities. In fact, "in the 1880s, when the first modern investigations of working-class family life were undertaken by the Massachusetts Bureau of Labor Statistics, one of the findings that most shocked and dismayed the middle-class male investigators was that working-class men would cook, clean, and care for the children while their wives were at work and they were not" (quoted in Coontz, 1988:306).

Immigration and Family Life

Many working-class families in the nineteenth century were immigrants. Between 1830 and 1930, over 30 million immigrants left their homes to come to the United States. The first wave of immigrants was predominantly from Northern and Western Europe—England, Germany, Ireland, and Scandinavia. Beginning in the early 1880s, immigration patterns shifted to Southern and Eastern Europe—Italy, Greece, Austria, Hungary, and Russia. Historians refer to the Slavs, Italians, Greeks, and Eastern European Jews who came to the United States at this time as the "new" immigrants. Frequently, the decision to emigrate followed economic or political upheavals. At the same time, immigrants were attracted to the United States by the promise of land and jobs.

The manner of emigration varied. Some immigrants, especially the Italians, Poles, and Slavs, came without families, planning to return home after making their fortunes. A Polish folk song conveys the enormity of disruption such families experienced when the father returned after several years: "There my wife was waiting for me. And my children did not know me. For they fled from me, a stranger. My dear children I'm your papa; three long years I have not seen you" (quoted in Daniels, 1990:219). Other unaccompanied immigrants hoped to earn enough to send for their families. Still others came with their families and

planned to settle permanently in the United States. To help ease their problems of adjustment, these new arrivals, whether alone or with families, sought out family, friends, or neighbors from their native country who were already settled here.

All immigrant groups faced a common set of problems: language barriers, periodic unemployment, difficulties in finding shelter, inadequate income, and often hostility from native-born workers, who feared the immigrants would take their jobs and lower the overall wage scale. Each group of immigrants developed distinct family and work patterns in response to these problems. At the same time, immigrants shared many common experiences with native-born members of the working class. Among the most serious of these was the need to have more than one breadwinner so that they could make ends meet.

The Economic Roles of Women and Children

Women and children in the working class contributed to the material support of the family in a variety of ways. Overall, a working-class wife did not work outside the home unless her spouse lost his job or was unable to work because of illness or injury. Maintaining a household was a full-time job. Working-class wives grew some of their own food, baked bread, carried water and wood for cooking and heating, managed the family finances, and coordinated the schedules of working members. Additionally, wives often supplemented family income by taking in boarders or by doing laundry or sewing in their homes. Working outside the home was more common among first-generation immigrant women whose husbands earned less than their native-born counterparts. The choice of occupation varied among ethnic groups. For example, Polish women chose domestic work over factory work, whereas the opposite pattern was true for Jewish women (Coontz, 1988).

Working-class children did not experience the luxury of a playful childhood. Children were employed in factories by the age of 8. Even though children and women worked as hard and as long as men, often in unhealthful and unsafe environments, they were paid considerably lower wages than men. "Until the end of the nineteenth century, women customarily received about one-third to one-half of the prevailing male wage, a sum seldom sufficient even for a single woman to support herself" (Kessler-Harris, 1981:62).

Ethnic and Racial Family Patterns

Racism and discrimination also made a profound difference in how work and family roles were constructed. For example, although immigrant Chinese males were recruited to build the railroads of America, they were not allowed to build families. The Chinese Exclusion Act of 1882 restricted Chinese immigration and thus restricted Chinese women from joining the men already here. "From 1860 to 1890 the sex ratio fluctuated from 1284 to 2679 Chinese men per 100 Chinese women" (Wong, 1988:235). Faced with this unbalanced sex ratio and prevented by law from marrying whites, single Chinese laborers were destined to remain bachelors if they stayed in the United States. Married Chinese laborers,

Sojourner Truth, born a slave in Ulster County, New York, was sold four times before she was 30 years old. She obtained her freedom in 1827. An electrifying public speaker, she became a forceful advocate for human rights for all people.

who were required to leave their families behind, could play the good provider role only minimally by sending money home to China. Sociologist Evelyn Nakano Glenn (1983) called this pattern of maintenance the "split-household family system."

With the end of slavery, black men, like white men, preferred that their wives remain at home. African American men had difficulties finding jobs, however, and the jobs they did find tended to pay very poorly. Thus, these men could not afford to keep their wives and daughters from working. "In 1900 approximately 41 percent of black women were in the labor force, compared with 16 percent of white women" (quoted in Staples, 1988:307). Sojourner Truth, a former slave, speaking as far back as 1851 at a women's rights convention in Akron, Ohio, eloquently addressed the exclusion of African American women from the "cult of true womanhood."

> That man over there says that women need to be helped into carriages, and lifted over ditches, and to have the best place everywhere. Nobody ever helps me into carriages, or over mud puddles, or gives me any best place! And ain't I a woman? Look at me! Look at my arm! I have ploughed and planted, and gathered into barns and no man could head me! And ain't I a woman? I could work as much as a man—when I could get it—and bear the lash as well! And ain't I a woman? I have borne thirteen children, and seen them most all sold off to slavery, and when I cried out with my mother's grief, none but Jesus hear me! And ain't I a woman? (Quoted in Schneir, 1972:94–95)

Mexican American Families

Similarly, Chicanos (Mexican Americans) were rarely able to exercise the good provider or domestic roles exclusively either. After the Mexican–American War in 1848, the United States annexed a considerable amount of Mexico's territory, an area that encompasses present-day Texas, New Mexico, Arizona, and California. The Mexicans who lived within this new region were granted U.S. citizenship and the right to retain ownership of their land by the Treaty of Guadalupe Hidalgo. Through the unscrupulous practices of some Anglos, however, many of the original Chicano landowners soon lost their land. The erosion of the Chicano agrarian economic base had a profound impact on Mexican American family life.

Family and Kinship One of the most distinctive features of the Chicano family was its emphasis on familism, "a constellation of values which give overriding importance to the family and the needs of the collective as opposed to individual and personal needs" (Bean, Curtis, and Marcum, 1977:760). Although the primary family unit was nuclear and patriarchal in form, there was heavy reliance on extended kinship networks for emotional and economic support. Another centuries-old source of support was the ritual kinship of *compadrazgo*, which linked two families together. Within this system, *madrinas*, or godmothers, and *padrinos*, or godfathers, were carefully chosen from outside the kinship circle to become members of the extended family, participating in all the major events of their godchildren's lives. In effect, they assumed the role of *compadres*, or coparents, providing discipline, companionship for both parents and godchildren, emotional support, and when needed, financial aid (Griswold del Castillo, 1984).

Marital Roles Chicano households tended to be large. In part this was due to a high fertility rate, but households also expanded in response to economic privation as kin and unrelated individuals, especially children, were taken in by other families. Households practiced a fairly rigid division of labor based on gender. Wives were expected to stay home and take responsibility for domestic chores and child rearing. They were also expected to be the carriers of cultural traditions and to organize celebrations of important rituals, such as baptisms, weddings, saints' days, and funerals.

In contrast, men were expected to protect and control their families and to perform productive work outside the household. This traditional male role is sometimes referred to as *machismo*. Although some writers have called attention to the negative aspects of this role, such as male infidelity and oppression of women (Madsen, 1964), most contemporary social scientists believe these aspects have been exaggerated. More recent research tends to focus on what has been called a "genuine machismo," characterized by bravery, courage, and generosity (Mirande, 1985).

Signs of Change White settlers bought up large tracts of land in the Southwest and instituted commercial agricultural production. The displaced Chicanos became a source of cheap labor. Much of this work was seasonal, and men experienced periodic unemployment. At times, men migrated in search of jobs in the mines or on the railroads. As a result, their wives became heads of families, sometimes on a permanent basis as a result of prolonged separation, divorce, or more frequently, desertion. Even when men worked full-time, their wages were often insufficient to support their families. Consequently, wives and mothers were drawn into the labor force, most frequently in low-paying domestic or agriculture-related work, such as canning and packing house work. Kinship structures were weakened as entire families left the area to find work. With the entrance of wives into the labor force and the frequent migration of families outside their familiar cultural area, the foundation of the patriarchal family structure began to erode. Working wives demanded more power in decision making, and by the twenty-first century a new balance in gender relations was already being observed. Like other families before them, the Chicano family was realigning itself.

FAMILIES IN THE TWENTIETH CENTURY

Although applicable only to certain groups, these idealized images of men as providers and women as homemakers continued to influence popular thought about the family well into the twentieth century. However, economic and political changes were already at work to undermine these roles. Technological innovations led to the mass production of goods and to the development of large-scale corporations. These developments affected almost every aspect of social relationships.

In this new work environment, the demand for child labor declined, and schools assumed more of the responsibility for the socialization of children. Young working-class women increasingly left domestic service for better opportunities in industry and in the expanding clerical fields. As a result, social contacts increasingly took place outside the family as women and men worked in proximity to each other. New products, such as movies, amusement parks, and the automobile, changed family recreation patterns. Young adults dated without chaperones and placed more emphasis on personal and sexual attractiveness. Women, dissatisfied with the restrictions of their domestic role, became activists for women's rights, particularly the right to vote.

The Emergence of the Companionate Family

These changes gradually led to a shift away from the nineteenth-century ideal of the family. In its place emerged the idea of a more personal and companionate model for heterosexual relationships, based on mutual affection, sexual fulfillment, and sharing of domestic tasks and child rearing. Personal happiness came to be viewed as the primary goal of marriage. New symbols—the observance of Mother's Day, for example—were created to celebrate family life. Although economic and social inequalities persisted across groups, this new model of the family took hold, and many of the distinct cultural differences among families began to disappear.

Other changes were helping reshape families. Medical advances reduced the rate of infant mortality so that couples felt less pressure to have large families to ensure the survival of some children. Life expectancy had increased. Thus, families were less likely to be disrupted by the premature death of spouses. In the short span of 40 years, from 1900 to 1940, the chances of a marriage lasting 40 or more years increased from one in three to one in two (Mintz and Kellogg, 1988:131).

There was another side to these changes in family life, however. As more people came to expect companionship and emotional fulfillment in marriage, they also became more willing to terminate an unhappy relationship. In a manner reminiscent of today's controversy over "family values," people in the 1920s and 1930s disagreed over the significance of these changes. Some saw the increase in the divorce rate, the decline in the birth rate, the increase in the number of married-women workers, and the change in sexual behavior as a sign of family disintegration and a breakdown of moral values. Others, however, interpreted these same patterns as signs of greater freedom of choice and as a continuing response to changing economic and social conditions in the larger society.

The Great Depression

In the 1930s, families were rocked by an economic crisis of staggering proportions. Millions of workers throughout the country were unemployed for periods of one to three years or longer. The consequences of joblessness were enormous. Some families became homeless and wandered from city to city in hopes of finding food and shelter; other families were forced to share living quarters. Young adults delayed marriage, couples postponed having children, and the number of desertions increased. The depression affected all members of the family, but it undermined the male breadwinner role in particular. This inability to support their families eroded the self-esteem of many fathers. Growing numbers of women became the major source of family income. Although all groups suffered economic hardships during the depression, the elderly, the poor, and those in low-paying, unskilled jobs—predominantly people of color—were hardest hit. Family stability was often a casualty of economic instability.

The severe problems confronting millions of families led to a shift in thinking about the family. No longer could the myth of the self-reliant family be sustained. Clearly, outside support was necessary if families were to weather the economic upheavals. The government responded to the depression by creating a series of social programs, known collectively as the New Deal, to aid distressed workers and their families.

World War II and Its Aftermath

No sooner was the depression over than another major upheaval confronted families. World War II brought about numerous changes—primary among them was the dramatic increase in the marriage rate. Between 1940 and 1946, it is estimated that 3 million more Americans married than would have been expected had rates remained at prewar levels (Bailey, 1978:51). There were many reasons for this upsurge. Some couples had postponed marriage because of the depression and were now financially able to marry. Others feared that if they did not marry now, it might prove too late later on. Some servicemen, fearing death in battle, asked women to marry them "to give them some happiness before going off to fight." Similarly, there was a dramatic increase in the birth rate as many couples decided to have a child right away.

Millions of families were disrupted by wartime migration to find work and by long-term separations for military service. These disruptions resulted in changes in family roles and functioning. With husbands and fathers off to war, wives, mothers, and teenagers went to work in war-related industries. During the war years, 250,000 women worked in plants manufacturing electrical equipment; 100,000 worked in ammunition plants; 300,000 built airplanes; and 150,000 worked as riveters, welders, and crane operators in the nation's shipyards (cited in Mintz and Kellogg, 1988:161). "Rosie the Riveter" became a popular image of the woman factory worker. These changes made conditions difficult for families. Although some preschool children were cared for in government-sponsored day-care centers, many mothers had to find child care on their own. As raw materials were diverted to support the war effort, many families faced shortages in housing and other consumer goods.

Although the majority of families experienced some dislocation during the war years, this experience was most intense for Japanese Americans on the West Coast, who were forcibly relocated from their homes to detention centers in isolated regions of several western states. This massive relocation was inspired by fear, prejudice, and economic jealousy, and resulted in depression, deprivation, and often family conflicts among the detainees.

Problems did not end with the cessation of hostilities. Families that had been separated for several years had enormous adjustments to make. Many reunited couples were like strangers to each other. Spouses had grown in different ways. Wives who had assumed both the financial and the economic responsibilities for their families had experienced a sense of independence, self-confidence, and self-sufficiency that was often at odds with their husbands' desire to return to a traditional family arrangement. Postwar housing shortages contributed to family strain as newly reunited couples found themselves living with other relatives in overcrowded conditions. Children who spent some of the war years as "latchkey" kids, taking care of themselves while their mothers worked, resented the new imposition of parental discipline. Many families were unable to survive the tensions and hardships created by the war and its aftermath. Divorce rates soared. In 1940, one marriage in six had ended in divorce; by 1946 the figure stood at one in four (cited in Mintz and Kellogg, 1988:171).

Changing Patterns of Immigration

After World War II, political and economic turmoil around the world led many other groups to leave their homelands in search of a better life. For example, the number of foreign-born people in the United States jumped from 10.3 million in 1950 to 19.7 million in 1990, increasing from nearly 7 percent of the population to about 8 percent. From 1990 to 2003, additional immigration brought the total to 33.4 million, approximately 11.7 percent of the population (U.S. Census Bureau, 2004–2005). Although historically most immigrants to the United States came from Europe, today more than half (53 percent) come from Latin America, 25 percent from Asia, but only 14 percent from Europe. Included in the newer arrivals are approximately 4 million immigrant and second-generation Muslims. Although some Muslims came to America with the Spanish in the late sixteenth century and some African Muslims were brought to America as slaves, the Muslim presence in the United States began to grow in the latter part of the twentieth century. Many Muslims came in response to the growing political and economic instability in the Middle East—the Arab–Israeli War in 1967, the Iranian Revolution of 1979, the Soviet invasion of Afghanistan, civil wars in Somalia and the Sudan, the ethnic cleansing in Bosnia and Kosovo, the 1991 Gulf War, and the American invasion of Iraq in 2003 (Maloof, 2003). These changing patterns of immigration have resulted in greater racial and ethnic diversity. Each group of immigrants arrived under different social and economic conditions, and each group brought some distinct family and kinship patterns. The frequent discrimination experienced by these newcomers forced many of them to adopt new survival strategies, often necessitating changes

During World War II, the image of Rosie the Riveter became popular. However, the ideology of women as men's helpmates had not changed, as evidenced in the language of this poster.

in their traditional patterns of family life. Current trends in immigration and differential patterns of fertility continue to change the composition of our population, adding to the rich diversity of family life in the United States.

Lessons from History

What lessons can we draw from this historical review? Five points seem relevant:

1. Although families have changed continuously over time, this change has not been in any single direction.
2. We cannot say with any certainty which changes have been good or bad. Rather, each change brings with it gains and losses. For example, the creation of childhood as a separate and distinct period created many opportunities for children's growth and development, but it also kept children dependent on parents for longer periods of time.
3. Throughout history there has never been a perfect family form that has protected its members from poverty or social disruption, nor has any one structure provided a workable model for how all families might organize their relations in the modern world.
4. Understanding the source of our idealized view of the "traditional" family can lead us to develop a more realistic sense of families, both in the past and in the present. Studying families in the past can help us see how they endured and adapted to historical changes. It also helps us realize that many of the changes we observe in contemporary families and that cause us concern, such as the increasing number of children living in poverty and unstable families, are not a result of changing family values, per se. Rather, they are more frequently reactions to rapid economic and social transformations taking place on an unprecedented scale. To take one example, within our lifetime we have witnessed the rise of a global economy, which has meant greater competition for the United States. Thus, today's families and the communities in which they live confront powerful forces that are redesigning and redistributing jobs, increasing inequality, and shifting population in and out of cities and regions across the country.

5. Given the past, it is likely that additional changes in family life will continue to occur as families continue to adapt to changing economic, social, and political forces. The more we understand these changes and their impact on families, the more likely we can develop social policies to assist families in adapting to these changes. We will explore these themes throughout the remainder of the text.

CONTEMPORARY PATTERNS IN MARRIAGES AND FAMILIES

Given this review of the history of families in the United States, today's patterns may seem more a continuation of trends rather than a startling new phenomenon. For example, over the last hundred years there has been a steady increase in the number of mothers of small children who are in the labor force (see Chapter 10) and in the percentage of couples who divorce before their children reach adulthood (Chapter 12).

In tracking these changes, the U.S. Census Bureau distinguishes between households and families. **Households** are defined as all persons who occupy a housing unit, such as a house, apartment, single room, or other space intended to be living quarters (Ahlburg and DeVita, 1992:5). Figure 1.2 reveals some of the changes in U.S. households between 1970 and 2003. One of the most significant changes is the increase in nonfamily households, which grew from 19 percent of all households in 1970 to 32 percent in 2003. According to the U.S. Census Bureau, nonfamily households are made up of individuals living alone; people of the same sex who share living quarters, often for financial reasons; cohabiting couples; adults who delay or forgo marriage; or those who are "between marriages."

Additional information on households and other marriage and family patterns can easily be accessed by visiting the U.S. Census Bureau Web site (www.census.gov). As the Internet Resources: Applying the Sociological Imagination box shows, households are getting smaller and the proportion of households consisting of one person living alone is

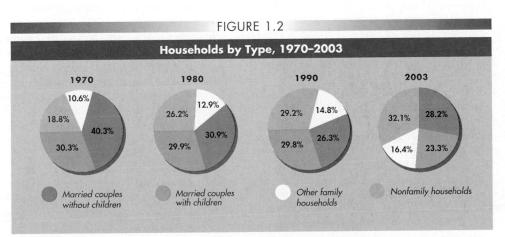

FIGURE 1.2

Households by Type, 1970–2003

Source: Adapted from J. Fields, 2004, "America's Families and Living Arrangements: March 2003," U.S. Census Bureau, *Current Population Reports*, Series P-20-537 (Washington, DC: U.S. Government Printing Office): 4, Figure 2.

APPLYING THE SOCIOLOGICAL IMAGINATION
U.S. Adults Postponing Marriage

- In the past three decades, the proportion of those who had never married doubled for women aged 20–24, from 36 to 75 percent, and more than tripled for women aged 30–34, from 6 to 23 percent.

- In 2003, 10 percent of the nation's households contained five or more people, down from 21 percent in 1970. Sixty percent of households had one or two people in 2003, up from 46 percent in 1970.

- The proportion of households consisting of one person living alone increased from 17 percent in 1970 to 26 percent in 2003.

- Between 1970 and 2003, the number of single mothers increased from 3 million to 10.1 million and then number of single factors increased from 393,000 to 2.3 million.

Begin with this Web page and then connect to other links on the census bureau

Web site to find out as much information as you can regarding the composition of households in the United States, comparing your generation with that of your parents'. What similarities and differences did you find between the experiences of the two generations? How do the data compare across race and ethnic groups? How do you account for these findings? http://www.census.gov/Press-Release/www/releases/archives//families_households/003118.html.

---

increasing. Individuals are delaying marriage for longer periods of time. Twenty-three percent of women aged 30–34 have never married, up from 6 percent in 1970. In addition, the number of single parents has increased dramatically. The number of single mothers rose from 3 million in 1970 to 10.1 million by 2003. During that same period, the number of single fathers climbed from 393,000 to 2.3 million. Each of these patterns will be examined in detail in subsequent chapters.

LOOKING AHEAD: MARRIAGES AND FAMILIES IN THE FUTURE

As we discussed earlier, many changes occurred in the composition of families over the last three decades. For example, In 2003, 39 million family groups in the United States included children, up from 30 million in 1970. The number of two-parent family groups with children remained relatively stable at about 26 million, but their proportion of all family groups with children declined from 87 percent in 1970 to 69 percent in 1995, and remained fairly level at about 68 percent from 1996 to 2003 (Fields, 2004). Nevertheless, the concerns that many people raised about the viability and future of families remain on the public agenda. Much of the debate centers on questions regarding the form that families should take, the degree to which divorce harms children, and the degree to which same-sex marriages would undermine the meaning of families when the real challenge ahead is how to help all people construct and maintain marriages and families that provide personal satisfaction and that contribute to the general welfare of society. Meeting this challenge requires solving several structural problems: insufficient well-paying jobs, lack of health insurance, inadequate educational opportunities, poor health care, inadequate and costly day care for working parents, lack of resources to care for elderly relatives, inadequate housing, discrimination, and

unrealistic expectations about marriages and families. Additionally, millions of families throughout the world have and are experiencing enormous suffering, loss, and deprivations because of terrorist acts and racial, ethnic, and religious conflicts. We will discuss how these structural factors and widespread violence both on local and international levels impact marriages and families throughout the remainder of this textbook.

THE SOCIOLOGICAL IMAGINATION

This brief review of the history of the family in the United States reveals an ongoing pattern of diversity and change. Sociologist C. Wright Mills (1959) observed that in an age of rapid change, ordinary people often feel overwhelmed by the events confronting them, feeling that their private lives are a series of traps over which they have little control. They feel that cherished values are being replaced with ambiguity and uncertainty. Mills argued that people can counter this sense of frustration and powerlessness and come to understand their own experiences by locating themselves within their historical period. By this he meant that we can understand our own life chances by becoming aware of those of all individuals in our same circumstances. Thus, Mills called on us to develop a **sociological imagination** to grasp history and biography and the relations between the two within our society. To do this requires asking three questions: (1) What is the structure of a particular society, and how does it differ from other varieties of social order? (2) Where does this society stand in human history, and what are its essential features? (3) What varieties of women and men live in this society and in this period, and what is happening to them?

The sociological imagination allows us to distinguish between what Mills called "personal troubles of milieu" and the "public issues of social structure." A "trouble" is a private matter, occurring within the character of the individual and within the range of her or his immediate relationship with others. An "issue," however, is a public matter that transcends the local environment of the individual. For example, any couple may experience personal troubles in their marriage, but the fact that in recent years approximately 1 million divorces occurred annually is an indication of a structural issue having to do with the institution of marriage and the family and with the other societal institutions that affect them. Mills argued that many of the events we experience are caused by structural changes. Thus, to understand the changes that affect our personal lives, we must look beyond our private experiences to examine the larger political, social, and economic issues that affect our lives and the lives of others in our society.

Although applying the sociological perspective offers many benefits, four general ones stand out: (1) It allows us to take a new and critical look at what we have always taken for granted or assumed to be true, (2) it allows us to see the vast range of human diversity, (3) it allows us to understand the constraints and opportunities that affect our lives and those of other people; and (4) it enables us to participate more actively in society (Macionis, 1991). Throughout the remainder of this textbook, we will stress the application of the sociological imagination in everyday life, focusing on social structure: How cultural values, historical context, economic and political changes, and various social-structural variables and social systems, such as race, class, gender, sexual orientation, and age, interact and affect the personal experiences of individuals and groups as they create, sustain, and change their marriages and families.

WRITING YOUR OWN SCRIPT

A course on the sociology of marriages and families usually invokes concern and interest among students about how the general principles and descriptions in the textbook apply to their own lives. As you have seen in the discussion of the sociological imagination, a guiding theme in the discipline of sociology is that individual lives are influenced, patterned, and shaped by large and powerful social forces beyond the control of any one individual. At the same time, individuals are not passive in this process. Individuals act in ways that influence these larger social forces. Therefore, there is a connection between our own personal and private experiences and the culture, society, groups, marriages, and families to which we belong. In this textbook, we stress the application of the sociological imagination in everyday life. That is, we stress the personal relevance of the topics, issues, and concerns addressed in this book with the goal of helping you, the reader, fully appreciate the connection between yourself (the individual) and society. In this context, we present in each chapter a box entitled "Writing Your Own Script" to reinforce your knowledge of the sociological imagination and your ability to apply it.

Writing Your Own Script is simply an exercise that utilizes an everyday life approach to the study of marriages and families. It encourages you to become directly involved in the learning process by using your own personal experiences (and those of others you know) as a way of understanding and critically examining or evaluating both the commonly shared elements as well as the uniqueness of your own personal life. Throughout our lives, all of us are confronted with life events, living arrangements, and other activities about which we must make decisions. Some of the most important of these decisions are those concerning marriage and family living. One way of doing this is to keep a personal journal of your thoughts and reactions to the material presented in the text.

In the Writing Your Own Script exercises you are provided with a more formalized process for reflecting on and planning your own life script. As you complete each chapter of the book, you are in a good position to reflect, examine, and evaluate your feelings and desires regarding the life choices you have

WRITING YOUR OWN SCRIPT

DEFINE IT, AND KNOWLEDGE FOLLOWS*

As you have seen in this chapter, the structure and lifestyles of marriages and families are diverse. However, for many people in the United States today, family is still defined in very narrow terms. According to Joan Ferrante (1995), narrow social definitions enable narrow legal definitions to persist, and both such definitions can cause pain and deprivation, or simply discomfort, for individuals. Thinking about popular cultural definitions of the family, as well as narrow legal definitions, where do you and your family fit?

Write a brief sociological description of your family. Some questions or issues to pay particular attention to are the following: How do you define family? Think about your own family and the individual members. What or who constitutes family for you? Does your idea of family include distant cousins (third and beyond) and great-great-aunts and uncles? Does it include people who are not related to you by blood, adoption, or ancestry? Is your definition of family consistent with that of other family members? If not, how does it differ? Do you make a distinction between the notion of "family" and that of "kinship"? If yes, how so? What is the structure of your family? What are the typical marriage types in your family? Marriage eligibility customs? Residential patterns? Family power patterns? You might want to make a family tree, starting with yourself and going back as far as you can.

*The title of this box is borrowed from the ideas of Joan Ferrante (1992) concerning the power to define.

made or will be making over the course of your lifetime. You can select only those exercises or marriage and family issues that are of immediate concern to you, or you can do them all. The exercises correspond to key topics discussed in each chapter; therefore, it is important that you understand and refer back to the chapter, if necessary, as you think about your own life. Even if you have already made some decisions, such as getting married and having children, these exercises can give you added or new insight into how well your decision making worked and can perhaps suggest other areas where improvements can be made. The exercises can also simply help you understand your life experiences and those of others within the sociohistorical and political contexts in which they occur.

To be sure, what you do now (how you write your own script) is not written in stone. The Writing Your Own Script exercises are simply one method among many that allow you to understand your life and begin making informed choices by applying the sociological imagination. Some of these choices, like becoming a parent, are permanent, whereas others, such as entering into or dissolving a relationship, can be altered. In addition, we should realize that the choices we make at various stages of our lives may affect later options. For example, a decision to delay marriage or childbearing into our 30s or 40s may result in fewer, if any, options to engage in these behaviors at a later date.

To best utilize the Writing Your Own Script exercises, consider the following: (1) the factual information presented in each chapter, (2) the key life events and activities around which the Writing Your Own Script exercises are built, (3) the options available to you in each area of decision making; (4) the larger social forces that may affect the range of options available to you, (5) the possible positive and negative consequences (advantages or disadvantages) of each option, and (6) how social forces and your own personal values may interact to influence your choices and those of others.

SUPPORTING MARRIAGES AND FAMILIES

Over the centuries marriages and families have undergone many changes. For most of human history, marriage was a way of ensuring economic and political stability. The belief that young people could choose their own mates and should choose them on the basis of something like love, which had formerly been considered a tremendous threat to marriage,

is only about 200 years old. Historian Stephanie Coontz (2005) argues that once this belief took hold, it created new demands—demand for divorce, the right to refuse marriage, even recognition of same-sex relations. The view that the old rules for marriage are not working has led some social critics to argue that marriages are in crisis. Although Coontz agrees that marriage has been weakened as an institution in that it has lost its former monopoly over organizing sexuality, male–female relationships, legitimacy, and political, social, and economic rights, she disagrees with those who think we can return to some idealized image of marriages and families. Instead, she argues that the main things that have weakened marriage as an institution are the same things that have strengthened marriage as a relationship. Marriage is now more optional because women and men now have equal rights in marriage and more equal economic opportunities. Thus, on the one hand, people can negotiate a marriage, making it more flexible and individualized and giving it the potential to be fairer, happier, more satisfying, and more fulfilling than ever before. On the other hand, these same forces allow people to choose to stay single or to leave a marriage that is unsatisfactory. Coontz believes that the marriage revolution, like the Industrial Revolution, is irreversible and that we have to learn from both the opportunities and the problems this raises for us. We would add one more thing. If we are serious in our belief that marriages and families are the foundations of our society, then it is all of our responsibilities to see that couples and families have the tools and societal supports to help them build and sustain satisfying and meaningful relationships and family lifestyles. At the end of each of the remaining chapters, we will briefly consider some of the possible ways to support marriages and families. These can range from governmental action, professional advice, community organizations, individual activists, and even commercial products. One quick example: illness places a huge stress on marital and family life, all the more so when families lack health insurance to help defray the cost. Today over 45 million people, the majority of them young, are without health insurance. A number of states have responded by creating KidCare, to provide low-cost coverage for children under 19 and, in some states, pregnant women. Payment is based on family income and size. Although this has helped numerous children and families, many people are unaware of the program, and thus do not apply; often states lack resources sufficient to cover all those in need.

SUMMARY

Marriage and family are among the oldest human social institutions. Each society develops its own patterns of marriage and family life, and these patterns vary considerably across and within cultures. In recent years, family values have become a topic for debate in the United States. Such debates are often clouded by mythology about the way families used to be. Myths are false, fictitious, imaginary, or exaggerated beliefs that can create unrealistic expectations about what families can or should be. Four of the most pop-

ular myths and stereotypes directly applicable to current debates about family life and gender roles are (1) the universal nuclear family, (2) the self-reliant traditional family, (3) the naturalness of the separate spheres of wives and husbands, and (4) the unstable African American family.

The discussion of mythical versus real families underscores the fact that not all families are the same; there is not now and never has been a single model of the family. Families are a product of their historical context, and at any given historical period families occupy different territories and have varied experiences. Race, class, and gender are three inter-locking categories of social experience that affect all aspects of human life; they shape all social institutions and systems of meaning, including the institutions of marriage and family, and the discussion of family values.

From the very beginning, the United States was eco-nomically, racially, religiously, and familially diverse. Native Americans, white ethnic settlers, Africans forcibly brought to this country as slaves, and Chicanos whose land was annexed by the United States all struggled to create and maintain a stable family structure in a new and often hostile environment. Over time, these and other immigrant groups confronted powerful economic and political forces, such as

industrialization, depressions, and wars, which led to major transformations in family life.

A course on the sociology of marriages and families can help us develop a sociological imagination and facilitate our understanding of how many of the concepts and issues per-taining to marriage and family lifestyles apply in our own lives, and at the same time are linked to social structure and historical circumstance. One way to appreciate fully the connection between our own personal and private experi-ences and the culture, society, groups, marriages, and fami-lies to which we belong is to engage in "writing your own script"—a process for utilizing the sociological imagination to reflect on and plan your own life script.

KEY TERMS

institution	cenogamy (group marriage)	modified extended family	myth
marriage	family	patriarchal family	institutional racism
monogamy	family of orientation	norms	kinship
serial monogamy	family of procreation	social structure	patrilineal
polygamy	nuclear family	status	matrilineal
polygyny	extended (multigenera-	role	households
polyandry	tional) family	socialization	sociological imagination

QUESTIONS FOR STUDY AND REFLECTION

1. In this chapter we have described some of the major functions of families, historically and presently. Do any of these functions apply to your family experi-ences? Describe how you have experienced these functions within your family. Be specific. What other social institutions (e.g., schools, government, reli-gion) have served as vital social functions for you or your family members? What, conflicts, if any, have arisen as a result of your or your family's participa-tion in these social institutions?

2. What is meant by the idea that race, class, and gender are interactive systems rather than individual variables? Think about your own family of orientation, and take one particular aspect of your family life as an example. Discuss briefly how race, class, and gender act simulta-neously to shape that aspect of your family life.

3. Given the tremendous number of immigrants this country has had, it is likely that you, a relative, class-

mate, neighbor, or someone else you know has migrated to the United States. Interview that person, focusing on the reasons for coming and the ways in which that experience has affected her or his life. To what extent, if any, have that person's family patterns and structures been changed as she or he adjusted to life in the United States.

4. Most people agree that marriages and families under-went major changes during the last half of the twenti-eth century; however, few people link these changes to larger societal changes that have taken place. Identify some of the major changes that have taken place during the past 50 years (for example, in trans-portation, technology, and social welfare policies) and discuss their impact on contemporary marriages and families. Reflect on your own family and consider how one such change has affected your family and/or families like yours.

ADDITIONAL RESOURCES

SOCIOLOGICAL

Coontz, Stephanie, Maya Parson, and Gabrielle Raley, eds. 1999. *American Families: A Multicultural Reader,* Boston: Rout-ledge. This anthology consists of a variety of articles that illustrate the diversity of American family life. It underscores the point that there is no singular model of marriage and/or family.

Foner, Nancy, Ruben G. Rumbaut, and Steven J. Gold. 2000. *Immigration Research for a New Century: Multidisciplinary Perspectives,* New York: Russell Sage Foundation. This collection of essays explores the rich variety of the immigrant experience, ranging from itinerant farm workers to Silicon Valley engineers. It also provides the fresh insights of a new generation of immigration researchers.

HAWES, JOSEPH M., AND ELIZABETH I. NYBAKKEN, EDS. 2001. *Family and Society in American History,* Urbana and Champaign: University of Illinois Press. An illuminating range of articles examines the changes that have occurred in American families from the eighteenth to the twentieth century that accompanied evolving social, political, and economic changes.

GORDON-REED, ANNETTE, 1997. *Thomas Jefferson and Sally Hemings: An American Controversy,* Charlottesville: University Press of Virginia. This compelling work provides a meticulous review of the evidence surrounding the Jefferson–Hemings relationship.

FILM

Romeo and Juliet. 1996. This is a modern version of Shakespeare's classic story of two teenagers who secretly fall in love and marry, but whose love is doomed from the beginning because their families, the Montagues and Capulets, have been fierce enemies for decades.

In America. 2003. Based in part on Director Jim Sheridan's autobiographical experiences as an Irish immigrant father, it captures the emotional ups and downs of a family struggling to make a life in a strange, new land.

LITERARY

HURSTON, ZORA NEALE. 1978. *Their Eyes Were Watching God,* Urbana: University of Illinois Press. This novel chronicles a proud, independent African American woman's quest for identity, through three marriages, on a journey back to her roots. It is an excellent demonstration of the intersections of race, class, gender, and culture and its impact on identity, self-concept, and intimate relationships. (Originally pubished 1937.)

BLAKE, MICHAEL. 2001. *Dances with Wolves.* New York: Ballantine Books. Posted to a desolate and deserted western outpost, Civil War hero Lt. John Dunbar becomes intrigued by the culture of the buffalo-hunting Comanche of the Plains. Over time they come to understand each other and develop strong personal and familial bonds.

INTERNET

www.cdc.gov/nchs/nvss.htm The National Vital Statistics System provides data on births, marriages, divorces and deaths in the United States.

www.lii.org The Librarians' Index to the Internet provides a well-organized point of access for over 16,000 quality Web sites, including many having to do with marriage and family issues.

www.migrationinformation.org The Migration Information Source provides data from numerous global organizations and governments, including the United States, and analyzes international migration and refugee trends.

www.mayflowerfamilies.com On this Web site you can find information on early colonial and Native American families and links to historical records and documents as well as resources to help you build your own family tree.

2

WAYS OF STUDYING AND EXPLAINING
MARRIAGES AND FAMILIES

IN THE NEWS

Washington, DC

Today, more than ever before, with issues confronting American citizens ranging from HIV/AIDS to genetic engineering to food additives and climate change, we are dependent upon the impartial perspective of science for solutions to these and many other social and biological problems.

Politicians have long acknowledged that government policies on a wide range of issues have been informed by the application of impartial and objective scientific research and analysis. However, according to a number of recent reports, news, and scientific journal articles, ever since President George W. Bush took office in 2001, the scientific community has expressed a growing concern over what they describe as President Bush's politicization of science. Scientists, doctors, and other experts both inside and outside the government have accused President Bush and his administration of suppressing or outright distorting scientific and medical information and facts when it conflicts with their policy objectives and/or in order to bolster their political agenda in areas ranging from abstinence education and condom use to missile defense and the environment. For example, among the purported abuses of scientific research by the Bush administration documented in a 40-page report released in 2003 and compiled by the minority staff of the House Government Reform and Oversight Committee's special investigation division (hereafter referred to as the House Report), is the revelation that "performance measures" used to determine the effectiveness of federally funded *abstinence-only* sex education programs were altered by the administration in ways that made it easier to say that these programs were effective. In addition, information about how to use a condom—along with scientific data showing that sex education does not lead to earlier or increased sexual activity among young people—was removed from a Centers for Disease Control and Prevention Web site. Similarly, the administration altered a National Cancer Institute Web site in a way that wrongly implied that there was good evidence linking abortions to breast cancer (Weiss, 2003).

Furthermore, according to two scientists who contributed to a study on the environmental impact of cattle grazing, the Bush administration manipulated the study's scientific data prior to announcing that it would loosen regulations limiting grazing on public lands. In an interview with the *Los Angeles Times,* Erick Campbell, a biologist who wrote the sections of the research report that addressed the effects of the Bush administration's new rules on wildlife, accused the administration of totally rewriting and watering down everything he wrote to cater to ranching interests—"they took all of our science and reversed it 180 degrees" (Quoted in BushGreenwatch, 2005:1).

Examples of the administration's manipulation of or tampering with scientific research abound in a host of news articles and reports in the mainstream press, in scientific journals, by major scientific organizations, and by a group of distinguished scientists since 2001: for instance, Alden Meyer (2004), writing in the *Catalyst Magazine,* reports that in 2002 an expert advisory committee to the Centers for Disease Control and Prevention (CDC) appeared ready to recommend a more stringent federal lead standard on the basis of new public health research data. However, just before the committee was to meet, the Bush administration took the extraordinary step of rejecting several qualified researchers nominated by the CDC scientific staff to serve on the committee and instead appointed two people handpicked by the lead industry. Other examples include the following: A respected scientist recently left the U.S. Department of Agriculture (USDA), claiming that he had been prohibited from publishing his research on potential hazards posed by airborne bacteria emanating from farm wastes. Before the beginning of the Iraq war, President Bush, Vice President Dick Cheney, and Secretary of State Colin Powell all claimed that Iraq had sought to import aluminum tubes for uranium enrichment centrifuges, disregarding the contrary assessments of experts in several national Department of Energy laboratories and the International Atomic Energy Agency (Meyer, 2004).

The Bush administration's imposition of its ideology is far-reaching, including not only the deletion of scientific facts on government Web sites but also the nomination of ideological extremists to senior positions at federal agencies and on key scientific committees. According to the House Report, for instance, the president has appointed numerous people with questionable credentials—political, rather than scientific, credentials—to key federal scientific advisory committees, and has favored candidates put forward by industry over those recommended by professional agency staff. For example, Jerry Thacker, a marketing consultant appointed by Bush to a presidential AIDS advisory committee, described homosexuality as a "deathstyle" and referred to AIDS as the "gay plague" (Platner, 2004; Weiss, 2003).

Much of the criticism of the administration's politicization of scientific research is not simply partisan politics. Rather, a wide range of the criticism can be heard from appointees of past Republican administrations as well as senior scientists who have advised administrations of both parties, all of whom suggest that the breadth and magnitude of the Bush administration's manipulation, suppression, and misrepresentation of science is unprecedented. Although the subjects involved cover a broad range, they share a common attribute: the beneficiaries of the scientific distortion are important supporters of the president, including social conservatives and powerful industry groups (Meyers, 2004; Weiss, 2003).

The integrity of scientific research relies on freedom of inquiry, and one of the hallmarks of that freedom is objectivity. According to U.S. Representative Henry Waxman, the Bush administration does not hold science to any test of objectivity. It looks at science as something to be changed, suppressed, or manipulated to preconceived results to reward its ideological supporters (cited in Platner, 2004). The misrepresentation of objective scientific knowledge has real-world consequences, resulting in misguided and even dangerous policies on a number of critical issues. According to several observers, the Bush administration's pattern of abuse of the scientific enterprise has affected scientific research and analysis ranging from mercury emissions, environmental issues—including global warming—missile defense, and nuclear weapons to worker safety, reproductive health and choice, and lead poisoning.

As more and more incidents of the Bush administration's political interference in the scientific process have been reported in news stories and editorials in scientific journals, they have generated widespread and deepening alarm within the scientific community. In 2004, for example, over 60 doctors and senior-level scientists, including some 20 Nobel laureates and 19 recipients of the National Medal of Science, issued a statement demanding that the distortion of scientific knowledge for partisan political ends cease if the public is to be properly informed about issues central to its well-being and if the United States is to benefit fully from its heavy investment in scientific research and education (Meyers, 2004).

WHAT DO YOU THINK? Do you find the administration's pattern of scientific manipulation troubling? If yes, why? If no, why not? Should scientific decisions be made on ideology alone? Explain. If you were asked to serve on a commission to study the politicization of scientific research, what recommendations would you make about how to protect scientific research from political interference? In your opinion, is science ever truly neutral or objective?

THE SOCIOLOGY OF MARRIAGES AND FAMILIES

Some of you might think that because you are already a member of a family, you know all there is to know about marriages and families. If this is the case, you might be asking what sociology can add to what you already know. The answer is that sociologists go beyond our individual experiences to study marriages and families in social, historical, political, and cross-cultural contexts. They have conducted thousands of studies on a variety of marital and family behaviors, relationships, characteristics, and problems, ranging from the sexual behavior of members of marriages, families, and other intimate relationships to fathers' involvement in child rearing and child care to the long-term effects of television viewing on the behavior of children. These studies have yielded a tremendous amount of data that have contributed significantly to what we thought we knew about marriages and families. For example, despite the apparent manipulation of research data pertaining to abstinence-only programs and comprehensive sex education by the Bush administration and various religious right groups, sociologists and other social scientists have well established through their scientific research findings that comprehensive sex education programs that teach both abstinence and birth control do not increase adolescent sexual activity, either by hastening the onset of sexual intercourse, increasing the frequency of sexual intercourse, or increasing the number of sexual partners. In fact, this research has found that such programs can help delay the start of sexual activity in teenagers and increase condom use among sexually active teens (see, for example, Bearman and Bruckner, 2001; Surgeon General, 2001; Centers for Disease Control and Prevention, 2002; Hauser, 2004). Similarly, some research findings have suggested that a significant majority of young people will engage in sexual activity before marriage no matter what kind of education and upbringing they have and that education about birth control can significantly reduce teenage pregnancy and infection rates. For example, comprehensive studies of teenage pregnancy have found that the teenage birth rate has declined steadily (approximately 30 percent) since the early 1990s. According to these research findings, approximately one-fourth of the decline was because teens delayed sexual activity, while three-fourths was due to the increased use of long-term contraceptives (see, for example, Manlove et al., 2000).

Furthermore, sociologists have generated a number of theories from their research that help explain issues like why and how marriages and families emerged, how they are sustained over time, how people involved in these relationships interact with and relate to each other, what effect children have on marriages, what significance marriages and families have for U.S. society, and how and why marriages and families change over time. In this chapter we examine the ways in which sociologists discover facts—do research—about marriage and family behaviors and devise theories or explanations of these behaviors. We begin with a consideration of the link between research and theory.

STUDYING MARRIAGES AND FAMILIES: THE LINK BETWEEN RESEARCH AND THEORY

Sociology involves observing human behavior and society and then making sense out of what we observe. Thus, both research and theory are involved. However, as the controversy and debate surrounding the administration's distortion of scientific data indicates, neither research nor theory is developed in a cultural or political vacuum. As that controversy shows, the social and political climate, as well as the ideological viewpoint of the researcher, has an impact on what is researched, how it is interpreted, and whether or not it is widely shared—or for that matter, how it is shared—with the public (such as which findings are stressed and which are omitted or downplayed). Politics aside, the link between research and theory is obvious: For example, research about marriages and families provides us with important observations about these intimate relationships. Various marriage and family theories and perspectives provide us with basic points of view or frameworks that help us analyze and understand these observations.

What exactly is a theory? A **theory** is an explanation of some phenomenon. Theories relate ideas and observations to each other as well as help explain them. They contain certain assumptions about the world and about the nature of society and human behavior. Different assumptions lead to different problems and questions and, potentially, to different answers or explanations about society and human behavior. In addition, most theories include stated or unstated value judgments concerning the topic or issues related to the topic. For example, if we use a theory that assumes that the family is a system held together through a basic harmony of values and interests and that consensus and stability are desirable in the family (a value judgment) because they facilitate this cooperation, then we are most likely to ask questions concerned with order, stability, and balance, such as how families function in an orderly and consensual way to maintain or preserve their families over time. And we are less likely to raise questions pertaining to disorder, disagreement, and open hostility in families.

Actually, if you think about it, no theory or perspective on human society and behavior is unbiased or completely value-free. Because they contain assumptions about the nature of human beings and their societies, all such theories implicitly or explicitly suggest that certain arrangements are desirable, good, or better than others. All social theories include these kinds of value judgments.

How do we know, then, if a particular theoretical perspective provides a viable explanation of its subject matter? The answer to this question lies in an understanding of the relationship between theory and scientific research. Theories are important sources of ideas for researchers to test. **Scientific research** provides us with empirical evidence as a basis for knowledge or theories. By **empirical evidence** we mean data or evidence that can be confirmed by the use of one or more of the human senses. Scientific research also allows us to test **hypotheses,** statements of relationships between two or more **variables**—factors that can have two or more values—to determine what is as opposed to what we think should be. As used in scientific research, the term *independent variable* is used to identify a cause—it is a variable that causes change in or affects another variable. The term *dependent variable* refers to the consequence of some cause—it is a variable that is changed or affected by some other variable.

All scientific research is guided by the **scientific method,** a set of procedures intended to ensure accuracy and honesty throughout the research process. An aim of the scientific method is to prevent our personal biases from distorting our research. The scientific method involves making systematic and objective observations (collecting information), making precise measurements, and reporting the research techniques and results to other interested parties. If followed, these procedures generally lead researchers to the facts of a situation or event, regardless of what we might hope or believe to be the facts. These procedures also permit others to repeat research studies to validate or invalidate previous findings, thereby allowing us to expose researcher biases where they might appear. Thus, any concerns about researcher bias can be addressed through a replication and validation of the study's findings.

Generally speaking, the scientific method refers to the procedures that science uses to (1) select or formulate research questions and operationalize (state in concrete terms) concepts, (2) select an appropriate research design, (3) collect data, (4) analyze the data, and (5) draw conclusions and report the findings. How these steps are actually carried out is dictated by a number of issues, including the particular research question under study and the researcher's

conceptual scheme. Research is also sometimes influenced by practical matters, such as the availability of funding, who funds the research (and publishes it), access to subjects, and time constraints. And as we have seen, research is also sometimes influenced by politics. Consequently, biases, compromises, selectivity, and other nonscientific issues often creep into the scientific research process and can have an effect from the beginning to the end of the process. A good example of this is the 1999 firing of the editor of the prestigious *Journal of the American Medical Association* (*JAMA*) for publishing a Kinsey Institute sex study showing that most college students did not consider oral sex as "having sex." This finding could have supported then-President Bill Clinton's definition of sex in the Republican-led impeachment process that centered largely around the president's intimate relationship with White House intern Monica Lewinsky. In the firing of the *JAMA* editor, political partisan issues surrounding the sexual conduct of a sitting president could well have played a role in the editor's firing, but more importantly, the firing could have influenced how the public viewed the Kinsey Institute's research.

How exactly are theory and research related? Theory provides insights, often in the form of abstract ideas, into the nature of individuals and society, and research provides the objective observations upon which theories are verified. It is a reciprocal, or back-and-forth, relationship. For example, theories that cannot be confirmed by evidence gathered through scientific research mean nothing. Similarly, facts have meaning only when we interpret them and give them meaning based on some theoretical perspective. Contrary to popular belief, facts do not speak for themselves. This is at the heart of the controversy over the attempt to include the teaching of intelligent design along with evolution in the science curriculum (see Debating Social Issues box).

METHODOLOGICAL TECHNIQUES IN THE STUDY OF MARRIAGES AND FAMILIES

People today are bombarded with information about marriages and families. We hear, for instance, that old-fashioned family moral values have disappeared, that children are having babies, that family and intimate violence are increasing, and that entire families are living on the streets. To ascertain what is really happening with marriages and families, we must therefore learn how to separate what is factual from what is not. As previously explained, scientific research enables us to see what is, as opposed to what might be or what we hoped would be. Most research, like theory, begins with the questions of why and how. A goal of research is to provide specific answers to these questions by gathering empirical evidence. Ultimately, the answers form explanations or theories about some aspect of human behavior and human society.

A potential problem for all scientific research is objectivity. Researchers have to be constantly aware of how their personal attitudes, expectations, and values might affect their

DEBATING SOCIAL ISSUES

SCIENCE AND/OR RELIGION: The Ongoing Evolution Wars

Thought you had heard the last of the challenges to the theory of evolution? Well, think again. Darwin's theory of evolution, presented nearly 150 years ago in *The Origin of Species*, has faced any number of efforts to invalidate it as a scientific theory. Early attempts were fairly crude and included the infamous "monkey trial" of 1925 in which Tennessee schoolteacher, John Scopes, was convicted for teaching evolution. At the time, Tennessee, Florida, and Oklahoma had laws that interfered with the teaching of evolution. In 1968, the U.S. Supreme Court struck down such laws and some states changed gears and began to require that "creation science" be taught alongside evolution. Later Supreme Court rulings (in 1982 and 1987) put an end to that, citing the teaching of creation science even as an aside violated the First Amendment's separation of church and state (Wallis, 2005). Today the controversy rages anew with the development of a new kind of creationist perspective under the name of *intelligent design*. At a time when American science is perceived as being under attack politically by the president of the United States and his administration, the issue boils down to the acceptance and teaching of a scientific theory of evolution confirmed by evidence gathered through scientific research versus a theory that has not been and cannot be confirmed with evidence gathered through scientific research. Theories that cannot be confirmed by evidence gathered through scientific research mean nothing.

Kansas State Board of Education hearing on teaching evolution or creationism.

Darwin's theory of evolution is widely regarded as one of the best supported theories in science, the only explanation for the diversity of life on Earth, grounded in decades of scientific research and objective evidence. Evolution by natural selection is a theory of gradual, incremental change over million of years, which starts with something very simple and works up along slow, gradual gradients to greater complexity. There is a huge amount of evidence for evolution not only in the fossil record but also in the letters of the genetic code shared in varying degrees by all species. Intelligent design, on the other hand, is a set of propositions suggesting

---

research. It is not possible, even when using the scientific method, to measure or observe social phenomena without committing themselves to some theoretical perspective. Theory is always implicated in the research process, although it is most often implicit—hidden from view. Therefore, we should be aware that researchers bring theoretical biases to the research process: the problems selected for study, the methods chosen to study those problems, the unique and individual observations made, and general assumptions about the world and about human behavior.

The methodological procedures followed have a great effect on the interpretation of the data. Although the scientific method minimizes research bias to a great degree, no one has found a way to eliminate it totally. Therefore, as consumers of massive amounts of research information, we must carefully examine the information we receive and be prepared for the possibility that what is presented as reality is not impartial. A good example in this regard is the controversy surrounding how one of the lead investigators of a 2001 National Institute of Child Health and Human Development

that living things are too complex to have evolved by a combination of chance mutations and natural selection. Rather, some aspects of living things are best explained by an intelligent cause or agent, as opposed to natural selection. Although few proponents of intelligent design come right out and say that the "intelligent cause" or "agent" is God, the implication is clear. They believe the hand of the designer of human life is self-evident. According to all who have examined the propositions of intelligent design, there is agreement that it is simply a more subtle way of purporting creationism and that the intelligent design movement is just the latest and most sophisticated attempt to discredit the theory of evolution (Wallis, 2005).

Based upon the results of recent polls, it seems that many Americans share the belief that the theory of evolution does not leave sufficient room for the influence of God as an explanation of the origins of the species. For example, 55 percent of the people responding in a 2005 Harris Poll said that students ought to be taught creationism and intelligent design along with evolution in public schools and 54 percent did not believe that humans had developed from an earlier species. These results are indicative of the growing prevalence of such beliefs among Americans as well as and the growing clout of the intelligent design movement. Proponents of intelligent design have been aggressive in challenging the teaching of evolution in public schools by targeting statewide curriculum standards. In 2005, for example, a series of new laws challenging the teaching of evolution in the form of so-called new science standards and in some cases altering the basic definition of science itself were pending or had been considered in 20 states. Some proponents recognize that

intelligent design is not a scientific theory—thus they advocate rather than teaching it alongside evolution as a scientific theory science teachers should instead teach about the problems and holes in the theory of evolution (Wallis, 2005).

Proponents of evolution say that there is really no debate—that members of the intelligent design movement have created a false, politically motivated debate between science and religion by creating confusion, to make it seem as if there is a real controversy about the validity of evolutionary theory. The scientific community has almost universally determined that intelligent design is not science. According to the U.S. National Academy of Science, for example, a conservative group of major research scientists and the most authoritative scientific voice in the country, intelligent design is unambiguously a religious position, not a scientific theory (National Center for Science Education, 2005a; Nelson, 2005). Biologists argue that intelligent design is a faith-based science that amounts to creationism by another name and both are simply sectarian religious viewpoints. Evolution, they say, is the cornerstone of modern biology and they stand by the scientific methodology on which the theory is based. They argue that there is overwhelming scientific evidence that supports the idea that all living things share a common ancestry. Intelligent design, on the other hand, is not a scientific theory; it has no scientific evidence to support it nor an educational basis for teaching it as science. It has neither the substantial research base nor testable hypotheses that are the hallmark of the scientific method. Far from a respectable scientific alternative to evolution, intelligent design is a clever attempt to sneak religion, cloaked in the guise of science, into the public school curriculum

(National Center for Science Education, 2005a and 2005b).

On the other side of the controversy is a devoted group of mostly religious Christians, including hundreds of scientists, engineers, theologians, and philosophers who support the viewpoint of intelligent design, some of whom have written papers and books, and contributed to symposiums on the perceived problems with Darwin's theory. Their detractors, however, argue that these scientists are not doing credible science. Rather, they are appropriating scientific-sounding arguments, many of which are written in scientifically abstruse, jargon-heavy language. Their goal is to advance a moral and political agenda into the public schools. Furthermore, they do not comply with the rules of science. That is, they do not publish papers in peer-reviewed journals and their hypotheses cannot be tested by research and the study of evidence. The bottom line, according to proponents of the theory of evolution: on a religious level one can believe in creation but that is not a scientific theory. Science is based upon certain standards: research and expert documentation (Wallis, 2005; National Center for Science Education, 2005b).

What do you know about the theory of evolution? What do you know about intelligent design? Familiarize yourself with the tenets of intelligent design. Why is it not a scientific theory? Review the steps of the scientific method and discuss why science provides us with a more valid base of knowledge than personal opinions, political perspectives, or even religious ideology or doctrine. Do you think intelligent design or any religious or political ideology should be taught alongside evolution theory as if it were science? Explain.

study of early child care reported the study's findings. The investigator was accused by several of his fellow investigators of monopolizing the press and making negative pronouncements about child care that were not based on "conclusive data." Some critics said that the investigator had a personal agenda that he had been pushing for some time; for years he had emphasized the negative aspects of child care to the exclusion of the positive aspects, which suggests that he may not have been completely impartial in how he presented the study's findings.

As pointed out earlier, because the study of marriages and families deals with everyday life, we often think we already know all there is to know about these issues. Most people, for example, probably believe that they know all there is to know about welfare and welfare recipients. Popular views of welfare include the notion that women who receive welfare have baby after baby as a way to collect higher payments. The findings of scientific research, however, tell a very different story. For instance, a profile of the welfare population shows that the fertility behavior of women on welfare does not differ from that of women in the general population. The majority of welfare recipients (74 percent) have only one or two children. And like the general population, the average number of children in a welfare family is less than two (Report from the Urban Institute, 1999; General Characteristics, 2005). Past research has shown that the longer a woman receives welfare, the less likely she is to have additional children.

Much of the research on welfare families to date reflects a white middle-class bias. Based on a mythical model of white middle-class families as a measuring rod, welfare families (often regardless of the empirical evidence) generally have been described as pathological, disorganized, lacking a work ethic, and locked into a way of life that perpetuates an endless cycle of so-called illegitimate births.

Before we accept such viewpoints as factual, we must carefully analyze the evidence presented to support the conclusions (see Internet Resources: Applying the Sociological Imagination box). This analytical process includes asking questions such as, Are the conclusions actually supported by the empirical evidence? Are the findings presented in such a way that they can be tested by others? What are the biases of the research, and does the researcher state them up front?

Basically, we should assess research in terms of its reliability and validity. **Reliability** is the degree to which the research yields the same results when repeated by the same researcher or other researchers. **Validity** is the degree to which the study measures exactly what it claims to be measuring. We should also keep in mind that conclusions are not final but are always open to question and reinvestigation.

In the remainder of this section we examine some of the primary methods used in marriage and family research: surveys, observation, case studies, and ethnographies. Researchers using each of these methods analyze the data they collect using either or both quantitative or qualitative analysis. **Quantitative analysis** is a process in which data can be analyzed using numerical categories and statistical techniques (for example, determining the percentage of respondents who report certain attitudes or behaviors). **Qualitative analysis** focuses on specific or distinct qualities within the data that show patterns of similarity or difference among the research subjects. Although each represents a different technique for analyzing data, quantitative and qualitative data are not necessarily at odds. Researchers often use both qualitative and quantitative methods to maximize our understanding of their research. Finally, we end this section with a look at who and what does and does not get studied by researchers, and why. In this regard, we pay close attention to issues of ethics and conscious and unconscious biases in the conduct of research on marriages and families.

Surveys

One of the quickest ways to find out what we want to know about people is to ask them. **Surveys** do just that: They enable us to gather information by asking people questions. Surveys are particularly useful when what we want to know about people is not easily observable, such as the private lives of married or cohabiting couples. The two basic

---

INTERNET RESOURCES

APPLYING THE SOCIOLOGICAL IMAGINATION
Some Characteristics of the Welfare Population

- Ten percent of welfare adults are married; 36 percent are separated, divorced, or widowed, and the remaining 54 percent have never married.
- Seventy-four percent of welfare mothers are in their 20s and 30s; 7 percent are under the age of 20 and 19 percent are 40 or older.
- The racial composition of welfare families is fairly evenly distributed across racial and ethnic groups: 30 percent are white, 36 percent African American, 26 percent Latina/o, 1 percent Native American, and 2 percent Asian.
- The average number of children in welfare families is two, which is consistent with the fertility patterns of the general public. Two in five welfare families have only one child and 1 in 10 families have more than three children.

- The majority of children receiving welfare stipends live with one or both parents; only 8 percent live with a grandparent.
- According to some research, women on welfare are more conscientious about using contraceptives while on welfare; they are less likely to want an additional pregnancy, and they are less likely to become pregnant while on welfare.
- Fifty-four percent of all welfare recipients have at least a high school education, including some who have attended college; 25 percent have a college degree.
- Over two-thirds of women who are on welfare had some recent work experience before applying for public assistance.

http://www.mothersmovement.org/resources/welfare.htm

http://www.tisszdv.uni-tuebingen.de/webroot/sp/spsba01_W98_1/denver2.htm

Use these two Web sites as starting points and find other Web sites or links that provide information about people who receive welfare benefits. Find the typical monthly welfare allotment for a person with two children living in your state. Imagine that this person is you and the welfare payment is all that you and your children have to live on. Using prices from the geographical area in which you live, develop a monthly budget to account for everything you have to spend to get by (day-to-day). What do you think your life and that of your children would be like? What does an exercise like this teach you about popular images of and attitudes about people who receive welfare benefits?

methods by which researchers ask their questions and receive answers are interviews and questionnaires. The **interview** usually involves one person, the interviewer, asking another person questions, with the interviewer recording the answers. The **questionnaire,** in contrast, usually provides autonomy to the person answering the questions. It is typically a set of printed questions that people read on their own and then record their answers. The survey is the most widely used method of studying marriages and families. It is likely that you or someone you know has participated in a survey regarding some marriage and family issue. You may even have conducted your own survey for a class assignment or some other project. For example, in marriage and family classes students are often asked to survey their parents or grandparents concerning the dating patterns of their youth.

A good example of the use of the survey in research related to marriages and families is Marceia Raffaelli and Lenna Ontai's (2004) study of gender socialization in Latina/o families. Using survey data collected from two groups—in-depth interviews completed by 22 adult Latinas, ages 20–45, and 166 self-report surveys completed by Latina/o college students (58 percent women; median age 21 years old)—the researchers found that among the first group, many Latina/o parents socialize their daughters in ways that are marked by "traditional" gender-related expectations and messages. Findings from the group of college students supported and expanded the findings from the first group. The female and male college student respondents in the second group described different experiences of household activities, socialization of gender-typed behavior, and freedom to pursue social activities or gain access to privileges. Raffaelli and Ontai used a combination of quantitative and qualitative analysis. On the one hand, they transcribed and coded each of the 22 adult female interviews identifying "typical" quotes and responses. On the other hand, they developed structured measures such as gender role socialization and conducted bivariate and multivariate analyses of a number of variables including parents' education, place of birth, and gender attitudes. Taken together, the researchers found three overarching themes related to gender socialization: differential treatment of girls and boys and privileging of boys in families with both daughters and sons, enforcement of stereotypically feminine behavior among daughters, and curtailment of girls' activities outside the home. For instance, daughters and sons were given different household chores, with girls expected to help around the house whereas boys were not. In addition, sons were typically granted more freedom than daughters to come and go without as much supervision. Many of the female respondents indicated that their parents encouraged them to act "feminine" and not do "guy" things. Although some degree of "tomboy" behavior was accepted in a number of families, as girls grew older parents tended to become less accepting of "unfeminine" behavior. Girls' freedom was curtailed far more than boys, with one female respondent describing growing up feeling as if she lived in a "little circle" delineated by her parents. Raffaelli and Ontai also found that Latina/o parental characteristics, particularly gender role attitudes, were linked to gender-related socialization. For example, mothers who held traditional gender role attitudes were more likely to encourage femininity in daughters and "manly" behavior in sons. And fathers who encouraged their sons to do chores and limited their sons' freedom regarding social activities tended to hold more egalitarian gender role attitudes.

Despite dramatic changes in gender roles that have occurred in the United States over the last several decades, based upon the findings of this survey research, it appears that many Latina/o parents nonetheless continue to engage in differential socialization regarding gender expectations for their children.

One of the major advantages of interviews and questionnaires is that they allow researchers to gather large amounts of information at a relatively low cost. On the negative side, the questionnaire method imposes the researcher's point of view on the people being studied by forcing them to respond to questions in terms of preestablished categories of answers. For example, a respondent might be given a choice of four categories to describe her or his socialization experiences that either is not appropriate or does not reflect the full range of her or his experiences. Another disadvantage is that survey methods must rely on people's ability and willingness to give accurate information, especially when the survey involves information about behavior that is typically considered private, such as sexual relationships or family violence. Thus, survey results are sometimes distorted because the respondents say what they think the researcher wants to hear. In the case of the Raffaelli and Ontai study, a potential limitation of the survey method is the retrospective aspect of the study, which required the adult respondents in the first study to recall experiences from their childhood and adolescence. Although a valid way of assessing family of origin experiences, recall bias can affect research results in ways not always determinable.

Observation

Surveys are good for telling us what people say they do. What people say they do and what they actually do are not always the same, however. An alternative to asking people questions is to observe their behavior systematically. Observational studies are useful when researchers have only a vague idea of the behavior they want to study, when they want to study people or situations that are not accessible to the general public, or when there is no other way to get the information. Researchers may observe behavior in a manner that does not intrude on the situation under study, or they may participate in or become a part of the interaction they are studying. This latter approach is referred to as *participant observation*. Regardless of the approach, observational studies require the researcher to develop a specific set of questions in advance of the study as a way to guide the collection of data.

An interesting example of an observational study relevant to the study of marriages and families is one conducted by researchers Pandora Pound, Caroline Sabin, and Shah Ebrahim (1999) in order to identify aspects of the process of care that might explain improved outcomes for patients on stroke units. The researchers knew from previous research that patients on stroke units have improved outcomes compared with those on general wards; that stroke units were associated with long-term reduction of death, dependency, and institutionalization, with benefits being independent of age, sex, or stroke severity. Based on their observation of 12 patients at each of three locations—a stroke unit, an elderly care unit, and a general medical ward—the researchers found that stroke-unit patients spent more time out of bed and out of their room and had more opportunities for independence than patients on the medical ward. There were more observed attempts in the stroke unit than on the general medical ward to interact with drowsy, cognitively impaired, or speech-impaired patients. Stroke-unit patients also spent more time with visitors. Similar aspects of care were also observed in the elderly care unit, where patients also spent less time sleeping or disengaged and more time interacting with nurses, and were given appropriate help more often than patients elsewhere. The researchers concluded that these aspects of patient care might help explain the improved outcomes on stroke units.

A major advantage of observation is that it is by far the best method for collecting data on nonverbal behavior. In addition, it not only allows researchers like Pound, Sabin, and Ebrahim to observe "process," but it also allows them to examine behavior or "process" in its natural environment (for example, a stroke unit, an elderly care unit, and a general medical ward). Observation is less restrictive or artificial than some other data collection methods, but the presence of the observer makes bias a real possibility. When people are aware that they are being observed, they frequently modify their behavior, either deliberately or subconsciously. This phenomenon is referred to by social scientists as the **Hawthorne effect.** Although the Hawthorne effect can sometimes be a serious drawback of observational studies, its limitations applies to all research strategies.

Other problems with observational studies include the following: (1) they usually take a long time and thus can be expensive, (2) they generally involve only a limited number of subjects, and (3) they offer the researcher little control over the research situation. However, the depth of understanding gained through observation research compensates for the disadvantages and has greatly added to our knowledge about marriages and families.

Case Studies

Sociologists who study a particular category of people or a particular situation typically do so as a **case study.** The case study is a detailed, in-depth examination of a single unit. Case studies use newly collected and preexisting data, such as those from interviews, participant observation, or existing records, for in-depth examination of a particular individual, group, or organization. Used in research on issues pertaining to marriages and families, case studies can provide a comprehensive and holistic understanding of behaviors within a single setting. Researcher John Bartkowski's 1999

study of how gender, domestic labor (that is, the allocation of financial provision, household tasks, and child-care responsibilities), and family power operate as processes within three white, relatively privileged, conservative Evangelical households is an example of the case study method applied to marriage and family issues. Bartkowski used the case study approach to trace how domestic labor issues emerged, were negotiated, and (at times) resolved through gender strategies employed by these couples. He found that contrary to the stereotypical view of conservative Evangelicals as rigid conformers to a traditional division of labor by gender, these couples exhibited both traditional and progressive gender practices.

Although the couples embraced the Evangelical ideology of wife–husband roles in the family (the dominant family discourse within contemporary Evangelicalism champions husband providership and wifely domesticity), they sometimes reconfigured or reversed their beliefs about gender, if only temporarily. For example, one husband whose wife worked outside the home indicated that he greatly appreciated the support that his wife provided both financially and emotionally, yet he also clearly believed that the financial provision for his family was his primary responsibility. Equality, per se, was not the guiding principle in the decision for his wife to work. Rather, in this husband's estimation, he should provide his wife with the "choice" to work or not, whereas he felt that he did not have a choice in the matter; it was his obligation.

According to Bartkowski, employed Evangelical wives and mothers may find themselves doubly burdened from shouldering both their traditional homemaking responsibilities—the dominant ideology of femininity within Evangelicalism—and their newly found co-provider role. For example, despite her best efforts, one wife in the study was unable to parlay her extensive labor force commitments into a lightened domestic workload in the home. The study found that, in dealing with their deviation from the prevailing definitions of Evangelical wifehood or motherhood, the women used a "both/and gender strategy" that entailed working two full-time jobs, as both co-provider and homemaker, during the family workday. This gender strategy seemed religiously motivated because it enabled these women to retain for themselves the "homemaker" label, which remains closely linked with femininity in their conservative Protestant circle despite its broader cultural devaluation. Bartkowski's findings underscore the importance of viewing gender and domestic labor as a product of interpersonal negotiation, while at the same time they highlight how gender relations are mediated by cultural forces such as conservative religious ideologies.

One of the advantages of a study like Bartkowski's is that it provides a great deal of detail about the research subject. In addition, the case study approach offers long-term, in-depth analysis of various aspects of the phenomenon being studied. A disadvantage is that each case study focuses on a very specific case and thus cannot be generalized to the larger population. For example, the Bartkowski findings apply to the specific conservative Evangelical families that he studied and not to all conservative Evangelical families. Furthermore, as with observation, the presence of the researcher may change how people act or interact. Overall, however, case studies have provided some significant insights into marriage and family processes. They have helped researchers understand and explain how families create roles, patterns, and rules that various family members follow, very often without even being aware of them.

Ethnography

In general, **ethnography** is a research technique for describing a social group from the group's point of view. Ethnography is not about pursuing or uncovering an objective reality (which is typically the focus of quantitative analyses). Rather, it is a technique for examining the many different versions of reality from the point of view, or through the eyes, of the researched. Therefore, by necessity, ethnographers use qualitative methods that, by design, allows the researcher to study conditions or processes that are hard to measure numerically. In essence, the ethnographer attempts to gain cultural knowledge from the people she or he is studying. Ethnographic research is particularly useful and relevant in areas of study where researchers have historically studied and measured other groups from the perspective of their own cultural, racial, or class biases. In this context, ethnography has special relevance as a technique for studying marriages and families that heretofore have been studied primarily from the cultural perspective of white middle-class male researchers.

An interesting example of ethnographic research in this regard is a study undertaken by Robin Jarrett in 1992 of low-income African American family life. Specifically, Jarrett explored hypotheses advanced by quantitative sociologists concerning the African American underclass, especially those put forth by William J. Wilson in his 1987 work titled *The Truly Disadvantaged*. Using aggregate data and statistical analyses of African American family structure and dynamics, these researchers had put forth a generalized profile of these families as dysfunctional. In contrast, utilizing ethnographic techniques, Jarrett found that inner-city African American family life is far more complex and heterogeneous than such a one-dimensional profile suggests. Jarrett used a two-step qualitative study that began with focus group interviews and moved to in-depth case studies based on participant observation and in-depth interviews of multiple family members. Her case study report of one of these families provides evidence consistent with other ethnographies of African American family life, which describe well-functioning families within impoverished neighborhoods. Jarrett's ethnographic research moves us beyond a one-dimensional view of inner-city African American families and documents the presence of various individual and family lifestyles within African American neighborhoods. She found that in response to neighborhood conditions, well-functioning African American families continue to live in and coexist with street-oriented lifestyles in impoverished areas despite the tremendous

odds that Wilson and other quantitative researchers articulate so well.

An advantage of ethnographic studies such as Jarrett's is that they provide firsthand accounts of those whose lives we are studying. Ethnographic research specifically and qualitative methods more generally provide an avenue for the voices of those we study—voices silenced by quantitative methodologies. Critics, on the other hand, contend that methodological biases limit the reliability and validity of qualitative data. They suggest, for example, that retrospective interviews can elicit idealized accounts of behavior or that the data may be compromised by memory lapses or the respondent's need to present a particular picture of self or the situation. The fact is, however, that all research methods are inherently limited. Therefore, to circumvent some of these biases, researchers should use a variety of strategies (such as in the case of the Jarrett study) to act as checks on potential threats to reliability and validity and to reduce some of the sources of researcher bias (Jarrett, 1992).

Scientific Methodologies Used by Feminist Researchers

Feminist scholars are interested in whom researchers study and how they study them, how conclusions are drawn, and what evidence those conclusions are based on. They are particularly concerned with how women have either been omitted from scientific research or have been studied according to male models of attitudes and behavior. Much of their work is a corrective to these problems.

You are probably wondering what is distinctive about the methods that feminists use. Are their methods fundamentally different from the scientific methods that other researchers use? In fact, no method of research is of itself a feminist method. According to feminist sociologist and researcher Marjorie DeVault (1990), what distinguishes feminist methods is what feminist researchers do—how they use the methodologies available to them. For example, feminist researchers generally avoid using the more abstract, impersonal methods that characterize quantitative methods. Rather, they rely heavily on qualitative methods. A person using quantitative methods to study rape might measure the rate of rape among various groups of women. On the other hand, one using qualitative methods might measure the reaction to rape or coping strategies devised by rape victims as recounted by the victims themselves. In particular, feminist researchers often use field methods such as the in-depth, face-to-face interview; participant observation; and ethnography. Although other researchers also use these methods, feminist researchers differ in how they define their research goals and how they view their own role as researcher.

A basic goal of feminist research is to present information that had been previously ignored or suppressed, and thus to make visible both the experiences of the people they study (particularly women) in all their diversity and the **ideologies,** or systems of beliefs, that have kept these experiences invisible. In this respect, gender is at the forefront of the analysis, with special attention paid to how race, class, gender, and sexuality interact and affect the lives of women and men. A major advantage to how feminists do their research is the way they define their role as researcher. As researchers they are conscious of the need to be respectful of the people they are studying, to be personal, collaborative, inclusive, and empowering.

These qualities characterize feminist methods because researchers consciously use techniques of data gathering that allow them to use the perspectives of their subjects. Instead of imposing their personal interpretations on the experiences of the people they study, feminist researchers develop theories and explanations that reflect the real-life experiences of their subjects, as reported by the subjects themselves. Ideally, feminist research is inclusive of the experiences of all women, not just a few, and it is empowering to the extent that it seeks to avoid defining women solely as victims. For instance, as we will see in Chapter 11, although women are often victims of violence and abuse, they are also survivors. So feminist researchers view women as actively involved in the world**s** in which they live.

An example of the feminist methodology applied to the people that researchers study can be found in the research on upwardly mobile African American women conducted by one of this text's authors, BarBara Scott. Scott (1988) used the life history method of collecting data about the experiences of these women. Her research showed that race and gender are important factors in upward mobility as well as family socialization. These women's self-reports of the process of mobility as they experienced it have greatly added to our knowledge about mobility, an area of research from which women and people of color were previously almost totally excluded.

The choice of the life history method reflects a central assumption of the feminist researcher that behavior can best be understood from the perspective of the persons involved. Scott assumed that her subjects understood their experiences better than other people did, and she respected their way of reporting and interpreting these experiences. Using this method, Scott avoided substituting her own interpretations for those of the women she studied. Her methodology was at once personal and collaborative. Scott was both the researcher and the researched in the sense that she, being an upwardly mobile African American woman, shared many of the experiences of her respondents.

The very features that feminist researchers consider advantageous and confirming have been singled out by critics as an important limitation of this research. Because this research is intentionally personal and collaborative, for example, critics immediately raise the question of objectivity. Many feminist researchers agree that their work is subjective in that it is research on people like themselves—other women. But, they argue, it is also objective in that women's experiences are explained in terms of the forces that shape their lives. Thus, like most research, which to date has been male-centered, feminist research clearly has a point of view and views social change as an important goal. They not only believe that their research and scholarship should be tied to social change but also that they have a responsibility to critique problems in the content and method of traditional research and scholarship. Sociologist

Howard Becker (1977) has addressed the role of values in sociological research and why researchers are sometimes accused of bias in their work. According to Becker, we can never avoid taking sides, but we can use research methodologies impartially enough so that the beliefs that we hold can be proved or disproved.

A CRITICAL LOOK AT TRADITIONAL RESEARCH ON MARRIAGES AND FAMILIES

Historically, sociology as a discipline has claimed as one of its major goals the improvement of social life. Today, most sociologists operate from this premise and believe the purpose of their research is to affect social policy and provide the impetus for social change. Some critics, such as feminist scholars, have argued that in practice sociology has not always lived up to this goal. Until the upsurge of feminist research and scholarship over the past few decades, women, their experiences, and their consciousness were largely absent from traditional sociological research and the theoretical paradigms that guide sociological thinking (Andersen, 2003). The same can be said for people of color. In addition, sociological researchers historically have failed to recognize groups other than the white middle class. That is, white middle-class marriages and families have been used as the norm against which other families are measured. When lower-class and working-class families differ from the white middle-class model, they are defined as deviant. At the other end of the class continuum, the upper classes have been the subject of little scientific research. Thus, although new and exciting research on families across race and class is currently being produced, much of what we know today continues to be based on a model of the family that represents only a small proportion of today's marriages and families.

A More Inclusive Sociology

Social science research often mirrors current issues and trends of society. In this context, scholars across academic disciplines are wrestling with new sensitivities and concerns with gender as a social construction and with issues pertaining to cultural diversity. Today, researchers are more cognizant of the intersections of social constructions such as race, class, gender, and sexual orientation, and are moving beyond conventional topics and traditional research methods to develop a more inclusive base of knowledge about marriages and families. Although traditional sociological research has provided important insights into marriages and families, there are important limitations. Whether intended or not, much of this research presents a skewed picture of marriages and families, one rooted primarily in white middle-class and/or male experiences that have rendered women and various groups of color and their experiences invisible, as if they did not exist. And when they were studied, it was often within a social pathology or sociology of deviance framework. Because of the tremendous impact of this research for our ongoing understanding of marriage and family life, it is worth noting some of these past limitations.

One way of exploring the limitations of traditional sociological research on marriages and families is to examine who does (did) and does not (did not) get studied.

Conventional topics studied by sociologists lead us to ignore issues that would illuminate women's lives. When women have been studied in traditional marriage and family research, for example, it has usually been in terms of a one-dimensional stereotypical model of women as nurturant caregivers and caretakers confined to the home. Most of this research has been conducted by men who use themselves as the standard. Gender is seldom considered a significant factor that influences behavior. Evidence of this trend recurs in traditional sociological studies that draw conclusions about marriage and family life based on investigations in which all the research subjects are male. This approach is particularly evident in research concerning issues of individual and family mobility.

The large-scale study of the U.S. occupational structure conducted by noted social scientists Peter Blau and Otis Duncan (1967), for example, was, until recently, the definitive statement in the mobility literature. Blau and Duncan concluded that social mobility was simply a function of education and social origins and that no other conditions affect chances for mobility in the United States. Clearly, this set of conclusions is obsolete today, ignoring as it did the reality of gender and race and their differing impact for women, men, and various racial and ethnic groups. In fact, Blau and Duncan's research study was based on a national sample of 20,000 men. No women participated.

Following this pattern, subsequent mobility research was primarily male-specific, measuring mobility strictly by comparing men occupationally with their fathers. When women's mobility was addressed, it was primarily that of white women, and it was measured by comparing the husband's occupational standing with that of the woman's father. In general, women's mobility was seen as a function of male status, that of either a father or a husband. This model of social mobility is particularly problematic for some women, including a large percentage of African American women, who historically have been required to work outside the home to help support their families. The percentage of women in the work force, across race, has risen dramatically over the last several decades, yet women's pay continues to lag behind that of their male counterparts. To be sure, this phenomenon has significant implications for current and future mobility studies.

Like feminist scholars, African American and other scholars of color have long criticized social science research for the negative and stereotypical ways in which African Americans, various people of color, women, and poor and working-class families have been portrayed. African American women scholars have been particularly vocal in their critiques concerning many myths and half-truths about African American women and their role in their families.

The longest lasting of these seems to be the myth of the "black matriarchy." One of the most widely publicized documents on African American family life, sociologist and government researcher Daniel Moynihan's 1965 study titled "The Negro Family: The Case for National Action," dramatically illustrates the use of social science methodology to promote ideas based on questionable data and oversimplification. Based on U.S. census data, Moynihan found that almost 25 percent of African American families were female-headed, a statistic he cited as evidence of a "matriarchy." Moynihan then explained the problems in the African American community in terms of this alleged structural feature of African American families. Although Moynihan recognized the historical fact of slavery and its impact on African American family life, he essentially placed the burden of an alleged family pathology squarely on the shoulders of African American women. However, even if one accepts Moynihan's notion of a black matriarchy, he failed to explain what is innately problematic or detrimental about matriarchies. Although the Moynihan Report, as it is often called, has been widely criticized in the social science literature, some contemporary sociologists argue that although the methodology was flawed and the findings overgeneralized vis-à-vis African American families, Moynihan nonetheless identified important trends. These trends, as we have found today, characterized not only the African American families he described but also white and various other racial and ethnic families as well.

In addition to women and African Americans, various groups of color are often overrepresented, misrepresented, or not represented at all in marriage and family research. For instance, compared with research about other groups in U.S. society, very little research has been done on Native American families; thus, little is known about these families. Because Native Americans are small in number and often live in remote areas of the country, they are, perhaps, the most invisible group of color. When they are studied, it is often either within erroneous or outdated models of family life that are generalized to a very diverse group of people or within a pathology/deviance model. In the 2000 census, 4.1 million people identified themselves as Native American and Alaska Native. These diverse peoples include Cherokee, Sioux, Chippewa, Navajo, Seminole, Lakota, and more than 500 other nations representing over 150 languages. Yet, traditional research continues to refer to Native Americans as if they were a homogeneous group. Traditional research on Native American families seldom presents family members as having agency, that is, initiating actions based on their own values and judgments rather than simply reacting to outside forces such as government pressure, exploitation, and oppression. Therefore, although we know much about the rates of alcoholism and suicide (alleged pathologies in response to oppression) in some of these families (though we are not exactly sure which families because these data too are often generalized), we know very little about their family relations or process. Furthermore, regional, cultural, and tribal differences are not distinguished when researchers have reported about Native Americans in generalized language. For example, some Native American families live in cities, others on reservations or in rural areas; some Native Americans have assimilated, some have not. These distinctions alone make for vast differences among and across Native American families.

On the other hand, although there is increasing attention to and research on Latinas/os (as one of the fastest-growing groups of color currently in the United States), the family patterns of these groups are also often misunderstood or misrepresented. A major problem in this regard is that popular images of and myths about Latina/o families sometimes merge with scientific research on such families. Moreover, according to Maxine Baca Zinn (1994), very often Latina/o groups are lumped together under the hybrid label *Hispanic*, which has the effect of obscuring important differences among various Latina/o groups. Although most Latinas/os share a common language and cultural ancestry, the diversity among Latinas/os makes generalizations about their family lifestyles exceedingly difficult.

Like other groups of color, Asian Americans are a diverse group with diverse family lifestyles. Yet researchers, especially since the 1970s, have focused almost entirely on the economic and educational achievements of some Asian American families, with the result being a rather widespread depiction or generalization of "success"—strong family ties, strong work ethic, academic excellence, self-sufficiency, and a low level of welfare dependency—to all Asian American families. This is not to say that such characterizations do not describe the realities of some Asian American families; however, the tendency, both in American popular culture and in scholarly research, is to put forth the notion of a monolithic "model minority" model of Asian American families. If nothing else, such a lumping of all Asian American families together obscures the legacy of racism and the difficulties associated with acculturation these families have experienced, with the result that not all Asian American families have been successful.

Although perhaps the most frequently researched of all families of color, much of the research on African American families focuses primarily on lower- and working-class families. As critics have pointed out, not only are most of the subjects of marriage and family research on African American families from the lower class, but they are frequently from the most deprived segment of the lower class. Little systematic research exists focusing on middle-class families of color, especially the upper middle class.

Even less is known about wealthy families across race. Thus, like gender and race, class is an important factor in who gets studied and how they are studied and in who does not get studied. Across race and gender little research is carried out on upper-class families. Power is an issue here. Because women, people of color, and the lower classes generally lack power, either they are largely ignored by researchers or they are easily accessible to researchers, some of whom allow their race, sex, and class biases to affect their research. Those individuals and families with considerable wealth and power can control researchers' access to them and thus researchers' ability to use them as subjects. Because there is so little information on the marriage and family lifestyles of the upper classes, Americans, hungry for a glimpse of such lifestyles, are fascinated with media portrayals of how such families live. Whether or not these portrayals reflect the real world of upper-class marriages and families is not readily known because there is so little scientific information against which to compare.

Estimates vary, but somewhere between 2 and 10 percent of the U.S. population is homosexual. Despite popular stereotypes and the increasing visibility of lesbians and gays,

Although we are sometimes afforded a glimpse into the social world of the wealthy through the mass media, there is little systematic research on the daily lives of upper-class families, particularly if they are not white Anglo-Saxon protestant.

we are only just beginning to learn about some aspects of their family lifestyles, such as their reproductive choices and ways of parenting. Traditionally, if lesbians and gay couples were referred to at all in research or textbooks, they were treated at best as an aberration of the "real" family and at worst denied family status overall.

Lesbians and gays are similar in their behavior, but they are not a monolithic group. They vary across race, class, age, and other important social characteristics. Yet the lesbians and gays that are studied are most often young, white, and middle class. Few studies focus on lesbians and gays of color or older lesbians and gays across race and class. Indeed, over the past decade, as we (the authors of this textbook) conducted research for each of the previous editions of this book, a major obstacle in our quest to be inclusive was the lack of research on diverse family groupings such as lesbian and gay families. When we did find research on lesbians and gays, for example, much of the traditional research was narrowly focused or concerned with their sexual behavior. Like others in the population, lesbians and gays are ongoing, active members of marriages, families, and intimate relationships. Thus, such narrowly focused research perpetuates many popular myths about homosexuality and is misrepresentative of the diversity of family lifestyles in the United States. Fortunately, this situation is changing as more researchers are broadening their focus to study diverse populations and a wide range of marriage and family structures and lifestyles.

Contemporary Marriage and Family Scholarship

Although sociology as a discipline has not always made good on its claim to give accurate accounts of the social world and its social problems, a growing number of sociologists and interdisciplinary scholars are using the perspectives that the discipline offers, including a feminist perspective, to develop and transmit more complete and accurate understandings of marriages, families, and intimate relationships.

Unfortunately, shoddy research methodologies, faulty generalizations, and researcher biases, myths, stereotypes, oversimplifications, and misrepresentations continue to affect some research on marriages and families. Much of this research continues to be heterosexist as well as sex-, race-, and class-specific, even though it is generalized as applicable to the largest possible population. Social scientist Marianne Ferber's observation on this subject seems appropriate here: "It is interesting to note . . . one significant difference between studies concerned with only men as opposed to those investigating women. The latter tend to be unmistakably labeled, while the former have titles which give no hint that they are restricted to men" (1982:293).

Scientific research on marriages and families does not exist in a vacuum. Its theory and practice reflect the structure and values of U.S. society. In a society where massive inequalities in power, wealth, and prestige exist among classes and racial groups, as well as between women and men, scientific research—its methods, content, and conclusions—reflects these inequalities. Given this reality, social research must be evaluated by who is or is not the researcher, who does and does not get studied, which theoretical paradigms and underlying assumptions are accepted, which methods are used and how, and what the research actually says and does not say about the subjects.

To their credit, contemporary family researchers exhibit a growing recognition of race, class, gender, and sexual diversity in marriage and family lifestyles. Although no research techniques are specific to people of color, women, poor and working-class people, or lesbians and gays, some existing methods seem more productive than others. For example, as we have already pointed out, various field methods, such as face-to-face interviews, participant observation, and case studies, enable the research subjects to tell their stories from their own point of view. In this context, contemporary scholarship has opened up a new and healthy discourse in the area of marriage and family research. This continuing discourse has greatly enhanced our knowledge of marriages and families. In addition, any attempt to understand marriage, family, and intimate relationships within U.S. society must necessarily be informed by the implications of the globalization of the world's societies. Thus, a new and increasing emphasis on cross-cultural and global research has increased our awareness of how global connections profoundly impact our lives and has provided further insights about marriages and families in the multicultural worlds in which humans live. In the "In Other Places" box in this chapter, we take a look, as an example, at a Kenyan-born sociologist, Wamucii Njogu, and her marriage and family research conducted in her native Kenya.

Now let us turn our attention to the other half of the scientific enterprise—namely, theories pertaining to marriages and families.

THEORETICAL PERSPECTIVES

Try as we may, we cannot separate theory from real life. The way we look at and understand society and human behavior depends on our theoretical perspective. In sociology, there is no single theory of marriages and families. Many different perspectives exist. By *perspective* we simply mean a broad explanation of social reality from a particular point of view. These perspectives provide us with a basic image of society and human behavior. They define what we should study, what questions we should ask, how we should ask them, what methods we should use to gather information, and how we should interpret the answers or information we obtain. In addition, theoretical perspectives often generate subtheories or theory models. Social scientist David Cheal (1989) describes a **theory model** as a minitheory, a set of propositions intended to account for a limited set of facts.

To understand properly the sociology of contemporary marriages and families, we should know something about the different views that are part of the discipline of marriage and family study. It is therefore worthwhile not only to describe the different theoretical perspectives but also to look at them with a critical eye to weigh their relative advantages and disadvantages as explanation systems.

In the remainder of this chapter we examine and critique some of the major theoretical approaches and perspectives used in the field of sociology. As you study these different approaches, pay particular attention to how the choice of a theoretical perspective will influence not only the way data are interpreted but also the very nature of the questions asked. Consider how a different theoretical perspective would lead to a different set of questions and conclusions about marriages and families.

Sociologists approach the study of human behavior and society with a particular set of theoretical assumptions. As in other disciplines, sociology contains not just one but a number of theoretical perspectives. Although there is some debate over how many sociological perspectives exist, there is general agreement that three basic perspectives form the backbone of what has been called mainstream sociology: structural functionalism, conflict theory, and symbolic interaction. In addition, we examine the social-constructionist, social-exchange, developmental family life cycle, and feminist theoretical perspectives. Most of these theories are broad, applying not only to marriages and families, but we examine them as they have been used to explain marriage and family life generally, or some specific aspect of marriage and family life in the United States.

Structural Functionalism

In the history of the sociology of marriages and families, structural functionalism has been one of the leading theoretical perspectives used to explain how families work and how they relate to the larger society. Basically, **structural functionalism** views society as an organized and stable system, analogous to the human system—that is made up of a variety of interrelated parts or structures. Each structure performs one or several functions or meets vital social needs. These

IN OTHER PLACES

MARRIAGE AND FAMILY PATTERNS IN KENYA

As family sociologists, one of our continuing messages is that there are diverse ways in which marriages and families are structured. Cross-cultural research is important in that it allows us to learn and understand cultures different from our own while at the same time appreciate how much all humans have in common. Learning about diverse cultural structures and lifestyles helps to deepen our understanding of sociological concepts. Comparisons and contrasts of diverse marriage and family lifestyles allow us to apply concepts and theories that broaden our understanding of their meaning. They also challenge ideas of a single model of marriage and family life and highlight the flexibility of humans in creating diverse cultures.

It is often said that social research interests are sparked by personal biography. Wamucii Njogu is a classic example. An associate professor of sociology, former chair of the Department of Sociology, African and African American Studies, Latino and Latin American Studies, and Women's Studies and currently an assistant provost at Northeastern Illinois University in Chicago, Dr. Njogu is an internationally known scholar and a member of the Union for African Population Studies, the International Union for the Scientific Study of Population, and the Population

Wamucii Njogu

Association of America. Born and raised in Kenya, she speaks three languages fluently, and received her Ph.D. at the University of Wisconsin at Madison. As a bilingual bicultural sociologist, she has been able to move back and forth between her native country and the United States and examine both cultures as an "outsider from within." Sociologically, this has had important implications for her research interests, the kinds of questions she asks, the issues that she finds problem-

---

structures, sometimes called *subsystems*, are the major social institutions in society and include the families, economy, government, and religion. Each of these structures has a function for maintaining society. Families, for example, through reproduction, provide society with new members, which ensures that society is ongoing. At least in theory, all institutions in society work in harmony for the good of society and themselves. Thus, a functional analysis examines the ways in which each part of a system (society or any one of its parts) contributes to the functioning of society as a whole. In this analysis, the terms *system* and *structure* refer to the interrelatedness or interaction of the parts. *Function* refers to the consequence or impact of something for itself and other parts of the system as well as the system as a whole.

Many Americans believe in a singular model of the family to which all families must conform. Those families that do not conform are seen as problematic. People who believe families must be structured in a certain way (for example, two heterosexual parents) to fulfill important family tasks and who see single-parent or female-headed families, lesbian and gay families, stepfamilies, and the changing role of women in marriages and families as threats to marriage and family life or as indicative of the demise of the family share a common view with structural functionalists. Are you a structural functionalist? Do you share these views?

The Family from a Functionalist Perspective   In analyzing the family, a person using the functionalist perspective would ask general questions, such as, What do families contribute to the maintenance of society? How does the structure of society affect families? How do families mesh with other institutions in society? Not only does this perspective view society as a system, but it regards families themselves as systems. Therefore, a functional analysis would examine such

atic, and the nature of her analyses and contributions to marriage and family theory and research. Some examples from her biography reflect this connection.

Dr. Njogu was first attracted to the study of sociology when, as an undergraduate student at the University of Nairobi, she was assigned to write a sociological research paper. Coming from a background in which her parents owned a large farm and employed a large number of poor rural workers, Dr. Njogu decided to focus on poverty among these workers and the question of how these people came to be where they were in the stratification structure. Her findings—namely, that these workers typically came from generations of such workers, that within these families some members (primarily women) were worse off generally than others, and that these families generally had a large number of children whom they could not adequately support economically—led her to her longstanding interests in stratification, gender inequality, fertility, family formation, and child fostering and informal adoption.

Her interest in gender inequality is also tied to the fact that she comes from a long line of female-headed households (which defies tradition in the patriarchal society into which she was born), including a paternal grandmother who, after the death of her husband, defied cultural tradition by refusing to marry her dead husband's brother. Remaining single, this woman raised her children alone and

instilled in them egalitarian values. Consequently, Dr. Njogu's father raised her and her male siblings as equals. Her research on female law students' participation in the classroom was shaped by her own experiences as a female student in high school and college in Kenya. Because of the preference for males in her culture, monies for school go first and foremost for boys' education. Dr. Njogu was thus, one of a small percentage of Kenyan women who attended high school and of an even smaller percentage attending college. She was an extremely bright student, which "was not the thing to do" in Kenya, she says. As a result, the boys called her names, such as "girl/boy," because only boys were supposed to be in school and to be smart. This helped her understand what sexism and gender inequality meant not just in abstract terms, but in terms of her actual personal experiences.

Most recently, Dr. Njogu has conducted research and written a series of papers on HIV/AIDS in Kenya. For example, using data collected in Kenya in 1998, Dr. Njogu studied the relationship between HIV/AIDS knowledge and risk prevention or safe sexual behavior. Although HIV/AIDS has killed individual family members and sometimes whole families, this deadly reality has not translated into safe sexual behavior, particularly for young women. In a report of her findings at the International Union for the Scientific Study of Population in Salvador,

Brazil, Dr. Njogu indicated that the gender gap is one of the greatest barriers to sexual behavior change in Kenya. For example, young Kenyan women are less likely than their male counterparts to know that AIDS can be transmitted through sexual intercourse or that condoms can protect them against infection. The difficulty experienced by women in implementing prevention strategies is another reason why AIDS knowledge may not necessarily lead to behavior change. Young women in Kenya consider their risk of contracting HIV/AIDS to be high, not because of their own behavior but because of their partners' past and current sexual behavior. This knowledge notwithstanding, unequal gender relations and other cultural traditions prevent women from protecting themselves against HIV infection.

According to Dr. Njogu, cross-cultural research not only fosters a better understanding and appreciation for cultural diversity but also often serves to debunk some of the myths created by research that uses Western culture as the model of marriage and family life.

What do you think? Is there a similar gender gap in HIV/AIDS knowledge in the United States? What role does gender play in risk prevention behavior among young American adults? What can we learn from cross-cultural research about the differential impact on family members of diseases such as HIV/AIDS?

---

issues as how families organize themselves for survival and what functions families perform for society and for their individual members. Take, for instance, the question of teenage suicide. A person using a functionalist perspective might ask questions about how the family functions vis-à-vis individual family members who contemplate suicide.

According to functionalists, family functions historically have been divided along gender and age lines. Women and men must perform different tasks, as must younger and older people. Particularly since the Industrial Revolution, an important family task has been to provide economic support for family members. If the family is to survive, someone has to earn money by working for wages outside the home—an *instrumental role*. At the same time, someone must work inside the home to maintain it for the wage earner as well as for other family members—an *expressive role*. This division of labor along gender lines is said to make women and men interdependent and characterizes what sociologists call the

traditional family, a family form that many conservatives believe to be the one and only true family form.

Functionalists are interested not only in the intended, overt, or **manifest functions** of social institutions such as the family but in the unintended, unrecognized, or **latent functions** as well. Thus, a manifest function of having children might be to continue the family lineage or to add to marital satisfaction. Because children can add stress to a relationship, however, the introduction of children in the early years of family life often has the latent function of decreasing marital satisfaction. In addition, not all features of a social system are **functional**—performing a positive service by helping to maintain the system in a balanced state or promoting the achievement of group goals. Some features of the system might actually hamper the achievement of group goals and disrupt the system's balance. Such features are said to be **dysfunctional.** A single feature can be functional and dysfunctional at the same time. For example, the movement of married women into the labor force might be defined as functional in that their salaries contribute to the family income but defined as dysfunctional in that their time with their families is limited. A classic example of the use of the structural-functional perspective to explain how marriages and families work is embedded in the "nuclear family model" popularized in the mid 1950s by the late sociologist Talcott Parsons.

The Nuclear Family Model   Recall from Chapter 1 that as Western societies became industrialized and urbanized in the late nineteenth and early twentieth centuries, the nuclear family emerged as the dominant family type to meet the needs of an industrial economy. Talcott Parsons (1955, 1964) agreed with the structural-functional assumption that the family is an adaptive system that performs essential functions for its individual members as well as for society as a whole. He argued, however, that in modern society the functional importance of the nuclear family has declined as many of its functions have been taken over and performed by other social institutions. This is particularly true in terms of the family's economic function. The modern nuclear family is no longer an economic unit. (This issue is often debated in the literature and will be discussed in more detail in Chapter 10.) According to Parsons, the two major functions of the modern family are now socialization of the young and personality stabilization of adults. Personality stabilization is the process whereby individuals internalize society's values and expectations concerning gender-appropriate behavior to the point where these values and cultural expectations become a consistent part of the individual's identity throughout her or his lifetime.

The nuclear family model places great emphasis on the isolation of the nuclear family from the extended family. It also emphasizes that a differentiation of gender roles within the family is a functional necessity for the solidarity of the marriage relationship. Parsons described the male role in this regard as instrumental and the female role as expressive. The personality traits needed to carry out these roles are quite different. **Instrumental traits** encourage self-confidence, rationality, competition, and coolness—qualities that facilitate male success in the world of work. In contrast, **expressive traits** encourage nurturance, emotionality, sensitivity, and warmth—qualities that help women succeed in caring for a husband, children, and a home.

Critique   Probably no other sociological perspective has been the center of as much attention, controversy, and criticism as structural functionalism. Parsons's nuclear family model has often been at the center of some of this controversy. Some of the major criticisms of this model are the same as those directed against functionalism generally: The model is specific to a particular time and place, does not use a historical context, and does not deal with the diversity of experiences that has always characterized U.S. families. What seemed true about marriages and families in the 1950s is less true today. The latest census data confirm that fewer and fewer families fit the Parsonian nuclear family model.

In addition, married-couple families often exhibit a diversity of structures and roles that the Parsonian model does not account for. Using this model, for instance, how can we explain the growing number of men today who are openly nurturant, caring, and sensitive—traits that Parsons describes as exclusively expressive and female? The nuclear family model is especially criticized for its rigid, exaggerated, and oversimplified view of marital interaction generally and of women's experiences specifically. It is also criticized for defining the family narrowly, through a white, male middle-class perspective (Andersen, 2003). For example, how does the nuclear family model apply to African American families under slavery, where legal marriage was prohibited and women's and men's roles were interchanged? Similarly, can it explain the diversity in Native American families, particularly those in which women exercised economic power in subsistence residential units that were the basis of their tribal economy?

Although functionalism has provided important insights, such as how marriages and families work and presumably why they exist, several important criticisms have been raised about this perspective generally. For example, although functionalism may be a useful framework for identifying a society's structural parts and the alleged functions of these parts, what function a particular structure serves, and why, are not always clear. What, for example, is the function of the division of labor in the family along gender lines? Is it efficiency and survival, as the functionalists maintain, or is it the perpetuation of the social dominance of certain categories of people—namely, men—and the subordination of others—namely, women? Another important criticism is the conservative bias of functional analysis. Critics argue that by assuming consensus lies at the basis of any social order, functionalists tend to promote and rationalize the status quo and to understate disharmony and conflict. Thus, they do not consider that something might be wrong with the system itself.

Although structural functionalism was the dominant theory in the field for over 30 years, the changing political consciousness of the 1960s brought about increasing criticism of this perspective. Today there is widespread recognition that structural functionalism generally and the nuclear family model specifically are limiting when used to analyze families in the United States and are therefore no longer representative of "mainstream" sociological thought on families. Consequently, functionalism has greatly declined in importance as a viable frame of reference for understanding society, its institutions, and its members. In fact, some of its strongest supporters during its peak now declare that it is "embarrassing" (Moore, 1978) and "dead," and that it should be abandoned and replaced by more enlightened perspectives (Turner and Maryanski, 1979). However, its impact, especially on the public, can still be detected. Today, when people talk about the family, they often have in mind the functionalist model of the nuclear family. For many people, the nuclear family remains the ideal form, even though such families are less prevalent today than they were in the past.

Conflict Theory

Since the 1960s, the conflict perspective has become increasingly popular and important in modern sociology and in the works of feminist scholars across academic disciplines. There are several different approaches to conflict theory; however,

Karl Marx

Max Weber

Emile Durkheim

Jane Addams

W. E. B. Dubois

Harriet Martineau

Patricia Hill Collins

Joe. R. Feagin

Chéla Sandoval

Although women and African Americans were involved in the early development of sociology, their contributions went largely unrecognized until the last two decades, when a movement for a more inclusive scholarship took hold. Today, women, people of color, and other theorists using a multicultural and inclusive approach to theorizing are gaining increasing visibility.

all of them have their roots in the nineteenth-century pioneering writings of Karl Marx. Thus, our discussion here is of a very general nature and combines various strands of thought on conflict theory today. First, however, we take a brief look at Marxian theory.

Karl Marx Karl Marx (1818–1883) was an economist, political agitator, and social theorist who did much to revolutionize social and philosophical thinking about human society. Appalled by the brutal treatment of workers and their families during the nineteenth-century Industrial Revolution in Europe, Marx sought to understand the causes of this condition, in hopes of changing it. Basically, he believed that the problem lay in the social organization of industrial societies. Such societies were capitalistic: The means of production were privately owned and were used to maximize profits.

For Marx, every aspect of social life is based on economic relationships. For example, he believed all industrialized societies are characterized by competition and conflict between two main groups: the capitalists (owners of the land and factories) and the proletariat (workers). These two groups have fundamentally opposing interests, as well as unequal power. Conflict arises because the capitalists can maximize their profit only by exploiting the proletariat. At the same time, it is in the interest of the proletariat to revolt and overthrow the capitalist system and to establish a classless society in which wealth and power would be distributed evenly. Thus, meaningful social change comes about only as a result of the struggle between competing groups. In essence, for Marx, economic power explains the structure of societies and social relationships. Order and balance are always tenuous in capitalist societies. Such societies are held together by the power of capitalists to dominate the workers.

Relative to the fundamental sociological question—What is the relationship between the individual and society?—Marxian theory addresses both structure and action. It deals with structural factors in that it stresses that the historical circumstances of capitalism limit most of the choices open to people. At the same time, it stresses the action element in that it recognizes the capacity of workers to join together as a class-conscious group to collectively change existing economic and social conditions (Light, Keller, and Calhoun, 1996).

Themes of Conflict Theory Like functionalism, **conflict theory** focuses on social structures and institutions in society. The basic assumption of the conflict perspective, and perhaps the one that most sets it apart from functionalism, however, is the notion that conflict is natural and inevitable in all human interaction, including family systems. Therefore, a complete understanding of society is possible only through a critical examination of competition, coercion, and conflict in society, especially those processes that lead some people to have great power and control and others to have little or no power and control. Thus, of major concern are the inequalities that are built into social structures or systems. Rather than focusing on interdependence, unity, and consensus, conflict theorists focus on society as an arena in which individuals and

groups compete over limited resources and fight for power and control. A key assumption here is that certain groups and individuals have much greater power and access to key resources than others do. From this perspective, disorder, disagreement, and open hostility among individuals and groups are viewed as normal, and stability is the condition that requires explanation.

For the purposes of our discussion, we can reduce conflict theory to three central themes: (1) Humans have basic interests or things they want and attempt to acquire. (2) Power is at the base of all social relationships, and it is always scarce, unequally distributed, and coercive. (3) Values and ideas are weapons used by different groups to advance their own ends rather than to define society's identity and goals (Wallace and Wolf, 2005). Given these assumptions, the conflict perspective leads us to ask questions about the sources of tension among individuals and groups with different amounts of power, the techniques of conflict control in society, and the ways in which those with power perpetuate, maintain, and extend that power. In short, a major underlying question of conflict analysis is, Who benefits from and who is systematically deprived by any given social arrangement?

The Family from a Conflict Perspective Whereas functionalists focus on the tasks that serve the interests of the family as a whole, conflict theorists see families, like all societal institutions, as a set of social relationships that benefit some members more than others. Thus, a conflict theorist might ask general questions, such as the following: How is social inequality built into the structure of marriages and families? What is the role of a marital partner or family member in promoting family disintegration or change? When conflict occurs in the family, who wins? Who loses? How are racial, ethnic, gender, class, and other inequalities perpetuated through the operation of the family?

From this perspective, marriages and families can be viewed as smaller versions of the larger class system, where the well-being of one class (men) is the result of the exploitation and oppression of another class (women). The family exploits women specifically by encouraging them to perform unpaid housework and child care so that men can devote their time to capitalist endeavors. Historically, those men who had the power to do so defined marriages and families in such a way that women were the sexual property of men. In consequence, marriage became a legally and socially enforced contract of sexual property. Although women in the United States are no longer legally defined as the property of men, other examples of male domination of women abound. For example, women continue to have major responsibility for and perform the major portion of housework and child rearing, even though most women are now in the paid labor force (Hochschild, 1997; U.S. Census Bureau, 2004).

In essence, then, the basic source of male dominance and women's subordination is the home and family. Although functionalists may view the family as a refuge, for the conflict theorist the question is, What kind of refuge is it, and whom does it benefit? The link between the traditional family and social inequality involves a number of conflicts that are discussed in some detail in later chapters of this book, including violence against women, children, and the elderly; divorce; female-headed families; and the feminization of poverty.

Critique For many people, especially those who experience oppression, the conflict perspective offers a concrete set of propositions that explain unequal access to resources in terms of institutional structure rather than personal deficiencies. A major strength of this perspective is the way in which it relates social and organizational structure to group interests and the distribution of resources. Furthermore, it provides a historical framework within which to identify social change: the major shifts in the distribution of societal resources and social and political power. By tracing social behavior back to individuals' interests and the purposeful way they pursue them, it suggests a model to explain social and political change. And finally, unlike functionalism, the conflict perspective does not treat norms, values, and ideas as external to, and constraints on, individual behavior. Rather, the conflict perspective views human beings as very much involved in using the system of norms, values, and ideas as much as being used by it. Those who have the power use these systems to further their individual or group interests.

Conflict theory is not without its criticisms. One major criticism is that the underlying assumptions that power is people's main objective and conflict is the major feature of social life are too narrow. Some critics argue, for example, that within the family, societal norms encourage certain behaviors that either prevent conflict or keep it under control. Thus, for example, disagreements among family members usually can be resolved without the use of physical force.

In addition, the conflict perspective is often criticized for explicitly advocating social change, thereby giving up some of its claim to scientific objectivity. Furthermore, conflict theory, like functionalism, raises the issue of value neutrality. Whereas structural functionalists evaluate social patterns in a system in terms of whether they are positive or negative, conflict theorists are purposely critical of society. Both of these positions pose a dilemma for value-free sociology. Most conflict theorists try to separate their value judgments from their analysis of society. However, when they focus on inequalities in society and claim, for instance, that a more equitable distribution of tasks and resources between the sexes is desirable, the inherent value judgment is quite clear. These problems notwithstanding, the conflict perspective is a useful framework for analyzing how factors such as race, class, gender, age, and ethnicity are linked to the unequal distribution of valuable resources in marriages and families, including power, property, money, prestige, and education.

Symbolic Interactionism

Functionalism and the conflict perspective both concern themselves with macropatterns (large-scale patterns) that characterize society or groups like families as a whole. In contrast, the **symbolic interaction** perspective focuses on micropatterns (small-scale patterns) of face-to-face interaction among people in specific settings, such as within marriages and families. This perspective is based on the notion that society is made up of interacting individuals who communicate primarily through the use of shared **symbols**—objects, words, sounds, and events that are given meaning by members of a culture—and construct reality as they go about the business of their daily lives. The most important set of symbols that humans use is language. People interact with one another based on their understandings of the meanings of words and social situations as well as their perceptions of what others expect of them within those situations. Thus, a major emphasis is on individuals and their social relationships, the subjective meanings of human behavior, and the various processes through which people come to construct and agree on various definitions of reality.

The Family from a Symbolic Interaction Perspective

When using the symbolic interaction perspective as a frame of reference for analyzing marriages and families, one might ask questions such as the following: How are marriages and families experienced? How do individual family members interact to create, sustain, and change marriages and families? How do family members attempt to shape the reality perceived by other family members? How do the behaviors of family members change from one situation to another?

According to the late sociologist Ernest Burgess (1926), the family represents a unified set of interacting individuals. That is, unity in family life comes about as a result of interactions among various family members. In this sense, the concern is with marriages and families as social processes rather than with their structure. Thus, a symbolic interactionist would argue that the reality of marriage and family life is not fixed but is *socially constructed* and is constructed differently by various family members with different roles, privileges, and responsibilities. The **social construction of reality** is the process whereby people assign meanings to social phenomena—objects, events, and characteristics—that almost always cause those who draw upon these meanings to emphasize some aspect of a phenomenon and to ignore others. These assigned meanings have tremendous consequences for the individuals involved, depending on how they interact with each other, what decisions they make, and what actions they take (Ferrante, 2005).

Taking this perspective, sociologist Jessie Bernard (1982) has argued, for example, that women and men are likely to view and experience their marriages differently. Referring to this phenomenon as "her" and "his" marriages, Bernard contends that due to traditionally different sex role socialization and expectations, women have less power than men in marriages and families. Married women, therefore, must make certain accommodations, some of which may have negative effects on their mental health. In this respect, the psychological costs of marriage are much greater for wives than for husbands, and the benefits are far less.

Social Constructionism

As the limitations of an objectivist explanation of social life have become more and more evident in postmodern society, many social scientists and other scholars (not only sociologists but also social workers, political scientists, lawyers, and historians) increasingly have sought to explain social life in terms of a subjectivist approach. These scholars use what is referred to as a *social-constructionist perspective*. **Social constructionism** is an extension of symbolic interaction theory, in which the analysis is framed entirely in terms of a conceptualization of the social construction of reality. A guiding principle is that human experience is not uniform and cannot be generalized to all people. The important facts of human social life are not inherent in human biology but are developed through a complex process of human interaction in which we learn both the attitudes and the behaviors appropriate to our culture and attempt to modify these scripted behaviors and attitudes to make them more palatable. Those using a social-constructionist perspective argue that the meaning of social reality is neither transhistorical nor culturally universal, but rather varies from culture to culture and within any culture over time. Some fundamental assumptions of this perspective and symbolic interactionism generally are as follows:

- Reality is invented, constructed largely out of the meanings and values of the observer.
- Language is a mediating influence on all constructions; we bring forth realities through our interactions with other human beings.
- We cannot know an objective reality apart from our subjective views of it.
- Culture, history, politics, and economic conditions all influence individual experiences of social reality.

Social Constructionism and the Family   Almost any subject related to marriage and family life can be analyzed within the context of the social-constructionist paradigm. One example of the application of the constructivist perspective that is especially relevant to the sociology of marriages and families can be seen in terms of the concept of gender. Gender is a socially constructed system for classifying people as girl or boy, woman or man, feminine or masculine (Chapter 3 is devoted to an in-depth discussion of gender within a broad context of social constructionism). Take masculinity, for instance: Men are not born to follow a predetermined biological imperative encoded somewhere in their physical makeup. Rather, to be a man is to participate in the social life of a culture as it defines manhood and masculinity. Thus, it is to participate in society as a gendered being. In this sense, men are not born but made by culture. Men also make themselves, actively constructing their masculinities within a social and historical context. Therefore, the reality of being a male in twenty-first-century U.S. society and its impact on marriage, family, and intimate relationships is quite different from that experienced by individual men, marriages, and families 100 years ago. It is also very different from being a male in South Africa, Sri Lanka, Southeast Asia, Bosnia, Kosovo, Albania, Israel, Palestine, or the former Soviet Union. In this same context, the roles of males as husband, father, brother, lover, worker, and so on, are all shaped by our cultural constructions and agreements about gender. The social construction of masculinity in the United States defines men's roles in the family as economic provider and protector of women and children. In New Guinea, among the Tchambuli, however, men are expected to be submissive, emotional, delicate, and dependent.

The social constructionist perspective is both historical and comparative. In the case of marriages, families, and intimate relationships, such a perspective allows us to explore the ways in which the meanings of social reality and of social experiences vary across marriages, families, and cultures, as well as how they change over historical time. This perspective enables us to better understand gender and its relationship in marriages and families. Thus, how culture and individual men construct masculinity has a very real impact on how men relate to women and children in marriages, families, and intimate relationships. The implication here is that all such relationships are social productions and have no intrinsic meaning. That is, they have no meaning outside that which is understood by the actors. As you continue to read this textbook, you will find that we apply the social-constructionist perspective wherever relevant. You will therefore find a range of topics, including violence, intimacy, gender, parenting, motherhood, fatherhood, race, ethnicity and sexuality, discussed within the framework of constructionism.

Critique   The symbolic interaction perspective brings people back into our analyses. Rather than seeing humans as passive beings who simply respond to society's rules, interactionists give us a view of humans as actively involved in constructing, shaping, sustaining, and changing the social world. It is a useful framework for examining the complexities of relationships and the daily workings of marriages and families, complexities that functionalism and the conflict perspective miss. One of the major advantages of this perspective is that it helps us understand how the roles we play are so important in our social constructions of reality.

Likewise, social constructionism is a useful approach for studying human social life and offers a viable alternative to traditional static, ahistoric, and deterministic theoretical perspectives. According to some scholars (for example, Rosenblum and Travis, 1996), an important advantage of a constructionist approach is that it enables us to understand that certain categories of human experience, such as race, sex, sexual orientation, and class, have social significance—that is, these categories are socially created and arbitrary. Instead of viewing people as essentially different by virtue of these labels, social constructionism leads us to question not the *essential* difference between categories, but rather the origin and consequence of the labeling or categorization system itself. Thus, as we will see throughout this textbook, categories such as race are not clear-cut; racial categories do not exist apart from the social and cultural milieux in which they operate.

Neither symbolic interactionism nor social constructionism are without limitations or critics. In focusing attention on the subjective aspects of human experiences and the situations in which they occur, both perspectives ignore the objective realities of inequality, racism, sexism, and the differential distribution of wealth, status, and power among various groups; they also minimize the impact of these phenomena on individuals and families. Criticisms directed specifically at social constructionism include the claim that it is inherently inconsistent, that its theoretical assumptions are contradictory. Some critics argue that there is no clear agreement about what constitutes constructionism. Most often those who criticize constructionism are objectivists who argue that (1) social constructionism springs from a particular set of moral and political values or biases, and (2) social constructionism is simply an exercise in *debunking* previously held truths (Best,

1995). These criticisms notwithstanding, a social-constructionist perspective provides a framework by which to make sense of what categories such as marriage, family, race, ethnicity, class, and sexual orientation mean in both historical and contemporary context; in addition, it heightens our awareness of the socially constructed nature of everyday life.

Social Exchange Theory

Probably the theoretical perspective most often used in the discipline to study marriages and families is **social exchange theory.** This theory adopts an economic model of human behavior based on costs, benefits, and the expectation of reciprocity; for this reason it is sometimes referred to as the *rational-choice perspective.* It tends to be very close to the way that many of us see and explain behavior in our everyday lives.

> *Have you ever wondered why some person you know or heard about remained in an unhappy relationship? Did you try to analyze this behavior by asking what the person might be getting out of the relationship versus whatever makes her or him unhappy (in other words, the pluses, or benefits, and minuses, or costs, of the relationship)? Did the person eventually leave the relationship? Did you wonder what finally made her or him end it? Was your answer that the costs finally became too great or outweighed the benefits? If you have ever engaged in this type of cost–benefit analysis to explain your own or other people's actions and relationships, you were using a basic social exchange perspective.*

Social exchange theory shares many of the assumptions of symbolic-interaction theory and thus in broad terms is another extension of interaction theory. Social exchange theory is so named because its underlying premise is that social exchange forms the basis of all social interaction. Exchange theorists view social interaction as an exchange of tangible or intangible goods and services, ranging from money or physical labor to social recognition, love, and respect. Humans are thought to be rational beings who, in making decisions, weigh the profits to be gained from a particular action against the costs it will incur. Only when people feel that the gains of their interactions outweigh the costs do they adopt the behavior. People, then, engage in those actions that bring them the greatest benefits at the least cost. They will continue to engage in these actions as long as they perceive them to be profitable.

The two best-known proponents of social exchange theory are George Homans and Peter Blau. Homans (1961) focused on actual behavior that is rewarded or punished by the behavior of others. According to Homans, humans react to stimuli based on need, reward, and reinforcement. Thus, in the various exchange relationships in which humans engage, the rewards will usually be proportional to the costs. Blau (1964), on the other hand, was more concerned with explaining large-scale social structures. According to Blau, not all exchange can be explained in terms of actual behavior. Rather, exchange, like other interactions, is a subjective and interpretative process. Blau agrees with Homans that humans want rewards, and in exchange interactions each person receives something perceived as equivalent to that which is given. Blau refers to this as "fair exchange." He contends, however, that our relationship choices and decisions are not made purely on the basis of the perceived rewards but are affected by various social influences, such as family and friends.

A good example of this can be seen in terms of various interracial relationships. An interracial couple might find their relationship mutually beneficial and satisfying, with the benefits far outweighing the costs. Social approval of the relationship may be very important to the couple, however. Thus, if family and friends strongly disapprove, the couple might decide to terminate the relationship.

The Family from a Social Exchange Perspective
Marriage and family literature is filled with examples of social exchange. Most experts agree that marriage and family life are characterized by an exchange of goods and services. Thus, most exchange analyses of marriage and family behavior focus on relations between couples. Typically, a person using an exchange perspective is concerned with questions like those previously asked of you. In the language of exchange theory, for example, we might explain the observation that when women work they gain power in the family (see Chapter 10) with the reasoning that in exchange for their economic contribution, working women share more equitably in decision making.

Family sociologists, particularly those concerned with dating, mating, and marital behavior, have long used exchange theory to explain this behavior. As we will see in Chapter 5, many sociologists use exchange theory to explain how people in the United States choose whom to date and marry. They contend that Americans search for the best possible mate (product) given their own resources (physical attractiveness, intelligence, youth, status, money). People in this situation weigh a range of costs and benefits before choosing a mate. As you read this textbook, think about the value of different types of resources and the exchange processes at work in understanding a variety of marriage and family behaviors and relationships.

Critique Exchange theory assumes that humans are rational, calculating beings who consciously weigh the costs versus the benefits of their relationships. A major problem with this notion of human behavior is that it cannot be disproved. Almost any behavior can be explained simply by saying that it must have had some value to the person involved, whether or not this is really the case. Furthermore, the notion of rational choice is limiting in that humans do not always act rationally, nor do we always agree on what rational behavior is. We do not always choose relationships or interactions simply because the rewards outweigh the costs. In fact, sometimes the reverse is true. One way of analyzing the "battered-woman syndrome" (discussed in Chapter 11) is to assume that women stay in abusive relationships not because the rewards outweigh the costs but because other factors, such as fear of physical violence if they leave, override all other considerations.

These criticisms notwithstanding, an exchange perspective provides us with a unique framework for explaining many face-to-face relationships. It provides insight into people's values, goals, and perceptions of reality. Exchange theory is probably most valuable for explaining people's actions when we want to know and understand the details of individual behavior.

The Developmental Family Life Cycle Model

Developmental family life cycle theory pays close attention to changes in families over time and attempts to explain family life in terms of a process that unfolds over the life course of families. Sociologist Paul Glick (Glick and Parke, 1965) was the first to analyze families in terms of a life cycle. According to Glick, families pass through a series of stages: (1) family formation (first marriage); (2) start of childbearing (birth of first child); (3) end of childbearing (birth of last child); (4) "empty nest" (when the last child leaves home); and (5) "family dissolution" (death of one spouse). Other life cycle theories identify somewhat similar stages.

According to such developmental theories, families change over time in terms of both the people who are members of the family and the roles they play. At various stages in the family life cycle, the family has different developmental tasks to perform. Each new stage in the family life cycle is brought on by a change in the composition of the family. These changes, in turn, affect various aspects of the family's well-being, including its economic viability. At each stage of development, the family is confronted with a distinct set of tasks whose completion is considered essential both for individual development and success at the next stage. One of the most widely used developmental theories in family sociology is an eight-stage model developed by Evelyn Duvall (1977).

> **???** As you study this model of family development, think about your own family and other families you know. How do these families fit into such a model? How do they differ? If they differ, does this mean that these families are abnormal or dysfunctional? (To pursue this activity, see the Writing Your Own Script box at the end of this chapter.)

Stage 1: Beginning families. At this first stage of development, the married couple does not have children and is just beginning married life and adjusting to it.

Stage 2: Childbearing families. The family is still forming in this stage. The first child is born, and women are deeply involved in childbearing and child rearing.

Stage 3: Families with preschool children. The family's oldest child is somewhere between $2\frac{1}{2}$ and 6 years of age. The mother is still deeply involved in child rearing. This stage lasts about 3 to 4 years.

Stage 4: Families with schoolchildren. The oldest child (or children) in the family is school-aged. With children in school, the mother is free to pursue other options, such as work outside the home.

Stage 5: Families with teenagers. In this stage, the oldest child is between 13 and 20 years old. The family must adjust to having adolescents in the home and adapt to their growing independence. This stage may last up to 7 years.

Stage 6: Families as launching centers. At this stage, the oldest child has been launched into adulthood. Families must develop adult relationships with grown children as they adjust to children leaving the family "nest." This stage lasts until the last child leaves home, usually a period of about 8 years.

Stage 7: Families in the middle years. This stage is sometimes called the "empty-nest" stage. It is a distinct new stage in the developmental cycle of the family and spans the time from when the last child leaves home to retirement or old age.

Stage 8: Aging families. Members of the family who work outside the home have retired at this stage. In this stage, families must cope with events related to aging, such as chronic illnesses and the eventual death of one of the spouses. The remaining spouse must then deal with the factors and experiences associated with widowhood.

Critique Although developmental family life cycle theory generally calls attention to the changing nature of family relationships over time, distinguishing a "typical" family life cycle is difficult, if not impossible. As family norms change, the stages of family development also vary. In fact, some scholars believe the stages of the family life cycle have become increasingly useful as indicators of change rather than as stages that all or even most families can be expected to experience. Although life cycle theories give us important insights into the complexities of family life, a shortcoming is that they assume most families are nuclear families with children. Thus, such theories present a "typical" family life cycle descriptive of the "conventional" family. As with structural functionalism, for example, *most* family life cycle theories do not incorporate the diversity of family lifestyles prevalent in U.S. society. Where, for example, do families without children, single-parent families, and remarried families fit in these models?

Moreover, families within various racial and ethnic groups develop through stages not recognized in these models. For example, due in part to their general disadvantaged economic position, many families of color and poor families across race take in relatives at some time in the family life cycle. In addition, a growing number of families in all classes are taking in and caring for aging parents. What does a developmental family life cycle model tell us about these families? Not only does such a theory omit these arrangements, but it generally implies a linear, or straight-line, progression in family life that few families actually experience. Families, for example, may progress through several of the early stages only to go back and repeat earlier stages, particularly if children are involved.

Furthermore, developmental theories such as Duvall's generally assume that developmental tasks, particularly those in the early stages, are gender-specific. Consider, for example, Duvall's first four stages. Each stage is defined entirely in terms of the presence of children and the role of women as caretakers and caregivers. Men and their parenting roles are totally omitted.

Feminist Theories and Perspectives

Feminist theory is not a single unified view; there is no single feminist theory. Rather, there are many types of feminist theory, just as there are many types of sociological theory. Nonetheless, this single label is often used to represent a diversity of feminist perspectives that contain certain common characteristics or principles. In this regard, feminist theory presents a generalized set of ideas about the basic features of society and human experience from a woman-centered perspective. It is woman-centered in three ways: (1) The starting point of all its investigations is the situations and experiences of women; (2) it treats women as the main subjects in the research process, that is, it attempts to view the world from the distinctive vantage points of women; and (3) it is critical and activist on behalf of women (Lengermann and Brantley, 2004).

A word of caution: Not all theories that deal with women or gender issues are feminist theories. To be considered feminist, a theory must reflect a feminist consciousness—an awareness rooted in a commitment to activist goals. In addition, it should adopt three basic philosophical approaches: (1) gender is the central focus; (2) status quo gender relations are viewed as problematic in that women are defined as subordinate to men; and (3) gender relations are viewed as the result of social, not natural, factors (Chafetz, 1988).

Basically, all feminist theories attempt to answer two fundamental questions. The first is, Where are women? The second is, Why is this situation as it is? In addressing these questions, feminist theories typically focus on the ways in which specific definitions of gender affect the organization of social institutions and patterns of gender inequality. Feminists have encouraged us to make the personal political. This helps us understand that individual behavior and experiences within marriages, families, and intimate relationships are part of and impacted by larger societal institutions and other social, political, and historical factors. Finally, a major objective of feminist theories is social change. Perhaps more than most theories, feminist theories are explicitly and self-consciously political in their advocacy of social change.

In general, feminist theories and perspectives demonstrate how traditional ideas and theories have been derived from the particular experiences of some men and then have been used as universal standards against which all others have been viewed and judged. Asking sociological questions and studying marriages and families from a feminist perspective transforms traditional models of inquiry. No matter the discipline, however, when men's experiences are the standard, women and other subordinated groups (including many men) appear incomplete, inadequate, or invisible. On the other hand, when women's experiences are taken seriously, new methods and theoretical perspectives must be established (Andersen, 2003). For example, feminist theories and scholarship make central considerations of the ways that race, ethnicity, sexuality, and class influence our marriage and family experiences. Feminist scholars, for instance, have revised our thinking about motherhood as a static universal category of experience. Scholarship such as Denise Segura's study (1994) of how heterosexual Chicana and Mexicana immigrant women balance work and family roles shows not only how the meaning and practice of motherhood are culturally constructed, and thus vary among different groups of women, but also that a white middle-class model of motherhood has been taken by some scholars to be a universal standard by which all other mothers are evaluated.

Although feminist theory is interdisciplinary, it is especially compatible with the sociological imagination because it links individual experience to social organization. Like other major sociological categories such as race and class, gender also influences the distribution of wealth, power, and privilege; how much we will learn and earn; how long we and our children will live; and how we are defined by others. As we have stated, there are many types of feminist theory and, as their various names imply, not all of them adopt the same focus. Listed below are brief descriptions of several prominent feminist theoretical perspectives. As you will find, we cannot always easily distinguish one from another.

- *Liberal feminist theory* assumes that at the basis of women's inequality is **sexism,** a set of beliefs about the superiority of men and inferiority of women that justifies prejudice and discrimination against women. Thus, the focus of this perspective is almost entirely on issues of equal opportunity and individual choice to the neglect of questions about how gender inequality emerged or the effects of race and class inequality in women's experiences. Its analysis for change, therefore, is limited to issues of reform relative to equal opportunity and individual choice.

- *Socialist feminist theory* rejects the reform orientation of liberal feminist theory. Rooted in classical Marxism, this perspective maintains that the sexual division of labor is the first form of class conflict. Thus, class and gender hierarchies become the base from which socialist feminist theorists explain systems of oppression such as capitalism, patriarchy, and domination. Of particular concern here are issues of production, reproduction, socialization, and sexuality and how they exhibit and maintain inequalities.

- *Marxist feminist theory* combines the classic Marxian class analysis and the feminist principle of social protest. This perspective begins with the premise that gender oppression is a reflection, first and foremost, of people's class position and only secondarily a reflection of gender itself. In general, women's inequality is explained in terms of class oppression and property inequality, exploited labor, and alienation. Marxist feminists advocate the abolition of capitalism (and thus class and class oppression) through revolutionary action as the solution to gender inequality.

- *Radical feminist theory* contends that oppression is pervasive throughout society. Most radical feminist theories see patriarchy as the basic cause of women's oppression, and in the process they downplay the impact of race and class oppression in women's experiences. A key point in these analyses is the description of patriarchy as physical and psychological violence practiced by men and male-dominated institutions against women.

- *Lesbian feminist theory* maintains that oppression of lesbians, like racial, class, and sexual oppression, is important in determining women's inequality. Lesbian feminists focus on the reasons for the dominance of heterosexuality. Adrienne Rich (1980), for example, argues that heterosexuality is political in nature in that it is "compulsory" in patriarchal societies and that lesbianism represents resistance and a threat to patriarchy. Some lesbian theorists have been among the first to explore how some women, themselves oppressed, actively participate in the oppression of other women; for example, white women oppressing women of color, heterosexual women oppressing lesbians. Thus, much of their writing calls for the eradication of prejudice and discrimination within the community of women itself. In addition, some lesbian feminists (as well as some nonlesbian feminists) advocate "separatism"—both the sexual separation of women from men and the wider separation of women from male culture and institutions—as a strategy of liberation. There is no common consensus, however, about how much separatism is necessary or how it will function.

- *Women-of-color feminist theory,* like other feminist perspectives, is an umbrella term for a wide range of viewpoints. Taking as a starting point that women of color have typically been omitted from all analyses, including *early* feminist analyses, women-of-color feminists begin their analyses by bringing women of color from the margins to the center of analysis (see, for example, bell hooks, 1984). A basic premise is that there is no common unified female experience. Rather, each individual woman is shaped not only by her experiences of gender and sexuality but also by her particular experiences of the intersection of race, class, and culture. Thus, a major emphasis is on forms of racism, sexism, and classism and how these factors are interrelated and affect the lives of all women.

- *Black feminist thought* has at its roots the goal of making African American women's standpoint visible. One of the more popular articulations of this theoretical perspective is Patricia Hill Collins's work, *Social Construction of Black Feminist Thought* (1989). Collins takes as a starting point that African American women's political and economic experiences have allowed them to develop a particular analysis of racism and sexism in the United States, as well as specific strategies of resistance. This perspective challenges the idea that oppressed groups are not conscious of their oppression and are somehow less capable than their oppressors of understanding the relations of ruling. More importantly, it goes far in challenging the notion that there can be and is one feminist theory or feminist perspective because people's positions in the social structure give rise to distinct standpoints or perspectives on the world. Thus, an inclusive feminist perspective takes into account the many distinct standpoints and diversity among women and men.

The Family from a Feminist Perspective

A feminist investigation of marriages and families asks both macro- and microlevel questions. Macrolevel questions include, What are the causes of women's inequality in marriages and families? How does the structure of marriages and families maintain gender inequality? How can change toward greater equality in marriages and families be brought about? Microlevel questions include, What social and interpersonal processes occur in families to generate gender differences and inequality? What roles do various family members play in perpetuating gender inequality? What kind of power structures exist within marriages and families, and how do they affect the distribution of tasks and resources in marriages and families?

Taking the position that women's subordination is based in the social relationships within marriages and families, the objective of an analysis of marriages and families is to explain the ways in which gender inequality is reinforced and maintained in these relationships. On a macrolevel, for example, a vast Marxist feminist literature asserts that women's oppression is built into and sustained by the patriarchal family structure. On a microlevel, a body of feminist theory exists that, by focusing on what these theorists refer to as the "reproduction of gender" in families, explains how gender inequality and oppression are reinforced and maintained (Chodorow, 1978). These theories suggest that gender identity and gender-specific behaviors are produced and reproduced through the socialization process as women expose their offspring to a

Chilean activist Isabel Allende captures the feminist principle that "the personal is political." Here, she testifies as a witness in a 1997 court case in Madrid concerning Spanish persons who "disappeared" during the dictatorship of Chilean General Augusto Pinochet, whose military junta ousted her father, President Salvador Allende, from office.

variety of gender-specific learning experiences during the child-rearing process. Recall, for example, our earlier discussion of of gender socialization in Latina/o families.

Critique There are many critiques of feminist theory. That feminist theory is woman-centered is the most frequent criticism, especially from mainstream sociologists. Basically, the criticism is that feminist theory is biased and excludes male experiences and perspectives. Feminist theorists respond to this criticism by asserting that the partiality to women in their work is necessary given the history of devaluation or exclusion of female experiences and perspectives in traditional social theories. They argue that the inclusion of female experiences and perspectives does not exclude men and male perspectives.

In addition, some critiques have come from feminist scholars themselves, who differ in their conceptualizations of the causes of women's oppression and the goals of feminist theory. For example, radical feminists criticize the liberal feminist notion that the major political goal for feminists should be equal opportunity for women and men. Critics contend that because this approach does not address such structural issues as class and race inequality, it would help only some women but would not help many others, particularly poor women and women of color. Marxist feminist theory is often criticized for its focus on women's oppression as a reflection of the more fundamental class oppression in society. This single focus on economic production largely ignores the importance of social and cultural factors.

One very important criticism of most feminist theories is that they are biased toward the experiences of white, middle-class, heterosexual women. In particular, feminist theory is criticized for not including an adequate analysis of race. Even when such theories deal with issues of race, class, and heterosexuality, they often focus primarily on the life experiences of the poor or working class, women of color, or lesbians. Such analyses cloud the fact that all women experience race, class, gender, and sexual orientation, albeit in different ways. In some cases, for example, women are economically disadvantaged and denied access to power and privilege because of their skin color, sexual orientation, or social class. In other cases, these same factors can enhance access to social and economic resources. For instance, women with white skin or a heterosexual orientation might enjoy certain privileges, whereas women with black skin or a homosexual orientation can suffer discrimination and be denied basic opportunities. No matter the specific critique, various feminist theories have contributed significantly to our current understanding of marriages and families and have made fundamental contributions to social change. One contribution of feminist scholars is the forging of new ideas and theories that are critical of preestablished thinking in traditional disciplines and their theories. This scholarship has touched every academic discipline, resulting in significant changes in the assumptions, theoretical frameworks, and research data on which these disciplines rest. In addition, feminist scholars have initiated legislation on family violence and they have worked for legislation that would provide both working women and men parental leave rights (Andersen, 2003). In the next section of this chapter, we briefly examine some of the contemporary literature on men and their roles in marriages and families.

MEN'S STUDIES AND MARRIAGE AND FAMILY RESEARCH

As we have seen throughout this chapter, there are many critical social and political issues related to explanations of marriage and family life in the United States. Whether or not we accept the feminist claim that their theories and research do not exclude the experiences or perspectives of men, since the 1980s a parallel movement has developed among some male activists and scholars who call for a larger, visible place in feminist analyses, one that pays attention to the oppression that males experience as a result of social conditioning and learning. They argue that the same values that have restricted women have also restricted men to their roles as aggressors. Not surprisingly, the ongoing inclusive work on women has given rise to men's studies, the academic arm of this movement. That this new field has gained momentum in recent years is evidenced by the fact that at least 500 colleges now offer courses on men and masculinity (Zernike, 1998). Although there is no specific masculinist theory, it is worthwhile to note the general viewpoint or perspective in this newest academic discipline, particularly as it relates to marriage, family, and intimacy.

One might say that we have always had "men's studies" because, historically, men have been at the center of most scientific analyses of human behavior and human societies. However, men's studies is not just about men and centering men in research and theory. Rather, it specifically challenges the patriarchal male bias in traditional scholarship, the existing sexist norms in society, and, like women's studies, it combines theory and practice to create a more just society. The line between men's studies and the men's rights movement is often blurred. However, men's studies looks primarily at the question long asked in feminist analysis: Why are

men the way they are? Recognizing that gender and sexism impact men's as well as women's lives, men's studies encompasses a critical examination of the functional and dysfunctional aspects of the traditional male gender role for men, women, children, and society at large. It begins with the basic premise that there is no hierarchy of oppression. Men, like women, are oppressed by a social conditioning that makes them incapable of developing and expressing a wide range of personality traits or skills and limits their experiences (Franklin, 1988; Zernike, 1998).

As with feminist theory, the network of men's studies consists of not one but several diverse perspectives. In fact, the theories and perspectives of much of men's studies parallel feminist theories and perspectives, so much so that some feminist scholars have declared that men's studies is explicitly feminist (see, for example, Andersen, 2003). Like feminist perspectives, then, perspectives in men's studies consider gender to be a central feature of social life—one of the chief organizing principles around which our lives revolve—examining how gender shapes men's ideas, opportunities, and experiences. Too often there is the tendency for the public and some in academic settings to assume that only women are gendered beings, as if men had no gender. We know, however, from women's and men's studies that this is not the case. Rather, gender affects the experiences of both women and men, albeit in different ways. Thus, as in feminist theories and perspectives, the perspectives of men's studies frame their analyses within the context of the diversity among men, recognizing, on the one hand, that not all men are sexist in their attitudes, beliefs, and behaviors and yet, on the other hand, that as a group, men benefit from gender privilege but this privilege varies according to race, class, and sexual orientation. Finally, as do feminist theories, men's studies view sexuality as an important component of the race–gender–class matrix of domination. Thus, scholars of feminist and men's studies alike analyze social, political, and cultural structures in societies that privilege heterosexuality and oppress lesbians and gays simply because of their sexual orientation (Andersen, 2003; Kimmel and Messner, 2001).

Men in Families

As we have indicated, a new politics of masculinity has emerged that claims men's oppression is often overlooked in theoretical analyses of marriages and families. Although many impressive analyses have documented the exploitation of women, little if any attention has been given to the massive disruption and destruction that contemporary economic and political institutions have wreaked on men or the kinds of constraints and inequities that society's gender stereotypes impose on men. Indicative of this growing movement to explore men's concerns is the emergence of the American Men's Studies Association (AMSA) founded in 1991 and of scientific journals, such as *The Journal of Men's Studies*, which premiered in 1992 and is devoted to research and theory on men's lives and issues. The 1990s also witnessed an explosion of scholarship on men, as well as the ways in which cultures shape or construct definitions and ideas about masculinity and how individual men embody it. Likewise, in the 1990s popular culture, a number of men's journals debuted with the purpose of exploring the contemporary masculine psyche and issues. In the movies, actor Arnold Schwarzenegger played a pregnant man in the movie *Junior*. And at the end of the decade, five TV sitcoms featured single dads. Today, television shows are increasingly showing more fathers who are involved in their children's lives. For example, a review of the 2004–2005 television season revealed that 86.5 percent of all TV children have a TV father figure involved in their lives, several of whom are portrayed as single fathers (Parents Television Council, 2005).

What does it really mean to be a man, a father, a friend, a lover in contemporary U.S. society? Scholarship in men's studies has increasingly delved into such questions. Relative to marriages and families, this scholarship examines how men actively construct masculinity within a social and historical context and explores their experiences—in marriage, fatherhood, and their emotional and sexual relationships with women and with other men. One of the most important issues for U.S. marriages and families over the past decade has been that of fatherhood. Debates centered around questions such as, Are men becoming more nurturing and caring fathers and developing parenting skills such as those we routinely expect from women? Men's studies scholarship on this issue has caused us to broaden our perspective about fatherhood, recognizing that the diversity of fatherhood is evidenced by different groups of men, such as gay fathers, Chicano and African American fathers, poor and working-class fathers, upper-class fathers, and immigrant fathers.

In his study of the lifestyles of gay husbands and fathers, Brian Miller (2001) reported among his findings that although these husbands and fathers perceived their gayness as incompatible with traditional marriage, they perceived their gayness as compatible with fathering. Gays in heterosexual marriages who leave their spouses and enter the gay world report that gay relationships are more harmonious than heterosexual marital relationships. They also report that fathering is more salient once they have left their heterosexual marriages. As more alternatives for fathering have become available within the gay community, fewer gays have become involved in heterosexual marriages and divorce. Adoption, surrogate parenting, and alternative fertilization are some of the methods that have expanded the opportunities for fatherhood regardless of sexual orientation.

On some levels, a "new father" has emerged. An increasing number of young husbands have joined their wives in birthing courses, have donned empathy bellies, and have taken part in the actual delivery of their children. There is little evidence, however, that these experiences by themselves produce a strong father–child (or wife–husband) bond or lead to greater participation by fathers with their children. As we shall see in Chapters 9 and 10, few new fathers assume a major role in child care and child rearing. According to the politics-of-masculinity perspective, for most men, no matter how much they would like to be more active in parenting, the demands of outside employment and the continuing definition of men and masculinity in terms of "work" and "family provider" preclude such participation.

Critique   A major criticism of the new politics of masculinity concerns those perspectives that view men as primary victims. Some feminist critics, for example, claim that the politics of masculinity is reactionary and sexist, depicting men as innocent victims of conniving and selfish women or of social structures and institutions that in fact they control. Another criticism is that although many of these analyses focus on the structural and institutional nature of men's exploitation and oppression, they have not clearly identified the alleged oppression or oppressors in society. Some feminist scholars argue that these perspectives as well as the men's rights movement, in general, are simply strategies for reaffirming men's authority in the face of the challenge presented by feminism (Carrigan, Connell, and Lee, 1987). Another criticism is that the new politics of masculinity is far more therapeutic (healing of men's egos) than political or activist.

Although recognizing the pervasive victimization of women, many proponents of masculinity theory nonetheless caution against the view of some feminists that being a male in and of itself and not the systems of social control and production is responsible for the exploitation of women. Although this point is well taken, according to critics it neglects to emphasize that the systems of social control and production in the United States are owned and controlled by men (albeit primarily white middle- and upper-class men). Thus, the issues of gender and the exercise of power cannot be separated.

In conclusion, we have seen that sociology offers a variety of theories and perspectives. Although each framework is somewhat distinct, the various frameworks are not completely incompatible with each other. Rather, they can and often do offer complementary insights.

WRITING YOUR OWN SCRIPT

THE FAMILY LIFE CYCLE: LOCATING YOUR FAMILY

Think about the developmental family life cycle theory model discussed in this chapter. Develop a life cycle model of your own family. Which stages of the model discussed in the chapter are applicable to your immediate family? Has it progressed directly through these stages? Have some stages been revisited? Which stages are not covered by the model? Why not? Describe some of the major roles, responsibilities, and adjustments that have been necessary at each stage of your family's life cycle.

SUPPORTING MARRIAGES AND FAMILIES

Few people would disagree that marriages and families are key components of American society and that our future depends on the health and stability of marriages and families. However, contemporary families are under considerable stress and strain due to a number of social and political factors such as war, economic downturns, outsourcing of jobs, unemployment, natural disasters, violence, and racism. If individual well-being depends on the well-being of our marriages and families, then we must be ever vigilant in seeking practical support to families so that they can survive such hardships and thrive. Support for marriages and families is needed perhaps now more than ever before as families and the country as a whole attempt to recover from both the ongoing pain and loss of family members as a result of the "war on terror" and the horror, mass devastation, separation, and dissolution of thousands of families in the aftermath Hurricane Katrina in 2005, the worse natural and unnatural disaster this country has ever experienced.

According to sociologists, the impact of a disaster such as Katrina on families depends on what the family was like before the storm. Strong families tend to go through such disasters together and come out stronger at the end. But for families that might have been having problems, even within their household or with other relatives, such disasters can make things worse. Thus families (some more than others) need serious help and support both before and after events such as hurricanes. Government policies and programs as well as community-based initiatives and programs should be implemented and supported to assist families in or responding to a particular crisis.

Scientifically sound research can play an important role in helping to identify marriage and family issues and suggest methods for assisting and supporting families. For example, sociological research on previous hurricanes have provided insights not only about the types of support families need after such a catastrophe occurs but also before such events happen. A team of faculty and graduate students in the Department of Sociology and Anthropology at Florida International University, for instance, studied the impact of Hurricane Andrew in 1992 and found that the disruption of families in Florida as a result of the hurricane took many different forms, including household and job loss or dislocation, extended commuting patterns, living in crowded and often deteriorated structures, the maze of paperwork and tasks associated with loss recovery and household reconstruction, as well as the lack of community infrastructure including parks and recreation facilities, and neighborhood stores and services. Daily living conditions made it extremely difficult for many families to regain domestic stability, and it could be expected that within the privacy of the home and its intimate relationships that stress and frustration were most likely to be openly expressed. This research and others also suggested that many of the problems in the aftermath of the hurricane were visible prior to the hurricane. For example, after Hurricane Andrew, researchers found strong evidence of racial differentials in insurance settlements, and clear evidence of insurance redlining of black areas in the South Dade County of Florida (IHC Research Activities, 2005).

To explore these issues, Betty Hearn Morrow and Elaine Enarson (1993), conducted what they entitled the Family Impact Study. Its purpose was to provide insights into the dynamics of family responses to disaster, with special emphasis on families that appeared to be having the most difficulties in the recovery process. They were particularly interested in the experiences of women and their children because women are the primary homemakers in most families. Their assumption was that wives, mothers, daughters, and grandmothers are most often in the best position to reflect on the effects of a disaster on household members. Yet community leaders seldom solicit these expert opinions when making policy and resource decisions which directly impact families and households. As part of their study, the researchers interviewed care providers, counselors, school and church personnel, and women's groups. In addition, they held focus group interviews with groups of women identified as having problems such as single mothers in public housing projects, low-income Haitian women, family day care providers, and battered women. Research such as this is important because it highlights the issues and areas in which families impacted by disasters need support and it can be used to develop concrete proposals for action by the government, communities, and individuals in support of marriages and families. Issues of long-term, pent-up frustration, marginalization, institutional racism, alienation, hopelessness, anger, and lack of social control as surfaced in the aftermath of Hurricane Katrina should be faced and dealt with in terms of proactive and supportive government policies and programs that address pre- and post disaster impacts on marriages and families such as individual and family poverty, poor educational systems, long-term chronic unemployment, racism and discrimination in housing, jobs, education and other sectors of American life. Family and parenting bodies such as The National Council on Family Relations, which provides a forum for family researchers, educators, and practitioners to share in the development and dissemination of knowledge about families and to work to promote family well-being, should be fully employed in the development of policies and programs that will support marriages and families.

SUMMARY

Sociology involves observing human behavior and then making sense out of what we observe. Therefore, both research and theory are involved. Theory is an explanation of some phenomenon, and scientific research includes a set of methods that allow us to collect data to test hypotheses and develop theories. The two are linked in that theory provides insights into the nature of human behavior and society, and research provides the empirical observations from which the theories are verified. Sociologists studying marriages and families have used a variety of research methodologies: surveys, observation, case studies, and ethnographies. Each of these methods has both advantages and limitations.

Although sociology as a discipline claims that the improvement of social life is a major goal, some feminist scholars have argued that in practice sociology has not lived up to this goal. A telling sign is who gets studied and how, and who is left out and why. Until recent times, conventional topics studied by sociologists and their theoretical perspectives had either ignored issues relevant to the lives of women, poor people, lesbians, gays, and people of color or studied them within white and male middle-class models. Given this history, new scholarship on marriages and families has emerged that recognizes race, class, and gender diversity in marriages and families.

Just as there is no single method for studying marriages and families, there is no single theory to explain these institutions. There are four mainstream theoretical perspectives that, while not specifically family theories, can be used to explain marriages and families. Structural functionalism and conflict theory provide frameworks for analyzing the determinants of large-scale social structure. Symbolic interaction theory allows us to focus on individuals within marriages and families and the interaction between couples or among family members. Social exchange theory is guided by the assumption that people are rational and logical, and that they base their actions on what they think is the most effective way to meet their goals.

Moreover, a number of sociological theories designed specially to address issues concerning marriage and family life are also being used. The most common are the nuclear family and the developmental family life cycle theories. Each is an extension of the larger, more encompassing functional perspective and thus provides both the advantages and limitations of a functional analysis. The nuclear family theory, popularized by Talcott Parsons, suggests that the family is an adaptive system that performs essential functions for its individual members as well as for society as a whole. In contrast, the developmental life cycle theoretical perspective focuses on changes in families over time and offers an explanation of family life in terms of a process that unfolds over the life course of marriages and families. Other theories that have important theoretical implications for studying marriages and families include social constructionism and feminist theories. Social constructionists speak of reality as invented or constructed out of the interactions between individuals in face-to-face interactions. It suggests that gender relationships within marriages, families, and intimate relationships are not uniform and universally generalizable to all people. Rather, they are social productions that have no meaning outside that understood and agreed upon by the actors. On the other hand, feminist theory is not a single unified view; rather, there are many types of feminist theory. A basic premise of all feminist theories is that women are oppressed and their lives are shaped by a number of important experiences, such as race, class, gender, and culture. However, different theories pay primary attention to different sets of women's experiences as causing or contributing to their inequality and oppression.

Finally, we have witnessed in recent years, a growing number of male voices advocating a larger and more visible place in feminist analyses, one that pays attention to the oppression that men experience as a result of gender role socialization. To date, however, very little effort has been made to extend these ideas into a practical agenda for social and political change.

KEY TERMS

theory	qualitative analysis	structural functionalism	symbols
scientific research	survey	manifest functions	social construction of reality
empirical evidence	interview	latent functions	social constructionism
hypotheses	questionnaire	functional	social-exchange theory
variables	Hawthorne effect	dysfunctional	developmental family life cycle theory
scientific method	case study	instrumental traits	sexism
reliability	ethnography	expressive traits	
validity	ideologies	conflict theory	
quantitative analysis	theory model	symbolic interactionism	

QUESTIONS FOR STUDY AND REFLECTION

1. Why do sociologists need different theoretical perspectives to explain marriage and family behavior? Why isn't one perspective sufficient?

2. Virtually every practical decision you make and every practical opinion you hold has some theory behind it. Consider any marriage and family behavior or event of interest to you. Develop a "minitheory" to explain the behavior or event. What are some of the major assumptions you make about human beings, society, marriages, families, women, and men? Is your theory a micro- or macrolevel explanation? Which one of the theoretical perspectives or theory models does your theory most resemble? After you have developed your minitheory, consider that you or some researcher wants to test it. What kinds of questions might you ask? Which research methodology would be most appropriate to test your theory? Why?

3. An implication of the social constructionist perspective is that social relationships are symbolic productions and have no intrinsic meaning. Do you agree with this

point of view? Why or why not? Can you think of some aspect of marriage, family, or intimate relationships that is not a social construction?

4. Identify a family from a culture other than the United States. Interview family members in terms of a range of issues including family values, norms, customs, and

rituals relative to marriage, childbearing, and child rearing. Compare your findings to families born and raised in the United States. How does your research help you to understand these sociological concepts and what does it tell us about the diversity of marriages and families?

ADDITIONAL RESOURCES

SOCIOLOGICAL

KIMMEL, MICHAEL, AND MICHAEL MESSNER, EDS. 2001. **Men's Lives,** New York: Macmillan. An anthology organized around specific themes that define masculinity and the issues that men confront over the life course. The authors incorporate a social constructionist perspective that examines how men actively construct their masculinity within a social and historical context. Related to this construction and integrated throughout the book are the variations that exist among men across race, class, and sexual orientation.

MARSHALL, CATHERINE, AND GRETCHEN B. ROSSMAN. 1995. **Designing Qualitative Research,** 2d ed., Thousand Oaks, CA: Sage. An excellent user-friendly guide for qualitative researchers that includes a number of vignettes from the educational fields studied by the authors as well as other researchers.

LADNER, JOYCE A., ED. 1973. **The Death of White Sociology,** New York: Vintage Books. Now a classic, this anthology presents the works of a group of African American writers and scholars who critique mainstream sociology for accepting white bourgeois standards as the norm and consistently treating all other social patterns—especially those found in African American cultures—as "deviant."

ZIMMERMAN, SHIRLEY L. 1995. **Understanding Family Policy: Theories and Applications,** Thousand Oaks, CA: Sage Publishers. In this book about family policy, the author offers several different ways of thinking about family policy and its effects on families. She introduces new theoretical frameworks as well as other family frameworks for assessing family well-being, including symbolic interaction, conflict, feminist and cultural theories. She also introduces various applications of theory that reinforce the link between family theory, policy, practice, and the everyday life experiences people have with the policy process. This book is an excellent resource for offering conceptual tools for analyzing family problems, policies, and consequences.

FILM

Kinsey. 2004. An excellent film biography of the life of Alfred Kinsey, the man who revolutionized our understanding of human sexuality. For years, Kinsey, an Indiana University professor and researcher, and his research assistants traveled across the country, interviewing and studying thousands of people about their sexual attitudes and behavior. According to this film portrayal, Kinsey was so consumed by statistical measurements of human sexual activity that he almost completely overlooked the substantial role of emotions and their effect on human behavior. This made him an ideal researcher and science celebrity whose scientific research revealed that sexual behaviors previously considered deviant and even harmful (homosexuality, oral sex, and so on) are in fact common and essentially normal in the realm of human experience, but whose obsession with the scientific method frequently placed him at odds with his research assistants as well as his understanding wife.

Miss Evers' Boys. 1997. A moving docudrama that deals with social and ethical issues as well as issues of racism in a medical setting during a historical period that spanned the civil rights movement. Set primarily in a Tuskegee, Alabama hospital, the film is presented from the point of view of an African American nurse, Eunice Evers, who was a participant in the infamous *Tuskegee Study of Untreated Syphillis in the Negro Male* sponsored by the U.S. Public Health Service and which ran 40 years (1932–1972) before it was stopped.

LITERARY

GERRITSEN, TESS. 1996. **Harvest,** New York: Simon & Schuster. An interesting novel about an "organs for cash" ring, run by an elite cardiac transplant team of doctors operating out of a prestigious New England hospital. Although this novel does not pertain to sociological research specifically, it does raise a number of important ethical issues that researchers and other professionals responsible for the well-being of human research subjects must consider.

DJERASSI, CARL. 1991. **Cantor's Dilemma,** New York: Penguin. This novel describes the fierce competition that drives scientific superstars as they strive to receive coveted recognition for their work. Of particular relevance are the ethical issues of scientific research.

INTERNET

www.census.gov   U.S. Census Bureau. An excellent resource for the latest statistical data on marriages and families. Pick a letter of the alphabet for a topic of interest to you (for example, fatherhood, motherhood, or parenting) and find the latest statistics on the topic.

www.NCFR.com National Council on Family Relations. The NCFR is the major scientific organization devoted to the study of marriages, families, intimate relationships, and children.

www.pscw.uva.nl/sociosite/TOPICS/theory.hmtl This Netherlands social science site provides links to pages with material on theoretical perspectives.

www.aecf.org The Annie E. Casey Foundation. This site features the Annie E. Casey Foundation's *Kids Count* data project. This project compiles data on children, the social conditions in which they live, and indicators of their well-being. Students may explore these data state-by-state.

3

IN THE NEWS

Montgomery, Alabama

On May 17, 2005, Alysha Cosby walked across the stage and announced her own name at St. Jude Educational Institute to applause and cheers from many of her fellow students. But as she headed back to her seat her mother and aunt were escorted out of the church by police. This took place at the end of the program when Alysha, who had been banned from graduation because of her pregnancy, announced her own name. Alysha was told in March that she could no longer attend school because of safety concerns, and her name was not listed in the graduation program. The school's guidance counselor delivered Cosby's degree to her house before the program but she still wanted to walk with her class. A fellow senior, the father of Cosby's child, was allowed to participate in the graduation ceremony ("Pregnant Student . . ." 2005).

WHAT WOULD YOU DO? If you were the principle of Alysha's school, would you have banned her from graduation or would you have allowed her to participate in the graduation ceremony? Would you treat the father of Cosby's child in the same way or in a different manner? Explain.

What are little girls made of?
Sugar and spice
And all that's nice,
That's what little girls are made of.
What are little boys made of?
Snaps and snails
And puppy dogs' tails,
That's what little boys are made of.

Anonymous nursery rhyme

Who has not, at one time or another, smiled on hearing this nursery rhyme? On one level we do not take it seriously, believing it just a cute and harmless caricature of girls and boys. Yet on another level it suggests that there are differences between females and males and that both sexes must therefore be treated differently. On the basis of this belief system, society constructs an elaborate sex–gender system that has serious ramifications for every facet of our lives, as the experience of Alysha Cosby so clearly revealed. This chapter explores the meaning of sex and gender, the process by which we acquire gender identity, and the role gender plays in marital and family relationships.

DISTINGUISHING SEX AND GENDER ROLES

If you were asked, Who are you? chances are you would reply by saying, I am a male, female, Latina/o, African American, Asian American, Native American; or a student, parent, daughter, son, wife, husband, mother, father, friend. Such responses reflect the statuses we have and the roles we play in the social order. Sociologists use the term *role* to refer to a set of expected behaviors associated with a specific status, the position we hold in society. These positions, by and large, determine how we are defined and treated by others and also provide us with an organizing framework for how we should relate to others. We are born into some of these statuses—for example, female, male, daughter, son, white, black—and therefore have little control over them. These are called **ascribed statuses.** Others are **achieved statuses,** acquired by virtue of our own efforts. These include spouse, parent, employee, student, teacher. Every status, whether ascribed or achieved, carries with it a set of role expectations for how we are to behave.

Role expectations are defined and structured around the privileges and obligations the status is believed to possess. For example, our society has traditionally expected males, especially fathers, to be strong, independent, and good providers. In return, they expect to be admired, respected, and obeyed. Females, especially mothers, are expected to be nurturing, caring, and self-sacrificing. In return, they expect to be loved and provided for. Such shared role expectations serve an important function in society. By making our behavior fairly predictable, they make social order possible.

Role expectations can be dysfunctional as well, however. They can be defined so rigidly that behavior and expression are seriously curtailed, to the detriment of the individual and the society at large. For example, because society fails to encourage or support fathers as primary-care providers for their offspring, many father–child relationships remain emotionally distant. Rigid role definitions often lead to the development of stereotypes, in which certain qualities are assigned to an individual solely on the basis of her or his social category. **Gender role stereotypes** refer to the oversimplified expectations of what it means to be a woman or a man. Stereotyping is used to justify unequal treatment of members of a specific group. For example, until recently, women serving in the military were believed unfit for combat and thus were denied the opportunity for career mobility associated with combat experience. Although today's military offers more opportunities to women, a good number of people still question the appropriateness of their full participation (see Debating Social Issues box). Similarly, in the past men were not hired as flight attendants, telephone operators, or receptionists because these occupations were seen as feminine. Although many stereotyped ideas such as these have been discarded as invalid, some individuals and groups still believe women and men are inherently unsuited for certain roles, a point we will return to later in this chapter.

The status of being female or male in our society affects all aspects of our lives; thus, sociologists regard it as a **master,** or **key, status.** For this reason, it is important to understand the dynamics associated with gender status and to distinguish between the concepts of sex and gender.

Sex refers to the biological aspects of a person—the physiological characteristics that differentiate females from males. These include external genitalia (vulva and penis), gonads (ovaries and testes), sex chromosomes, and hormones. These characteristics are the source of sex role differences—women menstruate, become pregnant, and lactate; men have erections and ejaculate seminal fluid. In contrast, **gender** refers to the socially learned behaviors, attitudes, and expectations associated with being female or male, what we call *femininity* and *masculinity*. Whereas a person's sex is biologically determined, gender behaviors and expectations are culturally constructed categories and, as such, change over time. Thus, gender is learned; we acquire gender through interacting with others and the social world (Wood, 1996). **Gender identity** is a person's awareness of being female or male. It sounds simple, doesn't it? We are either female/feminine or male/masculine, are we not? In fact, as we shall see, human development is not as simple as it first appears.

The Process of Sex Differentiation

Our biological sex is established at the moment of conception, when each genetic parent contributes 23 chromosomes to the fertilized egg for a total of 46 chromosomes (23 chromosomal pairs). One pair of chromosomes, the sex chromosomes, determines whether a fertilized egg will develop into a female (XX) or male (XY) fetus. Contrary to past belief, the father's genetic contribution determines the child's sex, in that he provides either an X or a Y chromosome, whereas the mother always provides an X chromosome. The process of sex differentiation does not begin until approximately the sixth week of embryonic development, however. Prior to that time, the XX and XY embryos are anatomically identical, each possessing a set of female ducts and a set of male ducts.

DEBATING SOCIAL ISSUES

SHOULD WOMEN SERVE IN COMBAT?

This question became a major issue with the introduction of the all-volunteer service in 1973 and the eventual demise of the separate female units in favor of integration into regular military units. Initially women were barred from many positions, including combat. Over time different branches of the military opened up more opportunities for women. For example, the Air Force began training women as pilots in 1976, as navigators in 1977, and as fighter pilots in 1993. Lt. Col. Martha McSally was the first woman to fly a combat sortie in a fighter aircraft and later flew 100 combat hours over Iraq in the mid-1990s. However, believing that in recent years the Army was violating the 1994 Department of Defense's (DOD) regulations exempting female soldiers from combat assignments, Representative Duncan Hunter (R-CA), chair of the House Armed Services Committee, reignited the debate when he sponsored an amendment to the 2006 Defense Authorization Bill that would have prohibited female soldiers from serving in smaller forward support companies that operate 100 percent of the time with land combat battalions such as the infantry. After congressional hearings at which top-level officers argued against this amendment, citing the potential loss of at least 21,000 combat support-related jobs, Duncan withdrew it in favor of a broader measure that strengthened reporting requirements on women in combat and on any changes that open or close positions to women. Twenty percent of U.S. combat support and service roles in Iraq are now performed by women serving as military police, medics, and truck drivers in military convoys. By March 2005, 35 women have died in Iraq and nearly 300 have been wounded. Today,

women constitute almost 15 percent of all active duty personnel.

Like Representative Duncan, people who oppose having women in combat positions believe that male soldiers would see them as a distraction and that their presence would lower a unit's morale. They further argue that women's physical characteristics (shorter height, less muscle mass and weight than men) put them at a disadvantage when performing tasks requiring a high level of muscular strength and aerobic capacity. Additionally, they believe that it is not practical for women and men to serve together for long stretches at a time as women may get pregnant and then need to be evacuated. And, if captured, there is the added risk that women POWs may be sexually abused. Opponents also believe that the public is not prepared to accept large numbers of female casualties that might occur if the United States should be involved in protracted conflicts.

On the other hand, those who favor allowing women to serve in combat maintain that women who are properly trained

have proven to be as capable as men. They point to the fact that mixed units in Panama in 1989, in the Persian Gulf conflict in 1991, and in Iraq in recent years performed as cohesive and effective teams when under fire. Moreover, serving in combat positions is the way to promotion and higher pay. Therefore, proponents argue, to exclude women from combat roles is discriminatory. Additionally, such exclusion would undermine their morale, hamper modern military operations, and likely dampen already low recruitment goals.

What do you think? A recent Gallup poll found that 67 percent of respondents favored women serving in combat zones as support for ground troops while 54 percent opposed their serving as the ground troops who are doing most of the fighting (Carlson, 2005). What do you think? Do you favor or oppose allowing women to serve in combat positions? What advantages and disadvantages would such a policy have for women, men, and the society at large?

The process of sex differentiation is as yet not completely understood. Genetic researchers have identified a sex-determining gene on the Y chromosome that appears to set in motion a chemical chain of events that leads to the development of testes, a prostate gland, and other distinctive male characteristics (Hoyenga and Hoyenga, 1993). Until recently, scientists were less clear about female development and assumed that the lack of the Y or male chromosome resulted in female development by default. Then, in 1994, molecular biologists at Italy's Padua University and at Baylor University in Houston, Texas, isolated a gene on the X chromosome called "dosage sexual sex reversal" (DSS), which sets in motion the development of ovaries and other distinct female characteristics. These researchers also discovered that the ovary gene, if present in excessive amounts, can override genes that ordinarily would produce males (Gura, 1994a).

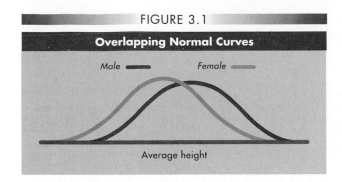

FIGURE 3.1

Overlapping Normal Curves

Male   Female

Average height

Gender Differences: The Nature–Nurture Debate

Because chromosomes and hormones play a critical role in sex differentiation, it is logical to ask whether they also play a role in the physical, behavioral, and personality differences that have been observed between women and men. For example, women, on the average, live longer and score higher on tests of verbal ability than men do. Men, on the average, are taller, heavier, more aggressive, and have better spatial skills than women. As Figure 3.1 shows, however, the differences within each sex are often greater than the differences between the two sexes. Thus, more variation in height occurs within a group of women (or men) than between the average female and the average male. This figure also shows that although most women are shorter than most men, some women are taller than some men. Most of the traits identified as masculine or feminine fit this pattern. The extent of sex differences actually found for most traits is typically quite small.

How much of our development and behavior is biologically based (nature) and how much is culturally based (nurture) remains controversial. On the one hand, sociobiologists, such as Edward Wilson (1975), believe genetic inheritance is responsible for many forms of social behavior, such as competition, aggression, cooperation, and nurturance. Most social scientists, on the other hand, believe the sociobiological approach is too simplistic. For example, studies show that when females are rewarded for behaving aggressively or when they experience certain environmental stresses, they can become just as aggressive as males (Hyde, 1984; Zuger, 1998). Similarly, researchers have found that differences in math and verbal ability based on sex do not manifest themselves much before adolescence and are not found in all societies (Harmatz and Novak, 1983; Fausto-Sterling, 1985). These latter findings suggest that cultural factors (nurture) also play an important role in sex differences. According to developmental biologist Anne Fausto-Sterling (1985), the biological and the cultural are not mutually exclusive categories; rather, they are two essential parts of an interconnected system. Biologist Ruth Hubbard vividly described the way that biology and environment work together to transform the organism so that it responds differently to other concurrent or subsequent biological or environmental influences.

If a society puts half its children in dresses and skirts but warns them not to move in ways that reveal their underpants, while putting the other half in jeans and overalls and encouraging them to climb trees and play ball and other outdoor games; if later, during adolescence, the half that has worn trousers is exhorted to "eat like a growing boy," while the half in skirts is warned to watch its weight and not get fat; if the half in jeans trots around in sneakers or boots, while the half in skirts totters about on spike heels, then these two groups of people will be biologically as well as socially different. Their muscles will be different, as will their reflexes, posture, arms, legs, and feet, hand-eye coordination, spatial perception, and so on. . . . There is no way to sort out the biological and social components that produce these differences, therefore, no way to sort nature from nurture. (1990:115–16)

This interconnectedness between biology and culture can be seen by examining a few of the sex/gender variations that exist in the human population—intersexuality, transsexuals, and multiple genders.

Although for the most part, the endocrine and hormonal systems mature and correlate with each other, occasionally a developing fetus is exposed to feminizing or masculinizing hormones at inappropriate times. As a result, an estimated 2 percent of babies are born with anomalous or unusual features; at times this makes it difficult to classify the infant as either female or male (Blackless et al., 2000). In the past, people with ambiguous genitalia were labeled *hermaphrodites;* scientists now refer to these individuals as **intersexed.** Although intersexuality occurs in every society, it has become standard medical practice in the United States to correct the ambiguity through sex reassignment using surgery and hormonal treatments. Although few in number, these cases suggest that biological sex alone does not determine gender identity; the sex in which a child is reared also plays a crucial role, as can be seen in the case of a genetic male (chromosomally XY) who was born with a tiny penis (1 centimeter long) and a urinary opening similar to that of a genetic female. The child's sex was surgically reassigned. The parents changed the child's name and reared the child as a girl. By age 3 the child showed "feminine" interests, playing with dolls and other toys considered girls' toys.

However, the case of an 8-month-old twin boy whose penis was accidentally burned off during a routine repair surgery shows that sex reassignment does not always work in the person's best interest. The physicians recommended that the child be raised as a female on the assumption that healthy psychosexual development depends on the appearance of the genitals. Over time, with the parents' agreement, they constructed female genitals to replace the lost penis. However, Joan, as she was called, realized she was different and preferred her twin brother's clothing and toys. Despite hormonal treatments and attempts at female role modeling, Joan was convinced she was a boy. Finally, realizing the depth of "her" despair, Joan's father told his son the full story of his life. After a double mastectomy, the construction of a phallus, and male hormone treatments, John, as he was now referred to, felt he had his identity back. The evidence indicates he adjusted well in school. As an adult, he married a woman with young children, whom he eventually adopted (Diamond and Sigmundson, 1997). After John Colapinto (2000) chronicled the John/Joan story in his book, *As Nature Made Him,* other individuals with similar experiences came forward to tell their stories. Although some people reported satisfaction with their sex reassignment, many others, like John, rejected theirs. As a result of these reports, an increasing number of scientists and physicians now criticize the practice of infant sex reassignment for putting cultural factors above medical ones and for failing to accept the fluidity of sex and gender as a normal part of the human condition, as do many other societies (Kessler, 1996). Rather than surgery following the birth of a mixed-sex child, these experts favor treatments centered more on psychological counseling (Dreger, 1998; Fausto-Sterling, 2000). This approach came too late for David Reimer, the Joan/John subject of Colapinto's book. He committed suicide on May 4, 2004, at the age of 38. According to Colapinto, David suffered bouts of depression related to his childhood experiences (Colapinto, 2004).

> *If you were born intersexed or with unusual genitalia, what treatment would you want to receive? Why? What do you see as the advantages and disadvantages of infant sex reassignment? What do you see as the advantages and disadvantages of psychological counseling? Who should make the decisions in these cases—medical personnel, parents, or the persons themselves when they are older? Explain.*

Another variation in the sex/gender linkage occurs in the case of **transsexuals,** persons who believe that they were born with the body of the wrong sex. These individuals cannot accept their assigned gender even though it is congruent with their biological sex. This dissonance between one's body and one's sexual identity is described as "gender dysphoria" or "gender identity disorder" (Kogan, 2004). Some of these individuals undergo surgery and take hormone treatments to achieve a body congruent with their own sense of gender identity. Two such cases received a great deal of publicity: that of reporter and writer James Morris (now Jan Morris), who chronicled the story of his transformation from male to female in *Conundrum* (1974), and that of 53-year-old Donald McCloskey (now Deirdre), a nationally renowned economic theorist at the University of Iowa ("Transgendered," 1997). To date, little is known about why

transsexualism occurs. And although there is controversy about the appropriateness of sex-reassignment surgery (SRS) and relatively little systematic research on the adjustment and satisfaction of postoperative transsexuals, evidence does suggest that the majority of postoperative transsexuals who have been surveyed are happy with their SRS results and report that SRS had improved the quality of their lives (Lawrence, 2003).

The third variation occurs in societies with multiple genders. Most of us are accustomed to thinking of sex/gender as consisting of only two categories: female/feminine and male/masculine. Yet, as sociologists Claire Renzetti and Daniel Curran (1995:71–72) point out, anthropologists have found evidence of multiple genders in other cultures. Certain Asian, South Pacific, and North American Indian societies recognized a third gender called the *berdache*, individuals who adopted the gender ascribed to members of the other sex. Although both females and males could become berdaches, it was more common for men to do so. Generally, men who chose to become berdaches did so at puberty, as an alternative to becoming warriors. These individuals lived, worked, and dressed as members of the other sex and were frequently thought to possess supernatural power. Among the Mohave, a Native American people who lived in California, women and men were allowed to cross genders. In that society, some boys preferred feminine toys and clothing. At puberty they could go through an initiation ceremony and become *alyha;* they would adopt feminine names, perform female tasks, and marry men. Females could pursue a masculine lifestyle by becoming *hwame*, dressing and living much like men, hunting and farming rather than performing domestic chores. Although the *hwame* could not aspire to leadership positions or participate in warfare, they could assume parental responsibility for children. In none of these societies were these individuals thought of as abnormal or deviant. Instead, these possibilities represent alternative ways for people to construct a gender identity. In sum, all three of these cases illustrate the fluidity of gender.

Although the nature–nurture debate has been framed as an either–or proposition, these data suggest that differences between females and males develop out of a complex interaction of biological and cultural factors and take a variety of

People often experience stress and anxiety when they don't live up to the gender stereotypes for their sex.
Source: Tribune Media Services, Inc. All Rights Reserved. Reprinted with permission.

In any given historical period, some people are likely to reject their society's definitions of appropriate gender role behavior. During the Civil War, a number of women, eager to fight for a cause they believed in, disguised themselves as men to enlist in the Union and Confederate armies. One such soldier was Frances Clalin, pictured here in nineteenth-century female attire and in her cavalry uniform.

forms. Before examining **gender role socialization,** a process by which people acquire the gender roles that their culture defines as appropriate for them, let us look at the content of these gender roles.

TRADITIONAL MEANINGS OF FEMININITY AND MASCULINITY

In Chapter 2 we discussed the theory of structural functionalism and the Parsonian dichotomy of expressive (female) and instrumental (male) roles. The assignment of these roles is based on the assumption that females and males are fundamentally different from each other and that the content of these roles reflects the biological differences between the sexes. Beginning in the 1960s and continuing to the present day, a number of studies have found a broad consensus among different groups of people regarding the existence of different personality traits associated with each sex. For example, a Gallup poll in which adults were read a list of ten personality traits and asked which were generally more true of women or men found that women were most often described as emotional, talkative, affectionate, patient, and creative. In contrast, aggressive, courageous, ambitious, and easygoing led the list of traits attributed to men (Newport, 2001). Women and men were in general agreement about the assignment of these traits but, with the exception of only one trait—aggressive—women were more likely than men to say that all the traits apply to their gender. In all cases, only a minority of respondents said that the traits described both genders equally. However, 40 percent of the women and 40 percent of the men said that one trait, intelligent, described both genders equally. The traits used to describe each sex are fairly consistent across cultures. A cross-cultural study of 25 countries found that in every country sampled, women were thought to be "sentimental" and "submissive," whereas traits such as "adventurous" and "forceful" were associated with men (Williams

and Best, 1990). More recently, an analysis of data from 26 cultures found similar patterns in people's perceptions of gender stereotypes (Costa, Jr., Terracciano, and McCrae, 2001).

Keep in mind that this type of research describes only the extent to which people possess an awareness of female and male stereotypes; it does not indicate whether or not they accept them as true or, for that matter, whether or not the stereotypes are actually true. Other research, applying a methodology that allowed respondents to rate the degree to which traits characterize both the typical woman and the typical man, found several interesting patterns. Two sets of adjectives became evident: First, there were those that represented prototypical traits (the clearest examples of each category—for women it was a niceness/nurturance dimension, whereas for men it was a potency/power dimension), and second, there were more peripheral traits, those less strongly associated with each category. Considerable overlapping occurred, with the core adjectives for one gender tending to fall in the periphery for the other gender (DeLisi and Soundranayagam, 1990).

Traditional Gender Roles: Female and Male

Historically, the female gender role clustered around family relationships and was patterned after the belief that a woman's place is in the home. Based on this belief, women are expected to marry; have children; and be nurturing, emotional, caring, and attractive. They should not be aggressive, loud, competitive, or independent; rather, they should be passive, submissive, and dependent on their husbands. If women are employed, their work must not interfere with family obligations. To ensure that women can be homemakers, men are to be providers and protectors. Thus, they are expected to be achievement-oriented, competitive, strong, aggressive, logical, and independent. They should not be emotional, expressive, or weak, and must be in control at all times.

Gender Variations: Race, Class, and Culture

Gender stereotypes—the overgeneralized beliefs about the characteristics associated with being female or male—are widely shared within a society and become a part of the rationale for the different treatment accorded women and men. In the United States, traditional gender roles have routinely been associated with white middle-class heterosexuals. Although only a limited amount of research on gender beliefs across race and class lines is available, from this research it does appear that people perceive different stereotypical traits in other groups. For example, one study asked college students to use a list of 23 adjectives to describe the characteristics of black and white middle-class women and black and white working-class women. The results revealed that race and class affect people's perceptions of gender roles. Although all four groups were depicted in ways consistent with the feminine stereotype, the ways in which white women and middle-class women in general were described were most like the traditional views of women. Black women were viewed as less passive, dependent, status-conscious, emotional, and concerned about their appearance than white women (Landrine, 1985).

These findings are consistent with other research showing that as a group, African American women are perceived as being strong and less deferential than white women (Halberstadt and Saitta, 1987). Relatively little information is available on gender stereotypes of other racial or ethnic groups. One study, however, suggests that Latinas generally tend to be viewed as more submissive and dependent, hence more feminine, than white women (Vazquez-Nuttall, Romero-Garcia, and DeLeon, 1987). Similarly, Asian American women have been described as very feminine and as making desirable brides because "they are cute (as in doll-like), quiet rather than militant, and unassuming rather than assertive. In a word, non-threatening" (Lai, 1992:168). Critics point out that the acceptance of these images can be problematic. For example, Tamara Beauboeuf-Lafontant (2005) argues that the dominant image of the "strong black woman" is a limiting rather than empowering construction of black femininity in that it rewards women for a stoicism that draws attention away from the inequalities they face in their communities and the larger society.

Anthropologist Margaret Mead (1935) was among the first to explore how concepts of masculinity and femininity vary across cultures. In studying three tribal groups, she found that both Mundugumor women and men behaved ruthlessly and aggressively, behaviors usually identified as "masculine." Among the Tchambuli, women were dominant and impersonal, whereas the men were more emotionally dependent, just the reverse of the patterns typically found in our culture. Arapesh women and men usually exhibited traits often described as "feminine"—caring, cooperative, and nonaggressive.

Similarly, other anthropologists have observed societies in which gender relations are not rigidly defined. For example, in Nepal, both women and men are expected to be nurturing, and both sexes provide care for children and the elderly (Wood, 1996). Shared child care is also characteristic of the Mbuti Pygmies of Zaire, a society in which both women and men hunt cooperatively. Among the Agta of the Philippines, both women and men hunt, fish, and gather vegetation (Estioko-Griffin, 1986). Tahitian women and men of the South Pacific are expected to be passive and cooperative (Gilmore, 1990). The women and men of Vanatinai, a remote island of 2300 inhabitants off the coast of Papua New Guinea, socialize, work, and raise children side by side in an almost equal manner. Both women and men participate in community decision making and the island's economy. Both women and men share access to social and economic power and prestige by participating in ceremonial exchanges of valuables, such as greenstone ax blades and coconut-leaf baskets, and by playing host to highly valued mortuary rituals. Older siblings, both female and male, learn to share in caring for younger siblings (Lepowsky, 1993). What are we to make of these findings? As Susan Basow points out:

> Gender is not the only variable by which people are stereotyped. Each one of us is situated in sociological space at the intersection of numerous categories—for example, gender, race or ethnicity, class, sexual orientation, and able-bodiedness. These social categories interact with each other in complex ways. A woman who is white, working-class, lesbian, and differently abled will be viewed very differently from a black, middle-class, heterosexual, able-bodied woman. (1992:4–5)

In sum, humankind is not composed of two homogeneous groupings—one feminine and one masculine. Rather, there is a rich diversity within each gender. To encompass this diversity, Harry Brod (1987), a pioneer in the field of men's studies, has suggested substituting the term *masculinities* for *masculinity*. The same argument could be made regarding the diverse forms of femininity. Although research has shown that Americans tend to adhere to a fairly consistent grouping of gender stereotypes, increasing evidence shows that some people are challenging these stereotypes and creating more flexible gender roles for themselves.

GENDER ROLES IN TRANSITION

Perhaps you find it difficult to identify with the traditional gender roles described in the previous section. Given the many changes that have occurred during your lifetime, that would not be surprising. Of special significance are certain demographic changes: patterns of continuing education for both women and men, the movement of married women into the labor force, delayed marriage and childbearing, high divorce rates, and increased life expectancy, especially for women. These changes, along with the liberation movements of the 1960s and 1970s, have challenged traditional gender roles. Thus, as we shall see throughout this book, there has been a definite shift from traditional to more egalitarian gender roles, at least ideologically if not always behaviorally in both the United States and in many other countries (Inglehart and Norris, 2003).

This shift in the United States is reflected in a recent poll. For the first time since Gallup asked the question, a majority of Americans (53 percent) say that women have equal job opportunities with men, up from 46 percent in 1976. However, men are more likely to believe that women have achieved equality of opportunity in the work force than are women (61 to 45 percent) (Jones, 2005). There is no doubt that the pay inequity between women and men has narrowed appreciatively over the past 30 years nor is there any doubt that women have more economic opportunities than before; nevertheless, as we will see in Chapter 10, women, on average, still earn considerably less than men regardless of levels of education or experience. Although the majority of adults believe women should have equal work opportunities, that increased gender equity has enriched both sexes, and that there should be gender equality in the home, there is also a widespread belief, as we shall see later that social and economic changes that altered traditional gender roles have made building successful marriages, raising children, and leading satisfying lives more challenging than in the past (Morin and Rosenfeld, 1998). Some of these challenges are suggested by current attitudes about who should take primary responsibility for child rearing. A recent survey found that although 41 percent of Americans believe it is ideal for one parent to stay at home solely to raise the children, with men slightly more supportive of that position than women (45 to 38 percent), 55 percent of those respondents feel it does not make any difference which parent stays home. Nevertheless, another 43 percent prefer that mothers stay home while only 1 percent prefer that fathers should stay home. Still, this is a noticeable shift from 1991, when 63 percent of the public believed that the mother should stay home to raise the children (Robison, 2002). However, in another survey when respondents were asked about their own preferences, 27 percent of men said they would prefer to stay at home and take care of the house and family while 68 percent said they prefer to have a job outside the home. The comparative figures for women were 42 and 53 percent ("The Gender Gap . . .," 2005).

Many women today have considerably more options in the workplace and exercise more control over their private lives. However, this pattern is not universally true. As we can see in the In Other Places box, women in Kenya are struggling to gain rights while women in Afghanistan and Iraq are experiencing an erosion in their status and losing rights they previously enjoyed. Men, too, are questioning their roles. For many men this means deemphasizing their work role and emphasizing their family role. Both women and men feel freer to express a much wider range of personality traits than the traditional gender roles would allow. Because changes in women's roles have been more open to public view than those in men's roles, we are more likely to be aware of assertive and strong women than of gentle and nurturing men. Research commissioned by the American Association of Retired Persons, however, revealed that men spend just as much time as women do at listening, handholding, and expressing concern in familial caregiving situations (Behrens, 1990). In fact, family caregiving is no longer predominantly a woman's issue. Men now make up 44 percent of the family caregiving population (National Family Caregivers Association, 2000).

Nevertheless, considerable controversy about these changes remains. Not all people are happy with their direction. Some find them confusing, and others prefer a return to a more traditional world. A 24-year-old truck driver complained, "My girlfriend drives me crazy at times. She wants to be paid the same as a man and to have every opportunity a man does. But she still wants to be treated like a woman. She doesn't believe women should be drafted, and if I don't open the door for her or help her with her coat, she gets upset." A 24-year-old medical student finds that some men feel threatened by changes in gender roles. "Jim and I dated in college. I thought he was a liberated male, but I found out differently when he took me to meet some of his friends. On the way he told me not to tell them I was going to be a doctor. He said he didn't want them to think his girlfriend was smarter than he was."

Other people support the movement toward gender equality in theory but have trouble implementing the ideas in their everyday lives. Several factors combine to make change difficult. First, people who hold privileged positions

Ex-police officer Tom Ashton, in his uniform and later as Claire Ashton, leaves a Shrewsbury courthouse where she claimed that she was unfairly dismissed from the police force because of her sex change.

IN OTHER PLACES

IN NORTHERN KENYA, WOMEN STRUGGLE TO GAIN RIGHTS

Over a decade ago, a group of women fled their homes and settled on a field of dry grasslands, establishing a village they called *Umoja*, which means "unity" in Swahili. Some of the women were fleeing abusive husbands, others were forced from their homes by their husbands after they were raped. Even though their wives were not responsible, their husbands said they brought dishonor on their family and community. Kenya is a patriarchal society where women have few rights and where young girls are often forced into marriages with older men. To protect themselves, the women, led by Rebecca Lolosoli, decided that no men would be allowed to live in Umoja.

To ensure their economic survival, the women started a cultural center and campsite for tourists visiting the nearby Samburu National Reserve. The men, angry at the women's behavior, attempted, although unsuccessfully, to build a rival tourist and cultural center of their own. At times they would attack the women's village by throwing stones, chasing the women into the brush or beating them up. Despite these threats and acts of violence, the women persisted. The revenue from the sale of crafts and the use of the campsite empowered the women and made it possible for them to send their children to school for the first time and to reject male demands for their daughters' labor and/or early marriage. In fact, the women were so successful that they were even able to hire men to haul firewood for them, a task traditionally defined as women's work. Over the years other women heard about the village and would come seeking help in getting a divorce or to escape troubled marriages. As word of the village spread, Rebecca Lolosoli was invited by the United Nations to attend a recent world conference on gender and empowerment in New York.

Although in Kenya women's rights are far from assured, a spate of new laws are being considered by Kenya's Parliament, covering such issues as women's rights to refuse marriage proposals, sexual harassment in the workplace, genital mutilation, and ways to prosecute rape, an act so frequent that Kenyan leaders call it the nation's biggest rights issue.

Source: Emily Wax, 2005, "In Kenya, All-Female Village Becomes an Outpost of Feminism," *Milwaukee Journal Sentinel* (July 17):23A.

. . . WHILE IN AFGHANISTAN AND IRAQ WOMEN'S STATUS AND RIGHTS ERODE

In the past, thousands of Afghan women studied at the University of Kabul; thousands more worked as teachers, doctors, and in other professional capacities. Then, in late 1996, Islamic Taliban militia captured the Afghan capital of Kabul and quickly imposed control over two-thirds of the country. Taliban's religious leaders barred girls from school and women from work. Because the vast majority of teachers were women, many boys' schools were forced to close as well. Afghan women had to wear a burqa (a head-to-toe covering) whenever they appeared in public. Violations brought swift and severe punishment. In 2001, the Taliban were driven out of power and limited freedoms were granted to women. Since then, however, a religious faction has reemerged and is again threatening even these limited freedoms.

Iraq, a former secular state under Saddam Hussein, is also a country besieged by war and chaos. Many Iraqis and outside observers fear that when the dust settles, whatever power sharing emerges will exclude women and that Sharia (Islamic law) will become the judicial standard with the effect that women vis-à-vis men will be disadvantaged in family, economic, and social matters.

What do you think? How do these three different societies inform the nature–nurture argument regarding gender roles and gender relationships? Can traditional gender roles be changed without causing a serious backlash? Explain. What do the experiences in Afghanistan and Iraq suggest about the permanency of gender roles?

have a vested interest in keeping them. Thus, some men may resist sharing power and authority with women at work and at home, whereas some women may resist sharing with men the aspects they most enjoy about the traditional role, such as nurturing children. Second, existing social arrangements tend to reinforce traditional gender roles. To take just one example, on average, women are still paid less than men. Thus, even if a couple should prefer an arrangement in which the husband is the primary parent and the wife the primary breadwinner, simple household economics might make this impossible. Third, as we will see in the next section, gender identities develop early in life, and much of what we learn from parents and other role models is still based on traditional gender norms. Although many women and men manage to challenge these norms successfully, gender socialization remains a powerful force in shaping gender identity. As family therapist Joan Zientek points out in the Strengthening Marriages and Families box, gender issues are often deeply embedded in the problems that families experience. When this occurs, family members must recognize and resolve those gender issues if the family is to function effectively.

THEORIES OF GENDER ROLE SOCIALIZATION

Although socialization is a lifelong process, it is especially significant in our formative years. Psychologists and sociologists have developed several theories to explain the socialization process with respect to the acquisition of gender roles.

STRENGTHENING MARRIAGES AND FAMILIES
Talks with Family Therapist Joan Zientek

RESOLVING GENDER ISSUES

Do Gender Issues Affect Family Functioning?

Indeed, they do. During the span of the twentieth century, our American culture, owing to evolving technology and a growing economy, has moved up Maslow's hierarchy of needs. Emphasis has shifted from physical survival to self-actualization. These changes have brought about economic independence for women, the necessity for many of a dual family income, and the lengthening of the work week for both women and men. These changes have had an extraordinary effect on gender roles in the family. Although there has been some gains in sharing household tasks and child care, the primary responsibility still falls on the shoulders of women even if they work outside the home. Even in families where the mom stays at home, when dad returns at the end of the day tired from the stress of the workday and mother is exhausted from the endless demands of clinging toddlers, tensions over household chores and child care can be intense.

In addition, women are no longer compelled to stay in unsatisfying or violent marriages. Economic independence can be a great bargaining chip when negotiating a more equal distribution of family tasks, thus forcing men to step up to the plate to take more responsibility.

One of the most salient gender issues occurs around the expression of affect in the relationship. The work of psychologist William Pollack suggests that by the age of 5, boys, unlike their female counterparts, have learned to mask their feelings and have come to view feelings as internal states rather than as a dynamic that exists between people. Later in life, this pattern sets up a dynamic game of pursuit and withdrawal between a couple. In a stereotypical fashion, the woman pursues the man and demands that he speak and reveal his inner life. The man, who many times does not have a clue as to how he should respond, withdraws and the game is set in motion, leaving both parties feeling isolated and dissatisfied.

Further, parents may become concerned about their son's behavior if the exhibited behavior tends to fall on what society considers to be the feminine side of the behavior continuum. Similarly, if daughters act too "tomboyish" or too "sexy," anxiety and arguments between parents about how the child should be raised can ensue. The issues can even become more intense if these behaviors persist through the teen years. Fear of having raised a gay child can dash the parents' ideals of how life should be. All these problems can be exacerbated further if the couple draws the extended family of in-laws and siblings into the mix. Although this can be done with the benign intention of looking for support, it often ends up creating sides and cementing differences.

How Can Family Therapy Help People in Such Situations?

Some issues can be resolved merely through an educational process. The work of Peter Salovey, Yale psychologist, on emotional intelligence coupled with the emerging neurobiological research have given us a new paradigm for helping couples manage conflict. Couples can be taught to prevent the limbic brain's "emotional hijacking" of rational thought. They can learn how to identify and shift brain-mediated emotional states, thus activating changes that pull them to greater intimacy.

The more difficult dynamic to change is the one in which couples are polarized relative to an issue. In this case, each party needs to identify their part in keeping the polarization alive and make the needed changes in their behavior instead of waiting for the other to change. At other times, work has to be done to help the couple create appropriate boundaries between the generations without alienating extended family members. Other issues may necessitate changing expectations, setting priorities, and/or negotiating commitments regarding the household division of labor. Marital problems that stem from unresolved issues from childhood are more difficult to resolve. For example, a man who has been raised by a controlling father may exhibit controlling behavior toward his wife. The family therapist helps the individual or couple navigate back and forth through the generations, looking both at unresolved issues from their family of origin, as well as current dysfunctional marital patterns. The process continues until resolutions are found for both the individual and the couple.

Psychoanalytic/Identification Theory

One prominent theory, known as **psychoanalytic/identification theory,** originated with Sigmund Freud (1856–1939), the founder of modern psychoanalysis. Freud believed that children learn gender-appropriate behaviors by unconsciously identifying with their same-sex parent and that they pass through a series of stages in their development. During the first two stages, the oral and the anal stages, the experiences and behaviors of girls and boys are similar. Both identify with the mother, who is their primary caretaker. However, in the third stage, the phallic stage, which occurs around the age of 3 or 4, the development of girls and boys proceeds in different directions. By this age children not only are aware of their own genitals but also that their genitals differ from those of the other sex. According to Freud, it is in this third stage that identification occurs. Children begin learning how to behave in gender-appropriate ways as they unconsciously model their behavior after that of their same-sex parent. Freud called the boy's development the *Oedipus complex*, based on the mythical Greek character who unknowingly killed his father and married his mother. According to Freud, the young boy experiences sexual feelings for his mother and sees his father as a rival for her affections. Hence, he wants to get rid of his father. At the same time, however, he becomes aware that he has a penis and that his mother does not. Unconsciously, he fears that if his father were to learn of his feelings for his mother, the father would castrate him. Thus, he resolves the Oedipus complex by identifying with his father (becoming like him) and giving up his desire for his mother. Thus, the boy acquires the appropriate gender role.

The path to feminine identification takes a different turn for girls. Freud called this development the *Electra complex*, after a mythical Greek woman who urged her brother to slay their mother, who had killed their father. According to Freud, a girl realizes that boys have something she does not—a penis. Because she is missing this organ, she develops a sense of inferiority and jealousy and blames her mother for this deformity, a condition Freud refers to as *penis envy*. At first she takes her love away from her mother, focusing on her father as her love object. Gradually, however, she realizes she cannot have her father, and she reestablishes her identification with her mother, with the goal of one day becoming a mother herself.

What are we to make of Freud's theory? Like Greek mythology, it makes fascinating reading, but because it maintains that the process of identification is unconscious, verifying it empirically is impossible. Other than psychoanalytical reports, which are subject to observer bias, there is little if any scientific evidence of either castration anxiety in boys or penis envy in girls. Furthermore, whether children that age understand the relationships between gender and genitalia is questionable. Finally, Freud's view of women as inadequate or incomplete contains an antifemale bias that later identification theorists sought to modify.

Karen Horney (1967) challenged the notion that women view their bodies as inferior and argued that a girl's psychosexual development centers around her own body rather than that of the male. She also argued that what women envy is not the male penis, per se, but what it symbolizes—men's higher status, freedom, and power. Erik Erikson (1968) suggested that male dominance is, in part, related to womb envy, the jealousy men have for women because of their unique ability to bear children.

Nancy Chodorow (1978, 1990), whose concept of "gender reproduction" was discussed in Chapter 2, sees gender identity as emerging from the social organization of parenting roles. Women mother; men do not. She sees this "asymmetrical organization of parenting" as the basis for gender inequality and the source of identification problems for boys. Boys must psychologically separate from their mothers and pattern themselves after a parent who is frequently absent. As a result, they form personalities that are more detached from others and in which emotional needs are repressed. Girls, on the other hand, continue their relationship with their mothers and, through this ongoing interaction, acquire the capabilities for mothering and emotional attachment behaviors. Implicit in Chodorow's work is the belief that shared parenting between women and men would

be beneficial to society. As with Freud's theory, the results of these theory modifications have yet to be tested and verified. In particular, research is needed to discover whether or not similar patterns exist across racial, ethnic, and social class groupings here in the United States. For example, Denise Segura and Jennifer Pierce (1993) question whether Chodorow's theory adequately accounts for patterns observed in Mexican American families, where child-rearing practices include multiple mothering figures, such as grandmothers, godmothers, and aunts. Finally, as we saw earlier, in some other non-Western societies both women and men participate in child care. Thus, Chodorow's developmental pattern provides insights into some Western families, but it cannot be applied universally to all families.

Social-Learning Theory

The perspective known as social-learning theory has its roots in behaviorism, the theory that human behavior is the result of a reaction to objective stimuli or situations. **Social-learning theory** asserts that gender roles and gender identity are learned directly through a system of positive reinforcement (rewards) and negative reinforcement (punishments) and indirectly through observation and **modeling,** learning through imitation. In direct learning, for example, parents reward their daughters with encouragement and approval for engaging in gender-appropriate behavior, such as playing with dolls and dressing up in mother's jewelry and high heels. If boys engage in this same behavior, however, they are punished and told, "Boys don't act that way." Research indicates that at younger ages girls enjoy greater flexibility in engaging in cross-gender behavior than do boys (Lynn, 1966; Martin, 1990). This finding is not unique to U.S. culture. Finnish parents also are more accepting of cross-gender behavior for girls than for boys (Sandnabba and Ahlberg, 1999). A girl can be a "tomboy," but a boy who engages in cross-gender behavior risks being labeled a "sissy." Sociologist David Lynn suggests that this harsher treatment of boys for acting "girl-like" leads boys to develop a dislike and contempt for females and femininity, which may explain their later hostility toward females (see Chapter 11).

Social-learning theory maintains that behavior that is regularly followed by a reward is more likely to be repeated, whereas behavior that brings forth punishment is more likely to be discontinued. Thus, children quickly develop an awareness that females and males are different and that separate gender roles are appropriate for each sex.

Children also learn which behaviors are appropriate for their gender by observing and imitating their parents and other adults, their peers, and media personalities. Social-learning theorists believe children initially model themselves after those who are readily available and perceived as powerful (who control rewards and punishment), warm and friendly (nurturing), and similar to the self (same sex). This modeling view of the same sex is similar to those of psychoanalytic/identification theorists. However, social-learning theorists do not accept the notion that behavior is fixed according to early learning patterns. Rather, they believe behavior and attitudes change as situations and expectations in the social environment change. As children grow older, the range of role models expands, and the work of crafting a gender identity continues.

A considerable amount of research supports social-learning theory. Nevertheless, social-learning theory alone cannot fully explain gender role acquisition. For one, modeling is more complex than the theory suggests. Children do not always model themselves after same-sex individuals. In addition, subcultural differences as well as differences in family structures may affect the variety and choice of available role models. Moreover, learning theory treats children as passive learners. In reality, parent–child interaction is two-directional, in that a child's behavior may have a significant influence on parental behavior as well.

Cognitive-Development Theory

Fundamental to **cognitive-development theory** is the belief that the child's mind matures through interaction with the surrounding environment. In contrast to social-learning theory, cognitive-development theory asserts that children take an active role in organizing their world. They manage this by creating schemas, or mental categories, that emerge through interaction with their social environment. Subsequently, as new information is encountered, it is processed and assimilated into these categories, or the categories are adjusted to fit the new information. Psychologist Lawrence Kohlberg (1966) adapted cognitive-development theory to explain the emergence of children's gender iden-

tities. Early on (about age 2 to 3) children become aware that two sexes exist; they can identify and label themselves and others as girls or boys. This labeling process, however, is based not on anatomical differences but on superficial characteristics such as clothes—girls wear dresses and pastel colors, whereas boys wear pants and bold colors. According to Kohlberg, at this stage children have not yet developed gender identity. This does not develop until children are 6 or 7 years old and have the mental ability to grasp the concept of constancy or permanency. Prior to this time they are too young to realize that all people can be so classified and that sex is a permanent characteristic that cannot be changed simply by changing clothes or hairstyles.

Cognitive-development theory maintains that once gender identity is developed, children are able to organize their behavior around it. That is, they strive to behave in a way consistent with their own sex, and they attach value to their behavior. Children come to view gender-appropriate behavior in a positive manner and gender-inappropriate behavior as negative behavior that should be avoided.

A considerable body of research gives support to cognitive-development theory. For example, researchers found evidence that children become more accurate at gender differentiation and labeling as they get older (Coker, 1984). In addition, cognitive-development theory helps explain children's, especially boys', strong preferences for sex-typed toys and for playing with same-sex peers (Zuckerman and Sayre, 1982).

Other researchers have criticized some aspects of cognitive-development theory. John Money and Anke Ehrhardt (1972) question the timing of gender identity. Their research implies that an important aspect of gender identity is present as early as 2 years of age; changing a child's sex after that age proves difficult. In a similar vein, other researchers have found that a great deal of sex typing—the degree to which men and women identify with societal definitions of masculinity and femininity (Basow, 1992)—and preference for sex-typed toys occurs before the age attributed to gender permanency (Downs, 1983; Bussey and Bandura, 1984). This apparent discrepancy may simply represent two different phases of gender development. The earlier sex typing may be due to differential reinforcement and imitation, whereas the sex typing that occurs later, after the development of the idea of gender permanency, may be a result of cognitive development (Basow, 1986).

The most serious criticism of cognitive-development theory is that it overemphasizes gender learning as something children do themselves and minimizes the role culture plays in gender socialization. Hence, as psychologist Sandra Bem (1983:609) writes, "The typical American child cannot help observing, for example, that what parents, teachers, and peers consider to be appropriate behavior varies as a function of sex; that toys, clothing, occupations, hobbies, the domestic division of labor—even pronouns—all vary as a function of sex." In a later work, Bem (1993) criticizes cognitive-development theory for minimizing the role of culture in gender role socialization and offers an alternative theory, the enculturated-lens theory, to explain gender role acquisition.

One of the ways children learn what is expected of them as they grow up is through imitating adults, as this 5-year-old is doing by dressing up in his father's clothes.

Enculturated-Lens Theory

In her **enculturated-lens theory** of gender role acquisition, Bem argues that hidden cultural assumptions about how societal members should look, behave, and feel are so deeply embedded in social institutions and cultural discourse and hence, individual psyches, that these behaviors and ways of thinking are systematically reproduced from one generation to the next. Although every culture contains a wide array of such assumptions, or *lenses*, as Bem calls them, her analysis focuses on three gender lenses: (1) *gender polarization*, whereby females and males are perceived as fundamentally different from each other—these differences, in turn, constitute a central organizing principle for social interaction; (2) *androcentrism*, which encompasses the beliefs that males are superior to females and that males and male experiences are the normative standard against which women should be judged; and (3) *biological essentialism*, which views the first two as natural and inevitable results of the inherent biological differences between females and males.

Bem argues that gender acquisition is a special case of socialization, or what she calls *enculturation*. Accordingly, individuals are constantly receiving *metamessages*, lessons about what is valued and important in their culture. For example, a metamessage about gender is being sent when children observe only mothers doing household tasks. As we will see in the next section, from birth on children quickly learn these social constructions and come to see them as natural, being unaware that other constructions are possible. However, Bem does not consider individuals passive in this process. Rather, she sees them as active, pattern-seeking individuals who evaluate themselves in response to these patterns and decide whether or not to conform to them.

Although Bem acknowledges that all societies must enculturate new members, she believes that the lenses of gender polarization and androcentrism must be altered. She proposes that parents begin this process by providing their children with an alternative lens for organizing and making sense out of the world, for example, an "individual differences" lens that would highlight the "remarkable variability of individuals within groups" (1983:613).

Empirical testing is required to determine how valid Bem's theory is. Nevertheless, an examination of the various agents of socialization—individuals, groups, and organizations that help form an individual's attitudes, behaviors, and self-concept—does provide us with insight into the content of gender messages and how they are communicated in our society.

AGENTS OF SOCIALIZATION

Gender role socialization begins at birth and continues throughout an individual's lifetime. In our interaction with parents, teachers, and peers, and through books, television, and movies, we are constantly taught values, attitudes, and behaviors that our culture sees as appropriate for each sex.

Parents

Parents provide children with their first exposure to gender learning and play a key role in helping children develop a sense of themselves as females and males. An extensive body of research indicates that parents think of and treat their daughters and sons differently, even though they frequently are not aware of doing so. This process begins early. Researchers found that many expectant parents relate to their fetus on the basis of whether they believe it to be a girl or a boy. Perceived female fetuses were thought of as "graceful and gentle," whereas the movements of perceived male fetuses were described as "strong" (Stainton, 1985). When asked by researchers to describe their newborns, parents described daughters as delicate, soft, and tiny, and sons as strong, big, athletic, and well coordinated, even though the infants did not differ significantly by sex on measures of weight, length, muscle tone, heartbeat, or reflexes (Rubin et al., 1974; Reid, 1994).

Consistent with these findings, other researchers have found that parents' gender influences the types of interaction they have with their children, particularly with infants. For example, across cultures, fathers spend less time with their infants (Parke, 2002). Further, fathers tend to engage in more rough-and-tumble play whereas mothers tend to be more containing and rhythmic in their behavior (Scher and Sharabany, 2005; Barnard and Solchany, 2002; Parke, 2002). Studies of father–child interaction also show that fathers play more interactive games with young sons, promoting visual, fine-motor, and locomotor exploration with them, whereas they have more verbal interaction with daughters and appear to encourage closer physical proximity with them. The consequence of this differential play activity may be that boys learn to be more independent and aggressive than girls do (Bronstein, 1988). In fact, traits of dependence and helplessness may be encouraged in girls as a result of parents acting on the belief that daughters need more help than sons (Burns, Mitchell, and Obradovich, 1989).

Not only do parents play differently with their children, they also communicate differently with them. Stories told to daughters tend to contain more emotion words than do stories told to sons. By the time they are age 6, girls typically use more specialized emotion words than do boys (Adams et al., 1995; Kuebli et al., 1995). In contrast, other researchers have found that mothers tend to speak to sons more explicitly, ask them more questions, and use more action verbs in conversing with them. Thus, sons seem to receive more of the kind of verbal stimulation associated with reasoning skills (Weitzman, Birns, and Friend, 1985), whereas the interactions with daughters encourage the development of emotional sensitivity to people's feelings and expressions (Goleman, 1996). As children get older, these patterns are likely to continue. For example, a study of middle-class parents and their sixth- and eighth-grade children found that parents, especially fathers, used less scientific language with their daughters than with their sons, regardless of their childrens' interest in science or the grades they received. In general, parents assumed that their sons were more interested in science than their daughters (Tenenbaum and Leaper, 2000). In an innovative study of family behavior in science museums, researchers found that both parents, but especially fathers, explained the content of interactive science exhibits three times more to sons than to daughters while parents were twice as likely to explain the content of interactive music exhibits to daughters than to sons (Crowley, 2000). In a similar vein, other research shows that when parents give unsolicited help with math homework to girls, they may be communicating the gender stereotype holding that math is a male domain and thereby undermine their daughters' confidence in their math ability (Bhanot and Jovanovic, 2005). This finding may help to explain why, even though achievement tests and class performance show that girls have the same math ability as boys, girls tend to express less confidence in their abilities than do boys.

Clothing   Parents also dress their children differently, initially perhaps to give clues to others so that they can be assured of responding appropriately on the basis of sex. The type of clothing children wear serves other functions as well, however. Frilly dresses are not conducive to rough-and-tumble play. Boys' clothing, by and large, is less restrictive than girls' clothing. Therefore, boys are encouraged to be more active and aggressive in their play than are girls.

Toys and Games   Studies of children's rooms revealed another way in which parents affect the gender identities of their children. The decor frequently reflected traditional gender stereotypes—florals and pastels for girls, animals and bold colors for boys (Rheingold and Cook, 1975; Stoneman et al., 1986). More important, however, the rooms contained a marked difference in toys. Boys had a wide range of toys (educational, sports, tools, objects, large and small vehicles), many of which promote outdoor play, whereas girls' toys were less varied in type (dolls, housekeeping objects, and crafts) and promote mainly indoor activities (Rheingold and Cook, 1975; Pomerleau et al., 1990). Market forces may play a role in these patterns. According to *PlayThings Magazine*, of the top ten toy licenses in 2003, only three (Barbie, Disney Princess, and Care Bears) were toys clearly marketed to girls; one was for a toy (Thomas and Friends) marketed to both boys and girls; the remaining six (Yu-Gi-Oh!, Power Rangers, Transformers, Star Wars, Spider Man, and Beyblade) were for toys clearly marketed to boys (cited in Golin, 2004). Although today's parents view more toys as gender-neutral than did their parents, seeing soccer balls and doctor kits as appropriate for both girls and boys, for instance, they still don't want their sons playing with Barbie dolls even though their daughters can play with action dolls like GI Joe. Fathers are more traditional in their enforcement of gender roles than are mothers and hence are still more likely to give their children gender-specific toys and occupational costumes (Abrahamy et al., 2003; Kulik, 2002). Some studies have also found that boys have more access to computers and the Internet in their homes and use them in more diverse ways than do girls. Even when girls have access to a home computer, male family members are likely to dominate its use (Gunn, 2003). A review of the literature on computer use found that although preschool girls and boys show equal interest in computer games, girls' interest and time investments in computer games have declined significantly by their teen years, (Agosto, 2004). Part of the explanation for this decline may be due to a lack of girl-oriented soft-

ware. Research has found that girls prefer storylines and character development in games whereas boys prefer competition between the forces of good and evil. A recent survey of computer games found that software creators have not responded in any major way to these gender differences in content preferences; 79 percent of the games reviewed were competitive in nature (Agosto, 2004).

These findings take on significance when we consider the way toys function in the learning process. Boy-specific toys for boys tend to promote exploration, manipulation, construction, invention, and competition whereas girl-specific toys typically encourage creativity, nurturance, and attractiveness (Lott, 1994). Thus, girls and boys may develop different cognitive and social skills based on play and game activities, which in turn may lead to very different opportunities as adults.

Chores   A distinction between inside and outside activities is also apparent in the chores assigned to children. Girls are expected to do inside work (wash dishes and clean the house), whereas boys are given activities outside the home (yard work and emptying the trash). Further, girls are assigned these chores at earlier ages than are boys (Leaper, 2002). Because girls' chores are daily ones whereas a great deal of what boys do is sporadic, girls spend more time doing chores than boys do. A study by researchers Teresa Mauldin and Carol Meeks (1990) of sex differences in children's time use found that boys spend more time in leisure activities and less time in household and personal care than do girls. There are some variations, however. Middle- and upper-income parents are less likely to assign gender-linked chores than are parents from lower-income backgrounds. The assignment of gender-linked chores occurs less frequently in African American homes, where both daughters and sons often are socialized toward independent and nurturing behaviors (Hale-Benson, 1986; P. H. Collins, 1991; Lips, 1993). From early on, then, patterns for a division of labor based on sex are formed and will likely carry over into adult marital roles. As we will see in Chapter 10, even when women work full-time, they still do the bulk of the housework.

Language

One of the first tasks facing a developing child is the mastery of language skills. There is growing agreement among social scientists that children's acquisition of gender identity and their perception of gender roles are strongly influenced by language. Research shows that the English language contains a number of gender biases. For example, the words *man* and *he* can be used to exclude females—"It's a man's world," "The best man for the job"—or they can be used generically to refer to both women and men, such as in *mankind*. In fact, the use of male terms frequently serves to exclude females. Think of the words *policeman, fireman, postman, chairman, spokesman, congressman, workman*. Whom do you visualize in these roles? Researchers have found that most people visualize men when such terms are used (Wilson and Ng, 1988). Other studies show that elementary schoolchildren give male-biased responses to story cues that contain the pronoun *he* (Hyde, 1984). When the masculine pronoun is used, as it frequently is in textbooks to refer to doctors, lawyers, and public officials, children tend to associate those roles with males. Thus, many children may limit their aspirations to what appear to be gender-appropriate occupations. To counter this restrictive influence, many publishers have moved to a more gender-neutral language, using *they, he or she, police officer, firefighter,* and *mail carrier.*

This trend toward more neutral language is not universal, however. For example, in the sports world, male teams are referred to by just the team name or mascot, such as the Bulldogs or the Bruins, but feminine tags are traditionally used to refer to women's teams, i.e., the Lady Bulldogs or the Lady Bruins. At a recent winter Olympics, a sportscaster, talking about a woman's bobsled team, referred to the woman in the forward position as a *front man.* The sportscaster was talking about a position, not a person. Critics of such patterns argue that if feminine tags are used for female teams, then masculine tags should be used for men's teams and that gender-neutral or inclusive terms should be used when talking about positions in order to convey the notion of equality, regardless of the sex of the athlete (Huppertz, 2002).

Peers

The games children play and the people with whom they play them also influence the acquisition of gender identity. At about the age of 3, a process of sex segregation begins. This process accelerates during the school years. Researchers have found that girls and boys both prefer same-sex groups. Psychologists Eleanor Maccoby and Carol Jacklin (1987) explain girls' same-sex preference as stemming from unrewarding mixed-sex play activities. Because boys play more roughly than girls and use physical assertion to resolve differences, they tend to dominate and bully girls in mixed-sex play groups. In contrast, girls enjoy more cooperation and mutuality in same-sex groups.

Boys also prefer same-sex groups, but their motivation is different. Aware of men's higher status, boys attempt to disassociate themselves from girls and anything that suggests femininity (Whiting and Edwards, 1988). Thus, girls and boys grow up in different peer subcultures that reinforce both real and perceived gender differences. Because opportunities for cross-sex interactions are so limited, most gender stereotypes go largely unchallenged. That such behavior exists and is reinforced by social approval is substantiated by a large body of research showing that from preschool to high school, children who engage in traditional gender role behavior are more socially acceptable to their peers than are children who engage in nontraditional roles (Martin and Fabes, 2001). Peers may play an even more significant role in the lives of African American males. Distinct bodily movements, athletic prowess, sexual competence, and street smarts, including how to fight and defend oneself, are lessons learned in the context of the male African American peer group (Hale-Benson, 1986). According to Richard Majors:

Black people in general, and the black man in particular, look out on a world that does not positively reflect their image. Black men learned long ago that the classic American

virtues of hard work would not give us the tangible rewards that accrue to most members of the dominant society. We learned early that we would not be Captains of Industry or builders of engineering wonders. Instead, we channeled our creative energies into construction of a symbolic universe. Therefore, we adopted unique poses and postures to offset the externally imposed "zero" image. Because black men were denied access to the dominant culture's acceptable avenues of expression, we created a form of self-expression—the "Cool Pose." (1995:82)

Play and Organized Sports

Sociologist Janet Lever (1978) observed and interviewed fifth graders about their activities and found many differences between girls' and boys' activities. She believes boys' activities better prepare them to succeed in modern industrial societies. Girls' games have only a few rules and frequently involve only a minimum of roles (for example, jumping rope or tag), whereas boys' play groups are larger, have complex rules, and involve a variety of roles. Girls' activities require more cooperation, whereas boys' games are organized around competition. Hence, boys' games provide more training for leadership and complex organizational roles than do girls' games.

Rarely has anyone questioned the physical, psychological, and social benefits that active play and organized sports contribute to boys' and men's lives. Only in the last decade, however, have researchers documented the enormous benefits of

Danica Patrick finished in fourth place at the 2005 Indianapolis 500 and was the fourth woman ever to qualify for this still largely male-dominated racing event.

sport participation for girls and women: physical (lower risks of obesity, heart disease, and osteoporosis), psychological (higher self-esteem, better body image, enhanced sense of competence and control, reduced stress and depression), and academic (better grades, higher standardized test scores, and lower risk of dropping out) (President's Council on Physical Fitness and Sports, 1997; Zimmerman and Reavill, 1998). Since the passage of the Education Amendment Act of 1972 and its Title IX provision, more money went into athletic programs for girls and women. The results of this investment are readily seen in the growing number of professional women athletes like Serena and Venus Williams (tennis), Laila Ali (boxing), Annika Sorenstam (golf), Lisa Leslie (basketball), Jackie Joyner-Kersee (track and field), Zoe Cadman (jockey), and the numerous athletes in the Olympic Games. Nevertheless, the athletic playing field is far from level. A gender gap remains in the media coverage and dollars devoted to women's and men's sports. Top women tennis players earn 59 cents for every dollar earned by their male counterparts; the gap is even wider in golf where women earn only 36 cents for every dollar men earn (Women's Sports Foundation, 2004). And, although women are 53 percent of the student body at Division I institutions, they get only 41 percent of the opportunities to play sports, 36 percent of overall operating budgets, and 32 percent of recruiting dollars. Women's sports opportunities at the high school level follow a similar pattern (National Association For Girls and Women in Sport, 2005). The Department of Education's recent clarification under Title IX (that schools may use an e-mail survey as the sole measure of women's interest in athletics) generated considerable controversy. According he National Collegiate Athletic Association (NCAA) an e-mail survey that may or may not be returned does not constitute an adequate indicator of women's interest in sports participation. Without serious enforcement of Title IX, the NCAA fears the growth of women's athletics will be stymied and possibly even reverse the progress made over the past three decades ("Statement from NCAA President," 2005).

Gender stereotypes and socialization experiences contribute to the gender gap in sports' participation rates. Boys and men may take more of an interest in sports to avoid the label of "sissy" and being viewed as unmanly. Some girls may avoid sports out of a fear of being thought unfeminine or labeled "lesbian."

Research has shown that playing with "masculine" (rather than "feminine") toys and games, playing in predominantly male or mixed-gender groups, and being considered a tomboy distinguished between women who later became college athletes and those who did not (Giuliano and Popp, 2000). In a similar vein, earlier research found that women in nontraditional occupations (for example, lawyers and physicians) were, as children, more likely to have played with boys and to have engaged in more competitive male activities than were women in more traditional occupations (for example, teachers and librarians) (Coats and Overman, 1992). Thus, breaking down gender-prescribed play in early childhood would most likely lead to more widespread female participation in sport and physical activity, providing them not only myriad physical and psychological benefits but wider career choices as well.

Teachers and School Organization

Teachers also play a major role in the socialization of children. If you were to ask teachers whether they treat girls and boys differently, most would probably say no, even though a wide range of research studies reveals differential patterns of interaction between teachers and their female and male students, often with negative consequences for both genders. Over the last two decades, a great deal of research focused on how schools and teachers shortchanged girls and the mechanisms for remedying these problems. The implementation of subsequent educational changes led to impressive results—girls improved their grades, expressed higher educational and career goals, enrolled in advanced placement courses more often, and undertook more and varied leadership positions. At the same time studies were pointing to girls' gains, researchers found that boys were experiencing a number of problems—they are more likely than girls to fall behind grade level, be diagnosed with emotional and learning disorders, use alcohol and drugs, be suspended, and less likely to go on to college (Kimmel, 2001; Goldberg, 1998). This has led some observers to proclaim the "myth of girls in crisis" and to suggest that there is a "war against boys" going on (Sommers, 2000). Others dispute this view and argue that girls and women still confront gender stereotypes that limit their opportunities. At the same, time, however, they recognize that boys suffer in this process as well and they argue that the answer to these problems is not to pit girls against boys but to examine the causes of these problems and to develop meaningful ways of addressing them. Two factors have been identified as major contributors to educational gender disparities: the organization of schools and teacher behavior.

A subtle but powerful messages is communicated simply by the organization of our schools—that of male dominance. In 1982, although 66 percent of all public school employees were women, men held the highest position—76 percent of administrators and officials and 79 percent of principals were male. Conversely, less than 2 percent of the clerical and secretarial positions were held by men. Eighty-four percent of elementary school teachers and 49 percent of secondary teachers were women (U.S. Census Bureau, 2005). Although men occupied the highest positions, in the elementary classroom, boys had few male role models to emulate. Much has changed in the past 25 years. By 2003, although women's share of public school employment had increased to 74 percent, the administrative positions were now more equitably balanced between females and males, with women accounting for 48 percent of administrators and officials and 52 percent of principals. During that same period, the percentage of men in clerical and secretarial positions doubled but still remained slightly less than 3 percent. Women now constituted almost 59 percent of secondary teachers but the percentage of male elementary school teachers dropped to 14 percent (U.S. Census Bureau, 2005).

Teacher behavior can send other gender messages to students as well. Studies at all educational levels found that teachers provided more assistance to and challenges for boys than for girls (Sadker and Sadker, 1994) and that males tended to dominant the learning environment (Lips, 1995).

Other studies show that boys receive more praise for creative behavior, whereas girls receive more praise for conforming behavior (Grossman and Grossman, 1994). Girls were encouraged to be quiet and neat whereas boys were rewarded for being boisterous and competitive (Orenstein, 1994).

Gender is not the only variable affecting student–teacher interaction. The race of the student may trigger different behaviors on the part of teachers. Overall, Asian American students are often perceived as the best students who therefore need little help or encouragement (Basow, 1992). Similarly, Latinas, especially those experiencing language difficulties, are often ignored (Orenstein, 1994). African American girls, compared with white girls, receive less in the way of teacher feedback and academic encouragement, and African American boys receive the most frequent teacher referrals to special education programs (U.S. Department of Education, 1997).

Messages like these are often reinforced by the curricular materials used in the classroom. Researchers Piper Purcell and Lara Stewart (1990), for instance, found many examples of gender stereotyping in children's readers. Although both sexes are depicted in a wider range of activities than had previously been the case, certain basic trends remain. Boys and men are featured more often than girls and women, and they tend to be portrayed in more active and powerful positions (Sapiro, 1999). And despite new guidelines for publishers, males are still primarily portrayed in stereotyped ways—that is, as competitive, aggressive, and argumentative (Evans, 2000). In fact, Geoffrey Canada (1998) argues that existing cultural images of men often give boys mixed messages. For instance, strength is confused with violence; virility is confused with promiscuity; adventurousness is confused with recklessness; and intelligence is confused with arrogance, racism, and sexism. Barney Brawer, director of the boys' segment of the Harvard Project on Women's Psychology, Boys' Development, and the Culture of Manhood, believes that a crisis in masculinity is occurring because, while society has become clear about what it wants for girls, it has not for boys (Rosenfeld, 1998). There is growing concern that our institutions are not preparing boys to survive in a world in which traditional masculine strategies that rely on physical strength and dominance are becoming outmoded.

At the college level, there is growing concern that the percentage of male students is declining, and although females are now enrolled in greater numbers, researchers have found that gender-stereotypical behavior is still quite common in some areas. For example, in many classes professors call on male students more often than on female students, they interrupt female students more than they do male students, and they are more likely to refer to female students as "girls" or "gals" while referring to male students as "men." Female students are not always taken as seriously as male students, particularly in fields traditionally dominated by males, such as math, science, and information and computer technologies (ICT) (Sanders, 2005; Myers and Dugan, 1996). A 22-year-old female student complained of discriminatory treatment by a math professor: "There were only two other women in the advanced calculus class I was taking. The professor didn't want us there. He made jokes about women not being able to balance their checking accounts, and he always seemed surprised when one of us solved his math challenges. I was going to drop his course because he made me feel like a freak for liking math, but my advisor encouraged me to stay with it." Her experience is not unusual. Female retention in ICT courses is positively related to their professors' positive attitude to female students and negatively related to their professors' belief that female students are not well suited to these majors (Cohoon, 2001). Other research shows that teachers often stereotype computer science as a male domain (Huber and Schofield, 1998). Such attitudes likely to contribute to the fact young women underestimate their computer skills as compared to their male counterparts. A survey of incoming freshman found a gender gap in computer confidence with males twice as likely as females to view their compute skills as above average (Sax et al., 2001). At one university where all students are required to have their own laptops and used them similarly, females still rated their skills as lower than the males (McCoy and Heafner, 2004). These patterns contribute to the fact that, as we will see in Chapter 10, women are significantly underrepresented in ICT occupations in the United States and in most countries around the world; this is a cause of concern among educators and public officials as well (Charles and Bradley, 2005).

In 2005, Harvard University President Lawrence Summers ignited a firestorm when he suggested the possibility that biological differences or differences in personal choices between women and men could be more important than either early socialization or some form of gender discrimination in explaining why there are fewer women than men in math and science professions. Recall your early and later school experiences. Did girls or boys do better in math and science? Who took advanced math and science courses in your school? Do you agree or disagree with President Summers? How can this question be studied scientifically?

The Mass Media

That the mass media play an important part in shaping the values, beliefs, and behaviors of modern societies is difficult to dispute. Let us take television as an example. More than 98 percent of U.S. households have at least one television set; 50 percent have three or more. Thirty percent of children from birth to 3 years of age and 43 percent of children from 4–6 years of age have a TV in their room (Rideout, Vandewater, and Wortella, 2003). The comparable figure for children 8–18 years of age is 68 percent. Boys are more likely than girls to have a TV (72 to 64 percent), video game console (63 to 33 percent), and computer (35 to 26 percent) in their bedroom (Rideout, Roberts, and Foehr, 2005). In the average home, the television set is on almost 8 hours per day. The average school-aged child watches approximately 20 hours of television every week. Even children under the age of 2 spend almost 3 hours in front of a screen. The average U.S. child spends 900 hours in school but 1023 hours

For Better or For Worse®   by Lynn Johnston

By the time children are in their teens, they have internalized images of the ideal body form for their sex.

Source: Lynn Johnston Productions, Inc./Dist. by Universal Press Syndicate, Inc.

watching television per year. It is estimated that children see 200,000 violent acts, including 16,000 murders on TV by the time they are 18. Additionally, children see 40,000 commercials per year and children as young as 2 develop brand loyalty; 97 percent of children 6 years and younger have products based on characters from TV shows or movies (cited in "Facts and Figures," 2005). Black children and adolescents watch more television than do their white peers, and children from blue-collar families spend more time in front of the television set than do children from middle-class families.

What gender messages do these children (and adults) get when they watch television? To answer this question, researchers employ a technique called **content analysis,** whereby they examine the actual content of programs. They do this by counting particular items within specific categories, such as the number of males and females featured in the program. As we shall see, most programming, from children's shows to prime time, casts its major characters in traditional roles.

Children's Shows   Content analysis reveals that children's shows are predominantly oriented to the white male, featuring more than twice as many male as female roles. This discrepancy implies that boys are more significant than girls, an image reinforced by the way in which female and male characters are portrayed. In a major study of commercial children's television programs, researcher Earle Barcus (1983) found that the sexes are presented in a biased and somewhat unrealistic way. Females are more likely to be found in minor roles with little responsibility for the outcome of the story and are rarely shown working outside the home. In contrast, male characters are depicted in a variety of occupations to which many boys realistically can aspire.

Many of these patterns are still evident over 20 years later, but they take more subtle forms. For example, an analysis of 10 episodes of *Teletubbies* and *Barney & Friends* found that, although there was an equal number of female and male characters in each show who often engaged in cooperative play, they still conformed to gender stereotypes.

Female characters were followers a majority of the time and played feminine roles (cooking, cleaning, and caretaking) while the male characters were the leaders and engaged in traditional masculine roles and occupations (Powell and Abels, 2002). Even in the popular and highly acclaimed *Sesame Street,* the major characters often portray a restricted view of female and male behavior.

Children are aware of these gender messages. In one study, 78 percent of children said there were more boy characters in cartoons; only 10 percent said more girls. Additionally, the respondents perceived boys in cartoons as violent and aggressive and girls as domestic, interested in boys, and concerned about their appearances. Such messages have consequences. Researchers found that children who were aware of the stereotypes in cartoons were more likely to report traditional gendered job expectations for themselves and others (Thompson and Zerbinos, 1997).

Prime-Time Television and Other Media   The situation is not much different on prime-time television. Although there has been an increase in the number of female roles, as well as more programming that deals with issues of gender equality (Dow, 1996), much of prime-time television still adheres to gender stereotypes (Signorielli, 2001). Besides appearing more frequently and having most of the major roles, male characters are older, more mature, and more authoritative than female characters. An analysis of all Sunday political talk shows illustrates this pattern. As Table 3.1 reveals, women constitute less than 11 percent of all guests. According to the White House Project (2001), by every measure, women make only rare appearances as experts or leaders on shows that play an important role in shaping people's perceptions of authority and leadership figures. Women's numbers represent far less than their availability; male peers appear much more often as repeat guests, receive more airtime on average, and are more likely to be in the earlier segments of the show. Thus, the public get a skewed view of who has the knowledge and ability to address political issues. Further, many of the guests are themselves politicians who are trying to connect with a constituency. By

TABLE 3.1

Guest Appearances on Political Talk Shows by Network, January 1, 2000 to June 30, 2001

Network	Total Guest Appearances	Number of Women	Number of Men	Women's % of Appearances	Men's % of Appearances
ABC	304	36	268	11.84	88.16
CBS	281	25	256	8.90	91.10
CNN	446	61	385	13.68	86.32
FOX	281	26	255	9.25	90.75
NBC	362	31	331	8.56	91.44
TOTAL	1674	179	1495	10.69	89.31

Source: Adapted from *Who's Talking? An Analysis of Sunday Morning Talk Shows.* 2001. New York: The White House Project, p. 23, Table 1A.

their absence from such shows, women are at a disadvantage in terms of the opportunity to be viewed as leaders and candidates.

Besides being younger, female characters are typically thin, physically attractive, and scantily attired. For example, one study found that 46 percent of TV female characters were thin or very thin compared with just 16 percent of male characters (Signorielli, 1997). Such findings may help explain reports of eating disorders in girls as young as 9. A survey of 6728 adolescents in grades 5 to 12 found that almost half (45 percent) the girls and 20 percent of the boys reported that they had dieted at some point. Additionally, 13 percent of the girls and 7 percent of the boys reported disordered eating behaviors (Neumark-Sztainer and Hannan, 2000). This gender differential reflects patterns observed in adults as well. According to a recent Gallup poll, a majority of women (57 percent) worry about their weight, while only 39 percent of men do. Age is a factor for women but not for men. Sixty-two percent of younger women (18–49) compared to 51 percent of older women (those aged 50 and older say they worry about their weight all or some of the time). Among men, 40 percent of younger men and 38 percent of older men say they worry about this often (Carroll, 2005). Further, women are much more likely than men to say they have tried to lose weight before. On average, women say they have tried to lose weight ten times while men say they have made an average of five attempts. Slightly less than half of men (45 percent) say they have never attempted to lose weight compared with only 23 percent of women (Carroll, 2005b). Similar patterns were reported in other countries, but the "gender gap" was smaller. In Great Britain, 49 percent of women but only 42 percent of men wanted to lose weight, while in Canada 59 percent of the women but only 45 percent of the men wanted to lose weight (McMurray, 2004). For women in particular, weight is perceived as a crucial indicator of their social acceptability. Although this perception seems to hold across all racial and ethnic groups, social classes, and sexual orientations, African American women appear less obsessed than white women about how much they weigh and about dieting (Celio, Zabinski, and Wilfley, 2002; Levine and Smolak, 2002). The most likely explanation for this difference is that African Americans have less restrictive definitions of female beauty, including how much a woman weighs along with support for the cultural image of strong black women. However, as Tamara Beauboeuf-Lafontant (2005) suggests, the stereotype of strong black women might also lead to problems of obesity, with eating acting as a coping mechanism for their having to care for others' needs to the neglect of their own.

Some 8 million Americans, the majority of them women, are estimated to have eating disorders (National Association of Anorexia Nervosa and Associated Disorders, 2001). Among the most common eating disorders are anorexia nervosa and bulimia. A person suffering from anorexia nervosa refuses to eat enough to maintain normal weight for her or his weight and height and has an intense fear of gaining weight. A person suffering from bulimia engages in binge eating and then to prevent weight gain induces vomiting or uses laxatives, diuretics, enemas, or other medications. Both disorders can be life-threatening.

Although we cannot assume a direct cause-and-effect relationship between television images and behavior such as eating disorders, there is mounting evidence to suggest that such a relationship does exist. In one study, for example, 15 percent of the girls and 8 percent of the boys reported that they had dieted or exercised to look like a TV character (Moore, 1995). Other studies of adolescent girls found that they frequently compare themselves to the thin-ideal images routinely provided in television and the print media. Many respondents in these studies reported that these comparisons led them to feel dissatisfied with their bodies, increased their desire to be thin, and, in some cases, motivated them to engage in eating disordered behaviors (Levine and Smolak, 2002; Thomsen, Weber, and Brown, 2001; Botta, 1999).

The public has long been aware of eating disorders in women, but it is only recently that attention has focused on boys and men. Increasingly males are being bombarded with media images of muscular, half-naked men and getting the message that muscles equal masculinity. Health officials are concerned that increasing numbers of adolescent and young adult males are suffering from muscle dysmorphia, an excessive preoccupation with body size and muscularity (Pope, Phillips, and Olivardia, 2002). This has led many males, not only athletes, to engage in strategies to increase muscles (McCabe and Ricciardelli, 2003), often risking their health through the use of body-altering steroids. Girls, too, in increasing numbers and some as young as 9, are using steroids. Like boys, some steroid use is to enhance their athletic performance, but for significant number of others, the purpose is weight control (Johnson, 2005).

A great deal of prime-time television programming continues to portray women and men in gender role stereotypes. A notable exception is ABC's new series *Commander-in-Chief*, starring Geena Davis as president of the United States. Recent polls suggest that voters in the United States are becoming more receptive to the idea of a woman president and predictions are that two prominent women, Secretary of State Condoleeza Rice and Senator Hillary Clinton, will be candidates in the future.

Gender role stereotyping is also evident in the content of the programs and their television characters. Although there are some notable exceptions (*Commander-in-Chief*, *Cold Case*), the vast majority of programs depict women in a limited range of roles—mostly in home or family situations, regardless of whether they are employed. When women characters are employed, their occupations are generally high-status ones, for example, lawyers, doctors, or business executives, a pattern not typical of the majority of working women. Thus, television distorts the reality of the working lives of most women and perhaps gives viewers an erroneous notion that gender barriers have disappeared.

In contrast, male characters are shown as powerful individuals, interacting in a wide variety of settings. Just as in children's readers, males are depicted as the problem solvers, whereas females generally are characterized as needing male help in solving their problems. There is one notable case in which women outperform men, however: They are seven times more likely to use sex or romantic charm to get their way (Condry, 1989). And there is one way in which male portrayals do not fare so well: Male characters are much more likely than female characters to use force or violence to get what they want and to commit crimes (Signorielli, 1997).

Stereotyping in the mass media is not limited to gender. Although racial and ethnic groups are more visible in programming today than in the past, they continue to be underrepresented both on and off camera. This is especially true for Asian Americans, Latinas/os, and Native Americans. And, despite increased Latino visibility, their characters are more likely to hold low-status occupations than other groups while Arab/Middle Eastern characters are more likely to be portrayed as criminals than members of other groups (Children Now, 2005; Coltrane and Messineo, 2000). Researchers found similar patterns in Canadian programming. Minorities made up 12 percent of characters—not far below their actual percentage in the national population, but they tended to be cast in secondary roles, low or unskilled occupations, and unstable domestic situations (Media Awareness Network, 2005).

In sum, gender stereotypes are presented in various degrees by all the agents of socialization. Even when parents make efforts to treat their daughters and sons equally, other socializing forces may undermine those efforts. As we have seen, rarely are either women or men portrayed in terms of the rich diversity and complexity that constitutes the human condition. Thus, it is not surprising that many children develop a stereotypic gender schema in the process of

APPLYING THE SOCIOLOGICAL IMAGINATION

Pediatricians have long been concerned about the public health risks posed by mass media images and messages directed at children and young adults as they try to develop their own gender identities. Thus, the American Academy of Pediatrics (AAP) developed a policy statement and guide for parents to suggests ways families can do media education in the home. Visit their Web site (www. aap.org/ pubed/ZZGVL4PQ7C.htm?&sub_cat=17) to get a full list of their suggestions. After reading them all, reflect on what media rules, if any, your parents established when you were growing up. How do they compare with those of the AAP? Do you think if parents follow their suggestions, there would be less gender stereotyping and fewer body image, weight problems, violence, and drug use among children and young adults? What is your reaction to their advice to keep TV sets, VCRs, video games, and computers out of children's bedrooms? What arguments can be made for or against this recommendation?

acquiring their gender identity. However, the socialization process itself does not tell us why one gender role is more highly valued than another. Although a discussion of the causes of gender inequality is outside the scope of this text, the theories discussed in the previous chapter, particularly structural functionalism and conflict theory, give some insight into how existing social arrangements define and support gender inequality. For now, let us turn our attention to the many ways in which our lives are affected by the cultural constructions of gender.

CONSEQUENCES OF GENDER STEREOTYPING

Studies show that each gender role has its advantages. Women live longer, can express their emotions more easily, and have closer interpersonal relationships than do men. Men have more power, both economically and socially, and greater freedom, and they experience less sexual discrimination or harassment than do women. However, this does not mean that all men enjoy these privileges or that men, as a group, escape any negative effect of gender socialization. Nevertheless, both women and men perceive the female role as having more disadvantages than the male role. A Gallup poll survey found that 62 percent of all the adults surveyed believe men in the United States have a better life than do women. In that same survey, 71 percent of the women and 52 percent of the men believe society favors men over women (Newport, 1993). A cross-cultural study of 22 countries found similar results, with respondents in 15 countries agreeing that society favors men over women (Gallup Poll, 1996). Indeed, that women and men are socialized differently has major consequences for individuals, families, and society at large. This is particularly true when existing social arrangements reinforce these differences, for example, institutionalized patterns of inequities in pay and job opportunities that disregard individual abilities. The scope of this book allows us to consider only a few of these consequences, so we will focus on lifestyle choices, self-esteem, self-confidence, mental illness, female–male friendships, and patterns of communication.

Lifestyle Choices

Although women have made major advances in a wide range of fields, from construction work to executive business positions, this progress is still more the exception than the norm. Current gender expectations continue to limit women's lifestyle choices. For instance, the choice of a single lifestyle by a growing number of women is still viewed as second best. Women who wish to combine career and family often must do so without much societal support. High-profile women who challenge the status quo are often suspected of undermining "family values." In 2001, when acting Governor Jane Swift of Massachusetts gave birth to twin girls, she was immediately criticized for putting her political ambitions ahead of her family.

Men, too, have found their lifestyle choices limited by traditional gender expectations. Not all men can or want to achieve "success" as defined by having a meaningful career or a high-paying job. Yet they are pressured to assume the role of the major breadwinner in the family. As a result, they may experience a serious conflict between their work and family roles. In addition, if they are not considered financially successful, they may be viewed as unsuitable marriage prospects.

Self-Esteem

Given that society values traits identified as masculine more highly than those identified as feminine, we might well expect to find gender differences in **self-esteem,** the overall feelings—positive or negative—that a person has about her- or himself (Alpert-Gillis and Connell, 1989). The research literature generally bears this out. As a category, females have lower self-images than do males. This does not mean, however, that all females have lower self-esteem than all males. At least two factors seem to play a crucial role in the relationship between gender and self-esteem: age and the degree of individual sex typing.

Age A major study by the American Association of University Women (AAUW) of a national sample of more than 3000 students in grades 4 through 10 found that not only did boys have higher self-esteem in elementary school than did girls, but that the gap between them widened in high school. In elementary school, 60 percent of the girls and 69 percent of the boys agreed with the statement, "I'm happy the way I am." By high school, only 29 percent of the girls and 46 percent of the boys felt that way. There were some interesting differences by race and ethnicity, however. Among elementary school girls, 55 percent of white girls, 65 percent of black girls, and 68 percent of Latinas reported being "happy as I am." By high school, only 22 percent of white girls, 58 percent of black girls, and 30 percent of Latinas agreed with that statement. The reason that black girls avoid such a drastic erosion in self-esteem compared with other girls is not entirely clear, but may have to do with parental socialization that emphasizes strength and independence for their daughters (cited in the AAUW Report, 1995:19, 21). This finding, documented in other studies as well (see, for example, McMullin and Cairney, 2004), is related to the conflicting expectations girls encounter when they reach puberty. Girls who were energetic, self-confident, and independent now experience pressure to behave in ways that will make them attractive to and popular with boys, even though this behavior might conflict with their own desires and abilities (Gilligan, 1990).

Early adolescence is a significant transition period for both sexes, but research reveals it to be a particularly difficult time for girls. Girls are growing up sooner than they did in the past. The age of a girl's first period, called *menarche,* has been falling for decades. Many of today's 10- and 11-year-old girls are at the same biological point that 16-year-olds were in 1800. In 1900, the average age for menarche was 14; by 1988, the average age had dropped to 12.5, and experts believe it will slip even lower (Creager, 1995). Researchers believe there is a correlation between how physically mature a girl looks and how people treat her. As

The United States has one of the highest incarceration rates in the world. Many experts believe that the large number of male prisoners today is a result of a national crisis in masculinity whereby boys and men receive mixed messages about what it means to be a man.

girls reach puberty, they are pressured to conform to gender roles more than they were before. The transition of little girl to young woman involves meeting unique demands in a culture that both idealizes and exploits the sexuality of young women. Thus, adolescent girls experience a conflict between their autonomous selves and their need to be feminine. Under these conditions, it is not surprising that many young women experience an erosion in self-esteem.

This does not mean, however, that males are unconcerned with their appearance. In a study of 1000 men over 15 years of age, researchers found that male self-worth is increasingly tied to body image, too. As we noted earlier, ads featuring images of the "ideal" steroid-enhanced bodies of actors and models are appearing more frequently on TV and in men's magazines. A recent study found that almost one out of two male respondents said they were unhappy with their overall appearance, up from the 1 in 6 reported in 1972 (Pope, Phillips, and Olivardia, 2002).

Sex Typing   The second factor that helps explain the observed gender differences in self-esteem is sex typing. Over the last several decades, social scientists have asked people to describe themselves using a list of personality traits thought characteristic of women and men. Scores are tallied and individuals are then categorized as masculine (high on instrumental traits, such as independence, strength, aggressiveness), feminine (high on expressive traits, such as understanding, emotion, dependence), or androgynous (having both instrumental and expressive traits). Researchers reported that the highest levels of self-esteem are found among both females and males who are high in masculine traits or who are androgynous (the latter's high self-esteem is attributed to the presence of instrumental traits). Conversely, feminine sex-typed individuals have considerably lower levels of self-esteem. This finding may help explain the observed differences in married women's and men's reaction to unemployment. In general, men report lower self-esteem and psychological health than women after becoming unemployed. Traditional gender roles associate masculinity with being a "good provider." When men lose this role, they perceive themselves as losing power and

status; however, unemployed women retain their nurturing role and hence much of their status (Artazcoz, 2004; Waters and Moore, 2002).

Self-Confidence

As with self-esteem, girls and boys differ in levels of self-confidence, and the gap widens with age. In response to the statement "I am good at a lot of things," 45 percent of elementary school females agreed, compared with 55 percent of their male counterparts. In high school, however, only 23 percent of the girls agreed, compared with 42 percent of the boys (AAUW, 1991). At least two patterns are associated with these perceptions. First, females tend to underestimate their abilities, whereas males overestimate theirs. In a small but insightful study, Edward Kain (1990:113) asked his students to grade their own papers. He found an almost perfect correlation between sex and grade estimation: The females gave themselves significantly lower grades, whereas the males gave themselves significantly higher grades. Kain concluded, "By the time students have reached college age, the cultural lessons about gender appear to be strongly internalized." Second, some activities may be avoided if they are seen as inappropriate for one's sex, regardless of ability. For example, as we saw earlier, females often consider themselves less competent in fields that have been traditionally defined as masculine, such as math and science, than males who have the same grades. Viewed in this light it is not surprising that, as one researcher discovered, "Preschool boys handle more tools, throw more balls, construct more Lego bridges, build more block towers, and tinker more with simple mechanical objects than do girls" (Kahle, 1990). In a similar vein, another study found that by third grade, only 37 percent of the girls, but over half of the boys (51 percent), had used microscopes, while by eleventh grade 17 percent of females compared with 49 percent of males had used an electricity meter (Mullis and Jenkins, 1988).

These play activities are not unimportant. They teach important mental and motor skills, and because girls are not encouraged—indeed, they may even be discouraged—from pursuing such activities, they are at a disadvantage as they

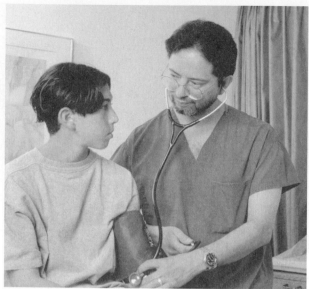

Today small but increasing numbers of women and men are entering nontraditional occupations. This male nurse examines his young patient.

grow older. These findings are significant, not only for their implications regarding self-confidence, but also for their economic implications. Society may be losing potential mathematicians and scientists simply because of narrowly defined gender roles. Similarly, society loses out when qualified men avoid entering fields deemed "woman's work" such as nursing, early childhood and elementary education (see Chapter 10).

Mental Health

Gender differences in mental health have long been observed. To take just one example, studies of both clinical populations and the general public consistently find that adolescent girls and women have higher rates of depression than adolescent boys and men do, a ratio of about two to one (Hazler, 2004; Cyranowski et al., 2000). There is considerable evidence that gender stereotypes play a pivotal role in these rates (Landrine and Klonoff, 1997). The higher rates of depression found among women may be a result of the fact that women are more likely than men to seek help for their problems (Klerman and Weissman, 1980). This behavior is consistent with traditional gender roles. The traditional feminine role grants women permission to seek help from others, whereas the traditional masculine role requires men to be strong and to "ride out" their problems (Real, 1997).

The attitudes and behaviors of mental health professionals are also important in understanding gender differences in mental illness. Historically, the mental health field has frequently reflected gender-related stereotypes. In one study, for example, researchers asked a number of clinicians to define a healthy woman, a healthy man, and a healthy, mature adult of no specified sex. Clinicians described a healthy woman as more emotional, more submissive, less independent, less aggressive and competitive, more easily excitable, more easily hurt, and more concerned with her

appearance than a healthy male. Significantly, when describing a healthy adult of no specified sex, clinicians listed a number of traits traditionally associated with the male stereotype, such as independence and assertiveness. Thus, women were viewed as possessing characteristics that are less positive and less healthy than those of a typical healthy adult (Broverman et al., 1970). Such an association implies that women who conform to the traditional feminine role do not measure up to the mental health standards of the general adult population.

Clinicians today are more sensitive to gender bias and are unlikely to list different characteristics for healthy adult females and healthy adult males. Nevertheless, some clinicians still hold an adjustment standard of mental health. Thus, women and men who conform to traditional gender roles are likely to be seen as healthier than those who deviate from these roles. Assertive and independent women and gentle and nurturing men may therefore be viewed as maladjusted (Robertson and Fitzgerald, 1990; Gilbert and Scher, 1999).

Marital status and level of marital power are also related to feelings of depression. Wives who share decision making with their husbands report lower levels of depression than those in unequal relationships (Whisman and Jacobson, 1988). As Susan Basow (1992) observes, women's lives themselves may add to their risk of being depressed. Women are more likely to be unemployed or employed part-time, poor, or in low-status jobs. As wives, they feel pressured to make sure that the household runs smoothly and the needs of all family members are satisfied, even when this means that their own needs go unmet.

Although, overall, men fare better on measures of mental health than women do, some aspects of the traditional masculine role can easily become detrimental. When taken to extremes, dominance and aggression can lead to psychologically and physically destructive behavior. Furthermore, the cultural connection between work and male identity can create considerable psychological stress for unemployed men. Lack of education, inadequate job skills, and discriminatory practices make this particularly problematic for poor men and men of color. Additionally, men's emotional lives are often deficient because of their inability to verbalize their love or show affection. Thus, rigid adherence to traditional gender norms may interfere with the development of good mental health for both women and men. This latter point raises an interesting question. Can both women and men benefit from becoming androgynous, that is, sharing masculine and feminine traits?

Research shows that masculine-oriented individuals (high on instrumental traits), both female and male, experience less anxiety, strain, depression, neuroticism, work impairment, achievement conflicts, and dissatisfaction in their lives than do feminine-oriented individuals (Nezu and Nezu, 1987; Long, 1989; Basow, 1992). Similarly, traits traditionally defined as feminine can be beneficial to women and men. The ability to express feelings and show sensitivity to those around oneself enhances interpersonal adjustment and the ability to form intimate relationships. For example, researchers Lawrence Ganong and Marilyn Coleman (1987) found that androgynous individuals are more expressive in their feelings of love, better able to self-disclose, and more tolerant of faults in their loved ones than are more traditionally oriented people. With this in mind, let us examine the meaning that friendship has in the lives of women and men.

Women, Men, and Friends

According to Lillian Rubin (1985:59), throughout most of the history of Western civilization, "men's friendships have been taken to be the model of what friendship is and how it ought to be. . . . Women's friendships didn't count, indeed were not even noticed." As recently as 1969, anthropologist Lionel Tiger hypothesized that men have a genetically based tendency to form nonerotic bonds with other males, and that these male bonds are stronger and more stable than those formed between women. An impressive array of research studies over the past 25 years, focusing on the similarities and differences between female and male friendship patterns, has not substantiated Tiger's hypothesis. Conversely, much of this research is consistent with Rubin's assessment: "The results of my own research are unequivocal: At every life stage between twenty-five and fifty-five, women have more friendships, as distinct from collegial relationships or workmates, than men, and the differences in the content and quality of their friendships are marked and unmistakable (Rubin, 1985:60–61).

Overall, women's friendships tend to be characterized by intimacy, self-disclosure, nurturance, and emotional support. Conversation is a central part of women's friendships (Walker, 1994; Johnson, 1996). Men's friendships, in contrast, focus more on shared activities such as sports, politics, and business, and tend to be less intimate than women's friendships (Inman, 1996). Definitive reasons for these gender differences have not yet been substantiated, but several explanations appear plausible. In contrast to men, women are more likely to be socialized to be more relationship-oriented. The emphasis on male competitiveness may make it difficult for men to self-disclose to one another, thereby making men feel vulnerable. Finally, the fear of being labeled homosexual may prevent men from developing emotional attachments to other men.

Despite these differences, both females and males report about the same level of satisfaction with their friendship activities (Mazur, 1989). Thus, although they may connect with others in different ways, both women and men share a common need for meaningful relationships with others of their sex. Although difficult to achieve, this need for connectedness sometimes manifests itself in cross-sex friendships.

Cross-Sex Friendships   A single parent who lives with her mother and her 9-year-old daughter told this story:

> Recently Jane had a male school chum over to the house. The grandmother was home and the mother was at work. The two children went up to Jane's room to play computer games. Upon realizing they went upstairs, the grandmother became excited and sent the boy home, telling her granddaughter that it was inappropriate for him to be there.

What do you think motivated the grandmother's behavior? No doubt you have observed mixed-sex groups of

As more women and men pursue similar occupations and work together, the possibilities for development of cross-sex friendships increase.

preschool children at play. However, this pattern begins to change in elementary school. Like this grandmother, adults become fearful that cross-sex friendships can become sexual. Thus, whether consciously or not, from early on society erects barriers to cross-sex friendships. Some of these barriers are reflected in the organization of elementary schools, with their frequent gender-segregated activities; others are embedded in the belief that women and men have opposite characteristics. As noted earlier, however, as children age, they exhibit more gender flexibility. One consequence of this is the tendency for cross-sex friendships to increase during adolescence and early adulthood. A study by Ruth Anne Clark (1994) of 10- to 16-year-olds found that as age increased so did the tendency to choose other-sex peers for interaction. In all grades, boys, but not girls, showed a slight preference for the other sex. The nature of the interaction, however, influenced the gender preference—both girls and boys preferred a male as a conversational partner for telling stories and joking, whereas girls were chosen as a preferred partner for cheering, advice, or suggestions on how to explain a complicated idea. These patterns continue in adulthood, when men more frequently choose women for conversational partners than women choose men (Reisman, 1990). College students have the highest incidence of cross-sex friendships (Werking, 1994). However, heterosexual marriage or a serious involvement frequently acts against maintaining cross-sex friendships. Lillian Rubin (1985) sees this response as keeping with the cultural expectation that romantic commitment and commitment to family must come before friendships. That our culture provides few models of enduring cross-sex friendships contributes to the difficulty in forming and maintaining such relationships (Rawlins, 1993). Gendered patterns of communication can also exaggerate both the perceived and the real differences between women and men and thus hinder the formation of cross-sex friendships.

Patterns of Communication

Linguistic scholars from Robin Lakoff (1975) to Deborah Tannen (1990, 1994, 2002) report that women and men often speak essentially different languages and have different communication goals and behaviors. These patterns begin early and have major consequences both for the society at large and in our interpersonal relationships. Let us take one example of the former context, the political arena. A recent study of adolescents and young adults, composed roughly of equal numbers of females and males with similar qualifications participating in a Model United Nations Program, found that male delegates spoke more, interrupted other speakers more frequently, and engaged in more aggressive and challenging behavior than did female delegates (Rosenthal, Jones, and Rosenthal, 2003). The presence of a female chair and a larger percentage of female committees made only slight differences in these patterns. These norms of male dominance have been found in a wide range of studies and suggest that politics is a masculine domain. Such findings may help explain the low percentage of women in public office and the difficulty women face in getting some of their needs on the political agenda. Gender differences in speaking styles can also affect workplace behavior, including who gets heard, who gets credit, and how work gets done.

Similarly, gender differences in communication styles affect interpersonal relationships. According to Tannen, women speak and hear a language of intimacy and connectedness, whereas men speak and hear a language of status and independence. She calls women's conversational style "rapport talk," the goal of which is to signal support, to confirm solidarity, or to indicate they are following the conversation. In contrast, Tannen sees men's conversational style as "report talk," intended to preserve independence and to negotiate and maintain status in a hierarchical order. These contrasting styles can be problematic in intimate relationships, especially in the realm of self-disclosure. As we will see in other sections of this text, men often find self-disclosure difficult, even to their wives.

Another linguist, Jennifer Coates (1986), concluded that women normally use conversation as an opportunity to discuss problems, share experiences, and offer reassurance and advice. Men, however, do not see the discussion of personal issues as a normal component of conversation. If someone discloses to them, they are likely to assume the role of expert and offer advice. Thus, in couple relationships women often complain that men do not express their feelings, and men say they feel burdened by such complaints. Such gender differences may result in stress and conflict in marriage.

> *Imagine for a moment that you had to spend the next year of your life as a member of the other sex. How would your life be different? What advantages and disadvantages would you experience as a female? As a male?*

CHANGING REALITIES, CHANGING ROLES

Whether we like it or not, the world we inhabit today is quite different from that of our parents and grandparents. Consider two examples that will be discussed in detail in later chapters: (1) More married mothers are working than ever before, many of them in sexually integrated work settings; and (2) increasing numbers of women (and some men) are finding themselves solely responsible for their family's economic and social welfare. Yet, as we have seen throughout this chapter, some of the agents of socialization continue to perpetuate traditional views of white middle-class femininity and masculinity, often in ways that have negative consequences for women's and men's development and self-esteem. Many of these patterns of socialization are not sufficient to provide solutions to the psychological and economic strains experi-

---

WRITING YOUR OWN SCRIPT

REFLECTIONS ON GENDER

As this chapter illustrates, gender is a significant factor in our lives. Social expectations about gender are so deeply woven into the fabric of our society that they often seem natural. Even when we are unhappy about some aspect of our lives, we often fail to see the connections between existing cultural assumptions and social arrangements and our own experiences. Take time to reflect on the role of gender in your experiences.

Questions to consider

1. How has being a male or a female affected your life to this point? Do you feel you missed out on anything because of your gender? What, if anything, would you change about being a woman or a man in today's society?

2. How satisfied are you with your physical appearance? If you could change any aspect of your appearance, what would it be? Why?

3. What are your friendship patterns like? Are you satisfied with the number of cross-sex friendships you have? What are some of the social barriers to developing and maintaining cross-sex friendships? What might you do to increase the likelihood of having more cross-sex friendships?

enced by many people today. Thus, it is necessary to seek new ways to socialize children, to enable them to make satisfying personal choices and to live full and satisfying human lives.

SUPPORTING MARRIAGES AND FAMILIES

A growing body of literature documents the fact that gender-stereotyped roles are bad for relationship stability and satisfaction (Johnson, 2003) and that establishing relationship equality provides a critical building block for balancing work and family life (Zimmerman, Ziemba, and Current, 2001), resulting in higher levels of emotional well-being and satisfaction with interpersonal relationships. Psychologist Sandra Bem (1983:613) offers two strategies that parents and other agents of socialization can employ to modify gender socialization patterns that lead to gender-stereotyped roles. The first strategy is to teach children that the only definitive gender differences are anatomical and reproductive. The second strategy is to help children substitute an "individual differences" schema that emphasizes the "remarkable variability of individuals within groups" for the gender schema they currently use for organizing and processing information. Classroom teachers can institute mechanisms for building gender equity inside and outside their classrooms. One quick example—two science teachers at a middle school created Science Chicks, an after-school club for seventh-grade girls to encourage girls' scientific interests (Cromer, 2005). The media can effectively assist in a move toward gender equality by featuring characters of both genders in substantial numbers in major roles that offer positive and competent role content. When children see females and males in nontraditional ways, they are less likely to see careers and personal options as gendered based. In the same manner, when people of color are portrayed in a diverse range of occupations, including those that are highly valued and respected, it helps erode racial and ethnic stereotypes and creates higher aspirations among children of color. Sociologist Hilary Lips (1993:397) sums up the possible benefits of such approaches: "As a society, we may finally come to the realization that the function and qualities stereotypically associated with each gender are valuable and necessary—and much more interchangeable and shareable than we used to think."

SUMMARY

Each of us occupies a number of statuses that carry with them expectations for behavior. Some of these are ascribed statuses, such as sex and race. Others are achieved by our own efforts, for example, becoming a parent or a teacher. Role expectations serve an important function in society in that they make behavior predictable. However, expectations can be defined so rigidly that they become dysfunctional for individuals and for society as a whole.

The status of being female or male in our society affects all aspects of our lives. Thus, it is important to distinguish between the concepts of sex (being female or male) and gender (the socially learned behaviors, attitudes, and the expectations associated with being female or male). From early on, we are taught to behave in gender-appropriate ways by parents, peers, teachers, and the mass media.

Psychoanalytic/identification theory, social-learning theory, cognitive-development theory, and enculturated-lens theory have been advanced by social scientists to explain how we acquire our gender identity. Although there is some empirical support for these theories, they do not explain why women and men are treated unequally. For this answer, we must examine existing social arrangements.

The traditional notions of femininity and masculinity are based on white middle-class definitions, and they do not accurately reflect the race and class variations in gender role perceptions. Traditional gender roles limit the lifestyle options of both females and males.

Gender roles are in transition as a result of new demographic and social patterns. Increasing numbers of individuals can be identified as androgynous, having characteristics of both genders. Research shows that both females and males who are high in instrumental (masculine) traits tend to have higher self-esteem and better mental health than those high on expressive (feminine) traits. Researchers have found that androgynous individuals are more expressive in their feelings of love, better able to self-disclose, and more tolerant of faults in their loved ones than are more traditionally oriented individuals.

Although they connect with others in different ways, both females and males have a common need for meaningful relationships with others of the same sex. Women's friendships are characterized by intimacy and self-disclosure, whereas men's friendships focus more on shared activities. Gendered patterns of communication exaggerate both the perceived and real differences between women and men and hinder the formation of cross-sex friendships.

KEY TERMS

ascribed status
achieved status
gender role stereotypes
master (key) status
sex

gender
gender identity
intersexuality
transsexuals
gender role socialization

psychoanalytic/ identification theory
social-learning theory
modeling
cognitive-development theory

enculturated-lens theory
agents of socialization
content analysis
self-esteem

QUESTIONS FOR STUDY AND REFLECTION

1. Distinguish between sex and gender. Why is it important to make this distinction? Many scientists today argue that sex and gender are fluid rather than dichotomous. What do they mean by this? What evidence is there to support this position?

2. Think back to your childhood as far as you can go. When is the first time that you can recall that you were aware of being a girl or a boy? (Hint: Sometimes these are painful events, for instance, when we asked for a toy and were told it wasn't appropriate for our gender or when we were criticized "for behaving like a member of the other gender.") How did you feel at the time? How would your life be different today if you were the other gender? Compare and contrast the theories advanced by social scientists to explain the process of gender acquisition. Using yourself as an example, which theory do you think explains how you acquired your gender

identity? Is any one of these theories, or are all of them combined, sufficient to explain the content of gender roles in our society? Explain your position.

3. Assume that you are entertaining visitors from another culture who are unfamiliar with the patterns of female–male relationships in the United States today and who do not want to make any major mistakes in their interactions during their visit. What would you tell them? What problems might they run into without this knowledge?

4. Consider the following proposition: Young girls and boys should be raised alike, with similar toys, play activities, and the same expectations regarding their education and future careers. Do you agree or disagree with this proposition? Explain and provide evidence to support your position.

ADDITIONAL RESOURCES

SOCIOLOGICAL

ANDERSON, MARGARET, AND PATRICIA HILL COLLINS, EDS. 2001. *Race, Class, and Gender: An Anthology.* Belmont, CA: Wadsworth. This anthology contains a collection of articles on gender along with the intersections of race and class.

FAUSTO-STERLING, ANNE. 2000. *Sexing the Body: Gender Politics and the Construction of Sexuality.* New York: Basic Books. Drawing on astonishing real-life cases, the author argues that individuals born as mixtures of male and female should not be forced to change their bodies to fit a flawed societal definition of normality.

KIMMEL, MICHAEL. 2000. *The Gendered Society.* New York: Oxford. The author presents a comprehensive examination of how gender functions in society and confronts gender inequities, suggesting the possibility of a "degendered society."

POLLACK, WILLIAM S. 1998. *Real Boys: Rescuing Our Sons from the Myths of Boyhood.* New York: Random House. The author argues that many of the problems that boys have stem from their early socialization experiences.

FILM

Bend It Like Beckham. 2002. A touching story about a teenage girl named Jess who lives in London and who must make a choice between following the traditions of her Indian family or pursuing her dream of playing soccer.

Mad Hot Ballroom. 2005. This insightful and fun documentary profiles a diverse group of 11-year-old girls and boys from three New York public elementary schools as they take a mandatory course in ballroom dancing that culminates in a citywide competition. In the process, the kids learn about each other, reveal their thoughts on the other gender, develop social skills, and improve their self-esteem.

LITERARY

NAFISI, AZAR. 2003. *Reading Lolita in Tehran.* New York: Random House. An engaging memoir of the personal and social changes experienced by a female professor in Iran and seven of her students who struggle to live under the strict laws governing the Islamic Republic.

GRAHAM, KATHARINE. 1997. *Personal History.* New York: Vintage. This memoir reads like a novel, telling the true story of a woman socialized to the traditional role of wife and mother who, after her husband's death, takes over the *Washington Post* and becomes one of the most powerful women in the world.

INTERNET

http://www.thewhitehouseproject.org This national nonpartisan organization works to advance a richly diverse critical mass of woman into leadership positions, up to and including the U.S. presidency. It features information about political and civic leadership programs for young women.

http://www.supportingoursons.org Supporting Our Sons is a national nonprofit membership organization dedicated to helping boys achieve their full potential. Its Web site contains research on boys and provides information and guidelines for parents whose sons want to pursue nontraditional gender roles.

http://www.media-awareness.ca This Canadian Web site provides information and research on how the media portray girls and women, boys and men, gays and lesbians, ethnic and visible minorities, whiteness and white privilege, and other important topics.

http://globetrotter.berkeley.edu/GlobalGender The International Gender Studies Resources features research and teaching materials relating to women and gender in Africa, Asia, Latin America, the Middle East and Arab world and among minority cultures in North America and Europe.

IN THE NEWS:

Paris, France

In a remarkable case of love transcending death, in February 2004, a 34-year-old Parisian woman, Christelle Demichel, married her dead lover. The bride, carrying a bouquet of yellow roses, was showered with rice as she left a town hall in Nice, France, where she had just married her fiancé, Eric Demichel, who died three years earlier. The wedding ceremony was followed by a reception at a local restaurant where more than 40 people helped the bride celebrate her nuptials with champagne whose bottles bore custom labels with the newlyweds' names. According to *New York Times* writer Craig Smith (2005), the only thing missing (beside a wedding cake) was the groom.

Although this scene might seem to some like a plot from the latest blockbuster movie or novel, the fact is that in France, it is possible to marry the dead thanks to a 1959 law enacted after the Malpasset Dam in southern France burst, killing hundreds of the townspeople. Visiting the town after the disaster, then French President Charles De Gaulle was approached by a young woman who begged him to let her follow through with her planned wedding even though her fiancé had drowned. De Gaulle promised to think about the young woman's request and later that month, the French Parliament drafted a law that permitted the young woman to marry her dead fiancé. Since that time, hundreds of Parisians have applied to marry their dead lovers. Anyone wishing to marry a dead person has only to formally request permission from the president, who then forwards the request to the justice minister, who, in turn, sends in on to the prosecutor in whose jurisdiction the surviving person lives. In this rather circuitous process, the prosecutor has the responsibility of determining whether or not the couple had actually planned to wed prior to the death and if the parents of the deceased approve of the postmortem wedding. If the answer is affirmative in both of these instances, the prosecutor then sends the recommendation back up the line to the president who, if so inclined, eventually signs a decree allowing the marriage to take place (Smith, 2005).

In the case of the newlywed Ms. Demichel, the bride received approval more than a year after her fiancé had been killed by a drunken driver and several months before the actual wedding took place. On what would have been her fiancé's 30th birthday, Ms. Demichel, dressed in a black pantsuit, stood in the ornate wedding room in Nice's town hall next to an empty orange armchair that represented the groom and, instead of repeating marriage vows, she listened as the mayor read the presidential decree that allowed the postmortem wedding. There was no exchange of rings, although the mayor asked the bride if she wanted to do something in this regard. According to the French law allowing Ms. Demichel to wed her dead lover, the marriage is retroactive to the eve of the groom's death. This allows her to carry his name and identify herself as a widow. According to Ms. Demichel, the marriage was otherwise of purely sentimental value. To avoid potential abuses, the 1959 law prohibits such spouses from any inheritance as a result of their weddings. Although as many as 20 such weddings take place each year and most are kept quiet, Ms. Demichel said she went public to help others who might not know that marrying a lost (more accurately, DEAD) love was an option.

Ms. Demichel's mother-in-law consented to the marriage because she believed Ms. Demichel was the only woman with whom her son had ever wanted to marry and start a family. After the wedding, Ms. Demichel took a few days off from her police officer duties and, in a honeymoon of sorts, spent a few days in Paris with her mother-in-law before returning home to her Nice apartment where she keeps her husband's ashes in an urn in her bedroom. According to Ms. Demichel, she has truly transcended death (Smith, 2005).

WHAT WOULD YOU DO? If you were planning to marry someone and before the nuptials could take place s/he died, if the law allowed, would you marry the person posthumously? Why? Why not? Could you live a satisfying married life without a living spouse? Sociologically speaking, what purpose does such a marriage serve? Would such a law allowing people to marry the dead be a contradiction to American ideas and values about what constitutes marriages and families?

"Love is blind." "Love makes the world go 'round." "Love is a many-splendored thing." "True love never dies." "Love at first sight." "Love conquers all." How many sayings like these can you think of? In Western societies, probably more than in any others, love is a central feature of life. It is such a major part of our lives today that most of us cannot imagine life and relationships without love. Most Westerners believe that love gives life meaning, that it is essential to a healthy and satisfying life. And as the In the News article opening this chapter shows, for some people *true love* never dies even after the object of our "true love" dies physically. In the United States, people of all ages devote much thought about and considerable time and effort to love and intimate relationships. Love is referred to or appears as a central theme throughout American popular culture, in the lyrics of all types of music, poems, sonnets, short stories, novels, films, plays, television, and art. The love affairs and love scandals of movie stars and other well-known people are mainstays in popular media, and we hunger for more and more of this "love" news. The advice columns of daily newspapers, daytime television talk shows and soap operas, as well as a popular literature and even academic courses on how to attract, impress, satisfy, keep, and even dump the lover of our choice all exemplify the extent to which love and intimacy occupy our thoughts and actions. Almost everyone at one time or another has been or will be in love. Yet, few of us can say exactly what love is.

Humans express many kinds of love, probably as many as there are types of people who love and are loved. Love encompasses a wide variety of feelings and behaviors, ranging from those we feel for our parents, friends, siblings, and children to those we feel for our spouses or partners. However, the type of love that is dominant in most of our lives, at one time or another, is romantic love. Although a common thread of caring is woven through all love relationships, the major difference between these feelings of love and romantic love is the element of *eroticism*—concerning or intending to arouse sexual desire. Although all types of love are important and merit discussion, our primary concern in this chapter is with romantic or erotic love.

WHAT IS THIS THING CALLED LOVE?

How would you respond to the question, What is love? If we asked 100 people to define love, we would probably get 100 different responses. Love, it seems, is an elusive emotion. Most of us insist that we experience it at some time in our lives, but we have extreme difficulty explaining it in words. Love is surrounded by myths and metaphors; we dream and hope of finding the love of a lifetime who will love us no matter what and who will transform an otherwise ordinary life into one of bliss. People have been known to do all sorts of things in the name of love: wage wars, forsake family and friends, sign away fortunes, or give up royal standing. We claim that love is blind, and so, blindly, we subject ourselves to a wide range of emotions from ecstasy to torment, and all in the name of love.

Because each of us expresses and experiences love differently, there are a variety of definitions and types of love. Some writers, for example, view love as an emotion that causes us to act irrationally. Other writers believe it to be an emotion that is much more centered on self than on another person; or a giving of the heart and soul, the giving of a person's total self; or an ideology that narrows people's perception of the world; or an innate undeniable aspect of what makes us human. Still other writers have defined love as a contrivance, a fantasy concocted by human beings over the centuries, a cultural delusion that originated in the twelfth century with wandering troubadours and knights in shining armor (Marriott, 2001). Some writers have even argued that love is a male invention used to exploit women. Definitions of love describe it in terms of any one or several of the following characteristics: deep emotional attachment, openness, self-disclosure, physical attraction, and personal growth. Although many social scientists steer clear of singular definitions of love because in their view love varies in degree, intensity, over time, and across social contexts, William Goode's definition of love is still perhaps the most widely cited in the scientific literature: "A strong emotional attachment, a cathexis, between adolescents or adults of opposite sexes, with at least the components of sex, desire, and tenderness" (1959:49). Although we agree that love defies a single definition, to facilitate a broader understanding of the concept, we will nonetheless use a more general and inclusive definition than that of Goode. In this context, we use the term **romantic love** to refer to, very generally, the intense feelings, emotions, and thoughts coupled with sexual passion and erotic expression that a person directs toward another, as well as the *ideology*—the set of beliefs—that upholds it.

Although romantic love is often considered unique to Western and modern cultures, anthropologists have found that it does exist in some "traditional" societies. For example, anthropologists William Jankowiak and Edward Fischer (1992) examined 166 traditional cultures and found evidence of romantic love in 88 percent of them. Individuals within these cultures sang love songs and even eloped; the folklore of many of these societies portrayed various types of romantic entanglements. Jankowiak and Fischer suggested that the reason romantic love has not been found in most traditional societies is because social scientists have either simply overlooked this aspect of traditional culture or they have not had sufficient access to these cultures to study love. Thus, they concluded that romantic love, which they equate with passionate love, constitutes a human universal, or at the least, a "near-universal."

 How do you define love? Is your definition of love consistent with that of your friends? Your parents and others around you? How many times have you been in love? How do you know when you are in love?

Love as a Social Construction

People tend to think of love as an individual choice fired by our biological engines. Although research from the biological sciences shows that biochemistry underlies our emotional behavior throughout every stage of human love, of interest to sociologists is how love is conditioned by the cultural context, historical period, and institutional structures in which it occurs. In this context, love emerges out of the unique context in which individuals encounter one another, but the feelings that develop between people are love only when they define it as such. And the criteria that people use to arrive at the conclusion that they are in love are social in origin.

Culture plays an essential role in this process, particularly in terms of whom we choose to love. In early childhood, we develop specific likes and dislikes in response to family, peers, experiences, cultural prescriptions, and definitions of love, beauty, and worthiness, so that by the time we are teenagers we have developed a mental picture of whom we will find attractive and fall in love with. Anthropologist Helen Fisher (1999) refers to this mental image that we carry around as an unconscious mental template, or **love map**—a group of physical, psychological, and behavioral traits that one finds attractive in a mate. Culture not only plays a critical role in whom we will find attractive but also in when we begin to court, where and how we court, and how we pursue a potential mate.

According to a social constructionist point of view, love can only be understood as symbolic or as a social construction that by itself has no intrinsic meaning. Feelings of romantic love and passion have a physiological component, but neither is based solely on our body reactions. Rather, they are also based upon the way in which we interpret and label our feelings and reactions. Take the classic example: You walk into a crowded room; your eyes lock on those of a stranger across the room; after a brief moment of staring you smile at each other; a short time later you find a reason to approach each other, and as you do so your heart begins to beat rapidly, you experience a shortness of breath, and you feel the blood rush to your face. What do these physiological responses signify? How do you interpret them? Do you have the flu? Have you had much too much to drink? Or is the room's thermostat simply out of control?

If you have grown up in the United States, you have learned from family, peers, and the mass media that what you are feeling can be interpreted in terms of love. These feelings do not have to be interpreted in terms of love, however. It is the context in which they occur (in a room where we have just locked eyes with a stranger) that leads us to that interpretation. The point here is that our emotional states are symbolic states and as such require interpretation and naming to give them meaning (Karp and Yoels, 1993). That is, the meanings of objects, emotions, and situations reside in our responses to and interpretations of them. In this sense, definitions of love vary because love is a social construction with no fixed meaning. What we define as love is rooted in both societal and cultural values as well as the values of the groups to which we belong.

Although no one has quite figured out why we fall in love, over half (54 percent) of American adults believe that it can happen at first sight. Perhaps you are among this 54 percent; maybe you have experienced love at first sight. Slightly more men than women (57 versus 52 percent) and more married than unmarried people (56 versus 51 percent) say they believe in love at first sight (Fox News Opinion Poll, 2005). When Gallup pollsters asked people about their past romantic behavior, four in ten Americans said that they had actually fallen in love at first sight, with men being slightly more likely than women to say they had fallen in love at first sight. Moreover, three-fourths of those polled believe that there is "one true love out there"—that there is "only one person that they are destined to fall in love with" (Carlson, 2001). In the harsh cold light of reality, however, sociological research shows that our "destiny" is tempered by formal and informal cultural norms and values concerning partner eligibility that filter out millions of potential lovers, one of who just might have been "our destiny" or "one true love." This research helps us understand and supports the constructionist point of view of love as a social and historical construction. As we stress throughout this textbook, systems of race, class, gender, and sexual orientation shape all intimate relationships. Thus, even something as abstract and hard to define as the concept of love illustrates the significance of historical context and the social construction of love in shaping intimacy. Therefore, as we will see in Chapter 5, an array of social factors including race, class, gender, age, sexual orientation, religion, and geographic location eliminate thousands, if not millions, of potential (or maybe *destined*) mates.

How Does Romantic Love Develop in Contemporary Society?

In the United States, love develops within the context of a popular culture that inundates us with messages about love: whom we should love, how, when, under what conditions, and how we should behave when we are in love. Based on an accumulation of research over the years, the typical developmental sequence of heterosexual love in the twenty-first century, particularly over the last 50 years, seemed to be as follows: Girl meets boy; they interact; they discover that they have common interests, values, and backgrounds; they find that they like each other; they begin to date; they are physically attracted to each other. Because they like and are physically attracted to each other, they date more frequently and grow more fond of each other. As the relationship continues and deepens, the couple typically progresses through stages of initiating, intensifying (falling in love), working out problems and making adjustments, and finally making a commitment to one another (Wood, 2004). At some point, they define their feelings as love. Feeling love for one another, they become engaged and plan to marry. The relationship may or may not include sexual activity, but if it does, sex is probably defined in terms of the couple's love for each other. This sequence is discussed in greater detail in Chapter 5. The development of lesbian and gay love relationships parallels that of heterosexuals, with stages of initiation, more frequent contact, intense infatuation, working out problems, and a maturing commitment (Wood, 2004).

Not all love relationships, of course, develop along this sequence. Perhaps far fewer couples today than in the past follow this sequence of love. For some people, love happens slowly over time; they seem to slide gently into love as they progress through these various stages. For other people, it is love at first sight; lightning strikes, and the heart palpitates. Thus, sometimes the stages are reversed; at other times some of them are omitted. Sometimes, for example, the sequence begins with sexual attraction. In addition, not all love relationships culminate in sex or marriage. In recent years, in fact, several of these stages may not apply to some couples who engage in a series of "involvements" that may or may not lead to marriage. And given that love is now advertised as something that can be taught in a classroom, a new developmental sequence may be emerging that begins with people taking a class in flirting or the art of falling in love. In any event, several social scientists have attempted to explain some of these newer modifications to the traditional developmental course of love. Later in this chapter we examine some of these theories. First, however, we must understand the history of love and its development in Western society.

Love in Western Society: A Historical Perspective

Romantic love has been portrayed in a variety of ways in Western cultures for centuries. Many of today's myths and legends about romantic love come from antiquity (Fisher, 1999). The love story of Isis and Osiris was recorded in Egypt more than 3000 years ago. Ovid composed poems to romantic love in the first century B.C. in ancient Rome. And the *Kuma Sutra* (Hindu words for "love" and for "pleasure and sensual gratification," respectively), a Hindu treatise on the art of love, including explicit sexual instructions, was composed sometime between the first and fourth centuries A.D.

As we have discussed, today romantic love is almost always linked to sex and marriage. The moment we think of any one of these concepts, the other two come to mind. For example, we refer to sexual intercourse as "making love" (some people refer to it as "the marriage act"), we marry because we are "in love," marriage is viewed as a "love relationship," and sex is said to be a "natural expression of love." And when we are no longer in love, we separate, divorce, or break up. We tend to think that one naturally follows another.

It has not always been this way, however. For much of human history, although marriage and sex were related, there was no conception of love as a necessary part of either. In most societies throughout history, and in many societies in the world today, people marry not out of romantic love but out of obligation to parents and family. In the typical case, a strong sense of family duty and obligation to parents is symbolically transferred on marriage to a spouse who is chosen by one's parents or grandparents (Coltrane, 1998). The linking of love with sex and marriage is a unique feature of romantic love, a type of love that is relatively new in human social history. It slowly developed in Western societies over many centuries, and its roots can be traced to ancient Greece and Rome.

Love in Ancient Greece   Most writers trace contemporary notions of romantic love to Greek society of the fifth century B.C. and the writings of the philosopher Plato. Plato defined love as the highest expression of human virtue because of its ability to inspire people to be kind, honorable, and wise. Plato distinguished several types of love: *Agape* is a selfless love; it is spontaneous and altruistic and requires nothing in return. *Eros* is a selfish love, with an emphasis on physical pleasure. It is based on sexual attraction and can be either homosexual or heterosexual. *Philos* is a deep friendship or brotherly love and includes a love for humanity.

The erotic love that Plato and other Greek philosophers idealized was a combination of the purely physical and the

Romantic love can be both exhilarating and practical. It often begins with love at first sight, passion, and exclusive attention to one another. However, over time, the practicality of long-term love sets in as couples must meet the requirements of everyday living.

Source: Reprinted with special permission of King Features Syndicate.

extremely spiritual. Although sex and beauty were its goals, it was not focused, however, on one's marriage partner. Marriages were arranged by families, and men married primarily to reproduce a line of male heirs. The primary role of women was to bear and care for children. Greek men often kept their wives locked up in their homes while entertaining themselves with cultivated prostitutes. Women were considered inferior to men and thus were generally uneducated and accorded low social status. Because the ancient Greeks believed high status made people attractive, and given that the emphasis of love was on mind and heart, women were considered unattractive and thus unfit for *agape*. As a result, ancient Greeks downplayed the significance of heterosexual love. Because only males were considered attractive and good or worthy companions, the highest form of love in ancient Greece typically involved an older man's infatuation with a beautiful adolescent boy. Male homosexual love was considered as natural as heterosexual love. Contributing to the prevalence of homosexual love relationships was that men who showed a love for or sexual interest in women were considered womanlike or effeminate (Dover, 1978; Murstein, 1974).

The Greek influence on modern ideas and practices of love can be found throughout our society. For example, we often hear people refer to relationships as "platonic." The idea of platonic love is rooted in the Greek emphasis that love is of mind and heart, and even today the term continues to mean essentially love without sex. The idea of platonic love is most often attributed to Plato; it thus, bears his name. Some contemporary researchers (for example, Solomon, 1981), however, have claimed that this attribution is misleading, as some of Plato's writings indicate that he recognized a connection between love and sex.

Love in Ancient Rome   Female and male relationships in ancient Rome were considerably different from those in ancient Greece. They therefore gave rise to a very different form of love from that described by Plato. Upper-class Roman women were more educated and worldly, and more socially and intellectually equal to Roman men than were their counterparts in Greek society. Thus, in contrast to ancient Greece, love in Roman society was oriented primarily toward heterosexual love. Love still was not connected to marriage, however. Marriages continued to be arranged by families and took place for the economic, social, and political advantages they accorded.

Love most often occurred in secret, outside these arranged marriages. It consisted primarily of meaningless flirtation and brief encounters between couples. The most important part of a love relationship was the seduction of a desirable person. To be desirable, potential lovers, especially women, had to be physically attractive. Love in this context had to be secretive: If exposed, men could be severely fined by the offended husband; women, however, could lose their lives. The severer punishments for women reflected a general sexual double standard that is still evidenced today by the fact that we define love relationships differently for each gender, as we will see later in this chapter.

The Early Christian Idea of Love   The arrival of Christianity promoted the idea of the love of God, a spiritual love that was different from Plato's ideal forms of love. The Christian church considered the overt sexuality and eroticism of the Greeks, Romans, and pagans as an immoral abomination. The early Christian idea of love was one of a nonsexual, nonerotic relationship, and the ideal person was expected to deny all desires of the flesh to attain holiness. If people could not control their desires of the flesh (that is, remain celibate) they could marry, but even between married couples, sexual desire and attraction were frowned upon. Noteworthy in this context are the Penitentials of Theodore, seventh-century Archbishop of Canterbury, which contained a list of punishments for those who could not abstain. For example, a man who had intercourse with his wife had to take a bath before entering the church, and newly married people or women who had given birth were likewise barred from the church for a period of time followed by a set penance (Queen, Habenstein, and Quadagno, 1985; Williams, 1993). As Christianity spread throughout the Western world, so too did the ideals of celibacy and virginity. From the Christian ideas about love and sexuality grew the notion that priests and nuns should live a celibate life, an ideal that is still part of the Roman Catholic faith but one that often has been not only challenged in recent times but also violated by some Roman Catholic clergy.

Although not the same, the Christian idea of love emphasized aspects of *agape*, especially the idea of honor and devotion to be directed to the spiritual community rather than to individuals. At the very least, the downplaying of eroticism in Christian love weakened the relationship between married couples, making it relatively easy for people to forsake personal relationships and devote themselves instead to the Christian community (Albas and Albas, 1989a).

Courtly Love   Not everyone accepted the Christian definition of love. In particular, many among the powerful nobility challenged the Christian notion and espoused a new idea of love—referred to as *courtly love*—that combined two basic ideas of the time period: male chivalry and the idealization of women. Courtly love, which emerged sometime between A.D. 1000 and 1300, involved flirtatious and romantic overtones that marked the beginning of chivalry and was the precursor to our modern version of romance—aptly called *courtship* (Collins, 1986; Coltrane, 1998).

The ideas and messages of courtly love were first heard during this period in the love songs and romantic poetry of French troubadours, a unique class of minstrel knights who traveled from one manor to another singing and reciting poetry and later sonnets in exchange for food and shelter. Their songs and poetry were directed toward aristocratic noblewomen whom they idealized in their lyrics and tales about beautiful and superior ladies who were inaccessible to their suitors. Courtly love was a break from earlier idealizations of love because in courtly love noblewomen were exalted, albeit in a spiritual sense. Their beauty and remoteness were worshiped as never before. As it is commonly referred to today, they were placed on a pedestal. One could flirt with a noblewoman and even have sex with her, but she remained unattainable as a permanent love object. Adultery, however, was common. Because noblewomen and their lords had not usually married out of love or developed a close personal relationship, erotic courtly romances frequently developed between ladies and visiting knights (or troubadours). The elaborate and mischievous seduction games of courtly love among the wealthy classes continued into the eighteenth century (Coltrane, 1998).

Although this form of chivalrous love was confined to a small segment of the population and was not associated with marriage, the courtly love rituals of the nobility laid the groundwork for more popular ideas about love and romance among the general population. As in the past, marriages were arranged. Love and romance were not considered essential elements of marriage and thus were most often found outside of marital relationships. In its popular manifestation, courtly love was often nonsexual. Sex was considered animalistic, dishonorable, and degrading, so courtly love required that there be no sexual relations between lovers. Couples could, however, and sometimes did, lie nude in bed together and caress each other, but they could not have intercourse. Sex was primarily for reproduction and thus generally reserved for marital relationships.

The emergence and development of romantic love was greatly influenced by a number of features of heterosexual relations during this period, most notably the idea that love should be reciprocal or mutual. With the emergence of courtly love, for the first time, women were considered an important part of the love relationship, worthy of the love and passion of men. Most researchers of the subject contend that a major contribution of courtly love was to raise women's status from that of a despised person to one worthy of being worshiped and loved. Many women today, however, insist that setting women apart to be worshiped and protected by men keeps women dependent on men for definitions of self and love and for care and protection. They thus, criticize the concept and practice of courtly love because it ignores the needs of women, limits women's expression and behavior, and impedes their progress toward gender equality (Cancian, 1991).

Whatever we might think of courtly love, its impact on Western thought and romantic behavior cannot be overstated. In fact, a number of the romantic ideas of courtly love are still apparent in contemporary notions of love. For example, the ideas today that you cannot love two people at the same time, that love makes your heart beat wildly, and that love can occur at first sight emerged from the period of courtly love. From these beginnings, romantic love became an institutionalized component of upper-class and then middle-class marriage and family life. Eventually, as Western societies became industrialized and urbanized, romantic love became institutionalized among the lower and working classes as well.

The Institutionalization of Love in Marriage

As the market economy developed and capitalism spread, the roles and functions of individuals and societal institutions changed, and the ideal of the family as a separate domestic sphere began to develop. For example, work became institutionalized outside the family, and separate institutions to educate the young and to provide religious training emerged. As the family lost or passed on to other institutions many of its old functions, industrialism created new demands, roles, and responsibilities for families and their members. The most relevant of these new responsibilities for the continued development and spread of romantic love was the responsibility of the family to provide emotional strength and support to its members.

Changing patterns of production and consumption encouraged within the family the development of both economic cooperation and marital love between wives and husbands. Although strongly influenced by the upper- (or noble-) class notion of courtly love, the emerging industrial middle class rejected the central idea that love is to be found outside marriage. Rather, love began to be viewed as a mutual caring that should occur *before* and continue to develop throughout the course of a marriage; it was supposed to last a lifetime. In many respects, love became a kind of emotional insurance that kept wives and husbands tied together "until death do us part." For this to work effectively, however, it was necessary to develop a new cultural attitude toward sex, one that connected it to love and kept it confined to marriage (Coltrane, 1998).

By the late nineteenth century in the United States, as the middle classes enjoyed more leisure time, courtship came to be extended over a longer period, and the idea of love and romance in such relationships had become widespread among all classes. By the early twentieth century, this concept of love was an essential part of the courtship process (see Chapter 5). Although love was now blended with marriage, it was not yet blended with sex. Romantic love and sex were considered almost polar opposites. For example, romantic love was thought of as tender, warm, and caring, whereas sex was thought of as crude and vulgar. The blending of love and sex ultimately grew out of the sexual revolution of the 1920s, an era that witnessed a marked increase in premarital sexual behavior. In addition, attitudes about sex changed noticeably as people began to tie it to love, intimacy, and marriage.

Today, romance, love, and sex are inseparably intertwined, and some people believe that the intimacy generated by one may actually enhance the others. Whether or not this is true, today it is believed that romantic love without sex is incomplete and sex without love is emotionally shallow and exploitative (Seidman, 1992). However, although most Americans believe that love is an important basis for beginning and maintaining a marriage, and that sex should be a part of a loving relationship, recent national polls indicate that they do not believe that sex should be necessarily reserved for marriage. Thus, they do not see premarital sex as wrong, but do see extramarital and casual sex as wrong. On the other hand, roughly about one-fourth of Americans find sexual activity recreational and do not need love or commitment as a prerequisite (Washington Post–ABC News Poll, 2003; Saad, 2001). Such attitudes highlight the degree to which our ideas about love, marriage, and sex have changed over time. They also alert us to the fact that the Western sequence of "love, marriage, and then comes the baby carriage" reflects several culturally based assumptions about the nature of intimate heterosexual relationships. These assumptions are by no means universally shared, particularly in non-Western cultures; even in Western societies, this sequence of love, intimacy, and marriage has not always prevailed. And as the discussion in the In Other Places box demonstrates, it is

IN OTHER PLACES

THE MEANING OF LOVE ACROSS CULTURES

Although romance and romantic love are not new to the world, their value among all classes of people (not just the elite) and their connection to marriage are a modern phenomenon, arising in industrial society (Luhman, 1996). In earlier times, both in Western and non-Western societies, because people's personal identities were not highly differentiated from the collective identity of their group, the social context did not provide the conditions under which romantic love could develop. However, as societies became industrialized, collectivism—the emphasis on the superiority of the group—gave way to *individualism,* an emphasis on promoting one's self-interest, personal autonomy, self-realization, individual initiative, and decision making. Some researchers have suggested that romantic love is most likely to emerge under these conditions of individualism (see, for example, Dion and Dion, 1998).

In any event, because romantic love figures so importantly in the culture and lives of people in many Western societies today, we tend to think of it as the only proper basis for forming intimate relationships. However, the concept of romantic love is not found in all cultures and, when it is, it is not necessarily the basis for establishing intimate relationships. Studies across cultures reveal very different attitudes toward romantic love and the ways in which it is channeled into long-term relationships. Among the !Kung of southern Africa, love is an important commodity for women, and it is intimately connected to their sexuality. A !Kung woman's sexuality is her primary means for negotiating the conditions of her relationships with men, and it is also believed to be an important

source for the mental well-being of women. According to the !Kung, if a girl grows up not learning to enjoy sex, her mind will not develop normally and, once she is an adult, if she does not have sex her thoughts are ruined and she is forever angry. In terms of loving relationships, a woman's sexuality attracts lovers and a loving relationship and maximizes her independence. By taking lovers, a !Kung woman proclaims her control over her social life, because in !Kung culture, women's sexuality is believed to be a major source of vitality and life for men; without it, they would die (Robbins, 1993).

In contrast, in traditional Chinese culture, romantic love and sexuality are far less important than other factors as a basis for intimate relations between women and men. Whereas !Kung women use their sexuality to attract lovers, the sexuality of Chinese women figures very little in their relationships with men, both before and after marriage. Unions between Chinese women and men are arranged by the heads of their families, and female virginity is both valued and necessary for a successful match. A Chinese woman's sexuality is not negotiable; rather, her value is in her potential to become a mother of a male child. In fact, becoming a mother cements her relationship with her husband (Robbins, 1993). The concept of romantic love does not fit very well in traditional Chinese society, where the individual is expected to take into account the wishes of others and the primary ties of love and intimacy are linked to family relationships—with parents, siblings, other relatives, and one's children. Romantic love, however, is not a totally foreign concept to the Chinese. In ancient feudal China, falling in love before marriage was not unusual, although parental consent was necessary before the marriage could occur. However, over the 2000-year period in

which the traditional Chinese family flourished, romantic love was considered dangerous and harmful to the development of a "good" marriage, in which women and men took on the proper roles of subservient daughter-in-law and respectful son (Queen, Habenstein, and Quadagno, 1985).

It is interesting to note that among recent cohorts of young adults in China and other Asian countries, there are signs of change toward greater valuing of love as a basis for marriage. In Japan, for example, the number of "love marriages" has increased significantly over the past four decades. Although the older generation of Japanese still hold on to traditional values, survey data indicate a strong desire among young Japanese women for "love" or "love-based" marriage. Similarly, after the revolution in 1949 in the People's Republic of China, and as a result of the increasing wage labor in mainland China's towns and cities as well as the growing Western influence, "love-marriages" have become the norm. Chinese women's roles are changing from passive compliance and obedience to their husbands and in-laws to a more active role in family and intimate relationships (De Mente, 1989; Dion and Dion, 1998; Leeder, 2004).

What Do You Think? How might intimate relationships be different if the U.S. view of love was similar to that of the !Kung? To that of the traditional Chinese? Explain. Which of the two views of love and intimacy presented here comes closer to approximating your personal viewpoint? Explain. Do you believe individuals in the United States have "free choice" in whom they fall in love with? Whom they date? Whom they "decide" to marry? If you do not believe Americans have free choice, then what do you think stands in the way of free choice?

important to take into account the cultural context and cultural and historical factors that contribute to the development of love and intimacy in a particular society.

The Importance of Love

Researchers have found that in U.S. society, love is extremely important both in terms of our physical as well as our emotional health and well-being. Numerous studies demonstrate

that love improves our health, that being in love romantically and/or being loved are positively related to good physical and emotional health. According to one medical expert, Joseph Nowinski (1980, 1989), a satisfying love affair is one of the best medicines for fighting off physical diseases. His claim is based on what he says are two well-known facts: (1) How we feel emotionally affects our health, and (2) being in love can create a natural emotional high. Nowinski says that a variety of studies show that married couples or those in a satisfying relationship have fewer psychological problems; single women, on the other hand, have the most. Many experts in the field today agree with Nowinski and contend as well that long-term love relationships (even if no longer passionate) appear to have a positive effect on the health of those involved (Pert, 1997; Ornish, 1998; Lacey, 1999). New research confirms the health-improving and life-affirming effects of love on the human body. For example, by studying the heart's rhythms, researchers have discovered that when we feel love, or any positive emotion such as compassion, caring, or gratitude, the heart sends messages to the brain and secretes hormones that positively affect our health. Love and intimacy also may help protect against infectious diseases. When we feel loved, nurtured, cared for, supported, and intimate, we are much more likely to be happier and healthier. We have a much lower risk of getting sick and, if we do, a much greater chance of surviving (Ornish, 1998). Conversely, being unloved has been shown to be related to heart disease and early death among unmarried people. Not being loved or the loss of love also has been linked to depression and can even lead some people to commit suicide (McGrath, 2002; Davis, 1985). Although feeling loved appears to benefit our health, giving love seems to do the same for our aging process. The results of a study of more than 700 elderly adults showed that the effects of aging were influenced more by what the participants contributed to their social support network than what they received from it. In other words, the more love and support they gave, the more they benefited (Lacey, 1999). According to Susan and Clyde Hendrick (1992), love may not be essential to life, but it certainly seems essential to joy. They contend that romantic love compensates for the drudgery and illness in our lives. By loving and being loved, we are *more* intelligent, attractive, and even saintly.

The importance of love in general can also be viewed within the larger context of human social development. Love is essential to the survival of human infants and the social, psychological, and emotional well-being of adults. Various sociological and psychological theorists have argued, for example, that from infancy through adulthood, humans have a need for love and attachment with other human beings. Early interactions with parents lead children to form attachments that reflect children's perceptions of their self-worth and their expectations about intimate relationships. These ideas about attachment are carried forward into later intimate relationships (Collins and Read, 1994). Sociological studies of children who have experienced extended isolation from other humans have found that the lack of bonding, attachment, and love with at least one other human being has a detrimental effect on the physical, psychological, and emotional development of the child. Later in their life cycle, these children are often unable to develop intimate love relationships because they did not experience such relationships when they were young. For adults, the experience of extended isolation often causes deep feelings of depression, anxiety, and nervousness (Feeney and Noller, 1996; Kennedy, 1999). A number of research studies (Shaver and Hazan, 1988; Shaver, Hazan, and Bradshaw, 1988; Feeney and Noller, 1996; Kennedy, 1996; Feeney, 1999a, 1999b; Collins and Sroufe, 1999; Moore and Leung, 2002) provide support for the

Loving bonds that develop during infancy are essential to the survival of human infants and for the social, psychological, and emotional well-being of adults. Parents, such as this father with his son, often exhibit an Agape love style that emphasizes nurturing and an unselfish concern for their children's needs.
Source: Joe Carini/Pacific Stock.com

relationship between attachment and romantic relationships, noting that the type of attachment pattern learned as an infant serves as a blueprint for later adult relationships, especially romantic love relationships. This research suggests that a person's attachment style is related to aspects of her or his childhood and remembered relationships with parents or other caregivers and is a predictor of the quality of her or his dating and marital relationships.

The experience of self-love or what some social scientists refer to as *self-esteem*, the personal judgments individuals make regarding their own self-worth, seems an important prerequisite for loving others. It has been suggested repeatedly in the literature that the ability to feel love, to express it, and to accept it from others is a learned behavior, acquired through our early experiences in infancy and childhood. Infants must be loved so that they can learn how to love. Like romantic love, self-love is tied to an individual's social situation. For example, several studies show that one's self-esteem is directly linked to the love expressed toward that individual by her or his significant others. When significant others give positive feedback, self-esteem increases; conversely, when feedback is consistently negative from significant others it lowers self-esteem. Thus, infants who are held, touched, caressed, and otherwise shown love develop a self-love—that is, they come to see themselves as important and worthy of love. In adulthood, the people most likely to succeed in their intimate relationships are those who have been socialized in childhood to develop their potential to love (Feeney and Noller, 1996).

Love not only dominates our everyday consciousness, it is also a yardstick against which we evaluate the quality of our everyday lives (Karp, Yoels, and Vann, 2003). The level of love we perceive as existing in our intimate relationships affects how we feel about ourselves and others. It seems,

APPLYING THE SOCIOLOGICAL IMAGINATION
Love as Big Business

In Western society, especially the United States, love is great for business. For instance, every February, long considered a month of romance, across the country, candy, flowers, and gifts are exchanged between loved ones, all in the name of St. Valentine. On Valentine's Day, the most romantic holiday of the year, Americans spend $400 million on roses, purchase more than $600 million worth of candy, and send more than 1 billion Valentine cards.

Did You Know?

- There are at least three legends about the origins of Valentine's Day. One legend, for example, has it that Valentine's Day originated to commemorate the anniversary of the death of St. Valentine, a Roman clergyman who was executed on February 14, about 270 A.D., for secretly marrying couples in defiance of the emperor.
- Americans began exchanging handmade valentines in the early 1700s. In the 1840s, Esther Howland, a native of Massachusetts, began selling the

nation's first mass-produced valentine cards. Today, approximately 1 billion Valentine's Day cards are sold in the United States each year.
- Valentine's Day is the third-largest retail holiday of the year.
- In 2005, Valentine's Day spending topped $13 billion. The average consumer spent approximately $100 on Valentine's Day.
- In 2003, men spent an average of $126 on Valentine's Day gifts, whereas women spent only $38.
- More than half of men (57.8%) buy flowers and one in five (18.1%) buy jewelry for Valentine's Day.
- In 2004, consumers purchased more than 175 million roses for Valentine's Day.
- In 2005, 8 billion pastel, heart-shaped candies with sweet sayings known as "conversation hearts" were made for Valentine's Day and 36 million heart-shaped boxes of chocolate were sold for Valentine's Day.
- There are over 28,000 jewelry stores in the United States. Jewelry stores sell

engagement, wedding, and other rings to lovers of all ages. In February 2004, these stores sold $2.4 billion worth of merchandise.

http://www.historychannel.com/exhibits/valentine
http://www.census.gov/Press-Release/www/factsheets.html
http://www.ecommerce-guide.com/news/trends/article.php/3309041

There are a variety of Web sites and links that provide facts and figures about love and issues related to love. For example, did you know that in criminal jargon, "getting a valentine" means receiving a one-year jail sentence? Or that the average person falls in love seven times before marriage and two out of five people marry their first love? Using the Web sites listed above as a beginning point, search the Internet for facts and figures about love. Pay attention to the reliability of the source and the validity of the data and figures. How do the facts and figures you gather fit what you thought you knew about love before you read this chapter and gathered additional information?

then, that those of us who are most happy with our lives define that happiness in terms of a loving relationship. We typically define a satisfying relationship as one in which there is an intense commitment to love. Attachment theory is an important framework for a sociological understanding of love because it reminds us that love is a learned emotion. It reminds us that we learn how to love not only from our culture but also from individuals, particularly those with whom we form our first intimate relationships (Wood, 1996).

HOW DO PEOPLE EXPRESS LOVE?

People express romantic love in a variety of ways. Some focus on commitment; some on passion; and others on caring, respect, or intimacy. Some people focus on a combination of these and other factors associated with love. This diversity in love and loving has inspired some social scientists to attempt to classify love in terms of its component parts or in terms of various types and styles of loving.

In his now classic book *The Art of Loving* (1956), psychoanalyst Erich Fromm popularized the notion that there are many different kinds of love, only one of which is erotic or romantic love. Other kinds of love Fromm identified include brotherly, maternal, paternal, infantile, immature, and mature

love. According to Fromm, love has four essential components: (1) care (we want the best for the people we love), (2) responsibility (we are willingly sensitive and responsive to their needs), (3) respect (we accept them for what they are), and (4) knowledge (we have an awareness of their needs, values, goals, and feelings). When people share these components, they then become a couple or a pair. Fromm cautioned, however, that contrary to popular belief, love is not a simple process. Finding the *right* person is difficult and requires a lot of work and practice. Fromm suggested that *falling in love* is very different from *being in love*, which involves facing the realities of living together. He further suggested that being a loving person is the best way to be loved.

Consider the following discussion of styles of loving and think about your own style of loving. Where does your definition of love and style of loving fit, if at all, in Lee's typology of styles of loving? Do you express only one style of loving or some combination of styles? Explain. What would be the best pairing of love styles? The worst? Why? Does Lee's discussion of romantic love help or hinder your understanding of love in general?

Lee's Six Styles of Loving

Whenever the subject of styles of loving comes up in the scientific literature, it is the research of Canadian sociologist John Alan Lee that is most often referred to. Using data from over 4000 published accounts of love in conjunction with 112 personal interviews, Lee (1974) concluded that there are many types of love relationships. Half of Lee's respondents were females and half were males. All were white, heterosexual, and under the age of 35. Based on findings from this group, Lee proposed six basic styles of loving. Using the analogy of a color wheel, he identified three primary styles of love relationships (analogous to the three primary colors of red, yellow, and blue): *eros, ludus,* and *storge.* In the same way that all other colors are a mixture or combination of the three primary colors, Lee contends that all other styles of love represent a combination of these three primary styles. The three most important compounds or mixtures of the three primary styles of love are *mania, pragma,* and *agape.* The six styles of loving are described here.

Primary Styles of Love   **Eros** is characterized by an immediate, powerful attraction to the physical appearance of another ("love at first sight"). Erotic lovers are often preoccupied with pleasing their lover, and sexual intimacy is strongly desired. In fact, they often engage in sexual relations soon after they meet a partner. This is the type of love that is presented to us, for example, day after day in soap operas, where the lovers eye each other, hear romantic music, glide toward one another, hearts pounding, collapse in each other's arms, and become sexually intimate. Nothing is more problematic for an eros lover than to have a partner who lacks her or his sexual enthusiasm. If the partner is not openly erotic, the relationship will usually be of short duration.

Throughout human history love has been expressed in a variety of ways. However, the type of love that is dominant in most of our lives, at one time or another, is romantic love.

In contrast to eros, **ludus** is a playful, nonpossessive, and challenging love, without a deep commitment or lasting emotional involvement. Ludus love is carefree and casual; it turns love into a series of challenges and puzzles to be solved. A ludus lover often has several partners simultaneously or encourages her or his partner to have other relationships to prevent the partner from becoming too attached. Unlike with eros, sex is not an integral part of the love relationship. The ludus lover engages in sex simply for the fun of it and not as a means to a deep emotional relationship. Thus, this style of loving seldom leads to a long-term relationship or marriage.

Storge (pronounced "stor-gay") describes a style of loving that is said to be unexciting and uneventful. An affectionate style of love with an emphasis on companionship, it usually develops slowly, beginning as a friendship and gradually developing into love. It is typical of people who grew up together in the same neighborhood. Storge is long-lasting, but it is not passionate. Sexual intimacy occurs late in the relationship and often results in marriage or cohabitation. Even if the relationship ends, storgic lovers often remain good friends.

Derived Styles of Love   Derived loves combine two or more of the primary styles. For example, **mania** combines eros and ludus. Manic love is characterized by obsession and possessiveness. It is a jealous and stressful love that demands constant displays of attention, caring, and affection from the partner. According to Lee, this type of love seldom, if ever, develops into a long-lasting, committed relationship. Marcia Lasswell and Norman Lobsenz (1981) have suggested that this style of loving might be associated with low self-esteem and a poor self-concept.

In contrast, **pragma,** which combines ludus and storge, is logical, sensible, and practical. A pragmatic lover rationally chooses a partner who shares her or his background, interests, concerns, and values. Compatibility is a must. Not surprisingly, computer dating and matching services are based on a pragmatic viewpoint.

Finally, **agape** (pronounced "ah-GAH pay"), a style of love that combines eros and storge, is selfless and giving, expecting nothing in return. It represents the classical Christian idea of love as altruistic, undemanding, and chaste. Agape lovers tend to advocate and adhere to sexual abstinence. It is a kind of love that is characteristic of saints. Lee reports that he did not find a single agape lover in his study.

According to Lee, although people generally prefer one particular style of loving, they often express more than one style. This can be true over many different relationships or within one particular relationship. For example, a relationship might begin with an erotic style of loving, but as the relationship matures, it might change to a friendship or companionate (storge) style. Lee also observed that the compatibility of styles of loving between two people is important to the success of a love relationship. That is, we have to find a partner who shares the same definition and style of loving as we do if we expect to have a mutually happy and satisfying relationship. The greater the differences between a couple in their style of loving, the harder it is for them to relate to each other.

Interestingly, in their extensive research on romantic love, social scientists Susan and Clyde Hendrick found a number of gender differences in styles of loving. According to the Hendricks (1983, 1987, 1995, 1996), women and men do not differ significantly on eros or agape, but gender differences on other love attitudes or styles consistently show up. For example, their research repeatedly shows that men are more ludic in orientation than women, and women are typically more storgic and pragmatic than men. In addition, women report a more manic orientation than men. Working with Nancy Adler (Adler, Hendrick, and Hendrick, 1987), the Hendricks found very few differences between male heterosexuals and male homosexuals in their love attitudes. They thus concluded that gay and straight men are similar in love styles. On the other hand, the Hendricks have found that women and men are similar in rating the typical features of love, and they are similarly passionate and altruistic in their love styles. In fact, although gender differences were apparent, the genders were more similar than different. Only more research in this area will enable us to determine if these differences are changing or shifting as the culture and society changes (Hendrick and Hendrick, 1996).

Moreover, Hendrick and Hendrick (1993) have also found that among many contemporary college students, lovers are also best friends. In written accounts of their love as well as their ratings on the Love Attitude Scale, research respondents described their relationship most often in terms of storge, or friendship, love. In one study, almost one-half of the respondents identified their romantic partner as their closest friend. These results certainly indicate the importance of storge or friendship in ongoing, contemporary heterosexual romantic relationships. In an investigation of the differences between people who are falling in love versus those who are not in love, the Hendricks found that people who were in love were more erotic, more agapic, and less ludic than people who were not in love.

Although Lee's typology is ideal (in the real world, no one's love style matches any of Lee's styles perfectly) and based on a sample of white heterosexuals under the age of 35, were you able to identify your style of loving in one or more of Lee's six styles? How close or how different are you and your partner's style of loving? Are you more similar than different or more different than similar?

> *A philosopher once said that we know the taste of love but few of us can distinguish the many flavors of love. Given the various types and styles of love it is possible to experience, how do we distinguish what we feel from true love, puppy love, friendship, liking, or infatuation? Perhaps the next section will help you answer this question.*

LOVE VERSUS FRIENDSHIP, INFATUATION, AND LIKING

How do we know when we are in love? Will we hear bells? Will our heart skip a beat? Will it last, or is it just a passing emotion? Are we old enough to know if it is love? If it is *true*

love? When we were young we were told our feelings of love were not really true love, that they were either "puppy love" or infatuation. Furthermore, we were told not to fret, because we would know when it was true love. Such responses imply that there is a "fake love" or that some other emotion can very easily be confused with love, but that love is some special feeling that we will recognize the minute we experience it. If this is the case, how do we tell the difference? How do we know if what we feel is not simply friendship, infatuation, or liking? And what happens to let us know when the feeling is love?

Close Friendship versus Love

Over the last several decades, a number of researchers have attempted to distinguish love from liking, friendship, and infatuation. Researchers Keith Davis and Michael Todd (Davis and Todd, 1985; Davis, 2004) compared close friendship and love and found that although the two are alike in many ways, there are crucial differences between them that make love relationships both more rewarding and, at the same time, more volatile. Davis and Todd's prototype of friendship includes the following eight characteristics:

- *Enjoyment:* For the most part, close friends enjoy being in each other's company.
- *Acceptance:* They accept each other for what they are; they do not try to change each other.
- *Trust:* They share the feeling that the other will act in her or his best interest.
- *Respect:* Each assumes that the other exercises good judgment in making life choices.
- *Mutual Assistance:* They are willing to aid and support each other; they can count on each other when needed.
- *Confiding:* They share feelings and experiences with each other.
- *Understanding:* Each has a sense of what is important to the other and why the other behaves in the manner that she or he does.
- *Spontaneity:* Both feel free to be themselves rather than pretend to be something that they are not.

Love, in contrast, is friendship and more: It is passion and caring. But it is also instability and mutual criticism. Some social scientists (Tennov, 1979; Davis and Todd, 1985; Davis, 2004) have described romantic love as unstable in that it involves an almost endless series of emotional highs (joys or positive emotions) and lows (despair or negative emotions). It includes all the characteristics of friendship as well as two broad clusters of characteristics not found in friendship: a passion cluster and a caring cluster. The *passion cluster* includes *fascination*, preoccupation with each other and desire to be together all of the time; *exclusiveness*, with top priority given to the love relationship, making another such relationship with someone new unthinkable; and *sexual desire*, the desire to be physically intimate with each other. The *caring cluster* consists of *giving the utmost*, caring so much for each other that each gives her or his all to the relationship; and being a *champion* or *advocate*, helping and supporting each other in all types of situations. Figure 4.1 illustrates the similarities and

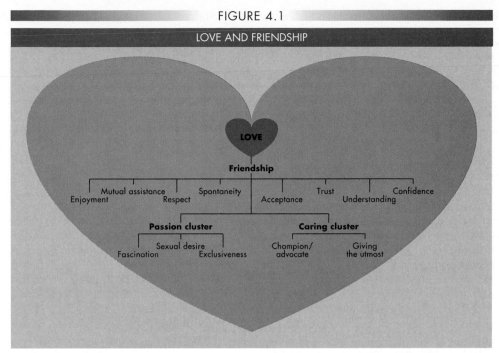

FIGURE 4.1

LOVE AND FRIENDSHIP

Source: Adapted from Keith Davis, 1985, "Near and Dear: Friendship and Love Compared," *Psychology Today* (February): 24. Reprinted with permission from *Psychology Today* Magazine. Copyright © 1985 by Sussex Publishers, Inc.

differences between friendship and loving using the model developed by Davis and Todd.

Social scientists have suggested that, like romantic love, friendship is important to our emotional and even physical well-being. It helps us maintain a sense of social reality and staves off feelings of isolation in a largely anonymous world. According to psychotherapist James Grotstein, "Friendship governs all intimate relationships and it is more profound than sex and love" (quoted in Sheehy, 2000). Like romantic love, the development and expression of platonic love or friendship is also heavily influenced by social factors. Research shows that friendship formation is largely a product of our daily interaction patterns rather than of chance or "good chemistry." Friendships tend to develop with the people we see most often—those with whom we work, go to school, are enrolled in the same class, or who are members of our church or synagogue, health club, and so on. Similarly, friendships tend to form among those who are in close geographic proximity. Like romantic love, friendship grows best out of similarity. We tend to build the strongest friendships with those who hold attitudes similar to our own. We also tend to connect with those who share our physical and social characteristics—appearance, income, educational level, race, and so on.

On the level of experience, various research studies show that the way in which we define and express friendship differs in terms of important social characteristics, such as race, gender, sexual orientation, and social class. Gender, for example, plays an important role in structuring intimate relationships—whether in same-sex or heterosexual relationships. Research in this regard shows this to be true in friendships as well as love relationships and those that include a sexual partnership. For example, some research indicates that the number of close friends that men have increases from adolescence until around age 30, falling off thereafter. In contrast, the research for women is mixed. Some research shows that for women, the number of important friendships rises gradually over the life span, whereas other research suggests that there is a slump in early adulthood followed by an increase beginning somewhere between the late 30s and 40s. Additionally, men are more likely to be intimate with women than they are with other men, even though they report more same-sex friendships than do women. Intimacy between men seems strongly influenced by the restrictive attitudes and sanctions in U.S. society

It is not always easy to distinguish love from close friendship because they share so many of the same characteristics. Couples in love, as well as close friends, often enjoy just being in each other's company.

generated by homophobia. Thus, for instance, fear of being seen as *gay* causes some men to distance themselves from friendships (at least close ones) with other men. In general, however, from middle to late life, a man is less likely to have a close friend the older he gets, whereas a woman's chance of having at least one such friendship does not change with age. Contrary to past assumptions that women's primary identity is attached to men, current research shows the important role that friendship between women have, including women who live within heterosexual relationships (Andersen, 2003). Although there are documented gender differences in friendship development and patterns, recent research indicates that women and men share many patterns and styles of friendship. Like women, for example, men rely on their male friends for emotional support and intimacy. In addition, many friendship activities such as seeing friends for dinner, sharing ritual events, and visiting are things that both women and men friends do (Walker, 1994, 2001). In fact, according to Barry Wellman (1992), there has been a widespread *domestication* of male friendship, with men seeing friends in their home in much the same way that women do (quoted in Walker, 2001).

In the past, most of the research on friendship has been conducted using white middle-class heterosexual females and males (usually college students). However, recent researchers have noted that women and men who are other than white, middle class, and heterosexual may have different types of friendships from that cited in much of the friendship literature (Franklin, 1992; Hansen, 1992). For instance, recent research indicates that for people of color, particularly women, *ethnic empathy* is a key factor in choosing friends. Although they often have cross-race friendships, their shared experiences with friends of their own race or ethnicity allow them to do what they feel they cannot do with friends of a different race—namely, share the experience of dealing with racism, the intersections of race, class, and gender, and the impact of these factors in their daily lives (Sheehy, 2000). According to Gail Sheehy (2000), this issue of ethnic empathy is compounded for people whose backgrounds are racially mixed. Similar to people of color, an important dimension of lesbian and gay friendships is a sense of shared history, a sense of sister/brotherhood, and a sense of shared marginal identity. And, like for many people of color, forming friendships with people with whom they can be themselves is important to lesbians and gays, given a cultural context that typically does not approve of that "self." Many lesbians and gays indicate a need to develop friendships with others like themselves who are out of the cultural mainstream (Rubin, 1986; Nardi, 2001).

Friendship studies focusing on social class show that working-class Americans conceive of friendship as an exchange of goods and services; gifts and favors indicate the strength of a friendship bond. In contrast, this kind of material exchange is not part of the middle-class definition of friendship. Middle-class individuals tend to view friendship as an emotional or intellectual exchange; they also frequently conceive of friendship simply as the sharing of leisure activities. Who our friends are also varies by class. Friends among the working classes are highly likely to be relatives—siblings, cousins, parents—whereas friends among the middle classes are typically nonblood relations. Further,

among working-class individuals, friendships are overwhelmingly same sex, most often local; friends have known each other for much longer periods of time than is typical of middle-class friends. Interaction among working-class friends is said to be more frequent than among middle-class friends, with some researchers suggesting that working-class friends interact, on average, once a week or more. In contrast, members of the middle classes are more open to cross-gender friendships and, because middle-class lifestyles often involve a high degree of geographic mobility, middle-class friendships are as often long distance as they are local. Not only are middle-class friendships often maintained after individuals move out of the immediate geographic area but also, because of geographic mobility, friendships among middle-class individuals often develop when people meet as they travel to different locales. As a result of this distance factor, middle-class friends typically report less frequent contact than do their working-class counterparts (Allan, 1989; Blieszner and Adams, 1992; Elles, 1993; Walker, 1995; Ruane and Cerulo, 1997). Research findings such as these support our contention that even the most personal of experiences such as love and close friendship are greatly influenced by the social worlds in which we live. Such findings illustrate the significance of sociological factors in the formation of intimate relationships and illustrate that friendship, like love, is socially and culturally mediated.

Infatuation versus Love

That warm and wonderful feeling that we are experiencing, is it love or merely infatuation? How do we begin to know and tell the difference? All too often we confuse these two emotions. **Infatuation** involves a strong attraction to another person based on an idealized picture of that person (Bessell, 1984). It usually focuses on a specific characteristic of the person and has a strong physical (sexual) element. Some social scientists have defined infatuation as passion without commitment. In contrast to love, infatuation is generally superficial and of short duration. It can, however, develop into love. The differences between infatuation and love are outlined in Table 4.1.

What do you think of the assessment of love and infatuation presented in Table 4.1? The author implies that love is a mature emotion whereas infatuation is a very immature emotion. Do you agree or disagree? Does it seem to you to be an overly biased conception of love? How would you define the difference between love and infatuation? Is there really a difference?

Liking versus Love

Liking has been described by some writers as friendship in its most simple form. Liking is generally distinguished from loving as the more logical and rational and the less emotional and possessive of the two emotions. It is believed that liking is the foundation for love. Although liking is closely related to love, several researchers have identified some differences.

TABLE 4.1
Differences between Love and Infatuation

- **Infatuation** leaps into your blood.

- **Love** usually takes root slowly and grows with time.

- **Infatuation** is accompanied by a sense of uncertainty. You are stimulated and thrilled but not really happy. You are miserable when she or he is absent. You can't wait until you see her or him again.

- **Love** begins with a feeling of security. You are warm with a sense of her or his nearness, even when she or he is away. Miles do not separate you. You want her or him near, but near or far, you know she or he is yours and you can wait.

- **Infatuation** says, "We must get married, right away. I can't risk losing her or him."

- **Love** says, "Don't rush into anything. You are sure of one another. You can plan your future with confidence."

- **Infatuation** has an element of sexual excitement. If you are honest, you will discover that it is difficult to enjoy one another unless you know it will end in intimacy.

- **Love** is the maturation of friendship. You must be friends before you can be lovers.

- **Infatuation** lacks confidence. When she or he is away, you wonder if she or he is with another woman or man. Sometimes you even check to make sure.

- **Love** means trust. You may fall into infatuation, but you never fall in love.

- **Infatuation** might lead you to do things for which you might be sorry, but love never will.

- **Love** leads you up. It makes you look up. It makes you think up. It makes you a better person than you were before.

Source: "How to Decide Whether It's Love or Infatuation." *Chicago Sun-Times* (1980): 2, Weekender Section.

The most frequently cited research distinguishing liking from loving was conducted in the 1970s by social scientist Zick Rubin (1973, 1974). According to Rubin, both liking and love consist of the same basic elements: care, respect, tolerance, need, trust, affection, and attraction. What sets the two apart is their differential emphasis on these components. For example, when we love someone the emphasis is on care, trust, need, and tolerance. In contrast, when we like someone the emphasis is on affection, attraction, and respect. The degree of emphasis we place on the various components of like and love is not absolute. Rather, it will vary in terms of intensity from one time to another, from one relationship to another, and sometimes even within a relationship over time.

Several other researchers have produced findings that are generally consistent with Rubin's conclusions (Dermer and Pyszczynski, 1978; Steck et al., 1982). However, the difficulty in distinguishing between liking and loving is expressed by researchers Elaine Hatfield and William Walster (1978), who contend that the only real difference between like and love has to do with the depth of our feelings and the degree to which we are involved with the other person.

As this discussion of love, friendship, liking, and infatuation reveal, much of the literature and research in this area of intimacy is somewhat dated. Not much research in this area has been conducted since the 1980s. Does this mean that Americans are less concerned with love and intimacy today than in the past and thus researchers no longer find it a hot topic for their research? What do you think? What factors might account for the diminished interest in romantic love among social scientists even though the public continues to be fascinated with the topic? Regardless of how we answer this question, a number of theoretical explanations (now considered classics) of why and how people fall in love are worth noting. In the next section we will explore a select sample of such theories.

SOME THEORIES OF LOVE

In recent decades, the works of several social scientists and researchers have provided us with significant insights into the nature of love. These works have laid the groundwork and become the benchmark for our current theoretical understanding of the topic. Some of the more insightful theories or explanations of love today include the wheel theory of love, love as a story, love as a social exchange, and limerence theory.

The Wheel Theory of Love

Generally, when we think about love we think about something unpredictable, sudden, and uncontrollable—something that happens somewhat haphazardly and out of the blue. For most of us, this is not how love happens. Rather, according to sociologist Ira Reiss (1960, 1971), love emerges and develops over time as we interact with the other person. Although there are more recent theories of love, Reiss's theory of love as a developmental process remains a classic. Stressing our need for intimacy, Reiss focuses on what he sees as the circular progression of love as a couple interacts over time. Describing this progression in terms of a wheel—the **wheel theory of love**—Reiss proposes that love involves four major interpersonal processes: rapport, self-revelation, mutual dependence, and need fulfillment. Each of these processes can be thought of as individual spokes on a wheel (see Figure 4.2).

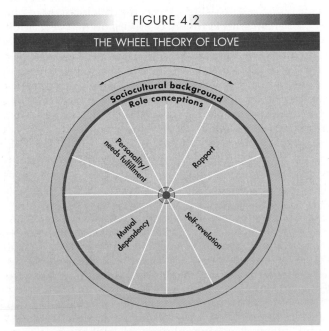

FIGURE 4.2
THE WHEEL THEORY OF LOVE

Source: Adapted from Ira Reiss, 1971, "Toward a Sociology of the Heterosexual Love Relationship," *Marriage and Family Living* 22 (May): 139–45. Reprinted with permission of Abbey Press, St. Meinrad, Indiana.

Rapport Love can develop only between people who relate to each other. Lovers must develop a sense of *rapport*—feeling at ease or relaxed with one another. A key factor here is social background. In general, we are more at ease and communicate better with people with whom we share a common background and lifestyle. Furthermore, we seem to feel rapport with people with whom we share ideas about social roles. Thus, for example, two people who believe that women's and men's roles are flexible and can thus be interchanged are far more likely to feel rapport than a couple in which only one of the partners feels this way.

Although similarity is important in the development of love, two people who are different are not necessarily precluded from developing a love relationship. Family sociologist Robert Winch and his colleagues (1954), for instance, have suggested that people who have different but complementary personality characteristics are attracted to each other—the notion that "opposites attract" (see Chapter 5). In addition, love relationships develop between people from different racial, ethnic, religious, and age groups. This fact notwithstanding, some researchers believe that a love relationship can develop only when both partners share certain fundamental values. It seems that if a couple share basic social values, then other differences are not as difficult to overcome.

Self-Revelation Ease of communication leads to *self-revelation*; the disclosure of intimate and personal feelings. People who feel at ease are more likely to open up and reveal things about themselves than they otherwise would. A couple who feels comfortable with each other want to know more about each other than the kind of superficial information we usually learn about people when we first meet. For example, they want to know what similarities and differences exist between them; how great or how small these similarities and differences are; and how, if at all, they will affect the relationship. As with the development of rapport, a person's background is critical to self-revelation, determining in large part what and how much she or he will reveal about her- or himself. Often, factors like race, ethnicity, social class, gender, and age are important determinants of how willing people are to disclose personal feelings. We often distrust people different from ourselves. Because of this attitude, factors such as race often present initial barriers to the development of trust. Unlike in fairy tales such as *Cinderella*, vast differences in two people's background and other social and cultural characteristics generally prevent the development of a successful love relationship. These characteristics act as filters when two people first come into contact. People tend to make snap judgments about another person's potential as a lover on the basis of them (Newman, 1995:237). If a relationship endures beyond rapport and self-revelation, the participants tend to grow closer and begin to think about the longevity of their relationship and making a commitment to one another.

Mutual Dependence As two people develop a sense of rapport and feel comfortable enough with each other to self-disclose, they develop what Reiss describes as a *mutual dependence*—a reliance on each other for fulfillment. At this stage, two people become a couple. They come to need and depend on each other to share their lives, their happiness, their fears, their hopes and dreams, and their sexual intimacies. They develop interdependent habit systems; ways of acting, thinking, and feeling that are no longer fun or fulfilling when done alone. For example, eating dinner without the other partner may become a lonely experience in that the pleasure of the meal now depends not only on the preparation and taste of the food but also on the presence of the other person. The social and cultural background of the couple continues to play an important role in this stage of love. For example, the forms of dependent behaviors that develop between a couple depend on the kinds of behaviors they mutually agree on as acceptable, which in turn are influenced by their backgrounds and value systems. Mutual dependence leads to the fourth and final stage in Reiss's wheel theory: the fulfillment of personality needs.

Fulfillment of Personality Needs Reiss defines the fulfillment of personality needs as the ability of each partner to satisfy the needs of the other. Reiss describes this stage in terms of a consistent pattern of needs exchange and mutual dependence that develops within a relationship. For instance, as the couple satisfies each other's basic needs, their sense of rapport increases, which leads to greater self-disclosure and more mutually dependent behaviors, which in turn lead to still greater needs fulfillment.

In his wheel analogy, Reiss captures this circular process of the development of love. All four processes are interdependent. Thus, a reduction in any one of them affects the development or continuation of a love relationship. As long as the wheel moves forward (the processes flow into each other), love develops and increases. However, when the wheel turns in the reverse direction—when there is a reduction in one of the processes—love may not develop, or if it has already developed, it may diminish. For example, if the partners in a couple are forced to spend less time with each other and they eventually develop divergent interests, their mutual dependence could weaken, which in turn could lower self-disclosure, which could lead to a reduced sense of rapport.

Reiss's pioneering theory of love as a process has sparked other researchers to extend or modify his theory using other metaphors besides the wheel. For instance, social scientist Delores M. Borland (1975) uses the analogy of a clock spring to explain how love develops in a series of windings and unwindings as love intensifies and ebbs. These windings and unwindings occur as each new event takes place in the couple's relationship and can lead toward a closer, more intimate, and mutually understanding relationship, or they may cause tensions that weaken the relationship. Essentially, such theories share with the Reiss model the notions that social background plays an important role in how and if love relationships will develop and that love is basically a matter of social as well as personal definition. Critics of these theories (for example, Albas and Albas, 1987) note that one of their shortcomings is that they ignore the variation in intensity among the different stages of a love relationship.

THE THEORY OF LOVE AS A STORY[1]

Love is often as unpredictable as the climax of a suspense novel. We might wonder from time to time why we or someone we know seem destined to make the same mistakes in love over and over, as if the fate of our intimate relationships were a written script. According to social scientist Robert J. Sternberg, in essence it is a script. As much as social scientists have attempted to explain the mysteries of love through their theories and scientific laws, Sternberg suggests that the best explanations of romantic love just may be *Wuthering Heights*, *Casablanca*, or the soap opera *General Hospital*. Sternberg believes that love between two people follows a story. Thus, if we are to understand romantic love, we have to understand the stories that dictate our beliefs and expectations of love. We begin writing these stories as children, and they predict the patterns of our later romantic experiences.

Sternberg is not new to the field of "love theories." His initial work on love, *The Triangular Theory of Love* (1986, 1988), which continues to be cited in most textbooks on marriages and families, suggested that love is composed of three interlocking components in a triangle-like relationship: intimacy, passion, and commitment (each component can be represented as one point on a triangle), with different loving relationships having different combinations of these elements. *Intimacy*, which rests at the top of the triangle, refers to the bonding and emotional closeness or connectedness that the partners in a couple feels for each other. *Passion* refers to the romantic feelings, desires, and arousal that partners feel for each other. And *commitment* refers to a person's attachment to another person. It develops over time and represents a couple's desire to be faithful to one another and to stay together. Love is not static, however. All love relationships undergo some change over time; thus, each vertex of the love triangle will not be equal. If, however, vertexes are very unequal—there is too much mismatch among the components—the relationship will fail. When gender role socialization is added to the mix, there is increased difficulty in maintaining equal vertexes (Lindsey, 1994). For example, according to this theory, women attach greater importance to the commitment vertex, and men attach greater importance to the passion vertex. Complete love requires all three components. The absence of all three components represents *nonlove*.

Although interesting, Sternberg's triangular theory of love has some limitations. Indeed, in recent years, Sternberg himself has indicated some dissatisfaction with this theory. For example, he now believes his theory leaves important questions about love unanswered such as, What makes people the kind of lovers they are? And what attracts us to other lovers? Based on research he conducted over the past decade with hundreds of couples in Connecticut, as well as ongoing research on the subject, Sternberg says that he found answers to these and other questions about romantic love in stories. He found that people describe love in many ways but their descriptions reveal their *love story*.

Love Stories

Sternberg identified 25 love stories that people tell: the sacrifice, police, travel, pornography, horror, recovery, gardening, business, fantasy, war, humor, and collection stories, for example (for the other story types, see Sternberg, 1998). Sternberg and one of his students developed this love story classification scheme after analyzing their research subjects' ratings on a scale of 1 to 7 of the extent to which a group of statements characterized their intimate relationships. Their highest-ranked statements indicated their personal love story. For example, people who strongly agree with the statement "I believe close relationships are like good partnerships" tell a *business love story*, whereas people who say that they "typically end up with partners who scare them"— or that they "like to intimidate their partner"—tell a *horror love story*. According to Sternberg, the most common love stories people tell are the *travel love story* ("I believe that beginning a relationship is like starting a new journey that promises to be both exciting and challenging"), the *gardening love story* ("I believe any relationship that is left unattended will not survive"), and the *humor love story* ("I think taking a relationship too seriously can spoil it"). The least popular or common love stories include the *horror* ("I find it exciting when I feel that my partner is somewhat frightened of me"), *collectibles* ("I like dating different partners simultaneously"), and *autocratic government* ("I think it is more efficient if one person takes control of the important decisions in a relationship") stories.

In essence, Sternberg's love story theory suggests that our love stories begin soon after birth as we start to form our ideas about love based on our individual personality, our early socialization experiences, our observations of our parents' relationships, as well as popular culture descriptions of love and romance in the mass media. We eventually seek to live out these notions of love in our personal lives. Sternberg posits that the course of love typically begins with a physical attraction and similar interests and values. Eventually, however, the couple may notice that something is missing in the relationship. Usually, the missing something is story compatibility. If a couple's stories do not match, there is an underlying lack of coordination to their interaction and their love relationship may not go very far. In contrast, when two people's love stories match, this is what keeps their love alive—it is the key to compatibility with a romantic partner.

Although no one story guarantees a successful love relationship, some stories do seem to predict failure more than others (for example, the business, collectibles, government, horror, mystery, police, recovery, science fiction, and theater stories).[2] The key to a happy healthy love relationship is that both partners have compatible love stories—that is, compatible relationship expectations. According to Sternberg, his ongoing collaborative research on the subject of love supports the idea that the more similar their love stories, the happier couples are together. Stories are compatible if they

---

[1]This description of Robert Sternberg's "love story theory" draws heavily from Sternberg's recent works (1998, 2001).

[2]Police ("I believe it is necessary to watch your partner's every move"), recovery ("I often find myself helping people get their life back in order"), science fiction ("I often find myself attracted to individuals who have unusual and strange characteristics"), theater ("I think my relationships are like plays").

include complementary roles in a single story, such as audience–comedian in the humor love story, or if the stories are similar enough so that they can be merged into a new, unified story. According to Sternberg, we end up with the same kind of bad partners in love relationships not because of bad luck but because we subconsciously find people to play out our love stories or we force our stories on the people we meet. Love story compatibility, however, is not the only thing needed in a successful romantic relationship. Once we understand the ideas and beliefs behind our love stories, we must analyze our stories: Decide which romantic tale we really want to tell and whether or not it has the potential to lead to a successful relationship, and, if not, determine what about it we like and don't like and what appears to not work for us and then set about changing our story for success. See if you can identify your love story in the Writing Your Own Script Box: Is There a Love Story for You?"

Love as a Social Exchange

Whatever our love story, it seems that it can be described in the language of social exchange theory (recall the discussion of social-exchange theory in Chapter 2). While Reiss's theory identifies the stages in the process of love and relationship development and Sternberg suggests that our love stories determine the patterns of our romantic experiences, family sociologist John Scanzoni (1980) uses some basic principles of economics to explain *why* we are attracted to and fall in love with some people and not with others and *why* we pursue and remain in some relationships and avoid or break off others.

Basically, Scanzoni argues that love, like any other commodity, involves an exchange of rewards between two interested parties. The process of rewarding each other and gratifying each other's needs is continuous and forms the basis on which the relationship rests. Some of the more obvious rewards of intimate relationships include love, caring, sensitivity, sexual gratification, companionship, liking, friendship, warmth, protection, and emotional and financial support. Some costs might be jealousy and conflict, the time and effort required to keep the other partner satisfied, and undesirable personal or social characteristics. Although these types of exchanges are not always acknowledged and usually do not seem as cold and calculating as the market metaphor makes them sound, according to social exchange theory, virtually every romantic encounter involves an implicit, if not explicit, exchange of sexual and emotional goods. As long as the love relationship is mutually rewarding it will continue, but when it ceases to be rewarding it will end. Thus, although people in love clearly care about each other, love is not totally altruistic. Research (for example, Rusbult, 1983) indicates that people who are happiest in their intimate relationships are typically couples who provide one another with far more rewarding experiences than costly ones.

Love as Limerence

Another pioneering theory of love comes to us from the discipline of psychology. Limerence theory, advanced by psychologist Dorothy Tennov (1979), provides important insights into the distinction between being in love and other types of loving. Tennov uses the term **limerence** to refer to a style of love characterized by an extreme attraction, a com-

When taken to an unhealthy extreme, love as limerence can become an obsessive compulsion. Such an obsessive compulsion with another person has been immortalized in popular films such as *Fatal Attraction*, a 1987 thriller film in which a married man (Michael Douglas) has an affair with a woman (Glenn Close) who refuses to allow it to end and becomes obsessed with him.

plete absorption or obsessive preoccupation of one person with another. She defines this emotion as being "in love" as opposed to "love," which she defines as caring and concern for another person.

Based on the findings from her study of the love experiences of over 500 people, Tennov concluded that limerence is a state of mind—that its most important features lie in the fantasies and ideas that one person has about another. Thus, the focus of limerence theory is on the experience of falling or being in love rather than on the relationship itself. Although some people never experience limerence, Tennov suggests that the majority do.

Limerence theory underscores the high level of intensity associated with romantic love; it describes and explains the extreme highs and lows that many people experience in their love relationships. Positive limerence can bring an elated feeling, whereas negative limerence can bring feelings of despondency, despair, pain, and depression. Limerence can be characterized by (1) its speed of occurrence at the onset, (2) its intensity, (3) whether or not the feeling is reciprocated, and (4) the length of time it lasts. As these characteristics show, there is no typical limerent experience. Tennov's description of limerent feelings encompasses a wide spectrum including incessant or continuous thoughts about the lover, mood swings depending on the lover's actions, being completely closed to the possibility of someone else as a lover, a fear of rejection, a preoccupation or

WRITING YOUR OWN SCRIPT

IS THERE A LOVE STORY FOR YOU?

Can you find your love story among the four stories here, taken from Robert J. Sternberg's book *Love Is a Story*. Consult his book for a full discussion of all his love story types.

Rate each statement on a scale from 1 to 9, 1 meaning that it doesn't characterize your romantic relationships at all, and 9 meaning that it describes them extremely well. Then average your scores for each story. In general, averaged scores of 7 to 9 are high, indicating a strong attraction to a story, and 1 to 3 are low, indicating little or no interest in the story. Moderate scores of 4 to 6 indicate some interest, but probably not enough to generate or keep a romantic interest. Next, evaluate your own love story. There are only four listed here; see Sternberg's book for more.

Story 1

1. I enjoy making sacrifices for the sake of my partner.
2. I believe sacrifice is a key part of true love.
3. I often compromise my own comfort to satisfy my partner's needs.

SCORE _____

The *sacrifice story* can lead to happy relationships when both partners are content in the roles they are playing, particularly when they both make sacrifices. It is likely to cause friction when partners feel compelled to make sacrifices. Research suggests that relationships of all kinds are happiest when they are roughly equitable. The greatest risk in a sacrifice story is that the give-and-take will become too out of balance, with one partner always being the giver or receiver.

Story 2

Object

1. The truth is that I don't mind being treated as a sex toy by my partner.
2. It is very important to me to gratify my partner's sexual desires and whims, even if people might view them as debasing.

3. I like it when my partner wants me to try new and unusual, and even painful, sexual techniques.

SCORE _____

Subject

1. The most important thing to me in my relationship is for my partner to be an excellent sex toy, doing anything I desire.
2. I can never be happy with a partner who is not very adventurous in sex.
3. The truth is that I like a partner who feels like a sex object.

SCORE _____

There are obvious advantages to the *pornography story*. The disadvantages are also quite clear. First, the excitement people attain is through degradation of themselves and others. Second, the need to debase and be debased is likely to keep escalating. Third, once one adopts the story, it may be difficult to adopt another story. Fourth, the story can become physically as well as psychologically dangerous. And, finally, no matter how one tries, it is difficult to turn the story into one that's good for psychological or physical well-being.

Story 3

Terrorizer

1. I often make sure that my partner knows that I am in charge, even if it makes her or him scared of me.
2. I actually find it exciting when I feel my partner is somewhat frightened of me.
3. I sometimes do things that scare my partner, because I think it is actually good for a relationship to have one partner slightly frightened of the other.

SCORE _____

Victim

1. I believe it is somewhat exciting to be slightly scared of your partner.
2. I find it arousing when my partner creates a sense of fear in me.
3. I tend to end up with people who sometimes frighten me.

SCORE _____

The *horror story* is the least advantageous of the stories. To some, it may be exciting. But the forms of terror needed to sustain the excitement tend to get out of control and to put their participants, and even sometimes those around them, at both psychological and physical risk. Those who discover that they have this story or are in a relationship that is enacting it would be well-advised to seek counseling and, perhaps, even police protection.

Story 4

1. I think fairy tales about relationships can come true.
2. I do believe that there is someone out there for me who is my perfect match.
3. I like my relationships to be ones in which I view my partner as something like a prince or princess in days of yore.

SCORE _____

The *fantasy story* can be a powerful one. The individual may feel swept up in the emotion of the search for the perfect partner or of developing the perfect relationship with an existing partner. It is probably no coincidence that in literature most fantasy stories take place before or outside of marriage. Fantasies are hard to maintain when one has to pay the bills, pack the children off to school, and resolve marital fights. To maintain the happy feeling of the fantasy, therefore, one has to ignore, to some extent, the mundane aspects of life. The greatest disadvantage of fantasy relationships is the possibility for disillusionment when one partner discovers that no one could fulfill the fantastic expectations that have been created. This can lead partners to feel dissatisfied with relationships that most others would view as quite successful. If a couple can create a fantasy story based on realistic rather than idealistic ideals, they have the potential for success; if they want to be characters in a myth, chances are that is exactly what they will get: a myth.

Source: Adapted from Robert J. Sternberg, 1998, Love Is a Story: A New Theory of Relationships (New York: Oxford University Press).

obsession with the lover to the neglect of other interests and concerns, and idealizing the lover.

Tennov's concept of limerence is very similar to that of infatuation. Both stress emotional intensity in romantic relationships, especially in the early stages and particularly for some people. In addition, Tennov's discussion of limerence shares many similarities with Davis and Todd's findings concerning romantic love. In fact, many of the features she identifies with limerence parallel those identified by Davis and Todd as characteristic of the passion cluster.

Do any of these attributes apply to a current or past love relationship in which you have been involved? Most of us can probably identify with one or more of these attributes, especially in the beginning of our romantic love relationships. At that point we will not believe anything negative about our lover; we cannot eat, sleep, or enjoy ourselves when we are away from our lover; we daydream about her or him; we feel hurt and dismayed at the thought that she or he may not return our feelings. Does this sound familiar?

Tennov's discussion of limerence calls to mind what could happen when limerence is taken to an unhealthy extreme. The almost obsessive compulsion with another person could develop into a full-fledged obsession that has been immortalized in films, novels, and other aspects of popular culture as a "fatal attraction" that is all too often a reality. Such full-fledged obsessions in the real world have had fatal consequences not only for the parties involved but often for intimates involved with the couple as well. Most people's limerence, however, does not go to this extreme. In fact, according to Tennov, if limerence is mutual it can lead to a love affair, a commitment, and ultimately to marriage.

LOVE ACROSS GENDER, SEXUALITY, AND RACE

Romantic love is often considered a universal feeling. As we have noted, however, not everyone experiences romantic love. Furthermore, when we do experience such love, a number of other important life experiences come into play, making love different for each of us. Probably the most powerful individual differences that affect how we experience love are gender, sexual orientation, and race. For example, do women and men experience romantic love similarly or differently? Do lesbians, gays, and heterosexuals experience romantic love similarly or differently? And how, if at all, does race impact the experience of love?

Gender Differences in Love Relationships

Although both women and men experience love and consider it an important experience and relationship, a large body of research shows, as we have already seen with styles of love, that females and males construct their realities of love generally in very different terms (Brehm et al., 2001). We should bear in mind, however, that, like friendship research, much of this research is also based on survey responses of white, middle-class, heterosexual couples.

Contrary to American cultural stereotypes that women are more sentimental than men, more likely to fall in love at first sight, and more likely to stick by their partners no matter what and that men are hard-hearted, rational, in control of their emotions, and able to fall out of love quickly, research on love and intimacy shows us that not only are these stereotypes wrong, but the opposite is actually true. Men are more romantic and give greater importance than do women to the desire to fall in love. Women, on the other hand, tend to initiate a breakup more often than men, and they seem better able than men to put aside feelings of rejection and to redefine their relationship as friendship (Peplau, 1994; Covel, 2003).

In studying the difference between liking and loving, Zick Rubin (1973) found that females distinguish much more sharply between liking and loving than males do. Rubin suggested that this is true because women are much more in tune with their feelings than men are. Given that men are socialized to be task-oriented as opposed to social-emotional, they are often unable to make the fine distinctions in their feelings that women are. Yet some researchers (Covel, 2003a, 2003b) have found that when men are in love, they tend to describe their love in slightly more passionate terms than do women.

In contrast to the popular view of women chasing reluctant men and coyly maneuvering them into an unwanted relationship (the notion of love as a feminine pursuit), it seems that men tend to start a relationship with a much more romantic perspective than females do (Sprecher and Metts, 1989). Although both women and men seem to enjoy the chase and are often stimulated by someone they find somewhat mysterious (Fisher, 1999), men tend to fall in love more quickly and earlier in their relationships, stay in love longer, have crushes, and fall in love with someone who does not love them in return more often than do women (Rubin, 1973; Hill, Rubin, and Peplau, 1976; Brehm et al., 2001). On the other hand, women are more likely than men to emphasize relationships and intimacy, but they are less impulsive than men about falling in love. Thus, women's love is more likely than men's to develop incrementally or practically (Hendrick and Hendrick, 1989; Wood, 1994). Once a relationship develops, women tend to form a more intense and lasting love bond and are willing to sacrifice more for love than men are (Walsh, 1991; Knox et al., 1999, 2000). Women also tend to be more expressive than men, fall in love harder and more intensely, more likely to idealize the love object, and prefer emotional closeness, whereas men prefer giving instrumental help and sex. For example, women express love by talking about and acknowledging their feelings for the other person, whereas men express their love through action—doing things for the other person (Murstein, 1986; Tavris, 2000).

In terms of intimacy, women generally regard intimacy, self-growth, self-understanding, and positive self-esteem as important benefits of romantic love, and loss of identity and innocence about relationships as important costs. Men, on the other hand, regard sexual satisfaction as an important benefit, and monetary losses from dates as an important cost. Furthermore, women tend to spend more time trying to cultivate and maintain love relationships than do men. However, as we have indicated, women are also the ones more likely to decide when to break off a relationship. Men are more resistant to breaking up and have a harder time recovering after a breakup. For example, once a relationship is over, men, more often than women, tend to feel sad, lonely, depressed, and unwilling to give up on the relationship. Men are also more violent and possessive when romantic relationships end (Herman, 1989; Hill, 1989).

These findings seem consistent with female and male socialization in U.S. society. Females are taught almost from birth to be loving, caring, and nurturant. Men, in contrast, are taught to be detached, independent, and unemotional. Obviously, these basic differences do not hold for every woman or man. Rather, they are general tendencies that are subject to change and have sometimes changed over time. The gender gap in the ways that women and men approach romantic love relationships, for instance, seems to be closing as women's and men's lives become more similar. For example, studies during the late 1960s and early 1970s (see, for example, Kephart, 1967) showed that women and men differed fairly significantly in terms of exercising control over their romantic feelings. For instance, when a sample of college students was asked "If someone had all the qualities you desired, would you marry them if you were not in love with them?" only one in four women said no, while two out of three men said no. This led the researchers to conclude that women exercise more control over their feelings and are more careful about falling in love than are men. However, as attitudes and behaviors have changed over time—as gender-specific socialization has loosened somewhat—responses to this same question in the 1990s (see, for example, Allgeier and Wiederman, 1991) indicated that women and men were equally committed to the idea that love is a prerequisite for marriage (nine out of ten women as well as nine out of ten men said that being in love is essential to marrying). Finally, there is some evidence that women's seeming superiority in love is not really as strong as it first seems. Many studies show small or guarded differences between women and men and, according to Francesca Cancian (1993), these studies are often biased against men and focus on verbal self-disclosure, a quality that is stereotypically feminine.

The Feminization of Love Discussions and investigations of gender differences in love relationships have led some sociologists, such as Francesca Cancian (1993), to call attention to how heavily gendered our ways of thinking about love are. According to Cancian, part of the reason that men seem so much less loving than women is because men's love behavior is measured with a feminine ruler. She describes the social organization of love in the United States in terms of the concept of the *feminization of love*—love as a central aspect of the female domain and experience and defined purely in female terms. Cancian's research demonstrates that social scientists generally use a "feminized definition of love" in their research. That is, only women's style of loving is recognized as love. At least since the nineteenth century, love has been defined primarily in terms of characteristics that women are thought to be particularly skilled in, such as emotional expression, self-disclosure, and affection. Such a definition typically ignores aspects of love that men prefer, such as providing instrumental help or sharing physical activities. It also presumes that men lack feelings and

emotional depth and that relationships and feelings are unimportant in men's lives. Men are thought of as incompetent at loving because the common view of romantic love overlooks the instrumental, pragmatic aspect of loving and stresses primarily the expressive aspect. And based on the myth that women both need love more than men do and are more skilled at loving than men are, love has become a preoccupation with women.

One of several problems with this incomplete and overly feminized view of love, says Cancian, is that it contributes to male dominance of women because it leads women to focus on interpersonal relationships while encouraging men to achieve independence from women and to specialize in the occupational activities that are more highly regarded in this society. She argues that ideally love should be **androgynous**—that is, it should include a wide range of attitudes and behaviors with no gender role differentiation. An androgynous view of love validates both feminine and masculine styles of loving and considers both necessary parts of a good love relationship.

What do you think? Do you agree with Cancian, or do you think that differentiation along gender lines in terms of love has disappeared? What evidence can you give to support your position? Try applying a sociological analysis to this issue. How close are your findings to what you already knew or have experienced?

Lesbian and Gay Love Relationships

Love is experienced not only by heterosexual couples but also by lesbian and gay couples. Despite the current controversy surrounding same-sex marriage in the United States, there are no reliable estimates of the number of American gay and lesbian couples. Survey data, however, indicate that between 45 and 80 percent of lesbians and 40 and 60 percent of gay men are currently involved in a romantic relationship (Kurdek, 2004). However, just as there is no distinct heterosexual style of loving, there is also no distinct homosexual value orientation toward love relationships. Instead, what appears to be more important than sexual orientation is one's sex—being female or male—and one's background. Women's goals in intimate partnerships are similar whether the partner is male or female. The same is true of men (Peplau, 1986). Regardless of the sexual orientation of the two partners, research indicates that most partners want to love and be loved, want to be emotionally close, expect fidelity in the relationship, and expect the relationship to be long-term. In general, patterns of lesbian and gay love are very similar to heterosexual love. Unlike heterosexual couples, however, lesbian and gay couples often feel compelled to hide their feelings of love because many people do not approve of such relationships. Although Americans tend to prize romantic love, they are generally hostile to love and intimacy between people of the same sex. Because of societal disapproval, gay lovers frequently look to each other to satisfy all their needs. Thus, gay love is often intense and sometimes possessive. In this sense, it is often both highly emotional and highly physical.

Social science research has traditionally been heterosexist and homophobic (Renzetti and Curran, 1999). Much of what was written about lesbians and gays before the 1960s was written by heterosexuals and discussed from a psychoanalytic and/or pathology perspective, which until recently focused almost exclusively on lesbian and gay sexual behavior. Although specific information and research on love among lesbians and gays continue to be limited, an emerging literature on lesbian and gay relationships across a wider span of social behavior is now being conducted by lesbian and gay social scientists, and their findings refute many of the common myths about lesbian and gay intimacy.

For example, one of the most long-standing stereotypes of lesbian and gay relationships is that they are fleeting, uncommitted, and primarily sexual. However, although gays do have more partners on average than heterosexual men, most establish enduring intimate relationships. And research indicates that lesbian couples generally have more stable and longer-lasting love relationships than either heterosexual couples or gay male couples. In the few studies that have included older lesbians and gays, researchers have found that relationships lasting 20 years or more are not uncommon. The long-term nature of these relationships often persists even after the couple is no longer "in love." For instance, research shows that when lesbian and gay partners break up, they frequently maintain a close relationship with one another by making a transition from being lovers to being friends (Blumstein and Schwartz, 1983; Weston, 1991; Kelly, 1995; Clark, 1999).

Another popular myth about lesbian and gay relationships is that they are unhappy, abnormal, and dysfunctional. However, a study of matched sets of lesbians, gays, and heterosexual women and men involved in a current romantic/sexual relationship found no significant differences among the three sets of couples in terms of love and relationship satisfaction. Like the heterosexual couples, lesbians and gays reported very positive feelings for their partners and generally reported that their relationships were highly satisfying and very close (Peplau and Cochran, 1981). Findings such as these negate the persistent negative cultural images of lesbians and gays as unhappy individuals who are unsuccessful in developing enduring relationships, who drift from one sexual partner to another, and end up old and alone. This is not to imply, however, that all lesbian and gay couples are euphorically happy and problem-free. Rather, the point is that lesbian and gay couples are no more unhappy, abnormal, or dysfunctional than are heterosexual couples.

As you have probably noted already, there are more differences between women and men in the expression and experience of love than there are differences between same-sex and heterosexual love. According to researchers Michelle Huston and Pepper Schwartz (1996), gender affects, and is affected by, the organization of lesbian and gay love. Gender identity and gender roles impact the dating process for lesbians and gays, the maintenance of romantic relationships, the ways in which lesbian and gay partners communicate with one another, as well as the organization of power and the division of labor within these relationships. In this regard, gay couple

relationships, but even more so in lesbian relationships, equality between partners is highly valued, and couples work hard to maintain an egalitarian relationship. Because many lesbians and gays do not allow themselves to be constrained by many of the conventional ways of organizing romantic relationships, they have created egalitarian schemes for dividing up responsibilities and rights within their relationships.

Huston and Schwartz suggest that heterosexual couples can learn much from the egalitarian models developed by lesbians and gays, which demonstrate that equality in a romantic relationship is not only rewarding but also quite possible. However, over and above the lessons we learn about equality in relationships, the study of lesbian and gay love relationships also gives us key insights into the contextual nature of gender. Although each of us is an individual, we are all part of a culture that holds very traditional and often rigid and stereotypical notions about what it means to be women and men. Sometimes these rigid gender roles are practiced in lesbian and gay relationships, but research indicates that most often they are not. Huston and Schwartz suggest that many lesbians and gays have overcome much of this socialization to become more androgynous, a lesson that heterosexuals can learn if they wish to change the current power imbalances prevalent in many of their relationships.

It is important to keep in mind that lesbian and gay relationships are not monolithic; there is no typical lesbian or gay couple or relationship. Rather, as with heterosexual couples, there is enormous variation among lesbian and gay couples. The emerging scholarship on lesbian and gay couples emphasizes this diversity. It also expands our existing knowledge base about love and intimate relationships by increasing the diversity of types of relationships studied to include same-sex partnerships and close relations.

Female–Male Relationships Across Race and Ethnicity

As with research on lesbians and gays, there is little systematic data on love and the organization of romantic relationships across race. To the extent that the American public is informed about such relationships among various racial and ethnic groups, often we have had to rely on a popular literature that may or may not accurately capture the essence and real-life experiences of these relationships, given that their bottom line is the selling of their product and profit. And to the extent that we hear about female–male love and intimacy other than among whites, it is most often about African Americans and it is most often in the context of pathology or crisis. This is perhaps not surprising given that there is little profit to be made by noting that the reality of African American intimate relationships are overwhelmingly nonpathological and stable; that African Americans overwhelmingly choose and marry each other and in most cases form stable, satisfying relationships (Hill, 2005). Thus, for example, over the past several decades, popular literature has repeatedly reported a crisis in African American female–male love relationships. According to several popular and scholarly writers on the subject, African American women and men have experienced some difficulty in developing and maintaining

Mass media portrayals of African Americans, such as the recent television program *My Wife and Kids* serve a useful purpose by counteracting popular stereotypes about African American families and female/male relationships.

meaningful love relationships. This is said to be due, in part, to the suspicions and mistrust generated by years of racism and exploitation, and the pitting of one sex against the other by forces outside their control. The African American struggle, along with other struggles such as the women's movement, has increased the levels of education and occupational mobility for African American women (and men) and has added to what some people describe as the aggressive, assertive, and self-sufficient nature of African American women. Contention over the strong *black woman* is a central theme in black popular culture and literature, with many African Americans embracing and idealizing patriarchal models of love and intimacy that is being abandoned by other races. While African American women are applauded for the active, strong, vital roles they play in their families and communities, they are contradictorily told that such roles are improper in their intimate relationships with men (Hill, 2005).

In turn, some African American women argue that it is difficult for them to develop a committed relationship based on equity because although the roles of women in society have changed, the attitudes of some African American men have not kept pace. Because racism has made achievement of a position of power in the larger society difficult if not impossible for many African American men, many of these men continue to hold on to the one venue where they have been able to exert power: their intimate relationships with African American women. They are said to hold on tenaciously to the ideology of male dominance and see controlling African American women as crucial to their claim to masculinity.

Contrary to this talk of a crisis, however, African American romantic relationships are no more or no less characterized by crisis than are such relationships for other racial and ethnic groups, and African American females and males fall in love as often and confront the same kinds of obstacles to their relationships as do individuals in other racial and ethnic groups. For example, like women in other racial and

ethnic groups, African American women perceive a lack of male commitment as a key obstacle to love and romance. In a poll conducted by *Ebony* magazine (cited in Hughes, 2001), African American women respondents reported that what they want in an intimate relationship is a supportive, romantic man who openly expresses his deepest love and feelings and listens attentively to theirs. Above all, they said, they want a lover who is not afraid of commitment. Some experts on African American love and intimate relationships refute the stereotype of African American men as noncommittal, nonpassionate, and afraid of responsibility. Instead, they argue convincingly that when they are in love, African American men are committed to the relationship and passionate about pleasing the women they love. On the other hand, they find that for African American men, as for men of other races, *romance* is a term that they hardly think about and they sometimes get it mixed up with "sex" (Hughes, 2001). According to sociologist Shirley Hill (2005), the dilemma facing African Americans is scarcely addressed in theories of heterosexual love and partner selection. To the extent that cultural theorists address the issue at all, they have fallen short of reconciling dominant societal traditions of love with the material realities and racial status of African Americans, often even insisting on the propriety of patriarchal relationships.

Although little scientific research has been conducted on differences in styles of loving across race in the United States, evidence suggests that there is a difference in the way various groups of color and whites view love. Research indicates, for example, that African Americans tend to have a more romantic view of love (Hughes, 2001). As with African Americans, the literature on Latinas/os and romantic relationships is practically nonexistent. According to some of the popular Latina/o literature, Latinas/os are more openly passionate about love and less afraid of falling in love and loving than most whites. On the other hand, like other groups, Latinas/os say that in love relationships, they look for someone who respects and treats them well; someone who is

DEBATING SOCIAL ISSUES

SHOULD SOCIETY PUT AN AGE LIMIT ON LOVE?

Romantic love does not always make sense, but should society put an age limit on love? That is a question that has repeatedly surfaced in the last decade or so as more and more youth under the age of 18 are involved in intimate relationships with adults. Although in popular culture the notions that love conquers all, that age is nothing but a number, and that older women and men make great life partners and loyal companions, in the face of both legal and cultural prescriptions about the appropriate age for love, sex, and marriage these adages do not hold up. In the twenty-first century, a person under the age of 18 is still legally and socially defined as a child. And in most states, sexual relationships between someone 19 years of age and older and someone younger than 16 is legally classified as statutory rape. In some states, such relationships are illegal even if the couple is married at the time. Furthermore, adults who engage in sexual relationships with a minor are considered sexual abusers and pedophiles. Nonetheless, adults romancing minors seems to have come of age in the United States.

In 2005, for example, Matthew Koso, a 22-year-old Nebraskan male who married his 14-year-old pregnant lover, was charged with statutory rape even though their parents' gave the marriage their blessing. The two became a romantic couple when she was 12 and he was 20. Unable to wed in their home state of Nebraska, which prohibits marriages of people under 17, the couple traveled to Kansas to marry, one of the few states that allow people as young as 12 to marry.

Back home in Nebraska, the Nebraskan attorney general accused Mr. Koso of being a pedophile but Koso said that what he and his bride have is *true love.* Outrage over the Koso case included a deluge of letters to the attorney general's office that opposed the prosecution and angrily urged the attorney general to leave the couple alone and spend more time putting "real criminals" in jail. Although legally Mr. Koso's sexual relationship with a minor is classified as statutory rape, most experts say it is extremely rare for a

man to be prosecuted for statutory rape when he has married his minor partner. This fact not withstanding, Mr. Koso faced up to 50 years in prison if convicted (Wilgoren, 2005). In a similar case but where the age of the couple was the reverse of the Nebraska couple, a 37-year-old pregnant Georgia woman, Lisa Lynette Clark, who married her 15-year-old lover in 2005, was charged with child molestation and jailed. The two were wed under a Georgia law that allows pregnant couples to marry regardless of

Barbara Hershey, 58, and her live-in boyfriend Noveen Andrews, 37.

sensitive, affectionate, exciting and who can be a companion in life. According to some of these sources, the stereotypical macho Latino in Latina/o intimate relationships is passé (Sigler, 2005). A search for data on love relationships among Asian/Asian Americans was equally sparse. Although beset by the limitations of popular literature, an insight into Asian/Asian American views about love can be gleaned from this literature. For example, in an Asian poem written by Mai Van Trang entitled "An Asian View of Cultural Differences" (cited in Selvaraj, 2005), the poet compares, among other issues, Asian/Asian American views of love with that of

Western society, citing some of the following examples: (Asians) marry first, then love. (Westerners) love first, then marry. (For Asians) marriage is the beginning of a love affair. (For Westerners) marriage is the happy end of a romance. (For Asians) love is mute. (For Westerners) love is vocal.

In any case, continuing racism and discrimination in U.S. society, coupled with the changing social roles of women and men, will no doubt continue to exert pressure on the development and maintenance of love relationships between African American women and men. As for other groups of color, the need for scientific research on love and intimacy is

age and without parental consent. Geared toward preventing out-of-wedlock births, the law dates back to at least the early 1960s (Dunwald, 2005).

Cases such as that of Koso and Clark along with a number of studies that show most babies born to teenage mothers are fathered by adults, have prompted many states to dust off seldom-used statutory rape laws that prohibit sex between adults and minors and to crack down on the older men. These studies of teenage pregnancy indicate that in two out of three births to teenage mothers, the father is 20 years of age or older, often much older than the mother; the younger the mother the wider the age gap. Although such studies provide revealing data on the incidence of intimacy between underage girls who get pregnant and their adult male lovers, they do not, however, indicate how many older men are sexual partners of teenage girls who do not have babies. Thus, the incidence of female minors and adult male lovers could be much higher. In any event, state legislators face more questions than answers as they debate what is exploitative and what is appropriate in love and intimacy. For example, if the adult is responsible and marries the minor, is the relationship all right? Are there certain cultural and social factors that must be considered? If so, what are they? An indication of how murky this issue can get is the variation among states in the age of consent—from 18 in most states to 14 in Pennsylvania and Hawaii (Navarro, 1996).

Historically, pedophilia, sexual abuse, and statutory rape have been generally thought of by most Americans as a male phenomenon. In the past, the most often publicized relationships between an adult and a minor have been those between an adult male and a minor female. However, in recent years there have been several cases nationwide involving alleged or proven love and sexual relations between adult females and male minors, particularly female teachers and male students. In recent memory, a flood of such cases seems to have begun with Mary Kay Letourneau, a Seattle teacher, who served 7 years in jail stemming from her relationship with a sixth-grade student. That relationship eventually produced two children and in 2005, after her second release from prison, Letourneau and her by then 22-year-old lover were married. One writer on the subject listed 50 recent cases in the United States involving women as old as 50 and minors as young as 11. And according to this writer, the United States is not alone in grappling with the issue of adult–minor intimate relationships. Australia is experiencing a similar rash of cases where adult women are having sexual relations with their male students (Kovacs, 2005).

Some people claim that the pairing of an older and younger partner is not new—it has always been around. They suggest that the increase in such romantic relationships is a result of today's increasing permissiveness and more relaxed social norms and that we should change the age of consent to accommodate these cultural changes. Others suggest that in the increasingly sexualized American culture, the lines seem to be increasingly blurred between what is appropriate and what is not relative to intimacy and the choice of partners. On one side of the issue of intimacy between adults and minors are those who argue that adults should not have romantic relationships, including sexual intercourse, with minors—those under the age of 18—who they believe know nothing about the complicated consequences of romantic love and involvement with an adult. On the other side of the issue are those who argue that not all adult–minor relationships are abusive, that, in fact, most are consensual and should not be classified as criminal. For example, a British professor who has been studying such relationships for the past 25 years concludes that sexual contact between an adult and a minor is not necessarily criminal and, in fact, can be a positive experience (WorldNetDaily, 2005). For those opposed to such pairings, two key issues involved in these relationships are trust and power. Therefore, they argue, even if such relationships are consensual, they are still coercive to some degree.

As older and younger people seek each other out at an increasing rate, centuries-old traditions about what is or is not an appropriate age for love, sex, and/or marriage might have to be reexamined and rethought. In an interview at a public school for teenage parents, a 14-year-old, 7-months-pregnant female who met her husband when she was 12 and he was 23, said that "it's nobody's business who you love and date" (Navarro, 1996).

What do you think? Are individuals under the age of 18 who are involved in romantic sexual relationships with adults victims of abuse or are they capable of entering a consensual relationship that should be recognized by the state? Are such relationships problematic solely because of the age difference between the two partners? Should such relationships be criminalized? Explain. How old is too old or too young for romantic involvements? Does it matter how old lovers are if they are happy? Explain. How much control should the state or federal government have over our personal lives?

even greater than that for African Americans. Indeed, this is an area of research that is sorely in need of the skills and insights of scholars across academic disciplines.

OBSTACLES TO LOVE AND LOVING RELATIONSHIPS

Few people thrive in an environment of social isolation, so we desire and pursue meaningful love relationships. Unfortunately, a number of individual and cultural factors serve as obstacles to the development and maintenance of love. Some of the most troublesome of these factors are demographic factors and social and cultural change, traditional gender role socialization, patriarchy, lack of trust, and jealousy.

Demographic Factors and Social and Cultural Change

As we have pointed out, race, class, gender, and sexual orientation are key factors that impact love and intimacy. A number of other demographic factors—such as age, income, occupation—are also key in shaping our love and intimacy experiences. For example, as you will find in Chapter 5, in the United States, age is a significant demographic factor that impacts whom we fall in love with, date, and eventually marry (if we marry) or cohabit with. In heterosexual relationships, for instance, women are expected to love, date, and marry men who are somewhere between 2 and 5 years older than themselves. Conversely, men are expected to love, date and/or marry women 2 to 5 years younger than themselves. Although there are no laws that require us to fall in love with, date, and/or marry people within this age range, informal norms and personal and public pressures operate to keep us typically within this age-related range.

On the other hand, formal norms or laws define when we are considered old enough to marry thereby defining (even if indirectly) when we are old enough and mature enough to fall in love. As we discuss in Chapter 8, each state has set a legal age for marriage, although the marriageable age for women and men is about the same in most states. In all but one state, the legal age at which marriage can be contracted without the consent of a parent is 18 for both women and men. In some states, couples under the age of 18 may marry with parental consent. In Georgia, for example, a female or male can marry without parental consent as early as 16 years of age. Such restriction is waived, however, if the female applicant is pregnant. In actual practice, age norms and laws around love, intimacy, sex, and marriage are not always followed. When such laws are violated, the consequences for the offending party can be grave, including long jail sentences. For example, in 2005, a 22-year-old Nebraskan male and his 14-year-old pregnant lover were wed with their parents' blessing yet he was prosecuted for statutory rape. Likewise, a 37-year-old pregnant Georgian woman who married her 15-year-old lover in 2005 was jailed on charges of child molestation. Moreover, a rash of news stories in recent years have reported on an increasing number of adult women who have fallen in love with and had intimate relationships with their underage lovers. This seemingly increasing phenomena of love knowing no age boundaries raises interesting and important questions about whether or not or to what extent love between minors and adults should be regulated (see the Debating Social Issues box).

Social and cultural change also shape our love and intimacy experiences. For example, as you will see in Chapter 5, with increasing technologies such as electronic mail, answering machines and voice mail, text messaging, Internet chat rooms, and computerized matchmaking services, a burgeoning love industry has developed that has had the effect of decreasing the incidence of face-to-face interactions and thereby depersonalizing love and intimacy.

Traditional Gender Role Socialization

As the discussions in Chapter 3 and throughout this chapter reveal, differential gender role socialization often creates very different attitudes and behaviors in females and males. Nowhere is this more evident than in the ways in which the two genders view love relationships. Research has shown that women and men seem to have different priorities when it comes to love relationships. Several researchers have found considerable evidence of an emotional division of labor within heterosexual love relationships, with one partner (usually the woman) more oriented toward the relationship than the other is. That is, the relationship and what it should consist of is more familiar to and central in the life and behavior of one partner than it is in that of the other. Likewise, homosexual couples tend to consist of one partner who is more oriented toward the relationship than the other is (Blumstein and Schwartz, 1983).

Researcher Robert Karen (1987) discussed this differential relationship orientation between women and men in terms of who gives and who gets. According to Karen, men get much more out of love relationships than they give. Women, because of the way they have been socialized, are able to be compassionate, to give support, and generally to be there for their partners. Men, in contrast, require emotional understanding and tenderness but have not been taught to give it. Thus, they often have less access to their feelings than do women. Consequently, it is often the woman who reaches out and makes emotional contact. Feeling this emotional inequality, some women console themselves with the belief that they can rely on their inner strength to make up for what they do not get from their partners. This emotional imbalance between women and men can be an obstacle to either the development or the maintenance of a loving relationship.

Patriarchy as an Obstacle to Lesbian Love

A number of scholars have identified the patriarchal structure of Western society as an obstacle to same-sex love. Focusing on lesbian love, some of these scholars contend that romantic love between women is outlawed and repressed because it is viewed by men as a threat to the patriarchal structure of intimate relationships and to heterosexuality generally. To these scholars, heterosexuality includes not only sex between women and men but also patriarchal culture, male dominance, and female subordination, all of which benefit men (Faderman, 1989). The centrality of patriarchy in mate selection is evidenced in the concept of heterosexuality and the notion that women are dependent on men for emotional as well as social and economic well-being. Some of the more common assumptions of patriarchy and heterosexualism are that women's primary love and sexual orientation are naturally directed toward men and that heterosexuality is ordained by nature. Thus, heterosexuals have seldom questioned these assumptions, even though there is ample evidence that lesbian love has existed throughout history and has been accepted at different times by various societies.

From a lesbian perspective, such assumptions not only legitimate heterosexuality as the norm but also denigrate women's romantic relationships with other women, defining these relationships as deviant or pathological. We need only to look at the social sanctions brought against women who love women (as well as men who love men) to understand how, through social control, heterosexuality is maintained as the norm and homosexuality is defined as deviant. For example, society subverts any public expression of homosexual consciousness or behavior, defining it with terms such as evil, sick, sinful, a crime against nature (Andersen, 2003). Such ideas and attitudes are detrimental both to lesbians' sense of self-worth and their ability to establish romantic relationships with other women.

Until women's and men's sexuality is freed from the constraints of patriarchy and heterosexism and society recognizes that there is no one right way to express love, women and men who choose to love people of the same sex will continue to face a wide range of obstacles to the development of romantic love relationships. In the meantime, however, a growing number of lesbians today openly choose other women as love objects even though the patriarchal system continues to define their behavior as deviant and severely restrict their ability to love other women. For many of these women, their selection of a partner is not just a personal choice but rather a political choice as well.

Lack of Trust

Do you trust your partner? Does your partner trust you? Is it important to your relationship that each of you trusts the other? Why?

Trust is probably important to your relationship because with it you and your partner can relax; you can feel secure about the relationship and not worry about whether it will continue. Social researchers John Rempel and John Holmes (1986) designed a trust inventory scale to address these questions. According to Rempel and Holmes, **trust**—the degree of confidence a person feels when he or she thinks about a relationship—is one of the most important and necessary aspects of any close or intimate relationship. Because trust can mean something different depending on what aspect of the relationship we are focusing on, Rempel and Holmes identified three basic elements of trust: predictability, dependability, and faith.

Predictability is the ability to foretell our partner's behavior, the knowledge that she or he will consistently act in our best interests. For confidence to grow and trust to develop, it is not enough simply to know in advance how our partner will behave. A sense of predictability must be based on the knowledge that our partner will act in positive ways. As the relationship progresses, however, we begin to focus more on our partner's specific qualities, such as dependability and trustworthiness, and less in terms of predictable behavior. This leads to the second element of trust, dependability. *Dependability* can be defined as the knowledge that our partner can be relied on when we need her or him. Both predictability and dependability are based on the assumption that people will behave in a fairly consistent manner (the same in the present as they did in the past). But because human behavior is changing, there is no guarantee that this will be so. Therefore, we often remain committed to a relationship based on sheer faith. Faith allows people to go beyond previously observed behaviors to feel assured that the partner will continue to be loving and caring. Faith is rooted in predictability and dependability, but it goes beyond what has actually happened in the past. Each of these components helps form the basis for a trusting relationship; none by itself is sufficient. Rather, the extent to which we trust our partner depends on the degree to which each component is interwoven with the others.

Jealousy and Envy

Although love can provide us with wonderful feelings and experiences, it often has a dark side as well: jealousy. Most of us have experienced jealousy at one time or another. Some of the most important relationships have been destroyed by it. In fact, for some people there can be no real love without jealousy. So what is this powerful emotion, what causes it, who is most likely to exhibit it, and what consequences does it have for our relationships?

As is the case with love, there are perhaps as many definitions of jealousy as there are people who experience it. It has been defined somewhat tongue-in-cheek as "a cry of pain," "the fear of annihilation," and "the shadow of love" (Adams, 1982:39). On a more serious side, however, most researchers on the subject define **jealousy** as an emotional reaction that is aroused by a perceived threat to a valued relationship or position and motivates behavior aimed at countering the threat. It is the fear of losing someone whom you love or who is very important to you and is usually an unhealthy manifestation of insecurity, low self-confidence, and possessiveness. To precipitate feelings of jealousy, the perceived threat of loss does not have to be real; instead, it can be potential or even completely imaginary. The key is that we *believe* the relationship is threatened (Farrell, 1997; Cano and O'Leary, 1997; Buss et al., 1992).

In response to such a perceived threat, jealous people try to protect themselves and/or their love relationship by thoughts, feelings, or actions. Researchers have also found that jealousy involves not one but a number of interrelated emotions including anger, anxiety, uncertainty, fear of loss, vulnerability, hatred, shame, sorrow, humiliation, abandonment, betrayal, loneliness, hopelessness, suspicion, insecurity, and pain. Although jealousy often brings about damage (psychological or physical), it is seldom the case that jealous persons actually mean to do harm. Rather, they usually are simply reacting to one or more of the emotions associated with jealousy, believing they are protecting either their relationship and/or the ego of the threatened partner. However, carried to the extreme, jealousy can lead to the greater probability of abuse and violence in an intimate relationship.

Jealousy is sometimes confused with or considered the same as envy. The two are, however, different emotions. **Envy** refers to unhappiness or discontent with ourselves that arises from the belief that something about ourselves (our personality, achievements, possessions) does not measure up to someone else's level. Envy involves feelings of inferiority, coveting what someone else has, rather than the fear of losing someone (Parrot and Smith, 1987).

A great deal of the research on the topic of jealousy has been conducted by psychologists and social psychologists and thus reflects their concern with the effects of interpersonal attributes on attitudes and behavior. In contrast, a sociological analysis of love and jealousy would focus far more on social-structural and cultural properties, such as norms or collective agreements of a particular society or of particular groups within the society, that govern whom and how we should love and under what circumstances we feel jealous. In this context, jealousy, like love, can be thought of

There are probably as many definitions of jealousy as there are people who experience this emotion. As with love, women and men differ in terms of how they view and experience jealousy.
Source: Reprinted with special permission of King Features Syndicate.

as a social construction, an emotion shaped by a person's culture. It is not biologically determined. Thus, what makes people feel jealous will vary from one culture to another and change over time even within a culture.

The Nature and Pattern of Jealousy The causes of jealousy vary from externally to internally induced factors. External factors include behaviors such as flirting or spending excessive amounts of time with someone other than the partner. Early studies such as those by social psychologists Ayala Pines and Elliot Aronson (1983) report that most episodes of jealousy arise from external factors. Some cases, however, stem from internal factors that reside in the individual personality and can include feelings of insecurity and distrust learned from previous experiences. Some studies have found, for example, that jealousy is closely associated with low self-esteem and a high level of dependence on one's partner. Other studies have found that among married couples the individuals who tend most often to be jealous are those who feel insecure about themselves and believe they would not be successful in getting someone else if their partner left them. The more insecure a person is about her or his relationship, the greater the chance she or he will feel jealousy (Marelich, Gaines, and Banzet, 2003).

The experience of jealousy varies greatly from relationship to relationship and from individual to individual. Researchers have found, however, that those who are most likely to be jealous are women, people in open or multiple relationships, people who are unhappy with their lives overall or with their love relationship, less educated people, younger people, and people who are unfaithful themselves (Pines and Aronson, 1983; Salovey and Rodin, 1989). Jealousy also varies from one historical period to another and from culture to culture. Examining research studies and records spanning a 200-year period, social psychologist Ralph Hupka (1991) found consistent differences across cultures in both the degree to which jealousy is present in a society and the ways in which it is expressed. This finding led him to classify societies as either high-jealousy or low-jealousy cultures.

Highly stratified societies and those in which heavy emphasis is placed on sexual exclusiveness, such as in the

United States, exhibit a high level of jealousy, whereas societies with little or no stratification, where individual property rights are discouraged and sexual gratification and companionship are easily accessible to all people, exhibit a low level of jealousy. A Native American group, the Apaches of North America, are an example of a high-jealousy culture. Among the Apaches, great emphasis is placed on female virginity and on male sexual gratification. Male sexual pleasure must be earned after a prolonged period of deprivation, and it must be judiciously protected from all intruders. Apache wives and children are so important to the status of Apache men that when the men are away from their families, they engage close relatives to watch their wives secretly and report their wives' behavior to them when they return home. In contrast, the Toda of southern India are an example of a low-jealousy culture. Jealousy in this culture is rare because there is little of which to be jealous. The Todas take a sharing attitude toward people and things; neither are defined as personal property. In addition, the Todas place few restrictions on sexual pleasure, and neither marriage nor heirs are prerequisites for social honor and prestige.

Based on his findings of high- and low-jealousy cultures, Hupka concluded that jealousy is not biologically determined; rather, it is a learned emotion. We learn what our particular culture defines as valuable and in need of protection. Hupka's findings are consistent with sociological research suggesting that jealousy is a social emotion learned through the socialization process. The existence and expression of jealousy depend very much on how love and love relationships are defined—which people, things, and relationships are valued in a particular society. In other words, jealousy is rooted in the social structure of a society insofar as cultural norms provide the cues that will or will not trigger it. For example, over a quarter of a century ago, sociologist Kingsley Davis (1977) argued that jealousy is the product of the practice of monogamy. If you are socialized in a society that practices monogamy, cultural norms require you to think of your partner in exclusive terms. Thus, adultery or nonexclusivity is resented and causes jealousy. An interesting example of the influence of socialization and cultural definitions of intimate relationships (that is, monogamy versus nonexclusivity) and the incongruence that sometimes occurs between ideological viewpoints and personal feelings about a valued relationship is provided in Candace Falk's (1984) examination of the life and ideology of Emma Goldman. Goldman, an early feminist (from the early twentieth century) known for her so-called radical political and social views, espoused, among other things, the notion of free love and freedom from sexual jealousy. Nonetheless, Falk reports that although Goldman spoke and wrote extensively about the perils and negative impact of jealousy, and the pettiness and small-mindedness of jealous people, Goldman herself was beset by jealousy of her lover, who, although he professed his love for Goldman, had a number of sexual liaisons with other women.

On the other hand, if you were born and raised in a culture such as ancient Japan, where extramarital sexual relationships (or nonexclusivity) was the norm for both women and men and acknowledged publicly, such relationships would not provoke sexual jealousy from either gender. Over time, however, cultural norms surrounding marriage and intimate relationships in Japan changed such that women were gradually prohibited from having extra lovers (extramarital sexual relationships), while men continued to engage in extramarital sexual liaisons with concubines. With this change in cultural norms and expectations, Japanese men could now express jealousy of their wives; however, wives were culturally prohibited from feeling jealousy of their husbands (Cherry, 1987).

Even today in contemporary Japan, while extramarital sexual liaisons are prohibited for both women and men, Japanese men (especially businessmen) nonetheless often seek out and utilize the services of prostitutes. According to Cherry, Japanese wives seldom if ever react to this behavior with jealousy. Rather, they tend to define such behavior as harmless because it does not involve love. In essence, Japanese women have learned within the cultural framework and constructs of their society that they should not be jealous of their husbands' indiscretions with prostitutes because such sex is "casual" and not a threat to their marriage. On the other hand, if the husband has a mistress, Japanese wives become extremely jealous. In this cultural context, a mistress is viewed as very threatening to a marriage in that Japanese men who have mistresses often have a second set of children as well.

In summary, the cultural basis of jealousy is well illustrated in the facts that (1) the basis for jealousy and the types of behavior appropriate to the expression of jealousy can and often do change over time; (2) the same behavior can provoke different feelings and actions in different cultures (for example, in the United States, given the cultural norm of exclusivity in marriage and intimate relationships, women and men alike are likely to feel and/or express jealousy if their partner has a sexual liaison with another person or persons, regardless of whether it is defined as "casual" or "nonthreatening sex"), and (3) within the same culture, the same behavior (for example, the extramarital sexual behavior of husbands) stimulates feelings and expressions of jealousy under one set of circumstances and does not under another set of circumstances.

Gender Differences in Jealousy   Although researchers have found that both women and men experience jealousy when their partners become emotionally or sexually involved with other people and that there is no gender difference in the frequency, duration, or intensity of this jealousy, they have found a gender difference in the causes of jealous. Women, for example, are more likely to become jealous if the partner is emotionally involved with another person, whereas men are more likely to become jealous if the partner becomes sexually involved with someone else (Clanton and Smith, 1986; Pines, 1998). Some of the more prevalent findings concerning the differences between women and men in the United States in terms of the ways that they feel and act when they are jealous include the following:

- Women feel jealousy more intensely than do men.
- Jealousy causes women greater suffering and distress than it does men.
- Men are less likely than women to stay in a relationship that makes them jealous (Pines and Aronson, 1983).
- Women are more likely than men to fight to win back a lost lover rather than give up the relationship. When men feel jealous they try to repair their self-esteem, whereas women try to repair the relationship (make themselves and the relationship better so that he won't desire another partner) (Shettel-Neuber, Bryson, and Young, 1978).
- Women's feelings of personal inadequacy lead to jealousy, whereas men feel jealousy first, which then leads to feelings of inadequacy, that something is wrong with them.
- Men are more likely than women to express their jealousy in the form of violence. They are also more likely to shift the blame for both their jealousy and their violent response from themselves to a third party (Hoff, 1990).
- Women more often consciously attempt to make their partner jealous as a way of testing the relationship (see if he still cares), of increasing rewards (get their partner to give them more attention or spend more time with them), of bolstering their self-esteem, of getting revenge, or of punishing their partner for some perceived transgression (White, 1980a).

 Are any of these gendered patterns of jealousy familiar to you? Are they consistent with your personal experiences with love and jealousy? If not, how do you account for any differences?

Destructive Jealousy   Although in the past jealousy was considered an indication or natural proof of love, today it is increasingly seen as destructive and as a sign of some deficiency in the individual or the relationship. Jealousy can be destructive in terms of the toll it takes on the individual psyche, in the form of deep depression, fear, anxiety, self-doubt, and low self-esteem. It can also be physically damaging and life-threatening when it is expressed in terms of anger, violence, and the desire for revenge.

Some researchers (for example, Clanton and Smith, 1986) have found that jealousy has some legitimate functions, such as to alert us to threats to our personal security and to our important relationships. Just as physical pain alerts us to threats to our physical well-being, the psychological pain of jealousy alerts us to threats to the security of our love relationships. Jealousy can also be a way of releasing pent-up anxieties and emotions that otherwise could lead to violence. More often than not, however, jealousy is destructive to our relationships.

Managing Destructive Jealousy If jealousy is such a damaging emotion, what can we do either to prevent it or to deal with it in a constructive manner? The options suggested by social researchers Lynn Smith and Gordon Clanton (1977) for dealing with jealousy continue to have relevance in today's intimate relationships. They suggest the following: (1) Get out of the relationship, (2) ignore or tolerate those behaviors that make you jealous, (3) attempt to change your partner's behavior, and (4) work on your own jealousy. How we manage jealousy depends on the type of jealousy we feel and our commitment to the relationship. If we are interested in maintaining our relationship, we must bring jealousy out in the open. This process involves self-examination: How does jealousy make me feel? How would I prefer to feel? Which actions cause me to feel jealous? Which behaviors or thoughts can I modify to reduce or eliminate my feelings of jealousy?

As we answer these questions, we must look beyond the specific incidents that disturb us to the underlying causes of our jealousy. For example, Is my jealousy caused by my partner's behavior, or is it rooted in my own feelings of inadequacy and low self-esteem? If the latter, perhaps I should try to discover ways to bolster my self-concept and develop self-confidence. We must also evaluate our situation realistically. For example, Is this situation the best for me? Does my partner return my love? If I decide the relationship is worth saving, perhaps I could move beyond my self-analysis of jealousy and share my feelings with my partner. We can share our goals for our relationship and reiterate or redefine what we expect from each other—the kinds of behaviors that are and are not acceptable. In this way, we can work together to change some of the behaviors and attitudes that spark jealous episodes. If these actions fail, both partners might consider counseling or therapy.

Moreover, if we understand the cultural basis of love and jealousy, we can also question the extent to which our personal feelings are rooted in cultural constructions and expectations about intimate relationships in the United States and thus the extent to which they are changeable. Whatever course is taken, it should be a collaborative effort. Both parties must agree on how they see the relationship and what they want for the future.

ROMANTIC LOVE TODAY

Heterosexual love and romance in the early years of the twenty-first century reflect the changes that have been evident in the roles of women and men since the emergence of the contemporary women's movement. In the past, female and male roles in love and romance were clearly, if not rigidly, defined, usually as a power relationship characterized by male dominance and female submission. Today, however, dramatic changes have taken place in the relationships between heterosexual lovers, especially among the middle classes. But at the same time, many traditional aspects of love, dating, intimacy, and mate selection remain firmly entrenched in U.S. society. The result is a great deal of anxiety and uncertainty as couples try to balance traditional norms with current developments in the absence of clear-cut rules and guidelines.

The contemporary women's movement and the subsequent rise in the level of education and employment opportunities for women, in combination with the sexual revolution, have affected the ways in which women and men relate to one another in their intimate relationships. Women have become more independent and more vocal about their desire to control their own destinies. Unlike their foremothers, many women today no longer define themselves in terms of a man or the lack of one.

The changing nature of female and male roles in intimate relationships has left some couples confused about how to relate to each other and has presented a number of problems that hamper the development or maintenance of love relationships. For other lovers or potential lovers, the challenge to traditional male-dominated intimate relations has set the stage for the development of a new, more equitable type of relationship. Many women and men are confronting the conflicts generated by changing gender roles by changing themselves. In general, women and men have accelerated the trend identified by social researchers in the 1980s and 1990s of dealing with each other in a new way, "not as one-dimensional entities who fit into narrow and rigid roles but as whole and complete human beings" (Simmons, 1988:139). If this trend continues as we progress through the twenty-first century, love relationships might be closer to the androgynous love ideal, and lovers may overcome many of the barriers currently caused by gender role stereotypes.

SUPPORTING MARRIAGES AND FAMILIES

According to some policymakers and various experts, marriages and families have become perhaps *the* most important domestic political issues of the twenty-first century. Whether this is the case, as we have already indicated, there is an ongoing need for social policies, principles, initiatives, and programs that support these primary and important institutions. As we have discussed in this chapter, love and intimacy bind society together; they are extremely important in providing both emotional support and a buffer against stress and thus, figure importantly in the preservation of our physical and psychological health as well. Therefore, it is important that there is a focus on the implementation of policies, principles, programs, and/or initiatives that allow love, loving, and intimate relationships to thrive as well as targeted measures that support these relationships in their variations and diversity.

WRITING YOUR OWN SCRIPT

A SOCIAL CONSTRUCTION OF LOVE

This chapter has examined the concept of love in Western society, paying particular attention to love as a social construction and the differential experiences of love and the organization of love relationships based on sex or gender, race, and sexual orientation. As the context of this chapter suggests, love is a complex phenomenon, as is our socialization into "love-appropriate" behavior.

Consider how you learned about romantic love and how you learned to behave in culturally appropriate ways within romantic love relationships. Think back to your earliest memories of cultural influences on your views. What did you learn about romantic love from your family? From popular culture? If you have siblings of a different sex, were they given the same messages about romantic love and the appropriate organization of such relationships in your family? In the larger culture? How does your economic class, race, sex/gender, sexual orientation, age, and historical location affect your attitude about and experience of romantic love? Do you agree that romantic love is a meaningless construct outside a cultural context? If not, why not? Write a brief analysis of a specific romantic love relationship you are currently in (if you are not presently in one, consider a previous relationship or that of someone you know) and critically reflect on it, using the following questions as a guide:

How would you describe each partner in the relationship in terms of gender role ideology: feminine, masculine, androgynous?

What, if any, impact does the organization of gender have on the way in which you and your partner relate to and love each other? Contribute to the success of the relationship?

Are there conflicts regarding intimacy (for example, over sharing intimacy)? Is one partner more self-disclosing than the other? Can this be related in any way to gender/gender role socialization? If so, how?

Think of, at minimum, two factors that contribute to one partner having more power in the relationship than the other.

If you are part of a same-sex romantic love relationship, relate two examples of how myths about same-sex love relationships impact your specific relationship. What effects does homophobia have on your relationship?

Is jealousy present in the relationship? If so, identify and evaluate the source of the jealousy.

Is the jealousy destructive to the relationship? What steps have you taken (or will you take) to change the situation? Think of, at minimum, two ways in which androgyny or egalitarian gender roles might result in increased intimacy and mutual satisfaction in the relationship.

Increasingly since the election of George W. Bush, this country has focused on and implemented policies and initiatives that are said to promote marriages and families. In 2003, for example, the United States Congress passed the *Personal Responsibility, Work, and Family Promotion Act*, the goal of which was to promote and support healthy marriages and families through such provisions as the awarding of grants to states for marriage promotion activities, the initiation of family self-sufficiency plans, the award of grants to public and nonprofit community entities for demonstration projects to test the effectiveness of various approaches to create a fatherhood program, as well as a host of other provisions that are defined as promoting and supporting marriages and families. Such initiatives may have merit, but it is well to keep in mind that healthy love and intimate relationships, including marriages and families, require more than a one-size-fits-all approach. Policies that sustain rather than demonize and/or deem inappropriate love, loving relationships, and intimacy that do not fit the "one size" model is what is needed.

Love, respect, and commitment are critical factors in marriages and families; thus to affirm love and intimacy and promote healthy love relationships is, in essence, the promotion of a wide variety of healthy intimate relationships including marriages and families. Social policies and programs are only one among many factors that impact the health and well-being of loving and intimate relationships. Such policies and programs are limited in what they can do to strengthen loving relationships and marriages and families but such policies should place these relationships as a critical component of public policy dialogue so as to support *all* opportunities to strengthen and support these relationships.

SUMMARY

Love is a central feature of life in Western societies. References to love can be found throughout popular culture. Because each of us expresses and experiences love differently, there are a variety of definitions of love and many different kinds of love. However, romantic love can be distinguished from other kinds by its erotic component. It can be defined as the intense feelings, emotions, and thoughts coupled with sexual passion and erotic expression that one person directs toward another, as well as the ideology that upholds it. According to a social-constructionist perspective, love can be understood only as symbolic or as a social construction of a particular historical time, location, culture, and people, having by itself no intrinsic meaning. Romantic love is relatively new in human social history. Its developmental roots in

Western societies can be traced to ancient Greek and Roman cultures.

Researchers have found that love is extremely important to our physical and emotional health and well-being. Studies of children and adults who have suffered extended isolation from other humans indicate the learned nature of love and our dependence on other people to provide us with the experiences of love. There is great diversity in the ways in which people express romantic love. Some researchers have attempted to define love by isolating its various components, whereas others have defined it in terms of several styles of loving. Still other researchers have distinguished love from friendship, infatuation, and liking.

Ira Reiss uses a wheel analogy to explain love as a developmental process, whereas Robert Sternberg theorizes that love is a story that dictates our beliefs and expectations of love. A popular sociological framework for examining love is social exchange theory. Using basic economic concepts such as reward, costs, and profits, social exchange theory explains why people are attracted to and fall in love with one another. Psychologist Dorothy Tennov uses the concept of limerence to refer to a style of love characterized by extreme attraction, complete absorption, or obsessive preoccupation of one person with another. Researchers have noted a variety of ways in which women and men differ in terms of how they feel and express love. For example, men fall in love more quickly than women and remain in love longer.

Love is experienced by lesbian and gay couples as well as by heterosexuals. In gay couple relationships, but even more so in lesbian relationships, equality between partners is highly valued, and couples work hard to maintain an egalitarian relationship. Because many lesbians and gays do not allow themselves to be constrained by many of the conventional ways of organizing romantic relationships, they have created egalitarian schemes for dividing up responsibilities and rights within their relationships. Regarding race, little research has been conducted that focuses exclusively on love and the organization of romantic relationships across race. According to the research that exists on African Americans'

love relationships, African American women, like most other women, want a lover who is supportive, romantic, openly expressive of his deepest love and feelings, listens attentively to theirs, and above all, is not afraid of commitment. Likewise, Latinas/os say that in love relationships, they look for someone who respects and treats them well; someone who is sensitive, affectionate, exciting, and who can be a companion in life.

A number of social and political obstacles hamper the development or maintenance of a loving relationship. These include demographic factors and social and cultural change, traditional gender role socialization, patriarchy, the lack of trust, and jealousy. For example, age norms and laws regulate the age at which love, sex, and/or marriage are acceptable. Jealousy is the dark side of love and can be detrimental to the development or maintenance of a long-term love relationship. As with love, jealousy can best be understood as a social construction, that is, as an emotion largely shaped by a given culture. In addition, as with love, there are gender differences in the expression of jealousy. We can manage or eliminate jealousy by looking inward and working out the problems that make us susceptible to jealousy, and we can talk to our partner. We can also share with her or him our feelings and expectations for the future of the relationship while coming to an agreement about what behaviors are and are not acceptable within the relationship.

Heterosexual romance today reflects the changes evident in the roles of women and men since the contemporary women's movement. In general, women and men in the 1990s accelerated earlier trends toward dealing with each other on a more equitable basis. If this trend continues as we progress through the twenty-first century, romantic love relationships might be increasingly androgynous or egalitarian in nature. Affirming love and supporting healthy loving relationships and intimacy is, in essence, promoting and supporting strong and healthy marriages and families. Thus, is an ongoing need for public policies, initiatives, and programs that recognize and support the diversity of loving relationships.

KEY TERMS

romantic love	storge	infatuation	androgynous
love map	mania	liking	trust
eros	pragma	wheel theory of love	jealousy
ludus	agape	limerence	envy

QUESTIONS FOR STUDY AND REFLECTION

1. What does being in love mean to you? Are love and romance necessary for a satisfying intimate relationship? Explain. Is there a relationship between love and sex? Explain. What is the difference between liking, loving, and infatuation? Have you ever loved someone without liking her or him? Is it important to like the person you love? To be her or his friend? Can a relationship last without these elements? Explain.

2. Messages about love and intimate relationships are deeply embedded in American popular culture. Consider greeting cards, for example, and the cultural messages and assumptions they contain about love, sex, intimacy, and appropriate intimate partners. Conduct a content analysis of romantic greeting cards such as valentine, engagement, wedding, and anniversary cards that express love and, using a sociological perspective,

analyze the messages and images they contain in terms of some or all of the following points: Do the cards contain the same or different messages for women and men about love and/or being in love? Can you tell if they are intended for a woman or a man or is the language neutral? How is love described in the cards? Do the cards make assumptions about sexual orientation? Does the cards' messages and images presume heterosexuality? Are there specific cards and/or messages for same-sex couples? What cultural assumptions do the cards make about love and intimacy between women and men of color? Are there specific cards and/or messages for couples of color? Do they differ from those for whites? What about interracial love? Are there cards that address interracial intimate relationships? If yes, how is the issue addressed? In your assessment, does the greeting card industry promote and maintain patriarchy, racism, sexism, and heterosexism? What changes would you suggest to those who create and promote greeting cards about love and intimacy?

3. Research indicates that our ability to establish and maintain love relationships is profoundly impacted by our childhood experiences and the development of self-love. In some families, children are given positive feedback and are often told verbally that they are important and that they are loved, while in others the expression of love is more subtle, or absent altogether. When you were growing up, did you receive positive feedback? Were you verbally told that you were loved? How were you shown that you were loved? Do you think these early childhood experiences have had an impact on your self-esteem? On how you show love today? Explain.

4. What do sociologists mean when they say that love, romance, and jealousy are socially constructed? What evidence do you see of this process in popular culture, particularly the media that you watch, hear, or read? If love is a social construction, what can heterosexual couples learn from lesbian and gay couples' organization of love relationships? Explain.

ADDITIONAL RESOURCES

SOCIOLOGICAL

ABRAHAM, LAURIE, L. GREEN, J. MAGDA KRANCE, J. ROSENBERG, AND C. STONER, EDS. 1993. *Reinventing Love: Six Women Talk about Lust, Sex, and Romance.* New York: Plume. An interesting personal account of six women's experiences of love, including first love, sex, romance, love partners, and problems in love relationships.

CLARK, DON. 1987. *The New Loving Someone Gay.* Millbrae, CA: Celestial Arts. A very good examination and discussion of lesbian and gay relationships.

NARDI, PETER M., ED. 1992. *Men's Friendships.* Newbury Park, CA: Sage. An excellent collection of articles and research pertaining to men's friendships, intimacy, sexual boundaries, and gender roles.

PINES, AYALA. 1998. *Romantic Jealousy: Causes, Symptoms, Cures.* New York: Routledge. A compelling discussion of and practical guide for dealing with the psychology of jealousy through a series of real life vignettes. The author suggests that jealousy is a natural, universal, and positive trait—indeed, the "shadow of love." There is no real jealousy where there is no love.

LITERARY

CANFIELD, JACK, MARK HANSEN, MARK DONNELLY, CHRISSY DONNELLY, AND BARBARA DEANGELLS. 2003. *Chicken Soup For The Romantic Soul: Inspirational Stories About Love and Romance.* Deerfield Beach, FL: HCI Publishers. This addition to the popular Chicken Soup series of books consists of a variety of stories about love ranging from humorous and poignant to emotional stories dealing with the loss of love and a loved one to discovering and renewing an old love relationship. It contains stories from both celebrities and ordinary people who share their experiences of love.

HOOKS, BELL. 2000. *All About Love.* New York: HarperCollins. A feminist theorist known for her penetrating and eloquent critiques of racism and sexism takes on the elusive subject of love in today's society and culture. hooks uniquely weaves her childhood search for love with society's misuse and dire need of it. The author provides

an excellent analysis of love and sex, and details the problems that arise from the confusion between the two.

FILM

Wicker Park. 2004. An interesting film that looks at what people will do when love seems either too close or too far away to believe in. The film touches on obsession on many levels. A young advertising executive believes a woman he sees in a cafe in his long-lost love who walked out on him without a word two years earlier. His conviction leads to obsession, while he puts his life on hold as he practically stalks his old flame.

Love Actually. 2003. According to this film, love actually *is* all around. The movie follows the lives of eight very different couples, loosely connected by friends of friends, family, and next-door-neighbors, as they deal with their love lives in various loosely and interrelated stories all set during a frantic month before Christmas in London, England. These couples' lives and loves collide, interrelate, mingle, and climax on Christmas Eve with romantic, and sometimes funny and bittersweet consequences, for anyone lucky (or unlucky) enough to be under the spell of love.

INTERNET

http://www.lovingyou.com This site provides a library of love stories, poetry, cards and dedications. It also includes a collection of other resources such as relationship advice, chat groups, horoscopes, message boards, free postcards, love games, romantic recipes, date night ideas, and a variety of links to other romantic-oriented sites.

http://www.heartchoice.com This Web site deals with matters of the heart that affect our choices in love and love-related issues. It is divided into six rooms, including "Right Mate," "Marriage Room," and "Divorce Room." In each room, visitors can find articles by professionals, resources, and links to other helpful sites on the internet.

http://www.electpress.com/loveandromance/lrlinks.htm The Love and Romance Express Web site provides tips, techniques, and ready-to-use material with which to express your love and affection to someone special in your life. On this site, visitors will find a mountain of romantic information that will help one communicate her or his innermost feelings. Some of the resources provided on the site include love letters and poems, word expressions, a gift emporium, a love and romance book shop, a relationship gallery, love and romance connection, love and romance links, and 89 ways to say "I love you."

http://www.dataguru.org/love/lovetest/findings This Web site contains a 68-item questionnaire designed to assess love and its dimensions. With Robert Sternberg's and John Lee's theories of love in mind, students can elect to take either one or both versions of *The Love Test:* The Concept version, designed to assess what people think love is and/or the Experience version, designed to assess people's experience of love. You will receive an analysis of your (and your partner's) love styles after the test is completed.

IN THE NEWS

Arlington, Virginia

College women looking for Mr. Right might be looking in the wrong place if they expect to find him on campus, so said a 2001 study titled "Hooking Up, Hanging Out, and Hoping for Mr. Right: College Women on Dating and Mating Today." The 18-month study of the attitudes and values of today's college women regarding sexuality, dating, courtship, and marriage, conducted by a research team led by sociologists Norval Glenn and Elizabeth Marquardt, found that college women are confused about the dating—mating game on campus, protesting that they basically have two options: "hooking up" briefly with a guy for casual sex, or being joined at the hip and virtually living together. They feel they either have too little or too much commitment, neither of which contributes much to finding a husband while in college, a goal 63 percent of the women studied at least partly embraced.

Since this study, all indications are that students on college campuses either say they have no time for serious dating or they continue to be more likely to go out in groups—the group has replaced the dating couple as a form of dating—than spend time with one significant other. Moreover, according research reported in 2004 (Wolcott, 2004), it appears that the notion of dating continues to be a dated concept as college women and men continue the trend of *hooking up* for sex. Significant shifts in college life continue to impact dating and intimate relationships among students on today's campuses. For example, women continue to outnumber men on college campuses, and coed dorms are still the norm at many universities. Intentional or not, researchers suggest that this phenomenon facilitates hookups and lessens the need for couples to socialize on dates. In addition, they say that marriage is a less immediate goal for students today than in generations past. Indeed, people are marrying at later ages than in the past and thus are statistically less likely to have met in college. The increased mobility of students after college further lessens the incentive for developing long-term relationships (Lehman, 2004; Wolcott, 2004). The frame of mind about traditional dating seems to be "no time," "no money," and "no need" (Wolcott, 2004:1).

Speaking about "Hook Ups" on college campuses, journalist David Brooks (2002) reports that many young college women have told him that they do not have time for a serious relationship, so they "hook up." However, they do not simply jump from the group-gathering or dating stage directly to hooking up. Rather, Brooks found that there is an intermediate stage called the "Hang Out," as in, *"Do you want to come hang out in my room?"* (Brooks, 2002:1). These Hang Outs begin in the dorm room with conversations ranging in topic, and may consist of one or more such encounters until the two partners move from the Hang Out to the Hook Up phase by engaging in sexual intercourse. As with Hook Ups, there are many different kinds of Hang Outs with infinite and ill-defined gradations of seriousness.

The hookup trend has led some today to call for the return of dating and courtship rules and a renewed role of colleges and universities in regulating sexual behaviors on campus. To counter what the media has described as a "postdating" or "undating" culture, some conservative groups such as the Independent Women's Forum have advertised in college newspapers, urging students to "take back the date" by buying someone dinner or flowers (Lehman, 2004:1). It should be noted that dating on college campuses is not entirely obsolete today. African American students at Howard University in Washington, DC, for example, report that *hookup* has a dual meaning for them, referring either to a sexual encounter or to a romantic dinner date (Lehman, 2004).

WHAT WOULD YOU DO? If you are single and open to dating, would you "hook up" or have you ever "hooked up"? If you are married, would you have engaged in this form of dating when you were single? As a parent, would you encourage or discourage your offspring from engaging in such dating practices? Some men blame women for this trend of hooking up and accuse college women of having destroyed romance by making it transactional. Although some women might agree that hooking up takes romance out of dating and may indeed be considered transactional, they argue that men have been doing this all along, so why shouldn't women? What do you think? Which position do you take? Explain.

Dating, coupling, and mating—these concepts call up a variety of images. Close your eyes. What images come to mind when you think about dating in U.S. society today? Do you think of youth, "swinging," sex, "singles," fun, marriage, or love? Do you think of college campuses where hundreds of young women and men rub elbows, and do you think of couples "hooking up" and "hanging out?" Many of these are familiar images associated with dating and mate selection in the United States, images that are relentlessly transmitted through the media. Do these images match the reality of your life? Do they match the reality of the lives of most unmarried people? Do they match the reality of mate selection for your parents? Your grandparents?

As this mental exercise might have illustrated, for many people the idea of dating and mate selection brings to mind love, marriage, and family. Traditionally, we have assumed that attraction leads to dating, dating to love, and love to marriage. Indeed, we have assumed that the major function of dating is to teach people to form intimate heterosexual relationships and to prepare people for marriage. As the Glenn and Marquardt research presented in the In the News story opening this chapter suggests, this sequence of attraction, dating, love, marriage, and family is still espoused and held onto by many, particularly college women. And Glenn and Marquardt themselves appear to fall into this camp as well, given that in the study's recommendations these authors stress that young people must be guided with sensitivity and support toward marriage. They posit that socially defined dating and courtship is an important pathway to more successful marriages. However, this is frequently not the viewpoint for many others, as research since 2001 suggests. Indeed, an increasing number of people are either delaying marriage or not marrying at all. Some are pursuing alternatives to marriage (see Chapter 7). Others, as the research indicates, continue to simply "hook up" and/or "hang out" with little hope that it will lead to marriage, if that is their goal. For still others, age is an important factor that impacts the dating experience. For many later-life individuals who are dating, for example, especially older women, love, marriage, and/or a long-term relationship is not necessarily the goal of dating. (See section on "Dating in Later Life" later in this chapter.) In addition, not all dating is heterosexual. As we discuss more fully later in this chapter, lesbian and gay couples, like heterosexual couples, date for recreational and entertainment purposes, but the development of love and long-term relationships are most often the goal. And finally, many dating relationships are based solely on material or sexual interests, not on notions of romantic love.

So what does this mean for current relationships among both heterosexual and homosexual couples? Is today's pattern of mate selection a continuation of trends of the past? Are dating relationships and mate selection really that different today than they were 50 years ago? A century ago? Are they the same around the world? Specific courtship procedures, like mate selection generally, have varied considerably from one culture to another and from one historical period to another. In the next section we explore some of the historical and cross-cultural trends in courtship, dating, and mate selection.

MATE SELECTION IN CROSS-CULTURAL AND HISTORICAL PERSPECTIVE

Did you know that dating is not a common practice in most countries? In general, when we speak of **dating** we are referring to a process of pairing off that involves the open choice of mates and engagement in activities that allow people to get to know each other and progress toward coupling and mate selection. In places such as China, India, South America, and most countries in Africa, dating is very rare. In addition, it is forbidden in most Muslim countries, including Iraq, Egypt, Iran, and Saudi Arabia. Only in Western countries such as the United States, Great Britain, Australia, and Canada is dating a common form of mate selection. In these countries, dating is perhaps the single most important method by which people get acquainted with each other, learn to interact heterosexually, and select a mate.

Sociologists use the term **mate selection**[1] to refer loosely to the wide range of behaviors and social relationships individuals engage in prior to marriage and that lead to long- or short-term pairing or coupling. An essential element in mate selection is **courtship,** a process of selecting a mate and developing an intimate relationship. Dating is simply one stage in the courtship process, a process that involves an increasing level of commitment that might culminate with the ultimate commitment, marriage. Whatever its end, mate selection is an institutionalized feature of social life. According to family sociologist Ira Reiss (1980), all known societies exhibit some form of courtship, marriage, and family that ensures the production and nurturing of young people. The process of mate selection ranges from agreements and arrangements among religious or community leaders or the families of prospective partners to choices made by the partners themselves with only limited consultation with parents or other relatives.

Mate Selection Cross-Culturally

How do people around the world select a marriage or life partner? As we have indicated, in Western societies some form of courtship and dating is the major process used to select a mate. However, most of the world's societies do not have the "open" courtship and dating system common in the United States and other Western nations. Rather, mate selection varies across a continuum of practices around the world. These customs range from arranged matches by village shamans who match mates according to astrological signs; to contractual arrangements between families (usually fathers), in which a mate may be required to serve as an indentured servant to the bride's parents; to the outright purchase of a mate; to the seemingly free choice of individuals

---

[1]The term *mate selection* is used consistently in marriage and family literature in descriptions of the process of dating and marriage. However, we thought it was worth noting an interesting and somewhat humorous request from a reviewer of this textbook, who asked if we could change our language from *mate selection* to *partner selection* because the term *mate selection* sounds rather like "two lions looking for each other out in the Kalahari Desert." What do you think?

Dating and mate selection rituals vary across cultures. Some practices, like those of the Wodaabe of Niger, Africa, where men dress as females to attract brides, may seem strange to North Americans. However, the liberal, unchaperoned dating and mating practices of North Americans appear strange to those whose customs include arranged marriages and the absence of courting.

based on criteria ranging from notions of love to physical attractiveness to economic considerations. In some cultures, mate selection begins as early as infancy, in others the process begins at 8 or 9 years of age, and in still others it begins in late adulthood.

Much of the literature on mate selection cross-culturally differentiates methods of mate selection according to a traditional/nontraditional or industrialized/nonindustrialized dichotomy. In most traditional (nonindustrialized) societies, for example, family and/or religious groups try to preserve cultural consistency, family unity, friendship, and religious ties through arranged marriages. For instance, among the Hopi, ancient Chinese, Hebrews, and Romans, mating was arranged by the head of the kinship group, who continued to exercise some degree of control over young people even after they married. These practices continue in many traditional cultures today. For example, in India, arranged marriages, complete with ostentatious receptions and large dowries provided by the bride's family, continue to dominate the mate selection process. To preserve family loyalty, marriages continue to be carefully arranged, with brides and grooms rarely choosing their own mate. Because most Indians look on marriage as a lifelong commitment and view divorce as a shameful tragedy, it is customary to call on the wisdom of family elders and ask them to search out and investigate potential mates, whose family background is just as important as individual personality traits (Lessinger, 2002). Many young people not only expect their elders to choose a mate for them, but prefer that they do so.

In this mate selection process, there is little or no opportunity for the couple to interact with one another, get to know each other before the matching, or freely decide to be a couple, remain a couple, or to marry. The goal is marriage, and potential mates do not typically meet until the day of

the wedding and, most often, have not even seen pictures of one another. Families negotiate issues of money, status, health, and even physical appearance so as to make the best or most profitable match. Arranged marriages serve important social functions. For example, they serve to extend existing family units and they reinforce ties with other families in the community, thereby strengthening the social order and organization of the community (Ramu, 1989; Bhopal, 1997; Remez, 1998).

The advantages of arranged marriages have been pointed out both by researchers as well as by various individuals who participate in this cultural pattern. According to researchers on the subject, arranged marriages tend to be very stable. Divorce is almost unheard of, except in cases where one of the persons is infertile. In addition, although romantic love is not a consideration in these matches, love grows between the couple over the years; the relationships are generally very harmonious; and because there is no courtship period, premarital sexual intimacy and pregnancy are minimal to nonexistent. Many Indians contend that arranged marriages are more successful than marriages in the West, particularly given the latter's staggering divorce rates. They argue that romantic love does not necessarily lead to a good marriage, and often fails once the passion dissipates. Real love flows from a properly arranged union between two individuals (Mathur, 2006). Many others who participate in a system of arranged mate selection, particularly those who immigrate to Western societies, find it preferable to "free-choice" mate selection. Women in particular say that arranged mate selection spares them the "hassle" or "silliness" of dating such as spending an inordinate amount of time trying to attract, snare, and keep a man; worrying whether you are attractive enough or whether you are too fat; wondering whether the man will discard you without any concern for your self-respect. Unlike in American dating, for example, in arranged systems of mate selection there is very little risk of being rejected (Temple, 1998).

Not all traditional societies subscribe to a pattern of arranged mate selection. And increasingly in some nontraditional societies some form of arranged marriage might be found. Political, social, and/or economic change, especially industrialization, in cultures around the world has brought about some significant changes in mate selection customs cross-culturally. For example, in some cities in India today, mate selection, particularly among some in the middle class, combines the traditional aspects of arranged marriages with various nontraditional methods. Traditional matchmakers or marriage brokers are often replaced by advertisements in newspapers and the use of computer dating services to find a mate. This modern method of arranged marriages can also be found in the United States, where advertisements in immigrant newspapers like *India Abroad* give an indication of how the institution of arranged marriages is changing and adapting to Western (American) culture. This process involves parents introducing suitable, prescreened potential mates to their offspring, who are then allowed a courtship period to decide if they like each other well enough to marry. This method allows parents to retain some control in the mate selection process while accommodating their children's desires for a "love relationship," fueled by both the Indian and American media (Lessinger, 2002). Researcher Johanna Lessinger (2002) points out how, within the framework of arranged marriages, these ads show a noticeable decline in the importance placed on caste, language group, and even religion in mate selection if people are otherwise compatible in terms of education and profession. In addition, increasing attention is paid to individual and personal qualities such as a sense of humor or weight and beauty.

In some societies, a shortage of marriageable women has significantly changed traditional patterns of mate selection. For example, while mate selection customs in traditional Chinese society consisted of parent-arranged marriages in which the bride's parents received a "bride price," the mating process changed considerably during the 1990s, when there was a dramatic decrease in the number of marriageable women. According to Chinese census data, the ratio of single men to women was about three to one. Although in the past the majority of Chinese adults were married by age 30, in the mid-1990s more than 8 million Chinese in their 30s had not yet married, and the ratio of men to women in this age group was a staggering ten to one. Moreover, it is estimated that there will be as many as 40 million single men in China by 2020 (McCurry and Allison, 2004). Among other things, this shortage of women in the pool of potential mates has led to a shift from traditional means of mate selection to new and unconventional means (by Chinese standards) of finding a mate. For example, some Chinese men are placing ads in major newspapers begging women to respond, with some men indicating in their ads that they have a "good bathroom"—the way to a modern Chinese woman's heart is a spacious apartment and a decent salary (McCurry and Allison, 2004). In addition, Chinese women and men increasingly use computer dating services to help them find a mate and even the government has gotten into the mate selection process with several government-sponsored computer dating and matchmaking services (Murphy, 2002).

Not surprising, the majority of those using computer dating services are males (70 percent). The scarcity of Chinese women has given them a newly found edge in a mate selection process that historically treated them as chattel. The down side of Chinese women's leverage in mate selection, and a jolting reminder of their continued oppression, can be seen in an observation made by Chinese sociologists and journalists: "With men unable to find wives as sexual partners there could be an increase in prostitution, rape, and among men, suicide" (Shenon, 1994:5). In addition, as a result of the shortage of Chinese women, there has been a significant rise in the numbers of bounty hunters, who kidnap city women and deliver them to rural farmers desperate for brides and the increasing reliance of many rural Chinese men on the booming trade in kidnapped women in Vietnam and Korea for a source of brides.

A transformation of the mate selection process as a result of the glut of single men is occurring in other nations as well. For example, based on figures put out by the United Nations, India, with nearly 900 million people, has a sex ratio among the single population of 133 men to every 100 women. As in China, Indian custom values males. The custom of arranged marriages in India has survived migration and modernization, remaining central to the fabric of Indian society. Although no exact figures are available, some 95 percent of all marriages in India are arranged, even among those in the educated middle class. In cities such as New Delhi, families routinely place ads calling for Indian women who are university graduates, who are tall, and who have a fair complexion. Thus parents with dark-skinned daughters have a harder task getting their daughters married. Although India's system of mate selection has adjusted somewhat to modernization, especially among the middle class, for millions of Indian women arranged marriage remains the norm. It is what defines India's status quo, which is ultimately male-dominated (Mathur, 2006).

Mate Selection in the United States: A Historical Perspective

Historically, mate selection in the United States has been based on notions of romantic love, a sentiment shared by both women and men. For most contemporary Americans, choosing a mate is the culmination of the process of dating, although not necessarily its goal. Although dating, by definition, is supposed to be separate from selecting a marriage partner, many Americans nonetheless expect that dating will provide them with valuable experience that will help them make an informed choice of a marriage partner ("Hooking Up, Hanging Out," 2001; Whyte, 2001). However, courtship and dating are about much more than simply leading one to a marital partner. They are also about economic relationships, family control (or the lack thereof), power dynamics, competition, popularity, having sex, recreation, and consumption patterns (Ferguson, 2001). Dating has been described by some social commentators (for example, Waller, 1937) as a "courtship game" that has its own set of rules, strategies, and goals. Over time, changing gender norms and power dynamics have contributed to adjustments, adaptations, and/or modifications in the rules and expectations of mate selection, culminating in the process we recognize today. Thus, contemporary patterns of mate selection are linked to our past.

Early U.S. Courtship and the Development of Dating

As in many societies around the world, mate selection in the United States has always centered on heterosexual pairing or coupling. Because the process was meant to lead to legal marriage, historical descriptions and early mate selection research focused only on heterosexual couples. Thus, the discussion that follows is based on historical and research data for heterosexual mate selection.

In the early history of the United States, mate selection was characterized by community, family, or parental control over the process. It included an array of activities, almost all of which involved couples keeping company under family or community supervision. In colonial times marriage was considered of utmost importance in bringing order and stability to daily family living. Thus, there was a stress on coupling and mate selection. During this period, couples came together through a variety of means, including matrimonial advertisements and third-party go-betweens. Demographic considerations as well as very precise cultural norms often dictated the ways in which couples came together (Ramu, 1989). For example, due to a severe shortage of women in the American colonies, different patterns of mate selection evolved. Some men cohabited with Native American women; others imported brides from across the Atlantic. Moreover, the requirement of parental approval of a mate, especially among the prosperous classes, put further constraints on the mate selection process for young people. For instance, throughout this period, young people tended to marry in birth order, and marriage to cousins was not uncommon (Ferguson, 2001).

Although parents could not legally choose a partner for their offspring, they continued to exercise considerable power over mate selection well into the eighteenth century. Daughters, in particular, were strictly supervised. If a young man wanted to court a young woman, he had to meet her family, get the family's permission to court her, and be formally introduced to her. In fact, colonial law required a man to secure the permission of a woman's father before he could court her. Even after a man gained permission to court a particular woman and the two people were formally introduced, they were often chaperoned (especially upper-class women) at social events.

This process of mate selection eventually assumed a formal pattern referred to as "calling." In this form of mate selection, the initiative and control were in the hands of women. For example, a male suitor would be invited to call upon a female at her home. He was expected to come "calling" only if he was invited to do so. The invitation usually came from the mother of the woman, but eventually the woman herself extended the invitation. If a woman had several suitors at one time, a man might be told that the woman was not at home to receive him. In this instance, he was expected to leave his calling card. If this happened many times, it was meant to give the man the message that the woman was no longer interested in him (Whyte, 2001). If a serious relationship developed between a couple, they advanced from calling to "keeping company." Keeping company was a very formal and upright relationship that developed only after people had become attracted to or felt romantic about each other. According to Martin Whyte (2001), keeping company was a precursor of the twentieth-century custom of "going steady." Unlike in calling, couples who kept company were expected to be monogamous—that is, a woman was expected to keep company with only one man.

Keeping company involved a variety of activities, and couples kept company in some unique and interesting ways. For example, in colonial New England, unmarried couples practiced bundling, in which they spent the night in bed together, wrapped in bundling blankets or separated only by a long wooden bundling board down the middle of the bed. Only the outer garments could be removed, and the woman sometimes was placed in a sack sealed at the neck. This arrangement evolved in response to harsh winters and the difficulty of traveling, both of which made it difficult for a young man to return home after an evening of courting. Although such a practice would seem to discourage sexual contact, it apparently did not. Researchers on the topic estimate that approximately one-third of all eighteenth-century brides were pregnant at the time of their wedding.

Significant for the evolving pattern of dating in the United States were industrialization; the rise of free, public, coeducational, and mandatory schooling; and the mass movement of women (predominantly working-class women) into the mills and factories, allowing them increased contact with men. These events helped loosen parents' hold on their children. However, the mass production of the automobile probably had the most profound impact on the course of mate selection in North America. The automobile increased the mobility of young people and made a number of activities and places accessible to them. It also gave young people a new and private place for **getting together,** a pattern of dating that involves women and men meeting in groups, playing similar roles in initiating dates, and sharing equally in the cost of activities. Initiative and control in the mate selection process shifted from women to men. Men now asked women out, instead of waiting to be invited to call upon women. And courting moved from the parlor to the front seats and backseats of cars, resulting in the emergence and institutionalization of dating. Some social scientists have gone so far as to suggest that the automobile became, in some sense, a "bundling bed on wheels."

Dating in the United States: The 1920s through the 1990s By the 1920s, amid the increased affluence and leisure of the white middle classes, dating became the major method of mate selection in this country. The affluence and leisure of the white middle class gave rise to a youth culture whose members were relatively free to pursue their personal interests and social life. The rigid Victorian sex ethic (see Chapter 6) of the past was replaced with a new sexual intimacy as part of the courtship process. Couples took the initiative to get to know each other; they dated for fun, pleasure, relaxation, and recreation rather than with marriage as the primary goal. This new method of mate selection moved from one controlled by parents to one based on the open and mutual choice of peers.

The term *dating* originally referred to a specific date, time, and place of meeting. Thus, to speak of "dating" simply meant that two people of the opposite sex met at a mutually agreed-upon place and time and engaged in conversation. Dating has not remained constant over the decades. A variety of sociopolitical and historical factors such as the Great Depression of the 1930s, World War II, and the middle-class prosperity of the 1950s helped to shape dating as we know it today.

During the 1920s and 1930s dating was especially visible on college campuses. Although college students represented only a small and select portion of America's youth—primarily white and middle class—their activities and behavior became the model for other youth. In a pioneering study of college dating patterns, sociologist Willard Waller (1937) described dating on college campuses in the 1920s and 1930s as a competitive system that involved rating prospective partners based on clear standards of popularity. Material signs included owning an automobile, possessing the right clothing, belonging to the right fraternity or sorority, and, of course, having money. By the 1930s, **going steady**—an exclusive relationship with one person—was a clear and entrenched part of the mate selection process. It was an intermediate stage between casual dating and engagement. With the stock market crash of the late 1920s, the prohibition of liquor, and the depression of the 1930s, the national mood changed dramatically. However, the changes that occurred in popular culture, and their impact on mate selection and dating, continued to be visible in later decades.

During the 1940s and 1950s, dating spread from college campuses to most cultural groups in the United States. During this period, dating became essentially a filtering process in the sense that a person dated many people before settling down with one person. Only then did serious dating or courtship begin, with the ultimate goal being marriage. Acceptance of the idea that dating should culminate in marriage seems to be reflected in the fact that the 1950s had the highest percentage of married adults on record (Ramu, 1989). According to researcher Ersel LeMasters (1957), dating involved six stages of progressively deeper commitment from the first date in the junior high school years to marriage in the late teens or early 20s. Going steady, the third stage, occurred somewhere in the late high school years and involved a transition from the first two stages, the noncommitment of casual dating in junior high school and the random dating in the early high school years. The fourth stage occurred in college, when the couple entered into an informal agreement to date each other exclusively. The final two stages were engagement and marriage. This sequential model of dating tended to be more common among the middle classes than among other classes. According to researchers, lower-income and working-class youth tended to speed up the process, generally marrying at an earlier age.

Like other cultural patterns, dating patterns incorporate many of the values of the larger society. Thus, dating in the 1940s and 1950s clearly revealed U.S. society's emphasis on traditional gender roles, marriage, and the sexual double standard, with the male being the aggressor and the female playing a submissive role. For example, it was up to the male to initiate the date, and the female, in a dependent mode, had to wait to be picked or asked out. The male then was expected to pick up the female at her home, take her to a place of his choosing, pay for all expenses, and return her to her home at a respectable hour. The sexual double standard was also evident in the desired outcomes of dating. For males a primary expected outcome of dating was sex, whereas for females it was commitment and marriage. Although women exercised some degree of control through their ability to give or withhold their affection and their bodies, the absence of parental control and pressure to respond to a man's initiatives put women in a weaker position than they had been under the earlier system of "calling."

During the 1960s and 1970s, changing sexual norms, the increasing availability of contraceptives, a decline in parental authority, and the increasing activism of young people helped reverse the conservative dating trends of the 1940s and 1950s. Dating was transformed into a casual and spontaneous form of courtship. Greatly influenced by the women's movement, women no longer waited to be asked out but instead began to initiate dates and intimate relationships. There was an increasing emphasis on each person paying her or his own way. This was particularly common among middle-class youth, who were financially more independent than poor and working-class youths (Ramu, 1989). Paying one's own way was seen as a way of reducing the exploitation of young women by males who, in the past, expected sexual favors in return for the money spent on dating. By the late 1960s, people were delaying marriage to a later age. Sexual intimacy, which had traditionally been closely confined to marriage or the courtship period that led directly to marriage, became a common part of dating. The increasing separation of sex from marriage during the 1960s and 1970s was probably most evident in the rising number of couples living together outside legal marriage. During the 1970s, *cohabitation*—living together without being legally married—became a common extension of the traditional dating continuum, especially on college campuses among urban middle-class whites, and served as either an alternative or adjunct to steady dating and engagement (Gwartney-Gibbs, 1986). Cohabitation is discussed in detail in Chapter 7.

In the 1980s and 1990s, dating started at an earlier age and lasted longer than it had in previous generations. Adolescents as young as 13 years of age participated in some form of dating or pairing off, representing a decrease in age of 3 years since World War I. If we consider the fact that the average age at first marriage in the 1980s was somewhere around 25, then the average person in the United States was dating and courting for over 10 years before getting married. As the age at first marriage continued to increase slightly in the 1990s, more people were spending more time in a number of dating relationships with a variety of people before marrying, if they married at all.

The longer period of dating for most people also contributed to a change in the ways dating in the last two decades of the twentieth century was structured and perceived. There is some consensus among sociologists that although most Americans continued to find mates through dating of some sort in the 1990s, dating was no longer what it was prior to the mid-1960s. Not only had the structure and content of dating changed, but so had the terminology. The terms *dating* and *going steady* became passé, replaced with terms such as *seeing, being with, going with someone, hooking up,* and *hanging out.* Although some people continued to date in the traditional pattern, in which each person has specific roles to play, most people preferred to say they were "going out" with someone. According to some researchers, not only did the terminology of mate selection change, but dating itself became passé. These researchers argue that dating was replaced by informal pairing off in larger groups, often without the prearrangement of asking someone out (Whyte, 2001; Peterson, 2001).

Contemporary Trends in Dating Although the term *dating* was less commonly used in the 1980s and 1990s, the practice nonetheless continues, albeit in different forms. For example, almost 60 percent of American adults are currently engaged in some form of dating or, at the very least, are interested in dating. By the time they reach their 16th birthday, 78 percent of girls and 83 percent of boys have been out on at least one date. Today, dating is based far more on

Dating is no longer necessarily the means to the end of marriage. Getting together, hanging out, or generally sharing fun activities on a date is now an end in itself.

mutuality and sharing than on traditional gender roles. The 1990s trend of dating as recreation and entertainment, with an emphasis on sociability, continues to cause a change in the pattern or progression of intimacy and commitment from initial meeting to marriage. Describing contemporary mate selection in the United States, a colleague of ours commented, with some degree of frustration: "People don't date anymore: they just get together; they just have sex, live together, and then go their separate ways." Although this was a nonscientific observation, it is nonetheless fairly consistent with scientific research that reports that contemporary dating patterns include considerably more casual sexual involvements and fewer committed relationships than in the past. Recall, for example, the research reported on at the beginning of this chapter. As was pointed out, women and men on college campuses today "hang out," spending time together, but rarely do they "date" in the old-fashioned sense. On the one hand, the dating pattern might be a "hookup," wherein two people get together briefly for casual sex without any emotional commitment. On the other hand, a college couple who is "dating" is sometimes in a fast-moving, highly committed relationship that includes sexual activity, sleeping at one another's dorm most nights, studying together, sharing meals, and more. Rarely, though, does it involve going out on "dates" ("Hooking Up, Hanging Out," 2001; Snapshots: Come Here Often? 2002; Lehman, 2004; Wolcott, 2004).

This dating pattern on college campuses notwithstanding, in general young adults believe current patterns of dating are more natural and healthier than they were in the past. Although, as in every generation, some couples still follow a traditional pattern, for many couples dating, sexual intimacy, living together, becoming engaged, and sometimes having a child have become a common part of heterosexual relationships that may or may not culminate in marriage. Moreover, today people are ever more aware that mate selection is not just a heterosexual phenomenon, nor is dating just for the young at heart. Dating (or whatever term we choose to use) involves lesbians and gays, the very young

as well as an increasing number of older people who either have never married or are divorced or widowed. Dating among older adults differs somewhat from dating among high school and college students, but many similarities exist. This is especially the case in terms of the purpose of dating.

Dating among the general population, like on college campuses, has become very time-contained, sometimes existing only for the moment for sexual or recreational purposes, with no pretense that it is a prelude to courtship or marriage. New dating trends in the twenty-first century have led some observers to suggest dating is no longer the self-evident activity that it was in the past. That is, what constitutes dating today has become so ambiguous that many singles, after "getting together" with someone they like, find themselves wondering afterward if it was a date or not. According to Jeff Wise, a self-defined "media coordinator" for the American Dating Association based in Los Angeles, there is such a thing today as a *nondate date*. When two people go out, if one person is not aware of the romantic intentions of the other, then it is a nondate date. Risk avoidance is at the base of this kind of getting together—avoiding getting hurt if the person you are getting together with ultimately rejects you (McKeough, 2001). Although some people are fed up with the direction of contemporary dating and yearn for dating patterns of old, most social demographers predict a continuation of the current trends, which they contend are pervasive and persistent across advanced Western societies (Popenoe and Whitehead, 2002).

Indeed, many scholars and others who study contemporary American dating patterns suggest that today's changed patterns of dating may be due to the reduced pressure to marry. Dating today, they say, is not oriented to marriage as it was in the past. The changing rules of dating or lack thereof have left many people confused about dating as the various studies of dating on college campuses suggest. However, this confusion in not limited to the young on college campuses, nor is it limited to fast-track young people in corporate America who are dating. As increasingly more older adults return to the dating scene, they are confronted with a different (sometimes radically different) oftentimes confusing set of rules and expectations about dating in today's society.

Although much of the discussion of contemporary dating patterns (as in the past) is descriptive of the white middle class, with some limitations it can be generalized to other groups. In the next section we discuss dating patterns among later-life adults. In addition, later in this chapter we pay particular attention to the intersection of race, class, gender, and sexual orientation in patterns of dating.

Dating Among Later-Life Adults

Typically in the United States when we think about dating, coupling, and mate selection we focus our attention on the young. However, dating and mate selection occurs throughout the human life cycle, albeit a somewhat different process depending on one's age. According to a growing body of research and popular articles on dating, the dating game changes significantly after the age of 40. In a dating world that has changed tremendously over the last several decades, the standard parameters of dating from your teens to your mid-20s are no longer the norm. For example, in 2005, Match.com, an online dating, relationships, singles, and personals service, reported that registrations on their dating Web site by people 50 years old and older had increased 340 percent since 2000 (Jayson, 2005).

The proportion of older people in American society has increased dramatically in recent decades. As life expectancy increases in years, the percentage of older Americans is expected to increase to around 20 percent of the population by the year 2030 (U. S. Census Bureau, 2003). Not only are Americans living longer and healthier lives, as they age they are more actively engaged in or looking for meaningful intimate relationships. Today, more than 40 million Americans over 40 are single, divorced, widowed, or never married. Not that all of them are seeking mates, but many are. Of these singles, more than one-half (25 million) are women, many of whom are more fit and health-conscious than their parents' generation, have a younger mind-set, and are seeking dating partners at record numbers. Traditionally, young women dated with the ultimate goal of getting married and having children. However, as women age, these become less and less an issue; they are no longer the primary focus and reason for dating. But reentering the dating scene when one is older is not an easy matter as the rules of the game have changed significantly over the past decade or more. Paula England, a 55-year-old Stanford University sociology professor and divorcée, for example, speaking of her dating experiences after her divorce, says that what she experienced after her divorce, was the feeling of being back in high school again, but the rules and conventions of dating had changed and she didn't know them (quoted in Jayson, 2005:4).

Older people, like their younger counterparts, date, fall in love, and behave romantically. Older adults tend to view romance similarly to younger people—consisting, for instance, of intimate activities such as candlelit dinners, flowers, candy, and other gifts. For many older men, as for many younger men, sex and romance are closely linked. However, there are unique challenges that older adults face that distinguish their dating experiences from those of younger people. Women, it seems, especially later-life women, face unique relational challenges in today's dating scene. For example, in a recent study of the dating and courtship experiences of 15 women 60 to 75 years of age, the researchers found three major themes: the need for independence, the need for companionship, and gender role conflict between dating partners. The dating experience for these women created dialectical tensions between themselves and their dates. The strongest tension perhaps was the need for independence versus the need for companionship. The women in this study clearly enjoyed and desired the companionship of their male dates, but they also prided themselves on their independence and did not want to give it up (Walker, Dickson, and Hughes, 2005).

In general, the women in the study said that they wanted to date; they enjoyed dating, but they did not see marriage as a viable option. Unfortunately, this created relational problems for them because most of the later-life men they met wanted to get married. Some of them reported losing good dating partners and losing very satisfying relationships due to their refusal to get married or cohabit. Interestingly,

these women chose their desire to remain independent over their need for companionship. They were willing to be lonely rather than give up their independence or become a caretaker for an older partner. The paradox is that the women also wanted to maintain the relationship at its present level of intimacy while not committing to a long-term, relationship (Walker, Dickson, and Hughes, 2005). For older women and some older men as well, remarriage, in their view, is fraught with complications, such as the eventual inheritances of children and risks to pensions and alimony of widows and divorcées. For these older adults, then, rather than mingle assets, they choose not to marry (Kilborn, 2004).

As we have indicated, dating today, whether among young or later-life couples, is much more casual, with fewer conventions and formalities. This means that women across age groups are setting the boundaries from whether he will open the door, whether to kiss on the first date, or whether to marry or not. This fact notwithstanding, even though older women are very often confident about what they want in an intimate relationship, not all are necessarily secure in the dating realm and some might not even be sure of what they want. Whatever the case, for those older women wishing to date, a significant barrier to dating and romance is the rather short supply of older men to date. According to U.S. Census Data, there are 20.6 million women 65 and older and 14.4 million men, or ten women for seven men. This means that many women are removed from the dating equation, not by choice but by chance. However, whether by choice or by chance, a good number of older women are finding that they can readily do without men. Some say they are simply looking for a date or for friends but not a commitment. Some older women are looking for marriage; others want a relationship without legal entanglements; and still others just want companionship (U.S. Census Bureau, 2000; Kilborn, 2004; Jayson, 2005).

To be sure, for singles of both genders, the dating game is more complex once you mature. Potential matches tend to have a past—children, former spouses, maybe old flames that have not quite died out. The need for understanding and compromise may be greater. With women outliving men and given that many older men often seek younger women to date and marry, there is a growing trend for older women to date younger men. A survey released in 2005 found that 56 percent of women and 51 percent of men say its acceptable for a potential date to be up to 10 years younger. Perhaps with a change in societal views of what are acceptable partnerships, older women will have a larger pool of eligible males to date in the future (Jayson, 2005).

Functions of Dating: Past and Present

Of all the stages in the mate selection process, dating is the one that carries the least commitment to continuing the relationship. So why do people date? The reasons are many and varied; however, researchers have identified some specific functions dating has traditionally fulfilled for the individual and, ultimately, for society's continuity. The meaning and functions of dating, of course, depend in large part on the person's age and sex and the particular stage in the dating

Dating in the twenty-first century takes many forms. Today it is not unusual to see homosexuals as well as heterosexuals enjoying each other's company. Some individuals prefer to share fun activities within a group setting.

process. One researcher, G. N. Ramu (1989), summarizes the functions of dating in terms of socialization, recreation, status grading and achievement, and mate selection leading to marriage. As you consider these functions of dating, bear in mind that they have been formulated primarily with young heterosexual couples in mind.

Socialization   The socialization function usually occurs in the early stages of dating. Through dating, people learn the norms, roles, and values that govern heterosexual relationships. One impact of the women's movement has been to change the ways in which some women and men define their roles in intimate relationships. Thus, for example, if a man finds he cannot accept an aggressive, self-confident, and self-reliant partner, or a woman finds that she will not accept a passive role, dating helps them to discover this and to realize what kind of roles they are willing to play in an intimate relationship. Dating is a competitive situation in which an individual can test and refine a number of interactive skills with respect to the opposite sex. For young people, dating also provides an opportunity for sexual experimentation and growth. Obviously, the socialization function of dating is not limited to heterosexual or young couples, nor does it end in our youth. Therefore, socialization continues to be an important function of dating in same-sex relations and as we grow older.

In addition, the socialization function of dating can serve to enhance the ego or sense of self. According to anthropol-

ogist Margaret Mead (1935), a major way that we develop a personality and gain a sense of self is through our relationships with other people. If a positive self-concept is attributable in part to successful experiences with others, then an important stage in an individual's personality development can occur during successful dating experiences. If the dating experience goes well, it can have the impact of enhancing our self-confidence and self-esteem.

Recreation   For most people, regardless of age, gender, and sexual orientation, dating provides an opportunity to relax, have fun, and enjoy themselves in the company of someone they like. However, social scientists distinguish between adolescent and adult patterns when discussing the recreational function of dating. The assumption is that dating in adolescence serves a recreational function (the seeking of fun and thrills): It is often an end in itself. In contrast, in adulthood it involves courtship, often directed toward finding a marriage partner.

Status Grading and Achievement   Most Americans view dating in positive terms. Thus, the more one dates, the more likely one's status and popularity will increase. Status grading and achievement in dating is a process whereby women and men are classified according to their desirability as dating partners. For example, very often on college campuses, people try to date those people who are rated as the most desirable on campus—females seeking to date the most popular athletes on campus and males seeking to date the most attractive females, to boost their own status and prestige.

Mate Selection   Mate selection is no longer the primary objective of dating, as we have said, but it continues to be the primary strategy for mate selection in the United States. The increasing divorce rates notwithstanding, Americans are still highly committed to marriage. Although dating thus initially brings people together simply for recreational and romantic purposes, over time it can become a means of socialization for marriage. An accumulation of dating experiences helps those who want to marry in their efforts to find a marriage partner. Given the longer dating period today, dating continues to fulfill the function that researchers S. A. Lloyd and R. M. Cote (1984) described as **anticipatory socialization**—socialization that is directed toward learning future roles, in this case marriage roles.

A person's primary reason for dating will influence that person's behavior in the dating relationship. The general change in the reasons that Americans date accounts for the significant changes we see in contemporary patterns of dating. Some researchers have suggested that a person's motivation for dating can be placed on a continuum ranging from completely expressive (dating as an end in itself) to completely instrumental (dating as a means to some larger goal). In addition, a person's emotional involvement in the dating experience may also be placed on a continuum ranging from no emotional involvement to complete emotional involvement. A person's place on these two continua is determined by her or his motive. If the primary motive is mate selection, the person will probably have strong instrumental orientation (dating should lead to marriage) and strong emotional involvement. In contrast, if the motivation is either recreation or status achievement, the individual is likely to have both low instrumental orientation and low emotional involvement. This research suggests that dating couples will

seek to continue their relationship if either the emotional involvement or the instrumental orientation is high.

THE INTERSECTIONS OF RACE, GENDER, CLASS, AND SEXUAL ORIENTATION

As with other social relationships, our dating experiences emerge from the social, political, and economic structure of a society. As we discussed in Chapter 1, race, class, gender, and sexual orientation are basic and central categories of experience that set particular limits on behavior and engender specific kinds of experiences. If we are to move away from an analysis that stems only from the experience of the white middle and upper classes, we must consider how race, class, gender, and sexual orientation influence dating and mate selection patterns.

We cannot provide a comprehensive picture of dating and mate selection for all groups, but we can provide some insight into these processes for some groups. Unfortunately, the literature in this area continues to be highly limited. Most of the literature on dating among groups of color deal with African Americans. Little work has been done on courtship among Native Americans, Asian Americans, and Latinas/Latinos. For example, although we know that family networks continue to make up the fabric of contemporary Native American social organization and are central to the day-to-day functioning of Native Americans, we do not know how these families are formed vis-à-vis courtship and mate selection. Nor do we know whether Native Americans have been affected by the larger cultural and changing patterns of dating and courtship. And despite the existence of a growing body of data on lesbian and gay relationships, most studies focus specifically on sexual behavior rather than more generally on the whole process of mate selection. For other groups such as Asian Americans and Latinas/os, the sparse literature on dating for these groups consists almost entirely of research, discussions, and data on interracial marriage among these groups with little or no discussion of patterns of dating and mate selection that may or may not lead, for instance, to marriage—interracial or otherwise.

Dating Patterns Among African Americans

The practice of dating among African Americans varies by region, historical period, social class, and age. According to Robert Staples (1991), a sociologist who has written widely on African American singles and mate selection, in the past, when African Americans lived in small, cohesive communities in the rural and urban South, what might be called dating behavior centered on the neighborhood, church, and school. As African Americans began to move to urban areas outside the South, however, the greater anonymity associated with urban life modified their dating patterns. The school and house party became major centers for heterosexual fraternizing, particularly among the lower class. Dating patterns among the middle class did not differ significantly from those of the larger society and included activities like movies, dances, and bowling.

According to most research, traditional dating patterns among blacks, as among other groups, is more prevalent among the middle and upper class than the lower class. For the African American middle class, dating is typically sequential, occurring over the course of several stages: getting together in the teen years; keeping company on the porch and eventually in the house under family supervision; group dating; and finally, individual one-on-one dating, engagement, and most often marriage (Scott, 1988). Research comparing black and white dating attitudes and expectations indicate that blacks are less flexible and more traditional than whites in several aspects of dating-related attitudes and expectations. For example, whites typically endorse more flexible role patterns in dating and seem less concerned with a traditional dating protocol (such as the expectation that males will bear the costs of dating) than do blacks (Ross and Davis, 1996). This fact notwithstanding, since the 1970s, blacks, like whites and several other groups, have been delaying marriage until later ages, which means they are dating, or getting together, for longer periods of time than in the past.

According to Robert Staples (1991), the historically low **sex ratio**—the number of men to every 100 women—in the African American community has traditionally limited the dating and mate selection options of African American women. Some researchers have suggested that the numerical scarcity inflates male value, giving them a decided advantage in the dating–mating game (Tucker and Mitchell-Kernan, 1999). Thus, African American men, whose marriage market value has been enhanced by their scarcity, apparently believe they can be "choosier" in terms of mate selection. The consequence is that many African American women who want to date may find themselves either left out of the game completely or having to settle for far less than their ideal. Moreover, compounded by the fear of sexually transmitted diseases, particularly AIDS, mating and dating has taken on new forms to facilitate the meeting of compatible members of the opposite sex. These and other factors appear to have contributed to a proliferation, in the 1980s and 1990s, of singles clubs and dating services aimed at African American urban professionals.

In addition, African American singles relied increasingly on the use of personal ads in African American and general singles magazines. A popular place to meet a potential mate, which continues today, became the "happy hour" at popular bars frequented by African American professionals. The black church also remains an important place to meet a dating partner. It seems that a large number of African American professionals are coming back to the black church and, according to Staples, these "buppy" (the acronym for "black urban professional") churches tend to sponsor special events that bring single people together for fun and relaxation. Some churches have even organized a singles auxiliary and publish a singles newsletter.

As African American women age, the already small pool of eligible males available to date shrinks even further. The perception among older women is that those single men who are out there are either dating younger women or dat-

Increasingly, African American women, especially the successful African American woman, say it is tougher than ever to find a mate and establish a long-term relationship. Many are taking an active approach to meeting men, often going to "singles socials" and other events to meet a potential mate.

ing white women. At the other end of the age continuum, research has found that African American high school students who date place more emphasis on materialistic factors than personality factors when choosing a partner, whereas white students rank personality traits more highly. However, at the college level, there does not appear to be a specific pattern of traits that African American students look for in a dating partner (Smith, 1996).

A notable characteristic of contemporary African American dating patterns is the significant increase in interracial dating, especially on college campuses. This pattern is attributed, in part, to the fact that many middle-class and high-status African Americans live and/or work in worlds that tend to be racially mixed or where there are few other African Americans. This has important implications for whom they meet and socialize with, which, in turn, is an important factor in the formation of dating and intimate relationships. It is also attributed to the desegregation of many of the nation's public school systems, workplaces, and other social settings. It is probably also due to the liberation of many white youth from parental control and the rejection of racist values conveyed throughout society. In the case of African American women, dating across race is also believed to be due, in some part, to the low sex ratio. In general, both within and outside the African American community, interracial relationships are viewed as a positive step toward smoother race relations by some, and as "sellout" behavior and denial of racial heritage by others. In any event, rates of interracial marriage continue to be a very low percentage of all marriages, with African American women being the least likely group of women to date and/or marry outside of their racial or ethnic group— further evidence that dating does not necessarily lead to marriage.

The intersections of race, gender, age, sexual orientation, and class are perhaps nowhere more apparent than in the dating patterns of heterosexual African American women. For example, the dating scene today for many African

American women, especially professional women, is consistently referred to in newspaper headlines as: "The Black Woman's Quandary" (see, for example, Jenkins, 2005). All dressed up but nowhere to go, the authors say, "successful sisters face a particularly tough challenge finding dates." Far outnumbering African American men, successful African American women are particularly hard pressed to find a date. According to historian Darlene Clark Hine, these women's affluence and success further separates them from potential dates and mates (quoted in Jenkins, 2005:64). Some of these women, like their predecessors in the 1980s and 1990s, are dating and marrying blue-collar or less affluent men. Others are said to be reluctantly looking outside the race for dates. Still others have quit the dating game altogether. This "quandary" has left some in the African American community wondering what this all means for the next generations' black middle class if large numbers of black America's best and brightest women are not finding dates and mates or are marrying so late that they have few children or none at all (Jenkins, 2005).

Most women and men of every racial or ethnic group today seem to have trouble hooking up and staying matched, but African Americans face special challenges that have led to the alleged "quandary" in their dating and mate selection patterns. Not only is there a significant shortage of African American men to date based on the low sex ratio, but African American women face competition not only from each other but from Latinas, white females, and Asian females as well. Although the women of all racial and ethnic groups bemoan the shortage of available men, it is a stark reality for African American women. For instance, whereas Latinos, white males, and Asian males in their 20s significantly outnumber the women in their racial and ethnic groups, there are only 91 black men for every 100 black women (see Figure 5.1). According to Darlene Clark Hine (and others), important social and lifestyle differences have also affected the ratio of marriageable (or dateable) African American men. The usual litany enumerated includes high rate of involvement with the criminal justice system, violence that claims young black male lives at disproportional rates, more black male high school dropouts, and fewer black men in college than their female counterparts (Jenkins, 2005:65). It is important to note that African American men are certainly not the only group afflicted by these societal problems. However, African American women feel these issues more acutely because of the numbers.

The Impact of Gender

Perhaps more than most relationships, dating is affected by gender roles and stereotypes. Society traditionally has conveyed certain messages concerning dating: We should mate with the opposite sex; women are supposed to want a masculine man; men are supposed to want a feminine woman; men should initiate the relationship and sexual behavior, although women may guide them by flirting; men should be dominant and women submissive; and sexuality is supposed to be more important to men, and love or commitment to women. As we shall see later in this chapter, although these messages are still widespread, they frequently do not reflect the realities of contemporary relationships.

Discussing gender differences in dating in the context of social-learning theory, social scientists contend that men's dating scripts focus on planning and paying for the date as well as initiating sexual behavior, whereas women's scripts focus on enhancing their appearance, making conversation, and controlling sexual behavior. However, more women today reject a passive role in their intimate relationships and seek to equalize more control in the dating relationship by initiating and paying for dates (Clark, Shaver, and Abrahams, 1999). On the other hand, many of us apparently have learned traditional sexual scripts well. For example, as you read in Chapter 4, researchers have documented that women and men have different orientations to romantic love and that this difference continues when they consider a prospective mate (Dion and Dion, 1998). Women and men have also differed in terms of the characteristics they look for in a mate. Women, on the one hand, prefer men who are well educated and have financial stability. Women tend to put less emphasis on aesthetic concerns and place greater value on qualities of a prospective mate such as working, saving, and paying bills. Men, on the other hand, especially upwardly mobile men, emphasize physical and sexual attractiveness (Fischer and Heesacker, 1995).

Other gender differences in dating and courtship behavior include differences in how women/girls and men/boys signal their interest in each other and initiate relationships. Recent research confirms the findings of earlier studies, which found that the genders differ in various tactics used to initiate courtship behavior. For instance, eye contact is the most frequently used initiation tactic for both genders, but women use indirect or subtle tactics more often than men, while men engage in direct verbal tactics more often than women. Men are also more confident in initiating a relationship and a greater percentage of men than women

FIGURE 5.1

SEX RATIOS BY RACE AND ETHNICITY

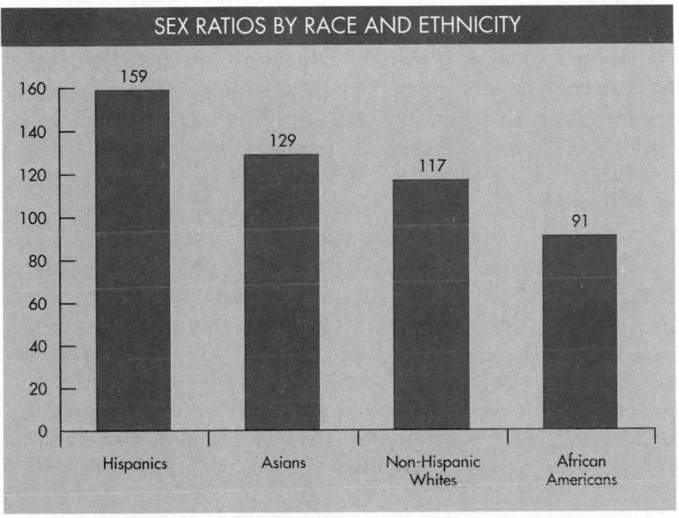

Source: Maureen Jenkins, 2005, "Black Woman's Quandry." *Chicago Sun-Times* (December 7): 64–65. U.S. Census Bureau, 2006, *Statistical Abstract of the United States* (Washington, DC: U.S. Government Printing Office): 15, Table 13.

seek sexual intimacy in the beginning stage of their romantic relationships. On the other hand, because of a fear of being rejected, women take a more tentative approach to initiating relationships and are more likely to rely on the man to initiate the relationship (de Weerth and Kalma, 1995; Clark, Shavers, and Abrahams, 1999). Interestingly, according to one set of researchers, when presenting themselves, men stressed personal characteristics traditionally interpreted as female-valued (such as tenderness) more often than women did, whereas women stressed characteristics traditionally interpreted as male-valued (such as being prestigiously occupied) more than men did. This apparent reversal in gender roles in dating can be linked to the changing function of courtship behavior and various societal developments relative to women and men's roles in the larger culture (de Weerth and Kalma, 1995).

Americans are not the only people who display gender differences in dating and courtship attitudes and behavior. According to a study of 37 cultures in 33 countries, regardless of the culture, most men want intellectually smart, good-looking, young wives. Women, too, want husbands who are intellectually smart, but they also want them to be a bit older, ambitious, and have bright financial prospects (United Press International, 1990). One implication of such studies is that the social construction of a dating reality, like other traditional realities, exaggerates differences between the sexes and constrains behaviors within the sexes.

The Impact of Social Class on the Dating Process

Although dating as a method of mate selection is a universal practice in the United States, social class, like race and gender, profoundly impacts whom we meet, whom we are attracted to, and who is available to date. As with race, there is a scarcity of research specifically focused on dating practices across class. The research that does exist is generally dated and focuses almost entirely on the "premarital" sexual behavior of lower-class youth. One comes away from this research with the sense that dating is essentially a middle- and upper-class phenomenon, and that mate selection is somehow problematic among the lower classes, especially among people of color in this class, but with little or no data or understanding of the *process of dating* for the two classes at each end of the class continuum: lower and upper classes. One thing we do know is that although social classes are not sharply delineated in the United States, people's location in the class structure vis-à-vis factors such as race, education, income, and occupational status is related to differences in attitudes, values, approach to life, behavior, and access to the means necessary to realize one's goals in life. So, how does social class affect dating and mating behavior? Individuals from similar social class backgrounds share similar interests and goals, which are the bases for dating and mate selection choices. Thus, most people in the United States date and marry within their social class.

Upper Class Dating within the upper strata of U.S. society tends to be far more regulated than it is for other classes.

According to the literature (for example, Whyte, 1990), children in upper- and middle-class families are more likely than children from working-class and poor families to be socialized to delay gratification and focus on education and career preparation rather than romance and sex. Thus, upper- and middle-class women and men tend to start dating later, delay intimacy, and marry later. This appears true across race. For instance, data from a study of upwardly mobile African American women reveal that these women, more often than not, were consciously socialized to delay dating and serious relationships until after they had completed a college education (Scott, 1988).

Moreover, social class is related to dating and mate selection in a number of other ways. Individuals from the middle and upper classes, for example, are generally viewed as more attractive dating partners and potential marital partners than those from the lower classes. Furthermore, upper-class families still exert considerable influence over mate selection. They tend to use their considerable resources to influence their offspring either to delay dating and marriage or to marry someone they consider a suitable mate and match for the family. For example, the 1990s on-again, off-again romance between the late John F. Kennedy, Jr. (son of the late president John F. Kennedy and the late Jacqueline Kennedy Onassis), and Daryl Hannah (a movie actress), for many years was reported to have been greatly influenced by Jacqueline Kennedy Onassis, who allegedly did not think that Hannah was right for her son. Thus, although the highly publicized couple romanced together over a number of years and Hannah allegedly pushed for a wedding, the couple never made it to the altar. John Jr. subsequently married the late Carolyn Bessette, an affluent and brainy suburbanite whose extraordinary looks, sophistication, and ambition, according to insiders, were strikingly similar to those of the late Jacqueline Kennedy Onassis (Bumiller, 1996). Many observers of the "rich and famous" claim it was Jacqueline Kennedy Onassis's disapproval of Hannah and her quiet influence over her son that prevented the two from marrying.

Many of the activities of young people in this class are closely supervised by parents or other adults who chaperone the young people's activities. Dates are sometimes arranged by parents, and dating partners are almost always selected from within their own ranks. Seldom do upper-class members date someone from the middle or lower classes, and dating a number of partners is the norm. Adults also exercise more control over the sexuality of young people than is true of other classes. When upper-class women reach 18, they are formally presented to society. After this "coming out," they engage in a number of activities, during which they encounter a number of eligible men. If the couple becomes engaged, the man presents the woman with an expensive ring, and the engagement is announced in the society pages of the print media. The wedding, which is generally a very formal and often lavish affair, is attended by the rich and famous, and is usually announced in the newspapers and the electronic media. For example, the 1999 wedding of Melissa Rivers, which is said to have cost her mother, comedienne Joan Rivers, over one million dollars, was attended by a long list of the "Who's Who" among this country's elite and celebrities.

Middle Class Dating behaviors among middle-class youths, at least traditionally, are fundamentally no different from those of the upper classes. Middle-class dating behaviors are likewise generally supervised by adults, although not to the same degree as are those of their wealthier counterparts. Dating activities among middle-class couples include going to sports events and engaging in sporting activities such as ice-skating and tennis, going to the beach, going out to dinner, and entertaining at home. On the one hand, going steady remains common among some segments of the middle classes and usually leads to an engagement. Engagements of middle-class couples, like those of wealthy couples, are usually announced in the print media. Weddings are fairly elaborate, expensive, and often performed in a church or synagogue. On the other hand, contemporary dating and mate selection patterns among middle-class youth include increasing freedom from parents' watchful eyes and supervision. For example, proms and homecoming parties often include a continuation of the celebration in rented hotel rooms and suites, where both same-sex groups as well as mixed-sex groups spend the rest of the night together, presumably under the watchful eyes of adults, although very often they are unsupervised. In addition, in some middle-class communities, **cruising**—where a group of teenagers (usually males) pack into a car and drive around the neighborhood looking for females to pick up—is a popular pattern in the mate selection process. Both these patterns of contemporary dating have caused parents and other community members some degree of alarm. In both cases, the youth involved are often accused of engaging in drinking alcoholic beverages, public littering and loitering, and loud and sometimes rude behavior.

Although the term *mixer*—an informal school dance designed to bring together people of both sexes so they can get acquainted with one another—may seem outdated to some (it was a method of mate selection common in the 1960s and 1970s), it is still a method used in heterosexual mate selection by both the middle and working classes.

Lower Class Most research on dating suggests that lower-class families tend to exercise the least control over mate selection. Dating among this group is most often very informal and often includes "hanging out"—getting out of often small and cramped living quarters in favor of such places as bowling alleys and local bars. Serious, unsupervised dating usually begins in the midteens and is most often exclusive or monogamous. Lower-class couples often skip the engagement phase and progress directly to marriage. When engagements occur, they are not usually announced in the press, and weddings are often small, inexpensive, and informal. Sometimes they are conducted in the home of one of the partners.

It should be noted that just as the lines separating various social classes are often blurred, so too are methods of dating and mate selection across class. Thus, methods of dating and mate selection are similar and sometimes overlap across social classes. For example, formal rites of passage such as coming-out parties can be found among both the middle and upper classes. Many middle-class groups present their daughters to the community and society by means of coming-out parties to signal the daughters' readiness to date and assume other adult responsibilities. In some middle-class African American communities, for example, this coming-out party is often in the form of a cotillion—a fairly elaborate formal affair and a very significant event in the life of a young middle-class African American female. Such an event involves family and friends and can cost parents several thousand dollars as their daughters make this very public and symbolic transition to adulthood. Likewise, in some Latino/a communities, the *quinceañera* represents a social and religious coming-out celebration for Latinas. It includes a religious mass followed by a reception for the young woman, who may begin dating after her *quinceañera*. Traditionally, these rites of passage activities have focused exclusively on females. However, recently, among some middle-class African Americans, the *botillion* has emerged as a rite of passage for African American males. As with the cotillion, parents present their offspring—in this case, their sons—to the community and society to signal their readiness to date and assume more adult responsibilities. Moreover, other methods such as cruising, school and church mixers, and hanging out are methods found among the lower and working classes as well as the middle classes, albeit sometimes in modified forms.

LESBIAN AND GAY DATING

We know very little about the dating and mating behavior of lesbians and gays because relatively little research has been done specifically in this area. Moreover, since the first edition of this textbook in the early 1990s, the research that exists continues to deal primarily with lesbian and gay sexual behavior and lifestyles. Because society continues to stigmatize homosexual behavior, much mate selection behavior is carried out in the privacy of homes and recreational establishments frequented only by lesbians and gays. According to the 2000 Census, there are almost 600,000 same-sex couples in the United States. Put another way, approximately 44 percent of all lesbians and 28 percent of gays are currently in a "partnered" relationship (Black et al., 2000). Like heterosexual couples, most lesbians and gays date for recreational and entertainment purposes, but the development of love relationships is also an important goal. In this regard, the function of dating for some lesbian and gay couples is to find a mate with whom they can share love, psychological and economic support, and perhaps children (Parrot and Ellis, 1985). Because lesbians and gays are legally prohibited from marrying in all but one state in the Unite States, for some lesbians and gays the ultimate goal of mate selection is a type of symbolic marriage, such as a domestic partnership, in which cohabiting lesbians and gays officially register as a couple. (Chapter 7 contains more detailed discussion of these topics.)

In a society where being lesbian or gay has challenges all its own, finding a partner and love can sometime be a daunting task. According to Michelle Huston and Pepper Schwartz (1996), in isolated, rural, and some urban areas, lesbian and gay meeting places are nonexistent. Even in urban areas where there are large homosexual populations, meeting a potential partner is not always easy. A large number of lesbians and gays remain "closeted"; thus, finding potential partners in gay bars and other gay-oriented meeting places limits the field of eligibles and potential partners to those lesbians and gays who feel comfortable in such settings.

As with heterosexuals, there appear to be some fundamental gender differences in the dating and mate selection attitudes and behaviors of lesbians and gays. For instance, lesbians, like their heterosexual counterparts, are less competitive and more relationship oriented than gay and heterosexual men, and both lesbians and heterosexual women are more likely than gays and heterosexual men to value their relationships more than their jobs. In addition, lesbian bars are not nearly as common as gay bars; therefore, women cannot always count on them as a place to meet potential partners. Further, lesbian bars serve primarily as a social gathering place for already-established lesbian couples, and the behavioral norms at these bars prescribe behavior that consists of couples socializing rather than individuals cruising and looking for a pickup. Because these bars tend to be frequented by couples, it is unlikely that one will meet an unattached person in these bars. Therefore, lesbians tend to meet their partners through lesbian friendship networks, mutual acquaintances, and participation in various lesbian and women's political and activist groups, with the period of courtship lasting on average 2 to 3 years (Stacey, 2003; Huston and Schwartz, 1996). Their partners tend to be women they have known for a while and with whom they have had no prior sexual relationship. Lesbians tend to practice a kind of serial monogamy in that they may have several partners over the course of their lifetime but are involved in only one intimate relationship at a time. In contrast, as we noted in Chapter 4, the courtship period for gays—as for heterosexual men—is often relatively short and is most often preceded by sexual relations.

The subculture of gay bars has been a prime place for gays to meet potential sexual partners but it has also acted to inhibit long-term partnerships. For example, research indicates that a major characteristic that gays look for in a potential partner is physical attractiveness; they prefer a partner who is very handsome—a trait that does not necessarily ensure a long-lasting relationship. Until recent times, the subculture of gay bars did not encourage gay men to form long-term relationships. In many places, singlehood rather than couplehood is still the norm (Huston and Schwartz, 1996). In general, there is no *one-size fits all* set of dating and mating patterns among lesbians and gays any more than there are among heterosexual couples. Lesbians and gays, like heterosexuals, are a diverse group representing many races, ethnicities, ages, religions, having diverse resources, values, attitudes, and dating and mate selection practices. Indeed, based on what we know about the patterns of lesbian and gay dating and mate selection, they do not appear to differ significantly from those found among heterosexual women and men. Thus, these patterns seem much more reflective of female and male socialization patterns than of patterns specific to lesbians and gays (Huston and Schwartz, 1996).

African American Lesbian and Gay Dating Research pertaining to lesbian and gay mate selection across race is especially scarce. Although it does not convey a comprehensive picture of the dating process, especially in the early twenty-first century, Vickie Mays and Susan Cochran's (1991) study of 530 middle-class African American lesbians nevertheless can provide us with some important data and insights into mate selection among this group. For example, the average age at which the women reported first being attracted to a woman was about 16. Their first lesbian experience did not occur until approximately age 19, however. Prior to their current relationship, almost all the women had been involved in a sexual relationship with another African American woman. In addition, two-thirds had at least one such relationship with an Anglo woman, and 39 percent reported a lesbian relationship with some other woman of color. The median number of sexual partners was nine, which is similar to that reported by research on white lesbians. Although two-thirds of the subjects were in a serious relationship, only one-third lived with their partner. In comparison, according to the 2000 Census, 85,000 African Americans self-identified as same-sex "partnered"—living together—couples representing 14 percent of all same-sex couple households. Although the census does not ask about sexual orientation or gender identity, it is assumed that those indicating that they were same-sex unmarried partners were in long-term, amorous relationships (Dang and Frazer, 2005).

Dating and mate selection among African American lesbians and gays may be influenced by sociocultural factors such as the unavailability of same-race, same-sex partners; residential immobility; fewer social and financial resources than whites generally and white gays specifically; and a general lack of employment opportunities. Thus, African American gays, like many African American heterosexual women, often have difficulty finding a potential partner. The traditional networks where mate selection takes place in the white gay subculture, such as gay bars, baths, and other public gathering places, are not always accessible to black gays due to actual or perceived racism. Thus, courtship among African American gays is more likely to center around home entertainment (Mays and Cochran, 1991). In addition, as in heterosexual relationships and lesbian and gay relationships generally, there are gender differences in dating and mating attitudes and behaviors among African American lesbians and gays. For example, African American lesbians are more likely than African American gays to report exclusively same-sex relationships. The Black Pride Survey 2000, for instance, found that 82 percent of the women surveyed reported having sex exclusively with women, while only 66 percent of the men reported having sex exclusively with men (Battle et al., 2002).

An interesting finding about African American gay sexuality comes from a 1978 study comparing the sexual behavior of black and white gays. In this study, Alan Bell and Martin Weinberg reported that black gays tend to be more bisexual in their behaviors than white gays. This finding implied that African American gays were dating both women and men either concurrently or alternately over some specified period of time. Today, such behavior is no longer implied but, rather, a documented reality. With the alarming increase in HIV/AIDS cases among African American women who have had unprotected sex with African

American men, health experts estimate that as much as 60 percent of African American gays infected with the HIV/AIDS virus are bisexual or living an alternative secret sexual life referred to as "down low." African American men living on the down low date and/or have sex with other men and also date and/or have sex with women, but they do not identify themselves as gay or bisexual. Such behavior is attributed to the intense homophobia alleged to exist within African American communities (we present a more detailed discussion of this behavior in Chapter 6).

Other comparisons generated by the Bell and Weinberg study of black and white gays include the following: Black and white gays reported equivalent numbers of sexual partners, both lifetime and over a 12-month period; black gays were significantly less likely than white gays to engage in brief relationships with anonymous partners; over two-thirds of the blacks reported that more than half of their partners were white men. This last finding is in stark contrast to white gays in the same study, none of whom reported that more than half of their partners were black. Over a quarter of a century later, according to the 2000 census, 21 percent of all African American same-sex couples were interracial compared to only 10 percent of white same-sex couples. Moreover, 11 percent of African American same-sex couples reported that at least one partner immigrated from another country, compared with only 6 percent of white same-sex couples (Dang and Frazer, 2005). Thus, it seems that similar to heterosexual African American women who date, a shortage of eligible potential mates may encourage African American lesbians and gays to couple with people of other races and ethnicities far more often than for whites.

THEORIES OF MATE SELECTION

Thus far we have discussed mate selection cross-culturally, historically, and within the context of U.S. society. We have also paid particular attention to issues of race, class, gender, and sexual orientation in dating behavior. A complete understanding of mate selection in these contexts requires a theoretical framework that shows how these and other social, economic, and political factors are variously related and influence mate selection. Obviously, no one theory can accomplish this. In the next section, we present some of the most frequently used theoretical explanations of mate selection: exchange theories, which include stimulus-value-role theory, equity theory, and filter theory.

Exchange Theories

Within the discipline of sociology, exchange theories are perhaps the most often used explanations of interpersonal attraction and mate selection. Although these theories were not developed specifically to explain mate selection, they provide some interesting insights into the process. You might recall from Chapter 2 that traditional exchange theory revolves around the notion that individuals attempt to maximize their rewards and minimize their costs to achieve the most favorable outcome possible. Applied specifically to mate selection, various exchange theories hold that people looking for mates try to maximize their chances for a rewarding relationship. In other words, we enter into and remain in an intimate relationship as long as we perceive that the rewards outweigh the costs. When our relationships are no longer rewarding, we discontinue them. If each person maximizes outcomes, then stable relationships will develop between people who have very similar levels of resources, because they will exchange comparable resources.

This principle is explained in the *exchange theory of homogamous mating*. According to this theory, within any pool of eligibles, a person looking to get married will seek out a person who she or he thinks will maximize her or his rewards. We therefore enter or do not enter into a romantic relationship depending on whether the other person possesses both tangible resources, such as money, and intangible resources, such as physical appearance. People with equivalent resources are most likely to maximize each other's rewards. Because couples with equivalent resources are most likely to have homogamous characteristics, mate selection is homogamous with respect to a given set of characteristics. As the relationship progresses, a couple engages in many other exchanges, including those involving power. Seldom are both parties equally interested in continuing the relationship. Thus, the one who is least interested has an advantage and is in a position to dominate (Edwards, 1969). Some researchers have described this as the *principle of least interest*, whereby, in essence, the person with the least interest trades her or his company for the other person's acquiescence to her or his wishes.

In traditional mate selection, men maximized their rewards because they generally had a range of rewards to offer, such as social status, economic support, power, and protection. In contrast, women generally had a limited set of resources, primarily involving their physical appearance and their ability to bear and care for children. Today, however, women have more rewards to offer and thus can be more selective in choosing a mate. Instead of the traditional male tradeoff of economic security, many women today are looking for men who are expressive, sensitive, and caring, and who are willing to share housework and child-rearing responsibilities. Men who do not possess these characteristics are finding themselves less desirable and sought out as a potential mate. Along the same lines, instead of the traditional female tradeoff of physical attractiveness and nurturance, many men today are looking for women who are assertive, creative, and self-confident, and who can contribute to the economic support of a family. So exchange theories help us understand how people develop a close relationship through an exchange of rewards. But why is it that some people develop an intimate relationship while others do not?

Stimulus-Value-Role Theory A popular variation of the general exchange theory of mate selection is Bernard Murstein's (1980, 1987) *stimulus-value-role theory* of interpersonal attraction. According to Murstein, in a situation of relatively free choice, attraction and interaction depend on the exchange value of the assets and liabilities that each person brings to the situation. In the mate selection process, couples move through three stages: stimulus, value, and role. They are first attracted to each other by an initial stimulus, and then they test their suitability for establishing a permanent relationship with each other by comparing their value orientations and agreement on roles. Responding to critiques of his theory by his colleagues, Murstein updated his theory such that the three stages are not mutually exclusive but rather work together to move a couple toward a committed relationship (Surra, 1991).

In the *stimulus stage*, two people are attracted to each other by some stimulus, such as good looks, the way one walks, or notoriety. Whatever the stimulus, it draws the two people together initially and tends to energize the relationship past the boundaries of simple friendship. If both partners feel the situation is equal concerning the exchange of resources, they will likely proceed to the value stage. In the *value stage*, the compatibility of the couple is tested with regard to a variety of mutually held beliefs and values, including religion, politics, marital and family expectations, attitudes about money and work, and lifestyle preferences. The more similar the two people's values, the stronger their attraction becomes and the more likely they will progress toward a long-lasting relationship. Couples with similar values may move on to the *role stage*. This stage provides each partner with the opportunity to see how the other acts out her or his roles in real-life situations. If mutual benefits at this stage are positive and fairly equal, the couple may choose to get married. That is, if the couple's roles are complementary—if their feelings and behaviors about issues such as power and authority in the relationship, the division of labor, and other expectations that they have for each other are the same or similar—then the couple might proceed to marriage. The key here is that these three stages act as filtering devices for evaluating a dating relationship to determine if it will continue or end.

Equity Theory   Yet another variation of exchange theory used to explain mate selection is *equity theory*. When used in this sense, the term *equity* signifies "fairness." Equity theory proposes that a person is attracted to another by a fair deal rather than by a profitable exchange. It argues that most people believe they should benefit from a relationship in proportion to what they give to the relationship. People are attracted to those from whom they get as much as they give. Two people do not usually seek the exact same things in a relationship; however, they are attracted by a deal that is fair to them. Values involved in judging equity range from physical attractiveness to family background to anything that a given person might value. If the relationship is inequitable, people will try to move the relationship to an equitable level. However, the greater the inequity, the harder it will be to move the relationship to an equitable level.

Filter Theories

As our discussion thus far indicates, mate selection involves a complex process of making choices within the context of a range of factors that can restrict or enhance our ability to choose. Some years ago, David Klimek (1979) described this process in terms of a series of filterings. As Figure 5.2 suggests, individuals use a series of filters to sort through a large number of potential mates to arrive at the final choice. Each filter, in descending order, reduces the pool of eligible mates until relatively few eligibles are left. We then choose a mate

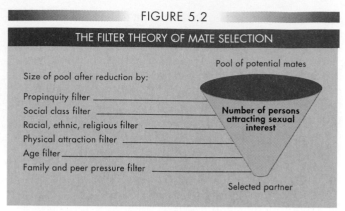

FIGURE 5.2

THE FILTER THEORY OF MATE SELECTION

Size of pool after reduction by:

Pool of potential mates

Propinquity filter _____

Social class filter _____

Racial, ethnic, religious filter _____

Physical attraction filter _____

Age filter _____

Family and peer pressure filter _____

Number of persons attracting sexual interest

Selected partner

Source: Adapted from David Klimek, 1979, *Beneath Mate Selection and Marriage: The Unconscious Motives in Human Pairing* (New York: Van Nostrand Reinhold): 13.

from among this group. *Filter theories*, or *process theories* as they are sometimes called, suggest that many factors are involved in the marital choice. In the next section we discuss some of the most prevalent of these factors, including the marriage squeeze and gradient, race, class, age, religion, sex/gender, propinquity, and family and peer pressure. After reading this section, you should be more conscious of the fact that contrary to popular belief, Americans do not have complete freedom of choice in mate selection.

MATE SELECTION: FINDING AND MEETING PARTNERS

"There's supposed to be more women than men, so where are they?" "I know there are a lot of good men out there—you just have to know where to find them." Do these comments sound familiar to you? Increasingly over the last couple of decades single women and men looking for "Ms. Right" or "Mr. Right" have lamented the mounting problem of finding someone to date or marry. And once they meet, how does each one know that the other is the right person? What attracts them to each other? What do they do once attracted to one another? How people meet and where, how or why they are attracted to each other and not someone else, are some of the most basic questions surrounding mate selection. As you will see in the following discussion, finding a mate has become almost a national pastime in the United

Do you know how your parents met? Was it love at first sight? How alike are they? What about you? Are you looking for a mate or partner? What characteristics do you look for in a mate? Character? Social conscience? A strong religious conviction? Money? Is it difficult to find someone who meets your standards? Think about your own dating and mate selection experiences and priorities as you continue reading this chapter. At the end of this chapter, you may find that your thinking has shifted, or perhaps you have become aware of priorities and feelings that you never realized you had.

States. Some people go to great lengths to meet a potential mate, as revealed later in the chapter in the discussion of where and how people meet potential partners.

The Marriage Market and the Pool of Eligibles

Throughout our history, various romantic theories of love and mate selection have suggested that when the time is right we will meet a "Fair Maiden" or "Prince Charming" without much effort on our part. Most such notions imply that mate selection is a rather unsystematic and random event determined by the "luck of the draw" or by a power higher than ourselves. In reality, meeting prospective mates, choosing partners, developing a dating relationship, and falling in love are not random activities but are predictable and structured by a number of social and demographic factors. For example, if you are a female college student in a dating relationship, without meeting you or your partner we could predict fairly accurately many things about your partner. For instance, he is probably a college student like you (or he has already completed college or attended college previously), he is probably of the same racial or ethnic background and social class as you, he is probably a little taller than you, a few years older, and as religious or spiritual as you are. We might even predict that you both are similarly attractive. And if he is not, you probably will not have a lasting relationship. Research shows that we are attracted to and tend to marry people who have a similar level of physical attractiveness. Most likely the two of you are similarly intelligent. Likewise, if you are a male student in a dating relationship the same predictions apply, with a few differences: Your partner is probably your age or 1 to 5 years younger, and she is probably your height or shorter. Although we may not be 100 percent correct, for many of you we are probably very close. The point here is that we have not randomly guessed about the characteristics of people who date and marry. Rather, we have used the knowledge that sociologists have provided us about the principles of homogamy, endogamy, and exogamy in mate selection.

Marriage Market   Historically, sociologists have described mate selection in terms of a **marriage market.** That is, they use the analogy of the commercial marketplace to explain how we choose the people we date, mate, live with, and marry. The marriage market concept implies that we enter the mate selection process with certain resources and we trade these resources for the best offer we can get. In this sense, the marriage market is not a real place but a process.

Regardless of how we choose mates, as exchange theory suggests, some sort of bargaining and exchange probably takes place. For example, in societies and subcultural groups where marriages are arranged by someone other than the couple, the parent or matchmaker carefully tries to strike the best possible bargain. Large **dowries**—sums of money or property brought to the marriage by the female—are often exchanged for valued characteristics in a male, such as high status. Indeed, valued resources like dowries can also act to make up for a person's supposed deficiencies. Thus, if a woman is considered unattractive but has a large dowry, she might be able to exchange the dowry for a highly prized mate.

Although the idea of swapping or exchanging resources in mate selection may seem distant and applicable only to those cultures in which marriages are arranged, this process is also very much a part of mate selection in the United States.

The nature of the marital exchange has changed, but the market has not been eliminated. Despite some improvements in their bargaining position, women remain at a disadvantage vis-à-vis men in the mate selection marketplace. Although women have entered the labor force in record numbers and have become increasingly independent, their actual earnings are far below those of their male counterparts, as is their ability to earn. Furthermore, many of the traditional resources that women could offer, such as child care, housework, and sexuality, can be obtained by men outside marriage and thus have less value in the marriage market today. Women are further disadvantaged in the dating and marriage market by the sexual double standard attached to aging: As women age they are considered unattractive and undesirable by men.

Does this description of the marital marketplace sound cold, calculating, and unromantic? Even if we are uncomfortable with the idea, most of us engage in the exchange of various personality and social characteristics (consciously or unconsciously) in our quest for a mate.

Pool of Eligibles   Theoretically, every unmarried person in the United States is a potential eligible mate for every other unmarried person. Realistically, however, not every unmarried person is equally available or accessible to every other unmarried person. The people whom our society has defined as acceptable marriage partners for us form what sociologists call a **pool of eligibles.** For almost all of us, the pool of eligibles consists of people of the same race, class, and educational level as ourselves. With amazing consistency, we are very much like the people we meet, date, fall in love with, and marry—far more so than can be attributed simply to chance. Sociologists refer to this phenomenon as **homogamy:** the tendency to meet, date, and marry someone very similar to ourselves in terms of important or desirable characteristics.

As we learned in Chapter 1, two of the most common sets of social rules governing mate selection and the pool of eligibles are exogamy and endogamy (see Figure 5.3). **Exogamy** refers to marriage outside a particular group. So, our pool of eligibles is first narrowed by society's exogamous norms. The most common exogamous norms in the United States are those that prohibit us from dating or marrying someone who is a family member or who is of the same sex. As you know from Chapter 1, the incest taboo is a universal norm that narrows our pool of eligibles by eliminating close blood relatives. Regarding same-sex partners, people of the same sex are considered socially unacceptable mates and are also excluded, at least theoretically. The opposite of exogamy is **endogamy,** marriage within a particular group. Endogamous norms can be formal, such as the laws in many U.S. states prior to 1967 that prohibited interracial marriage. Most, however, are informal. For example, social convention dictates that we marry someone near our own age.

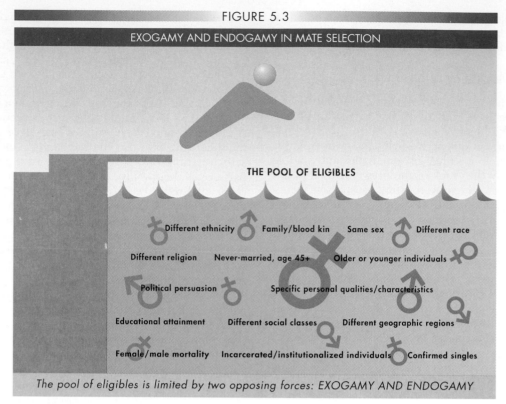

FIGURE 5.3

EXOGAMY AND ENDOGAMY IN MATE SELECTION

THE POOL OF ELIGIBLES

Different ethnicity　Family/blood kin　Same sex　Different race

Different religion　Never-married, age 45+　Older or younger individuals

Political persuasion　Specific personal qualities/characteristics

Educational attainment　Different social classes　Different geographic regions

Female/male mortality　Incarcerated/institutionalized individuals　Confirmed singles

The pool of eligibles is limited by two opposing forces: EXOGAMY AND ENDOGAMY

Source: Adapted from a drawing by John Chauncey Byrd, Chicago, 1993.

Freedom Versus Constraint in Mate Selection

We have increasing freedom and expanded options in choosing dating and life partners today compared to the past, but our freedom to choose a mate continues to be constrained by cultural norms that sort people according to race, ethnicity, religion, social class, residence, and related factors. The romantic belief that mate selection in the United States is based on love and our expanded mate selection options notwithstanding, these factors best predict who meets, dates, falls in love with, and marries whom. Let us look at how our pool of eligibles is loosely or closely organized around these factors. Although all of these factors are interrelated, we will examine each one separately. Two of the most important factors are the marriage squeeze and the marriage gradient.

The Marriage Squeeze Why do you think some people who want a mate and are actively looking cannot connect? Why do women complain more often than men about having difficulty finding a mate? Is there someone out there for all of us, no matter what resources we have to offer? Or will some of us not find a mate no matter how hard we look? In reality, there is not someone out there for everyone. If those people being advised to "sit tight and wait" are women born after World War II, they may be waiting for a very long time. Demographic data reveal that at any given time in the United States since World War II, there has been a greater number of women than men who are eligible for marriage and looking for a partner. Sociologists have defined this imbalance in the ratio of marriage-aged men to marriage-

aged women as a **marriage squeeze,** whereby one sex has a more limited pool of eligibles than does the other.

Demographic data indicate that the marriage squeeze reversed itself in the 1990s such that by the year 2000, never-married men outnumbered never-married women, 32.6 to 25.6 percent. More important, when we consider the total population of unmarried adults (never-married,

TABLE 5.1

Percentage of Unmarried Women and Men by Selected Age Categories, 2004

	Females	Males
Never-married 15 years and older	25.6 percent	32.6%
Unmarried (overall)* for selected ages		
20–24	78.3	87.7
25–29	49.8	61.4
30–34	36.2	41.4
35–44	32.7	34.3
45–54	33.1	28.9
55 and older	47.6	24.3

*Includes all categories of singles: never-married, separated, divorced, and widow/ widower.
Source: U.S. Census Bureau, "America's Families and Living Arrangements: 2004, Table A1. Marital Status of People 15 Years and Over by Age, Sex, Personal Earnings, Race, and Hispanic Origin, 2004." Published: June 29, 2005; http://www.census.gov/ population/www/socdemo/hh-fam/cps2004.html.

separated, divorced, and widowed), 15 years of age and older in 2004, as Table 5.1 shows, a greater percentage of unmarried men than unmarried women can be found in each of the four age categories: 20 to 24, 25 to 29, 30 to 34, and 35 to 44 (the ages family sociologists have designated as the marriageable years). This reversal of the marriage squeeze seems to be the case for blacks, whites, and Latinas/os. However, these percentages alone do not tell the whole story. Many women continue to find their options for dating and mate selection limited even though theoretically there are more eligible men than women. This might be accounted for, in part, by the fact that women tend to date and marry men who are 3 to 5 years older than themselves. Given this, when we look at the data in Table 5.1 we can see, for example, that although unmarried men outnumber unmarried women within their respective age categories, when we look at the percentage of unmarried women in a particular age category and compare it with the next highest age category of unmarried men, there is a noticeable decrease in the pool of eligibles for women (for instance, women 20 to 24 theoretically would date men in the 25 to 29 age category). Thus, according to Table 5.1, 78 percent of the women 20 to 24 are unmarried and theoretically form a pool of eligibles for men 25 to 29, where only 61 percent of this population or pool of eligibles are unmarried. Or put another way, in this pool there are only six unmarried men for every eight unmarried women. In addition, as women and men age, the pool of eligibles for women shrink even further, with twice as many unmarried women 55 and older (47.6 percent) as there are unmarried men (24.3 percent). Although the causes are different, as we noted earlier, countries like India, China, and Japan are experiencing a similar marriage squeeze, with high percentages of single men and a scarcity of single women.

Moreover, African American women, it seems, continue to be vulnerable to the marriage squeeze. In our earlier discussion of dating patterns among African Americans, we mentioned the historically low sex ratio in the African American community. In 2004, as we reported earlier, the sex ratio of African American men to every 100 African American women was about 91. According to some observers, the low sex ratio will continue to deny large numbers of African American women a comparable mate well into the future. Perhaps more important than the sex ratio itself, however, is a consideration of structural and attitudinal factors that work to limit the real (versus ideal) pool of eligibles for African American women. For example, if we take into account the lower life expectancy for black men (lower than for white males and all females), coupled with the increasing numbers of young black men who are victims of homicides (in 2002, the homicide rate for black males was 38.4 compared to 5.4 for white males; when we look only at black males in the marriageable years of 25 to 34, the homicide rate was a staggering 82.2 compared to 8.9 for white males) and the disproportionate numbers who are incarcerated (nearly one in three African American males 20 to 29 years of age are either in prison or jail, on parole, or on probation), the pool of eligible men—those who are desirable dating partners and mates—is drastically decreased (National Center for Health Statistics, 2004; ADPSR, 2004).

Women in Australia faced a similar marriage squeeze in the 1980s and 1990s when there were only 97 men for every 100 women. Today, the pattern of in-migration into New Zealand is causing a similar marriage squeeze as women of "marriageable age" are moving to New Zealand at rates of up to one-third higher than men. This is especially true for Asian migrants, with 53,000 more women than men in the age group 20 to 49. A recent study found that as a result of this gendered immigration, New Zealand has a higher ratio of women to men in the peak childbearing ages of 30 to 34 than any other industrialized country, with 9 percent more women than men. The ratio of women to men in this age group is as high as 32 percent for Asian women and even higher among certain Asian nationalities such as Thais and Filipinas/os. Although experts do not know the exact reasons for the influx of women into New Zealand, they think it may be one of the factors that has contributed to New Zealand having the second-highest rate of single-parent families in the world—because there simply are not enough marriageable men to go around. There is some speculation that New Zealand's changing economy calling for more nurse-aides, child-care workers, cleaners, and even prostitutes has brought in a predominantly female labor pool, particularly since the 1990s. Researchers note that the sex ratio in 2004 was more dramatic than the ongoing effects of loss of men in World War I ("New Zealand Attracting Young Female Immigrants," 2005).

The Marriage Gradient   Another factor that affects the availability of eligible mates in the marriage market is the marriage gradient. In general, the **marriage gradient** suggests that men marry women who are slightly lower down the social class continuum (younger, a little poorer, less educated). Accordingly, the pool of eligible mates for men increases as they get older, richer, and more educated while the pool of eligible mates decreases for women as they get older, richer, and more educated. For men, getting older, achieving more schooling, and becoming occupationally successful increases the number of women who consider them acceptable marriage partners. However, older, well-educated, successful women find that their choices are reduced because fewer men consider them acceptable partners.

The marriage gradient certainly shapes dating and martial choices for women and men, but it does so within culturally accepted limits. For example, in most cultures, including that of the United States, informal norms encourage women to marry men of equal or higher social status. Numerous studies of U.S. mate selection and marriage bear out this pattern. Various studies, for instance, estimate that only about 33 percent of women with 4 or more years of college marry men with less education, whereas 50 percent of men with 4 or more years of college marry less educated women. The fact is that when men marry outside their social class level, they more often marry downward than upward. Conversely, when women marry outside their social class, they most often marry upward. The tendency to marry upward in social status is referred to as **hypergamy**; marriage downward is known as **hypogamy**. Thus, in most cultures, women practice hypergamy and men practice hypogamy. Because women marry upward and men marry downward, men at the top have a much larger field of eligibles than do men at the bottom. The reverse is true for women: Those at the top have a very small pool of eligibles, whereas those on the bottom have a much wider range of men from which to choose. This pattern therefore works to keep some of the highest-status women and lowest-status men from marrying.

Although the marriage gradient traditionally provided most women with upward mobility, this is not necessarily the case today. The increasing economic independence of some women has made marriage less of a mobility mechanism. In particular, the growing gender gaps in college enrollment and degree attainment in the United States have led many popular writers and others among the lay public to ask, as the title of one article suggests, if "The College Gender Gap Could Mean Women Lose in the Mating Game" (see, for example, Sealey, 2002). In 2003, for instance, over 56 percent of college students were women. In every major age and race/ethnic group, women across the United States were enrolled in college, persisted in college, and graduated from college at considerably higher rates than men. As with the marriage squeeze, African American women express the greatest concern, and for good reason. For example, in 2000, for every 100 degrees awarded to African American men, African American women were awarded 188 associate degrees, 192 bachelor degrees, and 221 master's degrees. Similarly, Latinas earned nearly 130 degrees for every 100 degrees awarded to Latinos (McElroy, 2004). Thus, whether or not the shrinking pool of eligibles for women at the top of the education hierarchy is real or perceived, many of these women, across racial categories, are dating and marrying men who are less educated and earn less money than they do. For instance, a woman with a college degree was heard to say, "If I could find a kind plumber with a sense of humor, I'd marry him." Other women, although interested in dating and/or marriage, are not willing to settle for less than their ideal, so they neither date nor marry.

Not everyone agrees that women today face a marriage gradient. For example, according to Berna Torr (2005), the changing relationships between education, income, and marital status for women and men since the 1940s have created shifts in economic, social, and family life such that the old relationship between education and marriage has reversed. According to Torr, in the early part of this period when gender specialization in work and family life was more prevalent, high education levels impeded marriage for women. Today, however, that picture has changed as more and more women have entered the work force, their education levels have expanded, and work has become a normative part of women's lives. Torr calls this reversal for women the *marriage gradient transition.* Using a "gender revolution" theoretical approach, Torr suggests that as women's education, employment, and income patterns have become increasingly similar to men's, the relationship between economic status and marriage may become more similar for women and men, giving women increasing bargaining power in negotiating relationships. Women may also use their increased bargaining power to select marriage partners based on favorable noneconomic characteristics such as gender ideology or housework participation. Although the description here is of marital patterns, the same general trend

has been found to operate prior to marriage as well. This tendency has been called by some a *dating* or *mating gradient.*

Race Some of the most important norms in mate selection in the United States revolve around race and ethnicity. Because interracial dating and interracial marriage were outlawed or ostracized throughout much of American history, many sociologists today, as well as those among the lay public, consider interracial dating and marriage to be key indicators of the state of American race relations. Certainly one of the most public manifestations of race (along with gender and sexual orientation) is the choice of one's dating and/or marital partner. Citing the results of their respective surveys, many researchers today report that Americans have become much more racially tolerant. For example, the idea of African Americans and whites dating, once a highly divisive issue, is said to be broadly accepted today, at least in terms of attitude if not in terms of behavior. In the 1980s, for instance, a little less than one-half of the public believed it was all right for African Americans and whites to date each other. Today over three-fourths (77 percent) hold this belief. Similarly, in 1988, one-fourth of Americans said they had little in common with people of other races; today, only 13 percent say that (Pew Research Center, 2003).

Changes in attitude about interracial dating and people of other races are reflected in several major demographic and political groups. However, age is a major factor in American's racial attitudes. For example, although attitudes across generations have changed about interracial dating, there remains a persistent generation gap. According to researchers at the Pew Research Center for the People and the Press, succeeding generations of young people are moving into adulthood with more tolerant attitudes toward interracial dating than the age cohorts that preceded them (see Table 5.2). For example, the highest acceptance of interracial dating occurs among people born since 1977. Ninety-one percent of what researchers have dubbed "Generation Y" accept interracial dating, for example, compared to the World War II generation (people born between 1913 and 1927). There are reported differences for each succeeding generation. Differences in attitudes also continue to fall along geographic location lines. Although the South remains a more conservative region on racial issues, the differences between the South and the rest of the country appear to be narrowing. Compared to the 1980s, when roughly around three in ten Southern whites were open to African Americans and whites dating, today the number has doubled to six in ten being open to such dating. In comparison, 78 percent or roughly eight in ten whites living outside of the South hold such attitudes. These regional differences in racial attitudes are not confined to whites. African Americans in the South, for example, tend to hold a more conservative view on the subject than do their counterparts in other regions of the country. In the late 1980s, southern African Americans were 28 percentage points less likely than those living outside the South to approve of African Americans and whites dating. Today the attitudes have almost completely converged, with 89 percent of African Americans in the South compared to 94 percent of African Americans elsewhere approving of African American and white dating (Pew Research Center, 2003) (see Table 5.2).

TABLE 5.2

The Racial Landscape: Attitudes About Interracial Dating

Approve of Interracial Dating

Population at Large

	1987	2003
Public approval of interracial dating	48 percent	77 percent
All right for blacks and whites to date		
Blacks		93 percent
Whites		73 percent

Approve of African Americans and Whites Dating

Generations

	1987–1988	2002–2003
Generation Y (1977–)	—	91 percent
Generation X (1965–1976)	64 percent	85 percent
Baby Boomers (1946–1964)	59 percent	77 percent
Silent Generation (1928–1945)	41 percent	60 percent
World War II Generation (1913–1927)	31 percent	49 percent
Born prior to 1913	26 percent	—

Geographic Location by Race

Southern Whites	30 percent	59 percent
Southern Blacks	—	89 percent
Nonsouthern Whites	50 percent	78 percent
Nonsouthern Blacks	—	94 percent

Source: The Pew Center for the People and the Press, 2004, "The 2004 Political Landscape: Evenly Divided and Increasingly Polarized" (November 5). Washington, DC: The Pew Research Center for the People and the Press; http://people-press.org/reports/display.php3?PageID=754

Clearly, *racial attitudes* have changed, at least as they are reported to researchers and surveyers. However, the changing attitudes on interracial dating notwithstanding, we must be ever cautious in interpreting these surveys and other related data as evidence of more people dating across race lines. Despite such survey reports and the increasing depiction of interracial intimacy in the media, interracial dating and romance continues to be a significant taboo in American society. More importantly, attitudes (racial or otherwise) do not always translate into behavior. Although most surveys query the public about their attitudes, a survey conducted in April 2000 asked respondents about their actual dating practices and found that whites had the lowest rate of interracial dating (35.7 percent) and Asian Americans had the highest, with 57 percent of Asians reporting that they had dated someone outside of their race. Falling in the middle, 56.5 percent of African Americans and 55.4 percent of Latinas/os had dated interracially (Wellner, 2005). Overall, men and African Americans are more open to dating and marrying someone of a different race than are women and whites. According to Tom Smith, Director of the General Social Survey at the National Opinion Research Center at the University of Chicago, "Many people who are honestly accepting of equal treatment across a wide range of social interaction would finally draw the line when it came to (a romantic relationship) between the race groups" (quoted in Wellner, 2005:1).

Some experts believe the future of interracial dating can be best understood through the attitudes and behaviors of America's youth. An analysis of various survey results in the past show that younger people have historically been more open to racial integration and more positive about interracial dating than older people. The latest comprehensive survey of U.S. teens on the subject of interracial dating available found that more than one-half (57 percent) of teens surveyed who date said that they have dated someone of another race or ethnic group (white, African American, Latina/o, or Asian), and another 30 percent say they would have no objection to doing so. Interesting, and perhaps an important factor here, is parental and school acceptance of interracial dating. For example, nearly two-thirds (64 percent) of African American, Latina/o, or Asian teens who attended schools with students of more than one race said they had dated someone who was white. However, only 17 percent of white students who attended integrated schools said they had dated an African American, while 33 percent had dated a Latina/o and 15 percent had dated an Asian. Similarly, 38 percent of African American students had dated a Latina/o, and 10 percent had dated an Asian student (USA Today/Gallup Poll, 1997; Wellner, 2005).

Moreover, most of the teens polled (66 percent African American; 74 percent Latina/o; 75 percent white) said that interracial dating is "no big deal" at their schools, and in most cases parents are not a major obstacle. Sixty-four percent of teens said their parents either didn't mind that they date interracially or wouldn't mind if they did. Almost all teens (97 percent) said they or other teens date interracially because they find the person attractive and because they "care about the person they're dating" (91 percent). Interestingly, among those students who had not dated interracially, almost two-thirds (63 percent) of white students said they would consider dating someone who was not white and 58 percent of African American students said they would consider dating someone who was not African American. Most of the teens insisted that interracial dating is no different than any other kind and, in their opinion, it is here to stay (USA Today/Gallup Poll, 1997; Wellner, 2005). Several sociological factors can help explain this rising trend in interracial dating among young people:

- a heavy immigration of Latinas/os and Asians has increased the chances of meeting people of a different racial/ethnic background;
- the enrollment of students of color in public schools nationally has increased to a record high of 35 percent; and
- the growing acceptance of interracial marriage.

According to Karen S. Peterson (1997), as "Americans struggle with racially charged issues from affirmative action to record-breaking immigration," this emerging dating pattern among high school students could signal a shift in the way the nation will come to look at race. However, although attitudes are changing and interracial dating is more common than ever before, some racial barriers remain, particularly between African American and white teens. As we have

IN OTHER PLACES

INTERRACIAL DATING IN SOUTH AFRICA

Since the transition to democracy in South Africa in the 1990s, what are race relations there like today? Now, more than a decade since the end of apartheid, with the mingling of the races occurring at a level greater than ever before in the country's history, are more couples forming intimate relationships across race? Is there more interracial dating in the "new" democratic postapartheid South Africa? According to a 2001 news item on interracial dating in South Africa, such relationships, particularly public interracial relationships, are still unimaginable to some in South Africa. This is not surprising, given that the "new" South Africa, even after a decade, is still in its infancy and given the history of race, racism, and the legal bans prohibiting the intermingling of the races in South Africa. For decades, under the apartheid government, love, dating, and marriage across the color line were strictly forbidden. The first Afrikaner government came to power in 1948, and in 1949 interracial marriages were banned. Eight years later, in 1957, the apartheid government intro-

duced a new section to the country's Immorality Act that forbade sexual relationships between whites and nonwhites.

Although the ban on interracial dating was lifted in 1985, blacks and whites were still required by law to live in separate areas. Thus, couples who dated or married across race experienced harassment as well as other negative sanctions. Interestingly, the statistics on interracial marriage under apartheid in South Africa were strikingly similar to those in the United States today, where the ban against interracial marriage was lifted almost 40 years ago. For instance, in 1987, the South African government reported that about 2 percent of all marriages that year were interracial. The latest figures on interracial marriage in the United States indicate that about 5 percent of all marriages are interracial and that includes interracial marriages across all groups (not just blacks and whites).

True, the races are mingling more than ever before in South Africa. Black and white South Africans increasingly share public spaces, as well as office cubicles, suburban neighborhoods, and books in integrated classrooms. Indeed, some prominent blacks, including a former South African political prisoner, are married to

whites, and one of South Africa's most popular soap operas, *Isidingo*, features an interracial couple. However, the reality of the "new" South Africa is that most blacks and whites still live in very separate communities. Thus, not only interracial dating and marriage but also interracial friendships remain rare. And although interracial couples are no longer oddities in big cities, they are seldom visible in restaurants, shopping malls, or movie theaters. The postapartheid South African government does not collect statistics on the number of interracial marriages, but it seems that the new democracy and intimate relationships across race have not yet caught up with each other.

What do you think? Do people in a democratic society have complete freedom to interact with, date, mate with, and marry people of a different race? If not, why not? Although there are no longer laws in South Africa that prohibit interracial dating and marriage, why do you think it is still uncommon? Why do you think that the United States and South Africa have similar interracial marriage rates? Explain.

Source: "Sunday Q & A: Interracial Dating in South Africa," *New York Times* (May 27, 2001):16.

seen, interracial dating is still not accepted everywhere and by everyone, and it continues to be controversial in many areas of the country. Dating outside of one's race may be less taboo today than it was 30 or 50 years ago, but it still raises eyebrows and closes minds. Interracial couples still upset families, inspire stares and comments, and are often targets of hostility and violence. Although nearly two-thirds of whites say they approve of interracial marriage, as indicated earlier, such attitudes do not always translate into behavior. The gap between attitudes and behavior can be seen, for example, in a study of the online dating preferences of whites, which showed that one-half of white women and more than three-fourths of white men declare no racial preference in searching for a date. However, in practice, almost all (97 percent) of the women and men (90 percent) send e-mail queries to members of their same race/ethnicity (Tagorda, 2005).

Interracial couples are having a particularly hard time in the midst of rising racial and ethnic tensions in this country today. Since the 1980s, race relations have been particularly strained. Racial slurs, race riots, bigotry, the dramatic increase in the number of reported hate crimes during the 1990s, and the continued racially motivated violence, including widely publicized cases of African American men being

killed or beaten for associating with white women, have given many observers cause for translating the survey data on interracial dating and marriage with extreme caution. Not only do individual attitudes and behavior impact interracial dating, but various American institutions have also played a key role in manipulating who dates whom relative to race and ethnicity. For example, Bob Jones University, a fundamentalist Christian school in North Carolina, at one time in its recent history refused to admit African Americans but later admitted them under a restriction that there was to be no interracial dating or marriage (Arkes, 1991). In March 2000, however, in the wake of the controversy stirred by President George W. Bush's visit to the school a month earlier, the school's president, Bob Jones III, announced that he had met with school administrators and decided to end the ban on interracial dating (CNN, 2000). In a similar vein, the Department of Human Rights in Minnesota investigated the interracial dating policy at Pillsbury Baptist Bible College after it was publicized that the school's policy has discouraged dating between the races since its founding in the 1950s ("Probe Interracial Dating Policy," 1987).

Think about your own dating history and that of people you know such as family members. Use the exercise in the box titled Writing Your Own Script to analyze some of your own attitudes and those of people you know concerning the issue of race and intimate relationships. See the In Other Places box to see how interracial dating and marriage in South Africa, a formerly colonized country that prohibited interracial pairings until the 1980s, compares to the United States, which banned prohibitions to interracial marriage in the 1960s.

Social Class   Sociologists typically measure class using a composite scale consisting of level of educational attainment, occupation, and level of income. As we have seen, much of our behavior is affected by our location in the status hierarchy. People who share a similar social class background tend to share common interests, goals, lifestyles, and general behavior. These kinds of compatibility of interest and general homogamy are the bases of intimate relationships. As with race, Americans mate with people from their own socioeconomic class with far greater frequency than could be expected simply by chance. As you learned earlier, this is especially true among the upper classes of all races. It has often been observed that the upper classes expend more efforts to control the mate selection of their offspring than do other classes because they have much more to lose if their children marry outside their social class. Even on those occasions when a person marries someone of a different race, ethnicity, religion, or age group, the couple will most likely be from the same social class.

Because social researchers disagree on the nature and number of social classes in U.S. society, it is difficult to determine accurate statistics on class endogamy. We know, however, that courtships and marriages tend to be highly endogamous for such class-related factors as education and occupation. Educational homogamy is most observable for women with 4 or more years of college, who tend to marry men with comparable or higher levels of education, and for men who have never attended college (Bulcroft and Bulcroft, 1993).

Age   Are you involved in a relationship with a person who is much older or younger than you? Do you know others who are? What about your parents? Is your mother older or younger than your father? When you see a much younger woman with an older man do you think, "Gee, she must be looking for a father figure", or My God, he's robbing the cradle"? As we learned from our discussion of love in Chapter 4, age norms represent yet another important constraint on our freedom to fall in love and choose a mate. Although no laws require us to date, live with, or marry people within our age group, informal norms and pressures operate to keep mate selection fairly homogamous in terms of age. Most Americans mate with people from a closely related age group. For most of us this means that we date and marry people roughly within 2 to 5 years of our own age. Although the sanctions for dating or marrying someone very much older or younger (within the law) than oneself are mild, most people adhere to the age custom in selecting a mate. When they deviate, it usually goes unnoticed for the most part, unless, of course, the principals are wealthy or high-profile celebri-

ties. The case of former Playboy Playmate Anna Nicole Smith is a case in point. Still in her 20s, Smith met and married billionaire oil tycoon J. Howard Marshall, who was more than 60 years her senior. The match caused raised eyebrows and charges that she was a "gold digger." Despite her protests to the contrary, most Americans do not believe people extremely older or younger than their partner can be seriously in love. The marriage is still newsworthy, as Smith is suing her stepson for a portion of her now-deceased husband's fortune. In later marriages or remarriages, age differences are likely to be a little wider, although they continue to follow the general pattern of age homogamy.

Religion   How important is religion in your choice of a partner? Historically, religion has played a significant role in mate selection in the United States. Several studies conducted over the years have found that as many as 90 percent of people who marry select partners who are religiously similar to themselves (see, for example, Kerckhoff, 1976; Murstein, 1986; Shehan, Bock, and Lee, 1990). However, experts on the subject say that a growing number of marriages toady are interfaith or religiously heterogamous. It is estimated, for example, that one-third of Jewish, one-fifth of Catholic, about one-third of Mormon, and about two-fifths of Muslim adults and children in the United States live in interfaith households. Overall, approximately 15 to 20 percent of marriages today are between two people of different religions (Adler, 1997). Most of this research indicates that Jews in this country have been the most homogamous in terms of dating and marriage compared with any other religious group. However, since the 1960s, the proportion of Jews marrying non-Jews (or Gentiles) has risen steadily, from 11 percent of those who married prior to 1965 to 31 percent today. The intermarriage rate leveled off in the late 1980s and early 1990s to about 43 percent. Since then, it has climbed again slightly, with 47 percent of Jews who have married since 1996 choosing non-Jewish partners (Berkofsky, 2001). According to Joe Feagin and Clairece Feagin (1996), this trend toward interfaith marriages among Jews has led some observers to predict the disappearance of the American Jewish community within a few decades. This perceived threat to Jewish identity and culture has prompted some Jewish parents to actually arrange marriages for their children (Hartman, 1988). Moreover, some synagogues have started dating services and singles programs to discourage interfaith marriages. And since 1980 there has been a growing trend for interfaith married couples and their children to embrace Judaism and identify themselves as Jewish (Feagin and Feagin, 1996:187). Other religions as well either oppose or strongly discourage interfaith dating and marriage. As with race, many of these studies deal primarily with marriage; nonetheless, we can assume some degree of congruency between whom people date and whom they marry. Thus, religious homogamy is yet another factor that limits our pool of eligible mates.

Sex and Gender   When discussing factors that limit our pool of eligible mates, we cannot overlook sex. As we have indicated repeatedly, heterosexuality is the norm in mating, dating, and mate selection in the United States. Most Americans are so socialized into a heterosexual frame of reference that it is outside their scope of reality even to consider a same-sex relationship as an alternative. So important is the value of heterosexuality to many Americans that exogamous norms regulating this behavior have been encoded into law to ensure that people mate heterosexually. The stigma attached to same-sex relationships, legal constraints, and the physical abuse ("gay bashing") that such couples frequently experience can act as deterrents for some people who might otherwise choose a partner of the same sex.

Other Factors That Affect Mate Selection

As we have seen, mate selection in the United States is an individual decision, yet many social and structural barriers and limitations act to constrain our freedom to choose a partner. Besides race, class, age, religion, and sex, these barriers can also include propinquity and family and peer pressure.

Propinquity We have already touched on the subject of propinquity and its role in mate selection, particularly as we discussed racial and ethnic homogamy. **Propinquity** is used by sociologists to denote proximity or closeness in place and space. Traditionally, Americans met, were attracted to, dated, and married people who lived in the same community. This factor of residential proximity in mate selection was first introduced in a pioneering study of mate selection conducted by James Bossard in 1932. In his study of who married whom in the city of Philadelphia, Bossard found that more than half the couples who applied for marriage licenses lived within 20 blocks of each other. One-sixth lived only a block apart, and one-third lived within five blocks of each other. Subsequent research has reported similar results. Although we are no longer tied to our local communities in the way we were before mass transportation and the mass production of the automobile, residential propinquity continues to contribute to homogamy in mate selection.

Residential propinquity is closely tied to many of the factors we have already discussed: race, social class, sexual orientation, and to a lesser degree, religion. Historically, people of the same general social characteristics, for any number of reasons, have lived close together. For example, most U.S. cities are racially and ethnically segregated, and many are class-segregated as well. It is not unusual to go to a city and find very distinct racial or ethnic communities: the African American community, Little Italy, Chinatown, Greektown, Little Cuba. These residential patterns increase the likelihood that we will meet, date, and marry people of similar racial and social backgrounds. However, propinquity is not limited to place of residence. In a mobile society such as ours, propinquity operates as much, if not more, in schools, the workplace, entertainment venues, and other institutions as we increasingly move out of our communities for a good portion of each day. Nevertheless, the probability of meeting someone and establishing an intimate relationship still depends on the likelihood of

interacting with that person. And the likelihood of interacting with someone is a function of their nearness or close proximity to us.

Family and Peer Pressure Consider the following scenario:

> I am working on a doctorate; my boyfriend has never attended college. We love each other, but my family and friends insist that I should break off with him because he is not on my level. I think they might be right because sometimes even I am embarrassed by the way he speaks and carries himself. I feel so pressured by them. Can love overcome the prejudices of society?

Stated another way, this woman's question could well be: Can love overcome the pressures of family, friends, or peers? Who is or is not acceptable to parents and other relatives is of importance to most Americans. Parents in particular exercise direct and indirect influence on whom we meet and develop relationships with. Parents influence our choice of mate from the moment we are born through their teaching, their example, where they choose to live, which schools they send us to, and so forth. How, where, and when we are brought up has a profound impact on our views and decisions concerning dating, marriage, and family. Additionally, the closer we are to our parents and kin, the more likely we will consider their views.

Peers, too, can be powerful forces affecting both whom we meet and whom we decide to date or pair with. If our peer relationships are significant and close, we are far more likely to consider our friends' views and feelings about the people we date and marry. When you have completed the Writing Your Own Script exercise, you will probably have a greater awareness of just how influential parents, other family members, and peers can be in choosing a mate.

Personal Qualities and Mate Selection

As we saw in Figure 5.2, social factors such as those we have just discussed act as an initial screening. Once our pool of eligibles is determined, other factors come into play, such as the personal qualities or characteristics of the people we meet and consider as potential mates. The personal qualities we consider cover a wide range that includes physical appearance, lifestyle, ability to communicate, values and attitudes, personality, and family background, to name but a few. Probably the most important, at least initially, is physical appearance, because first impressions are often based on whether or not we find a person attractive. In addition, first impressions are often lasting impressions.

Attraction What does "Ms. Right" or "Mr. Right" look like? All of us have some image, vague though it may be, of who our ideal mate will be. Usually this image includes both physical and personality features, and we consciously or unconsciously rate or compare potential mates in accordance with these images. These ideas and images do not develop in a vacuum; rather, they are shaped in large part by the society in which we live. For most Americans, physical appearance is one of the most important ingredients in mate selection. Whether we admit it or not, how someone looks has a considerable impact on whether we choose that person as a friend or lover.

Researchers and pollsters have found a number of interesting points about physical attractiveness and its influence on mate selection. For example, Americans overwhelmingly agree that being physically attractive is a strong asset in the dating–mate selection game. Seven out of ten Americans believe that physical attractiveness is important in society today in terms of social life, happiness, and the ability to get ahead. In addition, we tend to think that we are better looking than other people think. When asked, almost no one says that they are below average in attractiveness or are downright unattractive. Furthermore, men are more likely than women to exaggerate their appearance, whereas less attractive females are more accurate in their self-evaluations. This is true, no doubt, because women get far more feedback about their appearance than do men. Likewise, younger Americans are much more likely than older Americans to ascribe above-average appearance to themselves, which suggests that older Americans may have bought into the popular notion that to be old is to be dowdy. In any event, once people meet and dating begins, personality characteristics become important considerations, although attractiveness does not decline in importance (Patzer, 1985; Newport, 1999).

Dating and marriage relationships tend to be endogamous for physical attractiveness. Various studies have documented our general tendency to look for and end up with partners whose attractiveness is roughly equivalent to our own. Attractiveness can impact the depth and duration of our relationships. For example, some researchers have found that couples who are similarly attractive are more likely to progress deeper into the relationship than are couples in which one partner is relatively more attractive than the other. In the dating game, people tend to shop around for an attractive partner. The greater our level of attractiveness, the greater our bargaining ability in the marriage market. Some of the physical similarities between people who become couples are probably the products of race and class endogamy. Some, however, are also probably a function of our definitions of what is physically appealing, including our assessment of where we fit in society's general definition of physical attractiveness.

Companionship Some demographers have predicted that many people who have married in recent times will likely stay married to the same person for the next 50 years or more unless death or divorce intervenes. If they are correct, then qualities such as compatibility and companionship are critically important in mate selection. It is essential to choose a mate with whom we can communicate; enjoy sexually and socially; and depend on for friendship, support, and understanding. The presence or absence of these attributes can have a tremendous impact on the quality and longevity of the relationship. Researchers have identified communication and sexual adjustment as the two most crucial personal attributes that contribute to companionship in an intimate relationship. These attributes are complex and depend on a number of factors: the partners' intellectual compatibility, their sensitivity and empathy toward each other, each partner's ideas about the other's sexual behavior, similarity in social class and other important social characteristics, and the importance to both partners of sexual relations in marriage (Ramu, 1989).

MEETING PARTNERS: WHERE AND HOW

"Looking for Mr. Right." "Suffering from a Man Shortage? Try Honey Hunting in the Boondocks." " Single Men from Coast to Coast Seek Sensible, Sensitive, Athletic and Sophisticated Mates." "A Few Good Men: Where?" "Where Are the Men?" "Where Are the Men for the Women at the Top?" "How to Meet Someone on the College Campus."

These quotes represent but a handful of the many titles that have appeared in recent popular and scientific literature. What do these titles suggest about contemporary mate selection? First, they suggest that single people in the dating market today face a great challenge, namely, finding a significant other. Moreover, they indicate that women more often than men express difficulty in finding a mate. Given what we already know about the marriage gradient and the sex ratios in some groups, this is not surprising. There are, however, many facts and figures that we probably do not know about dating or notions about dating we take as givens. Because most of the literature on dating continues to focus on college students, it perpetuates the myth that dating is still primarily a white, middle-class, college-aged phenomenon. The fact is, today people who date come from all walks of life, represent a wide range of ages, and are increasing in number. This fact has not gone unnoticed by an increasingly competitive service industry that has recognized and capitalized on this phenomenon. Dating is big business. One of the most significant additions to contemporary dating and mate selection is the highly developed dating technology that provides singles with increased opportunities to meet prospective partners by using a variety of new technologies. In this section we present a brief discussion of some of the traditional as well as new ways that those who want to date look for a partner. The Internet Resources: Applying the Sociological Imagination box provides some interesting statistics and facts about dating in American society.

School, Church, and Work

The high school or college campus is a traditional place where pairing and dating take place. Most high schools and colleges that used to be segregated by sex are now coeducational. Many campus dormitories are now desegregated, and

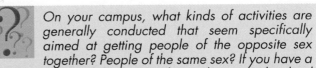
On your campus, what kinds of activities are generally conducted that seem specifically aimed at getting people of the opposite sex together? People of the same sex? If you have a significant other, did you meet her or him in high school or college? Is it difficult or easy to meet and establish relationships with people of your choosing on your campus?

APPLYING THE SOCIOLOGICAL IMAGINATION
The Dating Game: Playing by the Numbers

Have you ever looked at someone and were instantly attracted to her or him? Wondered what it would be like to date her or him? Have you ever wondered what the odds were of you meeting the perfect date or mate, falling madly in love, and establishing a long-term relationship? Have you wondered just how or in what way you would meet your mate? According to some observers of the dating scene, dating is a numbers game; there are statistics concerning just about every dating phenomenon that people have experienced. For example, did you know that most married couples (63 percent) were first introduced to one another through a network of friends? (Broussard, 2006). Or that the city you live in just might be the worst place in the world to find a date? To answer some of your questions about dating, consider the following statistics and facts:

- Almost one-half of adult Americans (44 percent) are single. Does this mean that there is somebody out there for you? Or does it give those who are looking, hope?

- By the time girls and boys in American society reach the age of 16, 78 percent of girls and 83 percent of boys have been out on at least one date.

- "Hooking up" with that ideal date is hard enough without the odds stacked against you because you live in the worst city for dating. According to a recent study, Austin, Texas, is the best city for dating and Kansas City, Missouri, is the worst.

- Statistically speaking, if we count the entire singles population of a city, the best place for single people seeking a date is New York, where 50 percent of state residents are unmarried, and Washington, DC, where a staggering 70 percent of the population is single. In contrast, the worst cities are in the states of Idaho, where 60 percent of the people are married, and Utah, where 59 percent of the people are married.

- Statistically, the "find-someone" odds favor men: There are 86 unmarried men for every 100 unmarried women, although in some regions of the country the gender ratio favors women.

- Got someone hot in your dating sights and want to reveal your interest? Fifty-one percent of singles say they use flattery as a tactic to reveal their interest in someone; 25 percent use touching, and another 23 percent send the word out through a friend.

- Think you are going to find a date sitting on a barstool? Experts indicate that only 9 percent of women and 2 percent of men say that they have found a relationship at a bar or club. Thus, if you are seriously looking for a date you need to explore other meeting places.

- If you are into online dating, you are hardly alone: In 2003, 45 million Americans used online dating services—that is about 40 percent of the entire U.S. singles pool. In the first half of 2003, consumers spent over $214 million for online dating services.

- On a date, first impressions do count: Men take only 15 minutes to decide if a woman is worth a second date. For women, the clock is ticking much slower—they take an hour or more pondering whether to get together again on a second date.

Sources: Meredith Broussard, 2006, "10 Dating Statistics You Ought to Know." Personalads.cc/full.php. Sperling's BestPlaces, 2006, "America's Best (and Worst) Cities for Dating." http://www.best-places.net/docs/studies/DatingCities.aspx. "Online Dating Fact Sheet," 2006, *Online Dating Magazine,* http://www.onlinedatingmagazine.com.

What is your dating IQ? Were you already aware of some of the facts and figures presented above? As with other topics we have studied, there are a wide variety of Web sites and links that provide facts and figures about dating. For example, Match.com regularly conducts surveys and provides interesting data about dating and issues related to mate selection. According to one Match.com survey, 98 percent of single men are looking for a long-term relationship and 94 percent say they are ready to balance both a serious relationship and a career (Match.com, 2005). Use Match.com and the Web sites listed in this box as sources to begin an Internet search for facts and statistics about dating. As we always caution when gathering data from the Internet, pay attention to the reliability of the source and the validity of the data and figures. Share the data you collect with your professor and classmates. How do the facts and statistics you gathered fit what you and your classmates thought you knew about dating before you read this chapter and gathered additional information?

---

even some fraternities have gone coed. These changes have increased the opportunities for heterosexual interaction and coupling. Students meet each other in the dormitories, in classes, or through friends. In addition, various groups sponsor activities such as dances, beach parties, and retreats to bring people together.

Obviously, high school and college campuses are insufficient places in and of themselves for meeting possible mates. Even on campuses we find those who want to date using a variety of other methods to meet people, such as being introduced by roommates, relatives, or friends; advertising in the college or local newspaper; and using computerized dating services. In the past, the church or synagogue frequently brought people together. Today, however, as church attendance generally has declined, particularly among young adults, religious institutions and services less frequently serve this purpose. Although the world of work at the turn of the century provided women with new and increased opportunities to meet and establish intimate relationships with the opposite sex in the sense that it got them out of the house and away from their parents' supervision, it no longer provides the same level of opportunities for pairing. As in the past, the work women do is often sex-segregated or predominantly female, such as elementary school teachers. Thus, it offers only limited contact with eligible males. In addition, the diversity of backgrounds that can sometimes be found in workplaces serves to limit the prospective pool of eligibles for women and men.

Singles' Bars and Gay Bars

Singles' bars reached their peak in popularity during the 1970s and early 1980s. Once symbolic of the singles' scene and a significant means of meeting potential mates, singles' bars today are rejected by many people who see them as nothing but "meat (not meet) markets." In the past and to some degree today, singles' bars have provided a space where people could feel comfortable and meet other single people. Studies of why people go to singles' bars indicate that the major reason is for companionship. Gay bars are similarly rejected by some lesbians and gays as meat markets. The motivations for attending gay bars are basically the same as those for attending heterosexual bars. Because of homophobia and discrimination against lesbians and gays, and because many lesbians and gays feel uncomfortable expressing or being themselves in a predominantly heterosexual environment, gay bars continue to serve a significant mate selection function.

Self-Advertising: Personal Ads

Are you Italian? Petite, attrac. DIF 40+, degreed, seeking S/DIM 40+, must be finan/emot secure. No drugs/alcohol/smoking. Must like music, din out and travel.

Attractive Aquarian. Gay, SWF, 33, tired of bar scenes. 5'5", 142 lbs., very romantic, honest, open-minded. Seeks honest open-minded gay SF, 30 to 40, nondrug user, for a long-lasting relat. Only serious need reply.

Sexy and Cute. SWF, 23, wants the best and won't settle for less! If you're attra., ambitious, prof. S/D white/Hispanic, fin secure please respond. Photo please.

SWM, 70, attract., very active, outgoing & sincere, looking for a SWF who desires companionship & romance.

Finding dating partners through the use of personal ads continues to be a popular way to meet potential dates. Such advertising allows individuals to find partners with matching interests and specific characteristics.

Although fictitious, these ads are typical of real ads found in many local newspapers around the country. Personal ads as an approach for finding mates is not a new phenomenon. For example, in the 1800s settlers in the Northwest used a mail-order system in which they advertised for a bride (Steinfirst and Moran, 1989). This type of advertising for a bride continues today in some circles. For instance, some American men use this approach to advertise for Asian brides. Some researchers and others have criticized these men, suggesting that they are looking to Asia for brides out of a stereotypical view of them as subordinate, subservient, and easier to control than American women. Furthermore, there is some evidence that personal ads appeared in newspapers during colonial times. Later, men moving across the frontier also advertised for brides in newspapers (Carlier, 1972).

Not until the 1980s, however, did the use of personals become widespread and public. Since the 1980s, it seems that using personal ads has become not only acceptable but a fashionable way to meet people, especially among educated people (Steinfirst and Moran, 1989). Today, people who use the personals are no longer considered either perverted or desperate. In fact, some experts consider the use of personal ads to be a healthy and creative adaptation to societal change (Bolig, Stein, and McHenry, 1984). In any case, with leisure time at a premium for many working people, with the dramatic increase in the numbers of singles, and with the sometimes difficult task of finding a partner through conventional means, an increasing number of people feel comfortable advertising themselves in the hopes of landing a mate.

Content analyses of personal ads indicate that men are twice as likely as women to place an ad seeking a partner (see, for example, Davis, 1990). Such analyses also consistently report gender differences in these ads. For example, women define or offer themselves as attractive more often than men, and men seek attractiveness and request photographs far more often than women. Men offer financial security much more than women while women seek financial security and more permanent relationships than men. Women's greater emphasis on resources and status translates into their preference for older men. In addition, personality or character is more important to women than men. Believing that they know what women want, men describe themselves in terms of their success, professional status, or as "caring" or "sensitive" or "loving." Women, on the other hand, emphasize their femininity (Smith, Waldorf, and Trembath, 1990; Fischer and Heesacker, 1995; Raybeck et al., 2000).

A recent content analysis of personal ads placed in a southeastern newspaper, a leisure magazine, a singles magazine, and a state magazine reported that the overwhelming majority of those placing ads were white, male, and heterosexual. According to the study, both females and males mentioned personality (for instance, intelligent, kind, honest, warm, sense of humor) most often as a characteristic they wanted in a potential partner. For women, the second and third most frequently mentioned characteristics were nonsmoking and a professional job based on a college degree. For men, the second and third most frequently mentioned characteristics sought in a potential partner were good looks and nonsmoking. The author of the study suggests that the women's movement and changing gender roles are having an influence on the search for potential heterosexual partners. Although good looks or attractiveness is still frequently mentioned in personal ads, more stress is put on personality characteristics. Women are now more educated, more professionally oriented, and more financially secure than in the past. Thus, it appears that men are beginning to place more emphasis on personality traits and somewhat less emphasis on looks. The

> *Do any of these findings surprise you? Can you determine the principles of endogamy and exogamy in the sample ads presented at the beginning of this section? Check your local or school newspaper. What do personals tell us about mate selection in the United States? In your city? On your campus? About the qualities that people look for in a mate? If you were to write such an ad, what would you say?*

concern with nonsmoking in a potential partner for both women and men may be a result of the increased knowledge about the health dangers of smoking (Lance, 1998). Today, it is fairly routine for single people using classified ads to dial an 800 number that puts them in contact with the person they have chosen to hear a more personalized message about that person's interests and attributes.

Dating Clubs and Dating Services

Dating clubs and services advertise and hope to attract those individuals who have difficulty meeting people through conventional routes or who are simply fed up with the commercialized nature of the singles' scene. A wide variety of dating clubs exist across the country that, for a fee, sort out compatible couples and bring them together. Rather than go the route of advertising in a newspaper or magazine, many people join or use the services of specialized dating clubs. A primary appeal of these clubs is they provide immediate visual stimuli (which is important to those concerned with physical attributes and appearance). They also save people from having to sort through pages of personals to find a person who fits what they are looking for in a mate

and then, sometimes through trial and error, having to arrange to meet. Many of these clubs are open to anyone interested in joining, but some are specialized and tailored to the interests of a particular group. Specialized dating clubs can be especially appealing because they cater to a specific clientele. A number of such clubs around the country specialize in attracting members of a specific group, for example, professionals, vegetarians, bisexuals, Catholics, Jews, African Americans, single parents, lesbians, gays, and people who like to travel. There is even a dating club for the wealthy that charges its members a fee as high as $100,000 to match them with a marriage partner.

Although dating and/or singles' clubs are common in the United States, they do not exist in some cultures, and in others they are a relatively new and unique phenomenon. For instance, until 1998 there was no such thing as a singles' club in the East African nation of Kenya. In that year, a Kenyan advice columnist opened the country's first singles' club. As definitions of women's and men's roles in marriages and families continue to undergo changes globally, traditional ways of mate selection in other non-Western countries may follow Kenya's lead and give way to Western trends, such as singles' or dating clubs, and even the widespread use of computer technology.

Computer Dating and the Internet

The technology explosion in the late twentieth century gave rise to incredible changes in the lives of Americans. In the social arena of dating and mate selection, millions of people have turned to computer technology in their search for a mate. Before the Internet, dating and mate selection was both simple and complicated. To meet a potential date, one actually had to see her or him. To get a date, you had to have chemistry. Today, millions of people can and do manage their social lives, including dating and mate selection, sitting at their computers. Millions of singles have joined computerized matching services that sell their members information on other members. For some online dating services, clients must complete a questionnaire covering a range of personal and demographic characteristics (sometimes as many as 200 traits) such as age, race, body build, religion, income, education, diet, tobacco use, political outlook, sense of humor, disposition, and sexual

The Internet, via the World Wide Web, has revolutionized the dating scene. However, it has also introduced some problems. On the one hand, the Internet increases one's possibility of interacting with and dating multiple partners. On the other hand, this could be problematic for users who are seeking a monogamous relationship.

Source: Reprinted with special permission of King Features Syndicate.

history. This information is fed into a computer, which matches it with other clients who have similar profiles. Members of computerized matching services pay a lifetime membership fee and then a separate fee for each computer match they receive. Such services do not guarantee a match; even if there is a match, some of the same risks one encounters in meeting potential mates in bars or other places are present such as noncompatibility or sexual aggression and violence.

Other people, who want more control over the mate selection process, use their personal computer to get in touch with prospective partners through dating networks called "dial-your-mate." People using these networks dial into a central computer and provide information similar to that contained in the questionnaires of the computerized matching services. Dial-your-mate services are geared toward heterosexual couples in that the information provided is compared with that of all opposite-sex participants and then ranked in terms of percentage of agreement. Subscribers can send information and messages back and forth on their computers, ignore the messages, exchange more information, or end the interaction at their discretion.

Dating in Cyberspace

Computer dating is not new. However, it has grown by leaps and bounds over the last two decades and is now estimated to be a billion-dollar social marketplace. There seems little doubt that the dating industry has changed dramatically as a result of new and increasing computer technology. Some observers say that a quiet revolution has overtaken the world of romance as the increasingly popular electronic bulletin boards have transformed into what some call "on-line pickup joints" (Baig, 1994). One thing is for sure, mate selection, by way of the computer and the Internet, has become pretty routine for a variety of today's singles. For example, many single professionals are looking for a mate in cyberspace. Modern life for the unmarried professional today is increasingly complicated and full, making finding a partner difficult, if not impossible, for those who are interested. Today's professionals are marrying later; they travel thousands of miles each year for business reasons; they relocate frequently as they climb the corporate ladder; they run in and out of health and other exercise clubs on a tight schedule on their way to the office; they rarely date colleagues on the job; and many of them are fed up with singles' bars, blind dates, and family and friend fix-ups (rarely does what they want in a partner coincide with what family and friends think they need). And, as we indicated earlier, the number of older single Americans is growing and they are increasingly using the Internet to hook up and hang out as well. For example, Match.com, one of the largest online dating services, reports that people aged 50 and older represent the fastest-growing segment of its members (Match.com Corporate, 2006).

It is estimated that by the year 2010 just about one-half of the U.S. population will be single. It appears, therefore, that more singles than ever before might be using computer technology to find a mate and that there will be a service out there in cyberspace for everyone. In this regard, some relationship experts predict that "niche dating sites" are the wave of the future for on-line dating. They say that as more new dating sites come on-line, the best chance for success is to focus on a particular niche. In fact, there are already hundreds of such niche dating sites currently on-line. These sites run the gamut from sites specifically for Seventh Day Adventists, Big, Beautiful Women, Christians, Singles who are Deaf, Military Singles and their Admirers, and Singles over 40 to Single Parents, Single and Widowed Seniors, and one for every possible racial/ethnic and religious group. There are no precise figures as to how many cyberspace dating services there are today and whether their growth has peaked. However, among those that exist, many promise to find their subscribers the perfect mate (or allow the subscriber to do it her/himself). Members can swing, place ads, search thousands of classified such as personals, view photos of potential matches, engage in live on-line romance chat, flirt using a cell phone, and even order a bride through mail order. Ironically, it is the same technology that some people feel isolates us and is too invasive that is also responsible for bringing people together (Cytrynbaum, 1995).

Online dating has advantages as well as pitfalls. Some of the advantages of online dating are its accessibility, autonomy, and increasingly low cost. Subscribers can sit in the privacy of their homes and access tens of thousands of eligible mates, sifting through them as often as they like by specific "niche" characteristics such as age, race/ethnicity, religion, or body type. They can also remain anonymous as long as they like, thus allowing people to portray the persona they choose until they are ready to get involved. This can lead to more open expression because people do not have to worry about seeing or running into each other if the on-line relationship does not work (Nichcolas and Milewski, 1999). It also saves the time and expense that might be spent on a bad blind or fix-up date, and it cuts out the need for barhopping. A pitfall is the potential for dishonesty and even harassment or violence if, for example, the on-line relationship does not work out. (See Debating Social Issues box.) When it does work, it can lead a couple to the altar. Although there is some debate today about the validity or accuracy of the statistics put out by some on-line dating sites about the number of matches they have made generally and the number of matches that have led to marriage specifically, it does appear that an increasing number of marriages are being made in cyberspace heaven. Match.com, for example, claims credit for over 1300 marriages since it began in 1995 ("Romance on the Web," 2003).

Moreover, not only are singles flocking to the Internet to find "relationship partners," but they are also using a variety of other—often unique—methods of hooking up. Text messaging via mobile phones, for example, has become an increasingly popular method of flirting or asking someone out on a date, according to a survey carried out by a Finnish wireless entertainment provider. According to the survey, nine out of ten women flirt with men using short messaging service (SMS) messages rather than talking. This method of flirting and hooking up is particularly popular among the younger generation. For example, 82 percent of the women 18 to 25 years of age said that they believed text messaging was the best way to ensure a man responded to them. Similarly, the majority of the men surveyed said that sending a

DEBATING SOCIAL ISSUES

TO REGULATE OR NOT— THAT IS THE QUESTION

Regulating Online Dating Services

Online dating services are a lucrative and growing industry that continues to draw concerns about the manner in which its members conduct themselves. Some politicians as well as many among the public at large believe there are inherent dangers throughout the entire Internet. They believe online dating sites, in particular, can be havens for unsavory people and indeed criminals, stalkers, and rapists who lurk on the Internet using dating services to gain access to people they would not otherwise have access to. This, they believe, poses a grave danger for dating service users, most of whom have no idea about the criminal background of the people they meet and are matched with through these services. In this context, a growing number of voices are calling for something to be done to protect Internet users of online dating services. As a result, an increasing number of U.S. states have responded to these concerns by proposing laws to regulate online dating services. This movement has created a debate over the merits of legislative regulation as opposed to self-regulation

through better business models and policies (Heydary, 2005).

Essentially, on one side of the debate are those who believe online dating sites should be regulated by government legislation to protect and increase safety for love seekers, who too often believe they are safe with someone dangerous they have met and gotten to know online (Farrell, 2005). Proponents include lawmakers across the country, many of who have drafted and introduced legislation that will require online dating services to conduct criminal screenings on its members or post prominent warnings on their Web site's

home page, all member profiles, e-mail communications, and personal advertisements accessible by the residents of the respective state stating that they have not conducted felony conviction or FBI searches on the particular individual (Heydary, 2005). Some states have proposed legislation that would require online dating service providers to conduct searches for felony and sexual offense convictions from a national database containing at least 170 million criminal and sexual offender records. These bills also set out specific wording that must be used in the warning and require that the warning be in bold capital letters in

---

text message was much easier than physically trying to talk with a woman. Both women and men indicated that they felt more comfortable sending text messages than speaking on their mobile phones (Telecomworldwire, 2001).

Another recent and unique matchmaking strategy in the increasingly popular speed dating industry is "8minuteDating," a matchmaking event popularized on such TV shows as *Frasier* and *Sex and the City*. The concept is rather simple. At the beginning of an 8minuteDating event, an equal number of women and men are given eight computer-generated dating combinations listed on a card. The participants then move from one table to another, revealing only a first name as they spend 8 minutes in pairs, getting to know each other, which amounts to a date. An 8-minute conversation may be all it takes to find true love, or at least a second date. Afterward, when the minidates are over, the singles decide who they would like to see again and submit the information to the organizer, who feeds it into a computer. If there is a match, the computer acts as a go-between, providing full names and contact information to the pair. Because the par-

ticipants stick to first names only and meet for brief conversations, the 8minuteDating events take much of the anxiety and pressure out of the dating process and avoids the awkwardness of a bad blind date (The 8 Minute Matchmaker, 2002).

The fast-growing speed dating industry caters to heterosexuals, lesbians, gays, and a number of racial, ethnic, and age groups and has spawned a number of companies with names such as "HurryDate," "Table for 6," "25Dates.com," "XDate," "8minutedating.com," "Speed Dater," "Speed Mingle," "BlinkDating.com," and "Fast Impressions." Organizers of 8 minuteDating events pride themselves on providing a comfortable social atmosphere in venues such as trendy bars and restaurants for people to see if there is chemistry with anyone they meet. It seems that such events are not only popular, but also many of the participants seem to have found that chemistry with someone they met on an 8-minute date. For example, 99 percent of singles say they enjoy the speed dating events and 90 percent of those who participate in such events say they met someone they would like to see again (The 8 Minute Matchmaker, 2002).

at least 12-point type. Providers that failed to comply would be fined each day they were out of compliance. These legislative initiatives would also have international legal consequences in that the mandates contained in them would apply to any online service provider, even those in foreign countries as long as the company in question was signing up members in the legislating state (Heydary, 2005).

Currently, True.com, is the only online dating service that conducts criminal background and marital status checks on all new members. The company's founder says legislation to regulate the industry would save lives, property, and heartache and prevent rapes, robberies and assaults. He and other supporters believe that online dating services owe it to their members to inform them of potential hazards and that such regulation of the industry would bring many more single people, currently not using online dating services, into the industry, once they perceived it as safe (Online Personals Watch, 2006).

Those either wavering or outright against such regulation argue that criminal background checks do not guarantee the safety of online dating service members. Various dating services such as Match.com oppose such legislation, arguing that criminal background checks are ineffective because national criminal databases are incomplete—thus criminals and those with unsavory pasts could avoid detection by signing up with a fake identity. Consequently, such a screening process could cause members to develop a false sense of security. Opponents accuse those in favor of such legislations of creating a problem where one does not exist, arguing that such laws would be "legislative overkill." They advocate instead for "self-regulation" of the online dating industry through better business models and policies. They argue that attempts to regulate the industry amount to special-interest legislation that takes a market differentiator of a particular online dating service and, through legislation, enforces it on the entire industry (Heydary, 2005).

According to the president of IDEA-OASIS, the Internet Dating Executive Alliance/Online Association for Social Industry Standards, the cure is worse than the problem; it forces the hand of online businesses and impairs the rights of free speech and free communication online. Other opponents, such as the CEO of Date.com, believe that criminal background checks give consumers a false sense of security with checks that are not 100 percent accurate. They contend that most reported crimes involving the Internet come from chat rooms, which would not be regulated by the proposed legislation. Thus, instead of requiring regulation through legislative action, responsible companies in the industry should continue to promote safety guidelines to those in the online dating community (Online Personals Watch, 2006).

According to True.com, a false sense of security already exists because there are users of online dating services who mistakenly believe that some of the larger dating services do perform background checks. While admitting that criminal background checks are not perfect, True.com and other proponents argue that such checks do, or will, provide some assurance to online dating service members (Heydary, 2005).

What do you think? Should online dating services be regulated by the government or should they be allowed to self-regulate? Do you think that the support for industry regulation by True.com Online Dating Service is simply a thinly veiled public relations ploy? If the industry is allowed to self-regulate, do you believe that it can and will do an adequate job of protecting its members from possible harm from lurkers who either have criminal backgrounds or misrepresent their marital status, or both? If not government regulation or self-regulation, what, if anything, do you think should be done? Have you ever used an online dating service? If yes, did you feel safe and comfortable with the people you were matched with?

Computer-based dating services may appeal to those concerned about AIDS, but consumers of this type of technology, especially women, must be careful and alert about the risks involved. As we have pointed out, there is the risk of meeting someone who may prove to be disappointing or, worse, violent or with a violent or unsavory past. Some observers estimate that men outnumber women in cyberspace six to one, while others say that the ratio is more like two to one. Whatever the case, more and more women depend on the Internet for business and recreation. Thus, as their use of on-line dating services and discussion groups increase, we can probably expect the problem of cyberspace stalkers to increase as well.

THE FUTURE OF DATING

What is the future of dating? We cannot be sure. It is a safe bet, however, that dating will be around for some time to come, albeit in an increasingly modified form. It is also a safe bet that single people looking for that "right" partner will continue to use traditional as well as creative new ways to facilitate their search. For example, some single heterosexual women today consider the food market a good place to meet a potential partner. They believe that if a man is there doing his own shopping, chances are he is single and may also be looking for a partner. In addition, some women suggest following him around the store to see the kind of items he buys. This should give one insight into the type of person he is—what he does and does not like. And according to recent news releases, devoted fathers are a hot commodity on the twenty-first century dating scene. Some single women, it seems, find the nurturing and vulnerable tendencies exhibited by single fathers to be powerful magnets in the mate selection market; they are attracted to single fathers because they see them as trustworthy, nurturing, and compassionate. In this context, public places frequented by unattached dads and their children such as public parks and outdoor and indoor playgrounds serve as new markets for meeting potential mates. Experts attribute this trend to an increasing number of fathers awarded custody of their children, theorizing that women are attracted to the male who proves that he can be involved (with his kids). Some outspoken critics of this new trend argue that such generalizations about single fathers are unfair and even sexist. They say that we should not reserve terms like "sweet, caring and nurturing" only for men with children. Rather, we should assume that all men possess these qualities. Society should not marvel over men who are attentive to their kids—rather, it should be expected behavior. It is ironic, they say, that kids are considered an asset for a single man, while they are often a liability to single women seeking a partner (Moyle, 1999).

Among some young urban professionals (sometimes referred to as "yuppies"), the local launderette has become a popular meeting place for singles. In many upscale urban neighborhoods where large numbers of single professionals live, establishments with a launderette in front and a bar next door or behind it enjoy increasing popularity with some singles. Today, singles can complete a sometimes unappealing chore (washing dirty clothes) while simultaneously enjoying the company of like-minded people, one of whom could potentially become a long-term partner. Along with the various methods of meeting a date that we have already discussed, today's singles also meet potential partners at singles' coffeehouses and on singles' vacations.

Whatever methods single people use to meet partners, as computer technology continues to advance people will continue to find creative ways to use the technology to meet potential partners. And whatever the future of dating, no doubt we as parents and grandparents some day will reminisce about the "good old days" when we were dating.

Although dating is often fun and can be a very positive experience in our lives, it can, and often does, involve negative experiences such as violence and abuse, and breaking up.

VIOLENCE IN DATING AND INTIMATE RELATIONSHIPS

Until the 1980s, the issues of date rape and violence received little public attention. Consequently, most people severely underestimated the extent of these problems. Since then, however, in part due to the women's movement and a more open social attitude toward sexual issues in general, the media have begun to focus on all forms of intimate violence. As a result, today we are now realizing just how widespread are abuse and violence within dating relationships. Because of the seriousness and high incidence of violence, abuse, and rape in marriages and families, we devote a full chapter (Chapter 11) to its discussion. Here we are concerned specifically with dating violence and assault.

Physical Abuse

Dating violence, the perpetration or threat of an act of violence by at least one member of an unmarried couple on the other member within the context of dating or courtship, encompasses any form of sexual assault, physical violence, and verbal or emotional abuse (National Center for Injury Prevention and Control, 2006). Dating violence

is a subject that few people like to discuss. Most people are reluctant to admit that it occurs. However, violent behavior that takes place in the context of dating or courtship is quite prevalent in U.S. society. Estimates vary because studies and surveys use different methods and definitions of dating violence. A review of dating violence research statistics, for example, shows that the rate of nonsexual courtship violence ranges from 9 to 65 percent, depending on how dating violence is defined—that is, whether threats and emotional or verbal aggression are included in the definition (National Center for Injury Prevention and Control, 2006). This also includes dating between same-sex couples, although most statistics have been gathered from heterosexual couples. However dating violence is defined, intimate partner violence is widespread, as national statistics indicate. For instance, according to the National Center for Injury Prevention and Control (2006), nearly 5.3 million incidents of intimate partner violence occur each year among U.S. women ages 18 and older, and 3.2 million occur among men. More specifically, more than four in every ten incidents of domestic violence involves nonmarried partners (Bureau of Justice, 2000). Some experts have suggested that violence among intimates is an epidemic whose casualties outnumber the Vietnam War in the amount of people killed (Kong, 1998).

Intimate partner violence affects all cultures, races, classes, occupations, income levels, and ages in society. However, according to most statistics, 85 percent of victims of dating violence are women and girls, and all too often the victims and perpetrators of dating violence are teenagers and young adults. The U.S. Justice Department (2002) has found that women ages 16 to 24 are the most likely victims of intimate partner violence. For instance, according to a February 2005 Lifetime Television survey of 600 women and men ages 16 to 24, intimate partner violence has personally touched their lives. Approximately seven in ten women (77 percent) and six in ten men (64 percent) also said they know or have known someone in an abusive relationship, and approximately six in ten said that they knew a woman who has been sexually assaulted. These statistics represent a dramatic increase in intimate partner violence over the past decade (Lifetime Television, 2005).

College campuses are prevalent sites where dating violence occurs. According to a variety of sources, the prevalence rate for nonsexual dating violence is between 32 and 53 percent among college students. A survey of college students at campuses across the United States indicate that three in five college students reported personally knowing friends, relatives, or someone else close to them affected by intimate partner violence (Roper Starch Worldwide, 1995). As in all cases of intimate partner violence, the gendered nature of such violence is apparent on college campuses, where one of every five females will experience some form of dating violence during their campus lifetime (U.S. Department of Justice, 2002).

Teen dating violence is particularly troubling. According to statistics from the U.S. Department of Justice (2002), about one in three high school students have been or will be involved in an abusive relation. Like their adult counterparts, girls are most often the victims of dating violence.

The most recent research on the prevalence of partner-inflicted violence on adolescent girls found that approximately one in five teenage girls were victims of partner assault. In addition, almost one-half of girls 14 to 17 say they know someone their age who has been hit or beaten by a boyfriend. Some studies of teenage violence suggest that both females and males inflict and receive dating violence in equal proportion, but the motivation for violence by women is most often for defensive purposes. Other studies have found that girls and women are victims of dating violence twice as often as are boys and men, and females suffer significantly more injuries than males. This abuse typically occurs in long-term relationships and is repeated; the victims do not terminate the relationship. Additionally, over 70 percent of pregnant or parenting teens are beaten by their boyfriends; about half of these teens say that the battering began or intensified after their male partner learned of the pregnancy (Domestic Violence Statistics, 2006; Borden, 1999). Even so, most often parents are unaware of the abuse. Hospitals report that these girls come in with facial injuries, such as a broken nose or black eyes, fractured wrists, and bruises on the neck and other parts of the body. Family therapists say that the pattern in these relationships is typically one in which male jealousy escalates into controlling and restrictive behavior, accusations, and suspicions that ultimately escalate into violence (Levy, 1992).

Although at first the physical abuse may seem relatively mild, such as pushing or grabbing, over time, as the couple becomes seriously involved, the violence escalates. Victims of dating violence report that the abuse takes many forms ranging from insults, humiliation, monitoring the victim's movements, isolation of the victim from family and friends, suicide threats, kicking, hitting, pushing, and grabbing to the use of a weapon such as a stick, gun, or knife and threats to harm family or property. The abuser also blames the victim for the abuse, or uses jealousy as an excuse.

Control and jealousy are often confused with love by both the victims and the offenders, who believe that the violence in their relationship is an indication of their love for one another and that it helps to improve the relationship. Victims who hold this "romantic" view of violence frequently blame themselves for their mistreatment, rationalizing that because their partners love them, they must have done something to "deserve" the abuse. Traditionally, females are taught to take responsibility for whatever goes wrong in a relationship. Thus, the abuser often convinces her that the abuse is her fault; that the violence used to control her is brought on by her less than perfect behavior; that she needs to be disciplined for her lack of consideration; that the discipline is for her own good; and that the abuser has a right to chastise her (Gelles and Cornell, 1990; Borden, 1999). Furthermore, it is rarely the case that violence in courtship is a one-time occurrence. Only about one-half of all couples in violent relationships end the relationship after the first act of violence. For female teens who remain in such relationships, if there is a child involved there is oftentimes an economic dependence on the male. Other factors are also involved when teen victims remain in their abusive relationships, including denial of the situation, fear of being alone or for one's life, shame, and peer pressure. Researchers have also found that health risks, such

as substance use, unhealthy weight control behaviors, risky sexual behaviors, and suicide are significantly linked with lifetime prevalence of dating violence. Although teen dating violence occurs in a variety of settings, it most often takes place in the home of one of the partners (U.S. Department of Justice, 2002; Silverman et al., 2001).

Various experts in the area of dating and courtship abuse have suggested that physical assault between teens is portrayed by the mass media as common and relatively harmless (see, for example, Reisman, 1998). Unfortunately, it is common, but harmless it most definitely is not. An extension of media portrayals of teen violence, as well as the romantic illusions about abuse, is indicated in the fact that most girls and women who are battered during dating hold the unreal belief that the violence will stop after the wedding. Unfortunately, it does not. The most recent information indicates that violence between teens who are dating or courting often precedes domestic violence or marital rape if the couple should marry. Teenage males are practicing their skills at sexual dominance and testing the boundaries of acceptable behavior. Thus, adolescent females in violent relationships before marriage or cohabitation can well expect that the violence will not disappear with the marriage vows or the moving in. Rather, the violence will likely be repeated and, in some cases, become more intensified. Most young women survive the violence they experience in their intimate relationships, but tragically many do not (Mignon, Larson, and Holmes, 2002).

Although statistics on violence in same-sex relationships do not specifically target dating relationships, the data shows that the prevalence of intimate partner violence among lesbian and gay couples is approximately 25 to 33 percent. Same-sex battering violence occurs within same-sex relationships with the same statistical frequency as in heterosexual relationships and, again, women are more often the victim (UIC Campus Advocacy Network, 2006). For example, a review of studies on same-sex domestic violence found that 22 to 46 percent of all lesbians have been in a physically violent same-sex relationship (Renzetti and Miley, 1996). There are many different types of abuse, some

In your opinion, what factors of life in the United States might account for the high incidence of dating violence? Why do you think that females are most often the victims of intimate violence? Are there battered males? What legal remedies could be enacted to deal effectively with dating violence? If you were asked to testify before the U.S. Congress on the subject of intimate violence, what would you say? How would you prepare for your testimony? What recommendations would you make?

of which are not obvious or physically harmful; however, all forms of dating abuse leave the victim (regardless of her or his sexual orientation) with scars. It is well to keep in mind, however, that while same-sex battering mirrors heterosexual battering both in type and prevalence, its victims receive fewer protections (Barnes, 1998).

Date rape is commonplace on college campuses today. In response to this growing problem, some colleges such as Hobart College in Geneva, New York, offer date-rape awareness workshops in an attempt to alleviate sexual assault in intimate relationships.

Date and Acquaintance Rape

Sexual assault is one of the most serious and fastest growing violent crimes in the United States. **Rape**—unwanted, forced, or coerced sexual intercourse—is the most extreme form of sexual abuse, although sexual assault includes (but is not limited to) treating a partner like a sex object, forcing someone to go further sexually than she/he wants to, and unwanted or uncomfortable touching. The Bureau of Justice Statistics reports that 94 percent of the reported incidents of sexual assaults in intimate relationships are committed by males, and 71 percent of these assaults are planned. According to the National Criminal Victim Center, one woman is raped every minute (National Crime Victimization Survey, 2005).

Just as our consciousness has become raised about intimate battering, we are also much more aware of the widespread sexual violence suffered by females in relationships with males whom they know and, in many cases, trust enough to date. This problem received national attention in the early 1990s when William Kennedy Smith, nephew of the late president John Kennedy, and Mike Tyson, former heavyweight boxing champion, were accused of sexual assault. In widely publicized trials, Smith was acquitted, and Tyson was convicted and sentenced to prison. The public debate surrounding these cases made many people aware that the majority of rapes are not committed by strangers. Rather, current estimates are that over 85 percent of all sexual assaults involve acquaintances or friends. Researchers report that in the United States, every year about 1.5 million women and more than 800,000 men are raped or physically assaulted by an intimate partner (Tjaden and Thoennes, 2000; Houston Area Women's Center, 1999). Rape of a person who simply knows or is familiar with the rapist is called **acquaintance rape.** And rape of a victim who is actually "going out with" the rapist is known as **date rape.** Acquaintance and date rape are a violation of a person's body and her/his trust. It is an act of violence and can be with someone a person has just met, or dated a few times, or even with someone to whom the vic-

tim is engaged. The force can come from threats or tone of voice as well as from physical force or weapons. These terms are so closely interrelated that they often are used interchangeably. Although most rapes are date or acquaintance rapes, most *reported* rapes are stranger rapes. The reason that most acquaintance and date rapes go unreported is because many people still believe that a sexual encounter between two people who know each other cannot be rape. Researchers have found that most young people do not define violence by an acquaintance or date as a problem; like older victims, they often do not recognize that they are victims of abuse (Ferguson, 1998).

A survey of adolescent and college students revealed that date rape accounted for 67 percent of sexual assaults. More than two-thirds of young women raped (68 percent) know the rapist either as a boyfriend, friend, or casual acquaintance. The younger the woman, the more likely that she knows the rapist. In 63 percent of reported cases of rape in which the victim was between 12 and 18 years of age and 80 percent of the cases in which the victim was younger than 12, the victim knew her attacker. Most of these rapes and sexual assaults (six in ten) occurred in the victim's own home or a friend or relative's home, not in a dark alley or parking garage (U.S. Department of Justice, 2002; Bureau of Justice Special Report, 2001).

Date rape and acquaintance rape cut across race, social class, and sexual orientation and can be found in all geographic regions. However, they are probably most commonplace on college campuses; rape is the most common violent crime reported on American college campuses today. For example, according to some reports, every 21 hours there is a rape on a college campus in the United States (UIC Campus Advocacy Network, 2006). Date and acquaintance rape occurs on virtually all campuses, public or private, urban or rural, large or small. Although most such cases go unreported (only 5 percent are reported to police), it is estimated that one in four college women have either been raped or suffered an attempted rape at least once since age 14. And almost one in four female students are victims of multiple rapes. Furthermore, nine in ten offenders were known to the college women victims, most often as a boyfriend, ex-boyfriend, classmate, or coworker, and the majority of the rapes took place on a date. Various survey data indicate that women ages 16 to 24 experience rape at rates four times higher than the sexual assault rape of all women, making the college (and high school) years the most vulnerable for women (Fisher, Cullen, and Turner, 2000).

Most females as well as males hold the attitude that the male use of force and aggression to have sexual intercourse is acceptable among acquaintances or dates, at least under certain circumstances, such as if the female arouses the male. Over a decade ago, researchers Crystal Mills and Barbara Granoff (1992) found that one in six male college students in their sample admitted to behavior that met the legal definition of sexual assault, while almost one in three (29 percent) admitted to continuing sexual advances after a women had said no. These findings are similar to an earlier study of sexual assault on college campuses conducted by *Ms.* magazine in which one in twelve college males admitted to having committed acts that met the legal definition of rape or attempted rape; that is, they admitted to having forced a woman to have intercourse or tried to force a woman to have intercourse through physical force or coercion. What is alarming is that almost none of these men identified themselves as rapists; 84 percent said that what they had done was *definitely* not rape. Equally alarming, of the women who were raped, almost three-fourths of them did not identify their experience as rape. In a 1999 survey, 35 percent of the men surveyed indicated some likelihood that they would commit a violent rape of a woman who had fended off an advance if they were assured of getting away with it (Rape Statistics, 1999). Recent rape and sexual assault surveys and research continue to report this gender gap: the great majority of college men who commit rape say that what they did was definitely not rape; over one-half of these men say they had sex again with their victims; nearly one-third say they are likely to have sex with an unwilling partner, if they thought they could get away with it; and 75 percent of young women think the issue is "extremely serious" compared to 57 percent of young men (Pennsylvania State University Sexual Assault Statistics, 2006; Lifetime Television, 2005; Fisher, Cullen, and Turner, 2000).

The incidence and prevalence of rape and sexual assault varies across types of college campuses. For instance, private colleges and major universities have higher than the national average rates of rape, while religiously affiliated institutions have lower than average rates. Also, students at two-year institutions are significantly more likely than those at four-year institutions to report having been forced during their lifetime to have sexual intercourse. That rape and sexual assault varies by school, type of school, and region suggests that there are perhaps certain schools and places within schools that are more rape-prone that others. Researchers have identified such features as frequent unsupervised parties, easy access to alcohol and drugs, single students living on their own, and the availability of private rooms as contributors to the high rape rates of women college students (Sampson, 2003). Historically, fraternities have contributed to coercive and often violent sex and sexual assault. According to some researchers, fraternities are very concerned with the expression of masculinity and seek to elevate the status of men above that of women. In this context, women are treated as commodities; that is, fraternity males knowingly and intentionally use women as sexual prey, creating a climate in which rape can and does occur. Despite this fact, many institutions of higher education have only recently begun to deal with sexual assault on campus.

Although the majority of the victims of campus rape and sexual assault are women, college men also report incidents of rape. However, college men who are raped are usually raped by other men and because so few men report their rape, statistical data is limited relative to the extent of the problem. Even current national data collection systems such as the FBI's Uniform Crime Report fail to provide data on male rape victims. The limited research that does provide such information is provided by recent surveys that suggest up to 10 percent of acquaintance rape victims on college campuses are men (Center for Problem-oriented Policing, 2003).

Finally, in the last decade of the twentieth century, Rohypnol, the "date rape drug," came to public attention. It has been used on many college campuses as well as at youth parties called "raves." The drug comes in pill form and is typically slipped unnoticed into a female's drink. The combined effect of the drug and the alcohol produces such intense intoxication that upon awaking from the drug-induced sleep, the victim is unable to remember what has happened. The seriousness of Rohypnol pushed Congress to pass the Drug-Induced Rape Prevention and Punishment Act in 1996, which made it a federal crime to give someone a controlled substance without her or his knowledge with the intention of committing a violent crime (such as rape). Currently, the penalty for a person found guilty of violating this law is up to 20 years in prison and a $250,000 fine.

Teen battering and date and acquaintance rape should not come as a surprise to us. Sociologically speaking, it is a reflection of the violence within relationships that is accepted socially and reflected in virtually every aspect of our mass culture—from movies to print and electronic advertisements to fiction as well as nonfiction to video games to MTV, BET Music Videos, and other popular music to daily talk shows to soap operas and most other forms of everyday television. In the context of a sociological analysis, rape is a behavior learned by men in the context of "masculinity." And, date rape can be considered an outgrowth of a cultural socialization into masculinity (Lindsay, 1995). Male socialization sets the stage for rape in that being aggressive is considered normal masculine behavior, being sexually aggressive is masculine, and rape is sexually aggressive behavior; therefore, rape is masculine behavior. Because American culture still supports female and male relationships that are stereotypically masculine and feminine—passive-aggressive and submissive-dominant—notions of masculinity are often associated with violence and force.

Many things can be done to reduce or eradicate courtship violence. Given that rape is learned behavior within the context of a masculine self-concept, it can be unlearned. We can teach future generations of males new roles that do not emphasize and exaggerate domination, aggression, and sexual prowess. On college campuses, administrators must deal with sexual aggression swiftly and punitively without blaming the victim. In addition, campus security police must work cooperatively with local police officials to expedite the prosecution of offenders. Furthermore, colleges should provide counseling and other referral services for both the perpetrators and the victims of both physical and sexual assault. Although some colleges and universities are responding proactively, positively, and efficiently in their attempts to prevent courtship violence or to alleviate its effects, much more remains to be done.

BREAKING UP

It sounds very pessimistic, but some researchers claim that nearly all romances fail. Some end before they get off the ground and others sputter out early. According to one survey, American adults have experienced a breakup of a romantic relationship at least twice during their lifetime, and almost one in four say that they have been "dumped" six or more times by a romantic partner (Mundell, 2002). Most serious dating relationships end after 2 or so years, and even if a relationship succeeds and the couple marries, the relationship still faces a 50–50 chance of breaking up (divorce). Couples who have the best chance of not breaking up are those who are equally matched from the start: equally committed, equally attractive, and of similar backgrounds (Manis, 2001). As with marriage, one or both dating or cohabiting partners may feel the need to get out of the relationship. Breaking up a relationship can take many forms: The partners drift apart or stop calling or coming by; they have a fight over a minor incident or something said in anger; or, in rare cases, both agree to terminate the relationship. Breaking up can be very painful, especially if the breakup is not mutually agreed upon.

As in other aspects of dating and courtship behavior, some researchers have found gender differences related to breakups before marriage. For example, most breakups are initiated by women; however, the chances of the breakup being amiable is far greater if the male initiates the breakup. As we pointed out in Chapter 4, men are more likely than women to report feeling depressed, lonely, unhappy, and less free after a breakup. However, men get over breakups more quickly than women. For example, men resume dating after a breakup much sooner than women do and women, more often than men, call friends and family members for consolation and comfort after a breakup (Fetto, 2003). No matter the gender, however, it is easier on a person when she or he is the leaver than the person being left. Leavers feel guiltier, but otherwise much less lonely or depressed than those who are left. In fact, often the happier one person is to get out of the relationship, the worse the other person feels about the breakup (Manis, 2001).

Some social scientists claim that breaking up before marriage is less stressful than breaking up after marriage, when the couple has to deal with legally ending the relationship and with possible custody issues. Furthermore, breaking up is viewed as a logical consequence of the courtship filtering process, whereby those who are incompatible eventually break up before they make the "ultimate" commitment: marriage. Even if this is true, breaking up is seldom easy and can have substantial consequences, no matter what the relationship or who makes the break. When people who are emotionally involved break up, they frequently experience feelings of insecurity, anxiety, low self-esteem, and guilt. "What's wrong with me?" "Will I find someone else?" "Will I be alone the rest of my life?" "What did I do to deserve this?" Unlike in marriage, there is no institutionalized means, such as divorce, to handle the breakup of a dating relationship; however, as our expert (family therapist Joan Zientek) tells us, like married couples, dating couples interested in strengthening and preserving their relationships and sorting through and dealing with anger and hurt, misunderstandings and miscommunications can avail themselves of the counseling and advice of family therapists.

SUPPORTING MARRIAGES AND FAMILIES

Dating, hooking up, going out, getting together—or whatever term one uses to describe the process of meeting and socializing with someone for possible long-term intimacy—is a common feature of American society. It may lead to marriage. But, whether or not one is on the way to the altar, dating is supposed to have a romantic, light, and fun quality. It is a form of recreation where couples go out to relax, enjoy themselves, and have fun. Dating and mate selection, however, is far more complex than merely two or more people engaging in recreational behavior or just "having fun." People who date and mate are members of families, and thus the impact of what they do and how they do it during the process of mate selection goes beyond the specific individuals involved.

Our ideas and feelings about love, intimacy, dating, and mate selection are influenced by cultural stereotypes about gender, race, and sexual identity. Unfortunately, many of the norms and values associated with dating and intimacy can, and often do, lead to unhealthy, addictive, and even lethal behavior. We spent some time at the end of this chapter discussing intimate partner violence, particularly that which occurs within dating relationships. Such violence has significant psychological, economic, health, and social consequences. The psychological harm to victims of violence includes shock, humiliation, anxiety, depression, substance abuse, posttraumatic stress syndrome, suicidal thoughts and behavior, loss of self-esteem, social isolation, anger, distrust of others, guilt, and sexual dysfunction. Economic consequences include the costs of providing health care and other services, increased absenteeism, decreased productivity, and lower earnings. For example, according to the Centers for Disease Control and Prevention, the annual health-related direct costs of intimate partner violence exceeds $5.8 billion each year. This figure breaks down to almost $4.1 billion spent on direct medical and mental health care services, just about $1 billion represents the lost productivity from paid and household chores, and $1 billion is lifetime earnings lost

WRITING YOUR OWN SCRIPT

PERSONAL BIOGRAPHY AND SOCIAL STRUCTURE

Selecting a Mate

Think about the structure of mate selection in U.S. society generally and in the various social groups to which you belong. Write a short essay that includes an analysis of your mate selection in terms of the following framework.

First, think about what initially attracts you to another person. Consider this question within the context of some or all of the following possibilities: physical attractiveness, race, age, sexual orientation, religion, residence, occupational status, popularity, social status, personality, character. Are you attracted to people very much like you, or the opposite?

Next, ask your parents or others with whom you are close and whose opinions you value, whom among the following they would object to if you dated or married:

Race: African American, white American, Asian American, Native American, Puerto Rican, Mexican American, other Latino, other race.

Age: 15, 20, 25, 30, 35, 40, 45, 55, 65, 75, 76 or older.

Educational level: Fifth grade or below, eighth grade only, some high school, high school graduate, some college, college graduate, graduate or professional school.

Religion: Catholic, Baptist, Methodist, Muslim, Buddhist, Mormon, Lutheran, Unification Church, Orthodox Jew, Jehovah's Witness, atheist, other.

Blood relatives: First cousin, second cousin, third or more removed cousin.

Gender: Same sex.

Also think about the following questions, and incorporate your responses in the essay. How do you feel about interracial dating and marriages? Do you know anyone who is dating or married to a person of a different racial group? What problems, if any, have they encountered? Have you ever been involved in an interracial relationship? If not, would you consider such a relationship? What barriers do you think you would encounter if you were a partner in such a relationship? Are any members of your immediate family dating or married interracially? If yes, how do you feel about these relationships? To what extent do parents, relatives, and friends' attitudes about interracial dating and marriage affect your dating and marital choices?

---

by victims of intimate partner violence. Furthermore, injuries sustained from violence perpetrated against girls and women by current or former dates, boyfriends, cohabitants, husbands, or former husbands result in 18.5 million mental and physical health care visits each year and the lost of 8 million days of paid work each year. This loss of days of paid work is the equivalent of 32,114 full-time jobs each year (Centers for Disease Control and Prevention, 2003; Sampson, 2002). From these figures alone, it seems clear that intimate partner violence generally and that against women and girls specifically places a significant burden on individuals, families, and society at large. It contributes to reduced quality of life of families and communities and decreased participation by women in democratic processes (Sampson, 2002).

Given that dating and other intimate partner violence exacts an enormous toll on individuals, families, and society, national policymakers, civil society, and communities must be galvanized to address the pervasive violence in society to protect individuals and strengthen American marriages and families. We must strengthen existing policies that pertain to intimate partner violence, ensure that there are ample resources available to respond to such violence, and increase ongoing efforts in this regard. It is important to explore cultural and societal policies and initiatives that will assist people, especially teens, in making and engaging in healthy love and dating relationships. For example, many of the issues that surround and contribute to teen dating violence include the fact that teens are often inexperienced with dating relationships, have romanticized views about love and intimacy, and are often pressured by their peers to have dating relationships. Moreover, teen dating violence is influenced by how teenagers view themselves and others. On the one hand, many young male teens believe that they have the right to "control" their female partners in any way necessary, that masculinity is physical aggressiveness, that their partner is their property, that they can and should demand—be in control—and that they might lose respect if they are attentive and supportive toward their girlfriends. Girls, on the other hand, believe that their boyfriend's jealousy, possessiveness, and even his physical and/or sexual abuse is "romantic," that abuse in intimate relationships is "normal" because their friends are also being abused, that they can change their abusive boyfriend, and that most often there is no one to ask for help (Cool Nurse, 2005). Policies, initiatives, and community programs are needed that will support teaching teens that they are valuable people and that will teach them how to choose healthy relationships.

Although increased resources are needed for effective responses to intimate partner violence, some of the most effective solutions for preventing intimate partner violence and methods for strengthening marriages and families lie in mobilizing communities to transform norms on the acceptability of violence within dating and other intimate relationships, including within families and at the cultural level, to transform norms that define women and girls as subordinate to men and boys and that narrowly define masculinity and femininity and how women and men should relate to each other.

SUMMARY

Mate selection refers loosely to the wide range of behaviors and social relationships that individuals engage in prior to marriage that lead to short- or long-term pairing. It is an institutionalized feature of social life and can be found in some form in all human societies, although the exact processes vary widely from one society to another. In the United States, the mate selection process, particularly for first marriages, is highly youth-centered and competitive.

Mate selection customs vary widely across cultures. Most researchers have divided mate selection customs along a traditional/nonindustrialized and nontraditional/industrialized society continuum. A review of mate selection cross-culturally reveals that many traditional societies now combine traditional and contemporary methods of selecting mates. Dating, an American invention that first appeared in the 1920s, is the focus of our courtship system and incorporates a wide range of social relationships prior to marriage. The history of mate selection in this country has ranged from highly visible parental involvement during the colonial and preindustrial periods to the informal, indirect involvement of parents today. Dating became a widespread phenomenon in the 1920s and 1930s; in the 1940s and 1950s it filtered down to high school students, who started to "go steady"; in the 1960s, 1970s, and 1980s it became a more casual process; and during the 1980s and 1990s dating underwent many changes that reflect contemporary social and gender roles. Today, dating is based far more on mutuality and sharing than on traditional gender roles. Given today's extended life expectancy, an increasing number of later-life Americans are entering and reentering the dating scene. Because dating and mate selection has changed considerably since some later-life adults have been in the dating game, many have to learn anew the rules of the dating game.

The functions of dating include socialization, development of self-image, recreation, and status grading and achievement. Like all other social behavior and organization, dating is deeply rooted in the social and historical conditions of life. Race, gender, class, and sexual orientation are basic and central categories in American life, and thus must be considered in any analysis of mate selection.

A wide range of theories exists that attempt to explain who selects whom and under what circumstances. These theories include explanations in terms of social exchanges and rewards, stimulus-value-role theories, and filtering theories. The process of mate selection can be viewed sociologically as a sequential or filtering process that stresses homogamy and endogamy. Mate selection in U.S. society is mediated by a range of structural and social factors: the nature of the marriage market, the marriage squeeze and marriage gradient, race, class, age, sex, religion, education, propinquity, family and peers, and cultural ideals about beauty and worth. Due to the impact of these factors, we are very much like the people we meet, fall in love with, and marry—far more so than can simply be attributed to chance. Computer technology has had a dramatic impact on the nature of mate selection around the world. Increasingly, couples are using cyberspace not only for recreation but also for serious mate selection. Many of these matches are leading to matrimony.

However, not all intimate relationships lead to marriage or long-term commitment. Couples often break up under the pressure of a variety of sociopolitical factors. Moreover, a large number of dating couples are involved in physically or sexually abusive relationships. Battering and abuse among young couples as early as elementary and junior high school has reached epidemic proportions. The same can be said for date and acquaintance rape. In both cases, the victims are overwhelmingly female. Most intimate relationships, however, survive the problems of human frailty. Couples wishing to strengthen and preserve their dating and intimate relationships can and do seek family counseling. Given that dating and other intimate partner violence exacts an enormous toll on individuals, families, and society, national policymakers, civil society, and communities must be galvanized to address the pervasive violence in society to protect individuals and strengthen American marriages and families.

KEY TERMS

dating	sex ratio	exogamy	propinquity
mate selection	cruising	endogamy	dating violence
courtship	marriage market	marriage squeeze	rape
getting together	dowries	marriage gradient	acquaintance rape
going steady	pool of eligibles	hypergamy	date rape
anticipatory socialization	homogamy	hypogamy	

QUESTIONS FOR STUDY AND REFLECTION

1. As you have read in this chapter, dating patterns in the United States have changed dramatically over the years. What are the current norms of dating in your community? On your college campus? Are these norms different or the same for each gender? Explain. What do you consider the advantages and disadvantages of such norms? What, if any, changes would you like to see in today's dating norms?

2. "Cupid's arrow does not strike at random." Explain this statement. Discuss the predictable factors that influence who meets, falls in love with, and marries whom in the United States.

3. Define the concepts of "marriage squeeze" and "marriage gradient." How are the two related? How would the marriage squeeze and marriage gradient be significant in the lives of a 35-year-old female with a Ph.D. and a 35-year-old male who is a high school dropout? Why is the marriage squeeze so significant for African American women? Find information about the marriage squeeze for other groups of women.

4. Think about the discussion in this chapter of violence in dating relationships. How prevalent is date rape and other intimate violence on your college or university campus? What are some of the attitudes, behaviors, and activities on your campus that encourage male physical and sexual aggressiveness and contribute to a climate that is conducive toward abuse? Is there any information about male victims of rape on your campus? Have you ever experienced relationship violence? If yes, how did you handle it? What institutional supports and services on your campus are there for victims of dating violence? In your community, city, and state?

ADDITIONAL RESOURCES

SOCIOLOGICAL

BECKER, CAROL S. 1988. *Unbroken Ties: Lesbian Ex-Lovers.* Boston: Alyson. An interesting case study approach to lesbian interpersonal relations, including separation.

KAUFMAN, MICHAEL. 1995. "The Construction of Masculinity and the Triad of Men's Violence." In Michael Kimmel and Michael Messner, eds., *Men's Lives*, pp. 13–25. New York: Macmillan. A provocative article that examines male violence in the social context of the construction of masculinity and the institutionalization of violence in the operation of most aspects of social, economic, and political life in the United States.

KIRKWOOD, CATHERINE. 1993. *Leaving Abusive Partners.* Newbury Park, CA: Sage. A compelling collection of stories by 30 formerly abused women told in their own voices.

WOOD, JULIA T., ED. 1996. *Gendered Relationships.* Mountain View, CA: Mayfield. An excellent set of readings on gendered relationships, focusing specifically on the reciprocal influence between gender and intimacy. The readings cover issues of communication, friendship, heterosexual love, lesbian and gay romantic relationships, sexuality and AIDS, intimate violence, sexual harassment, and gender issues in the workplace.

LITERARY

FIELDING, HELEN. 1999. *Bridget Jones's Diary: A Novel.* New York: Penguin. This lively paperback is witty and full of candor. It captures very well the way modern women teeter between being independent and a pathetic girlie desire to be all things to all men. It includes Bridget's quest for the right man, her affair with her charming cad of a boss, e-mail flirtations, as well as her mother's incessant attempts to arrange a date for Bridget with some guy that Bridget does not know. It is an excellent novel to get students talking about many of the issues discussed in this chapter. The book was made into a movie.

MCMILLAN, TERRY. 1997. *How Stella Got Her Groove Back.* New York: Signet Books. This novel is a chronicle of the dating and mate selection experiences of an African American divorced superwoman who has everything—except an intimate relationship with a man, something she is convinced she can well do without. However, much to her dismay, when she meets a man half her age while on vacation in Jamaica, she soon realizes that she must make some difficult decisions about her passions, desires, and dating, mating, and marital expectations. This novel is a good jump-off for a discussion of age differences in heterosexual intimate relationships, particularly when the woman is older than the man.

FILM

Must Love Dogs. 2005. A romantic comedy centered around the comic potential of Internet dating. After a recent divorce, a fortysomething woman, who is hesitant to get back into the dating scene, is pressured by her overly involved family to find a man by placing an ad for her in an on-line dating site. The movie touches on issues such as finding *the* love of one's life, the problems of on-line dating, a love triangle, the search for love and companionship after the death of a loved one, and the not so pretty side of love.

Pride and Prejudice. 1995. An adaptation of Jane Austen's classic romance novel about the prejudice that occurred between the nineteenth century classes and the pride that would keep lovers apart. Elizabeth Bennett is a strong-willed yet sensible young woman in a well-off but lower-class family with five sisters, a long-suffering but loving father, and a mother anxious to marry them to wealthy young gentlemen. At a local ball, she encounters one such wealthy young man, but he is arrogant, cold, and rude—it is hatred at first sight. However, as the characters succumb in many ways to pride and prejudice, Elizabeth learns that not all in matters of love is what it seems.

INTERNET

www.CollegeClub.com This Web site, part of the Student Advantage Network, allows students to connect with each other; it provides them with a variety of information and services from academics to love, dating relationships, and much more. For example, through its MatchU engine it allows students to meet and match up on-line.

www.meetmeonline.com Powered by AmericanSingles.com, this site is advertised as the best place on the Internet to meet someone. It boasts of a membership of 3 million high-quality singles.

www.agelesslove.com The first Web site exclusively devoted to older women and younger men/older men and younger women relationship support and intergenerational dating. A wide range of subjects are discussed in a number of forums regarding age-gap relationships.

www.match.com The world's largest on-line dating, relationships, singles, and personals service, offering its members a range of services including an on-line advice magazine, local personals, match international, and match mobile, a feature that will connect members anonymously with singles near them on their mobile.

IN THE NEWS

San Francisco, California

For most American teens, oral sex is not sex—so says a variety of recent studies and surveys of teenage sexuality. According to most of these studies and surveys, more teens today are engaging in oral sex than intercourse, perceive it as less risky, and are less likely to use protection while doing it. For example, researchers at the University of California—San Francisco (Halpern-Felsher et al., 2005) report that about one in five students said they'd had oral sex, compared with approximately one in seven who said they'd had intercourse. In addition, nearly one in three said they planned on having oral sex within the next six months, compared with one in four students who planned to have intercourse. The University of California—San Francisco researchers surveyed 580 ethnically diverse northern California ninth graders about their attitudes and behavior toward oral sex and their perceptions of the consequences of having oral sex as opposed to vaginal sex. On average, the teens perceived oral sex to carry fewer health and emotional risks and to be more socially acceptable than vaginal intercourse. For instance, they felt that oral sex was less likely to have negative social and emotional consequences such as a bad reputation, feeling bad about themselves, feeling guilty, or getting into trouble. Furthermore, they believed that having oral sex is less of a threat to their relationship with their partner. They also believed that oral sex is more acceptable than vaginal intercourse for adolescents their own age in both dating and nondating situations, that it is less of a threat to their values and beliefs, and that more of their peers were having and were likely to have oral sex rather than vaginal sex in the near future. Interestingly, girls and boys reported similar experiences and opinions about oral sex; both sexes view oral sex as not being a big deal. However, most surveys have found that in most cases of oral sex, it is girls doing the giving, often because they feel they must to keep their boyfriend (Lanzendorfer, 2002).

Although an increasing number of youths—some still in middle school—are having oral sex, they consider themselves virgins. In a dramatic reversal from what their parents believe, it seems that today's youth do not count oral sex as "having sex." They have convinced themselves that oral sex is not really sex, that sex is only vaginal intercourse (Remez, 2000). For instance, in a 2004 NBC News and *People* Magazine survey of 13- to 16-year olds, more than half of the teen respondents maintained that teens who only engage in oral sex are still virgins (MSNBC.com, 2005). Thus, although many teens might define themselves as abstinent and as virgins, they may be engaging in oral sex. Some observers of the teen sexuality scene have dubbed this attitude and behavior *technical virginity* and suggest it has become an important part of teens' sexuality equation today (Jayson, 2005a). They say that many of these teens are more casual about oral sex and view it differently than have other generations. Some teens view it so casually that it need not even occur within the confines of a relationship. They say it can take place at parties and in groups, possibly with multiple partners, and they do not see anything wrong with it. They also say, however, that most likely it occurs within an existing relationship (Jayson, 2005a, 2005b). Some surveyors have found that many teens will talk freely about what happens among their friends. For example, a 15-year-old in Green Bay, Wisconsin, reported that as early as sixth or seventh grade, children brag about having oral sex. According to this teen, the consensus at her high school is that oral sex makes girls popular, whereas intercourse would make them outcasts. Teens say that they engage in oral sex to let out sexual tensions, that it is something that happens at a party, whispered about between friends, and forgotten about the next week. Oral sex is just part of making out. Their attitude is, "What is the big deal?" (Remez, 2000).

That so many teens are having oral sex and view it as safe has important implications for the actual health risk of these teenagers. On the one hand, with oral sex there is no risk of pregnancy. However, on the other hand, the risk of sexually transmitted diseases (STDs) is definitely present. Oral sex puts young people in jeopardy of contracting sexually transmitted diseases, including the HIV/AIDS virus. In fact, a number of reports from family planning clinicians are showing evidence of dramatic increases in oral herpes and gonorrhea in the throats of teens. The American Social Health Association (ASHA) estimates the direct medical costs of the 9.1 million new cases of STDs in 2000 among youths aged 15 to 24 at $6.5 billion (Gardner, 2005). Part of the issue, according to one expert, is that Americans define sexual behavior in a very narrow way. We caution young people to abstain, but we are never clear as to what they should be abstaining from. Consequently, many young people try to think of anything they can do so they can say they are still virgins.

Does the data tell the whole story? For instance, what kind of oral sex do teens engage in, and does oral sex come first and vaginal intercourse at some later time? Or do the vast majority of teens who engage in oral sex also engage in sexual intercourse? We do not know the answer to questions such as these because most studies and surveys do not gather information about this intimacy sequence. Notwithstanding this fact, there is evidence that the trend of teens engaging in oral sex yet defining themselves as virgins transcends race, income, and family structure and is much more widespread than we might think. For some of these teens, intercourse is a huge leap from oral sex. For most teens, intercourse is something that is carefully thought through before acted upon. Unfortunately, there is not very good or consistent research on teen sexuality, especially oral sex, because until recently most major national surveys on teen sexual activity did not ask about oral sex and most did not question the youngest teens. In general, the University of California–San Francisco study and other recent studies and surveys on teen sexuality point out the problem inherent in classifying people as "sexually active" based on whether they have ever had vaginal intercourse (Peterson, 2000).

WHAT WOULD YOU DO? If you have teenagers or have a close relationship with teenagers, would you attempt to educate them about the risk connection between oral sex and STDs generally and HIV/AIDS specifically? Would you support sex education in the schools? As early as elementary school? Regardless of their relationship to you, would you counsel them on how to use condoms and how to get them? On how to talk with a partner about either abstinence or safe-sex practices? And would you counsel them on how to get tested for HIV and other STDs?

Sex continues to be the topic "du jour" in the early years of the twenty-first century. Continuing a pattern that emerged in the late twentieth century, sex and talk of sex, images of sex, sex scandals, and media and popular culture hype about sex are pervasive in the United States today. And no one is exempt from sexual scrutiny. For example, in the last decade of the twentieth century, a sitting president was involved in a highly publicized sex scandal with a young White House intern, in which he claimed, not unlike the teens described in the In the News opening this chapter, that oral sex was not having sex.

Sex is on television (prime time, soap operas, talk shows, comedians' dialogue), in advertisements, newspapers, the films we view, the music we listen to, the books and magazines we read, and increasingly in cyberspace. Even traditional women's magazines such as *Redbook* and *Glamour* have entered the fray. These and other women's magazines as well as other forms of the media have become increasingly brazen about dealing with the subject of sex, a trend most assuredly tied to the fact that our entire society is loosening up about sex. We are indeed talking about sex today more than at any other time in our history, and this makes sex more accessible than it has ever been.

Sex sells. It is titillating—most people are intrigued by any discussion of it, particularly when it involves other people's behavior and especially when the people are well known. However, probably no topic related to issues of marriage and family life is more shrouded with mystery, curiosity, intrigue, and controversy than is sex specifically and human sexuality more generally (see our definitions in the next section). The concept of human sexuality often is couched in terms of morality. The purpose of this chapter, however, is not to clarify or shape your morality, but rather to increase your understanding of the sociopolitical nature of human sexuality and in the process enhance your ability to make personal decisions concerning sexual behavior.

Because sexuality figures so prominently in marriage and family life, as well as in other intimate relationships, this chapter, in conjunction with the supplementary materials presented in Appendix A, concentrates on sexual attitudes and behaviors before, during, and after marriage or a committed relationship as well as throughout the life cycle. We begin with a brief discussion of the historical roots of Western sexuality, from the Judeo–Christian tradition to U.S. sexual codes in the early twenty-first century. We then consider the social basis of human sexuality by examining sexual learning and how sexual scripts vary across gender, as well as trends in sexual attitudes and behavior, including sexual orientation. In addition, we discuss physiological aspects of sexuality such as human sexual response and expression. We also examine various codes of sexual conduct and patterns of sexual relationships across the life cycle. Finally, we examine human sexuality within the context of sexual responsibility and protecting yourself and your partners from AIDS and other sexually transmitted diseases.

HUMAN SEXUALITY: PAST AND PRESENT

Often people use the terms *sex* and *sexuality* interchangeably. Thus, when someone talks about sexuality, we often assume that she or he is referring to sexual intercourse. On the other hand, when we speak of sex it is not always immediately clear whether we are speaking of sexual activity such as intercourse or whether we mean a person's genetic sex (that is, biologically female or male). Although neither of these uses is incorrect, for the purposes of clarification and consistency, we try to use the term *sexual activity* or *sexuality* to refer to a wide range of sexual behaviors, including intercourse. However, it is not always so simple a choice. In those cases, we use the term *sex*—not to refer to biological females or males but to refer to sexual intercourse or other sexual activities. We hope this does not confuse the reader.

Because human sexuality is so broad, no one all-encompassing definition is appropriate. In general terms, however, **human sexuality** refers to the feelings, thoughts, attitudes, values, and behaviors of humans, who have learned a set of cues that evoke a sexual or an erotic response. It includes behaviors well known to us, such as sexual intercourse and masturbation, as well as behaviors we do not readily identify as sexual, such as breast-feeding, giving birth, and talking affectionately with someone (Albas and Albas, 1989b). Furthermore, human sexuality involves issues of power, authority, and emotional and physical vulnerability in relationships (Boston Women's Health Book Collective, 2005), as you shall see in the discussion of gender differences in the experience of sexuality and, particularly, of the sexual double standard.

We are sexual beings, and a large proportion of our lives consists of sexual daydreaming, fantasy, and desire; reading about sexual activities or viewing a wide range of sexual behaviors; sexual pleasure, activity, joy, and pain. Given the fact that sexuality is such an important dimension of human experience, all societies are involved, in some way, in controlling the sexual behavior of their members. Although the ways in which sexual behavior is controlled have varied over time and from culture to culture, all societies have a set of rules or codes that define appropriate sexual behavior. Throughout U.S. history, Americans have been subject to one set of sexual codes or another. The codes we adhere to today have their roots in sexual attitudes and practices that existed hundreds, if not thousands, of years ago. Before we discuss the history of human sexuality in Western society, two points must be made:

1. Although the historical descriptions emphasize the sexual codes that were most prevalent during a given historical period, it is not our intention to imply that sexual ideas and behavior have progressed directly from very strict and repressive codes of sexual conduct to more liberal sexual norms. Rather, sexual ideas and behavior change according to cyclical patterns, with periods of extremely or moderately repressive norms followed by periods of more liberal norms. In addition, at any given time, many different sexual codes, ideas, and behaviors coexist.

2. Generalizations about human behavior are always risky. Human attitudes and behavior are so flexible that they are never the same for all people or all groups. Thus, there are many variations in sexual attitudes and behavior. The historical period in which people live; the political and economic climate; the social organization of race, class, and gender; and factors such as sexual orientation, age, and religion all affect human attitudes and behavior.

Consider, for example, the effects of gender on sexual behavior. Women historically have experienced sexuality in terms of reproduction, oppression (powerlessness), and vulnerability (victims of sexual assault). In contrast, men have experienced sexuality primarily in terms of power and control, passion and emotions, and freedom of sexual choice and behavior. Furthermore, sex and sexuality traditionally have been defined in terms of heterosexuality and monogamy, with homosexuality considered a form of deviance. Thus, for lesbians and gays, the experience of sexuality has been far more repressive and has involved a high degree of public concern and social control by outside forces such as the state.

Similarly, the sexuality of various racial groups (African Americans, Latinas/os, Native Americans, and Asian Americans) as well as poor people of all races has been defined primarily by outsiders. Thus, these groups have often been defined in scientific research or the popular culture as sexually promiscuous and uncontrolled. These definitions of sexuality often have been used in conjunction with other ideologies of racial inferiority to rationalize oppression and unequal treatment. These examples illustrate how human sexuality involves issues of power and authority and emotional and physical vulnerability. As you read this chapter, keep this point in mind. In addition, keep in mind that human sexuality is not static; rather, it is a dynamic, or changing, process that is continually being shaped and reshaped through the social organization of many diverse factors at any given time.

Jewish Traditions and Human Sexuality

Ancient Jewish tradition placed great emphasis on marriage and reproduction. Women and men who did not marry and have children were considered sinful. Marriage was the only appropriate context for sexual intercourse, the sole purpose of which was reproduction. Although in principle the norm of premarital chastity applied to both sexes, it was more rigidly applied to women. A woman was supposed to be a virgin at the time of marriage. If she was not, she could be put to death. Moreover, women could not own property, nor could they obtain a divorce without their husband's consent. A further restriction placed on women's sexuality can be seen in the rules surrounding menstruation. Because menstruation was considered unclean, menstruating women were isolated from their husbands and other family members and were forbidden to engage in sexual activities. Strongly forbidden by Jewish custom were nakedness, masturbation, and homosexuality. Although homosexuality was not mentioned in earlier Hebrew codes, it was made punishable by death in later Hebrew documents. Some scholars claim that early Judaism represented a transition from a more positive view of sexual behavior, a view prominent in ancient times, to a more restrictive view characteristic of the early Christian period (Harmatz and Novak, 1983).

The two ancient Jewish notions about human sexuality—reproduction as a married couple's obligation and male dominance over women in sexual relations—became a part of Christian as well as non-Christian doctrine and to some degree can still be found in contemporary U.S. sexual codes.

Christian Traditions and Human Sexuality

Although in the Gospels Jesus refers to marriage as a sacred union, values pertaining to women, marriage, and sexuality decreased as Christian ideas of chastity took hold. The early Christian sexual tradition seems to have been influenced most by St. Paul, who believed that celibacy is superior to marriage and that all humans should strive for a chaste life. A person who could not resist sexual temptation could engage in sexual intercourse, but only within marriage. In the fifth century, the Christian scholar St. Augustine continued Paul's tradition of condemning sexuality, and his influence lasted throughout the Middle Ages. St. Augustine believed that all sexual experience was lustful and shameful and would lead one to burn in Hell for eternity. He saw intercourse as animal lust to be tolerated for the sake of procreation. Celibacy, however, was the ideal, but for the weak-willed it was better that they marry than burn in Hell. Church documents of the eighth century specified that only the male-superior, or "missionary," position was to be used, because any other position might cause some enjoyment. People who engaged in other than the male-superior position faced a range of penalties. During the thirteenth century, the church, through the writings of St. Thomas Aquinas, renewed its position on sexuality. Sexual intercourse continued to be viewed as animalistic, an activity to be avoided except for reproduction. Celibacy and virginity were the ideals; masturbation, engaging in intercourse while unclothed, during the daylight, or in forbidden postures became sexual crimes that had to be confessed. In addition, nakedness, looking at parts of the body, dancing, singing, and touching other people were also considered sinful (Shriver et al., 2002).

The Protestant Reformation of the sixteenth century ushered in a diversity of views and attitudes concerning human sexuality. Religious reformer Martin Luther, for example, renounced celibacy as an unnatural and unrealistic goal for human beings. Leaving the priesthood to marry, he considered sex to be a natural and appropriate act when carried out within the context of marriage. Likewise, other theologians, such as John Calvin, argued against celibacy, believing sex was a holy act when it occurred within marriage. Although Christianity exerted considerable influence, not everyone adhered to its teachings concerning human sexuality. For instance, it has been noted that during most historical periods sexual behavior varies according to social class. Often the middle classes followed the prevailing sexual mores more closely than did the aristocrats (upper classes) or the peasants (lower classes).

Sexuality in the United States: An Overview

Puritan Sexuality In the seventeenth century, Puritan immigrants from England brought their Calvinist sexual traditions to the United States. The Puritans defined marriage as a covenant of God and thus the only legitimate mechanism for sex and procreation. Inside marriage, sex was an act that brought a wife and husband together morally and physically. The Puritans also believed that a husband was obliged to satisfy his wife physically. Outside marriage, sex was considered a sin and a threat to the institutions of marriage and the family. Sanctions against premarital and extramarital sex thus were very rigidly enforced. As in earlier historical periods, sexual codes of conduct were especially restrictive and rigid regarding female sexuality. Some of the Puritan views on sexuality can still be found in contemporary U.S. sexual attitudes and behavior. As late as the 1980s, many of the sex laws still on the books in various states throughout the country were a legacy of the Puritan forefathers. For example, in some communities it was still illegal to kiss on Sundays (a law

In early America, sanctions against premarital and extramarital sex were strictly enforced. The novel *The Scarlet Letter* illustrated the kind of punishment women could receive for violating their marriage vows. For example, women who engaged in extramarital sex were often forced to wear an "A" on their clothing to signify that they had committed adultery.

marital and extramarital affairs, was accepted (although not necessarily approved of), whereas similar behaviors by women were condemned (Shriver et al., 2002). Whereas single women were to refrain from sex altogether, married women were taught that sex with their husbands was their wifely duty—that they must tolerate and accommodate the animalistic nature of men. Given men's alleged greater sexual appetite and needs, wives were taught to look the other way when their husbands had extramarital affairs or engaged in sexual activities with prostitutes. Many of these Victorian ideas persist in some form in American society today. This differing set of norms based on gender is referred to as the **sexual double standard**.

According to some scholars, human sexuality during the Victorian era was characterized by contradiction, hypocrisy, and ambivalence. For example, sexual pleasuring activities such as masturbation were considered the cause of various maladies such as blindness and insanity. Given the Victorian views of sexuality, the Social Purity Movement in the United States began a campaign of sexual abstinence. Moreover, during this period there was an extreme ambivalence regarding homosexuality. Although in previous historical periods homosexuality had been considered sinful, in the Victorian era it became criminalized. Some writers have pointed out that the contradictory nature of the Victorian view of sexuality and the norms regulating it—despite the strict Victorian position regarding sexual virtue and restraint, prostitution flourished in the United States (for example, authorities counted 20,000 prostitutes in Manhattan, New York, alone in 1830) (Shriver et al., 2002).

The degree to which people adhered to the Victorian sexual codes varied from one social group to another. As in earlier periods, the rich and ruling elites basically ignored the restrictions and enjoyed considerable freedom in their sexual behavior. At the other end of the class structure, the poor were also exempted from the prevailing codes. As we indicated earlier, sexual purity was reserved for middle-class white women. Working-class, immigrant, and nonwhite women, on the other hand, were viewed as strongly sexual; in fact, they were defined as depraved and loose. This stereotype functioned as a rationalization for the continued mistreatment of these groups, especially the repeated rapes of African American women by white men (Basow, 1992).

Sexuality and Slavery   If Victorian norms regarding sexuality applied only to certain groups of whites, they did not apply at all to blacks. The lives and bodies of slaves were completely controlled by slave owners. Whereas for middle-class whites sex was considered sacred and ideally restricted to marriage, black female and male slaves were prohibited from legally marrying (although as we saw in Chapter 1 there were some exceptions), and they were routinely forced to mate with each other to reproduce and increase the slave population. Norms of white female purity were based on the need to establish the paternity of heirs to property; however, slaves did not and could not own property. Thus, such norms made little sense in the lives of slaves. The control and manipulation of slave sexuality, although oppressive for both sexes, was experienced differently by slave women and men. For men it took the form of being used as studs or

rarely enforced). In general, the Puritan codes of conduct continued to dominate U.S. sexual norms well into the nineteenth century, when the Victorians introduced a new and, according to some researchers, even more rigid set of sexual taboos (Harmatz and Novak, 1983).

Victorian Sexuality   The Victorian era was characterized by a number of sexual taboos. In general, sex, particularly premarital sex, continued to be viewed in negative terms. At the base of the Victorian view of sexuality was the notion that any kind of sexual stimulation, especially orgasm, sapped a person's "vital forces." Both women and men were fully clothed in several layers during sexual intercourse so that nudity and human flesh would not provide them with excessive stimulation.

According to the Victorian codes, sexuality was basically a male phenomenon. In contrast, women (specifically middle- and upper-class white women) were idealized and considered morally superior to men in matters of sexuality. The prevailing belief was that decent women did not experience sexual desire; decent women were delicate, passive, asexual, and passionless. Any expression of sexual desire, passion, and enjoyment in women was considered sinful and a woman who dared to express sexual feeling or enjoy sexual intercourse was considered to have loose morals. In contrast, males were considered sexual animals driven by their lust and desires whether inside or outside marriage. Because men were perceived this way, their sexuality, including pre-

being castrated to render them even more powerless and helpless. For women it included the experiences of concubine, mistress, and rape victim as well as the bearer of new generations of slaves. Slave women were robbed of sexual choice and had no legal protection from the rape of any white male who so chose to exploit them. In fact, laws made it legitimate for slave owners to "work out" their sexual desires with slave women (Shriver et al., 2002:11).

Sexual Attitudes and Behavior in the Twentieth Century and Beyond

In the twentieth century, sexual attitudes and behavior continued to change. Researcher Carol Darling and her associates (1989) have divided the century into three major eras in terms of sexual behavior. The first era lasted from 1900 to the early 1950s. Despite moral standards that defined sex as acceptable only in the context of marriage, this period witnessed an increase in the number of single women and men reporting sexual involvement before marriage. The sexual double standard, however, remained largely in force.

The second major era, from the 1950s to 1970, was characterized by greater sexual permissiveness. Darling refers to this period as an "era of permissiveness with affection" because sex outside marriage was acceptable as long as it occurred within a love relationship and the couple expected to marry each other. The prosperity of this era coupled with the ground-breaking work of sex researchers such as Alfred Kinsey, as well as William Masters and Virginia Johnson, sparked an exploration of alternative lifestyles and a new openness about sex, leading into the third era.

Since 1970, technological advances leading to greater travel and increased job opportunities for women and men resulted in a decreasing emphasis on the nuclear family and an increasing view that sexuality could be recreational as well as an expression of love. Women as a group became less sexually inhibited as they became more independent in other areas of their lives. As in the previous era, many people during this era viewed sexual intercourse as natural and expected for both women and men in love relationships. The difference in this era is that the couple did not have to plan marriage to justify their sexual conduct. Sex before marriage was no longer defined as deviant; rather, it became somewhat the norm.

> What about human sexuality and attitudes about sexual activities today? Would you add a fourth historical period to Darling's three eras? If yes, how would you describe it? How might contemporary issues such as hooking up and teens involved in oral sex figure in your description? What about HIV/AIDS and issues raised by the concept of "down-low"?

These changes in attitudes and behavior did not happen by chance. Not only did the mass movement of women into the labor force influence sexual attitudes and standards, but other major changes during the twentieth century such as advances in birth control technology (especially the Pill),

the contemporary women's movement, the 1973 Supreme Court decision (*Roe* v. *Wade*) legalizing abortion, innovative lifestyles on college campuses, the delay in marriage and childbirth, and the lesbian and gay liberation movements all helped move U.S. society toward less rigid sexual standards. These changes exerted a tremendous influence on sexuality, the family, and heterosexual and homosexual relationships. For example, improved birth control technology enabled women to spend less time bearing and raising children. This had the effect of separating sexual intercourse from reproduction, which in turn contributed to a wider acceptance of sex outside of marriage.

A Sexual Revolution? Do these fundamental changes in the sexuality of Americans represent a sexual revolution? Some people say yes, given the broad scope of the changes. Others contend that there has been no revolution, just the continued evolution of sexual norms. There is little doubt that attitudes and behavior have moved toward more liberal and permissive standards, but it is also a fact that many individuals and groups still hold securely to traditional sexual norms and values.

Researcher Morton Hunt (1974) has argued that a revolution has occurred only if institutional structures have changed such that traditional attitudes and behaviors have been replaced with a radically new set of attitudes and behaviors. In the case of sexuality, for instance, a revolution would include the displacement of vaginal intercourse by other sex acts or an increase in sexual activities that would alter the relationship between marriage and sex, such as mate sharing or swapping and mutually agreed-upon extramarital sex. According to Hunt, until such institutional change occurs, we cannot speak of a sexual revolution. Although Hunt's statement is more than 30 years old, his linking of revolution to major institutional change is still relevant.

By the middle to late 1980s, amid the growing awareness, concerns, and fears of sexually transmitted diseases, especially AIDS, many people began to rethink the wisdom, if not the reality, of the so-called sexual revolution. Some researchers were beginning to report either a decrease in unmarried sexual activity and a renewed emphasis on monogamous sexual relationships or a limiting of the number of sexual partners, if not both. However, for many people, the question of a sexual revolution remained open. Many Americans had come to believe that sex was rampant and that everyone (except themselves) was having lots and lots of sex, and those who were not were miserable misfits (Gorner, 1994b).

Sex surveys during the 1990s indicated that, though we did not know it, the sex lives of Americans had reached a turning point. Women and men were indeed moving away from casual sex and placing more importance on intimate relationships. Although several previous studies of sex in America helped create a popular image of casual sex, rampant experimentation, extramarital affairs, sex orgies and kinky sex, and young people gone wild with sexual activities, sex research during the 1990s painted a much more subdued picture of sexual practices in America. This research takes on added significance given that until its appearance, Kinsey's trailblazing research on sexual behavior in the United States had been, more or less, the definitive statement on America's sexual habits for almost

50 years without any serious challenge, and similar sex research had been almost nonexistent. Exceptions included the pioneering work of sex researchers William Masters and Virginia Johnson; Shere Hite's mail-in surveys on sexual behavior, including its methodological flaws; and a sprinkling of surveys using specialized groups such as college students as subjects, readers of popular magazines such as *Playboy* and *Redbook*, or focusing on sexual attitudes as opposed to actual sexual behavior. The 1990s studies overcame several of the flaws of Kinsey's research: For example, Kinsey's samples were not scientifically random, and the subjects were almost all white, well educated, and young. Few, if any, were at the poverty level, and the sample was geographically skewed, centering primarily on the Midwest and the Northeast, with few subjects from the South or West (Lyon, 1992).

The next section of this chapter, highlighting the sexual habits and attitudes of Americans in the 1990s, relies almost exclusively on data provided by sex researchers during that decade. Although the methodology and expertise of the researchers are reliable and unquestioned, the findings of these surveys have sparked endless debates about who is doing what to whom and whether or not people answered the survey questions honestly and openly. These debates notwithstanding, when reading the next section, bear in mind that these findings simply present a snapshot of American sexuality that is neither definitive nor precise. Moreover, the relatively small sample sizes of these studies show up in the data about people of color, women, and older people. In many subgroups, such as homosexuals and various racial groups, the numbers of respondents were too small to conclude much with any degree of integrity and accuracy. However, by the rules of science, the results of these survey will be the baseline information on American sexuality until such time as other good scientific studies are implemented and reported.

Sexual Attitudes and Behaviors in the 1990s

"Sex Study Shatters Kinky Assumptions." "What Is Normal?" "Generation X Is Not Generation Sex." "So, Now We Know What Americans Do in Bed, So?" "Now the Truth about Americans and Sex." "Sex in America Today." "Sex in America: Faithfulness in Marriage Thrives After All." These are but a sprinkling of the article titles reporting the findings of major sex surveys undertaken in the 1990s.[1] Given the

overwhelming attention paid to the results of these surveys, it is apparent that Americans are as interested as ever in what they and their neighbors are doing sexually. Most of us, at one time or another, have had the sneaky suspicion that people across the country were having more, livelier, and better sex in traditional places such as the bedroom as well as in exotic places like on the kitchen table, in a limo, in the bathtub or shower, and other places too scintillating to mention. At some time in our lives we have all probably eyed someone and wondered if that person has a sex life and, if so, what it must be like. As pointed out earlier, sex is everywhere we turn in America and, by and large, what we learn from popular cultural discussions and portrayals of sex is that it is primarily the province of young, attractive hard bodies who prepare for, recover from, or engage in an endless series of copulation (Elmer-DeWitt, 1994). But just how reality-based is this view of Americans' sex life? Researchers believe that the dearth of factual information about our sexuality reinforces fear, intimidation, anxiety, and a belief in popular fictionalized depictions of sexuality.

Although fantasies about sex are as old as humankind, the facts about what Americans do in bed, with whom, and how has become increasingly politicized, feeding into political skirmishes over homosexuality, same-sex marriage, abortion, sexual abuse, date and acquaintance rape, welfare reform, and even "family values" (Lewin, 1994b). Thus, given the political climate of the 1980s and 1990s, it is not surprising that those who had the power to control funding for major research such as on human sexuality were squeamish about such research, first inviting researchers to conduct the research and then refusing to fund it. So, what do these and other sex studies tell us about what Americans did in bed in the 1990s?[2]

Sex by the Numbers: Sexual Partners, Practices, and Fidelity By the mid-1990s, 97 percent of the adult population had been sexually active at some time in their lives (only 2 to 3 percent were virgins); approximately 1 percent had exclusively homosexual partners, and 5 percent had both homosexual and heterosexual partners; the rest had only heterosexual partners (Laumann et al., 1994). Although sexually active, Americans were largely monogamous, had few sex partners, a modest amount of sex, were true to their partners, and had less exotic sexual practices than reported by earlier sex surveys (especially the self-selective mail-ins for popular magazines). Although the spirit, if not overwhelming reality, of the sexual revolution was alive and well in the 1990s in

---

[1]One of these 1990s' studies is a national survey of Americans' sexual behavior and attitudes conducted in 1994 by Mark Clements for *Parade* magazine. The study, a follow-up to a similar 1984 study for *Parade*, covered a representative sample of the American population as a whole—1049 women and men, aged 18 to 65.

A second study, described as the most comprehensive and definitive study ever of Americans' sexual behavior and attitudes, is said to easily supplant the Kinsey studies of the late 1940s and early 1950s as the baseline for all comparable research because of the new study's high standards of methodology and the credentials of the researchers. This 1994 study was based at the University of Chicago's National Opinion Research Center (NORC) and was directed by a team of scholars headed by sociologists Edward Laumann, Robert Michael, John Gagnon, and Stuart Michaels. The research methodology included a voluminous questionnaire backed by face-to-face interviews with a random national sample of 3432 Americans aged 18 to 59, representing 97.1 percent of the adult population. The findings of this study provide a wealth of data about the sex lives of ordinary people.

[2]The following discussion draws heavily upon the following: Edward O. Laumann, John H. Gagnon, Robert T. Michael, and Stuart Michaels, 1994, *The Social Organization of Sexuality* (Chicago: University of Chicago Press); Tamar Lewin, 1994, "Sex in America: Faithfulness in Marriage Thrives After All," *New York Times* (October 7): A1, A11; idem, 1994, "So, Now We Know What Americans Do in Bed. So?" *New York Times* (October 9): E3; Peter Gorner, 1994, "Sex Study Shatters Kinky Assumptions," *Chicago Tribune* (October 6): 1, 28; idem, 1994, "What Is Normal?" *Chicago Tribune* (October 9): sec. 4: 1, 4; Trisha Gura, 1994, "Generation X Is Not Generation Sex," *Chicago Tribune* (October 9): sec. 4: 1; Philip Elmer-DeWitt, 1994, "Now the Truth About Americans and SEX," *Time* 144, 17 (October 17): 62–70; Mark Clements, 1994, "Sex in America," *Chicago Tribune, Parade* magazine (August 7): 4–6

As social taboos have fallen away, pornographic images have become more visible and explicit in our neighborhoods and our homes. The widespread dissemination of pornography and the heightened visibility of porn shops and billboards as well as the increase in sexually explicit Web sites on the Internet are believed by many to encourage violence and dominance and to put unwilling victims, especially children, at great risk.

some quarters—for example, approximately 17 percent of men and 3 percent of women reported having sex with 21 or more partners over their lifetime, with one man reporting having had 1016 partners and one woman reporting having had 1009 partners—overall the sex lives of most of us were not very exciting (Elmer-DeWitt, 1994). For instance, a typical woman in the 1990s had two sexual partners; a man six. When race is factored in, the typical number of partners over a lifetime for African Americans was four; for whites and Native Americans three, Latinas/os two, and Asian Americans one (Laumann et al., 1994).

Women and men who as children had been sexually touched by an adult were significantly less monogamous than the general population. Researchers and others have long suggested a link between child sexual abuse and adult sexuality. Data from the NORC survey give support to this thesis. For example, these women and men were more likely as adults to have 11 or more sex partners, to identify themselves as homosexual or bisexual, to express difficulties in sexuality (including anxiety, impotence, and inability to reach orgasm), and to report being unhappy. They also reported having participated in oral, anal, and group sex, as well as thinking about sex more often (Gorner, 1994a; Laumann et al., 1994; Lewin, 1994a).

When we consider people's sexual behavior by their religious affiliation, some interesting observations emerge. Roman Catholics were more likely than members of any other religious group to be virgins (4 percent). Jews had the most sex partners: 34 percent had ten or more, and over a lifetime Jews had, on average, six partners. The women most likely to achieve orgasm each and every time were conservative Protestants (Laumann et al., 1994).

How Often? Along with limiting the number of partners, Americans limited the number of times they had sex as well. On average, Americans reported having sex once a week, but clearly two-thirds of the population had sex less often (a few times a month, a few times a year, or not at all). Those

who reported having sex only a few times a year or not at all also said that when they did have sex it made them feel happy, loved, wanted, and cared for, thus putting lie to the myth that people who do not have sex frequently are unhappy and sexually frustrated.

Marital status and age appeared to have an important impact on the frequency with which people had sex. Although we tend to think of singles as sexually precocious and leading a "swinging" sexual lifestyle, the fact is that with the exception of cohabiting singles, married people have a more lively sex life than do their single counterparts and are the most likely to have orgasms. However, the majority of men (95 percent), either married or single, said that they usually or always had an orgasm. Cohabiting singles were the most sexually active, with over one-half (56 percent) reporting that they had sex twice a week or more (Laumann et al., 1994). On the other hand, the sexual reality of the older heterosexual population was quite different from its younger counterpart. For example, 22 percent of women and 8 percent of men 50 years old reported having no partnered sex in a year. And by the age of 70, fully 70 percent of women and 26 percent of men reported going for a year or more without partnered sex.

Among lesbians and gays, gays are far more sexually active than are lesbians. In the *Parade* magazine sex survey (1994), gays reported having 18 partners at some time in their lives, compared with 3 reported by lesbians. According to Philip Blumstein and Pepper Schwartz (1983) (still considered the best study that includes data on lesbian and gay sexuality), lesbian couples have sex less frequently than any other type of couple, and they are less "sexual" as couples and as individuals than anyone else. Furthermore, lesbians seem more limited in their range of sexual techniques than are other couples. However, a note of caution is warranted here: Until we are clear regarding the meaning of the words *sex* and *sexuality* for lesbians and whether or not the heterosexual model of these terms fits their experiences, we must be somewhat skeptical of research findings that reduce their

FIGURE 6.1

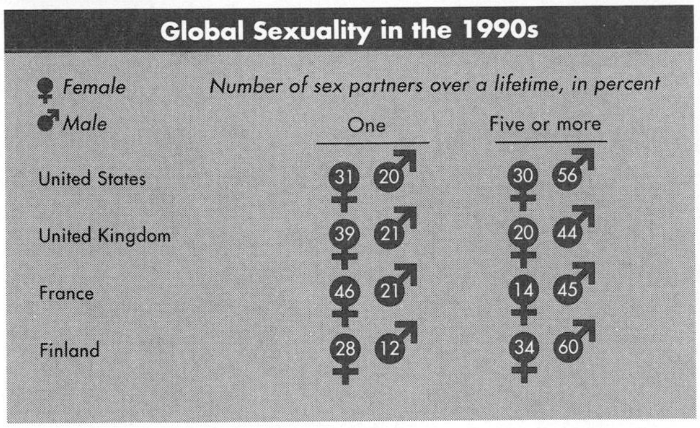

Global Sexuality in the 1990s

♀ *Female* *Number of sex partners over a lifetime, in percent*
♂ *Male*

	One ♀ ♂	Five or more ♀ ♂
United States	31 20	30 56
United Kingdom	39 21	20 44
France	46 21	14 45
Finland	28 12	34 60

Source: Adapted from Philip Elmer-DeWitt, 1994, "Now the Truth about Americans and Sex," *Time* 144, 16 (October 17): 64. © 1994 TIME INC. Reprinted by permission.

FIGURE 6.2

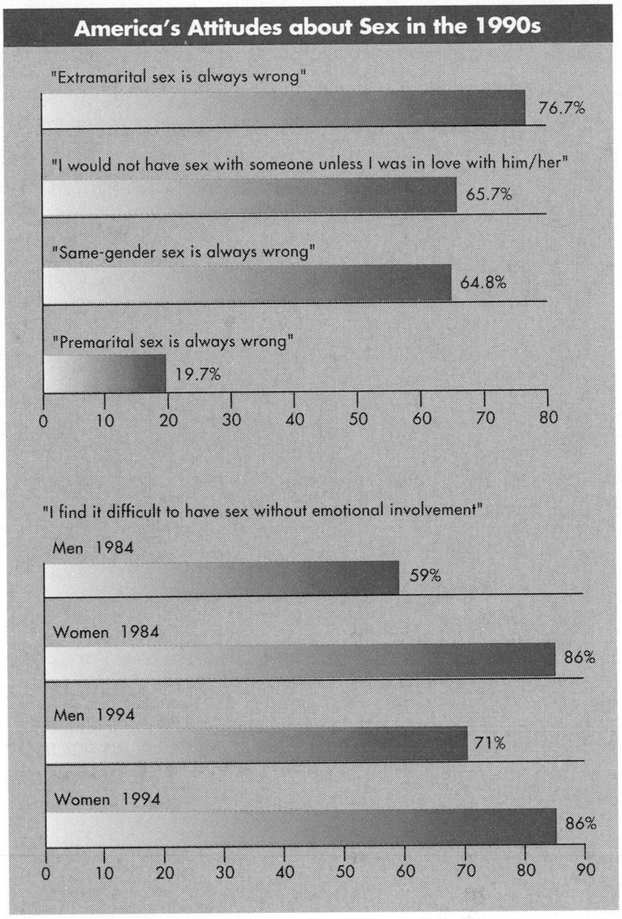

America's Attitudes about Sex in the 1990s

"Extramarital sex is always wrong" 76.7%

"I would not have sex with someone unless I was in love with him/her" 65.7%

"Same-gender sex is always wrong" 64.8%

"Premarital sex is always wrong" 19.7%

0 10 20 30 40 50 60 70 80

"I find it difficult to have sex without emotional involvement"

Men 1984 59%

Women 1984 86%

Men 1994 71%

Women 1994 86%

0 10 20 30 40 50 60 70 80 90

Source: Peter Gorner, 1994, "What Is Normal?" *Chicago Tribune* (October 9), sec. 4: 1; Mark Clements, 1994, "Sex in America Today," *Chicago Tribune, Parade* magazine: 4.

sexuality to numbers. (For a more detailed discussion of this point see, for example, Frye, 1995.)

How did Americans compare internationally during the 1990s? Studies of sexual behavior conducted in England and France show that during the 1990s, French women and men were a bit more sexually conservative than their U.S. counterparts. For instance, the average French woman and man had sex about twice as often as Americans did, but they tended to have somewhat fewer sex partners over a lifetime than did Americans (Gorner, 1994b) (see Figure 6.1).

Kinky Sex? Contrary to the assumption of widespread "kinky" sex, we, as a nation, seem to prefer only a few sexual practices. Heterosexuals overwhelmingly (96 percent) preferred vaginal intercourse and included it in almost every sexual encounter. The next two most appealing sexual practices were a distant second and third: watching a partner undress (an activity that many people may not have realized is a sex act) and oral sex, which many people have experienced but which is not a regular part of most adults' lovemaking (Gorner, 1994a). In fact, many older adults, like college students and teenagers, do not consider oral sex as "having sex" at all. In any case, however, men are substantially more likely to enjoy the latter two sexual practices than are women. Sexual practices such as anal intercourse, same-sex partners, group sex, and sex with strangers was appealing to only a minute percentage of the population. Here, as elsewhere, men reported more interest in these sexual practices than did women.

Despite the alleged permissiveness and liberalization of attitudes since the 1960s, Americans held fairly conservative attitudes about marriage and sexuality at the time of these surveys and were extremely faithful to their romantic partners. A majority of people said that they would not have sex with someone unless they were in love with the person. Men, in particular, were paying more attention to the emotional aspect of sex. The 1994 *Parade* sex survey reported that 71 percent of the men in its sample reported it was difficult for them to have sex without emotional involvement, up from 59 percent a decade earlier. The percentage

of women expressing this view remained constant over both studies, at 86 percent.

Finally, during the 1990s, most Americans viewed marriage and a long-term commitment as the goal of their intimate relationships; it appears to have regulated sexual behavior with remarkable precision (see Figure 6.2). Although attitudes about sex outside legal marriage may be somewhat permissive, it seems that once people marry they express a belief in fidelity as long as the relationship lasts (cited in Gorner, 1994b). In this context, Americans' sexual behavior in the 1990s was pretty consistent with their attitudes. Thus, contrary to the notion of a national wave of infidelity, adultery was the exception rather than the rule. More than seven out of ten people said that they disapproved of adultery; more importantly, despite seven-year itches and midlife crises, 85 percent of married women and more than 75 percent of married men said that they had never been unfaithful to their partners.

At What Age? According to responses in the NORC survey, white teens, both females and males, typically began having sex at age 17; black males typically began just before

16 and black females, just before 17. However, subsequent sexual encounters during teen years were sporadic. Teenagers in the 1990s typically had sex for the first time six months earlier than did their parents. It appears that as teens reach young adulthood, their sexual behavior becomes more conservative. For example, Generation X (young adults 18 to 30 years of age) told NORC researchers that they had less frequent sexual encounters and that the overwhelming majority of them practiced monogamy.

These data shatter our perceptions of young-adult sexual behavior. Most of our fantasies and ideas about delightful and delectable sex are based on what we thought were the sexual patterns of a wild and sexy Generation X. But as Trisha Gura (1994b) has stated, "Generation X is not Generation Sex." These young adults told sex researchers that they were engaging in sexual activity earlier, they were delaying getting married, and they were divorcing more frequently than did their parents. However, coming of age after AIDS, they actually were behaving far more conservatively than their predecessors. In general, they had only one sex partner at a time, they valued fidelity, they tended to marry by the age of 30, and many might marry more than once. In contrast, the parents of Generation X (the baby boomers), coming of age when they did, during a more sexually permissive and liberal period, were a much more sexually active group than their offspring. The percentage of adults, for example, who'd had 21 or more sex partners over their lifetime was significantly higher among the baby boomers than among other Americans.

Choosing Partners   Once Americans meet, with whom do they develop sexual relationships? From a sociological perspective, people bring to the sexual marketplace all of the characteristics of their makeup: education, occupation and earning potential, personality, looks, interests, diseases, children from prior marriages or liaisons, and so forth. As you learned in Chapter 5, the social world of mate selection—dating and sexual behavior—is constructed so that we meet, date, have sex with, and marry people very much like ourselves. According to Peter Gorner (1994a), personal ads and electronic dating services may work for short-term relationships, but they are rarely effective for long-term relationships. Sexual selection seems to rely more so on the same type of strategies that we use to buy a car, choose a college, or seek a job. In the same way that we consult with our friends, family members, and other advisors when, for example, choosing a college, we rely on our personal social networks when choosing sexual partners. It is not therefore surprising that, Americans typically have sex with, date, and marry people of the same race, educational background, religion, and similar age. They rarely cross lines of social class and upbringing when choosing sex partners or mates. Even if, as in the legendary romantic song, some enchanted evening we will meet and fall in love with a stranger across a crowded room, the odds are high that the room will be crowded with people very much like ourselves (Lewin, 1994b). In the NORC study, 93 percent of people who were married were married to someone of the same race, 82 percent were of similar educational level, 78 percent were within 5 years of each other's age, and 72 percent were of

the same religion. Not one woman with a graduate degree had a sexual relationship with a man who had finished only high school (Gorner, 1994a).

Sexual behavior is strongly affected by friends, family, and coworkers. For example, in the NORC sex survey, more than six couples out of ten were introduced by family or mutual friends. Only 8 percent of couples met in a bar or through a personal ad. Once introduced, contrary to popular media portrayals, people do not immediately fall into bed. Rather, the pattern is typically that of getting to know one another, first as a friend, building trust and taking the relationship slowly, then finally having sex, and for heterosexual couples, getting married. Couples who stay together are usually those who are sexually compatible, agree on the rules, and are faithful (Gorner, 1994a).

Gender Difference   Not surprisingly, women and men think and behave differently in terms of sex. For example, as noted earlier, men think about sex more than women do and are drawn to a wider range of sexual practices. During the 1990s, more than one-half of men said they thought about sex every day or several times a day, compared with 19 percent of women. Although a little more than two-thirds of women and men said that the actual sex act is better than foreplay, men were more likely (73 percent) to feel this way than women (58 percent). In this context, not surprisingly, more men than women said that sexual activity and orgasm were important; more men than women continued to rate themselves as having a high sex drive (Clements, 1994).

Perhaps the most alarming gender difference found in the NORC sex survey is the difference in female and male perception of what constitutes consensual sex. For example, 23 percent of the women reported having been forced by men to do something sexually that they did not want to do, including having vaginal intercourse, usually by someone that they knew well, were in love with, or married to. On the other hand, only about 3 percent of men said that they had ever forced a woman into a sexual act. Moreover, a little more than 4 percent of women reported being forced to have sex their very first time, compared with less than one-half of 1 percent of men. Although some of the disparity in the views of women and men on the subject of forced sex might be due to underreporting, it is far more likely that the disparity is because many men, given traditional male socialization, simply do not recognize just how coercive women find their behavior. Many feel they are entitled to demand sex from women and, if refused, to force it on them; and some women continue to feel dependent, pressured, and/or obligated to "give in" for the sake of "keeping their man" or maintaining the relationship. Thus, as you learned in Chapter 5, date and acquaintance rape are fairly common occurrences and of increasing concern among women.

In other areas of sexuality, however, women and men appear to be converging. This may be due, in large part, to the fact that over the last decade, men have shown more changes in their sexual attitudes than have women. For instance, almost 75 percent of men said it was easy to talk about sex with their partners, compared with 59 percent in 1984. Today, a similar percentage of women (70 percent) said that they found conversations about sex with a partner easy (up from 63 percent in 1984). And both women and men show a shift from seeking sex for recreation to seeking more emotional meaning in sex.

Understanding America's Changing Sexuality: Contemporary Patterns   As in the last two decades of the twentieth century, a majority of Americans today are monogamous and quite content with it, expressing satisfaction with their sex lives and a broad preference for emotional commitment in sexual relationships. Most Americans indicate that they prefer marriage to living single. As was the case during the 1980s and 1990s, more than one half of Americans report that their sex lives are traditional, 55 percent compared with 42 percent of those who describe their sex lives as adventurous. This fact notwithstanding, however, about one in six adults say that they have strayed from a committed relationship, including having sex outside the relationship and engaging in sexual activity other than sexual intercourse. Men admit cheating more often than women, 21 and 11 percent respectively. Those who cheat tend to be more uninhibited and more permissive—more likely to have watched sexually explicit videos, to have paid for sex, and to have had revenge or rebound sex. They are also more likely than noncheaters to approve of premarital sex and to believe that it is okay to have sex without an emotional relationship (45 percent of cheaters say so, compared with 19 percent of others) (Langer, Arnedt, and Sussman, 2004).

Although many of the patterns of the 1990s remain, it seems that in our increasingly sexed-up society, we are also acting upon sex in some distinctively different ways as well. We talk more openly and publicly about sex, and sexual acts once considered deviant are widely accepted now. Surveys of sexual behavior in the twenty-first century not only confirm much of what we already know about American sexuality, but it also ventures into new areas of American sexuality. For instance, more than one-half of Americans (57 percent) say they have had sex outdoors or in a public place. Almost one-third (29 percent) have had sex on a first date, and roughly the same percentage say they have had an "unexpected sexual encounter with someone new." Fifteen percent of men generally—and three in ten single men age 30 and older—have paid for sex; about one-half of women say they have faked an orgasm; and a number of women and men visit sex Web sites on a regular basis (Langer, Arnedt, and Sussman, 2004). In addition, it seems that politics can be found everywhere today, even in our bedrooms and beneath the sheets. For instance, a recent sex survey reports that more Republicans (87 percent) than Democrats (76 percent) who are involved in a committed relationship are satisfied with their relationship; and more Republications (56 percent) than Democrats (47 percent) are satisfied with their sex lives.

Today people are engaging in sexual behavior at earlier ages. For instance, three-fourths of all women and men by their late teens have had intercourse, and more than two-thirds of all sexually experienced teens have had two or more partners (Mosher, Chandra and Jones, 2005; Langer, Arnedt, and Sussman, 2004; Alan Guttmacher Institute,

2002a). And a recent survey of the sexual behavior of high school students indicated that 9 percent of these students had initiated sexual intercourse before they reached their 13th birthday. In every ethnic subgroup, males are significantly more likely than females to initiate sexual intercourse before age 13 (Grunbaum et al., 2002). At the same time, there is a noticeable increase in the number of people reporting that they are virgins. Research on high school students, for instance, shows an 11 percent increase in the incidence of virginity, driven by lower rates of intercourse for white and black male youths (Christopher and Sprecher, 2000). It seems to us that statistic might also be explained in terms of the increasing rate of teens who claim the status of virgin even though they have engaged in a variety of sexual activities other than vaginal intercourse (see In the News at the beginning of this chapter).

Although there is less insistence today that sex be tied to marriage (for example, eight of ten women and nine of ten men aged 20 to 39 are nonvirgins), premarital sex for both women and men is now more likely to occur within an affectionate, quasi-stable, if not permanent, relationship. Both women and men report feeling heightened sexual desire and pleasure when they share a mutually loving relationship with their sex partner. However, emotionally valuing a partner continues to motivate women, more than men, to engage in sexual intercourse (Christopher and Sprecher, 2000). In addition, the shift toward more relational sex and couplehood among gays continues today, although recreational sex is still more common among gays than among lesbians and heterosexuals. Further, whereas monogamy is highly valued among lesbian and heterosexual couples, non-monogamy is often an accepted part of gay men's culture (Peplau, Fingerhut, and Beals, 2004; Solomon, 2005). Recent research indicates that lesbians continue to be more likely than gays to seek emotional relationships, and to place greater value on mutual commitment and sexual fidelity. As a result, lesbians have fewer sexual partners than gays, and if living in a committed relationship, they are less likely to have sex outside that relationship (Solomon, 2005). Although still unacceptable to the general society, sexual lifestyles different from traditional heterosexual relationships such as homosexual and bisexual relationships have become more open, and there has been a decrease in the number of people who view homosexual behavior as morally wrong—43 percent in 2005, down from 65 percent in the mid-1990s and 53 percent in 2001 (Gallup Poll, 2006; Gallup, 2001). In general, it appears that a better understanding of one's own sexuality, rather than a simple pursuit of pleasure, is now an important sexual goal in many people's lives.

Although women and men continue to converge in some areas of their sexual behavior, the sexual double standard remains: Men are still more likely than women to think about sex daily, fantasize about it, be sexually active, have multiple partners, have sex on a first date, think that casual sex is acceptable, and be the initiator of sex (through both seduction or coercion), whereas women are still most often the one to refuse sex but are also still more likely than men to give in to sexual advances and to comply with sexual demands even when they do not want to have sex. Women are also more conservative than men about sex in other ways. For instance, women are more likely than men to say there is too much sex on television, they are less likely than men to condone sex before marriage, and less likely than men to sleep in the nude (Langer, Arnedt, and Sussman, 2004; Alan Guttmacher, 2002b).

Not only is there a gender gap in American sexual behavior, but also there is a generation gap. On the one hand, for example, later-life adults continue to be far more conservative in their attitudes about sex than are younger Americans. Only about one-third (30 percent) of people 65 years of age and older, for instance, approve of sex before marriage compared to 71 percent of people aged 18 to 29 who think it is okay. Yet when it comes to the issue of infidelity or cheating, more older than younger adults report having cheated in a relationship. Overall, however, young adults, whether single or in a committed relationship, are more progressive sexually; they are more likely to talk with their partners about their sexual fantasies, more likely to describe themselves and their partners as sexually adventurous, more likely to say that homosexuality is okay, and more likely to look at sexually explicit Web sites than are older people (Senior Journal, 2005).

On the other hand, according to a recent edition of *Newsweek* magazine (2006), single baby boomers are changing the way that older people look at sex, romance, marriage, and relationships. If we use baby boomers as a gauge, it seems sex is no longer the exclusive territory of the young, but a quality of life issue that continues well after the age of 50. Unlike earlier generations of older single Americans, baby boomers (who are now turning 60 years of age) are flaunting their sexuality. They desire fun, excitement, passion, and sex in their relationships. Boomer women in particular are increasingly more sexually confident, an observation consistent with research findings that report women's sexual confidence and self-knowledge increase as they go through life.

Clearly, today sex plays a much bigger role in some people's lives than others. Not everyone is actively engaged in sexual behavior. In fact, a growing number of people are publicly and actively disengaging in sex. Although there is some debate about who is a virgin and how we define virginity, the fact is that today there is a visible and aggressive movement to promote sexual chastity directed particularly at the nation's teenagers and young adults. For those in this movement, there is no debate; chastity and virginity means refraining from *all* sexual activity before marriage and being faithful to one's spouse after marriage (Abstinence Groups, 2000). In the early 1990s, True Love Waits, an international Christian organization that grew out of the Southern Baptist Convention, began asking young people in particular (teenagers and college students) to take voluntary chastity pledges committing to sexual abstinence until the day they enter a biblical marriage relationship (Schemo, 2001b).

The movement for sexual abstinence is not limited to a focus on youth. In a contemporary culture saturated with sexual messages and innuendo, a small but growing minority of older adults live sex-free lives (practice celibacy). Calling themselves "born-again virgins," they embrace abstinence not so much on moral or religious grounds but to cleanse themselves, recharge their spirit, and reassert self-control. There are no figures for how many Americans are born-again virgins. However, the bulk of them are women, with only a small number of men among the ranks. This newly chaste group ranges from purists, who refrain from all sexual activity, to those who tailor their celibacy to suit their tastes, permitting a degree of kissing and fondling but drawing the line at penetration. It is not clear, however, how many in the most sexually active years were celibate by choice (La Ferla, 2000).

Speaking of "born-again virgins," it seems that a growing number of women today are becoming, in a sense, born-again virgins not as a result of abstinence but as a result of getting cosmetic surgery on the most private part of their anatomy—their genitals. Genital cosmetic surgery—hymenoplasty specifically (recreating the intact hymen)—is not new. Historically it has been a big business for sexually active girls who come from families that place a high value on being a virgin at marriage. It is said to be especially prevalent among first-generation immigrants, especially Muslims. According to a Texas female board-certified obstetrician (Hailparn, 2005), there are typically three groups of women interested in hymenoplasty: (1) women who must be certified virgins before getting married or they may face being ostracized by their family or even death; (2) women who are raped or abused and striped unwillingly of their virginity and now want to give it willingly to a partner of their choice; and (3) women who simply want a "prettier look" or to give their significant other that "virgin-again" experience.

Recently, *New York Times* writer Mireya Navarro (Navarro, 2004) reported that as millions of American women today inject Botox, reshape noses, augment breasts, lift buttocks, and suck away unwanted fat, a growing number are exploring and getting genital plastic surgery to tighten vaginal muscles, plump up or shorten the labia, remove fat from the pubic area, and most notably, to restore the hymen, often against doctor's suggestions that such cosmetic surgery is unnecessary. Procedures that were once reserved to address medical problems such as incontinence, congenital malformations, or injuries related to childbirth are now being marketed by some gynecologists and plastic surgeons as "vaginal rejuvenation" and designed solely to enhance sexual satisfaction and improve the looks of the genitals. Some physicians as well as others believe that the cultural emphasis on a youthful look, fashions such as flimsier, more revealing swimsuits, the Brazilian bikini wax, and more exposure to nudity in magazines, movies, and on the Internet are key factors driving women to pay anywhere from $3500 to $8000 dollars for this surgery, the most popular of which is the tightening of the vaginal muscles, or vaginoplasty, and reduction of the labia minor, called labiaplasty.

Although many women are motivated to undergo vaginal cosmetic surgery to improve or increase their sex lives, there is no scientific evidence to suggest that such surgery will actually produce these women's desired results. To the contrary, after such surgery, for instance, the tightening of the vaginal muscles, sexual intercourse could be painful if the vaginal muscles are too snug. Other possible risks from genital cosmetic surgery are painful scarring or nerve damage that could result in loss of sensation or hypersensitivity. What about men? According to some doctors, men probably would be flocking to their offices for their own genital surgery if such procedures as penile enlargement were not fraught with complications and unintended outcomes.

> ?? *What do you think? Do you know women or men who have had genital cosmetic surgery? If yes, what reasons do they give for having such surgery? Would you consider such surgery for nonmedical reasons? If yes, why would you? If no, why not?*

Contemporary Sexuality in a Global Context How do Americans' sexual behavior today compare internationally? Over the last decade, global sex surveys have reported on a range of sexual behaviors in countries across the world. For instance, according to a 2005 Global Sex Survey (Durex, 2005), Greece is identified as the sexiest country in the world, with Greeks reporting having sex 138 times a year—well above the United States, with Americans having sex 113 times a year. Partners in Japan are the least sexually active, having sex just 45 times a year (see In Other Places box). The global average is 103 times a year, with men (104) having sex more often than women (101). It seems that 35- to 44-year-olds are the sexiest people on the globe, reporting having sex 112 times a year compared to just 90 times for 16- to 20-year-olds and 108 times for 25- to 34-year-olds. On average, people across the world who are engaging in sexual activities report spending about 19.7 minutes on foreplay, with men reporting spending more time than women—20.2 and 18.8, respectively. Contrary to stereotypes of the British as stiff and proper, the British report spending the most time on foreplay (22.5 minutes) compared to Americans (19.7 minutes) and the Thais, who spend the least amount of time (11.5 minutes). Globally, people are having sex with an average of 9 partners, with men having more sexual partners than women—10.2 compared to 6.9. Unfortunately, in a time when the rate of sexually transmitted diseases, including HIV/AIDS, has risen dramatically, almost half the sexually active world report having unprotected sex without knowing their partner's sexual history. Norway leads the way, with 73 percent of Norwegians having unprotected sex, compared to Americans, 51 percent of whom report having unprotected sex. Women are less likely to takes risks than men—45 percent have had unprotected sex, compared to 48 percent of men and older people (65 percent) are more likely to take risks than younger people (33 percent). Although Greeks are having sex the most often, they are second to Norway in having the highest percentage of people (70 percent) who report having unprotected sex. On a lighter note, it is interesting to learn where people feel most comfortable having sex. For instance, the most common place for adults to have sex outside their bedroom is in the car (50 percent), followed by toilets (39 percent).

In the United States, the car and the toilet are in a dead heat, with 70 percent of Americans reporting each as the most common place they have sex outside of their bedroom (see the box, Internet Resources: Applying the Sociological Imagination).

SEXUALITY AS SOCIAL LEARNING

Equally as important as the questions of what people do and with whom in the privacy of their bedrooms or in public places like parks and automobiles as well as whether or not a sexual revolution has occurred are questions such as, How do we become sexual beings? and, What factors contribute to changes in our sexual attitudes and behaviors? Anthropologists have long shown that human sexuality is defined and learned within a particular cultural context. What constitutes sexuality, then, will vary from one culture to another. In this section we consider sexual behavior as a learned social product.

Since the late nineteenth century, when Sigmund Freud first introduced his beliefs about the nature of human sexuality, the general public as well as professionals such as psychologists, social workers, and sex therapists have been influenced by his theories of human sexuality. According to Freud, the sex drive, which he viewed as a biologically determined force, is the motivator for all human behavior. In the mid-twentieth century, Alfred Kinsey's extensive sex research reflected his agreement with Freud that human sexuality is biologically determined. Both men believed humans have innate sexual desires that require gratification. Such desires cannot go unchecked in a society, however, or they would lead to uncontrolled sexual activity, which in turn would generate social chaos. Thus, through its sexual codes, society forces the individual to repress these desires or channel them into sexually appropriate behaviors. Even if an innate sexual drive exists in human beings, it seems clear from research across academic disciplines that this drive is given shape and direction by culture. The sexual feelings and desires that we experience may seem innate, natural, and beyond our control, but we are not born knowing how to think, feel, or behave sexually. Cultural norms *prescribe* (tell us what we should do) and *proscribe* (tell us what we should not do) our sexual behavior. They determine what is or is not sexually attractive and stimulating, why we should or should not engage in sexual behavior, and how we should or should not feel sexually.

Human sexual behavior is not unlike other behavior. It does not come naturally; rather, it is socially constructed (Gagnon and Simon, 1973, 1987). From this point of view, then, what Freud commonly referred to as the *sex drive* is really something we have learned in a particular social environment. Like other behaviors, our sexual behavior is guided by cultural scripts similar to those that guide the actions of actors. These **sexual scripts** are simply our society's guidelines or blueprints for defining and engaging in sexual behaviors. We begin learning these scripts very early in life through the process of socialization. In learning our culture's sexual guidelines, we in effect create or invent our capacity for sexual behavior.

IN OTHER PLACES

NO SEX, PLEASE . . .

In 2005, the number of deaths in Japan exceeded births. With a record-low birth rate, coupled with policies that virtually forbid immigration, the population shrank for the first time since Japan began compiling data in 1899 (Pesek, 2006). It seems, however, that the birth rate is not the only thing spiraling downward in Japan. Marriage and sexual intimacy is also on the decline. In a 2005 survey, condom maker Durex found that the Japanese have the least active sex lives. Japan ranked last among 41 countries in terms of frequency of sex: the average Japanese had sex only 45 times a year. Ranking number 37 out of 41, people in Hong Kong had sex only a bit more often—78 times a year (Global Sex Survey, 2005). In addition, according to some reports, condom shipments are down 40 percent in Japan since the early 1990s and love-hotel check-ins are down at least 20 percent since the end of the 1990s. Furthermore, it seems that an increasing number of Japanese who frequent the love hotels are not going there for romance. Rather, they are going because love hotels offer the cheapest access to karaoke machines and video games (Wiseman, 2004).

Japanese women and men are finding relationships today to be too messy, tiring, and potentially humiliating to bother with them anymore. According to some analysts, this downward trend in marriages, births, and "hanky-panky" has important implications for the country's future. For instance, in 2000, 54 percent of women and almost 70 percent of men between 25 and 29 years of age were unmarried. This behavioral pattern could have a devastating impact on the birth rate as conservative Japanese society frowns upon having children outside marriage. The declining birth rate means that fewer working-age Japanese will be around to support a growing population of elderly. In addition, Japan's faltering sex drive and record-low birth rates do not bode well for the country's economy. A declining work force will reduce tax revenue, making it harder to pay the country's national debt. Things have gotten so bad that a popular weekly Japanese newsmagazine exhorted Japanese youth to abstain, not from sexual activity, but from abstinence. That is, they were encouraged to have more sex. In response to a significant drop in the sale of condoms and business at Japan's rent-by-the-hour love hotels, the newsmagazine article cautioned young people to not hate sex (Pesek, 2006; McCurry, 2005; Wiseman, 2004).

The gender divide appears to be growing among Japan's young twenty-and-thirty somethings—women and men in their 20s and 30s are increasingly going their separate ways. Women, for instance, are off to designer boutiques and chic restaurants with their mothers or girlfriends while men are socializing with their buddies from work or spending their time in front of their computer screens romancing virtual women. Better educated, more widely traveled, and raised in more affluence than their mothers, Japanese women no longer feel bound by the cultural tradition that encourages marriage by age 25. A growing number of these women are either postponing marriage or deciding to not marry at all. They are weighing marriage against what they see as important shortcomings of love and marriage Japanese style: the husband works long hours and afterwards, instead of coming home, he parties late into the night with his buddies from work. The wife, on the other hand, is expected to stay home, do the domestic chores, and nurture the young. If the children are unruly, it is her fault—she is a "bad" mother. If her husband has an affair, she is a "bad" wife (Wiseman, 2004).

Although Japanese society still thinks that there is something wrong with women who are not married by the age of 25 or 30, the increasingly well-educated and career-oriented Japanese woman, seeking a career or already firmly established in one, is unwilling to give it up and lead the traditional life of a Japanese housewife. For their part, Japanese men seem bewildered by the rising assertiveness of Japanese women. Rather than risk rejection or expend the energy necessary to maintain a modern intimate relationship, many Japanese men simply pay for affection and sex in the country's massive sex trade—hostess bars and brothels. Others prefer virtual women online. Cybersex affords these men a quick way to get sexual satisfaction. In fact, it is estimated that as many as a million young Japanese males—the majority of whom are teenagers but increasingly older men as well—suffer from what the Japanese call *hikikomori*—a condition in which they seclude themselves in their rooms for weeks at a time (Wiseman, 2004).

The Japanese gendered sexual disconnect is most telling in the following statistics: (1) The rate of marriage is declining—54 percent of Japanese women in their late 20s are still single, a 74 percent increase since 1985. In a 2004 survey, one-half of single Japanese women between the ages of 35 and 54 said they had no intention of ever marrying. (2) The number of births in Japan have steadily declined since 2000—Japan's birth rate hit a record low of 1.29 in 2003 and remained unchanged in 2004—one of the lowest rates in the world. This rate is well below the minimum 2.08 needed to compensate for deaths. As a consequence of the declining birth rate, Japan's population is expected to peak soon and then decline rapidly. (3) The divorce rate has nearly doubled over the past decade, with some divorcing women blaming sexually inactive husbands for the breakup (McCurry, 2005; Foreign Press Center Japan, 2005).

Sexless marriages—a phenomenon that some experts describe as one of the factors pushing Japan toward a demographic disaster—have greatly exacerbated the problem between the sexes. For instance, a survey of Japanese women found that over one-fourth had not had sex with their husbands in the past year. Each year, 200 women seek clinical help because they have not had sex with their husbands in up to 20 years, and some have never had sex with their husbands. They love their husbands but the problem, it seems, is that their husbands have either lost interest in sex or did not want sex from the start. According to Kim Myong-gan, who runs clinic for women in sexless marriages, "Many men think of their wives as substitute mothers, not as women with emotional and sexual needs" (quoted in McCurry, 2005:1). In response to these women's needs, the clinic head offers them a short-term unconventional solution: After an initial, rather costly counseling session, he shows them photos of 45 men, the majority of whom are professionals in their 40s. The women are invited to go on dates with these men, and then, in almost all cases, can arrange regularly assigned meetings in hotel rooms. Accused of running nothing short of a male prostitution ring, the head of the clinic dismisses such charges, saying that the men are sex volunteers who pay half the hotel and restaurant bills, thereby there is absolutely nothing wrong with this arrangement (McCurry, 2005).

APPLYING THE SOCIOLOGICAL IMAGINATION

Much of what we know or think we know today about our own and others' sexual attitudes and behaviors is based on sex surveys conducted over the years dating back to the now classic Kinsey Reports. The most recent and definitive of such studies was conducted in 1994 by researchers at the University of Chicago. A decade later, in 2004, ABC News *Primetime Live* conducted a ground-breaking sex survey based on a random-sample telephone poll of 1501 adults that covered a range of sexual activities, fantasies, and attitudes in the United States from foreplay to fantasy—sexual issues rarely if ever covered in a representative national survey. The 2004 survey reported several surprising facts about Americans' sexual behavior while its other findings were consistent with previous sex research.

For those of us who are curious about the sexual practices and behaviors of people around the world, Durex, a popular condom maker, conducts a global sex survey of sexual attitudes and behavior annually that is considered the world's largest sexual health research project of its kind. In 2005, the survey covered 41 countries and the responses were analyzed by age and sex to give an in-depth global picture of sexual attitudes and behavior.

Consider the following selective findings from each of these two surveys:

From ABC News *Primetime Live* Poll: American Sex Survey (2004)

- Fifty-seven percent of Americans have had sex outdoors or in a public place.

- Twenty-nine percent of Americans have had sex on a first date, and about the same percentage have had an "unexpected sexual encounter with someone new." Looking at gender differences, 42 percent of men compared to 17 percent of women reported having had sex on a first date.

- Fifteen percent of American men—and three in ten single men 30 years of age and older—have paid for sex.

- Fifty percent of American women admit to faking an orgasm. Women, however, are not the only thespians: 11 percent of men also admitted to faking it.

- Weekly churchgoers have had half as many lifetime sex partners (median three) as have the "unchurched" (median seven). On the other hand, about 40 percent of churchgoers think about sex daily and have had sex outdoors; one-third describe themselves as sexually adventurous.

Sex on a Global Level (Durex 2005 Global Sex Survey)

- Forty-four percent of adults worldwide have had a one-night stand.

- Almost one-fourth of adults worldwide have had sex using vibrators; 20 percent have used masks, blindfolds, or other forms of bondage. Sex using vibrators is most common in Australia and the United States.

- Thirty-five percent of adults worldwide have engaged in anal sex and 15 percent have had sex with three in a bed.

Anal sex is most common in Chile and Greece, where 55 percent of adults in each country reported having anal sex, followed by Italians at 50 percent.

- Thirty-nine percent of adults worldwide have had sex in toilets, 14 percent in an alleyway, and 12 percent in front of a camera. Americans and Canadians lead the way for favoring sex in front of a camera (both 21 percent).

- Almost one-half (47 percent) of all adults globally have had unprotected sex without knowing their partner's sexual history. Women are less likely to take risks than men, and younger people (16 to 20 years of age) are less likely to take risks than older people (45 to 65 years of age). The lowest risk takers are people in India (21 percent), Hong Kong (24 percent), and Spain (27 percent).

http://www.metroactive.com/papers/sonoma/10.17.02/sex-0242.html
http://www.durex.com/uk/globalsexsurvey/index.asp

There are a variety of Web sites and links that claim to provide "facts" and "figures" concerning human sexuality. Using the Web sites listed above as a beginning point search the Internet for facts and figures about human sexuality, not only in the United States but also globally, Pay particular attention to the reliaability of the source and the validity of the data and figures. How does the information you gather fit what is presented above? Write a brief paper outlining what you have found about human sexuality and ask your professor if you can present it to your class.

Sources of Sexual Learning

In earliest childhood, as we are learning other important norms of our culture, we are also learning about our sexuality, first from **significant others**, such as parents, friends, relatives, and religious figures, who play an important role in our lives, and later from the point of view of **generalized others**, that is, the viewpoint of society at large. We also learn about our sexuality in school and from the mass media. Some of the cultural information about our sexuality is consciously presented and learned; much of it, however, we learn unconsciously.

Learning Sexuality in the Family   Many authorities on early childhood behavior believe the family is the first and most significant agent of socialization. Where sexuality is concerned, however, survey data during the last decade suggested that children learn very little from their parents. For instance, a 1998 *Time*/CNN telephone survey found that only 7 percent of teenagers reported learning about sex from their parents. Most teens reported that their parents either avoided the subject of sex, missed the mark by starting the discussion long before or after the teen's sexual encounter, or just plain stonewalled them (Stodghill, 1999). Mothers, on the other hand, say they are reluctant to discuss

Historically, parents have gone to great lengths to desexualize their children's lives, including presenting themselves as asexual. However, some parents model healthy aspects of love and intimacy whereby they openly touch and show one another affection.

sex and birth control with their children for fear that such discussions would embarrass their children or encourage them to become sexually active (Jaccard et al., 2000). Recent survey data indicate most young people rank their parents as their most preferred source of information about sex and sexuality. In one survey, 70 percent of the teens polled said they received some information about sexuality from their parents. This is quite a contrast to earlier teen responses to the question about the source of their information about sexuality. However, more than half of today's adolescents also learn about sexuality from television and other media, teachers, peers, girlfriends or boyfriends, and sex partners. And one in five teens says they receive information about sexuality from the Internet (Alexander, 2005; "Mass Media and Teen Health," 2003).

Although nearly all teens (87 percent) and adults (91 percent) agree that it would be easier for teens to delay sex and prevent teen pregnancy if teens were able to have more open, honest conversations about these topics with their parents (Albert, 2004), many parents still feel intimidated and fearful of broaching the subject with their teens. Many parents report that they do not know what to say to their children about sexuality, how to say it, or when to start the conversation

so they either say nothing or their conversations involve a brief discussion of rudimentary information about reproduction concerning "where babies come from" or the acknowledgment that females have a vagina and males have a penis. Some parents wait until their children reach puberty and then give them scant information on bodily changes, sometimes discussing menstruation with girls but rarely, if ever, mentioning things like *wet dreams* to boys. These conversations about sexuality are almost always the responsibility of mothers. Fathers are rarely expected or asked to provide direct sexual information to their children, especially their daughters (Carrera, 2004).

Because many parents feel uncomfortable about discussing sex with their children, they sometimes talk about sexuality in negative terms—sex is evil, nasty, dirty—or in the form of prohibitions (such as a negative response when a child touches her or his genitals). For instance, although research (Carrera, 2004; Knowles and Dimitrov, 2002; Packer, 1997) indicates that sexual play during late infancy and early childhood is both normal and positive preparation for adult sexuality and harms children only if reacted to negatively, many children are prohibited from engaging in such activities. Parents also give children a negative feeling about their sexuality by using euphemisms or silly names for the sexual organs (for example, *kitty cat, wiener, pocket book, ding-a-ling*). Children often do not learn the proper name for female and male sexual organs until they are taught by others outside the family. Studies of preschool-age children have found that almost none of the children studied could give the correct name for their genitals, although they could give the correct name to the nongenital parts of their body (Wurtele, Melzer, and Kast, 1992). Using improper names for the genitals conveys the message that the genitals are embarrassing, mysterious, or taboo whereas teaching children to use the proper names for their genitals instills a sense of comfort with all parts of the body and makes a positive contribution to children's overall sexual development (Sexualityandu.ca, 2004).

Researchers have also found that some parents go to great lengths to desexualize their children's lives. This often includes going out of their way to present themselves as asexual. They stop touching each other or showing any signs of intimacy when the children are around. They do not discuss sexuality around children except in hushed tones, and they often become embarrassed and speechless when their children ask them a frank question about some aspect of sexuality. Parents who avoid answering their children's questions concerning sexuality may teach their children that sex is something to be ashamed of. At the other end of this continuum, parents can be negative sexual role models if they are sexually promiscuous themselves; initiate sexual activities with youth; have children outside legal marriage; do not supervise their children's coed activities; and overemphasize the sexuality and physical appearance of their daughters, such as encouraging them at ages as young as 4 to 5 years old to dress and be seductive and adult-like (Haffner, 1999; Saltzman, 1999).

There are many parents who have little problem talking with their children and sharing factual sexuality information with them. They are open and nonjudgmental, putting the sex education of their children into a perspective that encourages asking questions, feeling good about themselves, embracing sexual feelings as a joyful part of life, and developing self-control and good judgment in sexual matters (Scott and Schwartz, 2006). Indeed, research indicates that when it comes to decisions about sex, parents are more influential than they think. When parents are open and encourage dialogue about sex, contraception, morals, expectations, risks, and responsibilities, adolescents can make better-informed decisions. When teens are given misinformation, no information, or threats about sex, they are far less likely to behave reasonably and responsibly (Rodriguez, 2006). Sociological studies continue to show that family and the social milieu play a significant role in the age at which teenagers will become sexually active. For instance, research shows that teens who have talked with their parents about sex are more likely to postpone sex and to use birth control when they do become sexually active. Teens of divorced parents are much more likely than those from families with two parents present to engage in premarital sexual intercourse; teens, especially younger teens, who feel close to their mothers are less likely to begin having sex early; teens whose parents value education are less likely to have sex. Conversely, teens whose mothers are highly religious are no less likely than other teens to start having sex (*Science Daily*, 2002; Palo Alto Medical Foundation, 2001; Rathus, Nevid, and Fichner-Rathus, 1997).

What did you learn about sexuality from your parents? Did they discuss the issue with you in an open and honest manner? What information did they leave out? What happened when or if you explored your body? What euphemisms did they use for the genitals?

On an often-hidden side of the family, thousands of children are sexually abused within their families every year. Although both sexes are victims of sexual abuse, females are more likely to be abused than are males (we examine child sexual abuse in more detail in Chapter 11). As we learned earlier in this chapter, such abuse often has a negative effect on the adult sexuality of these victims in a number of ways. In addition to those discussed earlier, a growing body of evidence indicates that childhood sexual abuse may desensitize an individual to her or his body. This might cause the person in adulthood to be either restricted or excessive in her or his sexual behaviors (Basow, 1992). Some research has even suggested a possible connection between female child sexual abuse and eating disorders in women (see, for example, Iazetto, 1989).

Gender Differences in Sexual Scripts Parents tend to communicate the content of sexual behavior to their children differently depending on the sex of the child. Despite changes in attitudes about gender-specific behavior, certain aspects of the double standard remain, and parents continue to pass these on to their children. For instance, girls and boys are given different sexual scripts for understanding how a sexual experience is supposed to proceed and be interpreted. Girls are more likely to have scripts that include romance whereas for boys sexual attraction tends to outweigh emotional factors. Furthermore, parents tend to be more open with daughters than with sons about reproduction and its relationship to sexual activities as well as the morality of sex. In fact, because females can become pregnant, the sexual scripts they learn tie sexual activity almost exclusively to reproduction and family life. Boys, on the other hand, learn that their sexuality is connected to society's notion of masculinity and their ability to achieve in different areas of life (Arnett, 2003). Many parents also practice a sexual double standard whereby they place more restrictions on their daughters' sexuality than on that of their sons. Thus, female movements, social activities, and friendships are far more guarded and chaperoned than are male activities. Researchers have identified several areas of gender difference in traditional sexual scripting including an emphasis on achievement and frequency of sexual activities for males and an emphasis on monogamy and exclusiveness for females (for example, a woman saving herself for the one right man in her life).

Despite the liberalization of sexual attitudes over the last several decades and the so-called sexual liberation of women, sexual scripts and gender socialization relative to human sexuality have changed very little. For example, women's bodies continue to be treated differently than men's in advertisements and other areas of popular culture (such as the exploitation of women's bodies in terms of nudity to sell products). Although there is increasing emphasis on and exploitation of male sexuality as well, women remain the primary objects of sexual exploitation. Some contemporary examples of the continued existence of the sexual double standard include the following: (1) the importance that insurance companies and advertisers have placed on male fertility and sexual health versus female sexual health (for example, Viagra, a male impotence pill, is widely publicized and promoted and insurance companies routinely cover the cost of such pills—around $10 per pill—but refuse to cover female contraceptives such as birth control pills, which cost far less than Viagra); (2) the reaction of the public and public officials to the public sexual harassment and rape of women (for example, the sexual assault and rape of dozens of women in New York's Central Park following the annual Puerto Rican Day Parade several years ago and the inaction of police in the park when some of the women reported these crimes to them); and (3) the female genital mutilation (FGM) of more than 2 million girls and women each year worldwide (FGM is a cultural practice in at least 40 countries, most of which are in Africa and the Islamic Middle East, and involves the partial or total amputation of the external female genitalia; we do not know of any such practice against the male genitalia) (Cocco, 1998; Campo-Flores and Rosenberg, 2000; Scott and Schwartz, 2006).

The gender-based differential sexual script is rooted in the cultural belief that male sexual needs are stronger and more important than female sexual needs. This represents a classic example of the greater power and status given males in American and most other cultures of the world. These messages and scripts continue to shape our sexual behavior. Research continues to show that both women and men accept this double standard. For instance, a recent study by Michaela Pichierri and Christine Corcoran (2005) found that males who engaged in premarital sex were viewed with a higher level of respect than females. Furthermore, males who engaged in premarital sex were perceived to be more assertive than females. Thus, as the old adage goes, the more things change, the more they remain the same.

Keep in mind that these are generalizations about sexual learning. Not all females and males learn the traditional sexual scripts. The exact content of sexual scripts varies according to a number of factors including race and ethnicity, social class, and religious orientation. Whatever sexual script we learn, then, our sexual behavior can change as our life circumstances change.

Peer Influence By the time children reach adolescence, the influence of the family diminishes and peers become the most important source of sex education, exerting a strong influence on each other's sexual values and behaviors. Next to physiological readiness, peer pressure is probably the single most important factor that determines when adolescents become sexually active (Thomsen and Chang, 2000). For instance, perhaps the strongest predictor of adolescent sexual

got wood?

If Americans knew that Bob Dole drops a "blue bomber" three times a week and knocks boots with Liddy for a solid hour, they would have elected Bob Dole president!

Don't miss your chance to make history. Order a big supply of Viagra today and stand up for what you believe in!

VIAGRA
America's Favorite Dick Medicine

The continued existence of the sexual double standard is blatantly visible in ads such as this featuring former U.S. Senator Bob Dole promoting Viagra, a drug used to increase male potency. Using words and phrases like "got wood," "blue bomber," and "rock back for a solid hour," the subtext of such ads encourages male dominance and control of sexual activities. In stark contrast, fewer research and advertising dollars have gone into finding and advertising ways to address women's sexual needs.

behavior is the perceived or actual sexual behavior of friends or peers. Adolescents who have close friends who are sexually active are much more likely to become sexually active as well. Teenagers frequently believe they will gain respect from their peers and be more accepted if they follow the perceived social norms—in this case if they are sexually experienced. Peer pressure to engage in sexual activity is especially strong among young males (Genuis and Genuis, 2006). In one survey, when asked why they had sexual intercourse for the first time, 13 percent of young males ages 13 to 18 cited pressure from their friends and 8 percent of young women the same age cited pressure from a partner. At the same time, almost one-half of teens who had experienced sexual intimacy said they had done something sexual or felt pressure to do something they weren't ready to do. Female teenagers were more likely than male teenagers to have had these experiences (Kaiser Family Foundation, 1998). Peers also serve as an important source of information concerning sexuality. Until around age 15, young people report learning about sex equally from parents, peers, and school. After this age, they learn almost twice as much about sex from peers than family; they get an increasing amount of their information about sex from the media and a decreasing amount from school (Gibbs, 1993a). Unfortunately, much of what peers think they "know" is actually inaccurate. Thus, peers frequently mislead and misinform each other. However, peers also provide positive sex socialization. For example, peers can and often do provide a forum wherein young people can openly and honestly discuss human sexuality, their own developing sexuality, if they cannot get this information and discussion in the family or in formal sex education classes.

The Mass Media Popular culture and the mass media play a key role in constructing, shaping, and transforming our views and knowledge about sexuality. The changes in media representations of sexuality over the last 50 years are astonishing. No longer do scenes of intimacy involve only married couples who occupy separated beds, where sexual activity is only subtly implied. The media-saturated world in which we live today is one in which sexual behavior is frequent and increasingly explicit as many advertisers have capitalized on the knowledge that "sex sells." Today we can hear and see sexual talk and portrayals in every form of media. Unfortunately, much of this social construction is inaccurate, distorted, inflated, misleading or outright false. It is most often a far cry from the ways in which average Americans experience sexuality.

One of the most visible manifestations of contemporary sexuality is the multibillion-dollar sex industry. Thousands of theaters feature nude or nearly nude exotic dancers and movie houses across the country continue to feature X-rated movies, even though X-rated cable television stations have garnered a significant corner of the sex market. Sex magazines like *Oui, Playboy, Hustler,* and *Playgirl,* though diminishing somewhat in popularity, still enjoy a wide readership. These and other print media, such as supermarket tabloids, exploit and sensationalize sexuality to make millions of dollars from a variety of readers, few of whom question the validity of the images or the power of those who transmit sexual messages.

Advertisers Advertisers routinely use sexuality—particularly female sexuality—in their advertising copy. Nudity or near nudity is now found in even the more established magazines today. It is commonplace to see undressed or scantily dressed women selling a variety of products, from heavy construction equipment to designer jeans, from candy and watches to cars, boats, and guns. For example, an ad for Swatch watches shows a woman in her underwear, her back to the viewer and her buttocks hanging from beneath her underwear, held by a handsome young man (who is fully dressed). On her arm (when you finally notice it) are several different watches. There is little clarification that it is the watches and not the female body that is "for sale." And ads in gun magazines routinely show women in skimpy lingerie or provocative evening wear clinging to men who are holding handguns or rifles. Although it is the female body that is most often sexualized and exploited in ads, increasingly men are shown in print ads and other media as sex objects with superattractive hard and muscular bodies that are unattainable for most men (Lindsey, 2005).

Moreover, advertisers are targeting increasingly younger consumers with sexually explicit and mature products—items that in the past were reserved for adult consumers, such as rhinestone bras and sexy, skimpy thong underwear. For instance, Abercrombe and Fitch—which is not new to controversy—was recently at the heart of a public controversy over its targeting of young girls 7 to 14 years of age with their Kids line, which included underwear that leaves the buttock exposed and is decorated with pictures of cherries and catchphrases such as "kiss me" and "eye candy." Many parents and other adults expressed outrage and described the underwear as pornographic, typical of the growing trend to sexualize America's youth. Abercrombe and Fitch defended the underwear line, saying that it was meant simply to be lighthearted and cute. Whatever Abercrombe and Fitch's intention, the ramifications of such sexualized marketing are great, especially for families with young children. For instance, children today have greater buying power and play a larger role in family buying decisions than at any other time in American history. Given that the average American child sees an estimated 20,000 ads each year, and that by the time she or he reaches adulthood the average adolescent has absorbed almost 300,000 ads, it is not surprising that teen spending (the 12 to 19 age bracket) tops $1.7 billion. Even when teens are not the intended target of advertisers' and retailers' sexualized messages, the ubiquity of such messages influences both the degree to which such advertising and marketing to increasingly younger audiences is acceptable and teenagers and others' receptivity to and demand for such products (Escobar-Chaves et al., 2004; Ramos, 2002).

Television Similarly, television, considered by some media scholars to be the most influential medium shaping our views of sexuality, routinely depicts sexual situations and behaviors. Sexual content is overt in the content of day-and-nighttime soap operas and talk shows, evening shows and movies, and perhaps most overt on cable channels devoted to sexual movies and shows. They present a never-ending stream of sexual liaisons between family members, friends, and strangers (anybody is fair game); explicit petting; references made to sex and actual simulations of sexual intercourse that are often so realistic that it is difficult to tell that it is just acting. By and large, these images are limited, stereotypical, and one-dimensional, depicting sex as an activity that is only acceptable for the young, single, beautiful, slim, and white heterosexuals. Some researchers, for instance, report that 70 percent of all television shows include some sexual content; over one-fourth (28 percent) of these include explicit sexual content, they average 5 sexual scenes an hour, and most of the sexual portrayals involve youthful characters from the ages of 18 to 24, with one in ten involving characters under the age of 18. In addition, most of the sexual action and language occurs between unmarried heterosexual characters. One study found that unmarried heterosexual characters engage in sexual intercourse four to eight times as much as married characters (Sexinfo, 2006).

On soap operas in particular, sex between unmarried partners, especially those with whom there is some tension or conflict, is romanticized, and few characters are sexually responsible, use condoms, or seem concerned about pregnancy and sexually transmitted diseases. On average, there is only one representation of a married couple engaging in sex for every 24 portrayals of unmarried characters engaged in sexual acts (Sexinfo, 2006). These images and messages about the sexuality of single people is grossly exaggerated based on what single people report in various sex surveys and research studies of American sexuality. In addition, when lesbian and gay characters are presented in television programming, they are presented at each of two extremes: either asexual—such as in television programs like *Will and Grace*, which presents images of asexual gay men—or consumed with sex such as in programs like *Queer As Folk*—which has been criticized for its use of stereotypes and emphasis on graphic lesbian and gay sex.

The sexual lessons of the media are particularly influential in shaping the sexual views and behaviors of America's youth. Young people in the United States today spend 6 to 7 hours each day, on average, with some form of media, mostly without parental oversight. Soap opera portrayals of sex have been found to be particularly influential for teenaged girls, who are heavy viewers of soaps and who develop their expectations of what their sex lives might or should be like from watching such programs. Soap operas are so influential because they are on every day and viewers identify with characters. Teenaged viewers, in particular, develop their expectations of what their sex lives might or should be like from watching the soaps (Sexinfo, 2006; Lindsey, 2005).

The sexual content of television is particularly pervasive in programming for youth. For instance, the shows most watched by adolescents in the 2001 to 2002 television season contained considerably higher amounts of sexual content compared to television as a whole: 83 percent of programs popular with teens had sexual content, and 20 percent contained explicit or implicit sexual intercourse (Brody, 2006). Despite increasing public concern about the potential health risks of early, unprotected sexual activity, only about one in seven of the television programs that include sexual content mentions possible risks or responsibilities. Sexually transmitted diseases other than HIV and AIDS are almost never discussed, and unintended pregnancies are rarely shown as the outcome of unprotected sex. For example, of the nearly 14,000 sexual references adolescents are bombarded with each year, only 165 of these deal with birth control, condoms, self-control, abstinence, or the risk of pregnancy or STDs. Abortion is a taboo topic, and homosexual and transgendered youth rarely find themselves represented in the mainstream media. Although a growing number of programs are either devoted entirely to lesbian and gay lifestyles or have incorporated lesbian or gay characters into their plots, what Adrienne Rich calls *compulsory heterosexuality* prevails (Sexinfo, 2006; Brown and Keller, 2000).

The clash between the media's depiction of sexual relations and the real-life experiences of young people contributes to the difficulties in making healthy sexual decisions. Although we still do not know the exact influence of the media on young people's sexuality, a large body of evidence indicates that besides imparting basic information about sex, media portrayals of sex, coupled with inadequate role models from other sectors, encourage unhealthy sexual attitudes and behavior (Brown and Keller, 2000). A Kaiser Family Foundation study (Kunkel et al., 2005) found that watching television with sexual content artificially ages children—those who watched more than average behaved sexually as though they were 9 to 17 months older; 12-year-olds who watched the most behaved sexually like 14- and 15-year-olds (Sexinfo, 2006).

Despite V-chips, movie ratings, and televised warnings of appropriateness for young people, American teenagers have no trouble getting access to graphic sexual representations and messages. Most have a television in their bedrooms; two-thirds live in homes with cable television; and all have access to music, movies, and the Internet.

Talk Shows Added to this mix is the influx of daytime talk shows that have deteriorated to a forum for a series of sexually dysfunctional people to air their dysfunctionalities (for example, "I had sex with my mother's husband while she fixed dinner and watched" or "I had sex with 12 bisexual midgets while waiting on the bus") publicly for hours upon hours every day on programs hosted by people such as Jerry Springer and Maury Povich. *The Jerry Springer Show*, with the largest share of the talk show audience at the beginning of the twenty-first century, not only focuses entirely on the sexual dysfunctionality of guests but also mixes insults and violence with the sexual content of the show. Guests routinely fight, tear off each other's clothing, expose themselves, and use sexual language that some people refer to as *gutter language*. Like soap operas, these talk shows attract a very large and youthful audience. Many of the young females in the live audience expose their breasts on camera and on cue to the wild applause of the audience. Many teens indicate that by the time their parents get around to talking to them about sex (if at all), they have already been indoctrinated by the sexual fare on television programs. One 14-year-old reported that he learned how to kiss at 8 years of age by watching television (Stodghill, 1999). Critics of these programs argue that the presentation of human sexuality in a sleazy and sensa-

tional manner makes the abnormal seem normal and provides audiences with distorted notions of sexuality and perverse role models for the young (Saltzman, 1996).

Pressured by critics and lobbies to present more sexually responsible media, some of the people responsible for television programming have begun adding more depth and accuracy to stories involving sex, ranging from stories about teenage pregnancy to coming to terms with being lesbian or gay. Shows like *Felicity*, which aired from 1998 to 2002, have included sensitive portrayals of homosexual youth, have provided explicit lessons in how to put on a condom, and have portrayed teenagers postponing sexual intercourse, with little apparent decline in viewer interest (Brown and Keller, 2000). Several soap opera executives have explored ways to make "love in the afternoon" more responsible as well. This would include showing that the use of contraceptives is essential, avoiding the linkage of sex with violence, and showing that not all encounters or even relationships result in sex (Stodghill, 1999).

Films Increasingly since the 1970s, sex and sexual violence have become so explicit in films that a rating system is used to determine the degree of suitability for audiences under a certain age. James Bond films (regardless of who plays Bond), which are highly popular among the young, routinely depict women being raped and enjoying it, rather than as an act of criminal violence, especially if the rapist is every woman's assumed dream man—James Bond himself. The sexual double standard is as apparent in the media as it is in other cultural institutions in American society. For instance, though films are full of nudity, women's and men's nude bodies are not shown in the same way. Women are often completely nude, and the view is almost always a frontal view, whereas men are generally semiclad as opposed to completely nude, or their backside is shown. Seldom, if ever, is the penis visible. Moreover, a whole genre of teenage films over the last two to three decades present sex in crude and vulgar detail for teenagers to emulate. These films, like much television programming, typically deemphasize sexual responsibility. As with television and music producers, a number of groups are working with Hollywood scriptwriters to encourage more sexually responsible film content.

Music Contemporary music, from popular ballads to rock, heavy metal, rhythm and blues, rap, and hip hop is full of lyrics that are either sexually explicit or convey messages about sexuality that are mixed with messages about love, hate, rejection, loneliness and violence (Scott and Schwartz, 2006). Popular music is being produced and marketed to younger teens and preteens while becoming more sexualized. It should not be surprising, then, that children as young as 3 or 4 years of age can be heard repeating lyrics such as "I want to sex you up," "Pop that coochie," "Shake yo ass," "I wanna bump and grind," and "Do it to me one more time." In addition, music videos are full of men grabbing or holding their crotch, and gyrating women and men in sexually suggestive clothing, positions, and situations. For example, in a content analysis of rock lyrics, Michael Medved (1992) counted 87 descriptions of oral sex and 117 explicit terms for female and male genitals in *one* album (*As*

Nasty as They Wanna Be by 2 Live Crew). Not much has changed since this analysis. Today sex, violence, and female victimization still go hand in hand in this medium. Sodomy or reference to it has become commonplace in these videos.

Sex has always been in music. But the increasing concern today is not so much that music artists are singing about sex but rather what they are saying about sex and how they are saying it. Much of this music is misogynistic, defining women as sex objects, "whores" and "bitches," and appropriate targets for male fantasy, hatred, and violence. Teenagers and other viewers are fed a constant diet of women asking, sometimes begging, to be raped and sodomized. The message, especially to young people, is that "everyone is doing it" so "let yourself go sexually." The increasing link of sex and violence in contemporary music makes sex seem like an act that should be done violently and to degrade women (Lynch, 2004). Song titles such as "Smack My Bitch Up" by Prodigy, "Stripped, Raped and Strangled" by Cannibal Corpse, or the phrase "Beat that bitch with a bat" included in the Ying Yang Twins' *Whisper Song*, and the following lyrics from "Bat a Bitch" by B.G. are typical of the rape, violence, objectification, and misogynistic themes of some of the best selling music today: "Pimpin' ain't easy, gotta keep these hoes from talking back, Hoe I'm your daddy respect it or get batted."

Moreover, a new wave of women's voices and lyrics have been added to the music mix. Women rappers are articulating sexual desire and activity in a manner that voices their irreverence for decorum as defined through cultural expectations of the proper behavior for "respectable" women and male expectations of female subordination (Perry, 1995). Female artists such as Lil' Kim, almost always nearly nude, prance both menacingly and sensuously through one video after another. With no respect for sexual taboos, Lil' Kim holds her crotch, grinds, gyrates, and speaks sexual language that seriously transgresses cultural boundaries of polite respectability and convention. Although some analysts have described this music as libratory, as a deconstruction of the phallocentric male rap and hip-hop lyrics, and as an inversion of the sexual gaze to make males the sexual object (Perry, 1995), the fact is, like their male counterparts, female rappers never give the slightest attention to sexual responsibility or safe sex while they are calling for every kind of sex act from cunnilingus to "buck wild" sex. The lack of a caveat concerning the sexual responsibility and protection of self that should accompany this new sexual liberation is problematic for those who emulate this behavior. There is a convincing body of research showing that many media consumers, particularly heavy television viewers, tend to uncritically accept media content as fact. Even if the content is negative, sexist, misogynistic, and/or racist, or if it distorts the reality of contemporary intimate relationships, it may nevertheless be accepted as accurate by a large segment of the viewing audience (Renzetti and Curran, 2002).

Internet   Finally, the diffusion of computer and Internet use has had a phenomenal impact, in a variety of ways, on contemporary sexuality. For example, using the selling power of female sexuality, each year Victoria's Secret, a well-known lingerie company, runs half-naked models across the information superhighway while broadcasting its fashion show live on the Web (the company made history with its first such Webcast in 1999). It is estimated that more than 2 million people log on to the Victoria's Secret Webcast to view supermodels strut down the catwalk in the retailer's latest and most titillating lingerie. There is little disagreement that the Internet has dramatically increased the availability of sexually explicit messages and content. Some researchers estimate that there are currently over 1 million exotic Web sites with chat rooms, video feeds, and cascading porn pop-ups on the Internet (Jerome et al., 2004). Hardly a day goes by that Internet users are not bombarded with hundreds of porn e-mails and pop-ups advertising a wide range of products and services from Viagra and penis-enhancement products (no matter your sex or gender) to invitations to have sex with someone with giant genitals. In fact, the word *sex* is said to be the most popular search term used on the Internet today.

The selling of sex (in a variety of manifestations) via the Internet is particularly troublesome when it comes to today's youth, who are spending a growing amount of time surfing the Internet. Through the Internet, young people (as well as older adults) have access to almost any sexual information there is, in one place, and at any time they want it. To date, it is far easier to find sexually explicit, unhealthy sites on the Internet than it is to locate those that promote sexually responsible behavior in an equally compelling way. According to a survey of young (10- to 17-year-olds) Internet users, one in five said she or he had been exposed to unwanted sexual solicitations while on-line in the past year. One in four reported inadvertently encountering explicit sexual content. This is particularly compelling given that by the year 2010, it is estimated that most homes with children in the United States will have access to the Internet (Brown and Keller, 2000). Although the Internet generally has many positive features, and cybersex specifically can be used positively to expand our ideas about sex and sexuality and to promote sexually responsible behavior, the dark side of cybersex is the increasing violence and victimization associated with it as a result of the increasing phenomena of on-line predation, cyberstaking, sexual harassment, pornography, pedophilia, and virtual rape. Almost three-fourths (70 percent) of young people 15 to 17 years of age have viewed pornography, much of it hard-core.

Knowledge of children's heavy involvement with computers has led some child pornographers and child molesters to use the Internet as a primary source for contacting children. One in four young people 10 to 17 years of age who are on the Internet regularly encounter unwanted pornography and one in five are exposed to unwanted sexual solicitations and approaches (Jerome et al., 2004). In 2000, Congress enacted the Children's Internet Protection Act; however, young people remain quite vulnerable and primary targets and victims of the cybersex stalkers and the cybersex industry. The bad news is that according to the small amount of research that currently exists on the subject, the constant exposure to pornography and other sexually explicit materials on the Internet may have the effect of distorting adolescent views about sex; they may wonder if it is okay to denigrate their partner and/or they may dissociate sex from intimacy (Jerome et al., 2004). The good news is that there is a growing number of Internet sites that promote healthy sexual behavior and provide sound advice on a wide range of intimate and sexuality issues (Brown, 2002).

SEXUAL ORIENTATIONS

It is impossible to discuss human sexuality without discussing sexual orientation. Contrary to popular belief, sexual orientation, whether heterosexual or homosexual, is not synonymous with sexual behavior. **Sexual orientation** involves not only whom one chooses as a sexual partner, but, more fundamentally, the ways in which people understand and identify themselves.

Although Americans tend to think of sexual orientation in terms of clear-cut categories—for example, heterosexual versus homosexual—various sex researchers have concluded that fundamental categories of sexual desire are nonexistent for most of us. Rather, sexual desire is constructed in the context of social relationships and identities (Andersen, 2005). Cultural historian and sex researcher Shere Hite (1976) believes we are born with a natural desire to relate to people of the same as well as the other sex. Society, however, teaches us to inhibit all of our sexual desires except those for partners with whom we can procreate. Regardless of whether we accept Hite's hypothesis, it is clear that U.S. culture historically has espoused **heterosexism**, the belief that heterosexuality is the only right, natural, and acceptable sexual orientation and that any other orientation is pathological.

Heterosexism is so strong in U.S. society that most sex research is based on the assumption of heterosexuality. This assumption overlooks the fact that many people have a homosexual orientation and even more people have engaged in homosexual behavior at least once in their life. For example, Susan Basow (1992) reported in 1992 that by age 45, somewhere between one-fifth and one-third of all men and one-sixth of all women have experienced at least one homosexual encounter. Furthermore, research suggests that sexual orientation forms a continuum with at least four recognizable levels of orientation (see, for example, Maier, 1984). According to this research, at the two extremes are exclusively heterosexual and exclusively homosexual orientations, with bisexuality and asexuality falling somewhere in the middle.

Heterosexuality

Heterosexuality refers to the preference for sexual activities with a person of the other sex. In a more sociological and political sense, heterosexuality also includes an individual's community, lifestyle, and core identity. It is difficult to know precisely how many people in the U.S. population are heterosexual. Research during the mid-1990s reported that 97 percent of Americans identify themselves as exclusively heterosexual (for example, Clements, 1994; Laumann et al., 1994). A decade or more later, in a report from the National Center for Health Statistics on sexual behavior in the United Sates, researchers reported that 90 percent of American women and men identify themselves as heterosexual (Mosher et al., 2005).

In describing a person's sexual orientation, most social scientists view sexual orientation, like other aspects of our identity, as an ongoing process that can vary considerably over the life course. Thus, they question whether it is more meaningful to emphasize a person's perceived attractions, her or his current sexual partners, her or his lifetime partners, or the description the person prefers for her- or himself (Laumann et al., 1994). **Sexual identity** refers to how a person describes her or his sexuality and how that person expresses that self to others. Typically, sexual identity will include an expression of a person's underlying sexual orientation. However, sexual orientation and sexual identity are not one and the same—they do not always match. One can have a homosexual orientation but choose to have a heterosexual identity (Palo Alto Medical Foundation, 2001). For instance, researchers have found that heterosexual and homosexual preferences do not always remain constant throughout people's lives. For any number of reasons, people sometimes change their sexual preference. Phillip Blumstein and Pepper Schwartz (1983), in their now classic study of American sexuality, for example, found that people often became homosexual after satisfactory heterosexual lives or became heterosexual after many years of homosexual identity and behavior. Moreover, some people who would prefer partners of their same sex might restrict themselves to heterosexual relationships because of religious, family, professional, or other social or political reasons. Conversely, in restrictive environments such as prison, people who are more attracted to members of the other sex might sometimes engage in sexual and other intimacy with members of the same sex (Shriver et al., 2002). For those who view human sexual orientation as fluid, the degree to which we identify ourselves as heterosexual reflects in part the extent to which we have internalized society's messages and definitions of what is and is not acceptable. Given the stigma associated with sexual orientations other than heterosexuality, it is not surprising that most people claim (at least publicly) to be exclusively heterosexual.

Social scientists using a feminist perspective maintain that in the United States, sexuality generally and sexual activities specifically that are associated with a heterosexual orientation are *phallocentric*, male-centered, and are defined almost exclusively in terms of genital intercourse and male orgasm (which might explain why so many people do not view oral sex as having sex). According to this point of view, the ideology of heterosexuality assumes that women exist for men, that their bodies and services are men's property. If a woman rejects this definition of normal sexuality, she is stigmatized no matter whom she chooses as a sexual partner (see Bunch, 1979). For men, the notion of heterosexual intercourse, with its assumptions of male power and control; male lust, passion, and aggression; and the male as the initiator of sexual activity, is the proving ground for acceptable male sexuality and identity in this society. It also provides the script that most men adopt, with some individual modification, as the foundation of both their masculinity and sexual activity. Some feminist social scientists such as Adrienne Rich (1980) have argued that making heterosexuality compulsory stymies or restricts the sexuality of males as well as females. Rich suggests that both heterosexism and **homophobia**—an extreme and irrational fear or hatred of homosexuals—act to inhibit the possibility of some women and men finding emotional and sexual satisfaction with same-sex partners.

Clearly, sexual orientation is much more complicated than simply identifying whom one sleeps with or even the label people use to identity themselves sexually. Although heterosexuality is the predominant sexual orientation, homosexuality exists in all known societies.

Homosexuality

Like heterosexuality, **homosexuality** refers to both identity and behavior. It is part of a person's core identity and includes whom she or he defines as an acceptable sexual partner, but it does not consist solely of sexual preference. Thus, as we have indicated in our discussion of heterosexuality, to label homosexuality entirely in terms of choice of sexual partner distorts our perception of lesbians and gays. We certainly do not define heterosexuals entirely or even primarily in terms of their choice of sexual partner. But what if we did? If you are heterosexual, how would you feel if people defined you entirely in terms of who you slept with? What if people routinely asked you questions such as, "When or how did you first realize that you were a heterosexual?" "Do your parents know?" "What do you think caused your heterosexuality? Is it possible that it is just a phase that you are going through?" "If you choose to have children, would you want them to be heterosexual, knowing the problems they would face?" "Why do heterosexuals put so much emphasis on sex?" "If you have never slept with a person of the same sex, is it possible that all you need is a good gay lover?" (see, for example, Rochlin, 1992). Would you find such questions offensive? Can you see and understand the indignity engendered when we routinely ask such questions of lesbians and gays?

As we have seen, some scientists explain both homosexuality and heterosexuality in terms of social learning, social experiences, and role models. However, no specific social experience or type of social relationship has been found to be significant in the development of human sexual preference (Bell, Weinberg, and Hammersmith, 1981). At the same time, there is no conclusive evidence to support the argument that sexual orientation is determined entirely by biology. Nonetheless, the debate over the relative roles of social environment and biology in determining sexual orientation continues to spark controversy among a number of groups in society, including scientists, gay activists, and religious and political leaders. In recent years, those who take a biological stance in this debate have received a boost from research results suggesting that sexual orientation (at least in men) is determined in large part by genetic factors. If it turns out that sexual orientation is genetically determined, then can we continue to define either homosexuality or heterosexuality as sexual preference?

How Widespread Is Homosexuality?
Like heterosexuality, the exact determination of homosexuality is unknown. Because homosexuality is still so stigmatized, self-reports as homosexual vary across time and type of sexual survey; responses are not always consistent with respondents' reported sexual behaviors. In the 1950s, Alfred Kinsey and his associates (1953) reported that 28 percent of their sam-

In contrast to popular images of the casual sexual behavior of lesbians and gays, many same-sex couples share long-term monogamous relationships that often include shared parenting.

ple of almost 8000 women had experienced a homosexual activity. Almost 25 years later, Shere Hite (1976) reported that 8 percent of the women in her sample said that they actually preferred sex with another woman. A few years later, in her study of male sexuality, Hite (1981) found that 11 percent of the 7000 men in her sample preferred to have sex with a person of their same sex. In 1994, *Parade* magazine reported that 1 percent of women and 3 percent of men identified themselves as homosexual. This finding was consistent with the 1994 NORC sex study in which 1.4 percent of the women and 2.8 percent of the men identified themselves as homosexual or bisexual. However, the number who reported having had same-sex experiences or same-sex attractions was considerably higher (8.6 percent for women and 10.1 percent for men). This disparity is evident in other, more recent national surveys. For instance, in a Centers for Disease Control and Prevention study of American sexual behavior, 2.3 percent of survey respondents 18 to 44 years of age identified themselves as gay. Additionally, in this same age group, 11 percent of females and 6 percent of males indicated that they have had same-sex contact in their lifetimes. Among the men who have ever had sexual contact with another male, one-half (49 percent) consider themselves heterosexual, and among women who have had sexual contact with another woman, nearly two-thirds (65 percent) consider themselves heterosexual. While the percentage of men reporting same-sex relationships remains relatively unchanged since the mid-1990s, the percentage of women who have had same-sex contact has tripled among women aged 18 to 29, from 4 or 5 percent in the mid-1990s to 14 percent currently. The authors of this report suggest that this dramatic increase in young women's reported same-sex behavior might be attributed to the fact that women might be trying to reduce their risk of STDs (Mosher et al., 2005).

In any event, as these statistics indicate, a definition of homosexuality is complicated by the fact that sexual preference, sexual attraction, and/or actual sexual behavior are not always consistent with one's sexual self-identity. An increasing amount of public focus, discourse, and debate around this issue has permeated the media and scholarly writings and discussions over the past several years, particularly as it relates to the African American community. For instance, it is claimed that many African American men who have sex with other men nevertheless think of themselves as heterosexual. Whites and Latinas/os are far more likely to report being gay than are African American women and men. For example, in the NORC survey, 3 percent of white men and 3.7 percent of Latinos identified themselves as homosexual or bisexual, compared with 1.5 percent of African American men. According to some analysts, machismo has always been a strong component of African American masculinity. The concept of being gay is seen as the antithesis of manhood. Thus, many African American men who have sex with other men do not consider themselves gay. While attempting to present a heterosexual image to the outer world, these men frequently engage in compulsive, high-risk sex with men while engaged in ongoing sexual relationships with one or more women. Experts in the field have dubbed this tendency the "down-low syndrome" when men have sex with other men but deny they are gay or even bisexual. Many believe this down-low behavior is a leading cause of the increasing incidence of HIV infections among African American women (Emory Health Sciences Press Release, 2004; Herbert, 2001a; Muwakkil, 2001).

The same discrepancy between how one self-identifies and what one actually does is also observable for women: 1.7 percent of white women and 1.1 percent of Latinas identified themselves as homosexual or bisexual, compared with less than 1 percent (0.6 percent) of the African American women in the sample. Findings such as these raise questions regarding the accuracy of statistics that purport to tell us the prevalence of homosexuality, heterosexuality, and bisexuality; they do not even begin to reveal the number of people who are transgendered. There does not seem to be much reliable data on transgendered people. The National Transgender Advocacy Coalition Web site estimates that between 2 and 3 percent of the American population is transgendered and that about 10 percent of them are homosexual.

In simple terms, **transgendered** refers to living life as the opposite sex. Complicating our ability to determine just how many people are transgendered is the fact that this group is not static; it includes heterosexuals, bisexuals, and homosexuals. In addition, some transgendered people are *transsexuals* (people who have undergone sex change surgery), others are *transvestites* (people who dress in the clothing of the opposite sex), and still others are masculine-appearing women and feminine-appearing men. Even those who feel they are the opposite sex, but do not express it outwardly, are considered transgendered. Like any other sexual orientation, transgender is also about identity; about expression—how a person feels about her or himself and how she or he wants to identity or present her-himself to other people.

Given the general difficulty of defining sexual orientation, what criteria, if any, should we use to classify people in terms of their sexual orientation? Do we use their behavior? Their attitudes? Both? How many female and male partners does a person need to have to be classified as heterosexual,

homosexual, or bisexual? Do we classify someone who has had 2 partners of the same sex and 15 of the other sex as heterosexual, homosexual, or bisexual? Or do we simply rely on self-labeling and what people feel rather than what they do? For example, how do we classify the person who feels gay, identifies as lesbian or gay, but never has same-sex sexual relations? Furthermore, given the prevalence of AIDS, the stigma associated with it, and its association to homosexuality, are people telling the truth?

Clearly from our discussion thus far it seems that the traditional sexual orientation dichotomy of heterosexual versus homosexual is misleading. According to Kinsey and his colleagues (1948), few of us are completely and exclusively heterosexual or homosexual. Rather, although many people would prefer not to entertain the thought, there are some aspects of both orientations in all of us. Kinsey expressed this idea with a rating scale (0 to 6) of heterosexuality and homosexuality, in which each number on the scale represents the degree to which people have heterosexual or homosexual experiences (see Figure 6.3). Using this rating, Kinsey found that almost 80 percent of 25-year-old white male respondents in his study were exclusively heterosexual, and 3 percent were exclusively homosexual. The remaining respondents fell somewhere along the scale from 1 to 5. Using the same scale, he later suggested that 2 percent of women have an exclusively homosexual orientation. He suggested further that somewhere around one-third of men and one-eighth of women had at least one homosexual experience leading to orgasm.

For sure, as with heterosexuality, we cannot speak of homosexuality as if it were a monolithic behavioral and attitudinal pattern. Homosexuality varies in terms of importance, organization, and actualization in people's lives. It is

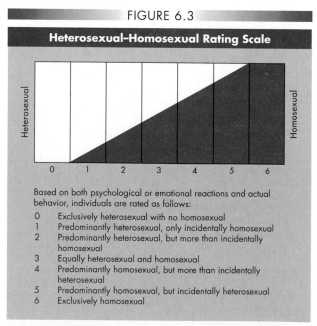

FIGURE 6.3

Heterosexual–Homosexual Rating Scale

Based on both psychological or emotional reactions and actual behavior, individuals are rated as follows:

0   Exclusively heterosexual with no homosexual
1   Predominantly heterosexual, only incidentally homosexual
2   Predominantly heterosexual, but more than incidentally homosexual
3   Equally heterosexual and homosexual
4   Predominantly homosexual, but more than incidentally heterosexual
5   Predominantly homosexual, but incidentally heterosexual
6   Exclusively homosexual

Source: From Alfred Kinsey, W. B. Pomeroy, and C. E. Martin, 1948, *Sexual Behavior in the Human Male* (Philadelphia, PA: Saunders): 470. Reprinted by permission of the Kinsey Institute for Research in Sex, Gender, and Reproduction, Inc.

sufficient to say here that, except for the sex or gender of one's partner, the sexual attitudes, behaviors, and relationships of lesbians and gays do not differ significantly from those of heterosexual couples. Although we provide a more in-depth discussion of lesbian and gay lifestyles in Chapter 7, lesbian and gay lifestyles, issues, and concerns can be found throughout the text.

Bisexuality

Although bisexuality is difficult to define, some researchers have suggested that it is more prevalent in American society than is homosexuality. On the one hand, as with other sexual orientations, bisexuality is subject to a variety of definitions, based on perceived attractions, current partnerships, past partnerships, or how a person self-identifies. On the other hand, **bisexuality** refers generally to individuals who do not have an exclusive sexual preference for one sex over the other. Rather, a bisexual has partners of both sexes, either simultaneously or at different times. It does not necessarily mean being equally attracted to both. Bisexuality also represents an identity and a lifestyle. As we have already noted, an important aspect of sexual orientation is how one defines oneself. Similar to homosexuality, it is difficult to know exactly how many people are bisexual. Some researchers suggest that this is so because bisexual is not a very well-defined social category. In a recent national survey, approximately 2 percent of women and men considered themselves bisexual—another 4 percent considered themselves "something else." Looking at bisexuality by gender: 3 percent of women and 2 percent of men identified as bisexual. According to some research, more men are bisexual based on their behavior than based on their self-identity. In short, as with homosexual men, some men who have sex with both women and men do not think of themselves as bisexual (Mosher et al., 2005; Shriver et al., 2002).

One of the difficulties in attempting to estimate the bisexual population is that many researchers and laypersons alike view bisexuals exclusively as homosexuals. For example, in the NORC study, statistics on bisexuals and homosexuals are collapsed. Although some people who engage in both same-sex and heterosexual relationships categorize themselves as either heterosexual or homosexual, many bisexuals do not see themselves in this either/or dichotomy; they do not see themselves as gay or straight, and their behavior does not correspond to either. Some sexuality researchers have claimed that part of the problem of counting bisexuals is because bisexuality is a temporary state that is subject to change. They suggest that people who are bisexual are either trying to deny their homosexual orientation, experimenting, or responding to circumstantial reasons, such as partner availability. Thus, in time, the bisexual behavior will be replaced with exclusively homosexual or heterosexual behavior. Other sexuality researchers disagree with this theory, arguing that many bisexuals have long-term bisexual behavior patterns (Shriver et al., 2002).

Like homosexuality, bisexuality is stigmatized in the larger society. In addition, bisexuals are often rejected by the homosexual community as well. Some lesbians and gays, for instance, view bisexuals with suspicion or hostility, perceiving their heterosexual behavior as indicative of a lack of commitment to the lesbian and gay community (Shriver et al., 2002). Many people do not believe people can really be bisexual; they have to be one thing (heterosexual) or another (homosexual). Shere Hite's (1981) suggestion that the terms *homosexual* and *heterosexual* be used not as nouns but as adjectives is noteworthy. Perhaps *bisexual* should also be used as an adjective to describe people's activities and not people themselves, particularly given that few people are completely bisexual.

HUMAN SEXUAL EXPRESSION

Sexual Response

The complex interaction of our biology and culture is evidenced in the fact that regardless of how we choose to express our sexuality, our bodies experience a physiological response pattern when we are sexually stimulated. Our physiological response to sexual stimuli can vary a great deal by our gender, age, and health. Generally, however, according to sex researchers William Masters and Virginia Johnson (1966), all people go through the same four phases of sexual response: excitement, climax, orgasm, and resolution.

During the first phase, *excitement*, the body responds to sexual stimulation; there is an increase in blood pressure, pulse rate, and breathing. For males, excitement often results in the swelling and erection of the penis and partial elevation of the testes; for females, it results in vaginal lubrication and clitoral swelling and the nipples may become hard. If sexual stimulation continues, both heart rate and blood pressure intensify. Sexual tension reaches a peak or *climax* and can last only a few minutes or for quite some time, leading to the third phase. The sexual emotions and excitement built up in the previous phases are released in an **orgasm**, the involuntary release of pelvic congestion and accumulated muscular tension through rhythmic contractions in the genitals of both women and men. In this third stage of sexual response, for most men orgasm usually includes **ejaculation**, the forceful release of semen. Women may feel contractions in the vagina, uterus, and rectum. In the final phase, *resolution*, following orgasm and the cessation of sexual stimulation, the body returns to its preexcitement physiological state. In females, the vagina decreases in size, and in males, the penis loses its erection. Both partners may experience physical and mental relaxation and a sense of well-being.

Although the discussion of sexual response patterns refers to heterosexual sexuality, from the point of view of physical pleasure we can relate erotically to either sex depending on our feelings (Hite, 1976). Heterosexual intercourse is simply one of many ways to express human sexuality. Human sexual expression covers a wide variety of behaviors ranging from activities involving only the self—**autoeroticism**—to activities involving one or more other individuals, such as "swapping" or group sex.

Autoeroticism

Some of the most common and recognizable forms of autoeroticism are masturbation, sexual fantasy, and erotic dreams. Until recent times, U.S. society placed particularly heavy restrictions on autoeroticism. Today, however, a range of such behaviors is considered acceptable. Nevertheless, recent surveys of America's sexual habits indicate that the majority of us do not engage in and enjoy a wide spectrum of exotic sexual practices. Rather, we are pretty conventional, most often engaging in only three different types of sexual activity.

Masturbation "Don't knock masturbation. It's having sex with someone I deeply love." This now classic statement by film director Woody Allen reflects the attitudes of many people in this society, for whom masturbation is a common form of sexual expression and enjoyment. **Masturbation** involves gaining sexual pleasure from the erotic stimulation of oneself through caressing or otherwise stimulating the genitals. Most people's first experience with sexual pleasure and orgasm is through masturbation. Masturbatory behavior is said to begin in infancy, when children accidentally discover the pleasure to be derived from rubbing, squeezing, caressing, or otherwise stimulating their genitals. For many people, this is the beginning of a lifelong way of expressing their sexuality. This fact notwithstanding, our culture is remarkably ambivalent about masturbation and other autoerotic behaviors. Some readers of this text might recall that Jocelyn Elders lost her position as U.S. Surgeon General in 1994 because she dared to publicly advocate that masturbation be discussed, and even promoted as "safe sex," as a part of sex education for young people. The outrage, anger, and loathing leveled at her for her position on masturbation cost her job but it also demonstrated how much we as a society deny the legitimacy of safe sexual expression such as masturbation for teens and our difficulty accepting sexual feelings and behaviors outside of a spiritual, religious, relational or reproductive context (Risman and Schwartz, 2002).

Masturbation is not limited to the self-stimulation of the genitals; it can also include the self-stimulation of other parts of the body such as the breast, the inner thighs, and the anus. Although masturbation is becoming more common among women, boys and adult men tend to masturbate more often than do girls and women. Sex researchers report that 42 percent of women and 63 percent of men say that they masturbate. Among those who masturbate, one man in four and one woman in ten report masturbating once or more a week (Laumann et al., 1994; Clements, 1994). In a study of undergraduate college students, 98 percent of men and 44 percent of women reported having ever masturbated. Undergraduate men reported masturbating an average of 12 times per month compared to undergraduate women, who reported masturbating an average of 4.7 times per month. As women and men age, they masturbate less frequently, but they do not stop altogether. One study found that as many as 43 percent of men and 33 percent of women in their 70s masturbate (Pinkerton et al., 2002; Laumann et al., 1994).

In addition to gender differences in masturbation rates, women and men also differ in terms of their attitudes toward masturbation. For men, masturbation functions more as a supplement to sexual life, whereas for women it functions more as a substitute for intercourse. Females tend to begin masturbation at much later ages than males, sometimes for the first time in their 20s or 30s, whereas males

typically begin to masturbate during early adolescence (Lindsey, 2005). Interestingly, Shere Hite (1976) found that most women have more intense and quicker orgasms with masturbation than with intercourse. Other researchers report that women who masturbate have significantly more single and multiple orgasms, greater sexual desire, higher self-esteem, and greater marital and sexual satisfaction; they become sexually aroused faster than women who do not masturbate (Shriver et al., 2002).

There are also significant differences in the rate of masturbation by age, race, and class (as measured by level of educational attainment). Young people 18 to 24 years of age are less likely to masturbate than are those who are 25 to 34 years of age. Further, the higher one's level of education, generally the greater the frequency of masturbation. For example, over 33 percent of the male respondents and 14 percent of the females in the NORC sex survey with a high school or college education reported that they masturbate on a regular basis, compared with 19 percent of men and 8 percent of women who did not graduate from high school. In fact, those most likely to masturbate are white and college-educated. Among racial and ethnic groups, African Americans report the lowest rates of masturbation. Sixty percent of African American men and 68 percent of African American women report that they have never masturbated (Laumann et al., 1994). Perhaps because this behavior does not conform to the stereotype of African American male sexuality, some observers have attempted to explain the low rate of masturbation among African American males by suggesting that these males shy away from such behavior because they view it as an admission of their inability to seduce a woman (Belcastro, 1985). Such interpretations should be viewed cautiously. This is clearly an underresearched area and, like other topics of human sexuality, may be an embarrassing or intimidating subject for people to respond to honestly and openly.

Although single, noncohabiting individuals report the highest rate of masturbation (41 percent for men and 12 percent for women), frequently people continue to masturbate after marriage. Husbands tend to masturbate more often than do wives. The majority of wives who masturbate rate their marriage as unsatisfactory (Petersen et al., 1983). Many married and nonmarried couples participate in mutual masturbatory activities rather than have intercourse. Others find that manual stimulation of the genitals during intercourse heightens the likelihood that both partners will reach orgasm. Furthermore, the NORC sex survey belies the myth that the majority of people who masturbate are those who are without a sex partner. According to the study, people who masturbate the most are people who have the most partnered sex (85 percent of men and 45 percent of women living with a sex partner reported having masturbated during the past year).

It is interesting that so many people engage in a behavior that not long ago was thought to cause blindness, dementia (insanity), and a host of other mental and physical ills. So intense were feelings about masturbation in our early history that children's hands and feet were often tied to bedposts to prevent them from masturbating during the night. Various "experts" in the late nineteenth and early twentieth centuries as well a variety of others blamed masturbation for every kind of human malady from brain damage to blindness, deafness, heart murmurs, and destroying the genitals to acne and bad breath. So entrenched were these ideas about masturbation that there was a large and active commercial market for a variety of devices to control masturbatory activities such as metal mittens to cover the hands, rings with metal teeth or spikes to wear on the penis, vulva guards, and alarms that were activated when the bed moved (Wade and Cirese, 1991).

Although many people still consider masturbation to be wrong, sex therapists have found that it serves some important positive functions, such as providing a means for people (especially women) to explore and determine in private what is most sexually stimulating for them (Gagnon and Simon, 1973). Despite the benefits of masturbation and the more liberal attitudes toward it today, many people find that their emotional needs are not met through self-stimulation.

Sexual Fantasy and Erotic Dream Sexual fantasy and erotic dreams, like masturbation, are common methods of autoeroticism. People use these activities to supplement or enhance a reality that is less exciting than the images they can construct in their minds. Some researchers have suggested that sexual fantasies might help prepare women for experiences that are erotically satisfying. Others suggest that they provide a harmless way for people to release pent-up sexual feelings or escape a boring sexual life (Patterson and Kim, 1991). Whatever their particular function, fantasies help maintain emotional balance in the individual. More males than females engage in sexual fantasy and erotic dreaming, and they do so more often. Over one-half of men (54 percent) report that they fantasize about sex several times a day. Another 43 percent fantasize about sex several times a week. In comparison, only 19 percent of women have sexual fantasies several times a day, while over two-thirds (67 percent) do so a few times a week. However, when it comes to talking with their partners about their fantasies, an equal number (51 percent) of women and men say they do so to enhance their sex lives (Langer, Arnedt, and Sussman, 2004).

Male fantasies appear to differ from female fantasies in that males tend to fantasize situations in which they are strong and aggressive and in which the sexual activity itself is basically impersonal. Women, on the other hand, tend to have more romantic, passive, and submissive fantasies (Patterson and Kim, 1991). The most frequent fantasies for both women and men involve oral sex and sex with a famous person (Patterson and Kim, 1991). Men also frequently fantasize about having sex as part of a threesome. Beyond the two similarities between the genders, there are some interesting differences in the frequency of different types of sexual fantasies (see Table 6.1).

Erotic dreams, often referred to as nocturnal dreams with sexual content, frequently lead to orgasm during sleep. This phenomenon is referred to as **nocturnal emissions** or **wet dreams**. Kinsey and his colleagues found that almost all men and the majority of women have nocturnal dreams with sexual content. Men tend to have more wet dreams than women: Four-fifths of all men, as opposed to one-third of all

TABLE 6.1

Common Sexual Fantasies Among American Women and Men

	Females (%)	Males (%)
Oral sex	43	75
Sex with a famous person	39	59
Using sexual devices	29	38
Sex in a public place	26	39
Sex with someone of another race	25	52
Multiple partners	24	57
Sex with a fictional TV character	20	30
Sex with dominance or submission	19	27
Sex with a much older person	15	34
Sex with a much younger person	15	39
Swapping partners	15	42
Anal sex	14	39
Sex with a physical object	11	15
Unexpected sex	10	20
A threesome	9	33
Workplace sex	7	12

Sources: Adapted from *The Day America Told the Truth* by James Patterson and Peter Kim. Copyright 1991 by James Patterson and Peter Kim. Reprinted by permission of William Morris Agency, Inc., on behalf of the author. G. Langer, C. Arnedt, and D. Sussman, 2004, "Primetime Live Poll: American Sex Survery," A Peek Beneath the Sheets, *ABC News.* http://abcnews.go.com/Primetime/News/story?id=174461&page=1 (Accessed: March 20, 2006).

females, had nocturnal dreams that led to orgasm. Between 2 and 3 percent of a woman's orgasms may be achieved during nocturnal dreaming. In contrast, for men that number may be as high as 8 percent. The content of such dreams can cover a wide variety of erotic or sexual possibilities, including any one or all of the items listed in Table 6.1. The dream need not be overtly sexual, but it is usually accompanied by sexual sensations (Strong et al., 2004).

Interpersonal Sexual Behavior

In contrast to autoerotic behavior, which involves an individual acting alone, interpersonal sexual activity involves two or more people acting in concert for the purpose of giving each other pleasure.

Pleasuring As far back as the mid-nineteenth century, women were describing what to them was sexually pleasurable. Elizabeth Blackwell, the first woman to earn a medical degree in the United States, suggested that both women and men could experience sexual pleasure from each other without penile–vaginal intercourse. This idea of giving and receiving pleasure without intercourse was described over a century later by Masters and Johnson as **pleasuring.**

Pleasuring involves a couple exploring each other's bodies. It is erotic behavior that involves one person touching, exploring, and caressing nongenital areas of her or his partner's body for the purpose of giving erotic pleasure. After a while, the partners exchange roles. This exchange can continue until orgasm, or it can function as foreplay followed by genital intercourse. However pleasuring is conducted, it seems that a large number of women find touching and caressing to be a natural eroticism and the most important part of sexual activity. More than three decades ago, women reported that one of the most basic changes that they wished for in their sexual relationships was touching and closeness for their own sake rather than only as a prelude to intercourse. One woman, for example, said that "general body touching is more important to me than orgasms." Another said, "You can't love sex without loving to touch and be touched. It is the very physical closeness of sex that is the main pleasure" (Hite, 1976:556). Although traditional sexual scripts define women as the passive recipients of pleasuring, they are now also more acting and reciprocating during this phase of sexual activity.

Petting and Oral Sex   **Petting,** which involves various forms of physical contact for the purpose of sexual arousal, is a common activity among adolescent girls and boys. Petting includes kissing, oral contact with the body, finger insertion, and fondling. Kinsey once said that petting was one of the most significant factors in the sexual lives of high school and college females and males. If that was true in the past, it is even more so today. The great majority of young people today have experienced some type of petting behavior before they reach adulthood (Christopher and Sprecher, 2000). Whereas in the past these behaviors were used most often as a substitute for copulation, for many couples today they are a prelude to copulation. For example, a high percentage of women and men say that they enjoy kissing, genital touching, mouth or hands on breast, body kissing, and mutual masturbation as preludes to copulation. Some couples use pornographic material, and others employ sexual devices before or during sexual activity to enhance their enjoyment (Shriver et al., 2002).

In many parts of society, oral–genital sex is an unmentionable subject and a taboo behavior. As late as the 1970s, social researcher Morton Hunt (1974) reported that oral–genital sex was still classified as a punishable crime against nature in the statutes of most states. By this time, however, **cunnilingus,** the oral stimulation of the female genitals, and **fellatio,** the oral stimulation of the male genitals, had become standard practices for a majority of white people of all social classes, single or married. Today, an overwhelming majority of women (86 percent) and men (87 percent) engage in oral sex, both giving and receiving. Although the percent of Americans engaging in oral sex increases with age, as we reported in the opening vignette, at the other end of the age spectrum an increasing number of adolescents and teens are also engaging in oral sex. Such behavior has been evident to a lesser degree among comparable samples of Latinas/os and African Americans. For instance, only 74 percent of Latinas/os and 79 percent of African Americans report engaging in oral sex. The practice of oral sex is particularly prevalent among married and cohabiting couples (92 to 93 percent) and white, college-educated men, 80 percent, compared with only 51 percent of college-educated African American males (Mosher et al., 2005; Laumann et al., 1994). Postfeminist writer Camille Paglia believes oral sex is a culturally acquired preference

that a generation of white college students picked up in the 1970s when they saw oral sex performed on the wide screen (in movies such as the X-rated film *Deep Throat*) (cited by Elmer-DeWitt, 1994:68). Although oral–genital sex has gained acceptance over the years, it may well be on the decline among some groups given the heightened sensitivity to various sexually transmitted diseases, especially herpes and AIDS.

Coitus   **Coitus** refers only to penile–vaginal intercourse. Other forms of intercourse such as anal intercourse are not included in this term. The U.S. patriarchal structure of heterosexual relations assumes that coitus is the most satisfying sexual activity for women and men. In this context, coitus is the primary method through which heterosexuals seek erotic pleasure. In every sex survey that the authors reviewed, both heterosexual women and men overwhelmingly identify coitus as *the most* appealing sexual practice. Coitus can occur with the partners in any number of positions. The most common is the "missionary position," in which the female lies on her back and the male faces her, lying on top of her. Some couples also adopt a position popularly called "69," in which the couple lie down with their heads in opposite directions and simultaneously perform oral–genital sex on each other. Because sexual intercourse is personal and private, people usually employ whatever positions they find mutually satisfying. Defining coitus as the sexual norm is problematic in that it is a limited viewpoint and it does not take into account sexual behaviors enjoyed and preferred by nonheterosexuals such as lesbians and gays.

Sexual Expression Among Lesbians and Gays

As with other aspects of behavior, there is little difference in homosexual and heterosexual sexual expression and physiological response. Like heterosexuals, same sex couples engage in kissing, caressing, sexual arousal, and orgasm. Because lesbians and gays are socialized with the same gendered sexual scripts as their heterosexual counterparts, their approach to sexual activity and intimacy reflects our culture's heavily gendered prescriptions for women and men. For instance, lesbians are more emotionally involved with their partners and are more likely to connect sex with love than are gays. They express affection before actual sexual activity begins, and they often reach orgasm through mutual masturbation and cunnilingus. Gays often kiss, caress each other's penises, and reach orgasm through anal intercourse or through fellatio (Strong et al., 2004). As indicated in Chapter 5, gays tend to have sex with more partners and in shorter-term relationships than do lesbians. Gays also tend to act on their sexuality earlier than lesbians do, just as heterosexual males act earlier than heterosexual females. Some research indicates that these behaviors have changed in recent years because of the spread of AIDS. However, many gays have been, and some continue to be, sexually active with multiple partners.

There are, however, some distinctive features of same-sex intimacy as well. For instance, researchers have found that same-sex couples, especially lesbians but gays as well, take much more time in their sexual relationships, holding and kissing each other. In addition, lesbians are less genitally oriented and less fixated on orgasm, compared to men. Romance and other emotional aspects of sexual intimacy are more central in their sexual activities. Contrary to popular belief, lesbians seldom use dildos or other objects in an attempt to simulate heterosexual intercourse, nor do they engage in rigid role-playing that imitates heterosexual sexual behavior. Rather, both lesbian and gay couples typically alternate active and receptive roles (Shriver et al., 2002). Such a belief is rooted in the heterosexist notion that heterosexual genital intercourse is the only normal way to express sexuality. Among other things, the use of a heterosexual model homogenizes sexual practices across sexual orientations and race. Although there continues to be a dearth of research on the sexual practices of lesbians and gays of color, we should not assume a universality of homosexual lifestyles or that heterosexual practices are adapted or adaptable to a lesbian or gay lifestyle or preference.

An increasing number of teenagers are engaging in some form of sexual activity, but we know very little about lesbian and gay teens' sexual behavior. Almost all survey studies of teenage sexuality presume that "sex" means heterosexual sex. Thus, there is little trend data available on teenage same-sex behavior, bisexuality or gay identity. Somewhere around 10 percent of teens in some sex surveys report being confused about their sexual identities. Researchers are unsure as to the cause of this uncertainty—whether it reflects typical adolescent struggles with identity or the decreased stigma attached to being gay, reflected in the mass media (Risman and Schwartz, 2002). Past research on lesbian and gay teenagers focused narrowly on self-identifying lesbian and gay teens who were routinely characterized as less emotionally healthy—as suicidal—than their nonidentifying same-sex-attracted and heterosexual peers. However, contrary to such popular negative stereotypes about young lesbians and gays, most same-sex-attracted teens are healthy, resilient, and mature, able to integrate their same-sex attractions into their emerging personalities as merely one aspect of who they are. In other words, lesbian and gay teens are not unlike other teens. As with adults, many teenagers today, despite having sex and relationships with same-sex partners, do not feel particularly "gay" (Savoie, 2005). Thus, categories of gay and straight, queer or not, are much more fluid among teens today than ever before. Many teenagers do not believe erotic attractions should or must remain stable while others—both gay and straight—hold fast to their sexual identities (Risman and Schwartz, 2002).

SEXUALITY ACROSS THE LIFE CYCLE

As we have indicated repeatedly throughout this chapter, sexual behavior for most people begins earlier and lasts longer over the life cycle today than at any other period in U.S. history. Adolescents at increasingly younger ages report being involved in some sort of sexual behavior. At the other end of the age spectrum, many people continue to enjoy sex well into old age. The following discussion is a brief examination of sexuality in several key periods of the life cycle.

Nonmarried Sexuality and Pregnancy

Although the terms *premarital sex* and *premarital intercourse* are commonly used in research studies of human sexuality, for a number of reasons they are outdated and inadequate for discussing contemporary sexuality. First, they imply that marriage is the norm, that human life consists of two periods: before marriage and marriage. They also imply that sexual intercourse does not normally occur until after marriage. As you have learned, neither of these assumptions is true any longer of the majority of the population. The fact is, an increasing number of adults (an estimated 10 percent) will never marry; many adults are separated, divorced, or widowed, and almost one-third of them will never remarry. Their sexual relationships, then, cannot be categorized with any reliability and validity, as "premarital." Furthermore, given that lesbians and gays are denied the legal right to marry in all but one state—Massachusetts—their sexual relationships certainly cannot be legitimately categorized as "premarital" either. Thus, whenever possible, we use the term *single* or *unmarried* whenever we refer to a nonmarried status.

The incidence of intercourse among singles increased considerably over the closing decades of the twentieth century. In addition, gender was no longer a distinguishing factor in unmarried sexual behavior. The behavior of white females dramatically illustrates both of these points. Over the last three decades, intercourse among single white females increased significantly, considerably narrowing the gap between them and their male peers. Among single African American women, a significant change also occurred, although it came primarily in terms of the earlier age at which coitus begins (D'Emilio and Freedman, 1988; Smith, 1999). At the end of the twentieth century, three-fourths of unmarried women had had sexual intercourse by the age of 19 and over four-fifths by the age of 29. The median age at first sexual intercourse for women was 16.9. Among men coming to maturity, the experience of sexual intercourse was nearly universal—95 percent. The median age at first sexual intercourse for males was 16.1 (Guttmacher Institute, 2005; Smith, 1999; Sonenstein et al., 1991).

This increased sexuality among the singles population is fairly consistent with the sexual attitudes and morals of the general population about sex outside a legal married relationship. For instance, in answer to a 2005 Gallup poll question about whether or not it is morally wrong for a woman and man to have sexual relations before marriage, 58 percent said it was morally acceptable and 39 percent said it was morally unacceptable. Over the years, the percent of Americans who view sex outside marriage as morally acceptable has grown but continues to vary by age. Anywhere from 60 to 67 percent of young adults and those 30 to 49 think sex before marriage is morally acceptable whereas older adults are much less liberal, with adults over 65 the least liberal on this question (Gallup Poll, 2006; Gallup Poll, 2001).

Added to the single's mix are adolescents whom we have already discussed in terms of the increase in their sexual behavior. As a result, some sex researchers are suggesting that American youth are in the midst of their own sexual revolution. Children as young as 8 years of age are asking teachers and others questions such as "What is oral sex?"

and "What is anal sex?" These researchers claim that television, entertainment, and even the news and children's cartoons have contributed to this sexual revolution; in addition, the pandemic openness about sex in the schoolyard, on the bus, at home when parents are not watching, and in the shopping malls has contributed to this revolutionary sexual behavior among today's youth. Teens today not only seem nonchalant about sex but also they seem to know more of the mechanics of sex than do many adults. For instance, a nurse at a Utah Teen Center reported that a 14-year-old couple came into the center for counseling because they had tried unsuccessfully to heighten their arousal during sexual intercourse. They wanted advice on the necessary steps that would lead them to a more fulfilling orgasm. In particular, the young man wanted to know how to get to his partner's G-spot. (For those who do not know, *G-spot* is a popular term for a particularly sensitive area within the vagina, about halfway between the pubic bone and the cervix at the rear of the urethra, named after gynecologist Ernst Gräfenberg [1881–1957], who first put forth a theory concerning this area.) Although this might sound unbelievable, the fact is that these young people, along with thousands of others, have clearly gone further sexually than many adults.

This sexual precociousness has led to a number of problems among youth, particularly in the nation's schools. Around the country, school officials have noted an increase in mock sexual behavior on buses carrying students to school. This behavior includes young people simulating sexual intercourse and simulating masturbation. Although girls reportedly initiate some of this conduct, in most instances the aggressors are reportedly boys. In response to this increasing display of sexuality among youths, some schools have instituted a sexual harassment policy to deal with the sharp increase in lewd language, groping, pinching, and bra-snapping incidents among sixth, seventh, and eighth graders. A by-product of this youthful sexual revolution is the presumption among many adolescent boys that sex is an entitlement—an attitude that fosters a breakdown of respect for oneself and others. A Rhode Island Rape Center study of 1700 sixth and ninth graders reported that 65 percent of boys and 57 percent of girls believed it was acceptable for a male to force a female to have sex if they have been dating for 6 months (Stodghill, 1999).

The statistics on adolescent sexual behavior should not lead us to assume that unmarried sexual activity (adolescent or adult) is synonymous with casual sex. According to most sex surveys and research, the majority of unmarried intercourse among adolescents as well as among adults occurs within an affectionate, serious, monogamous, and steady relationship.

Pregnancy and Single Motherhood A major practical issue associated with early coitus and declining and delayed marriage is an increase in childbirth among unmarried women. Although unmarried pregnancy is not a new phenomenon resulting from the so-called sexually liberated years of the 1960s and 1970s, births to unmarried individuals and couples have increased significantly over the decades. In 2004, childbearing by single women rose to a record high of 1.5 million births, a 4 percent increase from 2003. The proportion of all births to unmarried women increased to 35.7 percent, an almost eightfold increase since 1940. And those single mothers were most likely to be in their 20s. For instance, 55 percent of the births for mothers ages 20 to 24 were to single women. For those between 25 and 29 years of age, almost 28 percent of the births were to single women. The rate of birth among single women, however, decreases with age, with the proportion declining to 12 percent for single women 30 years and older. Although the proportion of births to single women typically decreases with age, in 2004, interestingly, there was a significant *increase* (9 percent from the previous year) in the number of births to single women 45 to 49 years of age. Considering that just 30 years ago, almost no one in that age group had babies at all, let alone without being married, this generation of women is turning that paradigm on its head (Ganahl, 2005). The percentage of births to single women also varies across race and nativity as well as level of education (see Figure 6.4). For instance, 24 percent of all births to Asian and Pacific Islanders were to single women, compared with 62 percent for African American women; 32 percent for Latinas; 62 percent for Native Americans, Eskimos, and Aleuts; and 25 percent for white non-Hispanic women. The proportion of births among foreign-born single women was considerably lower (26 percent) than among native-born women (33 percent). And the least educated single women had the highest rate of births (52 percent) compared to college-educated women (11 percent) (Dye, 2005).

Some observers have suggested that the increase in childbearing among single women is due to welfare benefits. Others have linked the rise in the number of births to single women to an increase in unmarried cohabitation, later-in-life marriage, and an increase in childbearing by older, unmarried women. Still others have concluded that economic factors, along with significant changes in societal attitudes about marriage, sex, and childbearing, are what explain increases in unmarried childbearing. Most agree, however, that more research is needed to determine whether efforts to strengthen families; to remove barriers to adoption, abortion, and marriage; to enforce child support orders; and to remove the marriage penalty in various tax and public assistance programs would substantially reduce out-of-wedlock childbearing ("New Report Explodes Myths," 1995).

Teenage Sexuality and Pregnancy According to the U.S. Census and other vital statistics data on reproduction and childbirth, the rate of pregnancy and birth for teenage girls has declined in the United States since the 1950s. The most dramatic decreases occurred during the 1990s, when in one year alone (1996–1997) the birth rate fell 4 percent, which represented a 17 percent decrease since 1990. In 2004, the teen birth rate reached a record low of 41 births per 1000 women aged 15 to 19, which was less than one-half the peak rate recorded in 1957, a 33 percent decrease since 1991, and was the lowest level ever reported for the nation. From 2003 to 2004, the rates fell 2 to 3 percent for non-Hispanic white and non-Hispanic black teenagers, and were

FIGURE 6.4

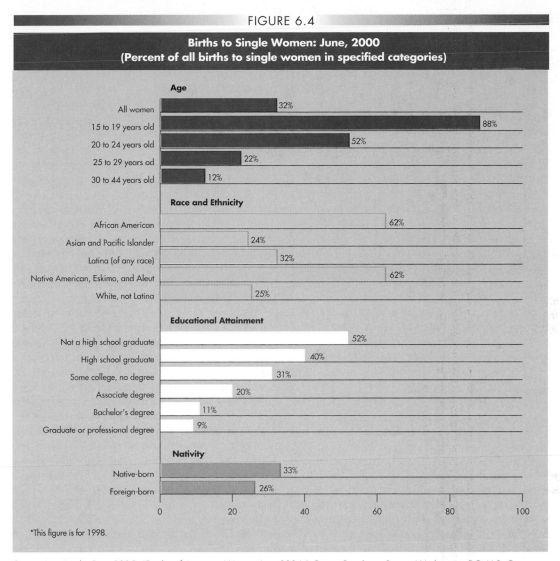

Births to Single Women: June, 2000
(Percent of all births to single women in specified categories)

Age

All women	32%
15 to 19 years old	88%
20 to 24 years old	52%
25 to 29 years od	22%
30 to 44 years old	12%

Race and Ethnicity

African American	62%
Asian and Pacific Islander	24%
Latina (of any race)	32%
Native American, Eskimo, and Aleut	62%
White, not Latina	25%

Educational Attainment

Not a high school graduate	52%
High school graduate	40%
Some college, no degree	31%
Associate degree	20%
Bachelor's degree	11%
Graduate or professional degree	9%

Nativity

Native-born	33%
Foreign-born	26%

*This figure is for 1998.

Source: Jane Lawler Dye, 2005, "Fertility of American Women: June 2004," *Current Population Reports* Washington, DC: U.S. Census Bureau: P20-555.

unchanged for Native Americans, Latinas/os, and Asian or Pacific Islanders. The most dramatic decrease in childbearing over the last decade occurred among African American teens. For instance, the 2004 birth rate for African American teens represented a decline nationwide from 115.5 in the early 1990s to 62.7—a 45 percent decrease. Overall, the birth rates are highest for Latina/o teens (82.6) and lowest for Asian and Pacific Islander teens (17.4), with non-Latina white (26.8 percent) and Native American teenagers (52.5) falling between these two groups. The birth rate for the youngest teens, 10 to 14 years old, also dropped from 1.4 births per 1000 during the early 1990s to 0.7 in 2004, the lowest level in more than 30 years. In general, however, the rate of births to teenagers increased in the majority of states, although the rate varied considerably from state to state. New Hampshire and Vermont, for instance, had the lowest rates at 18.2 and 18.9, respectively. And at the other end of the continuum, Texas (62.9), New Mexico (62.7), and Mississippi (62.5) had the highest teen birth rates. The rate for the District of Columbia declined from 83.5 at the end of the 1990s to 60.3 (Stolberg, 1999; U.S. Census Bureau, 2000; Ventura et al., 2001; Hamilton et al., 2005).

Despite recently declining teen pregnancy rates, the rate overall remains high, with more than four in five births to teenagers who are unmarried; 34 percent of teenage girls get pregnant at least once before they reach age 20, resulting in close to 1 million teen pregnancies each year. Consequently, the United States has the highest rate of teen pregnancy in the Western world, despite the fact that U.S. teens are no more sexually active than teens in other countries. Nevertheless, the U.S. rates are nearly double Great Britain's, two and a half times or more as high as Australia's and Canada's, more than three times as high as Germany's, nearly five times as high as France's, seven times as high as Japan's, and seven and a half times as high as the Netherlands' (United Nations, 2005; Teenpregnancy.org, 2004). The teenage birth rate is lowest in Japan, at 4 births per 1000 women, and is below 10 per 1000 in a number of countries (Ventura et al., 2001).

Historically, teenage mothers have been less likely to obtain their high school diplomas than nonparent teenagers. However, having a baby while in high school does not necessarily mean that teenage parents will not finish school. Although challenging, a growing number of teen parents today are juggling parenting and educational responsibilities. Researchers have found that most young women, like the one pictured here; who had a baby and remained enrolled in high school, are as likely to eventually graduate from high school as teens who did not have a baby and did not interrupt their schooling.

Perhaps we in the United States could take a lesson from some of these countries, particularly the Dutch. The Dutch are so unflustered by sex, sexuality, and birth control that some groups have proposed selling contraceptive pills over the counter. The high level of openness about all aspects of sexuality has given the Netherlands one of the world's lowest teenage pregnancy rate—9 per 1000 females (Alford and Feijoo, 2001). And it is not that Dutch teenagers are less sexually active than other teenagers. Rather, the low rate of teenage pregnancy is a function of a better-informed population concerning the consequences of sexual intercourse. The Dutch use what they label a *Double Dutch* method of birth control: the Pill to prevent pregnancy combined with condoms to prevent the spread of AIDS. In addition, there is open discussion of sexuality and childbirth in the family, schools, and the media. Teenage pregnancy cannot be traced to the liberal abortion laws in the Netherlands because they also have the lowest abortion rates in the world. Although the age of sexual consent is 16, Dutch family doctors sometimes prescribe contraceptive pills for girls aged 13 to 15 without informing their parents ("Dutch Have Lowest Teen Pregnancy," 1994:8).

Although most American teenagers do not have sex initially to reproduce, one in ten whites and two in ten blacks say that during their first sexual intercourse they neither thought about nor cared if they got pregnant. However, the majority of teenagers who are sexually active today report using some form of birth control, most often the Pill (53

percent) followed by condoms (45 percent). And as they become more sexually active, the more consistently they use birth control methods. So what explains the higher teenage pregnancy rate in the United States? Some experts argue that insufficient knowledge as well as our general discomfort with sex and sexuality may help explain why the United States has a higher rate of teenage pregnancy and childbirth than any other industrialized country. Unlike the Dutch, discussions of sexuality and childbirth and the dispensation of condoms and other forms of birth control in American schools are at the heart of a major divide in the United States today. When conservative Republicans in Congress tacked a last-minute amendment onto the 1996 Welfare Reform bill, earmarking $250 million over 5 years to promote sexual abstinence outside of marriage as the *only* acceptable standard of behavior for young people, they ushered the abstinence movement from its traditional home in the religious right into the American mainstream. This move also sparked a public debate about whether or not schools should promote comprehensive sexuality education or take a strict "abstinence-only-until-marriage" approach that is still evident today (see Debating Social Issues box).

On one side of the controversy are those who believe that American youth deserve to have an accurate and comprehensive education about sexuality, and given that over 60 percent of teens are already sexually active, they should have access to prevention and intervention programs that promote responsible teen sexual behavior. As already indicated, those on the other side of the debate believe that abstinence-only-until-marriage is the *only* strategy appropriate to teach young people about sexuality; any other sexuality education is an affront to the Christian value of abstinence until marriage. Although there are no scientific studies demonstrating that voluntary abstinence pledges succeed in bring more virgins to the marriage altar, and although there is widespread public and parental support for comprehensive sexuality education in schools, the government currently spends nearly $138 million per year for abstinence-only-until-marriage programs, in contrast to no federal money for comprehensive sexuality education programs (SIECUS Fact Sheet, 2004; ACLU, 2005). Not surprising, like most of the cultural wars in the United States, this debate has a political partisan divide. For instance, one-half of those who identify as Republican believe that abstinence-only programs are effective against HIV/AIDS and 46 percent believe that such programs counter unwanted pregnancies. Among Democrats, the numbers are considerably smaller, 39 and 28 percent respectively (Harper, 2006).

No matter which side of the debate one is on, teenage pregnancy is a particularly unsettling issue given that the majority of teen mothers live in or will live in poverty. Most teenaged parents, regardless of race, have low academic skills and high unemployment rates. They tend to come from poor families, most do not marry (at least not immediately), and they are likely to drop out of school, although black teenaged mothers are more likely than their white or Latina counterparts to continue attending school during and after pregnancy. According to sociologist Margaret Andersen (2005), regardless of their race and social class status, teenaged mothers value marriage as an ideal, but they do not see it as a viable option given expectant parents' general lack of economic resources.

In the final analysis, we should be very careful not to perpetuate myths about unmarried pregnancy or to lump single teenage and adult pregnancy together. As we have discussed, the majority of unmarried births are not to teenagers, nor are they to teenagers of color. The fact is that the majority of births to unmarried women occur among women who are 20 years of age or older. Equally important, we cannot assume that unmarried pregnancies are always unwanted, nor can we assume that the custodial parent or parents are incapable of providing for the newborn simply because of age or marital status. In other words, we cannot assume that single parenting in and of itself is "problematic" and damaging. As a reviewer of an earlier edition of this textbook so aptly pointed out, we should not "confuse unmarried pregnancy with teenage pregnancy. "People married at a younger age in the past but that didn't mean that they were prepared for childbirth. Unmarried pregnancies may not be a problem for those prepared for parenting" (anonymous reviewer, 1995).

Marital Sexuality: Does Good Sex Make Good Marriages?

Because marital sex is considered the norm, scholars have not paid much attention to this subject. However, based on some of the most recent data in this regard, the changes in sexuality we have discussed in this chapter have affected married as well as unmarried people. Most marriages today have moved toward greater variety in sexual behavior, more frequent intercourse, and higher levels of sexual satisfaction. For example, a comparison of married couples in the 1970s with those studied by Kinsey in the 1940s revealed that twice as many 1970s couples departed from the missionary position. Oral sex had been routinely incorporated into the sexual behaviors of married couples, except those of African Americans. Major surveys of women's sexuality during the 1970s and 1980s pointed out major shifts among heterosexual couples from penile–vaginal intercourse and simultaneous orgasm to a variety of sexual practices directed toward the needs and desires of women. These changes have weakened what some researchers have described as the male monopoly over the nature of sex (see, for example, Ehrenreich, Hess, and Jacobs, 1986).

Married couples are not only engaging in a variety of sexual behavior more frequently, they are also enjoying it more. How often married couples have intercourse varies depending on age, social class, how long they have been married, if there are children, as well as a number of other factors. For example, factors such as job demands, household chores and demands, monetary issues and concerns, number of adults living in the household—all may conspire to limit a couple's sexual life of spontaneity and frequency. However, for the majority of married couples, the rate ranges from two to three times a week (around 40 percent) to several times a month (close to 50 percent). Frequency of marital sexual intercourse typically decreases over time, with a sharp reduction after age 50 (Laumann et al., 1994; Call et al., 1995; Waite and Joyner, 2001). This is not meant to imply that the frequency of sexual intercourse leads to sexual satisfaction

and/or marital happiness. In fact, no such correlation has been found. Rather, it is not the quantity but the quality of their sexual lives that is important to married couples.

Sexual satisfaction is important to both wives and husbands, the majority of whom report both emotional and physical satisfaction in their sexual relationships and describe their sex lives as "very exciting" (Langer, Arnedt, and Sussman, 2004). Most research indicates that how a couple gets along sexually is an indication of how their marriage is going in general. Although most married people consider sexual activity important to their marriage, both wives and husbands report that the quality of the marriage relationship is more important than sex per se. Accordingly, most surveys show that approximately three of four people who are married are happy with their marital status compared with two of four single people. In most of these surveys, men generally report being more content with their marital status than do women and singles. Likewise, husbands also report greater sexual satisfaction than do wives. When couples define their sexual activities as satisfying, they generally define their overall relationship as satisfying as well.

Extramarital Sexuality

Along with other changes in patterns of contemporary sexuality has come a change in the value attached to sexual exclusiveness in marriage. Research indicates that since the 1950s the incidence of extramarital relationships has increased substantially. Researchers estimate that by the 1980s as many as 65 to 70 percent of males and 45 to 65 percent of females had been involved in an extramarital relationship (Stayton, 1984). However, in recent surveys, the majority of females and males report fidelity in their intimate relationships. Obviously, even with the increasing tolerance of different lifestyles, an accurate assessment of the number of married people involved in extramarital relationships is difficult to determine because many of these relationships are conducted in secret. Thus, at any given time we can assume that the reported rates of extramarital relationships are significantly lower than the actual rate.

Why do people seek intimacy outside their marital relationship? There are probably as many reasons as there are individuals who engage in such relationships. In general, the lower the marital satisfaction and the lower the frequency and quality of marital intercourse, the greater the likelihood of extramarital sexual relationships. Most people indicate that they became involved in an extramarital relationship because they felt that something was missing in their marriage or that their marital sexual life was boring. Early and later studies of marital infidelity, however, noted some important attitudinal differences between husbands and wives who engage in extramarital relationships. Most wives indicated that they were dissatisfied with some aspect of their marriage, most often the expressive area. Some wives reported that loneliness is the primary reason for engaging in an extramarital relationship. They also reported an improvement in their marital relationship, which they believed to be a direct result of their participation in an extramarital relationship. Husbands, on the other hand, more often

DEBATING SOCIAL ISSUES

ABSTINENCE-ONLY-UNTIL-MARRIAGE: The Only Approach to Safer Sex?

In 1997, the Franklin County, North Carolina, school board ordered chapters on sexual behavior, contraception, and HIV/AIDS and other STDs cut out of its health textbook for ninth graders. According to the school board, the deleted material did not comply with a new state law requiring public schools to teach abstinence until marriage in their comprehensive health education program for students in kindergarten through ninth grade. The school board also instructed teachers to discuss only failure rates in response to students' questions about contraceptives. If students were to ask teachers about AIDS, teachers were instructed to say only that the disease is caused by a virus transmitted primarily by contaminated needles and illegal homosexual acts. The school board's actions came after months of debate in the county about how to handle sex education in accordance with the state's new law, which allows school districts to offer more comprehensive sexuality education only after a public hearing and a public review of instructional materials (Donovan, 1998).

The board's new policy is a compelling example of the controversy raging in many communities today over not only what public schools should teach in sex education classes but also if public schools should be involved with dispensing condoms as part of their sexuality education programs.

The debate over school-based sexuality education is not new. Rather, it has been a major source of controversy in public schools at lease since the 1960s. However, since the early 1990s when the Southern Baptist Church sponsored a campaign aimed at teenagers to abstain from sexual intercourse, the controversy and debate over school-based sexuality edu-

cation has heated up once again. This debate centers on one crucial question: whether providing young people with full and accurate information makes them more or less likely to engage in sexual activity (Donovan, 1998). An added aspect of the debate centers on school-based condom availability programs. Condom availability programs operate today in over 400 public schools, generally in conjunction with comprehensive sexuality education. The programs have varied formats. Students in some schools may obtain condoms from a health counselor or from a basket; students in other schools may buy condoms from vending machines. Some schools impose no barriers to students' access to condoms; others limit access by requiring parental consent

or by offering an "opt-out" that allows parents to veto their children's participation (ACLU, 1998). As with every other aspect of this debate, in the controversy over condom availability programs, scientific, moral, religious, and political concerns overlap.

Religious Right political groups and others have fanned the flames of this debate first by urging opposition to comprehensive sexuality education and later changing their strategy by arguing that sexuality education in schools is very important as long as it tells young people, in no uncertain terms, to abstain from all sexual activity until marriage (Mehta, 2005). Proponents of abstinence-only sexuality education believe that youngsters need time-tested principles to live by; that

---

participated in extramarital relationships because of the sexual excitement of such a liaison or the sheer availability of another woman (Covel, 2003; Atwater, 1982).

Discussions of extramarital relationships are complicated by the diverse number of relationships included in this category. Extramarital relationships can range from a one-night affair to a lifelong relationship. A husband can be involved

with either a single or a married woman; likewise, a wife can be involved with either a single or a married man. A wife or husband can also have an extramarital affair with a person of the same sex. Thus, the frequency and nature of an extramarital relationship will vary not only with age, race, class, and other structural factors but also in terms of sexual orientation. Extramarital relationships are not just about physical sex. Nor

teachers should teach and reinforce pre-marital abstinence—unmarried teens should not be having sex. They argue that comprehensive sexuality education generally, and giving out condoms and birth control pills specifically, weaken the abstinence standard and encourage sexual promiscuity. Condoms, they say, are not the solution (Anderson, 1999). They also cite research saying that abstinence reduces the risks of unplanned pregnancy, STDs, and single parenthood.

The abstinence-only movement has been well-funded and supported in recent years by President George W. Bush. Each year under his presidency, abstinence-only programs have received increasing funding. By law, the exclusive purpose of these programs must be teaching the social, psychological, and health gains to be realized by abstaining from sexual activity. Programs that emphasize abstinence but also teach about contraception and prevention of sexually transmitted diseases (often referred to as comprehensive sexuality education) are not eligible for this money. Among the conditions for funding, abstinence-only programs must teach young people that a mutually faithful monogamous relationship within the context of marriage is the expected standard of human sexual activity and that sexual activity outside marriage is likely to have harmful psychological and physical effects (Scott and Schwartz, 2006). Interestingly, abstinence-only is now a multimillion dollar business complete with trinkets of every description from boxer shorts that say "Keep It" to mints that say "Sex is Mint for Marriage" to novelty ATM (Abstinence Till Marriage) cards that expire on the holder's wedding day (Kreinin, 2004).

On the other side of the debate, proponents of comprehensive sexuality education argue that abstinence-only education jeopardizes the health and lives of adolescents and teens by denying them information that can prevent unintended pregnancy and STDs, including HIV.

Whether or not young people abstain from sexual intercourse, they say, every young person needs to know how to avoid the potential negative consequences of sexual intercourse—they need to have accurate information about contraception and condoms. They argue that the implicit assumption in the abstinence-only approach that if young people do not learn about contraception or, if it is not made available to them, they will not have sexual intercourse is a dangerously faulty premise that can have highly negative consequences (Alford, 2001). They say that America's youths need sex education where they are—in schools—and that it should include information on heterosexual and homosexual relationships.

Those on this side of the debate further point out that although many factors are responsible for declines in teen pregnancy rates, many public health experts have put comprehensive sexuality education and HIV/AIDS education high on their lists of probable causes. The Centers for Disease Control and Prevention, for example, report that the changes in teenage sexual behavior correspond to a simultaneous increase in the percentage of students who have received HIV/AIDS education in their high schools. Moreover, recent studies show that comprehensive sexuality education programs are more effective than "abstinenceonly" programs at reducing risk-taking behavior by teens (ACLU, 1998). And a wide variety of respected health and health-related organizations such as the American College of Obstetricians and Gynecologists, the American School Health Association, and the National Medical Association have recommended that schools make condoms available to adolescents as part of a multifaceted approach to sexuality education. Comprehensive sexuality education proponents not only cite scientific research in support of such programs, but they also point out the growing body of research studies that demonstrates the importance

of these programs for teenagers' health. Several of these studies, for instance, have now shown that comprehensive sex education increases the rate of condom use during intercourse—and the likelihood that teens will be protected from infection and pregnancy—without increasing rates of sexual activity.

Many among those who support abstinence-only-until-marriage programs have falsely accused comprehensive sexuality programs and its proponents of not teaching abstinence, they have used flawed research studies to support their position, and they have framed the debate as one between the god-fearing and the godless; between those who want to give children values and those who want to give them condoms; between those who value families and those who value freedom of sexual expression; between the moral and the immoral (Kreinin, 2004). And despite the favorable research results and strong public support for condom availability programs in the schools, some conservative parents and organizations have challenged these programs in court. To date, such challenges have been rejected by the courts and the legality of condom availability programs has been affirmed (ACLU, 1998).

What do you think? Given the high rate of sexually active teenagers, do you think that abstinence-only sexuality education is a responsible way to address the increasing sexual precociousness among teens today? Do you agree with the 90 percent of Americans who are in favor of comprehensive sexuality education? If yes, why? If no, why not? Should such programs include the dispensation of condoms in school-based clinics? Why? Why not? If you are a parent, are you forthcoming and upfront with your children about their sexuality? If you are not a parent but plan to be one someday, how would you approach sexuality with your children?

are they always of short duration or meaningless. However, they are always about the violation of commitment, trust, and intimacy unless, of course, the couple has an *open* marriage in which they agree to have openly acknowledged and independent sexual relationships with persons other than each other.

What constitutes infidelity varies across gender, but both women and men agree that infidelity can include a range of

behaviors, sexual intercourse being only one. For instance, over two-thirds of women and around two-fifths of men believe that telephone sex and cybersex constitute infidelity in a committed relationship. And almost one-fourth of women and a little less than one-fifth of men agree that lustfully thinking about another person also constitutes infidelity (Covel, 2003). What is ironic about the incidence of marital infidelity is that, as a nation, we say that such behavior is improper and unacceptable. Yet, in 2001, for example, when U.S. Representative Gary Condit admitted to having an extramarital relationship with missing intern Chandra Levy, most Americans were not shocked. It was not the first time that an older, married, male political figure had admitted to having an extramarital affair with a younger female intern. Later the same year, Jesse Jackson, Sr., noted political and social activist, admitted to a long-term extramarital relationship that resulted in the birth of a daughter. In fact, it has become so routine in the lives of Americans to hear or read tabloid or other news accounts of the extramarital escapades of movie stars and other celebrities that many people no longer take notice.

Nevertheless, an overwhelming majority of Americans continue to say that extramarital affairs (no matter who the parties are) are morally wrong. That same year (2001), for instance, a Gallup poll reported that 89 percent of Americans said that "married men and women having an affair" is morally unacceptable. Continuing this trend, in 2005, 93 percent of Americans considered married women and men having an affair to be morally wrong. Gallup polls also show that more than one-half of Americans say that they know someone who has had an extramarital relationship, and two-thirds of the population believe that half or more of all married men have had an affair (Gillespie, 2001). Yet in most studies of American sexuality, the overwhelming majority of married women and men said that they have always been faithful, and almost all of the married people had at least been faithful to their partner over the prior 12 months. Clearly, then, despite the stigma of marital infidelity, there is an inherent conflict between Americans' moral ideals about marriage and sexual fidelity, what they say about their sexual behavior, and what they actually do.

> *Over two decades ago, researcher Lynn Atwater (1982) suggested that a primary reason for extramarital relationships is society's continued unrealistic views on love and the belief in the ability of one person to satisfy all the sexual needs of another person. Can one person totally satisfy another? Why do you think married people today enter into extramarital relationships? Are such relationships ever justified? Why or why not?*

Postmarital Sexuality

As divorce and separation rates have increased and a growing number of widowed people—particularly women—are living into old age without a partner, a larger number of adults than in the past are confronted with the task of adjusting to a postmarital life. Popular cultural images have these individuals living either a life of great excitement, entertainment, and sexual activity, or conversely, feeling depressed, devastated, and lonely, with no sex life. As we shall see, neither of these images is completely accurate.

Divorced People Most divorced people become sexually active within a year following their divorce, although older

people are somewhat slower in this regard than people under the age of 40 (Shriver et al., 2002). Among a sample of divorced, separated, or widowed respondents, researchers found that 31 percent of those not living with someone had not had a sexual partner during the previous 12 months, compared with only 1 percent of those who lived with someone. Additionally, 80 percent of those living with someone had one partner in the previous year, whereas only half that percentage (41 percent) of those not living with someone had had a sexual partner during that time (Laumann et al., 1994). Although divorced people appear to have a fairly active sex life and find postmarital sex more pleasurable and fulfilling than married sex, when people across marital statuses are asked whether intercourse is occurring frequently enough for their desire, divorced people are the most dissatisfied with the frequency (74 percent), compared to cohabitants and married couples (38 and 49 percent dissatisfied, respectively). In addition, next to single people (65 percent) over half (60 percent) of widowed people also report that they are dissatisfied with the frequency of sexual intercourse in their lives (Dunn et al., 2000). Such findings, however, should not cloud the fact that divorce often involves adjustments of many sorts, such as transition and recuperation, ending some relationships and developing new ones, and adjusting to nonmarital sex and a nonmarital lifestyle generally. Loneliness and anxiety sometimes accompany this transition, as do financial strains and concerns. Some people find the world of postmarital sex to be anxiety producing, particularly in terms of relearning the rules of dating and mate selection. Nonetheless, most divorced people manage to reintegrate their sexuality with their emotional needs. In fact, most divorced people will have sexual intercourse within one year of being separated from their spouses. Many of them enter into intimate relationships that endure and deepen over time and very often lead to remarriage.

Widows and Widowers Widowed women and men sometimes choose to abstain from sex after their spouse's death, but almost one-half of widows and widowers eventually engage in postmarital coitus. The death of a partner is a great emotional and social loss. Far less so than in the past, today's widows and widowers are not willing to resign themselves to a life without partner companionship and sexual activity. As we discussed in Chapter 5, for older heterosexual women who are also widowed, the problem becomes finding a suitable single man. Given the toll that HIV/AIDS has taken in the gay male community, many gays go through a similar mourning period and then a reentering or reintegration into a single's lifestyle. This might include dating, companionship, sexual activity, and even cohabitation. Because there is little or no specific research on the sexuality of separated and widowed people, much of the information about them is speculative. The prevailing view at this time is that their sexual behavior does not differ much from that of the divorced population.

Sexuality and Aging

The common stereotype of older women and men is that they are *asexual*—that is, as they age, they lose both interest in and the ability to engage in meaningful sexual activities.

In addition, those elderly who remain sexually active are frequently dismissed as "dirty old women" or "dirty old men." When you think about older people, how do you perceive them sexually? Can you imagine your grandparents or great-grandparents engaging in coitus or oral–genital sexual behavior? Given our views concerning aging and the elderly, many people in the United States believe women and men must give up sex as they age. Research on sexuality and aging, however, indicates that, in fact, sexuality is one of the last functions to be affected by age. In reality, people who are healthy and happy with their lives can continue to be sexually active well into their advanced years (Shriver et al., 2002; Hodson and Skeen, 1994).

It is true that as people become older they experience biological and psychological changes that can affect their sexual functioning. For instance, some older adults take longer to become aroused, are less sensitive to stimulation, and experience less intense orgasms than do younger people; however, the capacity to enjoy sex is not altered with age. Elderly people can be, and many often are, highly sexual beings with sexual thoughts and desires that continue into advanced age. A significant proportion of elderly people, for example, including those in nursing homes, remain sexually active. All too often, unfortunately, society does not deal well with this sexuality. Families, senior care facilities, and other caretakers often ignore or disregard the sexual needs and desires of older people. Sadly, some older adults accept cultural prescriptions about their sexuality and either discontinue their sexual activities or experience guilt, doubt, and shame about their desire for and engagement in sexual activity. Survey research indicates that women and men 55 to 65 years of age report that they have sex an average of five times a month. Over 60 percent of women and men in this age category say sexual activity is important, compared with 63 percent of those aged 18 to 24 (Shriver et al., 2002; Richardson and Lazar, 1995).

Older people may be sensual as well as sexual. As with younger people, older women and men rank hugging and kissing as top sexual pleasures. Older people also report having sexual fantasies, including engaging in such fantasizing while having sex with a partner and while masturbating. Although older Americans are just as satisfied with their life in general as are younger Americans, a higher percentage of older people report sexual problems, the most common of which are low sex drive, impotence, and difficulty achieving orgasm. Other sexual complaints, such as self-consciousness during sex and problems with a partner, decrease with age (Shriver et al., 2002; Clements, 1994).

Aging can necessitate some adjustments in a couple's sexual activity. Illness, for instance, might bring about a temporary loss of sexual interest or ability; however, it usually does not mean the end of people's sex lives. Rather, it might require different ways of giving and receiving sexual pleasure (Shriver et al., 2002). Most importantly, as people age, open and effective communication grows in importance. To maintain a comfortable and successful sexual relationship, the couple must communicate their sexual desires—what makes them feel good and what does not. In any event, the years of middle age and beyond can be a time for exploring sex at a deeper, more confident, and more satisfying level. The need for intimacy is never outgrown, and many older

A common cultural stereotype of the elderly is that they lose interest in sex along with the ability to be sexual. However, the reality is that sexuality is one of the last functions to be affected by age. Many people have healthy and active sex lives well into their advanced years.

adults report that their sex lives are warmer and more rewarding than ever before.

Women, Aging, and Sexuality As women age, their reproductive ability declines gradually. Somewhere around age 50, the menstrual cycle stops completely, marking the **menopause**. The onset of menopause and the symptoms that accompany it vary from woman to woman. Although menopause does not automatically signal the end of sexual interest and desire, some menopausal women experience anxiety because they fear that they will no longer be able to enjoy sexual activity. Experts disagree on the impact of menopause on female sexuality. Some studies suggest a decline in sexual interest and possibly the loss of female orgasmic response in the immediate postmenopausal years (Masters and Johnson, 1985). Other research (Starr and Weiner, 1981), however, suggests that despite these physiological changes, menopausal women are still capable of experiencing orgasm, their sexual interest may increase, and for many of these women, the quality of their sexual experience seems higher than when they were younger.

As we learned in Chapter 5, many later-life women feel less inhibited and more assertive sexually; many are more frank about expressing and meeting their sexual desires. According to an American Health Survey of baby boom women (ages 35 to 55), these daughters of the female sexual revolutionaries of the 1950s and 1960s are reaching midlife and changing the way that America thinks about what it means to be a middle-aged woman. These women typically reported that sex is better now than at age 25, primarily because they have become more comfortable with their bodies, their sexuality, and their partner. These women reported making healthy communication with a partner a priority and over one-half of them said that they discuss sexual issues with their partner. The result was that approximately one-third reported that they have sexual relations three to six times a week. This is in stark contrast to the three to six times a month typically reported in previous surveys of women in this age group.

That these women lead sexually healthy, vital, active, and imaginative lives is indicated in their reports of sexually titillating behavior—behavior that women a generation ago would probably not have acknowledged, let alone have tried. For example, more than four in ten baby boom women reported that they masturbate, 44 percent read sex self-help books, 38 percent surf into sex information Web sites or watch sex videos, 40 percent use vaginal lubricants or do Kegel exercises to strengthen vaginal muscles, and 21 percent reported that they have tried a vibrator. Not all women in this age group are this uninhibited. Among those who struggled with inhibitions in the American Health Survey, over one-half felt too fat for sex at some time in the year prior to the survey or they felt physically undesirable for some other reason (Hale, 1999).

Because of the sexual double standard, regardless of age, women are more likely than men to feel physically undesirable. Likewise, with society's double standard with regard to aging, we often have difficulty thinking of older people as sexually active and uninhibited, especially older women. For instance, men retain their sexual eligibility as they age, whereas older women are generally considered less desirable than their younger counterparts. This perception, we should note, extends beyond sexuality to many other ways in which women and men are valued or devalued.

Men, Aging, and Sexuality   Unlike women, men do not have a typical pattern of reproductive aging because there is no definite end to male fertility. Although the production of sperm abates after the age of 40, it continues into the 80s and 90s. Likewise, although the production of testosterone decreases after age 55, there is usually no major decrease in levels of sex hormones in men as there is in women. A very small percentage of men (approximately 5 percent) over the age of 60 experience what some sex researchers have labeled a *male climacteric*, which is similar in some ways to the female menopause. However, unlike women, some men father children when well into their 70s. For those who experience it, the male climacteric is generally characterized by some of the following: weakness, tiredness, decreased sexual desire, reduced or loss of potency, and irritability (Masters, Johnson, and Kolodny, 1992).

In general, males typically reach their peak of sexual function in their late teens or early twenties. Thereafter, their sexual function begins a gradual, progressive decline. Although sex continues to be important, as men age the urgency of the sex drive decreases and a reduced frequency of sexual activity is typical. Normal physical changes include a decline in the sensitivity of the penis, and some men experience an enlargement of the prostate gland. In older men, erections are also slower in developing, less precoital mucus is produced, the amount of semen is reduced, the intensity of the ejaculation is lessened, orgasmic reflex is shorter, and sensitivity to distractions increases (Masters, Johnson, and Kolodny, 1992). On the other hand, they tend to experience an increased capacity to delay ejaculation, which some men (and women) find satisfying. In general, men tend to stay sexually active longer than women, although this may be explained in part by the fact that women outlive men and that the older a woman is the less access she has to a sexual partner.

Women and men who were sexually active in their younger years typically remain sexually active into their 80s and 90s, although the frequency of intercourse is limited by their physical health and social circumstances, such as having an available partner. Although older people generally can and do remain sexually active, the existing evidence suggests that most forms of sexual behavior decline significantly for women and men after age 75. In any event, as we learned in Chapter 5, a rising number of older adults are romantically and sexually involved in relationships, and some choose to carry out their relationships in cohabitation with their partner. (Issues related to the elderly are examined in more detail in Chapter 14.) These relationships reportedly are generally satisfying and rewarding and provide a positive example that sexuality can be pleasurable into old age.

SEXUAL DYSFUNCTIONS

Like other aspects of human experience, sex is not always smooth and problem-free. Most available research indicates that sexual discord or maladjustment of some sort is a widespread phenomenon in the United States. Masters, Johnson, and Kolodny (1992) contend that some kind of sexual problem can be found in at least one-half of all marriages in this country. The fact is that almost everyone who is sexually active, even couples who are very satisfied with their relationship, experiences occasional sexual problems. These problems can range anywhere from lack of interest in sexual activities to an actual **sexual dysfunction**, the inability to engage in or enjoy sexual activities. Approximately one-third of the general population (not including the geriatric subgroup) experience some type of sexual dysfunction (Hedges, 1994). This fact notwithstanding, it is important to note that what is considered a sexual dysfunction is relative to time, place, and the individuals involved. That is, "a sexual dysfunction may be said to exist only if the person or couple is distressed by a particular aspect of their sexual response, rather than on the basis of some "objective criteria" (Shriver et al., 2002:217). Although a few cases of sexual dysfunction can be traced to physical problems, the majority of cases are the result of social-psychological factors that interfere with or impair people's ability to respond as ordinarily expected to sexual stimuli. These factors range from anxiety about sexual performance to general life stress. Sexual dysfunctions can be distinguished along gender lines. The most common sexual dysfunctions for women are related to penetration and orgasm: inhibited sexual desire, inhibited sexual excitement, inhibited female orgasm or anorgasmia, vaginismus, rapid orgasm, and dyspareunia. The most common sexual dysfunctions for men are related to erection and ejaculation: erectile dysfunction, premature ejaculation, inhibited male orgasm, priapism, dyspareunia, and inhibited sexual desire.

In American society a great deal of emphasis is placed on performance as a measure of people's personal worth. Sexual performance, like other performance, becomes a measure of our personal adequacy and value to others. Thus, when

STRENGTHENING MARRIAGES AND FAMILIES
Talks with Family Therapist Joan Zientek

TALKING FRANKLY ABOUT OUR SEXUAL NEEDS

What Kinds of Sexual Issues Do People Bring to Therapy? A couple's sexual relationship holds a very special place in the context of the total relationship. When sexual issues arise, then, tensions can permeate the entire relationship. These problems can result from sexual dysfunctions, such as impotence and premature ejaculation for the male, or vaginismus or orgasmic difficulties for the female. Issues such as these are usually addressed by a sex therapist or a medical doctor. More than likely, couples who come to marital therapy have sexual issues that stem from emotional problems in the marriage, such as boredom, differing sexual needs and preferences, sexual addiction, childhood sexual abuse, or affairs (either physical, emotional, or Internet sex). Because couples can experience a variety of sexual issues and marital problems, and because these two issues are often interwoven, therapists need to carefully evaluate the situation to determine how these problems best be treated.

It is only natural that the novelty and passion that was once part of marriage wears off over time. Even with all the self-help books starting with the work of Masters and Johnson in the 1970s together with the advice of Dr. Ruth and Sue Johanson, TV host of Sex Talk, couples still struggle with issues of sexual intimacy. At the heart of the struggle lies the misguided notion that sexual intimacy has more to do with mastering sexual skills and achieving orgasm than it does with deeply knowing and being known by one's partner. The latter requires that each partner in the marriage has a solid personal identity and is able to reveal him- or herself while risking the possibility that the other may not respond with empathy, validation, or delight.

What Are Some Strategies That Therapists Use to Help People with These Issues? The therapist generally begins by working in the here and now. This sometimes can be accomplished simply through education, problem-solving, and/or compromise. If the presenting problem is one of a difference in sexual desire, the therapist can normalize the couple's experience, conveying that these differences are normal and natural and may be due to each person's biochemical makeup. These differences are initially disguised because, according to some scientists, the euphoria of new love produces a hefty dose of PEA (phenylethylamine, a neurotransmitter), which elevates sexual desire. However, research also shows that the rapture of this infatuation burns out after 18 to 36 months, and couples then experience the natural differences in their need for sex. Understanding and accepting this natural phenomenon takes the sting out of worrying about the loss of desirability and the shame of refusal and places the couple in a better position to problem-solve and compromise in meeting their divergent sexual needs. Issues of sexual boredom or the use of sex as blackmail can often be resolved with these same techniques, along with enhancing the couple's communication skills.

Couples who come to therapy because of an affair, regardless of which person was unfaithful, need to explore the behavior of both parties that contributed to the marital context that made the affair possible, as well as working toward restoring trust in the relationship. With the guidance of the therapist, both parties either discover that they cannot recoup the marriage and need to work toward an amicable divorce or work through the marital crisis to achieve an even healthier and satisfying relationship.

If these interventions do not work, the therapist then turns to exploring the interpsychic blocks originating from past experiences, perhaps stemming back to childhood and early insecurities. Looking back to early experiences and working through the feelings and messages that accompany them, along with adapting new behaviors, is part of the long-term psychotherapy needed for issues of a deeper nature such as childhood sexual abuse and sexual addiction.

What Influences How Successful People Are in Solving These Issues? Different couples bring different strengths and resources for resolving their issues. One of the main issues is the strength of the love they have for one another. Some couples marry in a hurry and for the wrong reasons, only to wake up years later to discover they have grown apart. Other couples ignore the tensions in their relationship for years, gathering resentment and living parallel lives until a crisis such as an affair brings them to therapy. Also, if each person gets caught in blaming the other, and refuses to examine her or his own part in the problem, success can be stymied. On the other hand, if couples seek help when they first realize that their own efforts have not resolved the conflicts or when their own efforts only exacerbate the problem, there is a greater chance at success. When this is coupled with love, goodwill, and personal responsibility, most problems can be resolved.

people do not perform sexually as expected, they often feel embarrassed, guilty, frustrated, confused, and depressed. This can often cause problems in personal relationships as well as in other aspects of people's lives. We will not go into detail here regarding the specifics of these sexual dysfunctions. Rather, they are presented in some detail in Appendix A. Suffice it to say here that whenever people recognize that they have a sexual dysfunction they should seek the help of a qualified physician, psychiatrist, or marriage or sex therapist, depending on the problem (see the Strengthening Marriages and Families box).

We end this chapter with a discussion of sexual responsibility and protecting oneself from disease, particularly as these issues relate to AIDS.

SEXUAL RESPONSIBILITY: PROTECTING YOURSELF FROM AIDS AND OTHER STDS

Sexually transmitted diseases (STDs), diseases acquired primarily through sexual contact, are fairly common in today's society. Such diseases can be caused by viruses (AIDS, herpes, hepatitis B, and genital warts), bacteria (syphilis, gonorrhea, and chlamydia infections), and tiny insects or parasites (pubic lice). Approximately 340 million people worldwide are stricken with curable STDs each year, and in the United States an estimated 19 million new cases of STDs occur each year, almost half of them among young people aged 15 to 24. About one-half of all people will be infected by an STD sometime in their lifetime. The United States has the highest rates of STDs in the industrialized world. The CDC estimates that about 65 million Americans are currently living with a sexually transmitted disease. Women suffer more frequent and more serious complications from STDs than men (Banis, 2006; Centers for Disease Control and Prevention, 2005; National Women's Health Information Center, 2005). Some experts are claiming that the United States is in the throes of an STD epidemic in poor, underserved areas of the country that rivals that of some developing countries. However, the risk is not limited to this population. Recent data show that STDs are becoming increasingly common among teenagers, including those from middle- and upper-class families (each year, one in four teens aged 13 to 19 contracts an STD). There are over 25 identified STDS, the most common are chlamydia, genital herpes, genital warts, gonorrhea, hepatitis B, human papillomavirus, syphilis, and AIDS. Many cases of STDs go undiagnosed, and some highly prevalent viral infections, such as human papillomavirus and genital herpes, are not reported at all. For instance, it is estimated that as many as one in four Americans have genital herpes, and up to 90 percent are unaware that they have it. In addition to the physical and psychological consequences of STDs, these diseases also exact a tremendous economic toll. Direct medical costs associated with STDs, including human immunodeficiency virus (HIV), in the United States are estimated at $13 billion annually. All STDs can be improved by treatment, and some can be cured, but many people who are infected do not recognize the symptoms (Banis, 2006; Centers for Disease Control, 2004; Stolberg, 1998). Because of the risks to physical and mental health, we must become more knowledgeable about STDs, and more responsible to ourselves and others in our sexual behaviors. With the exception of AIDS, which we discuss next, STDs are examined in Appendix A.

AIDS

Women and men living in the United States today are perhaps more challenged in their exploration and enjoyment of sexuality than at any other time in our history. Protracted media, public attention, and information about responsible sexual behavior—abstinence, safe sex, and the use of condoms—reflect the new era of sexuality and sexual choices in America. In this new era of sexuality, HIV/AIDS continues to be a serious and deadly threat to women and

"How do I know you don't have herpes?"

Increasing public awareness and individual concern about sexually transmitted diseases have sparked a rise in humor about human sexuality. However, the contraction and transmission of STDs is a serious matter that should be discussed before having sexual relations.
Source: Reprinted with permission of V. G. Myers.© *Cosmopolitan*, 1982.

men, the young and old, rich and poor, heterosexual and homosexual, and across race and ethnicity. Experts estimate that close to 1 million people in the United States are living with HIV—which is believed to be the main cause of AIDS—and that more than half a million has died after developing AIDS. Identified in 1981, **acquired immunodeficiency syndrome (AIDS)** is a viral syndrome, or group of diseases, that destroys the body's immune system, thereby rendering the victim susceptible to all kinds of infections and diseases. People may have HIV without knowing it, given that the incubation period can be as long as 10 years and given symptoms of AIDS usually do not appear for a year or longer. Because the body is unable to fight off HIV/AIDS infections and diseases, they eventually kill the person. In 2001, marking the twentieth anniversary of the AIDS epidemic, experts and others expressed hope for a cure but, to date, there is still no cure for AIDS. People with HIV/AIDS are living longer and staying healthier on new medications, but the epidemic is still spreading and people are still dying.

Of the 944,306 people in the United States diagnosed with AIDS through December 31, 2004, 529,113 (56 percent) had already died (Centers for Disease Control and Prevention, 2004). Figure 6.5 illustrates the number of AIDS cases diagnosed and the number of AIDS deaths that occurred in selective years through 2004. A person who tests positive for HIV is regarded as infected and capable of transmitting the virus to others.

The Transmission of AIDS HIV/AIDS is transmitted through blood, semen, vaginal fluid, breast milk, and other body fluids containing blood. It can enter the body through a vein (such as intravenous drug use), the anus or rectum, vagina, penis, mouth, mucous membranes (such as eyes or inside of the nose), or cuts and sores. To date, the most common means of transmission is through sexual

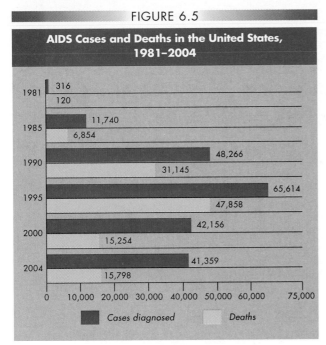

FIGURE 6.5

AIDS Cases and Deaths in the United States, 1981–2004

Year	Cases diagnosed	Deaths
1981	316	120
1985	11,740	6,854
1990	48,266	31,145
1995	65,614	47,858
2000	42,156	15,254
2004	41,359	15,798

Source: Adapted from Centers for Disease Control and Prevention, 2000, *HIV/AIDS Surveillance Report, Year-end Edition*, vol. 12, no. 2, p. 29, Table 20; Centers for Disease Control and Prevention, 2004, *HIV/AIDS Surveillance Report*, vol. 16, pp. 14,16, Tables 5a, 7.

still a deadly disease. Although new treatments have slowed the progression from HIV to AIDS and from AIDS to death, for many people the virus is nonetheless spreading and taking its toll on both old and new victims.

The intersections of race, class, gender, age, and sexual orientation are clearly revealed in various HIV/AIDS statistics (see Figure 6.6). People most frequently affected by HIV continue to be men generally and gay men more specifically, but increasingly there is a new face of AIDS: It is also an epidemic of the poor, which means it is increasingly an epidemic of some groups of color that are found disproportionately among the poor. For example, an increasingly high percentage of new HIV infections is occurring in African American women, particularly poor rural women. And although the number of new AIDS cases among white homosexuals has declined in several major cities since 1990, the rate of infection among homosexuals of color, especially African Americans, has surged significantly. No longer confined to gay men and intravenous drug abusers, AIDS in the United States is increasingly an epidemic of the heterosexual population as well (see Table 6.2).

More African Americans are living with HIV or are already dead from AIDS than any other single racial or ethnic group in the United States—a crisis one black AIDS activist calls "a state of emergency" for the African American community (quoted in Andriote, 2005). Researchers at the CDC estimate that about 1 in 50 African American men and 1 in 160 African American women are infected with HIV. By comparison, 1 in 250 white men and 1 in every

contact, as indicated in Table 6.2. For children under 13 years of age, the most common means of contracting the AIDS virus is from a mother either with or at risk for HIV infection (Centers for Disease Control and Prevention, 2004).

According to current evidence, HIV cannot be transmitted by casual contact. That is, AIDS cannot be transmitted through touching, coughing, sneezing, breathing, handshakes, or socializing, nor can it be spread through toilet seats, food, eating utensils, drinking out of the same glass, water fountains, or insects. And the risk of contracting AIDS through saliva (as in kissing) is said to be extremely low. However, there is little dispute that oral and genital sex are the most risky for the transmission of AIDS. This risk can be greatly reduced, however, with the use of latex condoms. Right now, the most basic ways to control the spread of the virus are believed to be through avoiding high-risk sex (either through abstinence, exclusive relationships, latex condoms) and through careful monitoring of transfusions of blood and other body fluids.

Who Gets AIDS? The Intersections of Race, Class, Gender, Sexual Orientation, and Age High-profile stars who have contracted AIDS, like Earvin "Magic" Johnson, the late Arthur Ashe, and former national heavyweight boxer Tommy Morrison, heightened Americans' sensitivity to the problem of HIV/AIDS. However, the appearance of these people as healthy and living a well-rounded life even with the virus, coupled with increasing news about people with AIDS generally living a longer and healthier life, has had the effect of dulling the sensitivity of some people to the continued crisis of HIV/AIDS—that it is

TABLE 6.2

Adult and Adolescent Reported AIDS Cases, by Exposure Category and Sex, Through December 2004*

	Females (%)	Males (%)
Adults		
Homosexual and bisexual men	—	55
Intravenous drug users	37	21
Homosexual male drug users	—	8
Heterosexuals	44	6
Hemophiliacs and recipients of blood transfusions	2	1
Other or undetermined	17	9
Totals	100%	100%
Adolescents		
Hemophilia/coagulation disorder	0	5
Mother with a risk factor for, or documented, HIV infection	94	89
Receipt of blood transfusion, blood components, or tissue	3	5
Other or undetermined	3	1
Totals	100%	100%

*The Centers for Disease Control and Prevention tracks diagnosis of AIDS in terms of two basic age groups: adult/adolescents (13 years of age and older) and pediatric (children under 13).

Source: Adapted from Centers for Disease Control and Prevention, 2005, *HIV/AIDS Surveillance Report, 2004*, Vol. 16 (Atlanta: U.S. Department of Health and Human Services, Centers for Disease Control and Prevention): p. 32, Table 17.

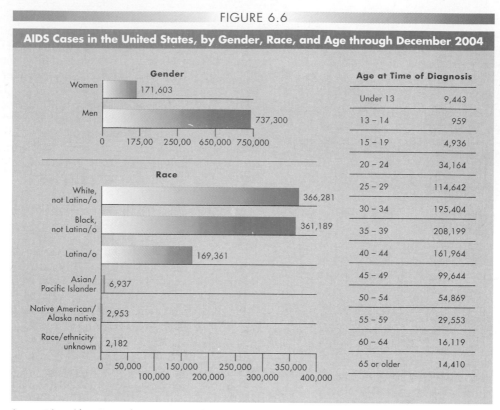

FIGURE 6.6

AIDS Cases in the United States, by Gender, Race, and Age through December 2004

Source: Adapted from Centers for Disease Control and Prevention, 2004, *HIV/AIDS Surveillance Report,* vol. 16, pp. 12, 32, 34, 36; Tables 3, 17, 19, 21.

3000 white women are infected. Among young people (ages 13 to 24), 65 percent of the new HIV diagnoses are among African Americans (Centers for Disease Control and Prevention, 2004; Herbert, 2001; Sack, 2001). And although the incidence of new cases among Latinas/os is lower than that for African Americans it is three times the rate for whites. As among all groups, the number of Latinas/os living with AIDS has increased, with males accounting for the greatest proportion (78 percent) of cases. Latinas/os include a diverse mixture of ethnic groups and cultures, and thus the incidence of HIV/AIDS varies across these groups (Centers for Disease Control and Prevention, 2004, 2000b).

Although there is a new face to HIV/AIDS, through December 2004 the preponderance of people with AIDS were still males who either have had intimate same-sex contacts or are intravenous drug users who have shared a hypodermic needle (see Table 6.2). According to federal health officials, each year another 40,000 Americans become infected with HIV. Of those infected, 70 percent are men and about 40 percent are men who have sex with men. Although the AIDS rates are lower for women than men, women now account for a little more than one-fourth (27 percent) of all newly diagnosed cases, more than three times the percentage since 1985 and a reflection of the ongoing shift in populations affected by the epidemic. Women of color are particularly vulnerable to the virus. For instance, African American and Latinas together represent less than one-fourth of all U.S. women, yet they account for 79 percent of AIDS cases reported to date among women.

An increasing percentage of women are becoming infected with the HIV virus through heterosexual transmission, and many have a history of sexually transmitted disease, intravenous drug use, or a sexual partner who is an intravenous drug abuser. Among the small number of Asian/Pacific Islander women who have AIDS, a little more than one-half (52 percent) contracted the virus through heterosexual contact. Comparable figures for African American, Latinas, Native American, and white women are 42, 49, 41, and 41 percent, respectively (Centers for Disease Control and Prevention, 2004; Manier and Obejas, 2001). Many women with HIV/AIDS are low income and most (76 percent) have important family responsibilities (e.g., children under age 18 in their homes), which potentially complicates the management of their illness. On average, women tend to die sooner after the diagnosis of AIDS than do men, which might reflect the disparities in their access to prevention, care, treatment, and support relative to men (Kaiser Family Foundation, 2004; Centers for Disease Control and Prevention, 2004; Sack, 2001).

HIV/AIDS and Risk   These statistics lead to a discussion of *risk:* Who is at risk, and why? Most observers of HIV/AIDS agree that certain kinds of behavior place people at greater risk of infection than other kinds of behavior. The highest-risk behavior is *anal sex.* Rectal bleeding, which often occurs during anal sex, allows the easy transmission of HIV from one person to another. Anal sex is often practiced by gay men (but is certainly not limited to gay men), some of whom

The AIDS gap between the sexes is one gap that women are not fighting to close. Unfortunately, although almost one-half of newly infected adults have been women, some health specialists warn that AIDS prevention is still too focused on men.
Source: Reprinted by permission of William Costello for *USA Today*.

have unprotected sex with multiple partners, putting these men, as a category of people, at greater risk than any other group. Data from the CDC indicate that almost half of gay men in their teens and early twenties had unprotected sex in the 6-month period preceding the survey.

Not only are African American women hit hard by HIV/AIDS, but so are African American youths. African American men who have sex with men (MSM) have proven particularly vulnerable to HIV infection, 15 percent of whom are newly infected with HIV each year—a rate that is six times greater than that for white gays (Andriote, 2005; Manier and Obejas, 2001). Because the incidence of AIDS remains high among gays, there is still some feeling that the rest of the population is relatively safe from exposure to the virus. However, this could not be farther from the truth. For example, estimates are that roughly one-fifth of gays marry heterosexually. Thus, heterosexual wives of gay men stand a high probability of being exposed to the virus. This does not include the possible exposure of women who are married to or have sexual relationships with bisexual males. In this context, of concern in African American communities is the increasing number of new HIV/AIDS cases that involve African American MSM but do not identify themselves as homosexual or bisexual. Such men are said to be "on the down-low," slang used to describe someone who has homosexual sex but hides it from friends, family, lovers, and sometimes himself. Some of these men are former prison inmates who may have been raped or started engaging in sex with men while incarcerated. Some observers believe this down-low behavior may be an important source of HIV/AIDS among heterosexual African American women.

On the other hand, female-to-female transmission of HIV/AIDS appears to be a rare occurrence. Of all the women reported with AIDS to date, only a very small percentage (2 percent) were reported to have had sex with women. Of those who reported having had sex *only* with women, 98 percent also had another risk—intravenous drug use in most cases. To date, there are no studies that have confirmed female-to-female transmission, either because

other risks were subsequently identified or because the women declined to be interviewed. Although these findings suggest that female-to-female transmission of HIV is uncommon, they do not negate the possibility because it could be masked by other behaviors (Hawkins, 2000; Center for Disease Control, 1999).

Finally, a highly risky behavior for HIV infection is related to *intravenous drug use* and the *sharing of needles* among drug users. Intravenous drug users who share needles account for one-fourth of all persons with AIDS, and the sharing of needles is a major source of transmission among women (see Table 6.2). In addition, people who have multiple partners over their lifetime are at far greater risk of HIV infection than those who have few sexual partners. According to the NORC survey, no other factor predicted risk more accurately than the number of sex partners an individual had in a lifetime. Because the majority of people who are at the highest risk of contracting the virus are members of categories that this society values least (gays, poor people, people of color, women), AIDS is a deeply divisive social and political issue. However, AIDS is first and foremost a critical public health issue that represents not one but multiple epidemics: an inner-city epidemic; a rural epidemic; and an epidemic among women, among intravenous drug users, among gay men, among African Americans, among Latinas/os, among non-Latina/o whites, and heterosexual women.

AIDS and Children   As we already know, age is an important factor in contracting AIDS. The number of children under the age of 13 with AIDS has steadily declined over the years. Between 2000 and 2004, the estimated number of AIDS cases decreased 61 percent among children younger than 13 years old. Ninety-one percent of children with AIDS contracted the disease from their mothers before, during, or after birth (for example, during breast-feeding). Of the remaining 9 percent of children with AIDS, 7 percent contracted the disease from blood transfusions or are hemophiliacs. Today, AIDS is the sixth leading cause of death in children under the age of 5. Almost five times as many African American as white children have AIDS. Thirteen percent of children with AIDS are white and 21 percent are Latino/a (Centers for Disease Control and Prevention, 2004). Often these children, across race, have mothers who are poor, are intravenous drug abusers, or have partners who are. These women also have little or no access to drug treatment programs or health care facilities.

At the other end of the age spectrum, elderly people are seldom thought of as HIV- or AIDS-infected. Women and men over the age of 55 account for 7 percent of all AIDS cases. A study of AIDS patients 60 years of age and older found that most HIV-infected persons in this age group acquired their infection through sexual intercourse or intravenous drug use. The study also reported that the HIV diagnosis in the elderly was usually not considered by clinicians until late in the course of the infection, even though a high prevalence of prior sexually transmitted diseases existed (Gordon and Thompson, 1995). Findings such as these on the treatment of HIV in older adults parallel those on women. They also vividly illustrate how our misconceptions about various social and cultural groups (in this case, our misconception about older Americans, especially their sexuality) have ramifications for various other aspects of our lives, including medical diagnoses for certain diseases and illnesses.

AIDS as a National and International Issue   The AIDS epidemic is not merely a U.S. problem. Some observers have described it as a global pandemic and disaster, given that, worldwide, an estimated 40.3 million people were living with HIV/AIDS at the end of 2005, an estimated 16,000 new cases are diagnosed every day, and, in 2005 alone, almost 5 million people were newly infected with HIV (UNAIDS/WHO, 2005; Ritter, 2001a). Approximately one-half of those living with HIV/AIDS are under the age of 25 and 43 percent are women–in more than 74 countries, with more than 95 percent in developing countries. The number continues to rise. At the end of 2005, 4.9 million new infections had been reported, and more than 25 million people around the world had died from AIDS since the beginning of the epidemic, over 4 million of them children. In the year 2005 alone, 3.1 million infected people died globally, a higher global total than in any other year since the beginning of the epidemic, despite antiretroviral drugs that have helped drive down the incidence of AIDS and AIDS-related deaths in the richer countries.

Although no country is untouched by HIV infection and AIDS, 70 percent of the world's adults and 80 percent of the children infected with HIV/AIDS live in Africa and another 20 percent of people living with HIV/AIDS are in Southeast Asia. Eighty percent of AIDS deaths are in Africa, and the pandemic has left 13.3 million orphans globally, 12 million of whom are Africans. In sub-Saharan Africa HIV is now more deadly than war itself. In 1998, 200,000 Africans died in war, but more than 2 million died of AIDS (AIDS in Africa, 2001). In 2005, the epidemic claimed the lives of an estimated 2.4 million people in the region. Botswana is one of the countries hardest hit by AIDS, where a staggering 37.3

Although no country is untouched by HIV infection and AIDS, today, the majority of global HIV/AIDS cases and AIDS-related deaths occur in sub-Saharan Africa and Southeast Asia primarily due to a lack of access to antiretroviral drugs that have helped drive down the incidence of AIDS and AIDS-related deaths in the richer countries. Critics say that rich countries could go a long way in helping the peoples of Africa and Southeast Asia by funding prevention programs and drug treatments. And drug companies could help by selling drugs to these nations at cost.

percent of adults are infected with HIV, the second highest in the world after Swaziland (Avert.Org, 2006; UNAIDS/WHO, 2005; AIDS around the World, 2001). According to some health experts and AIDS activists, AIDS is Africa's greatest social disaster since the transatlantic slave trade (Ritter, 2001b).

The HIV infection rate in South and Southeast Asia is also at epidemic proportions. It is estimated that there are close to 6 million adults and children living with HIV or AIDS in this region, more than the total number of people elsewhere in the entire industrialized world. The spread of HIV infection and AIDS in China, India, Thailand, and Cambodia, to name only a few, has been fueled by an extensive sex trade and the use of illicit drugs. In China, for instance, it is estimated that close to three-quarters of 1 million people were infected with HIV at the start of 2006, the majority of whom are intravenous drug abusers. According to UNAIDS, if current trends continue, there could be 20 million Chinese infected with HIV or AIDS by the end of 2010 (UNAIDS/WHO, 2005; AIDS around the World, 2001; Global Statistical Information, 2001).

Globally, women represent almost half (17.5 million) of the people living with HIV/AIDS; half (2.3 million) of all people (4.9 million) newly infected with HIV, the majority of whom are believed to be between 15 and 35 years of age; and nearly half of the total number of people who have died since the onset of the HIV/AIDS epidemic. As in the United States, the number of new cases of HIV/AIDS among women worldwide is increasing dramatically. This is because in many countries women are denied equal access to information, education, training, health care, and other social services, which makes it difficult to achieve effective preventive programs. In some poor countries where there are limited job opportunities, many women are forced to labor as sex workers (prostitutes); because of their poor economic situations they are unlikely to refuse clients who do not wear condoms. In many countries (such as South Africa, China, Thailand) large numbers of prostitutes have been infected with HIV and are blamed for its spread. It goes without saying that the impact of HIV/AIDS on women and their children, other family members, and their communities is devastating (Avert.Org, 2006; Global Statistical Information, 2001).

The social and economic consequences of AIDS are tremendous. AIDS has not only impacted the health of people around the world, but also education, industry, agriculture, transportation, human resources, and economies in general. AIDS has widened the gulf between rich and poor nations, and the United States and other wealthy nations have been criticized for completely ignoring or, at best, doing little to help fight the spread of the devastating virus in Africa. Critics say that rich countries could go a long way in helping the peoples of Africa by funding prevention programs and drug treatments. And drug companies could help by selling drugs to Africa at cost (AIDS in Africa, 2001; Ritter, 2001b).

AIDS Prevention and Sexual Responsibility   Like most other human choices and behavior, our sexual choices and behaviors carry with them an expectation of responsibility. Romanticized notions of sex and sexuality have sometimes caused us in the past to ignore or avoid these responsibilities. However, the AIDS pandemic has focused the spotlight on sexuality and sexual responsibility. A variety of groups have campaigned for **safe sex**. Such campaigns are geared toward informing people of how to protect themselves from AIDS and other sexually transmitted diseases through abstinence or by engaging in responsible sex. The major underlying theme is that abstinence is desirable and the only sure method of prevention, but that people who cannot or will not abstain should use protective methods, most notably condoms. Not all people agree with the premise of the safe-sex philosophy, however. Critics contend that the premise of safe sex promotes sexual promiscuity and does little, if anything, to promote abstinence. They argue that abstinence, not safe sex, should be the official public policy. The evidence on just how effective campaigns for safe sex or complete abstinence are is mixed. Although there was some evidence in the mid-1990s

Sparked by the AIDS crisis, posters, advertisements, and warning signs like these amusing condoms encourage the practice of safer sex.

that casual sex was on the decrease and sexual partners (from teenagers to the elderly) were practicing safe sex, primarily through the increased use of condoms, today there is some indication that, at least among some groups, casual sex or sex with risky partners without the use of condoms or other protective measures is on the rise again.

The fact is that most people will be sexually active at some time in their lives. Sex can be healthy, wholesome, and satisfying, but there are also constraints. In the final analysis, each one of us has a responsibility to engage in sex in a manner that is protective of both our own and our partners' health and well-being. In addition, the AIDS prevention agenda today and in the future must be global and must not focus exclusively on effecting changes in individuals' sexual behavior. More broadly, it must promote improvements in the overall status and quality of life of women, poor people, people of color, children, and those living in developing countries so that they have more control over when and how sex takes place. The AIDS prevention agenda must also work toward providing individuals and families with better medical care, regardless of whether or not they are impacted by HIV/AIDS or other sexually transmitted diseases. And it must encourage continued and improved funding for research on an AIDS vaccine that would be appropriate for use in developing countries.

WRITING YOUR OWN SCRIPT

IDENTIFYING SEXUAL VALUES

Thinking about your own sexuality, write a short essay outlining your values with respect to sexuality. What have been the major sources of sexual information for you? Consider major periods in your life, for example, childhood, adolescence, young adulthood, middle age, older. Who or what has been the major influence on your sexual values? Are your sexual values the same as those of your parents? If not, how do they differ? How tolerant are you of sexual lifestyles different from your own? If you have children, what will you teach them about sexuality? Will you be supportive of sex education in your child's school? If yes, why? If no, why not?

SUPPORTING MARRIAGES AND FAMILIES

Issues and concerns at the nexus of sexuality and marriages and families continue to claim the attention of scholars, policymakers, and citizens. People are engaging in sexual activities at earlier ages and remaining sexually active for much longer periods into old age. Although individuals, marital partners and families bear responsibility in promoting and living safe sexual lifestyles, the need for policies and programs that support marriages and families is nowhere more glaring than in the area of human sexuality. Whatever values and beliefs we hold individually about human sexuality, it is clear that as a nation, we cannot bury our heads in the sand and pretend that celibacy is the only answer to many of the pressing issues and problems that surround the sexual practices and behaviors of many Americans. Research, for instance, clearly demonstrates that the majority of both younger and older people no longer tie sexuality to long-term personal or institutional commitment. Teens and adults have sex before, during, and after marriage with a variety of partners over their life course (Risman and Schwartz, 2002). Therefore, in order to contribute to the strength of intimate partnered relationships, marriages, and families, there is a need for federal, state, and local policies that recognize these realities and that provide access to quality medical and social education that promotes responsibility and safety in terms of sexual practices and behaviors.

The overwhelming majority of Americans (84 percent) agree that preventing HIV/AIDS and other sexually transmitted diseases as well as unintended teenage pregnancies are public health issues that should rely on scientific evidence and not political or religious ideology (Advocates for Youth, 2006). Although sexual abstinence is a desirable objective, especially for youth, programs and policies must also include education and support for those who are already sexually active. Policies that deny the sexual realities of lesbians, gays, bisexuals, transgendered Americans, teenagers, and older adults, for example, and that teach that heterosexuality is the only valid sexual orientation and that abstinence is the only way to prevent pregnancy and disease, are biased, lack scientific support, and are counterproductive to the health and well-being of individuals, intimate partnered relationships, marriages, and families. Polices that (1) are ideologically motivated rather than empirically driven, (2) do not support access for all Americans to quality and affordable health care, as well as (3) support the investment of hundreds of millions of federal and state funds to programs that have little or no evidence of effectiveness, all constitute poor fiscal and public health initiatives and contributes to the weakening rather than the strengthening of American marriages and families. No matter how widespread politically and religiously popular and appealing policies, programs, and initiatives may be, the bottom line must be the efficacy in educating and modifying unsafe and risky sexuality behaviors and strengthening American marriages, families, and intimate partnered relationships.

SUMMARY

We are all sexual beings, and we spend a large amount of our time engaged in a variety of sexual behaviors. Although some people still believe the Freudian notion that our sexuality is biologically driven, sociologists stress the social basis of human sexuality. A sociological perspective of human sexuality focuses on the tremendous role that culture plays in creating and shaping the content of our sexuality. Like other behaviors, sexual behavior is guided by cultural scripts. In learning society's sexual guidelines, we in effect create or invent our capacity for sexual behavior. As we learn other important norms of our culture, we also simultaneously learn about our sexuality from a variety of sources including family, peers, and mass media.

There is some debate over whether a sexual revolution has occurred. Whatever the verdict, it is clear that drastic changes occurred in the approach to sexuality in the twentieth-century United States. The most dramatic changes occurred among women, across race, class, and age cohort. Americans have continued many of the sexual patterns and behaviors noted in the closing decades of the twentieth century. Over the last decade, global sex surveys have reported on a range of sexual behaviors in countries across the world indicating that Americans often fall somewhere is the middle of the average sexual practices of adults worldwide.

Although historically U.S. society has classified heterosexuality as the only acceptable form of human sexuality,

humans actually express a range of sexual orientations or preferences. According to Alfred Kinsey, these orientations fall along a continuum, with heterosexuality and homosexuality at each extreme, and bisexuality falling somewhere in the middle. William Masters and Virginia Johnson found that a variety of physiological factors are associated with sexuality and erotic arousal and that all people go through the same four phases of sexual response: excitement, climax, orgasm, and resolution. As with sexual orientation, sexual expression incorporates a variety of behaviors, ranging from activities involving only the self to those that involve two or more individuals. Masturbation and sexual fantasies and dreams are autoerotic activities in which the majority of people engage at some point in their lives. Petting and oral–genital sex are the most common sexual behaviors in which humans engage.

There have been dramatic changes in human sexuality in every phase of the life cycle. Unmarried people are engaging in sexual activities with little expectation that such relationships will lead to marriage. Teenagers in particular are increasingly sexually active. Within marriages, wives and husbands are experiencing a wider range of sexuality and are more satisfied with their sexual relationships than in the past. In addition, a growing number of married people are engaging in extramarital relationships. And although physiological changes cause changes in the sexual response of older adults, most enjoy satisfying romantic and sexual relationships well into old age.

The spread of HIV/AIDS is not just a concern in the United States. HIV/AIDS is a global pandemic affecting peoples in almost every country of the world. The hardest hit, however, are the peoples of Africa and South and Southeast Asia.

KEY TERMS

human sexuality	sexual identity	masturbation	menopause
sexual double standard	homophobia	nocturnal emissions	sexual dysfunction
sexual scripts	homosexuality	wet dreams	sexually transmitted diseases (STDs)
significant others	transgendered	pleasuring	acquired immunodeficiency syndrome (AIDS)
generalized others	bisexuality	petting	
sexual orientation	orgasm	cunnilingus	safe sex
heterosexism	ejaculation	fellatio	
heterosexuality	autoeroticism	coitus	

QUESTIONS FOR STUDY AND REFLECTION

1. For the most part, the media and mass advertising flaunt sexuality and define its content for all of us, including children. Consider how sexuality is presented in ads for popular products (cars, perfume, alcoholic beverages) as well as in rock and hip-hop videos. How have these images and definitions of sexuality affected your behavior? How closely do they resemble your everyday life? Is it possible to ignore the sexual messages of the media? Do you think there is a relationship between media emphasis on sexuality and the high rate of unmarried pregnancies? Explain.

2. What kind of AIDS awareness, if any, takes place on your college campus? Has awareness of the disease affected sexual behavior on your campus? Conduct a brief survey of students on your campus about their knowledge of HIV/AIDS and other STDs and their sexual behavior relative to HIV/AIDS and other STDs. Do you think that people who have AIDS should be isolated from those who do not? What do you think about mandatory AIDS testing in schools and in the workplace?

3. How do your views differ from those of people you know in your own generation and those of your parents and your grandparents concerning sexual activity or pregnancy outside of legal marriage, oral–genital sexual activity, extramarital sexual behavior, homosexuality, bisexuality, and sexual behavior among older adults? How do you feel about your body? Are your feelings different from those of people of younger or older generations? Explain.

4. What were your feelings when reading this chapter? Did some subjects or topics make you feel uncomfortable? How comfortable are you discussing topics such as masturbation, wet dreams, sexual fantasies, and positions in sexual intercourse with a significant other? Parents? In a classroom? Your answers to these questions can be used as a way of getting in touch with your own orientation toward sexuality.

ADDITIONAL RESOURCES

SOCIOLOGICAL

CARBADO, DEVON W. 1999. *Black Men on Race, Gender, and Sexuality.* New York: New York University Press. A collection of essays covering such topics as the legal construction of black male identity and sexuality, the role of black men in black women's quest for racial equality, and the heterosexist nature of black political engagement. It features the work of diverse African Americans males. It is an excellent source for discussions about the intersections of race, class, gender, and sexuality.

REINISCH, JUNE, AND RUTH BEASLEY. 1990. *The Kinsey Institute New Report on Sex: What You Must Know to Be Sexually Literate.* New York: St. Martin's Press. Over the years, the Kinsey Institute has received hundreds of questions concerning human sexuality. This book attempts to address some of the most commonly asked questions surrounding topics such as AIDS, other sexually transmitted diseases, and sexuality and aging.

RICH, ADRIENNE. 1980. "Compulsory Heterosexuality and Lesbian Existence." *Signs* 5:631–660. A classic and influential essay on the sociopolitical nature of female sexuality generally and lesbianism specifically.

ROSE, TRICIA. 2004. *Longing to Tell.* New York: Picador. A set of revealing and inspiring narratives from a variety of women of color—of various ages, and economic and educational backgrounds—who talk about sexuality, race, their sexual relationships, first sexual encounters with women and men, intimate clichés, and their coming of age as a woman. Tricia Rose sums up well the overall dynamics of the sexual ramifications that women of color encounter today.

FILM

Brokeback Mountain. 2005. This film presents an epic love story about a forbidden and secretive relationship between two young men—a ranch hand and a rodeo cowboy—who meet in the summer of 1963 herding sheep in the high grasslands of contemporary Wyoming and unexpectedly form a lifelong bond. The complications, joys, and tragedies of their relationship provide excellent text for a sociological analysis of same-sex love, heterosexual marriage, family, and American cultural confines, definitions, and expectations of masculinity—what it is to be a man.

TransAmerica. 2005. In this film, a preoperative male-to-female transsexual who works two jobs to pay for one last operation—gender reassignment surgery—that will make her a female, takes an unexpected journey when she learns that she fathered a son, now a 17-year-old teenage runaway hustling on the streets of New York. Although transsexuality is a topic that makes many people uncomfortable, this film is a good source for engaging students in a discussion of transsexuality and debunking the myths around this sexual orientation. For example, students might be directed in a critique of the way transsexualism is portrayed in the movie and whether or not it perpetuates stereotypes of transsexualism compared to the reality of life as a transsexual.

LITERARY

KUDAKA, GERALDINE, ED. 1995. *On a Bed of Rice: An Asian American Erotic Feast.* New York: Anchor. An interesting anthology of contemporary erotic prose and poetry by established and up-and-coming writers of Chinese, Filipino, Japanese, Korean, Vietnamese, and Indian descent explores the themes of sexual awakening, marriage, and interracial love. The stories range from haunting to humorous; some deal with the way that race and sex are intertwined in America, others with the myths about Asian American sexuality. This anthology is proof that sex and eroticism need not be taboo subjects for college students.

WILSON, BARBARA. 1990. *Gaudi Afternoon.* Seattle, WA: Seal Press. The author of this novel uses the mystery genre to explore a feminist perspective on sociologically relevant topics such as sexual orientation and identity, gender identity, and gender roles. It is an interesting lesbian crime novel that raises questions such as what makes a person straight or queer, femme or butch, lesbian or dyke, transgendered or translated. This novel provides professors and students with a rich narrative to examine, analyze, and critique the shifting debates that view gender and sexual identities as, in the words of gender theorist Judith Butler, "performative strategies of insubordination."

INTERNET

www.indiana.edu/~kinsey/index.html The Kinsey Institute, founded by noted sociologist Alfred Kinsey, sponsors this site, which is dedicated to supporting interdisciplinary research in the study of human sexuality. The site contains descriptions of the center's latest published research on human sexuality.

http://www.thebody.com This site, The Body, is a comprehensive multimedia HIV and AIDS health Internet site and information resource center. It provides information on more than 250 topics. Its stated mission is to lower barriers between patients and clinicians, demystify HIV/AIDS and its treatment, improve patients' quality of life, and foster community through human connection.

http://www.goaskalice.columbia.edu/ This site, Go Ask Alice!, is a health question-and-answer Internet service produced by Columbia University's Health Education Program. Its mission is to increase access to, and use of, health information by providing factual, in-depth, straightforward, and nonjudgmental information to assist users' decision making about their physical, sexual, emotional, and spiritual health.

http://www.guttmacher.org This site of the Alan Guttmacher Institute is committed to understanding issues of family planning, contraception, and social issues such as teenage pregnancy. Those who visit this Web site can search for a variety of information in the form of fact sheets as well as information about current research and family planning services.

LIVING SINGLE, LIVING WITH OTHERS: NONMARITAL LIFESTYLES

IN THE NEWS

The United States

Only a generation ago, parents whose children were becoming young adults, worried about how they would adjust to having an "empty nest" when the kids left home to be on their own. Today's parents are more likely to worry about how to get them to leave. In today's economy, with its tight job market, low starting salaries, high rents, and large student-loan debts, many young adults find achieving financial independence difficult. Divorce, mental illness, chemical dependency, and other problems also contribute to this phenomenon. Consequently, increasing numbers of young adults remain at or return to the parental home. Social scientists have dubbed this group, the "boomerang generation." According to the U.S. Census Bureau, approximately 18 million Americans between 18 and 34 (constituting nearly 27 percent of that age group) now live with their parents (Fields, 2003). Historically, the number of boomerang children increases when the economy contracts. Less than 8 percent of adult children aged 25 to 34 lived with parents in 1970; the rate increased when the economy slowed in the early 1980s, then decreased as the economy prospered in the 1990s. By 2003, when the economy again slowed, over 4 million (10.2 percent) of the 25 to 34- age group were living in the family home (Fields, 2003). In a recent online survey by MonsterTRAK.com, a job search firm, 60 percent of college students reported that they planned to move home after graduation. For most students, this was intended as a short-term living arrangement, but 22 percent said they planned to stay there for more than a year. Men are more likely to live with their parents than are women. This trend is not unique to the United States, but is raising concerns in Canada and England as well.

Given the cultural norm of independence in young adulthood, it would not be surprising to find both parents and adult children expressing dissatisfaction with such arrangements. This living arrangement can be stressful. Higher parental household bills and conflicts of lifestyles and values are common. Both generations complain about a lack of privacy. Regression is a likely result. Parents may want to know where their children are going and what they are doing, and adult children may revert to a high school mode, expecting their parents to cook and clean for them. Personal satisfaction and self-esteem can decline under these circumstances. One 23-year-old returnee expressed it this way, "I sort of felt like a loser. Everyone I graduated with was moving away to pursue careers or getting apartment with friends, and I couldn't afford to do anything. I was pretty depressed about moving home, at least initially" (cited in Eng, 2005). Many parents express ambivalence about these relationships as well. They do not want to be bad parents so they agree to the arrangement but sometimes feel trapped. As one parent said, "Once your kids are out of the house, you establish a schedule for yourself—eating, sleeping, etc. You have your own household rhythms. When the kids come home after college, they are not interested in your schedules. They see no problem with coming and going at all hours of the day and night. Parents are always aware of when a child is or is not in the house. You worry if they don't come home, and they're shocked that you worry" (cited in Levine, 2005).

Despite some of these difficulties, however, many parents report spending enjoyable time with their co-resident adult children. Parents were more likely to be satisfied having adult children living with them if the child was working and hence on the way to becoming independent. Conversely, parents with unemployed adult children are more likely to be dissatisfied with the relationship. To minimize difficulties, all parties must remember that they are now a collection of adults living together. Elina Furman (2005), a boomeranger herself and author of *Boomerang Nation*, suggests that parents and returning adult children discuss mutual expectations, house rules, chores, time limit for the stay, and shared financial responsibilities before the move to help all members of the family sort our the wrinkles of redefined relationships.

WHAT WOULD YOU DO? Do you or any of your friends plan to live at home after graduation? If not, under what conditions would you consider returning to or continuing to stay in your parental home? If you are a parent with adult children, would you entertain their returning home to live? What do you see as the advantages and disadvantages of living in your parental home as an adult child or, as a parent, having your adult children live with you? How could you and your co-residential parents (or adult children) minimize the potential conflicts in such a living arrangement?

Over the course of your lifetime you will be making a number of personal decisions, perhaps none more important than whether to marry. To make an intelligent decision, it is important to understand what the alternatives are and how they came to be. Although most Americans will marry at some point in their lives, increasing numbers of people are choosing to remain single into their 30s or even permanently. As indicated in our In the News opening to this chapter, many among this group are residing in the parental home. Still others are forming relationships that differ in significant ways from traditional family structures. This chapter examines the lifestyles of people who, for one reason or another, do not or cannot marry, as well as the economic and social trends that help or hinder the development of nonmarital lifestyles. As is true of marriages and families today, nonmarital lifestyles make up a diverse range of social forms. Among the most common forms are singlehood, heterosexual cohabitation, lesbian and gay relationships, communal living, and group marriages. Each of these lifestyles is examined from both a historical and a contemporary perspective.

Before we examine what it was like to be single in America's early years, we must clarify exactly what we mean by *single*. The term is frequently used to describe anyone who is not currently married—the divorced, widowed, separated, and those who have never married. Including all of these diverse groups under one heading acknowledges that their members are similar in that they do not have legal spouses. This practice, however, obscures the unique aspects of the lifestyles associated with each group. Thus, in this chapter we apply the concept of "single" to never-married people only. Those who were formerly married—the divorced, separated, or widowed—are discussed in separate chapters.

HISTORICAL PERSPECTIVES

Most of the data available on singles in colonial America refer primarily to white settlers. The marital status and lifestyles of Native Americans and African Americans, both free and enslaved, went largely unrecorded during this time. Therefore, we do not know how many individuals in these groups remained unmarried or what such a lifestyle might have been like for them. In addition, although there is a growing body of literature on single women in the eighteenth and nineteenth centuries, particularly middle- and upper-class women, scant information exists on the role of single men during this time. It is not that single men were nonexistent; in fact, quite the opposite was true. Single men made up a large proportion of immigrants to the United States at this time. But then as now, men's economic and political roles rather than their marital status were emphasized. Thus, the conclusions we can draw about the lifestyles of singles in America's past are indeed limited and cannot be assumed to apply to all of the diverse groups living here at that time.

A survey of America's past reveals that for much of this country's history marriage was the cultural ideal and the norm. In fact, positive views concerning the permanently single were rarely articulated. Instead, a social climate evolved that tended to devalue singlehood and to discriminate against individuals who remained unmarried. Although some negative stereotypes of the never-married still persist, today more people are choosing this lifestyle for longer periods of time (some even permanently), and in the process demonstrating that singlehood can be a rewarding and satisfying experience.

Singlehood in Early America

Being single in early America was not easy—unmarried people often faced personal restrictions. For example, N. B. Shurtleff's (1853/1854) examination of the Massachusetts Bay Company's public records found that the authorities mandated "every town to dispose of all single persons and inmates within their town to service or otherwise" (quoted in Schwartz and Wolf, 1976:18). This "disposal" took the form of placing single people in the home of a responsible family, the belief being that all people need to be associated with a family to ensure that they live a proper life. The assumption that unmarried individuals could not be trusted to lead a proper life on their own gave rise to the view that the unmarried, regardless of age, were somehow not mature adults. This belief that the progression from engagement to marriage and then to parenthood represents normal growth and development still exists among some life cycle theorists today (see Chapter 2).

Unmarried women and men were commonly seen as defective or incomplete and were often the subject of ridicule. After studying this period, one investigator concluded that "bachelors were rare and were viewed with disapproval. They were in the class of suspected criminals" (Calhoun, 1917, 1:67). Single women were not spared derogatory labels either. Those women not married by age 20 were referred to as "stale maids." Unmarried women 5 years older became known as "ancient maids." Even today, terms such as old maid and spinster convey negative connotations.

Why were single people treated this way? The devaluation of singlehood was in large measure a result of the high value attached to marriage, a value strongly associated with religious beliefs. The Bible stressed the importance of marriage and family life. For example, in the book of Genesis (2:24), men are enjoined "to leave father and mother and cleave to a wife." There were also practical considerations. The early settlers were concerned with economic and personal survival. Hence, there was an imperative to increase the population and to share the burdens of earning a livelihood in this new land. Writer Alice Earle (1893:36) took note of this in her reflection on New England customs: "What could he do, how could he live in that new land without a wife? There were no housekeepers and he would scarcely have been allowed to have one if there were. What could a woman do in that new settlement among unbroken forests, uncultivated lands, without a husband?"

In sum, marriage was seen as a practical necessity, and singlehood was not considered an acceptable alternative because "the man without a family was evading a civic duty . . . and the husbandless woman had no purpose in life" (Spruill, 1938:137). Despite the negative ways in which single people were viewed and treated in colonial America, their numbers in the general population gradually increased as political, social, and economic changes combined to create new opportunities for them, especially for women.

Singlehood in the Nineteenth and Early Twentieth Centuries

The percentage of single women began to increase in the last decades of the eighteenth century and continued to do

Like many women in her day, Susan B. Anthony (1820–1906) received several proposals of marriage. She refused them all, preferring her independence to being a wife and homemaker. She devoted her life to the pursuit of equal rights for women.

so into the nineteenth. At its height, the trend represented some 11 percent of American women, those born between 1865 and 1875 (cited in Chambers-Schiller, 1984:3). This historical increase is important to recognize, because we tend to think of developments in our own period as unique rather than as a continuation of long-term trends. Sociologist Edward Kain, in his book *The Myth of Family Decline* (1990), documents the fact that, contrary to popular belief, the increase in the numbers of never-married people since the 1970s is not a new phenomenon. Rather, it represents a return to historically higher levels of singlehood that began to decline markedly only after 1940. For example, in 1890, 15 percent of women and 27 percent of men aged 30 to 34 had never married. In 1940, the comparable figures for this age group were 15 and 21 percent, respectively; by 1970, they had dropped to 6 and 9 percent (Kain, 1990:75). By 2003, however, the rates had increased to 23 percent for women and 33 percent for men (U.S. Census Bureau, 2004–2005).

What accounted for the increase in the single population in the nation's early years? As we saw in Chapter 5, marriage rates are related to changing demographic, economic, political, and cultural factors. So, too, are changing rates of singlehood. In the early 1800s, industrialization created new jobs for both women and men, allowing them a measure of financial independence. Furthermore, some occupations were considered incompatible with marriage. For example, it was common for communities to have rules requiring teachers to resign when they got married (Punke, 1940). Thus, the choice to continue teaching was also a choice to remain single.

The Industrial Revolution was not the only event contributing to the growth of the single population. Earlier, the American Revolution gave rise to a new cultural ethos that emphasized individualism, self-reliance, and freedom of choice in pursuing one's goals. According to historian Lee Chambers-Schiller (1984), society's views of the unmarried woman moderated somewhat in this climate. Most Americans no longer thought of singlehood as a sin, even though to many it still seemed unnatural. An analysis of the professional and popular literature of the late nineteenth and early twentieth centuries reveals a changing attitude toward both singlehood and marriage (Freeman and Klaus, 1984). Some of that literature sounds quite modern, especially in terms of today's growing criticism of marriage and the perception that singlehood is preferable to a bad marriage. For example, in a Roper Organization survey (1990), 56 percent of single women and 59 percent of single men agreed with the statement, "I'm happier than most of my married friends."

The view that marriages should be happy rather than merely a duty evolved gradually during the early nineteenth century. The very title of Chambers-Schiller's (1984) study, *Liberty, a Better Husband*, provides insight into the decision to remain single. Marriage could now be viewed as an option, and more women chose not to marry; some even proclaimed their decision publicly. As one nineteenth-century woman explained: "I've chosen my life as deliberately as my sisters and brothers have chosen theirs. . . . I want to be a spinster, and I want to be a good one" (quoted in Freeman and Klaus, 1984:396). Other women saw their singlehood as a form of protest against the demands and restrictions of middle-class marriage and became advocates for women's rights. This criticism of marriage, the availability of employment, the opening of education to women, and the early women's movement all worked to the advantage of the unmarried, who were increasingly portrayed in a more positive light. Thus, there emerged a new ideology, called "the cult of single blessedness," which proved beneficial to families and the community at large. It became socially acceptable for unmarried women to care for aging parents, the orphaned, the sick, and the indigent members of the community. Over time, such work came to be seen as appropriate vocations for women.

Singlehood Today: Current Demographic Trends

Although marriage remains the most common living arrangement for Americans today, significant numbers of people are choosing to be unmarried for all or at least part lives. In 2004, 29 percent of all people 18 and over had never married, up from 15.6 percent in 1970 (Saluter, 1994; U.S. Census Bureau, 2006). Although this pattern holds true across race and ethnic groups, the proportion of nonmarried adults is lowest for whites (22 percent), highest for blacks (39 percent), with Latino/as in the middle (30 percent). Most Americans who eventually marry do so by their mid-30s. Thus, as age increases, the proportion who have never married declines. This can readily be seen in Table 7.1, which compares the percentages of both sexes remaining single beyond the usual ages of marriage. With the exception of the very latest years, the percentage of never-married men exceeds that of never-married women.

Among both sexes, African Americans and Latinos have higher rates of singlehood than do their white counterparts:

26 percent of white males, 42 percent of African American males, and 36 percent of Latinos were single compared to 18 percent of white females, 37 percent of African American females, and 25 percent of Latinas (U.S. Census Bureau, 2004–2005). Some social scientists attribute the higher rates among blacks and Latinos to the economic disadvantages and higher unemployment rates experienced by these groups, especially among men (Ooms, 2002). Demographic trends play an especially crucial role in the lower marriage rate of African Americans, especially of African American women. High incarceration and mortality rates among young African American men have dramatically decreased the pool of marriageable men. To be specific, while urban white men face a 2 percent change of being killed in street crimes, the rate is 10 percent for black men. In 2002, 12 percent of black men were either in prison or in jail compared to 4 percent of Latinos and nearly 2 percent of white men (Harrison and Karberg, 2003). Furthermore, African American parents often encourage their daughters to put education before marriage (Higginbotham and Weber, 1995). As we saw in Chapter 5, a greater number of black women than black men are college-educated. Many of these women may place a higher value on academic achievement and consequently may forgo marriage if they do not find a partner who meets their expectations (Perry, Steele, and Hillard, 2003). In addition, more African American men than women marry members of other racial or ethnic groups (Kinnon, 2003).

Comparable census data on the marital status of Asian American and Native American women reveal a similar pattern of delayed marriage. For example, in 1980, 24 percent of Asian American women and 21 percent of Native American women aged 25 to 29 had never been married. By 2000, the corresponding rates had increased to 41 percent and 42 percent, respectively (Lichter and Qian, 2004). Nevertheless, by midlife (ages 40 to 44) relatively few women across all race and ethnic groups are likely to remain single. In 2000, only 9 percent of white women, 7 percent of Latinas, and 8 percent of Asian American women were single. However, the rates were higher for Native American women (15 percent) and for African American women (18 percent), both rates related to a smaller pool of marriageable men in those groups due, in large measure, to factors mentioned earlier—restricted economic opportunities, higher mortality and incarceration rates.

The United States is not the only country to experience a growth in the never-married segment of the population. In fact, Britain is predicting that if present trends continue, married people will soon be in the minority. According to the government's Office for National Statistics, the percentage of married men is expected to fall from 53 percent in 2003 to 42 percent in 2031, while the percentage of married women will decline from 50 to 40 percent. The proportion of women who have never married is expected to rise from 28 to 39 percent between 2003 and 2031. The change in the percentage of never-married men is expected to be even more dramatic, increasing from 35 percent to almost 50 percent during that same period ("Marriage on the Rocks in Britain," 2005). Even in countries like Indonesia where marriage has been considered almost compulsory for most

TABLE 7.1

Never-Married by Age and Sex, 2004

Age	Sex	
	Males	Females
18 to 19 years old	98.6%	95.5%
20 to 24 years old	86.4	75.4
25 to 29 years old	56.6	40.8
30 to 34 years old	32.2	23.7
35 to 39 years old	23.4	14.6
40 to 44 years old	17.6	12.2
45 to 54 years old	12.1	9.3
55 to 64 years old	5.9	5.4
65 to 74 years old	4.4	3.7
75 years old and over	3.6	3.8

Source: Adapted from U.S. Census Bureau, 2006, *Statistical Abstract of the United States: 2006* (Washington, DC: Government Printing Office): Table 51, p. 50.

adults, statistical trends indicate that the incidence of delayed marriage is increasing rapidly. The proportion of never-married women aged 30 to 34 has risen from 2.2 to 6.9 percent between 1970 and 2000 while the increase for men was 6.1 to 11.8 percent, This trend was particularly marked in large cities. For example, in Jakarta 14.3 percent of females aged 30 to 34 had never married; the rate for their male counterparts was 21.1 percent (cited in Situmorang, 2005). Similar patterns have been reported in other Southeast Asian cities such as Manila, Bangkok, and Singapore. In Japan, women are delaying marriage or not getting married at all because they fear marriage will mean having to give up careers, financial independence, and personal freedom. Their behavior has triggered an unintended demographic crisis, a sharp decline in the birth rate in the traditional, male-dominated Japanese culture, which has government officials alarmed (Atoh, 2001).

DEMYSTIFYING SINGLEHOOD

In his analysis of the lifestyles of singles, sociologist Peter Stein (1976) observed that for many years most Americans, including social scientists, thought of single people as "those who fail to marry," believing that no one would want to remain single by choice. Stein's work has helped dispel this myth and shows that the decision of whether to marry or stay single is conditioned by psychological, social, cultural, and economic factors. He characterizes these factors as a series of **pushes,** or negative factors in a current situation, and **pulls,** or attractions to a potential situation.

Individual Decision Making

On the one hand, people are pushed toward marriage by pressures from parents, cultural expectations, loneliness, a fear of independence, and a feeling of guilt about staying single. On the other hand, parental approval, the marriages of friends, physical attraction and emotional attachment to another person, and a desire for security, social status, and children pull people toward marriage. In a similar vein, the perception of relationships as suffocating and as obstacles to self-development as well as an awareness of the high divorce rate may push people toward singlehood. Career opportunities, a sense of self-sufficiency, freedom, and the desire for psychological and social autonomy may pull people toward singlehood.

Although Stein's data represent common patterns of experiences, pressures, and desires, these are not necessarily experienced in the same way by everyone or even by the same person at different times in the life cycle. For example, some parents exert great pressure on their children to marry; others do not. Some people are self-sufficient in young adulthood but as they get older feel a greater need to be involved with someone else on a daily basis, as voiced by a 34-year-old male: "I've liked being single. It allowed me to travel to exotic places, change jobs several times, and really get to know who I am as a person, but now that I've done all that, I'm ready to share my life with someone."

The Influence of Social and Economic Forces

The decision of whether to marry is influenced by many factors. Many Americans no longer view marriage as an economic or social necessity. The stigma attached to singlehood has lessened in recent years, and there has been a corresponding reduction in the perceived benefits associated with marriage. Indeed, changes in gender role expectations (see Chapters 3 and 10) may make marriage seem more unattractive to both women and men. On the one hand, some women are putting careers before marriage, not wishing to undertake the conflict involved in balancing work and family. On the other hand, some men delay or forgo marriage because they are reluctant to share in household tasks and child care, now expected by increasing numbers of working women.

Economic factors play a critical role in the decision to stay single. A survey of 9100 college students found that their immediate concerns were finishing their education, establishing themselves in their chosen careers, and paying off their college loans. For now, marriage would have to wait. Nevertheless, most of those surveyed expected to marry some day (Levine and Cureton, 1998). So, too, do their younger counterparts. In a recent survey, a majority of teens (aged 15 to 19) agreed with the statement, "It is better for a person to get married than to go through life being single." Teen boys were more likely than teen girls to hold this view (68.9 to 54.2 percent). Although teen girls of different racial/ethnic groups favor marriage nearly equally (55.4 percent of Latinas, 54.4 percent of whites and 52.1 percent of blacks), the picture is different for teen boys. Black teens are less likely than white teens and young Latinos to favor marriage, 59.8 percent, 70.3 percent, and 74.7 percent respectively (Flanigan, Huffman, and Smith, 2005). Perhaps at this early age, girls already perceive that expanding economic opportunities have provided more women with the means to be financially independent outside of marriage. Research has shown that women in labor markets with favorable economic opportunities have lower rates of marriage than do other women (White, 1981) Researcher Judy Rollins (1986) found that most of her single respondents believe being unmarried will help them establish their careers. Similarly, increasing numbers of women in Southeast Asia are giving priority to their careers and a newly found sense of independence. Although many still retain a positive view of marriage and had expected to marry when they were younger, they now realize that they may have postpone marriage too long and are now unable to find suitable mates (Situmorang, 2005). Men may also delay marriage for the same reasons as women, choosing to devote their energy to finishing their education and establishing their careers. Declining economic fortunes, however, may contribute to an increase in the single population, especially for men. Women may perceive men who are unemployed or who earn low wages as less attractive candidates for marriage (Teachman, Tedrow, and Crowder, 2000), or such men may not want to undertake additional responsibilities until their job situation improves. Some people face other obstacles in finding a suitable marriage partner. People who have a physical or mental disability may find that their intimacy and sexual needs go unfilled because others may perceive them as unattractive or sexless (Kelly, 1995).

Other factors that affect the decision to remain single include the media's more positive images of this lifestyle. For example, TV programs increasingly depict attractive, stylish 30-ish singles on hit shows like *Sex and the City*, *Friends*, and *Will and Grace*, conveying the notion that being single is fun and exciting. And, the increasing visibility of older unmarried people leading satisfying and meaningful lives such as talk show host Oprah Winfrey and Secretary of State Condoleeza Rice has enabled younger adults to find a greater number of role models to emulate. Finally, over the last several decades, the liberalization of sexual norms and the availability of contraceptive devices have freed women and men to pursue an active social and sexual life outside of marriage. Nevertheless, controversy still shadows this liberalization and many Americans, especially those on the religious right, oppose easier access to some contraceptive devices (see Debating Social Issues box). And, as we have seen in Chapter 6, the fear of AIDS may constrain the expression of this freedom.

Despite increased opportunities to choose singlehood, not everyone who remains single does so by choice. As discussed in Chapter 5, some people find their desire for marriage frustrated by a marriage squeeze. The influence of these social and economic factors is reflected in Stein's typology of singlehood.

Types of Singles

Using the reasons that respondents gave for being single, Stein (1981) developed a typology of singlehood that places singles, including those who have never married and those who were formerly married, into four different categories based on the likelihood of their remaining unmarried:

- *Voluntary Temporary Singles* are currently unmarried and are not seeking mates. They remain open to the possibility of marrying someday, perhaps after completing their education or becoming established in a career.
- *Voluntary Stable Singles* choose to remain single and see themselves doing so on a permanent basis. Priests and nuns are included in this category.
- *Involuntary Temporary Singles* want to marry and are actively seeking mates.
- *Involuntary Stable Singles* desire marriage but have not yet found a mate. They tend to be older singles who have more or less accepted the probability of remaining single for life.

Sociologist Arthur Shostak (1987) also found four patterns corresponding to Stein's typology. However, he used more colorful terms to describe the same types of singles: ambivalents, resolveds, wishfuls, and regretfuls. Similarly, Robert Staples (1981b) developed a fivefold typology describing the variations among African American single men:

- The *free-floating single* dates a variety of people and is unattached.
- The *single in an open-couple relationship* dates others, but has a steady partner.

- The *single in a closed-couple relationship* expects her or his partner to be faithful.
- The *committed single* thinks of the relationship as permanent and may be engaged or cohabiting.
- The *accommodationist* is generally an older single who lives alone and who does not date.

Each of these typologies calls attention to the special characteristics of the single state: its heterogeneity and its fluidity. At any given time the population of singles is composed of individuals who either choose or hope to be single for only a limited period of time as well as those who plan to be or who will find themselves single for the rest of their lives. Perhaps not surprisingly, research indicates that individuals who are voluntarily single tend to have a better sense of well-being than the involuntarily single (Shostak, 1987).

Regardless of which category of singlehood nevermarried people find themselves in, they enjoy certain advantages and cope with some disadvantages resulting from this lifestyle. Before reading the next section, reflect on your perceptions of a single lifestyle.

 Using either Schwartz's, Stein's, Shostak's or Staples' typology, can you place yourself (if single) and/or your nonmarried friends in distinct categories? On what basis did you make those decisions? What do you see as the advantages/disadvantages of being single? How do your perceptions compare with those identified by researchers in the following section?

Advantages and Disadvantages of Singlehood

Studies have found a general agreement among single people regarding both the advantages and disadvantages of a single lifestyle. Among the most frequently cited advantages are personal freedom, financial independence, privacy, greater opportunities to pursue careers and other activities, and more time to develop a variety of friendships, including sexual relationships (DeMont, 2000). Consider what 34-year-old Vivian had to say about her life:

> My life is my own. I can do housework in the middle of the night, be a total vegetable all weekend, eat at ridiculous hours, or not eat at all. No one messes up my place when it's clean; no one gripes when it's dirty. I can keep fattening foods out of the house without depriving anyone. I can pig out without hiding. I see only the movies/shows/concerts I want to see. No one tells me how to spend my money. I may not be the best financial manager, but it's still my dough, and I'd rather spend it on clothes than stereo equipment. (Quoted in Lavin, 1991:3)

As we saw earlier in the case of Japan and other Asian countries, marriage in patriarchal societies often results in a considerable loss of personal freedom and financial independence for women. Thus, in those societies, women are increasingly reluctant to give up their single status. For example, women in Thailand are even getting certificates to

DEBATING SOCIAL ISSUES

SHOULD PLAN B BE MADE AVAILABLE OVER THE COUNTER?

In 1999, after much public controversy and debate, the U.S. Food and Drug Administration (FDA) granted Barr Laboratories, Inc., permission to sell its morning-after contraceptive levonorgestrel, marketed as Plan B, as a prescription-only drug. The contraceptive was called the morning-after pill because it must be taken within 72 hours after unprotected sex to prevent pregnancy. Plan B was to be used in emergency cases and never intended for use as a routine contraceptive In 2003, the company applied for permission to sell it over the counter to make it easier for women to obtain. In December of that year, an FDA expert advisory panel voted 23 to 4 in favor of the change. The then FDA commissioner Mark McClellan promised a decision in a "matter of months." However, reaction to the recommendation was immediate and intense.

Proponents praised the recommendation, citing studies that showed Plan B's safety and effectiveness in reducing unplanned pregnancy either due to unprotected sex or contraceptive failure and the fact that it would take away the embarrassment many women, especially unmarried women, had in having to obtain a doctor's prescription. Advocates of the recommendation also saw it as a victory for reproductive rights, indicating that women who could not or would not see a doctor after unprotected sex would now have access to Plan B. Additionally, supporters believed that easier access would eventually result in lower number of abortions as a result of a decrease in unwanted pregnancies. In contrast, opponents saw this proposed action as giving women more incentive to have unprotected sex and that it would encourage teenage sex. Jennifer Taylor of the anti-abortion Human Life International voiced the opinion that women who use emergency contraception show "an inability to control themselves in sexual situations" (cited in Bailey, 2005). Although the FDA does not consider the drug to cause an abortion, some opponents of the drug believed that under some circumstances it can cause a fertilized egg to die.

Former FDA Commissioner Lester Crawford

On May 6, 2004, the FDA rejected the recommendation for over-the-counter sale of Plan B, claiming it had not been tested in enough adolescent females to prove that it is safe for them to use. This set off another controversial firestorm. FDA staffers noted this was the first time this issue was raised and proponents of the recommendation viewed the FDA's action as a political move to appease the prolife constituency. Barr Laboratories was asked to submit more information and there was a suggestion that it seek permission for over-the-counter for women 17 and older and prescription-only sales for those younger than 17. However, on August 26, 2005, the newly installed FDA commissioner Lester Crawford announced a further delay on a promised final ruling, claiming that the proposed division by age poses "unique" regulatory problems that cannot be resolved with a formal

rule-making, which could take years (Kaufman, 2005). Susan F. Wood, assistant FDA commissioner for women's health and director of the Office of Women's Health resigned in protest, saying "I can no longer serve as staff when scientific and clinical evidence, fully evaluated and recommended for approval by the professional staff here, has been overruled" (cited in Kaufman, 2005). Critics of Plan B welcomed her departure. Crawford has since resigned his position. As of this writing, no final decision has yet been made on Plan B.

What do you think? Which side of this argument do you favor? Explain. Do you think it is the role of the FDA to decide on matters of values and morals—for example, should the FDA be able to rule on drugs on the basis of how someone will use them?

document their single status to safeguard their personal freedoms. Under Thai law, women lose many rights when they marry. For example, a married woman must have her husband's permission to conduct business transactions, while single women can do this freely on their own. Marrying a foreigner further disadvantages women because a foreigner is not allowed to buy land or own more than 49 percent of a business, nor can he give his wife permission to engage in such transactions (Gelken, 1999).

Given the negative view of singlehood in the past, it would be surprising if no disadvantages were associated with being single. Among the disadvantages that singles report are loneliness and lack of companionship, being excluded from couples' events or feeling uncomfortable in social settings involving mostly couples, not having children, and social disapproval of their lifestyle (Barker, 2005). Jeffrey Ullman, president and founder of Great Expectations, a national video-dating service, summed up the view of many singles: "Nothing is wrong with being alone. However, it has a very ugly, nasty and debilitating side, and that is being lonely when you don't want to be alone" (quoted in Pauly, 1992:5). Another disadvantage of living alone is more gender-specific. Interviews with single women reveal considerable concern about issues of safety. They report that decisions about where they live, their mode of transportation, and which leisure activities they engage in are influenced by their fears of assault (Chasteen, 1994). This finding is consistent with that found in a recent survey indicating that 50 percent of women respondents said there was an area within a mile of their homes where they would be afraid to walk alone at night. Only 19 percent of male respondents said there is such an area near their homes (Said, 2005).

These advantages and disadvantages are general categories and do not necessarily apply in every individual case or at all times in the life cycle. For example, not all singles are uncomfortable in social settings involving couples; some mix easily in such situations. Economic status also affects how singlehood is experienced, as singles with low incomes or singles who lose their jobs may not be able to implement the freedoms associated with being single. Additionally, changing family circumstances may alter a lifestyle in the direction of less freedom and more responsibility for others, as is often the case for single adult children who find themselves caring for sick or elderly relatives.

SINGLE LIFESTYLES

The major challenge facing single people through the ages has been building a satisfying life in a society highly geared toward marriage. Until recently, the general tendency in U.S. popular culture has been to portray singles as belonging in one of two stereotypical groups. On the one side is the "swinging single"—the party goer who is carefree, uncommitted, sexually adventuresome, and the subject of envy by married friends. Poles apart from this image is the "lonely loser"—the unhappy, frustrated, depressed single who lives alone and survives on TV dinners, a fate few people would envy.

How accurate are these images? Research on the lives of single women and men contradicts these stereotypes and reveals a wide variety of patterns. For example, one in-depth study of 73 white, never-married, college-educated women and men over age 30 found significant variation in how these singles went about organizing their lives. Although there was some overlapping of activities, six different lifestyle patterns were observed, each having a central focus:

- *Supportive:* These singles spend much of their time helping and supporting others and have careers in the teaching and nursing professions.
- *Passive:* These singles spend much of their time alone, have low levels of social participation and more negative outlooks on life, and show little initiative in shaping their lives.
- *Activists:* These singles center their lives around political or community involvement. They derive a great deal of satisfaction from working for social causes.
- *Individualistic:* These singles strive for autonomy and self-growth. They see their independence, freedom, and privacy as an environment in which to grow and develop as a whole person. They enjoy reading, hobbies, and other solitary pursuits.
- *Social:* These singles have extensive personal relationships and spend little time alone. Friends and social activities have a high priority in their lives. They are deeply involved in hobbies, organizations, and family activities.
- *Professional:* These singles organize their lives around work and identify with their occupational roles. Most of their time and energy is spent on their careers (Schwartz, 1976).

Another study of a representative sample of never-married women and men, including both whites and blacks, also revealed a rich diversity among this population. However, this research also found that, compared with married persons, persons who never marry are overrepresented in both extremes of social interaction. Thus, singles had higher rates of never interacting with relatives, friends, and neighbors as well as higher rates of seeing these support networks several times a week. Similar patterns were found among never-married women in urban centers in Southeast Asia (Situmorang, 2005) In contrast, married persons reported frequencies of interaction within these two extremes (Seccombe and Ishii-Kuntz, 1994).

Thus, the single population, like their married peer group, is not a homogeneous group. Singles differ not only in lifestyle orientation but also in the type of living arrangements they select. Earlier we discussed the boomerang generation, adult children who remain in or return to the parental home. The majority of this group has never married, although included in this group are some separated, divorced and even some widowed children. Overall, however, as adult children age, they are more likely to live alone. This pattern is more pronounced for women, especially in the later years when 17 percent of women live alone compared to 5 percent of men (see Figure 7.1). This is due in large measure to two factors: women live, on average, 5 to 7 years longer than men and divorced men are more likely to remarry than divorced women—and hence are more likely to be living with a spouse in their later years.

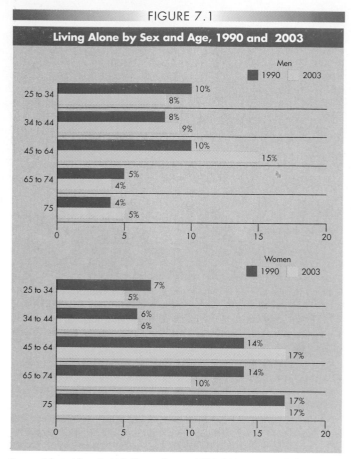

FIGURE 7.1

Living Alone by Sex and Age, 1990 and 2003

Source: Adapted from the U.S. Census Bureau, 2004–2005, *Statistical Abstract of the United States: 2004–2005.* (Washington, DC: Government Printing Office): Table 65, p. 54.

TABLE 7.2

Median Income by Household Type, 2000

	Married Couples	Single-Person Household	
		Male	Female
All Households	59,343	26,723	18,163
White	60,080	27,326	18,695
Black	50,729	21,286	14,825
Latina/o	41,116	20,597	13,295

Source: Adapted from the U.S. Census Bureau, 2002, *Statistical Abstract of the United States: 2002* (Washington, DC: Government Printing Office).

A number of unmarried people live in specially designed singles areas—apartments or condominiums developed to meet the perceived needs of this population. These areas offer access to swimming pools, health facilities, restaurants, and singles bars. Although these complexes have attracted a number of singles, especially younger ones, the majority of the never-married are dispersed throughout the general population. Some singles prefer the excitement of city living; others desire the less dense suburban areas or the openness of the countryside. With the changes in credit regulations beginning in the 1970s, more singles were able to get mortgages and become homeowners. According to the National Association of Realtors, single women bought 18 percent of all existing homes in 2004—up from their 14 percent market share in 1995. At the same time single men's share of the market fell from 9 to 8 percent (cited in Miller, 2005). The ability to buy a house, however, is dependent on income and, as we will see, as a category, single people do not fare quite as well as do their married peers.

Income

Earlier we noted that one of the perceived advantages of being single is financial independence. How well off are single people? Are they better off economically than married

people? These questions are difficult to answer because the needs of these populations may vary significantly. On the one hand, married people with children may need a larger living space than a single person does. On the other hand, singles may find that they spend more on food and traveling, as their married counterparts benefit from buying in quantity and sharing double-occupancy rates. We can, however, gain some insight into the relative status of single people by comparing their median income with that of their married peers. As Table 7.2 reveals, female householders living alone had a median income of $18,163; the comparable figure for male householders living alone was $26,723. In contrast, married couples with both spouses present had a median income of $59,343. There is also considerable variation in income across race and ethnicity with Latina and black single female householders having the lowest median incomes.

What factors explain these differences between the married and single populations? One possible explanation is that singles, as a whole, are younger and less experienced than are the married. This argument fails to hold up, however, when age differences are controlled. At the same age levels, singles still earn less than their married peers. Two factors are particularly significant in this regard. First, many married households have more than one wage earner, thus enhancing household earnings. Second, these earning differences may reflect a systematic bias against singles in the workplace. For example, certain data show that marital status affects men's wages. Numerous cross-sectional studies have documented the fact that, on average, married men earn more than men who have never married, with wage differentials found to range between 3 and 40 percent (Korenman and Neumark, 1991; Schoeni, 1995; Chun and Lee, 2001).

What accounts for this wage difference? Economists Robert Nakosteen and Michael Zimmer (2001) found evidence to support a selection hypothesis, i.e., men with higher earning potential are more likely to get married. However, British academics Elena Bardasi and Mark Taylor (2005) analyzed the hourly wages of men who have been interviewed annually since 1991 and concluded it was not selection but a specialization effect that explained the male marriage premium, i.e., as long as wives stayed home taking care of household tasks, husbands were free to concentrate on work and increase their productivity, and hence their wages. The researchers found that when wives went to work, the wage premium decreased or disappeared altogether.

More people today are delaying marriage or remaining single permanently. As their numbers have grown, so, too, has societal acceptance of nonmarital lifestyles. These single friends enjoy an afternoon bicycle trip.

Still other research suggests yet another factor at work—employer attitudes. According to this view, some employers assume that married men have greater financial needs than single men and reward them accordingly, while other employers believe married men are more stable, more dedicated to their careers, better able to get along with others, and less likely to cost the company money by changing jobs. Thus, they are more eager to hire married men and reward them more (Loh, 1996). An earlier survey of top executives found some support for that view. Although half of the top executive women were single, less than a tenth of the men were (Bradsher, 1989). In a similar vein, a 30-year-old graduate student told the authors about an experience he had looking for a job in public relations when he was 27: "When I was being interviewed, he [the personnel manager] kept referring to the social requirements of the job—entertaining, attending fundraisers and such. I could tell by his attitude that he wanted someone who was married, so I said I was engaged. The funny thing was, I didn't get the job, but I did get married a year later." Given the high percentage of men postponing marriage until their late 20s and early 30s, employer attitudes and behaviors, much like those of the larger society, have become more accepting of single lifestyles. Additionally, there is some evidence to show that the earnings premium paid to married men compared with never-married men is declining (Gray, 1997).

SUPPORT NETWORKS

As we saw in Chapter 4, everyone, regardless of marital status, has intimacy needs and must work at developing intimate and supportive relationships. Singles who live alone confront a greater challenge in meeting their need for intimacy. They respond to this challenge by establishing strong friendships. A growing body of literature reveals that singles, especially women, create their own "family," a support group of friends who function in much the same way as families do—exchanging services, traveling together, giving and receiving advice, celebrating birthdays and holidays, and

creating shared rituals and meanings (Inman, 1996; Johnson, 1996). Both women and men value friends, but in somewhat different ways. Women concentrate on establishing close, emotional bonds, whereas men focus more on sharing their interests and their values.

Another key intimacy need experienced by many people regardless of marital status is the bond that exists between parent and child. This need can present special problems for single people. Historically, great stigma has been attached to having children out of wedlock, and single women and men were denied the right to adopt children. However, changing attitudes as well as new reproductive technologies have made it possible for single people to bear and raise children and laws now permit single adults to adopt children (see Family Profile box). Consequently, more singles are becoming parents, a topic that will be discussed in Chapter 9.

Happiness and Life Satisfaction

No examination of the single lifestyle would be complete without a discussion of happiness and life satisfaction. How satisfied with their lives are never-married people? In the past, studies in the United States consistently found that married people reported higher levels of happiness and satisfaction than their never-married counterparts (Lee, Seccombe, and Shehan, 1991; Mastekaasa, 1992). Similar findings were reported in a large number of studies for different countries and time periods (see, for example Diener et al., 2000). The two most commonly reported explanations for the difference in happiness between married and never-married individuals relate to the benefits associated with marriage and a selection factor. In the first case, marriage is credited with providing financial security, ongoing companionship, psychological support, and increased self-esteem, in large part because marital status is positively valued in the larger society (Waite and Gallagher, 2000). In the second case, longitudinal data suggest that singles who get married are happier than individuals who stay single (Stutzer and Frey, 2003). Nevertheless, these data must be interpreted with some caution. Questions of happiness and life satisfaction are not always easy to answer for several reasons. First, happiness and life satisfaction depend on a number of factors other than marital status per se, such as good health, satisfying work, personal growth, financial security, love, family, and friends. For example, research has found that the more time spent socializing with friends, the happier the person regardless of his or her gender, age group, income group, and marital status (Powdthavee, 2005). Other research has found that physical health was the best single predictor of self-reports of happiness, followed by income, education, and marital status (Firebaugh and Tach, 2005).

Second, every living arrangement contains advantages and disadvantages. Some people may experience more of the advantages, whereas others with different life circumstances may endure more disadvantages. Third, life satisfaction is not static; perceptions of satisfaction may vary over time depending on the changes occurring in an individual's life and in the society at large. For instance, the percentage of married people reporting they were very happy declined between 1972 and 1988, whereas during this same time the

FAMILY PROFILE

VICKI, ALEX, AND KATE BYARD

Length of Relationship: 8 Years

Challenges of Being a Single Parent: I am a single lesbian who had breast cancer at an early age, so becoming a parent was difficult. When I began to research my options, I learned that the chemotherapy I had undergone made artificial insemination an ineffective and possibly unsafe choice. Also, many adoption agencies won't place children with an "out" homosexual, not to mention one who has had a major illness. Eventually, I found an adoption agency that places only African American and biracial newborns, and this agency welcomed my application. With the agency's full knowledge of my sexual orientation and cancer history, I adopted both my children as newborns. Alex is now 8 and Kate is 6 years old.

The greatest challenge I face as a single parent is that my family's well-being is limited to the resources of only one person: just my time, my finances, my energy, my emotional reserves, my wisdom, and at times, my lack of all these. Parents who have

Kate, Vicki, and Alex Byard

a partner or spouse tell me that I'm lucky to not have to compromise with anyone about my parenting decisions, yet I often envy the ability of two parents to divide the labor of rearing a family. I feel as if I work three shifts every day: teaching classes as a university professor while my kids are in school, being a full-time parent once school gets out until they're in bed, then doing much of my class preparation, grading, and domestic chores late into the night. Because my mother and siblings live in another state, when I'm sick, exhausted,

or simply cranky, there is no one else to take over.

Yet despite such difficulties, I know I have made the right decision in creating my family. Alex and Kate are inseparable playmates, and I'm blessed to have the companionship of such beautiful, funny, imaginative children.

Parenting Philosophy: Because our family is conspicuously nontraditional, one of my major parenting goals is to help my children feel comfortable with their own identities. We live in a large city that is racially and ethnically diverse, which lessens the stares we receive from strangers, and I would not consider moving to a more homogenous area. Together, we learn about and regularly celebrate my children's African American heritage. We've also developed friendships with other families like ours: interracial families, families formed through adoption, and/or families with homosexual parents. I also give my children a wide range of experiences to help them discover their own interests. My hope is that despite whatever struggles my children face as they grow to adulthood, they'll find comfort and strength in our love for each other.

---

percentage of single people reporting they were very happy increased (Glenn and Weaver, 1988; Lee et al., 1991). There is a relationship between the way society evaluates a lifestyle and the perceived desirability of that status. Historian Stephanie Coontz (2005:258) points out, "By 1978 only 25 percent of Americans still believed that people who remained single by choice were 'sick,' 'neurotic,' or 'immoral,' as most had thought it was in the 1950s. By 1978, 75 percent of the population thought that it was morally okay to be single and have children." As attitudes toward singlehood became more positive, never-married individuals were freer to think more positively about themselves and to express high levels of satisfaction and happiness with their lifestyle.

A popular belief in the United States is that singlehood may be an exciting and satisfying lifestyle for young adults but that the opposite is true for older singles. How accurate is this belief? The next section focuses attention on a rarely studied population, the never-married elderly.

The Never-Married in Later Life

Earlier in this chapter we discussed the fact that in the past marriage was perceived as the ticket to adult status. It was

also assumed that marriage was a means of achieving security and well-being in old age. Conversely, it was popularly assumed that elderly singles must be lonely and isolated individuals. Do you know any older singles? Is this view simply another version of the stereotyped images of singles, or does it reflect the lifestyles of the never-married elderly? To answer that question, let us first find out who the elderly singles are.

In 2003, nearly 36 million Americans were 65 years of age and older. Of that number, approximately 1.4 million had never married. Table 7.3 shows men are slightly more likely to have remained unmarried than women, except for those 85 and older. Just as with younger singles, numerous factors account for the marital status of older people. Although some older people are unmarried by choice, for those who want to marry, gender plays a role. A longer life expectancy and a marriage gradient that favors men mean that older women find a limited pool of eligible males in their age categories, and those males who are eligible often have few resources with which to attract a prospective mate. Older women are also more likely than older men to have responsibilities for caring for elderly parents, which limit their marital prospects.

TABLE 7.3
Never Married Elderly by Age and Sex, 2003

Age	Both Sexes	Men	Women
65 and Over	3.9	4.3	3.7
65–74	4.0	4.6	3.4
75–84	3.9	4.1	3.8
85+	3.7	2.8	4.2

Source: Federal Agency Forum on Age-Related Statistics, 2004, *Older Americans 2004: Key Indicators of Well-Being* (Accessed October 27, 2005; http://www.agingstats.gov/chartbook2004/tables-population.html#Indicators%203).

Our examination of the lifestyles of elderly singles is hampered by the fact that relatively little systematic research has been done on this population. Therefore, while instructive, the generalizations that we can make are limited and in need of further testing. Three decades ago gerontologist Jaber Gubrium (1975, 1976) reviewed what research had been done on elderly singles and concluded that (1) they tend to be lifelong isolates, (2) they are not particularly lonely, (3) they evaluate everyday life in much the same way that their married peers do (both groups are more positive than the widowed or divorced), and (4) due to their single status, they avoid the desolation of bereavement that follows the death of a spouse.

The "Lifelong Isolate" Reconsidered Later research has challenged some of these findings. For example, in his study of older men who live alone, Robert Rubinstein (1986) raises questions about the ambiguity of the meaning of "lifelong isolate." Rubinstein points out that the majority of the never-married men in his study spent many years living with other family members, particularly parents, and therefore could hardly be classified as isolates. These respondents did experience loneliness, but much less so than many of the widowers in his sample did. Although acknowledging that the married elderly may experience a unique form of desolation at the death of a spouse, Rubinstein argues that the death of a parent or sibling (and we would add friends) can be equally devastating to single people. We discuss how people cope with death and dying in Chapter 15.

Rubinstein's sample was small and exclusively male. Thus, we do not know if these patterns are typical of most older single men or to what extent these findings might apply to older women. Other research, however, indicates that there may be two distinct patterns among the older unmarried population. Some elderly people do experience a degree of isolation. Pat Keith (1986:392), in his analysis of census data, reported that about 33 percent of the elderly never see neighbors, about 30 percent never see friends, and 21 percent of the men and 14 percent of the women never see relatives. These findings must be interpreted carefully, however. Factors other than marital status may be better predictors of isolation in old age. Older singles with health problems, lower levels of education, and low-status occupations tend to be the most isolated. A second pattern appears more frequently: Many elderly singles lead active social lives. For instance, Keith found that more than 50 percent of all older singles interact with family, friends, and neighbors. More recent research also suggests that memberships in different types of social organizations help augment an older person's social network, reduces social isolation, and provides sources of identity and self-esteem (Arber, Perren, and Davidson, 2002).

Although a small sample, Katherine Allen's (1989) study of working-class women born in 1910 also shows the importance of family of origin in the lives of the elderly unmarried. Allen found that, like Rubinstein's respondents, the majority of the never-married women in her sample lived with one or both of their parents until their parents died. When this happened, however, they tended to replace the deceased parents with friends or other family members. Women appear to have an advantage over men in this regard due to early socialization experiences requiring them to concentrate more on developing interpersonal skills. Thus, single women often have a more extensive social support system than do single men. Allen also found that the majority of her respondents were pleased with their living arrangements, valued their independence, and had no regrets about not marrying. Later research has also found that never-married women are more involved in social organizations (Arber, 2004) and enjoy more practical and emotional support from family and friends than do their male counterparts (Aber et al., 2003).

Other researchers (for example, Kris Bulcroft and Margaret O'Connor-Roden, 1986) have examined heterosexual relationships and activities among older singles. They discovered that older singles, like their younger counterparts, enjoy movies, dances, travel, camping, plays, and romance. Like their younger counterparts, older singles take advantage of Internet Web sites designed to help them meet other people who share their interests. Additional research is needed to see how race, class, and gender influence the pursuit of such activities.

HETEROSEXUAL COHABITATION

People who are not married choose a variety of living arrangements. Some singles, like Vicki Byard (see the Family Profile box), are opting to share their life with an adopted child. These singles have much in common with other parents (see Chapter 9). Another arrangement that is increasingly popular among both the never-married and the formerly married is cohabitation, popularly referred to as "living together."

Historical Perspectives

In the past, the number of cohabiting couples was difficult to determine because such relationships were not publicly sanctioned; therefore, no systematic attempt was made to collect data on them. Nevertheless, such relationships did exist under a variety of forms. The people most likely to live together outside of legal marriage were the poor or those individuals involved in unpopular relationships, for example, couples with mixed racial, religious, or ethnic backgrounds. Because of the prohibition against lesbian and gay marriages, homosexual couples have often lived together as well. As frequently occurs, however, when living together became widespread among the white middle class, researchers and other social commentators "discovered" it and gave it a new label, one not associated with poor, working-class, and nonwhite groups.

One form of living together that was visible in America's past is **common-law marriage,** "a cohabiting relationship that is based on the mutual consent of the persons involved, is not solemnized by a ceremony, and is recognized as valid by the state" (Stinnet and Birdsong, 1978:84). In sparsely populated areas of the country, clergy or judges often were not readily available to officiate at marriages. Thus, couples intending to wed established a home together without any official ceremony. Later on, if the couple wanted legal recognition of their relationship, they had to prove that they had lived as husband and wife for seven or more years and that they were legally eligible to be married. By the 1920s, most states had abandoned the concept of common-law marriage. Today, only 13 of the 50 states (Alabama, Colorado, Georgia, Idaho, Iowa, Kansas, Montana, Ohio, Oklahoma, Pennsylvania, Rhode Island, South Carolina, and Texas) continue to recognize such marriages and several of them have established a cut-off date whereby only relationships existing before that date can be so recognized.

The Meaning of Cohabitation Today

The U.S. Census Bureau first began to collect data on unmarried-couple households, or what the Bureau calls POSSLQS, "persons of the opposite sex sharing living quarters," in 1960. Unmarried-couple households are defined as those households containing two unrelated adults of the opposite sex (one of whom is the householder) who share a housing unit with or without children under 15 present (Saluter, 1994:vii). There are some problems with this definition—it may miss cohabiting couples in households with more than two adults, and it may include noncohabiting adults who may be boarders, roommates, or employees living in the household. Thus, although this definition is useful for measuring the number of nonrelated adults sharing living space, it does not convey the full meaning of the concept of cohabitation. The 1990 census attempted to improve the estimate of the number of cohabiting households by adding the relationship category "unmarried partner" to the 1990 census questionnaire, defining it as "a person who is not related to the householder, who shares living quarters, and who has a close personal relationship with the householder."

Cohabitation is similar to marriage in that couples create emotional and physical relationships with each other, and in some cases they also bear or rear children. It differs from marriage, however, in that it lacks formal legal, cultural, and religious support. And although attitudes are changing—over half (52 percent) of adults in a national survey said living together was a morally acceptable lifestyle, compared to 41 percent who said it was morally unacceptable for an unmarried couple to live together (Saad, 2001)—it is likely that perceived parental or societal disapproval may still lead some couples to keep their relationship secret. Thus, our interpretation of past and current numbers of cohabiting couples must be somewhat tentative. In all probability, the census data underestimate the total number of cases.

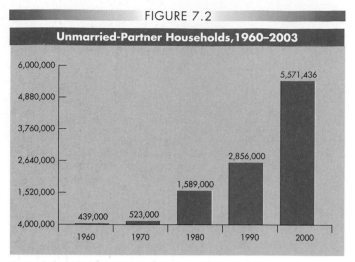

FIGURE 7.2

Unmarried-Partner Households, 1960–2003

Source: Adapted from the U.S. Census Bureau, 1991a "Marital Status and Living Arrangements: March 1990," *Current Population Reports,* Series P-20-450, (Washington, DC: Government Printing Office) 14, Table N; U.S. Census Bureau, 2006, Statistical Abstract of the United States, 2006 (Washington, DC: Government Printing Office) 52, Table 57.

Current Demographic Trends Figure 7.2 traces the growth in numbers of unmarried-partner households since 1960, when they totaled only about 439,000. By 2003, this number had increased to over 5.5 million, consisting of 4,869,703 (87 percent) heterosexual partners and 701,733 (13 percent) same-sex partners. It is easy to see how dramatic this change is when we consider that the number of unmarried couples living together increased tenfold from 1960 to 2000. In 1960, there was one unmarried couple for every hundred married couples; in 2000, there were nine unmarried couples for every hundred married couples.

Because these census data capture living arrangements only at a given point in time, they do not reveal the full extent of the cohabitation experience in the United States. However, when we consider the cohabitation experiences of women 15 to 44 years of age, a much stronger pattern emerges. Over 41 percent of these women have cohabited at some point in their lives. Among women 30 to 34 years of age, the figure is even higher; over 51 percent of these women reported having experienced cohabitation (U.S. Census Bureau, 2000). Sociologists Wendy Manning and Pamela Smock (2005) believe that current measurement strategies probably underestimate the extent of cohabitation. Their interviews with a sample of young women and men with recent cohabitation experience suggest that there is considerable fluidity between singlehood and cohabitation and that many people "slide" or "drift" into (and out of) cohabitation. For some people today, especially among the younger population, cohabitation has become an extension of the courtship process. This pattern is reflected in the changing attitudes of high school seniors. In 1975, a minority of these students (35 percent) agreed or mostly agreed with the statement that "it is usually a good idea for a couple to live together before getting married in order to find out whether they really get along." By 1995, the corresponding figure had climbed to 59 percent (Johnston, Bachman, and O'Malley, 1997). In a more recent study, about two-thirds of all teens aged 15 to 19 said it is okay for a young couple to live together while unmarried. Girls were only slightly less likely than boys to disagree with this position. Among both girls and boys, those who were sexually experienced were more likely to approve of cohabitation than those who were virgins, and those who grew up in two biological or adoptive parent households were more likely to disapprove of cohabitation than were their peers who grew up in other types of households (Flanigan, Huffman, and Smith, 2005). Today over half of all first marriages are now preceded by living together, compared to virtually none 50 years ago. Remarriages are even more likely to be preceded by cohabitation. These data reveal the extent of cohabitation today but do not tell us who the cohabitants are. Do cohabitants differ in significant ways from the noncohabiting population?

Characteristics of Cohabitants Although it is popularly assumed that those who cohabit are young college students, the majority of cohabitants (57 percent) are between the ages of 25 and 44; 18 percent are under 25; and another 24 percent are 45 or older. Most heterosexual cohabiting relationships are childless; only 34 percent of cohabitants have children under 15 years of age living with them, either born out of their current relationship or from a previous relationship. Cohabitants may also have children from a previous marriage who live with the other biological parent (U.S. Census Bureau, 2000). In general, cohabitants tend to be less educated, less likely to identify with an organized religion and/or to attend religious services, and more likely to be politically liberal, unemployed, live in large urban areas, have divorced or remarried parents, and become sexually active at younger ages than their noncohabiting peers (Seltzer, 2000; Amato et al., 2003; Simmons and O'Connell, 2003).

Although cohabitants are found among all classes, ages, and racial and ethnic groups, cohabitation is not uniformly distributed across these groups. For example, Native Americans and Alaskan Natives have the highest rate of cohabitation (17.4 percent) with African Americans a close second (16.9 percent). Asian Americans have the lowest rates (4.7 percent) followed by whites (8.2 percent); Latino/as are in the middle with 12.2 percent (Simmons and O'Connell, 2003). Race also adds an interesting dimension to cohabitation patterns when compared to marriage. An analysis of the 2000 U.S. census data found that across all groups—black, white, Asian, and Latina/o—unmarried-partner households consistently had higher percentages of partners of different races than did married couple households. Thus, research that does not examine cohabiting interracial couples significantly undercounts the extent of intimate interracial contact that exists in the United States today ("Love Is . . . ," 2000). It is probable that the higher rate of interracial cohabitation is due to the social pressure against interracial marriages.

Although we have comparative data on numbers and rates of cohabitation of these racial and ethnic groups, no systematic research on the cohabiting experiences of people of color has been done. Thus, we do not know if people of color attach the same meaning to this experience as do their white counterparts. We do know, however, that cohabitation is less likely to lead to legal marriage among black women than among white women (Oppenheimer, 2003). Additionally, black women and Latinas are more likely than their white counterparts to give birth in a cohabiting relationship. Thirty-five percent of white cohabitors, 54 percent of black cohabitors, and nearly 60 percent of Hispanic cohabitors have children present in the household (cited in Smock and Manning, 2004). These different patterns may reflect the fact that rates of cohabitation are higher among educationally and economically disadvantaged groups, including relatively disadvantaged white women (Bumpass and Lu, 2000). Thus, for these groups, cohabitation may serve as an alternative to marriage, or, as Judith Seltzer (2000) suggests, cohabitation is becoming more like formal marriage in that both are child-rearing institutions. Forty percent of cohabiting households include children, approaching the 46 percent for married couple households (Simmons and O'Connell, 2003). This pattern seems to be especially pronounced in northern Europe (see In Other Places box).

Reasons for Cohabitation

Perhaps some of you reading this book have had experience in a cohabiting relationship. Others of you may be contemplating such a relationship. Take a few minutes to reflect on why you (or others) might consider living together. The following discussion may help you illuminate thoughts you already have on the subject, as well as give you more of a sense of the variety of reasons people have for cohabiting.

Push and Pull Factors In an earlier section of this chapter we discussed Stein's model of pushes and pulls to analyze the decision to marry or to remain single. These conceptual categories are also appropriate for understanding the reasons people give for cohabiting. Among the push factors cohabitants report are loneliness, high costs of living alone, disenchantment with traditional dating and courtship, fear of marital commitment, awareness of the high divorce rate (and for the formerly married, fear of making another mistake), sexual frustration, and education or career demands that preclude early marriage. Among the pull factors are a strong physical attraction toward someone, being in a strong emotional relationship, desire for intimacy and sex on a regular basis, desire to experiment with a new living arrangement, desire for personal growth, example of peers, desire to test compatibility for marriage, and, today, perhaps to evaluate how likely a person is to be an egalitarian partner (Cherlin, 2000; Wilson, 2002).

Once again we can see the complexity of lifestyle choices. Cohabitation, like other options, is explained by a number of factors, both positive and negative. The meaning and experience of cohabitation varies considerably and reflects the different needs of individuals. For example, for some couples, living together is a new stage in a dating relationship, a "going steady" but with a live-in twist. A common pattern found among college students in the 1960s and 1970s was a gradual drifting into staying together, first spending the night, then the weekend, and then moving in (Macklin, 1972). For many, living together was a logical step in getting to know and share their lives with another person.

For other couples, cohabitation may represent a cheaper way to live. For example, sharing expenses might enable younger cohabitants to commit more time and energy to

IN OTHER PLACES

COHABITATION IN EUROPE

Cohabitation is not unique to the United States but exits in many countries around the world, including Australia, Canada, Latin America, Africa, and Asia. However, it is in northern Europe that we find a lengthy history of cohabitation. Records suggest that between the mid-eighteenth and mid-nineteenth centuries up to one-fifth of the population of England and Wales likely cohabited, either as a prelude to marriage or as an informal marriage without the sanction of church or state (Gillis, 1985). Sweden is also recognized for its long history of cohabitation. In the early twentieth century, many Swedish couples protested against the institution of church marriage and openly entered into "marriages of conscience." In response to this practice, the government created civil marriages in 1909 (Kiernan, 2002). Today approximately 30 percent of all couples in Sweden cohabit and it is generally within this cohabitation that first-born children enter the world (Ambert, 2005).

Although the majority of these cohabiting couples eventually marry, for a significant number of couples, cohabitation is replacing marriage. This is especially the pattern when cohabitation follows a divorce. Similarly, cohabitation and extramarital childbirth are also becoming more of a norm in Norway and Denmark, where 50 and 45 percent of births were outside of marriage (cited in Knox, 2004).

However, this pattern is far from universal in Europe. In the southern countries of Spain, Portugal, Italy, and Greece, along with Poland and Ireland, only a small percentage of the population cohabits. Other countries of Europe, including Great Britain, Belgium, the Netherlands, Luxembourg, Germany, and Austria, have midlevels of cohabitation, ranging from about 10 to 15 percent, rates similar to that of the United States and Australia (Kiernan, 2002).

Several factors may explain these different rates of cohabitation. In comparisons to most other countries, Scandinavian patterns of cohabitation are longstanding and seem to represent a substitute for marriage for many of these couples who tend to see

marriage as either having little value or as a huge commitment for which they are not yet ready. Government policies in these countries may also contribute to people's willingness to cohabit. For example, in Sweden and Norway, all parents, regardless of marital status, are eligible to receive a children's allowance from their respective governments. Further, many of these countries now provide benefits, such as insurance or pension rights, to cohabiting couples and some have laws regulating the distribution of property in the event of a breakup. Although there are state churches in the Scandinavian countries, religious attendance is low and there is relatively little religious pressure to marry. Finally, even though social acceptance of cohabitation is gaining in the United States and elsewhere in Europe, social approval for such relationships remains much higher in Scandinavia.

What do you think? Is the United States likely to follow the pattern of cohabitation that emerged in the Scandinavian countries? Why or why not?

---

education or career development. For older divorced or widowed people with grown children, cohabitation is sometimes chosen over marriage to avoid possible complications with social security or inheritance issues. Because there are many different motivations for cohabitation, partners should never assume agreement about where a relationship is heading. Like people entering into any relationship, the partners need to discuss and to understand each other's expectations.

Types of Cohabiting Couples Just as many reasons are given for cohabitation, the relationships established by cohabiting couples vary in terms of individual needs and degree of commitment. For some, the relationship is simply a *utilitarian arrangement* motivated by the desire to share expenses and household tasks or to avoid loss of financial benefits such as alimony, welfare, or pension checks. In such arrangements, intimacy may or may not be present. For others, there is *intimate involvement* with emotional commitment. However, they have no plans for marriage, preferring instead to take a "wait-and-see" attitude. In contrast, some cohabiting partners create a *trial marriage* to test their compatibility for a possible future marital commitment. Others go a step further. They have already decided to marry in the future and see no reason to live apart prior to that event, so for them cohabitation is a *prelude to marriage*. Despite these latter expectations,

research undertaken in the 1990s found that only 58 percent of cohabiting women married their partners (National Center for Health Statistics, 1996). Marriage following cohabitation was more likely for white and Asian women (about 61 percent) than for Latinas (54 percent) or African American women (41 percent) (Abma et al., 1997). These differences are most frequently attributed to economic factors, such as low earnings and periodic unemployment, which inhibit marriage. Further, because more cohabiting couples of color have greater rates of childbearing than their white counterparts, some social scientists are coming to see them as another family form rather than a prelude to marriage (McLanahan and Casper, 1995), or as Sharon Sassler's and James McNally's (2003) research suggests, for increasing numbers of couples, long-term cohabitation is becoming an alternative to marriage or being single. They found that of the cohabiting couples they studied, only about 40 percent ended up marrying within 4 to 7 years. They also found that, contrary to what some other studies have found, cohabiting men with the best economic prospects were the least likely to marry but were also less likely to breakup with their partners. A 39-year-old cohabiting architect reflects this pattern:

I am very cautious about marriage, having grown up around a not very pretty one. I am a tad cynical and a tad rebellious. I am not sure what I am rebelling against, but I really don't

For many people cohabitation has become a stage in the dating process. This couple enjoys sharing tasks together.

see a need for marriage. That isn't a statement about my feelings about the relationship, because there is no less strength of commitment. (quoted in Steinhauer, 1995:A9)

Given these reasons for and types of cohabitation, what, then, is gained or risked by living together?

Advantages and Disadvantages of Cohabitation

Among the most commonly reported advantages of living together are better understanding of self; greater knowledge of what is involved in living with another person; increased interpersonal skills, especially communication and problem solving skills; increased emotional maturity; better understanding of marital expectations; companionship; and the sharing of economic and domestic responsibilities. Although expenses may be shared, cohabitating couples are less likely than married couples to pool all their financial resources, preferring to maintain more independence.

Cohabitation is not without its problems, however. Among the disadvantages cohabitants report are lack of social support for their relationship, which for some contributes to a sense of guilt about their lifestyle; conflict with their partner over domestic tasks; the potential instability of the relationship; loss or curtailment of other relationships; differing expectations with partner; the emotional trauma of breaking up; and legal ambiguity—a point we will return to shortly. In addition, research shows that there is often less sexual fidelity between cohabiting couples than between

married couples, and cohabiting couples report less sexual fidelity and lower levels of happiness and sexual satisfaction than their married peers (Amato and Booth, 1997; Treas and Giesen, 2000).

Gender role expectations may also play a role in the degree of satisfaction with the cohabiting experience. In contrast to their married counterparts, cohabiting men are more likely to be unemployed, whereas cohabiting women are more likely to be employed (Fields and Casper, 2001). Furthermore, both women and men in cohabitating relationships may feel used when their partner gives no indication of making a marital commitment. Sharon Sassler and Jim McNally (2003) found that 42 percent of the cohabiting couples in their study disagreed about the future of their relationship. Conversely, some couples, rather than making a definite decision may slide into a marital relationship, i.e., marrying somebody they might not otherwise have married. Scott Stanley (2005) refers to this process as relationship "inertia."

Finally, spouses who cohabit before marriage exhibit a higher rate of verbal abuse and violent behavior than do spouses who did not cohabit (Cunningham and Antill, 1995; Cohan and Kleinbaum, 2002). Similarly, a study comparing 21-year-old females and males in dating and cohabiting relationships found that cohabitants were almost twice as likely as daters to be abusive toward their partners (Magdol, Moffitt, and Caspi, 1998). Although we do not have data on child abuse in cohabiting households in the United States, a study in Britain found that children living with cohabiting couples are 20 times more likely to be victims than children living with married parents. If the mother is living with a man who is not the father, the child's risk of abuse is even higher (Madigan, 1999). A variety of reasons contribute to this higher rate of violence: economic difficulties, isolation from family and friends, and differing levels of emotional involvement in the relationship.

Once again, we must not assume that each cohabiting individual experiences all of these advantages and disadvantages in the same way. The data on cohabitation, however, seem to suggest that regardless of the outcome, most individuals feel they learned something from the experience. Furthermore, because cohabitation has become more widespread, it is likely that fewer individuals now experience a sense of guilt about their living arrangement. For some couples, however, living together may go counter to their religious upbringing or to parental values; thus, their adoption of this lifestyle may trouble them. Such feelings may be intensified if a couple hides from family or friends the fact that they are living together.

Cohabitation and the Division of Labor

How do cohabitants go about the daily tasks of living? Do they behave differently from their married peers? Research suggests that the differences are relatively minor. For example, a Canadian study of cohabiting couples found that they were only slightly more likely to have a more equitable but not equal division of household tasks (Wu, 2000). Their U.S. counterparts also divide housework a bit more equitably and enjoy more similar earnings than married couples

(Brines and Joyner, 1999). However, despite the fact that many couples may start out sharing household tasks, over time traditional gender roles emerge, with women assuming a larger share of the cooking and cleaning. Numerous other studies have found more traditional patterns. Philip Blumstein and Pepper Schwartz (1983) reported that even when women worked full-time and earned as much as their partners, they did more of the housework. This is not unlike patterns found among married couples. Sociologists Beth Shelton and Daphne John (1990) analyzed data from the national survey of families and households, comparing cohabiting and married couples, and found that although cohabiting women may do less housework than their married peers, there was no difference between the amount of time married and cohabiting men devoted to housework or child care. This inequity in the household division of labor is often a source of conflict for cohabiting couples, just as it is for married couples, especially when both partners are working (see Chapter 10).

Cohabitation and Marital Stability

Earlier in this chapter we noted that one of the reasons cohabitants give for living together is that they want to test their relationship for marital compatibility. Thus, this becomes a critical research question. Is cohabitation a good predictor of marital success? To date the research in this regard has yielded some contradictory findings. Some early research found that cohabitants who married are more likely to remain together than couples who did not cohabit (White, 1987) while other researchers concluded that cohabitation has no clear effect on marital success or satisfaction (Watson and DeMeo, 1987). Despite these contradictory findings, the weight of the evidence seems to be that couples who engage in premarital cohabitation run a greater risk of divorce than do couples who do not cohabit prior to marriage. Depending on the specific statistical methods used, a wide range of studies found that couples who marry after a period of cohabitation are at a 35 to 50 percent greater risk of separating and/or divorcing than marriages without prior cohabitation (Seltzer, 2000; Teachman, 2002; Teachman, 2003; VanGoethem, 2005). Researchers found that premarital cohabitation was a significant risk factor for marital instability among Canadian couples as well (Wu and Penning, 1997). Research needs to continue in this area, but several explanations for the higher divorce risk of premarital cohabitants seem likely. Some cohabitants engage in behavior that in the long run is detrimental to marriage. For example, in the cohabitive situation they may put their best foot forward and share household responsibilities on an equitable basis. After exchanging marriage vows, however, one or both partners may, without consciously realizing it, change role expectations and fall back on traditional patterns in the division of household labor. There may be outside pressure as well. Parents and friends may be tolerant of a "live-in lover" because they do not want to jeopardize the possibility of marriage. After marriage, they may feel free to say or do things that could cause conflict between the now-married couple. Self-selection may also play a role. Cohabitants may hold more nontraditional views on marriage

and therefore be more accepting of divorce (DeMaris and MacDonald, 1993). Finally, people who cohabit may be less concerned about homogamous factors (see Chapter 5) in partner choice, factors that may increase the risk of divorce for couples.

Cohabitation and the Law

If you are part of an unmarried couple currently living in North Carolina, Virginia, West Virginia, Florida, Michigan, Mississippi, and North Dakota (or if you lived in Arizona and New Mexico prior to 2001), you are a lawbreaker and could be subject to fines and imprisonment. Such was the reality for 40-year-old Debora Hobbs, an unmarried woman who lost her job as a 911 dispatcher with the Pendar County Sheriff's office because she chose to live with her unmarried boyfriend in violation of a 200-year-old law that states, "If any man and woman, not being married to each other, shall lewdly and lasciviously associate, bed and cohabitate together they shall be guilty of a class 2 misdemeanor." Debora and her partner are not alone; there are about 144,000 unmarried couple lawbreakers living together in North Carolina. The law against cohabitation is rarely enforced. Only about three dozen cohabitation-related charges were filed in North Carolina between 1997 and 2004. The exact number of people convicted under the law is not clear (Hartsoe, 2005). The American Civil Liberties Union has filed a lawsuit on her behalf and is seeking to overturn the law. In January 2005, the North Dakota House, following similar action taken earlier by the state Senate, voted to uphold its cohabitation law.

Although living together is not illegal in the other 43 states, serious legal issues need to be considered by anyone choosing to cohabit. Cohabitation, like singlehood, can be temporary and fluid. Many cohabitants are together for only short periods of time. Half break up in a year or less, after which couples either marry or go their separate ways (Bumpass and Lu, 2000). Like their married peers, cohabitants end their relationship for many reasons: growing apart, loss of interest, unequal commitment, value conflicts, outside pressures, or the need to relocate because of work or other family commitments. However, unlike their married peers, cohabitants have fewer legal protections to guide them through their breakups.

What happens when cohabitants terminate a relationship? Who gets the apartment? The stereo? The children? Can cohabitants expect compensation for their unpaid work or other contributions while living together? What are the legal aspects of cohabitation? Even though you do not need a court decree to stop living together, there may be legal ramifications to ending a cohabitive relationship. Former live-in partners may file suit for what has come to be called **palimony,** a payment similar to alimony and based on the existence of a contract (written or implied) between the partners regarding aspects of their relationship. For example, if there were a promise of future marriage, of an economic partnership, or of support for a child, courts may hold a partner responsible for legally fulfilling these obligations or, conversely, may deny that such a claim has any merit. Twenty percent of court cases dealing with relationship dissolutions involve cohabiting couples, many with children (Hymowitz, 2003).

A Legal Response: Domestic Partnerships So far we have been talking about what happens when cohabitants break up. However, a number of other areas to consider when living together also have legal implications. For example, who is to be the beneficiary with regard to insurance and wills? Sometimes insurance companies require the beneficiary to have a conventional family tie. You cannot assume that because you live with someone you will be covered by her or his car or renter's insurance. Health benefits are problematic as well.

In an attempt to address these problems, some communities and organizations make provisions for extending benefits generally reserved for married employees to other employees involved in what have come to be known as **domestic partnerships,** a term referring to unmarried couples who live together and share housing and financial responsibilities. Although still relatively modest in number, a growing list of nonprofit organizations and private sector employers now recognize some form of domestic partnership, although the rights and benefits involved in these arrangements vary from place to place. Some benefits are minor, a membership in a gym or museum; others are substantial—including health insurance, family and funeral leave, family membership rates, and inheritance protection. To receive these benefits couples are required to register their partnership. Such registration provides public recognition of the union, thereby granting it a degree of legitimacy. Some agencies, however, restrict partnership benefits to those of the same sex, arguing that heterosexual partners can marry if they wish to receive such benefits. Currently, only a small number of countries and the state of Massachusetts recognize same-sex civil marriages. In December of 2005, a new law went into effect permitting civil partnerships for lesbian and gay couples in England, Scotland, Wales, and Northern Ireland. Some of the first to register were couples in long-standing relationships like 80-year-old John Walton and his partner of 40 years, Roger Raglan ("Gay Britons . . . ," 2005). Singer Elton John (59) and his partner of 11 years, David Furnish (43), were among the first couples to make their relationship official. It is estimated that as many as 22,000 couples may take advantage of the new law in the next 5 years (Lyall, 2005). The law permits civil ceremonies and gives same-sex couples legal rights similar to those of their married peers in areas like immigration, pension, and inheritance as well as responsibilities in areas such as child rearing. In the United States, in 2000, Vermont became the first state to offer civil unions to same-sex couples, granting them the same rights, privileges, and responsibilities as married spouses under state law. Connecticut followed a few years later, and in January 2005 California's domestic partnership law went into effect, providing a significant number but not all of the benefits and obligations conferred on married couples under state statutes. However, the actions of these four states can give no federal recognition or federal tax and

Singer Elton John and his partner of 11 years, David Furnish, were among the first couples to make their relationship official under Great Britain's new law permitting civil partnerships for lesbian and gay couples.

other benefits nor are they portable—recognized in other states. In fact, Congress and a majority of states passed laws that would block recognition of same-sex marriages should another state permit them. The lack of legal recognition of their union is particularly difficult for lesbians and gays who want to join a partner who has migrated to another country. Laws governing residence of a partner from another country most frequently require a blood or marital relationship, thus excluding homosexual couples (Binnie, 1997).

Further, without such recognition both heterosexual and homosexual cohabiting partners may have little to say in the medical treatment or other affairs of their partner. In case of death, who is to inherit property? Without a properly executed will, the state makes this determination, and the decision will likely favor family members over live-in partners. You cannot automatically claim ownership to any property that does not bear your name even if you helped pay for it. The status of children can be ambiguous in cohabitive relationships as well. If the biological parent dies and there is no provision for naming the live-in partner the legal guardian, again the court may decide the matter. Often it does so contrary to the wishes of the cohabitants. These are just a few of the items that cohabitants need to consider as they establish their living arrangements. Without a legally binding agreement, cohabitants may have few, if any, legal rights in these matters.

LESBIAN AND GAY RELATIONSHIPS

Many of the legal issues we have just discussed concerning cohabitants apply to lesbian and gay relationships as well. As with our discussion of heterosexual cohabitants, our focus here is primarily on social relationships constructed by lesbian and gay couples.

Homosexual behavior has existed throughout history and in every known culture. Nevertheless, cultures have varied considerably in their attitudes toward this behavior. Certain peoples in Melanesia, Central Africa, and Egypt viewed sexual relationships between older and younger males as part of the normal socialization process. Similarly, records of classical Greece and Rome reveal acceptance of same-sex bonding for men. Historians know less about women's relationships during this period but have discovered some evidence that female same-sex bonding occurred then, too.

In U.S. society, homosexuality historically has been considered a form of deviant behavior. Medical research into this "disorder" focused on its causes, with the emphasis on discovering a "cure." Among the treatments used to effect a "cure" were castration, hysterectomy, electric shock treatment, lobotomy, and estrogen and testosterone injections (Harvey, 1992). During the latter half of the twentieth century, some of these negative attitudes began to change as lesbians and gays began to organize to challenge laws and customs discriminating against them and condemning their behaviors. Although initially these groups were predominantly white, several African American, Asian American, and Latina/o organizations emerged in the 1970s and gave visibility to the ethnic and racial diversity that exists within the homosexual population. In 1973, an important step in the redefinition of homosexual behavior occurred when the American Psychiatric Association (APA) removed homosexuality from its list of psychiatric disorders. Experiencing prejudice and/or discrimination based on sexual orientation may cause lesbians and gays considerable stress (Mays and Cochran, 2001; Meyer, 2003); nevertheless, there is no reliable data to show that homosexual orientation per se impairs psychological functioning. Despite such findings, some psychotherapists and religious counselors still see homosexuality as an inherently deficient or sinful lifestyle and try to change lesbians and gays, especially teens, into heterosexuals through what is called reparative therapy or sexual conversion therapy. These efforts are being led and financed by groups on the religious right such as Focus on the Family and Exodus, an umbrella organization for more than 120 ex-gay ministries. Although these groups and therapists report having successfully changed the sexual orientation of numerous clients, the APA remains highly critical of this approach, citing its potential to do psychological harm and the fact that to date there are no systematic studies in peer-reviewed scientific journals that attest to the success of reparative or conversion therapy (Hausman, 2001). Additionally, child welfare advocates are concerned about the ethics involved in some of the techniques, especially those that place lesbian and gay teenagers, often against their wishes, in restrictive residential programs (Griffith, 2005).

Methodological Issues

Earlier in the chapter we noted the methodological problems surrounding the study of singlehood and heterosexual cohabitation. Similar problems of small, unrepresentative samples also limit the study of homosexual behavior. In addition, the long tradition of homophobia in the United States has kept many homosexual people from revealing their sexual orientation and from participating in research studies. Studies with small samples of Asian Americans (Liu and Chan, 1996), Latinas/os (Morales, 1996), and African Americans (Green and Boyd-Franklin, 1996) suggest that people of color may be even more reluctant to identify themselves as lesbian or gay because of the intense cultural disapproval of homosexuality in their respective communities. Thus, they may find themselves caught between two communities, facing double or even triple stigmatization with the potential for losing support in both the lesbian/gay community and in their gender/ethnic/racial community. For example, an African American may feel excluded from the gay community because of racism and rejected in the African American community because of homophobia. An Asian American female who interacts in the lesbian community may have to distance herself from her cultural community to avoid bringing shame and humiliation to her family.

Among many of these cultures, homosexuality is widely viewed as a white, Western phenomenon. This view may be changing, however, as countries like China now admit to having a sizeable homosexual population of their own. Official statistics suggest there are approximately 30 million homosexuals in mainland China. However, this is probably an undercount since few Chinese are willing to publicly acknowledge their sexuality for fear of being stigmatized. Nevertheless, attitudes are changing, albeit slowly. In 2001, China published a third version of its classification and diagnosis criteria of mental disorders and, for the first time, excluded homosexuality from the list ("Lesbians, Gays . . . ," 2005).

Finally, there are many variations in lesbian and gay lifestyles that have yet to be systematically studied. Some lesbians and gays live alone; others cohabit. Some have been involved in heterosexual marriages—one study puts the number at 33 percent for lesbians and 20 percent for gay men (Harry, 1988). Our focus here is on cohabiting same-sex couples, of which the Census Bureau counted over 594,000 in 2000. Additionally, many lesbians and gays are parents and grandparents. Some had their children when they were part of a heterosexual union; others elected to have children outside of a biological relationship through artificial insemination. In the 2000 U.S. census, 33 percent of female same-sex couple households and 22 percent of male same-sex couple households reported at least one child under the age of 18 living in the home. Lesbian and gay parenting is discussed in Chapter 9.

Demystifying Lesbian and Gay Relationships

What images do you have of lesbian and gay cohabitants? No doubt you are aware of some of the many stereotypes about lesbians and gays. Among the most prevalent images are those depicting lesbians as masculine or "butch" and gay men as effeminate. The major stereotypes involving cohabiting same-sex couples assume that these couples imitate heterosexual patterns, with one partner acting as "wife" (submissive female) and the other playing the "husband" (dominant male). Research, however, shows that these stereotypes apply to only a small minority of same-sex relationships, those in which partners tend to be older, male, and from lower socioeconomic and educational levels (Peplau and Gordon, 1983; Harry, 1984). In fact, partners in same-sex couples are less likely than those in heterosexual couples to assume gender-typed roles (Herek, 2000).

Richard Higginbotham (1991) argues that the problem with using the marriage model in studying lesbian and gay relationships is that it brings with it a set of expectations and norms that simply do not correlate with the realities of a same-sex relationship. Some researchers suggest that a friendship model, albeit with erotic and romantic elements, provides lesbians and gays with guidelines for their intimate relationships (Harry and DeVall, 1978). The difference between the two models is that the norms for friendship assume that partners will be relatively equal in status and power, as contrasted with traditional heterosexual marriage scripts, in which the husband is assumed to be the head of the family (Peplau and Gordon, 1983).

What, then, are lesbian and gay relationships like? First, it is important to recognize that just as there is tremendous diversity among heterosexuals who cohabit, there is rich diversity across race, ethnicity, religion, and social class among homosexual cohabitants (Stacey, 2003). Second, research comparing lesbian, gay, and heterosexual relationships shows that they are quite similar and operate essentially on the same principles, seek the same kind of mutually supportive, romantic, and emotionally intimate bonds, and confront the same issues in living together—division of household labor, finances, communication, and decision making (Herek, 2000). Lesbians and gays, like their heterosexual counterparts, experience the same fears of rejection, the same relationship problems, and the same problems with sexual functioning (Reinisch, 1990). However, compared to heterosexuals, lesbian and gay partners report fewer barriers to leaving a relationship (Kurdek, 1998). This finding is likely related to the lack of legal recognition and social acceptance of homosexual relationships.

Living Together: Domestic Tasks, Finances, and Decision Making

Because traditional gender distinctions are irrelevant to same-sex relationships, lesbian and gay couples are in a unique position to create living arrangements tailored to their needs and interests. How, then, do same-sex couples resolve the day-to-day requirements of living? Research shows that there is considerable discussion and conscious joint decision making in these areas. An early study found that over half of both lesbians and gays in the sample reported sharing housework equally (Bell and Weinberg, 1978). In one of the earliest studies comparing heterosexual and homosexual couples, sociologists Philip Blumstein and Pepper Schwartz (1983) found several factors that affect the division of household tasks. Among gay couples the number of hours spent at work determines the relative contribution

U.S. Representative Barney Frank, a Democrat from Massachusetts, openly acknowledges his homosexuality and provides a strong voice on behalf of equality and dignity for all people.

of each partner—the one with the fewer outside hours does more of the household tasks. There were some constraints on this pattern, however. For example, these authors found that "both heterosexual and homosexual men feel that a successful partner should not have to do housework" (1983:151). Although lesbian couples work harder than either gay or heterosexual couples to create an equitable distribution of tasks, overall for same-sex partners, individual interests, skills, or schedules take precedence over gender in determining how household tasks are divided (Peplau et al., 1996).

Decision making, like housework, is often related to income—that is, the partner with the highest income tends to have the most power. In a comparative study of heterosexual and same-sex couples, Blumstein and Schwartz (1983) found this to be true for gay and heterosexual couples but not for lesbian couples. In this same study, lesbian respondents reported less conflict over finances than did other couples. Among both heterosexual and gay couples, partners who feel they have equal control over how money is spent have a more tranquil relationship. An intriguing observational study of how lesbian, gay, and heterosexual couples behave in conflict interactions found that homosexual partners were less belligerent, less domineering, and exhibited less fear/tension and less whining than did heterosexual partners. Additionally, the data showed that the homosexual initiators of the conflict also demonstrated more positive emotions, more affection, more humor, and more joy/excitement when compared with the heterosexual initiators. The researchers speculate that the reasons for these observed differences is that homosexual couples value equality far more than do heterosexual couples and that because there are fewer barriers to leaving homosexual than heterosexual relationships, homosexual couples may be more careful in how they communicate with their partners (Gottman et al., 2003). However, these findings do not mean that conflict and violence are absent in lesbian and gay relationships. In fact, domestic violence occurs with the same or even greater frequency than in heterosexual communities (Peterman and Dixon, 2003) and takes many of the same forms (see Chapter 11). However, until relatively recently this behavior has been ignored both in the lesbian and gay communities and in the larger society as well. Even today victims of lesbian and gay domestic violence have fewer protections. Besides poor or inconsistent law enforcement, lack of access to family courts, and limited shelters and services, lesbians and gays may fear being "outed" to their families, at work, and in the community if they report the violence.

The Social and Legal Context of Lesbian and Gay Relationships

Same-sex couples experience the same disadvantages and advantages of cohabitation as heterosexual couples do in that they are generally denied legal and financial benefits such as community property rights, insurance coverage, tax breaks, leaves for the sickness or funeral of a partner, and inheritance protection. Additionally, both sets of couples confront many of the same issues when their relationship ends. However, in contrast to heterosexual couples, when lesbian and gay partners break up, they often maintain a close relationship with one another by making a transition from being lovers to being friends, and they often continue these relationships for many years (Weston, 1991). This finding is particularly significant given that same-sex relationships exist in a society that remains largely intolerant of their lifestyle.

Although there has been a positive shift in public attitudes towards lesbians and gays with growing numbers of the population opposed to discrimination in areas such as housing and employment, many people in the United States still consider homosexuality to be abnormal or sinful. Prejudice against lesbians and gays is particularly strong among men, the less educated, older adults, rural residents, those who hold traditional beliefs about gender roles and who have conservative religious beliefs. They are also less likely to have had any close relationships with an openly gay person. Conversely, heterosexuals with close friends who have acknowledged their sexual orientation are among those most likely to have positive and supportive attitudes toward lesbians and gays (Herek, 2000; Religious Tolerance.Org, 2003).

Although many work environments have improved considerably for people who are open about their sexual orientation, discrimination still exits. Despite the fact that lesbians and gays have long served in the U.S. armed forces, any open acknowledgment of (or even suspicion of) one's homosexuality can result in a dishonorable discharge. In 1993 President Clinton announced he would work with Pentagon and congressional leaders to end discrimination against lesbians and gays in the military. The resulting "don't ask, don't tell" policy adopted by the military was intended to be less punitive than the past policy of an outright ban, but it still denies gays and lesbians equal treatment with their heterosexual counterparts. In 2000, the armed forces discharged 1212 lesbians and gays, a 17 percent increase from the previous year and nearly double the number in 1993, the last year before the current policy went into effect (Marquis, 2001). However, the number discharged under this policy dropped by almost half (to 653 in 2004) since September 11, 2001 (Nieves and Tyson, 2005). Not only has the United States lost talented linguists

and bomb experts among those discharged, this policy harms the partners of those who remain in the military. Things that heterosexuals take for granted when they enter the military—help in keeping contact and communication with family and friends, establishing insurance beneficiaries, and completing wills—become dangerous minefields for lesbians, gays, and their partners. Most other Western industrialized countries allow lesbians and gays to serve openly in their military.

Lesbians and gays also confront other problems because of their sexual orientation. They are often the victims of name-calling, ridicule, and even violence. The incidence of "gay bashing" has been increasing in U.S. society over the last several years. According to the National Coalition of Anti-Violence Programs (2005), there were 1,792 incidents in 2004, up 3 percent from 2003. Violence against homosexuals is not confined to the United States. A report by Amnesty International documents abuses in 30 countries throughout Latin America, Eastern Europe, Africa, Asia, the Caribbean, and the Middle East. A few years ago Egypt arrested and tried 52 men for suspected homosexual behavior (MacFarquhar, 2001). In Chechnya, under the Muslim Shari'a code, men can be executed for homosexual acts (Leland, 2001). Because of the extreme prejudice and violence directed against homosexuals in their native countries, the United States grants asylum to individuals when their sexual orientation poses a serious threat to their lives. All too often, however, the asylum seekers face further rejection from their fellow countrymen who have migrated to the United States, bringing homophobic attitudes with them.

In such a climate, it is easy to understand why many lesbians and gays keep their sexual orientation hidden. Individuals who "come out of the closet" and acknowledge their homosexuality risk discrimination and alienating their family and friends. Given this context, lesbians and gays often create kinship structures of friends and lovers who provide the social and emotional support traditionally expected of biological kin. Even with this support, the issue of closeting or "coming out" has implications for the kind of personal relationships that lesbians and gays establish. For example, a study of 124 lesbians involved in a couple relationship found that closeting often has a negative impact on the couple's relationship quality. If couples can be open with family and friends, the quality of their relationship is likely to be higher. In particular, family behaviors—such as inviting a member's lesbian partner to family events and accepting demonstrations of affection between the couple—can enhance their relationship (Caron and Ulin, 1997).

Research on "coming out" suggests that patterns of disclosure and subsequent family reactions vary considerably (Merighi and Grimes, 2000). For example, mothers are more often told than fathers (D'Augelli et al., 1998). Lesbians and gays perceived more rejection and disapproval from families with high traditional values (those that emphasized religion, heterosexual marriage, having children, in addition to having a non-English language spoken at home) than those from families with low traditional values (Newman and Muzzonigo, 1993). Although some parents react negatively and distance themselves from their children, others are very supportive. A number of supportive parents formed Parents and Friends of Lesbians and Gays

(PFLAG), a nonprofit organization with 200,000 members and supporters and local affiliates in more than 500 communities across the United States and abroad.

Elderly Lesbians and Gays

No one can say with certainty how many lesbian and gay adults there are. Few national surveys ask about sexual orientation, and even when they do, older respondents are not likely to disclose their sexual orientation given the negative attitudes to homosexuality that they experienced over their lifetime. Estimates put the number of lesbian and gays 65 and older at around 1.75 million (Cahill, South, & Spude, 2000). The research that does exist on elderly homosexuals suggests that they face the same challenges of aging as do elderly heterosexuals. At the same time, however, lesbians and gays have unique life experiences stemming from their homosexual identity that create specific issues and needs. For example, many closeted elderly lesbians and gays are afraid to tell their doctors they are homosexual for fear their doctor will treat them differently or discriminate against them. Similarly when elderly homosexuals enter long-term care facilities, they may face hostility from other residents and/or if they enter a retirement facility with a partner, existing policies may require them to have separate rooms. Finally, lesbian and gay seniors are twice as likely (66 versus 33 percent) as their heterosexual peers to be alone (Davidson, 2001). Two factors are at work here. First the majority of lesbians and gays have never had children. Second, many others are estranged from their families because of disapproval of their lifestyle. These factors can lead to isolation and loneliness. Recently, developers have stepped in to address these problems. Although few in number at this time, retirement communities that take these issues into account in their design and policies are offering an alternative and welcoming environment for lesbian and gay elderly (see, for example, Scharnberg, 2005).

COMMUNAL LIVING AND GROUP MARRIAGE

Thus far, this chapter has focused primarily on single people who live alone or cohabit. Not everyone, however, is content to live alone or to cohabit with just one other person. Some people join a commune to satisfy their needs for intimacy and companionship.

A **commune** refers to a group of people (single or married, with or without children) who live together, sharing many aspects of their lives. Communes have existed from earliest times. In particular, they are likely to develop or expand in periods of political and social unrest (Mead, 1970). The communal movement in the United States originated around the end of the eighteenth century (Miller, 1998). Most of the early communes were religious in origin. Some, like the Shakers, named for the way they moved during prayer and song, believed monogamous marriage and the nuclear family were detrimental to the spiritual health of the community. Thus, they required all members, whether married or not, to live celibate lives.

Children share a meal on an Israeli kibbutz. Adults in this communal organization share many tasks of daily living, including child care.

Eighteen Shaker communes were established in Maine, New Hampshire, Massachusetts, Connecticut, New York, Kentucky, Ohio, Indiana, Georgia, and Florida. Membership reached its numerical high of around 5,000 souls during the 1850s. The only remaining active Shaker community, located in Sabbathday Lake, Maine, consists of a small group of women and men who care for the commune's 18 buildings, orchards, fields, and gardens. Besides spending their days in prayer and work, members often travel throughout the country, visiting museums and art galleries to tell the Shaker story as well as hosting visitors and students.

Marriage and sexual relationships took other forms in other of the early communes. The Mormons, for example, practiced polygyny. Still others engaged in free love whereby members could engage in sexual relationships with any other member of the group. The political instability in the years immediately preceding and following the Civil War produced about a hundred new communes. One of them, the Hutterites, a commune with a religious origin, still has members in the United States today. The economic turmoil of the 1930s and the political activism of the 1960s also led to new waves of communal development (Zablocki, 1980). It is estimated that today there are over 3,000 functioning communes worldwide ("The World Communal Scene," 2005). Among the better-known communes surviving in the United States are Sandhill Farm in Missouri, Twin Oaks in Virginia, and The Farm in Tennessee. To learn more about modern communes, see the Internet Resources: Applying the Sociological Imagination box.

Advantages and Disadvantages of the Communal Lifestyle

Have you ever considered joining a commune or wondered what motivates someone to adopt such a lifestyle? Studies of communes suggest that their members are motivated by a desire for egalitarian, personalized, cooperative, and satisfying

APPLYING THE SOCIOLOGICAL IMAGINATION
Understanding Communes: Daily Randomly Featured Communities

Alchemy Farm (Massachusetts, United States)

Alchemy Farm Cohousing combines the social design of cohousing with ecological forms of housing and agricultural use of our common landscape. Our mission is "to create and nuture a Cohousing Community where individuals live in integrity and harmony with each other and with nature, using sustainable agriculture and . . . .

Wholesome House (Oregon, United States)

We are a community focused on progressive political action, and grounded in mystical spirituality. Grounded in a belief that all beings are equally (and affirmatively) capable of direct connection with the divine, we dedicate ourselves to consensual democracy and the common good. We do this to live in Alignment . . . .

Monkton Wyld Court (United Kingdom)

Monkton Wyld Court is an educational charity run by a resident community of about a dozen adults, plus children and animals. The eleven acre grounds include a fifteen bedroom Victorian rectory, a converted stable block and other outbuildings, a large organic vegetable garden, terraced lawns, fields, woods and stream . . . .

Visit the on-line Communities Directory (http://directory.ic.org/), part of the Intentional Communities Web site, and follow the links to these and other communal groups. Examine their organizational structure and functioning. What kinds of people join communes? How do they earn their living? How do they raise their children? What kind of governance structures do communes have? Now that you have discovered more facts about communal living, do you think you would ever consider joining a commune?

---

intimate relationships—qualities they perceive are not readily available in the traditional nuclear family structure.

Among the advantages most frequently reported by members of communes are close intimate relationships with a variety of people; personal growth through group experiences; the sharing of economic resources, domestic tasks, and child care; companionship; social support; spiritual rebirth or strengthening; and a respect and reverence for nature. These advantages also create some disadvantages, including limitations on privacy, restrictions on personal freedom, limitations on parental influence and control, lack of stability, legal ambiguity, financial problems, and the possibility of sexual jealousy (Cornfield, 1983; Thies, 2000).

Most communes last for only short periods of time. Many of the problems encountered in communes center on conflicts over power, authority, and ideology. Those communes that survive the longest share certain characteristics: religious orientation, strict admission requirements, strong member commitment, controls on sexuality, adequate financing, time and space for privacy, and clearly defined authority and distribution of tasks (Cornfield, 1983; Kantor, 2005).

Communes, Shared Housing, and the Future

As with other lifestyles, communes are not for everyone, and we can only speculate on their future viability. Some writers believe that if the economy worsens or if new political turmoil develops, the number of communes will grow. Others predict that as populations age, some form of communal or group living will become a viable option for the elderly who otherwise might be forced to live alone (Dressel and Hess, 1983). There is some indication that this pattern is already well underway. For example, there has been a rapid growth of communes of elderly people in the Netherlands (Baars and Thomese, 1994). Here in the United States, one organization, the National Shared Housing Resource Center in Baltimore, a clearinghouse that helps people find ways to maintain their independence by living interdependently with others, keeps tabs on hundreds of shared-housing programs across the country. Shared housing usually takes one of two forms: group homes, in which several people share a residence, or matchups, where a homeowner and a home seeker agree to live together. Some programs are open only to the elderly; others are intergenerational.

Other experiments in cooperative living are also emerging. Two architects, Katie McCamant and Chuck Durret, intrigued by community developments in Denmark, founded the CoHousing Company in Berkeley, California, to introduce the idea in the United States. The concept of cohousing, or as some call it, "intentional neighborhood," is characterized by individuals or families living in their own private, self-sufficient units, but also sharing common spaces—a large dining room and kitchen, a garden, workshops, and a children's play area. Thus, members can share responsibilities like cooking and child care. Other benefits include ongoing support and companionship. Since their inception, 55 cohousing communities have been completed in the United States and Canada (Locke, 2001). If forms of shared housing are to be a viable option, however, critical issues of social policy will have to be reexamined. For example, many zoning laws restrict residential occupancy to individuals who meet the traditional definition of family. Such policies

WRITING YOUR OWN SCRIPT

THE MARITAL DECISION

Do I want to marry? The answer to this question represents one of the most fundamental choices we will make in our lifetime. As we saw in this chapter, people are more likely today than in the past to consider alternatives to traditional marriage. Nevertheless, pressure to marry remains intense, especially for young adults. The United States is still one of the most marrying societies in the world. Although increasing numbers of individuals are not marrying at all, delaying marriage to a later age, and divorcing at high rates, demographers predict that nine out of ten people born in the United States in recent years will marry at least once in their lifetime. Thus, one must weigh the merits of alternative lifestyles.

Questions to consider   If I decide not to marry, is this a permanent decision or will I reevaluate this decision at some later time? What lifestyle will I choose? Will I cohabit with a partner or live alone? What are the advantages and disadvantages of a single or nonmarried lifestyle? If I choose not to marry, will I be sexually active or remain celibate?

---

exclude the possibility of nontraditional households developing in many areas.

Group Marriages

Group marriages represent a variation of communal living. Sociologists Larry and Joan Constantine (1973:29) define **group marriage** as "a marriage of at least four people, two female and two male, in which each partner is married to all partners of the opposite sex." The actual number of documented group marriages has been small. One of the best-known experiments with group marriage was the Oneida Community in New York, founded by the Protestant minister John Noyes. It lasted from 1849 to 1881 and had about 300 adult members. Monogamous marriage and sexual exclusivity were not permitted. Children were reared in a communal nursery by specialized caretakers, and they were taught to consider all adults in the community as parents. Thus, the entire community was to be viewed as a single family. Hostile outside pressure contributed to the demise of this experiment in group marriage (Kephart, 1988).

No one knows for sure how many group marriages currently exist in the United States. Because group marriages are neither legal nor socially acceptable to most Americans, locating them is a difficult task. Extensive research on alternative lifestyles, including communes and group marriage, took place in the 1960s and 1970s, a period of social turmoil that included the Vietnam War, and various political and social movements (women's liberation, civil rights, and lesbian and gay rights). During this period, many people were publicly criticizing the institutions of marriage and the family as well as traditional gender roles and experimenting with alternative lifestyles. This climate provided a fertile ground for social scientists such as the Constantines, whose research on group marriages found that the most commonly reported reason respondents gave for their involvement was their dissatisfaction with traditional monogamous marriage. However, many of these relationships were short-lived, lasting on average only 16 months. Beginning in the 1980s, interest in and research on alternative lifestyles diminished dramatically. Only a few social scientists, such as Roger Rubin (2001), continue to raise questions about the continued practice and implications of these lifestyles.

SUPPORTING NONMARRIED ADULTS

As we have seen, being single in later life presents some of the same challenges that it does in earlier years. Meeting the demands of daily living alone while building supportive networks gives the unmarried of any age a tremendous sense of accomplishment and satisfaction. Nevertheless, changes in social customs and social policy could alleviate some of the problems encountered by the never-married as they grow older. For example, we are all familiar with the rituals, showers, and gift giving that accompany the marriage ceremony. Rarely, however, do we formally assist single people to establish their homes or symbolically, through a ritual celebration, recognize and give support to their lifestyle. Tax laws tend to favor homeowners (mostly married), heads of households, and parents. Singles are often at a financial disadvantage, especially today when homeownership and material goods require more than one income. As single people age, they may experience other disadvantages. If they are without children of their own, they may find themselves relatively isolated due to the age-graded character of our society, or they may feel some regret at not having children to carry on their legacy (Rubinstein et al., 1991). More opportunities for intergenerational contact and perhaps even intergenerational or some other form of communal living arrangements could be investigated as a means of providing support for never-married adults as they grow older.

SUMMARY

Over the last several decades the number of never-married people in the United States has grown. This increase is not a new phenomenon. Rather, it represents a return to historically higher levels of singlehood, which began to decline markedly only after 1940. In the past singlehood was a devalued status, and single people were often the objects of ridicule. Today there is greater acceptance of single people. Singlehood can be voluntary or involuntary, temporary or permanent. Singles engage in a variety of lifestyles. Some live alone, others live with relatives or friends, and some choose to cohabit.

In the past, cohabitation, or "living together," was more common among the poor. Today's cohabitants include people of all ages, races, and classes. Cohabitation, like living alone, can be temporary and fluid. For many, cohabitation has become an extension of the dating process. The number of unmarried-couple households has increased from 439,000 in 1960 to approximately 5.5 million in 2000. Cohabitation is similar to marriage in that couples create emotional and physical relationships with each other, and in some cases they also bear or rear children. It differs from marriage, however, in that it lacks formal legal, cultural, and religious support. Some couples choose to cohabit prior to marriage. The weight of research findings on the relationship of cohabitation to marital stability indicates that it increases the risk of divorce.

An increasing number of communities now allow lesbian, gay, and heterosexual cohabitants to register as domestic partners and receive some of the same benefits that married couples do. Lesbians and gays deal with the same issues of living together as heterosexuals: household division of labor, decision making, and finances. Additionally, however, they confront discrimination and social disapproval of their lifestyle.

Some individuals, seeking an alternative to traditional marriage, join a commune or participate in a group marriage. These arrangements generally meet with disapproval from the larger community, and most are relatively short-lived.

KEY TERMS

push/pull factors

common-law marriage

palimony

domestic partnership

commune

group marriage

QUESTIONS FOR STUDY AND REFLECTION

1. Identify and discuss the structural changes that have led to the increase in nonmarital lifestyles. What are some of the problems people face when they live a nontraditional lifestyle? What advice would you give to someone whose lifestyle meets with social disapproval?

2. Increasing numbers of people are delaying marriages into their late 20s and early 30s and some never marry at all. What social, demographic, and economic factors are responsible for this trend? What consequences, if any, exist for the larger society if a growing percentage of the population does not marry? Do women and men experience being single in similar or different ways? Explain. Do younger and older adults experience being single in similar or different ways? Explain.

3. Compare and contrast the legal status of married couples with that of cohabitants. What do you see as the advantages or disadvantages of the concept of domestic partnership? Do you favor or oppose granting domestic partnership status to heterosexual cohabitants? To homosexual cohabitants? What impact, if any, would this have on our understanding of marriages and families? Explain your position.

4. As noted earlier in this chapter, gay bashing, or attacks that are now called hate crimes, are on the increase. Has there been any such behavior on your campus, in your workplace, neighborhood, or city? What causes or triggers this behavior? What steps can be taken to minimize the likelihood of hate crimes from taking place in your immediate environments?

ADDITIONAL RESOURCES

SOCIOLOGICAL

ARNETT, JEFFREY JENSEN. 2004. *Emerging Adulthood: The Winding Road From the Late Teens Through the Twenties*. New York: Oxford University Press (USA). The author's interviews with young adults leads him to conclude that the majority of those coresiding with parents are not spoiled or self-indulgent as so often portrayed in the media but are trying to establish themselves in difficult economic times.

KANTER, ROSABETH MOSS. 2005. *Commitment and Community: Communes and Utopias in Sociological Perspective*. Cambridge, MA: Harvard University Press. The author provides an analysis of the nature and process of enduring commitment, utilizing early communes such as Oneida, Brook Farm, and the Shakers as well as present-day communes.

TRIMBERGER, E. KAY. 2005. *The New Single Woman*. New York: Beacon Press. A professor emirita of women's and gender studies,

Timberger interviewed women between the ages of 30 and 60 who have created full and satisfying lives. She found these women sharing six characteristics: nurturing home environments, satisfying work, comfort with their own sexuality, connections with the next generation, emotional intimacy with friends and family, and supportive communities.

WAITE, L. J., C. BACHRACH, M. HINDIN, E. THOMSON, AND A. THORNTON, Eds. 2000. *The Ties That Bind: Perspectives on Marriage and Cohabitation.* New York: Aldine de Gruyter. A readable volume that provides an excellent summary of recent data and current thinking on trends in marriage and cohabitation in the United States and Europe.

FILM

Brokeback Mountain. 2005. Ang Lee's epic western tells the story of two young cowboys who fall in love while working as sheepherders in the Wyoming high country. When their summer employment ends, they break up, both going their separate ways. Both marry and have children. Four years later, they meet again and their romance is rekindled. They spend the remainder of their otherwise straight lives concealing their love with tragic consequences for themselves and others they care about.

When Harry Met Sally. 1989. Harry meets Sally when she gives him a ride to New York after they both graduate from the University of Chicago. Over the years, they bump into each other from time to time and manage to carve out a genuine friendship, all the time struggling to keep it from becoming a romantic attachment.

LITERARY

KINGSOLVER, BARBARA. 1993. *Pigs in Heaven.* New York: Harper-Collins. A single woman finds and then adopts (perhaps illegally) a Cherokee child called Turtle and is faced with the possibility of losing her when a Native American lawyer enters the case.

BINCHY, MAEVE. 1992. *The Lilac Bus.* New York: Dell. Eight intriguing never-married women's and men's lives unfold as they ride the special Lilac Bus from Dublin to their families' homes for the weekend.

INTERNET

http://www.thetasksforce.org The National Gay and Lesbian Task Force provides data on lesbian and gay issues and links to other resources.

http://ilrg.com/forms/cohab-agreement.html The Internet Legal Research Group provides a nonmarital cohabitation/living together agreement form that can help couples address many of the issues they will face when living as an unmarried couple.

http://www.lifetimetv.com/reallife/relation/index.html This popular site examines issues that relate to personal relationships and the single life.

http://www.unmarried.org The Alternatives to Marriage Project advocates for equality and fairness for unmarried people and provides support and information for people who are single, choose not to marry, cannot marry, or choose to cohabit.

IN THE NEWS

Charlottesville, Virginia

Sigmund Freud once asked, "What do women want?" Modern feminists rephrased the question and asked, "What *should* women want?" In a controversial study published in 2006, two University of Virginia sociologists, Bradford Wilcox and Steven Nock, attempted to answer this compelling question, at least in terms of what contemporary women *want in marriage*. Using data from a comprehensive survey of married couples conducted between 1992 and 1994 (the National Survey of Families and Households), the researchers suggest that a new model of marital happiness has emerged, one in which wives stay at home and husbands are both good providers and emotionally engaged.

In the past, at least two-thirds of Americans believed that a focus on the domestic sphere of homemaking for wives and a focus on bread-winning for husbands made for a happy marriage. Influenced by the women's movement, by the 1990s, only one-third of the population embraced this traditional marriage structure. The new model of a happy marriage—in theory, if not in practice—became one of a partnership of equals who split marital responsibilities and tasks, both within and outside the home (Tierney, 2006).

Testing this model of marital bliss, Wilcox and Nock found that a husband's emotional engagement (affection and understanding) is crucial to a wife's happiness. So is a wife's belief that the housework is divided fairly. However, an equal division of labor does not make husbands more affectionate nor wives more fulfilled (Goodman, 2006). The happiest wives are those whose husbands contribute two-thirds or more of the couple's income. Even the most egalitarian wives (those who believe that duties and responsibilities should be equally divided in marriage) are happier with their marriage when their husbands are the chief earner. These wives, it seems, are ideologically egalitarians, but in practice they appear to prefer a more traditional marriage (Tierney, 2006). According to one of the researchers, Bradford Wilcox, "women want an equal division of labor at home but they still want their husbands to be providers who give them financial security and freedom" (quoted in Tierney, 2006:1). In addition, wives who have more traditional attitudes—who believe, for instance, that women should take the lead in caring for the home and family, and that men should take the lead in earning—have happier marriages. They report receiving more affection and understanding from their husbands, and spending more quality time with their husbands. Finally, wives who do not work outside the home report happier marriages than wives with outside jobs. A key finding in this study is that the happiest wives in the study are those who *perceive* that housework is divided fairly between them and their husbands. These same wives, however, also do more of the housework and their husband do more work outside home. Thus, according to Steven Nock, *what women want* is equity, which is not necessarily the same as equality (Tierney, 2006).

According to some observers, perhaps one of the most intriguing findings of the Wilcox and Nock study is that wives who work full time and have more progressive attitudes are more likely to be unhappy with the division of housework, which often spells trouble for them in terms of marital satisfaction. The happiest marriages are those in which men do more emotional work than they might choose and those in which women make an effort to expect less in household sharing. In essence, then, the researchers present what can be called a semitraditional model of marriage, where the husband expresses more feelings than his father did and the wife cleans more than her husband (Goodman, 2006). What do these findings mean for today's marriages? Do they mean that women who expect equality in marriage will have to lower their expectations or risk being in an unhappy marriage? Or does it mean that husbands will have to step it up a notch and become more emotionally engaged and share equally in household responsibilities and tasks?

Some critics of this study charge that it is flawed, that it is based on weak data collected some 15 years ago, and that it is so atypical of marriages today as to be an "outlier" (Rivers and Barnett, 2006). At best, critics say, there are several ways in which this data can be interpreted, depending on one's theoretical framework and perspective. Sociologists who have analyzed the same data used by Wilcox and Nock have found that the differences in happiness between working wives and stay-at-home wives are too small to really be significant. Sociologist Scott Coltrane of the University of California at Riverside analyzed the same National Survey of Families and Household data and did not find any differences at all. The bottom line is that the results of the Wilcox and Nock study are averages. There is a wide range of factors and arrangements that contribute to a happy marital relationship; an equal division of labor and emotionally engaged husbands are but two among many such factors or arrangements.

WHAT DO YOU THINK? Do you think that household and marital tasks and responsibilities should be equally shared? If you are (were) married or living in a long-term partnered heterosexual relationship, is it an egalitarian relationship, or would you describe your marriage or relationship as happy? Are the goals of an equal division of labor and a husband who is very emotionally engaged important to your marital or relationship happiness? Are you willing to forgo either one or both of these factors in your marriage or long-term relationship to be happy? If you are in a same-sex relationship, how, if at all, do these study findings correspond with your lived experiences? Is your relationship based upon an equal division of labor? Are one or both partners fairly equally emotionally engaged in the relationship? How important are these factors for your relationship happiness?

For those of us who have the choice, deciding whether to marry is one of the most important decisions we will make in our lifetime. This decision has implications for almost every aspect of an individual's life. Despite gender and sexual orientation, Americans continue to search for love and the "right" partner, to move in together, to vow to love each other, and, when legally allowed, to enter into marriages and often remarriages. And despite dramatic changes in marriages, families, and intimate relationships over the past half century (such as a significant rise in the divorce rate, in the number of couples who cohabit, in the number of people who choose either to delay marriage or to not marry at all, in ethnically mixed relationships, the preponderance of older couples, and the new visibility of same-sex unions) most people in the United States marry at least once in their lifetime. Approximately one-half of those marriages will last until one of the partners dies. Additionally, among those who do not marry, partnering with the expectation of a long-term or even lifetime commitment is still widespread; few people live through adulthood without at least one lengthy, intimate relationship (Yalom and Carstensen, 2002). However anxious we may be as a society in the face of charges that the institutions of marriages and families are dissolving and dys-

functional, surveys and other research consistently reveal that most Americans continue to view a happy marriage as either the most important goal or one of the most important goals in their lives. Most rank a good marriage at the top of their list of sources of satisfaction—above wealth, fame, good health, and a good job (Glenn, 2005; Waite and Gallagher, 2000). In addition, some researchers have predicted that the rates for both marriage and remarriage will continue to remain high in the foreseeable future (see Chapter 13 for a full discussion of remarriage).

These facts notwithstanding, as pointed out in Chapter 7, people in the United States today have more options with regard to marital roles than they did in the past. The women's movement of the 1960s and 1970s has had a profound effect on social attitudes concerning the roles of women and men both inside and outside of marriages and families. Shifts in gender roles and the growing demand for the right to marry among same-sex couples have altered not only how we view marriages and families but also how we experience them. In this chapter we focus on the ties between two people who commit to a long-term union, primarily, but not exclusively, within marriage. We examine the meaning of marriage in the United States in both traditional and contemporary terms, paying particular attention to the legal aspects of marriage and their effect on marital relationships. In addition, we examine the nature of marriage and other long-term relationships in the United States and the processes by which couples meet some of the many challenges of married life. Where appropriate, we also examine marriages cross-culturally.

WHY DO PEOPLE MARRY?

Why is it that amid much discussion and speculation about the decline in marriage and family values and that half of all marriages end in divorce, millions of Americans continue to marry each year? What is so attractive about marriage? What does it offer that other lifestyles do not? Recall the discussion of love in Chapter 4, where we indicated that most people in the United States believe that romantic love and marriage naturally go together—that marriage naturally follows falling in love. Given this notion about the interrelationship of love and marriage, it should not be surprising that the single most important reason people give for getting married is that they are in love. After love comes companionship, followed by a desire to have children, happiness, money, convenience, dependence, and the fear of contracting AIDS. Although most teens are just beginning to explore the complex world of dating and relationships, the majority, like their adult counterparts, also rate love as the most important reason to marry, followed by finances, compatibility, and common interests (Kiefer, 2004). For many Americans, marriage is a life-long commitment—a formal way for a couple to express their love, devotion, and commitment to each other and share their lives with the person of their choice. In this respect, marriage represents both a private and a public statement of commitment, trust, sharing, stability, intimacy, and the expectation of a permanent relationship.

However, love and commitment are not key aspects of a durable and long-lasting marriage in all cultures. In Japan, for example, although marriages, on average, are long-lasting, many married couples live without love. Based on interviews with Japanese couples living in a small community 200 miles southeast of Tokyo, *New York Times* writer Nicholas Kristof found that happiness and love are not key aspects of a durable marriage in Japan. For example, when describing her 40-year marriage, a 72-year-old Japanese woman said, "There was never any love between me and my husband. But, well, we survived" (Kristof, 1996:1). According to this woman, her husband used to beat her; he has never even said he liked her, never held her hand, and has never shown her affection in any way. Japanese couples are often perplexed when asked about love in marriage. For example, when asked if he loved his wife, a Japanese man who had been married 33 years furrowed his brow and looked perplexed, then responded, "Yeah, so-so, I guess. She's like air or water. You couldn't live without it, but most of the time, you're not conscious of its existence" (Kristof, 1996:6).

This is a common theme in the narratives of the people Kristof spoke with. According to Kristof, it does not seem that Japanese marriages survive because wives and husbands love each other more than American couples, but rather because they perhaps love each other less. Many Japanese couples believe love marriages are more fragile than arranged marriages. In love marriages, when something happens or if the couple falls out of love, they split up. Although the divorce rate in Japan is at a record high, it is still less than half that of the United States, and Japan is said to have one of the strongest marriage and family structures in the industrialized world.

Although the traditional married couple household is disappearing throughout most of the world, Japan is a prominent exception. Yet couples neither marry for love nor live with it during much of their marital life. In fact, based on answers to survey questions about politics, sex, social issues, religion, and ethics, a Japanese research institute found Japanese couples to have the lowest level of compatibility than couples in 20 other countries (see Figure 8.1). The example of Japan raises the obvious questions about what love is, as defined by whom, and its relevance or relationship to marital longevity. In short, it directs our attention to the socially constructed nature of love.

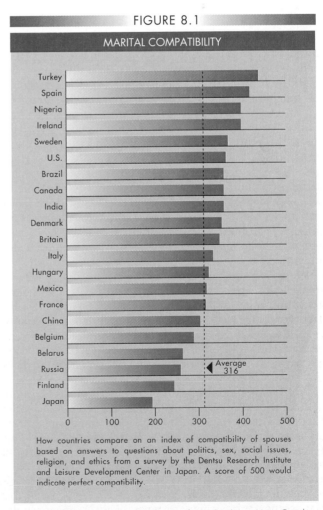

FIGURE 8.1

MARITAL COMPATIBILITY

How countries compare on an index of compatibility of spouses based on answers to questions about politics, sex, social issues, religion, and ethics from a survey by the Dentsu Research Institute and Leisure Development Center in Japan. A score of 500 would indicate perfect compatibility.

Source: Nicholas Kristof, 1996, "Who Needs Love? In Japan Many Couples Don't," *New York Times* (February 11): A6. Copyright 1996 by The New York Times Co. Reprinted by permission.

In addition to love and commitment, particularly in the United States, a number of social and economic reasons motivate people to marry. For example, although marriage does not ensure companionship, most Americans perceive it to be the greatest benefit of marriage. Many people believe being single inevitably leads to loneliness, even though there is no scientific evidence to support this view. In fact, some evidence suggests that people can be married and lonely; nonetheless, many people believe marriage offers the best opportunity for steady companionship. In a survey of never-married adults, for instance, 75 percent of the women and 80 percent of the men reported that what they would miss most if they never married would be companionship (Coontz, 2000; Edwards, 2000).

Some people marry for personal fulfillment while some marry purely for financial reasons, although this is less true in the United States today than in the past. For some individuals, the acquisition, maintenance, or extension of wealth, power, and status are strong motivations to marry. Financial marital arrangements sometimes occur among the upper classes, who build their lives around highly selective social encounters and relationships. It is also relatively common among many recently arrived ethnic groups, whose subcultural norms may include arranged marriages, dowries, and bride prices.

Because social norms, values, and ideologies often equate adulthood with marriage, for some people, achieving adulthood means getting married. People whose religious beliefs prohibit sexual intercourse and living together outside of legal marriage marry to legitimize and sanctify their relationship. And some people marry because of peer or family pressure. Women in particular are often pressured to marry by well-meaning relatives and friends who do not want to see them end up as "lonely old maids." Finally, some people marry to give legitimacy to a sexual relationship or to cohabitation, and others marry primarily for reproductive reasons—they want to have children or heirs who are recognized as legitimate by the state. Although an increasing number of people are having children outside legal marriage, most Americans indicate that they prefer to have children within the context of marriage.

Although in the United States we have considerable range to make a decision to marry or not, and although marriage is a personal choice and individual decision, larger sociopolitical and historical factors often shape our individual decisions of whether to marry. For example, economic factors are often key considerations. A variety of studies have indicated that during depressions and periods of high unemployment, men tend to put off getting married. However, when men have relatively good access to economic opportunities and resources they are more likely to make the decision to marry (Whitehead and Popenoe, 2004; Landale and Tolnay, 1991). Women's decisions to marry, on the other hand, are impacted by economic forces in a number of ways. On the one hand, the more economically independent a woman is, the more likely she will postpone marriage until a later age. On the other hand, some researchers have suggested that when women work, they are more likely to meet eligible men, and their economic independence might be an attraction in the marriage market (Jones, 2006; Kinnon, 2003).

Finally, race is an important sociopolitical construction that has a major impact on a person's decision of whether to marry. Several writers have suggested that the lack of employment opportunities, which hits poor people and people of color disproportionately, and the unlikeliness of a livable guaranteed minimum income often act as a deterrent to marriage. For example, the increasing economic marginality of many African American men has meant that marriage is often not a viable option. Given that men are still expected (consciously or unconsciously) to be the family "breadwinner," the disproportionately higher rates of African American male unemployment, sporadic or seasonal employment, and underemployment make marriage an unattractive proposition for many African American women and men (Jones, 2006; Kinnon, 2003; Mason, 1996). In this context, it appears that among low-income African American men, many men tend to postpone marriage until they feel they can support a family (fulfill the traditional "good provider" role).

Low income and economic marginality do not appear to affect the development and formation of intimate romantic relationships among these men. However, they do become factors in the decision regarding marriage. Various researchers, for instance, indicate that when there is economic prosperity among African Americans (for example, a high availability of jobs and/or when African American men have access to good-paying jobs), women and men are likely to marry and start a family and the chances of staying married increase dramatically (Hill, 2005; Kinnon, 2003). The intersection of race and family values also influences the decision to marry. For instance, individuals across race who come from families that place a high value on a college education will likely delay marriage until a later age than those who do not.

Sociological Perspective

On a theoretical level, there are several ways to explain why people marry. A dominant point of view in the field of sociology has been a structural–functional analysis that ignores individual motivation, and instead explains why people marry in terms of society's need or demand for legitimate children. The **principle of legitimacy,** the notion that all children ought to have a socially and legally recognized father, was first put forth by anthropologist Bronislaw Malinowski (1929).

According to Malinowski, although many societies allow individuals the freedom to be sexually active whether or not they are married, only a very few societies allow their members the freedom to conceive children outside of marriage. Almost universally, marriage is based on the official control of childbearing. Because women give birth, there is no doubt who is the mother of a child. There is, however, no visible means of identifying paternity. Thus, society must develop some means whereby men can be publicly (socially) and legally connected with their offspring. All societies, then, require that every child must have a man (a legitimately married father) who will assume the social role of father and protector and who will link the child to society. In essence, such an explanation implies that people marry solely to have children. We know, however, that this is not the case for most people. That a growing number of married couples do not have children gives us cause alone to question the viability of this principle to explain why people marry.

In contrast, a feminist perspective challenges theories such as the principle of legitimacy, maintaining that they place far more importance on the role of social father than mother in giving children social and legal status. Instead, a feminist perspective focuses on traditional gender role socialization, in which girls are taught to consider love, marriage, and children the ultimate goals for women and the most fulfilling roles they can play in society (see Chapter 3). Thus, a woman's decision to marry can represent, in part, a response to social pressures and expectations.

Whatever reasons people have for marrying, and whatever theories we use to explain why people marry, the fact remains that an overwhelming majority of us will marry at some time in our lives. Although marriage has declined somewhat over the last three decades, approximately 92 percent of Americans (down from 95 percent) still get married, and demographers predict that this trend will continue well into the future (Yalom and Carstensen, 2002; Smith, 1999). During a historical time when conservative pro marriage groups are attempting to influence legislatures around the country to repeal no-fault divorce laws (49 of the 50 states have such laws), when the U.S. Congress has approved financing for new marriage education programs, and when state courts in New Jersey and Washington contemplate rulings on same-sex marriage, what do you know about marriage in the United States? Although most Americans agree (and rightfully so) that marriage is not what it used to be, most of what "everyone knows" about marriage—what it used to be and just how it has changed—is not correct (Coontz, 2006). To find out how much you really know about marriage, try answering the true–false questions in the section titled "A Pop Quiz on Marriage."

THE MEANING OF MARRIAGE

As we have seen, marriage means different things to different people. Virtually everyone, however, regards marriage as a relatively permanent and committed relationship. In addition, given the fact that most marriages take place within some religious context, we can surmise that most people also view marriage as a sacrament. How many of us, however, think of marriage in terms of a legal contract?

Marriage is not an isolated event. Rather, it joins together both the couple involved and their respective families. The relationships formed by marriage sometimes become complex and can require some regulation. For example, to prevent conflict, the issue of inheritance and property rights requires a stable and consistent set of rules that prevails over time and applies fairly consistently across marriages and families. Thus, in the interest of order and stability, the state has set certain legal standards to which marriages and families must conform. These standards encompass such issues as whom we can marry, when we can

marry them, who is a legitimate heir, and who has property and inheritance rights. Although the specific laws regulating marriages and families may vary from state to state, in all states marriage is a legal contract with specified rights and obligations.

Marriage as a Commitment

Most researchers have found that commitment is a important factor in any intimate, emotionally satisfying, and meaningful relationship. When we pledge or commit ourselves to someone, we generally assume (or certainly hope) that the relationship will be long-term or permanent. According to some social scientists, human beings have a deep-seated need for secure, stable, and long-term relationships. Marriage is typically the type of relationship with which most people seek to fulfill this need.

In studies examining marital quality and longevity among couples who had been married 30 or more years, various researchers and writers found commitment to be a key factor in a long-term, enduring marriage. Couples who were highly committed to each other were usually also strongly committed to the institution of marriage. Researchers have also found that when couples are equal in terms of power in the relationship, there is a high rate of exchange and commitment to each other. Other factors found to contribute to marriage longevity include compatibility, mutual trust, friendship, honesty, faithfulness, and open and effective communication (Kalajian, 2006; Lawler and Yoon, 1996; Robinson and Blanton, 1993). Although important, commitment is not a single expectation or action. There are many aspects to commitment, some of which include the personal commitment between partners to each other, commitment to the relationship itself, commitment to the overall family unit, and long-term commitment. Commitment that includes these aspects tends to create individual as well as marital and family stability.

Marriage as a Sacrament

If you have not yet married but plan to in the future, what type of wedding will you have, and who will officiate at the ceremony? From a religious perspective, marriage is regarded as a **sacrament**—a sacred union or rite. In the past, the majority of people in this country who married for the first time did so under the auspices of some religious figure, such as a priest, rabbi, or minister. Although for economic and other considerations many people chose to bypass a religious ceremony, three-fourths of first-time marriages and three-fifths of remarriages among divorced people took place within the context of some type of religious ceremony. Even widows and widowers frequently remarried within the context of a religious ceremony (National Center for Health Statistics, 1988; Ravo, 1991).

However, according to a *USA Today* analysis of marriage license statistics, it appears that this trend is changing as fewer American couples who marry today see the need for religion's approval. Although there is no national data on how many marriages in this country are performed

A Pop Quiz On Marriage

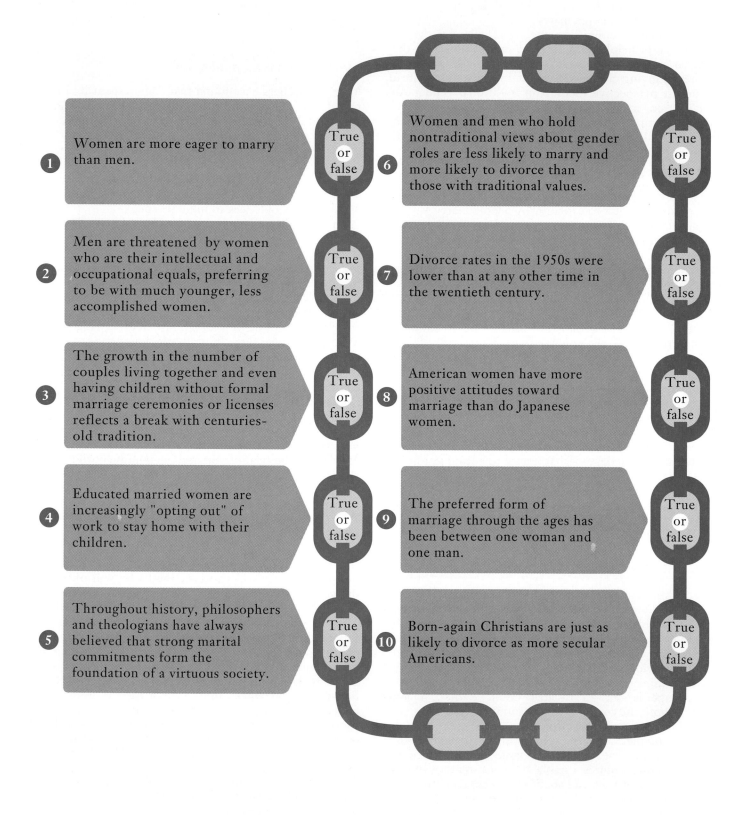

1. Women are more eager to marry than men.

   True or false

2. Men are threatened by women who are their intellectual and occupational equals, preferring to be with much younger, less accomplished women.

   True or false

3. The growth in the number of couples living together and even having children without formal marriage ceremonies or licenses reflects a break with centuries-old tradition.

   True or false

4. Educated married women are increasingly "opting out" of work to stay home with their children.

   True or false

5. Throughout history, philosophers and theologians have always believed that strong marital commitments form the foundation of a virtuous society.

   True or false

6. Women and men who hold nontraditional views about gender roles are less likely to marry and more likely to divorce than those with traditional values.

   True or false

7. Divorce rates in the 1950s were lower than at any other time in the twentieth century.

   True or false

8. American women have more positive attitudes toward marriage than do Japanese women.

   True or false

9. The preferred form of marriage through the ages has been between one woman and one man.

   True or false

10. Born-again Christians are just as likely to divorce as more secular Americans.

    True or false

ANSWER KEY

1. FALSE. From 1970 to the late 1990s, women's attitudes toward marriage became less favorable, while men's became more favorable. By the end of the twentieth century, more men than women said that marriage was their ideal lifestyle. And, on average, men become more content with their marriages over time, while women grow less so. A majority of divorced women and men report that the wife was the one who wanted out of the marriage.

2. FALSE. The gap in the age at first marriage between women and men has been narrowing for the past 80 years and is now at a historic low. By the end of the twentieth century, 39 percent of women aged 35 to 44 lived with younger men. Although men continue to rate youth and good looks higher than do women when looking for a mate, these criteria no longer outweigh all others. Men today are much more likely to seek a partner who has the same level of education and similar earnings potential. College-educated women are more likely to marry and less likely to divorce than women with less education.

3. FALSE. For the first thousand years of its existence, the church held that a marriage was valid if a couple claimed they had exchanged words of consent—even if there were no witnesses and no priest to officiate. It was not until 1754 that England began requiring issuance of a license for a marriage to be valid. Informal marriage and cohabitation were so common in early nineteenth-century America that one judge estimated one-third of all children were born to couples who were not legally married.

4. FALSE. The likelihood that college-educated women will drop out of the labor force because of having children declined by one-half from 1984 to 2004. And among all mothers with children under 6, the most highly educated are the least likely to leave their jobs, with that likelihood declining with each level of educational attainment.

5. FALSE. Ancient Roman philosophers and medieval theologians thought that loving your spouse too much was a form of "adultery," a betrayal of one's obligations to country or God. The ancient Greeks held that the purest form of love was between two men. In China, Confucian philosophers ranked the relationship between wife and husband as second from the bottom on their list of the most important family ties, with the father–eldest son relationship topping the list. Early Christians thought marriage was inescapably tainted by the presence of sex. According to the medieval church, virgins ranked higher in godliness; widows were second and wives a distant third.

6. TRICK QUESTION. Women with nontraditional values are indeed more likely to divorce than women with traditional views, but they are also more likely to get married in the first place. As for men, those with traditional values about gender are more likely to marry than nontraditional men, but they are also more likely to divorce. We do not precisely know why this discrepancy exists, but it probably has something to do with the fact that women's views on gender are changing more rapidly than men's.

7. FALSE. Aside from a huge increase in divorce right after World War II, divorce rates in the 1950s were higher than in any previous decade aside from the Depression. Almost one in three marriages formed in the 1950s eventually ended in divorce. Divorce rates rose steadily from the 1890s through the 1960s (with the dip during the Depression and a rise after World War II), soared in the 1970s, and have declined since 1981. Marriage rates, however, have also fallen significantly in the past 25 years.

8. TRUE. In 2001 schoolgirls around the world were asked whether they agreed with the statement that everyone needed to marry. Three-fourths of American schoolgirls agreed. In comparison, 88 percent of Japanese schoolgirls disagreed.

9. FALSE. The form of marriage that has been approved by more societies than any other through the ages has been polygamy—one man and many women. Polygamy is the marriage form mentioned most often in the first five books of the Bible. In some societies, one woman could marry several men—polyandry. In others, two families could forge an alliance by marrying off a daughter or son to the "ghost" of the other family's dead child. For most of history, the main reason for marriage was getting in-laws and managing property, not love or sex.

10. TRUE. Thirty-five percent of born-again Christians in the United States have divorced, almost the same as the 37 percent of atheists and agnostics who have divorced. In addition, 23 percent of born-again Christians have divorced twice. Among Pentecostals, the divorce rate is more than 40 percent. The region of the United States with the highest divorce rate is the Bible Belt.

Adapted from Stephanie Coontz, 2006, "A Pop Quiz on Marriage," New York Times (February 19): Section 4, p. 12.

by a religious figure versus a civil authority such as a notary, judge, or justice of the peace, statistics from those states that have tracked data for any significant period of time since 1980 suggest that the rate of civil marriage is on the rise across the United States. For example, there has been a growing and steady rate of civil marriages over the past 25 years—more that 40 percent of marriages in 2001, up from 30 percent in 1980. According to sociologist Pepper Schwartz, this trend toward civil versus religious marriage ceremonies might be attributable to high divorce and remarriage rates, more interfaith marriages, and more personalized ideas about spirituality. Other experts suggest that this trend could influence the larger debate in this country over same-sex unions—as fewer Americans feel a need for religious blessings on their marriage, they may be more inclined to support same-sex marriages (Grossman and Yoo, 2003). Is your choice of wedding ceremony consistent with these data or with past trends?

The trend toward civil marriages notwithstanding, most people in this country continue to at least regard marriage as a significant religious or holy institution based on a sacred commitment to each other and their God. In the Christian tradition, for example, the sacredness and joyfulness of marriage is often voiced in the story of Christ's first public miracle, which was said to have been the act of turning water into wine for a wedding celebration. In addition, marriage is considered a holy state ("holy matrimony") conducted under the direct authority of God ("What God has joined together let no man put asunder"). Marriage in the religious context is also considered a lifelong commitment. Recognizing that not all marriages will last a lifetime, however, some Protestant and Jewish denominations allow for the termination of marriage through divorce and sanctify remarriages based on the same principles of the sacrament. Some religions, however, most notably Catholicism, are quite literal in their interpretation of marriage as a holy union sanctioned by God. Thus, the Catholic Church does not recognize divorce as a valid means of terminating a marriage. Under certain circumstances, however, the Catholic Church may annul a marriage, declaring that the marriage never actually occurred.

Marriage as a Legal Contract

Some marriage and family researchers have distinguished between what they call legal and social marriage. **Legal marriage** is a legally binding agreement or contractual relationship between two people and is defined and regulated by the state. In contrast, **social marriage** is a relationship between people who cohabit and engage in behavior that is essentially the same as that within a legal marriage, but without engaging in a marriage ceremony that is validated by the state. Thus, the relationship is not, under most circumstances, legally binding. Cohabitation and common-law marriage, both of which were discussed in Chapter 7, are examples of social marriage.

Marriage in the United States is a legal and financial contractual agreement that, like most other contractual agreements, is regulated by certain legal requirements.

When two people marry, they agree to abide by the terms of the marriage contract. Although the marriage contract is very similar to an ordinary private contract, there are some very important differences. Unlike an ordinary private contract, the marriage contract is either unwritten or is not written in any one place. In addition, the terms and penalties of the contract are usually unspecified, that is, they are scattered throughout marriage and family laws and court decisions handed down over the years, or they are not very well known by the parties involved. In addition, the state, and not the married couple, specifies the conditions of the marriage contract. Therefore, unlike a private contract, where the parties involved may break, modify, change, or restrict the contract by some mutual action, a married couple cannot on their own change or break the marriage contract.

Most contracts cannot be changed while they are in effect without the knowledge and consent of the parties involved. In contrast, the marriage contract, because its terms are defined by various policymakers such as judges and legislators, can be changed without the direct knowledge or consent of married couples. No other contract operates in this fashion. Because no one sends married couples a notification every time marriage laws change, most of us are unaware of these changes unless, of course, we keep abreast of them through media and other reports. Thus, for example, some states have proposed legislation that would require a wife to secure the consent of her husband before she could have an abortion. Even though the couple had little or no input into the proposed legislation, if it becomes law they are legally bound by it.

The most important marriage laws are state laws. The U.S. government has both created and defined marriage, giving the individual states the responsibility for ruling marriages. Each state defines the rights and obligations of married couples through a myriad of marriage and family laws, and only representatives of the state may marry people and terminate marriages. Even when people choose to be married by a member of the clergy, only those clergy that the state has granted the right to officiate at marriages may do so. In addition, state marriage laws cover only the residents of the particular state. Thus, if a couple marries in one state and later move to another state, their marriage is covered by the laws of the new state as soon as they become residents. In a sense, then, the marriage contract is much less an expression of love for one's chosen partner and much more realistically a pact with the state. In this context, it is well worth noting that historically states have maintained social and legal control over women and children, defined women as property, and legitimized a gender-based division of paid and unpaid labor within society—women's labor is unpaid, men's labor is paid (Brownsworth, 1996).

Most people probably do not think of marriage in this way—as a legally binding contract ruled by individual states and that disadvantages one partner to the advantage of the other. Most of us are not aware of marriage laws and the extent of the state's role in marriage until separation, divorce, or death occurs, or when inheritance or property rights are at issue.

Some Legal Aspects of the Marriage Contract

Some of the more apparent legal aspects of the marriage contract specify who can marry whom and when. Every state in this country has laws that specify who can marry whom in terms of age and sex. In addition, until 1967 some states continued to specify who could marry whom in terms of race.

Sexual Orientation Marriage is a civil right that most heterosexuals take for granted. By and large, however, lesbian and gay couples do not enjoy this same civil right. Currently, in only one U.S. state can people of the same sex legally marry—Massachusetts. This is not surprising given that most states define marriage as a commitment by two people to carry on their lineage through conceiving and rearing children. The topic of same-sex marriages, almost unimaginable a few decades ago, is so potent a topic today that it is a major issue in many political campaigns and debates, public and popular discourse, and legal actions across the country. As an increasing number of lesbian and gay couples openly cohabit in long-term relationships, and are progressively more militant and litigious in their demand for the right to express their love and commitment to one another as do heterosexual couples, they have placed greater and greater pressure on business, government, religious institutions, the workplace, and law-makers to extend to them the same rights and privileges as heterosexual married couples. Although marriage between same-sex couples is legal in one state, and two others—Vermont and Connecticut—allow same-sex couples the rights and benefits of marriage in civil unions, and California has a domestic partnership law that provides similar benefits, same-sex couples are still a long way from enjoying all of the benefits and institutional privileges accorded heterosexual married couples (Scott and Schwartz, 2006) (see Figure 8.2).

Because marriages performed in one state are typically recognized by the others, the U.S. Congress passed the Defense of Marriage Act in 1996, which stipulates that no state can be forced to recognize another state's same-sex marriage, defines marriage in all federal policies, laws, and acts of Congress as a legal union of one woman and one man, and withholds federal marriage benefits from lesbian and gay married couples (104th Congress, HR 3396). Currently, 43 states have statutory Defense of Marriage Acts. Three of those states have statutory language that predates the 1996 Defense of Marriage Act, defining marriage as between a woman and a man. Nineteen states have defined marriage in their constitutions and seven states had a constitutional amendment on the ballot in 2006. Essentially, in more than two-thirds of the United States while the law sanctions heterosexual marriage it denies same-sex couples the same legal standing (see Figure 8.3).

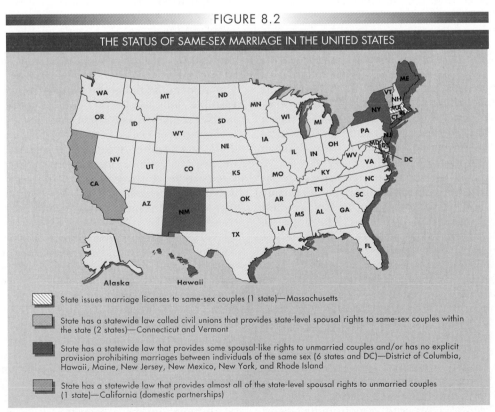

FIGURE 8.2

THE STATUS OF SAME-SEX MARRIAGE IN THE UNITED STATES

State issues marriage licenses to same-sex couples (1 state)—Massachusetts

State has a statewide law called civil unions that provides state-level spousal rights to same-sex couples within the state (2 states)—Connecticut and Vermont

State has a statewide law that provides some spousal-like rights to unmarried couples and/or has no explicit provision prohibiting marriages between individuals of the same sex (6 states and DC)—District of Columbia, Hawaii, Maine, New Jersey, New Mexico, New York, and Rhode Island

State has a statewide law that provides almost all of the state-level spousal rights to unmarried couples (1 state)—California (domestic partnerships)

Sources: Human Rights Campaign, 2005/2006, "Relationship Recognition in the U.S." and "Statewide Marriage Laws," http://www.hrc.org/marriage/; M. Daniels, 2000, "United We Fall," *World Magazine* 15 (June 17): 24, http://www.worldmag.com/world/issue/06-17-00/national_10asp.

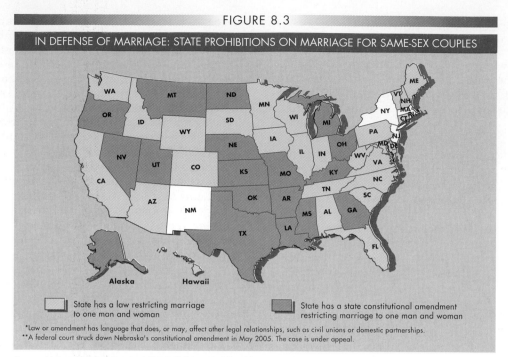

FIGURE 8.3

IN DEFENSE OF MARRIAGE: STATE PROHIBITIONS ON MARRIAGE FOR SAME-SEX COUPLES

State has a law restricting marriage to one man and woman

State has a state constitutional amendment restricting marriage to one man and woman

*Law or amendment has language that does, or may, affect other legal relationships, such as civil unions or domestic partnerships.
**A federal court struck down Nebraska's constitutional amendment in May 2005. The case is under appeal.

Source: Human Rights Campaign, 2005/2006, "State Prohibitions on Marriage for Same-Sex Couple," http://www.hrc.org/marriage.

As a consequence, defense of marriage laws are currently being challenged as a violation of the equal protection clause of the U.S. Constitution.

Lesbian and Gay Coupledom and Marriage According to recent census data, there are well over one-half million (594,391) reported same-sex households in the country—of those, 293,365 are female partners and 301,026 are male partners—and many of these couples would like to be married if marriage were an option. For example, in a recent survey, 85 percent of lesbians and gays said that legal marriage is "very" or "somewhat" important to them (Human Rights Campaign, 2003; Leland and Miller, 1998).

Given that most Americans view marriage as a significant religious and holy institution, it is not surprising that many lesbians and gays, like heterosexuals, want to sanctify their commitment to each other and their God. The desire to make a public commitment to one another in the church or synagogue of their choice is not only controversial but also a divisive issue within religious institutions.

Today, Presbyterians, Catholics, Jews, and members of other religions have been forced increasingly to grapple with whether to sanction same-sex unions and ceremonies within their faith, whether or not they are legally recognized by state and federal governments.

Some people feel that the legal prohibition of same-sex marriage prevents lesbian and gay couples from forming legal, religious, and public marital bonds that would secure their relationship rights, and it deprives them of a litany of benefits and protections, rights, and responsibilities. And this is certainly true. Although marriage has its drawbacks,

some of its most striking benefits include the right of a surviving marital partner to inherit property, the right to file a joint income tax return (married couples filing jointly are taxed at a lower rate than single people and married couples who file separately), and the right to share pension and health care insurance benefits offered by many employers to their employees. *Civil unions* for same-sex couples give them almost all of the rights and privileges of married couples (for example, joint property rights, inheritance rights, shared health care benefits, hospital visitation rights, and immunity from being compelled to testify against a partner) (Goldberg, 2001), but a major caveat is that, unlike traditional marriage unions, civil unions are only recognized in Vermont and Connecticut. Likewise, in states that recognize same-sex domestic partnerships, such recognition does not include the same legal rights that come automatically with marriage (see Table 8.1).

As homosexuality generally and gay marriage specifically have become more and more visible components of U.S. culture, same-sex domestic partners are gaining some legitimacy and protections. For instance, many states and cities, as well as many major corporations, offer medical and other benefits to the partners of lesbian and gay employees but not to unmarried heterosexual couples. In 1997, for example, San Francisco passed the first city ordinance in the nation that extended health insurance and other benefits to its domestic partner employees. Other cities, such as Chicago, Atlanta, New York, San Diego, and the District of Columbia, have followed suit. According to a survey of same-sex benefits in the workplace, 3400 private and public employers in the U.S. now provide domestic-partner benefits

TABLE 8.1

The Legal and Economic Benefits of Marriage and the Costs of Marriage Inequality

A marriage is not just a declaration of undying love; marriage also brings legal and financial benefits that partners share, and given that lesbians and gays do not have the same access to legal marriage, they are denied these same legally sanctioned benefits.

Some of the Benefits of Marriage

- Government benefits, such as Social Security and Medicare
- Joint insurance policies for health, home, and automobile
- Retirement benefits
- The status as next-of-kin and the right to make medical decisions for a partner
- Bereavement or sick or family leave to care for a sick partner or child
- Wrongful-death benefits
- Domestic violence protection orders
- Joint parenting, parental custody, and/or adoption
- Alimony
- Tax advantages
- Inheritance rights
- Divorce rights
- Hospital visitation rights
- Confidentiality of conversations
- Right to decide what to do with a partner's corpse

Some Costs of Marriage Inequality for Lesbians and Gays

- Same-sex couples pay more in federal income tax than married couples when one parent stays at home.
- Same-sex couples with children are far less likely to have access to employer-sponsored health insurance for their families than married couples—and those who do pay hundreds of dollars more in taxes for it.
- Denied Social Security survivor benefits that are made available to all married couples—When a gay or lesbian parent dies leaving a young child behind, the loss of Social Security survivor benefits to the family can range from $100,000 to $250,000, depending on whether state laws permitted both parents to establish a legal relationship to the surviving child.
- The lack of a marriage license may cost tens of thousands of dollars when a partner dies despite having paid taxes their whole lifetime at the same rate as other Americans. For instance, same-sex senior couples are more likely than married heterosexual couples to still be making mortgage payments on their home. The higher debt burden, combined with the financial losses that stem from being unmarried, means that the risk of losing one's home is greater for a surviving partner than for surviving heterosexual spouses. More than one in ten same-sex couples include a partner over 65, more than one in four include a partner over 55.
- Heavily taxed on any retirement plan—401(k) or IRA—they inherit from their partners, although married spouses can inherit these plans tax-free.
- Charged an estate tax on the inheritance of a home, even if it was jointly owned—a tax that would not apply to married spouses.

Sources: B. A. Robinson, 2001, "Legal and Economic Benefits of Marriage," *Religious Tolerance.org* (June 10): http://www.religious tolerance.org/mar_bene.htm (Accessed: April 19, 2006). Lisa Bennett and Gary J. Gates, 2004, "The Cost of Marriage Inequality to Children and Their Same-Sex Parents)" (April 13). Washington, DC: Human Rights Campaign Foundation. www.hrc.org. Lisa Bennett and Gary J. Gates, 2004., "The Cost of Marriage Inequality to Gay, Lesbian and Bisexual Seniors." (January 29). Washington, DC: Human Rights Campaign Foundation. www.hrc.org.

for lesbian and gay employees. These companies include the big three automakers (Daimler-Chrysler Corp., Ford Motor Co., and General Motors Corp), 165 of the 500 largest companies in the United States as listed in the Fortune 500 (such as IBM, Citigroup, Inc., AT&T, and Boeing), and a growing list of other large and small companies (such as American Express, Avon, Reebok, Walt Disney Company, Coca-Cola, the Gap, Microsoft, Time Warner, United Airlines, American Airlines, Apple Computer, Lotus Development, Nynex, Levi Strauss, Xerox, and Starbucks Coffee) (Robinson, 2000a).

Same-sex marriage is not a new concept, nor is it an issue unique to the United States. As we pointed out at the beginning of Chapter 7, a number of countries since 1989 have legalized same-sex unions, beginning with Denmark in 1989; most recently, in 2005, same-sex marriage was legalized across Canada. Other countries in which same-sex couples can marry include the Netherlands, Belgium, Germany, and South Africa, and those that offer legal status to civil unions or allow lesbian and gay couples to register include France, Iceland, Norway, Sweden, and several cities in Spain (Robinson, 2005). However, in the United States, most Americans view homosexual relations as immoral and oppose the legalization of same-sex marriages. For example, in a Gallup poll on morality, less than half (44 percent) of Americans believed homosexual behavior was morally acceptable, whereas 52 percent believed it was morally wrong, and most popular opinion polls consistently report that only 33 percent of Americans approve of legally sanctioned gay marriage (FOX News/Opinion Dynamics Poll, 2006; Gallup Poll, 2006).

Among those who oppose gay marriage, some believe it to be an oxymoron, an ideological invention designed to force societal acceptance of homosexuality. Those who hold this viewpoint believe marriage must be the joining of a woman and man only. They believe lesbians and gays should have the right to vote, to work, to inherit, to receive health benefits, to receive Social Security benefits from their partners, and to be free of violence—but not to marry. The most common argument against legalizing same-sex marriages is that it would subvert the stability and integrity of heterosexual marriage and family (Weiser, 1996; Associated Press, 2000).

On the other hand, those who support same-sex marriage argue that rather than weakening marriages and families, gay marriage would actually strengthen them. Giving lesbians and gays the same rights to marry as heterosexuals would reinforce the commitment of many gays to live within long-term, committed relationships and encourage others who might not otherwise to do so. In addition, permitting such marriages would not only benefit gay couples but would also benefit society at large given that research has consistently demonstrated that marriage encourages monogamy. And in a cultural and social environment where HIV/AIDS is a pandemic that disproportionately impacts gay men, encouraging gay monogamy is a rational public health policy. Most importantly, however, legalizing same-sex marriages would provide lesbians and gays with the fundamental American freedom of having the right to choose whether and whom to marry (Wolfson, 1996; Hartinger, 1994).

What do you think? Do laws prohibiting same-sex marriage violate the civil rights of lesbians and gays? Should lesbians and gays have the legal right to marry with all of the benefits that come automatically with heterosexual marriage? Should they be allowed to marry in their respective churches and synagogues, even if such unions are not legal in this country? Would same-sex marriage require a redefinition of marriage? If so, how might we redefine marriage? Should American children be taught to accept same-sex marriage as a "normal" marital lifestyle?

Whatever your position, the fact is that the issue of legal lesbian and gay marriage is not one that is likely to disappear. Rather, it will continue to be a prominent social and political issue far into the future. For what is at stake here? The debate is not just about abstract concepts such as the definition of a marriage and a family or the rights of a minority group. As we said earlier, marriage is not just about love and companionship. Marriage is also about legal and economic or financial benefits that a couple shares. Recall the somewhat detailed list of the kinds of benefits that are at stake for lesbians and gays seeking the rights and privileges of legal marriage presented in Table 8.1. Some proponents of same-sex marriages are optimistic that it will be a legal reality in all of the United States one day, with lesbian and gay partners sharing equally and consistently the legal and financial as well as social benefits of heterosexual marriage. Although the goal of gay marriage is not universally embraced among lesbians and gays, most gay couples feel they deserve the same rights that nongay couples take for granted.

In addition to requiring heterosexuality in marital relationships, marriage law also requires monogamy. Under legal statutes, people cannot have more than one spouse at a time. If an individual does, he or she can be prosecuted for **bigamy**—marrying one person while still being legally married to another. Although seldom enforced, many states have laws that prohibit **adultery**, extramarital sexual intercourse, and **fornication**, sexual intercourse outside legal marriage.

The Incest Taboo Not only does the marriage contract prohibit marriage between persons of the same sex, but it also prohibits marriage or sexual relations between a variety of relatives ranging from parents and siblings to non-blood-related in-laws. Although the specific set of blood relatives who we cannot legally marry or have sex with differs from state to state, no state allows us to marry a parent, a sibling, an uncle or aunt, a niece or nephew, a grandparent, or a grandchild. The majority of states prohibit marriage between half siblings and first cousins. Some states also exclude second cousins and, in a few cases, third cousins. In addition, some states go so far as to prohibit marriage between **affinal relatives**, people related by marriage, such as a brother- or sister-in-law, even though they are not related by blood.

As we discussed in Chapter 1, although the range of relatives covered by the incest taboo has varied over human history, some theorists maintain that this taboo serves an important social and political function for families and society. By forcing families to mate and reproduce outside the immediate family network, marriage helps create political and economic relationships vital to society's structure and survival.

Age Restrictions Marriage rules also define when we are considered mature enough to marry. In the past, the legal age at which people could marry was tied to puberty and the ages at which women and men could reproduce. If a person was old enough to reproduce, she or he was considered old enough to marry. Often the legal age for marriage was different for women and men. Today, however, the concern is whether a person is mature enough to marry, regardless of the ability to reproduce. To ensure that a person is both old enough and mature enough, each state has set a legal age for marriage. That age varies, however, according to whether the couple has obtained their parents' consent. The marriageable age for women and men, with or without parental consent, is the same in most states. For example, as discussed in Chapter 5, in every state except one the legal age at which marriage can be contracted without parental consent is 18 for both women and men. In Georgia, a female or male may contract a marriage without parental consent as early as 16 years of age. On the other hand, on the island of Puerto Rico, individuals cannot contract a marriage on their own until age 21. (See Appendix E for a list of marriage requirements by state.)

With parental consent, the picture changes. The typical age requirement for marriage with parental consent is 16. In as many as 5 states (Alabama, New Hampshire, New York, Texas, and Utah), however, females and males may marry as early as 14 years of age if their parents consent. Moreover, in a few states, parental consent is not required if a minor was previously married. And two states (California and Mississippi) have no age limits. In some states, minors may obtain a marriage license if the female is pregnant, if a child has already been born to the couple, or under what some states define as "special circumstances." In other states, a minor wishing to marry must not only have parental consent but must also get the permission of a judge. As we saw in Chapter 4, the interrelationship between age, sexual intimacy, and marriage is among several controversial issues in America's twenty-first century culture wars. Looking toward the future, an increasing number of older and younger people will be forming intimate bonds, so America as a society may be forced to reexamine traditions and state laws that define what is or is not an appropriate age for love, sex, and marriage.

Blood Test Regardless of age and whether parental consent is needed, when two people plan to marry they must file an application with the state and obtain a marriage license. In the majority of the states (approximately two-thirds), to obtain a marriage license a couple first must be tested to determine if they have a sexually transmitted disease. This procedure is commonly referred to as "getting a blood test." Usually there is a brief waiting period between the time people are tested and the time they receive the marriage license. In several states, individuals are tested for other diseases in addition to sexually transmitted diseases. For example, in 8 states, people (especially women) also must be tested for rubella (German measles) and their Rh blood type. In New York, certain applicants may be further required to take a test for sickle cell anemia, a condition that is far more prevalent among African Americans than among whites, before a marriage license is issued. If the sickle cell condition is present, a couple can be denied a marriage license unless it is established that procreation is not possible (World Almanac, 2000).

Although most states require some type of medical test for sexually transmitted diseases, there is little routine testing for AIDS prior to marriage. For a short period of time in the late 1980s, Illinois law required AIDS testing before a marriage license could be obtained. In 1989, however, the law was rescinded, partly because many people, unhappy with the law, crossed state lines and married in surrounding states. In addition, the tests proved extremely expensive and uncovered only a small number of AIDS cases (Marriage License Bureau and Cook County Clerk's Office, 1993).

One last point is that some individuals do not do any of the things discussed in the previous paragraphs, yet their relationship is recognized by the state as a legal, or common-law, marriage. As discussed in Chapter 7, although common-law marriages were once widely recognized, today only about one-fourth of the states recognize them. Thus, in answering the question "What is marriage?" we have seen that marriage encompasses a rather wide range of behaviors and issues. It includes a complex contractual agreement among not two but three parties: the couple and the state, but can also simply be a relationship defined by two people as a marriage.

CHANGE AND CONTINUITY IN THE MEANING OF MARRIAGE

One of the most fundamental and significant premises on which U.S. marriage and family laws have been based is the historical notion that the family is the property of the husband, and therefore he is the head of the household. The other side of this premise is the belief that women are the weaker sex and need the care and protection of men. This belief reflects the common-law concept of **coverture**, the idea that a wife is under the protection and influence of her husband—that the two become one at the time of marriage, and that one is the husband. From these assumptions flow many rights, obligations, and expectations about how a married couple should behave and relate to each other. Therefore, not surprisingly, we find that over the course of time many of the rules and laws surrounding marriage have treated women and men differently based solely on their biological sex. For example, the symbolic loss of a woman's identity once she marries is still evident today in the common practice of a married woman legally taking her husband's name when she marries, whereas the man's legal identity remains the same as it was before marriage. Many of the marriage traditions and rituals practiced around the world (see the In Other Places box) are also rooted in this premise.

Historically, marriage has extended the rights of men vis-à-vis women and children. Women, in contrast, lost many legal rights when they married, because their marital obliga-

tions and rights were defined primarily in terms of their service to husbands and children. Under this arrangement, for example, women have suffered a long history of violence at the hands of their husbands, who, until the late 1800s, could legally beat their wives if they did not fulfill their wifely duties. (Chapter 11 contains a detailed discussion of this issue.)

Provisions of the Modern Marriage Contract

The provisions of the modern marriage contract are similar to those based on the old principle of coverture. Over 30 years ago, social scientist Lenore Weitzman (1977) identified four basic provisions of the traditional marriage contract that have been incorporated into marriage laws in the United States: (1) the wife is responsible for caring for the home, (2) the wife is responsible for caring for any children, (3) the husband is head of the household, and (4) the husband is responsible for providing support for the family. In the language of marital rights and obligations, these provisions assert that the wife owes her husband domestic and companionship services, and in return the husband owes his wife protection and economic support. Although over the years marriage and family laws have become more equitable in the treatment of wives and husbands, these four provisions are not simply old-fashioned ideas that are no longer relevant. In many states, women continue to lose legal rights when they marry, and they continue to be treated as the property of their husbands. And among fundamentalist Christians and other Christian groups, women continue to be subjugated in marriage.

Today the specific conditions of the marriage contract vary from one state to another, but some common assumptions are evident. In the following discussion, we examine some specific beliefs and practices from the past in terms of their impact on current marital patterns, noting both continuity and changes where they have occurred.

Residence   In the past, a woman was expected to take her husband's surname and move into his domicile (place of residence). Although a wife is no longer required to take her husband's name, a husband retains the legal right to decide where the couple will live, and marriage law imposes an obligation on the wife to live in her husband's choice of residence. Therefore, when a woman marries, if her place of residence is different from her husband's, his place of residence automatically supersedes hers. If a woman lives in a different state from her husband and she does not take her husband's place of residence as her own, the legal ramifications are many. For instance, she must reregister to vote; she could lose the right to attend a university in her hometown as a resident student; and she could lose the privilege of running for public office in her home state (Renzetti and Curran, 1992, 2002). Laws pertaining to the marital domicile reflect traditional gender inequalities in other ways. For example, if a husband gets a job in another city and his wife refuses to relocate with him, she is assumed by law to have abandoned him. If, on the other hand, a wife gets a job in another city and her husband refuses to relocate with her, she is still defined by law as having abandoned him.

In this sense, men are still assumed to be the head of the household and can therefore determine where the family will live. Over the years, however, some equalizing of marital roles and obligations has occurred. Thus, in many states today a woman can establish a separate household for a specific purpose. In addition, at least one state court has ruled that a wife who is the primary breadwinner can decide where the couple will live (Renzetti and Curran, 2002).

Property Rights In the past, a woman's property rights also came under the control and management of her husband once she married. Not only did a husband gain control of his wife's property on marriage, but he could also do with it as he pleased, with or without her knowledge or consent. Today, however, women have considerable property rights, although the specifics differ across states. In some states, a wife and husband may own property individually, whereas in others their property may be considered community property.

Most U.S. states recognize the individual ownership of property. Whoever has proof of ownership of property owns it in the eyes of the law. If neither the wife nor husband has proof of ownership, however, most courts determine that the husband is the owner, particularly if the wife has remained in the home as a homemaker during the marriage. The court's rationale is that because the wife had no income with which to acquire the assets, they belong to the husband, who has simply allowed her use of them over the years. Thus, for example, in some cases a joint bank account has been deemed by the court to belong to the husband if the wife did not earn an income.

As this discussion makes clear, common-law property states, as they are called, give quite an advantage to husbands. It is ironic that those women who conform most closely to the patriarchal norms that surround marital roles are the ones who are hurt most by marriage laws and regulations pertaining to property ownership. Women who have spent their lives in service to their husbands (and children) end up with few assets of their own. Moreover, because of their dependency on their husbands, they are the most vulnerable during and after marriage. On the other hand, in the community property system, practiced in only a few states, wives and husbands own all assets jointly and equally whether or not the wife earns an income. This system does not penalize women for choosing to be full-time homemakers, although it does present other problems for wives, as discussed in more detail in Chapter 12.

As disadvantaged as married women were in the past and are today under the principle of coverture, men also were and still are restricted in several important ways as well. For instance, it has been argued that because marriage awarded a wife a right of inheritance, the husband's estate was reduced. In addition, marriage obligated a husband to support his wife and family, an obligation that poor and working-class men often found difficult to meet solely on their own. The continuation of this idea and the inequities it engenders for men are reflected in the fact that husbands today are still legally obliged to support their wives even if the wife works and earns a higher wage than the husband.

Given our discussion of marital rights and obligations thus far, are you wondering about the degree to which these principles are enforceable by law? We turn our attention next to an examination of this question.

The Law According to some experts on the subject, a husband's right to his wife's services is basically unenforceable by law in a direct sense. There are, however, some very important consequences of this provision of the marriage contract. One such consequence is a result that can be attributed to a husband's **conjugal rights**—rights pertaining to the marriage relationship. Because of this right and because, until recent times, rape statutes read that rape was forced sexual intercourse with a woman not your wife (in essence, granting husbands a license to rape), men had license to rape their wives. It was not until the 1970s, when some members of the women's movement argued for the elimination of this spousal exemption from charges of rape, that a married woman could charge her husband with rape. Although it took the next 20 years, marital rape is now a crime in all 50 states, under at least one section of the sexual offense codes (National Clearinghouse on Marital and Date Rape, 2005) (we will discuss this issue in more detail in Chapter 12). Furthermore, because the marriage contract obliges a wife to perform domestic labor for her husband, she cannot be directly compensated for her work; until recent times, her economic contribution to the marriage was not considered in the division of property at the time of divorce. Interestingly, although the husband has no legal obligation to compensate his wife for domestic services, if a third party injures the wife, the husband can legally sue the party for the value of the domestic services he lost.

Although a wife has a legal right to be supported by her husband, she has little control over the nature or amount of that support. Based on an accumulation of findings in various court cases, it seems that as long as a wife and husband live together the husband has a right to support his wife in whatever manner he chooses. If a wife feels she is not being adequately supported, she has little legal recourse.

The Marriage Contract Today

Since the 1970s, marriage and family law in the United States has changed substantially, although certain traditions and legal restrictions continue to leave women at a disadvantage. As pointed out, women no longer have to take their husband's surname. In many states, however, a wife who takes her husband's surname must seek his permission to return to using her birth name. In the past, the decision not to adopt the husband's surname often created legal problems and unnecessary difficulties for the couple. For example, insurance companies, banks, and other bureaucracies often had difficulty dealing with married customers with different surnames. Thus, such customers were sometimes denied services meant for married couples, or they were seriously inconvenienced. Today, however, legal and business establishments have caught up with this practice, and a woman's decision to retain her family name does not appear to cause as many difficulties.

Rather than give up their family name upon marrying, some women choose to hyphenate their name after marriage (for example, Lillian Brown-Johnson). This practice, however, is not without problems. For instance, how will the couple name their children? Will their children carry the father's surname only? Will they carry the hyphenated name? If so, when the children become adults, can they hyphenate their already-hyphenated name?

Other ways in which contemporary couples attack gender-stereotypic wedding rituals and traditions include brides having "best women" or best men, grooms having "men of honor" or women (rather than best men) stand up for them, both parents (as opposed to the father alone) giving away a daughter, one or both parents giving away the groom, or completely eliminating the ritual of someone "giving away" a human being.

Marriage Traditions in the United States

Marriage is a critical rite of passage in most cultures, and as demonstrated in the In Other Places box, in most cultures it is steeped with tradition and rituals. In the traditional sense, marriage in the United States is a culmination of the mate selection process: courtship, dating, engagement, parties for the bride and groom, and finally the wedding itself.

Engagement In the United States, if during the dating period a couple decides to take their relationship to another level, deciding that they will marry at some time in the future, they will typically end the formal and private dating phase of their relationship and move it to a more public expression of their relationship and intentions toward one another—the *engagement.* The engagement formalizes the couple's commitment to marry, and, until recently, it has been a formal phase in the mate selection process whereby the man gives the woman an engagement ring, a public announcement is made in the media (newspapers, newsmagazines) either by the couple or the couple's family, and family and friends are invited to share the couple's happiness and commitment to marry (an engagement party). Ideally, at this juncture in the relationship, each member of the couple is emotionally committed to one another, are sexually monogamous, are getting to know each other's family (if they not already know them), and are focused on planning the wedding.

Although the engagement functioned as a binding commitment to marry in the past, today it seems it is more symbolic and ritualistic than a binding commitment. And given that more people are delaying first marriage until later ages, a growing number of people are remarrying, and an increasing number of single people are cohabiting, engagements also have become far less formal. For some groups, engagement may not even be a ritual anymore. For example, the increasing number of couples who start their relationship by "hanging out," "getting together," or living together are less likely to become formally engaged. Rather, they typically will simply announce verbally that they plan to marry. This informal approach is less socially binding but consistent with the informal or casual nature of their relationship. The engagement phase of the mate selection process has changed in other ways as well. For instance, older couples may or may not go through a formal engagement period. Rather, they might forgo public announcements in the media and simply tell family and friends their intention to marry and then qui-

etly do so. Sometimes, particularly if both partners work, they will buy an engagement and wedding ring jointly. Likewise, couples who have cohabited before making the decision to marry often do not announce an engagement. For example, a couple we know cohabited for 14 years prior to making the decision to marry. Once they made the decision, they announced it to their family and close friends and within a week they flew to Las Vegas and wed.

Although engagements no longer necessarily follow traditional customs, they continue to perform several key functions. For example, the engagement helps the couple define the goal of their relationship as marriage, and it lets the rest of those in the pool of eligibles know that each person is now "spoken for," that they have entered into a commitment with someone and are no longer available. Second, it provides the couple with an opportunity to seriously and systematically examine their relationship—that is, their expectations about the reality of marriage on a day-to-day basis, including appropriate gender roles, children, money, friendships, religion, in-laws, and family traditions. Third, it gives the couple a period of time to become better acquainted with their future in-laws and to become integrated into each other's family. Fourth, it provides the couple with a reason to get information about their respective medical histories (for example, through the required blood tests; determining the Rh factor in each partner's blood, for instance, will be of major importance in any future pregnancy). Finally, an important function of engagement is premarital counseling. It can be quite useful for a couple to discuss their ideas, expectations, and plans with an objective third person such as a member of the clergy or marriage counselor (historically, the Catholic Church has made premarital counseling a prerequisite for getting married in a Roman Catholic church).

An increasing number of couples today are using the engagement period not only to define what their relationship with each other will be but also to define their economic and social obligations to each other during their marriage. They are doing this by writing their own **personal marriage agreement**—a written agreement between a married couple in which issues of role responsibilities, obligations, and sharing are addressed in a manner that is tailored to their own personal preferences, desires, and expectations.

Prenuptial Agreements Today, the marriage plans of many couples include the use of a personal marriage agreement in one of two ways. One is as a **prenuptial agreement,** developed and worked out in consultation with an attorney and filed as a legal document. The purpose of drawing up a prenuptial agreement in this manner is to negotiate ahead of time the settlement of property, alimony, or other financial matters in the event of death or divorce. The prenuptial agreement can also serve as a personal agreement between the partners, drafted primarily for the purpose of helping the couple clarify their expectations concerning their marriage. Formal or legal marriage agreements such as prenuptial agreements are not new. Wealthy and celebrity members of society have long used these agreements to protect family fortunes. It has been reported that before their marriage, the late Jacqueline Kennedy and Aristotle Onassis drew up a 170-point prenuptial agreement (Totenberg, 1985). Although

IN OTHER PLACES

MARRIAGE TRADITIONS AND RITUALS IN THE UNITED STATES . . .

Today, most Americans take the customs and rituals associated with marriage as givens and view them primarily within the context of love and romantic intrigue. However, as our discussion thus far has shown, in many ways the traditional marriage contract and the various rituals associated with "getting married" underscore the subordinate position of women in marriage and can be viewed as a transference of property among males, that is, from father to husband. Indicative of the property status of women was the practice in the past whereby a prospective husband had to receive the father's permission to marry his daughter. At the time of the wedding, the father gave his daughter to the groom, usually for a price. Today, fathers still *give their daughters away* in marriage; however, they do not consider it a transference of property but rather a symbol of their blessing of the marriage. If you are a married male, did you carry the bride over the threshold on your wedding night? It seems that the custom of *carrying the bride over the threshold* originally symbolized the abduction of a daughter who was reluctant to leave her father's home. Further, in ancient times, men sometimes captured or kidnapped women to make them their brides. A man would take along his strongest and most trusted friend to help him fight resistance from the woman's family and kidnap the woman he desired. This warrior friend was considered the best man among his friends and became the *best man* at his wedding, accompanying the groom up the aisle to help defend the bride (Olson, 2006). These are only a few of many marriage traditions that in some way reflect the unequal status of women and men.

How much do you know about other rituals and traditions surrounding marriage in the United States? For example, do you know why brides today need "something old, something new, something borrowed, and something blue"? This tradition apparently dates back to ancient Hebrew society, when brides wore blue ribbons on their wedding day to signify love, purity, and fidelity. In addition, the ancient Hebrews believed that if a bride wore an item borrowed from a married woman, the married

Marriage is a critical rite of passage in most cultures and includes a wide range of rituals and customs. For example, in the United States, following the bride's tossing of the bouquet, often the groom will remove and toss the bride's garter. According to tradition, the single make who catches it will be the next to marry.

woman's wedded happiness would transfer to the bride-to-be. There are, of course, multiple explanations for many of these traditions and some cannot be definitively traced back to their roots. The following are some of the most common and popular wedding traditions practiced by Americans and the stories about their origins.

The Bridal Shower

The first bridal shower is believed to have been held in Holland, when a father denied his daughter permission to marry a poor man with whom she had fallen in love. When the man's friends heard this, they gave the bride-to-be numerous gifts so that the couple could be married.

The Bachelor Party

The ritual of the bachelor party dates back to ancient Greece. The night before the wedding, a lavish dinner, called the "men's mess," was held for the groom-to-be.

The Ring

The first wedding ring might have been worn by the Romans, who believed a small artery, or "vein of love," ran from the third finger of the left hand to the heart. Thus, wearing a ring on this finger symbolized the joining of two hearts in destiny

and the ring itself is a never-ending circle that symbolizes everlasting love.

Why are engagement and wedding rings typically diamond? Medieval Italians used diamonds because they believed diamonds were created from the eternal flames of love.

The Wedding Veil

The tradition of the wedding veil cannot be traced to one single country; rather, it has its origins in many cultures. In general, to protect the bride from the evil wishes of her rivals, her face was covered on her wedding day. In ancient Rome and Greece, wedding veils were brightly colored, whereas the early Christian bride wore a white or purple veil to symbolize purity and virginity. After the marital vows were exchanged, the veil was pulled back from the bride's face to symbolize her new status as wife.

Standing Arrangements at the Wedding Ceremony

It is said that the custom that the bride stand to the left of the groom at the altar dates back to a time when men carried swords to protect themselves and their loved ones. The groom had to keep his right hand (his sword hand) free to be able to defend himself and his bride from his enemies or disgruntled in-laws.

Throwing the Bouquet

This ritual is said to have originated in England and has its basis in a bride's desire to save herself from an onslaught of wedding guests. In times past, it was the custom for guests to reach for the bride's garter. Moreover, women guests would try to rip pieces of the brides dress and flowers in order to obtain some of her good luck. One bride, tiring of the practice, decided that throwing the bouquet would be safer. Today, single women line up as the bride tosses her bouquet with the belief that the unmarried woman who catches the bouquet will be the next one to get married.

The Wedding Cake

The origin of the wedding cake is attributed to ancient Romans, who actually broke a specially baked cake over the head of the bride as a symbol of luck and fruitfulness. Wedding guests scrambled to catch pieces of the cake to share some of the couple's good luck. The story of the tiered-wedding cake has its origins in Anglo-Saxon times when guests would bring small cakes to the wedding and stack them on top of each other. Later, a clever French baker created a cake in the shape of the small cakes and covered it in frosting (Olson, 2006). The wedding cake continues to be an important part of traditional weddings today because it is a symbol of oneness through sharing. The bride and groom sharing the first piece of the cake is seen as a gesture of goodwill for the happy couple. (Does this include smashing the cake in each other's face?)

The Honeymoon

Did you ever wonder why newlyweds keep their honeymoon a secret? In fact, sometimes even the bride-to-be does not know where she is going for the honeymoon. It is probably not surprising that the honeymoon originated in France, a country synonymous with love and romance. Several hundred years ago, to escape relatives who opposed their marriage, the newlywed couple would seclude themselves in some secret place for a month until the opposition gave up and stopped looking for them. During this time of seclu-

sion, the couple drank a special wine made with honey while watching the moon go through all of its phases. Thus, the term honeymoon literally means "moon of honey" ("Wedding Traditions," 1988).

. . . AND AROUND THE WORLD

Sometimes we get so caught up in our own traditions we think that they are the same for all people. However, different cultures define marriage differently and have rituals and traditions that are based on their unique sociocultural and political experiences. People studying different cultures have discovered interesting marriage practices that demonstrate the uniqueness of each culture.

China

The Chinese have a perfect solution for individuals who do not marry in their lifetime: a posthumous wedding. The "spirit wedding" is an ancient custom that is being revived in the Chinese countryside today. It is supposed to ensure that people who die unmarried will have a partner in the afterlife. In this custom, an aging unmarried person buys a corpse in preparation for the "spirit wedding" when she or he dies. Upon death, the two will be "married" with a full ceremony and will be buried together (*Chicago Tribune*, 1991).

Iraq

In the 1950s, Elizabeth and Robert Fernea lived in an Iraqi peasant village and studied the women's lives in detail. In this culture, parents arranged their children's marriages, and a couple could not meet before their wedding. For women, virginity was essential and had to be maintained at all costs until the wedding day, when the couple consummated their marriage while their mothers, friends, and other relatives waited outside the couple's bedroom. When they finished, the mothers inspected the wedding sheets for blood from the young bride's broken hymen (a membranous fold of tissue partly closing the external opening of the vagina) and publicly announced the proof of the bride's virginity. If there was no blood, it was assumed the bride was not a virgin, and her family suffered great humiliation.

The bride herself was often put to death as a ruined woman (Fernea, 1965).

The Tiwi of Australia

Among the Tiwi, an aboriginal people on the islands off the coast of Australia, there is no such thing as an unmarried female. Females are betrothed by their fathers before they are born into a system of reciprocity among males. Tiwi males gain prestige through the number of marriage contracts they make. Thus, marriage contracts are highly valued, even if some are with brides who are not yet born or who are not yet old enough to join the husband's household. In this system of polygyny for males and serial marriage for females, because the husband must be an adult before an infant female can be married to him, females are likely to outlive their husbands. When a husband dies, the wife's father or next male head of family has the right and responsibility to make a new marriage contract for her. She can never be unmarried. Given the prestige for males of having many marriage contracts, all Tiwi women, including the elderly, are valuable as wives (O'Kelly and Carney, 1986).

The Islamic Custom of *Muta*

In the Islamic custom of *muta*, a man and unmarried woman agree to a temporary marriage, in which both the duration of the marriage and the amount of money to be exchanged are agreed upon in advance. *Muta* children are considered legitimate and are theoretically equals of half-siblings born to permanent marriages or contracts; however, Islamic law allows the father the right to deny his *muta* child's legitimacy. Government encouragement of *muta* increased with the deaths of hundreds of thousands of Islamic men in the Iran–Iraq war. Most Islamic men who enter into *muta* marriages do so as a sexual arrangement, while Islamic women's reasons vary widely (Lancaster, 1990).

What Do You think? Do you find any of the marriage traditions and rituals commonly practiced today to be demeaning to women? Do you think that following these rituals, regardless of what they symbolize, is okay for women and men today? Why, or why not? How do the roles of women and men reflected in these rituals correspond with the gendered division of labor in marriages and families? Explain.

With the number of millionaires rising steadily and new forms of wealth being developed every day, the number of marrying couples entering into prenuptial agreements have grown significantly. Popular movie plots such as that of the film Intolerable Cruelty, in which actress Catherine Zeta Jones portrays a revenge-seeking serial divorcee looking to marry a rich man (George Clooney) with the intention of making a killing in the divorce highlight the fact that marriage today is an economic as well as an emotional partnership and that prenuptial agreements, especially among those who have accumulated or inherited significant wealth, is a good way to protect their assets.

most prenuptial agreements are not that elaborate, they generally go far in protecting the assets of the persons involved as well as ensuring reasonable alimony and other financial payments agreed upon by the couple. For example, megarich property tycoon, Donald Trump, who believes that one should always have a prenuptial agreement, has signed such an agreement with each of his three wives. Trump's first wife, Ivana, unsuccessfully challenged their prenuptial agreement, which limited any divorce settlement to $25 million. And after a highly publicized divorce from second wife, Marla Maples, it was reported that she settled for $2 million per a prenuptial agreement (at the time, however, Trump was worth $2.5 billion). Although Trump and third wife, Melania Knauss, have a prenuptial agreement, the details of what is involved should they divorce are unknown.

Few topics in the modern-day marriage arena inspire more attention, headlines, discussion, and fury than the mention of the words *prenuptial agreement*. Asking your future life partner to sign a contract that limits her or his rights to your assets flies in the face of love and romance. Some people look on prenuptial agreements as cold, unromantic, businesslike, and an expression of greed. They think that such contracts are an indication of distrust on the part of the couple—that they imply one or both partners do not have faith in the relationship and that they care more about their bank account than their soon-to-be spouse. However, most marriage advisers suggest that premarital contracting does not mean that a couple does not love or trust one another. Rather, in many ways, a prenuptial agreement can show how much two people really care about each other. Marriage today is an economic as well as an emotional partnership. Thus, contemporary couples are advised to think

with their heads and not their hearts. A prenuptial agreement is not a bad idea, even for people who do not have a lot of money. Prenuptial agreements are like insurance policies, they are good estate planning, and they force couples to agree on how they want to handle their married life, including their money and other assets.

With the number of millionaires rising steadily and new forms of wealth being developed every day, the candidate pool for prenuptial agreements has grown significantly. It is estimated that somewhere between 5 and 15 percent of altar-bound Americans enter into prenuptial agreements each year, mostly those who have accumulated or inherited significant wealth of a million dollars or more (Potier, 2003; CNNmoney, 2000). However, it is not just the rich and famous but an increasing number of middle-class couples, elderly couples, and divorced people who are ensuring before the wedding that in case the marriage ends their assets will go or remain where they want them. For the first time, divorced women outnumber widowed women in their 50s and 60s, and given that half of all marriages end in divorce within the first 7 years, lawyers, financial planners, and others who deal with marriage and family issues strongly suggest that it is a good idea for anyone (not just the rich) who is planning marriage to consider a prenuptial agreement to be financially prepared should divorce or death occur.

Those embarking upon a second marriage are particularly urged to consider a prenuptial agreement to protect the inheritances of children from a prior marriage (see, for example, Friedman, 1999; Hobson, 2001). Rarely do couples break engagements because of disputes over prenuptial agreements. In almost every instance, the agreement is signed and the parties are married. For instance, it was widely reported in the news that before their well-publicized wedding, movie celebrities Catherine Zeta-Jones and Michael Douglas were squabbling over details of a prenuptial agreement and that the spat might end their marriage plans. Reportedly, she was asking for $4.5 million for every year they are married and a home for life if they split, and he was holding fast to an offer of $1.5 million a year and a house that would remain a part of his estate (ABC News, 2000). Although the exact details of the agreement are not public, the couple appears to have worked out the details as they are currently married and the parents of two children.

In addition to prenuptial agreements, some people enter into what are called *postmarital* or *antenuptial agreements*. These contracts contain provisions similar to those in premarital contracts but are drafted after the marriage has taken place (as opposed to before) but before either party separates, divorces, leaves, or dies. A married couple may seek to enter into a postmarital agreement after a significant financial change or after a reunification subsequent to a separation. A *marital settlement agreement* is a particular form of postmarital agreement that specifies the distribution of property and responsibility for debt between the respective spouses as part of a divorce. For cohabiting couples, many of whom have some or all of the same issues, concerns, and considerations as legally married couples in terms of the division of property and other assets, financial planners suggest that they draw up a *cohabitation agreement*. Such agreements can contain simple provisions about shared expenses and the acquisition of property, including real estate, or can be more elaborate specifying a specific distribution of certain assets and protections for the couple in the event of disability or incapacity of one of the partners.

Perhaps a sign of the times, the market, including the Internet, is flooded with information and materials about prenuptial agreements. Couples planning to wed can go on the Internet, where they will find an array of information from lawyers who will describe what prenuptial agreements are, discuss their importance, offer their legal services, to what judges and courts will enforce and what they will not, to advice on how to discuss an agreement with a partner, to what topics need to be addressed in an agreement to make it valid, to books with titles such as *Prenups for Lovers: A Romantic Guide to Prenuptial Agreements.*

A law called the Uniform Pre-Marital Agreement Act provides legal guidelines for those wishing to make a prenuptial agreement. Some 26 states plus the District of Columbia have adopted this act (and 2 more states were considering its adoption in 2005), and those that have not have similar laws. A few states have their own unique laws in this regard. For example, some states, including California, do not allow premarital agreements to modify or eliminate the right of a spouse to receive court-ordered alimony at divorce. Other states, like Maine, void all premarital agreements $1\frac{1}{2}$ years after the parties to the contract become parents, unless the agreement is renewed (MedLawPlus.com, 2006; Court TV's *Legal Cafe*, 1997). Although anyone can draw up a prenuptial agreement, for it to be upheld in court those involved must demonstrate that there was full, accurate, and fair disclosure of all assets at the time it was drawn up, that it was fair and reasonable when signed, and that it was signed voluntarily by both parties and entered into in good faith. To meet this criterion, parties should secure the services of an attorney familiar with state laws governing marriage and community property. Even then there is no guarantee that courts will uphold all of the agreement's provisions. The specifications in the agreement may be morally binding, but some, such as specifications concerning living arrangements, child custody, and/or the support of children, are not enforceable in court (CBS News, 2005).

Personal Contracts   The most popular version of the personal marriage agreement among couples today is the *personal contract*, created by the couple without advice or counsel from an attorney. Although these contracts serve primarily as guides to future behavior, they are sometimes filed as legal contracts. As with the more formal and legal pre-and postnuptial agreements, personal contracts are not new. At different times in history couples have used the personal contract to satisfy a range of personal needs. For example, in the late seventeenth century, Eleanor Veazel and John French drafted a marriage contract in which the provisions included promises by John to not take any part of the estate that Elizabeth had inherited from her former husband, to let Elizabeth sell their apples, and a promise to leave Elizabeth 4 pounds a year after his death, which could be paid in any number of ways, including in corn, malt, pork, or beef (Scott and Wishy, 1982). In the nineteenth century, suffragist and feminist Lucy Stone and her husband-to-be, Henry Blackwell, a well-known abolitionist, wrote their own personal contract in protest against the inequality of women in marriage, which they read and signed as part of their wedding ceremony. In addition, Stone refused to take her hus-

band's surname, preferring to be known instead as "Mrs. Stone" (Schneir, 1994).

Although there is a wide range of opinions about personal marriage agreements, many people find them to have several important benefits, including forcing a couple to communicate with each other their marital expectations, desires, and goals. A case in point was the 1995 premarital agreement drawn up by Rex and Teresa LeGalley of Albuquerque, New Mexico, that spelled out the rules of their life together in minute detail, including how often they would have sex (healthy sex three to five times a week), which gasoline to buy for their car (Chevron Supreme), and who was responsible for doing the laundry (Ms. LeGalley). This was Rex's third marriage and Teresa's second. The premarital contract, however, was the first for each, and it was Teresa's idea. The agreement was compiled from her notes taken over their one-year courtship (she took notes on their dates). Their 16-page, single-spaced premarital contract was a legally notarized document in which the LeGalleys attempted to cover almost every possible aspect of their lives. Examples from the agreement include the following:

- "Lights out by 11:30 P.M. Wake up 6:30 A.M., Monday through Friday."
- "Family leadership and decision making is Mr. LeGalley's responsibility. Ms. LeGalley will make decisions only in emergencies and when Mr. LeGalley is unavailable."
- Ms. LeGalley will be in charge of "inside house chores, including laundry," while Mr. LeGalley "will be responsible for inside repairs and will maintain the outside of the house, including the garage and cars."
- "If we get angry, we will count to 10 first."
- "We will make ourselves available for discussion 15 to 30 minutes per day and we will spend time together doing things 15 to 20 hours per week."
- "Ms. LeGalley will stay on birth control for 2 years after we are married and then will try to get pregnant. When both of us are working, she can have only one child. When one parent is free, she can have another child. When both of us are free, she can have one more child. After the third pregnancy, we will both get sterilized."

The LeGalleys even built in penalties for breaking the rules. For example, there was a monetary fine for overspending at the supermarket, and if one partner let the gas in her or his car fall below the one-half mark, she or he had to fill the other's tank.

In an interview a year after they were married, the LeGalleys said that the contract was working well. According to Rex, "Things couldn't be better. We worked out so many things before we married that we didn't have that transition period that most couples do in their first year of marriage." Teresa commented: "Writing the prenup was one of the best things we ever did because we discussed everything and learned a lot about each other." The document is probably not legally binding and the LeGalleys say they have no plans to enforce it. They said that it was simply "all about getting to know your partner." Although we do not have another update, Teresa was scheduled to have their first child in 1997. In their interview, Teresa said that the couple still planned to have their first child in 1997; "that's one item that's not negotiable" (Bojorquez, 1997).

Personal agreements are not always this detailed, nor are they limited to couples planning to marry or to heterosexual couples. Any couple who is committed to each other or who lives together, as well as couples who are legally prohibited from marrying, can benefit from such agreements.

As the LeGalleys' agreement demonstrates, prenuptial or personal marriage agreements can include anything a couple considers appropriate, such as the division of roles and tasks in the marriage or living arrangement, how often they will engage in sexual activities, and whether they will have children. Several celebrities have included items such as penalties if the wife gains weight, requiring a spouse to undergo random drug tests, with financial penalties for positive results, requiring a husband to pay $10,000 each time he is rude to his wife's parents, rules about football, and steep financial penalties for infidelity. For example, per her prenuptial agreement with ex-husband Charlie Sheen, Denise Richards was to receive a hefty $4 million if he was unfaithful. At the end of this chapter, in the Writing Your Own Script box, we invite you to write your own personal marriage or relationship agreement. We present several topics for your consideration. Are there other topics relevant to your relationship? Does the contract between the LeGalleys give you any ideas?

The Wedding

Today's couples tend to prefer traditional weddings, but increasingly they are infusing the wedding ceremony with a touch of personal style—from unusual or ethnic wedding attire to male bridesmaids and female groomsmen, to offbeat choices of locations for their wedding and receptions, to elaborate reception menus. For instance, every Valentine's Day hundreds of couples are married in shopping malls around the country. The weddings are typically promoted by local radio stations. Recently, a bride and groom in the United Kingdom got married halfway through London's 26.2 mile Marathon. The bride and groom ran 13 miles in their wedding outfits (the bride wore a full-length wedding gown with a train above her running shoes and the groom and his newly acquired father-in-law wore waistcoats, wing-collared shirts and cravats, with long shorts instead of trousers) to the ceremony on Tower Bridge. After an 80-minute service, the newlyweds returned to the streets to complete the marathon (Dalton, 2006). According to one observer, some weddings begin in the toilet. In January 1996, six Taiwanese couples married in a single ceremony in a custom-built one-million-dollar public bathroom (Bey, 1996). Other couples have gotten married as they were skydiving out of an airplane, and still others have wed via satellite with one partner in absentia. Every year, for example, the Reverend Sun Myung Moon marries thousands of couples simultaneously by satellite hookups between Korea and hundreds of sites around the world. Brides and grooms who cannot be present are represented by a photo. In 2000, for instance, Reverend Moon officiated over a mass wedding ceremony for approximately 450,000 couples. About 30,000 of the couples—some long married and others newly matched—from over 100 countries, including the United States, took part in the live ceremony in Chamsil Stadium in Seoul. The couples paid a predetermined fee to take part in the marriage ceremony sponsored by the Reverend and Mrs. Sun Myung Moon and the Unification Church. At the stadium, after sprinkling the

Although most couples prefer traditional weddings, an increasing number are choosing nontraditional locations and methods of getting married. For example, this photo, taken in 2000, captures one of the yearly mass wedding ceremonies presided over by the Reverend the Sun Myung Moon in which over 30,000 couples wed in Chamsil Stadium in Seoul, Korea while thousands of others were simultaneously wed by satellite hookups between Korea and hundreds of sites around the world.

A growing number of couples today are infusing the wedding ceremony with a touch of personal style. For many African American couples this includes mixing American and African dress styles in their wedding attire and a tradition of jumping the broom, which is said to be a tradition carried over from slavery.

couples closest to the podium with holy water, Reverend Moon asked the question, "Do you, as mature men and women who are to consummate the ideal of the creation of God, pledge to become an eternal husband and wife?" The crowd gave a resounding "Yes." Reverend Moon matches the newly wed couples, all of whom are total strangers, by age and education. The church believes that cross-cultural match-making will help unite the world. This belief notwithstanding, it is estimated that around three-fourths of these couples divorce (Associated Press, 1997; Baker, 2000).

Cultural or ethnic weddings are also quite popular. For example, many African Americans who marry today have what is defined as an African-centered wedding. Such a ceremony varies according to the individuals, but may include traditional African attire for the bride, groom, and other participants in the wedding made out of kente, Guinea brocade, or other expensive African fabrics; African and other cultural cuisine at the reception; African drummers and dancers; a wedding cake baked by an African or Caribbean baker; a Yoruba priestess or priest to conduct the ceremony; or "jumping the broom," a tradition carried over from slavery.

Weddings today are far more expensive than in the past. Over the last 25 to 30 years, the average age of the bride and groom has risen. Because the average couple is older, they tend to have more money to spend on an elaborate wedding. For example, the average bride is now 27 years old, her groom is 29, they have an estimated household income of $74,000, will be engaged for a period of 14 months, and their wedding will have about 165 guests. Weddings are big business in the United States. Somewhere around 2 and 2.5 million couples marry each year, spending anywhere from hundreds to tens of thousands of dollars on each ceremony. According to the experts, the average amount spent on weddings has increased to $27,852, an almost 100 percent increase since 1990. Over the last several years, almost all wedding expenses have increased by over 20 percent. This includes the bride and groom's wedding attire (up 30 percent), engagement rings (up 25 percent), and a 60 percent increase in the cost of the wedding music. Despite the increasing expense and the delay in marrying, by the end of 2006 it is estimated that 2.3 million Americans got married; an estimated 44,230 weddings occurred every weekend of the year with 23 million bridesmaids and groomsmen and 380 million wedding guests in attendance. Moreover, 81 percent of the brides in 2006 planned to take their husband's name after marriage and only 3 percent expected to sign a prenuptial agreement (CNNMoney.com, 2006).

The costs of a wedding, of course, will vary, depending on the quality and/or quantity of the items chosen for the wedding, the size and type of wedding, as well as where the couple marries. For example, a wedding in Las Vegas, Nevada, can cost as little as a $35 chapel fee to several hundred dollars for a chapel wedding package that includes any assortment or all of the following: chapel fee, wedding coordinator, organist or pianist, soloist, flowers, wedding photos, wedding album, professional video of the ceremony, custom marriage certificate holder, wedding garter, limousine service, bottle of champagne and champagne glasses, witnesses (if needed), and "Just Married" bumper sticker. At the other end of the continuum are the costs of the weddings for the rich and famous, who often spare no expense, spending enough money in one day to buy the average couple two or three new homes. For example, the short-lived marriage of Liza Minnelli and David Gest is reported to have cost $3.4 million. And one of the most expensive weddings ever is said to be that of multimillionaire Peter Shalson and wife Pauline, who allegedly spent $2 million alone just to have Elton John perform at their wedding. In addition, the couple spent $6 million on opulent touches such as live parrots and the finest champagne and caviar for their 300 guests (Burwell, 2006). The more unique the wedding, the more expensive it often is.

An interesting exercise, particularly for those planning a wedding now or in the near future, is to search the Internet to ascertain the costs for different types, sizes, and locales for weddings. (see Internet Resources: Applying the Sociological Imagination). After the wedding, for many couples there is the additional expense of the honeymoon. Today, couples planning a honeymoon will probably spend, on average, another $5,000 to $10,000, depending on whether they honeymoon within or outside the United States and how many days the honeymoon lasts.

Marriage Vows   As more people change their views of marriage, they are also changing or at least modifying many of the rituals and traditions of weddings. For example, although some people continue to recite traditional wedding vows when they marry, others have modified or rewritten those vows to accommodate their preferences and to make their wedding romantic, meaningful, and unique. Perhaps as much a sign of the times as the Internet blitz of prenuptial agreements and ways to save on wedding expenses is the wide range of Internet resources for writing your own wedding vows, from prewritten examples to custom wedding vows. Couples can add their own words or mix vows from different ceremonies. Even if they already have vows, they can find that one special line that adds an extra something to their wedding ceremony.

In Table 8.2 we present three sets of wedding vows: (1) traditional wedding vows, (2) a set of vows written by a white middle-class couple (Mary and Richard) who married in the 1970s, and (3) a set of prewritten vows found on the Internet. For the previous edition to this textbook (4th edition), we asked Richard to reread the vows that he and Mary had written in 1977 and tell us what meaning, if any, those vows had for him 22 years later in 1999. Lovingly, Richard indicated that "the beautiful sentiments expressed in the vows are still very much my sentiments today . . ." (Brewer, 1999). For this new edition, as Mary and Richard approached their 30th wedding anniversary, we thought it would be interesting to ask Mary to respond to the same question. Equally lovingly, Mary said, "We renewed our vows on our 25th anniversary and we will do so again on our 30th, not because we haven't followed them but because we live them. We know they work; they make the difficult times easier and they enhance the beauty and the joys we experience together. Love does grow deeper. Our love has" (Mary, 2006). Although personalized wedding vows do not ensure a long and successful marriage, they very often serve as a guide or a set of goals that silently guides a couple's life together, as Mary's and Richard's responses suggests.

APPLYING THE SOCIOLOGICAL IMAGINATION

The average price of weddings in the United States is $27,852, an almost 100 percent increase since 1990. Additionally, in some large cities such as New York, the increase is staggering, reaching as high as an estimated $40,000. The skyrocketing increase in almost every item associated with weddings and getting married has spawned a subcategory of wedding industry vendors, ideas, and Web sites designed to assist brides in finding creative ways to spend less money on their weddings and/or to spend the money they have more wisely by discovering low-cost wedding ideas—ways to have a beautiful wedding without spending a fortune. Some examples from these various Web sites include the following:

- Instead of buying an expensive wedding gown for several thousand dollars, order one from a discount bridal store or rent one from a "rental salon."
- Cut down on the number of guests you invite; consider a smaller, more intimate wedding.
- Avoid a Saturday wedding (Saturdays are the most expensive days to rent an event space—Sundays are always cheaper).
- Hold your wedding during the Christmas season or immediately after Easter, when a church will already be decorated.
- Stay away from planning a wedding on popular holidays like Mother's Day, Valentine's Day, when the cost of flowers is inflated, or New Year's Day, when band rates are inflated.
- Hire a DJ instead of a band.
- Use only in-season and readily available flowers. Stick to your budget and use the most inexpensive flowers.
- Make your wedding reception a lunch instead of a dinner.
- Choose a buffet rather than a sit-down dinner.
- Choose foods that are in season; serve more vegetables and less meat (also, chicken is cheaper than beef).
- Eliminate champagne toasts.
- Hire a professional photographer to shoot only during the wedding ceremony. For the reception, leave disposable cameras at each table.

http://weddings.about.com/od/weddingflowers/a/cheapideas.htm

http://www.confetti.co.uk/weddings/advice_ideas/wedding_you_want/budget_ideas.asp

http://store.yahoo.net/nmcs/etiquette.html

Beginning with these Web sites listed above, find other Internet sources that help brides budget for the wedding, as well as those that inform the bride of the proper protocol in terms of who pays for what wedding items, the types of wedding planners available and their costs, and different unique weddings and their cost. What other resources can you find that would aid someone planning her or his own wedding? You may also go to http://www.costofwedding.com and type in your zip code to find out the average cost of a wedding in your city.

After you have collected an ample amount of data, conduct a brief survey on your campus, asking questions of both married individuals and those who plan to marry. Your questions should include asking your respondents about their knowledge of Internet resources that assist brides and others in planning a wedding and if they plan to use such Internet resources. If they are already married, did they use such resources? Analyze your survey data and write a brief paper on the topic of weddings in contemporary America.

Although most women marrying today do not pledge to *obey* their husbands, the pendulum may be swinging back to vows of obedience, at least among the nation's Southern Baptists. At the close of the last decade, in response to what the leadership of the Southern Baptists viewed as a growing crisis in marriages and families, the nation's largest Protestant denomination (16 million members) issued a declaration on obedience to husbands. Those attending the Southern Baptists' 1998 national convention voted overwhelmingly to add a new article of faith, which declares that marriage is a lifelong covenant between one man and one woman, and the husband has the "God given responsibility to provide for, to protect, and to lead his family. A wife is to submit herself graciously to the servant leadership of her husband." This statement, with its emphasis on "one man and one woman," is also consistent with the Southern Baptists' campaign against homosexuality. Critics of the Baptists' declaration argue that focusing on wifely submission implies that women are inferior to men and could even offer a religious excuse for some men to abuse their wives (Kloehn, 1998; Niebuhr, 1998). Interestingly, the divorce rate for conservative Christians is significantly higher than for other faith groups, and for atheists and agnostics (Robinson, 2000b).

Personalizing the wedding vows, a personal marriage agreement, and the cost of weddings notwithstanding, what happens once a couple is married? What kinds of changes take place in their lives? Do women and men experience marriage in the same way? In the remaining sections of this chapter, we discuss marriage as it is experienced by women and men. In this regard, we examine gender differences in the marital experience, factors related to transitions and adjustments to marriage, some common typologies of marital relationships, heterogamous marriages, and the benefits of positive and open communication in marriages and intimate relationships.

TABLE 8.2
Telling Their Love: Marriage Vows for Different Preferences

Traditional Marriage Vows[1]

I, _____, take thee, _____, to be my lawful wedded wife [husband]. To have and to hold from this day forward; For better, for worse, For richer, for poorer; In sickness and in health; To love, honor, obey, and cherish; From this day forward; Till death do us part.

The Marriage Vows of Mary and Richard[2]

Mary [Richard], to manifest my deep love for you, I promise to cherish you, care for you, and to share with you the difficulties, the sorrows, and the hardships as well as the joys, the beauty, and the happiness that come our way. I promise you a warm home and a dear and understanding heart in it, so that we may grow with and for each other. I promise to work together with you to build and to maintain this home and this love.

Internet: Prewritten Wedding Vows[3]

I, _____, take you as my husband [wife], and promise to walk by your side forever, as your best friend, your lover, and your soul mate. This day is the first day for the rest of our lives. As husband and wife, we will face many challenges that we will overcome with trust, commitment, and love. I pledge my love to you, _____, now and forever, with a hug and a kiss every day that we are married. I promise to laugh with you, love you, and honor you; to support you and your dreams, comfort you, always hold you in the highest regard, and to be there for you for all of our lives. I give you these things today, and all the days of my life. I will always cherish you in good times and those times that aren't so good. You are the love of my life. You put the sparkle in my eyes, and the smile on my face. I come to you today just as I am, and I take you just as you are, my cherished husband [wife]. Let's never change, but always love each other the way we do today.

[1]Most couples, even if they recite the traditional vows, no longer vow to obey their partner.

[2]In addition to writing their own vows Mary chose to maintain her birth name.

[3]This set of vows was combined from the following two Internet sources: http://wedding-band-ring.com/weddingvowlist.html and http://www.weddingvowrings.com/customvows.html.

MARRIAGE AND GENDER

Marriage and family researchers across academic disciplines are acknowledging increasingly that marriage is experienced in different ways by women and men—that every marriage actually contains two marriages: hers and his. In her now-classic book *The Future of Marriage* (1972), sociologist Jessie Bernard detailed the different experiential realities of wives and husbands. When asked identical questions about their marriage, husbands and wives answered so differently that Bernard called their marriages "her marriage" and "his marriage." Even when asked basic questions like how often they had sexual relations or who made decisions, wives' and husbands' responses were so different it was as though they were talking about two different marriages. Though largely hidden, the female–male differences in the experience of marriage have a tremendous effect on the mental and physical well-being of wives and husbands.

"Her" Marriage

Does it surprise you that Bernard found wives were much less happy in their marriages than were their husbands? Some people believe that these are just a few disgruntled wives—that couples who love each other live in a kind of identical harmony and peace. Several of Bernard's findings challenge this

assumption. For example, although wives reported being happier with their lives than did single women, when compared with husbands they reported being less happy. In addition, married women reported much higher rates of anxiety, phobia, and depression than any other group in society except single men, and wives had a higher rate of suicide than did husbands.

Research continues to uncover women and men's different perceptions and experiences of marriage. Reporting on a study of married couples between the ages of 17 and 69, for instance, Daniel Goleman (1987) pointed out that husbands and wives differ dramatically in terms of how they evaluate their relationship. Men tend to rate almost everything as better than do their wives. They have a much more positive perception of marital sex, family finances, ties with parents, listening to each other, tolerance of flaws, and romance. Wives, on the other hand, tend to complain more about their marriage than husbands do. Moreover, although married women experience better health than singles do, they do not benefit in terms of health from marriage as much as men do. For example, women in traditional marriages (wherein the woman assumes the traditional role of wife and homemaker) are especially prone to higher rates of illness than are husbands (Flowers, 1991; Lauer, 1992).

Perhaps something about the nature or structure of marriage itself accounts for these gender differences. The structure of traditional marriage, particularly with regard to the housewife role, is revealing in this regard. For instance, the division of labor in traditional marriages leads to fewer sources of gratification for housewives than for husbands. The imbalance of power in traditional marriages further alienates the housewife from her wifely role. According to Bernard, the housewife role has a "pathogenic" effect on wives. Often when women marry they lose their legal and personal identity and become totally dependent on their husbands, which often leads to depression. Other researchers have concurred with this view, noting that the housewife role is so unstructured and devalued, restrictive, and stressful that wives often have low self-esteem, are highly self-critical, and are far more vulnerable to depression and unhappiness than their husbands are.

"His" Marriage

Many of you have probably grown up on tales of men running from marriage, going to great lengths to avoid being "trapped." This folklore actually runs counter to the reality, of women's and men's lives. In reality, men seem to prefer marriage to being single. For example, when asked if they would marry the same person again, they respond in the affirmative twice as often as their wives do. In addition, most divorced and widowed men remarry, and the rate of marriage for these men at every age level is higher than the rate for single men. Furthermore, when compared with single men, married men live longer, have better mental and physical health, are less depressed, have a lower rate of suicide, are less likely to be incarcerated for a crime, earn higher incomes, and are more likely to define themselves as happy.

Although marriage is beneficial for men overall, it imposes certain costs. Bernard contends that a major cost of marriage for men is that they must give up their sexual freedom and take on the responsibility of supporting a wife and family. Whether or not this is a *cost* is debatable. Nonetheless, the provider role is costly in other respects, including the fact that it forces many men to work harder than they might otherwise. This, however, is changing, as women and men have become more sexually free both within and outside of marriage and as more married women work outside the home and contribute to the family income. According to some social scientists, traditional marriage reinforces stereotypical masculine roles and may actually hurt men.

TRANSITIONS AND ADJUSTMENTS TO MARRIAGES

Getting married represents a significant change in the lives of a couple. The world of married couples is in many important ways different from the world of singles. As a married couple, two people must fit their lives together and meet and satisfy each other's needs. In simple terms, **marital adjustment** is the degree to which a couple get along with each other or have a good working relationship and are able to satisfy each other's needs over the marital life course. One major adjustment that a married couple must make involves being identified with a partner and thought of by the community as one unit, as opposed to the unique individual each was before the marriage. Another marital adjustment regards seeing and relating to a partner on a daily basis, and learning to live with that person and accommodate her or his wants, needs, expectations, and desires. Still other adjustments include sharing space, money, relatives, and friends with a partner; the division of tasks in the relationship; and adjustment to the partner's sexual attitudes and behaviors. Changing from a single to a married persona does not always run smoothly. Most couples, however, manage it with a minimum of problems.

Adjustment does not simply happen one day in a marriage; rather, it is an ongoing process. As pointed out in Chapter 2, some family sociologists hold that marriages and families move through a series of life events over the course of the marital life cycle. Research shows that couples must continuously make adjustments in marriage as they are confronted with new and different life course events.

A Typology of Marital Relationships

What makes a happy, well-adjusted marriage? Most contemporary studies have concluded that there is no single model for a well-adjusted marriage. Helpfulness, love, mutual respect, and selflessness are but a few of the many characteristics associated with successful marital adjustment. In a now-classic study of marital adjustment and happiness, researchers John Cuber and Peggy Harroff (1966) reported on 211 couples who had been married for 10 or more years and who expressed commitment to each other. Cuber and Harroff concluded that satisfying, well-adjusted, enduring marital relationships can vary a great deal from each other and from societal ideals of a happy marriage.

Although their work is over 4 decades old, and although it has been critiqued as a class-based analysis (the sample consisted only of upper-middle class couples, which certainly does not represent all marriages), it is still the most frequently cited research on adjustment and happiness in marriage. And until there is current and more representative research in this area, the Cuber–Harroff classification scheme continues to offer some useful insights into marriage and relationship types. Cuber and Harroff identified five distinct types of marriages, representing a wide range of communication patterns and interaction styles: conflict-habituated, devitalized, passive-congenial, vital, and total.

The Conflict-Habituated Marriage The first type, the conflict-habituated marriage, is characterized by extensive tension and conflict, although for the most part the tension and conflict are managed or controlled. Channeling conflict and hostility is so important to these couples that it becomes a habitual part of their marriage. The couple engages in both verbal and physical arguments and fights, usually in private but sometimes in front of family and friends. They see their fighting as an acceptable way to solve problems and do not see it as a cause for separation or divorce. However, fighting seldom solves their problems.

The Devitalized Marriage The devitalized marriage involves very little conflict. Rather, it is characteristic of couples who were once deeply in love and had a satisfying sexual relationship but over time have lost their sense of excitement and passion. In this type of marriage, the partners pay very little attention to one another. There are occasional periods of sharing and time spent together, but this is done out of a sense of "duty" not joy. Although the marriage lacks visible vitality, these couples remain together believing that their marriage is the way most marriages are.

The Passive-Congenial Marriage The passive-congenial marriage is similar in many respects to the devitalized marriage. The primary difference is that the passivity that characterizes this marriage was there from the beginning. Couples in this type of marriage began the marriage with a low emotional investment and low expectations that do not change over the course of the marriage. Although there is little conflict in this type of marriage, there is also very little excitement. Passive-congenial couples share many common interests, but their fulfillment comes from involvements and relationships outside the marriage. In fact, they feel their type of marriage facilitates independence and security and allows them the time and freedom to pursue individual goals.

The Vital Marriage The vital marriage contrasts sharply with the previous three types. Vital couples are highly involved with each other; their sharing and togetherness provide the life force of the marriage. Despite their enjoyment of one another, the vital couple does not lose their sense of identity or monopolize each other's time; rather, they simply enjoy each other when they are together and make this time the focal point of their lives.

The vital couple tries to avoid conflict; however, when it does occur, it is usually over a serious issue, and the couple makes every attempt to settle the disagreement as quickly as possible rather than let it drag on, as does the conflict-habituated couple.

The Total Marriage Finally, unlike the vital marriage in which the couple value their time together but maintain their individuality, the total marriage is characterized by constant togetherness and sharing of most if not all important life events. Couples in a total marriage often work together and share the same friends; the partners have few areas of tension or unresolved conflict primarily because tensions that do arise are dealt with as they occur. In fact, a defining characteristic of the total marriage is that when faced with tension, conflict, or differences, the couples deal with the issues without losing the feeling of unity and vitality paramount to their relationship.

Total relationships are rare, and the total couple is often aware of their exceptionality. Such relationships do exist, however. In fact, Cuber and Harroff report that they occasionally found relationships so total that every aspect of the relationship was mutually and enthusiastically shared. In a sense, it was as if these couples did not have an individual existence.

The researchers reported that the majority of the couples they studied fell into the first three categories. They labeled these marriages as *utilitarian*, because, in their view, the marriages appeared to be based upon convenience. They labeled the remaining two types of marriages *intrinsic marriages*, because these marriages appeared to be rewarding. One of several problems with this study and the categories used to describe types of marriages is the obvious bias in the choice of terms used to describe the marriages. For example, what criteria did the researchers use to determine if a marriage is intrinsic and thus rewarding? Could not a marriage be both convenient and rewarding? Do couples have an inferior or devitalized relationship simply because they are less passionate over time than at the beginning of their marriage? More recent research on marital adjustment and happiness has built upon the Cuber and Harroff typology, adding one or more new dimensions but essentially maintaining the typology elucidated by them (see, for example, the seven-point typology put forth by Lavee and Olson, 1993; or the four-point classification scheme of Wallerstein and Blakeslee, 1995; or the five types of married couples described by Olson and Olson, 2000, although this typology, too, has limitations as it is based on data from a sample that consisted largely of white couples).

Given the limitations of the study and the language used to describe marriage types, do you think that you fit into one of these types of marriages or intimate relationships? Why or why not? Do you know couples who can be described in terms of one or more of these relationship types? What about your parents? Your grandparents? Where do they fit (if at all)? What are the problems with attempting to fit couples into such a typology?

It is clear that the meaning of marriage as well as what represents marital happiness and adjustment differ among human beings. Cuber and Harroff stress the point that each of these relationship types simply represents a particular type of interaction in and adjustment to the marital relationship. Thus, people living in any one of the relationships described by Cuber and Harroff may or may not be satisfied. In addition, the categories are not mutually exclusive. Rather, some couples are on the border, and others may move from one mode of interaction to another over the course of their relationship. We should also keep in mind that the Cuber–Harroff typology represents relationships, not personality types. It is quite possible, for example, that a vital person could be living in a devitalized relationship, expressing her or his vitality through some other part of her or his life.

HETEROGAMOUS MARRIAGES

In addition to types of relationships, social scientists often classify marriages in terms of social characteristics such as race, ethnicity, and religion. Although people tend to select partners with whom they share these characteristics, some couples do come from different backgrounds or traditions. Marriages between people who vary in certain social and demographic characteristics are referred to as **heterogamous marriages.** Such marriages have become more common in recent years. The following section focuses on two major types of heterogamous marriage: interracial and interethnic marriages, and interfaith marriages.

Interracial Marriages

Race is only one of many characteristics—including social class, ethnicity, and religion—that affect the choice of a marital partner; however, race has always been a divisive feature in most aspects of American life. Although many people interpret interracial marriage as referring to black–white couples, interracial marriages actually involve a wide range of combinations, including not only whites and African Americans but also Native Americans, Asian Americans, and Latinos. Today, in fact, black–white marriages make up only seven-tenths of 1 percent of all marriages in the United States (U.S. Census Bureau, 2006). Interracial marriage is most common among college-educated, middle-income people of all races. However, the typical interracial married couple is a white person with a nonwhite spouse. In 2000, for instance, the most common type of interracial couple was a white husband married to an Asian wife (Pew Research Center, 2006).

According to some estimates, there are about 600,000 interracial marriages annually in the United States; however, this country has a long history of intolerance of marriage across racial lines. For instance, a half-century ago, in 1958, a Gallup poll found just 4 percent of whites approved of interracial marriage; blacks and other racial groups were not even asked. That same year, two black youths in North Carolina, a 7-year-old and a 9-year-old, were arrested after a white girl kissed the 9-year-old. Convicted of attempted rape, the 7-year-old was sentenced to 12 years in prison and the 9-year-old was sentenced to 14 years in prison. It was only after pressure from then-President Dwight D. Eisenhower that the two boys' release was secured (Kristof, 2005). In 1967, the U.S. Supreme Court's decision in the case of *Loving* v. *Virginia* (involving the marriage of a woman of African and Native American descent and her white husband) overturned antimiscegenation laws nationally.[1] Prior to that, as many as 39 states had laws that specifically prohibited miscegenation, or the interracial marriage of whites with other specific groups: Arizona, for example, prohibited marriage between whites and Native Americans; California, Utah, Wyoming, and Idaho prohibited white and Mongolian marriages; and Nebraska and Montana prohibited marriages between whites and Asian Americans (Kunerth, 1990). A year after the *Loving v. Virginia* landmark decision, public disapproval of interracial marriage was still overwhelming—73 percent of whites disapproved of such marriages. Thirty-five years later, a 2003 Gallup poll reported an overwhelming reversal of attitudes on the subject: 73 percent of whites now approved of interracial marriage and 23 percent disapproved. In the same survey, 86 percent of African Americans, 79 percent of Latinas/os, and 66 percent of white respondents said they would accept a child or grandchild marrying someone of a different race (Price, 2006).

As with interracial dating (see Chapter 5), younger Americans are much more accepting of interracial marriage than older adults. Moreover, in a Pew Survey conducted in 2005, 22 percent of Americans reported having a relative in an interracial marriage. African Americans (37 percent) were twice as likely as whites (17 percent) to have an immediate family member in an interracial marriage, while Latinas/os (27 percent) fell in the middle of those two groups. There was also a variance by age, with more than one-third (34 percent) of all 18- to 29- year- olds reporting that they have a family member or close relative is married to someone of a different race, compared with only 14 percent of those ages 65 and older (Pew Research Center, 2006).

As we indicated in Chapter 5, sociologists and others have interpreted contemporary survey data such as this (reporting on interracial intimacy) as showing that despite a history of intolerance and opposition to interracial intimacy, dating and marriage, over the years Americans have grown increasingly tolerant and accepting of such relationships. However, although the percentages of approval for interracial dating and marriage have increased over the years, as have the percentage of actual interracial marriages, there is still important opposition to such intimacy, particularly relative to African American–white marriages. For instance, the 1994 General

Social Survey conducted by the National Opinion Research Center revealed that 15 percent of the whites interviewed nationwide favored a law actually banning all marriages between African Americans and whites and, 3 years later, a Knight-Ridder poll reported that three in ten people opposed marriages between blacks and whites (James, 1997; Thackeray, 2000). By the end of the twentieth century, a Gallup poll reported that roughly four in ten people still disapproved of interracial marriages in general (Gallup Poll, 2000). And various surveys in the early 2000s still indicate that as much as 10 percent of whites still favor laws against marriages between African Americans and whites (Lee and Edmonston, 2005).

The paradox of white Americans' attitudes and behavior relative to interracial marriage does not go unnoticed, however. In the face of a history of forced race-mixing vis-à-vis the sexual exploitation and rape of African women under slavery, Native American women during the European conquest and colonization, and other women of oppressed and exploited racial and ethnic groups in this country, it is indeed paradoxical that, through legal prohibitions against interracial marriage, white Americans have outlawed race mixing until recent times. Interestingly, some sociologists, historians, and geneticists have estimated that 75 percent of all African Americans have at least one white ancestor, and another 15 percent have predominant white ancestral lines as a result of the rape of their ancestors. Concomitantly, 95 percent of "white" Americans have widely varying degrees of African heritage. Yet miscegenation laws meant to separate the races by prohibiting interracial marriages between whites and African Americans (and whites and Native Americans) began as early as 1661 and lasted until 2000. Although the U.S. Supreme Court decided in 1967 that laws prohibiting interracial marriages were unconstitutional, such laws remained part of the state constitutional language of South Carolina and Alabama until the end of the twentieth century. In 1999, South Carolina removed its ban on interracial marriages, and in the November 2000 election, voters in Alabama passed Amendment 2, which erased a section of the Alabama state constitution that read, "The legislature shall never pass any law to authorize or legalize any marriage between any white person and a Negro or descendant of a Negro" (Associated Press, 1999; "Voters Remove State Interracial Marriage Ban," 2000). This fact notwithstanding, the informal restrictions—sociocultural norms—concerning these marriages remain the most inflexible of all mate selection boundaries. Even though the number of interracial couples has increased considerably since 1970 from fewer than 1 percent of all married couples to 4 percent of all married couples today (U.S. Census Bureau, 2006), they still remain rare proportionately, relative to marriages between people of the same race or ethnic group.

As Figure 8.4 shows, racial endogamy in marriage is particularly strong for certain groups, such as African Americans. Thus, we cannot underestimate the power of informal social norms that operate in mate selection. For a better understanding, let us turn our attention to interracial marriages among various racial and ethnic groups in the United States.

---

[1]Historically, there have been controversies over interracial couples for reasons of racist origin, such as fears of "racial impurity." For example, during the 1930s, the racist and antisemitic Nuremberg Laws were enacted by the Nazis in Germany against the German Jewish community, forbidding marriages between Jews (considered "lower people') and German "Aryans" (considered "higher people"). As a result, many interfaith and intermarried couples committed suicide when these laws came into effect. Germany, South Africa, Canada, Australia, and the United States are only a few of the countries that have had regulations prohibiting interracial marriage. As of 2006, however, no countries have laws against miscegenation, but opposition to interracial marriages remains part of the programs for various groups, including hate groups such as the Klu Klux Klan in the United States ("Interracial Marriage," 2006).

FIGURE 8.4

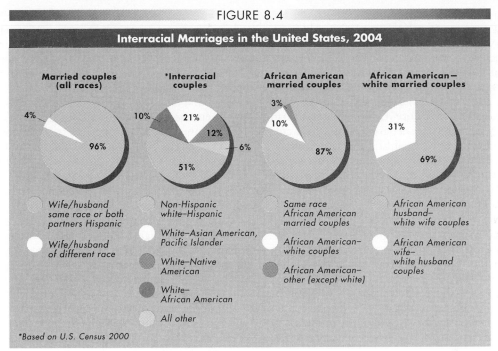

Interracial Marriages in the United States, 2004

Married couples (all races)
- 4%
- 96%
- *Wife/husband same race or both partners Hispanic*
- *Wife/husband of different race*

*Interracial couples
- 10%
- 21%
- 12%
- 6%
- 51%
- *Non-Hispanic white–Hispanic*
- *White–Asian American, Pacific Islander*
- *White–Native American*
- *White– African American*
- *All other*

African American married couples
- 3%
- 10%
- 87%
- *Same race African American married couples*
- *African American– white couples*
- *African American– other (except white)*

African American– white married couples
- 31%
- 69%
- *African American husband– white wife couples*
- *African American wife– white husband couples*

*Based on U.S. Census 2000

Sources: U.S. Census Bureau, 2000, *Statistical Abstract of the United States, 2000* (Washington, DC: U.S. Government Printing Office): 51, Table 54; U.S. Census Bureau, 2006, *Statistical Abstract of the United States, 2006* (Washington, DC: U.S. Government Printing Office): Table 54.

African Americans Among various groups of color in the United States, African Americans have the highest rate of endogamous marriages and the lowest rate of exogamous marriages. Of the total number of married couples in the United States in 2004, less than 1 percent were African American–white couples. Approximately 87 percent of all African Americans who are married are married to another African American. However, as shown in Figure 8.4, when African American women and men do marry interracially, most often (ten out of thirteen such marriages) their mate is white. Unlike any other race or ethnic group in the United States, African American men are more likely to marry outside the race than are African American women. For example, African American men (6.7 percent) are more than twice as likely as African American women (2.9 percent) to have a white mate. However, government statistics indicate that the number of African American women marrying white men is slowly increasing. For instance, the number of African American women married to white men doubled over the last 20 years.

In most cases, African American–white couples have been raised in racially sensitive homes; are more likely to have met through their jobs than in school, in their neighborhoods, in church, or through recreational activities; begin their courtship through repeated casual conversations rather than with immediate physical attraction, friendship over a period of time, or after close association with one another; are initially attracted to one another through their shared interests; and at least one partner in the marriage has been married previously. Some scholars have suggested that some African American–white couples might also belong to religions that encourage interracial unions, such as the Baha'i religion, which teaches that God is particularly pleased with interracial

unions. Moreover, the couples usually live far from their families of orientation; mothers of daughters tend to be more supportive of the relationship than mothers of sons, and fathers of sons are more supportive of the relationship than fathers of daughters (Zebroski, 1997). These marriages also are most likely to occur among highly educated persons. This is particularly true of African American men who marry white women. These men are typically well educated, have a high income, and are usually older than their mate. In fact, African

"I don't hate him because he's black. I hate him because he's my husband."

The rate of divorce for interracial marriages is only slightly higher than for same-race couples. When conflicts occur, they are more likely to arise from cultural, gender, class, social, and personal differences than from racial ones.

American men who have attended graduate school are the most likely to marry interracially (Kalmijn, 1999). Although African American–white couples have similar educations, white women who marry African American men nonetheless, "marry up" more often than those who marry white men. This is especially notable given that the pool of highly educated white men greatly outnumbers the pool of highly educated African American men. More than half of African American husbands with white wives have at least some college education compared to only two-fifths of African American husbands with African American wives. In this sense, some researchers have suggested that white wives get more than their "share" of well-educated African American husbands. It is also problematic for African American women in that it further reduces their chances, especially well-educated African American women, of marrying (qian, 2005).

In addition, the rate of interracial marriage among young African Americans under the age of 30 is about four or five times higher than for African Americans over the age of 60. Furthermore, the rate of divorce is lower for African American husband–white wife couples than for white husband–African American wife couples. Although attitudes and behavior regarding racial intermarriages have changed somewhat, interracial couples, especially African American– white couples, are still frequently subjected to a range of societal reactions—forms of antagonism and indignities from stares to cross-burnings to physical attacks and sometimes murder. According to some research, interracial couples say that the most pressing problem they face, both before and after marriage, is racism. The emotional wear and tear of social and cultural attitudes toward interracial couples is often enormous. For some of these couples, their way of coping with the indignities and nonacceptance of their relationship by family, friends, and/or the larger society is to not respond to the racism—to not let others make racism their problem (see, for example, the Schroeder family in the Family Profile box).

The widely publicized and horrific murder in 1955 of 15-year-old Emmett Till, an African American teenager accused of whistling at a white woman in Mississippi, symbolized the historically deep-seated views of some whites relative to the mere suggestion of racial mixing and intimacy. Although attitudes and behaviors have changed from such grotesque displays of disapproval, at least overtly, nonetheless, the FBI announced in 2005 that it had begun investigating the rising hate mail sent to prominent African American men married to white women. Clearly, then, such feelings run deep and can be found even among some of the nation's religious role models: the clergy. For example, in 2000 a pastor in Jasper, Ohio, shut the door on an interracial couple, refusing to marry them because she is white and her fiancé is African American. Although the nuptials had been scheduled in advance by the bride-to-be's brother, and although she was a member of the church, the pastor forbade the use of the building for an interracial marriage. The pastor refused to discuss the details of his decision; however, he did confirm that he prohibited the use of the church after learning that the groom-to-be was African American (Mahoney, 2000).

Reactions such as these reflect the importance that white Americans continue to attach to the preservation of racial segregation and the role of informal norms in shaping our behavior. Such statistics should not be taken to indicate that white Americans are the only group to oppose interracial marriage. There are those in almost every other racial group who also oppose such marriages. For example, many African Americans, especially women, oppose interracial marriages in the belief that it strains an already limited pool of eligible African American men. Others view such marriages as weakening cultural heritage and group solidarity. Likewise, Asian men, especially Chinese men, are opposed to interracial marriages, seeing them as a cultural and racial betrayal by Chinese women.

In addition to racial attitudes and beliefs that shape the informal endogamous norms surrounding mate selection in the United States, various structural features of American society also affect the rate of interracial marriages. For instance, interracial marriage rates vary across geographic regions and are highest in regions where relatively large numbers of people of color live, where the population is racially diverse, and where attitudes toward interracial relationships and race are relatively more permissive and tolerant than in other areas of the country. The rate of interracial marriages for African Americans, for example, is highest in the metropolitan Washington, DC, area, including the District of Columbia, Delaware, Maryland, and Virginia; not surprisingly, it is lowest in the South (Lee and Edmonston, 2005).

Native Americans If African Americans represent the most racially endogamous end of the marital continuum among people of color, Native Americans can be found at the other end of the continuum as they are the least likely to exhibit racial endogamy in marriage patterns. Native Americans are more likely than any other racial group to marry outside their group. They are more likely to marry a white American than another Native American and least likely to marry an African American. In fact, close to 60 percent of Native Americans are involved in interracial marriages. This trend of interracial marriage has increased steadily since the 1970s, and as with other racial groups, the rate of interracial marriages among Native Americans increases with education. For instance, husbands in interracial marriages have an average of 13 years of education, a year higher than for those in endogamous marriages. However, although older Native Americans in the past, had lower intermarriage rates than younger Native Americans, today such an age gradient is either small or absent. Moreover, unlike with some other racial groups (for example, Asian Americans and African Americans), interracial marriage does not appear to be associated with gender; Native American women and men are almost equally likely to marry a non-Native American (Lee and Edmonston, 2005).

A number of explanations for this marital pattern have been proposed. The most common is related to the size of the Native American population. Only about 2.5 million Americans today identify themselves as being of native descent (U.S. Census Bureau, 2006). Given the already small numbers of Native Americans, geographic areas with small Native American populations have significantly higher rates of interracial marriage than do those with large populations. The high rates of Native American interracial marriages are also linked to the increased migration of Native Americans to urban areas, expanding opportunities for education and employment in

FAMILY PROFILE

CHRISTOPHER, RANIMARIE BUEN-SCHROEDER, MAHAL, AND MATEO SCHROEDER

Length of Marriage: 10 years

Christopher Schroeder is an associate professor of English at Northeastern Illinois University. Ranimarie Buen-Schroeder is an art therapist (ATR-BC, LCPC). Their children, Mahal and Mateo, are 7 and 6 years of age, respectively. Because they do not compartmentalize their lives based on how others respond or do not respond to them as an interracial family, Christopher and Ranimarie profiled their lives below with what they describe as "a meditation about the cultural hybridity of our everyday lives."

Family Profile

We're like most. She stays up late. I get up early. How do we spend time together? She wants a house. I want a location. How do we afford both? Between us, we have two hearts and two brains.

We're not like most. My father visits for 36 hours. Her *tiyo* and *tiya* stay for weeks. On birthdays, we have pizza and *pansit*. Two hearts and two brains in bodies both brown and white.

We speak English. She understands Tagalog. I catch enough to barely keep up. She says that she can't keep up with me. I've learned to sit back when she speaks.

She hears Tagalog from nanay and tatay (her parents), who live ten minutes

Clockwise: Christopher, Ranimarie, Mateo, and Mahal Schroeder

away at her *ate's* (older sister's) house, and she responds mostly in English.

They were one of the reasons we moved from New York to Chicago. We wanted our kids to know their *lolo* and *lola* (grandparents), their *mga tiyá* and *mga pinsan* (aunts and cousins).

Once, before we moved, my kids and I were walking through a park where we often played. A woman asked how much I charge to watch children. I wondered how to explain that these were my children.

Last summer, we went to rural Illinois for my father's wedding, where they were the only brown in a church of white. My childhood family surrounded us after the ceremony. I longed for Chicago where difference is not as different.

Neither of our kids looks quite like us. Neither looks like each other. But together, we span a spectrum.

Mestiza means more than one, not none. Among us, we have four hearts and four heads in bodies kape (coffee) and cream.

nonreservation settings, and a generally more favorable attitude about Native peoples and their cultures. In this context, interracial marriage is much higher for Native Americans living in urban areas than for those living on reservations (Mindel, Habenstein, and Wright, 1998) and is more characteristic for those Native Americans who have left the reservation to pursue educational and occupational opportunities in cities. Researchers in the last decade found that approximately three-fourths of Native Americans living in 23 states were married to someone from another race. According to this research, except for those areas in which Native Americans live in enclaves, the Native American population is amalgamating rapidly. Current research is consistent with this research, indicating that the U.S. states with the highest proportions of white–Native American couples all have fairly

large Native American populations; these states include Oklahoma, Alaska, Montana, South Dakota, and New Mexico. Some researchers, such as Yellowbird and Snipp (1994), have suggested that the extremely high rate of interracial marriage for Native Americans may accomplish what disease, Western civilization, and decades of federal policies toward Native Americans failed to achieve.

Asian American Historically, social scientists have used the rates of interracial marriage with whites as an indicator of the acculturation or assimilation of various groups of color into the American mainstream. If that is the case, then Asian American families have become increasingly acculturated. As we have learned, antimiscegenation laws were very common in the United States prior to 1967. Although the first such laws were passed to prevent freed black slaves from marrying whites, many people soon saw Asian intermarriage with whites equally as threatening to American society and thus antimiscegenation laws were passed that prohibited Asians/ Asian Americans from marrying whites as well. These laws, part of the larger anti-Asian movement in this country, eventually led to the Chinese Exclusion Act in 1882 and other restrictive regulations against Asians that had an impact on the early interracial marital patterns that emerged, especially among Asian/Asian American men. Today, Asian Americans in interracial marriages are very common. Approximately 38 percent of all Asian Americans who are married are in interracial marriages, primarily with whites. This trend is particularly prevalent among younger Asian Americans. For example, 30 percent of married Asian Americans between the ages of 15 and 24 are married outside their race, and nearly one-half of those under the age of 35 are interracial couples. And those Asian Americans most likely to be in an interracial marriage are those who live in relatively small immigrant communities (suro, 2001).

Of course, Asian Americans are not a monolithic group—thus rates of interracial marriage vary from group to group. For instance, among the six major Asian American ethnic groups (Asian Indian Americans, Chinese Americans, Filipina/o Americans, Japanese Americans, Korean Americans, and Vietnamese Americans), Japanese and Chinese Americans have the highest rates of interracial marriage. For example, Japanese Americans have the highest rate, with over 50 percent marrying outside the group. This fact notwithstanding, the most revealing data on interracial marriage patterns among Asian Americans is that which presents rates by gender. According to some observers of the interracial marriage scene, the topic of interracial marriage is one of the most explosive social issues within the Asian American community today. The issue of Asian Americans, especially Asian American women, marrying non-Asian Americans, is said to be an emotionally divisive debate often loaded with charges of racism and sexism from within and without along gender lines due to the significantly higher numbers of interracial marriages among many Asian American women. For instance, contemporary U.S.-born Asian American women as a whole are far more likely to have a white husband than an Asian husband. Indeed, for several ethnic groupings of Asian women, wives are twice as likely to have a non-Asian husband than an Asian husband. In contrast, U.S.-born Asian American men lag significantly behind in interracial marriages, giving rise to a so-called *gender* disparity (Seraph, 2005). As Table 8.3 shows, with the exception of Asian Indian Americans, Asian American women in each of the remaining five largest Asian ethnic groups have nearly or more than twice the outmarriage rate as Asian men in these groupings. Across Asian ethnic groups and gender, by far the majority of those married interracially are married to whites. Basically among Asian women, the most likely to intermarry with whites are Japanese (33 percent), Filipinas (32 percent), and Koreans (28 percent). Conversely, among Asian men, the most likely to intermarry with whites are Japanese (14 percent) and Filipinos (12 percent). Although the number of interracial marriages with African Americans and Latinas/os are small, when Asian Americans marry within these groups, those most likely to intermarry with African Americans are Filipina,

TABLE 8.3

Interracial Marriage Among the Six Largest Asian American Ethnic Groups by Race, Ethnicity, and Gender of Spouse

Asian Indian Americans	Wives	Husbands
Asian Indians	92.1	88.4
Other Asians	3.9	4.0
Whites	2.8	6.9
Blacks	0.7	0.0*
Latinas/os	0.5	0.7
Chinese Americans		
Chinese	72.9	77.6
Other Asians	11.9	13.0
Whites	14.1	8.3
Blacks	0.1	0.3
Latinas/os	1.0	0.8
Filipina/o Americans		
Filipinas/os	55.6	75.6
Other Asians	6.9	9.4
Whites	32.0	11.9
Blacks	2.3	0.0
Latinas/os	3.2	3.1
Japanese Americans		
Japanese Americans	52.0	66.7
Other Asians	12.6	16.5
Whites	33.0	13.7
Blacks	1.1	0.0
Latinas/os	1.5	3.1
Korean Americans		
Korean Americans	62.6	86.4
Other Asians	6.7	9.2
Whites	28.2	4.0
Blacks	1.9	0.0
Latinas/os	0.6	0.4
Vietnamese Americans		
Vietnamese Americans	82.5	88.7
Other Asians	8.5	8.7
Whites	8.6	2.6
Blacks	0.0	0.0
Latinas/os	0.4	0.0

*Note: Although a percentage may be listed as 0.0, that does not mean that there are zero examples of these marriages in the overall U.S. population. Source of data for this table is Census 2000 Supplemental Survey.

Adapted from: C. N. Le, 2006a, "By the Numbers: Dating, Marriage, and Race in Asian America," Asian Nation. IMDiversity: http://www.imdiversity.com/villages/asian/ family_lifestyle_ traditions/le_interracial_dating.asp (Accessed: April 24, 2006).

Korean, and Japanese American wives, while Filipinas/os and Japanese men are more likely to intermarry with Latinas/os. Although often overlooked by researchers focused on interracial marriage patterns, the Pan-Asian intermarriage rate has grown over the years. Currently, Japanese and Chinese American women and men are most likely to marry another Asian American (outside their own ethnic group) (Le, 2006a).

Whether or not they are avoiding family complications as some researchers have suggested, the fact is that a large percentage of Asian Americans cohabit with an interracial partner. As with interracial marriage, a larger percentage of cohabiting Asian American women (55 percent) have a non-Asian partner compared to 37 percent of Asian American men. And, as with interracial marriage, the overwhelming majority of both cohabiting Asian American women and men live with a white partner, 40 and 27 percent, respectively (Le, 2006b). These patterns of interracial intimacy are believed to be causing a *marriage squeeze* for Asian American men, most of whom prefer to marry within their own race. The shrinking pool of eligible mates—the out-marriage of so many Asian American women—has caused deep resentments among some Asian American men. For example, it is reported that many Chinese men have strong feelings against interracial marriage and express a feeling of being betrayed and abandoned by Chinese women, whom they believe should be committed only to Chinese men (Guang, 1996). One consequence of the interracial marriage pattern among Asian Americans is the growing acculturation of Asian Americans into American society. Although there may be advantages to acculturation, the costs include a loss of ethnic tradition, heritage, and a distinct sense of Asian American identity as well as intergenerational strain and conflict between some Asian American parents and their interracially married children.

Whatever the implication, high rates of out-marriages among Asian Americans have led sociologists and other social scientists to theorize about why Asian Americans choose to intermarry with whites. A common theory emphasizes that marrying a white person is the ultimate form of assimilation and signifies full acceptance by white society. Thus, an Asian American may marry a white person because she or he (consciously or unconsciously) wants to be fully accepted in white society. A related theory of hypergamy also suggests that Asian Americans marry whites to increase their social status because whites generally occupy the highest sociocultural position in the U.S. racial hierarchy. As when applied to the higher rate of African American men than African American women marrying a white person, these theories are condescending in tone given the presumption that the only reason a nonwhite (in this case an Asian American) would marry (or cohabit with) a white person would be to fulfill a need for acceptance and an increase in social status (Le, 2006b).

Some Asian Americans argue that the cultural stereotype of or fetish for Asian women is a major reason that many males (particularly white males) are attracted to Asian women. In this context, Asian women are seen primarily as sexual objects that can be controlled and used by men. These critics point out that in most areas of American popular culture, rarely do you see the opposite happening—Asian males as the subject of infatuation or sexual desire by white women. Rather, Asian males have been and continue to be purposely portrayed as nonsexual martial arts experts, nerds and geeks, or evil villains, images that serve to eliminate them as potential rivals to white males for the affection of Asian women (Le, 2006b).

Interethnic Marriages

Latinas/os As we have already seen, like Asian Americans, Latinas/os represent a diverse group. Although inhibitions remain about marriages between African Americans and whites, Latinas/os, like Asian Americans, increasingly marry outside of their racial or ethnic groups. Some Latina/o groups are much more likely to marry non-Latinas/os than others. For instance, Puerto Ricans are most likely to be intermarried, followed by Mexicans and Cubans. Although the rates of interracial marriage vary from one Latina/o group to another, overall the rates have increased rather dramatically in recent decades. Marriage between Latinas/os and non-Latinas/os is one of the most prevalent types of intergroup unions, as Figure 8.4 shows. Currently, about 37 percent of all married couples of Latina/o origin are married to a non-Latina/o (U.S. Bureau of the Census, 2006). As with most every other nonwhite group, the majority of these marriages are between Latinas/os and whites.

As we have pointed out for other groups, most Latina/o interracial or interethnic marriages occur among young, higher-income, and well-educated individuals. In this context, two-thirds of Latinas/os who have attended or graduated from college marry outside their ethnic or racial group, as do one-third of all Latinas/os in top-income brackets. Interracial marriage is uncommon among Latinas/os who have less than a high school education. Latinas/os with a substantial income are five times more likely to marry a non-Latina/o than those who did not finish high school or college or who live in poverty. It is reported that in the trend-setting state of California, close to one in twelve non-Latina/o whites who "ties the knot" marries a Latina/o or Asian American. Interracial marriage is also closely linked to youth among Latinas/os, though to a lesser extent than among Asian Americans. About one-third of all married Latinas/os under the age of 35 are involved in an interracial marriage. Although concentrated among the young, there are also significant numbers of older Latinas/os in interracial or interethnic marriages. However, for most Latina/o groups, gender does not seem to be a factor in these marriages, as the rates are about the same for Latinas and Latinos. As with gender differences in interracial marriage for other racial groups discussed in this section, many factors contribute to gender variations in intermarriage, including demographic, cultural, and individual characteristics and personal preferences. In addition, like Asian Americans, native-born Latinas/os are much more likely than immigrant Latinas/os to marry a white person, with interracial marriage rates for all native-born married couples approaching 30 percent. And the longer a Latina/o has been in this country, the greater the prevalence of interracial or interethnic marriage.

The rates of interracial marriage are far higher in the West—in states that have a large Latina/o population—than in the rest of the country. For example, non-Latina/o whites and Latina/o marriages are approximately four to five times more common in California and Texas than in states that have relatively smaller Latina/o populations. The rates are also high in New Mexico, Arizona, and Hawaii, although Hawaii does not have a large Latina/o population. On the other hand, Latina/o interracial marriages are uncommon in states with small Latina/o populations such as North and South Dakota, West Virginia, Kentucky, Vermont, Maine, Mississippi, and Alabama (Lee and Edmonston, 2005; suro, 2001). Some researchers have suggested that this pattern of interracial or interethnic marriage among various Latina/o groups indicates that there is, perhaps, less "social distance" between Latinas/os and non-Latinas/os than among people from different other groups (Pollard and O'Hare, 1999). Others suggest that two demographic characteristics of Latinas/os appear to contribute importantly to their intermarriage with non-Latinas/os, especially non-Latinal/o whites. First, few Latinas/os identify as black, which greatly minimizes the white–black barrier to mate selection and marriage that historically kept interracial marriage rates low. Second, the rapid growth of the Latina/o population has likely contributed to the secular increase in racial and ethnic intermarriage (Lee and Edmonston, 2005).

Trends in racial and Latina/o intermarriage affects American society in a number of ways, and will continue to do so. The demographic impact is fairly clear and straightforward. However, the social and political affects are far less clear; they are much more complex and subtle. Certainly the increasing rate of interracial marriage among all racial and ethnic groups has contributed to the growing number of multiracial children and families in American society. In addition to the growing numbers of multiracial and multiethnic Americans, we can assume that as more people who identify as Latina/o also have non-Latina/o origins, the debate over how we will think about race in the future and how best to label and count the population by race and Latina/o status will be an important one. Already, the shift in the 2000 U.S. Census that allowed Americans to report more than one race has had an enormous impact on the composition of interracial couples and their children relative to how they reported their race. For instance, in the 2000 Census, over one-third of children growing up in interracial families were reported as more than one race. And among children of interracially married Latina/o couples, nearly two-thirds were reported as Latina/o (Lee and Edmonston, 2005; Tafoya, Johnson, and Hill, 2004).

Whites   Interethnic marriage among non-Latina/o whites is now so commonplace that most people do not pay much attention to it. Estimates are that three-fourths of U.S.-born whites are married interethnically. As with other groups, ethnic intermarriage among whites varies with age and region of residence. Although the data indicate that the rate of interracial marriage has been increasing and seems dramatic for some groups, we must be careful in drawing conclusions from them. Keep in mind that many of these statistics represent geographic- or age-specific groups and should not be generalized to a total population. We should not lose sight of the fact that, overall, interracial marriages are still an extremely low percentage of the total marriages in this country. In addition, we should remember that race and intimacy are not experienced in a vacuum. As we learned in Chapter 5, race is interrelated with many other social factors that combine to have a significant effect on if and whom we meet, fall in love with, cohabit with and/or marry.

INTERFAITH MARRIAGES

Marrying within one's own religion was the social norm in the United States until recently. Summaries of studies of interfaith marriages have consistently found Americans to be much like their partners in terms of religion. In the 1980s, for example, 93 percent of Protestants were married to Protestants, 88 percent of Jews were married to Jews, and 82 percent of Catholics were married to Catholics (Glenn, 1982). Most of these studies, however, simply divided religion into three categories: Protestant, Catholic, and Jewish. A problem with this classification scheme is that it overlooks the diversity within various religious categories. For instance, Baptists, Presbyterians, and Methodists are all Protestant denominations. If people from these different denominations intermarry, are their marriages endogamous or exogamous? Other problems arise in trying to define an interreligious couple. For example, if a Jew marries a Protestant who then converts to Judaism, is that an interfaith marriage, or do we consider it religiously homogamous? Or what if one partner is of a religious denomination and the other is an atheist or agnostic?

With these limitations in mind, recent statistics on who marries whom suggest that Americans are much more willing to cross religious than racial boundaries in selecting a partner. For example, religious intermarriage rates are much higher today than in the past among all religious groups except Fundamentalist Christians (Kalmijn, 1998). It is estimated that nearly one-third of Jewish, one-fifth of Catholic, 10 percent of Mormon, and 40 percent of Muslim adults and children in the United States today live in interfaith households (Adler, 1997). In recent years Americans have been moving toward more religiously tolerant attitudes, which might account, at least in part, for the fact that in a recent study of attitudes toward interreligious marriage, only 27 percent of women and 15 percent of men indicated that they would not marry someone of a different religious background (Knox and Zusman, 2001). Some scholars have suggested that the increase in religious intermarriage is because religion generally has lost some of its power and control over people's lives.

Like interracial marriages, interfaith marriages vary according to location and population. One researcher found, for example, that cities such as New York, whose population includes a large number of Catholics and Jews, have a higher than average incidence of cross-faith (Jewish–Catholic) marriages. Likewise, Catholics and Lutherans exhibit a higher than average rate of intermarriage in states such as Pennsylvania, Iowa, and Minnesota, where the population is almost evenly split between the two religious denominations (Pace, 1986). Gender is also a factor in some interfaith marriages. For instance, Jewish men are more likely to marry outside their faith than Jewish women. This could be due primarily to the fact that the home is the focal point for the practice of Judaism and women set the spiritual tone (Marshall and Markstrom-Adams, 1995).

Most religions actively encourage same-faith marriages. One reason is the belief that cross-faith marriages tend to weaken people's religious beliefs, values, and behavior, leading to a loss of faith not to mention a loss of church membership. The pattern of interfaith marriage is particularly evident today among Jews. Since 1945, the percentage of Jews in America has declined from 4 to 2 percent. In 1945, only one in ten Jews was married to a non-Jew, whereas one in two are today (Safire, 1995). Jewish rabbis, having long expressed a concern over the decline in the number of Jews, were so concerned about the high rate at which Jews were marrying non-Jews that in 1973 the Reform Judaism's Central Conference of American Rabbis denounced interfaith marriages, declaring that such marriages were contrary to Jewish tradition and discouraged rabbis from officiating at them. Consequently, many rabbis today will not officiate at an interfaith wedding. However, recently lay leaders of Judaism's liberal Reform Movement considered abandonment of the 1973 rabbinic statement, urging their clergy instead to rely on their individual consciences in deciding whether to officiate in interfaith unions. The lay trustees believe rabbinic officiation at interfaith weddings could actually work in favor of Jewish continuity because rabbis could encourage the interfaith couples they marry to keep a Jewish household and rear their children as Jews, which is, in fact, what a small number of Reform rabbis have long done anyway (Niebuhr, 1996).

Although interfaith couples are less often the victims of society's disapproval than are interracial couples cross-faith marriages are not without difficulties. Deeply held religious beliefs are an important part of our core personality. If we believe very strongly in a particular religious ideology, to what extent will we compromise? Partners from different religions must confront a number of issues such as choosing a religion for their children and deciding which holidays to observe. These are not insurmountable barriers, of course, but they do require that a couple closely examine the ramifications of marrying across faith and find solutions that are mutually satisfying.

Some studies indicate that racially and religiously heterogamous marriages have somewhat higher divorce rates and slightly lower levels of satisfaction than do homogamous marriages (see, for example, Kosmin, Mayer, and Keysar, 2001; Heaton and Pratt, 1990; Glenn, 1982). Other researchers, however, have found no evidence that interreligious marriages are any less satisfying or successful than religiously and racially homogamous marriages (see, for example, Shehan, Bock, and Lee, 1990). As with homogamous marriages, many factors affect the success of heterogamous marriages. Lack of familial, societal, and religious support; cultural hostility; and differences in background can often undermine the stability and success of these marriages. Two other critical factors in determining the success of all marriages, heterogamous and homogamous, are the ability to communicate openly and honestly and the ability to manage conflicts that arise within these relationships. The concluding section of this chapter focuses on the issues of marital satisfaction, communication, and conflict management and resolution in marriages.

MARITAL SATISFACTION, COMMUNICATION, AND CONFLICT RESOLUTION

Research has consistently found that married people, compared with unmarried people, report being happier, healthier, and generally more satisfied with their lives (Haring-Hidore et al., 1985; Glenn and Weaver, 1988; Colemen and Ganong, 1991), and new research shows that monogamous married couples enjoy greater sexual satisfaction than singles and non-monogamous marrieds (Clements, 1994). It should be noted,

Although there is disagreement over what constitutes a marriage and a family, conservative and liberals alike agree on the need to strengthen marriages and families. Increasingly, one way that couples prepare for this goal is by participating in marriage counseling or marriage preparation classes, which teach skills such as how to resolve conflict.

however, that the "happiness gap" between married and unmarried individuals has closed considerably over the last several years. Nonetheless, what is it about the quality of married life that makes it more satisfying than a single lifestyle? Researchers exploring the quality of married life have used a variety of terms, the most notable of which are *marital success*, *marital happiness*, and *marital satisfaction*. Throughout the literature, these terms are used interchangeably as key measures of the quality of married life. Because marital success is a relative concept—it depends on who is defining it—researchers have based much of their findings on marital satisfaction as reported by married couples and on the divorce rate.

Successful Marriage

How successful are American marriages? On the one hand, although the divorce rate leveled off in the 1990s, almost two-thirds of the marriages entered into in recent years are expected to end in divorce or separation. According to some researchers, these statistics are a clear indication of a decline in marital success, the causes of which are attributed to a number of factors: The motivation for marriage has become fairly selfish; individuals expect a lot from their partners in a marriage but are largely unwilling to give in order to get; the increased flexibility in marital roles has resulted in a breakdown in the consensus about what it means to be a wife or husband; the easing of moral, religious, and legal barriers to divorce has made people less willing and able to make needed commitments to and investments in marriage than they were in the past (Glenn, 1993).

On the other hand, general survey data repeatedly show that although the rate at which couples report marital

Women and men typically use different communication styles. A lack of understanding of these differences often leads to miscommunication and conflict.
Source: © Tribune Media Services, Inc. All Rights Reserved. Reprinted by permission.

happiness or satisfaction has declined in recent years, an overwhelming majority of married couples say that they are happy or very happy and describe their marriage as satisfying (Glenn and Weaver, 1988; National Opinion Research Center, 1992). Based on a variety of survey data, researchers have found that well over half of married couples say that if they had it to do over again, they would marry the same person (Patterson and Kim, 1991; Family First, 1999).

What are the factors that distinguish happily married couples from unhappy or dissatisfied couples? There is a vast literature on marital satisfaction, happiness, quality, and stability. Some of the more common factors elucidated in this literature are being in love; sharing aims, goals, and other important beliefs; sexual compatibility; financial security; having children; the amount of time spent together; family rituals; self-disclosure, open communication, and the ability to resolve conflict in a positive manner.[2] In fact, most research in this area has found open and effective or positive communication and successful conflict resolution to be essential to the success of marriages and other intimate relationships (for example, Gottman, 1994a, b).

Effective Communication

Indeed, effective and positive communication is essential to any relationship, married or unmarried. Two important components of communication are what is said and how it is said. You have probably heard the expression, "It's not what you say, it's how you say it." For instance, it is possible to say "I'm very happy in this relationship" several different ways. An individual could say it lovingly, sincerely, or sarcastically. In good communication, what we say should be consistent with how we say it. Also, communication involves not just words but gestures, actions, intonations, and sounds. Some-

times the messages that couples give to each other are misinterpreted, misread, or missed completely. Missed messages and misinterpretations can build on themselves and result in conflict and hostility in a relationship. Clinical psychologist Joel Block (1981) provides this example:

A couple have just taken a moonlight walk by the ocean. They sit down by the water's edge. The woman says, "Let's go inside, I'm sleepy." The man responds, "It's nice out here. Why don't we lie and rest here?" The woman, angry, storms into the house. The man, equally angry, gets dressed and drives off to a local bar.

What has happened here is miscommunication. When the woman suggested going inside because she was "sleepy," she was actually attempting to communicate to her partner that she wanted to make love in the house. Her partner, on the other hand, was attempting to communicate his wish to make love on the beach under the moonlight. According to Block, neither communicated her or his wishes directly; the evening thus ended with both partners feeling rejected and angry. When this type of miscommunication becomes a pattern of interaction in a relationship, a couple could find themselves continuously upset and irritated with each other. According to family therapist Joan Zientek, situations such as this could severely strain an already precarious line of communication and hamper the couple's ability to calmly and rationally generate options and select solutions that, at least in part, will meet each partner's needs (see the Strengthening Marriages and Families box). Because conflict is a natural and normal part of all relationships and the inability or failure to deal with it can be destructive, the field of family therapy has become an increasingly popular method by which couples seek to resolve relationship conflicts. It is estimated that close to one-half of American households seek some sort of counseling or therapy (*Better Homes and Gardens*, 1988).

Despite our best desire to communicate, many of us fall short. Some of the most common communication problems identified by researchers and therapists include not listening, blaming, criticizing and/or nagging, not responding to issues as they emerge, using scapegoats, using the silent treatment, and using coercion or physical threats. One of the ways that couples can learn to communicate directly

---

[2]It should be noted that the range of factors that can be used to measure marital satisfaction is immense, and the list of factors studied vary from one research study to another, thus producing different and sometimes contradictory results. Moreover, as we have pointed out, marital satisfaction is a relative concept. Although factors closely associated with marital happiness and satisfaction in the literature may apply to some marriages, it is quite possible and probable that some couples are quite satisfied with their marriages even though none or few of these factors are present.

STRENGTHENING MARRIAGES AND FAMILIES
Talks with Family Therapist Joan Zientek

COMMUNICATION, CONFLICT RESOLUTION, AND PROBLEM SOLVING IN MARRIAGES AND INTIMATE RELATIONSHIPS

How Often Is Communication a Factor in Marital Satisfaction? Communication is one of the most powerful factors influencing the quality of the couple's relationship. Whether it is verbal or nonverbal, communication cuts through all aspects of a couple's life. Couples who exhibit effective communication skills are better equipped to deal with the inevitable conflicts and problems that accompany cohabitation and the construction of a life together. Although the communication of facts and ideas is necessary just to carry out the business of the day, it is not enough. Couples who share on this surface level will, in time, find themselves growing apart. On the other hand, true intimacy in a relationship comes from sharing on a more personal level. The sharing of feelings, goals, dreams, worries, fears, and soon, is the emotional glue that binds couples together and gets them through the rough spots. This kind of sharing, of course, demands a certain level of vulnerability and can only occur in an emotionally safe atmosphere. Being a good listener is the complement to emotional sharing. Each party needs to listen without judgment or interruption. They also need to be able to give and receive feedback about their partner's behavior without fear of reprisal, retaliation, or the demand for change. Patterns of communication in a marriage are influenced by the family background of each partner. This includes their parent's communication patterns and the emotional climate of the home in which they were raised. Were conflicts avoided or confronted? Was there a supportive and encouraging atmosphere, or were the parent's depreciating, distant, or emotionally or physically absent? Each partner's birth order as well as their individual personality and level of maturity also play into the mix. Thus, the communication dyad is influenced by a multitude of factors.

What Kinds of Strategies Can Couples Adopt to Improve Communication? One of the most central communication skills is the ability to give and receive feedback from the other in a way that does not diminish either party. Speaking for yourself, giving messages that disclose the impact of the behavior of one person or the other is far more effective than using name-calling and negative labeling in an attempt to demonstrate displeasure. Being able to deal with feedback is also critical. Harville Hendrix, in his book, *Getting the Love you Want*, suggests a three-step process:

Mirroring: Paraphrasing your partner's comment.

Validating: Letting your partner know that what she or he says makes sense, at least, from her or his perspective.

Empathy: Being able to imagine your partner's feelings.

Though crucial, this is especially difficult to do when one party is giving feedback to the other about that person's behavior. In addition, couples need to treat their marriage as an entity in itself that needs nurturing. They need to take time for each other on a daily, weekly, and monthly basis and not merely give halfhearted attention to their partner as they attend to the needs of children or wait for vacation time to catch up with each other. Simple things like having a cup of coffee after dinner (without interruption from the children or the phone), going for a walk, or sharing a hobby can keep the communication lines open. In addition, the planning of positive exchanges or little surprises, doing small favors, sending cards or e-mails that show appreciation all make each party feel valued and appreciated and thus more open to the needs of the other.

Is All Conflict Bad for a Relationship? Conflict is a natural and normal part of all relationships. No two people will see a situation in the same way, have the exact same needs at the same time, or have the same priorities as they create a life together. The resolution of conflict in a positive manner can bring new life and direction to a relationship; it can prevent the storage of resentment on the part of one or both partners, thus allowing each problem its own day in court without the attachment of past unresolved issues. It can also bring a deeper understanding of the needs and vulnerabilities of each person and, many times, in the long run, lead to better decision making than if the decision in question were solely based on the views of only one of the partners.

What Strategies Can Couples Use to Resolve Conflicts? One of the main factors that impede the resolution of conflicts between partners is the lack of ability and/or skill to see a situation from another person's point of view. Couples waste much time demanding, convincing, and manipulating the other so they can get their way. This often results in anger, resentment, and the stifling of their creative energies that might, under more positive circumstances, stand them in good stead in resolving the conflict at hand. If they cannot control their emotions or if they are not able to express their feelings in such a way that they can be heard, they are not in a position to calmly and rationally generate options and select a solution that, at least in part, will meet the needs of both partners. Couples can learn the skills of "fair fighting," whereby they agree to talk about one problem at a time, refrain from interrupting, name-calling, counterattacking, blaming, and bringing third parties into the conflict. One or both parties may not be able to use these skills, not because they are incapable of learning them, but because they have a deep need to control the relationship. In these situations, therapy may be required to help each party work through personal fears so they can grow to truly be a partner in the relationship.

with each other is by conducting what Block calls "marital checkups." This involves identifying and appraising the assets and liabilities of the relationship. If done responsibly, the marital checkup can help the couple learn more about each other's needs, desires, and expectations.

Self-Disclosure

Self-disclosure is a important element in effective communication and higher levels of marital satisfaction. According to Susan Hendrick and Clyde Hendrick (1992), self-disclosure refers simply to "telling another person about oneself; to honestly offer one's thoughts and feelings for the other's perusal, hoping that truly open communication will follow" (1992:173). Research on self-disclosure consistently shows that reciprocal self-disclosure (when both partners self-disclose) is positively related to marital satisfaction. When couples are open and self-disclosing, it creates togetherness and closeness, and thus higher marital satisfaction. On the other hand, marital satisfaction is low when one partner is self-disclosing and the other is not, one is more self-disclosing than the other, or if neither partner is self-disclosing.

Some researchers have found that although marital satisfaction increases as the level of self-disclosure increases, there is a leveling off, whereby at the very highest levels of self-disclosure there is a decrease in marital satisfaction. One explanation for this phenomenon is that couples who exhibit high levels of self-disclosure tend to be more likely to express their opinions to and about each other more readily, whether positive or critical and disapproving. In turn, criticism and disapproval can become a problem in a relationship and can lead to lower relationship satisfaction (Schumm, 1986; Pearson, 1989; Moss and Schwebel, 1993). As in many other aspects of heterosexual relationships, women and men tend to differ in terms of disclosure, although the research findings are somewhat mixed. For example, some researchers have found women to be more disclosing than men (Arliss, 1991), whereas others have found no major difference between the sexes. According to Hendrick and Hendrick (1992), a major difference in female and male disclosure is in terms of the target person to whom they will disclose. Women tend to disclose more to same-sex friends, whereas men tend to disclose more to romantic partners. In contrast, research indicates that lesbians and gays are equally disclosing in their respective relationships (Nardi and Sherrod, 1994). Perhaps one of the greatest consequences of self-disclosure for marital (or intimacy) satisfaction is that when it is done well, it takes much of the guesswork out of interpersonal communication (Hendrick and Hendrick, 1992:175).

In general, successful communication includes a number of other conditions and skills. Two basic conditions are a nonthreatening, noncoercive atmosphere and mutual commitment. In addition, a couple must be willing to change as the needs and demands of the relationship change. Some of the key skills that are important for successful communication are the ability to identify, accept responsibility for, and resolve problems, as well as a willingness to listen and negotiate conflict. Based on now 25-plus years of observing couples interact in the "Marriage Lab" at his Seattle Marital and Family Institute, research psychologist John Gottman (1994a,b) argues that most marriages and similar

relationships fall into one of three categories: *validating partnerships*, which are dominated by affection and compromise; *volatile partnerships*, in which conflict is intense, but so is passion; and *others*, in which a pair of conflict-avoiders agree to disagree. All of these relationships can work and all require conflict, both as fuel and as a venting mechanism. More importantly, however, to be successful they all require many more acts of positive reinforcement than of negative interaction. According to Gottman, the real reason marriages succeed or fail is really very simple: Couples who stay together are *nice* to each other more often than not. That is, Gottman claims that couples who are satisfied with their relationship maintain a five-to-one ratio of positive to negative moments in their relationship (they are five times as nice as they are nasty to each other). Couples who are unhappy and/or dissatisfied with their relationship have let the ratio slip below one-to-one. Couples can improve their relationship with some simple practices during moments of conflict, such as take a deep breath, calm down, listen and speak nondefensively, try a morning leave-taking, a chat at the end of the day, or private time together without the children or other interferences. Gottman has found that successful relationships are not those that never have conflict, rather they are those in which the couple recognizes when there is a problem and tries to fix it.

Conflict and Conflict Resolution

No matter how happy or satisfying a marriage or other intimate relationship is, some conflict is inevitable. Good communication alone does not prevent conflict. Even when couples have positive and effective communication skills and high levels of self-disclosure, there are likely to be times of disagreement, conflict, and fighting. Several major areas of marriage and family life generally contribute to conflict in marriages: money, sex, children, power, loyalty, division of marital and family tasks, privacy, work, in-laws, friends, religion, and substance abuse. Gottman believes the four most destructive behaviors to marital happiness are criticism, contempt, defensiveness, and stonewalling:

Criticism involves attacking one's partner's personality or character rather than complaining about a specific behavior. For example, a healthy and specific complaint might be "I wish you would spend more time with me." A generalizing and blaming attack on one's personality or character might be "There's something wrong with you. You never spend time with me." The difference between these two approaches can be very significant to the listener.

Contempt involves intense and intentional negative thoughts about a person and can be manifest in a number of ways, for example, subtle or not-so-subtle putdowns, hostile jokes, mocking facial expressions, or name-calling. An example might be "You're getting old and stupid. I don't know why I married you."

Defensiveness is generally a response to being attacked or put down. It involves making excuses, tossing back counterattacks and insults, and denying responsibility. For example, a defensive response might be "Why is it that I'm the one who is always expected to initiate spending time together? What's wrong with you? Do you have a problem?"

Stonewalling means that the couple has essentially stopped communicating. They have reached a point where they refuse

Some conflict in intimate relationships is inevitable. However, such conflict does not have to be destructive. Researchers have found that successful partners find constructive ways to manage relationship conflict that allow each partner to maintain her or his differences while negotiating a solution that is mutually agreeable.

Consider the intimate relationships in which you are or have been involved. Can you distinguish particular patterns of communication in these relationships? What are or were the major barriers to communication? What strategies of conflict resolution have you and your partners employed in these relationships? Did you learn anything about conflict resolution from your parents' relationship? How can you improve communication and conflict resolution in your close relationships?

to respond to one another even in self-defense. According to Gottman, when a couple reaches this stage, one or both of them are thinking negative thoughts about the other most of the time, and, if their behavior is unchecked, the marriage will likely end in divorce.

When conflict arises in a relationship, as it inevitably does, it does not have to be destructive. Researchers have found that some conflict can be constructive. Conflict management is the key. When conflict is managed or resolved through negotiation and compromise, it can strengthen the bonds of affection between partners. When it is dealt with ineffectively, it can lower satisfaction and even contribute to the dissolution of the relationship. Social researchers Don Dinkmeyer and Jon Carlson (1984) suggest some of the following strategies to resolve marital conflict: Clearly define the problem, demonstrate a mutual respect for each other, agree to cooperate with each other, and agree to make decisions together.

Some social scientists (for example, Sprey, 1979) believe that couples in lasting marriages do not really resolve most conflicts in the sense that the conflict is settled forever with a clear winner and loser. Rather, they manage most conflicts through an ongoing process of negotiation. Couples in successful marriages find ways to manage conflict so that each partner can maintain her or his differences while working collectively to find a negotiated solution that is satisfactory to both parties. According to Gottman (1994), fighting, whether rare or frequent, does not have to be destructive. The important thing in a marriage is to find a compatible fighting style, not to stop fighting altogether. In fact, in many cases fighting can be one of the healthiest things a couple can do for their relationship. More important, the key to a happy and successful marriage or other intimate relationship is relatively simple: Learn to calm down, learn to speak and listen to one another nondefensively, validate one another, and practice the former steps over and over until they become routine, even in the heat of an argument

SUPPORTING MARRIAGES AND FAMILIES

Over the last three to four decades, American marriages and families have undergone profound and far-reaching transformation. Both the structure of marriages and families and marriage and family values, have changed; as a result, marriages and families today are very different institutions from those of the past. Yet there is a constant movement to reclaim mythical models of marriages and families that are believed to have existed in the *good old days*. This has led to hotly debated marriage- and family-related issues such as family values, the definition of marriage, the definition of family, a federal marriage amendment, and same-sex marriage. Although those who advocate a return to how families *use to be* claim they support marriages and families, their critics accuse them of trying to legislate morality through a variety of laws, ordinances, constitutional changes and amendments, and state and federal legislative actions. Many of these actions are extreme, and rather than supporting marriages and families, critics argue that they penalize those who fall outside such narrow definitions of marriages and families (see, for instance, the Debating Social Issues box). For example, lesbians and gays and cohabiting couples lack the institutional support that heterosexual and legally married couples have.

If we as a society are serious about supporting marriages and families, we must make the concerns and issues of marriages and families a central national, local, and community priority and not work to undermine them. Rather than develop and implement policies, and programs that discourage some forms of marriages and families and reward others, we should develop and implement policies, programs, services, and resources that encourage and support the diversity of marriages and families in today's society. The provision of state and federal monies as well as that of private organizations should included support for skill-based marriage and parenting education, premarital education and counseling, marriage education and counseling, and other services that would support marriages and families. Supporting marriages and families should be less about religious moralizing and more about providing tangible support such as marriage, family and couples or partner education courses, training, and other resources. Local communities can develop programs through various congregations and community organizations that help women and men in intimate relationships, whether legal marriage, cohabitation, or

DEBATING SOCIAL ISSUES

UNWED AND UNWANTED: SHOULD CITIES LEGISLATE MORALITY?

In 2006, a cohabiting couple, Olivia Shelltrack and Fondray Loving, purchased a five-bedroom three-bath house in Black Jack, Missouri, and moved into the home with their three children. However, the couple faced not only losing the house of their dreams but also being evicted from the city of Black Jack itself. It seems that Black Jack has a city ordinance that applies to unmarried couples with children. Under this Black Jack law, a home cannot be inhabited by three or more individuals not related by "blood, marriage or adoption." Unmarried and cohabiting with her boyfriend of 13 years and their three children, the couple was told that their household failed to meet Black Jack's definition of a *family*. Consequently, the couple was denied an occupancy permit for the house. According to Shelltrack, the law essentially means that you can have one child living in your house if you are not married, but more than that, you cannot. Shelltrack and Loving are engaged, but for financial reasons have delayed getting married so that they could buy a home and start a business (Kim, 2006; Goldstein, 2006).

The couple appealed the denial of an occupancy permit at a hearing before Black Jack's Board of Adjustment, where

Fondray Loving and Olivia Shelltrack

they were asked personal questions about their relationship, such as why they don't just get married; about their children, and their previous home in another city after which the Board denied the couple's request. Shelltrack then filed an appeal with the Black Jack municipal court. The ordinance has recently come under scrutiny because of Shelltrack's case, but it seems that Black Jack is not the only city

with such an ordinance that defines what *kind* of family can live within its limits. Most municipalities in the St. Louis, Missouri, area have similar, if not identical, rules. Shelltrack and Loving are not the first to challenge the Black Jack ordinance. In 1999, the unwed parents of triplets challenged the city's denial of an occupancy permit. However, the case was never resolved. Elsewhere, in 1985, the city of

other, develop and maintain healthy and stable relationships. The divisiveness over which marriage and family structure is valid, in the long run, is detrimental to all marriage and family forms.

SUMMARY

Although we have witnessed some important changes in marriage and family patterns, most Americans will marry at least once in their lifetime. People marry for a number of reasons, such as having a committed relationship and someone to share life with. Marriage means different things to different people. For some people, the key to marriage is commitment. For others, marriage is a sacrament, a sacred union, or holy state under the direct authority of their God. Most people do not think of marriage as a legal contract. When two people marry, however, they are agreeing to

abide by the terms of a marriage contract that they had no part in drafting. Although each individual state defines the rights and obligations of the marriage contract, all states specify who can marry whom and at what age they may do so. Marriage is a civil right that applies only to heterosexual couples in U.S. society. However, since 1991, several lesbian and gay couples have sued for the right to marry.

Historically, the marriage contract put women at a decided disadvantage. Although the process of marriage is different today, in many states women continue to lose legal

Ladue, Missouri, sued a couple for violating a city ordinance prohibiting an unmarried woman and man from living together if they were not related by blood, marriage, or adoption. A year later, the Missouri Court of Appeals upheld the ruling against the couple, who had lived in the home since 1981 (Kim, 2006; Goldstein, 2006).

The federal Fair Housing Act prohibits discrimination based on race, color, religion, national origin, gender, disability, and families with children. Most states include additional protected classes such as marital status. However, Missouri does not. Because some people believe the Black Jack ordinance crosses the line into discriminatory zoning, discrimination based on marital status and a denial of the right to live wherever one wants and can afford the ordinance has come under fire and the Black Jack city council is reviewing the ordinance. In what seems to be the latest battleground in the war on family values, various individuals and groups have drawn clear lines and as with most controversial issues, it has its supporters and detractors.

On one side of the issue are city officials such as the mayor of Black Jack and others who defend the ordinance. They claim that the ordinance is about overcrowding and has nothing to do with defining family, family values, religion, marriage, or unwed cohabitation. According to the mayor of Black Jack, it is what cities do to maintain the housing stock and to avoid overcrowding; you have laws on the books to preclude any situation. That is why it is there. Proponents of the ordinance claim that its sole purpose is to prevent overcrowding in houses and ultimately the schools of Black Jack—that it is designed to safeguard neighborhoods from everything from fraternities and group homes to crack houses (Goldstein, 2006).

On the other side of the issue, Shelltrack and others such as former Black Jack resident Amy Madson argue that the city is trying to regulate morality with the ordinance. Madson and her fiancé, who had lived for a year in the same house that Selltrack later purchased, was told that she and her fiancé were denied an occupancy permit for the home because they were not married. The couple was told that in God's eyes, they were not considered a family, even though those who were charged with enforcing the ordinance were hard put to explain what is meant by *family* (Kim, 2006). Given the history of the ordinance and its implementation, opponents contend that although the mayor and others deny it, the ordinance *is* indeed about marriage, family, and the city's attempt to legislate morality. Those against such ordinances argue that people should not be forced to marry just to live in their home. They also contend that Black Jack's definition of a family is too narrow and restrictive and is not compatible with the reality of intimacy and family life in twenty-first century America. For instance, in Black Jack, family is defined as "an individual or two or more persons related by blood, marriage, or adoption, or a group of not more than three persons who need not be related by blood, marriage or adoption, living together as a single nonprofit housekeeping unit in a dwelling unit" (Kim, 2006:2). It also discriminates against lesbian and gay couples and immigrants who often rely on living in larger groups to afford housing and who fall outside Black Jack's economically and heterosexually biased definition of family. Moreover, Shelltrack and others argue that a piece of paper—legal or otherwise—does not make a family. Shelltrack says that she, her fiancé, and her children are a family; her children are not children of an unmarried couple—rather they are children of two loving parents (Kim, 2006).

What do you Think? On which side of the debate do you fall? Explain your position. Is the Black Jack ordinance essentially an attempt to regulate morality? Should cities and/or the state be in the business of regulating morality? If yes, why? Who gets to define what is a family, what are family values, and so forth? Whose definitions should prevail? What other groups beside the unmarried are discriminated against by the Black Jack ordinance?

---

rights when they marry. Marriage in the United States is imbued with rituals and traditions, many of which date back to ancient societies. Although many people continue to abide by tradition when they marry, an increasing number of people are modifying, changing, or creating their own personal marriage rituals.

Like other relationships, marriage is experienced differently depending on factors such as race, class, and gender. For example, researchers point out that women and men experience marriage differently. This has led several researchers to describe marriage as containing two marriages: hers and his. The female–male differences in the experience of marriage, though largely hidden, have a tremendous effect on the mental and physical health of wives and husbands.

Getting married represents a significant change in the lives of a couple. Marital adjustment is an important part of the marriage experience. Couples must continuously make adjustments over the life course of the marriage. The success of the relationship depends, in large part, on the degree to which both partners are able to adjust. Satisfying, well-adjusted marriages vary a great deal. A typology of marital relationships representing marital adjustment includes the conflict-habituated, the devitalized, the passive-congenial, the vital, and the total relationship.

Whenever two people live together over some period of time, some conflict is bound to occur. Conflict does not have to be destructive, however. Couples in successful marriages learn to manage or resolve conflict in such a way that is satisfactory to both parties. An essential element in managing or resolving conflict is open, honest, and direct communication. If couples are committed to the relationship, they will try to manage or resolve conflict in a constructive way. Moreover, whatever problem-solving style a couple uses, the relationship can be successful as long as positive feelings and interactions outweigh negative ones by a ratio of five to one.

WRITING YOUR OWN SCRIPT

PREPARING YOUR RELATIONSHIP CONTRACT

The decision to marry or cohabit leads to a number of other related issues and areas of understanding that couples should consider, discuss, and resolve before to establishing their living arrangement. Many couples have found it useful to write personal contracts that clarify their feelings and expectations for the marriage or cohabitative relationship. To be most effective, this exercise should be done with your partner. It may be easier, however, if you and your partner write separate contracts and then compare and discuss each other's contract before writing a final version that represents your collective view and consensus. Prenuptial and personal contracts include the expectations the couple bring to their relationship. In the exercise that follows, we present the items commonly included in marriage and personal contracts. It is not necessary that you cover every item simply because it is here. Concern yourself only with those areas relevant to your particular situation. Or feel free to add topics or issues relevant to you and your life. (Note: If you choose to remain single, either permanently or on a temporary basis, many of these items will apply to you as well. Although you do not need to consider a partner, reflecting on these items can help you get in touch with yourself as well as build a more satisfying lifestyle.) Under each topic, we present some questions to consider. These questions are not exhaustive.

Relevant History

Couples often assume they know all they need to know about each other without really discussing their past. However, a lack of knowledge can sometimes lead to problems later on.

Questions to consider: Will we try to share all aspects of our history that might affect our intended relationship, for example, former marriages and our own and our families' health histories?

Division of Labor and Responsibilities

A source of difficulty for many couples is the perception of inequity in the performance of household tasks. Often partners have different assumptions about who should do these tasks. Some people believe household tasks should be allocated on the basis of gender even when both partners are employed full-time.

Questions to consider

1. What rights do we each have as individuals, and what role expectations do we have for each other? How will we divide household responsibilities? Who will cook, clean, make the shopping lists, shop, do laundry, make house and car repairs, do yard work, wash windows, plan entertainment, take out the trash, care for children, take care of finances, pay bills, and perform all the other tasks of daily living?
2. How will decisions be made—individually or jointly? How will we resolve differences of opinion?

Sexual Exclusiveness

One of the reasons some people give for dissolving their relationship is a partner's extramarital affairs. Such behavior can lead to feelings of betrayal, jealousy, insecurity, and anger. Often couples do not discuss their views on sexual matters until after they are married or cohabiting, and sometimes they find that they have conflicting values in this area.

Questions to consider: Will our relationship be sexually exclusive? What is our understanding about sexual access to each other? How will we communicate our personal desires? What are our feelings about outside relationships, both sexual and nonsexual? Would we feel threatened by outside relationships?

Money Matters

Money matters are issues that all of us have to deal with regardless of our marital status. Couples may not always share the same values concerning money and the things it can buy. As a way of keeping money and money management from becoming problems, it is wise for couples to discuss their values and expectations. Agreement on financial planning, spending, and management is a key ingredient in marital or relationship satisfaction.

Questions to consider

1. How will we handle the ownership, distribution, and management of property before and after marriage? How will we decide on the contribution of each person to the total family income and support? Will it matter if one of us earns more than the other?
2. As a couple, how compatible are our spending (including the use of credit cards) and savings patterns? Are we both comfortable with these patterns, or do we need to make changes in them? What are our financial goals? What plans can we make to achieve these goals? Should we have joint or separate savings and checking accounts? What are the advantages and disadvantages of each arrangement?
3. Who will manage the family finances? How will we decide on a family budget? How will we decide

KEY TERMS

principle of legitimacy

sacrament

legal marriage

social marriage

bigamy

adultery

fornication

affinal relatives

coverture

conjugal rights

personal marriage agreement

prenuptial agreement

marital adjustment

heterogamous marriage

how family money will be spent? Who will pay the bills and make the investments? How will we decide this? If one of us assumes this responsibility, how will that one keep the other informed about our financial matters? Will each of us be able to manage if something happens to the other?

Family Surname

Names are important symbols of identity. In some cultures a newly married couple incorporates both family names into their surname. The cultural tradition in the United States is for a wife to take her husband's surname. Many couples, however, are questioning this practice.

Questions to consider: Will we both carry the same surname? Will we hyphenate our name or use a new one? If we have children, what surname will they have?

Selecting a place to live

Where we live is an important decision that we make in adulthood. We spend a tremendous amount of time in the place we live. Thus, where and under what conditions we live is a major factor in how we perceive the quality of our lives.

Questions to consider   What type of housing do we want? How will we decide on our place of residence? How important are each of these factors in our decision: proximity to family, schools, work; convenience to community services and public transportation; the area's tax base; the overall safety and well-being of the neighborhood? What can we afford? Which is preferable for us, to buy or to rent?

Religion

Religion can be a source of comfort and support to couples, or it can be a source of conflict. If conflict occurs over religion, it may be because partners belong to different religions, have different values, or do not attach the same importance to religion.

Questions to consider: What role will religion play in our relationship? Are we religiously compatible? Is this important to us? Will we attend services together? Separately? Will we raise our children in a specific religion?

Relationships with Others

In many marriages today, couples often experience difficulty in trying to manage work, marriage, and other social responsibilities. Finding time to spend together may require making adjustments in the time devoted to other relationships.

Questions to consider: How do we feel about each other's relatives and friends? How much interaction do we want to have with them? How will we decide where to spend our holidays and vacations? How will relationships with others be determined? How will we manage to keep time for ourselves?

Conflict Resolution

Every couple will experience conflict in their relationship at one time or another. The critical factor in the relationship is not the experience of conflict but rather how the conflict is handled.

Questions to consider: What will we do when things do not seem to be working out right? What mechanisms can we create for resolving disagreements? Will we be willing to get counseling if we are having problems? What are our attitudes regarding divorce?

Renewability, Change, and Termination of Contract

People and conditions change over time. An effective contract allows for these possibilities. Couples are well advised to have periodic reviews of how the contract is working and what changes, if any, should be made.

Questions to consider: How will we provide for a periodic reevaluation and change (if necessary) in this contract? Under what conditions will we terminate this contract?
These are only a few of the many issues and decisions we all face in the course of our lives. For example, issues of work, jobs, or careers, or those concerning having or not having children are discussed in other chapters of this textbook. The decisions that are made will vary from one individual and family to the next. No single pattern can meet everyone's needs. Each individual and family must decide what arrangement is best for them. The most critical factor in all these areas is communication. All too frequently couples do not discuss these issues before becoming partners, with the result that they often begin a relationship with unrealistic expectations. Although communicating on these issues early in a relationship cannot by itself guarantee happiness or long-term stability, it can improve the probability of achieving these goals.

QUESTIONS FOR STUDY AND REFLECTION

1. Why do people marry? If you are married, why did you marry? If you are not married but plan to wed, why are you going to marry? Ask three different married couples—one in their 60s, one in their 40s, and one in their 20s—why they married and what were their expectations of marriage Do the women and men differ in their appraisals of marriage? Are there generational differences across couples? If so, how do you explain these differences?

2. Thinking about yourself, your parents, or some couple you are close to, do you (they) have a successful marriage? How important is communication to the success

of the marriage? What communication skills does each partner possess?

3. As you have read in this chapter, important changes have taken place in marriage and family patterns. If you have computer access, locate Web sites pertaining to marriage. Classify the types of Web sites that you find on this topic. What are the most salient issues covered in these sites? How do these issues relate to the topics you have read in this chapter? Which of these issues seem to be Internet-specific? Gender-specific? Race/ethnicity or class-specific? Are there issues that are different depending on one's sexual orientation? Explain.

4. Jessie Bernard's typology of marriages along gender lines is a classic in the field of sociology. Do you agree that marriages are experienced differently by women and men? Can you give evidence from your own experiences or the experiences of people you know to support or refute Bernard's argument?

ADDITIONAL RESOURCES

SOCIOLOGICAL

Johnson, Walton R., and D. Michael Warren, eds. 1993. *Inside Mixed Marriages: Accounts of Changing Attitudes, Patterns, and Perceptions of Cross-Cultural and Interracial Marriages.* Lanham, MD: University Press of America. An anthology of articles written by and from the perspective of couples in interracial or interethnic marriages.

Louden, Jennifer. 1994. *The Couple's Comfort Book: A Creative Guide for Renewing Passion, Pleasure, and Commitment.* San Francisco: Harper. A usable compendium of imaginative activities that couples can do together. It is cross-referenced so that you can skip around in the book and design your own program of relationship rebirth.

Nock, S. L. 1998. *Marriage in Men's Lives.* New York: Oxford University Press. In this provocative book, the author uses surveys to examine how and why marriage affects men's lives so much, and to study marriage as a means for developing and sustaining masculinity. The author draws some interesting and far-reaching conclusions about the nature of marriage and presents an interesting and innovative model for a new marriage.

Waite, L., and M. Gallagher. 2000. *The Case for Marriage.* Cambridge, MA: Harvard University Press. The authors focus on the benefits of marriage for all concerned: women, men, and children. It has an assortment of chapters covering a variety of relevant topics, including emotional well-being, sexuality, physical health, family violence, and children's outcomes.

LITERARY

McKinney-Whetstone, Diane. 1996. *Tumbling.* New York: Scribner (paperback). A delightful novel and heartwarming story of a young couple in Philadelphia during the 1940s and 1950s who are unable to consummate their marriage because of a horrible secret in the wife's past. Despite their problems, the couple care deeply for one another and they struggle to keep their unconventional marriage and family whole. This novel is suspenseful, tragic, humorous, and, above all, useful for a sociological study and discussion of marriage, family, and intimacy.

Nicolson, Nigel. 1974. *Portrait of a Marriage.* London: Futura. A lively and interesting personal account of the author's parents, each of whom had homosexual affairs and practiced "open marriage." Despite their marital lifestyle, they stayed together and loved each other in what was apparently an adjusted and satisfying relationship.

FILM

Bee Season. 2005. Based on the best-selling novel by Myla Goldberg, this film is about a wife and mother who begins a downward emotional spiral as her husband avoids their collapsing marriage by immersing himself in his 11-year-old daughter's quest to become a spelling bee champion.

Moonsoon Wedding. 2001. An insightful film about two young Punjabis from affluent Indian families coming together through an arranged marriage. The film consists of five intersecting stories, each dealing with different aspects of life and love as they cross boundaries of class, continent, and ideas of morality.

INTERNET

http://www.couples-place.com On-line since 1996, this site provides a learning community for solving marriage problems, improving relationship skills, celebrating marriage, and achieving happiness with your partner. The site includes practical articles about relationships, forums about marriage and couple life, bulletin boards, a relationship satisfaction quiz, and many other resources.

http://www.bridesandgrooms.com An interesting site that provides a free bookstore and newsletter and provides a variety of links to subjects ranging from guides and ideas for weddings and honeymoons, premarital counseling, wedding shopping, wedding attire, wedding styles, and wedding music to marriage encounters to surveys on sex and marriage.

http://www.gayweddings.com This site offers a range of wedding services and packages for a civil ceremony or a wedding event. The site offers ideas and planning for "Two Brides" or "Two Grooms" weddings, wedding etiquette, gay wedding and planning consultation, destination wedding packages, wedding invitations, discussion boards and forums, and access to wedding seminars.

http://www.covenantmarriage.com A Web site for conservative, Christian-based Covenant Marriage Movement members. The site provides a range of services, including a Covenant Marriage Online store, Sunday Promotion, Covenant Events, Covenant Legislation, Covenant Counselors, Cooperating Minstry, and Couple Support.

IN THE NEWS

The United States

A new kind of extended family is emerging in the United States and across the globe. These families are composed of "donor siblings" who share the same biological father whom, in all likelihood, they will never meet. Each year in the United States approximately 30,000 babies are born to mothers who conceived with the aid of anonymous sperm donors through a process called artificial insemination (AI), one of the earliest forms of reproductive technology. When AI was first introduced in the early 1970s, the procedure was used almost exclusively by infertile married couples. A great deal of secrecy surrounded it and children were usually not aware their father was a donor. Over time as its effectiveness was demonstrated and its popularity grew, AI became available to unmarried individuals. Today, approximately half the people using AI are single women and lesbian couples. As the number of households with no adult males grew, the secrecy surrounding AI began to crumble. Told about the nature of their conception, many children, as they grew older, wanted information about their biological fathers—Who am I? Where did I come from? Who do I look like? Now, with the help of the Internet-based Donor Sibling Registry, children of sperm donors who are over 18, their mothers, and donors themselves can register to find answers to those questions and maybe even to connect. According to information on www.donorsiblingregistry.com, membership has grown to 8281 with matches between more than 2077 half-siblings (and/or donors) facilitated.

Because sperm donors typically provide samples over a period of time, lasting anywhere from a couple of months to years, the probability that children conceived through AI have half-siblings is quite high. For instance, according to records of the California Cryobank, sperm donor 150 of the California Cryobank has fathered at least 4 children and possibly more. The dozens of women who bought Donor 150's sperm are not required to report when they have a baby. Two of his genetic daughters, each with different mothers, each living in different states, found each other through the help of the Donor Sibling Registry. The two families now have an ongoing relationship. Other groupings are even larger. One mother of a 7-year-old exchanges e-mail messages with 8 other mothers who have a total of 12 children from the same donor (Harmon, 2005).

Initial reports seem to indicate that the children are delighted to find that they have half-siblings and relish the fact that there are others like them who share physical and other characteristics. Their mothers, too, find common ground. One mother said of her relationship with 10 other women who conceived by using sperm from the same donor, "It's an emotional connection. We have a common base. Most of us are single. We all desired children and we were all attracted to the same donor" (quoted in Romano, 2006).

Now that it is easier for donor-conceived children to find half-siblings, some are advocating an end to the system of anonymity that surrounds AI and are calling for sperm banks to accept only donors who agree that their children can contact them when they turn 18, as is now the case in England and some other European countries. Some sperm banks are responding to these concerns by asking donors whether they would agree to be contacted by their offspring when they turn 18. They also charge more for the sperm of those who agree (Harmon, 2005).

Nevertheless, not everyone sees these developments as positive. Some sperm banks and medical ethicists are concerned about the real possibility that these Internet searches will violate the privacy of thousands of donors and end up discouraging others from donating sperm. Still others believe sperm banks are not sufficiently regulated. They argue that without records of how many children one donor may have fathered and where they are located creates the risk that, unknowly, half-siblings could end up marrying each other. One donor estimates that he donated between 150 and 200 specimens over a period of 7 years. He is now a pediatrician and he and his wife are expecting their first child. He made himself available over the Internet to answer questions that any children he fathered may have. He has been contacted and has seen pictures of some of "his" children. When asked by CBS reporter Steve Kroft if he had thought about the possibility of fathering children when he donated his sperm, he said,

> I guess I entertained the possibility of that. You know, I look at it a little differently. This may sound a little detached, but I don't really look at these children as my children or, you know, that I'm their father. I was somebody who provided a tool or a necessary ingredient for a family to have a child that was wanted" (quoted in "Sperm Donor Siblings," 2006).

Some critics of this flexible approach to parenthood believe it is not fair to children to deny them their father's identity and they suggest this technology serves the interests of adults without regard for children (see, for example, Marquardt, 2005).

WHAT WOULD YOU DO? If you were conceived through artificial insemination, would you want to know who your donor father is? Would you try to find him? Would you want to know if you had half-siblings? Would you try to find them? Explain. Would you favor legislation that would allow children who turned 18 to have the name of the donor father? Explain. Do you think this would affect the number of men willing to be sperm donors? How has artificial insemination affected the structure and functioning of families? Do you see this as a positive or negative development? Explain.

Fertility—the actual number of live births in a population—is both a biological and a social phenomenon. In all societies the timing and number of births are shaped by numerous social forces: the value attached to children and parenthood, marriage patterns and gender roles, political and economic structures, and knowledge about human reproduction, including reproductive technologies such as artificial insemination. Thus, fertility patterns vary greatly across cultures. For example, in some cultures children are highly valued as economic assets, and women are expected to have many children beginning at an early age. Other societies view children in terms of their emotional value. These societies promote small families and encourage women to delay childbearing until their middle or late 20s. In some societies, the birth of a first child precedes marriage; in others, a birth outside marriage is strongly condemned. Even within a given society fertility patterns may vary considerably across racial, ethnic, and class lines. And, as the cases of China and India make clear, cultural preferences for one sex, especially when abetted by new technologies, can dramatically alter the population structure and present new and unforeseen consequences for the well-being of a society (see Chapter 1).

This chapter begins with a brief historical review of changing fertility patterns in the United States and then proceeds to look at the many factors that influence the decision whether to parent. The remaining sections examine some of the issues surrounding conception, pregnancy, and parenthood.

HISTORICAL OVERVIEW: FERTILITY TRENDS IN THE UNITED STATES

Demographers use the term **fertility rate** to refer to the number of births per thousand women in their childbearing years (ages 15–44 in a given year). Evidence suggests that the fertility rate in early America was quite high. For example, the **total fertility rate** (the average number of children women would have over their lifetime if current birth rates were to remain constant) in 1790, when the first census was taken, is estimated to have been 7.7 (Gill, Glazer, and Thernstrom, 1992:41), in contrast to the estimated 2.09 in 2005 (CIA, 2006).

Figure 9.1 shows that by 1900 the total fertility rate had declined to half that of a century earlier. What happened to produce this dramatic decline? First, the transformation of the United States from a rural–agricultural society to an urban–industrial society lessened the economic value of

FIGURE 9.1

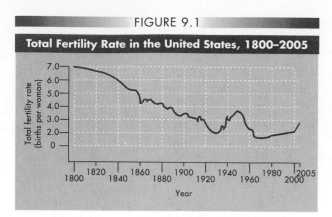

Total Fertility Rate in the United States, 1800–2005

Sources: Adapted from Richard T. Gill, Nathan Glazer, and Stephan A. Thernstrom, 1992, *Our Changing Population* (Englewood Cliffs, NJ: Prentice Hall): 41. Reprinted by permission of Prentice Hall, Englewood Cliffs, NJ; J. A. Martin, B. E. Hamilton, and S. J. Ventura, 2001, "Preliminary Data for 2000," *National Vital Statistics Reports 49*, 5 (Hyattsville, MD: National Center for Health Statistics): 4. CIA, 2006. *The World FactBook* (March 29). (Accessed April 17 http://www.cia.gov/cia/publications/factbook/index.html.)

children. Children are an economic asset in agricultural societies, where many hands are needed to cultivate the land. Second, the move to an urban–industrial society was accompanied by rapid advances in science and technology, leading to changes in people's views of the world. According to Robert Wells (1978), people came to adopt "modern values," which focus on planning and the future. Couples came to believe that controlling family size would have economic benefits. By having fewer children, couples could reallocate their resources from the basic costs of providing for children to investing more in their future. The changing technology of an urban–industrial society required a more educated labor force. Thus, not only did the economic value of children decline, but it also became more costly to raise and educate them. Over time, a general pattern has emerged—the higher the income, the lower the fertility rate. In contrast, lower-income parents generally see larger families as more beneficial than costly. These parents are less likely to go to college, more likely to marry early, and more likely to see children as a means of attaining adult status and identity.

In the first decades of the twentieth century, the fertility rate continued to decline, particularly during the years of the Great Depression, when couples limited family size because of economic hardship. Demographers had predicted that the number of births would increase after World War II as couples put the depression and the war behind them. However, no one anticipated the dramatic rise in the total fertility rate from about 2.5 in 1945 to a high of 3.8 in 1957. Between 1946 and 1965, a period called the "baby boom," 74 million babies were born in the United States. Although demographers do not agree completely on the causes of the baby boom, two factors seem to have played a major role. First, the expanding postwar economy enabled unprecedented numbers of people to marry and have children at an early age. Second, a number of government policies were aimed at helping young families get started. The GI Bill helped veterans get an education and hence better-paying jobs. Federal housing loans and income tax deduc-

tions for children and interest on home mortgages encouraged people to buy houses and start families.

The baby boom was not to last, however. In 1957, the total fertility rate again began to decline, falling by more than 50 percent in less than 20 years to a low of 1.7 in 1976. This rate increased only slightly in the 1990s. This drastic decline, called the "baby bust," was not anticipated either. Among the factors thought responsible for this change was a slowing of the economy, the introduction of the birth control pill in the early 1960s, the legalization of abortion, the continuing increase in women's labor force participation, and increases in both the age at marriage and in the divorce rate. However, the most likely explanation is that the baby boom was simply a short-term deviation from the long-term decline begun in the nineteenth century. Whatever the reasons for the decline, another baby boom of this magnitude does not seem likely in the foreseeable future. Nevertheless, the fertility rate rose 3 percent to 67.6 per 1000 women aged 15 to 44 years between 1999 and 2000 (Martin, Hamilton, and Ventura, 2001), dropped to 64.8 in 2002, and rose again to 66.3 in 2004 (Hamilton et al. 2005), most likely influenced by an improved economy. Although we do not yet know the reasons for this increase, demographers speculate that it was due to an improved economy.

Current Fertility Patterns

There were 4.1 million births in 2004, nearly 1 percent more than in 2003 and the total fertility rate was also slightly higher in 2004 than in 2003 (2.05 to 2.04). This rate is not uniform across all race and ethnic groups. As Figure 9.2 shows, Native Americans and whites have the lowest rates (1.74 and 1.85) and Latinas have the highest rate (2.82). However, there is great diversity even within these general categories. For example, in 2003, Mexican Americans had a total fertility rate of 2.96, Cuban Americans 2.06, women from Central and South America 2.73, and Puerto Ricans 1.84 (Martin et al., 2005). Age, cultural norms, and class combine to explain these rate variations. Asian Americans tend to marry later than other groups and they are

FIGURE 9.2

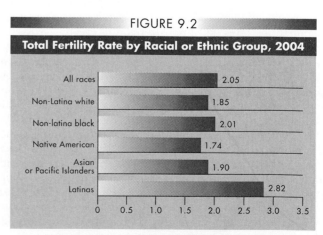

Total Fertility Rate by Racial or Ethnic Group, 2004

All races	2.05
Non-Latina white	1.85
Non-latina black	2.01
Native American	1.74
Asian or Pacific Islanders	1.90
Latinas	2.82

Source: Adapted from B. E. Hamilton, S. J. Ventura, J. A. Martin, and P. D. Sutton, 2005, *Preliminary Births for 2004*, Health E-stats (Hyattsville, MD: National Center for Health Statistics): Table 1.

more likely than other groups to delay childbearing until their late 20s and 30s. Asian Americans have the lowest fertility rate of any group in the 15 to 19 age category and they have the highest fertility rate of any group in the 35 to 39 age category. In contrast, African Americans, Native Americans, and Latinas begin childbearing at early ages. African American and Native American women have lower fertility rates in their late 30s than other groups.

As we have seen, the total fertility rate in the United States is now slightly lower than the 2.1 level required for the natural replacement of the population. Much of this decline has been attributed to the changing economic value of children, older ages at marriage, the decision of women to delay childbirth until their 30s, and the desire for smaller families than in the past. Of course, expectations are not always realized. In the next section we will explore the many factors that affect the decision to have children. Yet, despite these changing patterns, the population of the United States continues to grow as a consequence of immigration, both legal and illegal. In fact, immigration has become the major factor in population growth. Each year approximately 1.5 million immigrants arrive on our shore. That number, coupled with about 750,000 births to immigrant women, adds over 2 million people to our population annually (Camarota, 2002).

TO PARENT OR NOT

All too often the exposure most of us have to child rearing is of its romantic side. Advertisers surround us with images of gurgling, laughing, adorable infants and toddlers who say and do the most clever things. What we do not often see are the temper tantrums and the rebellious "No." Parenthood, like any other social activity, involves both costs and benefits that vary over the family life cycle and that people should consider before becoming parents. Even though people do sometimes change their mind after marriage, it is important to discuss the desire for children before marriage. Wives and husbands who disagree on whether to have children are likely to experience considerable marital conflict. If the issue cannot be satisfactorily resolved, the marriage may dissolve.

The Costs of Parenthood

In contrast to previous eras, when children worked at various jobs, particularly on farms and later in factories, children today are primarily consumers. Depending on level of household income (HI), parents can expect to spend anywhere from $139,110 (HI less than $43,200) to $190,980 (HI $43,200 to $72,600) to $279,450 (HI more than $72,600) to raise a child to the age of 17 (Lino, 2006). These figures exclude college costs, expenditures by others outside the household such as grandparents and other relatives, and indirect costs such as a parent, usually the mother, foregoing earnings as a result of staying home or working part-time because of the presence of children.

Time, Energy, and Emotional Costs Raising children involves more than financial outlays; it also requires a great investment of parental time and energy. Infants and toddlers are totally dependent on parents for meeting all their physical and psychological needs. As children enter school, parents are likely to find themselves enmeshed in rounds of school activities, organized sports, religious events, Scouts, music and dance lessons, family outings, and numerous other activities that compete for their time and attention. Raising children in today's environment also carries a high emotional cost in terms of parental worries over the easy accessibility of drugs, the lure of gangs, and random violence, all of which have taken a heavy toll on young people across all groups, but especially on the poor and children of color. An African American mother of two sons said, "I love my sons dearly, but if I had it all to do over again, I don't know if I would have children, especially boys. Every time my sons go out, my heart stops until they come home. Every day you read about some young African American male being shot or beaten up for being in the wrong place."

Lifestyle Disruptions The birth of a child can disrupt previously satisfying lifestyles. Not only do infants interrupt sleep and lovemaking and change household routines, they can alter a couple's social life and recreational pursuits. Babysitters are not always readily available, nor are babies easily compatible with work, hobbies, or leisure activities. Many parents find themselves in the position of having to forgo favorite pastimes at least until their children are much older. Although some parents find this a rather easy exchange to make, others are unprepared for the degree of change in their lives. Some parents become resentful and, as a result, both the marital relationship and the parent–child relationship may be negatively affected. Why, then, does anyone voluntarily become a parent? The answer to this question is twofold: Parenthood offers significant benefits to individuals, and society places enormous social pressure on its members to procreate.

The Benefits of Parenthood

Although all parents experience the costs of having children to some degree, most parents believe the benefits of parenthood outweigh the costs.

Emotional Bonds Children are not only consumers and takers; they also give love and affection to parents. Furthermore, for many married couples their children are a tangible symbol of the love they share and the means for establishing "a real family life" (Neal, Groat, and Wicks, 1989). Couples who recall happy childhoods and positive family life experiences are especially likely to want to reproduce those feelings through having children of their own. Children also enlarge the social interaction network of parents by providing connecting links to other family members (grandparents, aunts, uncles, cousins) and to the larger community via schools, churches, neighbors, and places of recreation.

Adult Status Many people see raising children as a means of achieving adult status, recognition, and personal fulfillment. From early on, girls are given dolls to play with to prepare them for the day they will become mothers themselves

Traditionally many fathers wanted sons who would someday join the family business. Today, it is not so unusual to include daughters in family enterprises.

and affirm their womanhood to the larger community. Men, too, are socialized to affirm their manhood through procreation and financial support of their families. Beyond that, however, rearing children provides parents with a sense of purpose and gives their lives meaning. By transmitting societal values to a new generation, parents feel they are making a contribution and leaving their imprint on society. Watching their children grow, and knowing they had a role to play in their children's development, gives parents a sense of pride and a feeling of immortality—that after their own deaths, part of them will live through their children and grandchildren.

Fun and Enjoyment Sometimes in the serious discussions of parenting another important benefit of having children is overlooked. Having children can be enormous fun. Through children, adults can reexperience some of the delights of their own childhood. They can recall their own sense of wonder of the world as they observe their children's new discoveries. The presence of children legitimizes many adult desires. Many parents delight in buying trains and other toys for their children so that they, too, can enjoy them. What adult has not at times looked wistfully on as children around them swing, swim, run, jump, and play games? Parents have the advantage of being able to do all these things with their children without needing to apologize or explain.

The Social Pressures to Procreate

Although many adults acknowledge the benefits of parenthood, these benefits alone are probably not sufficient to produce a steady fertility rate. Obviously, reproduction is necessary for the continuation of a society. Without a fertility rate approaching the replacement level and in the absence of immigration, a society would become, over time, extinct. Thus, it is in society's interest to promote a **pronatalist attitude**, one that encourages childbearing. Societies vary in their strategies for accomplishing this goal. For instance, France, worried about its low birth rate, increased the monthly stipend for parents who take unsalaried leave to care for a third child (Leicester, 2005). Since the late 1990s

Japanese prefectures, worried about low birth rates, have been organizing dating programs for single people (Turner, 2003). In the United States we celebrate parenthood by having special days to honor mothers and fathers. Federal and state governmental bodies show their support for childbearing by a tax structure that rewards earners with children through a system of tax deductions. Family members and friends often participate in encouraging childbearing by constantly dropping hints. "When are we going to be grandparents?" "Hurry up, our Jimmy wants a playmate [cousin]." Some religious organizations—for example, the Catholic Church—promote reproduction by teaching that the purpose of sex is procreation and that artificial means of birth control are contrary to that purpose.

The Child-Free Option

Throughout most of U.S. history having children was assumed to be the normal course of development for married couples. There were always some people who decided against childbearing, but until relatively recently a conscious rejection of parenthood was considered an unnatural and selfish act. About the only socially acceptable reason for not having children was biological incapacity. Those who were unable to have children were objects of pity and sympathy. Some psychoanalysts, like Sigmund Freud and Erik Erikson, believed that when couples decide not to parent, they are rejecting a major part of adult development that they may regret in later life.

However, researchers such as Marian Faux (1984) challenged this perspective. More recently, American writer Jennifer Shawne (2005), author of *Baby Not on Board: A Celebration of Life Without Kids*, and Britain-based writer Nicki Defago (2005), author of *Childfree and Loving It*, argued that many couples and women make conscious and rational decisions to remain child-free and do so without regrets. Among women 40 to 44 years old (who are nearing the completion of their childbearing years), 19 percent were child-free in 2004, almost double that of their age counterparts (10 percent) in 1976 (Dye, 2005). Just as there are numerous reasons for having children, there are many reasons for not doing so. Among them are career and marital considerations, the desire for personal fulfillment, uncertainty about parenting skills, environmental concerns, and the influence of antinatalist forces—policies or practices that discourage people from having children.

Career and Marital Considerations Couples vary in their choice of priorities in their lives. Some couples prefer not to have children because they want to focus their energies on constructing satisfying careers and they want to avoid the work–family conflicts typical of dual-career couples with children, a topic we discuss in Chapter 10. Other couples wish to concentrate their energies on the marital relationship itself. As one 43-year-old woman said,

> My sense is that marriages are frayed, not strengthened with children. I think that one can relax in one's relationship in a way that having kids makes hard, having to make sure that somebody's doing this, that, and the other thing,

and putting up with the craziness that goes on. And I don't see those marriages getting unfrayed. I see these things as permanent distances. I know it's alleged to be a cementing force, but I've only seen it go the other way. (Quoted in Morell, 1994, p. 115)

Personal Fulfillment Some couples prefer to invest the majority of their time and energy in hobbies, adult relationships, or in a variety of other activities they find personally fulfilling and satisfying. They contribute to society through working, performing volunteer activities, or interacting with and helping to support other people's children.

Qualifications for Parenthood In America's past the heavy cultural emphasis on having children rarely took into account the fact that most people can become biological parents but not all people have good parenting skills. The high incidence of child neglect and abuse, which we will discuss in Chapter 11, makes it clear that not all people are equipped to do a satisfactory job of child rearing. Some couples, remembering their own unhappiness as a child, do not want to repeat the kind of parenting they received. Others question whether they have the knowledge, patience, aptitude, stamina, communication skills, or role-model skills to be a good parent. Amy Showalter, 44, and her husband of 11 years, Randy Boyer, 45, concluded that they would not be good parents. Amy said, "We didn't feel we would be qualified" (quoted in Schodolski, 2005).

Antinatalist Forces Just as a society employs its institutions to encourage childbearing, it can also use them to discourage people from having children. To enforce China's one-child policy, local authorities have fined or imprisoned violators (Osnos, 2005). One example of an antinatalist tendency in the United States is the failure to develop a national system of child care. Without this support, some parents, mostly women, are forced to give up their jobs or reduce their hours if they cannot find alternative child care. Consequently, their standard of living is lower than that for couples without children. When both parents work, they confront many problems as they struggle to integrate work and family roles. If these conflicts remain unresolved, more dual-earner couples may decide that the costs of having children are too high.

Delayed Parenting

Delayed parenting (having a first child at 30 or after) is a relatively new trend in the United States, increasing from only 4 percent of American women in the early 1970s to over 26 percent in the late 1990s. Births to older women continue to increase. From 2003 to 2004 the birth rate for women aged 35 to 39 rose by 4 percent while the birth rate for women 40 to 44 years increased by 3 percent (Hamilton et al., 2005). Similarly, for the first time in England, the birth rate among women in their early 30s had outstripped women in their late 20s (Haynes, 2005). Couples who delay parenting are more likely to be white, highly educated, work in professional occupations, and earn high incomes. They also tend to overestimate the age at which fertility begins to decline (Madsen, 2003). Some in this later category seek help through assisted reproductive technology when it becomes clear that they have a reduced chance of conceiving, a topic we will turn to later. Western countries are not the only ones seeing an increase in delayed parenting. Japan is also experiencing a growing number of older first-time mothers. However, these mothers find less acceptance due, in large part, to traditional culture values that emphasize women's mother and homemaker roles as well as concern over Japan's low birth rate. However, since Crown Princess Masako gave birth to her first child just days before her 38th birthday, the stigma surrounding delayed parenting is beginning to erode in that country (French, 2001a).

Several factors have contributed to the pattern of delayed parenting. Among them are a greater cultural acceptance of singlehood as a positive lifestyle, changes in gender role expectations, apprehensions about the high divorce rate, improved contraception, and new reproductive technology that has made it possible for older women to bear children successfully. Although men can be fathers

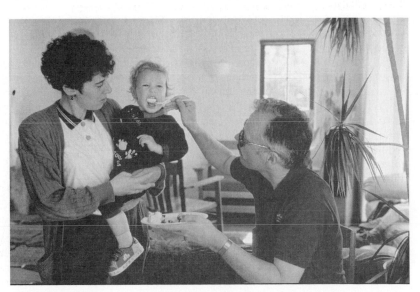

It is becoming more common for parents to delay childbearing until their 30s or 40s. As this couple is discovering, parenting at a later stage in the life cycle has its advantages and disadvantages.

at almost any age (for example, actor Tony Randall became a father at 77), it is only recently that it became possible for menopausal women to become pregnant using donated eggs. In 2005, a 66-year-old Romanian woman, Adriana Iliescu, became the oldest woman to give birth. Her daughter was born prematurely by Caesarean section after her twin sister died in the womb. A little over a year later, Janis Wulf, 62, gave birth to her 12th child. Wulf is the grandmother of 20 and the great-grandmother of 3. Cases like this have led some governments to restrict access to reproductive technologies for women over 50 and raised questions about the pros and cons of delayed parenting. Older parents may be more economically secure, more mature, and better prepared for the responsibilities of parenting than their younger counterparts, yet some older parents may lack the physical stamina needed to raise children. Children may benefit from having loving, involved older parents, yet some may find themselves caring for an ill or elderly parent while they are still in college.

Would you want to become a parent after age 60? What would be the advantages and disadvantages? Do you know anyone who became a parent at that age? Do you know anyone whose parent had her or him at that age? Were their experiences generally positive or negative? Explain.

CONTROLLING FERTILITY

The decision whether to have children is one of the most important decisions people can make, for it affects not only their own lives but the society in which they live. Throughout history many groups and societies have attempted to control the timing and number of births to ensure an adequate supply of food and other resources for the entire community. Early efforts to control fertility took many forms. Some groups tried creating contraceptive barriers made out of animal intestines and various roots and grasses, others ingested prepared herbs and potions thought to have preventive power. Over time, other techniques were also employed: celibacy, late marriages, abstinence from intercourse for prolonged periods of time, prolonged breastfeeding, physical actions such as jumping to dislodge the semen, and abortion. Because the process of human reproduction was not known until around the 1940s, many of these trial-and-error methods were unsuccessful. Thus, societies often resorted to other means to control their population. The most common mechanism of population control was infanticide. In countries where there is a strong cultural preference for sons, such as China and India, female infanticide is still practiced.

In contrast to these early methods, today efficient and safe methods of **contraception**—mechanisms for preventing fertilization—are readily available. Most of us take the availability of contraceptives for granted. However, the distribution and use of contraceptives in the United States were outlawed in the latter half of the nineteenth century and remained illegal in some states until 1965, when the Supreme Court, in *Griswold* v. *Connecticut*, invalidated laws prohibiting the use of contraceptives by married couples. Seven years later, in *Eisenstadt* v. *Baird*, the Court extended this principle to unmarried adults. In 1977, in *Carey* v. *Population Services International*, the Court extended the same constitutional right to privacy to minors, declaring that the state cannot deny them access to contraceptives.

Although couples today can choose from a wide number of birth control methods, they are not without controversy. Just as we saw with Plan B in Chapter 7, there is organized opposition to many forms of contraceptives, particularly when they are available to adolescents and unmarried individuals (see, for example, discussion of abstinence-only education in Chapter 6). Each contraceptive method carries with it advantages as well as disadvantages. Some have health risks but are extremely convenient; others are safer but less convenient. Some have only a temporary effect; others are permanent. Some are costly, others are relatively inexpensive. Although a particular birth control device may prevent pregnancy, it does not necessarily provide protection against AIDS and other sexually transmitted diseases. Thus, more than one form of contraception may be advisable at any given time. We will discuss each form of contraception and controversies surrounding them in Appendix D.

Contraceptive Use

In 2002, 62 million women were in their childbearing years (15 to 44). The majority of these women, 43 million (nearly 70 percent), were sexually active but did not want to become pregnant. The vast majority of these women, 38 million (62 percent), used a contraceptive, but 4.3 million (7 percent, up from 5 percent in 1995) did not use a contraceptive, leaving themselves at risk of an unwanted pregnancy. The remaining 19 million women (31 percent) did not need a contraceptive because they were infertile, pregnant, postpartum, trying to become pregnant, or were not sexually active. The most popular method was the Pill, used by 11.6 million women (31 percent), followed by female sterilization, used by 10.3 million women (27 percent). The male condom was third, used by 6.8 million women (18 percent). The partners of 3.5 million women (9.2 percent) had a vasectomy. Other contraceptive choices ranged from injections, implants, abstinence, and other devices (Mosher et al., 2004).

Contraceptive choices vary with age, education, marital status, race, and ethnicity. The Pill is the method most widely used by never-married women, women with a college degree or higher, and women under 30, especially those in their teens and 20s; by age 35, more women rely on sterilization. Sterilization is most commonly relied on by women with less than a college education and by women who are currently married or have previously been married. It is the leading method among African American women and Latinas, whereas white women prefer the Pill (Mosher et al. 2004). Whichever method a couple chooses should reflect their values, needs, medical history, and desires. Decisions concerning contraception is the responsibility of both parties and should not be left, as is frequently the case, to women simply because they are the ones who must worry about getting pregnant.

Almost half (49 percent) of the 6.3 million pregnancies in the United States that occur each year are unintended, the result of using unreliable or defective contraceptives, misusing contraceptives, or using no contraceptives at all ("Inducted Abortion," 2005). On a worldwide level, it is estimated that about 40 percent of the 210 million pregnancies occurring each year are unplanned (Dailard, 2000). Rates of unplanned births are particularly high in Latin America, Kenya, the Philippines, and Japan. Poor women in the United States and women in developing countries often do not have access to contraceptives or family planning services. Further, their ability to control whether and when to have children is related to gender roles within the family and society, their level of educational attainment, participation in the labor force, and the likelihood of being subjected to a domineering husband and even domestic violence. In many parts of the world, women's limited participation in reproductive decision making is a reflection of their second-class status in society. Given that there is a 2 to 4 percent chance of becoming pregnant after unprotected sex (which increases to 30 to 50 percent during ovulation), why do so many people risk the possibility of pregnancy by not using contraceptives?

Reasons for Not Using Contraceptives

As surprising as it might seem in this day and age, some young people believe they cannot get pregnant the first time they have intercourse. If they were lucky and pregnancy did not occur, they are likely to be tempted to have unprotected sex again, a pattern researchers Jerry Burger and Linda Burns (1988) call the "illusion of unique invulnerability." The reasons for not using contraceptives are the following:

- *Symbolism of sexual activity.* Being prepared with a contraceptive is a visible symbol of sexual activity, thus feelings of shame, guilt, fear, or anxiety may prohibit a person from using a contraceptive. These feelings may be especially strong for teens who took a pledge of abstinence but who later become sexually active.

- *Role of peers.* Friends share information and tend to behave in similar fashion. Those whose friends are not knowledgeable about or do not use contraceptives are also likely not to do so.

- *Role of parents.* Parents who have difficulty discussing sex with their children are more likely to have children who, if they become sexually active, will not use contraceptives.

- *Contraception is not romantic and/or not effective.* Some people complain that planning for and using contraceptives takes the spontaneity and romance out of a relationship. Some teens acquire incorrect information on the safety and effectiveness of contraceptives.

- *The nature of the relationship.* People are more likely to use contraceptives in the context of an ongoing, steady relationship than when they begin a new relationship.

As indicated in the foregoing sections, contraceptive devices are not always used and, when used, are not always successful. Thus, many women faced with an unwanted pregnancy seek an abortion.

ABORTION

Abortion refers to the premature termination of a pregnancy before the fetus can survive on its own. This can occur either spontaneously (a miscarriage) or can be induced through a variety of external methods (see Appendix C). Each year, more than half of unintended pregnancies worldwide—46 million, or two in ten pregnancies—are aborted (Dailard, 2000). Similarly, in the United States approximately half of all unintended pregnancies are terminated by abortions. In 2002, 1.29 million abortions took place, down from an estimated 1.36 million in 1996 ("Induced Abortion," 2005). The decline in the number of abortions is related to improved contraceptive use, particularly among teenagers, and to the use of the morning-after pill. Throughout the world, women give similar reasons for their decision to abort: they are too young or poor to raise a child; having a child would interfere with work, school, or other responsibilities; they are estranged from their sexual partner and/or they do not want to be a single parent. Additionally, about

Margaret Sanger, a public health nurse in New York City in the early 1900s, was alarmed at the high maternal and infant mortality rates associated with the large families of the working poor, who begged her for information about ways to prevent having more children. Sanger coined the term *birth control* as a positive description of family limitation and led the struggle to legalize contraceptive devices and to promote planned parenthood.

DEBATING SOCIAL ISSUES

SHOULD *ROE V. WADE* BE OVERTURNED?

Few issues in the United States are as contentious as the issue of abortion. It became even more so with South Dakota's recent abortion ban, which has set the stage for a court battle over the 1973 federal abortion law.

Proponents of overturning *Roe v. Wade*, popularly referred to as the prolife movement, argue that life begins at conception and therefore, in their view, abortion is a form of murder, which should not be allowed. People who see themselves as prolife believe abortion demeans the value and dignity of life and robs society of the likely contributions of a significant number of potentially viable human beings. They further argue that abortion psychologically damages women who have abortions. They use, as an example of this position, the experience of Jane Roe (not her real name), the woman involved in the original court decision, who later regretted her decision and now supports the overturning of *Roe v. Wade*. Many who support Jane Roe's current position believe that as women get older, they will likely regret their decision and will probably always carry guilt for their action and will forever experience a feeling of loss for

what might have been. Others who favor overturning *Roe v. Wade* do so because they believe some women are sexually careless and then use abortion as a means of birth control or they choose abortions because having a child would be inconvenient; they view such behaviors as morally objectionable. Many in the

prolife movement see abortion as a selfish act. Although they may agree that some women, especially young women, may not be ready to care for a child, they argue that there are many couples who are only too willing to adopt these infants. Many couples spend years trying unsuccessfully to adopt an infant or have to go

---

13,000 women have abortions each year following rape or incest ("Induced Abortion," 2005). Abortions are most common among young, white, unmarried women. However, the abortion rate for African American women is 3 times the rate for white women and the rate for Latinas is roughly $2\frac{1}{2}$ times that of white women, no doubt reflecting in large part the greater economic disadvantages they face. About 52 percent of women who have abortions are younger than 25, women aged 20 to 24 account for 33 percent of all abortions, and teenagers obtain the remaining 19 percent. Forty-three percent of women obtaining abortions identify themselves as Protestant and 27 percent identify themselves as Catholic ("Induced Abortion," 2005).

Induced abortion has been a method of birth control throughout human history and for a major part of U.S. history as well. However, today induced abortions are the subject of an emotionally charged and highly politicized debate involving conflicting values regarding women's reproductive rights and the question of when life begins (see Debating Social Issues box). In recent times, the struggle over the abortion issue has included violence against women's health

clinics and the murder of several doctors and women who provided abortion services. Yet such polarized views of abortion were not always the case in the United States.

Historical Perspectives

Until the nineteenth century, American laws concerning abortion generally reflected the tradition in English common law that abortion is permissible until "quickening"— the time (generally between the 4th and 6th months) at which a pregnant woman could feel the fetus moving in her womb. Abortions were advertised in newspapers, and recipes for abortifacients (anything used to induce abortions) were provided in popular books of the day. Estimates are that by the middle of the nineteenth century there was one induced abortion for every four live births (cited in Tribe, 1990:28). Connecticut was the first state to regulate abortion. It did so in 1821 not on any moral grounds but to protect women by prohibiting the inducement of abortion through the use of dangerous poisons. Over time, other restrictive measures followed, fueled in large measure by

outside the United States because there are so few infants available here. Rather than abort a fetus, they argue, women could help these couples by placing their babies up for adoption. The prolife movement is also concerned that *Roe* v. *Wade* allows minors, who are not yet emotionally, psychologically, and morally mature enough to make sound decisions, the means to have an abortion. Proponents of overturning *Roe* v. *Wade* also worry that if the law remains in place, advances in genetic testing may lead to more abortions if fetuses are identified as the wrong sex or less than ideal in some way. Finally, as taxpayers many people seeking to overturn *Roe* v. *Wade* do not want to see any of their tax dollars supporting a policy that they see as immoral.

On the other hand, proponents of keeping *Roe* v. *Wade*, those identifying themselves as prochoice, argue that abortion is not murder, that at conception there is potential life but the fetus is not a human being. They argue that women have a right to control their bodies, including deciding to abort a fetus that they are carrying and that government does not have the right to interfere in this decision. Citing women's experiences before *Roe* v. *Wade*, prochoice people fear making abortion illegal would mean a return to "back alley" abortions, putting women's lives and well-being

in jeopardy because the reasons women choose to abort would remain: incest, rape, the threat to a woman's emotional and physical health, poor economics, failure of contraceptives, inability to parent at that time, immaturity, birth defects, and a host of others. People in the prochoice movement agree that some women may suffer psychological damage as a result of having an abortion, but they believe that in most of those cases it is because of the stigma that some in society would put on them for choosing an abortion. Proponents of keeping abortion legal also point to data that show many young women have fared better academically, socially, and economically than their peers who gave birth and struggled to raise their children. They argue that one mistake can rob a woman of her childhood and limit opportunities for the rest of her life, not only at her expense, but of the child and the larger society as well. Prochoice advocates point out that giving a child up for adoption can be no less traumatic than abortion and women who do also suffer from regret, guilt, and a sense of loss that can last a lifetime. Finally, proponents of keeping abortion legal argue legal access is not the determining factor in abortion rates but rather it is the rate of unintended pregnancies. They point to research showing that abortion levels are high in countries where

small families are desired but contraceptive use is low or ineffective. For example, in most of Eastern Europe and the former Soviet Union, where desired family size was small and modern contraceptives were not generally available until recently, women relied on legal abortions to control family size. In recent years, contraceptives have been easier to obtain, and abortion rates fell by as much as 50 percent in some countries between 1990 and 1996. And in the Netherlands, where abortion is legal and contraceptive use is widespread, both abortion and unintended pregnancy rates are low (Dailard, 2000). Along these same lines, many in the prochoice movement echo former President Bill Clinton's desire to keep abortion legal, safe, and rare. To do this, proponents say, means providing programs for early and quality sex education, affordable and available contraception, affordable and quality child care, and living wages for women and their families.

What do you think? Should Roe v. Wade *be overturned or retained? What would be the likely consequences of overturning the federal law? Is abortion a matter for individuals or government to decide? Are there social policies that, if implemented, could make abortion, legal, safe, and rare?*

---

fears that the widespread use of abortion by white, married, middle-class women, coupled with the higher birth rates of ethnic immigrants, would upset the status quo. By 1900, abortion was illegal except when a physician judged it necessary to save a woman's life.

Criminalizing abortion did not end abortions. Rather, it drove them underground. Abortions became expensive, difficult to get, and often dangerous. Poor women who, unlike their wealthier counterparts, were unable to travel outside the country or have a physician diagnose the need for a therapeutic abortion suffered the most. Over time, stories about botched abortions resulting in permanent injury or death began to surface. Two events in the 1960s became a catalyst for a new debate on the abortion issue. The first involved Sherri Finkbine, a mother of four, who had taken the tranquilizer thalidomide while pregnant. When she discovered that the drug was associated with major birth defects, she elected to have an abortion rather than give birth to a seriously deformed child. After unsuccessful attempts to get an abortion in the United States, she went to Sweden, where she aborted a deformed fetus. The second event was a major

outbreak of rubella (German measles) during the years 1962–1965. The occurrence of rubella during pregnancy causes major birth defects. During this period, some 15,000 babies were born with such defects. The medical profession, increasingly conscious of these tragedies, changed its position from one of opposition to abortion to one advocating easing abortion restrictions. In 1973, the Supreme Court, by a seven-to-two vote in *Roe* v. *Wade*, struck down all antiabortion laws as violations of a woman's right to privacy. Women again had the right to choose an abortion. Since that time, however, there have been renewed efforts to restrict this right.

Race, Class, and Age

Although still legal, abortion has become increasingly less accessible. This is especially the case for poor women, women of color, and young women. In 1976, Congress passed the Hyde Amendment, which prohibited using federal Medicaid funds for abortions except in cases where the pregnancy threatens a woman's life. Over time, a majority of states followed the federal government's lead and prohibited state funding for abortions. Thus, although middle- and upper-class women, mostly white, are still able to choose whether to have an abortion, the rhetoric of choice is empty for poor women, regardless of race. In the late 1970s, the first laws were passed requiring that parents be notified or give parental consent when a minor seeks an abortion. Today, 34 states have such laws. An analysis of the impact of these laws in 6 states found that they had only a small impact on the number of abortions minors had in those states (Lehren and Leland, 2006). Supporters of parental involvement laws believe they bring parents and children closer together, allowing parents to play an important role in helping their children make important health care decisions. They also believe that in the long run, the law will result in fewer abortions. On the other hand, some abortion providers point out that it is often the case that the parents press their daughters to have an abortion rather than trying to stop them. Further, they say these laws often drive teenagers underground, sometimes with tragic consequences, as evidenced by the Becky Bell case. This Indiana teenager died as a consequence of an illegal abortion she had to prevent her parents from knowing about her pregnancy. Conversely, such restrictions may also result in forcing women to have a child they do not want.

Other state-imposed restrictive measures were challenged by abortion rights groups all the way to the Supreme Court. In 1989 the Supreme Court in *Webster* v. *Reproductive Health Services*, by a five-to-four vote, upheld Missouri's right to bar medical personnel from performing abortions in public hospitals. In 1992, in *Planned Parenthood* v. *Casey*, the Court narrowly upheld the right to abortion but at the same time allowed states to restrict the procedure.

The approach to abortion varies from country to country. Three countries ban abortion under all circumstances (El Salvador, Malta, and Chile). Fifty-nine countries, including Bangladesh, Columbia, Egypt, Indonesia, and Iran, allow abortion only to save the mother's life. Fifty-three countries, including Canada, France, Germany, Russia, South Africa, and Russia, allow abortion on demand. Many other countries allow abortion for other reasons: to protect the physical and/or mental health of the mother, in cases of rape or incest, or to eliminate an unhealthy child (Johnston, 2005).

Public Attitudes toward Abortion

According to a recent Gallup survey, almost a quarter of Americans (24 percent) believe abortion should be legal in all cases, a little over half (55 percent) say it should be legal in certain cases, and only 20 percent say it should be illegal in all cases. These attitudes are strongly related to both religion and political preferences. Overall, Christians have stronger anti-abortion views than non-Christians, those who attend church frequently have stronger anti-abortion views than those who attend less frequently, and Republicans are more likely than Democrats to oppose abortion (Newport and Saad, 2006). A FOX News/Opinion Dynamics Poll, taken shortly after the South Dakota legislature voted to ban abortion in all cases other than to save the life of the mother,

found that a majority of respondents (59 percent) opposed such a ban while 35 percent of registered voters would support the South Dakota ban in their own state (Hauser, 2006). However, that same poll showed that people continue to support abortions for "hard reasons": if the pregnancy puts the mother's life at risk (83 percent), in cases involving rape or incest (74 percent), or if the mother's mental health is at risk (62 percent). They are considerably less likely to support abortion if the pregnancy is unwanted (43 percent). In this poll, 41 percent considered themselves prolife whereas almost half (49 percent) considered themselves prochoice.

The abortion debate is not likely to end soon (see Debating Social Issues box). The United States could benefit by examining the history of abortion in other countries like Hungary and Russia that have lowered their abortion rates by providing effective family planning services. To date, little of the abortion debate in the United States focuses on strategies to prevent abortion. Until the two sides in the debate can come to some agreement about the need for this kind of action, it is likely that the United States will continue to have the highest percentage of unplanned pregnancies of any developed country in the West and, as a result, whether abortion is legal or not, will continue to have a significant number of abortions.

Thus far, we have treated the decision of whether to have children as one of personal choice and control. However, personal choices are not always realized. Just as some couples experience unwanted pregnancies, others want children but find they cannot have them.

INFERTILITY

The medical profession defines **infertility** as the inability to conceive after 12 months of unprotected intercourse or the inability to carry a pregnancy to live birth. Infertility affects approximately 10 to 15 percent of couples of reproductive age. When we examine who the infertile are and who is likely to seek and receive treatment for this problem, we find that race and class are critical factors. Although infertility problems occur in all race and ethnic groups, research shows that women who pursue medical help for fertility problems are a highly selective group who are more likely to be white, married, older, more highly educated, and more affluent (Stephen and Chandra, 2006). Infertility treatments are costly. Most insurance companies do not offer coverage for treatment, thus further limiting access to such treatment. Only 15 states have laws that require insurance carriers to cover fertility treatment ("National Survey Results," 2005).

Causes of Infertility

Because women show the visible signs of fertility—being pregnant—there is a tendency to view infertility, like birth control, as a woman's problem. This tendency is reinforced by a cultural tradition that has associated masculinity with fertility. For this reason, some men are unwilling to consider the idea that they could be infertile. However, men are as likely to experience infertility problems as are women. About 40 percent of fertility problems are traced to the male partner and an equal percentage to the female; the causes for the remaining 20 percent are unknown. Thus, if a couple is unsuccessful in their efforts to have a child, both should be examined for any possible problems. The causes of infertility are many and varied. Some of the same factors can affect both women and men. For example, prolonged exposure to toxic chemicals can produce sterility in both women and men. So, too, can sexually transmitted diseases. Other factors are specific to each gender.

The major causes of female infertility are failure to ovulate and blockage of the fallopian tubes. The major cause of male infertility is low sperm production. Additionally, the spermatozoa may not be sufficiently active (or motile), or the sperm-carrying ducts may be blocked. Regardless of the cause, however, infertility in either sex does not impede sexual performance.

Consequences of Infertility

During the process of growing up, it is common for children to imagine themselves as future parents. Few, however, ever question the possibility of being unable to have children. Thus, for couples wanting to have children, the knowledge that they cannot comes as a shock. Many experience a "crisis of infertility," an emotional state characterized by a feeling of loss of control over their lives. As a result, they experience a wide range of emotions: depression, disbelief, denial, isolation, guilt, frustration, and grief (Daly, 1999). Reactions to infertility vary by gender. Wives experience a deep sense of personal failure and often become preoccupied with the task of solving their infertility problems. Husbands are more likely to view infertility as an unfortunate circumstance. Their main concern with fertility focuses on their wives' unhappiness.

These different reactions can cause considerable strain in a couple's relationship. Some couples report an increase in conflict and a decrease in the frequency and level of satisfaction of sexual relationships after learning of their infertility. However, some of these same couples also report that the experience of confronting the crisis together improved the quality of their relationship (Greil, 1991).

For centuries about the only available solution for infertile couples was adopting someone else's children. Today, however, there is a scarcity of adoptable infants, especially white infants. Currently, only about 2 to 3 percent of babies born out of wedlock are given up for adoption, compared to a high of almost 80 percent in the past (Dunkin, 2000). This scarcity has created what sociologist Barbara Katz Rothman (1989) calls a "competitive market situation." We will discuss some of the legal and political issues surrounding adoption in Chapter 15. Although approximately 8 percent of women who are infertile adopt (Bachrach, 1986), many others who wish to have children seek medical help.

Historical records show that as early as the eighteenth century women actively sought help from the developing medical profession in having a child. Outside of providing advice to relax or to adopt children, doctors had little knowledge to offer women who wanted to conceive. It was not until 1940 that researchers had developed a clear understanding of the relationship between ovulation and the menstrual cycle. This knowledge breakthrough was immediately applied to attempts to reduce unplanned pregnancies by regulating conception, pregnancy, and menopause. The result of these efforts was the mass production of an oral contraceptive. With fewer unwanted pregnancies, fewer children were available for adoption and pressure grew to find ways to overcome infertility. AI and fertility drugs soon became common medical treatments. Another tool available today is **assisted reproductive technology (ART),** a general term that includes all treatments or procedures involving the handling of human eggs and sperm to establish a pregnancy. In coping with their infertility, couples must ask themselves how important becoming parents is for them as individuals and as a married couple, and how much medical testing, effort, expense, and marital tension they are willing to accept in seeking to become parents.

MEDICAL TREATMENTS AND REPRODUCTIVE TECHNOLOGY: IMPLICATIONS FOR THE MEANING OF PARENTHOOD

Considerable controversy has accompanied the development of medical and high tech means to treat infertility. In the United States the biological, rather than the sociological, aspects of parenthood have dominated thinking and social policies. Thus, as we shall see in the following section, artificial insemination and ART are challenging the traditional definitions of parenthood and family as well as raising numerous ethical and legal questions that are yet to be resolved.

Artificial Insemination

Artificial insemination (AI) involves the injection of fresh or frozen semen into the vagina or uterus of an ovulating woman. This process is one of the oldest and most successful of the reproductive technologies, initially having been developed in the animal husbandry field several centuries ago. Although conception can occur after one insemination, two to five inseminations are more common. Compared with other reproductive technologies, the cost of AI is relatively modest, averaging around $300 to $700. Although there are no national statistics on live birth rates after using AI, it is estimated that the success rate is around 20 percent and closer to 25 percent if fertility drugs are taken in conjunction with the procedure.

There is little controversy surrounding AI when the husband's sperm is used, because the resulting offspring is biologically related to both husband and wife. However, legal and ethical concerns are raised when AI donors (AID) are involved (see In the News). When husbands agree to AID and willingly accept paternal responsibility for any resulting offspring, most state laws view these children as legitimate and recognize the father's obligations to support them. Similarly, the courts have held separated lesbian partners accountable for children conceived in this manner. Other problems may arise, however. If the donor's identity is known, conflicts can later develop over parental rights even when those rights were initially disavowed. Alternatively, an anonymous donor may be used for a number of different inseminations, thus creating the possibility of future inbreeding when unsuspecting couples who share the same genetic father may marry.

Assisted Reproductive Technology (ART)

More than 48,000 babies were born in the United States as a result of ART procedures carried out in 2003, up from the 45,751 born in 2002 ("CDC Report," 2005). The most common ART procedure is in vitro fertilization.

In Vitro Fertilization   Sometimes called "test-tube" fertilization, **in vitro fertilization (IVF)** involves surgically removing a woman's eggs, fertilizing them in a petri dish with the partner's or donor's sperm, and then implanting one or more of the fertilized eggs in the woman's uterus. The insertion of multiple eggs increases the chances of pregnancy, but it also increases the likelihood of multiple births and with them increased medical risks of premature birth and low birth weight (see later discussion). Two recent variations of the IVF procedure increase the chances that the fertilized egg will implant in the uterine wall. The first variation, called *gamete intrafallopian transfer (GIFT)*, involves inserting both egg and sperm into the fallopian tube in the hope that conception will occur. In the second variation, called *zygote intrafallopian transfer (ZIFT)*, fertilized eggs are placed into the fallopian tube. In 1993, doctors began trying another technique, called *intracytoplasmic sperm injection (ICSI)*, whereby a single sperm is injected directly into an egg in a petri dish.

The first publicly acknowledged human success of IVF occurred in England in July 1978, with the birth of Louise Brown. Three years later, the first IVF baby was born in the United States. In 2003, overall, 28 percent of ART procedures resulted in the birth of a baby for women who used their own eggs. However, the age of the woman is a prime factor. The success rate was 37 percent for women younger than 35 but it decreased to 30 percent among women aged 35 to 37, to 20 percent among women aged 38 to 40, to 11 percent among women aged 41 to 43, and to 4 percent among women older than 43 ("CDC Report," 2005). The costs are high, though, ranging from $8,000 to $15,000 per procedure, out of the range of many couples.

Several objections have been raised to IVF. Some people question the "morality" of fertilizing more than one egg, given the possibility that the other fertilized eggs may be destroyed, a situation that they see as analogous to abortion. Sometimes the additional fertilized eggs are not destroyed but frozen with the idea that they will be implanted at a future date. This latter procedure, known as *cryopreservation*, has led to some complicated legal questions. For example, after an Australian couple died in a plane crash, the courts could not decide what to do with their frozen embryos. Who "owns" them? Do they have the right to exist, perhaps even inherit from their deceased "parents," or can someone (the doctor, a relative) decide to destroy them or implant them into an "adopting" party? These questions remain unanswered. Similarly, a divorced couple in Tennessee

fought over custody of their frozen embryos. The ex-husband asked the court to prohibit any use of the embryos without his consent, arguing that he should not be forced to become a parent against his wishes. The Tennessee Court of Appeals granted joint custody of the frozen embryos to the divorced couple, avoiding questions of whether the embryos are alive and deserving of legal protection, treating them instead as property of the marriage to be equitably disposed of in the event of a divorce. In a similar case, the New Jersey Supreme Court upheld a woman's right to bar the use of frozen embryos produced by her and her ex-husband, who wanted the right to implant them in another woman ("Court Upholds," 2001).

Embryo Transplant   **Embryo transplant** refers to a procedure whereby a fertilized egg from a woman donor is implanted into an infertile woman. This procedure has been refined and is now available to postmenopausal women who want to become pregnant as well as to women who want to avoid passing on a known genetic defect to their children. Criticism of embryo transplants revolves around two central issues. One is the possible exploitation of women donors. Although a woman may donate ova out of a desire to assist an infertile couple, some women, especially poor women, may feel pressured to sell their ova to help support themselves or their families. On average, donors are paid around $2000 to $5000. However, college women are the most coveted donors and they are being bombarded with ads in campus newspapers soliciting their eggs. Couples have placed ads in the *Stanford Daily* student newspaper offering $50,000 and $100,000 to intelligent and athletic young women for the donation of their eggs (Enge, 2000). Harvard Business School Professor Debora Spar (2006), author of the *Baby Business*, is calling for a national debate to bring order and safety to the infertility–industrial complex in which spending on everything from fertility drugs to eggs encompasses an estimated $3 billion a year.

The second issue raises questions of what constitutes biological motherhood—the contribution of genetic material (via the ova) or pregnancy and childbirth. This question has become even more complicated with the development of surrogate motherhood.

Surrogacy   In **surrogacy,** a woman agrees to be artificially inseminated with a man's sperm, carry the fetus to term, and relinquish all rights to the child after it is born. This is perhaps the most controversial of all the reproductive techniques, because, like AID, it involves a third party. Unlike AID, however, the donor is intimately involved in the reproductive process. Surrogate motherhood may develop in either of two situations. In the first, a third party is artificially inseminated with the husband's sperm (or donor sperm if he is also infertile). Here the term *surrogate* is somewhat misleading, because the woman who is inseminated is also the biological mother. In the second situation, the wife's uterus does not allow a fertilized egg to implant itself and develop. In such cases, the couple uses IVF, but the resulting embryo is then transplanted into a surrogate mother. The surrogate can be a relative or a stranger. In the

Reproductive technology raises many questions about the meaning of parenthood.

Source: © Tribune Media Services, Inc. All Rights Reserved, Reprinted by permission.

latter case, the woman and the couple generally sign a contract. Generally, the provisions of the contract include a fee payment $15,000 to $20,000 to the surrogate and coverage of all her medical expenses. Estimates are there are more than 1000 surrogate births annually (Cuda, 2005).

Questions inevitably arise regarding the motivations of the two parties in such an agreement. For the infertile couple there is a desire to have a child that is genetically related to at least one of them. Several motivational factors are probably involved in the decision to be a surrogate mother. Detroit psychiatrist Philip Parker conducted extensive psychological tests on over 500 surrogate applicants and found strong altruistic aspects in their willingness to be surrogate mothers. They wanted to give the gift of a child to those who otherwise would not experience child rearing (reported in Gladwell, 1988). More recent studies have also found that surrogates were motivated largely by altruism (Edelmann, 2004). However, some critics of surrogate motherhood see it as reproductive exploitation whereby poor women's reproductive capacity becomes a commodity that they are forced to sell to survive (Dworkin, 1987). Perhaps it is this that has created a growing fertility tourism trade. Increasing numbers of infertile couples from the United States and England are going to India because of the lower cost of treatments and lighter regulations (Spring, 2006).

The legal issues surrounding surrogate motherhood are many. What if the surrogate mother changes her mind and decides to keep the child? Research shows this is relatively rare and that any emotional problems experienced by some surrogate mothers in the weeks following the birth lessen over time. After the birth of the child, positive relations continued, with the large majority of couples maintaining some level of contact with the surrogate mother (MacCallum et al. 2003; Jadva et al. 2003). Nevertheless, when a surrogate mother changes her mind, the results can be traumatic for all parties. One well-publicized example was the celebrated case of Baby M, whose biological mother, Mary Beth Whitehead, changed her mind after giving birth and wanted to keep the child. After a lengthy court battle, the contract was ruled invalid. Custody of the child went to the biological father and adoptive mother, who were seen as more stable and capable of parenting than the biological mother.

In another case, the surrogate mother had no genetic relationship to the child but claimed that through pregnancy and giving birth she had bonded with the infant and was therefore the baby's mother. The judge disagreed and awarded custody to the biological parents, stating that genetics, not giving birth, constitutes parentage. The judge compared the role the surrogate provides to that of a foster parent who temporarily stands in for a parent who is unable to care for a child.

Other issues may also arise in surrogate cases. What happens if a child is born with a major physical problem? Can the contract then be rescinded? If so, does the responsibility for that child rest solely on the surrogate mother? What rights does each party have—the unborn child, the child's biological mother, the child's biological father, and the contractual parents? Do the contractual parents have a right to demand certain behaviors from the surrogate mother during her pregnancy—for example, maintaining a particular diet, refraining from drinking alcohol, or undergoing surgery to improve the life chances of the fetus? These questions have spurred considerable legislative activity in attempts to regulate surrogate parenting. Some countries, including Austria, Sweden, Norway, and Germany, ban surrogacy; others, like France, Denmark, and the Netherlands, ban payment to surrogates. The United States has not as yet developed a consistent legal view. Some states like New Jersey, Michigan, and Arizona have outlawed surrogacy; other states regulate it under certain conditions but most have not yet decided on how to approach this issue.

Another source of controversy has arisen with a relatively new ART procedure called **preimplantation genetic diagnosis (PGD)**, which allows physicians to identify chromosomal abnormalities such as Down syndrome or genetic diseases such as muscular dystrophy in the embryo before implantation. Thus, couples can avoid such "unhealthy" embryos. PGD can also be used to select an embryo that would be able to donate tissue to an existing sibling. To date over 1000 infants have been born using this technology. Public attitudes toward this technology are mixed. One survey found that 70 percent approved its used to avoid serious genetic disease and over 66 percent approved of using it to cure an existing sibling. However, less than 30 percent favored using the technology to choose a child's sex or other desirable characteristics such as strength or intelligence (Landhaus, 2004). To some critics, PGD is tantamount to abortion when "unhealthy" embryos are destroyed. Others point to the cost. PGD adds $3500 to $5000 to the IVF cycle and thus its benefits are likely to be realized by only the affluent. In sum, ART is charting new territory and extending the boundaries of what it means to be a parent or a sibling.

THE CHOICE TO PARENT

In the previous section, we examined the issue of fertility and various factors that affect the decision to parent. Once this decision is made, individuals and couples must turn their attention to matters of conception, pregnancy, childbirth, and child rearing. All of these activities effect considerable changes in the lives of the people involved.

"It's a girl." "It's a boy." Every year millions of parents hear these words as they strain to get that first glimpse of the miraculous new life to which they have contributed. Whatever their feelings concerning pregnancy and childbirth, a majority of Americans have at least one child in their lifetime. This fact notwithstanding, an increasing number of women are without children. However, as we have seen, fertility rates vary considerably among different groups, and individual cases vary greatly as well. For instance, according to the *Guinness Book of World Records* (Young, 1998), the largest number of children born to one woman is 69. From 1725 to 1765, a Russian peasant woman from Shuva (150 miles east of Moscow) and the first of the two wives of Feodor Vassilvev, in 27 different confinements, gave birth to 16 sets of twins, 7 sets of triplets, and 4 sets of quadruplets. We might assume that this woman made a conscious choice to have 69 children. Although most people do not choose to have 69 children, millions of people do make a conscious choice to parent. However, we should also point out that many people *do not choose* to parent, but rather, they become parents as a result of unwanted pregnancies or taking on the responsibility of parenting children of family or friends. Still others consciously choose not to parent and they take the necessary measures to ensure that they will not have children.

However, many children an individual or couple does have and no matter whether the choice is conscious or not, the process always begins with the fertilization of an egg by a sperm.

CONCEPTION

Pregnancy and eventual childbirth begin with **conception,** the process by which a male sperm cell penetrates the female ovum (egg), creating a fertilized egg, or **zygote.** At one time, penile–vaginal intercourse was necessary for conception to take place. As you have read in this chapter, however, today conception can take place not only inside a woman's uterus but also within a petri dish. For the purposes of this book, the term *conception* will encompass all forms of fertilization.

What makes conception possible is the process of **ovulation,** the release of a mature egg. The period of fertility in females normally begins with menstruation and ovulation and lasts until after menopause (which occurs somewhere between 45 and 50 years of age, on average). There are always exceptions, however. In the United States, girls as young as 10 years of age have conceived. The youngest female to conceive a child is recorded as a $5\frac{1}{2}$-year-old girl living in Peru; as we indicated earlier, the oldest is a 66-year-old Romanian woman (*Guinness World Records*, 2001).

Males participate in conception by producing sperm starting around puberty and continuing for some men into their 80s or older. Although millions of sperm are released with a single male ejaculation, only a few reach the fallopian tube that contains the egg. These sperm emit an enzyme that dissolves the outer layer of the egg, allowing one sperm to fertilize it. However, fertilization does not guarantee a successful birth. In fact, 18 percent of fertilized eggs are lost during the first week of pregnancy, and 32 percent are lost in the second week. It is estimated that only around 37 percent of human zygotes survive to become live infants (Norwitz et al., 2001).

Multiple Conception and Births

Multiple conceptions, in which two or more children are conceived at one time, used to be extremely rare. In recent years, however, the number of multiple births in the United States has skyrocketed. The most common form of multiple conception and birth is twins. The number of twin births has more than doubled since the early 1970s. Today, about 1 of every 32 births in the United States are twins (March of Dimes PeriStats, 2006). For reasons not clearly understood, the frequency of naturally occurring multiple births varies across race and ethnicity. For example, African American women have the highest birth rate of twins, followed by white women and Latinas. Asian American women have the lowest birth rate of twins. Although triplets and higher multiple births are still relatively rare, they have increased 200 percent over the last three decades. In 2003, about 1 in every 500 live births was triplets. Latinas and African American women have really low triplet (and larger multiple) birth rates. Quadruplets and larger sets of multiple conceptions, at each higher increment, occur less frequently (Zach and Pramanik, 2006; Pike, 1999). Not surprisingly, the mortality rate for multiple births is higher than for single births.

Two related trends have been associated with the rise in multiple births, especially with the rise of higher order multiples; older age at childbearing (women in their 30s are more likely than younger women to have a multiple birth, even without the use of fertility therapy), and the more widespread use of fertility-enhancing therapies. Although two-thirds of the increase in multiple births is due to fertility treatments (Martin et al., 2005; Pike, 1999), fertility drugs do not tell the whole story of the recent outburst of multiple births. According to some experts, where you live could make a difference. For example, the rate of twin deliveries in Massachusetts and Connecticut is 25 percent higher than the overall national rate. And the rate of triplets in Nebraska and New Jersey is two times the national average. On the other hand, the rate of multiple births in Hawaii is almost one-third below the overall U.S. rate. Interestingly, Nigeria holds the world record for the birth of twins and other multiple births. Most of the multiple births occur among women of the Yoruba ethnic group in the western part of the country, who have the highest number of multiple births in the world. Nigerians attribute their population's consumption of a specific type of yam to the record high number of twins and multiple births. Scientists have found that the yams grown in Africa contain a high level of a substance that is similar to the hormone estrogen, which could bring on multiple ovulations ("Facts and Figures," 2006; PRNetwire, 2002).

In the latter part of the 1990s, some American mothers made history with their multiple births. For example, in May 1997, the first recorded birth of sextuplets (six babies) to an African American couple in the United States occurred in Washington, DC. Delivered by Caesarean section, one girl among the five girls and one boy were delivered

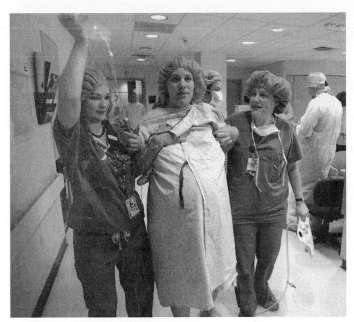

In an unusual pregnancy that attracted worldwide attention, after having five embryos implanted to increase the chances that at least one would hold, 25-year-old surrogate mom Teresa Anderson, for childless couple Luisa Gonsalez, 32, and her husband, Enrique Moreno, 34 (pictured), gave birth to quintuplets in April 2005. In a carefully choreographed delivery, which included 19 doctors, 15 nurses, family, a photographer, and a TV film crew, Ms. Anderson gave birth to five boys, believed to be the first quintuplets ever born to a gestational surrogate mother.

stillborn. The mother had not used a fertility drug. Later, in November 1997, the first completely successful septuplet birth in the United States occurred when a 29-year-old Iowa mother gave birth to seven babies—four boys and three girls—after taking fertility drugs. There are no other known living sets of septuplets in the world; the last septuple birth in the United States was in 1985, but only three of the babies survived. A Saudi Arabian woman gave birth to septuplets in 1997, but only one remains alive (Maxwell, 1997). In December 1998, a 27-year-old Nigerian-born mother gave birth in Texas to the only living octuplets (eight babies): six girls and two boys. Seven of the eight babies survived; one died a week after birth. The mother had used fertility drugs. More recently, in 2005, after having five embryos implanted to increase the chances that at least one would hold, a 25 year-old surrogate mother for a Phoenix, Arizona, childless couple gave birth to quintuplets (five babies), all boys. The birth of the quintuplets is believed to be the first to a surrogate mother (Roberts, 2005). Sociologically speaking, while joyful, such births can exert a tremendous drain on the health and well-being of a woman carrying three or more babies. Multiples have an infant mortality rate that is 12 times higher than that of single births. In addition, there is a tremendous emotional strain and financial burden caused by caring for a multiple set of children.

Media-highlighted cases of multiple births, such as those cited here, have contributed much to a growing public debate about the *ethics* of trying to carry an unprecedented six, seven, or eight children into the world, as well as the

morality of such a decision. One of the dangers of multiple births is that all of the fetuses must share the nutrients and blood supply of one mother. And they do not share the nutrients equally—thus one or more are shortchanged. Some people (including many doctors) believe that a woman should abort one or more of the fetuses to increase the chances of survival of some of the other fetuses. In London, the concern over multiple births following fertility treatments has caused fertility regulators to rule that doctors should normally transfer no more than two embryos at a time during IVF. This action is designed to reduce the number of British women giving birth to triplets or twins after fertility treatment. According to the regulators, the aim of infertility treatment should be the delivery of a single, healthy child (Ross, 2001).

 Should a woman who is carrying multiple fetuses abort some of them to increase the chances of survival of others? Explain. Is having multiple children immoral? Given that sociologists view morality as a social construction, frame your discussion within this theoretical framework.

Sex Preference and Selection

With increasing advances in reproductive technology, couples no longer have to leave the determination of their unborn child's sex completely up to chance. Gender clinics now offer parents-to-be a chance to increase the odds of having a girl or a boy, whichever their preference. From a sociological perspective, such genetic engineering has important social and political implications. Wherever and whenever males are valued more highly than females, such engineering is most frequently directed toward increasing the odds for a male child. The preference for a male child has led to sex-selective abortions and female infanticide in countries such as China and India, where women feel pressured to conceive a son. According to a study in the British medical journal *Lancet*, as many as 10 million female fetuses may have been aborted over the last two decades (cited in Gentleman, 2006). The preference for a male child has serious consequences for marriage, family, and community life, not to mention the girls who have escaped infanticide. As adults, these women may be forced to keep having children until they have a son, and other times they are forced to abort the fetus even though they want to keep the child. Both these practices can have profound health effects on the mother and, in some ways, represent a beginning cycle of violence against these women.

There is some indication that the trend toward assuring the birth of a male is carrying over to Indian and other South Asian immigrants to the United States. However, the cultural bias for males is not limited to Asians or Asian Americans. Despite the significant advances women have made over the past century and the increasing emphasis on gender equality, when it comes to having children, Americans today still prefer boys. For example, according to

TABLE 9.1

Folk Wisdom and the Art of Making Babies

	Girl	Boy
Sexual Position	A woman should initiate sex, try the missionary position, achieve orgasm first, and then sleep on her partner's left side.	A man should enter from the rear, penetrate deeply at climax, and achieve orgasm first.
Diet	A woman should eat vegetables, red meat, sweets, salty snacks, and a high-calcium diet.	Men should drink caffeinated coffee an hour before sexual intercourse to add speed to the male-producing sperm.
Timing	A couple should have sexual intercourse during ovulation—usually earlier than 14 days after a woman begins her period.	A couple should have sexual intercourse during ovulation—usually 14 days after a woman begins her period.
Temperature		Men should "keep it cool" and avoid hot tubs and tight clothing that lower sperm counts because heat kills less hardy male-producing sperm first.
String	In eighteenth-century France, men tied string around their right testicle in hope of producing a girl.	Men tied a string around their left testicle in hope of producing a boy. It was believed that male and female sperm came from the right and left testicle, respectively.
The Moon	Intercourse during a full moon increases the odds of conceiving a girl.	Intercourse during a quarter moon increases the odds of conceiving a boy.
Abstinence	Frequent intercourse until 48 hours before ovulation increases the odds for conceiving a girl.	Because male sperm are smaller and weaker, to increase the odds of conceiving a boy, couples should avoid intercourse if they are within four days of ovulation to increase the sperm count.

Source: Karen Springen, 2004, "The Ancient Art of Making Babies." *Newsweek* (January 26): 51.

recent research, over one-half of men surveyed indicated that they would prefer to have a boy if they could have only one child. Men are twice as likely as women to prefer a boy (Dahl and Moretti, 2004; Simmons, 2000). It is interesting to note some of the tactics people have used in the past to get the girl or boy of their dreams (see Table 9.1).

PREGNANCY

Pregnancy initiates many changes both physically and emotionally for a woman, her partner (if such a relationship exists), and the fetus. Major changes occur in the woman's hormone levels, body shape, and psychological state as the pregnancy develops. Pregnancy also brings about a variety of changes in the lives and relationship of the expectant parents. Their adjustment to the pregnancy is influenced to a large extent by whether the pregnancy was planned, their age at the time of pregnancy, their socioeconomic level, and their race and ethnicity.

Prenatal Development and Care

The attitudes and behaviors of a mother during pregnancy greatly influence the health and well-being of the fetus and later of the human infant. In addition, race, class, age, and gender experiences significantly affect maternal attitudes and behaviors during pregnancy (the prenatal period) and after (postnatal). Although early confirmation and quality prenatal care are important, they are not equally available to all women or couples. Many women of color and poor women, for example, often go without prenatal care because they do not have the resources or because of previous negative experiences involving the health care system. Often these women deliver their babies in public hospitals and teaching institutions that can be insensitive to their needs.

Pregnancy can be both a joyous occasion and one of concern. If the pregnancy is planned and/or wanted, the joy and excitement of impending parenthood can be tremendous. Pregnancy can bring a couple closer together as they adapt to this new stage in their lives and as they share common hopes and dreams for their future child. Pregnancy can also be a time of challenge. For example, a pregnancy can limit opportunities or it can place considerable strain on a relationship. Pregnancy can also be a time of discomfort, self-doubt, and low self-esteem. For instance, given the overwhelming emphasis we place on physical appearance in this society, it is no wonder that with the growth of a woman's body during pregnancy, some women feel ugly and unattractive. However, this is certainly not the case for all women. Some women are delighted with their appearance and believe they are more beautiful at this time than at any other time. This attitude is particularly apparent today among female celebrities. For example, recently, supermodel Cindy Crawford posed naked and proud in prenatal splendor on the cover of *W* magazine (a fashion magazine) when she was 7 months pregnant.

Moreover, pregnancy can create anxieties and fears concerning a number of issues, some of which include the pregnancy's effect on the couple's relationship, whether one or both partners will be good parents, the probability of carrying a fetus to full term versus a pregnancy loss of one kind or another, as well as concerns about the health and well-being of both the mother and the unborn fetus. If there is concern about the health or well-being of the fetus, prenatal testing can provide the couple with specific information about the condition of the fetus. Two of the most commonly used prenatal tests are amniocentesis and ultrasound. **Amniocentesis** is performed when there is some concern about a hereditary disease. It can also provide information about the sex of the fetus. **Ultrasound** allows a physician and the couple to observe the developing fetus directly by viewing electronically the echoes of sound waves pulsating through the pregnant woman's body. Not only can ultrasound be used to detect various birth defects, it can also be used to determine when a child will be born (within a couple of weeks) and whether or not the mother is carrying multiple babies. For many couples, one of the rewards of the ultrasound is the **sonogram,** which allows parents to see the fetus and any movements it makes.

As the end of the pregnancy period approaches, some women feel an enormous sense of urgency for it all to be over with. For others, it is a time of increased bonding with the fetus. Although maternal and infant health have been improving across the United States, according to the most recent data, the **infant mortality rate**—which is the rate at which babies die before their first birthday—is 6.9 deaths per 1000 live births. It is estimated that 2 million babies die within their first 24 hours each year worldwide; 2 million more die within their first month and 3 million are stillborn. The leading causes of infant mortality in the United States are congenital anomalies, disorders related to premature birth and low birth weight, sudden infant death syndrome (SIDS), birth defects, and maternal complications. Despite the steady fall in the infant mortality rate over the last several decades, the United States has the second worst newborn mortality rate in the developed world, with Singapore reporting the lowest recorded rate of infant mortality in history, with a rate of 2.5 deaths per 1000 live births. In 2006, as Americans celebrated Mother's Day, an estimated 5000 mothers mourned the loss of a newborn born that very day (Green, 2006; Save the Children, 2006). In addition, disparities in the United States remain high among racial and ethnic groups on many measures of maternal and child health. Although the trend in infant mortality rates among non-Hispanic blacks and non-Hispanic whites has been on an overall decline, the infant mortality rate among infants of non-Hispanic black mothers is more than double that for non-Hispanic whites. Babies born to African American mothers continue to have the highest rate of infant deaths at 13.5 per 1000 live births, while Asian/Pacific Islander Americans have the lowest rate at 4.8. The rate for Native Americans and Alaska Natives is 8.7 and for whites it is 5.7. Infants born to Latina mothers, who can be of any race, have an infant mortality rate of 5.6 (Matthews and MacDorman, 2006).

These facts notwithstanding, most often a pregnancy ends with the birth of a healthy baby. Nine out of ten babies born in the United States are healthy (O'Connor, 2004; Minino and Smith, 2001). Although the chances of having a healthy baby are good, most parents want to do all they can to make this a reality.

Prenatal Problems and Defects

Recent research findings are not entirely consistent concerning how many children in the United States are born with some sort of birth defect. Most estimates fall between 3 and 4 percent, but a few estimates are as high as 7 percent. Birth defects account for 20 percent of all infant deaths in the United States, more than from any other single cause (Matthews and MacDorman, 2006). Birth defects include any condition that causes or leads to death or the lowering of the quality of life. Birth defects usually can be traced to one or more of the following factors: (1) the influence of the prenatal environment on the fetus—for example, exposure to toxic chemicals and the use of drugs, including alcohol and tobacco, by the mother; (2) heredity—that is, the parents' genes; and (3) injuries sustained at birth. Regardless of their causes, all defects present at birth are referred to as **congenital.**

Protecting the Prenatal Environment   Only about one-fifth of birth defects can be traced to heredity. Research has shown repeatedly that experiences such as those of age, race, and class have important effects on **morbidity** (illness) and **mortality** (death). For example, although more women 40 and older are having children today than in the past, it is believed that the optimum age for pregnancy is between 20 and 35 years of age. Thus, women younger than 20 and older than 35 are at greater risk of having a miscarriage, a stillbirth, a premature birth, an underweight baby, prolonged and more difficult labor, or a child with a birth defect. Although the overall risks to maternal and fetal health for pregnant women over 35 have lessened in some areas of health and well-being, these women are still more at risk than are younger women. Women over 40, for example, have the highest rates of babies born with Down syndrome. At the other end of the age spectrum, the maternal death rate from pregnancy and its complications is 60 percent higher for adolescents than for mothers in their early 20s (Ventura et al., 2001).

Protecting the prenatal environment includes protecting the health of the mother. Each year, out of an estimated 120 million pregnancies that occur globally, approximately 600,000 women die from the complications of pregnancy and childbirth. One woman dies every minute from pregnancy-related causes. As in other areas of social life, race and class affect a woman's life chances when pregnant and/or delivering a baby. For instance, in Sub-Saharan Africa a woman has a 1 in 13 chance of dying in childbirth compared to women in industrialized countries, where the risk drops dramatically to 1 in 4085. Additionally, more than 50 million women suffer from a serious pregnancy-related illness or disability (United Nations Population Fund, 2004; UNICEF, 2003). In the United States, each year 30 percent of pregnant women have pregnancy-related complications before, during, or after delivery that often lead to long-term health problems. Approximately 1000 of these women die each year. Latina, Asian/Pacific Islander, and Native American/Alaska Native women suffer a significantly higher risk of pregnancy-related mortality than non-Hispanic white women, while African American women, with the highest risk of all racial and ethnic groups, are four times more likely as non-Hispanic white women to die in childbirth. Additionally, Asian and Hispanic immigrant women also have a much greater risk of pregnancy-related deaths compared to white women. Further, as women age, as with other risk factors, the risk of dying in childbirth increases. Younger women are the least likely to die from pregnancy-related complications, with white women under that age of 30 having the lowest risk of all groups (Martin et al., 2005).

In response to the high infant mortality rate in the United States, midwifery pioneer Ina May Gaskin initiated the Safe Motherhood Quilt Project, a national effort developed to draw attention to the current maternal death rates. The quilt is made up of individually designed squares, each one honoring a woman in the United States who has died of pregnancy-related causes since 1982. Each piece is personalized and may simply consist of the name of the woman or it may include the date and place of her death.

Moreover, the increasing cost of health care in the United States prevents many pregnant women, particularly those with limited economic resources and inadequate health insurance (if any), from receiving proper care during pregnancy. This problem is especially acute among Native Americans, Latinas, and African Americans. This situation highlights the larger and continuing problem in this country of an inadequate health care system for most individuals and families. The health of parents, particularly mothers before and during pregnancy, and the services available to them throughout their pregnancy, especially at delivery, are important determinants of the health status of their children. Infants whose health status is compromised at birth are more vulnerable to various health problems later in life. Although we cannot control heredity, we can, to some degree, control the prenatal environment. According to the March of Dimes "I Want My Nine Months" educational campaign, designed to prevent birth defects, premature births, and infant mortality, timely prenatal care and a healthy pregnancy is a major factor in reducing the risk of infant death (March of Dimes, 2006a). Some of the most prevalent prenatal concerns include nutrition, smoking, alcohol, drug use, and AIDS.

Nutrition Because nutrients pass from mother to fetus through the placenta, maternal malnutrition or an improper diet can have detrimental effects for the fetus—including congenital defects, small stature, and diseases such as rickets, cerebral palsy, and epilepsy; it can also cause a miscar-

riage or stillbirth. Various research studies show that girls who are inadequately fed in childhood may have impaired intellectual capacity, delayed puberty, and possibly impaired fertility and stunted growth, leading to higher risks of complications during childbirth (World Health Report, 1998). According to most authorities, maternal malnutrition is one of the leading causes of fetal death. The probability of malnutrition during pregnancy is highest among teen mothers and poor and working-class women regardless of age.

Smoking and Alcohol Consumption Not only is smoking detrimental to the health of the smoker, it also has been shown to be detrimental to the health of the fetus. Although the extent of damage caused by cigarette smoking during pregnancy is not fully known, since 1985 the U.S. surgeon general has cautioned that smoking during pregnancy increases the risk of miscarriage, premature birth, low birth weight, and the probability of sickness, convulsions, or death in early infancy. As a result, fewer women today are smoking during their pregnancy. However, the smoking rate varies across age, race, and level of educational attainment. Teenagers, for instance, are more likely than women of any other age to smoke while pregnant, with the highest rates for women 18 to 19 years of age. The youngest and oldest mothers (under the age of 25 and 40 to 49, respectively) have the lowest rate of smoking during pregnancy. Of all racial and ethnic groups, Native American women have the highest rate of smoking, followed by non-Latina white mothers; Latina and African American mothers have lower rates and Asian American and Pacific Islander women have the lowest rates of smoking of all groups. Smoking during pregnancy is also highly correlated with educational attainment. As the level of the mother's formal education increases, the likelihood that she will smoke during pregnancy decreases significantly (Matthews and MacDorman, 2006; CDC/NCHS Press Release, 2001). Smoking during pregnancy or exposing infants to secondhand smoke may contribute to such health problems as asthma, pneumonia, bronchitis, brain damage, and hearing problems. Parental smoking is also linked to behavioral problems and it may also be related to about 1000 cases of SIDS each year nationally (Lauer, 2001). Pregnant women who smoke are not the only ones to put the developing fetus in jeopardy. Research studies suggest that smoking by fathers may have an indirect and negative effect on the fetus. Male smoking can harm or impair sperms, causing a miscarriage and passing on a slight but significant legacy of cancer, tumors, and leukemia to offspring, even if the mother does not smoke (Williams, 1998).

As with cigarette smoking, maternal alcohol consumption can have considerable negative effects, both for the mother and the fetus. Alcohol use during pregnancy is the leading cause of mental retardation in children. An alcoholic mother can give birth to a baby who is also dependent on alcohol. Heavy alcohol use during pregnancy, either alone or in conjunction with smoking, can cause a range of disorders known as *Fetal Alcohol Spectrum Disorders (FASDs)*—an umbrella term describing the range of effects that can occur in an individual whose mother drank alcohol during pregnancy. One of the most serious effects of alcohol consumption during pregnancy is **Fetal Alcohol Syndrome (FAS)** or *Fetal Alcohol Effect (FAE)*, a lifelong condition that causes physical and mental disabilities characterized by growth deficiencies, skeletal deformities, facial abnormalities, organ deformities, and central nervous system handicaps.

FAS is one of the three leading known causes of birth defects in the United States. Each year over 40,000 American children are born with defects because their mothers drank alcohol when pregnant. The highest prevalence of FAS is found among Native American/Alaska Native newborns (30 per 10,000 live births) and is evidence of high rates of alcohol consumption during pregnancy. It is the leading cause of disability among these newborns. FAS occurs much less frequently among other groups of women: 6 percent of infants born to African American women have FAS, 1 percent of infants born to white women and Latinas have FAS, while fewer than 1 percent of the births to Asian American women have this condition ("Prevalence and Incidence of Fetal Alcohol Syndrome," 2006). A child with FAS or FAE may have speech and language delays, poor reasoning and judgment skills, difficulty paying attention in school, various learning problems, and a lower IQ; this child may also be hyperactive (CDC, 2006).

Experts have yet to agree on a safe level of alcohol consumption by pregnant women. Although many people believe an occasional glass of wine or beer is harmless for the fetus, most physicians recommend that a pregnant woman refrain from all alcohol consumption. FAS birth defects have no cure—thus the effects never go away. However, FAS defects are 100 percent preventable if a woman does not drink alcohol while she is pregnant.

Drug and Other Substance Abuse

The majority of drugs, whether street drugs, common drugs like caffeine and aspirin, or prescription and over-the-counter medications, contain chemicals that have been found to have some effect on the fetus. Almost all drugs taken or ingested during pregnancy cross the placenta. The fetus is particularly vulnerable to drugs in the first trimester, when the vital organs are forming.

A growing number of American women abuse drugs such as marijuana, cocaine, Ecstasy and other amphetamines, and heroin during pregnancy and thus endanger the well-being and lives of their children as well as themselves. Because most pregnant women who use illicit drugs also use alcohol and tobacco, it often is difficult to determine which health problems are caused by a specific illicit drug (March of Dimes, 2006b). In any event, most research suggests that women who use cocaine during pregnancy, for example, increase the risk of hemorrhage and miscarriage; they have significantly higher rates of premature and low-birth-weight babies, and an increased risk of lifelong disabilities such as mental retardation and cerebral palsy. Cocaine and other illicit drugs can cause a baby to be born too small; have smaller heads; which generally reflect smaller brains or to have birth defects or learning or behavioral problems compared with babies of nonusers. Babies exposed to narcotics in the womb are frequently born addicted, and the misery they suffer from withdrawal makes them difficult to care for. These babies are also at greater risk of suffering strokes, seizures, heart attack, brain damage, mental retardation, and

congenital abnormalities. The consequences of the mother's addiction to drugs can sometimes be fatal for the offspring. Some studies, for instance, suggest that cocaine-exposed babies have a greater chance of dying of SIDS (March of Dimes, 2006b). However, other studies suggest that poor health practices that often accompany maternal cocaine use also may play a major role in these deaths.

According to some observers, the overwhelming number of severely drug-damaged children is stretching to the limits the capabilities of most major societal institutions to provide assistance. What can society do? What, if anything, is the responsibility of parents? The state? The criminal justice system? These are questions of concern for a growing number of people in U.S. society who argue that the fetus has a right to be born with the best possible chance for a healthy and long life. Consequently, as the use and abuse of cocaine, particularly in the potent form of crack, has increased, drug-abusing women are being legally punished for the outcome of their pregnancies; they are being singled out and subjected to a sex-specific form of criminal prosecution for their drug use. Prosecutors in several states have brought cases against these women under statutes intended for other purposes. In 2000, the Ohio Supreme Court ruled that a baby born addicted to cocaine because of its mother's addiction is legally an abused child. And in 2001, in a landmark case, a 24-year-old mother of three gave birth to a stillborn infant and was charged with killing that child by smoking crack cocaine. After only 15 minutes of deliberations, jurors returned with a guilty verdict, making her the first woman in the nation to be convicted of homicide for killing an unborn child through drug abuse. Her sentence of 20 years, reduced to 12 years without the chance for parole, was the stiffest penalty yet for a woman who abused drugs while pregnant. This case has rekindled the debate about fetal rights and opens the door to future prosecutions of women for smoking, alcohol use, or other behaviors that could harm a fetus. Apart from the constitutional issues they raise, critics of such policies and practices charge that such cases could affect abortion rights and open the door to the prosecution of mothers who smoke, fail to follow their obstetrician's diet, or take some other action that endangers a fetus. Although prosecutors claim that such charges will encourage pregnant drug users to get treatment, in reality, critics say, it frightens such women away from the medical system (Sobey, 1997; Butler, 1999; Pressley, 2001). In addition, such policies fail to recognize the continuing need for drug treatment programs designed to meet the needs of women, particularly pregnant women.

AIDS and Pregnancy

Throughout this textbook we discuss the ramifications of AIDS for marriages and families. Here we limit our discussion specifically to the impact of AIDS on pregnant women and on the developing fetus. Women who are HIV-positive face not only the probability that the infection will develop into full-blown AIDS but also face severe restrictions on their behavior, particularly their reproductive behavior. One of the biggest problems for these women, when or if they do become pregnant, is how to take care of their health and at the same time prevent transmitting the infection to their infant. An HIV-positive woman can transmit the virus to her baby during pregnancy, labor and delivery, and through breastfeeding. It is estimated that approximately 25 percent of infants born to HIV-positive mothers contract HIV from their mothers during pregnancy or birth (vertical transmission); and, according to the CDC, this problem is more acute for pregnant HIV-infected women who do not receive preventive medication. If an HIV-positive woman takes no preventive drugs and breastfeeds, then the chance of her baby becoming infected is between 20 and 45 percent. The term AIDS Dysmorphic Syndrome or **HIV embryopathy** has been used by some researchers to describe specific facial malformations in infants who acquired HIV infection from their mothers. However, more recent research suggests that there is a lack of evidence for such characteristic facial malformations in these babies (Healthwise, 2001).

According to the World Health Organization, some 2000 babies are born every day with HIV because their virus-infected mothers do not get the treatment needed to stop vertical transmission. Fewer than 10 percent of the HIV-positive women in developing countries get antiretroviral therapy during pregnancy and childbirth, despite the fact that overall access to the drugs have increased over the past several years (MSNBC, 2006). In the United States, the problem of vertical transmission of HIV infection is exacerbated because most American women who are infected with HIV are not even aware that they carry the virus (March of Dimes, 2002). Because of their limited access to drug treatment programs, medical information, and quality health care, poor communities and communities of color are especially at risk for HIV/AIDS babies. This is unfortunate given that, to date, most research and clinical study trials of pregnant women with HIV/AIDS have shown conclusively that medical therapy treatments with modern drugs are highly effective in preventing HIV transmission from mother to child, and when combined with other interventions, including formula feeding, a complete course of treatment can reduce the risk of transmission to 2 percent or less. Even where resources are limited, a single dose of medicine given to mother and baby can cut the risk in half. However, vertical transmission is significantly increased in mother's with advanced stage AIDS (Kanabus, 2005; APAC, 2000).

We discuss other STDs such as syphilis and gonorrhea in Appendix A. These diseases can also affect a fetus and can be contracted by the newborn. As with the AIDS virus, STDs in pregnant women can cause miscarriage, brain damage to the fetus, problems with eyesight, and other medical problems.

EXPECTANT FATHERS

Pregnant women are considered to be in a special condition, and we generally give them all of our attention and support. But what about the expectant father? Given that we expect men to play an increasingly active role in childbirth and child rearing, what do we know about their experiences through pregnancy and the birth of their children? Exactly what is the father's part in the process of pregnancy? Are men's experiences entirely social and psychological, or do men experience physiological symptoms as well?

Historically, pregnancy has been viewed primarily as women's work. Expectant fathers were left in the background, unnoticed until the onset of labor. Few fathers participated in pregnancy and childbirth beyond offering general support to the mother. Today, however, a growing number of fathers are participating in the pregnancy and childbirth experience. Many prospective dads are joining their pregnant partners in prenatal classes and in the delivery room, where they help their partner with breathing and other relaxation techniques. Fathers are sometimes the first of the two to hold the newborn and a growing number of these men take some time off from work during the first few weeks after the baby is born to share in the caring for and bonding with the infant.

The Cultural Double Bind

In one of the few studies that examines the concerns and feelings of expectant fathers, psychologist Jerrold Lee Shapiro (1987) suggests that the pregnancy of a partner thrusts a man into an alien world. He is encouraged to be part of a process about which he knows little or nothing. He does not have role models because his father almost certainly did not participate actively in his mother's pregnancy. These problems are not insurmountable and can be overcome with care, preparation, and education. A more important issue is what Shapiro calls the "cultural double bind." On the one hand, men are encouraged to participate in the pregnancy and birth of their children; but on the other hand, they are treated as outsiders by everyone concerned. Although the expectant father's presence is desired, his feelings are not. At times, an expectant father might be as frightened, concerned, sad, and angry as his wife or partner. He needs to share these feelings and fears. But we allow only women to do this. The expectant father has neither the support systems nor the cultural sanctions for what he experiences during impending fatherhood.

Some men unconsciously compensate for this by developing physiological aspects of pregnancy, such as morning sickness, weight gain, or backache, but such symptoms are generally treated humorously by family and friends. When expectant fathers develop symptoms similar to those of the pregnant woman, it is sometimes referred to as a sympathetic pregnancy, or more formally as **couvade**. However humorous the pregnant-father syndrome may seem, many child psychologists believe that the more involved a man is with the pregnancy and birth of his child, the more likely he is to be involved in child rearing. Sociological studies support this viewpoint. For example, various studies have found that fathers who were involved with their partner's pregnancy and were present at delivery showed more interest in looking at their infants and talking to them than did fathers who were not involved with the woman's pregnancy and were not present at the delivery.

The exclusion of fathers-to-be in both the prenatal and postnatal processes reinforces the cultural notion that pregnancy, childbirth, and parenting are exclusively the domain of women. This perpetuation of sex role stereotypes does not facilitate gender equality. The good news, however, is that since Shapiro's pioneering study, the popular and sometimes humorous image of expectant fathers and fatherhood is

In times past, expectant fathers paced nervously in hospital waiting rooms, anxious to hear news of their child's birth. Today, fathers not only are present at the birth of their children, but many actively participate, as this father does, by cutting the umbilical cord.

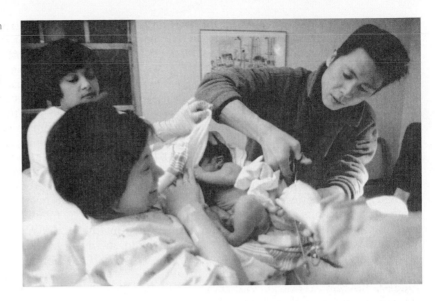

shifting. Today, an increasing number of fathers are speaking out and saying that they are more than simply sperm donors. Rather, they experience a wide range of emotions and there should be greater recognition that expectant fathers also experience things unique to that special time of life. Since the mid-1990s, the number and variety of resources available to these and other dads to prepare them for fatherhood and how to parent have skyrocketed. Hospitals across the country are reaching out to men by letting them play more active roles in their children's births. For example, hospitals across the country now offer classes geared especially for expectant dads called "Boot Camp for New Dads," where expectant fathers can get advice and encouragement from "veteran" fathers and get to spend time with their own babies. Some of these hospitals also offer expectant father classes each month, providing a place where men can talk openly about issues of concern to them as expectant fathers (Marshall, 1999). Equally important, fathers-to-be now routinely witness and/or participate in the birth of their children in such roles as breathing coach or moral supporter. Even in the case of a Caesarean birth, fathers often attend the surgery (Woodard, 1998). When men witness their babies entering the world, they almost always become active fathers, and it gives them a sense of self-worth and feeling of inclusion in the birth and life of their child.

At the end of pregnancy and the birthing process, parents embark on another set of experiences that often change their lives and their relationship with one another forever. In the last section of this chapter, we present a selective review of some of the experiences parents have after the birth of a child.

PARENTAL ADJUSTMENTS, ADAPTATIONS, AND PATTERNS OF CHILD REARING

Parenting is one of the most challenging roles that individuals and couples face in their lifetime. Parents are often unprepared for the changes that this new family member will bring to their lives. Research has shown repeatedly that the addition of children to a relationship increases stress and lowers relationship satisfaction, particularly when children are still young and dependent. The addition of a new and dependent person requires that the couple make major lifestyle adjustments. Either one or both parents, or someone acting on behalf of the parents, must constantly be available and responsible for the care of the child.

The ways in which people parent are significantly tied to how parenting roles and gender roles are culturally defined and the degree to which parents accept these definitions. As in other areas of social life, experiences such as age, race, class, gender, and sexual orientation interact to make the experience of parenthood different for different individuals and groups. After the birth of a child, parents must develop a mother or father identity. Also, particularly in the early months after the baby is brought home, parents have to adjust their sleeping habits to coincide with those of the newborn. Getting up in the middle of the night can be disruptive and exhausting and can affect the parents' job performance. Financial obligations also increase with the birth of a child, as do household and child-care responsibilities. All of these changes can increase stress within the family unit.

For some women, these stresses can show up in **postnatal depression** (sometimes referred to as "the blues" or "postpartum blues"), a condition characterized by mood shifts, irritability, and fatigue. It is estimated that 10 to 15 percent of women who give birth experience a significant level of depression in the first 6 months that follow (McAllister-Williams, 2005). Until recently, postnatal depression had been considered a "woman thing." However, fathers are vulnerable to similar emotions, especially if they are in primary caregiver situations. For example, one study of postnatal depression in fathers found that about one in ten fathers gets serious postnatal depression. Researchers believe a variety of factors contribute to male postnatal depression. The most common are *fear of fatherhood*, *financial concerns*, and *role anxieties*. Added to the stress that men feel during this time is the fact that men are socialized not to share their fears; rather, they are often admonished to "act like a man" and deal with it. Because of this differential gender socialization, when men experience such depression they seldom seek help (Mistiaen, 1994; Kleiman, 2001).

Additionally, a couple often has to adjust their private and intimate time together to the schedule of a child. The sexual lifestyle of a couple may change drastically when a new child arrives. However, there is no set standard of sexual desire or behavior after childbirth. Thus, sexual activity varies greatly from couple to couple. Childbirth does not preclude the early resumption of sexual activities. But, after childbirth, sexuality often loses its spontaneity as couples must now arrange sexual activities around working hours and at times when the newborn is asleep. Such adjustments can be long-term in that as children get older couples often continue to arrange sexual activities around times when the children are at school or otherwise away from home.

Parental Roles

Traditionally, U.S. culture has made a clear distinction between motherhood and fatherhood. Both of these concepts reflect our ideas about gender-appropriate behavior and heterosexuality: Women are perceived as nurturant, caring, and supportive, and men as authoritative, strong, and protective. However, this idealized notion of women, men, and parenting does not fit contemporary reality. As with other aspects of social life, a social constructionist perspective would direct us to view parenting as a social construction. The roles of women and men, mothers and fathers, are not innate; women and men are not "born" to perform certain roles. Rather, what seems natural or real in terms of parenting depends on time, place, and social location; the meaning of motherhood and fatherhood changes in response to different social, cultural, and historical circumstances. In this sense, parenting is socially constructed. This would help to explain why we give different meanings to the same or similar behavior depending on whether it is performed by women or men—mothers or fathers. For example, when women are nurturant, caring, and protective of their children, it is called *mothering* and considered women's duty or responsibility—it is not seen as out of the ordinary. On the other hand, when men are nurturant, caring, and protective of their children, it is not called *mothering* (for fear of de-masculinizing men). More importantly, we celebrate their actions as extraordinary and think that they are wonderful human beings. The attitudes and beliefs that people hold toward appropriate gender roles have a significant influence on how they parent. Researchers have found that, for many people, the transition to parenthood means taking on more traditional gender roles.

Motherhood Traditional notions about motherhood are rooted in a Eurocentric (a worldview that places European culture at the center of analysis) middle-class ideology that emphasizes mothering as a woman's highest achievement and fulfillment in life. If we believe that motherhood is the only true and worthwhile role for women, then, by implication, those who consciously choose not to have children or who for various medical reasons cannot have children are less than complete women. Some researchers (for example, Hoffnung, 1998) have referred to traditional ideas about motherhood as the **motherhood mystique**—which proposes that (1) the ultimate achievement and fulfillment of womanhood is through motherhood; (2) work assigned to mothers—caring for children, home, husband—fits together in a noncontradictory manner; (3) to be a good mother, a woman has to enjoy being a mother and all the work that is defined as part of the mothering role; and (4) a woman's attitude about mothering will affect her children. The optimal situation for children is when women are devoted to mothering. According to Hoffnung, this social construction of motherhood and mothering is narrow and limiting, and it is harmful not only to women but also to men and children. For one thing, it conflicts with other important aspects of women's lives—productive work, companionate marriage, and economic independence. Although traditional motherhood has benefits, it has substantial material cost for women as well.

Some benefits of motherhood include the joy of intimate contact with a growing, developing infant, the sense of importance that nurturing holds for many women, and the personal growth that comes from facing and mastering a new developmental life stage. However, the pressures that push women to devote their major energies to the family and child rearing can have negative economic consequences for women individually and for their families. For example, women who work often select jobs around the scheduling needs of their families rather than according to their own career development. They are pushed to give up what they have accomplished for "mother-work," or to spread themselves very thin. The resulting part-time or intermittent employment patterns they develop contribute to the large wage differential between women and men and limit their economic contribution to their families (Hoffnung, 1998).

In addition, the motherhood mystique also instills guilt in some women if they do not measure up to this ideal. Women who work outside the home, for instance, are often made to feel guilty for not giving their children their undivided attention. Significantly, no such expectation is made of fathers who work. The myth that children need their mother's exclusive and continuous attention also serves to make women the scapegoat for whatever happens to children and serves to support traditional gender roles that define women as subordinate to men. According to Hoffnung: "It is not enough for women to be able to do men's work as well as *women's*, it is necessary to reconsider the value of mothering and to reorder public priorities so that caring for children counts in and adds to the lives of women and men. Until children are valued members of society and child care is considered work important enough to be done by both women and men, the special burdens and benefits of motherhood will keep women in second place" (1998:278).

Evelyn Nakano Glenn (1994) reminds us that mothering is not just gendered but is also racialized in that the concept of mothering as universally women's work disguises the fact that it is further subdivided, so that different aspects of caring are assigned to different groups of women. For example, poor women of color are often employed to care for the children of middle-class white women. Furthermore, according to feminist sociologist Patricia Hill Collins (1991), the basic assumptions that underlie the traditional view of motherhood apply primarily to white middle-class families and most often do not reflect the realities of African American families and other families of color. As an alternative to this view, Collins has proposed a model of African American motherhood that consists of four basic themes:

- **Bloodmothers, othermothers, and women-centered networks.** Within African American communities, the boundaries distinguishing biological mothers (bloodmothers) and other women (othermothers) are nebulous. In such communities, a network of bloodmothers and othermothers (mothers, grandmothers, sisters, aunts, cousins, and friends) shares responsibilities for the others' children. This responsibility includes temporary and long-term child-care arrangements that, when necessary, can turn into informal adoption.
- **Providing as part of mothering.** African American women make an essential economic contribution to the financial well-being of their families. They have long integrated economic activities into their mothering role, a combination that is looked on favorably in the African American family.
- **Community othermothers and social activism.** African American women's experiences as othermothers in their extended family networks are generalized to the larger community, where these women feel accountable for all of the community's children.
- **Motherhood as a symbol of power.** Because mothers not only raise their own children but also serve as community othermothers, motherhood is a symbol of power in the African American community.

In recent decades, the demographics of motherhood have changed considerably. Thus, contemporary women's views on motherhood can be seen as falling along a continuum identified by Collins. At one end of the continuum are traditionalists who want to retain the centrality of motherhood in women's lives; at the other end are those who want to eliminate what they perceive as a cultural mandate to mother. In the middle are large numbers of women who argue for an expanded but not essentially different role for women. In their view, women can be mothers as long as they are not just mothers. Many of these women are opting for both a career and motherhood. They continue to see motherhood as fulfilling but not as the only route to personal fulfillment. The motherhood mystique notwithstanding, the reality is that women can and do find satisfaction in a variety of roles. Not all women find motherhood fulfilling. In fact, not all women desire to mother. The best circumstance is one in which a woman freely chooses this option.

Fatherhood The traditional notion of fatherhood emphasizes an instrumental role of father as breadwinner and authority figure: the father is expected to go out to earn money to support his family. He is expected to come home, play with the children a bit, but basically a traditional father must leave the nurturing, caring, and rearing of children to the mother. The father steps back in at later stages, disciplining, guiding, protecting, and exposing his children to the outside world. According to Nancy Gibbs (1993b), American culture perpetuates this traditional definition of fatherhood in a number of ways, one of them being the many messages we transmit to men about fatherhood and fathering that say they are not up to the job—that we not only do not trust them to be parents but also we do not really need them to be. A classic example can be seen in the fact that teachers and other professionals often treat fathers as if they are incapable of parenting. For example, when a father takes his child to the doctor's office, often the doctor will give him instructions about the child's care to pass on to his wife or partner, the assumed caretaker.

Critics of today's families claim that fatherhood has diminished as a social role for men and they call for a return to the traditional family structure with fathers as head of the family—the protector and breadwinner. David Blankenhorn (1998), president of the Institute for American Values, for example, has advanced a conservative critique of the contemporary family, arguing that it has undermined the father's role in the family and weakened the bond between men and their children. Supporting a traditional view of fatherhood, Blankenhorn claims that traditional fatherhood has become smaller, devalued, and decultured and a new fatherhood has emerged—caused by men being more devoted to their work than to their families, by women having increasing power within the home, and by high divorce rates. There is a wide body of literature that critiques such conservative views of families and fatherhood. Most researchers agree that the traditional concept of fatherhood is as limiting as the traditional concept of motherhood. However, until recently, public policy, societal sentiment, state and federal legislation, and family law all echoed a traditional view of fatherhood. Today, for a growing number of people the word *fathering*, once a word that meant mainly to sire a child, now describes the life of a caring parent. For these people, fatherhood is increasingly that which one does and less what one simply is.

Until the last decade, fathers were virtually ignored in research on children and families, and government statistics reflected this bias. To overcome the scarcity of reliable data,

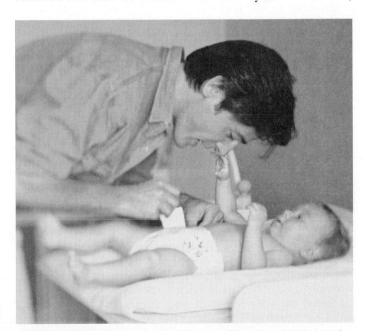

In the past, when it came to fatherhood, much of popular culture assumed that fathers were inadequate as caregivers. Today, however, many fathers are disproving such cultural stereotypes by increasing their involvement in their children's lives, including changing diapers

APPLYING THE SOCIOLOGICAL IMAGINATION

The idea of Father's Day originated with Sonora Dodd of Spokane, Washington, while listening to a Mother's Day sermon in 1909. Dodd wanted to honor her father, William Smart, a widowed Civil War veteran who raised his six children by himself on a rural farm. June was chosen for the first Father's Day celebration—proclaimed in 1910 by Spokane's mayor—because it was the month of William Smart's birth. The first presidential proclamation honoring fathers was issued in 1966 when President Lyndon Johnson designated the third Sunday in June as Father's Day. It has been celebrated annually since 1971 (Census Bureau, 2006:1).

Father's Day Facts

- Nearly 95 million Father's Day cards were given in 2005 in the United States, making Father's Day the fourth-largest card-sending occasion.
- Fifty percent of all Father's Day cards are purchased specifically by sons and/or daughters; nearly 20 percent are purchased by wives for their husbands; the remaining cards are bought for grandfathers, sons, brothers, uncles, and "someone special."
- In 2006, seventy-two percent of Americans said they planned to celebrate or acknowledge Father's Day.
- Neckties lead the list of Father's Day gifts. Sales at the nations nearly 11,000 men's U.S. clothing stores exceeded $800 million in 2005.

Facts About Fathers

- There are approximately 26 million fathers in married-couple families with their own children under the age of 18. One in ten are raising their own infants under age 1; 4 percent of married couple fathers are over the age of 55; and 22 percent have an annual family income of $50,000 or more.
- Three in ten children under 18 live with their single father and his unmarried partner. In contrast, only one in ten children who live with their single mother share the home with mom's unmarried partner.

- Eighty-eight percent of children under 6 years old who live with married parents are praised by their fathers at least once a day.

Begin an investigation of fatherhood in the United States starting with the Web sites listed in this box. Which aspects of the U.S. family system foster the gendered division of labor for mothers and fathers? What evidence is there to support the idea that there are gender-based inequalities in marriages and families? How involved are fathers in child rearing? What impact do fathers have on the successful socialization of young children? What, if anything, should be done to reduce or eliminate gender-based inequalities in parental responsibilities?

http://www.census.gov/Press-Release/www/releases/archives/factsfor features_special_editions/006794.html; http://www.census.gov/Press-Release/www/releases/archives/facts_for_features_ special_editions/001792.html; http://dadsandgrads.about.com/od/celebratingdad/a/aadadsday.htm

---

President Clinton issued a 1995 memorandum to all federal agencies directing them to make a concerted effort to include information on fathers in their research programs where appropriate. The increasing concern about child well-being, the push for fathers' rights by various individuals and groups, and the demand of some fathers, especially divorced fathers, to become more actively involved in their children's upbringing have pushed some social scientists to conceptualize, reconceptualize, measure, and gather information from and about men and fathering beyond their traditional emphasis on nonmarital childbearing, child support, and child poverty (see Internet Resources: Applying the Sociological Imagination). Consequently, a new and growing body of research on fatherhood and fathering has emerged in which a primary emphasis is on the quality and quantity of father involvement and its effect on children and families. This research calls into question the traditional notion of fatherhood and the popular assumption that the primary, if not only, role of fathers is that of economic support.

Based on a review of the literature on fathering, Michael Lamb (1987) identified three types of fathering: (1) *engagement*, which includes actions such as feeding children, playing with them, bathing them, and helping them with homework; (2) *accessibility*, which essentially involves being near the child but not directly engaged in child care;

and (3) *responsibility*, being the one who makes sure the child gets what she or he needs. When mothers work, fathers become more engaged and accessible but not more responsible for their children. Although fathers today define their roles in many different ways, some researchers have suggested that there are five major views of fatherhood that coexist, with some degree of overlap: (1) the aloof and distant father; (2) the father as breadwinner; (3) the father as moral teacher; (4) the father as a gender role model for the couple's children; and (5) the father as an active, nurturant parent. Many of today's fathers are far more tightly bonded to their children than were their fathers and grandfathers.

Although there is ample evidence that the number of fathers defining their role in terms of this "new father" ideal is growing, the traditional view of fatherhood remains the dominant view. In her research on two-job couples in the San Francisco Bay area, for example, Hochschild (1989) found that only about one in five of the working husbands in her sample fit the "new father" model of fatherhood in the sense of fully sharing the care of children and home and fully identifying themselves as men through this sharing. Even those fathers who actively participate in child care still see "breadwinner" as their primary role. They also see themselves as a helpmate assisting the main caregiver, the mother (Hochschild, 1989; Mederer, 1993). According to

IN OTHER PLACES

SHARED PATERNITY

Western social scientists historically have predicated their work on the assumption that a child can have only one biological father. However, universality of a human sexual arrangement whereby a male provides for his mate (or mates) and offspring in exchange for female fidelity and paternity certainty has now been called into question. Researchers have identified 18 widely separate and distinct cultures in South America whose members engage in the practice of "partible," or shared biological fatherhood. These South American societies are not isolated cases. Other examples of shared parenting are being discovered in indigenous societies in New Guinea, Polynesia, and India.

According to Pennsylvania State University anthropologist Stephen Beckerman, the general belief system underlying the practice of multiple fatherhood is that all of the men who have sex with a woman around the beginning of her pregnancy as well as during her pregnancy share the biological paternity of her child. The fetus is believed to grow and gain strength by repeated contributions of the men's semen. Although patterns of shared parenting vary from one society to another, anthropologists believe this concept may function as a strategy with real benefits to the welfare of those societies that practice it. For example, studies of the Bari of Venezuela and the Ache of eastern Paraguay found that, in both societies, children with multiple fathers were more than twice as likely to survive to their adolescent years as children born to a single father. The explanation for this may be simply that the secondary fathers contribute additional food and protection to the mother and her children.

Another interesting finding of Beckerman's study is the lack of sexual jealousy among the Bari. Beckerman offers a plausible explanation for this by making an analogy to a life insurance policy: When a woman takes a lover, her husband knows that if he dies, there will be another male who has at least a residual obligation to her children, who most likely belong to the husband.

What do you think? Does the concept of shared parenting make sense? Are there any instances of shared parenting in Western societies? What are the belief systems underlying the Western conception of sole biological fatherhood? How does it function as a strategy in modern societies? Would our society benefit from expanding our views of parental responsibilities beyond the boundaries of biological parenthood?

Source: Kim A. McDonald, 1999, "Shared Paternity in South American Tribes Confounds Biologists and Anthropologists," *The Chronicle of Higher Education* (April): A19, A20.

---

some people, the "new father" is simply the latest adaptation of the nuclear family model. They suggest that people other than biological fathers can be and are equally beneficial to a child. For example, lesbian mothers who conceive children through artificial insemination or heterosexual mothers single by choice or necessity are legitimate alternatives to the "new father." Others, like Arlie Hochschild (1999), point out the contradictions between the ideal of the "new father" and the reality of what fathers actually do. Nonetheless, it would be erroneous to assume that fathers do not play a significant role in child rearing. The importance of fathers in the lives of their children is well documented in some South American countries, where the role of father is often shared (see In Other Places box).

Gender Differences in the Experience of Parenthood

Regardless of the division of labor before the birth of a child, after a child is born mothers are typically more involved in child-care activities than fathers are, with the possible exception of stay-at-home dads. New mothers find themselves with increased housework expectations and responsibilities. Mothers of babies and young children spend more hours on their family roles than do nonmothers or mothers with older children. This is true regardless of whether or not a woman works outside the home (Bianchi, 2000).

There is little dispute that more and more fathers want to spend time with their children; they desire a deeper emotional connection with their children. In a recent survey, 70 percent of fathers said they would take a pay cut to spend more time with their families (Newman, 2000). However, their actions often lag behind their attitudes. Fathers may be bonding more with their children but they continue to be far less involved in the day-to-day care of their children than mothers. Indeed, surveys show that the world over, fathers spend only a small fraction of the time that mothers, even employed mothers, spend on child-care activities. Men have generally claimed that the reason they do not participate more fully in child rearing is because of their job commitments and their general exhaustion at the end of a workday. In fact, however, women who are employed manage to do both. Although mothers spend more time taking care of children than fathers do, fathers spend more time than mothers in play behavior. The net result is that mothers' energies are more divided than fathers' energies, and their lives are more stressful.

Although many women experience stress and ambivalence about motherhood, they generally feel the rewards of parenting outweigh the negatives. However, as we will see in Chapter 10, some women, especially working mothers, express resentment at their partner's general lack of involvement in parenting. Research suggests that marital satisfaction often decreases after the birth of a child due to role conflicts and restriction of freedom (Twenge, Campbell, and Foster, 2003). In recent years, there has been a decrease in the number of working mothers in the labor force. Some observers attribute this action to more women choosing to

Although a growing number of fathers are participating in child rearing today, mothers continue to be the primary providers of child care.

Source: Baby Blues Partnership. King Features Syndicate.

be stay-at-home moms. However, many researchers conclude women are leaving the labor force not because of a change in attitude but because combining work and family is becoming more difficult. This, in turn, they say, is related to the fact that many couples are delaying the arrival of their first child. For example, in 1979, 28 percent of women ages 33 to 37 had children under 6. By 2004, about 37 percent of that age group had preschoolers at home (Porter, 2006). These statistics suggest that midway in their work life, these women are adding more child-care responsibilities.

The work-and-family juggling act—once seen as the sole burden of mothers—is now increasingly performed by men, not out of duty but out of desire. From the 1970s to the early 1990s, when women went to work in record numbers, only 15 percent of men reported difficulty reconciling work and family compared with 70 percent of all working mothers. By the early 1990s, the gap had narrowed until, by the end of the twentieth century, there was no difference at all between genders (Rubin, 2000). These issues will be discussed in more detail in Chapter 10. For now, however, it does seem that further reallocation of household work and child care will be necessary if families are to have dual earners, which is a necessity for many families. It also means other institutions, like business and government, will have to provide added support for working families.

Current research points to a number of ways in which parenting in the United States continues to be gendered even among those couples where fathers take on the "new father" role. For example, mothers clearly spend more time "doing" for children, including the emotional work of caring and worrying about them, than fathers. In short, mothers are always on call for their children, whereas men are not. In addition, fathers across race, class, and religion tend to spend more time with sons than with daughters. Although children become just as attached to their fathers as to their mothers and fathers are just as sensitive to their infants as mothers, women and men interact with their children in different ways. For example, fathers tend to emphasize "play" over "caretaking"; they spend a larger proportion

of their time together playing (40 versus 25 percent for mothers), and their play is more likely than mothers to involve physical and arousing play activities (Parents Forever, 2001). In addition, children's views of their parents typically fall along gender lines as well. For instance, children often view their fathers as stricter and more likely to use punishment than mothers.

What consequences does this unequal gendered division of labor and parenting have for children? Some scholars claim that family organization is based on very real biological differences between women and men, and "parental androgyny" (mothers and fathers playing essentially the same social roles) is neither good for children nor marriage generally (Popenoe, 1999; Glenn, 1997). Other scholars argue that such gender ideology is harmful and that equitable social arrangements within marriages and families is a must and a definite improvement over the traditional division of roles because such arrangements provide increased opportunities for adult self-fulfillment (Barnett and Rivers, 2004; Stacey, 1996).

Styles of Parenting

How parents rear their children and the effects of various child-rearing strategies are the subjects of a substantial literature. Professionals and the lay public alike dispense advice and analyses of what works and what does not. As a consequence, parents today are far better informed about child development and behavior than were parents at any other time in our history. Just as every pregnancy and child is different, so too are parenting styles. However, sociologists have identified some common patterns of parenting among families in the United States, especially within particular social classes.

Because one of the basic elements in sociological definitions of class is occupation, studies of parenting styles across class often examine the kinds of attitudes and values associated with different occupations and how these attitudes and values are related to child-rearing strategies. A classic statement using this approach is sociologist Melvin Kohn's (1977) discussion of parenting styles in terms of self-direction versus conformity parental-value orientations. According to Kohn, middle-class occupations require or allow workers much more self-direction in the ordering of activities and the selection of methods than do working-class jobs, which are more often routine and subject to strict supervision. In addition, middle-class occupations tend to call for individual action, whereas working-class occupations more often call for coordinated group or team action. These occupational differences are reflected in general differences in values and parenting strategies among various social classes. According to Kohn, the *traditional* or *conformity value orientation* is more commonly found among working-class and lower-class parents who emphasize order, authority, obedience, and respectability. In contrast, the *developmental* or *self-direction orientation* most commonly found among middle-class parents, stresses the child's motives and the development of self-control. Emphasis is on internal qualities such as consideration, curiosity, and initiative rather than on external conformity.

Some social scientists, like Diane Baumrind (1968, 1979, 1991), have incorporated Kohn's findings into a model that divides parenting styles into three general categories: authoritarian, permissive, and authoritative. The *authoritarian style* demands absolute obedience from children and often involves the use of physical punishment to control behavior. Although this style of parenting is commonly associated with working-class parents, variations do exist. Working-class fathers who experience autonomy at work and who have high self-esteem, for instance, are more accepting of their children and less likely to try to control them psychologically than are working-class fathers whose jobs carry less autonomy and who have lower self-esteem (Grimm and Perry-Jenkins, 1994). Some parents, particularly those who live in certain environments (high poverty, high crime), believe authoritarian measures are necessary to protect their children from danger. For example, some African American parents realize that if their children make a mistake, they are less likely than white children to be given a break by public authorities. Thus, they may feel the need to be a little more controlling in their parenting style (Hill, 1995).

The *permissive style* of parenting, more typical of middle-class parents, involves giving children autonomy and freedom to express themselves, and downplays conformity. Permissive parents generally have few rules and regulations, make few demands on their children to conform, and most often use reason instead of physical punishment to modify their children's behavior. However, permissive parents sometimes exercise too little control in conflict situations with their children and allow them to grow up with little self-control or discipline. The *authoritative style* also encourages children to be autonomous and self-reliant. Authoritative parents generally rely on positive reinforcements, while avoiding, as much as possible, punitive and repressive methods of discipline. These parents are in control of their children's behavior while at the same time they allow the children much more freedom than do authoritarian parents.

Recent research on American and British youth shows that parenting style has important consequences for psy-chosocial development in adolescence, with an authoritative style apparently the most effective regardless of socioeconomic background or family structure (Shucksmith, Hendry, and Glendinning, 1995). Similarly, Nancy Hill (1995) found in her study of African American families that authoritative parenting was related to such positive family characteristics as cohesion, intellectual orientation, organization, and achievement. Additionally, this style was positively related to expressiveness for fathers and negatively related to family conflict. A study of African American students between the ages of 5 and 18 supported the idea that students with parents who used an authoritarian (high-control, low-nurturance) parenting style had lower grades than students whose parents practiced an authoritative style (high-control, high-nurturance). Students with permissive parents (low-control, high-nurturance) also had lower grades (Taylor, Hinton, and Wilson, 1995). A more recent study of Korean American college students found similar results. Authoritative parenting styles and the number of years lived in the United States were predictive of higher academic competence whereas authoritarian and permissive parenting styles were predictive of lower self-reliance (Kim and Chung, 2003).

In general, these parenting styles often overlap depending on a number of factors, such as the number of children, the unique personalities of the parents and child, parents' attitudes concerning child rearing, and the structure of the family. As we saw in Chapter 1, although some of the child-rearing functions of families have been taken over by other societal institutions, parents remain the major socializers of their children. Thus, their styles of parenting have important consequences for children and the larger society. This notion is reinforced in Annette Lareau's (2003) research on middle- and working-class families, which found that middle-class families engage in practices of *concerted cultivation*, whereby parents actively foster and assess their children's talents, opinions, and skills and facilitate their children's activities, which are often quite extensive. The conversational style middle-class parents use with their children helps the children to learn negotiating skills with adults and the back-and-forth mode allows children to challenge adults and to engage in reasoning and problem solving. This pattern fosters a sense of entitlement that helps middle-class children navigate the educational system from elementary school to college. In contrast, working-class and poor families engage in child-rearing practices that Lareau calls the *accomplishment of natural growth*, whereby parents provide their offspring with food, shelter, and clothing but development comes spontaneously and parents organize their children's lives so they spend time around the home. Children have more autonomy and initiate their own informal play activities with neighborhood peers, but there is less conversation and little emphasis on negotiating. Lareau concludes that both practices have benefits but she argues that the middle-class approach gives children advantages in terms of learning to assert themselves and to interact in a variety of settings with all kinds of people, behaviors that are rewarded in our economy. More research is needed to see if these patterns hold up across a wider spectrum of classes, races, and ethnic groups. It does suggest, however, that if all children are to have equal opportunities for social rewards, efforts must be made to help parents gain the tools they need to equip their children with the appropriate skills.

> *What style of parenting did you experience growing up? What did you like or dislike about it? Is it a style you wish to replicate if you have children? Given Professor Lareau's findings, what, if anything, do you think should be done to increase opportunities for working-class children?*

Discipline A major issue for many parents is how to change their children's behavior when it is unacceptable. In the United States, it is commonly believed that physical punishment is sometimes necessary to discipline a child, with more men favoring this view than women. These attitudes are in line with reported behavior. For instance, 94 percent of parents report spanking their 3- and 4-year-olds, 50 percent hit their 12-year-olds, and 13 percent hit their 17-year-old children (Strauss and Stewart, 1999). Experts on child care are somewhat divided on the efficacy of spanking. On the one hand, psychologist Diana Baumrind argues that many studies do not distinguish the effects of spanking as practiced by nonabusive parents from the impact of severe physical punishment and abuse. Her analysis of data from a 12-year study of over 100 families found that mild to moderate spanking had no detrimental effects when such confounding influences were controlled (Goode, 2001). On the other hand, Murray Strauss (2001), a nationally recognized researcher on family violence, points out the harmful consequences of spanking:

- The more frequently a child is spanked, the more aggressive the child is likely to become.
- Spanking erodes the bond of affection between parent and child.
- Spanking teaches a child what not to do, not what is the right thing to do.
- Parents who were spanked as children are more likely to spank their own children.
- Spanking can get out of hand and escalate into physical abuse. Spouses who received harsh punishment as children are more likely to be abusive to their spouses and children.

To avoid these negative effects, child experts recommend alternative methods of discipline that include removing temptations that lead to misbehavior, establishing reasonable and consistent rules, modeling appropriate behavior, praising good behavior, treating children with respect, and providing emotional support by expressing love, warmth, and acceptance (Angermeier, 1994; Leach, 1994).

These alternative methods of discipline are viewed with skepticism by a number of immigrant groups, who perceive American parents as too lenient with their children. Many immigrant parents, among them Nigerians, West Indians, Dominicans, Mexicans, and East Europeans, are separated from their extended families, who previously helped in the socialization and control of their children. Here in the United States they must work long hours away from home. Their concern for the safety of their children often leads them to impose harsh forms of discipline for any misbehavior. As one West Indian parent said, "If I cannot beat them and they get out there, the police will shoot them when they do wrong. I love my children more than the system loves them" (quoted in Dugger, 1996).

Questions about parenting styles, including methods of discipline and control of children's behavior, loom particularly large and relevant today when so many of America's youth express feelings of conflict, anger, and alienation. There is a growing debate about the influence of parents on their children and parents' ultimate responsibility for their children's attitudes and behavior, particularly in the wake of the increasing gun violence of some of America's youth. Given the obvious troubled nature of many of today's youth, an increasing number of people have expropriated the African proverb that so often served as a guiding principle in African American communities: "It takes a village to raise a child." Using this concept, they argue that parents, regardless of parenting style, need help from "the village"—a community or network of individuals and group support—to raise a child. A number of research studies support this notion of extended parenting. For example, various research shows that when teachers and parents work collaboratively and begin intervention early in children's lives, it has a significant long-term, positive effect on children's behavior and their academic achievement (Brody, 1999).

Married and heterosexual people are not the only ones who have children or face special challenges during pregnancy, childbearing, and child rearing. As we have emphasized often, the interrelationship of the axes of social structure such as race, class, gender, sexual orientation, and age shape the experiences of *all* people in this country. Thus, it is instructive to consider some of the ways in which these structures shape the reproductive and parenting experiences of a number of groups in U.S. society. Although these general parenting styles can be found among the total population, there are some differences, modifications, and adaptations associated with race, class, age, and sexual orientation.

Race and Class

African Americans African American families have historically experienced issues that many other families have only recently become attentive to—combining work and family roles, single parenthood, and extended family relationships. Their experiences can be instructive for other families.

Family Structure African American families represent a variety of household types and structures. Although African American families reflect the general American culture of families and structures, they have also formed some distinctive structures for surviving and getting ahead in response to a history of racism, discrimination, poverty, their own cultural heritage, and a variety of other social and political factors. In terms of family type or structure, just under half of African American family households (47 percent) are married-couple families, 44 percent are female-headed families, and 9 percent are male-headed families. Like most other married-couple families, African American married-couple families are smaller than in the past; 88 percent of these families have two or fewer children living at home under the age of 18. Although the poverty rate for African Americans in 2000 was at its lowest since 1959, African American families today are still more likely than white families to live below the poverty level (22 and 8 percent, respectively, in 2004). In addition, African American children have a greater likelihood of growing up with only one parent (primarily mother-only) than children of other races and ethnicities (for example, less than one-half—41percent—live with both parents). Such families tend to be disproportionately poor compared to two-parent African American families. However, contrary to popular myth, the majority of these families have a working head-of-household (U.S. Census Bureau, 2006).

It is important to keep in mind that although African Americans families share many commonalities, there are also important economic and social differences among African American families. For example, African American families differ by class, region of the country they live in, age and gender of family head, and number of family members, to name but a few. However, as we discussed in Chapter 1, the one thing that African American families typically are not is the stereotypic, mythical, and/or negative images commonly applied to them in both popular culture and in some scholarly research.

Dispelling African American Family Myths   Contrary to popular myth, African Americans value family life and parenthood. According to some research, African Americans believe very strongly in the institution of the family, the majority (90 percent) reporting that they are satisfied with their spouse and/or family life. This is particularly true of the middle class, who report that family life is their greatest source of life satisfaction (Bowman, 1993; McAdoo, 1993; Taylor, Jackson and Chatters, 1997). Other research has consistently shown that motherhood and child rearing are among the most important values in the African American community and that strong kinship bonds have had a significant impact on African American parents' ability to parent successfully in an environment that is so often negatively impacted by male sexism and white racism. Among African Americans, caring for kin is shared among female and male adults, elders, and children, so that single parents, for example, are not generally left alone to raise their children. They can often rely on the assistance of family members and/or fictive kin. Both two-parent and single-parent families are more likely than white families to live in an extended family household. Additionally, in two-parent families African American husbands are more likely than white husbands to share in household chores and child-care responsibilities (John and Shelton, 1997; Xu, Hudspeth, and Estes, 1997). Furthermore, caring is often reciprocal, whereby members may be recruited to take care of other kin who cared for them earlier (Stack and Burton, 1994).

According to Robert Staples, raising an African American child is not, and has never been, an easy task (1999:152). Given the obstacles they face, African American parents have done a tremendous job in rearing their offspring, and they have generally done so with fewer resources than most other parents. African American parents face a dual responsibility in parenting: They must teach their children the folkways of their own culture and what it means to be "black" in a racist society; at the same time they must also socialize their children into the values of mainstream American culture to adapt successfully to mainstream group requirements and institutions. Given the poor social conditions under which many African American children are raised, it is not surprising that some of them fail in life. What is surprising is that so many more succeed given the adverse circumstances they encounter in the larger society (Staples, 1999).

Social Class Differences   Because most African Americans have encountered racism and discrimination in some form, African American child-rearing practices and aspirations for their children tend to be similar across class boundaries. At the same time, however, they also exhibit class differences similar to those found among other groups in society. For example, African American middle-class families have a value orientation characterized by high achievement motivation, social striving, and a high regard for property ownership. In fact, one-half of African Americans in 2004 were homeowners versus renters, and this figure increases to 71 percent for married-couple families (U.S. Census Bureau, 2006; 2000b). African American middle-class families also have high educational and occupational expectations for their offspring. Thus, they try to teach their children positive attitudes toward work and thrift. These families tend to be more egalitarian than patriarchal. Parents stress conformity, chastity, and fidelity and are more inclined to use persuasive approaches to elicit obedience and conformity than to use coercion and physical punishment. Yet they demand a high degree of respect for parental authority (Staples, 1999). In addition, researchers have found that African American fathers generally, and middle class African American fathers particularly, are often integrally involved in parenting such as monitoring and supervising their children's behavior, teaching them life skills, stressing academic achievement, and generally being warm and loving and only moderately strict disciplinarians (McAdoo, 1993; Toth and Xu, 1999; Wagemaar and Coates, 1999).

African American working-class families hold similar attitudes concerning basic family goals, but their value orientation is much more affected by the constant struggle for survival, and they take great pride in the fact that they are self-supporting. The parenting style in working-class families includes an emphasis on respectability: Parents demand that their children behave well and not get into trouble with the police. Like their middle-class counterparts, they stress conformity and obedience. They typically make every attempt to buffer their children from exposure to the negative influences of drugs, gangs, and other problem behaviors by strictly monitoring their children's time and friendships (Jarrett, 1995). Like their middle-class counterparts, working-class parents socialize their children to exercise self-control and succeed in school. Lower-class African American parents are often regarded as the most ineffective in their role as parents because of their reliance on physical punishment to control their children's behavior. However, what is missing from this assessment is the fact that most lower-class parents, across race, combine heavy doses of emotional nurturance with their physical measures of punishment. Some researchers suggest that this combination of child-rearing practices may be more beneficial for a child's development than the middle-class practice of withholding love if the child does not behave correctly (Staples, 1999).

Perhaps the greatest class differences in parental attitudes and parenting styles are those between the African American poor and middle class. Many poor African Americans are disenchanted, disillusioned, and alienated, and see little progress and even fewer possibilities for breaking out of their low economic status (Blackwell, 1985). As a consequence, according to some sociologists, many poor African American parents are generally limited in their ability to guide their children and often have little control over their children's behavior. Parental values and behaviors generally are those that are most expedient and offer hope of a livable or tolerable existence at the time. Although female-headed families make up a large proportion of the African American underclass, some of whom are perhaps the basis for many of the stereotypes and myths about African American families generally, it is erroneous to assume that such families are synonymous with problems, including a lack of family values. In fact, several scholars of African American families have suggested that single African American mothers may be particularly strong not only in terms of valuing and keeping their families together but also in protecting themselves and their offspring and coping in a world of chronic poverty, racism, sexism, and male violence (Sudarkasa, 1993; Edin and Lein, 1997).

African American Fathers   African American fathers all too often are portrayed as uninterested and uninvolved with their children. However, as we have indicated, research that focuses on African American male roles in the family does not support such stereotypes. According to Lora Bex Lempert (1999), by accepting popular myths and cultural stereotypical images of African American families as "matriarchal," where African American men are either absent or peripheral to the family, and by focusing research attention almost exclusively on female-headed African American families, researchers have all but ignored the significant role that African American men play in supporting their families and communities.

In an interesting analysis of research data reported by African American grandparent caregivers, Lempert extends Patricia Hill Collins's work on *othermothers*—which speaks to the centrality of women in African American child rearing and extended families—to describe the role of African American men in extended family constellations. Collins cautions against assuming that the centrality of women in child rearing is predicated on the absence of husbands and fathers, noting that men may indeed be physically present and/or have well-defined and culturally significant roles in the extended family.

Lempert uses the concept of *otherfathers* to present an alternative perspective on African American community

caring and childrearing that highlights the central role of African American men in the lives of African American children. *Otherfathers* are men who, as family members and/or as community members, actively engage themselves as providers, protectors, role models, and mentors in the lives of the children of other men: They may assume financial responsibility, in part or in whole, for these children, and serve as models of honesty, respectability, dignity, social wisdom, and race pride as they maintain a positive, interactive presence in the children's lives. An example of this type of *otherfathering* can be seen in a recent rare ruling by the Illinois Appellate Court. The case involved a 15-year-old youth whose mother was a drug addict and whose biological father was not much involved in his life. After the young man's grandmother died, the father of his half-sister (Kenneth Clair, a felon as a result of an 11-year-old gun possession conviction) petitioned the court for custody of his daughter and later asked the court to appoint him as the young man's legal guardian as well. Denied by a lower court based on an Illinois statute that prohibits felons from being appointed guardians, Clair's lawyer immediately appealed the decision to the higher court. In the rare ruling, the Appellate Court Justice indicated that a strict interpretation of the Illinois statute would not be in the best interest of the 15-year-old and named Clair guardian (Patterson, 2005:15A). This case, as does Lempert's research, demonstrates that while some African American children may be growing up without the care of their biological parents, they are not growing up without love and nurturing, protection, and provision from *otherfathers* as well as *othermothers* (Lempert, 1999).

Family Strengths and Resiliency   Historically, social science research on African American families has focused almost entirely on the so-called pathology of African American families and has almost completely ignored the diversity, strengths, and resilience of these families. Beginning in the 1970s, in response to this unbalanced depiction of African American families, a group of African American scholars across academic disciplines began to develop a corrective scholarship that debunked many of the pathology myths of traditional social science research on African American families. A pioneer in this regard, sociologist Robert Hill (1972) pointed out in his book *The Strengths of Black Families* that contrary to popular stereotypes, although some African American families experienced myriad social problems, the majority of them exhibited strong kinship bonds, a strong work orientation, a strong achievement orientation, a strong religious orientation, and flexible family roles. Twenty-five years after his pioneering work on the strengths of African American families, Hill (1997) revisited those strengths, suggesting that conventional depictions of African American families in the media and social science research continued to be unbalanced; the typical focus continued to be on the weaknesses or deficiencies of a disadvantaged minority of African American families, with little or no consideration of the majority. According to Hill, there continues to be a fixation on the nonworking poor (or underclass) that excludes an examination of the larger working class who often live in the same communities, or excessive attention is paid to the two out of ten African American families on welfare or on the one out of ten African American teenagers who had a baby outside of legal marriage. Little or no attention is paid to the majority of low-income African Americans that achieve against the odds. Despite economic adversity, the effects of continuing entrenched racism and discrimination, disproportionately high rates of unemployment, poverty, and incarceration of young African American males; and the street violence, as well as gang and criminal activities of a minority in the community, most African American families (whether married-couple or single-parent) are family-oriented, love their partners and their children, and teach their children to have self-respect, to be self-sufficient and achievement-oriented, and to be proud of their cultural heritage (Hill, 1998; St. Jean and Feagin, 1998).

Native Americans Native American families are perhaps the least studied families compared to other families living in the United States. Therefore, researchers often rely on aggregate data that yield a generalized picture of Native American individuals and families. As a group, for example, resulting from a history of legal and social domination, oppression, and, at times, total neglect, Native American families have among the highest rates of poverty, unemployment, poor health, infant mortality, suicide, and alcoholism of any racial or ethnic group in the United States. The average life expectancy of Native American women is 46 and of Native American men 45. Despite some important economic gains in recent years, the majority of Native Americans still remain in the bottom tenth of the economic hierarchy and at the bottom of the class hierarchy (Scott and Schwartz, 2006).

Family Structure Currently, less than 1 percent (0.7) of all households in the United States consists of Native American peoples. Of all Native American households, 73 percent consist of families, and of these family households, 61 percent are headed by a married couple, 28 percent are headed by a female, and 10 percent are headed by a male. Native American families typically consist of two children and are among the nation's youngest households. They are also among the country's poorest, with a poverty rate of 26 percent (Ogunwole, 2006). According to the National American Indian Housing Council, 40 percent of the homes in tribal communities are overcrowded and have serious physical deficiencies (National Congress of American Indians, 2002). There has been a considerable migration of Native Americans from reservations since World War II. More than half of Native American families today live outside tribal lands, and although separated from their traditional tribal cultures, they typically fare better economically and socially than those who remain on reservations. Moreover, with the increasingly large numbers of Native Americans marrying non-Native Americans, a growing number of children in these families are biracial. Those who marry other Native Americans tend to marry within their respective tribal groups. As we have noted elsewhere, the high rates of interracial marriage, however, have caused some Native Americans to question whether or not Native American families will maintain their ethnic identity and familial traditions.

Differences and Commonalities in Parenting Styles These generalizations about Native Americans notwithstanding, and despite their common history of racism and oppression, Native Americans are a heterogeneous people, perhaps more heterogeneous than any other group in the United States (for example, there are 569 federally recognized Native American cultural groups plus an unknown number of cultural groups that are not federally recognized). Specific social and economic characteristics, family structures, contents, and behaviors therefore vary considerably from group to group. Among the Navajo, for example, parents operate on the principle of the inviolability of the individual, which some researchers have translated as a principle of permissiveness. Navajo parents discipline their children through persuasion, ridicule, and shame rather than coercion and physical punishment. In addition, supernatural sanctions are used to control children's behavior (John, 1998). On the other hand, Native American groups such as the Hopi, Zunis, and other various descendants of the ancient Anasazi continue today to be loyal to their matrilineal clan systems and religious ceremonies, and they emphasize sobriety and self-control (Coltrane and Collins, 2001).

Although there is considerable variation among different tribal groups, Native American families share a strong sense of tribalism, family identity, and pride, and parents of all backgrounds tend to stress to their children a sense of family unity, tribal identity, self-reliance, and respect for elders. Children are viewed as assets to both the family and the group. Some researchers have suggested that child rearing among Native Americans frequently is nonverbal: Parents communicate by giving stern looks or by ignoring inappropriate behavior. Furthermore, children are socialized by example and are expected to share with others, to be quiet and unassuming, to show deference to their elders, to control their emotions, to be self-reliant, and to make an economic contribution to the family from an early age (John, 1998).

Interdependence and interfamily exchange are important family patterns, especially on reservations. In this context, extended families are significant. And elders typically hold a special place in Native American families. Not only are children taught to respect elders, but, also, elders expect family members to take care of them when needed (Yellowbird and Snipp, 1994).

Some of the recent literature on Native American families indicates that socialization practices among Native Americans have changed in recent times from "cohesive and structured" households characterized by high-dominance–high-support parent–child relations to "loosely structured" households with low-dominance–low-support parent–child relations. Today, rigid gender roles are loosening, and more Native American women are working outside the home.

Family Strengths and Resiliency Similar to African American families, much of the popular attention and scholarly research on Native Americans focus on the social and economic problems of this group and ignore its strength and resiliency. However, like every group, Native American families exhibit important strengths. Although the problems, particularly as they are manifest on reservations, have yet to be resolved, the diversity and strengths of Native

American families—extended family networks, interdependence and interfamily exchange, value of individuals and the group, group cooperation, tribal support systems, and preservation of culture and family traditions—promote a pan-Indian identity and facilitate the maintenance of strong tribal and family identities across the numerous tribes.

Latinas/os Like Native Americans, Latinas/os are a highly diverse people whose marriage and family behaviors vary, sometimes considerably, from group to group. Thus, the following brief description of Latina/o family structure represents a generalized view of structural features that Latina/o families share.

Family Structure The structure of Latina/o families is more likely than African American families but less likely than Asian and white families to consist of two parents. About two-thirds (67 percent) of Latina/o family households consist of married-couple families and nearly one-fourth (23 percent) are female-headed. Forty-six percent of married-couple families have one to two children, and 20 percent have three or more children. Like most other groups in the United States, however, a growing number of Latina/o children are living in families with only one parent present. Currently, 30 percent of Latina/o children live in single-parent families, the overwhelming majority of which are headed by a female. For some Latina/o groups such as Puerto Ricans, some of the increase in children living in single-parent households is due, as we noted earlier, to the increasing number of children born outside legal marriage. Like African and Native Americans, Latina/o families generally are more likely than others to live in poverty (23 percent). On the other hand, in 2004, 34 percent of Latina/o families had an income of $50,000 or more. And almost one-half (47 percent) of all Latinas/os owned their own home (U.S. Census Bureau, 2006; DeNavas-Walt, Proctor, and Lee, 2005). Generally, Latina/o family households consist not only of immediate but also extended family members, an increasing number of mothers are working outside the home, and young children in these families are increasingly less likely to be under the exclusive care of their parents (del Pinal and Singer, 1997).

Parenting in Puerto Rican Families Although there is little research that focuses specifically on child-rearing patterns among Latinas/os, one can glean from existing research that some Latina/o groups, such as Puerto Ricans, exhibit an emphasis on family interdependence and unity. Among Puerto Ricans, females are charged with the responsibility of creating and maintaining these values in offspring. In general, the Puerto Rican parenting style can be characterized as authoritarian. Children are rarely consulted on matters that directly affect them. They are viewed as passive people whose attitudes and behavior must be completely shaped by the parents. Good behavior is taken for granted, and reasons for punishment are seldom offered. Physical punishment is frequently used, especially by parents with the least social mobility and status. Parents born in Puerto Rico, more so than those born or raised in the United States, tend to per-

petuate, although with some modifications, a double standard of conduct between the sexes. Females are trained to be modest, and overt expressions of affection are more common with girls than boys. Furthermore, mothers tend to be warmer and more playful with children than fathers are and interact more frequently with daughters than with sons.

Parenting in Mexican American Families Machismo, sex, and age grading characterize Mexican American families and child-rearing patterns. For example, female children are socialized into the roles and skills of wife and mother early on because they will carry them out both in the absence of the mother and as a future wife and mother. In contrast, after puberty the eldest male has authority over the younger children as well as his older sisters because he is expected to take on the responsibility for the family in his father's absence and for his own family as a future father (Becerra, 1998). Although Mexican American child rearing is mother-centered, some scholars have suggested that contemporary Mexican American fathers share more in child care than in the past as more Mexican American mothers enter the work force (Zavella, 1987; Mirande, 1988).

Parenting in Cuban American Families Cubans, on the other hand, particularly second-generation Cubans raised in the United States, show a lesser inclination to embrace machismo or traditional sex roles. Because Cubans value lineality, children are expected to conform and to obey their parents and elders in general. In addition, Cubans have been found to endorse a "doing" orientation that emphasizes success-oriented activities, which are usually externally measurable. As a result, they tend to judge themselves and others by what the person achieves (Suarez, 1998). This value, no doubt, is transmitted to offspring during the socialization process.

Family Strengths and Resiliency Like other families of color who have experienced racism, prejudice, and within-group social problems such as gang membership and violence, male violence, drug abuse, a high school dropout rate, teenage pregnancy, and female-headed families, Latina/o families exhibit amazing strength and resiliency. They have maintained family values and ties and adapted positively to a variety of changing social, political, and economic circumstances. This is particularly true for Latina/o immigrants who must not only learn a new language but also adjust to a new and sometime hostile environment. Some researchers have identified a number of family strengths characteristic of Latina/o families, including family unity and cohesion, extended family support networks, a strong family focus and ethnic identity, religious orientation, and flexibility of family roles (Vega, 1995).

Asian and Pacific Islander Americans Perhaps more than for any other racial or ethnic group in the United States, it is difficult to talk about Asian American and Pacific Islander family type and structure, even in general terms. Although they are often lumped together, these two groups include people from a wide variety of countries (20 or more) whose cultures (representing more than 60 different ethnicities), including language (more than 100 different languages), religion, and customs, differ greatly. With this in mind, the following represents a brief discussion of Asian and Pacific Islander family structure in aggregate terms.

Family Structure Along with whites, Asian and Pacific Islanders have the highest percentage of married-couple families (81 percent) and the lowest percentage of female-headed families (11 percent) than all other major racial or ethnic groups in the United States. Asian and Pacific Islander families tend to be somewhat large; for instance, roughly one-fourth (23 percent) of married-couple families have five or more members. In most Asian and Pacific Islander families, a language other than English is spoken at home by both the younger and older generations. And in cities such as New York, one out of five Asian children in the public school system has limited English proficiency. About 20 percent of Asian American family households include at least three wage-earning workers, many of whom (particularly Asian immigrants) work in industries with low wages and long hours. On the other hand, in 2004, over half (53 percent) of all Asian and Pacific Islanders (regardless of marital status) lived in families with incomes of $50,000 or above; and a similar percentage (52 percent) of these families lived in owner-occupied housing (U.S. Census, 2006).

Although in the aggregate only 10 percent of Asian and Pacific Islander families live below the poverty level, this figure masks the considerable variation among various populations of Asian and Pacific Islander Americans. Factors such as the country that the family migrated from, the era in which they migrated, and the education and skill levels of adult family members contribute to whether or not an Asian or Pacific Islander family will live at, below, or above the poverty level. For example, families consisting of less advantaged migrants from Southeast Asia (e.g., Laos, Cambodia) with low education and skill levels have very high levels of poverty and welfare dependency, whereas families consisting of Japanese and Taiwanese immigrants, as well as those consisting of second and third or more generations of Asian Americans, tend to have very low levels of poverty ("Half-Full or Half-Empty?," 1999; NWHIC, 2000; U.S. Census, 2000b; U.S. Census, 2006).

Asian and Pacific Islander American Parenting Styles: Commonalities and Differences Parenting styles among Asian and Pacific Islanders vary according to the degree that parents are acculturated into U.S. society. Newly immigrated or first-generation parents typically use traditional approaches based on authoritarian methods. In general, family values and child-rearing practices are similar across Asian and Pacific Islander families. Obedience and conformity, responsibility, obligation, and loyalty to the family as well as self-control and educational achievement are expected. Socialization practices are characterized by a strong parent–child bond; in traditional families there is a rigid division of roles and tasks, and children are taught to defer to their parents' wishes and commands. Discipline is typically strict and involves physical punishment. In contrast, acculturated parents are generally more nurturing and verbal and give their children more autonomy (Kitano and Daniels, 1995; Min,

1998). Like Native American and other families in the United States, parenting styles and child-rearing practices vary among Asian and Pacific Islander families by social class as well as degree of acculturation. For example, older Korean immigrant parents whose children were born in Korea are more authoritarian and controlling of their children's behavior than their younger middle-class counterparts. The more educated Korean parents are, the more liberal they are in their child-rearing practices. Although somewhat moderated from practices in Korea, Korean American parents engage in very rigid, gender-based socialization practices for their daughters and sons. For example, Korean American mothers feel that certain chores, such as setting the table, should be done only by girls (Min, 1998).

Likewise, among Chinese Americans, some of the old traditional ways of child rearing have been maintained by recent immigrants. For example, parental authority, particularly the father's, is absolute. The extended family, if present, plays a much more significant role than typically is found in middle-class or more acculturated Chinese families. In upwardly mobile and middle-class Chinese families, the father maintains his authority and respect by means of a certain amount of emotional distance from his children. The mother does not interact with the children but commands and decides what is best for them, and the children are expected to obey. Although on the surface Chinese parents are seen as more indulgent with their young children than are parents in other racial and ethnic groups, discipline is much more strict than in the typical American home. Punishment is typically immediate and often involves removal from the social life of the family or the revocation of special privileges or objects rather than physical punishment. Moreover, Chinese parents stress independence and maturity in their children early on. Older children are expected to participate in the rearing of their younger siblings—serving as role models of adult behavior (Wong, 1998).

Acculturation shapes socialization practices in a number of ways. For example, among the Issei, or first generation of Japanese Americans born in Japan, male dominance, a stronger parent–child than husband–wife bond, a rigid division of gender roles and discipline of children, and the precedence of family over the individual characterize child rearing in these families. By the Nisei, or second generation, husband–wife relations take precedence over parent–child relations, and parents are less rigid in their child-rearing practices. The Sansei, or third-generation Japanese American families, are extremely likely to be interracial with biracial children. Because this generation marries, on average, later, parents tend to be, on average, older and increasingly less rigid in terms of gender role socialization and life expectations for their female and male children. However, for both the Nisei and Sansei generations of parents, close family ties and family loyalty, socialization for social control, including obligation and duty, continue to be part of the socialization practices of parents (Mirande, 1991; Takagi, 1994; Ferguson, 1995; Kitano and Kitano, 1998).

Myths and Facts One of the greatest stereotypes that Asian American families face is that of the "model minority." This stereotype can be harmful in that it does not acknowledge the differences within Asian and Pacific Islander families and thus masks many of the unique problems and strains that some of these families face. Some researchers have pointed out that the model minority myth also creates and fuels tensions and conflicts within and across Asian American subgroups as well as across other racial and ethnic groups; it camouflages ongoing racism and discrimination in U.S. society (though more subtle today) by suggesting that the United States is a meritocracy in which Asian and Pacific Islanders are the model of unparalleled achievement and success—the model for pulling oneself up by the bootstraps that all other groups should emulate. In this context, other groups are judged by the myth of the model minority, and if they have not been as successful it is due to factors endemic of them as a race and not U.S. policies and ongoing structural and institutional racism (Do, 1999; Aguirre and Turner, 2001). As has been amply pointed out in many other places, not all Asian and Pacific Islanders are as uniformly educated, acculturated, and financially successful as the myth of the "model minority" would have us believe. Like other communities, families, and individuals, Asian Americans run the gamut in terms of achievement and success.

According to the Coalition for Asian American Children and Families (1999) some facts to contradict the model minority myth include the following:

- Asian American individuals are twice as likely to be poor as non-Hispanic whites, and they have an illiteracy rate that is five times that of non-Hispanic whites.
- Asian American women have the highest suicide mortality rate among all women between the ages of 15 and 24.
- In New York City, one of the five urban centers where most Asian Americans live, almost one-half (48 percent) of Asian American births are paid for by Medicaid, indicating that the mothers are either poor or near poor.
- Twenty-four percent of Asian Americans over age 25 do not have a high school diploma and 36 percent of Asian American students in public high schools drop out or do not graduate on time.
- The number of Asian American youths arrested for major felonies increased 38 percent between 1993 and 1996.
- 17 percent of Asian American boys in fifth through twelfth grade reported physical abuse, as compared to 8 percent among white boys, and 30 percent of Asian American girls in the same grades reported depressive symptoms compared to Latinas (27 percent), white girls (22 percent), or African American girls (17 percent) in a 1998 survey by the Commonwealth Fund.

Family Strengths and Resiliency Although they have experienced a history of prejudice and discrimination in terms of U.S. policies and practices, resilience marks the character of Asian and Pacific Islander families. Asian American families have managed to maintain strong family values and ties that are transmitted to each new generation and, in some cases, high economic and educational success. Characteristics such as family obligation and loyalty to family and culture, respect and care for the elderly, an extended family network of support, a high value on education, close family ties across generations, a low divorce rate (which is considered a hallmark of family stability), and a complex system of other positive values and behaviors have helped Asian and Pacific Islander families to successfully adapt to their environments in the United States and to counter some of the deleterious effects of racism and discrimination many have experienced.

Lesbian and Gay Parents

No one knows with any certainty how many lesbian and gay parents there are because many choose to keep their sexual orientation hidden in fear of discriminatory treatment. However, we do have some estimates based on the latest census data. Of the 701,733 same-sex couples in 2003, 34 percent of female unmarried-partner households and 22 percent of male unmarried-partner households had at least one child under the age of 18 living with them. Sixty-two percent of the children are white, 17 percent are African American, and 25 percent of all children living with same-sex couples are Latina/o (Simmons and O'Connell, 2003; gaydemographics.org, 2003). Prior to the 1980s, the children of lesbians and gays were primarily the product of a heterosexual marriage that ended. From the 1980s on, many children were brought into a same-sex household through adoption or through use of AI or assisted reproductive technology, including surrogacy. On the high side, estimates are that between 6 and 14 million children have at least one lesbian or gay parent (Johnson, and O'Connor, 2002). A more conservative estimate is that between 1 and 9 million children ages 19 and under are being raised by a lesbian or gay parent (Stacey and Biblarz, 2001). These numbers challenge traditional notions about families and parenting while at the same time they point out that many lesbians and gays, like their "straight" counterparts, view parenting as a rewarding endeavor (Macionis, 2005).

The body of research on lesbian and gay parenting and the outcome of their child-rearing practices is still relatively small, but growing. Among the general population there is still considerable controversy over lesbian and gay parenting. However, credible scientifically conducted studies have found no harmful effects on children who are raised by lesbian and gay parents. In fact, the American Academy of Pediatrics (Perrin, 2002), the American Psychological Association (Patterson, 1995), the American Academy of Family Physicians (2002, 2003), and the National Association of Social Workers (Vallianatos, 2002) have all concluded that lesbian and gay parents perform just as well as heterosexual parents. According to Charlotte Patterson (1992), there can be positive effects of being raised by lesbian or gay parents. For example, having a nontraditional adult role model gives children a greater appreciation of diversity. In addition, having a parent who is different can make it easier for a child to be different and independent. The child might be more tolerant, accepting, and less judgmental because she or he has been taught to accept social and personal differences in others. This seems to be true for the sons of gay men studied by clinical psychologist Orson Morrison. These men reported feeling more multifaceted and freer from rigid gender roles than children of heterosexual parents because their fathers provided an alternative model of masculinity (cited in Kuzman, 2005).

More recently, Jennifer Wainwright and her colleagues (2004) compared 44 adolescents being raised by female same-sex couples with 44 being raised by heterosexual couples and matched the children from the two groups on many traits. They found that across a wide range of assessment, the personal, family, and school adjustments of adolescents living with same-sex parents did not differ from that of adolescents living with heterosexual parents. When problems do arise, often it is due not to the sexual orientation of the parents but rather to outside influence and interference and the degree to which society accepts the negative stereotypes of lesbian and gay parents. As one young woman said, "It wasn't having a gay father that made growing up a challenge, it was navigating a society that did not accept him and, by extension, me" (Garner, 2002).

Findings such as these notwithstanding, many people continue to believe that growing up in a lesbian or gay household is problematic—it is emotionally unhealthy for children and can cause confusion about their own sexuality. However, rather than a negative influence on their children's development, research indicates that the outcomes for children in these families tend to be better than average. Lesbian mothers and their children (of both sexes), for instance, have similar patterns of gender identity development to children of heterosexual parents at comparable ages, and they display no differences in intelligence or adjustment. Children of lesbians and gays are generally understanding, adaptable, and accepting of their parents' lifestyle, and they are as well adjusted as children who grow up in heterosexual households. This does not mean that there are no differences between children raised in lesbian and gay households and children raised in heterosexual households. For example, in a systematic review of the research on lesbian and gay parenting, sociologists Judith Stacey and Timothy Biblarz (2001) found that children of same-sex couples are as emotionally healthy and socially adjusted, and are at least as educationally and socially successful, as children raised by heterosexual parents; but these researchers also found that children raised by lesbian and gay parents feel less confined by gender roles and are more likely to have had or considered same-sex relationships even though they are not more likely to self-identify as lesbian, gay, or bisexual than children of heterosexual couples. They also found in a few studies that sons of lesbians play less aggressively, that children of lesbians communicate their feelings more freely and aspire to a wider range of occupations, and that sons of gays are also less likely to show aggression than are sons of heterosexuals.

Thus, it seems clear from most studies that quality parenting and not sexual orientation is the critical determinant of children's development (Wainwright, Russell, and Patterson, 2004). As we will see when we consider divorce in Chapter 12 and remarriage in Chapter 13, it is not family structure per se that determines outcomes for children, but rather it is the quality of the parenting. Children who have a close relationship with their parents fare better than children who do not, regardless of family structure or their parents' sexual orientation.

Not all lesbian and gay parenting is "out" in the open. In the past and still today, some lesbian and gay parents have remained secretive and protective of their children, fearing that open disclosure might cost them custody of their children. For instance, gay parents Steven James and Todd Herrmann, worry that their sons, Greg and Max, 4, might be taken away from them if they travel to visit Steven's parents in Oklahoma, one of 11 states that do not recognize adoptions by same-sex couples (Dingfelder, 2005). Thus, as long as homophobia continues to exist, getting a representative sample of children of lesbian and gay couples will remain problematic. Clearly, more research is needed if we are to understand the full range of lesbian and gay parenting. Most of the current research consists of white, middle-class samples, partly due to their greater visibility and willingness to participate in research. Relatively little is known about upper class lesbian and gay parents with the exception of celebrities like Rosie O'Donnell. The same is true for working-class and lesbians and gays of color. Although we know that children of lesbians and gays studied to date do not differ in significant ways from children raised by heterosexuals, we still cannot say with certainty whether the children studied are typical of the general population of children raised by lesbian and gay couples (Meezan and Rauch, 2005).

Single Parents

The number of single-parent families has increased dramatically over the past two decades as both the divorce rate and the number of children born outside of legal marriage have increased. As we have indicated, more than one-third of all births in the United States are now to single mothers. Although the percentage of single parents has increased most dramatically in the last 20 to 25 years, the fact is that the percentage of births to single women in this society has been steadily increasing since the 1950s. According to some experts, half of the children born today will live in a single-parent family before they reach adulthood.

Popular images of single parenthood present a dichotomous picture of these parents as primarily women who are either white, affluent, college-educated professionals, near or at the end of their childbearing years, or girls who are black, poor, young (teenaged), and high school dropouts. However, the data call these assumptions into question. As we discussed in Chapter 6, although the majority of single mothers are poor or working class, poorly educated, and have few marketable skills, they are also both racially and ethnically diverse and are more frequently in their 20s and 30s. Nonetheless, regardless of race or gender, single parents must accomplish the same parenting tasks and goals as two-parent families. These families face many of the same challenges and rewards of parenting as other types of families. However, the situation of single parents, particularly for female single parents, carries a unique set of challenges, not the least of which is related to their economic position. A family's resources are strongly influenced by the number of parents and/or wage earners in the household.

Female-headed families, are of concern not because they are inherently problematic but because people living in female-headed families typically have access to fewer economic or human resources than people in married-couple families. There are fewer potential earners in female-headed families, which partially explains their lower household income. Another part of the equation is the differential

Actress and single mom Angelina Jolie, pictured with her two adopted children Maddox (Cambodian) and Zahara (Ethiopian), is an example of a growing number of single women, especially celebrities, choosing single parenthood. Although Jolie gave birth to her third child (first biological), fathered by boyfriend Brad Pitt, in May 2006 and the couple said they planned to adopt more children, the actress remained single. Unlike Jolie, however, most single mothers are poor or working class, poorly educated, and have few marketable skills.

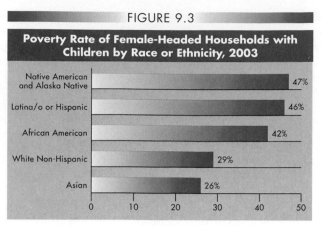

FIGURE 9.3

Poverty Rate of Female-Headed Households with Children by Race or Ethnicity, 2003

Native American and Alaska Native	47%
Latina/o or Hispanic	46%
African American	42%
White Non-Hispanic	29%
Asian	26%

Source: M. Mather, K. Rivers, and L. Jacobsen, 2005, "The American Community Survey," *Population Bulletin.* 60, 3 (September): Figure 7, p. 16. Washington, DC: Population Reference Bureau.

earning power of women and men in the American labor force (we discuss this issue in more detail in Chapter 10). In addition, delinquent child support payments from absent fathers also erode economic resources available to many female-headed families. In 2000, only about 35 percent of female-headed families with children reported receiving child support or alimony payments (Annie E. Casey Foundation, 2003, 2005). Given this context, children living in female-headed families are particularly vulnerable to poverty. In 2003, for instance, about 37 percent of families maintained by women with children were poor, nearly six times the rate for married couples with children. Poverty rates were highest for female-headed families headed by Native American and Alaska Native women, Latinas, and African American women and lowest for Asian American and white non-Hispanic women (see Figure 9.3). As we have observed elsewhere, the high poverty rates for Native Americans reflect, in part, the geographic isolation of many Native American ethnic groups in rural communities and on reservations that are cut off from employment opportunities. Furthermore, children in lower-income families (families with income below 200 percent of the official poverty level) are more likely to live with a single mother and less likely to live with two married

parents than are higher-income children (Mather, Rivers, and Jacobsen, 2005).

Whether the single parent is divorced or never married seems an important indicator of the quality of life for children in these families. For example, children living with divorced single mothers typically have an economic advantage over children living with a mother who has never married. This might be accounted for, in part, because divorced parents are typically older, have higher levels of education, and have higher incomes than parents who never married. In terms of race and ethnicity, white single-mother families are more likely to be the result of a marital disruption (50 percent were divorced) than having never married (30 percent), whereas African American single mothers are the most likely to be never married (65 percent) and the least likely to be divorced (17 percent). African American and Latina single mothers are also more likely than white single mothers to live in an extended family household (Fields and Casper, 2001).

These trends have important implications for the well-being of children and families and the programs and policies that relate to welfare, family leave, and other areas of work and family life. Studies show that children reared in these families tend to drop out of school, to become delinquent, to have emotional problems, to get pregnant as teenagers and give birth outside of legal marriage, to be at greater risk for drug and alcohol addiction, to end up on welfare, to be poor as adults, and to get divorced more often than children from two-parent families (Whitehead, 1993; Worthington, 1994; Potok, 1995; Wallerstein and Blakeslee, 1996). Moreover, the economic challenges that single mothers face are exacerbated by race. Women of color are confronted with the same challenges as white women but added to these is the challenge of institutional racism.

Although these problems are typically attributed to the absence of a father, according to Andrew Cherlin (1981), the most detrimental aspect of the father's absence from female-headed families is not the lack of a male presence but rather the lack of a male income. Recent research confirms that poverty and inadequate income are major threats to children's well-being and development regardless of how many parents are present. Although child poverty is much higher in the United States than in other Western countries, it is not an unalterable fact of nature that children born to single mothers have to grow up poor. Whereas social policies in the United States express disapproval of single parents, social policies in other Western countries support the well-being of the children (Skolnick and Rosencrantz, 1994).

Single Fathers As the number of married-couple families generally as well as those with children have decreased, as marital and relationship breakups and unmarried pregnancies have increased, there has been an explosion in the number of single-father homes. For example, in about 1 U.S. household out of every 45, a father is raising his offspring without the mother present. This represents a 62 percent increase in such households from 1990 to 2003—to 2.3 million compared to an increase of just 25 percent in single-mother homes and a 200 percent increase since 1970 (from 0.7 percent to 2.3 percent). And if we add to this those fathers who are sole caregivers to their children on a part-time basis, we have a formidable population (Davis, 1998; National Center for Policy Analysis, 2001; Census Bureau, 2004). Recent census data indicate that a little less than one-half (42 percent) of these single fathers are divorced, 39 percent have never married, 15 percent are separated, and 4 percent are widowed. The increase in single-father parenting has occurred across all racial groups; however, white fathers (22 percent of all white single parents) are twice as likely as African American fathers (10 percent of all African American single parents) to be the sole head of household (U.S. Census Bureau, 2000a). Nevertheless, a growing number of African American men who are divorced, widowed, or who have never married are confronting the economic and social challenges of single parenthood and are willingly providing a loving and nurturing environment for their children. According to many observers, on any given day, African American single fathers cook, clean, do dishes, potty train, comb hair, and perform other family chores without the help of a partner.

Some experts say that fathers' desire to be involved with their children is to the twenty-first century what women's desire to be in the workplace was to the twentieth century (Goldberg, 2001). These fathers are shattering the myth that fathers lack nurturing skills. Still, men are far less likely than women to take family leave, and despite the surge in the number of stay-at-home fathers, they remain a much rarer breed than stay-at-home mothers (Rubin, 2000).

Compared with single-parent mothers, single-parent fathers tend to be older, better off financially, have a higher level of education, hold full-time professional or higher-level jobs, and have a much higher median income than their female-headed counterparts (Census Bureau, 2006). They also tend to be highly motivated parents. Some experts believe, however, that an important factor contributing to the increase in single fathers is not just more men wanting to be involved with their children but rather a growing willingness on the part of mothers to cede primary custody. For example, fathers typically get custody of their children belatedly. That is, most courts in the United States are still more likely to award custody to mothers than fathers; thus, when a father does get custody it is usually with the mother's consent.

A recent trend in unwed parenting is unmarried fathers who are fighting for babies placed for adoption by the birth mother. Although one in every three American babies has unwed parents, the fact is that fathers' rights are an unsettled area. For example, what are the rights of unmarried fathers when the birth mother chooses adoption? In most states, unwed fathers who show a desire for involvement when the birth mother chooses adoption are required to put their names on a registry. In some states, an unwed father must actually claim paternity; in others, just the possibility of paternity. The deadlines range from 5 to 30 days after the birth of the child or any time before an adoption petition is filed. In most states, fewer than 100 men register each year, primarily because most have never heard of the registry. For instance, in 2004, the Florida registry had just 47 registrants for the 89,436 unwed births that occurred in the state that year. One exception is the state of Indiana, where men are notified of the registry when a birth mother names them as the father. Consequently, in that state, more than 50 men per week register (Lewin, 2006). Although there are no reliable statistics on how many unmarried fathers seek to raise babies the birth mother relinquished to adoption, recent publicized cases of fathers fighting for their rights to either raise their children or be a part of their lives might be a growing trend.

The flip side of unwed fathers fighting to raise their babies, are those unwed fathers who are unwilling to become fathers. Recently, for instance, a Michigan man, who says he was tricked into fatherhood, sued, he said, to establish his and other men's right to decide whether or not to have children. Supporters of the man are calling his case "*Roe* v. *Wade for Men*"—a precedent-setting case that could define a man's right to choose parenthood (Graham, 2006:3). The man, 25-year-old Matthew Dubay, claims that he told his girlfriend that he was not ready to have children. The girlfriend allegedly responded that she was infertile and on birth control pills just in case. However, when the woman became pregnant she refused his request that she terminate the pregnancy. After the birth of the child she obtained a court order requiring Dubay to pay child support. Subsequently, Dubay sued back, claiming that men have a constitutional right to "avoid" procreation. Dubay's case is the first to test the constitutional freedom to choose not to be a father under the equal protection clause of the U.S. Constitution. Dubay is one of a small number of men who argue they were duped into having children they never wanted and then forced to assume financial responsibilities for which they are unprepared. It seems that, to date, the courts have been very clear on this matter, ruling that the child's interest in receiving support overrides any interests the father may have. According to many experts in this area of reproductive rights, the argument that men do not have the same reproductive rights as women is an artificial argument. They argue that if a man wants to avoid parenthood, there are many steps he can take beyond accepting the word of a woman or expecting a woman to take sole responsibility for the prevention of pregnancy. For example, what about men accepting responsibility—like using condoms? (Graham, 2006).

In any case, like single mothers, single fathers must balance the added demands of child care and maintain a satisfactory relationship with the noncustodial parent. Fathers who adapt well typically have higher incomes, had been involved in housework and child care during the time they were married, and actively sought custody of the children at the time of the breakup. They are also more likely to have the mother actively in the picture, sharing involvement with the children on a regular basis. This means that single fathers can often come very close to approximating an intact or nuclear family. Single mothers, on the other hand, often have to go it alone. When these factors are not present, fathers are more likely to experience difficulty in parenting.

Although there is an increase in fathers parenting alone, for a significant number of families, fathers are absent. In addition, in whole neighborhoods fathers are scarce. According to statistics reported by Carol Jouzaitis (1995), about one in four children living in single-mother families were living in areas where single-mother families constituted more than one half of all families. This phenomenon is a growing trend in states around the country. In Illinois, one in eight children live in a neighborhood where fathers are scarce, compared with the national average of one in fourteen. The Illinois rate is surpassed in states such as Alabama, Maine, Massachusetts, Michigan, Mississippi, and New York. In fact, New York has the highest rate of all states, with one in six children living in communities that consist predominantly of single mothers. These data underscore the connection between poverty and family structure. One of the primary reasons that many fathers are absent from the home is unemployment and low wages. According to Jouzaitis, the median wages for young men between the ages of 25 and 34 have fallen 28 percent over the past two decades. Many of these young men lack the education and skills to successfully compete in today's labor force and thus to be able to contribute to the support of their children.

All too often the focus on single-parent families is on the problems they face. This gives the impression that single parenting is inherently problematic and that there is absolutely nothing positive about the experience. We know, however, that this is not the case. The amount of resources and availability of support systems available to single parents, like other parents, will determine the degree to which parenting will be more rewarding than challenging. Studies have identified many benefits of growing up in a single-parent family. One of these benefits is that there are more opportunities for the children to be androgynous—they experience less pressure to conform to rigid gender-appropriate roles and more opportunity to experience a wide range of social roles. Studies have also consistently shown that children raised by a single parent tend to be more mature and have a stronger sense of self than children in two-parent families (Lauer and Lauer, 1991).

Teenaged Parents

As we have indicated, teenage pregnancy is particularly unsettling given that the majority of teen mothers live in or will live in poverty. Unfortunately, however, rather than develop programs that adequately address this issue, as a culture we blame unmarried teenaged parents, especially mothers, for the majority of family and societal problems. The current trend of delayed marriage and childbearing, especially among the middle and affluent classes, is used as a measuring rod against which teenage fertility and parenting are inappropriately judged (Scott-Jones, 1996).

As in many other areas of life, teenage pregnancy is exacerbated by race and class. The typical teenaged mother in the United States today is white, in her late teens, and she is more likely to have a child outside of legal marriage than her counterparts in other industrialized countries. However, a disproportionately higher percentage of teenagers and young adults of color, particularly African Americans, Native Americans, and Latinas, are unmarried teenage mothers. In addition, a major factor impacting teenage mothers, particularly those of color, is a high unemployment rate and declining wages for both women and men. Some critics of teenage pregnancy and childbearing attribute its incidence to the availability of welfare. They suggest that welfare is a substitute for a husband's income and encourages teenage pregnancy, especially among poor teenagers. However, research studies show that the role of welfare is relatively small. There is very little evidence to support the conclusion that many unmarried teenagers deliberately allow themselves to become pregnant to collect welfare payments. Nonetheless, significant challenges to the traditional welfare system that began in the closing years of the twentieth century continue today.

In any event, early motherhood places tremendous demands on teenaged mothers who, like their adult counterparts, are generally raising their children without much support (financial or emotional) from the fathers. Like older mothers, teenaged mothers are responsible for managing the developmental tasks of parenting. Many young mothers manage these tasks quite well. Continued education, as well as social and financial support from family and friends, appear to be some of the predictors of the unmarried teenager's ability to successfully meet the unique challenges of childbearing and child rearing. Most teenaged mothers are no less nurturant and caring than are adult mothers. However, some early research (for example, Miller and Moore, 1990) found that some unmarried teenaged mothers interact less frequently and are less expressive with their children than are many older mothers. According to this research, teen mothers are also much more likely to have financial problems and other stresses and less likely to be able to control their emotions in the child rearing process.

As with single mothers generally, however, research shows that although a male role model in single-parent families may be needed to meet the challenges of parenting, their importance may be overrated. For instance, a national study by researchers at Ohio State University, comparing teens raised in single-parent households, found that children raised by single mothers were doing just as well as those raised by single fathers. These findings counter the notion that children in single-mother households are disadvantaged simply because there is no father present. The sex of the single parent does not play a crucial role in raising children, but time spent with children and the opportunities and stability provided them makes a significant difference. The most critical factor in a child's well-being in any form of family is a close, nurturant relationship with at least one parent. In sum, what matters in children's well-being is the parent's economic and interpersonal investment in her or his children, not her or his gender (Parenting, 1999).

Teenaged Fathers   Like adult unmarried fathers, teenaged unmarried fathers are all too often left out of the parenting equation, both in terms of our perspectives on parenting and their responsibilities in parenting. We continue to see teenaged fathers in terms of stereotypes and myths of them being streetwise, gangbangers, or potentially so—macho males who sexually exploit a long string of women; count their offspring as notches in their belt of armor of manliness; are often illiterate, unemotional, and incapable of caring about another person; have only a passing and casual relationship with the mother; do not support the child financially by choice; and do not want to be emotionally involved in the rearing of their children.

Research on single fathers generally and teenaged fathers specifically is limited. However, according to the research

Teenage fathers, especially unwed fathers, are often ignored in discussions of teenage pregnancy and childbirth. However, many young men not only want to be, but are actively involved in child rearing. Like this father trying to study and care for his son, they sometimes find they must juggle multiple roles.

that does exist, contrary to popular belief, many young teenage fathers acknowledge paternity of their children and actively seek to be involved in the rearing of their children. Many are at the hospital at the time of the birth of their children, and many sign records indicating their paternity. And, many provide some child-care support as their financial situation allows. In one study of young fathers, many of the young men studied negotiated a set of rights and responsibilities with the mothers before the birth of their children. These rights and responsibilities included not only themselves but oftentimes their own parents as well. Although these relationships were often fragile, in many cases the young father began support and care for the child during pregnancy, and he and his family, usually his mother, worked out a process of child care and support after the child was born (Lerman and Ooms, 1993). A report on Latino gang members acknowledges the strong family ties among gang members and how parenthood among some male gang members reversed their behavior during impending fatherhood, the result being that they consciously sought to be a part of the childbirth and child-rearing process. One gang member cited, for example, divested himself of gang symbols such as tattoos and a bald head and actively sought legitimate work when his 17-year-old girlfriend became pregnant with their child (Mydans, 1995).

Although our knowledge of parenting styles among teenaged unmarried fathers is limited, as we have already indicated, we do know that in general fathers who are involved in the socialization of their children—who are involved in child care—have a more positive impact on their children than fathers who do not and, in turn, these fathers experience a greater degree of emotional and psychological benefit and well-being from the parent–child interaction than do traditional fathers. Research has shown consistently that children who are highly interactive with their fathers (whether teenaged or older adult) are characterized by higher levels of cognitive competence, increased empathy, and less sex-typed beliefs and behaviors.

Teenage childbirth affects many areas of social life, and as we have indicated, it is not limited to racial and ethnic groups of color. It is deeply rooted in many of our society's social problems and cannot be understood simply on an individual level. From a sociological perspective, in analyzing teenage births and parenting, we must consider structural and institutional factors such as the continuing individual and structural racism, sexism, and class bias that is extant in U.S. society; the bleak economic picture for many individuals and families in the twenty-first century, especially teenagers of color; the proliferation of drugs in the United States, especially in those communities that are least able to fight them; and a mass media that continues to romanticize and popularize sexual themes and set standards about appropriate sexual behavior, often encouraging sexual intercourse and pregnancy, to name but a few. When we consider the link between individual experiences of unmarried childbirth and social structure, it helps us understand the socially constructed nature of teenage childbearing as a social phenomenon and directs us to seek remedies in terms of institutional and structural change rather than focusing on alleged individual pathologies.

WRITING YOUR OWN SCRIPT

TO PARENT OR NOT?

A major life choice many of us will make regardless of whether we choose to marry is whether we will parent. Choosing to parent will have significant consequences for us in terms of the time, energy, and resources required to perform this critical task. The parenting decision not only affects our personal lives, but also affects the life of the society. Fertility rates and the consequent size and composition of a nation's population have enormous social implications. In the past, it was almost a foregone conclusion that a woman would reproduce. Deciding whether or not to parent today is much more a matter of choice than it was in the past.

Questions to Consider

1. Do you want children? For what reasons? What do you have to offer children? What do you expect to receive from the children you may have? How many children do you want? If you or your partner are infertile, will you consider alternatives for having children? Would you consider adoption? Any of the new reproductive technologies?
2. What advantages and disadvantages are there to being child-free? What are your options if you or your partner have an unwanted pregnancy? Are there any conditions under which you would consider abortion? Putting a child up for adoption? If you do not want children now or in the future, will you use contraception? What kind? How will you reach agreement on this with your partner? Explain.
3. What kind of parenting style did you experience in your childhood? Looking back, are you satisfied with this parenting style? What parenting style do you think you would be most comfortable enacting with your own children? Why?

SUPPORTING PARENTS AND CHILDREN

Clearly, today's marriages and families do not fit the mold forged by 1960s and 1970s family sitcoms. For instance, in 2003, a single gay father and his three adopted sons were honored as the National Adoption Center's Family of the year. This recognition is not so earth-shattering in-and-of-itself, rather it is indicative of the profound changes in the structure and definition of family occurring in today's society—a change that some people find heartening and others horrifying (Crary, 2003). No matter one's position on this issue, the fact is that all types of marriages and families deserve support.

Although many individuals and families receive sustained support from their families and friends, federal, state, local, and community policies are needed to supplement that support for those who need it. More community and private initiatives such as the Alternative to Marriage Project (AtMP)—a national nonprofit organization advocating equality and fairness for unmarried people, including people who choose not to marry, cannot marry, or live together before marriage—are needed to embrace the diversity of American marriages and families and provide them support. Moreover, politicians must work to reverse or eliminate legislation that discriminates against and/or excludes marriages and families based on definitions biased by conservative politics. This would include granting same-sex partners the same rights and responsibilities as married heterosexual couples and not limiting their right to adopt children. In addition, there is a pressing need for federal, state, and local policies as well as various initiatives aimed at improving the health of mothers and reducing the increasingly high infant mortality rate in this country. We must also find ways to educate individuals, especially youth, to practice safe and responsible sexual behavior and, when pregnancy does occur, to provide the support that these parents (females and males) need to have healthy and sustaining lives.

That an overwhelming majority of parents today rate their parenting as fair or poor is indicative of the fact that parents across diversities are struggling with issues of parenting. A recent national survey revealed a significant gap between parents' efforts to teach their children *good* values and their perceived success in so doing. Most parents believe it is essential to the viability and strength of families to teach children self-discipline, self-control, and honesty. Yet most parents do not think that they have succeeded with these parental tasks. Interestingly, over one-half of today's parents think they are doing a worse job at parenting than did their own parents (Matthews, 2006). Data such as these suggest that despite parents' desires and efforts, they are having trouble parenting and they point all the more to the need for both internal and external support for families and children. Along with government policies and support, communities can play important roles in helping individuals, marriages, families, and parents succeed even in high-risk areas by providing programs for prenatal health care, parental education, job training, child abuse prevention, and other support services. It really does "take a village to raise a child."

Finally, for the most part, throughout most of our discussions of supporting marriages and families, we have stressed the role of social institutions and social policies that can help support marriages and families. There are, however, growing examples of how private enterprise is helping to support marriages and families by helping overextended families. For example, a persistent complaint of working parents is the lack of time they have to spend with family members. Working, grocery shopping, planning and preparing nutritious dinners can be overwhelming for many. More often than most parents would like, family meals end up being take-out pizza or other fast foods. Now there is another option. Cook-and-carry companies, such as Dinners Together, Dream Dinners, and Dinner by Design, are springing up all across the country. They are taking over the tasks of menu planning, shopping, chopping, slicing, and cleanup so that families can spend their time enjoying a meal together without all the time and work that is usually required in preparation. Customers, both females and males, can go into commercial kitchens run by these companies, choose which menus they want and then, following the recipes, assemble dishes like cheesy chicken casserole and Salisbury steak from ingredients that have already been prepared for them. At Dream Dinners, for instance, customers can make 12 dinners for six in about 2 hours for $200. Among the several advantages of this kind of support is that spouses and children can easily help with getting dinner on the table. Of course, not all families can afford this service, but for many families the expenditure for two weeks of healthy meals prepared this way is less than what they spend at fast-food restaurants or for take outs and the time saved can be spent enjoying the companionship of all family members.

SUMMARY

At the beginning of the nineteenth century, the U.S. fertility rate was quite high. Since that time it has steadily declined to its current low rate, with the notable exception of the "baby boom" of the late 1940s and 1950s. Fertility rates vary across race and class; people of color and low-income groups have the highest rates.

Deciding whether to parent involves an evaluation of both the costs and benefits. Increasing numbers of people are deciding to be child-free or to delay parenting until their 30s or even 40s and beyond. During the mid-nineteenth century the use of contraceptives and abortion became illegal. After a long struggle, the Supreme Court invalidated laws prohibiting contraceptives, and in 1973 in *Roe* v. *Wade* it recognized a woman's right to an abortion. Since that time many efforts have been made to restrict abortion, and abortion has become a major issue in states like South Dakota as well as in national politics.

The decline in the fertility rate, the legalization of abortion, and the tendency for more unmarried mothers to keep their babies have led to a scarcity of infants available for adoption. New reproductive technologies have been developed to help infertile couples achieve their desire to have children. These new reproductive techniques present many legal, ethical, and social challenges and raise questions about the nature of parenthood and the meaning of families. Social policy is only slowly emerging to deal with these questions.

Conception, pregnancy, and childbirth have a tremendous effect on the lives of individuals and couples. Conception begins with the fertilization of an egg by a sperm. Once pregnancy is confirmed, the woman should get immediate and continuous prenatal care. Research indicates that a number of factors, especially age, race, and class, affect the prenatal attitudes and behaviors of pregnant women. Poor women and women of color are at a higher risk of receiving inadequate prenatal care because of a lack of economic resources. As a consequence, babies born to these women are at greater risk of birth defects, diseases, and other physical or medical problems. Some of the most common risks to the prenatal environment are poor nutrition, smoking, and drug and alcohol use. In addition, AIDS and other sexually transmitted diseases can harm the fetus.

In focusing on the pregnant woman, we often forget about the expectant father. Many expectant fathers now participate in their partner's pregnancy through a variety of actions, including taking a paternity leave for the birth of their child. Becoming a parent is a major transition in a person's life. Not all people experience parenthood in the same way. Rather, parenthood varies for individuals and groups within as well as across a number of important areas of experience: race, class, gender, age, sexual orientation, and marital status. Within all groups, however, females and males seem to experience parenting differently. Although many individuals and groups no longer adhere as strongly to the traditional gender division of labor, women nonetheless tend to spend far more time in child-rearing and housework activities than do men. In the final analysis, no matter who does the parenting, more support is needed for parenting and for those who parent.

KEY TERMS

fertility
fertility rate
total fertility rate
pronatalist attitude
antinatalist forces
contraception
abortion
infertility

assisted reproductive
  technology
artificial insemination
in vitro fertilization
embryo transplant
surrogacy
preimplantation genetic
  diagnosis

conception
zygote
ovulation
amniocentesis
ultrasound
sonogram
infant mortality rate
congenital

morbidity
mortality
fetal alcohol syndrome
HIV embryopathy
couvade
postnatal depression
motherhood mystique

QUESTIONS FOR STUDY AND REFLECTION

1. Trace and explain the changing fertility rates in the United States over the last 3 centuries. Project the patterns of fertility among various age, marital status, race, and class groupings that are most likely to develop in the first half of the twenty-first century. Explain the rationale for your projections. Discuss the implications of these changes for the society at large.

2. Discuss the legal and ethical issues surrounding assisted reproductive technology. How have these technologies affected our understanding of parenthood and families? Explain. U.S. bioethicist Daniel Callahan sees the open market in sperm as an acceptance of the systematic downgrading of fatherhood, in that men can now produce children and have no responsibility for them. Do you agree or disagree with Callahan's view? Explain. Overall, what guidelines would you recommend be established for each of the assisted reproductive technologies? Explain.

3. According to some, as a political, legal, and social issue, same-sex marriage now seems to be where interracial marriage was a half century ago. Comparing the history of interracial marriage in the U.S. with same-sex marriage, do you agree that same-sex marriage is on the same trajectory as interracial marriage or is it so fundamentally different that it will never be legalized? Explain your position.

4. What is your idea of a good mother? A good father? How do you rate yourself as a parent or prospective parent? What do you think are some of the important questions that people should ask themselves before they decide to become parents? Can men mother? Why? Why not? Does a person have to be legally married to be a good parent? Why? Why not?

ADDITIONAL RESOURCES

SOCIOLOGICAL

BENKOV, LAURA. 1994. *Reinventing the Family: Lesbian and Gay Parents*. New York: Crown. Compelling personal stories provide a close-up look at the changing face of the modern family. The author examines the growing numbers of lesbian and gay parents, discussing issues such as how to raise a child in a homophobic world, child custody, foster parenting, and child development, and presents detailed advice on a number of topics including coming out.

COLTRANE, SCOTT. 1996. *Family Man: Fatherhood, Housework, and Gender Equity*. New York: Oxford University Press. An in-depth look at the role of men in the family. The author explores and refutes many of the commonly held myths about shared parenting and examines the changing nature of the typical American family, the reasons for this change, and their implications for family roles in the future.

DEFAGO, NICKI. 2005. *Childfree and Loving It*. London: Vision. Numerous people from around the world tell the author why they chose not to have children; others tell why they wish they had not had children and the reasons for their regrets.

TONE, ANDREA. 2001. *A History of Contraceptives in America*. New York: Hill & Wang. The author provides an eye-opening look at the development of the U.S. contraceptive industry and its resilience in the face of militant attempts to suppress it.

FILM

Offspring. 2001. A documentary by Barry Stevens depicting his search for his donor father and his discovery of half-siblings.

A Midwife's Tale. 1996. An excellent docudrama based on historian Laurel Ulrich's Pulitzer Prize–winning book by the same name. The movie, about birth, healing, and love, traces the life and work of eighteenth-century midwife, Martha Ballard, a mother and wife who cared for many sick people, more than a thousand women in labor and their infant children.

LITERARY

ATWOOD, MARGARET. 1996. *The Handmaid's Tale*. New York: Fawcett Columbine. An interesting view is presented of a future society where women have lost their reproductive rights and no longer have control over their own bodies.

PARENT, MARC. 2001. *Believing It All: What My Children Taught Me about Trout Fishing, Jelly Toast & Life*. New York: Little, Brown. Wonderful poetic, contemplative, from-the-heart honest reflections of one man's journey of raising children through an incredible time and a unique view of life in the United States at the beginning of the twenty-first century.

INTERNET

http://www.resolve.org   The RESOLVE Web site offers information on issues of infertility.

http://www.100.com/Top/Parenting   A unique Web site that offers links to 100 different parenting sites. A sampling includes Movie Mom, a guide for choosing quality movies for your family; *Father Magazine*, an on-line parenting magazine for men; and At Home Mom, a site that provides resources compiled by stay-at-home parents.

http://www.babynotonboard.com/links.html   This Web site offers articles related to being child-free and provides links to resources and ways to contact others who are child-free.

www.childtrends.org   Child Trends is a nonprofit, nonpartisan research organization that produces information about a number of marriage, family and child-related issues in order to improve the decisions, programs, and policies that affect children and their families. The Web site includes a data bank indicator, press releases, a newsroom, a variety of publications, projects, and research.

IN THE NEWS

Washington, DC

In late August 2005, Hurricane Katrina, one of the costliest, most destructive, and deadly natural disasters ever to hit the United States, left an estimated 1.5 million Americans homeless along the Gulf Coast region, adding to the estimated 3.5 million American women, men, and children already homeless across the country (National Law Center on Homelessness and Poverty, (2005). Although many homeless people from the Gulf region were able to find housing with relatives and friends, hundreds of thousands had to seek emergency shelter through public and private agencies. Months after the hurricane struck, thousands of individuals and families were still living in tents, cars, barns, and the remnants of their destroyed homes. At the same time, thousands of trailers purchased by the Federal Emergency Management Agency (FEMA) sat idle because communities refused to have them in their neighborhoods (Regan, 2005).

Today's homeless population is diverse and encompasses every age, race, religion, and marital status. The homeless inhabit every region of the country, from inner-city neighborhoods to the rural countryside. If you spend any time in parks or public facilities, be they bus or train stations, libraries, or airports, you will encounter the homeless. What you will observe if you look closely is a population that includes the young and the old, the unmarried and family groups, veterans, as well as the working poor. How many Americans are currently homeless? No one can answer this question with certainty because there is no agreement on how to define homelessness. Sociologist Peter Rossi (1989) distinguishes two kinds of homelessness. The "literally homeless" are those who already live on the streets. The "precariously housed" are those who are in danger of losing their homes or who have lost their homes but have found temporary shelter. Extended families often provide support by taking in homeless relatives, sometimes exhausting their own resources in the process. Therefore, if we use the first definition only, the number of homeless we count will be smaller than if we expand our definition to include those who are poorly or only temporarily housed. Most studies of the homeless have used the first definition, thereby understating the extent of the problem. That homeless people tend to move in and out of shelters and public view on a regular basis also makes counting them difficult. Finally, we can count people only if we can locate them. Not all homeless people are in shelters. Many live in parks, cars, cardboard boxes, doorways, or other places not readily accessible to researchers. Thus, any published figures on homelessness must be interpreted with caution.

According to recent surveys of many of America's cities, one of the fastest growing segments of the homeless population is families with children, accounting for 40 percent of the homeless population. Forty-nine percent of the homeless population is African American, 35 percent Caucasian, 13 percent Latina/o, 2 percent Native American, and 1 percent Asian. Twenty-two percent of homeless people are considered mentally ill, 30 percent are substance abusers, and 11 percent are veterans. Employment does not always protect against homelessness, as evidenced by the fact that 15 percent of the homeless population are employed, and many of these are full-time, year-round workers (U.S. Conference of Mayors, 2004; Lowe, 2005).

Although experts may disagree on the exact numbers of the homeless population, researchers, social workers, public officials, and community activists are in general agreement that homelessness occurs as a result of a number of distinct but interrelated factors. First and foremost is the increase in poverty brought about by eroding employment opportunities for large segments of the workforce, including stagnant or falling wages and jobs that offer little security and few benefits. To compound this problem, in 2005, Congress failed to increase the minimum wage of $5.15, the real value of which in 2004 was 26 percent less than in 1979, worth only $4.42 in real dollars (The Economic Policy Institute, 2005). Second, there has been a rapid decline in the availability of affordable housing in recent decades. According to the National Low Income Housing Coalition Homeless (2005), in all 50 states, more than the minimum wage is required to afford a one- or two-bedroom apartment at fair market rent. During 2005, requests for emergency shelter assistance increased by an average of 6 percent over the previous year. Third, there has been a serious decline in the value and availability of public assistance. An average of

14 percent of the requests for emergency shelter by homeless people overall and 32 percent of the requests by homeless families alone are estimated to have gone unmet during 2005 (Lowe, 2005). Other factors also contribute to homelessness: mental illness, compounded by a shortage of adequate services and government policies of deinstitutionalization, family violence, adolescent runaways, substance abuse, and discrimination.

Given the many factors that contribute to homelessness, these numbers are likely to continue to increase in the years ahead. Because homelessness has many causes, no quick and easy solutions are likely. Only by a concerted effort to reduce poverty by expanding jobs that pay a living wage, increasing the supply of affordable housing, and providing support for those who cannot work can we hope to bring an end to homelessness.

WHAT WOULD YOU DO? If you suddenly found yourself homeless, where would you go? Who would you contact? What problems would you encounter on a daily basis? How would you attempt to solve them? What is your reaction when you meet a homeless person on the street? Do you think your attitude reflects that of most other people? To what extent is homelessness a personal problem or a structural problem? Do you think private efforts can solve the problem of homelessness? How is the structure and functioning of a family affected by homelessness? Whose responsibility is it to try to end homelessness? Explain.

In our society, we frequently think of work and family life as separate spheres, but as the problem of homelessness makes clear, the availability and rewards of work are major factors in the structure and functioning of families. For example, unemployment and minimum wage or declining wages for those who are employed have put decent, affordable housing out of the reach of many. When families are homeless, virtually every aspect of their lives is disrupted. Families may be separated as a result of shelter policies that deny access to older boys or fathers. Children may be placed in foster homes when their parents become homeless. In 56 percent of the 27 cities surveyed in 2004, homeless families had to break up in order to enter emergency shelters (U.S. Conference of Mayors, 2004). Throughout this chapter, our focus will be on how work and families are being transformed in the United States.

THE WORK–FAMILY CONNECTION

Research shows that the worlds of work and family affect each other in significant ways. The quality and stability of family life are dependent to a large extent on the type of work available for family members. Work provides income that determines a family's standard of living.

Because of changing economic and social conditions, a single income is no longer sufficient for most families. Many

In the aftermath of Hurricane Katrina, evacuees walk back and forth between the rows of cots at the Astrodome in Houston, Texas, holding signs with the names of their relatives in hope of finding them. Months after the hurricane, many families were still separated and others were still seeking permanent housing.

husbands remain major providers, but increasingly wives are sharing this role. As we will see throughout this chapter, reactions to these changes are mixed. Although many women want to work outside the home, some feel that doing so saddles them with a double burden—besides outside employment, they still do the majority of household and family work. Some men, relieved at not having to be the sole provider, are participating more in housework and child care. Others, frustrated by the erosion in their breadwinning role, are dispirited, especially when their working spouses make demands on them to share household tasks and child care and to be more emotionally involved in family relationships. Additionally, growing numbers of families are headed by a single parent who must fulfill both the breadwinner and homemaker roles.

Work affects families in other ways as well. It can have *spillover effects*, either positive or negative, on family life. An example of positive spillover is the carryover of satisfaction and stimulation at work to a sense of satisfaction at home. Similarly, increases in marital satisfaction are related to increases in job satisfaction (Rogers, 2003). Negative spillover involves bringing home the problems and stresses experienced at work, making adequate participation in family life difficult (Voydanoff, 1987). Family life can affect work in important ways. Family obligations can provide motivation for working hard, but problems at home, such as a child's illness, can hinder job performance as well.

This chapter focuses on the interconnection between families and work, beginning with an examination of the changing composition of the labor force, notably the increasing participation of married women with small children and the impact of this change on marriage and family structures and functioning. We also examine today's growing inequalities of wealth and resources as manifested in low income, poverty, unemployment, and underemployment, all of which have contributed to a sense of unease and perceptions of future economic uncertainty among many working families. Despite government reports of a growing economy and new job creation, recent polling data suggest that the majority of Americans are concerned about current economic conditions. As 2005 came to a close, only 39 percent of respondents rated the economic conditions in this country as excellent or good; 61 percent rated them as only fair or poor. Fifty-six percent of respondents thought that economic conditions were getting worse. These attitudes contrast with more optimistic views exhibited just 5 years ago when 63 percent of respondents rated economic conditions as excellent or good ("Consumer Views of the Economy," 2006). Similar concerns were observed in a recent Gallup poll that found that four in ten Americans said they were worried about their financial situations. It probably comes as no surprise that Americans residing in low-income households were much more likely to say they are worried than are those living in upper-income families. Sixty-four percent of adults living in households earning less than $30,000 a year said they were worried about their finances compared to 41 percent living in households earning between $30,000 and $74,999 a year and just 24 percent of those in households earning $75,000 or more per year. Women were considerably more worried than men (48 to 36 percent); and

adults 30 to 49 years old, the age group most likely to have small children, were more worried (46 percent) than were their 18- to 29-year-old peers (41 percent) or their 50- to 64-year-old peers (35 percent) (Carroll, 2005a).

People's concerns about their economic future are not unfounded. In recent decades both the U.S. and world economies have experienced major changes that have adversely affected many family budgets, often leading to declines in family functioning and family stability. For example, in the early 1990s many high-paying jobs disappeared in the United States. Between 1991 and 1992, 5.5 million workers lost jobs because their plant or company closed or moved, there was insufficient work for them to do, or their positions or shifts were abolished (Gardner, 1995). Although approximately 75 percent of those workers found work, slightly less than a third found full-time jobs with earnings the same as or higher than those of the lost job. During the 1980s and well into the 1990s, the real earnings of most male workers remained stagnant or fell. A study by the Economic Policy Institute found that only in 1997 was the typical American family able to match the income it enjoyed in 1989. This recovery came not from an improvement in real wages but through an increase in the number of hours worked, an estimated 247 more hours per family, or approximately 6 additional weeks of work (Choo, 1999). Many of these extra hours came as a result of workers taking on more than one job.

By 1999, the U.S. economy had recovered and grown, resulting in one of the country's lowest unemployment rates in more than 25 years (4.2 percent). However, in 2001 another economic slowdown was under way. Between 2001 and 2003, 11.4 million workers were displaced from their jobs. Among them, 5.3 million had held their job for 3 or more years. Yet only two-thirds of the displaced had found jobs by January 2004 and 57 percent of those displaced from full-time wage and salary jobs and who were reemployed in such jobs had earnings lower than those on the jobs lost. About one-third experienced earnings losses of 20 percent or more (Bureau of Labor Statistics, 2004). Taking just one state as an example, Idaho lost more than 8000 manufacturing jobs since 2000. The top 7000 of those jobs had an average annual wage of $40,939. Over the same period, more than 22,000 service jobs were created, but two-thirds of those had an average salary of just $19,278. As a result, 34 percent of the state's working-age population went without health insurance during all or part of 2002–2003, and lingering credit problems forced many families deeper into debt and contributed to a record 9000 bankruptcy filings in 2003 ("Loss of High-Paying Jobs . . . ," 2005). Not all families are affected equally by the experience of job loss. African Americans are more likely to be affected by job loss than are white workers and the consequences of job loss appear more severe for blacks who, on average, have fewer economic resources to sustain them during periods of unemployment. In the past, white-collar workers and professionals were less likely to be affected by economic downturns. This is much less the case today. Announcements by leading American corporations like Ford and General Motors of massive layoffs and United Airlines defaulting on its pensions along with the news of Enron's and WorldCom's collapse with the dislocation of thousands of

FIGURE 10.1

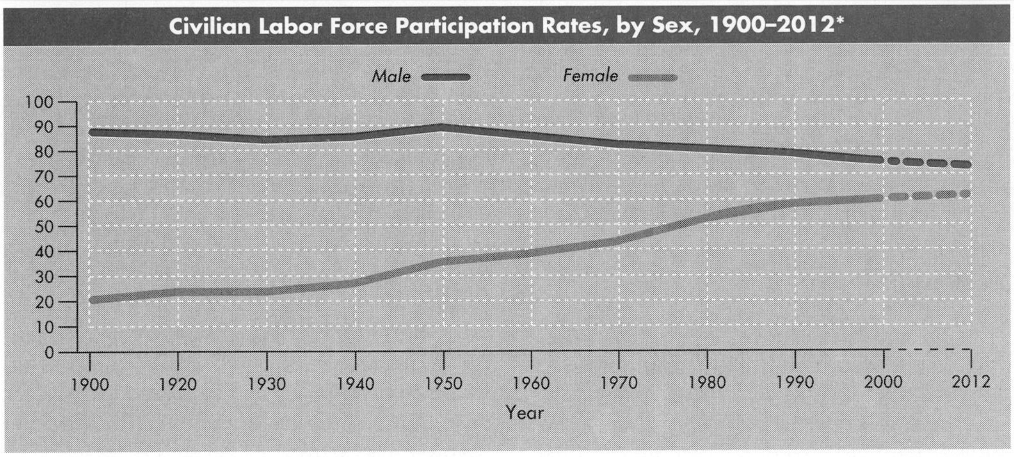

Civilian Labor Force Participation Rates, by Sex, 1900–2012*

Male ▬▬ Female ▬▬

[Line graph showing male and female civilian labor force participation rates from 1900 to 2012, with y-axis from 0 to 100 and x-axis years 1900, 1920, 1930, 1940, 1950, 1960, 1970, 1980, 1990, 2000, 2012. Male line starts near 88 and declines to about 75; female line rises from about 20 to about 62. Dotted lines represent projections for 2012.]

Year

*Dotted lines represent projections for year 2012.

Sources: Adapted from U.S. Census Bureau, 1975, *Historical Statistics of the United States, Colonial Times to 1970*, bicentennial ed., part 1 (Washington, DC: U.S. Government Printing Office): 131–32; U.S. Census Bureau, 2006, *Statistical Abstract of the United States, 2006* (Washington, DC: U.S. Government Printing Office): Table 577, p. 387.

workers has added to the anxiety among many employed workers. We will discuss these trends in more detail throughout this chapter and conclude it with an assessment of the kinds of changes that need to be made in the organization of work and in social policies to help individuals maintain a decent standard of living while also maintaining a balance between the demands of work and family.

THE TRANSFORMATION OF WORK AND FAMILY ROLES

The idealized images of men as providers and women as homemakers continued into the second half of the twentieth century despite the fact that these roles were already being undermined. Figure 10.1 traces the changes in women's and men's labor force participation rates from 1900 to 2000. The **labor force participation rate** refers to the percentage of workers in a particular group who are employed or who are actively seeking employment. If people are not employed and are not actively seeking work, they are not counted in the labor force. As the twentieth century opened, only 20 percent of women aged 14 and older were in the labor force, compared with approximately 86 percent of men in that age category. The comparable rates 100 years later were 60 percent for women and 75 percent for men 16 years of age and over. Thus, during the twentieth century the labor force participation rates for women and men have moved in opposite directions, with the result that women now constitute 47 percent of all workers, up from 18 percent in 1900. This gap between the proportion of female and male workers is expected to narrow even further in the twenty-first century, as an even higher percentage of women (61.6 percent) and a lower percentage of men (73.1 percent) are expected to be in the labor force by 2012.

The decline in the male participation rate reflects a number of changes in the U.S. economy. On the one hand, improvements in pension and other retirement benefits

have allowed older men to retire early; on the other hand, the labor market demands for better-educated workers have kept younger men in school longer and led to the displacement of workers with low levels of education and marginal skills, especially men of color.

The narrowing gap between women's and men's participation rates reveals only part of the story, however. According to historian Alice Kessler-Harris (1982), a marked shift occurred in the participation patterns of women. Prior to World War II, the majority of women workers were young, single, poor, and women of color. As Figure 10.2 shows, as late as 1975 only 36.7 percent of all married mothers with children under 6 years of age were in the labor force. However, a much higher percentage of black mothers (almost 55 percent) than

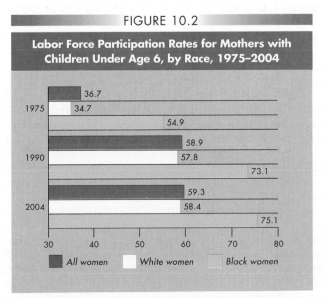

FIGURE 10.2

Labor Force Participation Rates for Mothers with Children Under Age 6, by Race, 1975–2004

[Bar graph with values:
1975: 36.7 (All women), 34.7 (White women), 54.9 (Black women)
1990: 58.9 (All women), 57.8 (White women), 73.1 (Black women)
2004: 59.3 (All women), 58.4 (White women), 75.1 (Black women)
x-axis from 30 to 80]

■ All women   □ White women   ▨ Black women

Source: Adapted from U.S. Census Bureau, 2006, *Statistical Abstract of the United States, 2006* (Washington, DC: Government Printing Office): Table 587, p. 393.

white mothers (about 35 percent) were working. Three decades later, almost six out of ten (59.3 percent) married mothers with preschool children were in the labor force. However, the gap between the percentages of working black and white mothers decreased only slightly, 75.1 to 58.4 percent. Even more noteworthy is that 54.7 percent of white married women but 70.7 percent of black married women with children 1 year old or younger were in the labor force, compared with 29.2 and 50.0 percent, respectively, in 1975.

Variations by Race, Gender, and Marital Status

Historically, labor force participation rates varied by race as well as by gender and marital status. In the past, white women were less likely than women of color to be in the labor force. As white women began to delay marriage and to divorce in greater numbers, however, their rates became similar to those of other groups of women. In 2004, the labor force participation rate for black women was 61.5 percent, followed by white women with 58.9 percent and Asian women with 57.6 percent. Latinas had the lowest rate of participation, 56.1 percent. These differences are expected to continue well into the new decade. The participation rate for white women is expected to increase slightly to 59.2 percent while black women are expected to increase their rate to 64.0 percent. Asian women's expected participation rate of 61.3 percent will surpass that of white women. Although Latinas are expected to increase their participation rate to 58.6 percent by 2012, they will continue to trail all other groups. For men, the differences in participation rates are more pronounced across race and ethnicity. Latinos lead with 80.4 percent, followed by Asian men with 75.0 percent and white men with 74.1 percent. Black men have the lowest labor force participation rates, 66.7 percent. By 2012, black and Asian men are expected to increase their participation rates, albeit slowly, while the participation rate for white men is expected to decline slightly (U.S. Census Bureau, 2006).

Reasons Women Work

Rarely do we ask men why they work—we assume they have no choice. They are expected to be family providers. But because the homemaker role was believed to be the traditional role for women, any departures from this role required explanation. According to the U.S. Department of Labor (1993), the majority of women (56 percent) work for the same reasons men do—to support themselves or their family; an additional 21 percent work to bring in extra money. Other reasons women give for working are interest and self-fulfillment.

Additionally, during the last half of the twentieth century the economy was undergoing rapid change and there was an increased demand for women workers to fill the expanding number of jobs in the service sector, such as teaching, health care, social services, government, and real estate. The women's movement and affirmative action legislation also enhanced employment opportunities for women and people of color. Additionally, social attitudes have become more accepting of working women. These factors, combined with the desire for a higher standard of living, led many women into the workplace. No single factor can explain the dramatic changes in women's labor force participation rates. Rather, a complex interplay of demographic, economic, social, political, and personal factors have contributed to these changes. For example, in contrast to women in previous eras, women today are better educated, have fewer children, and live longer. Women who postpone marriage and childbearing to increase their level of education and to begin work are more likely to remain in the labor force after the birth of their children. Advanced education influences women in much the same way that it influences men. Not only does education offer better job possibilities but it also raises awareness of personal options and creates a desire for self-expression and self-fulfillment. Women today also have more time in their total life span to pursue activities other than child rearing.

WORK AND FAMILY STRUCTURES

The rapid entrance of married women with children into the labor force has altered family life in many ways. A variety of work and family structures have emerged as a response to these economic and social transformations, creating both opportunities and problems for family members.

Traditional Nuclear Families, Including Stay-at-Home Dads

The highly idealized family structure consisting of a working husband, a wife who is a full-time homemaker, and one or more children currently represents only 7 percent of all households in the United States (Population Reference Bureau, 2003). Smaller in numbers but similar in structure are households in which husbands and fathers (popularly called househusbands) stay home to care for home and family while their wives work. The exact number of stay-at-home dads is unknown. According to the U.S. Census Bureau, there are 143,000 stay-at-home dads (Facts for Features, 2006). Others put the number as high as 2 million, claiming that the definition used by the U.S. Census Bureau is too limiting, counting only fathers with children under 15 who have remained out of the labor force for more than a year primarily to care for the family while the mother works. Thus, those who left the work force less than a year ago are not included nor are fathers who earned money whether from some home venture or part-time work. The United States is not the only country with stay-at-home dads. In 2002, Canada had about 110,000, a 25 percent increase from a decade earlier (Lai, 2005) and in the Republic of Korea the government reported there were 128,000 male homemakers ("Househusbands on the Increase," 2004).

Most men take this role on a temporary basis when they are unemployed, going to school, or able to do their work from home. In some cases, the comparative earning power of spouses dictates who stays at home. Today, one out of four wives earns more than her husband. If a wife's earnings are substantially higher than his, the family budget is improved if Dad is the one who stays home. Other stay-at-home men are retired; still others have remarried younger women and now want the opportunity to participate more fully in childrearing activities. Although most men find great personal satisfaction in caring for their children, many complain that they receive relatively little support from the larger society and often find their masculinity questioned by others. Dads like Arkady Lapidus, a former banker who cares for 11-month-old Erik, complain that people's biggest misconception is "that I can't find a job." Jeff Brice, a 35-year-old father, notes that "everybody thinks we don't know what we're doing. That's frustrating" (cited in Kepner, 2005). However, many moms, like, Darla Stencavage, a captain in the U.S. Army stationed in Fort Rucker, Alabama, know better. When they leave for work, they go with the assurance that their children will be well carried for by active and loving stay-at-home dads. According to Darla, "He is a wonderful caregiver and nurturer for me and my daughter and it really eases my mind. It was important for us to raise our own children, and I would have had to quit work if he had not been willing to stay home." Peter Stencavage not only assumed full-time parenting, he took on the role of the supportive spouse of an Army commander and participates in his wife's unit's family support group, often the only male in attendance. His public role is changing the way some people think about family roles. After he joined the club for spouses, the officers changed the name from "Officers Wives' Club" to "Officers and Civilians Spouses' Club" ("Dad of the Month," 2006).

This stay-at-home dad keeps in touch while taking his children on an outing to the park.

These men, like their female counterparts, engage in activities that some authors are now calling "home production," the nonmarket production of goods and services, usually for the family but occasionally on a volunteer basis for schools, churches, or other groups. According to sociologists Randy Hodson and Teresa Sullivan (1995), what is traditionally known as "housework" is only one aspect of home production, which also includes household budgeting, grocery shopping, care of dependents, and other tasks that go beyond cleaning and laundry. They point out the enormous value to families of these activities. If these nonpaid home production "workers" were compensated for their labor, their compensation would amount to billions of dollars per year.

Like all social roles, the role of home production worker (traditionally known as "housewife") has both costs and benefits (Oakley, 1974). On the positive side, it provides the possibility of scheduling activities to suit one's own priorities and the opportunity to watch children grow and develop on a daily basis. Many parents, including some women and men currently in the labor force, would prefer to stay home at least while their children are young. In a 2005 survey, 53 percent of women said they would prefer to stay home compared to 42 percent who said they would prefer to work, up from 45 percent who said they preferred to stay home in 2001. More men are reporting a preference to stay at home as well, 27 percent in 2005 compared with only 12 percent in 1985 (Moore, 2005). Given that previous polls have fluctuated on this issue, it is too early to tell if the 2005 responses represent significant attitudinal changes or temporary concerns about their current personal and family situations.

Among the disadvantages of the home production role are the repetitive and sometimes boring nature of activities such as cleaning and doing laundry and the overall social devaluation of housework, often reflected in the phrase, "I'm just a housewife." Important financial costs as well become major burdens for families with only a single source of income and become particularly significant when divorce or death disrupts the family. This is particularly the case when the disruption is unexpected, as happens when accidents, natural disasters, or terrorist attacks result in the untimely death of the major breadwinner. Homemakers are economically dependent on their partners. Unlike homemakers in several European countries, U.S. homemakers are not covered by pensions, insurance, or social security. Thus, when a marriage is dissolved in the United States the displaced homemaker frequently suffers downward social mobility (see Chapter 12).

The Two-Person Career

One variation of the traditional nuclear family–work relationship is what some writers have called the "two-person career" (Papanek, 1973; Mortimer and London, 1984). This pattern, considered by Hanna Papanek to be a "structural part of the middle-class wife's role" (1973:857), incorporates the wife into her spouse's job through the expectation that she will be available to entertain his business associates, engage in volunteer activities that will enhance his organization's image, attend company parties and other events, socialize with her husband's coworkers off the job, and at the same time attend to the children and keep the household functioning smoothly. Much of the research on the two-person career focuses on middle- and upper-class occupations. Many business, professional, and political wives, for example, the first lady, are often viewed as typical examples of the two-person career. Thus, men in these families symbolically bring two people to their jobs (Kanter, 1977). However, when women hold similar positions, husbands are rarely expected to perform these duties. One notable exception was Charles T. Hunt III, a stay-at-home dad and husband of former Massachusetts Acting Governor Jane Swift, who agreed to take on some of the responsibilities usually delegated to first ladies such as giving tours of the governor's mansion. Recently, initial segments of the ABC series *Commander-in-Chief* depicted a likely scenario for a first husband. Actor Kyle Secor, playing Rod Calloway, husband of the first woman president of the United States, was expected to play the supportive helpmate, deciding on dinner menus and White House décor and staying out of political decision making. Given traditional definitions of masculinity, it is not surprising that the script had him experiencing frustration, humiliation, and anger with this limited role. However, as more women climb the political ladder, it is only a matter of time before the country must grapple with this issue.

The two-person career marriage, like all others, has advantages and disadvantages. On the positive side, employers benefit by having additional "workers" without having to pay for their efforts. Many husbands owe much of their career advancement to the social skills of their wives. Because the husband is away from home much of the time, the wife becomes the exclusive home manager. Fulfilling this role gives wives status and a sense of accomplishment, leaving their husbands free to devote most of their energy to work. Among middle- and upper-class wives, the financial rewards for taking on this responsibility may be significant—a secure lifestyle, travel, and opportunities for cultural enrichment. On the negative side, many wives experience unhappiness in this role. Like other nonemployed homemakers, these wives may believe their role is not appreciated or respected by the public. Wives may feel enormously limited in their behavior, constrained in their choice of friends, and restricted in their own occupational goals because of the demands of their husbands' careers (Papanek, 1973; Kanter, 1977). In addition, the husband's work often takes priority over family life, thus limiting the time spouses have to be together.

Economic shifts that require multiple family earners as well as the changing aspirations of women and men have led to a decline in the two-person career strategy. The traditional nuclear family of working husband, homemaker wife, and children is being replaced by dual-earner families, or as some writers prefer, "two-paycheck couples."

Dual-Earner Families

Dual-earner families are not new; there have always been families where both spouses were employed outside the home. However, in the past, dual-earner families tended to be concentrated among the poor. In contrast, today dual-earner couples are the norm and cut across all class race, and ethnic lines.

Nevertheless, dual-earner families do not all follow the same pattern. There is considerable variation in their commitment to work. At one end of the continuum are couples in which one of the spouses, usually the wife, works part-time. At the other end is a small (approximately 7 percent) but growing number of couples in which both spouses are highly committed to work. These are what social scientists call dual-career couples. These households differ from other dual-earner households in their approach to work. Rather than simply having a job, these couples invest in careers, which have several identifying characteristics. First, they require extensive training, usually a college or professional degree. Second, careers are more structured than are jobs, containing specific paths of upward mobility. Finally, careers involve commitment beyond a 9-to-5 workday.

Later in this chapter we will see that couples in dual-earner marriages experience satisfaction as well as stress and conflict as they struggle to solve important relationship problems such as the "problem over who will do the 'family work,'" the housekeeping and child care that formerly was the work of the housewife" (Lauer and Lauer, 1991:326).

Commuter Marriages

Some couples work in different geographic locations and because of distance must maintain two separate places of residence. Social scientists refer to these arrangements as **commuter marriages.** Although the exact number of commuter marriages is unknown, one estimate puts the number of such relationships at around 1 million and rising ("Managing the Miles . . .," 2004). By contrast, estimates are that in the central region of Thailand 41 percent of all couples live apart after marriage due to economic, occupational, or educational needs (quoted in Schvaneveldt, Young, and Schvaneveldt, 2001). One form of commuter marriage has existed for a long time. Couples in which one spouse, most frequently the husband, is a politician, professional athlete, traveling salesperson, seasonal worker, prisoner, or serves in the military, have had some experience with living apart while maintaining a marital relationship. Today, however, 15 percent of active-duty military personnel are women who have entered military life for many of the same reasons men do—better job opportunities than in civilian life, opportunities for education, travel, and adventure, patriotism, and a sense of duty. Many of these women are married; some have children who they have had to leave in the care of spouses, partners, or other relatives when called to serve in Afghanistan, Iraq, or other locations.

Dual-residency patterns were and continue to be common among low-income families around the world, where one spouse motivated by economic necessity migrates to another country, either making occasional visits home, such as many Latina/o migrants in the United States do, or works to reunite the family in her or his new location. Today, many commuter marriages develop because both spouses pursue careers but find that suitable jobs for each spouse are unavailable in the same location. Sometimes, too, the requirements of a job call for a transfer to a new area, and for whatever reason the other spouse cannot or will not relocate. According to industrial relations expert Linda Stroh, about 7 percent of corporate relocations end up creating commuter marriages (Franklin, 1999). Researchers found that women were more willing to relocate to another city for a spouse's or partner's career; only 14 percent of female respondents, compared to 34 percent of male respondents, said they would not move. Men's reluctance to move was related to a belief that a move would hurt their careers and/or earning power. Women were concerned that a move would disrupt strong family ties to their current community ("Men Won't Budge . . . ," 1997). When couples do commute, they are most likely to see their accommodations to their careers as a temporary lifestyle arrangement (Stewart, 1999). Generally, the geographic distance involved determines the length of separation. Some couples are able to be together on weekends; others can manage only monthly reunions. These arrangements are more stressful for younger couples, especially those with children, those who have been married for only a short time, and those who feel insecure in their relationship. Couples in these relationships are pioneers. Few guidelines exist to help them, and they receive little social support, because living apart is contrary to the traditional U.S. vision of married life.

Commuter couples, of necessity, have developed coping strategies for maintaining a sense of family. Many of these strategies require significant outlays of resources, particularly frequent telephone calls and travel to each other's place of residence. Many commuter couples use e-mail to keep connected on a daily basis. Research comparing commuting and noncommuting dual-career couples found that commuters are more satisfied with their work life and the time they have for themselves but are more dissatisfied with family life, their relationship with their partner, and with life as a whole (Bunker et al., 1992). This finding appears constant across diverse racial and ethnic groups (Jackson, Brown, and Patterson-Stewart, 2000; Schvaneveldt, Young, and Schvaneveldt, 2001).

Implications for the Corporate World   Given the changing nature of the American economy, it is expected that the number of workers involved in commuter marriages will increase. Research on such workers found that, in general, commuters work more hours than their noncommuter colleagues and also demonstrate a high level of organizational commitment (Ferk, 2005). Thus, employers are well advised to develop accommodations that will attract and retain this particular category of employee such as scheduling meetings to avoid weekends or late in the day on Fridays, permitting more flexible work schedules as well as flexplace that allows the commuting partner to work from a location besides the office.

> Would you be comfortable as a partner in a commuter marriage? Consider some of the unique problems you would face in such a relationship. How would you handle social events? Would you attend events alone or in the company of a same-sex or an other-sex friend? How would you convey emotional support and intimacy from a distance?

THE IMPACT OF WORK ON FAMILY RELATIONSHIPS

Much of the research conducted in the past on the impact of work on family life has been sex-segregated—that is, based on the assumption that work has a different meaning for women than for men. For women, paid work was thought an option that had to be weighed against the disruption it would cause their families; for men, it was considered a given. Men might have choices in the type of work they selected but not in whether they would work. Therefore, outside of their earning power, there is "a dearth of empirical research on the effects of fathers' employment on father–child interactions and their children's behavior" (Barling, 1991:181).

Studies of working women, in contrast, focused on different questions. Recall, from Chapter 2, Talcott Parsons's functionalist view that a woman's role in the family is expressive and a man's is instrumental. According to Parsons, stepping outside these roles leads to family instability. Thus, before 1960 researchers assumed that the entry of mothers into the labor force would have negative consequences for the family, leading, for example, to children getting into trouble at school or with the law.

These traditional role definitions no longer (if they ever did) adequately reflect the work and family experiences of women and men, especially those in dual-earner families. A new theoretical model is required that acknowledges the labor force participation of both women and men. Thus, sociologist Joan Spade (1989) called for a sex-integrated model to understand the impact of work on the family. Such a model asks how the type of work women and men do shapes their orientations and behaviors in the home.

Given the increasing number of dual-earner families, this question takes on major significance. The attempts by dual-earner couples to integrate work and family experiences affect many aspects of family life: power relationships and decision making, marital happiness, and the household division of labor. In short, by examining dual-earner couples we can learn how gender roles in the family are changing in response to both spouses taking on paid employment.

Marital Power and Decision Making

One of the most consistent findings relating to the impact of work on family life deals with the relationship between income and power in decision making. Money frequently translates into power. When both spouses work, the traditional pattern of male dominance in the marital relationship shifts to one of greater equality in terms of more joint decision making (Godwin and Scanzoni, 1989). Spouses, most frequently wives, who do not contribute financially in general, have little power in the relationship. The consequences of this may be severe. If the marriage is an unhappy one, the spouse without independent financial resources may feel compelled to stay in the relationship, whereas working may give an unhappy spouse the ability to leave the relationship. This relationship between independent resources and choice is illustrated by one of the respondents in a study of Chicana cannery workers: "It wasn't that my working hastened my divorce, in that it made my marriage worse, like Mario claims to this day. But rather it allowed me the freedom from a bad marriage" (Zavella, 1987:147). A more recent examination of data from the National Survey of Families has provided empirical support for her observation that women's employment does not destabilize happy marriages but increases the risk of disruption in unhappy marriages (Schoen, 2002).

This pattern of wives gaining more power as a result of their economic contribution holds true across most racial and ethnic groups. Researchers Jose Szapocznik and Roberto Hernandez (1988), for example, observed that Cuban women who migrated to the United States often found jobs sooner than their husbands did. Their economic contributions were then translated into gains in family decision making, thereby weakening the traditional Cuban patriarchal family structure. For the first generation of Cuban Americans, these changes were often disruptive. Second-generation Cuban American couples, who grew up in the United States, are less troubled by the greater equality in decision making and have tended to construct family relationships that are less male-dominated than those of their parental generation (Boswell and Curtis, 1983; Szapocznik and Hernandez, 1988). Similar patterns have been observed among Chinese American and Korean American families (Min, 1988; Wong, 1988) and among couples in Mexico (Attanasio and Lechene, 2002). Furthermore, given the consistently high level of labor force participation of African American women, it is not surprising to find that egalitarian decision making is common in African American families as well (McAdoo and McAdoo, 1995).

There are significant exceptions to these patterns. Differences in economic power and decision making are often reinforced or offset by ideological considerations. In a study of women in second marriages, Karen Pyke (1994) found that some remarried women stopped working and became full-time homemakers, yet increased their power in the marital relationship. According to Pyke, the meaning couples give to women's paid employment or unpaid household labor is key to determining the woman's power in the relationship. Thus, if unpaid household labor is valued by the working spouse, egalitarian power sharing between spouses is likely. Conversely, if couples believe men should be the primary breadwinners and, correspondingly, have the final say in most decisions, then the man will have more power in the relationship regardless of the earnings of either spouse (Benjamin and Sullivan, 1996).

Marital Happiness and Satisfaction

Are couples with one earner happier than those with two? The results of research on this question are inconsistent. Some earlier studies have found homemakers to be happier than working wives (Stokes and Peyton, 1986; Saenz, Goudy, & Frederick, 1989). However, these researchers found that much of the dissatisfaction the working wives felt was attributable to the quality of the jobs they held—jobs with low pay, little status, and considerable stress. Later research also found a correlation between a stressful job and lower levels of marital adjustment (Sears and Galambos, 1992).

Other research found that working wives reported higher levels of happiness than did nonworking wives. Similarly, research has consistently found that wives in dual-earner couples are healthier, less depressed, and less frustrated than their homemaker counterparts (Coontz, 1997). This finding is probably related to the fact that a wife's income contribution gives her more power within the family as well as being a source of satisfaction and self-esteem. However, a more recent study, albeit a controversial one, discussed in Chapter 8, suggests that wives are happier when their husbands are the main breadwinners, as well as emotionally engaged in the marital relationship (Wilcox and Nock, 2006).

More important than work per se, however, is the couple's attitude toward work. If the couple disagrees about spousal employment or if the wife works only because of economic necessity, some tension and conflict are likely. Some wives who desire only a domestic role may be embittered about their need to work, whereas some husbands who adhere strongly to the good provider role might feel threatened or inadequate as a result of having a working wife. This is especially the case for some husbands whose wives earn more than they do (Minetor, 2002). According to the U.S. Bureau of Labor Statistics, in 2003, 25 percent of working wives whose husbands also worked earned more than their husbands, up from 18 percent in 1987. If we count working women married to men who are unemployed, the percentage increases to 32, up from 24 percent in 1987. Not all men feel threatened by higher-earning wives, however. One husband, when asked if his wife's making more money would be a problem for him, responded, "No, it would be fun to have more money" (quoted in Sahadi 2003).

The experience of marital happiness is related to another constraint confronting dual-earner families: finding time to be together, especially recreational time. "Couples with less time together express less satisfaction with their marriages" (Nock and Kingston, 1990:133). This lack of time together grew more acute in the 1990s as Americans added nearly a full week to their work year, working 1979 hours (an increase of 36 hours from 1990) or nearly $49\frac{1}{2}$ weeks a year on the job. In comparison, Japanese workers (long the leader in working hours) worked 1842 hours, Canadian workers 1767 hours, British workers 1719, and German workers 1480 (Greenhouse, 2001). These differentials are due to variations in cultural practices and economic situations. Traditionally, European employers have granted European workers 4 to 6 weeks of vacation each year, compared to the 2 to 3 weeks most Americans receive. In the 1990s, the European economy grew much more slowly than that of the United States. European governments responded by reducing the official workweek in an attempt to pressure employers to hire more workers while U.S. employers met their needs by adding overtime work. According to Ellen Galinsky (2004), President of the Families and Work Institute, the majority of employees (67 percent) say they don't have enough time with their children while 63 percent say they don't have enough time with their spouses. Children reflect these views as well. A nationally representative group of children, aged 8 to 18, reported that their number one wish to improve their lives was that their parents were less tired and stressed.

Time is also related to two other important aspects of family living: household tasks and the care of children. Parsons's model of the family assumes that these are the wife's responsibilities and that they complement the husband's breadwinner role. Parsons did not anticipate the contemporary widespread need for two incomes, however. What happens to housework and child care when wives share the breadwinner function? Do husbands reciprocate and share domestic responsibilities?

Husbands and the Division of Household Labor

As more wives entered the labor force, social scientists began to investigate the degree to which husbands increased the amount of time they spent doing household work. Data collected from the 1960s to the mid-1970s show that family work remained almost exclusively the province of women, whether or not they were employed. For example, a study of 1296 New York State families found that husbands spent about 1.6 hours per day in family work compared with 8.1 hours per day for housewives and 4.8 hours per day for working wives (Walker and Woods, 1976). It is not surprising, then, that compared with their spouses, wives experienced more **role overload,** a situation in which a person's various roles carry more responsibilities than that person can reasonably manage. As a result of role overload, women have less free time for themselves and experience a diminished sense of well-being (Robinson, 1977; Hochschild, 1997). This pattern led sociologist Arlie Hochschild (1989) to describe women's dual role of worker and housewife as a "second shift."

Two recent studies have documented a shift to a more equitable, albeit not equal, division of labor, with men doing slightly more work and women doing less work than was the case in the 1970s. According to a 2004 Time Use Study by the Bureau of Labor Statistics (2005), on an average day 84 percent of women but only 63 percent of men reported spending some time doing household activities such as housework, cooking, lawn care, or financial and other household management. Women reported spending 2.7 hours on such activities while men spent 2.1 hours. However, only 19 percent of men reported doing cleaning or laundry compared to 54 percent of women. Men were somewhat more involved in food preparation and cleanup, with 35 percent of men and 66 percent of women reporting doing these activities. In households with the youngest child under age 6, women averaged 2.7 hours for primary child-care activities while men averaged 1.2 hours. A slightly earlier study of dual-earner couples by the Families and Work Institute also found that men's involvement in household chores and child care has increased steadily since 1977. Then employed fathers spent an average of 1.3 hours on household chores compared to 3.7 for employed mothers. By 2002, the comparable figures were 2 hours per day for fathers and 3 for mothers. Likewise, there has been a narrowing of the nurturing gap. In 1977 employed fathers spent 1.9 hours per workday with their children whereas employed mothers spent 3.3 hours. By 2003, the comparable figures were 2.7 hours for fathers and 3.5 hours for

mothers (Bond et al., 2003). Similarly, the general conclusion of most but not all studies of children's home responsibilities is that girls spend more time than boys doing household chores (see for example, Cheal, 2003). Given that this gendered pattern is learned in childhood, it is not surprising that it is reproduced in adulthood.

Data from a cross-national study of 13 countries reflect similar patterns to those in the United States. In only one country, Russia, did spouses say housework was shared about equally. In the other 12 countries, spouses reported that wives did more housework than husbands (Davis and Greenstein, 2004). Individuals' and couples' characteristics were found to influence the division of household labor. In households where wives were employed outside the home and/or had education levels equal to or above that of their husbands, husbands were reported to perform about half of the household labor. However, other research found that macro-level factors such as a country's level of economic development, female labor force participation, and gender ideology are equally important in the dynamics of how housework is divided between spouses. Overall, women in less egalitarian countries benefit less from their individual-level assets such as earning power and educational level than do women in more egalitarian countries (Fuwa, 2004). For example, Jeanne Batalova and Philip Cohen (2002) found that husbands in Japan do considerably less housework than do husbands in the Scandinavian countries and in the United States.

Sharing the Load: Emergent Egalitarian Relationships
Inequity in family work can affect the satisfaction found in marriage. Among wives there is a clear and positive connection between an equitable division of family work and marital and personal well-being (Rogers and Amato, 2000; Frisco and Williams, 2003; Wilcox and Nock, 2006). Dutch wives, like their U.S. counterparts, are dissatisfied when their husbands' participation in household labor is only minimal (Kluwer, Heeskink, and Van De Vliert, 1996). Data on couples in Moscow revealed similar patterns (Cubbins and Vannoy, 2004). Wives whose husbands do their share of family work are more satisfied with marriage than are other wives. According to a 1990 national opinion poll, next to money, "how much my mate helps around the house" is the single biggest cause of resentment among women who are married or living as if married, with 52 percent of the respondents reporting this as a problem (Townsend and ONeil, 1990:28). Fifteen years later, wives still believe dads could do better. Forty-five percent of respondents wanted their husbands to provide more help with the kids and with household chores ("Voice of Mom Report," 2005).

Thus, there seems to be some consensus among both women and men for the need to alter traditional gender roles. That some of this is occurring, albeit slowly, is indicated by Audrey Smith and William Reid (1986) in their study of role-sharing marriages, by Rosanna Hertz (1986) in her study of dual-career marriages, by Pepper Schwartz (1999) in her study of peer marriages, and by Shelley Haddock and her colleagues (2002) in their study of couples who perceive themselves as successful in balancing family and work. Hertz argues that dual-career couples generally do not start out with an ideology of equality in marital roles, but

FAMILY PROFILE

THE PARKINSON FAMILY

Karen, Craig, and Brody Parkinson

Length of Relationship: 10 years

Length of Marriage: $4\frac{1}{2}$ years

Challenges in Parenting: Karen and I became first-time parents when our son, Brody, was born on September 17, 2005. For the most part, we both felt ready to take on the challenges of parenting and saw the challenges as the next exciting phase of our relationship. Karen and I have a great understanding of each other and that allows us to minimize the challenges of parenting, although we know more challenges are on the way as Brody grows up.

The first challenge we faced, and are still facing, was finding quality alone time for just us as well as alone time with our friends as individuals. As new parents, we sometimes second guess our decisions to go out to dinner or go out with our friends because we are away from Brody and wonder what he is doing or whether or not going out was the right decision. Time spent with friends on an individual basis is reduced when a baby arrives and I often find myself thinking about Brody when I am at a sporting event or at the movies. As parents, we have found that alone time is important for keeping our relationship strong, but we really have to pick-and-choose our opportunities.

The other key challenge to this point has been sharing the responsibilities of

having an infant. Karen and I see each other as equals in parenting. Being first-time parents we really must have a plan for almost every scenario, but must be able to react to anything that could happen. We always discuss who is going to care for Brody (whose turn is it to feed first at night, whose turn is it to change him, whose turn is it to put him to bed, and so on) and that has allowed us to address the

---

that it often emerges out of the opportunities and constraints they experience on a day-to-day basis. In contrast, the couples in Schwartz's study had strong ideas about building a marriage based on equity and equality and made conscious efforts to achieve their goal—"marital intimacy that comes from being part of a well-matched, equally empowered, equally participatory team" (1999:162). Other couples have altered traditional gender roles in the family as well. However, as Francine Deutsch (1999) discovered in a study of 150 dual-career couples with children, most couples had a work-centered family in which work and career advancement, usually the husband's, was the priority. Nevertheless, 41 couples in her study (nearly 25 percent) had child-centered families in which their children's needs were the central focus for both parents. By fully sharing all responsibilities, these parents managed to have successful work lives and well-balanced family lives. Craig Parkinson and his wife Karen tell us how planning and ongoing communication help them

to achieve partnership and a balance between work and family (see Family Profile box). Their story also illustrates the important role social policy can play in helping parents achieve these goals. The Parkinsons are fortunate. As public school teachers, they are both eligible for parental leaves. Many other workers are not. As we will see at the end of this chapter, the United States lags behind other developed countries in the benefits available to parents.

The Impact of Gender Ideology, Social Class, and Race and Ethnicity Research shows that men in dual-earner families who see themselves as co-providers with their wives do more domestic tasks than do men who still believe in the good provider role (Perry-Jenkins and Crouter, 1990). Social class also seems relevant here. Spouses with higher levels of education are more likely to share domestic tasks, especially when the wife has high earnings and a professional status (Perry-Jenkins and Folk, 1994; Spain and

difficult decisions that must be made. We both believe in the same styles of parenting and know that communication is essential to being good parents. I am sure that will be tested as Brody gets older.

The next challenge Karen and I will face is the decision regarding job status. Both of us are teachers (Karen, first grade, and I, eleventh grade) and we thoroughly enjoy our jobs. However, both of us grew up in households where our mothers stayed home with us as we were growing up. I will continue to teach and we will explore Karen's options. I know she loves to teach but also feels strongly that she wants to be the one home with him daily. That both of our mothers made the decision to stop working after we were born plays an important role in our decision making. No final decision has been made as yet whether or not Karen will be staying home with Brody next school year. We are keeping our options open and we will continue to discuss our feelings about the decision. I will fully support whatever final decision Karen makes because I know she will always put the needs of our son first.

As for taking care of Brody after birth, Karen took the first 15 weeks of his life as her maternity leave and has since returned to work and I am currently on my six weeks of paternity leave. It seems strange being home when I know my students are at school attempting to learn U.S. history without me, but Karen and I wanted to make it as long as we could before we would send Brody to day care for the remainder of this school year.

As a father being home, the experience has been absolutely worthwhile—although a bit different. Some days are exciting while others are frustrating to the point where I think I would rather be back teaching. There are a few things that I constantly wonder in my head as each day passes. First, am I on his schedule for feedings and naps or can that schedule change? I have tried to change the schedule a couple of times and that led to the frustrating days. Each time he cries I wonder what I am doing wrong and, yes, have even called Karen at work a few times to find a solution. Second, can I take him places and be all right? I have found that some of the best times have occurred when we do go to the mall or to grandma's work. Sitting at home all the time takes its toll on your mind and can add to the frustration.

My experience of being on paternity leave has been one of great joy and I am grateful that Karen and I decided to both take leaves from work. As for being a father and taking time off of work, my coworkers were very supportive of me. I even think some of the other male teachers wished they could have taken time off to be with their child after hearing I was going to leave for six weeks. The principal of my school reacted with some shock but in the end was supportive of my decision. He knows I am not one to miss a day of work and he wondered if the advanced placement U.S. history courses at school would survive, but they will. There is not a day that goes by when I do not think about my students at school, but I know I made the right decision, especially when I see that smile on my son's face. Many people say family comes first and then make decisions that do not correspond with that philosophy, but I wanted the opportunity to be with my son and have enjoyed it.

I am learning two things as a stay-at-home dad. First, you must get other household jobs done while you are home during the day. If not, your evenings will be very hectic. Second, Brody does nap quite a bit so it has been important for me to find a hobby for that down time.

Relationship Philosophy: Our relationship philosophy since Brody was born has always been that he now is our first priority. At the same time, we both believe that continuing to do some of the things we have always liked to do is still important and keeps our relationship fun and interesting. We understand that a balance must be kept and from this point on Brody will always come first. Karen and I are extremely proud of what we have accomplished both in our marriage and to this point as parents. We are thankful to all of our friends and family who have been and continue to be supportive.

Bianchi, 1996). Like their U.S. counterparts, urban Chinese husbands with higher educational levels and whose wives' earnings are close to theirs have the highest rates of participation in household labor (Lu, Maume, and Bellas, 2000). The affluence of these couples, however, also allows them to hire others to do their household tasks and/or child care. Although this solution may work well for them, it often creates problems for the families of domestic workers who find themselves sacrificing time with their families to accommodate the family needs of their employers. This situation reflects the traditional racial and ethnic divisions in the United States. Historically, African American women and white ethnic immigrant women made up the core of domestic workers; today, more and more Latinas are filling these positions (Hondagneu-Sotelo and Avila, 1997).

Race and ethnicity are also factor in how family work is divided. Research has found that African American husbands are more likely than white husbands to share in household tasks (John and Shelton, 1997. Lillian Rubin (1994) found that Latinos and Asian American men, especially those who live in ethnic neighborhoods where traditional gender roles remain strong despite women's employment, are less likely to share household work. However, other research on Mexican American couples found husbands participated more in domestic tasks if the wife's earnings equaled or surpassed that of her husband (Coltrane, 1996). Such findings underscore the complex nature of the work–family linkage. More research is needed to determine the various ways in which micro-level and macro-level forces interact to produce different patterns of work and family role tradeoffs.

Nevertheless, one dominant theme that cuts across all of these studies regards the expectations that women and men bring to their roles as partners, parents, and providers. If women and men are to share equally in home production work, then women must redefine the value of their jobs or careers as providers and men must redefine the meaning of domestic work as something beneficial, not demeaning (Lorber, 1994). William Beer (1983), in a study of house-husbands, redefined housework, incorporating masculine images:

> A day of cooking, cleaning, child care and household man-agement is not unlike climbing a mountain. Some of it is sweaty, grueling work, but the pleasures, such as sunlight through the mist on Mount Washington, or seeing a toddler learn a new game, are constant enough to make it worth it . . . . Housework may not be Everest, but it is an adventure that awaits any man who wants to forge ahead and meet the challenges of unexplored territory. (xxi)

Child Care

When a couple has their first child, their life changes dra-matically. Workloads increase. Often without conscious planning, many couples move to a more traditional division of household tasks, with women taking on more tasks. One study found that the time devoted to work responsibilities increased by 64 percent for mothers and 37 percent for fathers after childbirth (Gjerdingen, 2004). To avoid conflict and marital dissatisfaction, it is important that parental spouses regularly evaluate and negotiate a division of labor that satisfies both their and their children's needs.

That some of this is happening is evidenced by the fact that fathers are spending more time with their children than fathers did 20 years ago (Lewin, 1998a) and, as we saw ear-lier, a considerable number of fathers are stay-at-home dads. Although men's parenting activities appear to be increasing, women still take the major responsibility for child care in the United States. This situation puts working women at a competitive disadvantage with male colleagues, who are freed of this responsibility by their spouses. For women, having children constrains their labor market activities. Women with small children have lower labor force partici-pation rates, and when they are employed, they are more likely to work part-time. This is especially true of poor women with limited education and skills. Finding a job that pays an income sufficient to cover child-care costs is prob-lematic for them. In 2002, the average weekly cost of child care was $92.00 for families with children under 15. In fam-ilies with a monthly income under $1500, the costs of child care typically consumed over 24 percent of their monthly income. In comparison, families with a monthly income of $4500 and over paid only 5.8 percent of their income on child care per month (Johnson, 2005).

Some couples respond to the difficulties of child care by split-shift employment and split-shift parenting, thereby enabling one parent to be home while the other is at work. Approximately one-third of dual-earner couples with chil-dren have one spouse working late or rotating shifts. Addi-tionally, more than 66 percent of all dual-earner couples have at least one spouse working some time over the week-end. Both of these patterns are more common among low-income families and families with preschool children (Presser, 2003). These patterns also hold true for single mothers as well. Although a 24/7 economy provides a great deal of convenience for consumers and travelers, it creates serious problems for families whose members must work nonstandard hours. Often these hours mean that one parent is unavailable during dinnertime hours, a time that usually allows for meaningful family interaction. This lack of time together can cause tensions between spouses that can affect children as well. This is especially true for couples where one spouse works the late shift, as they have substantially less quality time together and experience more marital unhappiness. Although neither an evening shift nor week-end work seemed to affect the stability of marriages, couples with children where one spouse worked late night hours were more likely to separate or divorce than other couples. However, on the plus side, split parenting allows children to see their parents as coproviders and if the separate time period each parent is at home overlaps somewhat with the children's waking hours, children are likely to experience care from both parents.

Single working mothers and couples who work the same shift face a different set of problems, the most serious of which is finding alternative child care. In winter 2002, 9.8 million preschoolers lived with employed mothers, up from 8.2 million in 1985. In 1977, 13 percent of employed women with a child under 5 years of age used organized day care. Twenty-five years later, 24 percent were using such facilities. Relatives remain a major provider of child care for working mothers. Figure 10.3 shows the distribution of primary-care arrangements for children with working mothers in 2002. Eighteen percent of the preschool children were cared for by fathers, down from 20 percent in 1991; grand-parents provided care for 19 percent of preschool children while siblings and other relatives cared for another 6 percent. Another 17 percent received care from a nonrelative. Three percent of children under age 5 were cared for by their mothers either while working at home or on the job. These mothers were frequently employed as private household workers or were themselves child-care workers who took in other children while caring for their own at home. Thirteen percent of preschoolers have some other or no regular arrangement, including self-care (Johnson, 2005). The type

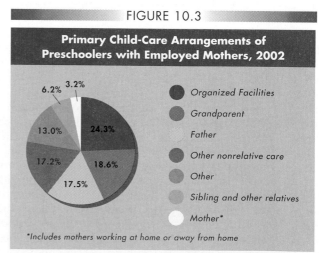

FIGURE 10.3

Primary Child-Care Arrangements of Preschoolers with Employed Mothers, 2002

- Organized Facilities
- Grandparent
- Father
- Other nonrelative care
- Other
- Sibling and other relatives
- Mother*

*Includes mothers working at home or away from home

Source: Adapted from Julia Overturf Johnson. 2005, *Who's Minding the Kids? Child Care Arrangements: Winter 2002.* Current Population Reports, P70-101. U.S. Census Bureau. Washington, DC: Government Printing Office, Table 3, p. 9.

A major concern of dual-earner families is finding adequate child care. In split-shift households one parent, like this father fixing dinner with his sons, takes primary responsibility for child care while the other parent is at work. In some cases, the child-care dilemma is resolved when one parent, like this executive, takes her child to work.

of child-care arrangements available to parents depends heavily on their resources and family systems. When families are poor or on government assistance, they must rely on relatives more so than other families. African American and Latina/o children are more likely to be cared for by grandparents and other nonparental relatives and less likely to be in organized facilities than white children.

Regardless of the type of child-care arrangement in use, the majority of families who need child care confront two major problems: high cost and limited availability. These problems stem, in large measure, from cultural attitudes that see child care as primarily a private matter requiring a private solution. In other words, if couples have children, the reasoning goes, it is their responsibility to care for them. However, as we will see at the end of this chapter, some employers are reconsidering this attitude as many of the new entrants to the labor force are mothers. To attract and keep these employees, an increasing number of companies (around 10,000) are providing on-site day care so that parents can visit their children during work or lunch breaks, thus relieving them of worry over how their children are managing without them. However, employer-sponsored child care in the United States is available to only one in eight employees (13 percent), and even programs that offer tax savings for those able to pay for their own children are available only to three in ten people (Heymann et al., 2004).

Reexamining the "Mommy Track"   The notion that child care is still considered primarily a woman's problem was highlighted when corporate consultant Felice Schwartz (1989) wrote an article for the *Harvard Business Review* outlining a controversial approach to the problem of child care and working women. She suggested that employers divide women into two groups based on whether they are career-primary or career-and-family women. Schwartz described the former group as women who are willing to put their careers ahead of family needs. She advised companies to identify these women early and put them on the same career track as talented men. The other women would make good workers, but to keep them Schwartz recommended that companies provide considerations for their parental responsibilities, such as part-time

employment, maternity leaves, and so on. The media labeled this position the "mommy track."

Criticism was swift to Schwartz's proposal. Some writers argued that such an approach would create a two-tiered system of women workers, with working mothers receiving fewer rewards for their work efforts and perhaps placing limitations on opportunities for career advancement, especially if they take time off to fulfill child-care responsibilities. A recent study found evidence that this criticism was warranted. Among respondents who took family leave, an overwhelming majority (70 percent) felt positive when they left their full-time jobs but their optimism dropped sharply when they tried to reenter the workplace later on. Many women felt frustrated or depressed by their job search. Eighty-three percent of the job seekers took either a comparable role or a lower role than they had held previously; only 17 percent reentered their field at a higher level and most women returned to work in smaller companies or changed industries altogether (Ramachandran, 2005).

Reacting to the perceived gender inequity of Schwartz's proprosal, Ronnie Sandroff (1989) questioned why the adjustment for having children would fall only on female workers. Rather than a "mommy track," she argued there should be a "parent track" but without current economic penalties. In fact, some fathers want to give more priority to their families. A national survey found that men between the ages of 20 and 39 were more likely to value family over career success. Eighty-two percent put family first and 71 percent said they would sacrifice part of their pay to have more time with their families (Rayman, 2000). A more recent study in Canada found that 90 percent of mothers and fathers with preschool children would prefer to stay home and raise them. Additionally, 90 percent of mothers and 84 percent of fathers who are married and employed would work part-time if they could afford to do so. And almost all employed mothers who are divorced, separated, or cohabiting agree (Bibby, 2005).

Choice Versus Reality   Despite these stated preferences, choice and reality often collide. Let us look first at the experiences of mothers and then those of fathers. A literary firestorm erupted after the appearance of media stories about the increasing numbers of mothers "opting out" of the work force (see, for example, Belkin, 2003; CBS News, 2004; Hirshman, 2005). According to the U.S. Census Bureau, the percentage of mothers with infants working or seeking employment increased steadily from 1976 (31 percent) to 1998 (58.7 percent) and then began to fall, declining to 52.9 percent in 2004. Explanations for this downward trend vary. Some analysts see it as a response to a distressed economy with contracting job and wage opportunities; others believe women are reacting to the pressures and stresses inherent in workaholic job cultures. Still others view this pattern as a failure of feminist goals, arguing that the public world had changed to include women but that what women really value is home and motherhood, not success, money, or power. Because the news stories focused primarily on women who graduated from schools like Yale and Harvard, some dubbed this an "elitist debate," noting that these women, mostly white, enjoyed family incomes that allowed them the option to stay at home while mothers at the other end of the income range have little alternative but to go to work.

It is certainly too early to know whether a so-called opt-out revolution is really underway or whether these numbers represent a temporary blip. One thing does seem pretty clear, however—an increasing number of both mothers and fathers want to spend more time with their children and have more of a direct influence on their lives, especially in the critical early formative years. This is true across race, ethnic, sexual orientation, and class lines. Thus, the assertion that this is only an "elitist" phenomenon, while having some validity, probably overstates the case. Stay-at-home mothers of color have largely been invisible in this so-called "opting out" behavior. One illustration can serve to make this point here. Women of color who are stay-at-home moms often feel invisible. Historically, economic circumstances have forced many women of color into the labor market. Compared to white women, the proportion of women-of-color stay-at-home moms has been considerably lower and thus more difficult to identify. Even today, the experience of Adrienne Foster, an African American mother, is not unique. When she takes her children to story hours or play groups, she is often the only African American woman present. Tammy Greer Brown, another African American stay-at-home mom, feels compelled to respond in such situations by saying, "No, I'm not the nanny" (Leas, 2003). Mocha Moms, founded in 1997 to provide support for women-of-color who "opt" to be stay-at-home moms as well as for those who struggle to balance work and family, now has 120 chapters all across the United States with a membership of more than 1,000 mothers.

Turning to fathers, a Census Bureau survey found that only 2 percent of employed fathers with preschoolers adjusted work schedules for child-rearing considerations. Overall, European fathers have access to more paid leave than their American counterparts and use it more readily, yet even then many men are still reluctant to take time off from work. In France, after the government passed legislation creating two-week paid paternity leave in 2002, 59 percent of dads took advantage of it. In Sweden, where leaves are more generous, dads account for only 17 percent of all parental leave taken. In the Netherlands, the number of men who opt to take leave fell slightly from 13 percent in 1998 to 12 percent in 2001. In Germany, where 20 percent of men said they would like to take parental leave, only 2 percent did so. Danish law allows both parents to share 32 weeks of state benefit-supported leave during the first nine years of their child's life, yet men account for only 5 percent of all parental leave taken (James, 2004). Why do so many European men reject what on the surface seems like a great opportunity to spend time with their infants and young children? The answer, according to some men, is found in the structure and culture of work. Steen Broust Nielsen, a 36-year-old marketing director in Denmark, was reluctant to take the leave to which, as a new father, he was entitled because, as he said, "We have an interim report coming up, so I can't possibly stay away too long, perhaps half a day here and half a day there when it's convenient." His reluctance was echoed by a 38-year-old Dortmund-based management assistant, who said, "When you are on your way up, you can't take a time out. That will set you back no end career-wise" (quoted in James, 2004). Men in the United States share these views. Although the concept of paternity leave is gaining public acceptance, many Americans who have access to such leave do not act on it. According to a survey by the U.S. Department of Labor (2000), 42.6 percent of men who were considering paternity leave cited "fear of hurting career advancement" as the primary reason for not doing so; 31 percent feared they might lose their jobs if they took a leave. Their concerns are not unwarranted. Research shows that men who take advantage of family medical leave are considered less conscientious employees than those who do not (Wayne and Cordeiro, 2003).

Other employer behavior also contributes to men's reluctance to take leave. Employers who do not promote leave policies to their employees communicate a silent message that, for men at least, taking leave is not an appropriate career move. Conversely, when employers actively promote parental leave for both genders, the results are quite different. When New Jersey's XPMG company sent e-mails at work and letters home explaining the company's parental leave policy and how to apply, 30 percent of eligible fathers took a leave in 2002. The following year, 87 percent of eligible fathers took leave. In fact, 58 percent of all people taking leave that year were males (Earls, 2003). Other factors may influence a father's decision to take leave. If wives do not ask their husbands, or at least discuss the possibility with them, men may conclude they do not care or do not want them to take leave. As we saw in Chapter 9, men may experience more pressure to be a breadwinner with the birth of a first child or additional children. And if there is an economic downturn, men may be more apprehensive of taking any action that may jeopardize their current position.

In sum, the United States has not yet resolved the dilemma surrounding the gendered ideology of the family that assigns housekeeping and child rearing primarily to women and assumes that balancing work and family needs is a personal matter. Much of the material discussed throughout this textbook suggests, and, as other researchers have forcefully argued, that cultural myths, about the appropriate roles for each gender, internalized by both women and men, can harm relationships, children, work, and the larger society (Barnett and Rivers, 2004). To phrase this dilemma as one of individual choice ignores the reality that current structures prohibit many parents from making satisfying choices, thus preventing many women from exercising full partnership with men in economic and political arenas as well as precluding many men from full partnership with women in family life. We will consider some structural changes that can help to overcome this problem at the end of the chapter.

INEQUITIES IN THE WORKPLACE: CONSEQUENCES FOR FAMILIES

Although the labor force participation rates of women and men are converging, women still confront issues of inequity in the labor market. These issues, in turn, can have a profound effect on women's sense of worth and their family's economic well-being. Three issues are of special significance: occupational distribution, the gender gap in earnings, and sexual harassment.

Occupational Distribution

Occupational distribution refers to the location of workers in different occupations. Although the media like to highlight stories of women and men who are in nontraditional occupations, for example, women construction workers and male nurses, many occupations are still perceived as either women's work or men's work. Table 10.1 shows the percentage of the work force in selected occupations. Even work traditionally thought of as women's work such as cooking, when done outside the home and "professionalized," often becomes a male specialty. Only 18.9 percent of chefs and head cooks are women. Even though slightly more

women than men are working in a professional specialty (50.3 percent), women tend to be working in the lower-paid professions such as nursing or elementary school education, whereas men are more concentrated in the higher-paid professions of law, medicine, architecture, and engineering. In 2004, only 29.4 percent of lawyers, 29.4 percent of physicians, and 13.8 percent of architects and engineers were women. Women and people of color are more heavily concentrated in low-paying clerical or service jobs, whereas men are concentrated in the higher-paying jobs of craft workers and operators.

The good news is that in the last three decades increasing numbers of women have entered many occupations traditionally thought to be exclusively male, for instance, computer and mathematical occupations (27.0%) and the clergy (15.0 percent). Women have been less successful in breaking other barriers, for example, only 5.3 percent of women are aircraft pilots and flight engineers. An even smaller percentage of women are electricians (2.1 percent) and carpenters (1.8 percent). Men, in contrast, have been more reluctant to enter "women's" occupations in any significant numbers. Thus, some job categories remain overwhelmingly female—for example, preschool and kindergarten teachers (98.1 percent) and nursing (92.2 percent)—although men have made gains as social workers (22.3 percent) and librarians (16.8 percent), once thought to be the domain of women. To eliminate gender-segregated jobs in the United States, approximately one-half of all female workers would have to change jobs (Renzetti and Curran, 1995). We can see that race and ethnicity also play a role in occupational distribution. Although African Americans make up 11.3 percent of all employed civilians, Latinas/os 10.3 percent, and Asians 4.3 percent, they often are underrepresented in the higher paying jobs and overrepresented in lower-paying jobs.

TABLE 10.1

Percentage of Work Force in Selected Occupations, by Sex, Race, and Ethnicity, 2004

	Women	African American	Asians	Latinas/os
All occupations	46.5	10.7	4.3	12.9
Aircraft pilots/flight engineers	5.3	1.7	1.5	3.2
Architecture and engineering occupations	13.8	4.9	8.4	5.7
Carpenters	1.8	5.2	0.8	21.8
Chefs and head cooks	18.9	11.5	10.7	20.9
Child-care workers	94.5	17.8	2.1	16.5
Clergy	15.0	11.6	5.1	6.0
Computer and mathematical occupations	27.0	7.5	14.0	5.5
Electricians	2.1	6.5	1.2	13.6
Lawyers	29.4	4.7	2.9	3.4
Librarians	83.2	5.6	4.5	4.6
Physicians/surgeons	29.4	6.1	16.5	5.3
Preschool/kindergarten teachers	98.1	15.2	2.5	8.2
Registered nurses	92.2	10.1	6.8	4.4
Social workers	77.7	20.4	2.9	10.9

Source: Adapted from U.S. Census Bureau, 2006, *Statistical Abstract of the United States, 2006* (Washington, DC: Government Printing Office): Table 604, pp. 401–404.

FIGURE 10.4

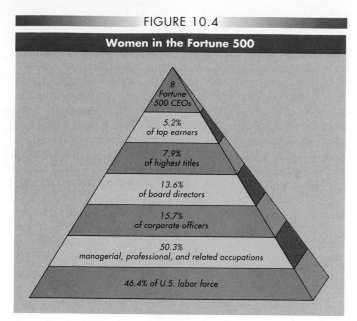

Women in the Fortune 500

8 Fortune 500 CEOs

5.2% of top earners

7.9% of highest titles

13.6% of board directors

15.7% of corporate officers

50.3% managerial, professional, and related occupations

46.4% of U.S. labor force

Source: Catalyst, 2003, "The Catalyst Pyramid: U.S. Women in Business, 2003" (accessed January 11, 2006 www.catalystwomen.org/files/fact/ COTE%20Factsheet%202002updated.pdf).

As Figure 10.4 clearly shows, women have fared even less well in business. Although women make up almost half of the U.S. labor force (46.5 percent), in 2003 there were only 8 Fortune 500 CEOs. And, despite gains since 1999, only 5.2 percent (118 out of 2259) of the nation's top earners were women and only 13.6 percent of women were Fortune 500 board directors (Catalyst, 2003). A recent survey showed that although women occupied only 8 percent of corporate boardroom seats across Europe, there were some interesting differences. Norway and Sweden led with 22 and 20 percent. Italy had the lowest representation, with just 2 percent. France, the Netherlands, Germany and the United Kingdom had rates ranging from 6 to 10 percent ("Women and the Board . . .," 2006). Norway's top position is not accidental. Gender equality is part of Nordic traditions. As long ago as Viking times, women ran farms and businesses while men were away at sea. In recent years women have held approximately 40 percent of cabinet and parliamentary positions. However, concerned with an underrepresentation of women in higher levels of business, Norway called on its top corporations to meet a goal of 40 percent women on their boards. If the corporations fail to comply, the government may initiate action against them.

Women face many obstacles in reaching top positions. Among them is the fact that women are poorly represented in line positions, those jobs with profit-and-loss responsibilities that are the traditional route to executive promotion. Surveys of executives in the United States point to gender-based stereotyping as a major barrier to women's advancement (Prime, 2005).

As these data demonstrate, occupational segregation has consequences for the well-being of workers and their families. First, it restricts the options of both women and men. Men are less likely than women to enter a sex-atypical occupation. Second, when workers enter occupations that are not traditional for their race or gender, they often encounter prejudice and hostility, resulting in high levels of stress. For women and people of color, this hostility often takes the form of exclusion from the informal work groups so necessary to successful job performance and advancement. In contrast, men in nontraditional occupations experience prejudice from people outside their occupation, but are less likely than women to experience discrimination at work. Sociologist Christine Williams (1992) found that although women often encounter a "glass ceiling" that limits their advancement, men in sex-atypical occupations experience a "glass escalator" that propels them to higher positions in that field. Finally, occupational segregation results in an earnings gap between women and men and between whites and people of color that limits the resources families receive when female members work.

The Race–Gender Gap in Earnings: Good News and Bad News

No matter how earnings are measured, women's wages are lower than men's, regardless of race and ethnicity. Similarly, men of color are disadvantaged in comparison with their white counterparts. In the first quarter of 2006, the median weekly earnings for female full-time wage and salary workers were $600, nearly 81 percent of the $744 median for their male counterparts. In 1979, when comparable earnings data were first available, women earned only about 63 percent as much as men did. However, white workers of either gender earned more than their black or Latina/o colleagues. The differences among women were considerably smaller than those among men. White women earned $607, 10.7 percent more than black women ($542). In contrast, white men outearned their black counterparts by 24.4 percent ($763 to $577). Overall, the median earnings of Latinos who worked full time ($487) were lower than those of blacks ($560), whites ($688), and Asians ($766). The female-to-male earnings gap was widest for Asian and whites, with these women earning only 71.1 and 79.6 percent, respectively, as much as their male peers. Black women earned 93.9 percent and Latinas earned 86.6 percent as much as their male counterparts. Age, occupation, and education all impact wages. By and large, older workers (those 45 to 65) earned more than younger workers. Persons employed in management, professional, and related occupations had the highest median weekly earnings, $1,160 for men and $816 for women. Full-time workers age 25 and over without a high school diploma had median weekly earnings of $420 compared with $592 for high school graduates and $1019 for college graduates. Yet, even at the highest levels of education, the highest-earning 10 percent of male workers made $2899 or more per week, compared with $1904 or more for their female counterparts (U.S. Department of Labor, 2006).

The narrowing of the race–gender earnings gap in recent years can be attributed to a number of factors: women's increased investment in education and professional training, entry into higher-paying nontraditional occupations, fewer and shorter interruptions in their work lives, and a decline in men's wages. However, the gains many workers made in the 1990s as a result of low unemployment, low inflation, and the increase in the minimum wage started to erode in the economic downturn beginning in 2001. The terrorist attacks on September 11, 2001, the war in Iraq, and natural disasters like Hurricane Katrina have exacerbated this trend as affected industries, particularly those that cater to business and tourist travel, laid off thousands of workers.

For years researchers have struggled to explain why the wage gap persists even when workers are matched on the basis of years of experience, number of hours worked, education, occupation, and union membership. The general consensus of many of these studies is that discriminatory treatment is the major cause of the earnings gap between women and men and between whites and people of color (Cherry, 2001). Discrimination takes many forms—lack of access, denial of promotions, assignment to lower-pay jobs, violations of equal pay laws, and devaluation of women's work. Additionally, researchers have found that family responsibilities contribute to women's lower wages. For example, childbearing can lead to career interruptions that hinder women's overall advancement (Taniguchi, 1999).

Consequence of the Earnings Gap Gender and racial inequalities in pay deprive families of greater purchasing power. According to a joint study of the American Federation of Labor–Congress of Industrial Organizations (AFL-CIO) and the Institute for Women's Policy Research (IWPR), America's working families lose a staggering $200 billion of income annually to the wage gap—an average of more than $4000 per family, even after taking into account differences in education, age, location, and number of hours worked ("Equal Pay . . .," 1999). Much of the race–gender gap could be eliminated by more vigorous enforcement of current equal pay laws as well as implementation of the principle of pay equity—equal pay for work of equal value. To put this principle into practice requires evaluating jobs in terms of education, experience, and skill requirements, as well as the job's value to the community.

I WISH WE COULD PROVIDE YOU WITH HEALTH INSURANCE, MA'AM, BUT YOU HAVE A PRE-EXISTING CONDITION: YOU'RE FEMALE. SHOULD YOUR SITUATION EVER CHANGE, GIVE US A CALL...

Although the earning gap between women and men has narrowed in recent years, gender discrimination in employment still deprives women of many benefits enjoyed by their male colleagues.

The income analysis conducted by the AFL-CIO and IWPR found that if married women were paid the same as comparable men, their family incomes would rise by nearly 6 percent and their families' poverty rates would fall from 2.1 to 0.8 percent. Similarly, if single working mothers earned as much as comparable men, their family incomes would increase by nearly 17 percent, and their poverty rates would be cut in half, from 25.3 to 12.6 percent. Despite such potential gains, there is strong opposition to **pay equity** among employers who claim it would be too expensive to implement. Nevertheless, a number of unions have successfully negotiated pay equity programs for their members, albeit primarily with local and state government bodies. A study of several states' efforts to reduce pay inequity in state employment found that both women and men had benefited from wage adjustments in at least 12 states. For example, in Iowa, where wage adjustments for affected workers averaged about $3500, men were 41 percent of the beneficiaries ("Fact Sheet: How Equal Pay Helps Men," 2006).

The Union Difference

Strengthening protections for workers' right to organize in unions and to bargain collectively with their employers would be another potent tool for eliminating some of the current disparity in wages and thereby improving the well-being of families. Data from the Bureau of Labor Statistics (2006) show that in 2005 the median weekly earnings of union members were $801, considerably higher than the $622 earned by their nonunion counterparts. With the exception of Asian men, this union wage advantage holds true across all race and ethnic groups and holds true for women as well. In 2004, 89 percent of union workers in private industry participated in medical care benefits, compared with only 67 percent of nonunion workers. Additionally, union members are more likely to enjoy paid holidays, vacation pay, pay for jury duty, and other benefits than are their nonunion counterparts. In an economy where higher-paying jobs are disappearing and are often being replaced with lower-paying jobs, the role of a union may be even more critical than in the past. Union membership for workers in low-wage occupations may be the difference that keeps them out of poverty. For example, union cashiers earn, on average, $11.22 an hour, thus bringing their yearly wages to $23,338, considerably above the poverty level for a family of four. However, nonunion cashiers, earning, on average, only $8.63 an hour or $17,950 per year, fall below the poverty level. Similar comparisons can be made for a wide variety of low-wage occupations. Despite union advantages, union membership is at a historic low in the United States. Less than 13 percent of today's workers belong to a union. This is in contrast with many other countries—Italy (34.8 percent), Canada and the United Kingdom (both 30.4 percent), and Germany (23.2 percent). France, however, has an even lower rate of union members than the United States (7 percent) (Glader, and Maher, 2005). Here in the United States workers in the public sector are more than four times as likely to be union members as private-sector employees—36.4 percent to 7.9 percent (U.S. Census Bureau, 2006).

IN OTHER PLACES

SEXUAL HARASSMENT

Sexual harassment as a legal concept is still unknown in many parts of the world where women, lesbians, gays, and minorities have few rights. Even among the countries where it is recognized, there is still no universally agreed upon definition as to what constitutes sexual harassment. Therefore, it is difficult to quantify the experiences of sexual harassment and to compare the prevalence from one country to another. Nevertheless, there are movements in this direction. After a survey revealed that close to 50 percent of European women reported that they had been victims of sexual harassment at some point in their lives, the European Union Parliament called on its member states to investigate the extent of sexual harassment in their countries and to develop policies to remedy it (Moline, 2002). Although not strictly comparable, reports from various countries show that sexual harassment is a problem in all corners of the world.

- In Italy, 56 percent of women report they have been victims of verbal sexual harassment, 23 percent victims of exhibitionism, and 24 percent victims of physical harassment.
- In Malta, 7.5 percent of women and 4.2 percent of males report being victims of sexual harassment.
- In the Netherlands, 78 percent of women reported verbal incident of harassment; 54 percent reported being victims of minor physical contacts, and 5 percent reported they were victims of physical assault.
- In Spain, 1 to 18 percent of respondents reported sexual harassment, depending on level of severity (The Irish Presidency of the European Union, 2004).
- In Sweden, 22 percent of medical students reported at least one incident of sexual harassment (Larsson et al., 2003).
- In Australia, 41 percent of women and 14 percent of men had experienced sexual harassment, two-thirds in the workplace ("Paying Out . . .," 2004).

What do you think? Why does there appear to be such extensive patterns of sexual harassment in the United States and around the world? What strategies would you suggest for combating sexual harassment? Is the experience of sexual harassment the same or different for women and men?

Several factors combined to produce a decline in union membership. Chief among them were periodic recessions, which led to massive layoffs in the highly unionized manufacturing sectors. In an effort to prevent further job cuts, unions agreed to give back some hard-won benefits, angering many rank-and-file members. President Ronald Reagan's firing of striking air traffic controllers in 1981 encouraged many employers to develop more aggressive antiunion campaigns. The country's shift to a more conservative mood and some well-publicized corruption scandals involving union officials turned some people against unions. Lastly, but very importantly, unions lost members as a result of their success. As union members income increased, they sent their children to college and professional schools, traditionally not union strongholds. In the past when children followed their parents into the factory or other work settings, unions regenerated themselves. Long-term employment for even one generation is no longer the norm. Whether unions will be able to regenerate themselves in the future is an empirical question. Recent surveys indicate that there is some change in the public's view, with 38 percent of respondents now wanting to see unions have more influence, up from 30 percent in 1999 (Jones, 2005), and indications are that more people would be willing to join unions, if given the opportunity.

Sexual Harassment

Another problem workers may experience is some form of **sexual harassment**, unwanted leers, comments, suggestions, or physical contact of a sexual nature that the recipient finds offensive and causes discomfort or interferes with academic or job performance. Sexual harassment occurs in all types of educational and work settings. Because of the sensitive nature of sexual harassment, accurate data on its extent are difficult to collect. However, numerous studies both in and outside the United States indicate that it is an enormous problem (see In Other Places box). Here in the United States the Equal Employment Opportunity Commission (EEOC), established by the passage of the Civil Rights Act of 1964, is charged with investigating alleged violations and enforcing the laws against sexual harassment. In 2003, the EEOC resolved 13,786 sexual harassment charges and recovered $37.1 million in monetary benefits for charging parties and other aggrieved individuals, not including monetary benefits obtained through litigation (Equal Employment Opportunity Commission, 2005). At about the same time, across the ocean, Britain's Employment Tribunals Service, judicial bodies that resolve employment-related disputes, handled 14,284 sexual harassment and discrimination claims (Capell et al., 2004). Public and private employers that ignore the problem of sexual harassment can pay a high price. For example, a Dade County jury awarded a female employee hired as a pastry chef $1.5 million in damages on her claims of sexual harassment and retaliatory discharge ("Dade County Jury . . .," 2005). In Britain, Merrill Lynch & Company paid a former in-house lawyer $900,000 in an out-of-court settlement after an executive allegedly made lewd comments about her breasts and sex life (Capell et al., 2004).

Sex, Race, Sexual Orientation, Age, and Marital Status

Sexual harassment appears to be more prevalent in male-dominated occupations, where some male workers seek to maintain control over women rather than recognize them as equals. For example, women soldiers, physicians, lawyers, coal miners, and investment bankers have all reported high levels of sexual harassment (see, for example, Meier, 1996; Gruber and Morgan, 2004). One 29-year-old returning woman student provided a personal illustration of harassment at the job site: "I worked as a carpenter for 7 years. Many nights I came home and cried. I was the only woman on my first job. The men didn't want me there. They used to hide my tools and put obscene notes in my lunch bucket. My next job was easier. There was another woman at the job site, and we ate lunch together. It helped to know I wasn't alone. After the men saw we could do the job, they left us alone; a few even became my friends after a while."

Although still quite low compared with that of females, sexual harassment of males may be increasing. Men' claims now account for 15 percent of all sexual harassment charges being brought to the EEOC, up from 9 percent in 1992 (Equal Employment Opportunity Commission, 2005). Juries are taking men's complaints seriously. A jury awarded a male prison guard $750,000 in actual damages and $3 million in punitive damages after he claimed he was sexually harassed by a female guard. The employer denied the allegations, saying the situation was nothing more than two coworkers who did not get along ("Female on Male Sexual Harassment," 2004). Although the perpetrators in male complaints include both women and men, the overwhelming majority of the claims by men are male-on-male harassment. Men, either gay or straight, who do not conform to masculine stereotypes are frequently the target of harassment from other men.

Women of color are more likely to experience sexual harassment than are white women, and the harassment is likely to include racial stereotypes (Fain and Anderson, 1987). Single, divorced, and younger women report being sexually harassed more often than then married and older counterparts. Lesbians, like gays, experience physical and verbal harassment because of their sexual orientation. Sexual harassment of lesbians and gays in the workplace has been reported in a wide variety of countries (see, for example, Jarman and Tennant, 2003).

Although sexual harassment violates equal-employment laws, enforcement is difficult. Many victims are afraid to report the harassment for fear of losing their jobs, or being blamed for bringing it on themselves. All too often, victims do not believe anything can be done or they do not trust the organization to take any meaningful action to change the situation. Fighting sexual harassment is even more difficult in countries where women's rights have yet to be recognized and where they have little legal protection.

Workers who are sexually harassed report a number of problems both physical (chronic neck and back pain, gastrointestinal disorders, sleeplessness, and loss of appetite) and psychological (feelings of humiliation, helplessness, and fear). Recent research suggests that experiences of sexual harassment may lead to use of alcohol and prescription drugs (sedatives and antidepressants) as a means to self-medicate the distress engendered by sexual harassment (Richman and Rospenda, 2005). Harassment victims frequently bring these problems home with them (recall the spillover effect discussed earlier), thereby adding tension to family relationships. Thus, it is in everyone's interest, from employers to government to families, to take steps to end sexual harassment.

THE ECONOMIC WELL-BEING OF FAMILIES

All parents share a common desire to provide a decent standard of living for themselves and their families. To accomplish this goal, an increasing number of couples have made the decision to become a dual-earner family. Women's wages play an important part in the economic well-being of families. In families where both husband and wife work full-time throughout the year, the wife's wages account for an average of 40 percent of family earnings. In 2003, the median income for all married-couple families was $62,281; half of those families had an income higher than that and half of those families had lower incomes.

Table 10.2 reveals how important family structure has become to the economic well-being of families and the amount of money available to families to meet their ongoing needs. Dual-earner couples had incomes of $75,170, compared to the $41,122 of married couples where the husband was the sole breadwinner. Single householders, whether male or female, made less than their married counterparts even when the wife was not working. And, as we have seen before, female householders made considerably less than male householders. This aggregate figure, however, conceals important differences by race and ethnicity. For example, the median income for all white families in 2003 was $55,768, but only $34,369 for African American families, and $34,272 for Latinas/os families. Asian/Pacific Islanders had the highest medium income at $63,251. Their earning power and the fact that, in general, Asians Americans have higher levels of education than other groups, has led many observers to see them as a "model minority." However, this stereotype obscures the diversity within the Asian American population and the processes involved in reaching that income level. For example, Asian American household income generally reflects multiple wage earners, not necessarily high salaries per worker. Asian Americans, although becoming more dispersed in recent years, still tend to be concentrated in a small number of cities (San Francisco, Los Angeles, New York, Chicago, and Honolulu) where salaries, but also cost of living, are higher. Further, approximately half of the Asian American population is composed of the highly educated immigrants who came to the United States in the 1960s. Asian refugees who came to the United States after the Vietnam War were fleeing wartime persecution and had few resources. In 2004, 49.4 percent of Asian Americans aged 25 or older had

TABLE 10.2

Median Income of Families, by Type of Family, 2003

Total married-couple families	$62,281
Wife in paid labor force	$75,170
Wife not in paid labor force	$41,122
Male householder, no wife present	$38,032
Female householder, no husband present	$26,550

Source: U.S. Census Bureau, 2006, *Statistical Abstract of the United States, 2006* (Washington, DC: Government Printing Office): Table 682, p. 465.

a college or professional degree compared to 28 percent of whites, 18 percent of African Americans, and 12 percent of Latinas/os (U.S. Census Bureau, 2006). However, in 1990 almost 67 percent of Cambodian, Hmong, and Laotian adults did not have a high school education (Lee, 1998). Recent Census data indicate that in 1990, 47 percent of Cambodians, 66 percent of Hmong, 67 percent of Laotians, and 34 percent of Vietnamese were impoverished, compared with 10 percent of all Americans and 14 percent of all Asian Americans (Thrupkaew, 2002). Similarly, there was considerable variation in educational levels among Latinas/os, with 24 percent of Cubans having college or professional degrees, Puerto Ricans (14 percent), and Mexicans (8 percent). Thus, it is well to remember that the notion of a "model minority," like all stereotypes, hinders our understanding of the reality of people's lives and thus prevents the development of sound policies that can address their needs.

These statistics take on even more significance when we look ahead to the future. Today immigrant children and children of immigrants are now about 14.1 million, one in five of all Americans aged 18 and under, and their number is rapidly growing (Portes, 2002). Although most immigrant parents have high educational expectations for their children, they often lack the resources required to achieve this goal. Consequently, their children are likely to go to poor schools, live in unhealthy and even dangerous neighborhoods, and when adults are quite likely to be unemployed and even unemployable.

Economic Uncertainty: The Widening Income Gap

The latter part of the 1990s saw real gains in income for most Americans. Inflation and unemployment were at their lowest in many years. However, many of these gains proved be short-lived as the economy slowed in 2001. Many workers lost their jobs as companies reduced their labor costs by outsourcing jobs to other countries and introducing more automation in the workplace. Automation is not only changing the factory floor but it has made inroads into the service sector. Just as consumers learned to pump their own gas, they are now learning to check out and bag their own groceries, and cashiers are almost extinct in parking garages.

Although there is some evidence that the economy is recovering, the financial benefits are concentrated among a smaller segment of the population. At the same time that many families lost economic ground, there was a financial resurgence among the world's wealthy. According to the 2004 World Wealth Report, there were an estimated 7.7 million high net worth individuals (HNWIs)—people with financial assets of at least US $1million, excluding home real estate—at the end of 2003, up 7.5 percent or a net of 500,000 people compared with the previous year. The ranks of HNWIs or millionaires in the United States stood at 2.27 million at the end of 2003, up 14 percent. China, at 12 percent, and India, at 22 percent, outdistanced the gains in Europe, the Middle East, and Latin America. The study also found that in the United States and Canada, the number of ultrarich, those with investment assets of more than $30 million, climbed to 30,000, about the same number of people that live in Juneau, Alaska's capital. These gains were due to a number of factors—chief among them were rising stock markets and wealth-friendly tax cuts (Frank, 2004).

Figure 10.5 shows that the disparity between rich and poor families grew ever wider during the last two decades.

Automation and new technology have eliminated many service jobs. Like many other consumers, this woman is checking out and bagging her own groceries at her local supermarket.

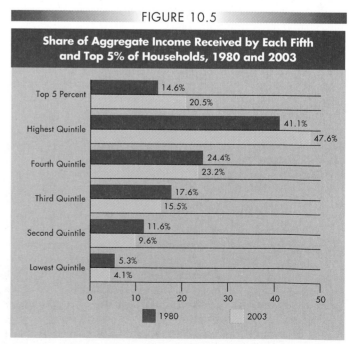

FIGURE 10.5

Share of Aggregate Income Received by Each Fifth and Top 5% of Households, 1980 and 2003

	1980	2003
Top 5 Percent	14.6%	20.5%
Highest Quintile	41.1%	47.6%
Fourth Quintile	24.4%	23.2%
Third Quintile	17.6%	15.5%
Second Quintile	11.6%	9.6%
Lowest Quintile	5.3%	4.1%

Source: U.S. Census Bureau, 2006, *Statistical Abstract of the United States, 2006,* (Washington, DC: Government Printing Office): Table 680, p. 464.

In 1980, the richest fifth of all families received 41.1 percent of all aggregate income, compared to the 5.3 percent received by the poorest fifth of all families. By 2003, the gap had widened to 47.6 and 4.1 percent, respectively. Families at all other income levels, with the exception of the wealthiest families (the top 5 percent), who saw their share of income jump from 14.6 to 20.5 percent, experienced a decrease in their share of aggregate income.

Economists attribute this trend toward greater inequality to a number of factors: the loss of high-paid manufacturing jobs, the decline in union membership, the growth in low-paid service sector jobs, the higher salaries paid to people with higher education and technical skills, the increase in families with two high-wage earners, and the increasingly popular practice of rewarding executives with stock options and bonuses. An analysis by two research groups, United for a Fair Economy and the Institute for Policy Studies, found that in 2004, the average CEO of a U.S. corporation earned an astonishing 431 times the average wage of a blue-collar worker, up from 301 to 1 in 2003 and 42 to 1 in 1982). The average blue-collar worker earned $27,460; the average CEO brought home $11.8 million. If the minimum wage had risen as fast as CEO pay since 1990, the lowest paid workers in the United States would be earning $23.03 an hour today, not $5.15 an hour (Anderson et al., 2004). As the Internet Resources: Applying the Sociological box shows,

Yahoo! co-founders David File (left) and Jerry Yang (right) sit with company chief executive Terry Semel (center) during an interview at the NASDAQ before ringing the opening bell to celebrate the tenth anniversary of the Internet search engine in New York City. Semel is among the highest paid CEOs in the United States.

INTERNET RESOURCES

APPLYING THE SOCIOLOGICAL IMAGINATION

Pay Watch Fact Sheet: H. Lee Scott, President and CEO, Wal-Mart Stores

Total 2005 Compensation Plus Stock Option Grants: $17,542,908

CEO-to-Worker Comparisons	Annual	Weekly	Daily	Hourly	Per Minute
H. Lee Scott	$17,542,908	$337,363	$67,472	$8,434	$140
Minimum-Wage Worker	10,712	206	41	5.15	0.09
Average Worker	25,501	490	98	12,26	0.20
President of the United States	400,000	7692	1538	192	3.21

How Many Years to Equal H. Lee Scott's 2005 Compensation

Minimum-Wage Worker	1637 years	Completion Date 3642 A.D.
Average Worker	687 years	Completion Date 2692 A.D.
President of the United States	87 years	Completion Date 2092 A.D.

This information can be found at http://www.aflcio.org/corporatewatch/paywatch/ceou/database.cfm?tkr=WMT&pg=6 Follow this and the related links to determine how your current income or your expected income after graduation compares with the CEO of your choice.

Think for a moment about how your life would be different if you had the $25,000 income or the $17.5 million. Where would you live? What changes would you make in your lifestyle? What do you think about the growing income gap between top executives and rank-and-file workers?

Is this trend something Americans should be concerned about? Explain. A growing number of shareholders and groups like Responsible Wealth have proposed that there be a maximum ratio between CEO and worker earnings. Do you agree or disagree with this concept? Explain.

H. Lee Scott, President and CEO of Wal-Mart, made over 17 million dollars in 2005. However, his compensation pales in comparison to that of Terry Semel, Yahoo!s CEO, whose total compensation was $109,301,385 in that same year. Mr. Scott does not even make it to the top ten most highly paid CEOs but his company, Wal-Mart, is one of the largest employers in the United States and has been the subject of considerable controversy over the pay and benefits his employees receive.

Who Are the Poor?

As we have just seen, all families do not share equitably in America's wealth. In 2000, 6.2 million families (8.6 percent of all families) were poor. However, as the economy slowed in recent years, the number of poor families increased. In 2004, 7.9 million families (10.2 percent) were living below the poverty level (U.S. Census Bureau, 2006). Each year the federal government calculates the minimum level of income necessary to meet basic subsistence needs of families according to size and type. In 2005, the poverty level, as determined by the federal government, was $19,350 in annual income for a family of four. Even so, many economists believe this threshold is too low because it does not take into account the variation in costs of living in different regions of the country nor the special needs some families have for elder or child care. A minimum-wage worker would have to work more than 72 hours a week, 52 weeks per year, just to keep her or his family of four above the poverty line. Recall that there is no state, county, or metropolitan area in the nation where someone working 40 hours a week at the federal minimum wage can afford the fair market rent for a two-bedroom unit.

Poverty rates are not randomly distributed across the population. They vary by family type, race, and ethnicity. Married-couple families have a relatively low poverty rate (5.5 percent) compared to families with a female householder, no husband present (28.4 percent). Although families with a male householder, no wife present, fared better, their poverty rate was still high at 13.5 percent. Families headed by women accounted for the largest portion of the increase in poor families since 1970. Over 60 percent of the children born since 1980 will spend some part of their life in a single-parent household, and hence are vulnerable to the risk of being poor. This increase in the numbers of women and children who are poor is referred to as the **feminization of poverty.** In 2004, the overall poverty rate among children was 17.8 percent (13 million children), reversing the downward trend of 2000, then at the lowest level since 1979 at 16.2 percent (11.6 million children). The poverty rate remains alarmingly high for African American and Latina/o children, 33 and 28 percent, respectively. Although in absolute numbers most poor children are white, white children had one of the lowest poverty rate overall (10 percent). Only Asian children had a lower rate (9 percent). Having immigrant parents increases a child's chance of being poor. Twenty-six percent of children of immigrants are poor compared to 16 percent of children whose parents are native born (Fass and Cauthen, 2005). The poverty rate for chil-

dren under 18- remained higher than that of 18 to 64-year olds (11.3 percent) and that of people aged 65 and over (9.8 percent).

Although many believe people are poor because they are lazy and do not want to work, the reality is that the majority of people living in poverty are in households where individuals work full-time but make very low wages. They are called the **working poor.** According to a team of Penn State researchers, as many as 25 percent of all jobs in the United States pay less than a poverty-level income. In some states as many as 30 percent do not pay a living wage. Of the more than 35 million persons classified as living in poverty, the majority are children, disabled, or elderly, but 7 million of them are women and men, the majority over the age of 24, who work but who do not earn a sufficient wage to support themselves and their families (Glasmeier, 2005). Although the working poor live in every state of the union, in 17 states the majority of working poor totals more than 50 percent of the working age population. These states are concentrated in the Farm Belt, where economic decline has been going on for the last two decades, and in the West where, according to the Penn State researchers, population growth has helped to keep wages low. Additionally, the South and Southwest, states traditionally with low union membership, have high concentrations of working-poor families with children. Thus, being employed is not always sufficient to avoid poverty.

Many jobs pay only the minimum wage and offer few, if any, benefits. Many are part-time or temporary jobs. Although educational and skill deficiencies contribute to the employment problems of some poor workers, two-thirds of poor workers have high school diplomas. Thus, for many, it is not a lack of basic skills but a scarcity of higher-paying positions that keeps them in poverty. This is especially disturbing when we consider that in spite of the economic gains of the 1990s, child poverty increased in full-time working families. More than seven out of every ten children had at least one employed parent in 2004 (Children's Defense Fund, 2005). At the same time that poverty rates are going up and the wealthy are receiving significant tax cuts, Congress is cutting billions from the federal budget, mostly in programs that will adversely affect poor and low-income children. Many factors are creating an atmosphere of economic uncertainty in the United States and putting more individuals and families at risk of poverty, especially workers with less than a college education, people of color, particularly African Americans and Latinas/os, families headed by women, and a significant proportion of children and the nation's elderly who already live close to the poverty line. Among the most significant risk factors for the nation as a whole are growing trade deficits, accumulating individual and national debt, loss of high paying jobs, reduced returns to investments in education, and the lack of a living wage. Despite repeated attempts, Congress has failed to raise the minimum wage. Lack of congressional action and recognition by state legislatures that poverty rates are increasing among their citizens has led to many state efforts to raise the minimum wage or to seek what is being called a "living wage" (see Debating Social Issues box).

UNEMPLOYMENT AND UNDEREMPLOYMENT

To this point we have dealt with the complex connections between work and families. But what happens to families when this connection is broken or nonexistent? To date, the U.S. economy has been unable to provide jobs for everyone who wants to work. In 2005, the U.S. unemployment rate was 5.1 percent (7.66 percent million people), a slight decrease from the rate of 5.5 percent in 2004. This was a relatively low rate compared to those of other industrialized countries whose rates ranged from a low of 4.7 in Luxembourg to a high of 18.8 in Poland (see Figure 10.6). The level of unemployment in any country depends on a number of factors: structural transformations (economic growth or slowdowns, global competition, mergers, and new technologies), political events, governmental policies, as well as consumer confidence.

Any one set of figures, however, does not tell the full story of unemployment in this country. In any given year, hundreds of thousands of other people are not counted among the unemployed. Some cannot seek work at any given moment because of family responsibilities, illness, or disability, or because they are in school. The Bureau of Labor Statistics does not count these individuals in their monthly unemployment rate and they are considered "marginally attached" to the labor force. These numbers rise and fall with business cycles as people withdraw from the labor force when job opportunities contract and they return when job opportunities expand. Others, unsuccessful in their job quest, give up looking for work altogether, convinced no one would hire them. The federal government calls these individuals "discouraged workers." In January 2005, the

BLS estimated that there were 1.8 million marginally attached workers, with 515,000 listed as discouraged, an increase over previous years (cited in Pack, 2005). If marginally attached workers were counted in Bureau of Labor Statistics calculations of the unemployment rate, it would increase by one or two percentage points.

> *Have you ever been unemployed when you wanted to be working? Do you know anyone who is currently unemployed? How do the unemployed see themselves? How does society view them? How are family relationships changed when one or more members are unemployed?*

Unemployment affects individuals and families in many ways. Clearly, the immediate result of becoming jobless is the loss of or at least a lowering of income. This loss of income puts a severe strain on family budgets and in extreme cases can lead to homelessness, as we saw in the chapter opener. Unemployment can also have a negative impact on family and social life. For example, things we take for granted—home entertaining, going out with friends for dinner or a movie, exchanging cards and presents—may no longer be possible. Children may feel isolated and rejected when they cannot participate in the activities of their friends.

Regardless of the causes, the impact of unemployment on family members can be enormous. To understand how devastating the experience of unemployment can be requires an appreciation of the role work plays in our lives. Paid employment is a means for earning a living, for providing food, clothing, shelter, and other basic necessities for ourselves and our families. Success or failure at this task is often the yardstick by which individual self-worth is measured. The unemployed repeatedly describe themselves as "being nothing," as "being looked down on" or as "having self-doubts." Joblessness can erode a person's self-esteem which, in turn, can lead to other problems.

Some people who lack this ordering in their lives frequently feel psychologically adrift and may seek to escape these feelings through alcohol or other drugs. Other reactions to unemployment can be deadly. One researcher has statistically correlated the increase in the aggregate unemployment rate with increases in deaths, suicides, homicides, admissions to state mental hospitals, and sentences to state prisons (Bluestone, 1987). Research in other countries have found similar results. For example, increases in unemployment in Scandinavian countries had a positive and significant effect on property crime (Edmark, 2005).

Unemployment and Marital Functioning

In addition to causing distress for individual family members, unemployment can affect the functioning of the family as a unit. Many researchers have found that unemployment is associated with lower levels of marital satisfaction, marital adjustment and communication, harmony in family relations, and even divorce (Hetherington and Kelly, 2002; Kalil, 2005). Joblessness can also lead to a disruption in previously

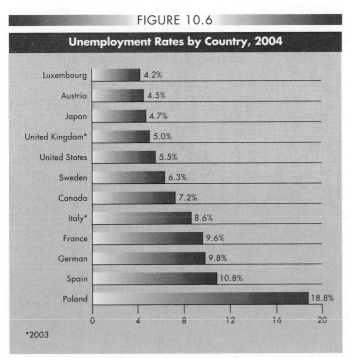

FIGURE 10.6

Unemployment Rates by Country, 2004

Country	Rate
Luxembourg	4.2%
Austria	4.5%
Japan	4.7%
United Kingdom*	5.0%
United States	5.5%
Sweden	6.3%
Canada	7.2%
Italy*	8.6%
France	9.6%
German	9.8%
Spain	10.8%
Poland	18.8%

*2003

Source: Adapted from U.S. Census Bureau, 2006, *Statistical Abstract of the United States, 2006,* (Washington, DC: Government Printing Office): Table 1342, p. 881.

DEBATING SOCIAL ISSUES

SHOULD CONGRESS RAISE THE MINIMUM WAGE?

No doubt you have noticed that over the last few years you are paying more for goods and services. Although few of us like to pay more for the things we need on a daily basis, many of us manage because our wages and salaries are higher than inflation. However, the minimum wage is not indexed for inflation. Therefore, a significant segment of the population (over 7 million people), who work for the minimum wage fall further behind other workers. Congress has not raised the minimum wage since 1997 and its purchasing power has eroded dramatically. An individual working full-time at the current minimum wage only makes $10,712 per year, slightly over half of the poverty level for a family of four. Several attempts have been made to raise the federal minimum wage in recent years but all have failed.

Proponents of raising the minimum wage see it as a simple matter of social justice and good economics. Specifically, they argue that America has become a two-tiered society with the rich getting richer and the poor getting poorer. Although other employees can reasonably expect to get raises as their tenure on the job increases, keeping others at a mini-

Minimum wages jobs are often difficult and dangerous

agreed-upon family roles, resulting in dissatisfaction for one or both partners. For example, Patrick Burman (1988), in his study of unemployment in Canada, found that when wives were unemployed, the egalitarian norms they had negotiated with their spouses disappeared. Consequently, the wives were forced back into the traditional role of housekeeper. As one of his respondents reported, "When I was working, it was more of a joint effort between my husband and I [*sic*] to get it done. . . . But when I was off then—I don't know if it was me or just the way things went—it became more my responsibility, which I really hated. There was no escape from . . . there would always be something to do. . . . I hate it" (quoted in Burman, 1988:171). Burman also found that when husbands were unemployed, they tended to do more housework, but not significantly more. A more recent study in the United States found similar patterns. A common complaint was expressed by a transportation planner who works all day and said, "There hasn't seemed to be a commensurate increase in housework with the decrease in paid work, and it can lead one (me) to feeling a little screwed. I want to come home to a clean house and dinner" (Minetor, 2002).

When parents are psychologically stressed by unstable work and unemployment, they may show less emotional warmth toward their children that, in turn, can lead to academic and emotional problems for their children. Additionally, parental unemployment can have intergenerational aspects. If children perceive their parents' labor market experiences in pessimistic ways, they may disengage from school and/or work and eventually be in the ranks of the unemployed themselves (Kalil, 2005).

Variations in Family Responses to Unemployment As in other areas of family life, families differ in their ability to respond to a member's unemployment. In some cases, families can absorb the loss of income and provide emotional and physical support for their unemployed member until such time as new work is found. How family members react to unemployment depends a great deal on how the family functioned prior to the onset of unemployment as well as on the reasons for the unemployment. Patricia Voydanoff (1983) uses family stress theory to explain the conditions under which unemployment contributes to family crisis or disrupts

mum wage increases the income gap. Currently, the United States is experiencing the widest income gap on record and the percentage of poor children living with a full-time year-round working parent is growing. For too many working families a full-time job does not provide enough money to support a family. The consequences of this fact are enormous and can even prove to be deadly as low-income parents confront choices no parent should have to make: Do I skip paying the utility bills and risk cutoff of electricity, heat, or phone services? Do I miss rent payments and risk eviction, perhaps having to move into substandard housing or even becoming homeless? Do I buy food or medicine? Can we leave the children alone instead of using spare dollars for child care? Those who favor a minimum wage increase believe this action would increase a family's ability to pay for the basic things every family needs—food, shelter, clothing, and health care—thereby improve the overall quality of life for working families. According to this argument, other benefits would follow as well. Any increased purchasing power of working families, would, in turn, put more money into the local economy, thus helping the whole community. Finally, proponents point to national surveys indicating that there is broad support for increasing the minimum wage. For example, a recent Gallup poll found that 86 percent of Americans are in favor of "Congress passing legislation that would raise the minimum wage." Support for raising the minimum wage has consistently exceeded 75 percent over the past two decades. Although traditionally Democrats have taken the lead on this issue, there also is strong support among Republicans. Ninety-three percent of Democrats favor raising the wage compared with 80 percent of independents, and 74 percent of Republicans (Jones, 2006).

Opponents of raising the minimum wage argue that such an action would hurt the economy. Their reasoning is that it would increase labor costs that would cause businesses, especially small businesses, to go out of business or to reduce the number of workers they carry on their payroll. According to this line of reasoning, unemployment would go up, the tax base would shrink, and the community at large would suffer. Strongly related to this argument is their belief that wage levels are best established by the market and that it is inappropriate for the government to set wage levels. Opponents also believe that the poor, who most likely have low levels of skill and education, are not well served by minimum wage legislation because employers, forced to pay higher wages, will in turn look for more skilled workers, thereby lowering job opportunities for the less skilled worker. Relatedly, those opposing increasing the minimum wage see it as an ineffective tool for fighting poverty in that some minimum wage workers are not poor but rather students, teenagers, and additional family wage earners. According to this view, such workers take entry-level jobs for the purpose of gaining experience and training and developing work habits that will then lead to higher paying jobs in the future.

Because of the failure to increase the federal minimum wage, a growing number of states have taken the initiative to raise the state level. Some states and local governments have gone beyond increases in the minimum wage and set living wages, wages that would lift people above the current poverty level. In 2005; this requires an hourly wage of $9.31.

What do you think? Should the market or the government determine a minimum wage level? Explain. Should characteristics of the working poor (for example, age, gender, student status, family income) be taken into account in setting minimum wage standards? Do you or did you ever work at a minimum wage job? If so, how did it affect the quality of your life? Do you favor or oppose increases in the minimum wage? Do you favor or oppose the concept of a living wage? Explain.

family functioning. The model she uses is Reuben Hill's (1958) formulation of the A, B, C, X model of family crisis. A is the event (unemployment) that interacts with B (the family's crisis-meeting resources) that interacts with C (the definition the family gives to the event). This produces X (the crisis—the degree to which family functioning is affected).

Unemployment (A) hits some families harder than others. Families who receive unemployment compensation or severance pay or who anticipate new employment might experience fewer financial and psychological hardships than families lacking these benefits. Among the unemployed, women are least likely to have these benefits. Families also differ in the number and effectiveness of the resources (B) they have for coping with stressful events. Family savings, homeownership, additional sources of income, good communication, and problem-solving skills can minimize the problems associated with unemployment. Research shows that marriages based on a sharing model, in which both partners can perform economic and household labor competently, are more flexible and therefore better equipped to respond to the unemployment or loss of a partner than marriages based on strict gender specialization (Oppenheimer, 1997). Additionally, how the family defines unemployment (C) is critical to the outcome. "If the family perceives the event as a crisis-producing situation, the likelihood of crisis is increased; if the family considers the event to be normal or manageable, family vulnerability to crisis is reduced" (Voydanoff, 1983:244). A graduate student confirmed this assessment when he told the authors, "I was laid off after 15 years of working for one company. I was angry and scared. But my wife and kids were great. We agreed to cut back on expenses while I went back to school. I always wanted to be a teacher but got sidetracked into business where the pay was better. I'm now a tenured teacher and will have my master's degree in another semester. I am happier now than I ever was in my old job and my son now says he wants to be a teacher, too."

Implicit in the family stress model are mechanisms for minimizing the negative consequences of unemployment. Leaving aside the need for more jobs, adequate financial assistance in the form of unemployment compensation and health insurance would help families get through a period of

TABLE 10.3
Unemployment Rates by Sex, Age, Race, and Ethnicity, 2003

	Age	
	16 and over (%)	16–19 (%)
Total	5.5	17.0
Sex		
Males	5.6	18.4
Females	5.4	15.5
Race/Ethnicity		
Whites	4.8	15.0
Blacks	10.4	31.7
Latinas/os	7.0	20.4
Asians	4.4	11.5

Source: U.S. Census, 2006, *Statistical Abstract of the United States, 2006* (Washington, DC: Government Printing Office). Table 610, p. 409.

unemployment with fewer difficulties. In additional, educational or counseling programs aimed at improving family functioning would help families cope with the stresses of unemployment. Finally, knowledge about the structural causes of unemployment would help families define unemployment in a realistic way and lessen the tendency to blame individual members for the problem.

Age, Race, Ethnicity, and Unemployment Table 10.3 shows that like social rewards, unemployment is unevenly distributed throughout the population. In 2004, the unemployment rate for teenagers between the ages of 16 and 19 was 17.0 percent, compared with 5.5 percent for the population 16 and over. The problem was even more severe for youth of color. The unemployment rate for black teenagers was 31.7 percent, over twice that of white teenagers (15.0 percent). Latinas/os were in the middle, with an unemployment rate of 20.4 percent. Teenaged girls had slightly lower unemployment rates than their male counterparts (18.4 to 15.5 percent). Youth unemployment is troubling for a number of reasons. First, a family may depend on income contributions from teenaged members for its economic well-being. Even when teenagers' earnings go directly toward meeting personal needs—clothing, books, and entertainment—this contribution is likely to relieve some of the pressure on household budgets. Second, research indicates that adolescents who have a job are less likely than their unemployed counterparts to become involved in illegal activities such as drug dealing and theft. Finally, if this high unemployment rate continues, the likelihood that these teenagers will establish stable marriages and make long-term commitments to the labor force will diminish.

Similarly, in adulthood the burden of unemployment continues to fall more heavily on people of color despite the progress in civil rights and affirmative action of the last three decades. Among the hardest hit by unemployment are Native Americans. According to the U.S. Census Bureau (2003), the unemployment rate for Native Americans/ Alaska Natives was 15.1 percent, over two and one-half times the national average. However, this figure underrep-

resents the extent of the problem because large numbers of Native Americans live on reservations where few employment opportunities exist. This is also true among tribes that have legal gaming, even though for those tribes there are somewhat more employment opportunities. On some reservations as many as 50 to 80 percent of the tribe's adults may be unemployed and/or have given up looking for work. Thus, many Native Americans fit the profile of "discouraged workers."

Additionally, significant numbers of people experience what economists call **underemployment,** a situation in which a worker is employed but not in the desired capacity, whether in terms of compensation, hours, or level of skills and experience. Underemployment takes several forms. Some of the underemployed are people who are employed part-time but who want to work full-time, a condition called *involuntary part-time employment.* Reliable statistics on underemployment are not easy to find. Government statistics do not differentiate between people who have jobs and those who have jobs below their skill set. However, a recent employment survey by CollegeGrad.com (2004) found that underemployment affected 18 percent of recent college graduate job seekers. Two recent graduates expressed their frustration. One, a finance major complained, "You spend years in school working hard, expecting it to pay off and graduate with a cozy job and a great salary. Then after graduation reality hits; you have to work even harder to get a job." The other, a computer science graduate, said, "I have a very technical degree from a great university and I have had to go back to a line of work I did before I got my degree" (quoted in CollegeGrad.com, 2004). Underemployment is not the province of recent college graduates; it can hit long-term employees as well. Jose Carlos Cavazos, a 37-year-old telecommunications worker with a bachelor's degree in mechanical engineering and an MBA., lost his high-paying job and after an 8-month search took a job throwing mail on the night shift at a U.S. Postal Service distribution center for $13 an hour. It was not only the pay differential that bothered him. "My daughter came home yesterday with a group homework assignment and I had to write a paragraph about what I do for a living. Here I am throwing mail with an MBA. I was totally embarrassed. I'm just grateful my daughter is still too young to understand how tough this is for me" (quoted in Konrad, 2002).

Underemployed workers face serious problems; they are more likely than regular full-time workers to earn minimum wage and much less likely to receive health and pension benefits. In addition, such workers, like Jose Cavazos, are likely to be dispirited. Like the unemployed, those who are underemployed worry about family finances and may experience low levels of marital and family satisfaction as a result.

This discussion of unemployment and underemployment illustrates C. Wright Mills's distinction between personal troubles and social issues (see Chapter 1). Unemployment of this magnitude is not simply a personal trouble of affected families; it is also a social problem. Thus, solving the problem of unemployment and underemployment requires action on the part of the larger society to create more jobs or to provide meaningful alternatives for those who cannot work.

BALANCING WORK AND FAMILY: RESTRUCTURING THE WORKPLACE

Throughout this chapter we have seen how the relationship between work and families has changed drastically. However, a gap still exists between the current structures of families and the way other institutions continue to relate to them. For example, one of the major problems working parents face is getting children off to school in the morning and having a parent there to greet them when they come home. We are probably all familiar with stories of "latchkey children," children who return home after school to an empty house. According to one government study, approximately 7 million children between the ages of 5 and 14 (18 percent) care for themselves after school (Smith, 2000). This is probably a low estimate given that many parents are reluctant to admit to leaving children home alone. Children who are home alone confront many issues. For example, should they answer the doorbell? If they do, someone will know they are home alone. If they do not, someone will assume the house is empty. Both could lead to serious problems. Parents worry about this and other safety issues, so they use the telephone to keep in contact and to monitor their children's activities. Telephone companies report an increase in calls around 3 P.M. as children return from school.

Some school districts offer after school programs to assist working parents, but most do not. Without outside support, families frequently find they must solve this problem by having one parent, usually the wife, work part-time rather than full-time. The economic consequences of this approach include low pay, few benefits, and little or no mobility for the affected worker.

Family-Friendly Policies and Benefits

Given the low birth rates of the past two decades and that the majority of new entrants into the labor force are women and people of color, many employers are increasingly aware that they must institute organizational changes and provide family-friendly benefits to help employees balance work and family demands. One indication that this is happening is the increase in the number of companies identified and ranked as family-friendly businesses. In 1986 *Working Mother* magazine began compiling of list of family-friendly companies. Only 30 companies made the initial list; by 1992, 100 companies made the list, and each year since then the magazine has been able to run a list of the 100 best companies for working parents. To see which companies are family-friendly, go to www.workingmother.com. Among some of the most popular family-friendly benefits are child and dependent care, job sharing, flextime, and family leave.

Child- and Dependent-Care Programs In the past, employers were reluctant to offer on-site day care because of cost. However, over time employers began to realize that employee concern about their children and other dependent relatives was a drain on productivity and morale. This growing realization was reinforced by a recent study that found a positive relationship between the availability of child-care centers, and employee's performance, attitudes, and retention rates (Connelly, DeGraff, and Willis. 2004). Employers and public officials should take special note of one of the study's major findings. A majority of workers said they would be willing to contribute, on average, between $125 and $225 to subsidize on-site day care whether or not they used the benefit themselves. Respondents explained their willingness as both a concern for working parents and a concern to see their company stay profitable by reducing the rates of turnover and absenteeism and increasing worker productivity.

Job Sharing Another innovation allows workers more time for family matters through is **job sharing,** in which two workers split a single full-time job. Each job sharer gets paid for half-time work, although most usually contribute more than a half-time performance. Thus far, the existing evidence suggests that companies would benefit by getting more than half-time performances for half-time wages.

Flextime This represents yet another approach to meeting family scheduling needs. **Flextime** arrangements allow employees to choose when they arrive at and leave work within specified time limits. Flextime is especially helpful when one parent can start work early and arrive home early, while the other works a later shift. To date, only about 28 percent of U.S. workers have flextime, compared with more than 50 percent of the work force in Western European countries. However, this benefit is not evenly distributed among workers. Approximately 29 percent of white workers and 27 percent of Asian workers are on flexible schedules compared to 20 percent of African American workers and 18 percent of Latinas/os.

Family Leave Until recently, the United States was one of the few industrialized countries that did not have a national family leave policy. Finally, in 1993, after two previous failed attempts, Congress passed the **Family and Medical Leave Act** (FMLA), which allows either parent to take up to 3 months of unpaid leave for births, adoptions, and family emergencies. The bill excludes workers in companies with fewer than 50 employees, thus, almost 41 million Americans, more than 40 percent of the private-sector work force, are not eligible. Because it provides only for unpaid leave, it is of little help to low-income workers. The benefits fall far short of those in other countries. Australia is the only other industrialized country that does not have paid maternity or parental leave for women, but it does guarantee a full year of unpaid leave to all women in the country. According to a Harvard University study, 163 countries around the world offer some guaranteed paid leave to women in connection with childbirth and 45 countries ensure that fathers either receive paid paternity leave or have a right to paid paternal leave. For example, in European countries, childbirth-related leave ranges from a low of 3 months to a high of 18 months and the percentage of wage replacement ranges from 50 to 100 percent. In many European countries, for example, the Netherlands, Norway, Denmark, Finland, and Germany, both parents can share parental leave. Additionally,

139 countries provide paid leave for short- or long-term illnesses, with 117 providing a week or more annually. The United States provides only unpaid leave for serious illnesses through the FMLA, which does not cover all workers. Forty-two countries guarantee leave for major family events; in 37 of these countries, the leave is paid (Heymann et al., 2004).

Furthermore, unlike all other advanced industrialized countries, the United States has no statutory provision that guarantees a woman pregnancy leave, either paid or unpaid, or that guarantees that she can return to her job after childbirth. In the United States, pregnancy leaves are covered by the **Pregnancy Discrimination Act of 1978,** which requires that pregnant employees be treated the same as employees with any temporary disability. One obvious limitation to this law is that employers that do not offer disability insurance to their other employees are not required to provide pregnancy leaves to their workers. Family sociologist Joseph Pleck (1988) points to an additional problem with using disability as the mechanism for dealing with childbirth: It excludes fathers from parental leave.

CONTINUING PROGRESS OR RETRENCHMENT?

Although the last three decades have brought considerable changes to the workplace, demographic trends (increases in number of dual-earner couples, in single parents, and in the elderly) argue that more change is needed. Yet the volatility of the current economy may jeopardize existing benefits as companies struggle to contain costs and maximize profits. Some studies show a diminishment of benefits while others show some increases. For example, a study by the Society for Human Resources, a widely respected research organization, found in the 600 companies they surveyed that the number of companies offering paid family leave dropped from 27 percent in 2001 to 23 percent in 2003; those offering flexible work hours fell from 64 to 55 percent, while job sharing dropped from 26 to 22 percent (Armour, 2004). Conversely, the Families and Work Institute's 2005 National Study of Employers (NFE) found no statistically significant decrease in flexibility nor in leaves of absences. In fact, the NFE found that in 2005, 31 percent of employers allowed at least some employees to change starting and quitting times, up from 24 percent in 1998 (the time of the previous study). There was also an increase in the opportunity to work a compressed work week, up from 37 percent in 1998 to 44 percent in 2005. The NFE also found that there was no statistically significant differences in the types of child-care assistance as assessed in 1998 and 2005. Additionally, employers were more likely to provide information about elder care resources to employees, increasing from 23 to 34 percent during those 7 years. At the same time, however, 37 percent of employers reported shifting a greater proportion of the costs of health care to employees from 2003 to 2005. Additionally, fewer employers were contributing to employees' retirement plans and fewer companies provided defined benefit pension plans that guaranteed a specific benefit on retirement (Bond et al., 2005).

WRITING YOUR OWN SCRIPT

WORK–FAMILY DECISIONS

As we have seen in this chapter, the link between work and family is complex and constantly changing. Most families can no longer expect to survive with only the traditional male wage earner. Thus, partners in a relationship have to make considerable personal adjustments if both are working, especially if they have children.

Questions to Consider
1. Do my partner and I want jobs or careers? Will one of our jobs or careers take priority over the other? How will we make employment decisions that involve the other partner? How will we deal with career moves, including geographic relocation, especially if one of us does not want to relocate? If we both work, how will that affect our division of household labor? How will it affect our decision if and when to have children?
2. If our family does not need two wage earners, will we both work anyway? Can either of us consider staying home to take care of the children? Why or why not? If we both need to or want to work, what options do we have for quality child care? What can we do to reduce the stress of work–family conflicts? Some working parents have tried to resolve their work–family conflicts by working at home. Would one or both of us want to work at home? What would be the advantages and disadvantages of this for our personal and family relationships?

SUPPORTING MARRIAGES AND FAMILIES

Family values are often discussed in the United States and many public officials pay lip service to these values when they are on the campaign trail, but the reality is that the United States lags behind most other countries in providing benefits that would help working families live less stress-filled lives. To overcome this situation requires major efforts. Resolving work and family conflicts can no longer be seen as primarily a mother's issue, in which the solution puts the major responsibility on her, requiring her to reduce work hours or to leave the labor force entirely, thus becoming a low earner or even non-earner. However, to move to a more egalitarian culture requires women to share some of the more enjoyable aspects of parenting as well as their authority in the domestic sphere with men and it requires men to share power in the public square as well as to share more fully in family work. Nevertheless, changes in personal attitudes alone are insufficient. The larger society must more fully recognize and reward women's competence in the public spheres as well as men's competence in the private sphere of family life. In her book, *Restructuring Gender Relations and Employment: The Decline of the Male*

Breadwinner, British sociologist Rosemary Crompton (1999) outlines a "dual-earn/dual-career" society in which women and men engage symmetrically in market work and in caregiving work. To achieve this does not require wives to become like husbands who work 40+ hours outside the home but rather that both wives and husbands equalize paid work hours and unpaid caregiving hours.

The ability for couples to implement more egalitarian attitudes and arrangements depends on structural changes in the workplace, including but not limited to the following:

- Revising work schedules that would allow for a shorter work week and allowing both female and male workers to request reduction in hours for a prorated reduction in wages and benefits as well as paid family leave for the birth or adoption of a child and for major family emergencies.

- Providing a living wage for all workers and eliminating the existing discrimination in wages among different categories of the population.

- Providing a national system of affordable and quality day care.

- Ensuring a safety net for all workers and their families by providing universal health care and adequate retirement benefits.

Unquestionably, such policies would be expensive—thus they are likely to be opposed by employers and even many taxpayers. However, implementing such benefits is not impossible. Many other countries have had similar benefits in place for many years (see, for example, Gornick, 2002; Appelbaum et al., 2002; Heymann et al., 2004). These countries provide lessons in how to provide benefits. None of these countries rely on individual employers providing wage replacement for their own employees. Rather, paid leaves are funded through a variety of social insurance plans and/or general tax revenues. Because these proposals stand to benefit all segments of the population, the expenses should also be borne by all segments of the population. Imagine the possibilities if employers, public officials, union leaders, worker representatives, and religious leaders agreed to work together to create and share the costs of a family-friendly work environment.

SUMMARY

Although we frequently think of work and family life as discrete activities, research shows that the worlds of work and family affect each other in significant ways. The quality and stability of family life depend to a large extent on the type of work available to family members, and work can have spillover effects, both positive and negative, on family life.

In 1900, only 20 percent of women aged 14 and older were in the labor force, compared with approximately 86 percent of men in that age category. One hundred years later, 60 percent of women and 75 percent of men 16 and older were in the labor force. Before World War II, the majority of women workers were young, single, poor, and women of color. As late as 1975, only 36.7 percent of married women with children under 6 were in the labor force. By 2003, the comparable figure was almost 60 percent.

Women work for many of the same reasons men do, particularly to support themselves and their families. The rapid entrance of married women with children into the labor force has altered family life in many ways. The traditional

nuclear family consisting of a working husband and a full-time homemaker with dependent children is in the minority today. The typical family today is a dual-earner, or "two-paycheck" family. The attempts by dual-earner couples to integrate work and family experiences affect many aspects of family life: decision making and power relationships, marital happiness, and the household division of labor. Working couples often experience role overload and role conflict as they struggle to balance the demands of work and family. Lack of affordable quality child care is particularly stressful for working parents of preschool children.

Although the labor force participation rates of women and men are converging, women still confront issues of inequity in the labor market. Among them are occupational segregation, a gender gap in earnings, and sexual harassment. Parents differ in their ability to provide a decent standard of living for themselves and their families. The disparity between rich and poor families grew even wider during the last two decades due to loss of high-paid manufacturing jobs, the decline in union membership, the growth in low-paid service sector jobs, the increase of in families with two-wage earners, tax cuts that primarily benefited the wealthy, and the increasingly popular practice of rewarding executives with stock options and other financial benefits. An increasing number of families are living in poverty. Being employed is not always sufficient to avoid poverty. Nearly two-thirds of all people living in poor families with children live in families with a worker.

The experience of unemployment or underemployment can have severe negative impacts on marital functioning. Unemployment is unevenly distributed throughout the population. It is particularly high among teenagers and people of color.

The United States is one of the few countries that does not offer paid maternity leave for its workers. Although many employers are becoming more sensitive to the family needs of their employees, the volatility of the current economy has led to decreases in some family-friendly benefits. Some programs that have been introduced to help workers are job sharing and flextime. Given the widespread movement of mothers into the labor force and the growing number of workers caring for elderly parents, pressure will likely build for improved work–family policies. However, this is likely to come about only when work–family conflict is seen as a problem for both women and men.

KEY TERMS

labor force participation rate	occupational distribution	working poor	Family and Medical Leave Act
commuter marriage	pay equity	underemployment	Pregnancy Discrimination Act of 1978
role overload	sexual harassment	job sharing	
	feminization of poverty	flextime	

QUESTIONS FOR STUDY AND REFLECTION

1. Describe the major changes in the characteristics of the U.S. labor force during the last half of the twentieth century. How have these changes affected the quality of family life in the United States? Today, approximately 70 percent of families have two earners. For this reason, many people argue that the United States needs a national family policy. To what extent do you think the federal government and employers have a responsibility for resolving some of the problems confronting working parents? Would you be willing to see tax dollars subsidize all or a portion of child care for all working families? Explain.

2. How were household tasks divided in your family of orientation? What was the basis for this division of labor? Did family members perceive this division as equitable? Do you plan to replicate this division of labor in your family of procreation? Why or why not? How is the division of household labor related to marital functioning and satisfaction?

3. How have recent economic, social, and political trends, including acts of terrorism, impacted your lifestyle? Have they caused you to be optimistic, unenthused, or pessimistic about the future of the national economy? How has the evolution of a global economy affected the structure and functioning of families throughout the world? Discuss the pros and cons of the global economy that has developed in conjunction with the spread of capitalism. How do you feel about corporations relocating jobs to other parts of the country and to other countries to save on labor costs? Do they have an obligation to employees to pay living wage regardless of their geographic location? Explain.

4. In the section on Supporting Marriages and Families, we call for changing our cultural ideas about gender as a way to balance work and family. Do you agree or disagree? In your answer, consider the likely consequences of such a change, both positive and negative. Do you agree or disagree with the suggestions for changing the workplace environment? Are such proposals achievable? Under what conditions?

ADDITIONAL RESOURCES

SOCIOLOGICAL

CHERRY, ROBERT. 2001. *Who Gets the Good Jobs? Combating Race and Gender*. New Brunswick, NJ: Rutgers University Press. Cherry provides a readable and provocative synthesis of the theoretical, historical, and cultural material that sheds new light and understanding as to why discriminatory barriers faced by women and people of color persist even when they conflict with profitability measures.

DRAUT, TAMARA. 2006. *Strapped: Why America's 20- and 30- Somethings Can't Get Ahead*. New York: Doubleday. If you are feeling financial strapped, Draut provides statistical data to show that you are not alone. The author argues that depressed wages, inflated educational costs, and credit card debt are making it difficult for young adults to reach financial independence and she advocates political action to reverse these trends.

MOEN, PHYLLIS, Ed. 2003. *It's About Time: Couples and Careers*. Ithaca, NY: Cornell University Press. Based on the Cornell Couples and Careers Study of 2216 workers from 20 to 73 years of age, 93 percent of them with a spouse or partner, 33 contributing authors analyze various aspects of dual-career couples' lives. Moen calls for visionaries who understand the new work force and who can help reshape the lock-step social organization of careers by providing a range of alternative career paths and work hours, benefits, reward structures, and opportunities to fit today's workers and their families.

STRINGER, LEE. 1998. *Grand Central Winter*. New York: Seven Stories Press. This riveting chronicle of one man's homelessness and addiction to crack puts a human face on a growing problem.

FILM

The Corporation. 2005. This film explores the nature and dramatic rise of the dominant institution of the modern era while raising critical questions about the proper role of business in society.

North Country. 2005. Based on a true story, this film powerfully tells the experiences of a working mother who became a miner on the Minnesota iron range and suffered sexual harassment at the hands of her male colleagues. Her experiences inspired the first sexual harassment class action lawsuit.

LITERARY

SINCLAIR, UPTON. 1981. *The Jungle*. New York: Bantam. Sinclair provides one of the most important and moving works in the literature of social change as he tells the story of Jurgis Rudkus, a young Lithuanian immigrant who arrives in America with dreams of wealth, freedom, and opportunity, but instead encounters injustice and "wage slavery" in the turn-of-the-century meat-packing industry. This grim indictment led to government regulations of the food industry.

WALDMAN, AYELET. 2005. *The Cradle Robbers*. New York: Berkley. This is the latest in the "Mommy-Track Mysteries" whose protagonist, Juliet Applebaum, a former public defender turned a stay-at-home mom, uses her knowledge and skill to investigate murders and crime.

INTERNET

http://www.familiesandwork.org The Web site of the Families and Work Institute provides data to inform decision making on the changing work force, changing family, and changing community to improve working conditions and family lives.

http://www.bls.gov The U.S. Department of Labor's Bureau of Labor Statistics provides up-to-date information on the economy, employment, and earnings.

http://www.studtentsagainsthunger.org The goal of the National Student Campaign Against Hunger and Homelessness is to end hunger and homelessness by educating, engaging, and training students to meet individuals' immediate needs while advocating for long-term systemic solutions. Their Web site provides information and links to many other resources and provides information for how you can get involved.

http://www.eeoc.gov The Equal Employment Opportunity Commission Web site provides information on laws and various types of discrimination, policies for eliminating discrimination from the workplace, and guidelines and other aids for filing sexual harassment claims.

11

POWER, ABUSE, AND VIOLENCE IN INTIMATE RELATIONSHIPS

IN THE NEWS

Hastings, Minnesota

Although statistically rare, **parricide**—the killing of one's parents—occurs approximately 300 times a year in the United States. In the aftermath of one such recent case of parricide—in February 2006, 17-year-old Matthew Niedere and his high school friend, Clayton Keister, pleaded guilty to the first-degree murder of Matthew's parents, Peter and Patricia Niedere on October 8, 2005. The reverse of American society's stereotypical view of the type of youth that might be involved in such family violence, Matthew and Clayton were members of upper-middle-class, intact families, went to a private faith-based high school, and attended church regularly. Two weeks before to the murders, the two teenagers, together with a third co-conspirator (who was charged with involvement), secretly met several times to plot the murders. According to authorities, Matthew was the driving force in the plot to kill his parents, while his friend Clayton was the tactical leader for the plan and supplied the weapons used in the killings.

The murders of Peter and Patricia Niedere was not the first attempt by Matthew to kill his parents. After a failed preplanned attempt on the lives of his parents at their home the night before the actual murders, Matthew enlisted his friend Clayton to come back to Hastings the next day to help him kill his parents, this time at the family-owned auto glass business. The plan was to take some money from the cash register to make it look like a robbery. According to authorities, the physical evidence along with witness and participant statements indicate that once inside his parents' store, Matthew shot his father five times with a 22-caliber semiautomatic handgun. He then shot his mother four times with the same handgun. Unlike her husband, none of the four shots fired by Matthew were life-threatening. However, while trying to save her dying husband, Matthew's friend Clayton Keister shot her in the head at almost point blank range with a 12-guage shotgun, causing instantaneous death. After the murders, Matthew and Clayton each went home to dress and prepare to attend their high school homecoming dance later that evening.

Although the real motive may never be known, Dakota County Attorney James C. Backstrom speculated that the motive for the crime lay in a mixture of Matthew's quest for freedom from his parents, whom he viewed as too strict and too overbearing, and his greed. His friend, Clayton, participated out of a warped sense of loyalty. Matthew planned to use the proceeds from his parents' estate to pay off his co-conspirators for their help and to move to the new life of freedom he so desperately sought.

To some people's surprise, County Attorney Backstrom announced that he would not pursue a conviction for premeditated murder, which carries a mandatory sentence of life in prison without any possibility of parole. Rather, according to the attorney, after what he describes as lengthy and emotional discussions with members of the Niedere family, a review of the co-conspirators statements and psychological reports on the two teens, as well as dozens of letters he received from members of Clayton Keister's family and friends asking for mercy, he chose to pursue a conviction of life in prison with the possibility of parole after 30 years. The county attorney's decision seems also based, in part, on his knowledge of the workings and development of the human brain, which he believes does not fully develop until a person reaches her or his mid-20s, and that the last portion of the brain to fully develop is the frontal lobe, the region that governs impulse control.

WHAT WOULD YOU DO? If your parents were murdered by a sibling, would you be sympathetic to her or him? If yes, would you ask for mercy for your sibling? If no, why not? If you were the mother, father, sister, brother, or a member of the extended family, would your feelings be different? Explain. Do you agree with the criminal justice process that places the ultimate decision of what type of conviction to pursue in cases such as this in the hands of correctional professionals? Do you agree that 16- or 17-year-olds of basic intelligence who are not suffering from any serious mental illness or psychosis should be tried for murder as an adult? Explain.

A father who wanted to avoid paying child support injected his infant son with HIV-tainted blood. The boy subsequently developed full-blown AIDS. Recently, a New York mother of seven children starved her 4-year-old to death, allegedly because she neither wanted nor loved her. A 33-year-old man was charged with attempted murder after beating his girlfriend's 14-month-old son into unconsciousness. A father killed his son by repeatedly punching him in the stomach because he was making too much noise during a televised football game. A mother of seven children was charged with manslaughter after her 15-year-old son, weighing only 23 pounds, died from pneumonia and apparent malnutrition. Until recently, most people in the United States probably would have shaken their heads in wonderment at these stories, thinking that they were isolated and unusual acts of cruelty that only the most deranged person could commit. Families, after all, are "havens in a heartless world" (Lasch, 1977:8).

Unfortunately, this picture of families as havens of nonviolence is inaccurate. Instead of havens into which we can retreat for comfort, safety, and nurturing, families are increasingly places of danger for many of us. Although most family members do not inject us with HIV-tainted blood, starve us to death, or beat us into unconsciousness, every year millions of Americans intentionally injure, abuse, assault, or murder members of their own families. Domestic or intrafamily violence is interwoven into the very fabric of U.S. society. It is believed the most common yet least reported crime in this country. In no other U.S. institution or group is violence and abuse more of an everyday occurrence than it is within the family.

THE ROOTS OF FAMILY VIOLENCE: A HISTORICAL CONTEXT

Many people think of family violence as a uniquely American phenomenon that has come into being only in recent decades. Records show, however, that as early as the 1640s Americans recognized the existence and seriousness of family violence and abuse and attempted to prevent or punish such behavior (Pleck, 1989). But the extent of family violence in America's past is difficult to ascertain because official records were not always kept. Likewise, we know very little about the history of violence across cultures because most cultures around the world have not officially recorded such data. Nonetheless, based on his examination of cultures around the world, anthropologist David Levinson (1981) concluded that family violence is not rare. Furthermore, wife beating is the most common form of family violence. Levinson's findings are consistent with those of most social science research into family violence in the United States, which finds that women are far more often the victims of violence and offenses against family members than are men. Recent statistics reveal that approximately 85 percent of the victims of domestic violence in the United States are women. In fact, domestic violence is the single greatest cause of injury to women, exceeding rape, muggings, and auto accidents combined (Family Violence Prevention Fund, 2006a; National Coalition Against Domestic Violence, 2006a).

Violence against Women

The historical subordination of women and children is linked to their experiences of violence and assault in the family. Historical accounts by colonists and missionaries as well as anthropological studies inform us of the extent to which violence against women has been a part of the institutional structure of various societies throughout history. Consider for a moment the following historical facts about women and violence:

- Under Roman law, a husband could chastise, divorce, or kill his wife for adultery, public drunkenness, and other behaviors.
- According to the Decretum (c. 1140), the first enduring systematization of Christian church law, women were "subjects to their men" and in need of punishment to correct their supposed inferiority and susceptibility to the influence of the devil.
- Well into the seventeenth century, in many European countries, including England, a man could legally kill his wife for certain behaviors.
- English common law held that men had a legal right to beat their wives as long as the stick they used was no thicker than the husband's thumb. (This law is the basis of the contemporary saying "rule of thumb.")
- The eighteenth-century Napoleonic Civil Code, which influenced Swiss, Italian, French, and German law, gave men absolute family power. Under this code, men could legally use violence against women up to the point of attempted murder.
- In the 1800s, in both Europe and the United States, men could use "reasonable" physical force against women, which included black eyes and broken noses.
- Sexual assault, as well as severe physical beatings, was an integral part of the female slave experience in the United States.
- A nineteenth-century Mississippi court declared that husbands could use corporal punishment on their wives. Not until 1883 was wife beating banned in the United States.

The folkways and mores of various cultures show the universality of violence in women's lives. According to feminist philosopher Mary Daly (1978), such practices as the binding of young women's feet in China, the Indian suttee (the burning of Indian women on the funeral fires of their husbands), European and American witch burnings, the mutilation of African women's genitals through female circumcision,[1] and past (and some present) gynecological practices in the United States such as unnecessary surgery and forced sterilization, are all variations of the same thing: violence against women.

As in the past, women continue to be the primary victims of violence. And violence against women continues to cross many geographic lines and borders. For example, despite

---

[1]Female circumcision takes many forms. The mildest form involves cutting the hood of the clitoris in a manner similar to the practice of male circumcision. The most severe form of female circumcision involves the removal of the clitoris, labia minora, and most of the labia majora, after which the vagina is stitched closed except for a very small opening to allow for the passage of urine and menstrual blood. Perhaps the most common form of female circumcision involves removing the clitoris and part of the labia minora. This latter type of circumcision is currently practiced in about 40 countries, including East and West Africa, Asia, the Islamic Mideast, and South America. It is not uncommon for as many as 90 to 98 percent of the female population to have undergone one or another form of circumcision without the aid of anesthetics (Renzetti and Curran, 1992; State of the World Population, 1997).

the termination of military rule in Latin America, the deregulation of India's economy, and the end of apartheid in South Africa, physical and sexual assault of women is still widespread. The violence against women globally is so intense that the United Nations has described it as a "global epidemic of violence against women." Other observers call this violence "terrorism in the home." By whatever name, violence against women is global and "epidemic." Worldwide, for instance, one in three women have been beaten, forced to have sex, or abused in other ways during her lifetime. Violence against women crosses all borders. For example, every 83 seconds a woman is raped in South Africa; in many Third World countries, 500,000 or more women a year die from pregnancy-related problems, including botched abortions (Family Violence Prevention Fund, 2006a; Wallace, 2004).

In the United States, although women are less likely than men to be victims of violent crimes overall, women are five to eight times more likely than men to be victimized by an intimate partner. It is estimated that every 9 seconds a woman is battered; every 6 hours a woman is battered to death; somewhere between 4 and 6 million women experience a serious assault by an intimate partner during an average 12-month period; 17.7 million women have been raped or been a victim of attempted rape during their lifetimes; every day in the United States four women die as a result of domestic violence, a euphemism for murders and assaults by husbands and boyfriends (Centers for Disease Control and Prevention, 2006b; Bureau of Justice Statistics Crime Data Brief, 2003; Clark County Prosecuting Attorney, 1999). On and on the violence continues (see Table 11.1 for other examples of the global nature of violence against women), and one by one lives are lost, families are shattered, and communities are ripped apart. In the United States, intimate partner violence ranks as one of the nation's most expensive health problems. The cost of intimate partner violence annually exceeds $5.8 billion, including $4.1 billion in direct health care expenses. Businesses forfeit another $900 million in lost wages, sick leave, absenteeism, and nonproductivity, and $900 million in lifetime earnings (Centers for Disease Control and Prevention, 2003).

Violence against Children

Throughout history, children also have frequently been victims of violence and abuse, including sexual assault. Violence against children is linked to cultural values and attitudes that have defined children as the property of families. In many societies, families were ruled by fathers who virtually held their children's lives in their hands. Historian Samuel Radbill (1980) reports that in ancient times a father had the power to withhold the right to life from his child by abandoning the child to die. Although there are no clear records of the actual number of children who died as a result of such practice, **infanticide**—the killing of infants and young children—appears to have been widely practiced throughout much of history. In some societies infants would be killed if they cried too much or if they were sick or deformed. Infanticide has been practiced by a wide range of groups, including some early Native American cultures, where newborns were thrown into a pool of water and declared fit to live only if they rose to

TABLE 11.1
The War against Women: Domestic Violence around the World

- Approximately one-fourth of the world's women are violently abused in their own homes.
- Seventy percent of all murdered women worldwide were killed by their male partners.
- Every day 36,000 women in the Russian Federation are beaten by their husbands or partners; every 40 minutes a woman is killed by domestic violence.
- In Bangladesh, 47 percent of adult women report physical assault by a male partner. Throwing acid to disfigure a woman's face is so common in Bangladesh that it warrants its own section of the penal code.
- Approximately one-fourth of Australian women who have ever been married or in a de facto relationship has experienced violence by a partner at some time during the relationship.
- In a nationally representative sample of Canadian women, almost one-third (29 percent) of those ever married reported being physically assaulted by their current or former partner.
- In a survey in the Kisii District of Kenya, 42 percent of women reported being "beaten regularly" by their partners.
- In South America, a study found that 70 percent of all crimes reported to police were of women beaten by their husbands.
- In India, more than 5000 women are killed each year because their dowries are inadequate—according to their husbands.
- In countries of the Middle East and Latin America, husbands are often exonerated from killing an unfaithful or disobedient wife.

Sources: Commonwealth of Australia, 2004, "Women in Australia 2004," Australian Government, Department of the Prime Minister and Cabinet, Office of the Status of Women, http://ofw.facs.gov.au/womens_safety_agenda/index.htm (Accessed July 8, 2006); Amnesty International, 2004, "Making Violence Against Women Count: Facts and Figures," http://web.amnesty.org/library/Index/ENGACT770362004 (Accessed July 8, 2004); Charlotte Bunch, 1999, "Violence against Women and Girls: The Intolerable Status Quo," in Cheryl Albers, *Sociology of Families: Readings* (Thousand Oaks, CA: Pine Forge Press): 296–298.

the surface and cried. Even adult children did not escape the power of fathers. In France, for example, fathers had the legal right to kill an adult son or daughter under certain conditions.

Historically, girls and children born to unmarried parents have been the primary victims of child violence, abuse, and murder. Like their adult counterparts, girls have been far more vulnerable to family violence and abuse than have boys. Female infanticide continues even today in some societies, such as in parts of China, where male babies are preferred. In the past, much of the violence against children was socially acceptable. Although such treatment is not generally acceptable today, some level of violence against children by parents continues to be condoned (or certainly tolerated) in the United States. Unlike in Sweden, where a parent can be imprisoned for a month for striking a child, in the United States many parents believe in and use corporal punishment when disciplining their children.

Violence against the Elderly

Another group frequently victimized by family violence is the elderly. Little is known about the historical incidence of elder abuse. However, we do have examples of societal violence directed against the elderly: Older women were the common targets of witchcraft trials, and older men were the most frequent murder victims. During the sixteenth, seventeenth, and eighteenth centuries, elders controlled the economic resources of the family, and independence for adult children came only with the parents' death. Elderly parents were thus frequently the targets of violence and abuse from adult children who sought to express their frustration or to take control of family resources. Following this period came the industrial era, during which adult children had opportunities to become independent of their parents. Parents often became financially dependent on their children rather than the other way around. This period seems to have witnessed relatively little reported elder abuse (Sigler, 1989). The situation has not changed very much today. Many elderly continue to suffer neglect and abuse in silence out of fear or embarrassment. Therefore, many of these cases go undetected, unless, of course, the victim dies and the media picks up the story. (We will return to a more detailed discussion of contemporary elder abuse later in this chapter.)

Violence against Siblings

Another kind of violence that has occurred within families throughout history is sibling abuse. To date, however, few systematic studies of nonfatal sibling violence in the United States have been conducted. One of the problems involved in documenting sibling violence and abuse is that historically parents have considered sibling conflict to be "normal" behavior and therefore have not generally reported it. Even today there is little information on or public awareness of sibling violence.

How much do you know about family violence? More likely than not, you probably know someone who is either a victim or perpetrator of such behavior. Moreover, it is possible that you have been or will be a victim of family violence yourself. Why is violence of all types so common among members of the most intimate of all human groups—the family? In the following pages, we explore this and other questions about family violence. To begin, we look at domestic violence and assault within the context of U.S. culture.

MYTHS ABOUT VIOLENCE AND ABUSE

A number of oversimplifications, myths, and distortions continue to block our understanding of the nature and extent of marriage, family, and intimate violence. Most of these myths involve issues of gender, race, class, sexual orientation, age, marital status, and the mental state of the abuser. Although research has shown many of these beliefs to be overstated or blatantly false, many people continue to believe them. As a consequence, much family violence and abuse goes unrecognized and unreported. Consider the following:

Myth: **Family violence is rare.**

Fact: **Family violence occurs in epidemic proportions in the United States.**
- Acts of family violence occur every 12 to 15 seconds, more frequently than any other crime in the United States (Eric County Coalition Against Family Violence, 2003).

Myth: **Men are equally victims of domestic violence.**

Fact: **Approximately 85 percent of the victims of domestic violence are women (Family Violence Prevention Fund, 2006a)**
- While it is acknowledged that men also suffer from abuse, women are five to eight times more likely than men to be victimized by an intimate partner and experience chronic domestic violence.
- 95 percent of all spousal or partner assaults are committed by men.

Myth: **Domestic violence occurs only in poor, poorly educated, minority, or "dysfunctional" families in urban inner-city communities.**

Fact: **Domestic violence crosses all boundaries, whether social, economic, professional, religious, geographical, or cultural.**
- Domestic violence is not confined to poor, poorly educated, or so-called dysfunctional families. It happens in urban and rural communities, in wealthy high-rise apartment buildings and middle-class suburbs, in white as well as other racial or ethnic minority families, and to people who speak all languages. It happens regardless of sexual orientation and religion, and victims range in age from less than 1 year old to over 65 years of age.
- Educated, successful men, such as lawyers, doctors, ministers, politicians, and business executives, beat their wives as regularly and as brutally as do men in other classes (Clallam County Courts, 2006).
- Violence will occur at least once in two-thirds of all marriages. Violence is the reason stated for divorce in 22 percent of middle-class marriages.
- Every year, 1 to 4 million children between the ages of 3 and 17 are abused (punched, kicked, beaten, or attacked with a knife or gun) by parents, stepparents, and guardians.
- Each day more than four children die as a result of child abuse in the home and three out of four of these victims are under the age of 4.
- Three out of five cases of elder abuse occur in the senior's own home at the hands of family members.

Andrea Yates (middle) sits with her attorneys as the not guilty by reason of insanity verdict is read in her retrial 26 July, 2006 in Houston, Texas. Yates admitted to murdering all five of her children by drowning them in a bath tub in her suburban home in 2001 and pleaded guilty by reason of insanity.

Myth: **Domestic violence is a "loss of control" and only mentally ill or "sick" people abuse family members.**

Fact: **Domestic violence is rarely caused by mental illness, but mental illness is often used as an excuse for domestic violence (Coalition to End Family Violence, 2006).**

- Violent behavior is a *choice*. Perpetrators use it to control their victims. Domestic violence is about batterers *using* their control, not *losing* their control. Their actions are deliberate.
- Only a small percentage of abusers are actually mentally ill. Whatever we think of their behaviors, most abusers are "normal" in the psychological sense of the word.
- Most men who assault their partners are not violent outside the home. They do not assault or abuse their bosses, colleagues, or friends. If abusive men were truly mentally ill, they would not limit their violence in this way.
- Most people who suffer from various forms of mental illness do not engage in violent or aggressive behavior (Wallace, 2004; Women's Health Care House, 2002).

Myth: **Domestic violence is more common in heterosexual than in same-sex relationships.**

Fact: **Domestic violence and abuse occurs in approximately 30 to 40 percent of LGBT relationships, which is the same percentage of violence that occurs in heterosexual relationships. It is a myth that same-sex couples do not batter each other—or if they do, they are just "fighting" or it is "mutual abuse."**

- Two in five gay and bisexual men experience abuse in intimate partner relationships, comparable to the rate for heterosexual women.
- Intimate partner violence is the third most severe health problem facing gay men behind HIV/AIDS and substance abuse.
- Almost one-half of lesbians have been abused by a partner in their lifetime.
- Domestic violence occurs in lesbian and gay relationships without regard to age, race, class, lifestyle, and socioeconomic boundaries and with the same statistical frequency as in heterosexual relationships. However, lesbian and gay victims receive fewer societals protections.
- Many battered lesbians and gays fight back to defend themselves—it is yet another myth that same-sex battering and abuse is mutual (National Coalition Against Domestic Violence, 2005; NPR, 2002; Fulcher, 2002).

Myth: **If the victim did not like it, she would leave; anyway, "It's their own fault—they bring it on themselves."**

Fact: **Victims of domestic violence neither ask for nor like the abuse. Many victims stay in the relationship for any number of reasons, including fear. However, most victims eventually leave.**

- Violent behavior is solely the responsibility of the violent person. Perpetrators of violence *choose* violence; victims do not "provoke it."
- The decision to leave an abusive relationship places the victim at great risk. For example, 75 percent of women murdered by their abusive partners are killed in the attempt to leave or after they have left (Trauma Intervention Programs, 2006).
- Leaving an abusive relationship is not easy. However, despite the risk and many obstacles, almost all battering victims leave at least once. Battered women leave, on average, seven times before leaving permanently. Most do leave their abusers permanently and succeed in building a life free of violence.

FAMILY VIOLENCE AND U.S. CULTURE

Even a cursory look at any of the national and local media reveals that we live in an increasingly violent culture and world. Crime statistics alone do not capture the full range of violent crime in this country. Statistics from an assortment of Uniform Crime Reports indicate that one violent crime is committed in this country every 21 seconds; an aggravated assault occurs every 37 seconds; a forcible rape occurs every 6 minutes; a robbery occurs every minute; and a murder occurs every 26 minutes. Today, almost one-fourth (21 percent) of all reported crimes are crimes of violence (U.S. Department of Justice, 2006a). Despite our fears to the contrary, it is not a stranger but a so-called loved one or an acquaintance who is most likely to assault, rape, or murder us. In fact, Americans are more likely to be hit, beaten up, sexually assaulted, and killed in their own homes by other family members than anywhere else or by anyone else. Forty-three percent of all murders in U.S. society are perpetrated by one family member or acquaintance against another, and violent assaults within families have been estimated to account for nearly one-fourth of all serious assaults. Every 5 years the death toll of persons killed by relatives and acquaintances equals that of the entire Vietnam War (Fayette County Government, 2004).

These statistics notwithstanding, only in recent decades has the American public gained an informed awareness of the seriousness, magnitude, and multifaceted nature of domestic violence. This awareness is due, in part, to the efforts of the women's movement (very broadly defined), but also to a number of events that have brought family violence into our living rooms on a daily basis. Consider, for example, the infamous O. J. Simpson trial in 1995 with the widely publicized 911 tapes that were interpreted as evidence of Mr. Simpson's history of stalking his wife and his verbal and physical abuse of her. Public opinion polls and surveys comparing "pre- and post-O. J. attitudes and behavior" show an increase in the number of women who identify themselves as victims of domestic violence, heightened public awareness of spousal or partner abuse, more public condemnation of domestic violence, as well as uncertainty about how to create violence-free families and communities after the Simpson trial (Family Violence Prevention Fund, 1999).

Since the Simpson trial, numerous local and nationally publicized cases of family violence have reached our living rooms. For instance, in 2006, while vacationing with his wife and two children and celebrating his 10th wedding anniversary, an Illinois doctor killed himself and his two sons. The 43-year-old radiation oncologist and head of the cancer center at a hospital in Godrey, Illinois, threw his 8- and 4-year-old sons off a 15th-floor balcony at a posh hotel in Miami Beach, Florida, and then jumped. He did not leave a suicide note. However, according to an unsealed search warrant, before killing himself and his children, the doctor had accused his wife of having an affair with the family's gardener (Suhr, 2006). Contrary to the popular belief about the perpetrators of such family violence, the doctor did not suffer from mental illness and was not on any sort of medication.

Likewise, incidents of severe child abuse or murder have become almost daily news items. Recently, a Queens, New York, couple was charged with brutally abusing their 6-month-old infant son, beating and burning him and tying his hands so he could not remove his pacifier. After a week in which the father beat the boy several times, the couple tried to abandon the boy in a hospital, when they were arrested. The 6-month-old's severe injuries included a fractured skull and collarbone and third-degree burns to his hands (Fahim, 2006). A few weeks later, an 18-year-old Brooklyn mother and her 23-year-old boyfriend were charged with criminal neglect homicide and manslaughter in the beating death of the mother's 3-year-old daughter (Fahim, Farmer, and Moynihan, 2006).

According to a growing number of observers, violence is not only as American as apple pie, it is often as homemade (Wallace, 2004:5). Violence, abuse, and assault are deeply rooted in U.S. history and culture, beginning with the founding of this country. The early European American settlers subjected the native populations to widespread violence, abuse, and other atrocities, forcing them off their homelands and onto barren-land prisons called "reservations." Similarly, the American slave system was created and maintained through systematic violence and oppression.

The Media

Today, violence pervades U.S. popular culture. Violent films, for example, comprise almost two-thirds of all films released (Abelard, 2001). Among our most popular films are westerns, war movies, and crime dramas that contain (and sometimes romanticize) widespread death and destruction. The heroes of these films frequently are violent "macho" males. Crime dramas in particular often center around violence perpetrated by males against females. In these films, women are almost routinely terrorized, physically and sexually assaulted, and murdered. Many of these films are so popular they have been developed into movie series with a cult-like following. Film characters such as Jason of *Friday the Thirteenth* and Freddie Kruger from *Nightmare on Elm Street* are classic examples of film characters that have made violence a successful enterprise for movie producers (Wallace, 2004).

Television, like film, presents a constant stream of violent images. One of the largest content analysis of television violence to date found that nearly two out of three TV programs contained some violence, averaging about 6 violent acts per hour. Fewer than 5 percent of these programs featured an antiviolence theme or prosocial message emphasizing alternatives to or consequences of violence to the victim, perpetrator, and victim's family (Kaiser Family Foundation, 2003). Various other research studies have concluded that people, especially the young, become immune to the constant images of violence and gradually come to view violence as an acceptable way to solve problems. Prime-time television is especially violent and the later into prime time the more violent it is. Moreover, 67 percent of prime-time programs, 64 percent of basic cable programs, and 92 percent of premium cable contain violent content.

Violence is even more prevalent in children's programming. For example, research on violence in children's television shows report that over two-thirds of the shows have violence, they contain anywhere from 14 to about 20 violent acts each hour, and two-thirds of the time violence is presented in a humorous fashion. Although they portray killing less

frequently than other programming, cartoons depict the highest number of violent acts and episodes of any kind of television program. On any given Saturday morning, the airwaves are filled with animated violence. Of particular concern are the combat cartoons in which violence is central to the storyline. The villains and superheroes in these cartoons routinely use violence as an acceptable and effective way to get what they want, and the perpetrators are valued for their violent combat abilities. By the time the average American child finishes sixth grade (approximately 13 years old), she or he will have watched 100,000 acts of televised violence, including 8000 depictions of murder (Parent's Television Council, 2006; Kaiser Family Foundation, 2003; Abelard, 2001). Added to this television landscape are the popular trashy talk shows, such as the *Jerry Springer Show*, that cater to sex, violence, and hostility.

Similar trends appear in contemporary music, particularly heavy metal rock and rap videos. Violence is a recurrent theme, as are rape, mock rapes, the implication of rape, and the anticipation of rape and conquest by males. According to those who study media violence, much of this music is misogynistic, defining women as sex objects and appropriate subjects of male fantasy, hatred, and violence. In addition to the visuals, the language itself is often violent and sexually explicit. The audience for these videos includes many teenagers and young adults, who are thus exposed to these attitudes and behaviors as they are growing up. Many experts believe that children emulate what they are exposed to.

Moreover, pornographic films are big business, outnumbering other films three to one and grossing over $3.5 million a year in the United States alone. Research indicates that the major themes of pornographic films are consistent with those in other media: sex, violence, and domination of one person by another, usually women by men. In one study of X-rated films, over four-fifths of the films included scenes in which one or more men dominate and exploit one or more women; three-fourths portrayed physical aggression against women; and one-half explicitly depicted the rape of one or more women (Wood, 2004).

Although the media in general are not pornographic, they do perpetuate themes of sex, violence, and male domination of women. These same themes are pervasive elements of our everyday lives, in which men dominate in number, status, and authority. The pervasiveness of sex and violence toward women in the media acts to desensitize both women and men to the seriousness and unacceptability of violence and assault against human beings. A particularly compelling fact in this regard is the growing body of evidence indicating that exposure to sexual violence through the media is related to greater tolerance, or even approval, of violence (Wood, 2004). For example, one study of television violence on MTV found a strong relationship between women's viewing of sexual violence on MTV and their acceptance of sexual violence as part of *normal* intimate relationships; the more they viewed such violence the more likely they were to define violence as a natural part of female–male relationships and the less likely they were to object to violence perpetrated against them or to defend themselves from violent attacks. In essence, heavy exposure to violence in the media tends to normalize it such that violence and abuse come to be viewed as natural parts of love, sex, and romance (Dieter, 1989).

Detractors argue that there is no clear link between media content and actual behavior (see Social Policy Debate box).

Added to the traditional media methods of transmitting violence are the new and changing technologies of the Internet and video games. Violence on the Internet, or its potential for violence, has increasingly become a concern, particularly as it relates to children. However, the actual incidence of violence on the Internet is difficult to quantify because the technology has moved faster than our capability to monitor it. Currently most of the data on Internet violence are anecdotal, but the Internet's potential as a mechanism that leads to violence is evidenced in the increasing number of documented cases of cyberspace seduction by pedophiles in which children have been lured by on-line predators into traveling to locations hundreds of miles from their homes where they are then sexually assaulted. In addition, not only do a number of Internet sites market a wide array of violent products to children including those with age restrictions due to violent content, but also anyone, child or adult, can find a variety of violent materials on the Internet that give a formula or recipe for violence and destruction. For example, the Oklahoma bomber obtained a copy of the *Turner Diaries*, a book that advocates the violent overthrow of government, off the Internet ("Facts about Media . . . ," 1997).

Moreover, video games, which constitute a multibillion-dollar industry in the United States, are increasingly violent, yet increasingly popular, particularly among America's youth. For example, more than 90 percent of children play video games, on average for about 30 minutes daily. Children no longer are merely passive witnesses to violence that happens in the media. Now they are actually becoming involved in violent scenarios by way of video games and they are being rewarded for their violence (Weber, Ritterfeld, and Mathiak, 2006). In games such as Grand Theft Auto, women are the primary targets of violence. The violent nature of these games has been the subject of intense scrutiny in recent years, and was brought to public attention with the revelation that the young Columbine High School mass murderers, Dylan Klebold and Eric Harris, were addicted to them. Top-selling games such as the "Mortal Kombat" series encourage players to engage in a wide range of violent acts, including tearing off their foes' heads, ripping out their hearts, and ripping off the skin of an opponent, leaving only a bloody pile of muscle. Although it is important to note that research linking media violence and the violent behavior of Americans is inconsistent, there is a consistency in the research suggesting that a constant diet of these kind of games, as well as media violence generally, desensitizes the habitual player or media observer to violence and its consequences, or at least makes it more tolerable. Such findings have spurred a number of civic, religious, and other activist groups to publicize the most violent video games list to alert unwary parents and grandparents to the violent blood-soaked and antisocial content of the games that might otherwise be purchased for children (see Table 11.2).

Moreover, the popular depiction of the violation of women contributes to what has been called a **rape syndrome** or men's proclivity to rape—the group of factors that collectively characterize men's likelihood to rape. For example, the unwanted, unsolicited pinch on a woman's behind, the wolf whistles and lewd remarks directed at women when they walk down the

TABLE 11.2
The Ten Most Violent Video Games, 2005

- **Resident Evil 4**—The player is a Special Forces agent sent to recover the president's kidnapped daughter. During the first minutes of play, it is possible to find the corpse of a woman pinned to a wall by a pitchfork through her face.
- **Grand Theft Auto: San Andreas**—The player is a young man working with gangs to gain respect. His mission includes murder, theft, and destruction on every imaginable level. He recovers his health by visiting prostitutes, then recovers funds by beating them to death and taking their money.
- **God of War**—The player becomes a ruthless warrior, seeking revenge against the gods who tricked her or him into murdering her or his own family. Prisoners are burned alive and the player can use 'finishing moves' to kill opponents, like tearing a victim in half.
- **NARC**—The player can choose between two narcotics agents attempting to take a dangerous drug off the streets and shut down a KRAK cartel while being subject to temptations including drugs and money. To enhance abilities, the player takes drugs including pot, Quaaludes, Ecstasy, LSD, and "Liquid Soul"—which provides the ability to kick enemies' heads off.
- **Killer 7**—The player takes control of seven assassins who must combine skills to defeat a band of suicidal, monstrous terrorists. The player collects the blood of fallen victims to heal her- or himself and must slit her or his own wrists to spray blood to find hidden passages.
- **The Warriors**—Based on a 1970s' action movie that set new standards for "artistic violence," a street gang battles its way across New York City in an attempt to reach its home turf. The player issues several commands to her or his gang, including "mayhem," which causes the gang to smash everything in sight.
- **50 Cent: Bulletproof**—This game is loosely based on the gangster lifestyle of rapper Curtis "50 Cent" Jackson. The player engages in gangster shoot-outs and robs the bodies of victims to buy new 50 Cent recordings and music videos.
- **Crime Life: Gang Wars**—The player is the leader of a ruthless street gang, spending time fighting, recruiting new gangsters, and robbing. The player can roam the streets and fight or kill anyone in sight for no apparent reason.
- **Condemned: Criminal Origins**—The player is an FBI agent who hunts serial killers. The game emphasizes the use of melee weapons over firearms, allowing players to use virtually any part of their environment as a weapon.
- **True Crime: New York City**—The player is a New York City cop looking for information regarding the mysterious death of a friend. The player can plant evidence on civilians and shake them down to earn extra money.

Source: Brendan Sinclair, 2005, "10 Most Violent Games Named" (November 28): http://videogames.yahoo.com/newsarticle?eid=416427 (Accessed: July 11, 2006).

street, and the unwelcome compliments about a woman's anatomy are all acceptable behaviors among various groups of men. When we tolerate these so-called minor acts, other acts of aggression and violation seem more acceptable.

Violence in popular culture has become so epidemic that in September 2000, the Federal Trade Commission addressed a U.S. Senate committee regarding the marketing of violence, particularly in the entertainment industry and particularly to young people under the age of 18. Some critics of the FTC report and others in the media industry complain that the media have become too sanitized. Whether or not this is the case, since the violence of the terrorist acts of September 11, 2001, many of those who have the power to control media content have either tacitly or overtly agreed to tone down the amount of violence they present in their respective medium. Whether or not these actions are enough is debatable.

DEBATING SOCIAL ISSUES

VIOLENCE AND MISOGYNY IN THE MASS MEDIA: IS REGULATION THE ANSWER?

The media-saturated world in which we live is increasingly one in which sex, violence, brutality, and misogyny are common features. Media critics and the public at large have been long concerned about violence in the media, and its impact on behavior. Today, however, that concern has intensified with what some view as an escalation of violence in the media, which all too often is sexualized, misogynistic, and sexist. Indeed, violence against women—women as the victim of men—has become a media mainstay. Despite the film industry's rating system, television's V-Chip, and rap music's adult advisory indicating that a song has explicit lyrics, young people are exposed to a steady diet of violence, sex, misogyny, and homophobia in today's media. Rape and/or the threat of rape is a regular feature of films, no matter their rating. Most often rape is presented as romantic, titillating, sexy, and justified because of some behavior on the part of a female (for instance, the way she walks, talks, or otherwise acts provocatively, or by leading a man on) instead of as a criminal act. These film perpetuate the "rape myth"—the idea that women enjoy sexual violence and that it leads to positive consequences—that the female victim is "turned on." The popular film *Swept Away*, for example, depicts a woman who falls in love with a man who rapes her (Neil Malamuth, cited in Center for Media Literacy, 2003). Other films, such as *Indecent Proposal*, eroticize male domination expressed in the exchange of women, as well as the subjugation of other men, through brutal violence (hooks, 1994).

Likewise, much of contemporary music is misogynistic, defining women as whores and bitches and appropriate objects of male fantasy, hatred, and violence. Sodomy or reference to it has become commonplace in music videos, and teenagers and other viewers are fed a constant diet of women asking, sometimes begging, to be raped and sodomized. In his critical examination of MTV, the music industry, and music video representations of

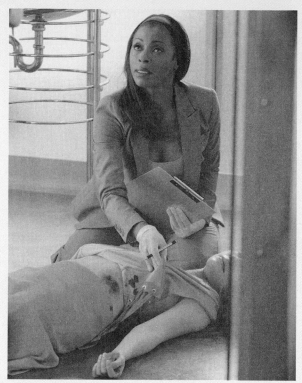

Voilence against women—women as victims of men—have become a media mainstay as exemplified in this scene from the popular CBS television crime drama "CSI: Miami"

PHYSICAL ASSAULT: THE CASE OF BATTERED WOMEN

A spaniel, a woman, and a walnut tree
The more they're beaten the better they be.

—*Old English proverb*

In this section we consider both the patterns of abuse and the strategies of resistance by victims of violence. Because 95 percent of all spousal or partner assaults are committed by men, we pay most attention here to woman assault or battering. Woman assault has several dimensions. Those most commonly discussed in the literature are battering and sexual assault. As we have indicated, battering, in fact, is the single-most common cause of injury to women—more frequent than automobile accidents, muggings, burglaries, and rapes combined (Family Violence Prevention Fund, 2006a). Often, the physical assault of women is accompanied by sexual assault, and it sometimes ends in the murder of the victim. This point is nowhere more poignantly illustrated than in the anonymous letter featured in Table 11.3.

Most experts agree that woman battering is probably the most common and one of the most underreported crimes in this country. The lives, health, and well-being of 51 percent of women in the United States and their children are endangered on a daily basis due to brutal acts of violence committed by an intimate partner. Injuries that battered women receive are at least as serious as injuries suffered in 90 percent of violent felony crimes, yet under state laws, they are almost always classified as misdemeanors. As we have

women, Sut Jhally (1995) argues that the images of women and girls in music videos are limited and have a negative effect on men's understanding of women and women's understandings of themselves.

In a recent analysis of television violence, Northwestern University Media Professor Jeffrey Sconce argues that television content increasingly presents a variety of images and depictions of women being raped, chained, butchered, or brutalized for the public's pleasure and entertainment. According to Sconce, *sadistic* is the only word to describe many of the prime-time television shows today. In his examination of the 2006 season, for instance, program content included gruesome shots of women being brutalized and terrorized in very graphic and extended ways. For example, the opening scene in Fox television's *Killer Instinct* shows a homicide of a woman paralyzed by venomous spiders, then raped while she is immobilized and powerless to do anything. In CBS's *Close to Home*, a woman's husband puts a dog collar on her as punishment (cited in Jones, 2006).

As with most issues in American society today, a line in the sand has been drawn separating two camps around the basic question of whether or not media violence actually causes real-life violence. On one side are those who link media violence to societal violence; they argue that constant exposure to the increasingly blatant violence, brutality, and misogyny in the media has a negative effect on both child and adult behavior. Therefore, the media should be regulated. Proregulation adherents argue that decades of research concludes that exposure to violence against women can lead to subsequent viewer aggression, especially among boys and younger children. Recent research, for example, has found that males who were heavy viewers of violence as children are twice as likely as other males to push, shove, or grab their spouse, and three times more likely to be convicted of criminal behavior by the time they are in their early 20s (Swanbrow, 2003). Further, proponents of regulation argue that when people are exposed to violence and hatred toward women over a long period of time they will come to be more accepting of the violence against women in the real world.

On the other side of the debate, those who oppose more media regulation argue that the data upon which those who call for more regulation is based is flawed, inconsistent, or incomplete. They see media regulation as simply a euphemism for more censorship or a smokescreen hiding the root causes of violence in society. More importantly, they see such regulation as an infringement upon First Amendment rights.

Increasingly, the focus of the debate is on the "culture of violence" and the normalization of aggression, violence, brutality, and hatred of women, and a lack of empathy, compassion, and respect for human life, especially that of women and girls. Those who call for more regulation of the media argue that media violence creates a climate in which violence is more acceptable in real life. Some proponents argue that media violence has become so embedded in the cultural environment that it is part of the "psychic air" that children and adults constantly breathe. Such an environment of violence, profanity, crudeness, misogyny, and brutality erodes civility in society by demeaning and displacing positive social values (Media Awareness Network, 2006).

Those who are opposed argue just as strongly that just because a form of the media has a murder scene or sexual violence against women for that matter does not mean that people will go out and commit those same acts. They argue that proponents for media regulation overstate the power of the images and media content and underestimate the power of parents or adults to decide what to watch and what not to watch. Opponents of regulation argue that it is ultimately up to the viewer to decide what to watch. If a person does not like violence, misogyny, or sexual assault, they say, then turn off the TV or do not spend money on the movie or music video.

What do you think? In your opinion, should the media in all forms be regulated? If yes, by whom? If no, why not? Is there a difference between regulation and censorship? If yes, what is the difference? How do you feel about the content, images, and depictions of women in contemporary mass media? Do these viewpoints represent the reality that you live and experience? How so? How not? Is the problem simply one of the First Amendment right to free speech? Because women do not live in a vacuum, how, if at all, do media images and depictions of poor men and men of color parallel or are connected to those of women?

---

already indicated, a woman is battered approximately every 9 seconds. While you are reading this paragraph, four women will be severely beaten. Physical abuse by an intimate partner is the leading cause of death among women.

The person responsible for raising our consciousness on this subject is Erin Pizzey, whose pioneering work titled *Scream Quietly or the Neighbors Will Hear* (1974) shocked many people and made public the problem of intimate violence. Since Pizzey's book, woman battering, along with child abuse, has received a greater share of public, professional, and scientific attention than any other form of family violence. Perhaps because the issue of intimate violence was overlooked until recent times, early research on the topic often grouped all battering against women as "wife battering." In fact, violent treatment is not restricted to married women. Rather, women in all marital categories are battered by men that they date, are related to, cohabit with, or simply know.

Another limitation of the mainstream literature on woman battering is that most often it fails to represent the experiences of women of color and lesbians. Like other experiences, the experience of intimate violence is not the same for all women. How exactly it differs, however, is unclear from most research. Although some of the research indicates that race, class, and to some degree sexual orientation are important factors in the incidence and nature of intimate violence, seldom do such discussions provide clear documentation. Researchers have yet to investigate systematically, for example, whether there are any issues unique to women of color in violent relationships.

TABLE 11.3

I Got Flowers Today

I got flowers today. It wasn't my birthday or any other special day. We had our first argument last night, and he said a lot of cruel things that really hurt me. I know he is sorry and didn't mean the things he said, because he sent me flowers today.

I got flowers today. It wasn't our anniversary or any other special day. Last night, he threw me into a wall and started to choke me. It seemed like a nightmare. I couldn't believe it was real. I woke up this morning sore and bruised all over. I know he must be sorry, because he sent me flowers today.

Last night, he beat me up again. And it was much worse than all the other times. If I leave him, what will I do? How will I take care of my kids? What about money? I'm afraid of him and scared to leave. But I know he must be sorry, because he sent me flowers today.

I got flowers today. Today was a very special day. It was the day of my funeral. Last night, he finally killed me. He beat me to death.

If only I had gathered enough courage and strength to leave him, I would not have gotten flowers today.

Source: Anonymous

Much the same can be said about sexual orientation. Most of the research on intimate violence either fails to mention the sexual orientation of the people included in the sample or acknowledges that only heterosexuals were studied. The social pressures that contribute to family violence affect women and men of all sexual orientations and races. Because of the continued prejudice against homosexuals, however, much of the violence that occurs in lesbian and gay relationships goes unreported. Moreover, many lesbians deny the very existence of lesbian battering. However, as the statistics on same-sex violence cited earlier reveal, lesbians and gays are not exempt from abusive relationships. This denial is no doubt grounded in the desire to maintain an image of lesbian relationships as violence-free and egalitarian. Unfortunately, this approach has left many lesbians vulnerable, isolated, and at high risk of being a victim of violence (Levy, 1991).

What Is Woman Battering?

In the family violence literature, the terms **woman battering** and *woman assault* are used interchangeably to refer to a range of behaviors that includes hitting, kicking, choking, and the use or threatened use of objects and weapons such as guns and knives. Because many battered women are also sexually abused, some discussions of woman battering include **sexual assault**—violence in the form of forced sexual acts, including vaginal, oral, and anal penetration; bondage, beating; torture; mutilation; bestiality; and group or gang rape. Still other discussions include emotional as well as physical assault. In either case, domestic violence is always about power and control. One partner uses violence to intentionally gain power over her or his partner (see Figure 11.1).

In general, the pattern of the battering experienced by women is referred to as the **battered-woman syndrome** and is defined in terms of frequency, severity, intent to harm, and the ability to demonstrate injury. Following a classification scheme presented in 1979 by social scientist Murray Straus, most researchers today define and classify battering in terms of severity. Battering is said to be severe if

it has a high likelihood of causing injury, causes the victim to seek medical treatment, or is grounds for arrest. Certain forms of battering like slapping, pushing, shoving, grabbing, and throwing objects at the victim do not fit this category.

Battering is generally cyclical in nature. Family violence researcher Lenore Walker (1984) proposed a *cycle of violence theory* that is still often cited today. The equality wheel illustrates the concepts of equality in a relationship. The outside dark area of the wheel is the non-violence that is or should be used in a relationship. The inner spokes are forms of non-violent interactions and behaviors. These sections are held together by the use of respect, equality and non-violence. Moreover, Walker is often called upon as an expert witness in court cases involving woman abuse. The cycle of abuse includes three stages: (1) tension building, in which tension escalates gradually, making the woman increasingly uncomfortable in anticipation of the impending abuse—as the male becomes more violent, the female feels less able to defend herself; (2) acute battering, in which the woman is the victim of severe physical and verbal abuse; and (3) loving contrition, in which the man apologizes for his behavior, professes his love, and promises that he will never do it again. After a time, however, the remorse and contrition disappear, and the cycle starts all over again (Walker, 1978, 1984). In contrast to this cycle of violence and abuse, a group of battered women in Duluth, Minnesota who had been abused by their male partners and were participating in the Domestic Abuse Intervention Project—a community-based intervention program, developed a wheel that illustrates what nonviolence and equality in intimate relationships should look like (See Figure 11.2).

Although defining woman battering to include every possible type of physical violence is difficult, the limitations of current definitions should not be overlooked. Limiting battering or assault to discrete physical actions excludes a wide range of violence that women experience. For example, battering is often accompanied by verbal abuse, psychological abuse, and threats or actual violence toward children and other loved ones. Children whose mothers are victims of battery in the home are twice as likely to be abused themselves as those children whose mothers are not victims of abuse. In fact, as violence against women becomes more severe and more frequent in the home, children experience a 300 percent increase in physical violence by the male batterer. Ignoring "mild" or "less severe" violence overlooks the fact that any use of violence in a marriage or intimate relationship can have long-lasting detrimental effects on both the victim and the couple's relationship (Wallace, 2004). In the simplest language, the bottom line is that abuse is abuse whether or not it is severe (by someone else's definition). We concur with Linda Rudnick, executive director of South Shore Women's Center in Plymouth, Rhode Island: "The dynamics are the same—someone is misusing power and controlling someone else's life. It is a pattern of coercive control" (quoted in Haddocks, 1995). According to Julia Scott, violence in the broadest sense against women is any violation of a woman's personhood, mental or physical integrity, or freedom of movement, and includes all of the ways our society objectifies and oppresses women (1994:20). Thus, a definition of battering that takes into account a fuller range of the violence and abuse is very much needed.

FIGURE 11.1

Power and Control Wheel

Physical and sexual assaults, or threats to commit them, are the most apparent forms of domestic violence and are usually the actions that allow others to become aware of the problem. However, regular use of other abusive behaviors by the batterer, when reinforced by one or more acts of physical violence, make up a larger system of abuse. Although physical assaults may occur only once or occasionally, they instill threat of future violent attacks and allow the abuser to take control of the woman's life and circumstances.

The Power & Control diagram is a particularly helpful tool in understanding the overall pattern of abusive and violent behaviors, which are used by a batterer to establish and maintain control over his partner. Very often, one or more violent incidents are accompanied by an array of these other types of abuse. They are less easily identified, yet firmly establish a pattern of intimidation and control in the relationship.

Developed by:
Domestic Abuse Intervention Project
202 East Superior Street
Duluth, MN 55802
218.722.4134

Produced and distributed by:

NATIONAL CENTER
on Domestic and Sexual Violence
training · consulting · advocacy
4612 Shoal Creek Blvd. · Austin, Texas 78756
512.407.9020 (phone and fax) · www.ncdsv.org

Source: National Center on Domestic Violence, http://www.ncdsv.org/publications_wheel.html.

How Prevalent Is Woman Battering?

Official statistics on the prevalence of woman battering rely largely on crime statistics, FBI and police reports, scattered hospital emergency room records, and records from shelters. Although many women report domestic violence only to family, friends, relatives, churches, synagogues, private physicians, and nurses, these sources of information are not included in national crime surveys. In addition, most reports do not show the number of violent incidents experienced by individual battered women and their children.

Since 1972, a major source of information on family violence is the National Crime Survey sponsored by the Department of Justice. Although an improvement over previous sources, estimating the incidence of woman battering remains difficult, primarily because it typically occurs in private and more often than not goes unreported. Added to this is the fact that women who are battered or assaulted "only once" are rarely labeled as battered. Thus, some researchers estimate that the true incidence of woman battering may actually be double the rates reported in most studies.

FIGURE 11.2

Equality Wheel

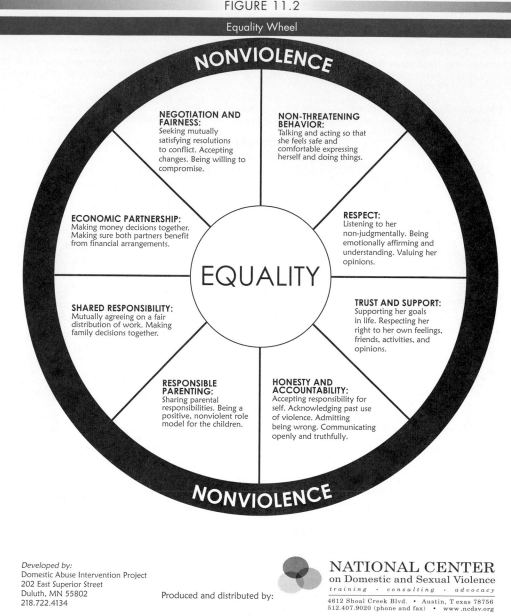

Developed by:
Domestic Abuse Intervention Project
202 East Superior Street
Duluth, MN 55802
218.722.4134

Produced and distributed by:

NATIONAL CENTER
on Domestic and Sexual Violence
training · consulting · advocacy
4612 Shoal Creek Blvd. · Austin, Texas 78756
512.407.9020 (phone and fax) · www.ncdsv.org

Source: National Center on Domestic Violence, http://www.ncdsv.org/publications_wheel.html.

The difficulties of painting an accurate picture of the prevalence of woman battering notwithstanding, what available statistics reveal about woman battering is alarming. For example, every year more than 1 million women seek medical assistance for potentially lethal injuries caused by battering. The overwhelming majority of these women will have additional or repeated injuries requiring treatment within the year (Family Violence Prevention Fund, 2006a; Amnesty International, 2004). In addition, women who are pregnant are also at great risk of abuse and injury—they are at twice the risk of battery than nonpregnant women. Studies reveal that 37 to 59 percent of pregnant women are physically abused. Almost one-half of all assaults on women by their male partners begin during the first pregnancy. Women are four times more likely to suffer increased abuse as a result of an unintended or unwanted pregnancy. Pregnant adolescents

(ages 13 to 17) have a particularly high risk of violence from their partners. Battery and abuse during pregnancy is a focused attack that puts not just one, but two (or more) lives at risk. The results of this type of battering include hemorrhaging, fetal fractures, rupture of internal organs, placental separation, miscarriages, birth defects, low-birth-weight babies, and stillbirths (National Coalition against Domestic Violence, 2006a; Pan-American Health Organization, 2006). In all too many cases such battering is fatal. For example, murder is the second most common cause of injury-related death for pregnant women after car accidents. Over a 14-year-period ending in 2004, 1300 pregnant women were murdered, most of whom were shot to death while the rest were stabbed or strangled. Over three-fourths of these murders occurred during the first trimester of the victim's pregnancy. Added to these statistics is the fact that incidents of battering and abuse among women with disabilities may be as high as 85 percent (Chang et al., 2005; St. George, 2004; Lehman College Art Gallery, 1998).

Moreover, a woman's relationship to the abuser is a key variable. Over two-thirds of violent victimizations against women were committed by someone known to them: husbands, boyfriends, acquaintances, or other relatives. In contrast, victimization by intimates and other relatives accounts for only 5 percent of all violence against men. Men are significantly more likely to be victimized by acquaintances (50 percent) or strangers (44 percent) than by intimates or other relatives. Research shows that women who are physically violated by intimates face a much higher risk of being recurring victims of violence than do women who are victims of a stranger's violence. Yet, ironically, women victimized by intimates are six times less likely than those victimized by strangers to report their violent victimization to police, because they are afraid of reprisal by the offender (athealth, 2006).

When woman battering is compared across marital status, married women experience battering less often than single, separated, divorced, and never-married women. Marriage also reduces the likelihood of violent crime among men. Never-married men are more likely to commit assault, and they suffer most (60 percent) assaults. They are also five times more likely to rape and commit other violent crimes than are married men (Maginnis, 1995). Women who cohabit are more likely to experience battering than are either single or married women. In fact, cohabiting women are twice as likely to suffer severe battering or violence than are married women. Experts in the field say the violence reported by cohabiting women ranges from pushing or slapping to using a knife or gun (Haddocks, 1995). How might we account for this? Possible explanations are that cohabiting women may simply report battering more often, that violence against cohabiting women is more likely to be labeled as battering than is violence directed against married women, and that cohabiting women may be less willing to accept a battering situation because they are less dependent economically and may not have children. In any case, concern about cohabiting violence is becoming significantly more important as more and more couples choose this lifestyle. Finally, women aged 16 to 24 are the most vulnerable to nonfatal intimate violence, whereas women aged 35 to 49 are the most vulnerable to murder by an intimate partner (U.S. Department of Justice, 2006a). Vulnerability includes those women who have never married or are separated and have low incomes. Typically, their offenders are someone known to them, and the violence usually occurs at or near their home.

Although we have addressed the myth that battering and abuse is limited to lower-class families, to understand the relationship between social class and family violence, we must be aware of the factors most closely associated with woman battering. According to researchers, violence against women is most likely when the following circumstances are present:

- The husband is unemployed or employed only part-time, usually in manual labor, or he is a high school dropout.
- The husband is under the age of 30.
- The wife is a full-time housewife; she has a high school diploma or less education.
- Two or more children are present in the home, and disagreements over the children are common.
- Family income is at or below the poverty line and both spouses are worried about economic security, or the wife is strongly dissatisfied with the family's standard of living.
- Either one or both individuals use and/or abuse alcohol and other drugs; and the husband uses alcohol or other drugs as an excuse for violence and aggression (Wallace, 2004; Gelles, 1995).

These factors tend to be more characteristic of lower-income families for a variety of reasons; rates of violence among such families may therefore be slightly higher. However, these statistics should not mask the fact that battering and abuse occurs regularly across class categories—it is not confined to the lower and working classes. For example, psychotherapist Susan Weitzman (2001) has shattered the cultural myth that emotional and physical violence in the home is confined to couples of a lower socioeconomic class. Weitzman coined the term "upscale violence" to describe domestic abuse among the affluent, something that has been ignored and denied in research on the subject. According to Weitzman, of the millions of women each year nationwide that are victims of domestic violence, an unknown proportion of them are well educated, with at least a bachelor's degree; they live in the top 25 percent of this country's neighborhoods; they see themselves as upper-middle-class or upper-class; and their combined marital income exceeds $100,000.

Theories of Spousal or Partner Abuse

What causes one human being to physically, emotionally, or otherwise violently abuse another human being that she or he professes to love? Perhaps if we had a definitive answer to this question we could eradicate this form of violence. Unfortunately, to date we have no such answer. However, various scholars across disciplines and professions have attempted to respond to this question. In this section, we present a brief and selective review of some explanations.

Social Stress   Increasingly, life in the United States is characterized by high levels of stress, both for individuals and families. Various structural and environmental forces—such as crime and violence on the streets, gangs and gang warfare, carjackings, downsizing of jobs, jobs moving to other countries, rising unemployment and underemployment, increasing intolerance and racism, fiscal mismanagement, poor social and community services, higher interest rates, decreasing credit power, and increasing personal and property taxes—converge on us, causing an untold amount of stress. This increased level of stress, in turn, finds an outlet in the family or other intimate relationships. Very often we respond to these stresses in our lives by using violence—all too often directed at the person closest to us, a partner or spouse, and all too often in the form of physical assault. This explanation does not suggest that stress causes violence. Rather, it suggests that violence is one of many responses available to people who suffer from stress.

Power   The use and abuse of power and the imposition of one's will over another is a major characteristic of spousal and partner abuse. Prominent characteristics of both the abuser and the abused are encapsulated in the concept of power. Men generally possess greater physical, social, and political power than women and do have an advantage in this regard. If a man abuses power and control in intimate relationships, there is a significant potential for violence; as victims of this violence, women often feel power*less*. Research has demonstrated that couples who share power or conduct themselves as equals in their relationship have the lowest level of conflict and violence. When they do experience conflict, they are better able to resist violence. When dealing with intimate or family violence, *feminist theories* focus on this issue of power and gender inequality and encourage us to examine the influence of gender and gender-structured relations on the institution of the family and the violence and abuse within it. A key to comprehending this phenomenon using one of these perspectives is understanding the historical subordination of women to men. Although women have made significant historical contributions to society, men continue to control all major aspects of society (the patriarchal tradition). Thus, feminist perspectives encourage us to examine the social structure that is designed to condone, perhaps even encourage, and perpetuate the superordination (power) of men over women as well as encourage violence toward women.

Dependency Historically, the institution of marriage has fostered women's economic dependency on a husband. Although this is changing to some degree, women often find themselves dependent on their partner not only for financial support but for emotional and other support as well. Very often, too, there are children involved, which complicates the woman's ability or willingness to leave an abusive relationship. Accordingly, this dependency makes a woman particularly vulnerable to physical abuse and increases her tolerance for it. Research on dependency and violence indicates that the more dependent a woman is, the more likely she is to suffer physical violence from her husband. Dependent wives or partners have fewer alternatives to marriage and fewer resources within the relationship with which to cope with or modify the abuser's behavior. According to Harvey Wallace, "This dependency is a pair of 'golden handcuffs' that binds the spouse to the abusive partner" (2002:186).

Alcohol "He had too much to drink." "He's not responsible." "He's really a nice quiet guy when he's not drinking." "When he's sober he wouldn't hurt a fly." Sound familiar? People in this society typically associate violence with alcohol consumption. Various social scientists have suggested that there is indeed a link between the two but have been unable to establish a causal relationship. *Disinhibition theorists* suggest that alcohol releases our inhibitions and alters our judgment, making us capable of behavior that we would not otherwise engage in. *Social-learning theorists* suggest that violence is a learned behavior; we learn violence by observing people who drink and become violent. We rationalize that they are not responsible for their violence because they were *drunk*. Some social-learning theorists suggest that people use alcohol as a means of increasing their power and control over others. An *integrated theoretical perspective* suggests that it is

not just the consumption of alcohol but the drinking mixed with a number of other factors that leads to violence—for example, conflict in the relationship and the cultural notion of drinking as an acceptable male behavior. The fact is, although alcohol can make it easier for a man to be violent, the real cause is not alcohol but the abuser's desire for power and control over his partner. As with the claim of mental illness, abusers often use alcohol as an excuse to avoid taking responsibility for their violent behavior. Each of these explanations gives us some insight into drinking and violence, but none is definitive (Wallace, 2004).

Even from this cursory and selective review of theories of spousal or partner abuse, it is clear that much more study and research are needed before we can fully understand the determinants and dynamics of spousal and partner abuse and be able to predict the risk for women who enter into intimate relationships. Until such time as we are able to do this, it is instructive for all of us to recognize and understand some of the characteristics of this kind of abuse. Researchers have noted a number of variables that seem to be conducive to violence in intimate relationships. We have already discussed several of these factors in our discussion of the relationship of social class to abuse. Other variables include the following:

1. *A high level of family or intimate conflict.* Conflict is present for any number of reasons, including conflicting expectations, activities, or interests; gender-stereotypic role expectations; high levels of individual or family stress.

2. *A high level of societal violence.* As pointed out elsewhere, American society is characterized by a high level of violence. Violence within families and intimate relationships may simply be an extension of this external violence.

3. *Family socialization in violence.* Growing up in or living in a family that uses violence to resolve conflicts, release stress, or as a principal means of securing compliance teaches us that such behavior is acceptable.

4. *Cultural norms that legitimize family or intimate violence.* Although physical and sexual assault are illegal, various cultural norms including the historical rights of men in marriage tend to legitimize wife or woman battering and chastisement.

5. *Gender-stereotypic socialization and sexual inequality.* Many families continue to socialize females and males into rigid gender-stereotypic roles that reinforce a sexual double standard and inequality between the sexes. In marriage, this means that the husband is the family head and women and children are his subordinates. A husband's right to use physical force to "control" his wife and children for the most part remains unchallenged. This arrangement of roles and role expectations makes women and children particularly vulnerable to physical and emotional violence. According to some scholars, this kind of violence is a logical extension of a patriarchal system in which the husband is defined as the ruler and head of the family with a right to use whatever means he deems necessary to extract obedience from family members (Eshleman and Bulcroft, 2005).

6. *The privacy of the American family.* Because we believe that "what goes on behind closed doors" (especially if those doors are within the family residence) is not our concern, many people, including friends, relatives, and other family members, tend to ignore the signs or evidence of violence and abuse by rationalizing that it is a "private" matter between a husband and wife (or two intimate partners) and

they have no right to interfere. It is curious, for example, how so many people, including close family members, knew that Nicole Brown Simpson was a battered woman yet no one spoke up until after her violent and tragic death.

Researchers have found that these variables are interrelated and do not act alone in leading to family and intimate violence. Rather, they are mutually supporting and reinforcing in producing spousal or partner violence (Utech, 1994:125–26).

Why Do Women Remain in Abusive Relationships?

If the violence and abuse are so bad, why do women stay in these relationships? This question is often raised and is indicative of our lack of information concerning battered women. A more appropriate question would be "Why does he abuse her?" or "Why can't he be stopped from hurting his family?" Instead, the question—"Why does she stay?"—puts the responsibility back on the victim, and is often followed with the statement, "She must like it" (ACADV, 2006). Battered women bear the brunt of considerable **victim blaming**— essentially, justifying the unequal treatment of an individual or group by finding defects in the victims rather than by examining the social and economic factors that contribute to their condition. As we have pointed out, many people believe that female victims of domestic violence are somehow responsible for their mistreatment, or are masochists who enjoy being beaten, which explains their unwillingness to leave the relationship. However, there is no empirical evidence to support this anachronistic psychological viewpoint. The fact is that women do not enjoy, provoke, or deserve battering. No one deserves to be beaten. Victim provocation is no more common in domestic violence than in any other crime. The reasons women remain in violent relationships are far more complex than a simple statement about their strength of character. Victims of domestic violence desperately want the abuse to end and engage in a variety of survival strategies, including calling the police or seeking help from family members, to protect themselves and their children. Enduring a beating to keep the batterer from attacking the children may be a coping strategy used by a victim, but it does not mean that the victim enjoys the battering. Leaving a battering situation is not as simple as just packing up and leaving. Leaving could mean living in fear, losing child custody, losing financial support, and experiencing harassment at work, or, as we have said, losing her life. But not leaving does not mean that the situation is okay or that the victim wants to be abused.

Battered women often make repeated attempts to leave violent relationships, but are prevented from doing so by increased violence and control tactics on the part of the abuser. Research and other scholarship in this area indicate that women remain in battering relationships for a variety of reasons. One of the most common is fear. Battered women may stay in a violent relationship because they think the situation is inescapable. They typically feel helpless about getting out of the relationship and fear that any action on their part will contribute to more violence, perhaps even their own death. A battered woman may also be concerned for the well-being of her children. She may fear that she will lose custody of her children or cause emotional or physical harm to them if she tries to leave. She may even fear that her abuser will kill himself if she leaves. Given the statistics relative to the number of women who are murdered by their abusive partners when they attempt to leave or after they have left the abusive relationship, this fear is not unfounded.

In addition to fear, a woman may have limited or no financial resources, access to alternative support, or skills to secure work. Economic dependence and a lack of viable options for housing and support can keep a woman in an abusive relationship. Even if a woman leaves, economic necessity may force her back to her abusive partner, who might retaliate with even more severe violence and abuse. Or she may face the risk of becoming homeless. Nationally, 50 percent of all homeless women and children are fleeing abusive and violent households. Even if a woman is financially secure, she may not perceive herself as being able to deal with economic matters outside of the relationship.

Sometimes women remain in battering relationships because of religious beliefs. They feel that their faith requires them to keep their marriage and family together at all costs and to honor and obey their husband, submitting to his will. And if she leaves or divorces her partner, her religious community may not support her. They not only believe that it is their responsibility to make the marriage or relationship work but also that leaving the abusive situation would be an admission of failure. In addition, some women stay because their family and friends may not support their leaving. Their partner or husband may have convinced their family and friends that everything is good in their relationship, that any problems are "her fault" or "in her head" (Avon Foundation, 2006; Wallace, 2004). They often come to believe that they caused or deserved the battering. Other times women remain in such relationships because they sincerely believe in the notion of the "cult of domesticity" and family harmony. Even though their situation does not fit this ideal, they continue to believe that they can reach the ideal. They often feel physically and emotionally trapped by society's expectation of them: Society labels them stupid if they stay in the relationship and a failure if they leave. Still other women remain in battering relationships because they believe that children must be raised in a household with a father present. Thus, they endure physical and emotional abuse to keep the family together for the children's sake. Very often it is when the violence is directed at the children that a woman will take them and leave. More than half of the children whose mothers are battered are also victims of physical abuse.

In some cases the fear of being alone keeps women in an abusive relationship. Often women in battering situations have no meaningful relationships outside their marriage or intimate relationship. The husband or lover may have systematically cut off all her ties to family, friends, and other supportive people. Having nowhere to go and no one to turn to, she remains with her abuser. In fact, being withdrawn and isolated is one of the primary telltale signs that a woman might be in an abusive relationship (see Table 11.4). Other times, a woman may feel shame about being abused and reluctant to let anyone know that abuse is occurring in her relationship or it may be that she grew up with violence and abuse—so she may consider her own violent and abusive relationship normal. Sometimes women in abusive relationships do not know who to

TABLE 11.4

Telltale Signs That a Woman Might Be in an Abusive Relationship

- She is withdrawn and isolated from her friends and family.
- Whereas she was once an active participant in social activities, she is no longer active.
- She displays poor self-esteem, poor self-concept. She speaks poorly of herself.
- She seems aloof and detached and she will not make eye contact when talking.
- She appears nervous, especially when her partner is around, and she never accepts an invitation or a responsibility without getting his approval or okay first.
- She calls her partner frequently during the workday or whenever she is away from him.
- She is excluded from decision making at home and seldom has money of her own.
- Her husband or partner will not let her drive or learn to drive, go to school, or get a job.
- She has many "accidents," some of which seem illogical and suspicious.
- She has unexplained bruises, marks, scratches, or welts. She is often vague about how she got these injuries.
- She wears a lot of makeup or sunglasses, indoors as well as outdoors. She also wears a lot of turtlenecks, scarves, long sleeves, and slacks.
- She may complain of nonspecific aches and pains that are constant and recurring. These are stress-related problems.

Sources: M. D. Pagelow, 1984, Family Violence (Wesport, CT: Praeger); Salt Lake Community College, 2004, "Abuse," http://active.slcc.edu/hw/docs/abuse.pdf (Accessed July 15, 2006).

turn to for help or where to get assistance or they may face language barriers to seeking help or independence, and may fear deportation. Although some people might not understand this, some women in abusive relationships remain because of pity—they feel sorry for their abuser. They believe he really loves them but he simply cannot control himself. In other cases, low self-esteem keeps some women in an abusive relationship. As the battering continues, the abused loses confidence in herself, and her self-value and self-worth decline.

Finally, a common reason women remain in violent relationships is love. Most people enter a relationship for love, and that emotion does not magically disappear in an abusive relationship (Domestic Abuse Shelter, Inc., 2006). Many women want the violence to end, but love their partner and want the relationship. They believe he loves them as well and their love will change the abuser. Each of these factors acts as a barrier to a woman trying to leave an abusive relationship. Although most battered women actively seek help from a variety of sources in ending the cycle of violence, very often the failure of various professionals and systems to provide adequate support keeps women in violent relationships. In spite of all the reasons why some women remain in abusive relationships, most battered women work hard to leave; most do, in fact, leave their abuser at some point, even if only temporarily. As we have already indicated, battered women who leave the battering situation do so, on average, seven times before they leave permanently. Those who make it beyond the barriers and do not go back are the fortunate ones who find support for their leaving the abuser, and most of them go on to lead healthy, happy, and productive lives.

Mentally put yourself in the shoes of a battered woman. Would you leave? Where would you go? How many services are available for women who are victims of courtship or marital violence at the college or university you are now attending? Are there offices you can go to? People you can talk to? Do you know women who are in battering relationships? What reasons, if any, do they give for remaining in such relationships? Are the reasons similar to or the same as some of those found above?

Confronting Intimate Violence

Do you know someone who is in an abusive relationship? Do you know what to look for? Table 11.4 lists some of the factors that might indicate a woman is in an abusive relationship. If you know someone who is abused, have you tried to help? What have you done? Many individuals and groups are urging the public—relatives, friends, and neighbors—

Talking with a female relative or friend who we know or suspect is a victim of violence and abuse is never easy. We often remain silent for fear that we will not say the right thing in just the right way. Given that one out of every three murdered women is killed by her husband or boyfriend, our relative or friend may not have the luxury of waiting until we find the right words.

to get involved, to take a stand against abuse, to help stop intimate violence, to intervene to help battered women and their children. For example, in a series of powerful public service announcements depicting the plight of abused women and children, begun in 1994, the San Francisco-based Family Violence Prevention Fund (FUND), has conducted a highly successful education campaign designed to prevent and reduce family violence. Using the theme There's No Excuse for Domestic Violence, the FUND has developed public service announcements such as the one shown on page 378. Another, designed to encourage intervention with batterers, reads,

> It's Hard to Confront a Friend Who Abuses His Wife, But Not Nearly as Hard as Being His Wife.

Additionally, a radio announcement features a woman talking about her struggle to find the right words to say to her abused friend. The announcement concludes: "I just knew if I said the wrong thing, I'd lose her friendship. So I didn't say anything. And instead . . . I lost my friend" (New PSA's against Domestic Violence, 1996:2). These public service announcements go to the heart of the problem of society's silence about intimate violence. Although we are increasingly aware of the devastation of intimate violence, too few of us know how to help battered women and children. Today, the FUND, along with a variety of other organizations and sources, regularly publicize domestic violence information and prevention strategies on the Internet with easy-to-read steps for simple, safe, and effective ways in which battered women can begin taking steps to leave their abusive relationships as well as how we, the public—family, friends, neighbors—can help battered women and children. This information includes tips on a range of interventions that include reaching out to women you suspect are being abused, helping children who face violence in their homes, teaching young people that violence against women is never acceptable, and approaching men you know or suspect are batterers.

THE SEXUAL ASSAULT OF WOMEN

Battering is not the only form of abuse experienced by women in intimate relationships. Millions of women in the United States and around the world have suffered or will suffer some form of sexual assault. Sexual assault is a broad term that incorporates any behaviors, either physical or verbal, intended to coerce an individual into sexual activity against her or his will. Violence against women, including sexual assault, is a problem in every country in the world. For example, in 9 Latin American countries, a rapist who marries the victim stays out of jail (Domestic Abuse Shelter, 2004). Globally, one in five women will be a victim of rape or attempted rape in her lifetime (Amnesty International, 2004). Sexual assault is extremely widespread in U.S. society, with women and children representing the majority of the victims. In fact, over two decades ago, statisticians claimed that the average woman was as likely to suffer a sexual attack as she was to be diagnosed as having cancer or to be divorced (Johnson, 1980). Looking at today's statistics on rape and the sexual assault of women, it seems that this statistic has changed little.

One of the most extreme forms of sexual assault is rape. Every 2½ minutes, a woman is raped somewhere in the United States (RAINN, 2006). Rape is legally defined as sexual assault in which a man uses his penis to vaginally penetrate a woman against her will, by force or threat of force, or when she is mentally or physically unable to give her consent. This definition overlooks the fact that men and boys are sometimes victims of rape as well. Some states have broadened the legal definition of rape by removing sex-specific language to include males (who are almost always victimized by other males). According to recent statistics, 1 in every 10 rape and sexual assault victims is male and 1 in 33 (about 3 percent) men has experienced an attempted or completed rape in his lifetime, compared to 1 in 6 women. In addition, it is estimated that 1 woman in every 12 *will be* a victim of rape or attempted rape during her lifetime. As these figures reveal, the overwhelming majority (9 in every 10) of rape victims are female (RAINN, 2006). Contrary to what some people believe, rape is not about sexual arousal. Rather, it is about the violent abuse of power. Whether an attempted or completed sexual assault, it is an act of violence instigated by one or more persons against another human being (Doyle and Paludi, 1997). In essence, some observers have described rape as a terrorist tactic, a tangible and symbolic way for men to keep women in a subordinate position (Soroka and Bryjak, 1999). A typical female rape victim, for instance, is raped nearly three times a year, often by her husband or domestic partner. In fact, contrary to popular myth, the rapist is not typically a "masked man" or stranger. Rather, rapists are typically people known to the victim. For example, two-thirds (67 percent) of female rape victims know their assailant, who is either a friend or acquaintance (47 percent), an intimate (17 percent), or some other relative (3 percent). In addition, the rapist is not typically hiding in the bushes. About 42 percent of all rapes in the United States take place in the victim's home and another 23 percent take place in the home of a friend, relative, or neighbor. Of those rapes that do not occur in the victim's own home or in that of a friend or relative, more than one-half occur within one mile of where the victim lives (U.S. Department of Justice, 2004).

Rape is the most frequently committed violent crime in the United States. It is also the least reported of all such crimes. It is estimated that as many as two-thirds of rapes and sexual assaults are not reported to law enforcement officials (U.S. Department of Justice, 2004). Thus, statistics on rape are considerably understated. Estimates of rape would be even higher if they included assaults on young girls by their fathers, stepfathers, and other male relatives (usually categorized separately as incest), cases of statutory rape, and cases of male rape both within and outside of prison. Statistics on rape provided by the FBI do not include these categories, nor do they include date and marital rape.

Females of all ages have been victims of rape. That no age is immune to rape is indicated in the findings from a study of a Washington, DC, hospital in which those treated for rape ranged from a 15-month-old baby girl to an 82-year-old woman (Benokraitis and Feagin, 1986). Approximately one of every seven victims of sexual assault reported to law enforcement agencies are under the age of 6. Adolescent and young adult women are at the highest risk, however. Risk peaks in the late teens: Girls 16 to 19 years of age are about four times more likely than the general population to be victims of rape, attempted rape, or sexual assault (Childhelp, 2005; U.S. Department of Justice, 2001b). Data concerning the likelihood of rape indicate a link between a woman's economic status, her race, and rape. The majority of rapists are under the age of 25, and their victims are typically white women, also under the age of 25, divorced or separated, poor, and unemployed or a student. Among people 12 years and older, 83 percent of rape victims are white, 13 percent are African American, and 4 percent are of other races (RAINN, 2006; U.S. Department of Justice, 2001b). However, women of color are at greater risk, with African American, teenaged, and urban working-class girls running the greatest risk of being raped (FBI, 1999). According to some researchers, the risk of rape for African American women is so great that elderly African American women are just as likely to be raped as young white women (Gollin, 1980, cited in Doyle and Paludi, 1995:159). These statistics are all the more significant given that, in general, when violence in the African American community is discussed, its impact for African American women is usually minimized relative to the focus placed on the street violence suffered or perpetrated by African American males. Although the street violence associated with African American males is significant and has a devastating impact on African American women, the most devastating form of violence in the life of African American women is sexual assault and domestic violence. There is a significant difference among women across race in the reporting of rape and physical assault. For example, Native American and Alaska Native women are most likely to report rape and physical assault victimization, while Asian/Pacific Islander women are least likely (RAINN, 2006).

Furthermore, divorced or separated women have been found to be more vulnerable to rape than women who have never been married. Married women are much less likely to be raped than divorced, separated, or never-married women. The likelihood of being raped is also higher for female heads of households and has a direct relationship to the amount of time a woman spends in public places (Andersen, 2005). The perpetrator of rape or sexual assault is typically white (52 percent) and 25 years of age or younger. Interestingly, 22 percent of imprisoned rapists report that they are married. And in about one in three sexual assaults, the perpetrator was intoxicated either with alcohol or other drugs (RAINN, 2006; U.S. Department of Justice, 2001b). Men and boys are at greatest risk of being raped under conditions of incarceration (although this is not the only environment in which the rape of males occurs). And they are even less likely than women to report that they have been raped. Gay men, like their heterosexual counterparts, seldom report this type of victimization. We will discuss male battering and rape in more detail later in this chapter.

Rape Myths

As with battering, an enormous amount of myth surrounds rape. Many people, female and male alike, hold erroneous notions about rape, rape victims, and rapists. You have probably heard most of these myths, and you might even believe some of them. Two of the most persistent rape myths are that male sexual violence is caused by the attitudes and behaviors of female victims, and African American males are the primary perpetrators of rape. In the following discussion, we examine these two myths more closely.

Rape and Race

Because of the relentless link of African American males to violence and crime, many people mistakenly believe the majority of rapists are African American males who are usually strangers to their victims. In fact, as we have seen, in most cases the rapist knows her or his victim. Statistics reveal that most rapes, especially those of white and young female victims, occur within the same race. Therefore, the myth that African American men commit the majority of rapes is just that—a myth. Nevertheless, the myth of the African American male rapist, especially of white women, persists. As some scholars have pointed out, such a myth is dangerous in that it diverts the attention of white women away from the most likely sources of their sexual assault: white men. At the same time, it serves as a justification for negative attitudes toward and treatment of African American males.

Blaming the Victim

Another common myth surrounding rape is that most (if not all) women secretly desire to be raped, that it is their greatest sexual fantasy. According to this belief, rape victims have generally acted in a manner that "invited" the rape; for example, they were a tease, had a sexy smile, were out too late, were too friendly, or were dressed seductively. Actually, women fear rape—in fact, they fear it more than any other crime. Researcher Susan Griffin (1979), for example, expresses the view that continues to be held by most women today:

> I have never been free of the fear of rape. From a very early age I, like most women, have thought of rape as part of my natural environment . . . something to be feared . . . like fire or lightning. (Quoted in Doyle and Paludi, 1995:160)

Women must constantly act defensively; they must try not to be alone in public, especially at night. In one study, 40 percent of women said they avoid going out at night, while fewer than one in ten men avoid doing so (North Carolina Coalition against Domestic Violence, 2002). Such fear acts to pressure some women into accepting their oppression and subordination. See Table 11.5 for a detailed list of common rape myths. Both women and men promote these myths. Do you now or have you in the past held any of these beliefs? They are all myths—there is no scientific or systematic data to support any of the myths listed. The fact is, no matter how a woman dresses, walks, or talks, when she says no she means no—not yes or maybe. A man who has forced sexual intercourse with a woman who says no is exercising his power and ability to dominate her, and he is committing the violent crime of rape.

Marital Rape

Marital rape is a taboo subject in countries around the world, including the United States. It is rarely acknowledged or discussed publicly. Yet it affects millions of women. According

TABLE 11.5
Common Rape Myths

- A woman who gets raped deserves it, especially if she agreed to go to the man's house or ride in his car.
- It wasn't rape, it was just "rough sex." Women like it that way. Other women simply enjoy rape.
- Women say "no" when they really mean "yes."
- Women provoke men by the way they dress, walk, talk, and behave, "leading men on." They thus deserve whatever happens to them.
- When men are sexually aroused, they must have sex. Once they are aroused, they can't control themselves.
- Rape happens only to certain kinds of women: women who are sexually active and promiscuous, women who are poor, women who take risks, women who like to party, women who previously have been abused.
- If a woman is not a virgin, she can't be raped.
- Women who don't fight back have not been raped. If they had resisted, they could have prevented it.
- If the man did not have a gun or knife, then the woman has not been raped.
- If there are no bruises, she must have consented.
- Sex is the proper repayment for a man who takes a woman out to dinner or pays for a movie or drinks.
- Women are asking to be raped when they go out alone at night.
- Women generally exaggerate about rape. Most times they make up rape stories to get revenge against a man who rejected them.
- Men who rape are mentally ill and out of control.
- When a husband rapes, it is because his wife withheld sex.

Sources: Adapted from Robin Warshaw, 1988, *I Never Called It Rape* (New York: Harper & Row); Liz Kelly, 1988, *Surviving Sexual Violence* (Minneapolis: University of Minnesota Press): 35–36.

to some estimates, 10 to 15 percent of women in the United States report being raped by their husbands. Marital rape occurs across age, social class status, education, race, and ethnic origin. There is a considerable and growing literature on domestic violence and sexual assault, but little if any literature on marital rape (Ghista, 2005). Victims of marital rape are often referred to as "hidden victims" because they seldom report their experiences. In one of the few systematic studies of marital rape, David Finkelhor and Kersti Yllo (1995) found a rather blasé attitude toward marital rape: respondents viewed it as simply a matter of the husband wanting it but the wife does not. In essence, the husband's response is that's too bad, I'm going to do it anyway, and he does. This kind of attitude, as well as the shame and intimidation of the victim, makes it extremely hard for the wife to come forward and report her husband's assault. Marital rape is typically not a random act; it generally occurs within the context of an abusive and exploitative relationship. Women who are raped by their husbands are likely to be raped many times. They experience not only vaginal rape, but also oral and anal rape. According to Finkelhor and Yllo, marital rape has very little to do with sex and much more to do with anger, resentment, humiliation, and degradation.

The impact of marital rape is no less serious and is sometimes more frightening, humiliating, and degrading than that of rape by strangers. Some researchers have found, for example, that the closer the association or prior association of the victim and the rapist, the more violent the rape

tends to be. Consequently, wives who are raped suffer greater and longer trauma than other female rape victims. According to Kersti Yllo (1999), when a woman is raped by a stranger, she lives with a frightening memory, but when she is raped by her husband, she lives with the rapist. Marital rape can be classified in terms of the following categories: (1) *force-only rape*, wherein the husband controls the type and frequency of sexual activity within the marriage; (2) *battering rape*, in which a husband humiliates and degrades his wife; and (3) *obsessive/sadistic rape*, which involves sexual fetishes, sadism, and forcible anal intercourse—husbands use torture or perverse sexual acts. Often pornography is involved (Finkelhor and Yllo, 1995). Whatever the classification, when a woman submits to sexual acts out of fear or coercion or implied harm based on prior assaults causing the woman to fear that physical force will be used, *it is rape* (Ghista, 2005). According to the Center for Constitutional Rights, every woman has the right to control her own body and to make decisions about having sex, using birth control, becoming pregnant, and having children. She does not suddenly lose these rights when she marries (Wellesley Centers for Women, 1998).

Researchers have identified several factors associated with marital rape. Among these factors, four have been most important: (1) the historical foundations of marriage in the United States, (2) the establishment of marital exemption in rape laws, (3) the socially and economically disadvantaged position of women, and (4) the violent nature of U.S. society and its "rape culture" (Pagelow, 1988). The last two factors were discussed under family violence. Let us briefly examine the first two. At the beginning of this chapter we pointed out the historical foundation of violence, which is firmly linked to the historical foundation of marriage. As you might recall from that discussion, in the past, husbands had absolute power over wives, including control over the wife's body. This idea, in conjunction with the British common-law notion that marriage represents a merger of husband and wife into a single identity—namely, that of the husband—provided the rationale for failing to legally recognize the concept of marital rape. Historically, then, laws prohibiting rape contained spousal exemption clauses, which meant that a husband could not be prosecuted for sexually assaulting his wife. In essence, such clauses granted husbands a right to rape.

Although it is perhaps difficult to conceive of today, in the past there was considerable resistance to the passage of laws that would allow a wife to charge her husband with rape. Until the mid-1970s, marital rape was legal in every state in the United States. In 1977, Oregon became the first state to repeal the marital exemption clause in its rape statute. In 1993, marital rape became a crime in all 50 states. Additionally, marital rape is a crime under international law. However, cultural norms and the perceived social stigma attached to rape often discourage the reporting of marital rape and prosecution for marital rape is rare in most countries including the United States. In fact, a number of states have actually broadened their marital rape exemptions to prevent the prosecution of a man who rapes the woman with whom he is living. This cohabitor's rape exemption or voluntary social companion rape exemption further limits women's ability to pursue rape cases in the criminal justice system.

THE CRIMINAL JUSTICE RESPONSE TO WOMAN ASSAULT

Every part of the criminal justice system—police, prosecutors, judges, jurors—is critical to eliminating family violence generally and woman abuse specifically. Unfortunately, the system has refused to intervene on women's behalf, except when the violence is extremely severe or death has occurred. It is often said that women are doubly victimized: first by their assailant and second by the criminal justice system. A major reason for this is that the criminal justice system, like society in general, has historically considered family violence to be a private matter, not a criminal issue. Consequently, offenders rarely have been arrested or punished, and victims have received little, if any, protection or support.

Attitudes and Behaviors

The attitudes of police officers who respond to calls of family and intimate violence are critical in determining how these victims are treated. Although progress has been made toward sensitizing police to the issues and concerns of battered and sexually assaulted women, many police still do not understand the battering cycle. They often resent having to respond again and again to the same violent household, and some simply do not want to get involved in what they believe is a private matter.

Although for more than 2 decades now almost all states have some sort of laws relative to domestic violence, most police calls for battering still do not result in arrest. Some police officers are reluctant to arrest an abuser, believing his arrest would cause an economic hardship for the family. Others think an arrest of the abuser is a waste of time, given the low probability that he will be prosecuted and given the leniency of the courts toward abusers even if they are prosecuted (Wallace, 2004). When arrests are made, the offenders are generally released after a few hours. Very often they go home and continue their violent behavior. On the other hand, it is sometimes the case that the victim does not want the police to arrest the abuser. In this circumstance, police can do little save admonish the abuser and leave him with his victim.

IN OTHER PLACES

GLOBAL RESPONSES TO VIOLENCE AND SEXUAL ASSAULT AGAINST WOMEN

Nepal: Where the Consequences of Rape Result in Imprisonment of the Victim

In 1997, at age 13, Min Min Lama, a young girl from Nepal, was raped by her sister-in-law's brother and became pregnant. Scared and not knowing what else to do (given that in her society people would disapprove of her pregnant condition), she chose to have an abortion in a country where abortion is illegal. She was arrested and sentenced to 21 years in prison; her rapist went free. The International Planned Parenthood Federation (IPPF), in collaboration with other groups, worked actively for Min Min's welfare and release, including sending a mercy petition to the king of Nepal requesting him to grant Min Min amnesty for a crime she did not commit. Two years after her incarceration, at age 15, Min Min was officially released from Central Jail in Kathmandu. The Family Planning Association of Nepal, an IPPF member, along with the IPPF South Asia Region, produced a film titled *For the Sake of Our Women* on the abortion law in Nepal and its conse-

quences on women's rights and health (IPPF, 1999; Mandate the Future, 2002).

Ethiopia: Where Rape Is a Marriage Proposal

In some areas of Ethiopia, abducting and raping a woman is the customary way to procure a wife. If a man wants a wife, he kidnaps her and then rapes her until she becomes pregnant. According to tribal tradition, once the abducted girl is pregnant, the man can put his claim on her. Village elders then act as mediators between families and negotiate the bride's price. Recently, 14-year-old Aberash Bekele, still a virgin, was abducted by seven men in southern Ethiopia, taken to a remote hut, and repeatedly beaten and raped by the gang's leader. On the second day of her kidnapping, taking with her a gun she found in the hut, the young girl tried to escape, but her rapist soon caught up with her. Frightened and trembling, Aberash fired three warning shots in the air, but the rapist kept advancing toward her. She lowered the gun and shot and killed him. Aberash was arrested for murder and brought to trial. The incident created a major rift between her parents and the abductor's family, who said, "Many people marry through abduction. He abducted her for marriage, not to be killed by her."

Although abduction is illegal in Ethiopia, it is a common practice and police typically turn a blind eye to it. It is almost always a matter left to the village elders to resolve. In Aberash's case, the village elders sent the young rape victim into exile in an orphanage and ordered her family to pay compensation for the abductor's death. With the assistance of the Ethiopian Women's Lawyers Association, Aberash became the first woman ever to challenge and resist this kind of violence. Although the village elders were furious, after 2 years of tedious legal proceedings, the judges hearing the case were convinced that Aberash acted in self-defense and she was acquitted. Unfortunately, Aberash is not completely free. Dissatisfied by the judges' decision, the village elders decreed that Aberash remain in exile. Their ruling supersedes the power of the law. Meanwhile, the six men who participated in Aberash's abduction remain free ("Where Rape Is a Proposal of Marriage," 1999).

Batman, Turkey: Where Honor Killing Is Replaced with Honor Suicide

In Batman, Turkey, a small city of 250,000, when a woman (or girl) is suspected of engaging in sexual relations out of wedlock, her male relatives convene a family

That the attitudes and behaviors of some police and related personnel toward victims of battering and sexual assault continue to be problematic is evidenced in a recent study of domestic violence and sexual assault in Washington, DC, conducted by the District police department. According to the 20-page report, police officers often fail to report or follow proper investigative procedures when handling domestic violence cases. Battered women often encounter spotty investigative work and insensitive dispatchers and, at times, belligerent officers who do not take their complaints seriously. Attitudes and behaviors such as these often deter victims from contacting police again. The upside of this report is that the Washington, DC, police department has reorganized the enforcement, training, and investigation of domestic violence cases, including requiring domestic violence training for officers. In addition, it has formed a domestic violence enforcement unit with a centralized command and oversight of domestic violence investigations (DeMillo, 2001).

Moreover, those involved throughout the criminal justice system have not been immune to the racist, sexist, and homophobic ideas prevalent in U.S. society. Thus, women have often been faced with police who believe that women provoke men into violent acts and then stay with these men because they like to be beaten. African American women and lesbian and gays are often further confronted with police and others who dismiss intimate violence as a natural part of African American or lesbian and gay culture. The reactions of police to victims of lesbian and gay violence frequently have ranged from skepticism to outright hostility and violence.

Although some studies report that today more rapes lead to jail time than just a few years ago, the overwhelming majority of rapists still remain free. Because two-thirds of sexual assaults go unreported to the police, those rapists, of course, never serve a day in prison. If the rape is reported to the police, there is roughly a 50–50 chance that an arrest will be made. If an arrest is made, there is an 80 percent chance of prosecution. If there is a prosecution, there is a 58 percent chance of a felony conviction. If there is a felony conviction, there is a 69 percent chance that the convicted will spend time in jail. Thus, even in the one-third of attacks reported to police, there is only a 16 percent chance the rapist will end up in prison. When we factor in unreported

council to decide her sentence. Female offenses can range from stealing a glance at a boy to wearing a short skirt, wanting to go to the movies, having consensual sex, or being raped by a stranger or relative. Once the family's shame, brought on by the woman's behavior, is known in the community, the family typically decides that the only way to restore family honor is to kill the woman. Hoping to join the European Union (EU), Turkey officials have been warned that its failure to make progress on women's rights (for example, putting a stop to honor killings) would impede its drive to enter the EU. In response, Turkey has tightened the punishment for attacks on women and girls by revamping its penal code and imposing life sentences for honor killings, regardless of the killer's age. But the violence against women has continued—honor killings have simply gone underground. What seemed like progress for women in fact is not as some families have taken other steps to achieve the same traditional goal of honor killing such as forcing their daughters to commit suicide or killing them and disguising the deaths as suicides. In a 6-year period between 2000 and 2006, there were 165 suicides or suicide attempts in Batman, 102 of them by women. In the first 7 months of 2006 alone, some 36 women had killed themselves. A United Nations investigation of the suicides revealed that

some few were authentic, but most appeared to be "honor killings" disguised as a suicide or accident. And the deaths keep coming. Every few weeks in Batman and the surrounding area, which is poor, rural, and heavily influenced by conservative Islam, a young woman is coerced by her family into attempting suicide. She is admonished to kill herself and clean the family's shame or they (a family member) will kill her first. Other females are stoned to death, strangled, shot, or buried alive. Thus, although the laws have been changed, tradition has not (Bilefsky, 2006).

Cape Town, South Africa: Where Men March against Rape

According to a number of sources, South Africa has one of the world's highest rates of rape and other crimes against women. Johannesburg, for example, has a reputation of being the world's "rape" capital. Fifty-two thousand rapes are reported each year in South Africa; many of the victims are young girls. Unreported cases would push this figure much higher. In 2000, led by the Anglican archbishop of Cape Town and other religious leaders, more than 2000 men took part in a march to condemn South Africa's high rate of violence against women. The archbishop told the marchers that real men do not rape, and

he urged the men to take a stand and act as role models for boys in the fight against violence against women. The men marched to parliament, where they gave the welfare minister a document stating that women were equal to men and that women and children were entitled to be safe and have their rights protected (BBC News, 2000).

What do you think? Do you think that antiabortion laws, even in the case of rape, are fair to women? Do you think that Nepali women such as Min Min should be imprisoned for making a choice about their own bodies? Who do you think should have the right to develop legislation that affects women—their bodies, their reproduction, their lives? Using sociological concepts and analysis, how would you explain why Min Min is guilty of a crime but her rapist is not? That a Turkish female should die when she is raped but the rapist faces no penalty? How might women and other persons combat cultural traditions and practices such as those in some parts of Ethiopia that have institutionalized rape and violence against women? Do you think that men marching against violence against women is enough for men to do in the fight to eliminate violence against women? Tie your answer to this question to the exercise in the Internet Resources: Applying the Sociological Imagination box.

rapes, about 6 percent of rapists—1 out of 16—will ever spend a day in jail; 15 out of 16 will walk free (RAINN, 2006). Even men who kill their wives or partners and are convicted of homicide often do not get lengthy jail sentences. Moreover, men who kill their wives or partners are less severely punished than are women who kill their husbands or partners.

If a woman's case gets to court, she often finds that she as much as her assailant is on trial. She is often questioned as if she did something wrong and "caused" the violence. Unfortunately, today there still are many judges who are insensitive to or uninformed about the nature of domestic violence. This helps explain why the conviction rate for male offenders is still very low. Notably, some states such as California have adopted a zero tolerance policy toward domestic violence such that the abuser is required to stand trial for his abuse and the victim is required to testify against him whether she wants to or not. In Los Angeles County, the penalty for partner abuse is up to 6 months in jail and a fine of $1000.

Have We Made Progress?

There is no clear-cut answer to the question of progress. The answer is both yes and no. One battered, violated, or sexually assaulted woman is one too many. However, there are signs of progress. On the national level, due in part to the vigorous efforts of a variety of individuals and groups, as well as the support of former President Bill Clinton, the Violence against Women Act was included in the Violent Crime Control and Law Enforcement Act of 1994. Under this landmark act, administered by the Department of Health and Human Services and the Department of Justice, the federal government adopted for the first time a comprehensive approach to fighting domestic violence and violence against women, including improvement of official responses to violence against women by combining tough new penalties with programs to prosecute offenders and assist women victims of violence. It also offers incentives to states that arrest spouse abusers and triples the amount of federal dollars available for battered-women's shelters.

Moreover, the treatment of rape and battered victims has improved somewhat in recent years. Since the 1970s many state legislatures have changed their laws so that women no longer have to prove that they "fought back" or produce extensive evidence to corroborate their lived experience of rape or assault. Also, several states have passed "shield laws" that prevent the victim's previous sexual experiences from being used as evidence in the trial. In addition, most police officers now receive some type of training to sensitize them to the trauma of victims. Other indications of progress include the fact that some statistics show a decline in the incidence of rape, attempted rape, and sexual assault in the mid-1990s; more and more survivors are speaking out publicly, helping to lessen the stigma associated with battered women and rape victims; an increasing number of victim support and advocate services have appeared throughout the country; advocates,

APPLYING THE SOCIOLOGICAL IMAGINATION
Men Challenging Woman Abuse and Violence

Although we know that men are the primary perpetrators of violence against women and children and even against other men, most often our challenges of and activism against domestic violence is aimed at women—the victim. While it is certainly necessary for victims of violence to empower themselves and actively work to eliminate male violence, men must also be held accountable for their violence and abuse and to take responsibility in the fight to end domestic violence.

The Texas Council on Family Violence (TCFV), one of the largest domestic violence coalitions in the United States, is doing just that. TCFV works to end violence against women through partnerships, advocacy, and direct services for women, children, and men. One of its major projects is the Men's Nonviolence Project, which pursues safety and justice for women, works to hold men accountable for their violence and abuse, and strives to eradicate the sexism from which violence against women

grows. It seems that a growing number of men all over the world (see In Other Places box) are choosing nonviolence and challenging other men to do the same. There is a plethora of Web sites for organizations and coalitions that focus on men's violence against women and challenge men to not only stop their own individual acts of violence toward women and children but also to get involved with collective action against domestic violence. According TCFV's Web page,

- Women decided long ago that they wanted men's violence against them to stop. Men, as a gender, have not made that decision. When men decide and act on that decision, violence against women will end.

- American institutions provide systemic support for men's violence against women.

- Men's violence against women will not end as a result of the work done by

battering intervention and prevention projects alone. The number of batterers is too large and the resources too limited. What is required is a social change movement that will address the root causes of men's violence against women.

http://www.tcfv.org/education/mnp.html
http://www.mensnonviolence.org/

Use these two Web sites as starting points and find other Web sites or links to organizations or coalitions led by men who are working to eliminate male violence and abuse. What kinds of programs, campaigns, and other actions are conducted by these groups? Can you ascertain their effectiveness in raising awareness about domestic violence? What kinds of men are involved in these efforts? Is there a comparable organization on your college campus? In your city? Would your campus benefit from such a group? Why? Why not?

Thousands of women die each year in honor killings perpetrated by family members, usually fathers and/or brothers, to avenge the shame the women or girls allegedly brought on their families. With increasing world attention to this form of violence against females, in some countries honor killings have gone underground—made to look like suicide. Pictured here, a Turkish father of a 14 year old girl who allegedly "committed suicide" in 2006 holds photos of her while standing with his wife and sons in front of their house in a village outside of Batman, in Southeast Turkey.

prosecutors, and survivors are finding ways to work together in states across the country to change laws and statutes; and more men are taking a public stand on domestic violence (U.S. Department of Justice, 2000b, 2004, 2006a). Men challenging domestic violence has become an increasingly visible phenomenon both in the United states and in places such as South Africa, a country dubbed the *rape capital of the world* (see In Other Places box and the Internet Resources: Applying the Sociological Imagination box).

THE EFFECTS OF PHYSICAL AND SEXUAL ASSAULT ON WOMEN

A growing body of research deals with the psychological effects of physical and sexual violence against women. There is also a growing recognition of battered women as "survivors." The harm that men inflict on women takes many forms and has a wide range of effects. Research indicates that violent abuse exacts a tremendous toll on women: physically, psychologically, emotionally, and financially. The physical effects are perhaps the most obvious and can range from bruises and temporary pain to scars, permanently broken bones, disfigurement, and even death. Less visible but perhaps more damaging are the psychological and emotional scars brought on by abuse. Low self-esteem, self-hate, economic and emotional dependence on others (especially on those who perpetrate the violence), fear, self-destructive behavior such as alcohol and drug abuse, and suicide are common among abused women.

Given traditional gender role socialization, many abused women attribute the violence and abuse to something they

did or did not do and therefore believe that they deserve to be treated violently. They frequently try to change themselves or the situations that they believe lead to the abuse. However, they usually come to realize that the abuse is unpredictable and could be triggered by almost anything they do. It is not surprising that women suffering under such conditions have a low sense of self-worth and a high sense of helplessness and hopelessness. Women who have been victims of incestuous assault as children report feelings of severe depression throughout their lives, often to the point of suicide. Probably the most extreme manifestation of battered women's self-blame and recrimination is their tendency toward self-destructive behavior. Self-destructiveness can be considered both an effect and a coping strategy that abused women use to deal with their violent life experience.

COPING AND SURVIVAL STRATEGIES

As with any stressful situation, coping with violence and abuse requires a variety of skills, survival tactics, and resources. Research shows that battered women have developed a wide range of strategies, both constructive (seeking help, leaving the violent situation) and destructive (substance abuse, suicide, murder). Although the ways individual women cope vary from situation to situation, their coping and survival strategies can be classified in the following ways: psychological and emotional, self-destructive, and fighting back.

Psychological and Emotional Strategies

One strategy employed by battered women is avoidance or prevention of violence. Victims of abuse sometimes develop plans to avoid future attacks. Sometimes they use sex (to the degree that they still have some control over their sexuality) in an attempt to change the batterer or to avoid further beatings. Some battered women cope by trying to make the relationship work in spite of the obstacles, and others manage to cope and survive by insisting that the violence is not serious enough to end the relationship. Some women resort to dreams or fantasies that can range from being in a violence-free relationship to killing their mates. Still other women block out or repress their experiences of violence, though these experiences often resurface at some future time.

Self-Destructive Strategies

For many battered women, self-destructive behavior is not only a consequence of battering and abuse; it is also a way of coping with the situation. Various addictions such as alcohol and drug abuse, overeating, and suicide are all forms of coping, although most people would consider them unhealthy, unwise, and ineffective. Battering appears to be the single-most important context for female alcoholism, suicide attempts, and a range of mental health problems. For example, battered women account for 42 percent of all attempted suicides. As previously stated, more than 25 percent of all female suicide attempts reported by hospitals are associated with battering. Of these women, 80 percent have a history of suicide attempts and have been seen in the hospital for at least one abusive injury prior to their first suicide attempt (Abbott et al., 1995; Frazer, 1995; RAINN, 2006a). For African

American women, fully one-half of those who attempt suicide are abused. Indeed, the association among the experiences of violence, low self-esteem, depression, substance abuse, and suicidal tendencies is quite strong among all female victims of violence (McNeal and Amato, 1998).

Battering is also closely associated with female alcohol and drug abuse. Some researchers caution that it is unclear whether substance abuse is the context or the consequence of stress precipitated by violence. That is, some researchers contend that alcohol abuse may contribute to a climate that makes abuse more likely. Other researchers respond that the rate of alcoholism among battered women is significantly greater than among nonbattered women. An examination of the recorded onset of alcoholism and of abusive injury among battered women reveals that three-fourths of the alcohol cases emerged only after the onset of abuse, suggesting that abuse leads to alcoholism among battered women, and not the reverse. Similarly, whereas drug abuse is no more common among battered women than nonbattered women before the onset of abuse, after abuse the risk of drug abuse is nine times greater than would normally be expected (Stark and Flitcraft, 1988; Brown and Anderson, 1991).

Sometimes the self-destructive coping behavior of battered women is manifested in addictive behaviors such as overeating. Although a causal relationship between abuse and addiction to food has not been established, some battered women seem to use food as a way of coping with the violence in their lives (Dutton, 1988; Iazetto, 1989).

Fighting Back

Some women who cannot escape abusive relationships cope by fighting back. Most often their self-defense takes the form of hitting or shoving the batterer. Only occasionally is women's self-defense more violent, such as pushing the batterer down a flight of stairs, biting him, kicking him in the groin, cutting him, or even shooting him. A growing number of women today are taking self-defense classes to protect themselves against male attackers. A small number of women who fight back eventually kill their abuser. Although a few of these women are acquitted by the courts on the grounds of self-defense, most are convicted and jailed. The majority of those convicted serve many years in prison despite their claims of self-defense and despite a large amount of evidence indicating that they had been severely abused by the men they killed. Some people consider women who respond to male violence by fighting back and who are then imprisoned to be political prisoners (see, for example, Bannister, 1991). Whatever term we use to describe these women, the fact is that killing an abuser is more the exception than the rule. Only a small percentage of battered women use this strategy to end the abuse they suffer.

Any discussion of domestic violence is necessarily depressing, given the high rate of victimization in the United States. However, many victims of violence are also survivors. They are not passive and defeated victims. As we have indicated, some victims fight back; others seek the assistance of family, friends, professionals, and institutions. Still others find ways, sometimes after years of victimization, to leave their abusive relationships, very often at great personal risk. Through individual and collective actions, they resist, challenge, and/or change the violent forces impacting their lives. Many victims of domestic violence have developed interesting and self-fulfilling methods by which to celebrate their survival. One such creative method is the *Clothesline Project*, which originated in Hyannis, Massachusetts, in 1990. The Clothesline Project is about direct, personal violence against women and provides an opportunity for women to bear witness to their personal experience of violence and celebrate their transformation from victim to survivor in a powerful statement of solidarity. It consists of a clothesline hung with shirts designed by survivors of assault, rape, and incest using paint, magic markers, crayons, or elaborate embroidery to create their shirt. Families and friends of women who have died as a result of violence can and do make shirts to express their deep loss (Clothesline Project, 1995).

A COMPARATIVE LOOK AT BATTERED MEN

A 30-year-old man moved out of an apartment it had taken him ages to find because of the couple who lived next door. What was it about the couple that made this young man give up his hard-won apartment? He said it was the fights: the shouting, the verbal abuse, and what sounded like physical abuse that resounded from the apartment next door. What he found most disturbing was the fact that, in his view, the woman was the abusive and violent partner (Sims, 1989).

What evidence exists for female violence and male victimization? The suggestion that men are battered by women probably sounds implausible, if not silly, to some people. For others, the image of a skinny little henpecked man chased by a large, buxom wife with a rolling pin in her hand might immediately come to mind. In fact, some research during the 1970s and 1980s suggested that the phenomenon of battered husbands was as prevalent as that of battered wives. Suzanne Steinmetz (1977) was one of the first to call attention to this issue by claiming that more women battered husbands than vice versa and that husband abuse was the most underreported of all forms of family violence. Studies based on national survey data in the 1980s found that in homes with couple violence, approximately one-fourth of the respondents indicated that men were victims and not perpetrators of violence, an additional one-fourth reported that women were victims and not offenders, and the remaining one-half reported that both wives and husbands were violent. Some recent studies suggest that there is a higher degree of female violence and aggression than previously thought. For example, although the percentage of males arrested in California for domestic violence decreased 10 percent over the 10-year period from 1988 to 1998, the percentage of female domestic violence increased 10 percent during the same period (Wallace, 2004).

Critics of the idea of widespread husband abuse caution that statistics such as these and those of Steinmetz can be seriously misinterpreted. A major problem with claims that women use violence as often as men is that there is little or no clarification of how many of the women who use violence are actually acting in self-defense or retaliating against an abusive partner. Data from studies of violent relationships in which the police intervened clearly indicate that men are rarely the victims of battery (Gelles, 1997). Research also clearly shows that men initiate violence in the majority of cases. Moreover, men who kill their partner do so in self-defense far less frequently than do women who kill their partner. Further, rarely do battered women report initiating violence. The most frequent motive for violence in their self-reports is "fighting back," and the violent acts that they report tend, most often, to be protective or self-defense actions.

Given that women are, on average, smaller and physically weaker than men, the abuse inflicted on them is far more severe and life-threatening than those instances of male or husband battering. In addition, not only are battered men less physically injured than battered women, but they are also less trapped in an abusive relationship than women because men typically have greater economic resources and can more easily leave an abusive relationship as they usually do not have responsibility for children. Although some men are injured by a wife or lover, most women are unable to defend themselves effectively against male batterers. In fact, most battered women find it far safer to submit to the battering than to fight back and risk being seriously injured or even killed. In light of this fact, it seems inappropriate to generalize women's behavior in this regard as "husband abuse" or "battering." This is not meant to trivialize male battering where it exists. And it does not alter the fact that domestic violence in all forms needs to be investigated and understood. Frequently during the last decade, media-generated sensationalism drew our attention to women's abuse of men. Because women are overwhelmingly the victims, we sometimes find it difficult to think of them as perpetrators of violence. But, in 1998, comic

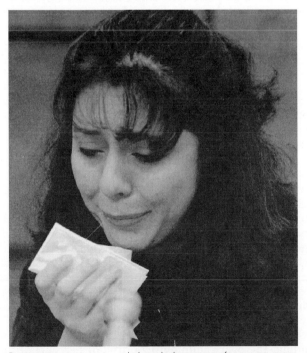

Because women are overwhelmingly the victims of intimate partner violence, we sometimes find it difficult to think of them as perpetrators of violence. However, frequently in recent times, media-generated sensationalism has drawn our attention to women such as Lorena Bobbitt who stood trail and was acquitted in 1993 of malicious wounding—a charge stemming from the fact that she cut off her husband's penis after he raped her, an act of violence to which she had been regularly subjected throughout their marriage.

Phil Hartman of *Saturday Night Live* and *NewsRadio* was shot to death in his $1.4 million mansion by his wife, who then killed herself. More recently, in 2003, Asia Gray, the fiancée of William Green—a running back for the NFL's Cleveland Browns—was arrested and charged with assault and domestic violence. She was accused of stabbing Green in his back during a fight (Family Violence Prevention Fund, 2006b).

An interesting development in male abuse and a fact that perhaps few people know is that every year, thousands of men turn to women's rape crisis agencies because there is no other place for men who have been sexually assaulted. Unlike in the case of female rape victims, however, the perpetrators of male rape are not the opposite sex. They are overwhelmingly other men. Nonetheless, this is an important form of violence that a growing number of men face. Many of the issues with male and female rape victims are the same. Both generally feel guilt, shame, and self-blame. Like women, men must also deal with "rape myths," which add to the emotional trauma of dealing with rape. Perhaps the foremost myth is that men cannot be and do not get raped. This myth prevents many men from reporting their rape. For example, during 1993 and 1994 in Chicago, a serial rapist who targeted teenaged boys and young men was never caught, partly because most of his victims suffered in silence. According to some authorities, in cases of rape, men's emotional needs are often ignored as cultural norms do not permit men to be victims. In an early study of male rape victims, a team of Memphis gynecologists found that in one free clinic for rape victims in Memphis, Tennessee, over a 2-year period, 6 percent of the clients were male. More than one-half of these men had been abducted before the assault, and only two knew their attackers.

Perhaps the most common myth is that male rape occurs only within the context of prison or that it is related to a male's sexual orientation. The fact is, rape is rape. It is a crime of violence whether the victim is female or male. It goes without saying that most advocates for abused males believe the incidence of male rape is much higher because most male rapes go unreported and because the prison population was not included in these figures. Men are generally silent about their rape because they think most people will not believe them or because they think most people will think that they are gay. Their silence about their victimization relative to rape contributes to the myth that rape affects only women and homosexuals. Research suggests that, as with women, most rapes of men are not prompted by sexual desire. Rather, it is an issue of power and control (Edelhart, 1995).

CHILD ASSAULT AND ABUSE

Although child abuse has existed throughout human history, in the United States it attracted public interest only in the early 1960s. At that time Dr. C. Henry Kempe and his associates (1962) published a national survey that described for the first time the series of behaviors known as the **battered-child syndrome.** They defined this syndrome basically as "a clinical condition in children who have received severe physical abuse, primarily from a parent or foster parent" (Kempe et al., 1962:17). Even then, however, child abuse was not widely acknowledged to be a major issue until the

1980s, when expanded media coverage brought the problem to the attention of millions of Americans. Public opinion polls conducted in the 1970s revealed that only one in ten Americans considered child abuse a serious problem. By the 1980s, the nation's awareness of the impact of crime and violence against children changed dramatically, as reflected in the change in that figure to nine out of ten. Interestingly, however, only one in three reported abuse when confronted with an actual situation (Childhelp, 2005; Gelles and Strauss, 1987).

As well, we as a nation should not only be aware of but also consciously concerned about the escalating violence in this country, especially that directed at children at younger and younger ages. Today, hardly a day goes by without news of another child (or children) who has been severely abused, neglected, starved, or murdered, usually by a parent or close relative. Consider the following statistics related to children and violence in the United States: *Every 10 seconds a child is reported to authorities as abused or neglected; every 20 seconds a child is arrested; every 44 seconds a child is born into poverty; every 4 minutes a child is arrested for drug abuse; every 8 minutes a child is arrested for a violent crime; every 2 hours a child is killed by a firearm; every 3 hours a child is a homicide victim; every 4 hours a child commits suicide; every 5 hours a child dies from abuse or neglect* (Children's Defense Fund, 2001b). The epidemic of violence against children is global. However, three out of four child killings in the industrialized world happen in the United States, and child suicide rates in this country are twice those of the rest of the industrialized world ("Violence Kills More U.S. Kids," 1997).

As with woman victimization, the maltreatment of children takes many forms, including physical battering and abuse, child endangerment and neglect, sexual abuse and assault, psychological or emotional abuse, exploitation, murder, children thrown away, child runaways, and child abduction by parents and by strangers. Until recently, the greatest threat to children was believed to be stranger abductions. However, today a substantial body of research has documented that, of the thousands of children each year classified as missing or abducted, parents, not strangers, are responsible for the vast majority of these abductions—every day 559 children are kidnapped by a parent or other family member. In addition, the largest category of missing children today are runaway, thrown away, and homeless youth, a substantial number of whom have been victims of prior physical or sexual abuse in their homes. Their life on the streets continues this pattern of violence (Mignon, Larson, and Holmes, 2002).

Moreover, new manifestations of child victimization have emerged over recent decades. For example, Munchausen syndrome by proxy is a rare form of abuse that is relatively new to public awareness and involves an adult, usually a white, middle-class mother with some knowledge or experience with medicine or nursing, who assumes the sick role indirectly (for example, by proxy) by feigning or inducing illness in her child (usually an infant or toddler). It can include making a child think that she or he is mentally ill, having the child committed to a mental hospital, claiming that the child suffers from depression or anxiety, inducing apnea (a cessation of breathing) by suffocating the child to

the point of unconsciousness, scrubbing the child's skin with oven cleaner to produce a blistering rash, and various behavioral problems exhibited only in the presence of the perpetrator. The mother's motives range from a desire for attention from people—family, friends, and community—as the heroic caretaker of a tragically ill child, dislike or hatred for the child, to monetary returns from insurance. Because it takes many years of illness before the secret of Munchausen by proxy is discovered, the mortality rate for this form of child abuse is 9 percent (Parnell and Day, 1998; Asher-Meadow, 2001; Feldman, 2001).

Although not a new phenomenon, many Americans are only just beginning to recognize shaken-baby syndrome (SBS) as a form of child abuse. SBS is a form of child abuse in which the perpetrator, usually a parent or adult caretaker, shakes a child so violently that the brain sustains significant injury. Although the percentage of injuries to children as a result of SBS is not currently known, the syndrome is recognized as the most common cause of child maltreatment fatalities and accounts for the most long-term disability in infants and young children. Some of what we do know about SBS is that every year somewhere between 1200 and 1600 children in the United States are victims of SBS. About 25 to 30 percent of infant victims with SBS die from their injuries. Nonfatal consequences of SBS include varying degrees of visual impairment (e.g., blindness), motor impairment (e.g., cerebral palsy), and cognitive impairments (Barr, 2005).

Moreover, advances in technology now present serious threats and potential harm to children that we did not even imagine 10 or 20 years ago. Video cameras are increasingly used to produce homemade child pornography; personal computers with access to the Internet are used to instantly disseminate child pornography around the world and to solicit children for sexual encounters. The power of the Internet and the pervasive concern about electronic virtual sex involving unsuspecting children have led to a new generation of child protectors, including the U.S. Congress, which has repeatedly tried to impose special restrictions on Internet speech to protect children. Recently, a unique case of virtual rape of a child came to public attention when a 51-year-old New Jersey man acknowledged that he had made obscene phone calls to 12 girls, ranging in age from 8 to 14, and pleaded guilty to multiple counts of child endangerment. What made this case unique was that the man was also charged with aggravated sexual assault because he had persuaded one of his victims, a 10-year-old girl, to insert her finger into her vagina. The man never met his victim, his only contact was by phone. Nonetheless, he was convicted of aggravated sexual assault and given a 12-year sentence, part of which will be served at the state's sex offender treatment center. According to Wendy Kaminer (2001), this case may change the way we think about rape. The growing threat of telephone and on-line sexual predators notwithstanding, the overwhelming majority (90 percent) of juvenile sexual assault victims know their attacker—30 percent are family members and 60 percent are acquaintances (U.S. Department of Veteran Affairs, 2006).

Just as for most types of violence and sexual assault, trying to determine the overall incidence of child abuse is a difficult task. However, the data do indicate, as we said earlier, that child victimization in the United States is an epidemic of national scope and importance and it involves children of all ages, races, classes, sexual orientations, and both sexes. Each year in the United States, it is estimated that millions of children directly experience or witness violence in their homes, neighborhoods, and schools. It is estimated that as many as 3.3 million children are exposed to violence against their mothers or female caretakers by family members alone. In homes where partner abuse occurs, 40 to 60 percent of men who abuse women also abuse children. Considering the various forms that child abuse takes, by far the majority of reported cases of child abuse are due to child neglect (61 percent) or physical abuse (19 percent). Some children, however, suffer more than one type of maltreatment (RAINN, 2006; American Psychological Association, 2001).

In some ways, child abuse is even more difficult to deal with than woman abuse. Although there have been significant legislative changes relative to child victimization, children still have limited legal rights and are subject to the authority of their parents. Parents have a right and obligation to discipline their children, and few restrictions are placed on how they may do so. Perhaps more so than even woman abuse, parental violence against children historically has been considered a "family matter" with which the larger society should not interfere, except in extreme cases. The remainder of our discussion of child victimization takes a brief but closer look at the physical and sexual assault of children. However, this is not meant to diminish the seriousness or prevalence of other forms of child abuse.

The Physical Assault of Children

Because adults have great latitude in the methods they may use to discipline children, violence against children must be serious before it is labeled as abuse. (How many Americans recognize spanking as a form of violence?) (see Figure 11.3). Of all the types of child abuse, physical abuse is probably the most likely to lead to intervention by outside forces because it most often leaves visible evidence (such as bruises, lacerations, and broken bones) that can be introduced into a court of law as evidence of maltreatment.

Prevalence   As already noted, because of a high rate of underreporting, the incidence of child assault is difficult to assess. Notwithstanding this fact, the statistics we have on child assault and abuse are alarming. National surveys that ask Americans about violence in their homes have found considerable violence directed toward children. Most parents admit to using some kind of violence on their children, including beating up a child at least once, using severe forms of punishment, and threatening to use or actually using a gun or knife (Straus and Donnelly, 2001). Each day in the United States, more than 4 children die as a result of child abuse in the home. Indeed, parental violence is among the five leading causes of death for children 18 years old and younger. More than three-fourths of these children are under the age of four; 44 percent are under the age of one. Child homicide risk is greater in the first year of life than in any other year of childhood. Infants are most likely to be killed by their mother during the first week of life but thereafter are more

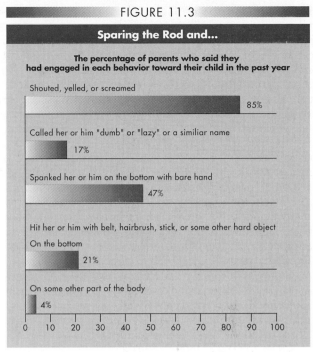

FIGURE 11.3

Sparing the Rod and...

The percentage of parents who said they had engaged in each behavior toward their child in the past year

Shouted, yelled, or screamed — 85%

Called her or him "dumb" or "lazy" or a similiar name — 17%

Spanked her or him on the bottom with bare hand — 47%

Hit her or him with belt, hairbrush, stick, or some other hard object
On the bottom — 21%

On some other part of the body — 4%

Source: Adapted from Tamar Lewin, 1995, "Parents Poll Finds Child Abuse to Be More Common," *New York Times* (December 7). Copyright © 1995 by the New York Times Co. Reprinted by permission.

likely to be killed by a male, usually their father or stepfather (Childhelp, 2005). Maltreatment deaths are more associated with neglect (38 percent) than any other form of abuse. Most of these victims (81 percent) were maltreated by one or both of their parents. One of the most striking differences between maltreatment fatalities and other types of maltreatment is that maltreatment fatalities are less frequently perpetrated by just one parent acting alone (U.S. Department of Health and Human Services, 2001a).

It is estimated that as many as one-third of all abuse and neglect cases go unreported or undetected, especially if they involve middle-class or wealthy families. We can safely assume that like most family violence, child abuse is often hidden in the privacy of the home, and most people do not admit to it. Furthermore, as with most statistics on violence, child assault statistics rely heavily on self-reports and on the reports of various professionals such as doctors, nurses, social workers, teachers, child-care workers, and police. Even though the reporting of suspected child abuse has improved significantly in recent years because of increased training, awareness, and legislation, perhaps one primary reason that a significant amount of child assault continues to go unreported is that many of these professionals refuse to "get involved." Very often their biases concerning race and class affect their decision on whether to report suspected cases of child assault. For example, doctors are twice as likely to label a black child a victim of abuse as a white child. Similarly, they are twice as likely to miss abuse in two-parent families, compared with single-parent families, and they are more likely to label a case as abuse if the child is from a janitor's family than if the child is from a lawyer's family (Jenny et al., 1999).

Who Are the Abused? The intersections of race, class, gender, and age are important considerations in any discussion of child physical assault. Current statistics indicate that the majority of victims of maltreatment are white in all categories of maltreatment except one—medical neglect. The highest percentage of medical neglect victims are African American (44 percent), with whites a close second (41 percent). However, when we look at victimization within the same race, more than one-half of all victims of child maltreatment are white (54 percent), one-fourth (25 percent) are African American, 17 percent are Latina/o, 2 percent are Native Americans and Alaska Natives, and 1 percent are Asian and Pacific Islanders. For most racial categories, the largest percentage of victims suffer from neglect (American Humane Fact Sheet, 2006; U.S. Department of Health and Human Services, 2004; Mignon, Larson, and Holmes, 2002).

Although child maltreatment occurs in all socioeconomic groups, poverty and other socioeconomic disadvantages such as unemployment are key risk factors. As with other forms of violence and abuse, reported cases (and this is key) are disproportionately from among economically and socially disadvantaged families, particularly families receiving public assistance. Children in families with incomes under $15,000 a year are far more likely than children in families with yearly incomes over $30,000 to be victims of some form of neglect or abuse. In addition, they are also more likely to be both emotionally and educationally neglected. Economic stress and poverty also appear to be related to the severity of abuse. Children whose families earn less than $15,000 per year compared with those whose family income is $30,000 or greater are more likely to be harmed by some variety of abuse, to be seriously injured by maltreatment or abuse, and to die from some type of maltreatment or abuse. According to some studies, serious or fatal injuries to children are more prevalent among families whose annual income is below the poverty level than any other income group (U.S. Department of Health and Human Services, 2004; Barnett, Miller-Perrin, and Perrin, 1997).

Research results are mixed as to who receives more physical abuse, girls or boys. However, the most recent data show that 52 percent of abused children are female compared to 48 percent for males (American Humane, 2006; U.S. Department of Health and Human Services, 2001a). Because younger children are the most frequently reported victims of child abuse, until recently little attention was paid to abused adolescents. However, along with infants and toddlers, the highest rates of physical injury occur among adolescents (Barnett, Miller-Perrin, and Perrin, 1997). Many people do not see adolescents as being particularly vulnerable because, unlike small children, they can run away, protect themselves, and get help. They are often viewed as an accomplice in their abuse because of their size, strength, and/or behavior. In fact, however, every year an unknown number of adolescents are abused. Many run away to someone or someplace, but most end up on the streets, unprotected and vulnerable to the abuse of a variety of unscrupulous people such as pimps, pornographers, and drug dealers.

Sometimes abuse increases during adolescence as children experience independence and personality changes. Such changes can at times cause some parents to feel a loss of power and control and they compensate for this by increasing the abuse. Sometimes adolescents fight back. Some researchers estimate that almost 2.5 million teenagers commit acts of violence against their parents every year. Approximately 2000 parents die each year at the hands of a teenage son or daughter, often in self-defense or in retaliation against abuse. However, as we saw in the In the News at the beginning of this chapter, sometimes parricide has little or nothing to do with parental violence and abuse. Nonetheless, parricide is said to be most common during adolescence (Gelles and Straus, 1987; Wallace, 2004). Almost all murders of parents are committed by sons. In the few cases that involve daughters, often a male accomplice is recruited. One common scenario of parricide involves a drunken, physically abusive father who is killed by a son who sees himself as the protector of the family. According to one source on parricide, 63 percent of boys aged 11 to 20 who commit homicide murder the man who was abusing their mother. Overall, however, teenagers are more likely to employ physical violence against mothers than against fathers (National Coalition Against Domestic Violence, 2006a; Wallace, 2004).

Current research indicates that certain characteristics predispose a child to being abused. Children born to unmarried parents; premature infants; children who are congenitally malformed or mentally retarded; twins; children born during a mother's depressive illness, to parents with a history of domestic abuse, or into large families (with four or more children); and children whose parents are substance abusers are most vulnerable to abuse. It is estimated that one in every four children in the United States live in a household with an alcoholic adult and an estimated 40 to 80 percent of the families who become child protective services cases have problems with alcohol or drugs. In addition, children with disabilities are also at risk for abuse (about 7 percent of abused children) as are children in foster care (Centers for Disease Control and Prevention, 2006a; Childhelp, 2005).

Usually only one child in a family is abused. That child most often is the youngest, followed, in terms of frequency, by the oldest. Before the age of 10 or 11, boys are more frequently abused than girls. At that point, the incidence of abuse of girls becomes greater. Research also indicates that between 30 and 42 percent of abused children come from single-parent homes (Tower, 2004). In addition, they are more likely to have young parents and few siblings, to have been separated from their parents during the first year of life, and to have parents who were themselves abused as children. Some research suggests that teenage mothers are more likely than older mothers to be abusive because of a number of factors, including poverty, economic strains, substance abuse, and lack of parental skills and abilities (Gaudin et al., 1996; National CASA Association, 2000; Children's Defense Fund, 2001b).

The impact of child physical abuse is multifaceted. Abused children tend to have emotional scars and problems that they take into adulthood, such as low self-esteem and a tendency to abuse alcohol and other drugs. Moreover, children who grow up in abusive families, observing violence directed toward a parent, exhibit emotional problems and are likely to be "juvenile delinquents." In this context, nearly 2 million appear to have suffered (and more than 1 million still suffer) from posttraumatic stress disorder (PTSD) a long-term mental health condition often characterized by depression, anxiety, flashbacks, nightmares, and other behavioral and physiological symptoms (Family Violence Prevention Fund, 2006a; U.S. Department of Justice, 2004, 2001b). Furthermore, of children who witness family violence, 60 percent of the boys eventually become batterers and 50 percent of the girls become victims; 73 percent of male abusers were abused as children and at least 80 percent of men in prison grew up in a violent home (National Coalition against Domestic Violence, 2006a; Childhelp, 2005; National CASA Association, 2000).

Who Are the Abusers?   In 90 percent of child abuse cases, the abuser is a member of the immediate family, typically a person between the ages of 20 and 39. According to various studies and crime statistics on violent offenders and their victims, 97 percent of offenders who commit violent crimes against children are male; 25 percent are 40 years or older; 70 percent are white; only about 10 percent of these offenders of child victims receive life or death sentences; and the average prison sentence is shorter than that received by those who abuse adults (U.S. Department of Justice, 2006a; U.S. Department of Health and Human Services, 2001a). Half of the reported cases of parental physical violence against children involve women and half involve men, but most of the literature on child abuse claim that mothers are more likely than fathers to abuse their children, despite the small difference between the two. This finding should not be taken to mean that women are, by nature, more violent than men. Rather, women's general lack of power in the family, their iso-

lation in the home, and the emotional tensions of mothering all lead to situations in which abuse is likely to occur. In fact, if we controlled for the amount of time spent in contact with children, rates of abuse would be higher for men.

Some researchers have found that women who are abused by their husbands or lovers are most likely to use severe violence against their children, although these women account for only a small overall percentage of such cases. Other researchers have found a positive relationship between women's work and child abuse, with women in the paid labor force (compared with all mothers) exhibiting the lowest rates of overall violence toward their children. Fathers whose wives work (compared with all fathers) also have the lowest rate of violence toward children (Gelles and Hargreaves, 1987). It seems, too, that a person's occupation is significantly related to the probability of abuse. People in working-class occupations are more likely to use physical punishment and abuse their children than are their counterparts in white-collar occupations. Moreover, children in homes where the father is either unemployed or working part-time are more likely to be abused than are children in homes where the father works full-time. Finally, stepfathers and boyfriends of single mothers are frequent abusers of children, especially sexual abusers (DHHS, 2005; Wiese and Daro, 1995).

The Sexual Assault of Children

Child sexual abuse is a major problem today, and public concern about this issue has been heightened by both numerous reports by adult survivors of its impact on their lives and the unfolding saga of sex abuse in the Catholic church. On the one hand, celebrities and other public figures are calling attention increasingly to child sexual assault by sharing their childhood experiences of abuse. For example, the extremely successful talk show host Oprah Winfrey revealed that she was only 9 years old when she was raped by a 19-year-old cousin, the first of three family members to sexually assault her before she reached adulthood. On the other hand, one of the most public and controversial sex abuse scandals in American history involves priests and the Catholic church. Reports of Catholic priests who have sexually abused children have come to light in virtually every major U.S. city. Over the past 25 or more years, for instance, more than 400 priests in the United States have been identified as child sexual abusers. The majority of their victims have been boys (many of whom served as altar boys), who as adults, like Oprah Winfrey and other women victims of incest, gained the courage to come forward and report the abuse that occurred during their childhood (Scott and Schwartz, 2006). Approximately 35 percent of women and 20 percent of men in the United States were victims of sexual abuse as children, and almost half report that they kept the abuse to themselves (Mendel, 1995).

There is no one single definition of child sexual abuse. In general, the term *child sexual abuse* refers to the use of a child for the sexual gratification of an adult. A central characteristic of any abuse is the dominant position of an adult, which allows him or her to force or coerce a child into sexual activity. Child sexual abuse or incestuous behavior is not confined to sexual intercourse. It may include nudity, disrobing, genital exposure, kissing, fondling a child's genitals and/or

Joaquin Aguilar Mendez holds a press conference in 2006 outside the Superior court in Los Angeles where he filed charges of sexual abuse and cover up against several Mexican priests: Cardinals Roger Mahony and Norberto Rivera the Diocese of Tehuacan Puebla and Father Nicholas Aguilar. Mendez, along with several U.S. lawyers and members of the Chicago-based Survivors Network of Those Abused by Priests, called the news conference to reveal details of his civil lawsuit that alleges that as a 12-yearold alter boy, Mendez was raped and sodomized by Father Rivera and the Cardinals acted to cover up the crime.

other body parts, masturbation, oral–genital contact, digital penetration, sodomy, as well as vaginal and anal intercourse. Child sexual abuse is not limited to physical contact; such abuse can include noncontact abuse, such as exhibitionism, voyeurism, child pornography, deliberately exposing a child to the act of sexual intercourse, and masturbating in front of a child. In addition, child sexual abuse can include sexual exploitation such as engaging a child or soliciting a child for the purposes of prostitution; using a child to film, photograph, or model pornography (American Humane Fact Sheets, 2004; American Psychological Association, 2001), and as we discussed earlier in the case of "virtual rape," it can include coercion via telephone.

Such abuse can be divided into two basic categories depending on who the abuser is: familial abuse and extrafamilial abuse. Familial abuse is generally referred to as **incest**—the sexual abuse by a blood relative who is assumed to be a part of the child's family. Most definitions of incest include stepfathers and live-in boyfriends. Because most child sexual abuse is perpetrated by family members, our discussion focuses on familial rather than extrafamilial abuse. Sexual abuse progresses over time and in intensity. It might begin with an adult undressing in front of the child and progress to the rubbing of the perpetrator's penis on the genital or rectal area of the child. Not every case of sexual abuse progresses in the same way. No matter what the cyclic order of child sexual abuse, however, it involves an adult using her or his powers to force, coerce, or cajole compliance from a child who participates out of awe, fear, trust, respect, or love for the adult (Tower, 2004).

Prevalence   Because of the extremely sensitive, embarrassing, and outrageous nature of incest, victims and perpetrators often keep it hidden. Family members and others outside the family cite personal reasons for not reporting known instances of child sexual abuse. The most common reason cited by adults is their reluctance to believe a child's claim of abuse and their hesitance to accuse an adult of such behavior. Thus, official reports of incest severely underestimate its actual occurrence. Despite the underestimation of the true magnitude of the problem, of all victims of sexual assault reported to law enforcement agencies two-thirds (67 percent) are juveniles under the age of 18 at the time of the crime. Between 10 and 20 percent of American children are victims of sexual assault by a parent or parent figure and 90 percent know their attacker. Only 10 percent of child molesters are strangers to those they abuse (6 percent for children under 6 years old). About 30 to 40 percent are family friends or trusted adults. Typical child sex abusers—50 to 60 percent—are fathers, stepfathers, uncles, grandfathers, and brothers. The percentage of women who sexually abuse children is low. The majority of incest cases involve stepfather and stepdaughter or father and daughter; only a small proportion of incest cases involve fathers and sons, and even more rare are cases that involve mother and son (National Coalition against Domestic Violence, 2006a; Childhelp, 2005; Stevens, 2005). It is estimated that 20 to 40 percent of adult women in the United States were sexually abused before the age of 18. For men, the range is 10 to 20 percent. That is 24 to 48 million women and 11 to 22 million men (Stevens, 2005).

In the late 1990s, a survey of the health of adolescent girls and boys (Schoen et al., 1997a, 1997b) found that 7 percent of young girls and 3 percent of young boys in grades 5 through 8, and 12 percent of "older" girls and 5 percent of "older" boys in grades 9 through 12, said they had been sexually abused. Furthermore, about one of ten pregnant adolescents reported becoming pregnant as a result of a sexual assault, primarily incest. Consistent with current research and crime data, most of child sexual abuse occurs at home, particularly for girls, and is recurrent. The sexual abuse of boys takes place less often in their homes and less often is the perpetrator a family member. Although most sexually abused children often remain silent about their abuse, boys more often than girls say they did not talk to anyone about the abuse. Many of these children express a fear of being in their homes and want to leave.

The Sexually Abused Child and the Abuser   We have already made some generalizations concerning which children are sexually abused and who abuses them. For instance, the typical victim of sexual abuse is female and girls are more often sexually abused within the family and boys outside the family (for example, by the clergy or athletic coaches). Some researchers, however, dispute these conclusions, saying they are misleading because boys, who are taught early to be "strong" and "macho," are less likely to report a sexual assault no matter where it occurs. Recent research, in fact, suggests that boys are almost equally as vulnerable to incest as are girls (Tower, 2004). At the very least, these studies indicate that the incidence of abuse among male children is significantly higher than we imagined or is reported.

The underreporting of male child sexual abuse notwithstanding, we do know that, in general, boys, like girls, are most likely to be victimized by men. In addition, boys are more likely than girls to be one of a number of victims of the same perpetrator; boys are more likely than girls to be victims of both sexual and physical abuse; and boys are also more likely to be subjected to anal abuse than are girls (Mignon, Larson, and Holmes, 2002). Some researchers have pointed to a cycle of sexual abuse that they describe with the term **transmission of victimization**—abuse carried from one generation to the next. The cycle is as follows: sexually abused girls often have mothers who were also sexually abused as a child. A significant proportion of women who were abused as a children grow up and marry or live with partners who abuse them and may also abuse their daughters, thus transmitting victimization from mother to daughter. Children who live with an abused mother are twelve times more likely to be sexually abused (McCloskey, Figueredo, and Koss, 1995).

As with physical assault, white children are more likely than either African American or Latina/o children to be sexually assaulted by a family member within the household rather than someone outside the household. Among victims of child sexual abuse, 75 percent of white children are assaulted by a member of the household, as opposed to 13 percent of African Americans children and 9 percent of Latina/o children. In addition, the abuse of boys generally takes place for a shorter period of time. Furthermore, sexually abused boys are typically from poorer socioeconomic backgrounds than are sexually abused girls, and abused boys from families where the mother has less than a high school education are more than twice as likely as boys in families where the mother has higher education to report abuse. Moreover, Asian American boys are three times as likely as white boys to report sexual abuse (9 vs. 3 percent). Latinos also report higher rates of sexual abuse than white boys. The sexual abuse rates among African American and white boys are very similar (Schoen et al., 1997b).

The Effects of Child Abuse Researchers have only recently begun to focus on the long-term consequences of child abuse. We already know that the most serious short-term effect is death. Among the findings on long-term effects are that a large percentage of sexually abused children become prostitutes or drug users and that sexually abused female runaways are more likely to be involved in deviant or criminal behavior than are nonabused females (Andersen, 2005). In addition, victims frequently suffer any one or more of a wide range of ailments, which can include the following (1) physical ailments, such as bruises, genital pain and bleeding, problems walking or sitting, eating disorders, headaches and stomachaches, brain injuries, infants and toddlers who have been shaken violently sometimes suffer bleeding within the brain; (2) emotional problems, such as anxiety, fear, guilt, nightmares, depression, temper tantrums, hostility, aggression, perfectionism, or phobias; (3) cognitive problems, including learning disabilities, poor attention and concentration, and declining grades in school; and (4) behavioral problems, such as social withdrawal, sexualized behavior or sexual preoccupation, regression or immaturity, hyperactivity, and family or peer conflicts (Barnett, Miller-Perrin, and Perrin, 1997).

Food, sex, alcohol, and/or drugs deaden painful memories of the abuse and expel reality, at least temporarily. Bulimia and anorexia are also forms of self-punishment, eventually leading to the ultimate self-victimization, suicide. When child victims of sexual abuse become adults, they often have problems with their sexuality; many avoid intimacy and emotional bonding; and many become abusers themselves or victims of spousal battering and abuse (Karp et al., 1995; Chandy, Blum, and Resnick, 1996; Wilsnak et al., 1997). Less is known about the gender-specific consequences of sexual abuse for male victims. According to some researchers, one of the consequences for male victims is linked to the fact that definitions of masculinity in U.S. culture can compound the consequences of male sexual victimization. For example, some studies have found that the most common reaction of boys is to try to reassert their masculinity, often inappropriately. This can take the form of disobedience, hostility, aggression, fighting, violence, and destructiveness, or these boys may experience some confusion about their sexual identity (Mignon, Larson, and Holmes, 2002). Finally, it should be pointed out that not all children who are sexually abused follow a deviant or self-victimization life course. With the support of parents, family members, friends, appropriate therapies, as well as individual interpersonal strength and resiliency, many of these children build healthy and constructive lives (Ambert, 2001).

ELDER ABUSE IN THE UNITED STATES

As our earlier historical account of family violence illustrates, abuse of the elderly by their adult children (and sometimes grandchildren or other relatives) is not new, nor was it always

viewed as a problem. Recently, however, elder abuse has gained widespread public attention and has been defined by some people as a major social problem. For example, a *Chicago Sun-Times* survey on elder abuse estimated that in the city of Chicago alone, each year over 21,000 people 60 years of age or older are victims of abuse, or one such person every 24 minutes (Fornek, 2001). The fact is, each year hundreds of thousands of older persons are abused, neglected, and exploited. Many victims are people who are frail and vulnerable, and cannot help themselves, and they depend on others to meet their most basic needs. Although at greater risk, it is not just the frail, infirm, or mentally impaired elder that is vulnerable to abuse. Legislatures in all 50 states have passed some form of elder abuse prevention laws. Laws and definitions of terms vary considerably from one state to another, but all states have set up reporting systems.

As we shall see in Chapter 14, a growing percentage of the U.S. population is over age 65. In fact, according to most estimates, the number of elderly people living in the United States will increase dramatically over the next several decades. This is particularly true for people of color. For instance, it is projected that the number of white elders will increase by approximately 97 percent compared to 265 percent for African American elders and 530 percent for Latinas/os (Administration on Aging, 2001). Given these statistics, some people have suggested that, in general, older people of color might be at greater risk of abuse and neglect than white elders primarily because they are more often less able to advocate for themselves because of cultural, language, or educational

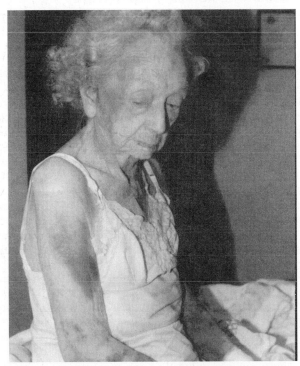

Like other low-status groups in the United States, older Americans are highly vulnerable to neglect and abuse. Although many older people are independent and healthy, as life expectancy increases more of the elderly population will spend some time in either a convalescent center or in their homes dependent on family members as caretakers. According to data on reported cases of elder abuse, family members are reported to be the perpetrators in nine out of ten cases.

barriers. Although there is little current research that examines race- or ethnic-specific cases of in elder abuse or the factors involved, some observers have suggested that among specific racial or ethnic groups, African American elders might be at slightly higher risk than whites, because, for example, African American seniors, especially grandmothers, are more likely than whites to take in needy children, grandchildren, and even great-grandchildren. Therefore, given their increasing numbers in the population and their greater propensity to take in children, at least in theory they are thought to be at greater risk of abuse (Wallace, 2004).

In any event, the greater longevity and visibility of older people have increased our awareness of and sensitivity to the many problems they experience, including violent treatment at the hands of family members. Every year an estimated 2.1 million older Americans are victims of physical, psychological, or other forms of abuse and neglect. And these statistics may just be the tip of the iceberg. Like all other forms of family violence, elder abuse is greatly underreported. Experts estimate that only one in six incidents of elder abuse is ever reported to the authorities. Recent research indicates that elders who have been abused tend to die earlier than those who are not abused, even in the absence of chronic illnesses or life-threatening disease (American Psychological Association, 2006). Like other forms of violence and abuse, elder abuse is a complex problem continues to gain recognition worldwide. Both the United Nations Economic Council and the World Health Organization have launched initiatives to increase awareness of elder abuse as a human rights issue.

What Is Elder Abuse?

The term **elder abuse** is an umbrella term referring to any knowing, intentional, or negligent act by a caregiver or any other person that causes harm or a serious risk of harm to an older adult including physical, psychological, and material maltreatment and neglect. Although many older Americans are independent and in good health, the chances of poor health and dependency increase with age, as does the potential for victimization in any one or more of the following forms: physical violence (such as inflicting, or threatening to inflict, physical pain or injury, physical restraint, overmedication, or depriving them of a basic need—withholding medicine, food, or personal care), emotional or psychological abuse (such as verbal abuse, threats, intimidation, isolation, and neglect), sexual maltreatment (such as and rape or other sexual assault), material abuse (such as theft or concealment or misuse of assets, money or other personal property), neglect (such as the refusal or failure by those responsible to provide food, shelter, health care, or protection for an elder), abandonment (such as desertion by anyone who has assumed the responsibility for care or custody of an elder), and personal violation (such as placement in a nursing home against the person's will).

Who Are the Abused and the Abusers?

As with women and children, some older adults run a greater risk of being abused than others: women, older people with physical or mental impairments, and those dependent on a caretaker to meet their basic needs. Current research suggests that over three-fourths (77 percent) of the victims of elder abuse and neglect are white, compared to 16 percent African American, 5 percent Latina/o, 0.7 percent Asian American/Pacific Islander, and 0.6 percent Native American (Cecil, 2006). In addition, female elders, especially those 80 years of age and older (43 percent), are the most likely victims of elder abuse. In fact, older women are more likely than younger women to experience violence for a longer period of time, to be in current violent relationships, and to have health and mental health problems Overall, older women are far more likely than men to suffer from abuse or neglect. For example, two out of every three (66 percent) of elder abuse victims are females compared to 34 percent for males. Among married elderly couples, violence and abuse are typically perpetrated by the male spouse and are often a continuation of an earlier pattern of abuse. Elderly women who abuse their husbands may be enacting revenge for previous abuse by the husband. This probably reflects women's general lack of strength, their general lack of power, their devalued status, and the fact that they outnumber elderly men. Not everyone, however, agrees that elderly women run a greater risk of abuse than elderly men. One set of researchers, for example, found little difference in the victimization rates of older women and men, but the abuse inflicted by husbands was much more severe and serious than that inflicted by wives (National Center on Elder Abuse, 2005, 2006; Wallace, 2004).

Although violence and abuse occurs across race, class, gender, age, sexual orientation, gender identity, and religion, the greatest amount of attention of domestic violence has been on heterosexual victims, primarily heterosexual women. Lesbian, gay, bisexual, and transgender elder abuse victims of domestic violence have been frequently overlooked and/or ignored. Although the issues facing LGBT elders may be different than non-LGBT elders, nonetheless, as we have already reported, about one in four LGBT persons are battered by a partner (FORGE, 2006). As with elder abuse in general, this omission is related to the devaluation and lack of respect for elder people as well as the negative cultural and societal attitudes towards LGBT individuals, including homophobia.

Contrary to popular belief about the perpetrators and location of elder abuse (aided by sensational stories in the media of nursing home abuses), studies repeatedly show that the overwhelming majority of confirmed cases of elder abuse (89 percent) occur in domestic settings. Although the picture is still inconclusive, family members alone are reported to be the perpetrators in seven out of ten substantiated cases of elder abuse and/or neglect. More specifically, the abuser is most often an adult child (33 percent), a spouse (11 percent), or some other family member (22 percent). Perpetrators of elder abuse are almost evenly female (53 percent) and male (47 percent) (Cecil, 2006). Among children who abuse their parents, sons are most likely to use physical violence whereas daughters are more likely to practice elderly neglect, and the most frequent offenders are adult daughters. This probably reflects the fact that because of gender role socialization, daughters most often have the responsibility of caring for an aging parent or other relative.

Often, adult children who abuse their elderly parents were themselves abused and thus learned that violence toward intimates is acceptable behavior. In some cases, they may be acting in retaliation against an abusive parent (Wallace, 2004). In other cases, the abuser is financially dependent on the older person, and the abuse stems from this dependency and lack of power in the relationship.

Although over two-thirds of U.S. states have enacted mandatory reporting laws to deal with elder abuse, some people question the effectiveness of these laws, given that they address the problem only after the fact. Critics have suggested that a more successful strategy might be to provide adult children with greater institutional assistance and support in caring for their elderly parents. (Chapter 14 contains a fuller discussion of the elderly.) Indeed, the abuse of the elderly is part of the larger problem of structured inequality. Like other low-status groups in U.S. society, older Americans are highly vulnerable to abuse.

SIBLING ABUSE

Given the enormity of the statistics we have presented in this chapter, who do you suppose most commonly abuses children? Perhaps surprisingly, the answer is not mothers or fathers or other adults, but siblings. Although the media, the public, researchers, social workers, and other relevant professionals have focused our attention on child and woman abuse, seldom have they discussed sibling violence and abuse. This fact notwithstanding, according to some authorities on the subject, it is perhaps the most common form of family violence. Indeed, it is probably even more common than child abuse (by parents) or spouse abuse. Like other forms of victimization, sibling abuse involves a number of forms of maltreatment including mental, emotional, and sexual abuse. It is estimated that 53 children in 100 are *dangerously violent* toward a brother or sister. It seems that when abusive acts occur between siblings, they are often not perceived as abuse.

However, siblings hit, slap, kick, and beat each other so frequently that few of us pay much attention to this behavior or consider it to be a form of family violence. Indeed, such behavior is so commonplace that it is almost normative. For example, most of us have probably at one time or another during our childhood engaged in some type of altercation with a sibling: pulling hair, pushing, name-calling, biting, pinching, poking, scaring, and so on. Parents (and society at large) often do not take these behaviors seriously, viewing them as normal childhood behavior, labeling it sibling rivalry. In fact, critics agree with parents, arguing that much of the aggressive behavior between siblings is not really serious and thus should not be labeled as abusive. Although research confirms this argument, finding that the majority of violence between siblings could be classified as nonabusive, the fact remains that a high frequency of violence does occur between siblings that can definitely be classified as abusive (Perozynski and Kramer, 1999; University of Michigan Health System, 2005). Statistics on sibling violence suggest that we reexamine our thinking about this behavior as "natural," "inevitable," and "nonabusive." A complicating factor in

sibling violence is that in some cases, siblings may switch back and forth between the roles of abuser and victim.

A 1980 survey that included 733 families with two or more children found that 82 percent of the children between 3 and 17 years of age reported having used some type of violence against a sibling in the previous year (Straus, Gelles, and Steinmetz, 1980). By the late 1980s, researchers suggested that every year at least 3 percent of siblings confront each other with lethal weapons, such as knives and guns (Gelles and Straus, 1988). In 1988, Mildred Pagelow reported that almost one-half of the 1025 college students whom she studied indicated that when they were adolescents, they, along with their siblings, were either the aggressors or the victims of violent acts of abuse such as kicking and punching. One in ten reported that their siblings beat them up, and 4 percent stated that their siblings had threatened them with a weapon such as a knife or gun or had actually used a knife or gun against them. Other studies estimate that upward of 29 million siblings physically abuse each other every year. These acts are not minor acts of hitting. Rather, over half of them could have resulted in legal prosecution had they been perpetrated by someone outside the family. Added to this is that one in ten murders in families is committed by siblings. Coupled with physical violence between siblings, sibling sexual abuse or sibling incest is also seldom talked about but is perhaps a more common occurrence than parent–child incest. Sibling sexual assault is typically brother-to-sister initiated or coerced, but sometimes it occurs between same-sex siblings as well. Sibling victims are often much younger than the perpetrator. Sibling sexual abuse perpetrated by adolescents often occurs repeatedly and over a longer period of time than adolescent-perpetrated abuse against nonfamily members. This is due primarily to the ready availability of a sibling and the convenience of being at home. Even in old age, siblings often abuse one another. Some scholars suggest that it is often the case that, like elderly spouse abuse, sibling abuse in old age tends to be a continuation of earlier family violence (American Psychological Association, 2006; Mignon, Larson, and Holmes, 2002). Because of the historic acceptance of sibling violence, we are unable to ascertain whether such behavior is becoming more or less common. Like the public, researchers have long ignored this pattern of violence.

Who most often initiates sibling violence? Boys of all ages are more violent than girls, but the difference is relatively small. The highest rates of sibling violence tend to occur in families with only male children. Families with all daughters have lower levels of sibling violence and, in fact, the presence of girls in the family reduces the level of sibling violence. Sibling violence is also higher among children in families in which child and spouse assault also occur. Sibling violence is more common during the youngest ages, when siblings are home together, and decreases as children get older and spend less time at home and with each other. Some children both physically and sexually abuse their younger siblings. Various research studies have reported a significant amount of overlap between the various forms of sibling abuse, with emotional abuse between siblings most common, followed by sexual abuse and then physical abuse (Wieche, 1990; Worling, 1995).

WRITING YOUR OWN SCRIPT

RECOGNIZING ABUSIVE BEHAVIOR

As you have learned from reading this chapter as well as from simply being a member of contemporary U.S. society, violence and abuse in intimate relationships are of serious concern. Because they often occur in the privacy of our intimate relationships and in the privacy of our homes, we sometimes do not know what to do or where to go if we or someone we know is a victim of intimate violence.

If you are involved in an intimate relationship, consider your relationship for a moment. Is it a violence-free relationship, or is it bad for your health? Is it heading into dangerous territory? Has your partner ever been abusive? With the high incidence of verbal, physical, emotional, and sexual abuse in intimate relationships, it is very important to know as much as possible about our partners in terms of the likelihood that they could be or are abusive or violent. Although there is no specific profile of an abuser, the data presented in this chapter suggest certain characteristics or factors that are prevalent among abusers, such as poor self-esteem, rigidity, and excessive dependency. Are these characteristics familiar to you? If they are characteristic of you or your partner, they should alert you to the possibility that the person with such characteristics could become abusive or violent. (This is not to say that this will happen, but you should

be alert for other signs of abusive behavior and seek help before violence occurs.)

Take the following test to find out if your relationship is violent or headed toward violence. Answer each of the following categories of questions. If you answer yes to more than two of the categories, you should seek help. Do you know or suspect that someone you know is in a violent relationship? Share these questions with that person and then help her or him get appropriate assistance.

Is your partner someone who . . .

1. Is obsessively jealous, aggressive, and possessive toward you; won't let you have friends; checks up on you; won't accept your leaving him or her?
2. Tries to control you by being very bossy, giving you orders and demanding that you follow them; makes all of the decisions; or doesn't take your opinion seriously or doesn't allow you to have an opinion at all?
3. Is threatening and whom you are afraid of? Do you worry about how this person will react to things you do or say? Does this person ever threaten you, or use or own weapons?
4. Is violent? Does this person have a history of violence: losing her or his temper, bragging about mistreating others? Has the person assaulted someone within or outside of the family or has the person committed some other violent crime?
5. Pressures you for sex, is forceful about sex? Accepts no when you say no? Thinks that women or girls are sex objects, attempts to manipulate you or make you feel guilty by saying things like, "If you really loved me, you would . . . ?" Does the person get too serious about the relationship too fast for comfort?
6. Abuses alcohol or other drugs and/or pressures you to take them? Does the person use alcohol or other drugs as an excuse for aggression?
7. Mistreats you and then blames you for the mistreatment? Tells you that you provoked it, that you brought it on yourself?
8. Has a history of bad relationships and blames the other person for all of the problems?
9. Has very traditional views about women's and men's roles; believes that men should be in control and powerful and that women should be passive and submissive?
10. Has hit, pushed, slapped, choked, kicked, forced sex with you, or otherwise abused you?
11. Isolates you from your family, friends, neighbors, and the community? Makes your family and friends concerned about your safety?

Source: Adapted from the Mount Auburn Hospital Prevention and Training Center and the Dating Violence Intervention Project.

Little is known about the reasons for sibling violence. Some researchers have suggested that it is a learned response. Children raised in a violent environment learn that physical punishment is an appropriate way to deal with certain situations. In contrast, children raised in an environment free of violence learn other ways to resolve conflicts with siblings and later with other intimates (Gelles and Cornell, 1997).

STRENGTHENING MARRIAGES AND FAMILIES

Based upon all available data, family violence is of epidemic proportions in the United States. As we have shown, women and children are particularly vulnerable to this type of violence. According to Amnesty International, domestic and family violence is a fundamental violation of human rights

and is not acceptable in any form. It cannot be justified by any political, religious, or cultural claims.

Systemic and systematic inequality and discrimination against women allows violence to occur daily and with impunity. If we are serious about strengthening marriages and families we must individually and collectively take responsibility and help eradicate violence against women and children so that they may achieve lives of equality and dignity. Individuals, national, state, and local government agencies, and community social service agencies must work to provide better and more comprehensive responses to domestic violence, no matter who the victim. The development of partnerships between advocacy and direct services for women, children, and men are needed. This would include providing more funds for additional shelters and more services within these shelters. Policies and programs are needed to provide parenting education and training to both women and men that address the batterer who is both a caretaker of the children and the person exposing them to violence and abuse. Additionally, changes in laws and the way the criminal justice system works are needed as well as the development of effective strategies to make batterers accountable for the well-being and safety of children in their families. These strategies should be built upon an accurate data collection system that allows decision makers to begin understanding the presence of violence in families. Given

that much of societal and family violence is tied to sexism and male power, we must reconsider and reconceptualize our current thinking and practices in terms of women's and men's roles in marriages and families to eradicate the sexism from which violence against women grows. A narrow devotion to traditional gender roles heightens, in our view, the potential vulnerability of women, children, and the elderly in marriages and families.

SUMMARY

Family and intimate relationship violence are deeply rooted in human history and widespread in contemporary society. The family is the major context within which most violence in this country occurs. A number of myths about family violence, ranging from the notion that it is a rare occurrence to the idea that women secretly desire to be raped, obscure our view of and knowledge about its pervasiveness.

Although any family member can be abused, women and children are the most common victims. Woman battering is perhaps the most common and one of the most underreported crimes in this country. Its cyclic nature has been described in terms of the battered-woman syndrome. Although we do not know a lot about battering across race and sexual orientation, we know that it can be found among all groups.

Family violence includes not only battering but also sexual assault. Here, too, women and girls are the typical victims. Although information on the incidence and prevalence of marital rape is limited, there is a growing public awareness that husbands can and do rape their wives. This fact notwithstanding, the criminal justice system generally is

unresponsive to battered and sexually assaulted women except in cases of severe violence or death.

Some of the most visible effects of violence against women are low self-esteem, self-hate, economic and emotional dependence on others, fear, anxiety, and self-destructive behavior. Victims also develop a number of survival strategies, some of which, such as overeating and substance abuse, are self-destructive. In addition, a growing number of women are dealing with their violent situation by fighting back. Women sometimes use violence against men, although they most often do so in self-defense against a threatened or actual physical attack.

Men are also victims of violence. However, because men often do not report their abuse we cannot be sure of the prevalence of male abuse.

Women are not the only major victims of family violence: Somewhere between 1 million and 4 million children are abused each year by parents or someone close to the family. We are only beginning to appreciate the extent of this problem today. Other, less visible victims of family violence include siblings, the elderly, and lesbians and gays.

KEY TERMS

parricide	woman battering	victim blaming	transmission of victimization
infanticide	sexual assault	battered-child syndrome	
rape syndrome	battered-woman syndrome	incest	elder abuse

QUESTIONS FOR STUDY AND REFLECTION

1. Do you have siblings? Same sex or different sex? Did or do you engage in behaviors that can be defined as abusive? When does behavior between siblings become abusive? What should we do about sibling abuse? Should the abusers be subject to the same penalties as other abusers? Why or why not? What if your 7-year-old son sexually assaulted your 3-year-old daughter? What would you do?

2. Which child-rearing philosophies and economic and social factors contribute to the prevalence of child abuse in the United States today? Should children be spanked? In your opinion, is there a difference between spanking and child abuse? Have you ever hit a child

with something other than your hand? Do you think your behavior constituted battering? Why or why not?

3. In your opinion, is it possible for a man to rape his wife? A woman to rape her husband? Why or why not? To what degree would you be willing to remain in a marriage if your spouse raped you or you raped your spouse?

4. What factors might explain why some societies are more likely than others to abuse their elderly members? What possible reasons do you think a person could have for battering an elderly parent? Have you ever been physically or psychologically abusive to one or both of your parents? How might we deal with the problem of elder abuse?

SOCIOLOGICAL

BEATTIE, ELISABETH, AND MARY ANGELA, SHAUGHNESSY. 2000. *Sisters in Pain: Battered Women Fight Back.* Lexington, KY: University Press of Kentucky. This book is based on interviews with seven of ten battered women in Kentucky who, in the 1980s and early 1990s, stood up to their brutally abusive husbands and boyfriends, and were subsequently convicted of killing, conspiring to kill, or assaulting the men who had abused them for years. The media began referring to them as the "Sisters in Pain," a name they embraced. In 1995, when Kentucky's Governor Brereton Jones learned of the Sisters in Pain and their stories, he became convinced the women had acted in self-defense. In a controversial move, Jones granted all of the women clemency on his last day in office. This was only the third mass clemency for battered women in U.S. history. Among the many topics of violence discussed, this book provides an example framework for students to address the relentless question: *Why don't abused women just leave?*

KIMMEL, MICHAEL S., AND MICHAEL A. MESSNER. 1995. *Men's Lives.* Boston: Allyn & Bacon. An excellent anthology focusing on the male experience. The book is organized around specific themes that define masculinity and the issues that men confront over their lifetime. Part 6 deals with men and women, including some poignant articles on the American context of male violence and the rape of women.

RENZETTI, CLAIRE, AND MILEY CHARLES, EDS. 1996. *Violence in Gay and Lesbian Domestic Partnerships.* New York: Harrington Park Press. An excellent compilation of studies and literature reviews of research on intimate violence among lesbian and gay couples.

WEISS, ELAINE. 2000. *Surviving Domestic Violence: Voices of Women Who Broke Free.* Sandy, UT: Agreka Books. The book consists of the collective stories of 12 women from across the United States who are survivors of domestic violence and abuse; they left their abusers and went on to reconstruct their lives. The stories are at once painful and humorous, insightful, uplifting, and indicative of the remarkable courage of these women survivors. A domestic violence survivor herself, the author presents a clear picture of women as both victims and survivors of domestic violence. An excellent context for faculty to engage students in a discussion of human agency.

FILM

Domestic Violence 2. 2002. Zipporah Films. This documentary about domestic violence is long, painful, and sometimes difficult to watch. Educators should preview the film before using it and be prepared to deal with the emotions generated by viewing extreme violence. The film is based on filmmaker Frederick Wiseman's experiences following the Tampa, Florida, police as they responded to domestic violence calls, and spending time with women in a shelter for abused women. Although it does not offer solutions to the problem of domestic violence, it does provide an excellent framework for students to examine and come to understand the systemic nature of domestic violence—the system through which violence works and through which it is perpetuated.

Swoon. 1992. New Line Home Video. Although almost 90 percent of violence and abuse occurs within marriages and families, we cannot ignore the 10 percent that is termed "stranger violence." This film, based on the real-life murder of a young boy (Bobby Franks) by gay lovers Nathan Leopold and Richard Loeb, is a compelling drama that is historically accurate. It will allow students to confront cultural myths about who commits such crimes by putting a different face on violence against children. That Leopold and Loeb are white college students from well-to-do families provides a beginning basis for students to confront the myth of lower-class and minority violence. The film also boldly examines homosexuality and its impact in the lives of the two murderers.

LITERARY

DRISCOLL, FRANCIS. 1997. *The Rape Poems.* New York: Pleasure Boat Studio. The author of this book of poetry believes that we are the stories we tell. The book includes poems that recount the author's experience with rape in a highly detailed way. In one poem, for example, the poet describes her postrape physical examination "inch by inch." In another, she describes a woman who was looking for someone to call to talk about her rape. The book consists of a set of compelling poems that can be used to analyze the experiences and consequences sexual assault against women.

HAULSEY, KUWAMA. 2001. *The Red Moon.* New York: Villard, a Division of Random House. Among the many sociologically relevant topics this novel deals with are the complex subjects of female circumcision, ritual circumcision, and routine domestic violence in a reclusive Samburu culture in rural Kenya. It is an excellent novel to help students understand the connection between women's subordinate status and violence.

INTERNET

http://www.nomsv.org Web site maintained by the National Organization on Male Sexual Victimization. This site is designed to meet the needs of adult male survivors of sexual abuse through the provision of a number of resources, including a chat room, a newsletter, books, news updates, and a directory of clinicians and therapists.

http://www.silcom.com/~paladin/madv/ Sponsored by the Paladin Group Grant Mentors, this is a practical research-oriented site that offers advocacy and information as well as a variety of other resources including addresses of shelters.

http://www.stopviolence.com/domviol/menagainst.htm This Web site offers a variety of resources to raise men's awareness about the problems of men's violence and to end their silence about it. Because the vast majority of violence against men is also committed by other men, some of the resources on this site explore problems with masculinity and how to find ways of "being a man" without being violent or homophobic. It is a good site for students to explore information about men who are working, both individually and collectively, to reduce the violence of men.

http://www.ojp.usdoj.gov/bjs The U.S. Department of Justice Web site provides statistics, data, and reports on crime and victims, criminal offenders, law enforcement, prosecution, courts and sentencing, expenditures, and other topics related to domestic violence and child abuse.

12

IN THE NEWS

Little Rock, Arkansas

After 31 years of marriage, Governor Mike Huckabee of Arkansas and the former Janet McCain upgraded their wedding vows to that of a covenant marriage before thousands of onlookers gathered for a "Celebration of Marriage" in a North Little Rock sports arena on Valentine's Day, 2005. The governor, a former Baptist minister, hoped to set an example for others in his state to join the movement to a covenant marriage as an alternative to traditional marriage. The distinguishing characteristics of covenant marriage include an oath making a lifelong commitment to marriage and premarital counseling. Divorce is only allowed for a narrow range of problems such as abuse, adultery, imprisonment, and abandonment. Additionally, if there are problems, a couple in a covenant marriage can only divorce after counseling and a waiting period of about 2 years. In 1997, Louisiana became the first state to pass a covenant marriage law allowing couples to choose either a regular marriage or the more restrictive covenant marriage. Arizona followed with its own law in 1998 and Arkansas passed its version in 2001. Political leaders in all three states were reacting to the fact that their states had some of the highest divorce rates in the nation.

In 2004, Nevada, the perennial leader in divorce among the 50 states, had a divorce rate of 6.4 per 1000 population, nearly twice the rate of the entire country (3.7). Arkansas ran a close second, with a rate of 6.3 (U.S. Census Bureau, 2006). Over the last 5 years, a number of studies documented the fact that many of the states with the highest divorce rates are located in the Bible Belt, whose populations contain large numbers of Baptists and evangelical religious sects, known for their social conservatism and family-values orientation. By contrast, in states such as New York, Connecticut, Massachusetts, and Pennsylvania, generally considered to be socially liberal and whose populations include high percentages of Roman Catholics, the divorce rates are considerably lower.

Reactions to these findings were swift and sometimes emotional. Some people pointed the finger at religion, questioning the effectiveness of how its leaders minister to families. Anthony Jordan, executive director of the Baptist General Convention in Oklahoma, seemed to agree, noting that the Catholic Church does not recognize divorce and that Protestant evangelists, in attempting to be compassionate, do not place the stigma on divorce that should be there. He also believes that ministers give more attention to helping young people plan a wedding than to helping them plan a marriage (Harden, 2001). Stewart Beasley, president of the Oklahoma Psychological Association, believes that the Christian teaching that there is to be no sex before marriage puts pressure on young people to marry early, thus increasing the risk of marital instability (Veith, 1999). Other analysts view such reasoning as a logical fallacy, arguing that besides a high number of evangelicals, these states have other factors that contribute to a high divorce rate. Prime among them is the fact that these states rank at the bottom of the country for household income.

Although earlier in his term Governor Huckabee declared a "marital emergency" in his state and vowed to cut his state's divorce rate in half by 2010, the divorce rate remains high and relatively few couples choose covenant marriage. Some 112,000 couples married in Arkansas in the first three years of the new law, but only 800 of them (less than 1 percent) selected a covenant marriage license. Similarly, fewer than 3 percent of couples in Louisiana and Arizona opted for the stricter marriage requirements (Monkerud, 2006). In the past several years, over 20 other states considered adopting convenant marriages but failed to do so. Given the extensive media coverage devoted to family values and the proliferation of efforts to build a covenant marriage movement, why have there been so few takers? Critics point out that as laudable as these efforts may be, they do not attack the primary structural cause of marital strife— lack of sufficient economic resources to maintain a family (Latham, 2000). Other research suggests that the answer to this question lies in the differences between the couples choosing covenant marriages and those choosing standard marriages. Laura Sanchez and her colleagues (2002) studied newlywed couples in Louisiana and found that covenant married couples are substantially different from standard married couples in several ways. People who choose covenant marriage are much less likely than others to have cohabited or had children with someone other than their current marriage partner. They tend to be more educated, hold more traditional attitudes, and are more religious in both faith and practice than their standard married counterparts. Finally, while covenant and standard married spouses share similar negative emotional reaction to conflict in their marriages, covenant married spouses are far more likely to choose positive communication strategies than do spouses in standard marriages. It is too early to tell if covenant marriage will be associated with a lower divorce rate over the long haul. However, if it is, it may not be due to the legal requirements of the covenant marriage contract but rather to a self-selection process; that is, those who select covenant marriage may also be the couples who are least likely to divorce.

WHAT WOULD YOU DO? If you were the governor of a state with a high divorce rate, would you be willing to publicly take (or upgrade) wedding vows in a covenant marriage? Given where you are today, would you consider entering (or upgrading to) a covenant marriage? Do you advocate making it more difficult to get divorced and/or to get married? How much responsibility do you want government and organized religion to have in preparing people for marriage and/or for reducing the likelihood of divorce? Explain.

The vast majority of people who promise to love, cherish, and comfort their spouse "until death do us part" really mean it. How, then, can we account for the fact that over 1 million married couples in the United States divorce each year?

That divorce is so common today has led many to conclude that the family is a dying or at least a critically wounded institution. This thinking reflects the myths discussed in Chapter 1, that in the past, marriages were happier, families were more loving, and members treated each other with respect. People who feel this way tend to see divorce in a negative light, as a recent social problem that must be overcome. In contrast, some people see divorce as a solution to the problem of unhappy and sometimes abusive marriages. Both schools of thought find abundant evidence to support their positions. As with so many social phenomena, however, the reality concerning divorce lies somewhere in between. Regardless of the quality of the marriage they left, few people undergo separation or divorce without experiencing some pain. In fact, some divorced people never get over the trauma they experience with the breakup of their marriage. This is especially true for the spouses who did not want the divorce. Conversely, divorce allows people who were unhappy in their marriages to move on and build satis-

Arkansas Governor Mike Huckabee and his wife, Janet, accept congratulations from Pulaski County Circuit Court Clerk Pat O'Brien after they upgraded their wedding vows to that of a covenant marriage in a "Celebration of Marriage" observance in Little Rock.

fying new relationships. To appreciate more fully these divergent outcomes of divorce, we need to see how the current institution of divorce came about. In this chapter we examine the historical controversies surrounding divorce, with an eye to understanding current divorce laws and social policies. We also discuss how divorce rates vary from place to place, as illustrated by the higher divorce rates in the Bible Belt (see In the News), who divorces and why, and the consequences of divorce for family members, as well as its implications for the larger society.

HISTORICAL PERSPECTIVES

Contrary to popular belief, divorce is not a modern phenomenon. It has been a part of U.S. history since 1639, when a Puritan court in Massachusetts granted the first divorce decree in colonial America. This does not mean, however, that divorce was socially acceptable to all the early settlers. In fact, throughout U.S. history conflict has existed between those who favor divorce and those who oppose it.

Divorce in Early America

Although early in their history the New England colonies permitted divorce, the grounds for divorce varied from one colony to another. Divorces were often adversarial in nature—one partner was required to prove that the other was at fault and had violated the marriage contract. Thus, friends, relatives, and neighbors were called as witnesses and, in effect, were forced to choose sides in what often became an acrimonious procedure. The finding of fault became the basis for harsh punishments for the "offending" party: fines, whippings, incarceration in the stocks, prohibition from remarrying, and even banishment from the colony. This faultfinding also became the basis for **alimony,** a concept originating in England in the 1650s, whereby a husband deemed at fault for the dissolution of the marriage was required to provide his wife with a financial allowance. Conversely, if a wife was judged at fault, she lost any claim to financial support. Then, as today, however, the law was one thing and its implementation another in that courts did not always enforce the payment of the award. We will never know the true extent of divorce in colonial America, however, because many records are incomplete or lost.

The population of the time included Native Americans and African Americans. Nevertheless, their marriages were rarely recorded in the white courts. Thus, it is likely that few Native or African Americans sought an official divorce. However, one researcher did uncover the record of a divorce granted in 1745 to a slave living in Massachusetts on the grounds of his wife's adultery. The same researcher also found that in 1768, Lucy Purnan, a free African American woman, received a divorce decree on the grounds of her husband's cruelty (cited in Riley, 1991:14). In addition, Jesuit missionaries complained about frequent divorce among the Native Americans they came to convert (Amott and Matthaei, 1991:39).

Divorce was granted more infrequently in the middle section of the colonies than in the north. Most of the middle colonies did not enact explicit statutes regarding divorce, and records show that only a few divorces were granted in the colonies of New York, New Jersey, and Pennsylvania. For the most part, the southern colonies did not enact divorce legislation until after independence was achieved. The reluctance of these colonies to legalize divorce should not be interpreted to mean that marriages were happier and more tranquil there than in the rest of the country. Formal and informal separations seem to have been widespread in these colonies, including Native Americans and African Americans both free and enslaved; evidence of marital discord can be found in southern newspapers of this period, which carried disclaimers of spousal debt, stories and advertisements of runaway spouses, and other forms of marital strife.

Why did these early marriages dissolve? Historian Glenda Riley (1991) sees a variety of social and economic factors interacting to put strains on marriages and families. The growing mobility of the colonists, the movement west, and the emergence of a market economy along with new technology all combined to alter the role of the family as an economic unit, and thus to undercut to a degree a couple's sense of interdependency and common purpose. In addition, the resistance to British rule and the ideology of the Enlightenment, with its emphasis on liberty, justice, and equality, caused people to examine their own level of personal well-being. On the individual level, people sometimes made errors in their choice of spouse or married under duress of an unplanned pregnancy, only to regret their actions later on. Whatever the causes, on the eve of the American Revolution, divorce was fairly well established in the social fabric of the nation.

Divorce in Nineteenth-Century America

The period following the American Revolution was a time of rapid social, political, and economic change. Each state assumed jurisdiction for divorce. Although there were individual differences among the various states, the general trend was to liberalize divorce laws and expand the grounds for divorce. Two major exceptions to this rule were found in New York, where adultery remained the sole ground for divorce, and in South Carolina, where divorce was not permitted. These restrictive laws led to "migratory" divorce, whereby residents of one state would travel to another with more liberal laws. To discourage people from coming into their state solely to obtain a divorce, many of the more liberal states instituted minimum-residency requirements.

Data on the number of divorces were not systematically collected until the end of the nineteenth century. Newspaper accounts and scattered divorce records, however, suggest that increasing numbers of people were using the liberalized divorce laws. The apparent increase in the divorce rate sent shock waves across the United States. Passionate debates were carried on in newspapers and legislative chambers and from pulpits. Those opposing divorce, like newspaper editor Horace Greeley, saw it as immoral and responsible for most of the social ills of the day, and argued that restricting divorce would deter hasty or ill-advised marriages.

On the other side, social critics of the day argued that marriage, not divorce, needed reform. Women's groups spoke out against wife abuse, which had gained public visibility by the 1850s. Female divorce petitioners frequently cited cruelty, including sexual abuse, as the reason for wanting to end their marriage. Proponents of divorce, like Indiana legislator Robert Owen, saw personal happiness and fulfillment as the primary purpose of marriage; they believed that a marriage ought to end if these goals are frustrated.

In 1887, Congress responded to these public debates by authorizing Commissioner of Labor Carroll D. Wright to undertake a study of marriage and divorce in the United States. Wright found that 68,547 divorces were granted between 1872 and 1876, representing an almost 28 percent increase over the 53,574 divorces granted between 1867 and 1871 (cited in Riley, 1991:79). He noted several interesting patterns in these data: Women obtained two-thirds of the divorces (a pattern still evident today); desertion was the most common ground for divorce; and western states granted the most divorces, and southern states the fewest. Although people in all classes and occupations sought divorces, more divorces occurred among the working class than among the middle and upper classes.

Although much of the public reaction to divorce focused on its frequency and availability, other problems connected with divorce were becoming evident. After divorce many women, especially those with custody of children, became impoverished. Although alimony was often granted by the courts, enforcement was difficult. Child custody was another problem area. The traditional view in colonial America was that children belong to the father; therefore, he should automatically get custody if a marriage was dissolved by either death or divorce. Thus, some women stayed in unhappy marriages rather than risk losing their children. With industrialization and the consequent notion of separate spheres for women and men, however, judges came to adopt the "tender years" principle that children under the age of 7 were better off with their mothers. This principle was based on the assumption that women are by nature more adept at nurturing than are men.

Men did not always agree with this interpretation. Sometimes, heated custody battles ensued, especially if the mother was seen as the spouse at fault. Judges occasionally split siblings, giving girls or younger children over to the care of mothers and boys or older children to fathers. This decision, called **split custody,** is still made by some judges, albeit in a small number of cases. As we shall see later, the divorce reforms of the twentieth century have not been completely successful in resolving the debate over which parent should have custody of the children. In the reform efforts of the twentieth century, the principle of tender years was modified, and child custody was, in principle at least, based on the best interests of the child.

Americans were also troubled by the destructive consequences that often accompanied divorce. Most of the criticism, however, focused on the divergent laws and procedures that existed in the various states. Many sought a solution to these problems by proposing a uniform divorce law that would encompass the entire country.

Twentieth-Century America: Efforts at Reform

Generally, those favoring a more restrictive and uniform approach to divorce saw it as a moral evil to be stopped. This moral–legal view was challenged by a group of scholars in the newly developing social sciences. These analysts believed divorce originates not in legislation but rather in the social and economic environment in which marriage is located. The changing patterns of divorce seemed to support this view. The divorce rate jumped considerably after World War I, when many marriages, some hastily conceived in the midst of war, floundered under the stress of economic and political uncertainty and the strains of separation and reunion. This war-related increase in divorce was not a new phenomenon; it had been observed earlier in the United States in the period following the Civil War (and following all subsequent wars, including the war in Iraq). Industrialization, the decline in economic functions of the family, employment and financial independence of women, weakening of religious beliefs, and the declining social stigma of divorce were also viewed as causes of divorce.

By the 1960s, the focus of the divorce debate began to shift once again. Although still concerned with the high rate of divorce, public attention increasingly turned to the effects of divorce on spouses and children. Numerous voices were raised against the adversarial nature of divorce, and various proposals for divorce by mutual consent were put forth, culminating in California's **no-fault divorce** bill signed into law by Governor Ronald Reagan (who was himself divorced) in 1969 (Jacob, 1988). Over the next 25 years, state after state adopted its own version of no-fault divorce, believing the most negative consequences of divorce would be eliminated by this measure. Spouses no longer had to accuse each other of wrongdoing; instead, they could apply for a divorce on grounds of "irretrievable breakdown" or "irreconcilable differences." Indeed, no-fault divorce removed much of the acrimony of divorce while also lowering its economic cost. As we shall see later in this chapter, however, after nearly four decades of experience with no-fault divorce, we know it is not the panacea its advocates anticipated. Issues of spousal support, division of marital property, and child custody remain problematic. Today, some critics of no-fault divorce are working to reform the process while others are working to eliminate it altogether (see Debating Social Issues box).

What lessons are to be learned from an examination of the history of divorce in the United States? Perhaps the most important is that neither marriage nor divorce can be understood apart from its social context. As Roderick Phillips (1988:640) observed, "It is entirely futile to expect marriage to remain constant or to have a consistent social meaning while social structures, economic relationships, demographic patterns, and cultural configurations have undergone the massive changes of past centuries." The historical record also makes it abundantly clear that efforts to eliminate divorce will in all likelihood fail. Therefore, it is probably more effective to focus social efforts on strengthening marriages and creating compassionate and fair systems of helping people whose marriages have failed.

DEBATING SOCIAL ISSUES

IS IT TIME TO ABANDON NO-FAULT DIVORCE?

A new movement to toughen state divorce laws has emerged over the last several years in response to concerns over the impact of family breakups on children and the high incidence of poverty in single-parent households. The principal target is the no-fault divorce statutes adopted by every state over the last 25 years. Supporters of abandoning no-fault divorce laws argue that the current rules encourage a casual attitude toward the dissolution of marriage and thereby have weakened the legal and social protections available to family members under more stringent laws. Thus, they argue, no-fault divorce empowers the spouse who wishes to leave, but wreaks havoc on the spouse being left behind. Their view, then, is that no-fault divorce is something of a misnomer and should more accurately be called unilateral divorce on demand. Those who want to end no-fault divorce believe it has contributed to an increase in the divorce rate and has lessened our culture's commitment to marriage as a social institution and as a contract between two parties. They advocate legislation that would put pressure on couples to remain together and that would deny a divorce when one spouse opposes it unless the plaintiff can show that a spouse was physically or mentally abusive, had a problem with alcohol or drugs, had committed adultery, had deserted the home, or had been incarcerated.

On the other hand, those who oppose abandoning no-fault divorce fear that doing so could mean a return to the anger, lies, and distortions required to obtain a divorce before no-fault, resulting in more pain for children as parents engage in a legal blame game. Going back to establishing fault would be costly and hurt those who can least afford litigation. In addition, they believe that without no-fault divorce, couples would be discouraged from getting married in the first place, thereby increasing

the incidence of nonmarital births, leaving more women and children economically and socially vulnerable. Family expert Barbara Dafoe Whitehead (1997) argues that the divorce revolution was a cultural rather than legal phenomenon, growing out of a complex set of social, economic, and cultural factors that created an ethic that emphasized individual well-being. In the process, divorce came to be seen as a healthy response to marital discontent. Thus, she cautions legal sanctions will not stop divorce and that the desire to do away with no-fault divorce is misplaced.

There is concern that making divorce more difficult to obtain would force people to stay in unhealthy and even abusive relationships. Rather than forcing people to stay together, those who oppose aban-

doning no-fault laws emphasize a focus on reducing the economic stresses that contribute to the high rate of breakup, including requiring absent parents to meet their child support obligations. Some opponents of divorce law reform believe this effort is directed at the wrong target. They argue that if you want to minimize divorce, make getting married more difficult and require couples to go through counseling before they get married.

What do you think? Does no-fault divorce increase the likelihood of people's getting divorced? Explain. Do you favor or oppose efforts to outlaw no-fault divorce? Explain. Should marriage laws be strengthened to make it more difficult to get married? Explain.

CURRENT TRENDS: HOW MANY MARRIAGES END IN DIVORCE?

If you have been paying attention to news-grabbing headlines, you may be tempted to say that one in every two marriages ends in divorce. This figure is based on a simple but flawed calculation: the ratio of divorces to the total number of marriages. For example, in 2005, there were approximately 2.2 million marriages and although we do not as yet have a corresponding figure for the number of divorces owing to nonreporting in some states, they numbered a little over 1 million in recent years. Hence, we get a figure of

50 percent or one out of two marriages ending in divorce. This interpretation is problematic—a little bit like comparing apples and oranges—because this marriage statistic represents only couples married in a particular year, whereas the divorce statistic refers to all couples who divorce during that same year, regardless of when they married. According to demographers, the divorce rate in the United States, although the highest in the Western world, never reached one in every two marriages, although in past years it came closer to that figure (Kreider, 2005).

A more meaningful and commonly used measure of divorce is the **crude divorce rate** (CDR), the number of divorces per 1000 people in the population. This statistic has two advantages. It is easy to compute and it allows us to see whether the number of divorces is increasing or decreasing over time. Its disadvantage is its sensitivity to population characteristics. Since children are included as well as single people, this reduces the divorce rate because they are not eligible to divorce. And, even though more young and middle-aged adults may be divorcing, an increase in the number of elderly may mask what would otherwise be an increase in the divorce rate. Conversely, an increase in marriages in earlier years can raise the divorce rate in later years. The number of marriages increased dramatically in the 1970s as a large number of "baby boomers" took on adult roles. In subsequent years, many of these couples divorced. This pattern can be seen in Figure 12.1. In 1950 the CDR was only 2.6, whereas by 1980 it had more than doubled to an all-time high of 5.2. Thereafter the divorce rate began a gradual decline down to 3.6 in 2005 (National Center for Health Statistics, 2006).

Another more accurate way to measure divorce is the **refined divorce rate** (RDR), the number of divorces per 1,000 married women age 15 and over. This statistic focuses on individuals who realistically are potential candidates for divorce. Figure 12.1 allows us to see the differences between the crude and refined divorce rates. Using the RDR allows us to examine changes over time and to investigate how the frequency of divorce is affected by economic and political events. For example, the divorce rate declined during the depression of the early 1930s, when couples simply could not afford to get divorced. The rate was 7.5 in 1930 and dropped to 6.1 by 1933. It increased dramatically during and immediately after World War II, because of an improved economy and because couples previously separated by the war had to readjust to living together. When the United States entered the war in 1941, the RDR was 9.4; a year after the war ended (1946), the rate climbed to17.9. As the country returned to peacetime, the rate began to fall and stayed relatively stable through the 1950s and the mid-1960s, when it again began an upward march; it reached a high of 22.6 in 1980, after which it started to drop, falling to 17.7 in 2004, considerably lower than was the case between 1975 and 1990. What accounts for some of these changes? No doubt, as we saw in Chapter 10, the increasing economic pressures that led many wives to enter the labor force in the 1970s and 1980s strained marital relationships, thus adding to the divorce rate. By the 1990s, cohabitation was well established. Many couples who otherwise would have married and then divorced broke up instead, remaining outside the official statistics. Additionally, during the last decade, considerable media attention has been given to the issue of

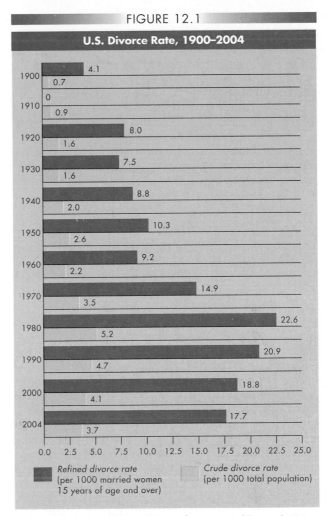

FIGURE 12.1

U.S. Divorce Rate, 1900–2004

Sources: A. A. Plateris, 1973, *100 Years of Marriage and Divorce Statistics: 1867–1967* (Rockville, MD: National Center for Health Statistics): p. 24, Table 4; National Center for Health Statistics, 2005, "Marriages and Divorces, 1900–2004, found at www.print.infoplease.com/ipa/A0005044.html; Refined Divorce Rate (RDR) for 1960–2004 cited in Barbara Dafoe Whitehead and David Popenoe, 2005, "The State of Our Unions: The Social Health of Marriage in America" (accessed March 4, 2006 from www.marriage.rutgers.edu/Publications/SOOU/TEXT50042005.htm).

divorce. This awareness may have encouraged couples to put more effort into making their marriages work.

A third way of determining the divorce rate, one preferred by most demographers, is to calculate how many people who have ever married subsequently divorced. According to a recent study using 2001 data, the highest rate of divorce was 41 percent for men between the ages of 50 and 59, and 39 percent for women in the same age group (Kreider, 2005). There is a tendency to use figures such as these to project into the future, that is, four out of ten marriages will end in divorce. However, such predictions assume that social conditions remain constant. In a rapidly changing society like ours, this is unlikely. For example, the covenant marriage movement, discussed earlier, may increase marital stability by making divorces more difficult to get and/or lead people to work harder to save a troubled marriage. Conversely, if we assume that we will return to the marriage patterns of the late 1970s, our divorce projections will be higher. A word of caution is in order here. Some people are concerned that public awareness of high divorce projections can serve as self-fulfilling prophecies, the tendency of people to respond to and act on the basis of information, whether it is accurate or not. They reason that couples having marital problems may opt to divorce because so many marriages fail anyway (see, for example, Scott, 2003). Obviously, people do not have to go along with prevailing societal trends. One way to guard against this tendency is to be as well informed as possible and to recognize that there are a number of risk factors involved in divorce, many of which can be avoided. To this end, let us examine the question of who divorces and why.

WHO IS LIKELY TO DIVORCE?

As Table 12.1 illustrates, divorce is not evenly distributed across all segments of the population. However, women are more likely to be divorced than are men across all major race and ethnic groups. This pattern is largely because men are more likely to remarry than are women and they are also more likely to remarry more quickly after divorce than are women, a topic we will discuss in greater detail in Chapter 13. Keep in mind that this table reflects the percentage of people who were divorced in 2004. If we consider people who were ever divorced, but who subsequently remarried, the percentages would be higher. For example, in 2001, 23.1 percent of women and 21.0 percent of men had been divorced at least once (Kreider, 2005). A second pattern is also evident in this table: variations by race and ethnicity. African Americans have the highest percentage of divorced persons followed by whites and Latinas/os, with Asians having the lowest rates. A somewhat similar pattern exists in the rate of marriage dissolution. Forty-seven percent of first marriages of African American women end within 10 years compared with 34 percent for Latinas, 32 percent for white women, and 20 percent for Asian women (Bramlett and Mosher, 2002).

Divorce among African Americans

How do we explain the different rates of divorce among racial and ethnic groups? In the past, some analysts have viewed the higher rate of divorce among African Americans as the legacy of slavery (Frazier, 1939). Subsequent scholarship, however, has found that the increase in African American marital instability is a more recent development, accelerating in particular since 1960 and corresponding to a decline in the economic situation of large numbers of African Americans (Cherlin, 1981; Gutman, 1976). Numerous studies support the argument that higher divorce rates among African Americans reflect greater economic hardships (see, for example, Teachman, Tedrow, and Crowder, 2000). One statistical analysis showed that a significant amount of black–white differences in marital stability can be explained by differences in levels of education and income among the two groups (Jaynes and Williams, 1989). Studies in other countries have also found a strong relationship between unemployment and high divorce rates (Lester, 1996). In addition, there is a higher rate of teenage pregnancy and premarital pregnancies among African American women than in women in other groups, a factor that, in itself, increases the risk of marital dissolution across all groups (Garfinkel, McLanahan, and Robins, 1994). Finally, as we saw in Chapter 1, African Americans often rely on the extended family for social support. Thus armed with the knowledge that there will be help for them, couples may be less reluctant to divorce than others whose communities offer less support and acceptance for divorcing couples (Blake and Darling, 2000).

Divorce among Latinas/os

Because Latinas/os also experience higher rates of poverty and unemployment as a result of discrimination, we might

TABLE 12.1
Percent of Divorce Population by Sex, Race, and Ethnicity, 2004

	Total (%)	Male (%)	Female (%)
All Races	10.2	8.6	11.5
White	10.1	8.7	11.4
Black	12.2	10.0	13.7
Latina/o	7.5	6.3	9.3
Asian	4.4	3.2	6.4

Source: Adapted from U.S. Census Bureau, 2006, *Statistical Abstract of the United States,* 2006 (Washington, DC: Government Printing Office): p. 49, Table 50.

Compared to African American and white couples, Latina/o couples have lower rates of divorce. Nevertheless, a growing number of Latinas are single parents.

assume that the Latina/o divorce ratio would be closer to that of African Americans than to that of whites. In fact, as Table 12.1 indicates, Latinas/os rate of divorce was low in comparison to whites and African Americans. Two factors are often cited to explain the relatively high level of marital stability among Latinas/os: a cultural tradition that emphasizes the importance of the family unit and a religion (Catholicism) that prohibits divorce. According to a national survey, Latinas/os were less likely to see divorce as acceptable (57 percent) than the general population (66 percent; Deane et al., 2000).

Demographers Hugh Carter and Paul Glick (1976:246) raise another issue that may be relevant here. In their analysis of 1960 Census data, they found that the lowest ratios of divorced to married persons for a major group were among the foreign-born white population. They speculated that lack of familiarity with the U.S. legal system and a reluctance to become involved in court actions probably led many foreign-born couples to tolerate marital problems that might have resulted in divorce among native-born groups. These conclusions might apply to those Latinas/os who have arrived in the United States most recently.

Although all these factors may contribute to the lower divorce rates found among Latinas/os, the Latina/o ratio itself presents several problems. It does not distinguish among the diverse categories of Latinas/os whose economic status and rates of marital stability might vary. Among Latinas, for example, Puerto Rican women are the most likely to be divorced and Cuban women are the least likely. The rate for Chicanas falls somewhere in between the other two groups (Sweet and Bumpass, 1987). One possible explanation for these differences is the greater economic stress experienced by Puerto Ricans; they have higher unemployment rates and less income than the other groups.

Divorce among Asian Americans

According to the U.S. Census Bureau, Asian Americans are less likely than the total population to be separated or divorced. In 2000, 9.7 percent of the population age 15 and older were divorced, but only 4.2 percent of Asian Americans in that age category were (Reeves and Bennett, 2004). There are several factors that explain the lower rate of divorce among Asian Americans. First, both women and men tend to marry later than other groups. They are thus a bit older and likely to be more mature and settled at the onset of marriage. Second, Asian Americans tend to rank higher on numerous indicators of socioeconomic status, all of which can contribute to marital stability. For example, in 2000 a higher proportion of Asians (44 percent) than of the total population (24 percent) had earned at least a bachelor's degree. Similarly, Asians were more likely to be employed in management, professional, and related occupations than was the case for the total population (45 to 34 percent). And, as we saw in Chapter 10, the median annual income of Asian American families was higher than that of families in other groups. Finally, many Asian Americans are relatively new to the United States. Seventy-six percent of the foreign-born Asian population came to the United States over the past two decades compared to 70 percent of others in the

foreign-born population. Forty-three percent of the foreign-born Asian population entered the United States between 1990 and 2000.

Many Asian Americans brought cultural traditions of strong family ties with them, including living with or near extended and multigenerational families. However, as is the case with any racial or ethnic category that includes people with diverse languages, religions, customs, and countries of origin, a global figure obscures differences within the larger category. For example, Thai, Japanese, and Filipino divorce rates (7.4, 6.7, and 5.2 percent) are considerably higher than the 4.2 percent global rate for Asian Americans. Conversely, Pakistani, Hmong, and Asian Indian rates are considerably lower than the global rate (2.1, 2.3, and 2. 4 percent, respectively). Many Asian American community leaders are concerned that as Asian Americans become more assimilated into mainstream U.S. culture, their traditional family patterns will change and divorce rates will rise. That this may be happening is indicated by more recent Census data; the divorce rate among Asian Americans increased to 5 percent in 2002 (Associated Press, 2003).

The need for further research is apparent if we are to understand the interactive effects of economic status, race, and ethnicity on marital stability. In particular, more data are needed on groups such as Native Americans who often are not included in major surveys. One of the few studies to examine marital stability among Native Americans found that in 1980, 48 percent of Native American women and 43 percent of their male counterparts were no longer in intact first marriages (Sweet and Bumpass, 1987). Again, it is likely that these high rates, in large part, were related to high rates of unemployment and poverty, but we lack recent comparable data to assess whether or not marital situations are improving for this segment of the population. In a similar vein, we have little systematic data concerning marital stability among other groups whose numbers are small and/or who are more recent arrivals to the United States, for example people from the Middle East.

Race and ethnicity are, of course, not the only factors affecting divorce rates. The next section examines a variety of social and demographic factors that affect the likelihood of divorce.

FACTORS AFFECTING MARITAL STABILITY

If you are like most Americans, you are probably concerned by the high rate of divorce. Perhaps the thought has occurred to you that you or people close to you are likely to end up divorced. Although no one can say with any degree of certainty which marriages will end in divorce, based on existing patterns, researchers can predict the statistical probabilities for different groups. The likelihood of any given couple getting divorced depends on a wide range of factors, including age at marriage, premarital childbearing, education, income, religion, parental divorce, cohabitation, and the presence of children. By understanding how these factors can influence a marital relationship, people contemplating marriage can better evaluate their chances of a successful marriage. For example, knowing that the age at marriage can increase or decrease the likelihood of divorce may lead people to evaluate their readiness for marriage more realistically.

Age at First Marriage

Younger brides and grooms, especially those who are still in their teens when they marry, are more likely to divorce. Forty-eight percent of marriages of women who married under age 18 dissolved within 10 years compared with 24 percent of marriages of women at least 25 years of age at marriage (Bramlett and Mosher, 2002). Social scientists also attribute the higher divorce rates found in the Bible Belt states (see In the News) to the tendency for couples to marry at younger ages than their counterparts in other states. Similarly, marrying at a late age (35 plus) can increase the probability of divorce during the first 15 years of marriage (Booth, White, and Edwards, 1986). The reasons for marital instability among the young come easily to mind: immaturity, lack of adequate financial resources, different rates of personal growth, and often the pressures of early parenthood, particularly if it involves premarital childbearing. Numerous studies document a negative relationship between premarital childbearing and the risk of divorce after first marriage (Norton and Miller, 1992; Teachman, 2002). According to demographers, the likelihood that first marriage will break up when the first birth is within 7 months of marriage is 23 percent for white women, 26 percent for Latinas, and 36 percent for African American women (Bramlett and Mosher, 2002).

By later ages, however, those problems should be resolved. Although fewer data on late marriages are available, some evidence suggests that late marriages tend to be more heterogamous and thus potentially more conflictual. Also, the pool of eligible marital partners becomes more restricted with increasing age. Thus, older people wishing to marry may have to accept greater differences in values, ages, and educational and economic status in their partners than do younger people. It is also likely that late marriages involve a remarriage for one or both spouses; rates of divorce for remarriage are higher than those for first marriages. We examine the dynamics of remarriages in Chapter 13.

Education

Overall, individuals who graduate from college have more stable marriages than those with a high school education (Kreider, 2005). This pattern reflects a number of different factors. Individuals with only a high school education are more likely to marry at an early age and to hold low-paying jobs. Thus, financial pressures on the marriage are likely to be substantial. Moreover, those who persist in school tend to marry later, have higher incomes, and in general probably are better equipped to work out problems as they occur. This pattern holds for both women and men.

Income

In an earlier section, we observed that low income and its accompanying stresses are a major factor in the higher divorce rate found among some groups. The significance of income is shown, for example, in its impact on early marriages. Young couples with sufficient financial resources had more stable marriages than similar couples with inadequate resources (Spanier and Glick, 1981). Poverty and low incomes, regardless of age, are risk factors for divorce (Amato and Previti, 2004). In their book, *For Better/For Worse*, E. Mavis Hetherington and John Kelly (2002) describe how the lack of money can corrode a marital relationship, particularly when the husband is unemployed and cannot find or hold a job. The husband may feel inadequate as a breadwinner, and if the wife complains, his self-esteem may decline even further. Both may become resentful.

Religion

Historically, many religions have either prohibited or tried to discourage divorce among their members. On this basis, we would predict that more religiously involved people would have lower rates of divorce, a view supported by a considerable body of research. Studies from the 1980s on have documented a significant pattern. Among Americans, those who attend church regularly are less likely to divorce than those who attend less frequently or not at all (Wilcox, 2005). Furthermore, couples who share the same religion are less likely than interfaith couples to divorce (Mullins et al., 2004). One possible explanation for this pattern is that religious homogamy increases the commonality spouses share in values and traditions. Membership in a religious organization also promotes social cohesion (Durkheim, [1897] 1951) and provides a source of support in times of difficulty. This support helps couples work through problems that otherwise might lead to divorce.

Data from the General Social Survey showed a different tendency to divorce among various religious groups. Among U.S. adults, 53 percent of respondents identifying themselves as religiously unaffiliated were separated or divorced. Among the religiously affiliated, 53 percent of black Protestants, 42 percent of Evangelicals, 39 percent of mainline Protestants, 36 percent of Jews, and 35 percent of Catholics were separated or divorced (Wilcox, 2005). Among the Protestant denominations there is also considerable variation, with Baptists and Pentecostals having higher divorce rates than Presbyterians and Episcopalians. Some caution is required in interpreting this last finding, however. The differences in rates may be the result of an interactive effect between religious membership and other factors such as education and income. Baptists and Pentecostals tend to have lower levels of education and income than do Presbyterians and Episcopalians. Tennessee, Arkansas, and Oklahoma, each with high percentages of residents belonging to Baptist and Pentecostal denominations, also tend to be among the states with the lowest levels of household income (U.S. Census Bureau, 2000).

Although religion continues to be a factor in people's willingness to divorce, there are indications that organized religions are no longer as effective in restricting divorce as they had been. For example, in the past, Catholic countries in Europe did not permit divorce. Now virtually all do, leaving Malta the only European country still imposing such a ban. In 1995, voters in Ireland, where 95 percent of the population is Catholic, narrowly approved a constitutional amendment to allow couples to divorce if they have lived apart for at least 4 of the previous 5 years. The previous ban on divorce did not mean that Irish couples stayed together: According to Irish officials, about 80,000 people were separated but unable to divorce at the time of the referendum. In fact, many of them were living with and had children with a new partner (Moseley, 1995). Chile, another predominantly Catholic country, made divorce legal for the first time in 2004. When the law went into effect, more than 500,000 people were separated (Ross, 2004).

Parental Divorce

Can the parents' divorce influence the outcome of their children's marriage? The answer apparently is yes. People whose parents divorced have higher divorce rates than do children who come from intact families (Amato and DeBoer, 2001; Wolfinger, 2000). Two factors may combine to produce this outcome. First, from their parents' example, children learn that divorce can be a solution to marital difficulties. They thus may be more ready than their peers from intact families to seek a divorce when problems start. Second, after a parental divorce children often experience downward social mobility, which in turn may limit college attendance and contribute to early marriage, putting them at increased risk of a divorce themselves. However, gender seems to play a role here. Daughters from both middle and lower socioeconomic families are at greater risk for divorce than sons from divorced parents of middle-class background. Parents are still more likely to encourage sons to go to college than daughters and therefore provide more resources for sons to continue their education (Feng et al., 1999).

Several other marital patterns have been observed in adult children whose parents were divorced. Parental divorce raises the likelihood of teenage marriage. However, if these children do not marry before age 20, they are likely to remain single or to cohabit. If they do cohabit, however, they are unlikely to marry their partner (Wolfinger, 2001, 2003). For the most part, research on the impact of parental divorce has been limited to their immediate offspring. A recent study suggests that the effects of parental divorce extend into the third generation. Sociologists Paul Amato and Jacob Cheadle (2005) examined data collected on divorced families covering a span of 20 years and found that the grandchildren of divorced couples had less education, more turbulent marriages, and more distant relationships with their parents than did grandchildren of still married couples. This was especially true when the middle generation also experienced these divorce-related consequences.

Cohabitation

As we saw in Chapter 7, studies consistently show that people who live together before they marry are more likely to divorce. Attitudes and behaviors often interact to make premarital cohabitation risky. Cohabitation often involves less commitment than marriage, and when less committed couples drift into marriage, the experience of a less secure, committed, and even faithful cohabitation may shape their mar-

ital behavior (Dush et al., 2003). Additionally, cohabiting couples may bring into their marriage the attitude that relationships, including marriage, are temporary in and of themselves (Smock and Gupta, 2002). Other researchers report that, in the first two years of their marriage, couples who had cohabited had somewhat less positive problem-solving behaviors and were less supportive of each other on average than couples who had not cohabited (Cohan and Kleinbaum, 2002). This could be related to cohabiting at an early age and/or to the insecurity and low commitment level of their initial relationship. Thus, many marriage experts caution against thinking that cohabitation realistically represents a "trial" marriage.

Although the weight of evidence continues to show that couples who cohabit before marriage are more likely to divorce than couples who do not cohabit, some researchers are questioning whether this divorce gap will narrow or even disappear in the future. An Australian study of recent cohorts of people who marry after cohabiting seems to indicate that possibility. Researchers found that the risk of subsequent divorce was greatly reduced for more recent cohabitants compared to those who had cohabited and married in the 1970s. Two factors seem to account for this. The first was related to measurement of duration of relationships. Including the period of cohabitation and marriage together reduces the differences in length of marital stability between cohabiting and noncohabiting couples. Second, after researchers removed the effects of different characteristics of those who cohabit and those who marry directly, they found that the contemporary marriage survival or separation outcomes of the two groups were next to indistinguishable (Vaus, Qu, and Weston, 2003). Clearly, more research is needed in this area to test the possibility that the experience of contemporary cohabitation has or will have different outcomes than that of cohabitation in earlier decades.

Presence of Children

A consistent research finding is that marital disruption is most likely when the marriage is child-free (Tilson and Larsen, 2000; Wineberg, 1988) and least likely when there are preschool children (Previti and Amato, 2003). This finding should not be construed to mean that marriages with children are happier than those without. In fact, couples with children still at home tend to be less happy than either childless couples or those whose children have left home (Twenge, Campbell, and Foster, 2003). Rather, parents who are having marital problems often delay divorce until all the children are in school. The likelihood of divorce increases when children reach their teens (AARP, 2004; Heaton, 1990). Two plausible explanations for this behavior come readily to mind. Parents may believe that teenaged children are more capable of handling this family disruption, or it may be that coping with adolescent children puts additional strain on an already weakened relationship.

Increasingly, married couples are less likely to stay together because children are present in the home. More than 1 million children have been involved in divorce annually since 1972. Thus, increasing numbers of children are spending part of their childhood in a single-parent family. A

APPLYING THE SOCIOLOGICAL IMAGINATION
Are You at Risk?

This exercise is designed to help you assess some of the risk factors of divorce that may be present in your life. Answer yes if the question accurately describes you or those close to you.

1. Did you marry or do you plan to marry before your 20th birthday?
2. Are your parents divorced?
3. Are any of your close friends divorced?
4. Do you attend religious services only occasionally?
5. Are you likely to drop out of college before graduating?
6. Did you or will you consider marrying someone who did not graduate from college?
7. Did you or will you want to cohabit with your partner before marriage?
8. Will both you and your spouse work?
9. Do you have difficulty managing money?

Scoring

Add up the number of times you answered *yes*. The higher the number of *yes* answers, the more risk factors you have for becoming divorced. However, this does not automatically mean you will be divorced at some point in your life. Rather, it indicates that you have some of the characteristics that researchers have found to be associated with a tendency to divorce.

Go to www.cdc.gov/nchs/data/series/sr_23/sr23_022.pdf and read the article, "Cohabitation, Marriage, Divorce, and Remarriage in the United States." Do the authors suggest that there are any factors that can act as marriage protectors? What do they identify as risk factors regarding the likelihood of divorce? How can knowledge of these risk factors be used by couples and by social institutions in attempts to develop strategies to lessen the likelihood of marital dissolution?

---

study of 17 Western countries found that in all the countries studied childhood exposure to single parenting is more often caused by parental separation than out of partnership childbearing (Timberlake and Furstenberg, Jr., 2003).

Research has also found that a child's gender is a factor in divorce. Overall, parents of girls are more likely to divorce than are parents of sons (Bedard and Deschenes, 2005). Economists Gordon Dahl and Enrico Moretti (2004) found that parents of a girl are nearly 5 percent more likely to divorce than the parents of a boy, and the more daughters, the bigger the effect. Parents of three girls are almost 10 percent more likely to divorce than the parents of three boys. Dahl and Moretti also found this same relationship, although with much higher effects in Mexico, Columbia, Kenya, and Vietnam. Researchers attribute this to a greater preference of fathers for sons. Graham Spanier and Paul Glick (1981), who reported the same pattern over two decades ago, suggest that it is related to a man's desire to have a son carry on his name, a desire especially strong among traditional fathers. In addition, they speculate that mothers of sons might resist a separation in the belief that raising sons without a father would be more difficult than raising daughters alone. Finally, it should be noted that the birth of a first child can create considerable stress for new parents. Seventeen women interviewed by Hilary Hoge (2002) in her thoughtful book, *Women's Stories of Divorce at Childbirth: When the Baby Rocks the Cradle*, detail how the transition to parenthood became a personal crisis leading to marital disruption. We examine the effects of divorce on children later in this chapter.

Thus far, we have examined a number of risk factors associated with divorce. Take a minute to see whether any of these risk factors apply to you (see Internet Resources: Applying the Sociological Imagination box). Obviously, these factors do not tell us about the process of divorce or why individuals decide to divorce. What happens to marriages that look so promising when they begin? Although every marital disruption has its unique features, social scientists have identified several common stages through which most divorcing couples pass.

THE PROCESS OF DIVORCE

Divorce does not just happen. It is a complex social process in which a basic unit of social organization—marriage—breaks down over time, culminating in a legal termination of the relationship. Nonetheless, this process can vary significantly from culture to culture (see In Other Places box).

Stages in the Divorce Process

Divorce involves more than a legal decree officially symbolizing the end of a marriage. Some researchers, like Constance Ahrons (1980) and George Levinger (1979), identify three stages in the divorce process: (1) a period of marital conflict and unhappiness, (2) the actual marital dissolution itself, and (3) a postdivorce period. James Ponzetti and Rodney Cate (1986) see divorce as a four-step process: (1) recognition by one or both spouses of serious marital problems; (2) discussion of these problems with the spouse and possibly with family, friends, or counselors; (3) initiation of legal action to dissolve the marriage; and (4) the postdissolution period, which involves adapting to a new status. Although both spouses go through the same stages, the timing may be different for each spouse, depending on who initiates the divorce.

IN OTHER PLACES

DIVORCE ON DEMAND TO NO DIVORCE PERIOD

Cultures vary significantly in their degree of acceptance of divorce and the rules governing who can initiate a divorce. In some cultures, like the Hopi Native Americans of the Southwest, both women and men could initiate divorce. Among the Yoruba of West Africa, however, only women could initiate divorce; and for centuries among many Muslim and Asian cultures, only men could ask for a divorce.

Similarly, some cultures allow divorce on demand. For example, researchers who studied the matrilineal Hopi 50 years ago found a high divorce rate: about one out of three marriages. The divorce process was easy. A wife could initiate divorce simply by placing her husband's belongings outside their dwelling. A divorcing husband simply moved back into his mother's house. If the couple had children, they stayed with the mother (Queen, Habenstein, and Quadagno, 1985:49–50). In some countries, like India, a Muslim man can divorce his wife in a matter of minutes in a practice known as "triple talaq," or instant divorce, by saying three times in a row, "I divorce you." This can be done over the phone, by mail, or through mobile phone text message. The husband does not have to give her reasons or have a face-to-face meeting with his wife (Pandey, 2004). The practice of instant divorce is banned in several Islamic countries including Pakistan, Bangladesh, Malaysia, and Indonesia.

Men in Egypt have a unilateral and unconditional right to divorce and they do not need to go to court to end their marriages. However, women who want a divorce must go to court to divorce their husbands, using one of two options. A

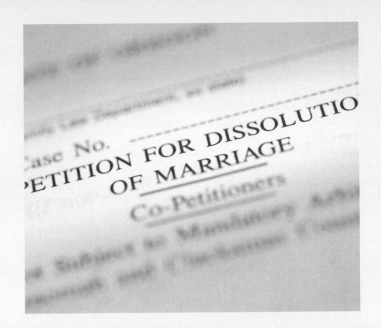

woman can seek a fault-based divorce, which can provide financial rights, but to gain it, she must show harm inflicted by her husband during the course of their marriage, including eyewitness testimony in allegations of physical abuse. The second option is no-fault divorce. This also requires a woman to petition the court, but here she must agree to forfeit her financial rights and repay the dowry given to her by her husband upon marriage. Court proceedings can take years and a noncooperative husband can appeal the court's decision, prolonging the process (Levinson, 2005).

In two countries, the Philippines and Malta, both predominately Catholic, divorce is not a legal option. Recent attempts to change the situation in both countries failed. The Family Code of the Philippines provides for a legal separation or annulment due to "psychological incapacity" of a marriage, but not divorce. Because the marriage is still valid under a legal separation, remarriage is not permitted. An annulment, which allows a couple to remarry, is difficult and costly to obtain (Wilson, 2005). Maltese citizens who are married to foreigners and living abroad can obtain a divorce in the country in which they are living and have it registered in Malta if the marriage took place there (Ameen, 2006).

What do you think? What is your reaction to these different approaches to divorce? How do they compare with practices in the United States? Do you think there is any merit to making divorce as easy as it is for the Hopi or as difficult as it is for the citizens of the Philippines and Malta? Explain.

Although these researchers propose different models, they all agree that the dissolution of a marriage occurs through a series of stages. The majority of separations and divorces follows a period of personal unhappiness, conflict, and deliberation, during which time individuals make decisions based on three types of criteria: (1) an evaluation of the attractiveness of the relationship itself (the material, emotional, and symbolic rewards a spouse provides); (2) an evaluation of the costs and benefits of a divorce (monetary, social, and psychological); and (3) an evaluation of the attractiveness of possible alternatives, including new relationships (Levinger, 1965). These processes are illustrated in numerous studies of divorce here in the United States and in other countries as well. A study of people's open-ended personal accounts of why they stay married found that individuals perceived the cohesiveness of their marriages in terms of rewards and barriers. People who reported barriers only, compared with people who reported rewards only, were more likely to divorce. However, in some case this process took place only after many years (Previti and Amato, 2003).

Similarly, the narratives of Israeli women and men who were married for 15 or more years show that divorce for these respondents was not a spontaneous or impulsive response to any immediate event but was rather the process of marital deterioration over time (Rokach, Cohen, and Dreman, 2004).

The Six Stations of Divorce

Anthropologist Paul Bohannan (1970) has identified not one but six divorces that couples experience in dissolving their marital relationship. These he calls the **stations of divorce**: emotional, legal, economic, coparental, community, and psychic divorce.

The **emotional divorce** can be present in the marriage for a long time before any legal action is taken to end the relationship. Here one spouse, or both, questions the viability or quality of the relationship and at some point shares this view with the other. There is often a period during which one or both partners withdraw emotionally from the relationship. A loss of mutual respect, trust, and affection follows. During this period both spouses may hurt or frustrate the other deliberately. Yet despite the deterioration of the relationship and talk of separation, one or both may not want a divorce for a variety of reasons: fear of living alone, concern about the children, desire to fulfill marriage vows, or the economic and social costs involved. This process is well illustrated by Fran Welch, who divorced her alcoholic husband after 36 years of marriage. "I had never lived on my own," she said. One evening during dinner with friends, her husband's obnoxious behavior pushed her to the edge. "I knew at that point that was it. I wasn't going to listen to or watch or see this kind of behavior anymore. I just couldn't do it. And that was the end," Welch said (quote in Smith, 2005). Thus, some marriages may remain intact in form but not in substance for extended periods of time. Other spouses take action to move to the next stage. This may involve one spouse walking out or a mutual decision to begin a period of separation.

Gender plays a role in the decision-making process. Women appear to take a more active role in preparing and planning for divorce or separation. They are more likely than men to think about divorce after a spousal argument, and they are more likely to make specific plans to discuss divorce or separation with their spouse and/or with others (Crane, Soderquist, and Gardner, 1995).

The **legal divorce** officially ends the marriage and gives the former partners the right to remarry. Legal divorce generally follows a period of months or even years of deliberation. Sociologists Graham Spanier and Linda Thompson (1988:331) interviewed 50 separated and divorced people (22 women and 28 men) and found that the median length of deliberation between thinking that divorce is a possibility and the certainty of divorce was 12 months for the men and 22 months for the women. Women thought about divorce earlier than men. The divorce itself can be an adversarial process, especially when children and property are involved. In attempting to settle these issues, the divorcing couple may lose control of the process itself to lawyers who advocate their client's interest generally without regard to the needs of the other party. In addition, legal divorce can be an expensive proposition. When lawyers are involved, the average cost of a divorce in the United States is around $20,000 and this only takes into account the legal costs and consequences. It does not include the emotional and familial costs, which are so much higher (Skul, 2005). For individuals who are able and willing to use the Internet, a "do-it-yourself" divorce can cost as little as $50.

The **economic divorce** involves the settlement of property, a process that often involves considerable conflict. Most states now have laws specifying that both spouses are to receive an equitable share of the marital property. Equity is not always easy to determine, however. Tangible items like the house, the car, income, and bank accounts, whose values are easy to calculate, can be divided without great difficulty. But what about the current and future earning power of each individual? Should this be considered in a divorce settlement? For example, spouses with advanced degrees or special labor market skills are at a real advantage after a divorce. Considerable controversy exists over what constitutes a fair return on an investment in human capital. This question arises in cases where one spouse (most frequently the husband) earned a degree or learned a skill while the other spouse (most frequently the wife) played a major supportive role in making that possible, earning the money to pay for the spouse's education. Increasingly, courts are wrestling with issues like this. Retirement funds represent an important asset, the value of which changes dramatically over the years. Former spouses often return to court long after the divorce is final to try to renegotiate financial settlements. This is especially the case as children grow and develop and have more expensive needs.

The economic station of divorce is less often applicable than some of the other stations. It assumes that all couples have tangible assets to divide. Although this is certainly true for middle- and upper-class couples, it is generally not true for the poor and for many working-class couples who live in rental units and depend on public transportation. According to Judith Seltzer and Irwin Garfinkel (1990), 40 percent or more of divorcing couples do not make any property settlement because they have nothing of value to divide.

The **coparental divorce** involves decisions concerning child custody, visitation rights, and the financial and legal responsibilities of each parent. This station can also be a source of conflict, particularly when parents are engaged in a custody battle. We will return to the topic of child custody later in this chapter.

The **community divorce** involves changing social relationships. It can involve a loss of relatives and friends who were previously shared with the spouse. In one study of 60 divorced mothers, over three-fourths reported losing former friends, usually during or immediately after the divorce (Arendell, 1986). The withdrawal of friendship may occur for several reasons. Those who were friendly with both spouses may not want to be drawn into taking sides. Others may see the divorce as a threat to their own relationships. For most of the women in the study, the loss of friends was an unexpected occurrence that was painful and emotionally confusing. In this stage of divorce, people may feel lonely and isolated.

The **psychic divorce** involves a redefinition of self away from the mutuality of couplehood and back to a sense of singlehood. This process takes time and involves a distancing from and an acceptance of the breakup. Many people go through a mourning process similar to that experienced by people who lose a spouse to death (see Chapter 15). The time this takes and the degree of difficulty with which this station is passed through varies considerably from individual to individual.

We examine some of the dynamics of these stations of divorce in more detail when we discuss the consequences of divorce later in this chapter. Before we examine the causes of divorce, we need to recognize that there are several other ways to dissolve a marriage. Many of the causes we will consider are applicable to these forms of marital dissolution as well.

OTHER FORMS OF MARITAL DISRUPTION

Thus far our discussion has focused on the legal concept of divorce. However, marriages can be disrupted by separation, desertion, annulment, and death.

Separation refers to the termination of marital cohabitation and can take a variety of forms. Sometimes one of the partners simply moves out. This can be the result of an individual or a mutual decision. Its goal may be to give one or both partners some space and time to think about the relationship, or it may be the first step toward divorce. Because this is an informal arrangement, the courts are not involved, and the couple remains legally married.

In other cases, when the couple does not want to divorce or to continue living together, the courts order legal separation with specific regulations governing the couple's interactions, including custody, visitation rights, and economic support. Such separation orders may also provide for counseling or therapy and give a stipulated time frame for the duration of the separation. This can give the couple an opportunity to reassess and possibly learn to alter problem areas in their relationship. Couples may reconcile or divorce at the end of the legal separation. Researchers have found that close to 10 percent of currently married couples have separated and reconciled (Wineberg and McCarthy, 1993). A study of African American women found that women who were separated after age 23 were more likely to reconcile than their younger peers. Greater maturity and a greater investment in the relationship were seen as key characteristics in the pattern of reconciliation (Wineberg, 1996). The desire to have day-to-day contact with children also provides an incentive for a couple's reconciliation. For some couples, however, a legal separation may become permanent. Some people reject divorce on religious grounds and therefore agree to live apart until the death of one spouse. Although either party may begin new relationships, neither is free to remarry.

Desertion refers to the abandonment of a spouse or family. The partner simply leaves, often without a word of warning. Desertion has sometimes been called the "poor people's divorce" because it frequently occurs when the family is experiencing economic hardship. However, desertion occurs among all classes, races, and ethnic groups. Although both women and men desert, men do so in greater numbers. This is perhaps the most difficult of all marital disruptions because the family is left without the financial and domestic support of the other spouse, and the courts cannot intervene unless the whereabouts of the deserting spouse are known. At the same time, the deserted spouse is not legally free to remarry until a specified number of years have passed. Thus, the family's life is overshadowed by uncertainty and ambiguity.

An annulment has quite a different meaning from the other forms of disruption we have been discussing. In divorce, separation, and desertion there is agreement that a legal marriage had existed. In contrast, a civil **annulment** legally states that the marriage never existed and thus the parties are free to marry at will. Generally, the basis for an annulment is that the couple did not meet the legal requirements for a marriage in the first place—they were underage, the degree of kinship was too close (first cousins, for example, are not legally permitted to marry in some states), the marriage was never consummated, or some form of fraud was involved. A civil annulment is distinct from the religious annulment granted by the Catholic Church. The church, after investigation, may decide that a religious marriage did not take place. In the eyes of the church, the individuals are free to marry, but to do so legally they must obtain a civil annulment or a divorce.

Finally, the death of a spouse brings an end to many marriages. Throughout much of U.S. history marital disruptions were generally caused by death, not divorce. This was due primarily to shorter life expectancies, harsher living conditions, and cultural patterns that discouraged divorce. Today widowhood most commonly occurs at later ages in the life cycle. We discuss the concept of widowhood in Chapter 14.

THE CAUSES OF DIVORCE

Although we now know how couples end their marriages, we still do not have an answer to the most frequently asked questions about divorce: Why? What went wrong? What causes people to evaluate their relationships as problematic or unsatisfactory? People who respond to someone's divorce by asking these questions frequently assume that some specific event or events disrupted the relationship. An important assumption here is that by eliminating the cause of the problem, the marriage could have been saved. Yet, as our historical review made clear, divorce is a complex phenomenon that needs to be understood in the context in which it occurs. Thus, changes in social structures, economic relationships, demographic patterns, and cultural configurations all play a role.

Societal Factors

Several macro-level factors have contributed to the long-term trend of a rise in the divorce rate (White, 1991). Perhaps the most influential factor is a change in attitudes. Although divorce is still seen as an unfortunate occurrence, it has become far more socially acceptable than in the past. Sixty-three percent of Americans view divorce as morally acceptable (Robison, 2002). Indeed, all major social institutions, including religion and the family, have become more tolerant of this behavior. These attitudinal factors have been reflected in more liberal divorce laws, which many people believe have made divorce more accessible to a wider share of the population. Since the advent of no-fault divorce in all 50 states, the divorce rate has increased in all but 6 of them (Nakonezny, Shull, and Rodgers, 1995). We will see later that there is a movement under way to tighten up on divorce legislation. These changes in attitudes became possible as a result of transformations taking place in the organization and functioning of major social institutions. As we discussed in Chapter 1, the advent of industrialism weakened the family as an economic unit and placed more emphasis on the personal relationship between spouses. Spouses were less likely, under these new conditions, to remain in a union that was not personally fulfilling.

Similarly, as we saw in Chapter 10, changes in the economy led to major transformations in the relationship between work and family and in the gender roles of husbands and wives. Among the most striking changes in this regard is the increase in the labor participation of women in this century, especially from 1970 on. Numerous studies show that marital instability has increased along with women's labor force participation (Cherlin and Furstenberg, 1988; Spitze, 1988).

What is less clear, however, is why this relationship exists. One interpretation suggests that among marriages that are unsatisfactory for whatever reason, the costs of divorce are lowest for wives who are capable of self-support (Hiedemann, Suhomlinova, and O'Rand, 1998). Other explanations have been tied to changing gender role ideology. As discussed in Chapter 10, some husbands may find it difficult to adjust to a co-provider role, and some wives may feel overburdened by working outside the home while still being expected to do the bulk of the housework (Rogers and Amato, 2000). In a nationally representative sample of individuals involved in dual-earner marriages, researchers found that unfair perceptions of the division of household labor not only decreases women's marital quality but also leads to role strain that makes them more likely to end unsatisfying marriages (Frisco and Williams, 2003). However, not all women respond to these inequities in the same way. Theodore Greenstein (1995) found that nontraditional women who saw marriage as an egalitarian partnership viewed such inequalities as unjust, whereas traditional women did not perceive these inequalities as inherently unfair. Nontraditional women experienced more stress in their relationships as a result of trying to resolve the inequities.

Nevertheless, the relationship between the employment of women and divorce is not a simple cause-and-effect relationship. Other factors are at work here as well. For example, Greenstein (1990) found that the conditions under which wives work is the fundamental issue. He reported that divorce is less likely when the wife's earnings and her share of family income represent a significant part of a family's budget. Having two wage earners may relieve financial tensions that often contribute to divorce; thus, a wife's employment may contribute to greater marital stability. Under different circumstances, however, female employment can increase marital instability. As with men, for example, women in high-stress jobs frequently find that work-related pressures carry over into domestic situations and intensify marital difficulties. In addition, employment outside the home can provide women with greater opportunities for alternative relationships, which can weaken the marital bond. Clearly, then, we must avoid simple generalizations concerning the relationship between female employment and divorce.

The United States is not alone in experiencing these macro-level changes. Other countries confront similar changes and consequently they are also experiencing higher divorce rates. For example, a cross-cultural study found that 25 out of 27 countries saw divorce rates rise between 1950 and 1985 (Lester, 1996). What is particularly noteworthy is that this trend is not confined to Western countries. Even in some of the more traditional societies in Asia, marital dissolution has increased in recent years. For example, in traditional Taiwanese society marriage was expected to last a lifetime. Divorce did occur, but historically divorce laws favored men with respect to property and child custody, leaving women reluctant to seek a divorce. However, as the economy changed, so, too, did gender role expectations. As women entered the labor force in large numbers, they became less accepting of unhappy relationships. Over two decades ago, just one in seventeen marriages ended in divorce (under 6 percent). Estimates are that in recent years 25 to 30 percent of marriages in Taiwan end in divorce (Warmack, 2004). Similarly, divorce rates have doubled in mainland China over the last two decades as economic reforms put pressure on traditional marriages by giving women and men more personal freedom and life choices than they had previously known. In the past, Chinese couples who wanted to divorce had difficulty in breaking through the bureaucratic wall of refusal (Goode, 1993). Today it takes only 10 yuan (US$1.20) and less than 20 minutes to get a divorce at a local civil affairs department (Weihua, 2006). The growing divorce rate is a reflection of the rising expectations that women now bring to marriage. Presently about 70 percent of divorces in China are initiated by women.

Similarly, a cross-cultural study examining the reasons for divorce in a sample of 312 Muslim Arabs in Israel found a combination of modern and traditional sources of marital tension. On the traditional side, respondents complained of interference by relatives and male violence governed by a gender ideology giving husbands power over their wives. On the modern side, over two–thirds of both spouses reported communication problems and a failure to get along, problems commonly found in the United States and other Western countries (Cohen, 2003).

Although a discussion of these societal factors helps us to understand the context in which divorce takes place, it does not tell us what happens on the personal level. For that we have to look to the divorcing couples themselves or to the therapists who work with them.

From the Perspective of Divorced People

Paul Rasmussen and Kathleen Ferraro (1991) interviewed 32 divorced people, in most cases both husband and wife.

Sexual infidelity, a major factor in many divorces, is often the story line in prime-time television programming. In an episode of the popular *Desperate Housewives*, actors Eva Longoria and Jesse Metcalfe fear their extramarital affair is about to be discovered.

Their findings raise questions about how we look at the causes of divorce. The behaviors most commonly cited as leading to divorce were poor communication, extramarital sex, constant fighting, emotional abuse, drug or alcohol problems, and financial mismanagement. Twelve years later, Paul Amato and Denise Previti (2003) classified 208 open-ended responses to a question on why respondents' marriages ended in divorce and found similar causes, with infidelity the most commonly reported cause, followed by incompatibility, drinking or drug use, and growing apart.

Did these behaviors, however, actually "cause" the divorce? Many respondents in the Rasmussen and Ferraro study considered these activities to be aftereffects of crises or problems that derived from other sources. Other respondents reported that these behaviors had occurred prior to dating, during dating, and during the marriage. Many of the spouses had remained committed to marriages in which such offending behaviors were present and openly acknowledged. Rasmussen and Ferraro concluded that these behaviors may exist for years without leading to divorce or even creating any serious problems. Supporting evidence for this observation can be seen in a study of spouses' reactions to their partner's extramarital affair (EMA). The change in marital satisfaction because of the EMA increased the probability of divorce, but it was not the only determinant. The presence of dependent children in a family and good marital quality before the discovery of the EMA lowered the proba-

bility of divorce (Fan and Lui, 2004). Conversely, Rasmussen and Ferraro also found that these same behaviors may be totally absent when divorce occurs. According to Rasmussen and Ferraro (1991:387):

> Husbands and wives who share strong emotional ties require . . . [a] significant crisis to break the bond. While the typically listed causes of divorce played an important role in all the divorces studied, it was in their use as tools to facilitate the divorce rather than as direct causes. The "knife of crisis" used as a means of ending a marriage was often adultery, heavy drinking, or financial ineptitude. Spouses either indulged in or complained of problem behaviors in building a case for divorce.

Thus, it appears that divorced people may not have a single reason for their divorce. Rather, a wide variety of "causes" are cited that pertain to a spouse's behavior, to perceived difficulties in the marital relationship, or to the impact of social and economic factors existing in the larger society. This does not mean, however, that researchers are unable to code categories of complaints. For example, one sociologist was able to arrive at 13 causes reported by her respondents, ranging from clear-cut justifications, such as abandonment or "becoming gay," to rather fuzzy references to personality differences, poor communication, or simply the need to find a happier situation (Johnson, 1988). More recent studies found similar complaints (Carrere and Gottman, 1999; Lowenstein, 2005; Rubin, 2001).

From the Perspective of Family Therapists and Matrimonial Lawyers

A 1981 survey asked members of the American Association of Marriage and Family Therapists to rate the frequency, severity, and treatment difficulty of 29 problems frequently seen among couples experiencing marital difficulties (Geiss and O'Leary, 1981:516–17). The therapists were asked to rank the areas they considered most damaging to couple relationships and those most difficult to treat. The ten areas rated as most damaging were (1) communication, (2) unrealistic expectations of marriage or spouse, (3) power struggles, (4) serious individual problems, (5) role conflicts, (6) lack of loving feelings, (7) lack of demonstration of affection, (8) alcoholism, (9) extramarital affairs, and (10) sex. The ten areas rated as most difficult to treat successfully were (1) alcoholism, (2) lack of loving feelings, (3) serious individual problems, (4) power struggles, (5) addictive behavior other than alcoholism, (6) value conflicts, (7) physical abuse, (8) unrealistic expectations of marriage or spouse, (9) extramarital affairs, and (10) incest.

Although that survey was conducted more than 25 years ago, its findings remain relevant. A recent survey of matrimonial lawyers found many of the same problems in the clients they serve: extramarital affairs, family strains, emotional and family abuse, midlife crisis, addictions, and workaholism (Skul, 2005). For more insight into how a therapist views the causes of divorce and the way therapy may help in resolving them, see the Strengthening Marriages and Families box.

STRENGTHENING MARRIAGES AND FAMILIES
Talks with Family Therapist Joan Zientek

RESOLVING PROBLEMS

In Your Practice, What Do You Find Are Some of the Problems that Lead to Divorce? A good percentage of divorcing couples come from families that lacked good models of spousal interaction. Thus, as children they did not learn the skills necessary to make a relationship work. Then when they grew up and married, they often selected a partner much like one of their parents, perhaps unconsciously using their marriage to work out their family of origin issues. If their partner comes with the same level of emotional health, the marriage lacks the resources to work out the natural conflicts that come from two people blending their lives together. When offspring are added to the mix, the picture becomes even more complex, resulting in three generations of issues living in one household. Recent studies show that couples who cohabit before marriage are more likely to divorce. In these cases, couples often just slide into marriage, acting

on the next logical step without a strong commitment to the relationship.

Other problems can arise when people marry without allowing time to get to know their partner. They can initially be drawn by the sexual energy that exists between them but when this wears out, they realize they have selected someone with whom they have little in common. This results in a conflict of values and priorities that is difficult to compromise and thus resolve. One of the main complaints of divorcing couples is the lack of communication stereotypically demonstrated by nagging by the wife and lack of affection on the part of the husband.

Sometimes a couple faces a trauma, such as the death of a child, where one partner's grief is too intense for the other to bear as she or he is also struggling with grief. In situations like these, one party or the other may turn to someone outside the marriage for comfort and support; an affair may ensue, and in time the marriage may dissolve. This is especially true if, as

psychologist John Gottman (1994b) suggests, they do not have an "emotional ecological balance," that is, engage in more acts of positive emotional interactions than of negative interaction. Gottman found that couples who have a five-to-one ratio of positives to negatives have the greatest chance of marital success.

Are Some Problems More Difficult to Solve than Others? Yes. One of the most difficult situations to manage is when one partner diagnoses the other as the source of the problem and refuses to see her or his contribution to the conflict in the marriage. It may take some time before the blaming person feels safe enough to begin to understand that feedback about her or his behavior need not be taken as harsh criticism, but instead as an opportunity to create changes that furthers closeness in the relationship. Another very difficult situation to confront occurs when one partner struggles with an addiction, whether it be alcoholism, gambling, or a sexual addiction.

Implications for Strengthening Marriage Understanding the causes of divorce implies that certain constructive measures can be taken to strengthen marriages. First, therapists can intervene in distressed relationships to help people improve their communication skills (see Chapter 8). Improved communication skills can help each partner understand the perspective of the other and perhaps avoid unnecessary conflict. Couples can also take certain steps to avoid entering marriage with unrealistic expectations of their relationship or each other. Discussion and negotiations (perhaps formulating a marital contract) before getting married, as well as ongoing discussion and renegotiations, are necessary if couples are to achieve satisfaction and agreement on their roles and responsibilities. Finally, recognizing that some problems, like alcoholism, are difficult to treat effectively may encourage some people to take action sooner. For example, if a prospective spouse has a drinking problem or is abusive, perhaps marriage should be postponed until this problem has been addressed through counseling or some other means. Unfortunately, couples seeking help typically wait 6 years from the time marital problems surface before seeking professional advice and, by then, the anger and hurt are often too deep to allow resolution. Furthermore, studies show that 5 to 25 percent of divorcing

couples did not seek any kind of counseling (reported in Barnes, 1998).

THE IMPACT OF DIVORCE ON SPOUSES

The consequences of divorce are many and varied. Although some of these are experienced by both spouses, a number of factors are gender-specific. We will begin this section by looking at those issues that commonly affect both spouses, and then we will isolate those features of divorce that affect women and men in distinctly different ways.

Common Consequences of Divorce

Charles Dickens could just as easily have been talking about divorce and its aftermath as about eighteenth-century London and Paris when he wrote, "It was the best of times; it was the worst of times." For most divorcing couples, both statements are true. On the positive side, divorce can free people from unhappy, conflict-ridden, or unsatisfactory relationships; it can also be a means to achieving personal growth. On the negative side, however, divorce can produce considerable pain, guilt, and uncertainty. This duality is clearly visible in Cheryl Buehler and Mary Langenbrunner's (1987) research. They

Addiction places enormous strain on the relationship. The resulting problems are often very intense and affect every aspect of family life, from lack of money to emotional withdrawal and even violence. The path to recovery is rarely smooth or easy. Even with the assistance of all the support groups that are now available, the impact is often more than the marriage can bear. An affair can also have a devastating affect on a marriage. Not only is the present condition of the relationship in question; an affair touches the meaning of the entire relationship—past, present, and future. The deception, the shattering of trust, the questioning of the relationship, and the loss of hope for a future together are all difficult issues to manage.

Can Counseling "Save" a Marriage?

When a couple enters treatment, there are no guarantees about the outcome. Much depends on the strengths that each brings to the task. If, in therapy, each party is capable of observing her or his own behavior, if they speak directly to each other and not solely to the therapist, and if they refrain from placing the blame at their partner's feet, and if they have a lot invested in the marriage, such as children, a shared history, financial investments, or

friends, they have a good chance to work out their problems. These behaviors act as a cushion, absorbing the pain as well as providing the energy and support needed to resolve the problem. Also, couples need to have realistic expectations relative to the time it may take to resolve their issues without crying "divorce" when the road gets bumpy. They need to be willing to change their behaviors, to learn and practice new patterns of behavior as they relate to each other, and to sustain these changes after the therapy has ended. Some controlled studies of marital therapy outcomes have shown that only 50 percent of couples significantly improve their marriages, while 30 to 40 percent of those who do improve relapse within 2 years. This, in part, can be due to the fact that some couples enter therapy too late. Dysfunctional patterns have been ingrained and the hurt is too deep. Other factors also contribute to this low rate of success. Some therapists working with couples are not trained in marital therapy and many insurance policies do not cover marital therapy, or if they do, provide for too few sessions to make a difference.

When Couples Decide to Divorce, Can Counseling or Mediation Help Make the Process Easier?   When parties divorce,

they can become involved with three types of professionals: a lawyer, a mediator, and a therapist. Rather than dealing with the expense of two lawyers, which often creates an adversarial situation, couples often seek the services of a mediator. The mediator serves as a guide to the parties as they define the issues in dispute and negotiate an agreement that includes the division of marital property and finances and decisions regarding child custody arrangements. Therapy, on the other hand, can help a couple resolve the emotional issues that may block the efforts of the mediation process. Many mediators come from a therapy background, and the two areas may overlap. Having a third party involved in the dissolution of the marriage brings not only an objective point of view to the process, but it also provides a structure and sets limits that allow the couple a means for containing the anxiety and strong emotions that surround the situation. It also can prevent the children from becoming pawns in the process and ensure that their interests and well-being will be protected. In addition, today couples can find help by going to a variety of Web sites that provide lists of local and national self-help organizations, programs, workshops, and support services.

---

asked 80 divorced people whose divorces had been finalized 6 to 12 months earlier to identify which of 140 items they had experienced since they separated from their spouses. The results showed that divorced people are almost equally likely

TABLE 12.2	
Most Frequently Reported Experiences of Divorced Persons	
I have felt worthwhile as a person	96%
I have experienced personal growth and maturity	94%
I have felt relieved	92%
I have felt closer to my children	89%
I have felt competent	89%
The cost of maintaining the household has been difficult	87%
I have felt angry toward my former spouse	87%
I have felt insecure	86%
My leisure activities have increased	86%
I have been depressed	86%
Household routines and daily patterns have changed	85%

Source: Cheryl Buehler and Mary Langenbrunner, 1987, "Divorce-Related Stressors: Occurrence, Disruptiveness, and Area of Life Change." *Journal of Divorce and Remarriage* 11:35. Reprinted with permission of The Haworth Press, Inc., Binghamton, NY, 1987.

to report both positive and negative outcomes. The most frequently reported items appear in Table 12.2. Although this research is almost 20 years old, the results are still valid today. A recent study of 1147 people ages 40 to 79 who had divorced between the ages of 40 and 70 found they made similar assessments of their divorce experience (AARP, 2004).

Are you surprised to find that the most frequently occurring responses are positive? Many people are. However, this finding should not be interpreted to mean that the negative consequences are inconsequential. They are not. People in the process of divorce frequently encounter a number of problems. The most common problems experienced by both women and men are health problems (both physical and psychological), loneliness, the need for social and sexual readjustments, and financial changes in their lifestyles (AARP, 2004; Amato, 2000). This latter problem is more common to women than to men, so we will consider it later under gender-specific problems.

Health Problems   Many people experience depression and sometimes despair in the wake of a divorce. The process of divorce involves a number of major lifestyle alterations: loss of a major source of intimacy, the end of a set of daily routines, and a changed social status—going from a socially approved category (married) to a still somewhat disapproved category (divorced). Based on her research with 104 separated and divorced respondents (52 women and 52 men), sociologist Naomi Gerstel (1990) found that the stigma of divorce has not completely disappeared. Gerstel argues that although divorce is now less deviant in a statistical sense than it was in the past, and although the divorced are no longer categorized as sinful, criminal, or even wrong, the divorced still believe they are the targets of informal relational sanctions—they are excluded from social events, blamed for the marital breakup, and sometimes held in low regard. These feelings are especially true among members of various immigrant groups for whom a divorce is still seen as losing face for the whole family. A college student whose family is from India and whose parents divorced after a 24-year marriage said at a conference on Indian divorce stigmas, "Some people might think it's selfish. Marriage is a holy institution. Marriage is highly regarded, and to break that is taboo in itself" (Qamruzzaman, 2006:1). Hence, many divorced people respond to their new status with feelings of stress, guilt (especially for the initiator of divorce), and failure (especially for the partner who was asked for the divorce). Compared with their married peers, divorced people exhibit lower levels of psychological well-being, greater risk of mortality, more negative life events, greater levels of alcohol use, and lower levels of happiness and self-acceptance (Amato, 2000).

Loneliness   Although people who live alone are not inherently more lonely than people who live together, a period of loneliness often accompanies the transition from being a part of a couple to being single again. This is especially true for childless couples and older couples whose children have already left home. However, divorce can involve more than the loss of a spouse. Relationships with former in-laws can be strained or broken off completely. Ann-Marie Ambert (1988) studied 49 separated and divorced spouses and found that only 11 percent of the respondents maintained positive relationships with their former in-laws after the separation. Conversely, blood relatives might choose to retain contact with the ex-spouse even against the wishes of their own kin. The latter pattern often creates social distance among family members.

Social and Sexual Readjustments   Feelings of isolation and loneliness can lead to physical and psychological problems. Thus, divorced people are well advised to maintain old friends and companions or to seek new ones to offset the possible losses in their support network and to restore their self-esteem. In this regard, one of the major adjustments divorced people face is getting back into circulation. Dating is not easy at any age, but it is particularly problematic for older divorced people.

Newly dating divorced people must deal with two key issues: how to explain their unmarried status and whether to be sexually active. Divorce does not lessen social or sexual needs. Studies from Alfred Kinsey, Wardell Pomeroy, and Clyde Martin (1948) through those of today show that most divorced people have sex within 1 year of being separated from their partner. Besides filling a physical need, providing intimacy, and exploring a new-found freedom, sex is often

used to validate a sense of self-worth that may have been seriously eroded during the divorce process. Both women and men need to know that others find them attractive and sexually desirable. Some need to test their sexual adequacy, especially if their performance was criticized by their previous spouse.

These needs are not always adequately met, however. Sexual encounters are not always satisfying. Women in particular often feel exploited by men who assume that because they are divorced, they will automatically welcome any casual sexual relationship. Although both divorced women and men are sexually active, overall men have more sexual partners than do women.

Gender Differences in Divorce

As discussed in Chapter 3, the U.S. sex/gender system structures women's and men's marital and family experiences in markedly different ways. In her study titled *The Future of Marriage*, Jessie Bernard (1972) observed that every marital relationship contains two marriages that are often widely divergent. She called these "his" and "her" marriages. The same social structures and gender expectations that create differential marriage experiences for women and men also act to create differential divorces. These can be described as "her divorce" and "his divorce."

"Her" Divorce   The most striking, even startling, difference between women and men following a divorce is a monetary one. Media headlines about the divorce settlements of the rich and famous, like Donald Trump, suggest that women are the recipients of huge alimony payments. Volumes of research over the last two decades reveal a markedly different pattern, however. The standard of living for children and their custodial parents (predominantly women) drops sharply after a divorce.

Downward Social Mobility   In a pioneering study of the economic impact of California's no-fault divorce law (discussed earlier in this chapter) on divorcing spouses, sociologist Lenore Weitzman found a larger discrepancy. Weitzman analyzed 2500 California court records covering a 10-year period, some before and some after the enactment of the law. She found that within a year of the final divorce decree the standard of living of women and their children declined by an average of 73 percent, whereas that of ex-husbands improved by an average of 42 percent (Weitzman, 1985:339). Other researchers have arrived at somewhat different numbers, but the general pattern they found is the same: downward social mobility for women and children, often to the point of impoverishment (Peterson, 1996; Raymond, 2001). This pattern holds across all racial–ethnic groups and can extend for long periods of time. A recent study found that 6 or more years after divorce, the family income of the average child whose custody parent remains unmarried is 45 percent lower than it would have been in the absence of a divorce (Page and Stevens, 2004).

Women and children do not fare much better in other countries. British wives, who initiate 75 percent of divorces in their country, face similar financial difficulties. A longitu-

TABLE 12.3

Child Support Awarded and Received, 2002

	%	Average Amount Due	Average Amount Received	% Receiving Full Amount	% Receiving Any Amount
Custodial Mothers	63.0	$5138	$3192	45.4	74.7
Custodial Fathers	38.6	4221	2881	39.0	67.4

Source: Adapted from T. Grall, 2003, *Custodial Mothers and Fathers and Their Child Support: 2001.* Current Population Reports, P60-225. (Washington, DC: U.S. Census Bureau).

dinal study over a 10-year period found that men's disposable income increased by 15 percent while women and their children experienced a 28 percent drop. Less than half of the fathers pay the full child support that was awarded and nearly one-third will pay nothing at all (Sarler, 2000). Similar patterns were also found in Scotland and Wales (Hill, 2000). In Australia, even after 12 years of improved payment of child support, 44 percent of divorced mothers and their children were below the poverty line while men were better off or just as well off as before their divorce (Horin, 2000).

The decline in living standard following a divorce may push older women into poverty as well. In 1960, only 1.5 percent of older women and 1.6 percent of older men were divorced. By 2003, 8.6 percent of older women and 7 percent of older men were divorced and had stayed single (U.S. Census Bureau, 2006). With first marriages lasting an average of 8 years (Krieder, 2005), the number of women who do not meet the 10-year marriage requirement that allows them to share in their husband's pension is increasing. Thus, it is expected that the proportion of economically vulnerable elderly women will increase when baby boomers retire. Divorced elderly women face a 20.4 percent poverty rate as compared to 4.3 percent for married women (Anzick and Weaver, 2001).

Overall, this downward mobility for women and children is explained by two key factors: the earnings gap between women and men (see Chapter 10) and the failure of courts to award—and ex-husbands to pay—alimony and child support.

The Legal System and Women's Financial Well-Being According to sociologists Frank Furstenberg and Andrew Cherlin (1991:48–49), "When marriages dissolve, the shift in family responsibilities and family resources assumes a characteristic form. Women get the children and, accordingly, assume most of the economic responsibility for their support. Men become nonresidential parents and relinquish the principal responsibility for their support." These patterns are directly related to U.S. legal practices in granting alimony (also called "spousal support" or "spouse maintenance"), child custody, and child support.

The Census Bureau stopped reporting on alimony in 1992; thus, national statistics on alimony awards are scarce. According to one study, the courts routinely award alimony in only 15 percent of all divorce cases) and thereafter alimony is actually received in far fewer cases than the awards indicate (Hanna, 1996). Both women and men are eligible to receive alimony from their former spouses. In practice, however, because men are usually the higher earner, they are less likely to be awarded alimony.

Similar patterns exist in child support awards. In 2002, an estimated 13.4 million parents had custody of 21.5 million children under 21 years of age whose other parent lived somewhere else. Slightly over 84 percent of custodial parents were mothers and nearly 16 percent were fathers, figures largely unchanged since 1994. About 56 percent of custodial mothers were white, 27 percent were African Americans, and 15 percent were Latinas. The majority of custodial fathers (71 percent) were white, 15 percent were African Americans, and 11 percent were Latinos. However, only 7.9 million of these parents (59.1 percent) had some type of support agreement or award for their children. Custodial mothers were more likely than custodial fathers to be awarded child support, 63 to 39 percent (Grall, 2003). However, as Table 12.3 shows, awards and receiving them may be two different things. Custodial mothers were more likely to receive awards than were fathers; white custodial parents had significantly higher award rates than African Americans or Latinas. The awards, in and of themselves, were not large and the majority of custodial parents worked. Custodial mothers were more likely than their male counterparts to work part-time. And although the poverty level of custodial mothers declined over the last decade, it was still significantly higher than the rate of custodial fathers (25 to 15 percent). Additionally, working full-time, year-round was not enough to keep 7.8 percent of custodial parents out of poverty.

Why do you think so many parents (both mothers and fathers) fail to make child support payments? Although there are laws allowing states to withhold child support payments from the noncustodial parent's paycheck, compliance remains a problem. What do you think could be done to get more noncustodial parents to pay child support? Would you support legislation like that pending in Kansas that would deny a hunting or fishing license to a deadbeat parent? Many Internet sites now post photos of deadbeat parents. Do you think this is an effective technique to reach these parents? Explain.

Causes of Inequality between Divorced Women and Men What explains this economic discrepancy between divorced women and men? Weitzman (1985) attributes it to the provisions of the no-fault divorce laws, which require that husbands and wives be treated equally. In the abstract this sounds eminently fair. In reality, however, it overlooks the fact that women historically either were not in the labor force, or they received lower wages than did men if they were. Thus, simply dividing marital property equally without regard for the resources (professional degrees, skills) or the earning power of the respective spouses puts women at a real disadvantage vis-à-vis men. Women's advocates point out that by assuming responsibility for the majority of housework and child care, women sacrifice their own employment and earning power (see Chapter 10) and enhance that of their husband. Thus, these advocates argue that an equitable divorce settlement would take into account women's contributions to a husband's present and future earnings.

The Consequences of Divorce for Women What happens to women who experience this downward mobility? Many women, especially those in traditional marriages, suffer a loss of status, identity, and their domestic sphere—the home. Under the doctrine of equal division of property, homes are often sold so that both spouses can receive their share of the value of the house. The sale of the home often means moving out of a familiar and comfortable neighborhood into a smaller, less expensive place in a different neighborhood. Consequently, school, neighborhood, and friendship ties are often disrupted when they are most needed. Even when the house is not sold, financial strains may make maintenance and a comfortable style of living difficult.

Women with sole custody of children are often doubly burdened—they must be full-time parents as well as economic providers. In the process, they must watch their children do without many things that were taken for granted in

The economic aspects of a divorce can be quite daunting, often necessitating the sale of the family house. Having to relocate to another neighborhood can add to the trauma of divorce for family members, especially for children.

the past. As the sole parent, divorced women may find little time for themselves or for social activities with peers. All of this exacts a toll and many women lose a sense of the future and feel trapped by their economic circumstances.

Despite their economic stress, evidence suggests that women fare better in terms of divorce adjustment than do men. According to Judith Wallerstein (1986), women improve the emotional and psychological quality of their lives more than do men. For example, women are more likely than men to experience a sense of growth in self-esteem after a divorce (Baruch, Barnett, and Rivers, 1983). One explanation for women's and men's differing reactions may be that as women take on more instrumental roles, for example, becoming the sole provider and family head, they feel more confident about their abilities. Such changes were expressed by a female respondent: "I'm learning how to do things. . . . There's no mystery about it now, I can get out an electric drill . . . . I got satisfaction from putting a bookcase together" (quoted in Riessman, 1990:168). Men, on the other hand, lose some of those roles. The roles they add, such as housekeeper and cook, are not highly valued in this society, and hence adoption of these roles does not generally increase self-esteem (Gecas and Schwalbe, 1983).

"His" Divorce On the basis of a growing body of literature, it does appear that men are better off economically after a divorce than are women. This is a result of many factors. Traditionally, society has placed greater value on male workers and therefore paid them higher wages. Even when men pay child support, these payments often represent only a relatively small amount of their take-home pay. A combination of anger, emotional pain, irresponsibility, other debts, ongoing conflict with the former spouse, and remarriage often leads to noncompliance with court-ordered child support. Legal efforts to enforce compliance are often plagued by heavy caseloads, inadequate budgets, a shortage of personnel, and, until quite recently, a societal indifference to the plight of divorced women and children. Thus, a divorced husband typically has more discretionary income to support himself than his ex-wife has to support both herself and their children. Despite this finding, many divorced men feel they have been victimized by the divorce process and the aftermath of divorce (Arendell, 1995; Lehr and MacMillan, 2001).

As we saw earlier, divorced people suffer more health problems and are more depressed than people who are married. In fact, divorce can be lethal, especially for men. An analysis of U.S. mortality data found that divorced men are two and one-half times more likely to commit suicide than married men. Divorced white men and older men are the most vulnerable (Kposowa, 2000). Several factors are likely to contribute to this pattern. First, given that women tend to initiate divorce, men may feel more responsible for the breakup and/or were unprepared for it. Research suggests that the spouse who is left suffers more, at least initially (Sweeney, 2002). Second, because women are more likely to get custody of the children, men lose not only the husband role but a day-to-day father role as well. Third, norms of masculinity preclude many men from building effective social support networks that could help them during and after a divorce.

Although the number of single-parent fathers has increased slightly, divorced men typically do not have custody of their children. Therefore, whether men desire it or not, divorce frees them from child care. Because they have more discretionary money, they are freer than their ex-wives to pursue social and leisure activities. Men's opportunities for remarriage are also greater than women's. Unencumbered by children, they are freer to date and to begin new relationships. As we will see in the next chapter, men remarry at higher rates and more quickly than do women.

Dating for divorced men is not problem free, however. Divorced men may feel uncomfortable in this new role and may hold back because of a fear of rejection. They confront other problems, too. One man explains these problems this way: "The relationships are shallow, let's put it that way. They're not long-range. I don't know how to put it to you. If you just get into bed with someone (names women), I suppose it satisfies your basic needs, let's put it that way. But it's not meaningful. That's the best way to explain it. So, in a sense you have your freedom. You can play the field, you're on the circuit, on the tour, as we call it. But I find that they're basically shallow. So I guess your freedom is basically shallow, as far as that goes" (quoted in Riessman, 1990:193). Many divorced men, especially those from traditional marriages, have trouble establishing a satisfying home environment and maintaining a household routine on their own. Because this was considered a wife's domain, many ex-husbands feel overwhelmed by shopping, laundry, cleaning, and cooking.

Although loneliness can be a problem for both women and men, divorced fathers without custody may feel it more intensely. Even with visitation rights, they miss out on the day-to-day contact with their children and may miss the ritual of family celebrations of special events and holidays. Dennis Meredith (1985) reports that some noncustodial fathers exhibit a child-absence syndrome, feeling depressed, anxious, and cut off from their children's lives. For some divorced fathers, this triggers negative reactions. Visits with their children become more sporadic or stop completely, or the fathers become psychologically distant from their children (Amato and Booth, 1996; Weissbourd, 1994). According to a recent study, 42 percent of the male respondents, compared to 15 percent of the female respondents, said their worst fears after the divorce was that they would lose contact with their children (AARP, 2004). Their fears seem well founded. In one study, researchers found that, on average, nonresidential fathers see their children only four times per month following divorce and about 20 percent of children have no contact with their fathers 2 to 3 years after the divorce. Nonresidential mothers, on the other hand, visit their children more frequently and are less likely to stop contact with them (Kelly and Emery, 2003). This is a critical issue because when fathers do not maintain contact with children, they are less likely to pay child support (Maldonado, 2005).

Divorce also has a negative effect on men's contact with their adult children and on their perceptions of their children as potential sources of support. When men relinquish ties to their children during childhood, even when they have provided child support, rarely do they resume those ties later in life (Furstenberg, Hoffman, and Shrestha, 1995).

For example, in one study, over 30 percent of middle-aged divorced fathers had lost contact with one or more of their adult children, a situation almost nonexistent for never-divorced men (Cooney and Uhlenberg, 1990). Ninety percent of the never-divorced older fathers had weekly contact with at least one of their adult children; this was true for only one-third of the divorced fathers. A similar pattern exists for fathers who divorce later in life. Over 20 percent of today's divorces involve couples married more than 15 years (Cooney, Hutchinson, and Leather, 1995). One study of adult children whose parents had recently divorced after many years of marriage found that they had less intimate and more distant relations with their fathers than their peers from nondivorced families (Cooney, 1994). Overall, the evidence suggests that divorced fathers are at greater risk for problematic relations with offspring regardless of the child's age. These studies raise questions about the degree to which family ties exist for divorced men as they age.

In sum, although men appear to benefit more than women do from divorce, particularly economically, they also experience dislocation from the breakup. Social policy must address divorced men's concerns as well as those of divorced women.

Recovering from Divorce

Given that the majority of divorcing couples face serious economic, social, and psychological problems, you may well wonder whether people ever recover from the trauma of divorce. Most do, although the process usually takes several years. For example, a study conducted over a period of 10 years by Judy Wallerstein and Sandra Blakeslee (1989) of 60 families disrupted by divorce found that women take an average of 3 to 3.5 years and men 2 to 2.5 years to reestablish a sense of external order after the separation. Not everyone recovers at the same speed, however. Wallerstein and Blakeslee found that some of their respondents had not recovered 15 years after their divorce. However, a more recent study found a gradual recovery usually begins by the end of the second year; 6 years after divorcing, 80 percent of both genders have moved on to build reasonably or exceptionally fulfilling lives (Hetherington, 2002). Similarly, a study of people who divorced at midlife or later found that three out of four respondents (75 percent) said they made the right decision and used words like freedom, self-identity, and fulfillment to describe their current situation (AARP, 2004).

Why do some people adjust more quickly than others? Do certain characteristics enable some people to cope with divorce problems more effectively than other people? An emerging body of research has begun to identify certain factors that affect people's ability to adjust to divorce. Robert Lauer and Jeanette Lauer (1988) found that those who successfully coped with their divorce were able to redefine the divorce as an opportunity for growth. They did things like going back to school, building new social networks, becoming involved in community affairs, and learning to be more effective parents (Hetherington, 2002). Both women and men, but especially women, talked about gaining greater self-esteem and developing new competencies. Jane Burroughs, who married at 19 and divorced after more than

30 years of marriage, said, "After getting my divorce it was like going back and doing things I should have done when I was a teenager. I learned how to look within myself for happiness. It's a new experience, and I have found that I do it quite well" (quoted in Enright, 2004). Other research suggests that women and men who are nontraditional in their gender orientation adjust better and more quickly to a marital breakdown. The explanation for this is that androgynous women and men have better coping skills with which to handle the trauma of divorce than do women and men who behave according to traditional gender role expectations (Chiriboga and Thurnher, 1980; Hansson et al., 1984). This latter point has major implications for how we socialize children to prepare them for adult roles.

THE IMPACT OF DIVORCE ON CHILDREN

With the relatively high divorce rate over the last three decades, more and more children have been drawn into the process. Writing in 1985, Sandra Hofferth estimated that nine out of ten African American children and seven out of ten white children (and most likely growing numbers of Native American and Asian American children) would spend part of their childhood in a single-parent household, mainly because of divorce and births to unmarried mothers. In 2004, 28 percent of all children under 18 lived with only one parent, up from 12 percent in 1970. Nearly 22 percent of white children, 56 percent of African American children, and 31 percent of Latina/o children lived in one-parent families (U.S. Census Bureau, 2006).

Some social theorists and many public and religious leaders argue that the intact, two-parent family is necessary for the normal development and well-being of children. Thus, divorce is assumed to be contradictory to these ends. This view is most evident in structural-functional, social-learning, developmental, and symbolic-interaction theories (see Chapter 2), all of which see the family as one of the primary agents of socialization and role modeling for children. However, these theoretical perspectives ignore the fact that the effects of disrupted families on children might be short-lived, that the role of an absent parent might be filled by significant others (as was the case in much of human history), that the custodial parent might be warm and supportive, or that parental separation may be better for children than remaining in a conflict-ridden family (Ahrons, 2004; Campbell, 2001; Kelly, 2000).

Short-Term versus Long-Term Effects of Divorce on Children

There is an extensive body of literature on the effects of divorce on children. For the most part, there is agreement about the short-term effects of divorce, some of which resemble those experienced by divorcing parents: rejection, anger, denial, sadness, despair, and grief (Kelly and Emery, 2003). Children frequently feel guilty, blaming themselves for the divorce, especially if their parents have quarreled over them. Children often entertain fantasies about reuniting their parents.

A child's reaction to divorce can be similar to that of divorcing parents—it often includes feelings of denial, anger, sadness, rejection, despair, grief, and loneliness.

Just as with adults, these stresses can result in health problems, both psychological and physical. Research shows that the physical health ratings of children from divorced families are poorer than those of children from intact families (Amato, 2000). Children living with their mothers are more likely to lack health insurance, making timely and quality health care problematic. Children with divorced parents see themselves as less competent and exhibit more depression and withdrawal than children from intact families (Najman et al., 1997). The duration and intensity of these feelings depend in some measure on parental behavior. If parental conflict continues after the divorce, the adjustment process for children may be prolonged.

In contrast, many of the findings of long-term effects on children are not as clear-cut or consistent. On the one hand, some researchers like Judith Wallerstein and her colleagues (2000) conclude that the effects of divorce are long-lasting and interfere with normal social-emotional development. Twenty-five years after her 1971 study of 131 children whose parents divorced, Wallerstein interviewed 93 of the original subjects, now 33 years old on average. She found that in comparison to a control group of 44 adults similar in age and socioeconomic status but whose parents had not divorced, the adult children of divorced parents experienced greater anxieties and more failures in their interpersonal relationships. More recently, Elizabeth Marquardt (2005) drew a similar conclusion based on her study of adults whose parents divorced when they were children. On the other hand, sociologists like Andrew Cherlin (2000) have cautioned against reading too much into long-term effects without a knowledge of the state of the parental home prior to the divorce. He points out that 50 percent of the fathers and close to half of the mothers in Wallerstein's study suffered from serious mental or addiction problems. Thus, it is possible that these adults would have had the same or similar problems even if their parents had not divorced. Other researchers have come to similar conclusions, noting that many of the estimated effects of divorce are not as strong as some researchers claim (Amato, 2003). According to psychologist Robert Emery (2004) the vast majority of children from divorced families are indistinguishable from children whose parents remain married.

The fact that a number of longitudinal studies of children found that as many as half of the behavioral and academic problems of children in marriages whose parents later divorced were observed 4 to 12 years before the separation suggests that troubled families and not divorce, per se, may be more responsible for long-term negative effects (Cherlin, 2000; Kelly, 2000). Similarly, other research has found that marital conflict is a more important predictor of children's problems than is divorce itself (Buehler et al., 1998). Further, symptoms commonly found in children of divorced parents (low self-esteem, depression, and school and behavioral problems) also are more often found in children of high-conflict marriages than in children of low-conflict marriages (Vandewater and Lansford, 1998).

Stephanie Coontz (1997) reminds us that although some children of divorced parents do have problems, the majority do not experience severe or long-term problems. Andrew Cherlin (1992) believes that children, by and large, regain psychological equilibrium 1 or 2 years after the divorce and then continue on a "normal pattern of growth and development." It may be that children's age at the time of divorce has an impact on the degree to which they experience disruption in their lives. The lives of younger children may remain more stable than those of older children, who may be more aware of changes in their family's economic and social status. Cross-sectional studies limited to comparisons of differences between children from disrupted homes and those in intact families, with no control for variables of changed economic status or quality of family relationships before the divorce, are not conducive to sorting out short-term versus long-term effects. Accurate assessments of the long-term impact of divorce require more study and more precise control for the complex variables that promote or hinder growth in children's lives.

How Does Divorce Affect Children's Behavior?

Researchers report that children of divorce are absent from school more, do poorer schoolwork, are more likely to use alcohol, cigarettes, marijuana, and other drugs, and have a greater risk of dropping out of school and experiencing a premarital pregnancy than children from intact families (Coleman, Ganong, and Fine, 2000; Crowder and Teachman, 2004). College attendance is also affected by divorce. A government study found that 71 percent of the children from intact families went to college, compared with 54 percent of those whose parents were divorced (Mathews, 1996).

Again, however, these findings must be interpreted cautiously. It is estimated that the declining economic status of disrupted households accounts for as much as half of the adjustment problems found in children of divorced parents (McLanahan, 1999).

Gender and Divorce

While earlier studies found that within divorced families boys had more behavioral problems and had more difficulty adjusting to divorce than girls (Demo and Acock, 1988, 1991), other studies did not find gender differences specifically linked to divorce (Hetherington, 1999; Vandewater and Lansford, 1998). In the population at large, school problems, run-ins with the police, and aggressive behaviors have been found to be more common among boys than girls regardless of family structure. Additionally, some of the general and assumed gender-specific problems attributed to divorce may instead be a result in a decrease in parental supervision (McLanahan, 1999). For example, when divorced fathers are more involved with their children, the children do better academically and have fewer school problems than children with less involved fathers; there are no significant differences in performance and achievement between them and children in intact families (Nord, Brimhall, and West, 1997). These findings have important implications for divorcing parents: When ex-spouses provide appropriate supervision and emotional support to their children, their children are more likely to adjust better and more quickly after the parental divorce (Emery, 2004).

Not all research on the effects of divorce has found negative effects. In female-headed families, both mothers and children develop more androgynous behavior as they reorganize the household after the father has left. Additionally, assuming more responsibilities leads children to greater maturity and feelings of competence (Gately and Schwebel, 1992). Finally, of course, children may feel relief to be out of a conflictual and possibly abusive family situation. A study of 330 undergraduates at a large southeastern university found that almost a third (32.9 percent) reported a positive effect of their parents divorce (Knox, Zusman, and DeCuzzi, 2004). Children living in a stable single-parent family are emotionally better off than if they remain in a conflict-ridden two-parent family (Kelly, 2000).

Children and Divorce in Other Countries

To date, most of the research on the effects of divorce on children has been conducted in the United States and other English-speaking countries, where the findings have been fairly consistent. However, in countries like China, divorce has traditionally been condemned and those who divorce are stigmatized. As globalization has increased, especially in countries where women's roles are changing, divorce tends to be increasing as well. Whether children in countries with diverse cultural and economic patterns will respond to parental divorce in the same way as children in Western countries is an intriguing empirical question and one that leaders in those countries must address if they are to be prepared to meet the needs of their newly divorced families.

Although there has been relatively little cross-cultural research on this topic, it does seem that there is at least some initial support for the belief that findings from the United States may be generalizable to other cultures. Researchers have found that Chinese children of divorced parents, like their U.S. counterparts, are more likely to be aggressive, to be withdrawn, and to have more behavioral and social problems than children from intact families. Also, divorced parents report more mental and physical health problems for their children than do nondivorced parents (Liu, Guo, and Okawa, 2000). Further support that there are at least some universal factors that affect children's reactions to family conflict and divorce comes from Croatian researchers (Cudina and Obradovic, 2001). However, these two studies also suggest that there are culture-specific factors that also affect divorce outcomes. Additional research in a variety of cultures and economic settings will help clarify our understandings of the process and effects of divorce.

CHANGING PATTERNS IN CHILD CUSTODY

In any marital disruption involving children, a question that must be resolved is, "Who gets the children?" We examine this difficult question by focusing specifically on the issues of sole custody, joint custody, and visitation rights.

Sole Custody

In divorce cases, for much of U.S. history, courts have almost always awarded **sole custody,** in which one parent is given legal responsibility for raising the child. Earlier we noted that in colonial America, fathers were far more likely to get custody of their children following a divorce. Over the years a cultural belief evolved that women are inherently better at nurturing than are men. The courts adopted the view that children, especially in their early years, need to be with their mothers. So entrenched did this view become by the mid-twentieth century that the only way a father could get custody was to prove his wife an unfit mother (Greif, 1985). Since then, however, a noticeable shift has occurred in child custody cases. Although most fathers still do not request custody, today those who do so have a good chance of being successful. According to the U.S. Census Bureau (2005), fathers have sole custody in 9 to 12 percent of single parent families. Research shows that fathers increased their odds of receiving sole custody when they were the plaintiffs and when a friend of the court investigation was undertaken. Thus, fathers often have to exert extra legal efforts to strengthen their claims. The odds of fathers gaining custody are enhanced when they pay child support, when the children are older, and when the oldest child is male (Fox and Kelly, 1995). According to the U.S. Census Bureau, there are 2.2 million mothers who lack custody of their children (National Association on Non-Custodial Moms, Inc., 2006). Some of these mothers have voluntarily relinquished custody. Given the traditional view of women as nurturers and homemakers, women who agree to give custody to the father frequently are portrayed as unloving, uncaring, selfish, and unwomanly. In her research, Catalina Herrerias (1995) found that these negative images have little to do with the woman's actual reasons for giving up custody: inadequate finances, child's preference for living with father, difficulty in controlling children, threats of legal custody fights, and physical or emotional problems experienced by the woman. Although these women did not have custody, 97 percent actively maintained a relationship with their children; 71 percent described their relationships as close and caring.

Not all women who lose custody do so voluntarily. In one study of over 500 noncustodial mothers, almost 10 percent reported losing their children in a court battle or relinquishing custody to avoid conflict (Greif and Pabst, 1988:88). Women's groups have expressed concern that some of these decisions could set precedents that would weaken women's chances for gaining custody. They point to cases in which the judge's decision was based primarily on the father's better financial position (Max, 1985). Using financial means as a criterion for child custody puts women at a real disadvantage because in the vast majority of cases fathers are better off economically.

Money is not the only issue over which custody battles are fought or decided. The sexual orientation of a parent is also an issue. In the past, lesbian and gay parents' custody of their children was often challenged and threatened solely because of their sexual orientation. A 1995 decision in a child custody case in Tallahassee, Florida, is an especially eye-opening example of the prejudice and discrimination lesbians and gays faced, and sometimes still do, in child custody cases. In this case, a Florida judge took an 11-year-old girl from her mother simply because the mother was a lesbian and awarded custody to the father, a convicted murderer and accused child molester. A judge in Illinois, relying on allegations of lesbianism, denied the mother's request for custody and ordered that the mother not visit with her daughter in the presence of any woman with whom she may happen to be living.

Such judicial decisions were often based on the mistaken belief that children raised in a lesbian or gay household would "naturally" adopt a gay or lesbian lifestyle or that they would suffer some psychological harm. As we saw in Chapter 9, such beliefs are contradicted by research findings that children raised by lesbian and gay parents have no significant psychological damage nor proclivity to be homosexuals themselves. These attitudes are changing and today most state courts require evidence of adverse impact before a parent's sexual orientation or involvement in a nonmarital relationship can be used to limit custody or visitation rights. This adverse impact test, also referred to as the *nexus test*, requires a clear connection between a parent's actions and harm to the child before a parent's sexual orientation can assume any relevance in the custody determination (National Center for Lesbian Rights, 2002). Nonetheless, these times of struggles are not over. As we shall see in Chapter 15, some states are gearing up to restrict the rights of lesbians and gays to adopt children. At the same time, however, a California court has expanded same-sex parents' rights in three separate cases, effectively saying that same-sex partners could both be the legal parents of a child born through assisted reproduction. Justice Joyce Kennard ruled "being a legal parent brings with it the benefits as well as the responsibilities" as she ordered a former partner to pay child support (Liptak, 2005).

Joint Custody

Spurred in part by fathers' rights advocates, who argued that the legal system discriminated against them, California passed the country's first joint-custody law in 1979. Currently, the vast majority of states allow for some form of joint custody. **Joint custody** means that both parents are involved in child rearing and decision making. Joint custody

In recent years, increasing public attention has focused on the high rate of divorce in the United States, particularly with respect to how divorce affects children. This young boy indicates his displeasure with the process by sticking out his tongue at his father during a custody hearing. Reprinted with permission of the Daily Breeze © 2002

can take two forms: joint legal custody, in which both parents are to share decision making on such issues as education and health care, and joint physical custody, an arrangement in which children spend from one-third to one-half of their time with each parent. The increased role of fathers in child rearing has led to some creative joint-custody living arrangements, one form of which is known as *bird-nesting*. Here the children stay in the family home and the parents alternate living there, with each parent having another place to stay on their off time (Navarro, 2005). However, full joint custody in this latter sense is still relatively rare. In practice, most joint custody involves shared legal custody, with physical custody remaining with one parent, usually the mother. In that sense, joint custody varies little from sole custody except for the assumption that decisions about the children's welfare will be made by both parents (Glendon, 1987). About 18 percent of total custody cases presently involve joint custody (U.S. Census Bureau, 2005).

Which Is Better, Sole or Joint Custody?

Before we can answer this question, we need to ask, "Better for whom and under what conditions?" Our focus here will be on children. It is not that the needs of parents do not matter, but they are likely to be quite different from their children's in this regard. If children had a good relationship with both parents before the divorce, they probably want regular contact with both parents to continue. The divorcing parents, on the other hand, may wish to avoid contact with their former spouse.

Earlier we examined the impact of divorce on children and found that raising a child as a single parent is extremely difficult. All things being equal, the evidence suggests that being raised in a loving, intact family provides the most beneficial arrangement for children. Thus, the motives behind the movement to increase joint custody are to provide children with continuing contact with both parents and to relieve one parent of the total burden of child care. A recent study comparing child adjustment in intact families with that in joint physical or joint legal custody and sole-custody settings indicate that some of these benefits are being realized. Children in

joint-custody arrangements had less behavioral and emotional problems, had higher self-esteem, and had better family relations and school performance than children in sole-custody arrangements. In addition, these children were as well-adjusted as intact family children on the same measures, most likely because joint custody provides the child with an opportunity for continuing contact with both parents (Bauserman, 2002). Other research found that there was a higher compliance rate of paying child support in cases of joint custody compared to cases of solo custody (Grall, 2000). In addition, fathers with joint custody were more likely than fathers without joint custody to have at least weekly contact with their children, including overnight visits (Selzer, 1998). However, other earlier studies have found that outside the regular child support payments, there were few differences in adjustment between children in sole versus joint physical custody (Johnston, 1995; Pruett and Hoganbruen, 1998).

Because joint custody is relatively new, an evaluation of its effectiveness in minimizing the adjustment problems of children over time is still open to debate. Some experts, like Mary Ann Mason (1999), a professor of law and social welfare and author of *The Custody Wars*, are critical of the joint custody trend. Mason argues that the push for joint custody grew more out of a concern for the rights of parents, particularly fathers, rather than out of a concern for children's rights. Based on her years of experience practicing family law and her extensive research, she concludes that joint custody rarely works because it requires parents to cooperate, which she believes is more than most divorced couples can manage. Although Mason concedes it would be difficult to achieve, she would like to see the court assess objectively which parent, regardless of gender, is "primary" in terms of both caregiving and emotional attachment.

Joint custody is not for everyone. It works successfully only in cases where divorcing couples have a fairly amicable relationship and desire a pattern of shared parenting. In the absence of these two characteristics, joint custody may simply perpetuate the conflict that led to the divorce in the first place. All too often children have little or no voice in how custody decisions are reached. This may change, however, in light of a recent court cases. Juvenile court judge Thomas

Kirk granted 12-year-old Gregory Kingsley's request that the parental rights of his natural mother be terminated, thus allowing the boy's foster parents to adopt him. This ruling is believed to be the first time in which parental rights were ended based on a legal suit brought by a minor. Judge Kirk based his ruling on what he deemed the best interests of the child. Gregory's mother, an unemployed waitress, had given him up for foster care three times because of economic difficulties. Gregory testified that he had lived with his mother for only 7 months in the last 8 years and that for almost 2 years while he was in foster care his mother never visited, called, or wrote him. More recently, 17-year-old Olympic gymnast Dominique Moceanu filed suit in a Texas court to be declared a legal adult, claiming that her parents drove her to succeed and then squandered her earnings. Dominique won her case. These cases will likely set a precedent for giving children legal standing in their own right in cases where there is a clear pattern of abuse and neglect, rather than relying on adults to initiate cases for them.

Regardless of the form custody takes, provisions for visitation of the other parent must be agreed on. Noncustodial parents with visitation rights enter into a new set of interactions with their children. Often both the parent and the child are uncertain how to behave in this situation; thus, visitation itself becomes a source of stress. Logistics are a problem, too: Where to go? What to do? Whom to include? Often the spontaneity of parent–child relationships is transferred to a recreational relationship, with the time together being spent in a constant round of activities, for example, going to the movies or the zoo. Noncustodial fathers who engage in this pattern are referred to as "Disneyland dads."

Parents and children often perceive the visits in different ways. Parents may think that by engaging in recreational activities they are being loving, whereas children may feel rejected because the relationship seems artificial and as such does little to enhance children's sense of well-being (Stewart, 2003). Thus, in the best of circumstances problems can occur with visitation. The visits can become a source of real stress, especially in the period immediately after a divorce if parents have not worked through their own feelings. Visitation can then become a battleground through which ex-spouses carry on their conflict with each other. This takes many forms: The noncustodial parent often overindulges the children to look good in their eyes; both parents may grill the children about the other parent's new lifestyle or speak ill of the other parent; one or both parents may consistently violate the spirit of the visitation agreement by changing plans at the last minute, not having the children ready on time, or bringing them back late. Child experts agree that such behaviors have a negative impact on children. Parents are more likely to avoid these behaviors if they reflect on the rights of children caught up in divorce situations as they have been identified by the judicial system. All children have the following rights:

- To have a continuing relationship with both parents
- To be treated not as a piece of property, but as a human being with unique feelings, ideas, and desires
- To receive continuing care and proper guidance from each parent

When children are involved, divorcing couples must negotiate visitation rights for the noncustodial parent. If parents can cooperate with each other in this regard, children are less likely to feel caught in the middle and can benefit from a relationship with both of their parents.

- To not be unduly influenced by either parent to view the other parent negatively
- To freely express love, friendship, and respect for both parents, without feeling shame or a necessity to hide those emotions
- To be given an explanation that the parents' divorce was in no way caused by the child's actions
- To not be the subject and/or source of any arguments.

Colorado legislators passed a bill with these rights in mind. The legislation changed the terminology from "custody" to "parental responsibilities" to remove the psychological barrier often associated with being the noncustodial parent. The law also requires parents to file a court-approved parenting plan as a piece of the final separation agreement. Other states are considering similar legislation in an attempt to find ways to reduce conflict between the divorcing parents and to put the needs of children first (Graber, 1999).

Noncustodial parents are not the only ones concerned about visitation rights. Grandparents can play an important role in helping their grandchildren adjust to a divorce. Grandparents symbolize stability and continuity. Because of the acrimony of some divorces or the geographic relocation of the custodial parent, however, grandparents may be unable to fulfill this role. Studies have revealed certain trends in relationships between grandparents and grandchildren following divorce. In general, the custodial grandparents (parents of the custodial parent) have an advantage in maintaining ties with their grandchildren. Andrew Cherlin and Frank Furstenberg (1986a) found that several years after the divorce, 58 percent of noncustodial grandparents saw their grandchildren less frequently than before the divorce, compared with only 37 percent of custodial grandparents. Because women are more likely to receive custody, relationships between maternal grandparents and grandchildren tend to be maintained and even strengthened, whereas ties with paternal grandparents frequently are weakened.

Visitation rights are not the norm in all countries. In Japan, for example, joint custody is not legal. In the past, fathers got the children most of the time. Now that most women work and can support their children, mothers routinely get custody of their children. However, the usual pattern is that the other parent does not visit or is not allowed to visit her or his children. Although some parents engage in informal visitation, according to a 1997 survey, there was no contact with the noncustodial parent in nearly 40 percent of divorces and only minimal contact in another 18 percent. When Prime Minister Junichiro Koizumi and his wife divorced over 20 years ago, Koizumi got custody of their two sons, and his wife got custody of their as yet unborn son (Tolbert, 2001).

When Things Go Wrong: Family Abduction

It should be clear by now that process of divorce can involve ongoing conflict between the divorcing spouses. All too often children can end up in the middle of the fight. When this happens, a child might be abducted by a parent or other family member in an attempt to protect the child from abuse, to get back at the other parent, to gain control, or to use the child as a pawn in a divorce settlement. According to the U.S. Department of Justice (2002), **family abduction** is the taking or keeping of a child by a family member in violation of a custody order, a decree, or other legitimate custodial rights, where the taking or keeping involved some element of concealment, flight, or intent to deprive a lawful custodian indefinitely of custodial privileges. It is estimated that 350,000 children are victims of family abduction each year in the United States. Fathers are significantly more likely to abduct children than are mothers. Fortunately, in almost half of the cases the children were gone for less than one week. However, some children are taken out of the country, presenting political as well as legal difficulties in getting them back. This is especially the case when the abducting parent is a national of another country.

REACHING ACCORD: COUNSELING, COLLABORATIVE LAW, AND MEDIATION

Thus far, we have seen that divorce can cause a variety of problems, not only for the divorcing couple but also for their children, their extended family, and their friends. Because of the emotional content, most divorces can easily become bitter and acrimonious affairs, leaving deep emotional and psychological wounds. Therefore, a growing number of marriage counselors and other professionals have shifted some of their practice into **divorce counseling.** Essentially, their goal is to replace the adversarial and often destructive aspects that can accompany the legal divorce with a more cooperative spirit. At the same time, they try to help people withdraw and distance themselves from the relationship so that acceptance of the loss and subsequent healing can take place. When these goals are accomplished, people are better able to begin new relationships. Divorcing couples or individuals may seek such counseling during the process of the divorce or at a much later stage in their life. Some states, however, require **conciliation counseling** before the courts will consider granting a divorce. The purpose behind this kind of counseling is to see whether the marital problems can be resolved and the couple reconciled.

When reconciliation is not possible, couples often find themselves caught up in an adversarial divorce proceeding. Concerned by the destructive impact this causes, Stuart Webb, a prominent Minnesota divorce lawyer, instituted a practice called **collaborative law**—where the attorneys for both parties to a family dispute agree to assist in resolving the conflict using cooperative techniques rather than adversarial strategies and litigation with the goal of reaching an efficient, fair, and comprehensive out-of-court settlement of all issues. If the process fails and either party wishes to have the matter resolved in court, both attorneys withdraw and disqualify themselves from further representation except to assist in the orderly transfer of the case to adversarial counsel. In his first two years of collaborative practice, Webb handled 99 cases, reaching full settlement in all but 4 (Florence, 2000). Today, a large number of national, regional, and state collaborative law groups exist and there is now an International Academy of Collaborative Professionals.

Divorce mediation has a related but somewhat different emphasis. It is a procedure designed to help divorcing couples negotiate a fair and mutually agreed-on resolution of such issues as marital property distribution, child custody, visitation rights, and financial support. Divorce mediators generally have backgrounds in law, social work, counseling, or psychology. In any given divorce, one or more mediators may be involved. For example, divorce lawyers may work with counselors or therapists to help the couple reach accord. Some states actively encourage and even sponsor divorce mediation. Mediated settlements must be approved by the court to become legally binding on the parties involved.

Although divorce mediation is still relatively new, having emerged as a distinct practice only in the 1970s, evidence suggests that all parties benefit from the process (Hahn and Kleist, 2000). Couples can learn negotiating skills that will help them deal with each other in the future. Children do not see their parents embroiled in a constant struggle over them. Because the spouses have helped to forge the agreement based on their own needs and those of their family, they are more likely to adhere to the terms of the agreement, thereby reducing the likelihood of future conflicts (Grebe, 1986). Another key benefit appears to be that fathers stay more involved in their children's lives as a result of the experience of divorce mediation (Emery, 1995). This latter point is most likely the result of fathers feeling they have more of a say in the decisions concerning their children. Finally, mediated divorce agreements cost considerably less than adversarial divorces because less time and labor are required (Werland, 1999).

THE RENEWED DEBATE: SHOULD PARENTS STAY MARRIED FOR THE SAKE OF THEIR CHILDREN?

In recent years, findings from a number of studies have revived this question. As Paul Amato (2001) observed, before the 1970s, divorce was viewed as catastrophic for children who were said to be from "broken homes," and at risk for a wide range of behavioral and emotional problems. People in unhappy marriages were expected to do the right thing and stick it out for the sake of the children. Then along came the 1970s, opening an era characterized by an emphasis on personal choice and self-fulfillment. Staying in an unhappy marriage, especially one marked with conflict, was viewed as bad for children. It was assumed that if parents were happy, so, too, would the children be. The divorce rate climbed. This liberalizing period was followed by a new wave of conservatism and religious renewal. Concern for the perceived breakdown of the family began to and continues to dominate public discourse, and with it a renewed concern about the negative impact divorce can have on children and society at large.

Earlier we reviewed studies examining the impact of both short-term and long-term effects of divorce on children. We will not repeat those findings here except to note that the studies finding long-term effects of divorce on children are a critical part of the current debate. For example, in her well-publicized book, *Between Two Worlds: The Inner Lives of Children of Divorce*, Elizabeth Marquardt (2005) found significant differences between children who grew up in intact families and children who experienced their parents' divorce and who said they felt like they grew up in two families, not one. However, what seems to be at the core of this question is the finding that many divorces involve low-conflict marriages, even marriages in which spouses say they were happy but perhaps experiencing a midlife crisis, were not feeling self-actualized, were bored, or were looking for new experiences. Thus, the question, can these marriages be saved? And should saving these marriages become a goal of public policy?

These are not easy questions to answer. Much of the public discourse on this issue seems to pit the happiness and welfare of children against the happiness and welfare of adults. A recent longitudinal study tracking unhappy marriages over a 12-year period found that long-term, low-quality marriages have negative effects on overall well-being. Remaining unhappily married is associated with significant lower levels of overall happiness, life satisfaction, self-esteem, and health. The study also found evidence that staying unhappily married is more detrimental than divorcing as those who remained unhappily married scored lower on measures of well-being than people who divorced and remained unmarried (Hawkins, 2005). This finding notwithstanding, it is also likely that some divorces need not have happened. When asked in a recent survey "Do you wish you had worked harder to save the marriage?" only one-third of the respondents said "no." When asked do you wish your ex-spouse had worked harder to save the marriage, 62 percent of ex-wives and ex-husbands answered "yes" (DiCaro, 2005).

 What do you think? Should people in low-conflict (or unhappy) marriages be encouraged to stay married for the sake of the children? Would you? Under what conditions? How do you think staying married in these kind of relationships would affect children? Explain. Should there be a public policy to encourage people to stay married? If so, what should that policy look like?

SUPPORTING MARRIAGES AND FAMILIES

The first step in formulating support for married couples and their families is to recognize that inevitably some marriages will not survive and that there are some relationships so abusive that for spouses and children to remain in them is

---

WRITING YOUR OWN SCRIPT

EVALUATING RELATIONSHIPS

Although no one likes to consider the possibility that a loving relationship will come to an end, we do have to face the reality that over 40 percent of first marriages will end in divorce. We also know that divorce is more common among certain groups and that every couple will experience problems and conflicts at one time or another. The critical factor in the relationship is not the experience of problems or conflicts in themselves but rather what resources and skills are available to help resolve them.

Questions to Consider

1. *What will my partner and I do when things do not seem to be working out right? Can we create mechanisms for resolving disagreements before they occur? Will we be willing to get counseling if we are having problems?*

2. *Have our parents, siblings, or any of our friends been divorced? What are our attitudes regarding divorce?*

3. *What resources can we establish for meeting unexpected problems, such as unemployment, financial difficulties, or illness?*

4. *If we have children, what do we see as our responsibilities toward them should something happen to our marital relationship?*

a threat to health and even life itself. That being said, it is also reasonable to assume that other married couples could be helped to avoid divorce. There is considerable evidence that premarital and postmarital counseling, if undertaken early enough, can help couples to improve their communication and parenting skills and thus lesson sources of marital stress. Such counseling needs to be affordable and readily available in schools and in the community. Parents who make the decision to divorce should be encouraged to learn more about how divorce affects children and what they can do to lessen the risks their children face. If the goal of saving marriages is to improve the welfare of children, it will require strategies to create jobs that pay a decent wage so that household income will increase (see Chapter 10). Parent absence, particularly father absence, has been found to be a major factor in problems many children encounter after a divorce and in some ongoing marriages as well. A part of any program to foster and stabilize marriages and families needs to promote activities that keep parents and other adults connected with children at all ages.

SUMMARY

Contrary to popular belief, divorce is not a modern phenomenon. It has been a part of U.S. history since 1639, when a Puritan court in Massachusetts granted the first divorce decree in colonial America. As public concern grew over the perceived consequences of divorce, reform efforts were debated.

Divorce rates vary from group to group and are associated with a wide range of factors. Among the most frequently cited factors are race and ethnicity, age at marriage, level of education and income, religion, cohabitation, parental divorce, and the presence of children.

Divorce does not just happen. It is a complex social process in which a basic unit of social organization, marriage, breaks down over time, culminating in a legal termination of the relationship. Researchers have identified several stages in this process: a period of marital conflict and unhappiness, the actual marital dissolution itself, and a period of adjustment following divorce. Both women and men in the process of divorce face some common problems: a decline in health, loneliness, and the need for social and sexual readjustment. However, there are also gender differences. Although women suffer more economic distress than men, they may fare better in terms of overall adjustment.

Increasing numbers of children are affected by divorce. Researchers generally agree that children experience some of the same short-term effects their divorcing parents do: rejection, anger, denial, sadness, despair, and grief. There is less agreement about the long-term effects. Some researchers believe that children gain equilibrium 1 or 2 years after the divorce; others feel that the effects are long-lasting and interfere with normal social-emotional development for a significant number of children.

Although the courts typically award one parent, generally the mother, sole custody of the children, more judges are awarding joint custody. It is still too early to assess the effectiveness of the latter approach for the welfare of children. Establishing fair and appropriate visitation rights for noncustodial parents (and increasingly for grandparents) is not an easy matter. Conflict over visitation rights can prolong the trauma of divorce. As a reaction to many of the problems associated with divorce, a number of legislatures across the country are debating proposals to change existing divorce laws. Divorce counseling, conciliation counseling, collaborative law, and divorce mediation are being used increasingly in an effort to reduce some of the conflicts in the divorce process.

KEY TERMS

alimony	emotional divorce	separation	divorce counseling
split custody	legal divorce	desertion	conciliation counseling
no-fault divorce	economic divorce	annulment	collaborative law
crude divorce rate	coparental divorce	sole custody	divorce mediation
refined divorce rate	community divorce	joint custody	
stations of divorce	psychic divorce	family abduction	

QUESTIONS FOR STUDY AND REFLECTION

1. Historian Eric Sager, commenting on the growing ranks of singles, points out, "It is often said that divorce today performs the function that death did in the past. The promise to live together for better or worse, so long as you both shall live, means something very different if you anticipate a married life of 60 years, as opposed to a married life of 25 years." Do you agree or disagree with Sager? Is the goal of lifetime marriage realistic in today's

society? What role, if any, does an increase in life expectancy play in marital stability? Explain.

2. Most marriages start out with many rituals. Among them are the engagement, the bridal shower, the bachelor party, the rehearsal dinner, and the wedding ceremony itself (often religious in nature). Friends and relatives offer their support by cards, gifts, and attendance at these events. Divorce, on the other hand, is often a solitary experience. In fact, the partners are not even required to be physically present when the divorce decree is issued. Yet divorce, like marriage, marks a new beginning in a person's life. Do you think society should initiate divorce rituals aimed at helping people move on with their lives? Marianne Williamson (1994) provides one example: At a ceremony, the divorcing couple can face each other and, in turn, say, "I bless you and release you. Please forgive me; I forgive you. Go in peace. You will remain in my heart." Other variations include readings and the return of wedding rings. What is your reaction to such rituals? Could they serve a useful purpose for the divorcing couple? Their children and other relatives? Society at large? Or do you think they would encourage more couples to divorce? Explain. Consider in your answer the benefits that rituals provide in many other aspects of our lives.

3. Consider both the positive and negative consequences of divorce. On balance, do you think restricting divorce through more stringent laws would be a wise public policy? Explain. Should couples who are experiencing marital difficulties be required to undergo counseling before being allowed to file for divorce? Should couples with children meet stricter standards for divorce than child-free couples? Conversely, should marriage licenses depend on receiving premarital counseling? Explain.

4. As we have seen, children suffer many consequences in the aftermath of a divorce. What steps could be taken to lessen the trauma of divorce for children? How and what should children be told about their parents' divorce? Who should tell them? What reactions should parents expect from children during and after the process of divorce? Would the trauma of divorce be lessened for children if parents followed the judicial guidelines covering children's rights? Explain.

ADDITIONAL RESOURCES

SOCIOLOGICAL

AHRONS, CONSTANCE. 2004. *We're Still Family: What Grown Children Have to Say About Their Parents' Divorce*. New York: HarperCollins. Relying on interviews with the adult children (now between the ages of 21 and 47) of her original 1979 probability sample of divorced couples, Ahrons shows how divorce reorganizes a family but does not destroy it.

McGRAW, PHILLIP C. 2000. *Relationship Rescue: A Seven Step Strategy for Reconnecting with Your Partner*. New York: Hyperion. The author presents a readable, down-to-earth guide for diagnosing, repairing, and maintaining relationships.

HETHERINGTON, E. M., AND JOHN KELLY. 2002. *For Better or For Worse: Divorce Reconsidered*. New York: W. W. Norton. Based on extensive research, the authors present both sides of the divorce question, pointing out its pain and problems but recognizing that many people reach happiness after divorce.

RICCI, ISOLINA. 1997. *Mom's House, Dad's House*. New York: Simon & Schuster. Divorced and remarried parents will find this a practical guide for navigating through the hassles and confusions of setting up a strong working relationship with their ex-spouse to make two loving homes for their children.

FILM

The Squid and the Whale. 2005. Writer-director Noah Baumbach's semiautobiographical story provides a moving account of two teenage boys who struggle with the painful reality of their parents' divorce while at the same time facing the dilemmas of growing up and coming to terms with their emerging sexual selves.

Kramer vs. Kramer. 1979. Although this film was made over two decades ago, it is still an insightful exploration of how a just-divorced man must learn to care for his son on his own and then must fight in court to keep custody of him.

LITERARY

CORMAN, AVERY. 2005. *A Perfect Divorce*. New York: St. Martin's Press. A fast-moving novel by the author of *Kramer vs. Kramer* that packs an emotional punch as it reveals the efforts of an urban, middle-class, dual-career couple who attempts to structure a "perfect divorce" for their son, only to find their expectations dashed when their son goes off the tracks.

KATCH, ELISE E. 2001. *The Get: A Spiritual Memoir of Divorce*. Deerfield Beach, FL: Simcha Press. Readers of all faiths will be fascinated by the real-life experience of a modern woman who is pressured to participate in an ancient Jewish Orthodox ritual to end her 30-year marriage.

INTERNET

www.fambooks.com/daads.htm Dads at a Distance provides suggestions and support on how to improve long-distance relationships with children.

www.divorceinfo.com/children.htm This Web site provides basic pointers to help parents make their children's lives easier when experiencing their parents' divorce.

www.divorcesupport.com This site provides divorce information on family law topics such as divorce, child custody, child support, visitations, property division, and state divorce laws.

www.prepare-enrich.com The mission of Life Innovation is designed to help build strong marriages and healthy relationships; it offers programs for professionals as well as couples seeking to enrich relationships.

IN THE NEWS

Louisiana

When 9-year-old Blake Brunson played his last basketball game of the season, he had his own cheering section— eight grandparents. Blake's maternal and paternal grandparents divorced before he was born. According to gerontology professor Merril Silverstein, this pattern is no longer unusual. Today nearly half of all American families have at least one set of grandparents who have been divorced, compared with just one-fifth in the mid-1980s (Harmon, 2005). This trend adds new complications to family structures and functions as a third generation is added to that part of the family tree. Blake and his family illustrate how this family formation can work to everyone's advantage. For example, Blake's paternal grandmother remembers crying before the baby shower when her daughter-in-law was pregnant with Blake because she dreaded meeting her former husband's wife for the first time. "I didn't want this strange woman to share my grandchildren," she remembers thinking. But her son gave her strict orders to be nice. Blake's mother also expected her divorced and remarried parents to be civil to all parties attending family events. Blake's father said, "They all understand that if they want to be a part of his life then they need to get along with everybody" (quoted in Harmon, 2005). Now, without fighting, the four couples, who live within a few miles of one another, share not only Blake, but his younger sister as well. Nevertheless, everything is not always smooth sailing. Holidays are still daunting because each biological grandparent has steprelationships with members of the new spouse's family. The solution the Brunson family arrived at is to have independent celebrations with each biological grandparent and her or his spouse over a realistic period of time. Mrs. Brunson is clear: "Like my sister says, 'That's what happens when people get a divorce.'"

Not all families are as fortunate as the Brunsons. Adult children whose parents divorced when they were children themselves and then remarried may have lost contact with a parent as they were growing up. As they themselves become parents, they may feel the loss over again as they realize their children will not experience the doting grandparents that they may have known when they were children. In addition, if tensions were strained between them and their stepparent(s), it will take effort to overcome those feelings. This is particularly difficult if there is geographical as well as emotional distance between the generations. The grandparents living far away may envy the interactions between other sets of grandparents and their grandchildren that are made possible by close physical proximity. Children, however, do not seem to discriminate as to biological or steprelationships. Babies and toddlers are likely to bond with anyone who demonstrates love toward them and cares about them like Blake did. As he says about his grandparents' marital histories, "That was before I was born" (quoted in Harmon, 2005). If this attitude is to continue to exist, however, parents (and grandparents, too) must refrain from bad-mouthing and blaming someone for the marital breakdowns in front of the children, not always an easy task, especially if a divorce was acrimonious. Stepgrandparents as well as emotionally distant biological grandparents are well advised to proceed slowly in building a relationship, especially with older children who may be meeting them for the first time or only on special occasions. This is nothing like bonding with a baby; it takes time and patience to gain the trust and affection of older children. Adolescence is tough enough without all that is involved in adding new relatives to the old mix. One problem is names. How do you distinguish among four biological and four stepgrandparents? Generally speaking, experts suggest that the stepgrandparent and stepgrandchild come up with a name that is comfortable for both of them. Blake has different names for all eight of his grandparents, ranging from simple first names to "grandpaw," "pawpaw," and other terms of endearment for his special cheering section. But Blake and his sister are not the only beneficiaries of this involvement. Blake's parents, although not gaining their childhood fantasies of their parents reuniting, can now include them both in family events and rituals of their own making. They also enjoy having babysitters on call in case of emergencies or when they want to be by themselves as a couple.

WHAT WOULD YOU DO? If you were in Blake's parents' shoes, would you include all of the stepgrandparents in your children's lives? If so, how would you go about it? Would you talk to them to establish rules? If so, what would the rules be? How would you handle a biological parent who might view such inclusion as a betrayal? What do you see as the advantages and disadvantages of this type of family formation? Do you or any of your friends have stepgrandparents as well as biological grandparents? How many of each? How has your family (or theirs) coped with this situation, especially around major holidays?

In the previous chapter, we discussed the high divorce rate in the United States. Some writers have erroneously interpreted this high rate of marital dissolution to mean that marriage is no longer a popular institution among Americans. The remarriage statistics tell another story, however. The pattern of marriage, divorce, and remarriage has become well established in the United States today. About 38 percent of recent marriages involved a second marriage for at least one of the partners (Kreider, 2005). The United States has the highest remarriage rate in the world, but stepfamilies are also becoming the fastest-growing family types in Great Britain (Ferri and Smith, 2003). In England and Wales in 2003, only 59 percent of marriages were to first-time brides and groom; 19 percent of all ceremonies were remarriages for both parties, and another 22 percent were first marriages for one partner only (Govan, 2005). The number of remarriages are also increasing in other parts of the world (see In Other Places box). Here in the United States, over half of the population is now or will be in one or more steprelationships during their lives, and by the year 2007, estimates are that stepfamilies will outnumber nuclear families (Mitchell, 1998). Thus, like Blake, it is statistically likely that you (or a number of your classmates) have stepgrandparents or lived or will live part of your life in a remarried family.

For purposes of our discussion in this chapter, we will use Esther Wald's (1981:2) definition of a **remarried family**: "A two-parent, two-generation unit that comes into being on the legal remarriage of a widowed or divorced person who has biological or adopted children from a prior union with whom he or she is regularly involved. . . . The children may or may not live with the remarried couple, but, in either case, they have ongoing and significant psychological, social, and legal ties with them."

Despite the large number of remarriages, however, social and legal changes have not kept pace with this new family form. The general societal approach to these relationships is to view them in much the same way as first marriages. However, although all families share some of the same characteristics and face many of the same problems, families formed as a result of remarriage face additional problems that must be addressed if these relationships are to survive. A 1998 study by James Bray and his colleagues found that unrealistic expectations were a major factor in the divorce rate of remarried couples. To prepare themselves for the day-to-day reality of living in a remarried family, couples need to know about the structure and functioning of remarried families. Figure 13.1 illustrates some of the complexities of remarried families. William Beer (1989) identified ten fundamental ways in which the remarried family is different from the nuclear family:

1. **Complexity.** Remarried families take many forms: divorced individuals/single partners, divorced individuals/widowed partners, divorced individuals/divorced partners. The presence of children increases the families' complexity.

2. **A Changing Cast of Characters.** Remarried families may have shifting membership. Some of the stepchildren may live together permanently, others will come and go depending on visitation arrangements, still others may appear rarely, if at all.

3. **Unclear Boundaries.** Membership boundaries often are ambiguous in remarried families. For example, children may not include a noncustodial parent's new spouse in their definition of family. Unlike in Blake's situation, a stepparent's parents may or may not view themselves as stepgrandparents or be viewed that way by stepgrandchildren (or they themselves might have brought other people into the family as they themselves remarried). The boundaries become further confused if there is a second divorce. Then, is the divorced stepparent still a member of the family?

4. **Undefined Rules.** Remarried couples often find it difficult to agree on rules regarding discipline, money, and parenting responsibilities.

5. **Unclear Laws.** Although the biological parent–child relationship is legally well defined, there still is considerable

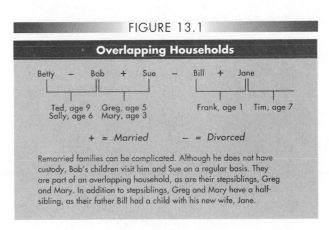

FIGURE 13.1

Overlapping Households

Betty — Bob + Sue — Bill + Jane

Ted, age 9   Greg, age 5   Frank, age 1   Tim, age 7
Sally, age 6 Mary, age 3

+ = Married   − = Divorced

Remarried families can be complicated. Although he does not have custody, Bob's children visit him and Sue on a regular basis. They are part of an overlapping household, as are their stepsiblings, Greg and Mary. In addition to stepsiblings, Greg and Mary have a half-sibling, as their father Bill had a child with his new wife, Jane.

IN OTHER PLACES

REMARRIAGE: A GROWING TREND IN ASIA

In the last chapter we discussed how divorce was on the increase in countries like Korea and China, in part because of more liberal divorce laws and changing social and economic conditions. The presence of a large number of divorced people, in turn, is eroding the stigma attached to marrying for a second or even third time, especially in Korea. In 2004, there were 44,355 remarriages, up 16.1 percent from the previous year (Sung-jin, 2006). Remarriage has become so popular in Korea it is creating a whole set of new industries. In 2004, Petit Wedding, a wedding hall dedicated to second weddings, opened in southern Seoul and was quickly followed by others. Similarly, matchmaking firms have been established dealing only with divorcees. Hotels also cater to these new clients. Second marriages account for about 10 percent of the total weddings in five-star hotels. Wedding planners specializing in remarriages report that their clients tend to be financially more independent than younger couples marrying for the first time and they plan smaller but more elite weddings than was the case for their first marriages ("Remarriage Industry Sees Rapid Growth", 2006).

Although remarriage rates are also increasing across all age groups in China, concern exists that there are still obstacles preventing many elderly from remarrying. This is causing consternation among government officials as they anticipate an aging society. In 2004, China had an elderly population of 142 million, or 11 percent of the total population; estimates are that it will reach 200 million by 2015 and increase to 400 million by 2040 ("China's Elderly Population," 2005). Part of this an increase remarriage is a result of the one-child policy adopted in the late 1970s (see Chapter 1). Many elderly people report being lonely and desirous of finding a companion. A nationwide survey published in the *Chinese Women Weekly* found that 35 percent of people over 60 lost their spouse to divorce or death. Of those, 37.6 percent were interested in

This Chinese couple found companionship in their later years

remarriage but only 6.9 percent had remarried (Wei, 2005). Although some elderly people, many of whom cared for an ailing spouse, do not wish to remarry, others do but are reluctant to do so because of social tradition, the objection of children, and the fear of being ridiculed by others. Many older Chinese still believe that a person should marry only once and that to marry again is a betrayal of the deceased spouse. Some adult children share these traditional views, but they also oppose their parent's remarriage out of fear of losing their inheritance. Many social traditions remain strong in China, and elderly people who remarry are often the subject of gossip and socially ostracized by neighbors.

The government of China is taking steps to address these problems. In 2001, the National People's Congress added an amendment to its marriage laws, calling for children to respect their parents' right of marriage. Children are not allowed to interfere in the remarriage of their parents or their life after remarriage. Clauses protecting elderly marriage partners have been added to the local laws of 22 provinces and municipalities. Some

children, responding to these new laws, have come to see the social, emotional, and health benefits that attach to a parent's finding a partner and are actively supporting their parents' efforts to do so. Recently, the Shanghai Women's Activities Center organized a matchmaking meeting for elderly singles in that city. Similar matchmaking programs are occurring in other parts of China as well. The government, too, has actively promoted community service aimed at the elderly, including matchmaking services for the widowed and divorced. Media programs are also dealing with this topic in an effort to reduce the stigma associated with remarriage in later life. These efforts seem to be working, albeit slowly, as there has been a slight increase in the rate of remarriage among the elderly.

What do you think? Should the Chinese government actively intervene to change the norms of remarriage in China? (Explain). What do the patterns of remarriage in Korea and China tell us about how social change occurs? How does the situation of the elderly in China and in the United States compare? Explain.

ambiguity regarding the legal rights and duties involved in stepparent–stepchild relationships.

6. *A Lack of Kinship Terms.* American culture has relatively few kinship terms, and in remarried families the same word is used to denote very different relationships. For example, the word *stepparent* applies to a person who has married either a custodial parent or a noncustodial parent. It also refers to a new spouse of an elderly parent, even though no parent–child relationship ever existed for this spouse. The new spouses of each biological parent may see each other frequently and join in negotiations over stepchildren. Yet there are no kinship terms for their relationship to one another.

7. *Instant Families.* Remarried families come ready-made, often without appropriate time for members to establish emotional bonds with one another.

8. *Guilt.* New spouses may have unresolved feelings about their previous marriage. Children may feel guilty for showing affection to the stepparent, believing this to be disloyal to the noncustodial biological parent.

9. *Grieving.* Remarried families have undergone a loss before their formation, and some members may not have completed the grieving process. Children may be particularly affected because they must now relinquish the dream of reuniting parents.

10. *Myth of the Recreated Nuclear Family.* Stepfamilies are not like nuclear families. Complex stepfamilies often feel less like one family and more like two separate families than do first-married families (Banker and Gaertner, 1998, 2001). The more a remarried couple tries to make the stepfamily into a family like any other, the more likely they are to be disappointed.

These differences are being recognized, albeit rather slowly. Thus, there are as yet few clearly defined role models for stepfamilies to follow. Consequently, the participants generally lack preparation for the special complexities of remarried family life (Papernow, 1998, 2001). Members of stepfamilies often find themselves questioning their feelings and experiences, uncertain of how typical or "normal" their family situation is. In this chapter we will explore the history and cultural meanings of remarried families, their special characteristics and problems, and strategies for strengthening these families.

HISTORICAL PERSPECTIVE

In the previous chapter we discussed the fact that divorce has been a feature of American family life since 1639. Remarriage has also been a part of family life from this country's beginnings. During the seventeenth and eighteenth centuries, the proportion of remarriages among all marriages was approximately 20 to 30 percent (Ihinger-Tallman and Pasley, 1987). The circumstances leading to remarriage were quite different then, however. Whereas in early America the overwhelming majority of remarriages followed the death of a spouse, today remarriages typically involve divorced individuals. In the early colonies, the climate and harsh conditions as well as the lack of medical knowledge took a heavy toll on the inhabitants. For example, in Charles County, Maryland, marriages were likely to last an average of only 7 years and had only a 33 percent

chance of lasting 10 years before one spouse died (Carr and Walsh, 1983). In Virginia, 25 percent of children by the age of 5 had lost one or both parents; this figure rose to 70 percent by age 21 (Fox and Quitt, 1980). No group was immune to early death. For example, the fathers of Patrick Henry, Thomas Jefferson, George Washington, and James Madison all married widows (Calhoun, 1917).

Given the value attached to marriage in colonial America, remarriage following the death of a spouse was not only common but socially expected for both women and men, especially for those with young children. Little is known about the nature and quality of early remarried families. They were considered the same as first families; no special records were kept on how well they fared. However, it is likely that remarriages, then as now, faced some problems not encountered in first marriages.

CULTURAL IMAGES OF STEPFAMILIES

One basic problem stepfamilies throughout history have had to contend with is their cultural image. The original meaning of the term *step* in *stepfamily* comes from Old German and Old English terms associated with the experiences of bereavement and deprivation. The earliest designations of *step* referred to a child who was orphaned. Later, the term was expanded to include the replacement parent, whether a stepmother or stepfather.

The terms *stepchild*, *stepparent*, and especially *stepmother* have conveyed negative connotations from earliest times. Most of these images derive from folklore and fairy tales that through the medium of storytelling sought to provide guidelines for daily living. An analysis of children's fairy tales found that stepmothers along with bears, wolves, giants, ogres, and witches were the most frequent representations of evil (Sutton-Smith, 1971). Other analyses confirm the consistent image of the stepmother as a cruel and evil person (Dainton, 1993; Ganong and Coleman, 1997). For centuries children have been entertained and/or frightened by *Hansel and Gretel*, *Snow White*, and *Cinderella* with their tales of maternal loss and cruel replacement.

Professionals and laypeople alike need to be aware of the fear and anxiety such images can create, especially for young children, who today increasingly live in stepfamilies. Such images also complicate the stepmother role, making it difficult and ambiguous. Negative images also imply that "step is less," as conveyed in the metaphor that anything of lesser value is "like a stepchild" (Wald, 1981). Writer Jim Warda (2000), a stepfather, describes his pain at hearing a coworker say, "Jim, they're treating our department like a red-headed stepchild." Warda says that the comment implies that a stepchild is less than a biological child, someone whom a parent can like, and possibly love, but never to the same degree as his or her own biological child.

Such images can affect the perceptions people have of stepfamilies. Margaret Crosbie-Burnett (1994/1995), for example, has written about the bias against stepchildren and stepparents that frequently exists in the educational system. Even today, counselors and teachers may be quick to assume that if students in remarried families are having difficulty, it is because of

Throughout history, many nursery rhymes and children's stories have depicted stepmothers as wicked and cruel.

a faulty family structure. She therefore recommends that school personnel receive professional training about both the strengths and challenges associated with living in a stepfamily.

In an attempt to correct negative stereotypes, many stepparents, children's writers, and family professionals are publishing more accurate representations of today's stepfamilies. One result of this is an attempt to create more neutral terms to describe stepfamilies: *reconstituted, blended, merged, binuclear,* and *remarried families.* Some of these terms, however, create problems of their own. The notion of reconstituted, blended, or merged families implies that all members get along and fit comfortably into the new family structure. In fact, such a situation may never be achieved, or at least might not be achieved for a number of years. The pressure felt to measure up to such standards may add further stress to a remarriage. Thus, we prefer the term *remarried families,* agreeing with Wald (1981:33) that this term is "accurately descriptive, nontechnical, and value-free, and does not imply goals achieved." Throughout this chapter we will use the term *remarried families* when referring to the family as a whole. However, because

> *What images come to mind when you hear the term stepfamily? Are these images positive, negative, or a combination of both? How did you first learn about stepfamilies? Perhaps you live or have lived in a stepfamily. If so, do you see any differences between your stepfamily and biological families? What differences did you observe? As you read the remainder of this chapter, evaluate the accuracy of your views of stepfamilies with that conveyed in the sociological literature.*

there are as yet no newly agreed-upon terms for relationships within remarried families, we will follow common practice and refer to them as steprelationships.

THE PROCESS OF REMARRIAGE

Over time, most divorced and widowed persons are able to relinquish their strong emotional ties to the past. This, of course, does not imply that they do not have warm memories of the past or that they never think about their former partner. Rather, it means that they are able to focus on the present and plan for the future. When this happens, the widowed or divorced individual confronts the issues of whether to date and perhaps whether to remarry.

Dating and Courtship Patterns

Are dating and courtship different the second time around? Older adults report many of the same anxieties about dating that adolescents do: appropriate behavior for the first date, what to talk about, who pays, whether to be sexually involved, and how to end the relationship if it is going nowhere. Adults with children may find dating even more complicated. Children often have difficulty accepting a parent's decision to date. When the parental loss was due to death, children may interpret the surviving parent's dating as an act of disloyalty to or betrayal of the deceased parent. When the loss was due to divorce, children may fantasize about their parents' getting back together again and thus react negatively to a parent's dating. In addition, children may feel displaced by the dating partner, so they may attempt to sabotage the relationship by behaving obnoxiously. Conversely, they may pressure parents by promoting the relationship in hopes of finding a new parent.

Children are not the only ones to react to the resumption of dating. Relatives of a deceased spouse may feel hurt or betrayed if they believe the surviving spouse is dating too soon following the death of their loved one. Ex-spouses may also be hostile to their former spouse's dating. They may be jealous themselves or fear someone else will replace them in their children's eyes. Thus, they may withdraw cooperation over visitation rights and delay or even end financial support.

We might assume that dealing with these complications would lengthen the courtship process. The opposite pattern seems to be the case, however. Divorced and widowed individuals who remarry tend to spend only half the time in dating and courtship that they did preceding their first marriage (Ganong and Coleman, 1994).

Other researchers suggest that more than time distinguishes dating and courtship before first and second marriages. For example, Frank Furstenberg and Graham Spanier (1987) found that dating among their divorced respondents was guided more by pragmatic than by romantic considerations. The style of dating among the divorced is more informal, and courtship often involves living together before marriage. Couples often believe the experience of cohabitation gives a marriage a better chance to succeed, but as we saw in Chapter 7, couples who cohabit first have a higher likelihood of divorce than those who do not cohabit. Yet approximately 60 percent of divorced people cohabit before remarrying (Bumpass, Sweet, and Castro-Martin, 1990).

The high prevalence of cohabitation after divorce has led some researchers to argue that the definition of stepfamilies should be expanded to include cohabitation with a child or children of only one partner and should recognize that step-families include those formed after nonmarital childbearing as well as after marital disruption. Estimates are that over two-fifths of children will spend some part of their child-hood living with cohabiting parents (Bumpass and Lu, 2000). And, although we do not know the precise percent-age, a substantial number of recent remarriages were pre-ceded by cohabitation (Spearin, 2006).

Beyond this cohabitation strategy, however, most individuals do little to prepare themselves for living in a remarried family. Only 38 percent of the women and 25 percent of the men in the Ganong and Coleman study sought professional counseling, although many more reported getting advice from friends and self-help books. Furthermore, many couples did not use the dating or courtship period to discuss potential problems in a remarriage. For example, only 56 percent of the couples discussed the most serious problem observed by stepfamily experts, namely, children from a previous marriage. Less than 25 percent discussed the second most serious problem: finances. A full 13 percent reported that they did not discuss any issues very seriously. As a result of this lack of preparation, many people enter remarriage with nonverbalized expectations that, if not realized, become sources of conflict and disappointment (Papernow, 2001).

The Decision to Remarry

Given the pain and trauma surrounding many divorces, and given the complications of resumed dating, why do so many Americans choose to remarry? First and foremost, marriage remains an important cultural value, and it is still perceived as the normal way to form an intimate connection with another person. Many of the reasons women and men give for remar-riage are similar to those given for first marriages: conven-ience, social pressure, love, companionship, support, and for some, pregnancy. Some divorced individuals want to alleviate the feelings of failure that accompanied the dissolution of their previous marriage (Ganong and Coleman, 1994). Fur-thermore, given the persistent economic inequalities between women and men and the downward mobility experienced by many divorced and widowed women, remarriage may also be a rational economic decision that results in an improved stan-dard of living. Numerous studies show that women and chil-dren are almost always better off financially after remarriage (Nielsen, 1999; Page and Stevens, 2004). Finally, divorced and widowed custodial parents may be motivated to remarry so they will have help raising their children.

Patterns of Remarriage

As we saw earlier, remarriages have always been quite com-mon in the United States. In the 1950s, two-thirds of divorced women remarried within 5 years; today only about 54 percent do (Casper and Bianchi, 2002). Remarriage rates declined dramatically during the 1970s and continued to decline throughout the 1980s and 1990s, although at a much slower rate. For instance, between 1970 and 1984 there was a 16 percent drop in the proportion of people who remarried within 5 years of their divorce. This did not mean, however, that divorced people did not enter new relationships. During this same time there was a 7 percent increase in the propor-tion who formed a union through cohabitation (Bumpass, Sweet, and Cherlin, 1991). A number of factors affect if and when people remarry: age, sex, marital status, social class, race and ethnicity, religion, and the presence of children.

Age, Sex, and Marital Status   Data consistently show that groups remarry at different rates with widowed and divorced men having the highest rates and widowed women the lowest. Widows are less like to remarry than divorced women, prima-rily for two reasons. First, widows, unlike most divorced women, may continue to hold a strong emotional attachment to the previous spouse. Thus, they may not be interested in establishing another relationship (Talbott, 1998). Additionally, if women did the bulk of the household labor, they may be reluctant to take that on again, preferring their new-found independence to a second marriage. In contrast, widowers, with positive attitudes toward marriage, are more likely to miss the benefits of having a wife. Second, widow-hood usually occurs at older ages than divorce. Although some widows might prefer to remarry, they may find them-selves disadvantaged by norms that encourage men to marry younger woman. Remarriage is more likely among women

Thirty-eight percent of all marriages today involve a second marriage for one or both partners.
©Tribune Media Services, Inc. All Rights Reserved. Reprinted by permission

who were under age 25 at divorce than among women ages 25 and over at divorce. Ten years after divorce, 81 percent of women who were under age 25 at divorce have remarried compared with 68 percent of women age 25 years and older at divorce (Bramlet and Mosher, 2002).

Divorced men are considerably less likely than divorced women to have custody of children. Thus, men tend to have more resources and leisure time that allows them to reenter the dating scene more easily. The greater resources at men's command also make them more attractive in the marriage market. Despite these differences, half of the women and men across all major race and ethnic groups who remarried after a divorce did so within about 3 to 4 years. The median duration of second marriages that ended in divorce was about 8 years for women (about the same as for first marriages) but slightly longer for men at 9 years. Approximately 3.1 percent of women and 3.2 percent of men remarry after a second divorce (Kreider, 2005).

Social Class and Education   For both women and men, however, age may be less of a factor in the decision to remarry than social class. Men with higher incomes are more likely to remarry than men with lower incomes. For men with low incomes the added burden of supporting two households may be prohibitive. Conversely, inadequate income may motivate some single mothers to remarry. As we saw in the previous chapter, divorce adversely affects women's and children's economic well-being. Remarriage, by adding another (often higher) wage earner, reverses this process (Page and Stevens, 2004).

Social Class, Race, and Ethnicity   Rates of remarriage vary across social class, race, and ethnicity. For example, lower-income African Americans are less likely to remarry than their white counterparts. In fact, remarriage rates for African American women across all socioeconomic levels are lower than those for their white counterparts. As Figure 13.2 shows, within 6 years of divorce, 58 percent of white women,

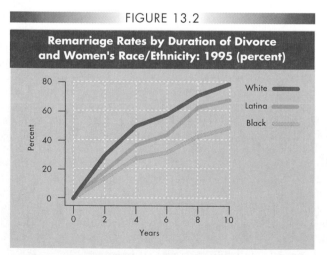

FIGURE 13.2

Remarriage Rates by Duration of Divorce and Women's Race/Ethnicity: 1995 (percent)

White
Latina
Black

Source: Adapted from M.D. Bramlett and W.E. Mosher, 2001 *First Marriage Dissolution, Divorce, and Remarriage: United States.* Advance Data from Vital and Health Statistics, no. 323 (Hyattsville, MD: National Center for Health Statistics): 10, Table 8.

44 percent of Latinas, and 32 percent of African American women have remarried. Ten years after divorce, 79 percent of white women, 68 percent of Latinas, but only 49 percent of African American women have remarried. Studies suggest that these differences are most likely related to higher rates of unemployment, incarceration, and mortality; lower levels of educational attainment and earnings; previous experiences as children of unmarried or less educated parents; and higher rates of poverty and lack of job opportunities in the communities in which African Americans live (Bramlett and Mosher, 2001, 2002). This overall disadvantaged economic position has led many African Americans to see the marital relationship as less effective than the larger kin network in providing support. In addition, as we saw in Chapter 5, a sex ratio imbalance places limits on the opportunities for remarriage among African American women.

The rates of remarriage for Latinas are between those of African American and white women. However, considerable variation exists among Latina/o groups. According to the latest available census data, Puerto Rican women have the lowest rate of remarriage and Cuban men have the highest. Similar variations in rates of remarriage have been found among Asian Americans, with Korean women and men having the highest rates and Vietnamese men the lowest. Native American women and men have fairly high rates of remarriage compared to other groups (Sweet and Bumpass, 1987). Relatively little research has been done on remarried families of color. The reasons, then, for the varied patterns across racial and ethnic groups are not entirely clear. However, it is likely that part of the answer is to be found in the different economic positions of the various groups, the availability of support from kin members, and increased acceptability of cohabitation as an alternative to marriage.

Religion   As we saw in the last chapter, religion is one of the factors affecting patterns of divorce. Within 20 years of a first marriage, 48 percent of Catholics are divorced, compared with 49 percent of Jews, 56 percent of Protestants, and 59 percent of persons with no religious affiliation (Hout, 2000). Despite the Catholic Church's opposition to divorce and its ban on remarriage except in cases involving a church annulment (see Chapter 12), at least half of all divorced Catholics will eventually remarry. This pattern is similar to that for people of other faiths (Hornike, 2001). Among the 51 million Catholic adults in the United States today, 16 percent are currently divorced or separated and another 9 percent have been divorced in the past but are now remarried, up from 7 percent in the 1980s. Divorced Catholics contemplating remarriage face the added dilemma that a decision to remarry can mean the loss of a beloved church and parish family. Seventeen to 20 percent of divorced Catholics leave the Catholic Church as a result of their remarriage (Hout, 2000). Despite the Catholic Church's official policy on remarriage, many members of the clergy have instituted a variety of programs to help remarried Catholics, including support groups, second-marriage preparation classes, and a Rainbow Program for children to help them cope with the loss and grief they experience following a parental divorce.

The Presence of Children   Earlier research found that age and the presence of children affected the likelihood of remarriage for women and men in different ways. Divorced men with custody of children tended to remarry sooner than their female counterparts. Perhaps because they represented such a small minority and had not been socialized to be the primary caretaker, custodial fathers felt the need for a partner to assist them with child care. Among women, those with young children and those with fewer children were more likely to remarry than those with large families or older children (Glick and Lin, 1986). More current research found that children under age 6 tended to reduce the remarriage prospects of single mothers relative to childless women, whereas having children older than 18 increased the likelihood of their remarriage. However, having a child older than 18 years reduces the prospects of remarriage for men, relative to childless men (Sweeney, 1995). A logical explanation for this finding is that older children require less of a mother's time but may require more of a father's finances. More research is needed today to see to what extent the presence of children may lead more divorced parents to cohabit rather than to remarry.

Across all these factors, the decision to remarry begins a complicated series of adjustments that must be made if the new relationship is to survive.

The Stations of Remarriage

In Chapter 12 we discussed the complex process of exiting from a marital relationship, using Paul Bohannan's (1970) six stations of divorce: emotional, psychic, community, parental, economic, and legal divorces. Ann Goetting (1982) found that there is a similarity between the developmental tasks that must be mastered in the divorce process and the many personal changes and adjustments that accompany the process of remarriage. Looking at remarriage this way makes it clear that remarriage involves more than the exchange of wedding vows. It requires individuals to adopt new roles, to unlearn old expectations from previous relationships, and to cope with an ambiguous legal status.

Goetting has identified six remarriages derived from Bohannan's stations of divorce. Each station of the remarriage process presents a challenge to the formation of a new couple and a new family identity. Keep in mind that, as is the case for the stations of divorce, the six stations of remarriage do not affect all remarrying people with the same intensity, nor do they occur in exactly the same order for everyone. The presence of children, for example, can affect the intensity as well as the number of stages people experience in remarriage.

The term **emotional remarriage** refers to the process of reestablishing a bond of attraction, love, commitment, and trust with another person. This can be a slow and difficult process for both the widowed and the divorced. The nature and quality of the previous marital experience affect the relationship with the new partner in different ways. On the one hand, people who were happily married and then widowed may idealize the deceased spouse and thus see the new partner in a less favorable light. Such people can become overly critical of the new partner's behavior if it does not measure up to this ideal. On the other hand, people who have been hurt and disappointed in previous relationships may be oversensitive to spousal criticism and may sense rejection by the new spouse when none is intended. For example, an intended compliment may be judged suspect because a former partner used similar comments as putdowns. Both the widowed and the divorced must be careful not to let the experiences of the first marriage unduly influence their new relationship. If children from a previous marriage or marriages are involved, a couple must make special effort to constantly renew and strengthen their emotional bond as a couple (Wisdom and Green, 2002).

The process known as **psychic remarriage** requires moving back from the recently acquired identity of single person to a couple identity. This transition varies in intensity and perceived difficulty. For individuals who have accepted more traditional gender roles, regaining the status of husband or wife may be especially gratifying and their adjustments to couple identity may be relatively minor. Other people, however, especially women who experienced a new sense of autonomy and personal independence after widowhood or divorce, may feel constrained after taking on a marital role.

Just as with a community divorce, a **community remarriage** involves changes in social relationships. Following the dissolution of a marriage, individuals often find that the nature and frequency of contact with relatives and friends is disrupted. As we have seen in Chapter 12, relationships with other married couples often suffer following a divorce. As a result, couple friends are often replaced with new, unmarried friends. Often these friendships are deeper and more intimate because they are selected on the basis of one's personal interests and needs, not those of a couple. Reentering the couple world may result in reverting back to less intimate and more couple-oriented relationships that can be shared more easily and "fit" more readily into a couple's lifestyle. Additionally, remarriage means that new in-laws must somehow be integrated into the family network. These changes, involving both gains and losses in the social network, carry with them both joy and sadness for all affected parties.

Remarriage in which one or both spouses have children from a previous relationship is known as **parental remarriage.** This station of remarriage generally receives the most attention in social science literature and in the media. More than half of all remarriages involve minor stepchildren living in the household. In 2001, 15 percent of children (10.6 million) lived in blended families. The U.S. Census Bureau defines *blended families* as families formed when remarriages occur or when children living in a household share only one or no biological parents; the presence of a stepparent stepsibling, or half-sibling designates a family as *blended*. About half of these children, 5.1 million, lived with at least one stepparent; 2.9 million lived with neither of their parents, including 0.3 million children living with one or more foster parents (Kreider and Fields, 2005). Relatives, usually grandparents, often cared for children who were living with neither parent, a topic we will discuss in Chapter 14. Sixty-seven percent of stepchildren under 18 were white, 12 percent were African American; 15 percent were Latina/o. Native Americans and Asian Americans each represented slightly over 1 percent of all stepchildren (Kreider, 2003). However,

Individuals who plan to marry someone with children are well advised to build a friendship with those children before assuming a stepparent role.

often confounded by the presence of the nonresidential biological parent. The attitudes and behavior of the ex-spouse, if hostile, jealous, or uncooperative, may slow the integration of the stepparent into the family unit.

An **economic remarriage** involves the establishment of a unit of economic productivity and consumption while at the same time working out mutually agreeable earning and spending habits. The presence of minor stepchildren can complicate the establishment of an economic plan for the new family unit in several ways. First, the remarried couple may be dependent, to a degree, on the economic behavior of people outside their immediate relationship. For example, when custodial parents remarry, they may be receiving alimony and child support from their ex-spouses. As we saw in the previous chapter, child support might become sporadic or stop entirely after remarriage, adding a dimension of uncertainty to the family budgeting process. Second, new spouses may themselves be noncustodial divorced parents who are paying alimony and child support to their ex-spouses, thus diminishing the financial resources available to the new family unit. Friction may develop over resource distribution: Who should get how much of what is available?

Handling issues of financial equity, need, and flexibility may prove a daunting task. The nature of the financial arrangement may have an impact on the degree and speed of family integration. Some couples choose a common-pot approach, putting all wages and child support together and then allocating resources according to need rather than source of income. Others choose a two-pot arrangement, in which each spouse contributes a fixed amount to running the household but each biological parent is responsible for her or his children's expenses. Barbara Fishman (1983) found that the common-pot approach is more likely to unify the stepfamily, while the two-pot system tends to reinforce biological loyalties and individual autonomy. Couples who have used the "one-pot" method generally reported higher family satisfaction than those who kept their money separate (Bray and Kelly, 1998).

Other financial issues must be dealt with as well. If either partner has assets such as property, stocks, bonds, family heirlooms, insurance policies, the use and final disposition of those assets needs to be discussed. Each party may have different expectations about what happens to these assets in

as Figure 13.3 shows, Native American/Alaska Natives had the highest percentage of children living in blended families (17.3), with African Americans having the second highest (16.5 percent). Whites and Latinas/os were in the middle, with 14.7 and 14.2 percent. Children of Asian Americans/Pacific Islanders were the least likely to live in blended families (5.1 percent). The lower rate among Asian Americans is generally attributed to the lower rates of non-marital childbearing and divorce among Asian American adults compared to other groups.

Establishing good working relationships with stepchildren is perhaps the most challenging and emotionally trying aspect of remarriage. Both stepparent and stepchild confront the emotional challenge of moving from the role of stranger to that of family member. This process takes time and is primarily one of trial and error. Such adjustments are

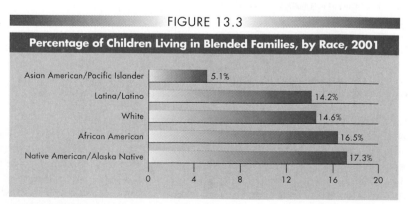

FIGURE 13.3

Percentage of Children Living in Blended Families, by Race, 2001

Race	Percentage
Asian American/Pacific Islander	5.1%
Latina/Latino	14.2%
White	14.6%
African American	16.5%
Native American/Alaska Native	17.3%

Source: Adapted from Rose M. Kreider and Jason Fields, 2005, *Living Arrangements of Children: 2001.* Current Population Reports, P70-104. (Washington, DC: U.S. Census Bureau): 8, Table 6.

a remarriage, especially when the remarriage involves different sets of children. Although many financial experts recommend prenuptial agreements so that children from a previous marriage are protected, asking for a prenuptial agreement can itself become a cause of dissension.

Just as in a first marriage, a **legal remarriage** establishes a legally recognized marital relationship with all its responsibilities and privileges. However, it also requires people to make a number of adjustments. Taking on new responsibilities as a spouse does not absolve one from responsibilities that accompanied the first marriage. Court-awarded payments of alimony and child support remain in effect. Other responsibilities to the first family are not as clear-cut, however. For example, do nonresident biological children or an ex-spouse have a right to any health or life insurance, retirement benefits, or inheritance from a noncustodial parent or former partner? Because these issues are not clearly dealt with in most states, increasing numbers of couples sign a premarital agreement, declaring which assets belong to the remarried family and which should be directed toward the ex-spouse or nonresidential children. These agreements notwithstanding, conflict may develop if circumstances change and one spouse feels that too many resources are being diverted to the other spouse's former family.

Additionally troubling is the legal ambiguity surrounding stepchild–stepparent relationships. Only a few states have laws that obligate a stepparent to support a stepchild. This legal vacuum may create tension in several ways. On the one hand, some stepparents may resent being asked to assume responsibility for someone else's children. On the other hand, biological parents may feel guilty asking for help to support their children, or they may resent their new spouse's reluctance to help in this regard. A further complication for remarried families is stepparents' lack of legal rights concerning stepchildren. For example, in most states stepparents are not permitted to authorize medical treatment for stepchildren, nor do they have legal rights to custody and/or visitation of stepchildren who lived with them before the dissolution of their remarriage.

Another area in which the legal system has failed to provide adequate support and guidelines for remarried families is in the area of sexual relations. Although all 50 states prohibit marriage and sexual relations between persons closely related by blood, few make similar provisions for family members in a remarriage, for example, between a stepfather and stepdaughter or between stepsiblings. Although a sexual relation between a minor stepchild and a stepparent is considered a criminal offense, and although sexual relationships between stepsiblings are not socially condoned, neither behavior is defined as incest. This differential treatment of sexual relations in first marriages and remarriages can lead to tensions and even sexual exploitation in remarried families. All of these problems have led some people to argue for changes in the law that would prompt greater legal clarity for stepfamilies (see Debating Social Issues box).

Remarrying a Former Spouse

You may recall that in Chapter 12, we discussed the fact that a number of former spouses wished they had tried harder to save their marriages. Overall, that is what it remains, a wish. However, in a small number of cases some ex-spouses decide there was more to their relationship than they had thought and try again. According to Les Parrott, a clinical psychologist and coauthor of the book, *Saving Your Second Marriage Before It Starts*, "Most of the time these . . . are people who say, 'We've grown, we've learned new skills and we're ready to make a commitment again.' It's not done out of haste" (quoted in Hahn, 2006: Sec. 5, 1). Pepper and Ron Miller, who divorced in 1996 and remarried in 2006, exemplify this process. The two met by accident and realized they were still attracted to each other. During the course of dating, they dealt with the problems that led to their breakup. Each recognized their need to change and move toward the other. This activity is necessary to succeed in a remarriage. As psychologist Parrot observes, "It can't just be. 'Well I've dated, and I can't find anyone better, so I'm willing to settle'" (quoted in Hahn, 2006:7).

THE DEVELOPMENT OF REMARRIED FAMILIES

The process of remarriage takes time. According to James Bray and John Kelly (1998), all stepfamilies experience up and down patterns, with the first two years being the most difficult as they attempt to master the basic tasks of stepfamily life: parenting, managing change, separating a second marriage from a first, and dealing with the nonresidential parent. This stage is followed by a leveling off of the initial difficulties; the next three or four years become more tranquil as compromises are negotiated. However, a third cycle can see the reemergence of stress and conflict, as children and parents confront issues relevant to the adolescent years.

REMARRIED FAMILIES: ROLES, INTERACTIONS, AND REACTIONS

The dynamic interrelationships among these stations will become clearer as we examine the roles, interactions, and reactions of various members of remarried family households, beginning with stepchildren. Children whose parents decide to remarry often experience fear and anxiety about what this means for their own place in the family. Thus, couples contemplating remarriage are well advised to consider including children from a previous marriage in the wedding ceremony.

Children and the Remarriage Service

Even though the wedding itself may take a simple form, planning for a remarriage ceremony when children are involved can be a delicate matter. Unlike a first marriage, which is usually a union between a woman and a man, a remarriage when children are involved is really a merging of families. Yet until recently, relatively little attention was given to how to include young children in the service itself except to have them stand next to or behind the couple during the

DEBATING SOCIAL ISSUES

SHOULD LAWS BE CHANGED TO MAKE STEPPARENTS LEGAL PARENTING PARTNERS IN STEPFAMILIES?

Today as many as one in three children will spend some part of their childhood years living with a stepparent. However, family law has been slow to recognize the many changes families have undergone over the past decades. Today, there are many overlapping families, families in which parenting roles are shared by custodial and noncustodial parents, biological parents, and stepparents. Yet, for the most part only biological parents are legally and financially obligated to support their children, usually until the age of 18. However, with respect to stepparents, there is no uniform treatment regarding their financial responsibilities to stepchildren. Although marriage to a child's parent would seem to create a legal relationship to the child, it does not. Many employers do not recognize stepchildren as an employee's dependents. To date, about the only way to resolve the legal ambiguities of the stepparent role and establish a legal parent–child relationship is through stepchild adoption. However, for that to happen the noncustodial parent's legal rights must be terminated by court order or by voluntary consent. Few natural parents are likely to give this consent and a court order can be a traumatic step for all concerned.

The courts have not as yet readily accepted the position that it is in the child's best interest to have more than two legal parents. According to many family advocates, this norm of exclusivity does not serve the interests of children and it also denies recognition and respect to the adults who participate in their lives and who voluntarily contribute to their support without any legal rights. Thus, these advocates recommend that the courts recognize a contract establishing a legally recognized stepparent–stepchild relationship

Courts are increasingly being asked to settle complicated family issues.

specifying rights and duties during marriage (and postmarriage in case of parental death or divorce), in effect creating a legal parenting partnership with the biological parent (see, for example, Malia, 2004). Such a contract would be negotiated between the custodial parent and the stepparent and could include such rights as giving stepparents access to school and medical records, the right to authorize permission for children to attend various events, the right to claim stepchildren as dependents for insurance and income tax purposes, the right to be named legal guardian if something happens to the custodial parent, and, in case of divorce, visitation rights as well as the obligations to provide financial support and care. Proponents of such a legal contract argue that this would strengthen stepfamilies by creating greater incentives for stepparents to become more involved in their stepchildren's lives and, hence, in the event of marital dissolution, it would also increase the likelihood that the stepparent would remain involved with her or his stepchildren. Advocates also believe a

legal contract would reduce family boundary ambiguity and give children more of a sense of belonging to a family.

Those who oppose such a contract are concerned that it would undermine the role of the noncustodial parent by putting her or him in competition with the stepparent. Other opponents see proposals such as these as further undermining the concepts of marriage and family by suggesting that children can have more than two legal parents. Some opponents fear that extending family law to include nontraditional family structures would open the door to same-sex marriages.

What do you think? Should family law be broadened to be more inclusive of diverse family structures? Explain. How would giving stepparents legal rights and expecting certain obligations from them in return affect their roles and functions within the stepfamily? If you were a biological noncustodial parent, would you support or oppose such a contract? If you were a biological custodial parent, would you support or oppose such a contract?

Family therapists have long stressed the symbolic importance of rituals in family health and child well-being (see, for example, Kiser et al., 2005). And, creating new family rituals in remarried families is especially critical. For children, participation in a formal ritual can make the new family seem more "real" and can give them a sense of belonging.

Celebrating the wedding ritual together as a family serves another key function. A remarriage ceremony can be the basis for the first collective memory that the new family will share. However, for some children the prospect of a parent's remarriage may be painful, and some older children may decline an invitation to participate in the ceremony. They may even refuse to attend the wedding. Although couples may be hurt and disappointed by this reaction, it is generally best to let children decide this matter for themselves. Often when children know the decision is really theirs and that they will be welcome if they change their minds even at the last moment, they do decide to reverse their position and attend. Forcing children to attend against their wishes may set up a power struggle that will have a long-term negative impact on the quality of family life.

The remarriage of Grammy- and Oscar-winning rapper Eminem and his wife Kim Scott was short-lived. Three months after their January 14, 2006, remarriage, Eminem filed for divorce. The couple first wed in 1999. The relationship ended in 2001 after an acrimonious legal fight over custody of their daughter.

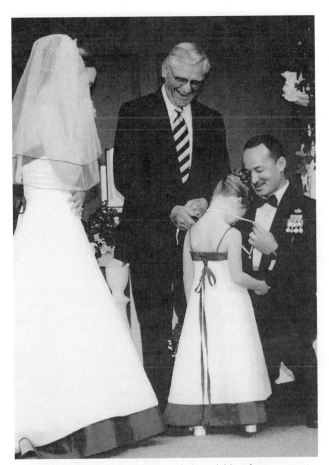

Increasing numbers of couples are including children from previous marriages in their wedding ceremony. Here the parent and stepparent are placing a family medallion around the daughter's neck to symbolize their commitment to building a strong family unit, inclusive of all parties.

ceremony, or if old enough, serve as bridesmaids or groomsmen. Today, as a result of the pioneering efforts of Dr. Roger Coleman, chaplain of Pilgrim Chapel in Kansas City, many religious bodies have modified their wedding rituals to include the children from previous marriages. Every year thousands of couples use Dr. Coleman's Family Medallion ceremony to help foster a new family bond between children, parents, and stepparents. Even a very young child can take part. After the couple exchanges wedding rings, their children join them for a special service focusing on the family nature of this remarriage. Each child is given a gold or silver family medallion with three interlocking circles, a symbol that represents family love in much the same way that wedding rings symbolize conjugal love. Just as the two individuals exchange vows with each other, as parents and stepparents they promise to care for all the children in the family.

Remarriages can also affect adult children who are celebrating their first marriage. Whether a biological father, a stepfather, or both should walk a bride down the aisle or whether a divorced parent's spouse should be an invited guest can be difficult and emotionally loaded issues even years after the parental divorce.

> *Have you attended any remarriage ceremonies where children were included? If so, what was the ceremony like? What do you see as the advantages and/or disadvantages of including children in their parent's wedding ceremony? Have you or anyone you know had to deal with whether or how to include divorced parents and/or stepparents in planning a wedding? What were the problems? How were they resolved? What advice would you give to someone planning to remarry?*

Children and the Honeymoon

More parents are giving thought to how children should be integrated into the wedding ceremony but they sometimes overlook another area that can be equally problematic, the honeymoon. For example, in one family, a man with four children, ages 5–12, married a woman who had not been married before:

> Toward the very end of the wedding reception, one of the older children came to his father and asked, incredulously, "Are you going on your honeymoon without us?" The answer was "yes." The couple had never said anything directly to the children about their plans because, as the father said, "In our wildest imaginations such a thought had never crossed our minds, so we didn't think of saying anything to my children about our plans. It never occurred to us that the children would think they were included." (quoted in Visher, 2001)

Children in Remarried Families

Throughout this text we have emphasized that all families are influenced by persons and events outside the immediate family unit. This is particularly true for remarried families formed after a divorce. Although members of nuclear families generally share one household, divorce creates two separate but **overlapping households,** with children having membership in both households.

This dual membership can have both positive and negative consequences for children. On the one hand, if one or both biological parents remarry, children have more adult role models to guide, love, and nurture them. Interacting in two households, each with distinct members, expectations, activities, traditions, and family culture, can provide a richness of experience not found in any one household. On the other hand, this dual membership can be a source of conflict and confusion for children. Each household has a set of rules, so children must behave differently from one household to the next. For instance, one of the author's young friends who is involved in an overlapping household complained,

> When I'm at home, I can go to bed anytime I want. Mom doesn't care as long as I get up right away when she calls me in the morning. When I'm at Dad's house, they make me go to bed when the other kids do, around 9 o'clock. I don't think that's fair. I'm older than they are.

Adults in both households need to understand that adjusting to two sets of rules is not easy for children; there must be time and space to allow for the transition from one to the other. Mixed emotions in these circumstances are not unique to children. Both parents and stepparents may feel insecure and jealous when children visit the other household and they may communicate these feelings to their children who, in turn, may feel that to enjoy being in the other household is somehow disloyal to the other biological parent.

Whether overlapping households are beneficial to children depends, in large measure, on the attitude and behavior of the adults involved. If all parental adults cooperate in matters of visitation, refrain from criticizing each other in front of the children, and give children permission to care about and enjoy their other family household, the positive benefits of dual household membership are likely to outweigh the negative consequences for both children and other family members. For example, a study of adolescent family life satisfaction in remarried families found that adolescents who perceived their families to be more flexible reported greater satisfaction with both overall remarried family household and the parent–stepparent subsystem. This flexibility allowed them to meet the expectations of multiple elements of the extended-family systems (Henry and Lovelace, 1995). For more information of how to work successfully across households, see the Internet Resources: Applying the Sociological Imagination box.

Nevertheless, children, too, play a role in determining the nature and quality of overlapping households. They can cooperate or be a source of friction. A major factor in their behavior is the way in which they come to define family membership.

Who's In, Who's Out? Boundary Ambiguity in Stepfamilies When social scientists investigate who is in and who is out of the family system, they refer to this as **boundary ambiguity.** Initially most studies of boundary ambiguity relied on adult perceptions. Penny Gross (1987) conducted one of the first studies on children's perceptions of family membership involving 60 Canadian children, 30 females and 30 males between the ages of 16 and 18. Each had two living divorced parents, at least one of whom had remarried. Using a structured interview that focused on parent–child relationships, Gross asked the children who they considered family members. Four patterns emerged: retention, substitution, reduction, and augmentation.

Retention Twenty children (33 percent) defined the family in terms of its composition prior to the divorce—that is, with both biological parents but not the stepparent. Thus, some children lived with a stepparent but did not consider that person part of their family; nonresidential parents continued to play an important role in the lives of their children. Sons were more likely than daughters to include the nonresidential father as a family member.

As a result of the remarriage of both sets of his grandparents, Blake Brunson, 9, finds his cheering section at basket ball games has doubled (see In the News)

Source: Lori Waslchuk/The New York Times

Substitution   Eight children (13 percent) excluded one biological parent and included at least one stepparent in their definition of family. This was most common when children lived with the remarried parent. For these children, the household membership and the family were synonymous.

Reduction   Some children included fewer people than the original family. Fifteen children (25 percent) excluded their nonresidential biological parent as well as the stepparent, considering only the custodial parent as family. In most cases, the custodial parent's remarriage had occurred recently, and the children still had negative feelings about it. These children were the most dissatisfied with their lives and revealed emotional stress during the interview.

Augmentation   Seventeen children (28 percent) added to their original family by including both biological parents and at least one stepparent as members. Most of these children lived with their biological fathers and their stepmothers but continued to have regular contact and a strong relationship with their biological mother. They felt free to move back and forth between the overlapping households without the fear of being disloyal to either biological parent.

A similar survey conducted in the United States also found variations in children's definitions of family membership. When asked, "When you think of your family, who specifically do you include?" Ten percent of the children did not list a biological parent, and 33 percent omitted a stepparent (Furstenberg and Spanier, 1987). Such research suggests that the realities for children involved in remarriages vary considerably. It also challenges definitions of the family that assume an overlap with household membership. In the eyes of both children and parents, families may include more or fewer people than current household members. More recent research finds that boundary ambiguity in stepfamilies remains a critical issue; it can have a negative impact on the quality of a couple's relationship and the stability of the union itself. Boundary ambiguity is even more likely in stepfamilies formed as a result of parental cohabitation, where children are even more likely to experience family instability (Raley and Wildsmith, 2004; Stewart, 2005). Further research is needed to examine the relationships among stepsiblings and half-siblings in both cohabiting and remarried families and the degree to which children incorporate these relationships into their subjective views of family.

Consequences of Parental Remarriage for Children

How do children react to the remarriage of their parents? Do they experience more stress or behavioral problems than children in other family structures? To date, studies reveal no consistent and clear answer to these questions. A number of early studies found that stepchildren experience more stress, have more difficulty in school, and have higher

---

INTERNET RESOURCES

APPLYING THE SOCIOLOGICAL IMAGINATION
Working Successfully Across Households

Stephen F. Duncan, a professor in the School of Family Life at Brigham Young University, suggests three major principles for parents to follow when there is some form of shared custody that allows children contact and co-residence with their biological parents at alternating times:

■ Create a parent coalition.
■ Accept continual shifts in household composition.

■ Build relationships with extended family members.

Go to www.foreverfamilies.net/xml/articles/step_working_success_across.aspx and read the entire article. How can these ideas be put into practical terms? What are some of the likely difficulties biological parents might encounter when implementing these ideas? How much of a role should children play in the establishment

of overlapping households? Have you or anyone you know lived in overlapping households? To what extent did they meet Duncan's three principles? With what effect? Visit some of the links connected to this Web site. Evaluate the type of help and support available to stepfamilies. Does the type of information you are finding enhance your understanding of this marriage form?

rates of delinquency and emotional problems than children living in their original families (Hetherington and Clingempeel, 1992; Peterson and Zill, 1986; Santrock and Sitterle, 1987). Yet at the same time other studies suggested that in the long run stepchildren are only slightly more troubled than children in original families and that most stepchildren eventually adapted and emerged as reasonably competent people (Ganong and Coleman, 1994; Hetherington and Jodl, 1994). Marilyn Ihinger-Tallman and Kay Pasley (1987) found that children in stepfamilies are similar to those in intact families in self-esteem, psychological functioning, and academic achievement. More recent research shows similar patterns. On the one hand, Nicholas Wolfinger (2005) found that children of divorce and later remarriage were twice as likely to struggle academically, behaviorally, and socially as children of first marriages. On the other hand, E. Mavis Hetherington and John Kelly (2002), in their 20-year study, found that the vast majority of divorced children and stepchildren built productive and satisfied lives. How are we to reconcile these divergent findings?

Some researchers find fault with how some studies are done, arguing that they focus on the problems and stress in stepfamilies and ignore the positive behaviors that make them function effectively (Coleman et al., 2001). Closely related to this is the argument that many of the differences reported between children in stepfamilies and children in first-marriage families tend to be small and that, in fact, there are more similarities than differences among children from different family structures (Coleman, Ganong, and Fines, 2002). Other researchers have found that children in remarried families do quite well if conflict between parents is minimized and if stepfamilies build satisfactory relationships (Braithwaite et al. 2001). Thus, family structure per se may be less important than the kind of relationship that exists within it. Also, time may be a factor here. There is a growing body of evidence that men who become stepfathers more recently may be more involved with stepchildren than men in prior decades. This is significant because close bonds between stepfathers and stepchildren are associated with better child outcomes (Pryor and Rodgers, 2001).

Stepfamilies, like all families, face many challenges and various factors are at work that influence whether the outcome will be positive or negative. The first step in trying to understand this process is to recognize the timing and complexity of divorce and subsequent remarriage. As one research team observed, "Empirical findings suggest that the age of the child at the time of parental divorce and remarriage, sex of the child, and sex of the stepparent are important factors for understanding and predicting the influence of family change on children" (Ihinger-Tallman and Pasley, 1991:461).

Age Studies suggest that if parental remarriage occurs early in the child's life (before age 5), it has few adverse effects. In contrast, school-aged children experience more stress after a residential parent remarries, and schoolwork and social behavior are frequently adversely affected (Arnold, 1998). In comparison with younger children, older children find it more difficult to adjust to new people and new places, and they experience a complex set of emotions regarding both. As adolescents struggle to become more autonomous, the addition of another "parenting" adult in the household may be perceived as threatening (Skaggs and Jodl, 1999). This may be especially true for the oldest child in a single-parent family. In that position, the child may have had considerable authority over younger siblings and may have acted as confidant for the custodial parent. For some children, relinquishing this responsibility may be a relief; others may resent the loss of power and status.

Sex When sex differences are taken into account, interesting patterns emerge. Research has consistently shown that boys have more problems adjusting to divorce than do girls. In contrast, in stepfamilies girls experience more adjustment problems and report poorer relationships with parents than do boys (Ganong and Coleman, 1994). For example, after a parental divorce there is an upswing in drug use among boys but not among girls. However, the pattern is reversed following a remarriage; there is increased drug use by girls but reduced use by boys (Needle, Su, and Doherty, 1990). Recent research suggest that boys have closer relationships to stepfathers and nonresident fathers than girls (King, Harris, and Heard, 2004) and that close father–child relationships are predictive of less delinquency and substance use among adolescents, more so for sons than for daughters (Bronte-Tinkew et al., 2006).

Observational studies have found that compared with stepsons, stepdaughters are more sullen, withdrawn, and direct more negative problem-solving behavior toward stepfathers (Hetherington, 1989). Other researchers report similar findings, particularly in mother-custody stepfamilies (Vuchinich et al., 1991). Part of the explanation for this pattern lies in the nature of the relationships established after divorce. The most common structure in remarried families is a biological mother, her children, and a stepfather. This pattern is because in the United States divorced mothers overwhelmingly get custody of their biological children. Girls often become closer to the custodial parent after a divorce and view the stepfather as an intruder or the stepmother as competition. In fact, closer mother–stepfather relationships are associated with more behavior problems in girls. Additionally, the adolescent stepdaughter–stepfather relationship may be confusing for both parties. The emerging sexuality of adolescent girls may cause both to be uncertain about the appropriate way to express affection for each other. Girls may feel uncomfortable with a nonbiologically related adult male in the household (Hetherington, 1989). These tensions are reflected in the fact that girls in stepfamily households leave home to marry or live independently at an earlier age than those in either single- or two-parent households (Goldscheider and Goldscheider, 1993). This tendency is more pronounced in households containing stepsiblings (Aquilino, 1991). Similarly, in a British study of young adults, respondents were asked why they left their parental home. Those who had lived in stepfamily households were more likely to say they left because of "friction at home" than those in other types of households (Kiernan, 1992).

Boys, on the other hand, are initially angry that dad was "sent away," but then they become comfortable with another male presence in the household. The presence of a stepfather often eases the mother–son problems that resulted from the divorce. Boys now find themselves with a source of support and companionship. E. Mavis Hetherington (1989) found that preadolescent boys who enjoy a close supportive stepfather–stepson relationship display fewer behavior problems and increased social competence.

Although stepparent–stepchild relationships can be troublesome, most of these problems disappear by the third year into the remarriage. Perhaps the best advice for parents in such situations is to be patient.

Stepsibling Relationships: Rivalry or Solidarity? As with the role of children in remarriages, stepsibling relationships have rarely been studied utilizing the perspective of children themselves. This is a critical omission for, as we will see later in this chapter, children can affect the stability of the remarriage. As we have just discussed, part of the difficulty lies in the relationship between stepparent and stepchild. However, a significant part of the tension in remarried families is centered on stepsibling relationships. Why is this the case? What is it like to be a stepsibling? How are stepsibling relationships different from sibling relationships in intact families?

William Beer (1988) reviewed the literature on remarried families and found only indirect references to the subject of stepsiblings. When stepsiblings were discussed, it was generally in relation to one of four themes: (1) stepsibling rivalry, (2) changes in age order, (3) stepsibling sexuality, and (4) the role of half-siblings. The following discussion relies heavily on his work.

Stepsibling Rivalry   One of the main differences between siblings and stepsiblings is the origin of their relationships. In the idealized pattern, children arrive after the marital relationship has been solidified. They share two biological parents and hence a sense of belonging to the same family unit. This does not mean, however, that their relationships are always harmonious. In fact, siblings sometimes experience intense rivalry for parental love.

Stepsiblings, however, start out in a different place than children in intact families. They were part of a family unit disrupted by death or divorce. Since that disruption, they have formed close relationships with the custodial parent prior to a remarriage. Now they are asked to share this parent not only with another adult but with other children as well. Family therapist Emily Visher (1994) stresses the importance of maintaining one-on-one parent–child relationships. When a parent spends time alone with a child, it increases the security a child is likely to feel in the relationship. One of her clients complained:

Before my dad got married again, I liked it. We had a lot of free time together. We played Nintendo games and we

stayed up late and watched TV on Friday nights, and sometimes we went out to eat pizza. Now we have to take Kate and Shawna and Kathy with us. I liked just the two of us. (Quoted in Visher, 1994:334).

In addition, children are asked to share living space, property, and other possessions that may be in short supply. Sharing space is less of a problem when the remarried family moves into new, neutral housing, where no one has yet established territorial claims. This option, however, requires a degree of affluence that is absent for many remarried families. Thus, the more common pattern is for one part of the remarried family to move into the residence of the other. When this occurs, the former are likely to be seen as intruders and to feel like unwelcome guests. As an 8-year-old stepdaughter reported:

We feel like guests in Jim's house. We are careful of what we do. It is like we are intruders. And I feel very bad that we took Tommy's room. They fixed up a room for him in the basement, with posters and all, but he's still mad at us for taking his room. (Cited in Fishman and Hamel, 1991:442)

Consequently, neither party is really comfortable with this arrangement, at least in the beginning, and it may give rise to stepsibling rivalry.

 Imagine you were Tommy. How would you react? What can remarried families do to minimize such disruptions when households are merged?

Several other factors contribute to stepsibling rivalry. First, there is often a feeling of "them" and "us." Children see their ties to their biological parent as giving them a greater claim in the competition for love and other resources: "She's my mom, not yours." Second, when the families were separate, both units had their own rules. After remarriage, stepparents may try to impose all the rules

Integrating members of two different families can be difficult. Remarriage can also provide emotionally satisfying relationships for stepsiblings, however.

impartially on all stepchildren, both those living in the same household and those who only visit. This attempt at impartiality, however, may not be perceived as equitable by the stepchildren because the rules are often more familiar to one set of children than the other. Third, differential treatment by others can lead to feelings of rejection, hostility, and envy. For example, grandparents may provide generous gifts to their biological grandchildren and ignore their stepgrandchildren. Excluding some children in gift exchanges weakens the chances for establishing a sense of family integration as it reflects the image that some are "outsiders."

Changes in Age Order   In intact families, the natural order of family births determines the age order and age interval of siblings that, in turn, provide a relatively stable ranking system for children. Each position carries advantages and disadvantages for its occupant, and the children know where they fit in. However, when two sets of siblings are combined through remarriage, some siblings may find their age order positions in the family altered. Some of these changes are easier to accept than others. For example, when an only child becomes the oldest child, a position of privilege is retained. To a degree, benefits also accompany the transition from being an only child to becoming the youngest child or "baby" of the family. The most difficult change is losing the position of being the oldest to another child, especially one of the same sex. Although these changes often cause tensions in the short run, over time children learn to adapt to the new sibling social structure.

Stepsibling Sexuality   When the new sibling social structure includes adolescents of different sexes, drawing and maintaining sexual boundaries may become a critical task for remarried families. Sexual tension is usually a greater problem in remarried families than in first marriages. Several factors interact to create this atmosphere. First, the parent–stepparent union is relatively new. As a couple, they are still likely to be in a honeymoon stage, showing affection for each other, which may be sexually stimulating for adolescents. In first marriages, parents have already worked out patterns for privacy over the years. By the time their children reach adolescence, most parents no longer display sexuality overtly (Visher and Visher, 1982). Second, when a teenaged girl and boy who have not grown up together come to live in the same residence, they may become sexually attracted to each other. Parents may unintentionally contribute to this process by encouraging mutual activities as a way of bringing the children together. Third, stepsibling relationships are not covered by the same incest prohibitions as are sibling relationships. This lack of clear rules may cause confusion and uncertainty in remarried families. Given these conditions, it is not surprising that some sort of romantic or erotic attraction sometimes develops between stepsiblings. Nevertheless, at the present time there has been no systematic attempt to measure the extent of such behavior. What information we have on this behavior comes primarily from clinical reports of family therapists and social workers. However, not all sexual feelings between stepsiblings are acted out. A more likely pattern is for adolescents to convert this eroticism into expressions of hostility. Parents often report that stepsiblings seem to "hate each other." This anger can be temporary or long-term; if too severe, it can threaten family stability. A more positive outcome results when children can convert their erotic feelings into warm, supportive relationships. Which outcome is more likely depends, to a large extent, on parental reaction. Open and honest discussions with the involved stepsiblings, reassuring them of the normality of such feelings and making clear that there is a difference between feelings and acting on those feelings, can reduce the possibility of a negative outcome.

The Role of Half-Siblings   As a result of tensions among siblings, it is often difficult for remarried family members to feel like a "real" family. One way in which remarried parents try to overcome this perception and create a cohesive family is by having a mutual child that will provide a blood tie among all members of the remarried family.

The decision to have a mutual child is quite common and occurs soon after remarriage. According to Canadian family demographer Heather Juby (2003/2004), roughly half of stepfamily couples cement their union by having a child together. The youngest stepfamily couples are the ones most likely to decide to have a child together; an additional child is born within about two-thirds of stepfather families created when a young, unmarried mother marries (or moves in with) someone other than her child's father. Next come couples in stepmother families—around half of the women who first experience motherhood as a stepmother later have a child of their own. Only one-third of the other types of stepfamily couples—stepfathers with separated mothers, and those in which both have children from a previous relationship—expand their family by adding a common child. The rapidity with which the birth of a mutual child takes place often causes confusion and adjustment problems for the other children. Although both adults may be biological parents in their own right, they are stepparents to each other's children, and they may or may not share responsibility for them. The birth of a mutual child adds a new role, a shared parental role.

Although this new role may help solidify the couple relationship, it is not problem free. A pattern may emerge whereby both parents exert authority over mutual children but only biological parents assert authority and take responsibility for their own children. This layering of authority and responsibility is a unique feature of remarried families and can produce problems, especially when disagreements over parenting styles arise (Giles-Sims, 1984). When this happens, there is often a tendency to form alliances—each parent siding with her or his biological offspring or criticizing the other's children, to produce what Emily Visher and John Visher (1982) have called the "two-family-under-one-roof" syndrome.

Stepchildren may see the birth of a mutual child as adding yet another competitor for parental attention. Conversely stepchildren may have positive feelings about the birth of a half-sibling, believing that because they are now all related by a blood tie, they finally all belong to a "real" family. Some support for the beneficial role of having a mutual child comes from the pioneering research of Lucile Duberman (1973). Forty-four percent of her parent respondents who had a mutual child reported that relationships between the siblings were excellent, compared with 19 percent of those without mutual children. Later research supports this finding; half-siblings come to see each other simply as siblings (Ganong and Coleman, 1994). These relationships are likely to be strongest when the mutual child comes at a time when the remarriage is well established and when there is only one child from each of the two prior marriages.

In sum, we have seen that stepsibling and half-sibling relationships can be conflictual. However, that is only part of the story. The dynamics of living in a remarried family with stepsiblings and/or half-siblings can also have positive effects. Just as in first families, stepsibling rivalry can help children distinguish themselves from others in the family, thereby giving them a strong sense of personal identity. For example, if an older stepsibling is active in sports, a younger stepsibling may turn to music to express her or his individuality. Competition among stepsiblings in some areas does not prevent them from cooperating in other areas. Just as in intact families, solidarity among stepsiblings is a likely outcome of ongoing family dynamics (Ganong and Coleman, 1994).

Stepsibling Relationships over Time   Sociologists Lynn White and Agnes Riedman (1992) undertook the first empirical research on adult step/half-siblings, focusing on their relationships after they grow up and leave home. In general, they found evidence of continued contact and interaction. Although contact was more frequent among full siblings (one to three times a month) compared with the several times a year that step/half-siblings were seen, less than 1 percent of the respondents in that study were so estranged that they did not even know where their step/half-sibling lived. Contact among step/half-siblings was affected by three key factors: race, gender, and proximity. As true among full siblings, African Americans, females, and those who lived near one another had the most frequent contact.

To date, we have relatively little information about the quality of these relationships. However, Marilyn Ihinger-Tallman (1987) hypothesizes that stepsibling bonding occurs most rapidly under conditions of similarity (age, sex, experience, shared values), interdependency, perceived mutual benefit of association, few perceived personal costs, and approximate equality in relinquishing aspects of a former lifestyle. Confirmation of this hypothesis awaits further research.

Adult Children's Reaction to Parental Later-Life Remarriages

It is not only younger children who get caught up in the dynamics of stepfamilies. As we saw in Chapter 12, the divorce rate is increasing among older adults. Thus, children who are independent adults can find themselves suddenly thrust into the world of adult stepfamilies. Estimates are that about 500,000 Americans over the age of 65 remarry each year; 266,600 were cohabiting in 2000 (cited in Cohn, 2005). In these situations, both parents and children are often surprised by the emotional reactions this process engenders. Parents often assume that since their children are grown and leading their own lives, a parental remarriage or cohabiting experience will be problem free. Yet, adult children may have some of the same fears as younger children—fear of being abandoned by their parents, displaced by the new spouse or partner, or losing an inheritance. They may express these fears by anger or by limiting their contact with the new couple. If the new spouse also has children, there may be jealousy, confusion, and perceived loyalty conflicts. Like in any stepfamily, boundaries need to be identified and expectations clarified. However, if adult children can come to terms with this new family form, they often find they have gained a friend and an ally who will be there as their parent gets older and needs more help. Conversely, stepparents acquired in later life may not be seen as family members and thus adult children may feel that norms of family obligations do not apply to them and they have little or no contact with them after their biological parent dies (Ganong and Coleman, 2006).

Children are not the only players in determining how well remarried families function. Stepparents also play key parts. Let us first look at stepmotherhood. The most typical form of stepmothering in the United States is part-time, occasioned by the weekend and holiday visits of children to their remarried biological father.

Stepmothers: A Bad Rap?

To what extent are the cultural images of the wicked stepmother valid? Although research does not substantiate the fairy tale image of the "wicked" stepmother, it does suggest that stepmothers have the most negative image of any family member and are often perceived as being less affectionate, good, fair, kind, loving, and likeable (Recker, 2001). In one longitudinal study involving 1400 divorced families, only about 20 percent of adult stepchildren reported feeling close to their stepmoms (Hetherington and Kelly, 2002). Children who have negative images of stepmothers may not develop a positive relationship with their new stepmother. In turn, children's unpleasant behavior may cause stepmothers to be more critical of stepchildren (Berger, 1998). Real-life stepmother and stepdaughter Kali and Elizabeth Schnieders (2005) provide insight into the dynamics of this type of behavior in their book, *You're Not My Mom: Confessions of a Formerly "Wicked" Stepmother*. In it they reveal their up- and down struggle for over ten years to build a meaningful relationship.

Deciding how to approach the new stepmother role is not easy. Margaret Draughon (1975) suggests three possibilities: (1) "other mother," or second mother; (2) primary mother, who assumes major responsibility for day-to-day caregiving; and (3) friend, who is supportive and caring but does not try to be a substitute mother. According to Draughon, the choice of role should be based on the degree of emotional comfort the stepmother feels as well as on the child's emotional state at the time. Draughon believes if the child is still mourning the loss of the biological mother, whether through death or divorce, the role of friend works best. If, however, mourning has ended, the primary-mother role is probably more appropriate. This role, however, must be defined carefully. Generally speaking, defining it to mean primary caretaker instead of a replacement for the biological parent is likely to minimize stepparent–stepchild conflict. Draughon sees no particular advantage to the other-mother model. Later research supports her position. Stepfamilies in which the stepmother plays the other-mother role are the most likely to experience tension and conflict (Kurdek and Fine, 1993). A more recent study of nonresidential stepmothers identified three roles enacted by stepmothers similar to Draughon's categories: mothering but not mother roles, other-focused roles, and outsider roles. The choice of role to enact depended on a variety of issues related to biological mothers, spouses, stepchildren, biological children, and the stepmother's own ideology of motherhood (Weaver and Coleman, 2005). Stepmothers, whether residential or not, face a difficult dilemma—doing mothering things but not being a mother.

Stepmothers and Mothering How do stepmothers fare in the mothering role? Much of the research on stepmother–stepchild relationships shows that these relationships are more tentative and difficult than are stepfather–stepchild relationships (MacDonald and DeMaris, 1996; Pasley and Ihinger-Tallman, 1987). This is due, in large part, to the greater expectations placed on women in families. Women are expected to take primary responsibility for the well-being of the family, especially in the area of child care, regardless of whose children they "mother." Such expectations can be more distressing for a woman who chooses a marital role but not necessarily a parenting role when she marries a noncustodial father. After remarriage she may find that his children visit more frequently than anticipated or that child custody has shifted unexpectedly to him. Furthermore, the expectations for

women regarding nurturing are so strong that stepmothers themselves often assume that "instant love" of stepchildren should be possible. For this reason, stepmothers frequently feel guilty when they do not as yet feel a strong attachment to their spouse's children. One stepmother writing in for advice said,

> I feel like a stereotypical wicked stepmother when I complain about my stepchildren because they are good kids. They really are. I understand that the irritating things they do are totally normal for kids their age and I think that maybe if I loved them then perhaps I wouldn't care so much about the stuff that bugs me. But I don't know how to make that happen. I don't love them now and I don't think I ever will. To be completely honest, sometimes I even feel disgusted by them. (Quoted in Tennis, 2005).

In addition, a stepmother's attempt to create a close-knit family structure may be misinterpreted. The biological mother may accuse her of trying to take her place. The stepchildren may also perceive her behavior as a threat to their mother's position. On the other hand, if the stepmother chooses a less involved approach toward her stepchildren, she may be accused by them and her spouse of not caring enough or not being a good mother. A common reaction to these situations is stress. Stepmothers report significantly greater role strain than do stepfathers (Nielsen, 1999). Melady Preece (2003/2004) suggests that this greater stress stems from traditional gender ideology. Many husbands view the caring for children as their wives' responsibility, even when the children are his, not hers. When stepchildren visit, the stepmothers, and not the fathers, usually acquire extra work, such as housecleaning and cooking.

We should remember, however, that not all stepparenting situations are alike. In a study of 109 stepparents, Anne-Marie Ambert (1986) found that having live-in stepchildren is less divisive than having children who live with the other parent come for visits. The former situation allows the couple more control over their lives. Wives felt more "appreciated" by their spouses because of their child-rearing contributions and felt less threatened by the biological mother. Stepmothers developed a closer and deeper relationship with their live-in stepchildren than with stepchildren living elsewhere. These research findings are significant in that they offer an explanation for why stepfathers seem to have fewer problems in their role. Most stepfathers, in contrast to most stepmothers, have live-in stepchildren. What role, then, do stepfathers play in remarried families?

Stepfathers: Polite Strangers?

In an earlier section of this chapter, we discussed the cultural images of the "wicked" stepmother. Although no comparable image or body of folktales exists for stepfathers, they are often stereotyped as indifferent or even abusive, the latter exemplified in the 2001 film, *Domestic Violence*, which depicts a violent and ruthless stepfather. Newspaper accounts of lethal assaults on children by stepfathers as well as an extensive body of research on domestic

Remarried families are complex. The members of this family include a son from his first marriage, a daughter from her first marriage, and the child they had together. A major decision for these parents is who should be the disciplinarian.

violence involving stepfamilies (Daly and Wilson, 1994; Weekes-Shackelford and Shackelford, 2004) continues to contribute to a popular perception of a dysfunctional family structure. However, a considerable amount of social science research focused on stepfather families and the specific role of stepfathers in these families provides a substantially different view.

A fairly consistent image of stepfathers has emerged from these investigations. Overall, stepfathers tend to be more positive and responsive and less negative and directive toward children than are biological fathers (Hetherington and Henderson, 1997). Samuel Vuchinich and his colleagues (1991) characterize such behaviors as the "sociable polite stranger" role. This pattern of stepparenting might explain the finding that stepfathers in stable stepfamilies generally enjoy better relations with their stepchildren than do stepmothers (Ganong and Coleman, 1994). In a recent study, 63 percent of children reported having a good or very good relationship with their stepfather (Smith, 2004). However, this finding should not be interpreted to mean that stepfathers do not encounter problems in this role. They do. Elizabeth Einstein (1985) identified three areas of difficulty for stepfathers: sex, money, and discipline.

Sex Stepfathers may feel uncomfortable in the presence of sexually developing adolescent stepdaughters. To prevent any misinterpretation by the stepdaughter or her mother, stepfathers often remain emotionally distant from their stepdaughter, with the result that the stepdaughter may perceive him as uncaring.

Money Finances may be a source of conflict for stepfathers in a number of ways. If he is a noncustodial biological parent, he may feel guilty for not playing a more active role in his own children's lives. Thus, he may give his children money or expensive gifts to compensate for his absence, thereby creating envy among his stepchildren. This behavior may also cause friction with both his current spouse, who feels the money is needed elsewhere, and with his ex-spouse, who fears he is buying his children's love by spoiling them. In other cases, the economic demands of a second family may be so severe that he stops supporting the children from his first family. Despite these very real problems, many stepfathers invest significant financial resources in their children. This is especially the case when the stepfather's biological children and his stepchildren are living in the same household with him (Anderson et al., 2001; Hofferth and Anderson, 2003).

Discipline Issues involving discipline revolve around two key questions: Who should discipline? Under what conditions? The answers to these questions may be far from clear not only on the part of the stepfather but in the minds of other family members as well. The wife and mother in the remarried family may voice a desire to share authority with her new spouse, but when he takes her up on it, she may be emotionally unprepared to relinquish any of her authority over her children. Earlier research showed that it took approximately 18 to 24 months for stepparents to achieve an

equal "co-management" role with the biological parent (Visher and Visher, 1982). More recent research suggests it may take longer, as long as 5 to 7 years for stepfathers to form good relationships with their children (Cohn and Merkel, 2004). Rather than disciplining children from the outset, many stepfathers gradually slide into the role over time (Marsiglio, 2004).

Stepchildren, too, may hold contradictory views regarding discipline by a stepfather. They may resent his efforts to make them behave. Yet if he does not try to discipline them, they may perceive him as indifferent and uncaring, and respond angrily, "You don't care what I do; you don't love me." Researchers have found a correlation between stepchildren's perception of being loved by a stepparent and whether the stepparent makes them behave (Bohannan, 1985). The dilemma of discipline appears to be lessened in cases where children are young or where a friendship has been established first between the stepparent and the stepchild. When friendship exists, stepchildren are more likely to accept discipline from the stepparent. A study of 20 well-functioning stepfamilies confirmed this finding. These stepparents found that things work best when the stepparent does not arrive as a disciplinarian right away (Kelley, 1995).

Lesbian and Gay Stepfamilies

Lesbian and gay stepfamilies existed long before same-sex marriage became a political issue. A parent may have realized (or came to accept) that she or he is homosexual only after being in a heterosexual marriage. After a divorce, she or he may have moved in with a same-sex partner. Lesbian and gay parents who form same-sex unions confront the same challenges facing heterosexual stepfamilies. However, because of their sexual orientation, their very existence as a family unit is often questioned. Thus, lesbian and gay stepfamilies may lack the support given to heterosexual stepparents and often face prejudicial and discriminatory treatment (van Dam, 2004). In fact, Roni Berger (2001) considers lesbian and gay stepfamilies a triple stigmatized group. First, they are stigmatized because of their homosexuality, which is still regarded as deviant or a sin by many people. Second, gay parenthood is stigmatized because many people perceive lesbians and gay unfit to be parents and view their family structure of a stepfamily as deficient compared with nuclear families. Finally, within the homosexual community itself, lesbian and gay parents may suffer stigmatization from those who emphasize the primacy of the partner relationship and who perceive children as a threat to couple relationships.

Although no precise figures exist on the number of children being raised in lesbian and gay stepfamilies, the fact that reproductive technology and changes in adoption laws allow more lesbians and gays to become parents suggests there are and will continue to be an increasing number of people functioning in such units. As we observed in previous chapters, studies on lesbian and gay lifestyles, particularly family lifestyle issues, are just beginning to emerge. One such study examined lesbian stepparent roles and found three distinct patterns: (1) the coparent family, in which the nonbiological mother takes the role of an active parent and committed family member by being a helper and supporter of and consultant to the biological mother; (2) the stepmother family, in which the lesbian stepparent fulfills many of the traditional mothering tasks while the biological mother functions as the decision maker, a pattern similar to the traditional heterosexual stepfamily model; and (3) the co-mother family, where both mothers share responsibilities in the day-to-day decision-making and child-rearing tasks (Wright, 1998). Similarly, other studies show that lesbian and gay stepfamilies are diverse and flexible in constructing family roles (see for example, Lynch, 2000).

Ex-Spouses: Do They Fade Away?

Divorce ends a marriage, but it does not necessarily end the relationship between the former spouses. This is especially true for couples with children. How do couples come to view each other after divorce? One study of divorced fathers and their new wives found that most of these couples identified the children's mother as a major source of stress in their marriage. Both the ex-husband and their wives described the ex-wife in negative terms (Guisinger, Cowan, and Schuldberg, 1989). This finding seems to support the popular image of ex-spouses as warring factions. In other studies, however, researchers found that only a fraction of the sample of divorced couples fit that description. Such couples were classified as either "angry associates," whose relationships are characterized by bitterness, resentment, and ongoing conflicts over visitation and support payments, or "fiery foes," whose relationships are extremely antagonistic. The lingering acrimony of their divorce made it impossible for them to cooperate with each other on any matter.

In contrast, a number of divorced couples maintained cordial relationships, with each other as "cooperative colleagues" who are friendly and mutually concerned about their children's' welfare. They managed to make decisions and celebrate their children's major life events together. A smaller number of ex-spouses remained "perfect pals." Their divorce was amiable; they continued to like and trust each other, and they worked cooperatively to maintain a positive environment for their children. Finally, there are the dissolved duos, ex-spouses who have little or no contact after the divorce (Ahrons, 1994).

A recent study of 1791 previously married women and men in the Netherlands found that 10 years after divorce, almost half of the respondents report contact with their former spouse and that the number of former couples with antagonistic contact decreases strongly over time. However, couples with joint children have both more friendly contact and more antagonistic contact than other couples (Fischer, de Graab, and Kalmijn, 2005). As we discussed previously, the nature of the relationship between former spouses is an important factor in how well their children adjust to a parent's remarriage and in the frequency and kind of contact children have with the nonresident parent.

Thus far, our discussion of remarried families has tended to focus on the numerous adjustment problems members face. This should in no way be interpreted to mean that there are few benefits to living in remarried families. Quite the opposite is true, as we will see in the next section.

THE STRENGTHS AND BENEFITS OF REMARRIED FAMILIES

The identification of strengths in remarried families is a relatively new phase in social science research. Patricia Knaub and her colleagues (1984) were among the first to undertake an empirical study of what makes remarried families strong. They asked 80 randomly selected remarried families to indicate what strengths were most important to their families. Their respondents listed love and intimacy (caring, affection, closeness, acceptance, understanding), family unity (working together; shared goals, values, and activities), and positive patterns of communication (honesty, openness, receptiveness, and a sense of humor), characteristics important to all families.

Further insight into the strengths of remarried families comes from a study of remarried couples in central Pennsylvania (Furstenberg and Spanier, 1984). These couples felt their current marriage was stronger than their first marriage in three important ways. First, they had better communication skills. Second, they were more realistic about the existence of conflict in marriage, and perhaps as a result of having better communication skills, they reported having fewer conflicts in their second marriage. Third, the balance of power in decision making was more equal in the remarriage. A review of studies conducted in the 1990s supports the finding of equitable power sharing and decision making by spouses in stepfamilies (Coleman, Ganong, and Fine, 2002). A comparison of 111 remarried and 111 matched first-married spouses also found that remarried spouses endorsed more autonomous standards in child rearing and finances and remarried women endorsed greater autonomy regarding friendships and family. The division of household tasks also appeared to be less traditional in remarried families (Sandin et al., 2001).

Actor Bruce Willis joins his former wife Demi Moore and her new husband Ashton Kutcher at a family gathering. Like many divorced parents, Willis and Moore are staying in contact so that both can be involved in the lives of their three children.

In addition, John Visher and Emily Visher (1993), two therapists who work with remarried families, identified six behavior patterns associated with building successful step-families: (1) developing realistic expectations, (2) allowing children to mourn their losses, (3) building and maintaining a strong couple relationship, (4) proceeding slowly in constructing the stepparent roles, (5) creating their own traditions and rituals, (6) developing satisfactory rules and arrangements for children living in overlapping households. Dawn Braithwaite and her colleagues (2001) found similar dynamics at work by which remarried families came to "feel like a family," and a review of 50 years of research on naturally occurring family routines and rituals found that the establishment of family routines and rituals contribute to parenting competence, child adjustment, and marital satisfaction (Fiese et al., 2001). Establishing new routines and rituals early on is especially critical to the success of setting family boundaries of inclusion in remarried families.

Finally, other researchers have also documented the importance that a strong couple relationship plays in the success of remarried families. When children see a stable and well-functioning relationship between their parent and stepparent, it reduces their fears about the possibility of another breakup and also provides them with role models who can resolve problems in a rational and nonthreatening manner (Kheshgi-Genovese and Genovese, 1997).

Remarriage offers a number of benefits to family members. A custodial parent gains a partner with whom to share family work as well as financial responsibility. In exchange, the new stepparent shares in the joys of family life. For the new spouses, remarriage restores the continuity of a sexual relationship and provides companionship and a sense of partnership. Additionally, although it might be viewed as a mixed blessing, the ambiguity of roles in remarried families offers family members the opportunity to create new ones that may prove more satisfying in the long run. For example, stepparents do not have to try to replace parents; instead, they can be friends, counselors, teachers, or companions to stepchildren. Both stepparents and stepchildren can benefit by interactions that are less encumbered by unrealistic expectations of instant family love and unity.

THE QUALITY OF THE REMARITAL RELATIONSHIP

When remarried people are asked about the quality of their relationships, the results show a mixed picture. Despite all the problems we have just discussed, most remarried couples, overall, seem to find happiness in their new relationship. In reviewing the literature on remarriage, Coleman and Ganong (1991) found that there were very few differences between spouses in first marriages and those in remarriages. A more recent study comparing first-married and remarried military couples found that remarried couples reported lower marital satisfaction than first-married couples (Adler-Baeder, Taylor, and Pasley, 2005). However, like earlier studies, the difference between the two groups was small.

When gender is examined, however, larger differences in levels of happiness and satisfaction emerge. In both first marriages and remarriages men report higher levels of satisfaction than women. For stepmothers, the perception of child-care inequities were the strongest predictor of marital dissatisfaction over time (Pasley, Dollahite, and Ihinger-Tallman, 1993). The help of the biological father in child-care and household tasks was associated with better adjustment to the stepparent role (Guisinger, Cowan, and Schuldberg, 1989). These findings resemble data obtained from two-income couples discussed in Chapter 10.

As is true with first marriages, the presence of children in stepfamilies can affect the quality of family happiness. Studies of middle- and upper-middle-class families with adolescents reveal that the quality of the stepfather–stepchild relationship had a greater impact on family happiness than did the quality of the marital relationship (Crosbie-Burnett, 1984). Remarried couples with children from previous marriages are more likely to divorce than are remarried couples without stepchildren (Pill, 1990).

Other studies reinforce the view that successful stepfamilies require partners who not only can cope with the usual stresses of stepfamily living but who can successfully relinquish traditional gendered parenthood roles (White, 1994). When there is disagreement over discipline, house rules, and financial resources, remarried spouses are likely to express more marital dissatisfaction (Coleman et al., 2002). In her study of well-functioning stepfamilies, Patricia Kelley (1995) found general agreement among the respondents that it works best not to define gender roles as distinctly as they are in many families. Thus, both spouses took on nurturing and provision functions. These stepparents found that discipline and primary nurturing are usually best done by the biological parent, not the stepparent, regardless of gender.

Other factors can also impact a remarried couple's relationship. Among them is the form the stepfamily takes. For example, several researchers found that marital satisfaction was higher in mother–stepfather families where the stepfather had no children from a previous marriage than in stepfamilies where the stepfather coparented children from another marriage with an ex-spouse (Clingempeel and Brand, 1985; Giles-Sims, 1984). These authors explain this qualitative difference in terms of the nature of the coparenting relationship that exists with ex-spouses. If the relationship is one of conflict over ongoing issues, for example, child support, discipline, or visitation rights, the stress created by these issues is likely to have a negative impact on the remarried couple's relationship. However, if the stepparent and ex-spouse have resolved their emotional problems and are able to relate to each other and to their children on a nonconflictual basis, then this situation should not exert stress on the remarriage.

In sum, then, what can couples do to facilitate happiness in remarriage? Remarried couples who accept their children's loyalties to noncustodial parents, accept their spouse's ongoing coparenting relationship with an ex-spouse, and resolve the problems raised by their prior marriage are likely to have a happy remarriage. However, as we shall see in the next section, happiness in the remarried couple relationship may not, in and of itself, be sufficient to ensure the stability of the remarriage.

Stability in Remarriage

Songwriters Sammy Cahn and James van Heusen popularized the notion that "love is lovelier the second time around." Conventional wisdom would have us believe that second marriages should be more successful than first marriages. People often assume divorced people possess characteristics that should translate into more effective relationships. On average, the divorced are older and seemingly more mature and experienced than those entering marriages for the first time. Thus, the argument goes, they should make more intelligent choices, have more realistic expectations, and have more negotiating skills with which to handle the stresses and strains that arise in married life.

But do they? Overall, research shows that first marriages are somewhat more stable than remarriages. An analysis of divorce rates found that the cumulative probability of first-marriage dissolution after 10 years of marriage was 33 percent, whereas the probability of second-marriage dissolution after 10 years of marriage was 39 percent. After 10 years of remarriage, 48 percent of African American women's remarriages, 39 percent of white women's remarriages, and 29 percent of Latina remarriages dissolved (Bramlett and Mosher, 2001).

Factors Affecting Stability   Several factors combine to explain divorce among remarried couples. First, as we have already observed, remarriage is a complex process, requiring a number of adjustments that are outside the scope of first marriages and for which most remarried couples are not well prepared. To cite just one example, kinship terms and interactions may be a sticky point for all those affected by remarriage. Because stepchildren already have biological parents they call "Mom" and "Dad," forms of address for stepparents must be worked out. In her study of well-functioning stepfamilies, Patricia Kelley (1995) found that most of the children called their stepparents by their first names. According to Kelley, by not having a mandate to love and obey, steprelationships could more easily flourish, and love often did develop between stepparent and stepchild.

Another potential source of divisiveness centers on how to integrate multiple sets of grandparents into holiday and family celebrations. What happens to previous family customs and traditions? Sociologist Andrew Cherlin (1978) argues that "remarriage is an incomplete institution" that does not provide answers to these questions. Consequently, remarried families are left adrift to find their own solutions to these problems. Without institutionalized patterns of family behavior and support, family unity is likely to be precarious.

Outside Support and Pressures   In addition, the attitudes of relatives, friends, and community members can affect the stability of remarriages. Positive and supportive reactions from friends and relatives contribute to successful remarriages. Conversely, disapproval of the remarriage by significant others can put added stress on the relationship. Sometimes the announcement of a remarriage may be greeted with little enthusiasm on the part of relatives. As one stepmother said in an interview,

> My mother was thrilled for me when I told her I was going to marry, but her manner changed completely when I told her he had a child. She was wary for me, she wanted me to think about it. It was not the dream she had for my marriage. (Smith, 1990:30)

In addition, sheer numbers can add to the challenges facing remarried couples. A stepfamily can have an unusually large extended family. For example, as Donald Duncan (2001) observes, a divorce and remarriage of a couple with three children could generate as many as 100 possible kin relationships. Stepfamilies need to think creatively about how to develop relationships with all their extended kin. Holidays can be especially problematic when children must be shared between families.

Attitudes toward Divorce   Moreover, the familiarity with the divorce process itself may remove some of the social barriers to a second divorce. Having survived a first divorce, some remarried people are less likely to stay in an unhappy or deteriorating relationship. Furthermore, because they have already dealt with the reactions of family and friends to their first divorce, they are likely to be less fearful of an adverse public reaction to their course of action.

This seems especially true for some groups. For example, remarried white men are more likely to redivorce than remarried white women (Glick, 1984). This seems strange, given that women tend to report less happiness in second marriages than do men. Yet, the reverse pattern is found among African Americans. More African American women than men divorce a second time. The most frequently cited explanation for these opposing patterns focuses exclusively on economic motivation. According to this argument, African American women come closer to having economic equality with African American men than white women do with white men. Consequently, remarriage may not represent the same level of financial security for African American women as it does for white women. This interpretation clearly ignores many noneconomic factors. It may be that many African American women, having been socialized to be assertive and self-sufficient (Hale-Benson, 1986), simply are less willing than other women to stay in an unhappy relationship. It could also be that the African American community does not view divorce with the same stigma that the white community does.

The Presence of Children   Children may play a pivotal role in the parental decision to redivorce. Women who have children at the time of remarriage are more likely to experience second marriage disruption than woman who do not have any children, and if the children were unwanted, the probability of disruption is even higher. After 10 years of remarriage, the probability of disruption is 32 percent for women with no children at remarriage. For women with children, but none of whom were reported as unwanted, the probability is 40 percent, and for women with children, any of whom were reported as unwanted, the probability is 44 percent (Bramlet and Mosher, 2002). On the other hand, stepfamily couples who have a mutual child together stay together longer than those who do not. Nevertheless, compared with other children, those born within most types of stepfamilies are more likely to experience their parents' separation before their 10th birthday (Juby, 2003/2004). Marilyn Ihinger-Tallman and Kay Pasley (1991) suggest three ways in which children can contribute to the dissolution of remarriages: personal adjustments, discipline problems, and disruptive behavior.

The presence of children makes adjustment harder for a remarried couple. Children limit a couple's privacy and their opportunities for intimacy. Couples may agree on aspects of their personal relationship but be at odds over what constitutes appropriate child behavior. This is especially likely considering the different parenting histories of each partner. As we saw earlier, another source of conflict for remarried couples with children is discipline. Stepparents may feel that discipline was too lax in the "old" family and that new rules are in order. Stepchildren may resent such changes, and biological parents may feel caught in the middle. Consequently, all parties are likely to experience stress.

The behavior of children can be a powerful force in disrupting the marital relationship. Children can manipulate the biological parent into taking sides against the stepparent or stepsiblings. If children refuse to cooperate in matters of daily family living, they can create a tense and hostile environment. Time is often required to resolve these issues.

Time   Patricia Papernow (1993, 2001) cautions stepparents to be realistic about the time involved in solidifying stepfamily relationships. She divides the process of becoming a stepfamily into three major stages, each with its own set of developmental tasks. Tasks in the early stages involve becoming aware of fantasies such as "instant love" and letting go of or grieving for unrealistic hopes as well as learning about one's own and others' needs in the new family. In the middle stage members must actively confront differences between family cultures and generate new stepfamily rituals, customs, and codes of conduct in which all members of the family participate. The later stage, generally less conflictual, finds members enjoying the family's new boundaries and relationships and functioning well.

Here, too, however, the awareness process must continue as new issues arise. According to Papernow, families differ in the length of time it takes them to complete the stepfamily cycle. Fast-paced families move through the early stages quickly, and they take about 4 years to complete the cycle; average families take about 7 years; and slow families take about 9 years. These latter families get stuck in the early stages, taking longer to resolve their fan-

tasies and grieve their previous losses. Some families never complete the cycle.

Researchers can gain a better understanding of how stepfamilies fare over time by using *longitudinal studies*, in which the same people are studied at different periods in time. Comparisons of stable remarried families with those that have dissolved should help us to identify ways to help remarried families cope with the unique aspects of remarriage. For example, the therapists' experiences show that it takes a minimum of 4 to 9 years for remarried families to begin to stabilize and develop their own customs, rituals, and history. Knowing that this is a normal pattern for remarried families, some remarried couples, who might otherwise contemplate divorce, may be able to stay together and wait for the "storms" to pass. Support groups for stepfamilies are increasing around the country. This should also help to stabilize this emerging family form.

In the meantime, however, existing research findings on stepfamilies suggest a number of ways in which social policy and enlightened individuals could be enlisted immediately to help support the growing number of stepfamilies in the United States.

SUPPORTING REMARRIAGE AND REMARRIED FAMILIES

Before any social policy can be effective, it must first have a clear view of the targeted population it wishes to serve. As we have discussed throughout this text, many American family policies are still based on a traditional nuclear family model. Yet only a small percentage of families currently fit this model. The processes of divorce and remarriage (and cohabitation) have created a wide variety of household forms. Thus, conceptualization of what constitutes a family must change to include these households. Several steps can be taken immediately to help meet the needs of remarried families.

First, legislators can modify state laws to include a form of legal guardianship, with the custodial parent's agreement, allowing stepparents to function more effectively in families. For instance, stepparents then could be allowed to sign school permission slips, view student records, sign emergency medical forms, and authorize driving permits.

Second, evidence shows that premarital counseling contributes to more stable marriages. Efforts should be made to offer (and to fund) premarital counseling for individuals contemplating remarriage, using remarried couples to share their experiences. Similarly, schools can do their part to recognize stepfamilies as one of a variety of families by including them in curricular materials and teacher preparation courses that reflect their organization and functioning. This process would minimize perceptions that stepfamilies are somehow "lesser" family structures. Popular media depictions of stepfamilies need to be more realistic than old TV program, *The Brady Bunch*, or the romantic comedy *Yours, Mine, and Ours*, where problems are resolved in short order and everyone lives happily ever after. In addition, more should be done to encourage the normalization of stepfamily relationships. For example, the exchange of greeting cards on special occasions has become an expected pattern of behavior in American culture. However, the greeting card industry, like many other businesses, has been slow to recognize the diversity of the American population. In the past, it was difficult to find cards representing people of color outside of ethnic specialty shops. Today, most stores stock these cards. Nevertheless, it is still difficult to find cards like the one depicted in Figure 13.4 that represent other than traditional family forms.

Visit your neighborhood card shop. Does it carry cards for stepfamilies? What does the selection of cards in the section marked "relatives" reveal about our culture's attitude regarding stepfamilies? Do you think there should be greeting cards specifically for stepfamilies? For other types of relationships? Why or why not? What purposes does the exchange of cards serve? Explain.

Third, many stepchildren are members of overlapping households. Both households spend money on food, shelter, clothes, entertainment, travel, and many other items. Currently, however, dependent children can be claimed as a tax deduction for only one household. If the tax code were revised to allow stepparents to deduct more of their cost of shared child support, it would give them some financial assistance. Besides the obvious monetary benefit, this change would symbolize society's recognition of the contribution stepparents make to the well-being of children and hence to the community at large.

FIGURE 13.4

APPLYING THE SOCIOLOGICAL IMAGINATION

There was a time when I was afraid—afraid that once you came into our family there would be less love, less understanding, less "family" than before. But you showed me how love can blossom in a caring relationship, how an understanding heart can smooth a painful transition, how a family can be more than a matter of birth.

You have shown me so much friendship, so much caring, so much love that I want to thank you for being you—a wonderful stepparent, a wonderful person.

Joan L. Stone

WRITING YOUR OWN SCRIPT

THINKING ABOUT REMARRIAGE

Consider these facts: One-third of all U.S. children under the age of 18 are connected to a stepfamily; approximately 43 percent of first marriages and over 50 percent of remarriages will end in divorce. It is thus possible that you or someone you know will spend at least part of your life in a remarried-family household.

It is important to be aware of the complexities of remarried families and not to assume that they will be like intact nuclear families.

Questions to Consider

1. What factors would you take into account in determining whether to remarry? How would you go about preparing for a remarriage?

2. What expectations do you have for how a remarried family should function? How do you think each of the following roles should be constructed in a stepfamily: (a) the biological parent, (b) the stepparent, (c) stepchildren, (d) step-in-laws, (e) biological and stepgrandparents?

SUMMARY

The pattern of marriage, divorce, and remarriage has become well established in the United States. Today, however, most remarriages involve divorced individuals, whereas in previous eras most remarriages involved widowed people.

Despite the high rate of remarriage, relatively little is known about this family form, especially among different classes, races, and ethnic groups. Remarried families differ from nuclear families in fundamental ways: They are more complex, they have a changing cast of characters, their boundaries are unclear, and their rules are often undefined. Laws regarding remarried families are ambiguous, and there is a lack of kinship terms to cover all affected parties in a remarriage. Members of remarried families often feel guilty or are still grieving over previous relationships.

Divorced people who remarry tend to spend less time in dating and courtship than do people who marry for the first time. Like couples marrying for the first time, divorced people spend little time discussing issues such as finances and children. The reasons for remarriage are similar to those for first marriage. Men remarry more frequently and sooner than do women. Men with higher incomes are more likely to remarry than men with lower incomes. College-educated women are less likely to remarry than other women. Whites have the highest rate of remarriage of any racial and ethnic group in the United States.

Children of remarried or cohabiting parents often experience boundary ambiguity when defining who is and who is outside their family. Many children whose parents divorce and then cohabit or remarry find themselves living in overlapping households, having to adjust to two different sets of rules. Although stepchildren often have difficulties adjusting and may experience stepsibling rivalry, they also benefit from new extended families. A half-sibling may be yet another source of competition for a parent's attention, but may also help stepchildren feel they are now part of a "real" family.

Both stepmothers and stepfathers face difficulty in establishing relationships with stepchildren, although stepmothers experience more stress than do stepfathers. Remarried couples report levels of marital happiness similar to those reported by those in first marriages. However, due to the greater complexity of remarriages, especially those with children, the duration of remarriages is shorter than that of first marriages.

KEY TERMS

remarried family
emotional remarriage
psychic remarriage

community remarriage
parental remarriage

economic remarriage
legal remarriage

overlapping households
boundary ambiguity

QUESTIONS FOR STUDY AND REFLECTION

1. Discuss the significance of viewing remarried families as entities that are distinct from nuclear families. In a similar vein, some sociologists have argued against referring to remarried families as reconstituted or blended families. How might these latter terms cause problems for individuals living in remarried families? Should biological parents who are cohabiting with a partner be considered stepfamilies? Explain.

2. Andrew Cherlin has referred to remarriage as an "incomplete institution." What did he mean by that? Do you agree or disagree? What would be necessary to make remarriage a complete institution? Explain.

3. The divorce rate is higher in second marriages than in first marriages and even higher in third marriages. What factors are involved in these lower rates of marital stability? Do you see any as more important than the others? Explain. What can individuals and the community do to help improve the duration of remarriages? Explain.

4. To what degree do you think remarried families are seen as a legitimate family form in the United States today? Be specific. Consider their relationships to other social institutions like schools, laws, government, and the media. What changes, if any, would you make in these institutions regarding remarried families? Explain.

ADDITIONAL RESOURCES

SOCIOLOGICAL

ANNARINO, KAREN L. 2003. *Stepmothers and Stepdaughters: Relationships of Chance, Friendships for a Lifetime.* Berkeley, CA: Wildcat Canyon Press. These personal accounts of dozens of women highlight the difficulties and triumphs of the stepmother–stepdaughter relationship.

GANONG, LAWRENCE, AND MARILYN COLEMAN. 2004. *Stepfamily Relationships: Development, Dynamics, and Interventions.* New York: Springer. This volume provides a comprehensive, multidisciplinary look at the variety of relationships within stephouseholds as well as between households, focusing on internal family dynamics while emphasizing the diversity and complexity of stepfamilies.

PHILIPS, SUSAN. 2004. *Stepchildren Speak: 10 Grown-Up Stepchildren Teach Us How to Build Healthy Stepfamilies.* AWYN Publications.

Ten people in their late 20s and 30s who grew up in stepfamilies describe how it feels to juggle in between households and to navigate homes with different values. They don't pull any punches. They talk candidly about both good and bad experiences.

STAHLMANN, ROBERT F., AND WILLIAM J. HIEBERT. 1997. *Premarital and Remarital Counseling.* San Francisco: Jossey-Bass. The authors provide helpful guidelines to couples for what to expect from any therapist and therapy in general and examine the plusses and minuses of group counseling.

FILM

The Parent Trap. 1998. This movie captures the fantasy of many children whose parents divorce—getting them back together.

Stepmom. 1998. Anna and Ben must cope with the divorce of their parents and learn to adjust to the new woman in their father's life. At the same time, their biological mother and new stepmother struggle to come to some kind of accommodation.

LITERARY

Louie, Al-Ling. 1996. *Yeh-Shen: A Cinderella Story from China.* New York: Putnam Publishing Group. This Chinese version of the story Cinderella predates the European version by almost a thousand years and contains many familiar details—a poor overworked girl, a wicked stepmother and stepsister. But rather than being handed gifts from a fairy godmother, Yeh-Shen earns her good fortune through kindness to a magic fish.

Joanna Trollope. 2000. *Other People's Children.* This is not your typical *Brady Bunch* story. It is a rough-and-tumble depiction of what most stepfamilies are, in fact, like. It is the emotionally messy world of children and adults who must deal with divorce and remarriage and all the ups and downs they entail.

INTERNET

www.rainbows.org This organization offers training and curricula for establishing peer support groups in churches, synagogues, schools, and social agencies for children and adults of all ages and denominations who are grieving a death, divorce, or other painful transition in their family.

www.saafamilies.org The Stepfamily Association of America is a national nonprofit membership organization dedicated to successful stepfamily living. It provides information, support, articles, and links to other resources.

www.secondwivesclub.com The Second Wives Club is an on-line support community for second wives and stepmothers. It provides practical advice for succeeding in these roles as well as relevant articles about a range of issues for people in remarried relationships.

www.stepfamily.org The Web site of the Stepfamily Foundation provides information on stepfamily research, counseling, and many other resources.

IN THE NEWS

Davis, California

New experimental housing for the elderly is opening across the country. Among the latest is Glacier Circle, the first self-planned housing development in the United States. Twelve old friends, now average age 80, spent 5 years conceiving and designing their own community. They found and bought property together, hired an architect, worked out insurance issues, lobbied local government for a zoning change, and planned how to live independently as well as communally together (Brown, 2006). Four couples, two widows, and two singles live in eight individual town houses grouped around an inner courtyard. When complete, the complex will have a "common house" with a living room and a large kitchen and dining room for communal dinners; upstairs will be a studio apartment. The plan is to rent the studio at below market value to a skilled nurse who will provide additional care for the group when needed.

The residents of Glacier Circle have known each other for many years, earlier living and raising children in the same neighborhood and attending the same local church. They have weekly meetings and they begin them by pledging to "listen deeply and thoughtfully to each other." The 12 friends, all retired, had professional careers, owned homes that appreciated in value over the years and thus were able to invest approximately $400,000 each to build their commune. Each person or couple owns their own unit and contributes $350 in monthly dues to cover expenses for maintaining common areas. Some in the group now suffer from a variety of chronic ailments and need assistance—they recognize that over time things will change. Their homeowners association, with a representative from each unit, has the right of first refusal to buy any home when a vacancy occurs for whatever reason, or for what one of the residents casually refers to as a visit from "the great father in the sky."

Not all new housing for the elderly is on this scale, but there is a growing movement to offer the elderly more options for noninstitutional living in their later years. ElderSpirit, in Abingdon, Virginia, is one such example. Founded by Dene Peterson, a 76-year-old former nun, and three other former Glenmary sisters, ElderSpirit offers subsidized affordable housing to about 37 elderly people. A unique feature of this complex is its "spirit house" used for ecumenical prayer and meditation. Other Elder-Spirit communities in Florida and Kansas are in the planning stages.

WHAT WOULD YOU DO? Imagine yourself at age 70 or 80. Would you invest in a commune like Glacier Circle? Explain. What do you see as the advantages and disadvantages of living in Glacier Circle? Do you think it is possible to build similar facilities for the less affluent? If so, who should do it? Explain.

In 1990, the United Nations General Assembly designated October 1 as the International Day for the Elderly, also known as the "International Day for Older Persons." The United Nations created this holiday to highlight the challenges and opportunities presented by the world's rapidly aging population, both in absolute numbers and in its percentage relative to the younger population. According to U.N. estimates, there were some 200 million persons age 60 and over throughout the world in 1950. By the end of the century, that number had jumped to 600 million, one out of every ten persons. In another 50 years it is expected that one out of five persons will be 60 years or older (United Nations, 2000). In 2005, Japan was the world's oldest nation, with 21 percent of its population aged 65 and over, surpassing Italy's 20 percent. The ratio of people 15 or younger in the total population was the world's lowest, at 13.6 percent ("Asia," 2006). Populations are aging even faster in the developing world. Asia, Latin America, and the Caribbean are the world's fastest aging regions, with the percent of elderly in these regions expected to double between 2000 and 2030 (United Nations Population Division, 2005). A major concern of both developed and developing countries is how to meet the challenges of a growing elderly population at a time when traditional family support systems for elderly members are under considerable stress from a variety of quarters: falling fertility rates resulting in fewer children as caregivers, higher divorce rates, both among the elderly and their offspring, geographical distance between family members, changing norms of familial support with greater acceptance of institutional care for the elderly, and increasing economic pressures.

Like these other nations, the United States is undergoing a major demographic transition. In 1900, only 3 million people in the United States were age 65 or over, representing just 4 percent of the total population. By 2003, nearly 36 million people were in this age group, constituting 12 percent of the population. By 2030, the number of elderly is expected to climb to about 87 million, 20 percent of the population (He, Sengupta, Velkoff, and DeBarros, 2005). If the demographic projections are correct, 1 in 5 persons in the United States will be 65 or over in 2030, compared with 1 in 25 in 1900.

The signs of this revolution in longevity are everywhere. Television programs, movies, and commercials portray older people in active and productive roles. Not only are people living longer but they are creating new ways of living to meet their needs, as evidenced by the 12 friends who built Glacier Circle. At the same time, public officials debate the budget implications of an aging population. For the first time in history, middle-aged adults are dealing with the benefits and the burdens of being part of a multigenerational kinship structure. According to one survey, 70 percent of midlife couples are part of four-generation families (Task Force on Aging Research, 1995). And in 2000 there were 3.9 million multigenerational family households, nearly 4 percent of all households in the United States (U.S. Census Bureau, 2001a). Members of such families are pioneers with relatively few role models to guide them. Consequently, there is a great deal of confusion and uncertainty as well as excitement and joy. For the oldest relatives, great-grandchildren can be a source of pride and delight. They can also be a source of conflict and confusion, however, because different generations often adhere to different values and behaviors. The primary focus of this chapter is on what family expert Timothy Brubaker (1990) has called "later-life families"—families beyond the child-rearing years.

CHARACTERISTICS OF LATER-LIFE FAMILIES

Later-life families possess several characteristics that make them fascinating to study but that also have practical implications for developing meaningful social policies on aging. According to Brubaker, later-life families exhibit three characteristics: (1) they are multigenerational, (2) they have a lengthy family history, and (3) they experience a number of new life events for which they may have little preparation, for example, grandparenthood, retirement, and widowhood. As we will see throughout this chapter, these characteristics greatly influence the nature and quality of family interactions.

In this chapter, we look at some of the changes in family composition over time and at the new developmental tasks that accompany these changes. In this regard, our approach uses the theoretical model of the family life cycle introduced in Chapter 2. Evelyn Duvall's (1977) last two stages in the life cycle incorporate "later-life families." These stages encompass middle-aged parents who must deal with the "empty nest," the period after the last child leaves home; and the aging family, whose tasks include adjusting to retirement and the death of a spouse.

The Sandwich Generation

The middle-aged generation, sometimes called the **sandwich generation** because of the pressures its members experience from both ends of the age spectrum, finds itself playing many roles. Middle-aged parents must meet the challenges of their own lives—their own aging and approaching retirement from work and all the adjustments these entail. As their children reach adulthood, parents expect to be free from major family responsibilities and to have more time to spend on their own pursuits. For many parents, however, the economic realities of recent decades have put some of these expectations on hold. As we saw in Chapter 7, many young adults find achieving financial independence difficult. Consequently, increasing numbers remain at or return to the parental home. Not only do middle-aged parents frequently have adult children living at home, but they often must care for elderly parents as well. Increasing life expectancy, combined with lower birth rates, has brought about a major shift in the amount of time people spend in various roles. The middle generation, for example, will spend on average more years with parents over 65 than with children under 18. According to a recent study,

Maria Esther de Capovilla of Guayaquil, Ecuador (born September 14, 1889), was named the "World's Oldest Person" by Guinness World Records on December 9, 2005. Her claim as the oldest living supercentenarian was verified by various documents. By the year 2050, more than 1 million Americans are expected to be 100 years of age or older.

44 percent of adults between the ages of 45 and 55 find themselves still providing support for their children as well as caring for aging relatives (Dessoff, 2001). Thus, the empty-nest stage is more a myth than a reality for increasing numbers of middle-aged parents.

Although many middle-aged adults confront such changes, recent research indicates that popular images of a "midlife crisis" are largely overdrawn. A 10-year study of nearly 8000 Americans, aged 25 to 74, by the MacArthur Foundation Research Network on Successful Midlife Development, found that, for most respondents, the midlife years appear to be a time of good health, productive activity, psychic equanimity, and community involvement. Only 23 percent of the respondents reported having a "midlife crisis" and, of that group, the majority tied the crisis to a specific event in their lives, for example, a divorce. Only one-third described the crisis as a time of personal turmoil related to their realization that they were aging (Goode, 1999). According to social psychologist Orville Brim, "Normal people recognize that the lifespan, regardless of age, brings change and that a healthy response to change is to make the necessary adjustments that are required. When a change is connected to an event, and an appropriate accommodation is made, this can be called a turning point" (quoted in Kotulak, 1999:1).

To a degree, being old is a matter of self-definition. Some people may feel old at age 60; others may not feel old at age 80.

Source: FOR BETTER OR FOR WORSE © 2007 Lynn Johnson Productions. Dist. by Universal Press Syndicate. Reprinted with permission.

Diversity in the Family Life Cycle

As we saw in Chapter 2, the family life cycle model has some inherent limitations that we will try to avoid. For example, our discussion of later-life families does not assume a nuclear family model. Child-free couples, single-parent families, and families that have taken in other kin or friends—a pattern common among families of color—must also make changes and confront new tasks as their members grow older. Additionally, like families at other stages of development, later-life families take diverse forms. They include couples in a first marriage, mothers who have never married, widows and divorced people who have not remarried, and people who have remarried, some more than once. Diversity is further enhanced by the fact that these households cut across all social, economic, racial, and ethnic groups. Our discussion incorporates the diversity among and within later-life families to the extent that the existing data permit. Here again, however, much of the existing research involves white, middle-class families. Thus, our ideas concerning how the poor (and for that matter the rich) and people of color experience many of these later-life stages remain largely undocumented.

For much of the twentieth century, U.S. culture has emphasized youth. Consequently, many Americans have developed negative stereotypes of the elderly. Robert Butler, the former director of the National Institute of Aging and author of *Why Survive? Being Old in America* (1975), coined the term **ageism** to describe these stereotypes and the discriminatory treatment applied to the elderly. Coined over a quarter of a century ago, the concept is still relevant today. According to a recent poll, 62 percent of respondents say older persons face discrimination in today's society and fewer than half (46 percent) think older people are viewed with respect in America (Research! America, 2006). **Social gerontology,** the study of the impact of sociocultural conditions on the process and consequences of aging, shows us that the impact of aging on marriages and families is multifaceted. Some older family members are frail and in need of care, whereas others are living independent, healthy, active lives. Some of America's elderly live in isolation in single-room occupancy hotels, but many others enjoy happy lives, interacting with family and friends and engaging in numerous new and exciting activities. Our goal throughout this chapter is to present these differing realities of America's elderly and their families. This approach requires that we balance the strengths and satisfactions of the elderly with the real problems many of the elderly confront on a daily basis.

Changing Age Norms

In general, life course development tends to follow specific **age norms**, expectations of how one is to behave at any stage in life. These age norms currently show signs of being less restrictive than in the past. For example, today it is not unusual for people to marry for the first time in their 20s, 40s, or even 60s. Similarly, women are becoming mothers at both younger and older ages. Not only are teens giving birth but, due to new reproductive technologies, so too are menopausal women (see Chapter 9). Divorced and remarried men in their 40s and 50s are starting new families. As late as the 1960s, students typically attended college for 4 years, starting at age 18 and finishing at age 22. Today, your classmates may be 20, 30, 50, or even 70 years old, and they may take 4, 5, or even 8 years to complete their degrees. Although more people are opting for early retirement at age 55, others begin new careers at age 70. As these examples indicate, there has been an ongoing shift toward a loosening of age-appropriate standards of behavior. As a result of falling mortality rates, most of us can expect to experience many of these later-life events—launching of children and the period of the empty nest, job changes, retirement, parental care, widowhood, and, particularly for females, an extended period of solitary living. By reflecting on the experiences of the generations ahead of us, we may better prepare ourselves to deal with these events. It is also useful to anticipate how long we can expect to live and to begin to prepare for our own aging experience (see Internet Resources: Applying the Sociological Imagination).

APPLYING THE SOCIOLOGICAL IMAGINATION
How Long Can You Expect to Live?

To answer this question, go to http://www.fastfa.com/life.jsp and use the Life Expectancy Calculator to determine your anticipated life expectancy. Were you surprised by that number? Are you satisfied with that number? Explain. Now that you have an estimate of how long you might live, reflect on the factors that influence the number of years you will likely live. What factors are due to your family background? What factors are due to your lifestyle choices? Is there anything in these factors that you should change to improve your chances for a longer life? Ask your friends and parents to use the calculator. Compare your findings. What patterns do you find? Would you like to live to be 100? Why or Why not? What is your ideal of a normal life span? Explain.

THE DEMOGRAPHICS OF AGING: DEFINING "OLD"

Who are today's elderly? When does old age begin? One easy answer is at age 65, which was arbitrarily selected by government officials in 1935 as the age at which a worker could receive full social security retirement benefits. Defining old age is more complicated than this, however. Consider, for example, the active 78-year-old friend of ours who explained why she does not care to go to her local senior citizen center: "The people there are all so old." By that she meant they are in their 80s and 90s and less active than she is. Her experiences confirm what many researchers have come to call **functional age**—an individual's physical, intellectual, and social capacities and accomplishments. People grow old at different rates. One person may be "old" at 60, whereas another is "young" at 75.

Although the elderly share some common experiences, we will see in the following discussions how social characteristics such as age, gender, and marital status interact in ways that lead to different experiences for different groups of elderly.

Age Categories of the Elderly

Including everyone over 65 in a single category called "the elderly" obscures significant differences in the social realities of older people. Recognizing the diversity among older people in terms of physical and social functioning, gerontologists now speak of three distinct categories: the young-old (ages 65 to 74), the middle-old (ages 75 to 84), and the old-old (ages 85 and over). The older population itself is aging at a rapid rate. Figure 14.1 shows the projected changes expected in these age categories for 2005 and 2050. In 2005, only 14 percent of the elderly were expected to be 85 or older, but in only another 45 years, 24 percent of the elderly will be that old. The oldest-old make up the most rapidly growing elderly age group. In 2005, the expected 65 to 74 age group (18.6 million) was eight times larger than in 1900, but the 75 to 84 group (12.9 million) was more than 16 times larger and the 85+ group (5.1 million) was over 35 times larger. Additionally, 71,000 centenarians (people 100 years of age or older) were expected to be living in the United States, up from the 1990 figure of 37,306. By 2050, that number is expected to exceed

1.1 million (U.S. Census Bureau, 2006). These demographic changes present both opportunities and challenges. On the one hand, families and the society at large have much to gain by using the experience and wisdom of the older population. On the other hand, families and social planners must also prepare to meet the anticipated health care requirements and other service needs of an aging population.

Gender and Marital Status

The gap between the number of women and men narrowed during the last several decades due to changing migration patterns and declining male death rates, bringing the overall sex ratio (the number of males per 100 females) to 96.9 in 2004, up from 94.5 in 1980 (U.S. Census Bureau, 2006). However, among the elderly population, especially those in the oldest category, women significantly outnumber men. This pattern has led some researchers to characterize old age as primarily a female experience (Longino, 1988). This, however, is a relatively recent development. Only around 1930 did women's life expectancy begin to increase more rapidly than men's as female deaths connected with pregnancy, childbirth, and infectious diseases declined dramatically. Table 14.1 shows the change in the sex ratios in the

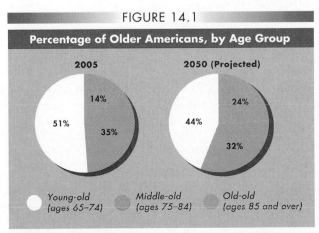

FIGURE 14.1

Percentage of Older Americans, by Age Group

2005: 51% Young-old, 35% Middle-old, 14% Old-old
2050 (Projected): 44% Young-old, 32% Middle-old, 24% Old-old

Young-old (ages 65–74)
Middle-old (ages 75–84)
Old-old (ages 85 and over)

Source: Adapted from U.S. Census Bureau, 2006, *Statistical Abstract of the United States, 2006* (Washington, DC: Government Printing Office): Table 12, p. 14.

TABLE 14.1

Changing Sex Ratios in the Older Population, 1980, 1990, and 2004

Age Category	Sex Ratio		
	1980	1990	2004
Young-old (65–74)	76.5	77.9	83.9
Middle-old (75–84)	58.9	59.7	67.3
Old-old (85+)	43.7	38.5	44.9

Source: Adapted from U.S. Census Bureau, 2006, *Statistical Abstract of the United States, 2006* (Washington, DC: Government Printing Office): Table 11, p. 13.

different age groups of the elderly from 1980 to 2004. Women clearly have a longevity advantage over men. Why this should be the case is not fully understood. Science has not yet unraveled all of the reasons for the gender difference in mortality rates. Gerontologist Erdman Palmore (1980) attributes half of the difference to genetics and the other half to social roles and environmental factors.

Longevity for women, however, can be a mixed blessing. On the one hand, it allows for a rich and meaningful life, and it provides an opportunity to share in the socialization of new generations. On the other hand, it often means years alone, as husbands, male relatives, and friends die at earlier ages. As Figure 14.2 shows, older women are much less likely to be married than older men—43 compared to 74 percent. Women are three times as likely as men to be widowed (44.3 and 14.3 percent, respectively). As we saw in Chapter 13, men are more likely to remarry after widowhood than are women. Only 8 percent of all older people were divorced in 2003. However, this proportion represents a considerable increase form the 1.6 percent of elderly who were divorced in 1960 and this increase is likely to continue into the future as divorced baby boomers grow older. By age 75 and over, the marriage rates decline for both women and

men but they drop off more sharply for women, with only 31 percent married while 70 percent of men are still married at this age (U.S. Census Bureau, 2006).

These differences in marital status also vary significantly by race and ethnicity. Among males 65 and older, African Americans were the least likely to be married with spouse present (57 percent), compared with 73 percent of whites, and 69 percent of Latinos and Asians. Similarly, among elderly women, 25 percent of African Americans, 43 percent of whites and Asians, and 40 percent of Latinas were married with spouse present (He et al., 2005). These patterns are directly related to the different rates of marriage, divorce, and remarriage among the different racial and ethnic groups, as discussed in earlier chapters, as well as differences in mortality rates.

Gender differences in survivorship rates are significant because older women across all racial and ethnic groups have fewer financial resources and are more likely to experience poverty in old age than are elderly men. In Chapter 10 we noted that historically women have been disadvantaged in the labor market. They earn less money, are segregated into less prestigious jobs, and are more likely to work part-time and to have their work life interrupted by child rearing than are men. Consequently, women have less access than men to pension plans and receive fewer benefits when they do have access. The median income of female householders 65 and older, who were living alone in 2003, was $13,775 for females and $17,359 for their male counterparts (He et al., 2005).

Race, Ethnicity, and Class

In 2003, the overall racial composition of the population 65 and older in the United States was 82.5 percent white, 8.4 percent African American, 5.7 percent Latinas/os, 2.7 percent Asian, and 1.1 percent all other races alone or in combination, including Native Amerians and Pacific Islanders (Figure 14.3). Together, people of color make up approximately 18 percent of the elderly population, and their numbers are

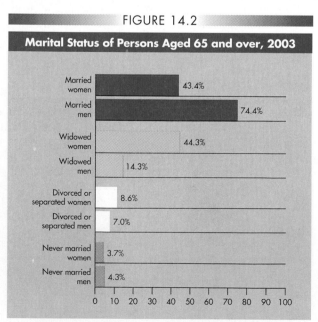

FIGURE 14.2

Marital Status of Persons Aged 65 and over, 2003

Married women	43.4%
Married men	74.4%
Widowed women	44.3%
Widowed men	14.3%
Divorced or separated women	8.6%
Divorced or separated men	7.0%
Never married women	3.7%
Never married men	4.3%

Source: W. He et al., 2005, "65+ in the United States: 2005," *Current Population Reports,* P23-209 (Washington, DC: U.S. Census Bureau): Table 6-1, p. 146.

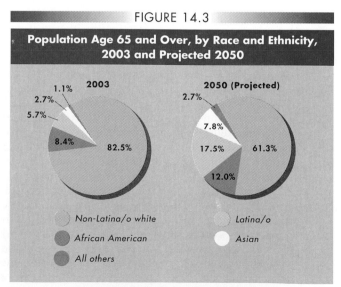

FIGURE 14.3

Population Age 65 and Over, by Race and Ethnicity, 2003 and Projected 2050

2003: 1.1%, 2.7%, 5.7%, 8.4%, 82.5%

2050 (Projected): 2.7%, 7.8%, 17.5%, 12.0%, 61.3%

Non-Latina/o white · Latina/o · African American · Asian · All others

Source: Adapted from Federal Interagency Forum on Aging-Related Statistics, 2004, *Older Americans 2004: Key Indicators of Well-Being,* Appendix A: Detailed Tables, Table 2 (Accessed May 2, 2006 http://www.agingstats.gov/chartbook2004/tables-population.html).

increasing at a faster rate than those of the white elderly, primarily because of higher fertility and immigration rates. This trend is likely to continue well into the twenty-first century. Projections are that by 2050 people of color will constitute about 40 percent of the population aged 65 and over in the United States. Although all groups will experience change, the highest growth rates will be among Latinas/os and Asians. By 2050, nearly one in six elderly is likely to be Latina/o.

Although the gap in life expectancy rates for the white population and people of color is narrowing, these rates remain lower for people of color. In 2000, for example, life expectancy at birth was 80.0 for white females and 74.8 for white males. In contrast, it was only 75 for African American females and 68.3 for African American males (U.S. Department of Health and Human Services, 2001b). Native Americans and Latinas/os also have lower life expectancies than do whites.

What accounts for these differences? One major factor, of course, is social class. In general, families of color have fewer economic resources in old age than do their white counterparts. This is mainly because of the disadvantages they faced in the labor market in earlier years: low-paying jobs, longer and more frequent terms of unemployment, and racial discrimination. Thus, they tend to have fewer health insurance or social security benefits than do the white elderly, and they are less likely to have supplementary retirement incomes from private pensions. In 2003, white households containing families headed by persons aged 65 to 69 had a median household income of $35,798, compared to $20,503 for African Americans and $19,962 for Latinas/os. The gap narrowed somewhat for households, with a householder aged 75 and over; nevertheless, whites continued to lead with a median income of $20,298, followed by Lainas/os ($15,685). African Americans had the lowest medium income at $13,903 (He et al., 2005)

Poverty among the Elderly

Although median income gives us a general picture of the economic situation of families headed by the elderly, it does not allow us to see the range of differences among elderly families. Not all elderly are poor, nor are all elderly of color poor. In 2000, for example, approximately 28 percent of households headed by an individual age 65 or older had incomes of $50,000 or more. Nevertheless, the more typical pattern was one of low income. Almost 34 percent of such households had incomes of less than $25,000. Twelve percent had incomes of less than $15,000 (Administration on Aging, 2001).

Although a smaller proportion of elderly is poor today than in the past, poverty remains a problem for millions of elderly, especially for the old-old. Table 14.2 shows the changes in the poverty rate over the past four decades. In 1959, 35 percent of the elderly over 65 were poor; by 2003, only 10.2 percent were so identified, although many others had incomes only slightly above the poverty line. The poverty rates for people of color are significantly higher than those for whites. Additionally, women had higher poverty rates (12.5 percent) than men (7.3 percent). Older people who live alone or with nonrelatives were more likely to be poor (19.2 percent) than were older people living with families (4.9 percent). Latinas living alone or with nonrelatives had the highest poverty rate (41.8 percent), followed closely by black

TABLE 14.2

Poverty Status of the Elderly by Race and Latina/o Origin, 1959–2003

Years	All Races (%)	White (%)	African American (%)	Latina/o (%)
1959	35.2	33.1	62.5	NA
1970	24.6	22.6	48.0	NA
1980	15.7	13.6	38.1	30.8
1990	12.2	10.1	33.8	22.5
2003	10.2	8.0	23.7	19.5

Sources: Adapted from the U.S. Census Bureau, 1991, "Poverty in the United States: 1990" *Current Population Reports*, Series P-60, no. 175 (Washington, DC: U.S. Government Printing Office): Table 3, pp. 18–19; W. He, M. Sengupta, V. A. Velkoff, and K. A. DeBarros, 2005, "65+ in the United States: 2005," *Current Population Reports*, Series P23-209. Washington, DC: (U.S. Census Bureau): Table A-4, p. 207.

women (40.4) compared to 18.6 percent for white women. Some of the explanations for these differential rates have to do with discrimination in the workplace (see Chapter 10).

The initial decline in poverty rates was due to the nation's efforts to win the "War on Poverty" in the 1960s. Many new social programs were instituted for poor people of all age groups, including the elderly. Although many social welfare programs were reduced or eliminated during the last two decades, programs that benefit the elderly remained largely in place because of effective politically lobbying by groups such as the American Association of Retired Persons (AARP), which has over 35 million members. During this period, Social Security benefits were improved by providing for increases in the cost of living. Many companies instituted private pension plans for workers, thus providing workers with additional retirement income and numerous businesses instituted discount programs for senior citizens regardless of economic need. However, in recent years, the economy slowed and many companies struggling to remain competitive in an increasingly global economy cut many employee and retiree benefits. If these trends continue, it is likely that poverty rates among the elderly will increase in the future.

LIVING ARRANGEMENTS

If you are like most Americans, you probably share the fear that when you get old you will be sent to a nursing home. Perhaps your parents have asked you to promise never to put them in a home. Disturbing stories of the plight of elderly in nursing homes frequently appear in the pages of newspapers. This may account for the widely believed myth that most aged persons end up institutionalized. In fact, only a small proportion of older Americans live in an institutional setting. At any given time, only 5 percent of the elderly are in nursing homes, and they are primarily the infirm old-old (Cockerham, 1991:27). In 2000, only 1.1 percent of persons aged 65 to 74 were in nursing homes, compared to 4.7 percent of persons 75 to 84 and 18.2 percent of those 85 and older (Administration on Aging, 2001). Americans are entering nursing homes at a later age than in the past. The average age on admission increased from 81 years in 1985 to 83 years in 1997, and nursing home stays were shorter in 1997 than in 1987. It is likely that these changes reflect more use of home health care, assisted-living arrangements, and/or the use of nursing homes for short-term rehabilitation (National Center for Health Statistics, 2001). Because the old-old are the fastest growing part of the elderly population, however, we can predict an increased need for quality nursing home care over the next several decades. Thus, many more families, perhaps yours included, will have to face the difficult decision of how to care for an elderly dependent relative. Some cultural groups have more problems making these decisions than others, however. Among U.S. Muslims, for example, there is a strong aversion to nursing homes. At the same time, however, like other immigrant groups before them, first- and second-generation adult siblings in Muslim families are often geographically separated and struggling to balance the demands of dual-income families with both children and elderly parents. To meet this need, some mosques are initiating plans to build assisted living quarters for the elderly nearby so that their religious practices and cultural traditions can be maintained insofar as possible (Clemetson, 2006).

As Figure 14.4 shows, the vast majority of older people maintain their independence in the community, living alone or in a household with their spouse. Living arrangements show a clear gender and race or ethnic difference. Men are more likely than women to be living with a spouse across all race and ethnic groups and women are more likely to live alone across all race and ethnic groups. Living with other relatives is less common among whites than among any other group. Widowed Asian American women and men were more likely than any other group to live with their adult children. Latinas/os were the second-most likely group to do so. Among the old-old, African American elderly are more likely to live with their children than are white elderly. Similarly, in Chile and Mexico, most unmarried elderly women, even

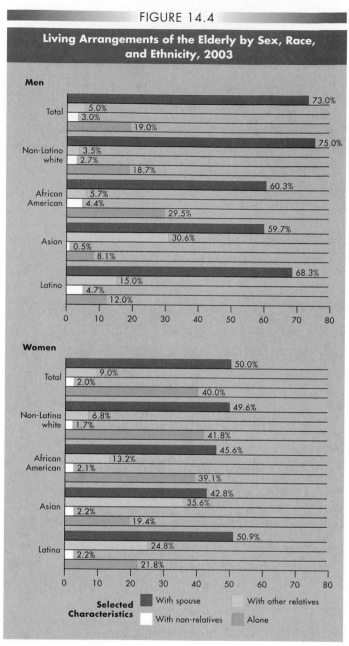

FIGURE 14.4

Living Arrangements of the Elderly by Sex, Race, and Ethnicity, 2003

Source: Adapted from Federal Interagency Forum on Aging-Related Statistics, 2004, *Older Americans 2004: Key Indicators of Well-Being,* Appendix A: Detailed Tables, Table 5a (Accessed May 2, 2006 http://www.agingstats.gov/chartbook2004/tables-population.html).

When independent living is no longer possible, some elderly people must move to nursing homes. Although the quality of life in nursing homes varies considerably, the elderly living in homes with programs that meet their social and intellectual needs as well as physical needs do quite well. This home provides a strong arts and crafts program for its residents.

those without children, live with relatives, often nephews, nieces, or siblings (De Voss, 2000). Economic need and a cultural emphasis on the extended family are the most common explanations for these different patterns. Increasingly, however, even among Asian Americans there is a trend away from coresidence with adult children. Greater numbers of Asian American women are now in the labor force, and today more Asian American couples pursue dual careers, leaving them less time and energy to care for elderly parents. This is upsetting to traditional parents, but others who have become more accustomed to independent living do not expect or want to live with their children. Business is responding to this change. Several years ago Aegis Assisted Living, a company based in Redmond, Washington, opened Fremont Aegis Gardens, the first for-profit assisted-living community for Asians, offering ethnic foods and activities. The trend away from multigenerational households in the Asian American community is likely to continue (Kong, 2002). There is concern in Chile and Mexico that the patterns now developing in the United States and other Western countries will find their way across the borders. Public officials and family experts are hoping to find a balance between retaining valuable kin ties and respecting increased autonomy for all ages.

Housing Patterns

Of the elderly who live independently, the majority reside in their own homes. Homeownership offers a number of advantages: security and familiarity, lower cash outlays for shelter, a possible source of income when the home is sold, and a sense of control in one's life. The elderly are far more likely to own their own homes (80.5 percent) than other age groups, except householders aged 55 to 65. Married couples are more likely to own homes (92 percent) than are older persons who lived alone (69 percent) (U.S. Census Bureau, 2003). Given these rates, at first glance we may be tempted to conclude that the elderly have few housing problems. A closer look reveals this is not the case, however. First, homeownership varies from group to group. Only 66 percent of African American, 65 percent of Latina/o, and 63 percent of Asian elderly householders are homeowners compared to 83 percent of whites and 74 percent of Native Americans, Eskimos, and Aleuts (U.S. Census Bureau, 2002).

Obviously, income is a factor. Elderly homeowners have annual income almost twice that of renters—($23,465 compared with $12,356 (He et al., 2005). Second, although overall today's elderly are less likely to be living in physically deficient housing than past generations, a significant portion of the housing occupied by the elderly is old and requires constant maintenance that is often too costly for people on fixed incomes. According to a study by the U.S. Department of Housing and Urban Development (1999),17 percent of older African American households lived in inadequate housing, compared with about 11 percent of older Latina/o households and 4.3 percent of older white households. Because of these housing problems, the elderly are often exploited by unscrupulous individuals who promise to do home repairs but flee with the money without doing the work. Finally, there is concern that in the future, fewer elderly will own their homes because an increasing number of younger and middle-aged adults are unable to afford to purchase a home of their own (Savage, 1999).

The situation for renters can be worse. Renters typically live in apartments, including public housing of various quality. Some renters are boarders, and others live in residential hotels, including single-room occupancies (SROs). Increasingly, SROs, especially those that cater to low-income elderly men, have been demolished to make room for urban renewal projects. Not only does the destruction of SROs displace elderly residents, but, as we have seen in Chapter 10, it also contributes to homelessness.

Today's families are smaller in size than in the past, resulting in fewer people to meet the needs of elderly members. Further, given that women live longer than men, increasing numbers of elderly women, like the woman above, are likely to spend their last years living alone.

Although younger Americans tend to be mobile, middle-aged and older people prefer staying in a familiar environment. Housing is more than a place to live. For many, it symbolizes continuity, independence, family history, and a sense of belonging. The majority of the elderly have lived in their current residence for 20 or more years. As the family life cycle changes, however, so, too, do housing needs. Houses can become too big, too isolated, too expensive, or too difficult to maintain for a retired couple or the widowed after children have left home. In addition, housing that once was satisfactory may become inadequate as a result of the resident's illness or disability. The affected person may no longer be able to use stairs, reach cupboards or counters, get in or out of bathtubs alone, or maneuver a wheelchair through narrow halls or doorways. Sometimes, remodeling or the intervention of outside help can take care of these problems. In other cases, relocation to more suitable housing is the only alternative. When a change is voluntary, the personal and psychological disruption it causes is likely to be relatively minor because the perceived benefits outweigh the costs. When the elderly are forced to relocate, however, the result is often trauma, confusion, grief, and a sense of helplessness and isolation. When asked which living arrangements they prefer, the elderly consistently say they want to be independent. An 80-year-old widow told us,

> My daughter feels I should not be living alone. We are very close, but she and her husband have their own lives. They both work. They have a lovely home, but it is in a suburb with no sidewalks or public transportation. I'd be isolated and dependent on them for going anywhere. I like my independence. Here I can walk to the store and the bank, and I can see people every day. We keep in touch by phone, and I know they will come if I need them. That's all I want.

MARRIAGES IN LATER LIFE

Imagine being married to the same person for 50, 60, or even more years. Given current life expectancies, many married couples can expect to celebrate their golden wedding anniversary (6 percent) and beyond. What can we expect of a marital bond that endures this long? Does the quality of the relationship change over time? Is the poet Robert Browning correct in saying, "Grow old along with me/The best is yet to be"? We shall try to answer these questions by looking at two issues: marital satisfaction and adjustment to retirement.

Marital Quality and Satisfaction

Does marital quality improve with age? According to John Rocchio, aged 101, and his wife, 99-year-old Amelia, the answer is a definite "Yes." They have been married for 82 years and quite likely are the world's longest married couple (Associated Press, 2005). Nevertheless, to researchers, the answer is not so clear-cut. In an early review of more than 25 studies, no consensus was found on this question. Some studies reported little or no change in marital quality in later life. Couples who were happy in earlier years were likely to be happy in later years; early unhappiness remained in later years. Other studies found a gradual pattern of decline in marital love and companionship over the years. A third set of studies showing improvement in marital quality revealed a pattern whereby couples start out with high levels of satisfaction, "the honeymoon phase," followed by the childbearing and child-rearing years, during which stress and anxiety levels may be heightened, leading to a decline in marital satisfaction. Once the children are grown and leave home, couples can concentrate on each other again and rediscover or develop common interests and interdependence, resulting in increased feelings of affection and companionship (Ade-Ridder and Brubaker,1983). More recent studies support this curvilinear relationship between family stage and the perceived marital quality of both spouses (Glenn, 1990; Vaillant and Vaillant, 1993). However, this does not work equally well for all couples. For example, a study of three generations of Mexican Americans found that marital satisfaction declined for women after their children left home. Middle-aged and older Mexican American women also experienced a decline in marital satisfaction as they took on caretaking responsibilities for older relatives (Markides et al., 1999). In general, the ability to make smooth role transitions depends on a couple's prior adaptability and their earlier degree of marital satisfaction. Couples who have long-lasting marriages, including the 6 percent of all married couples who celebrate golden wedding anniversaries, tend to characterize their marital relationship as based on trust, intimacy, shared values and belief systems, the ability to negotiate with each other, and a willingness to make adjustments (Parron, 1982; Arp and Arp, 2001). Jean and Harry Gottlieb, who have been married for 65 years, provide a good illustration of these dynamics (see Family Profile).

What are we to make of these different findings? Some of the differences may be related to the particular methodological techniques used in the studies themselves. Much of this research involved studies of small samples of older couples taken at only one point in time. Comparisons of changes are difficult to make unless the same couples are retested at different times and unless a standardized measure of marital quality is used.

Throughout this text, we have examined a number of factors that influence a couple's level of marital satisfaction. For example, in Chapter 6 we discussed sexuality among the elderly. Marital satisfaction is positively related to sexual behavior among older couples who are still sexually active. This does not mean, however, that couples no longer sexually active have poor-quality marriages. Rather, for those still active, this intimate expression adds another satisfying dimension to their marital lives. Another important factor that affects later-life marriages is the way in which couples deal with retirement.

Adjustment to Retirement

Retirement, as a distinct phase in the family life cycle, is a modern phenomenon. Before the twentieth century, American workers typically worked until they died or were physically unable to continue working. When they stopped working, there was no pension or Social Security for their later years, and their welfare most frequently depended on other family members (Markides and Mindel, 1987). In the wake of the Great Depression, however, this situation changed. With the establishment of Social Security in 1935, the institution of retirement became part of the national culture. Nevertheless, not all elderly are retired, and those that do retire do so at different ages. In 2003, the elderly made up 3.3 percent of the U.S. labor force. Altogether, 4.8 million people 65 and over were working or actively seeking work—18.6% of men and 10.6 % women in that age category (He et al., 2005). These numbers are likely to increase in the future. A recent *USA Today*/Gallup poll found that a majority of Americans are looking forward to working beyond retirement age—63 percent of nonretirement-age adults say they plan to work when they reach retirement age, 51 percent say they will work part time, and 12 percent say they will work full time (Saad, 2006). People are motivated to work beyond retirement age primarily for two reasons: their enjoyment of working or the need to make money.

Like so much of social life in the United States, the experience of retirement is affected by an individual's gender, race, and class. Years ago it was common to hear housewives say, "I married him for better or worse, but not for lunch." Such a line usually produced chuckles in the listeners because they could easily envision a newly retired man who suddenly has time on his hands wandering aimlessly around the house, interfering with his wife's daily routines. However, today it can as easily be a retired wife who is disrupting the household system. Thus, to understand the impact of retirement today, we must ask, whose retirement?

Types of Retirement With approximately 60 percent of all women of working age in the labor force, couples must deal with more than one retirement. Given that men tend to be older than their wives, the timing of retirement, especially for employed wives, might be a source of friction. Brubaker (1985) has identified four patterns of retirement among older couples:

- *Single or traditional retirement:* Here, one spouse, usually the husband, has been employed and thus only one spouse retires from paid employment.
- *Dissynchronized—husband initially:* In this situation, the husband retires before his wife. She continues to work because she is usually younger or started her career after his.

FAMILY PROFILE

THE GOTTLIEB FAMILY

Jean and Harry Gottlieb, their children, and grandchildren

Length of Relationship: 65 years

Challenges of Later Life: The challenge is to maintain a real and caring interest in the world around us—in our children's and friends lives as well as the more public events of the day—even though we are less in the mainstream and more like watchers on the riverbank. We must remain convinced that we can continue to make a real contribution to the world we live in. We have the long view and should be the all-important living link between a historic past and a still-mysterious future. We have fewer constraints on our own lifestyle and can do more things on impulse.

Relationship Philosophy: We never take each other for granted. Our relationship has always been based on trust, a compatible sense of humor, close family ties, and good old romantic love. After

65 years of marriage, we love and respect each other more than ever. We are confidants, best friends, co-conspirators, and last—but not least—lovers. We spend more time together now, but we each have our own interests and activities

as well as some mutual endeavors. When we have differences, we try not to go to bed mad. Although our life remains vibrant, we are saddened by the death of dear old friends and are aware of our own mortality.

- *Dissynchronized—wife initially:* This pattern, in which the wife retires first, is rare. It may be that she has health problems or is needed to take care of an older relative.
- *Synchronized retirement:* In this situation, both the husband and wife were employed, and they retire at the same time.

Most of the studies conducted on retirement have not taken into account these variations, yet it is likely that marital satisfaction is affected in different ways not by retirement itself, but by the circumstances of retirement. For example, researchers found that synchronized retirement is most conducive to marital satisfaction while dissynchronized retirement is negatively related to marital happiness (Moen, Kim, and Hofmeister, 2001). Two possible explanations for these relationships come readily to mind. First, one partner is still employed, the time the couple has available to pursue joint social and recreational activities is limited. Second, if the husband retires first, a common practice because husbands tend to be older than their wives, he may only marginally increase his domestic labor. As we saw in Chapter 10, perceived inequality in the division of household tasks is often a source of marital dissatisfaction.

Other factors also affect the quality of life after retirement. In 1986, Congress passed legislation ending mandatory retirement for most employees. Prior to that time, most workers were forced to retire at age 65 whether they wanted to or not. Despite the change in the law, 30 to 40 percent of early retirements are "forced," often the result of a company's downsizing, relocating, or going out of business or of an employee's or spouse's poor health (Henkens and Van

Dalen, 2003). Unanticipated and involuntary retirement is likely to produce stress and depression. In contrast, when people want to retire and make plans to do so, retirement is more likely to be a positive experience (Van Solinge and Henkens, 2005). In general, when people control the timing of their retirement, they are more likely to feel satisfied with this stage in their lives. However, the degree to which workers have this control varies considerably. African American workers are less likely to experience voluntary retirement than are their white counterparts. Although financial readiness is a major factor in the decision to retire for whites, poor health and disadvantaged labor force experiences are more likely to affect the retirement decision for African Americans. Compared with whites, African Americans are more likely to retire at earlier ages, retire because of poor health, be forced to retire, be unemployed in the 12-month period before retirement, and report job dissatisfaction and job search discouragement prior to retirement (R. Gibson, 1991, 1996). Thus, it is not surprising to find that African American and Latino workers express less confidence about their retirement prospects and financial preparations than workers overall, and are more likely than other workers to say they will rely most heavily on Social Security for retirement income (Employee Benefit Research Institute, 2003).

The concept of retirement has little meaning for individuals whose jobs do not provide old-age benefits. They must keep working until they become physically incapacitated. This is particularly true for unskilled white workers and people of color, especially African American women, who often work to an advanced age. Little systematic data exist on the retirement experiences of other people of color, especially Native Americans and Asian Americans.

Finally, satisfaction during the retirement years also depends on the couple's financial status and health. If retirement income is sufficient to enable couples to pursue desired activities, retirement is likely to promote satisfaction. However, if couples have been unable to save much in the earlier years of married life or if their earnings have been so low that they receive only minimal social security benefits, they may experience considerable downward mobility with retirement.

INTERGENERATIONAL RELATIONSHIPS: CONTACT AND SOCIAL EXCHANGES

That most elderly live alone or with their spouse gave rise to a belief that most old people are neglected by their children. On the contrary, a recent national study found that 65 percent of respondents who have a living parent say they live within an hour's drive of that parent and 42 percent of adults say they see or talk with a parent (usually, it's Mom) every single day compared to just 32 percent of adults in 1989. Another 44 percent report seeing or talking to a parent at least once a week. There are some variations by race and ethnicity. More blacks (59 percent) than Latinas/os (42 percent) or whites (39 percent) are in daily contact with at least one parent, again usually Mom. Members of all three groups are equally likely to report a close relationship with their mother, but among those whose father is still living, whites (78 percent) are more likely than blacks (60 percent) to report a close relationship with their father (Pew Research Center, 2006). In another study, 68 percent of grandparents said they see a grandchild every one or two weeks; another 24 percent reported seeing a grandchild once a month to once every few months. Eighty percent of grandparents contact a grandchild by telephone at least once every couple weeks (American Association of Retired Persons, 2002). No doubt, the increase in and frequency of contact observed in these studies is, in part, a by-product of the changing technology that makes communication easier and less expensive than in the past.

Although there is considerable diversity, both around the world (see the In Other Places box) and within the United States, in the way different generations relate to one another, family interactions are shaped to a large degree by the norm of reciprocity or complementary exchanges. Contrary to popular belief, older people are not primarily dependent recipients of aid; in many cases, they are primarily donors. Older parents often remain a resource for their adult children, providing financial assistance, advice, and child-care services. This is especially the case when adult children have stressful problems, for example, getting divorced or becoming widowed. In exchange, both generations expect that adult children will assist their parents in times of need (Bengtson and Harootyan, 1994; Hogan and Farkas, 1995). Social class, however, may influence the direction of tangible aid. For example, wealthier older people are likely to continue giving financial assistance to middle-aged children, whereas working-class parents are more likely to be receiving assistance.

Evidence suggests, however, that several decades of high divorce rates (see Chapter 12) are having negative effects on intergenerational exchange and contact. For example, research has found that widowed parents engage in more intergenerational transfers than divorced parents and that remarried parents are less likely to receive informal care from their children. Divorced men are particularly likely to lack intergenerational support in later life as a result of weaker ties with their children. And families containing only stepchildren have lower rates of financial and time transfers and lower rates of intergenerational co-residence than families with biological children (Pezzin and Schone, 1999). Additionally, stepparents acquired later in life frequently are not perceived as family members and thus norms of family obligations are not applied to them (Ganong and Coleman, 2006). If these patterns become more pronounced, they will have widespread repercussions on the economic and social well-being of the elderly in future years.

Quality of Relationships

Although we know a great deal about the frequency of intergenerational contact, we know less about the qualitative aspects of these relationships. Frequency of contact in and of itself does not ensure a strong emotional bond. Nevertheless, researchers have found that most adult children and their elderly parents like one another and express satisfaction with their relationships. Research indicates that this is also true for grandparent–grandchild relationships (Wiscott and Kopera-Frye, 2000). Gender seems to play an important role in this regard. For example, mother–daughter relationships tend to be particularly close and intimate during all phases of the life span (Pew Research Center, 2006). In contrast to sons, daughters are more likely to be chosen by the aging parent as a confidante and to stay in closer contact with parents (Aldous, 1987). The maxim that "A son is a son until he takes a wife, but a daughter is a daughter all of her life" seems to have some empirical support.

EVOLVING PATTERNS OF KINSHIP: GRANDPARENTHOOD

Changing mortality and fertility rates can have enormous consequences for the kin network. As recently as 1900, families with grandparents were rare. An analysis by Peter Uhlenberg (1980) showed that families in which three or more grandparents are alive when a child reaches age 15 increased from 17 percent in 1900 to 55 percent in 1976. Further increases in life expectancy make it now common for grandchildren to have all four grandparents (or even more as a result of divorce and remarriage, as we saw in the case of Blake Brunson in Chapter 13) alive throughout childhood. In 2002, there were about 90 million grandparents. Seventy-five percent of all people 65 and over are grandparents, and nearly half of all these grandparents will become great-grandparents and some will become great-great-grandparents. Twenty percent of women who die after the age of 80 are great-great-grandmothers (Barber and Tremblay, Jr., 2004). Nevertheless, the

IN OTHER PLACES

THE ROLE AND STATUS OF THE ELDERLY: VARIED AND CHANGING

A considerable amount of mythology surrounds the role of the elderly in both industrial and nonindustrial societies. In industrialized countries, there is the myth that the elderly are isolated and alone. In nonindustrialized countries, there is the myth that the elderly are always respected and cared for by the next generation. What we find when we examine these and other myths is that the empirical reality is a lot more varied. In the United States, for example, although a significant minority of elderly struggle to survive, there is extensive intergenerational contact. Additionally, the government provides economic security and health care for many of its elderly citizens.

How do the elderly fare in other places? Nancy Foner (1993) examined ethnographic reports for a wide range of nonindustrial cultures and found in many cases a strong ethic of intergenerational caregiving. Let us look at some examples from her review. Among the Kirghiz herders of Afghanistan, the younger son (and his family) looks after aged parents, remaining in the parental household. In exchange, he inherits the family herd, tent, and camping

ground. When traditional healers and health workers of the Akamba tribe of Kenya were asked to choose between a dying old man over 60 and a dying 25-year-old man when there was only enough medicine to cure one person, many favored saving the old man, even where the young man was first in line. A man from among the Gonja of West Africa said, "When you were weak (young) your mother fed you and cleaned up your messes, and your father picked you up and comforted you when you fell. When they are weak, will you not care for them?" Similarly, among the Samia of Kenya, adult children care for parents just as the elders cared for them when they were small. Australian aborigines consider it callous and reprehensible for family members to desert an ailing elder. The Twareg pastoralists of Niger believe the elderly should be fed and served. In the 1980s, despite a severe 3-year drought and an inadequate supply of food, the Twareg daughters or granddaughters continued to feed and care for the physically weak elderly. Among the !Kung of Botswana, those who are generous to the old are likely to be honored.

Unfortunately, in many of these societies today, limited resources combined with rapid social change are undermining the reciprocal relationships that have characterized intergenerational relationships, espe-

cially for elderly without children. These elderly are often neglected, since they have not been part of an exchange relationship. Some parents take on a childless role when their children migrate to other places in search of work. According to Foner, limited resources sometimes lead to extreme behavior—gerontocide or the abandoning or killing of the elderly. In some societies, there is an understanding by both generations that when the old are no longer productive and a drain on the community, it is time to go. Among the Mardudjara hunters and gatherers of Australia, when life was too difficult, some of the elderly asked to be left behind to die. The elderly Eskimos of northern Canada would go off by themselves onto the icy tundra to die.

In sum, a cross-cultural perspective helps us to understand that kinship structures and functioning are complex phenomena and that they can be understood only by examining cultural belief systems as well as social and economic factors.

What do you think? Which society would you prefer to live in as an elderly person? Explain. What obligations do you think the younger generation should have toward the older generation in the United States? How effective do you think this nation is at meeting the needs of all age groups?

---

social role of grandparent, let alone great-grandparent, is a fairly recent one and one that is still evolving.

Styles of Grandparenting

There is great diversity in the timing of grandparenthood. Given the incidence of teenage pregnancies, some parents become grandparents as early as their 30s. Other parents who had children later in life may not become grandparents until into their 60s or 70s. This diversity in ages of grandparents contributes to the ambiguity surrounding this role. Although a great deal of folklore is connected with grandparenting, there is little agreement on how to fulfill this role. Thus, most of us will construct our grandparenting role out of our own childhood memories of our grandparents, our perceptions of the way our parents acted as grandparents, and the attitudes we pick up about grandparenting from the media and from those around us, especially our adult children.

Over the years, researchers have investigated the role and meaning of grandparenthood and in the process have identi-

fied several styles of grandparenting. Bernice Neugarten and Karol Weinstein (1964) studied 70 middle-class grandparent

One of the roles grandparents can fill is that of a family historian. Here Chinese grandparents share family photos with their granddaughter.

couples and classified their interactions with their grandchildren into one of the following five categories:

- *Formal:* Grandparents follow what they see as a prescribed role for grandparents.
- *Fun seeker:* Grandparent–grandchild interaction is characterized by informality and playfulness.
- *Distant figure:* Interaction is limited to holidays and special occasions.
- *Surrogate parent:* Grandparents assume caretaking responsibilities for grandchild.
- *Reservoir of family wisdom:* Grandparents are the dispensers of special skills or resources.

Neugarten and Weinstein also found that age is a factor in the development of grandparenting styles. Younger grandparents were more likely to be fun seekers, whereas older grandparents were more likely to adopt the formal approach.

This study and other early descriptions of grandparent roles have been criticized for their unidimensional approach (Roberto, 1990). In Neugarten and Weinstein's study, each respondent was placed exclusively into one of the five categories. No provision was made for overlapping styles of grandparenting or changes in styles over time. Two decades after the Neugarten and Weinstein study was published, Andrew Cherlin and Frank Furstenberg (1986b) analyzed telephone interviews with 510 grandparents (and personal interviews with 36 of them) and found three styles of grandparenting:

- *Remote:* Grandparents interacted infrequently and maintained a ritualistic or purely symbolic relationship with their grandchildren.
- *Companionate:* Grandparents had an easygoing, friendly style of interaction with their grandchildren.
- *Involved:* Grandparents took an active role in rearing their grandchildren, exerted substantial authority, and imposed definite and sometimes demanding expectations.

These three styles correspond roughly to Neugarten and Weinstein's grandparenting styles of distant figure, fun seeker, and surrogate parent. However, Cherlin and Furstenberg's analysis takes into account the dynamic quality of such relationships. They found that grandparent–grandchild relationships can change over time. For example, grandparents may have a fun-seeking relationship with young grandchildren, but when the children reach adolescence, the time spent together may decrease dramatically. Years later, the relationship may change again with the arrival of great-grandchildren. Also, the same grandparent may exhibit different grandparenting styles with different grandchildren. For example, a grandparent may have a close companionate role with one grandchild and a remote relationship with another. Numerous factors influence the kind of relationship grandparents have with their grandchildren: age, health, and employment status of grandparents, physical proximity, economic need, relationships between the grandparents and their adult children, number and ages of grandchildren, birth order, gender, and personality differences.

Benefits and Conflicts

The grandparent role has the potential to benefit all three generations. Grandchildren enrich their grandparent lives in many ways. Grandchildren contribute to a sense of immortality—something of the grandparent will continue after death. Playing the role of teacher, family historian, and resource person enhances the self-esteem of grandparents. Grandparents can take pride in the achievements of their grandchildren and boast about them to friends. Through social contact with grandchildren, grandparents can keep up-to-date on cultural and social changes and have great fun in the process. Later on, older grandchildren can provide assistance to grandparents—shopping, lawn care, and doing household chores.

In exchange, grandparents can provide grandchildren with love and guidance minus the intensity, responsibility, and tension that frequently exist in parent–child relationships. Grandparents can give children a sense of continuity, identity, belonging, and values as they share with the children stories about the family's history. In so doing, they often can help younger people understand their parents, and they frequently act as mediators between the two generations. Additionally, grandparents can be role models of successful aging for both their adult children and grandchildren. Finally, the parent generation can benefit by having someone they can trust assist them in their parenting role and, if necessary, act as surrogate parents in time of need. In this latter regard, grandmothers have played a key role in the lives of adolescent mothers, especially in aiding them in the care of their infants during the early months of the infant's life (Harvey, 1993). In their study of inner-city unwed adolescent mothers, Nancy Apfel and Victoria Seitz (1991) found that the presence of grandmothers often had a stabilizing effect on both the young mothers and their children. Grandparents frequently care for infants and toddlers of young working mothers (Vandell et al., 2003).

Such benefits, however, can also produce tension and conflict. Parents and grandparents may disagree about child-rearing strategies. Parents may resent what they perceive as grandparental interference or be jealous of the child's affection for the grandparent. Older grandchildren may become preoccupied with their own lives and forget to call or visit grandparents. As a result, grandparents often feel hurt and ignored. These problems notwithstanding, much of the research on grandparenthood shows that both grandparents and grandchildren tend to be satisfied with their relationships.

Research also indicates that there is more contact with maternal grandparents; maternal grandmothers are consistently listed as the grandparent to whom grandchildren feel closest. The main factor contributing to this pattern is parental divorce. As we saw in Chapter 12, mothers are more likely to have sole custody of children than fathers, and many fathers lose contact with their children following a divorce. Thus, it is not surprising to find grandchildren losing contact with paternal grandparents. This pattern, however, may be a function of the timing of the divorce and the age of the grandchildren. Teresa Cooney and Lori Smith (1996) found that parental divorce was not associated with levels of affective, functional, or associational solidarity between adult grandchildren and grandparents. The issue of custody is not a factor with adult children, and they are more able than younger children to manage relations with their grandparents on their own; they no longer need the mediating role of their parents.

In the past and to a great extent today, helping and caring for grandchildren are more traditionally associated with grandmothers. Earlier research suggested that grandmothers were more satisfied with the grandparenting role than were grandfathers (Thomas, 1986). However, today gender differences in satisfaction with the grandparenting role seem to be diminishing. Grandfathers who have frequent contact with grandchildren report similar levels of satisfaction with their role as do grandmothers (Peterson, 1999). A recent study in New Zealand found that many grandfathers attach great importance to the grandfather role, seeing it as an opportunity to experience the contact with babies and young children that they missed out on with their own children (Wilton and Davey, 2006). This seems the attitude of many American grandfathers as well. Increasing numbers of fathers in the United States are more involved in child care than were their fathers and we expect they will also become more involved in the grandparenting role than was the case for grandfathers in the past.

Race and ethnicity also play a role in the degree of involvement in the grandparent role. Some research suggests that African Americans, Asian Americans, Italian Americans, and Latinas/os are more likely to be involved in the lives of their grandchildren than are other groups (Cavanaugh, 1993). The apparent greater involvement of ethnic grandparents may be a result of the greater extended kin network among these groups. For example, in a study of 48 African American and 51 white grandfathers aged 65 and older, Vira Kivitt (1991) found that the grandfather role was more central in the lives of African American men than it was for white men.

A high level of grandparent support has been found among Native Americans. Besides caring for grandchildren of working parents, grandparents often ask their children to allow the grandchildren to live with them for a period of time so that they can teach their grandchildren about the Native American way of life (Weibel-Orlando, 2000). In particular, grandfathers are active in transmitting a knowledge of tribal history and cultural practices through storytelling (Woods, 1996). However, there is concern that the role of the elderly in Native American families is being eroded by geographical mobility of children, high poverty rates, and diminished social resources.

Unplanned Parenting Many grandparents routinely provide child-care services for their grandchildren, but in a growing number of cases, grandparents have assumed sole responsibility for their grandchildren. In effect, they become surrogate parents. In 2002, 5.6 million children were living in households with a grandparent present; the majority of these children (3.7 million) lived in 2.4 million grandparent-headed households. Approximately 1.3 million children were being raised entirely by grandparents with no parents present in the household (Fields, 2003). Grandparent-headed households have grown over 105 percent since 1970 (Hudnall, 2001). Grandparent-headed households cut across all races and ethnic groups. Although the largest number of children

living in grandparents' homes is Caucasian, their percentage (4 percent) is lower than that of African Americans (9 percent), Latinas/os (6 percent), and Asian and Pacific Islanders (3 percent) (Fields, 2003). In addition, large proportions of Native American children are being raised by grandparents —with some Native American tribes estimating up to 60 percent of their children in this living situation. Another 1.5 million children in the United States are living with other relatives (Goyer, 2005). As high as these numbers are, the numbers are even higher in Africa and other nations where grandparents and other relatives struggle to provide basic subsistence for their grandchildren. In the United States and these other countries, grandparents are increasingly taking on this parental role as a direct result of the incapacity of the middle generation to care for their children because of parental unemployment, death, poverty, disease, substance abuse, AIDS, incarceration, divorce, or increasingly today in the United States, military deployment.

Unplanned parenting produces both positive and negative outcomes for the caregivers. In one study of 114 grandparents who provided daily care to their grandchildren, nearly two-thirds of the custodial grandparents reported that caring for their grandchildren provided more of a purpose in their lives and kept them young, active, and "in shape" (Jendrek, 1996). Others want to keep their grandchildren out of foster care, a system they often distrust (Adler, 2005). Despite positive feelings about their involvement, the assumption of such responsibility is emotionally and financially exhausting for many grandparents. In some cases, the grandparents must abandon or fight their own children to provide their grandchildren with a healthy and stable environment. Keeping up with young grandchildren can be physically exhausting. Retired grandparents on a fixed income may find their household budget severely strained by the unexpected expense of children. Custodial grandparents are more likely to live in poverty than noncusdodial grandparents and they are more likely to be in poorer health and less educated than non-relative foster parents (*Forging Connections*, 2004). Adequate housing, particularly a lack of space, is also a problem and the reality of unplanned parenting can be psychologically difficult to accept. The dreams these older couples have for spending time together, taking vacations, and pursuing other interests may be lost forever. Custodial grandparents may also experience profound changes in their friendship networks as their lifestyle is altered to fit the needs of children, babysitters, and finances. As one grandmother who has been living with a grandchild for about 8 years, said,

> In our age bracket most of our friends don't have (young) children and as a result a lot of times we don't accept invitations to go because our children (the grandchildren) are not invited . . . . Most of the time it doesn't bother me . . . . Our close friends are still the same. We don't see them as often. (Quoted in Jendrek, 1996:299)

Although more communities are establishing programs to help these surrogate parents, many of these programs are underfunded, inadequately staffed, and are able to provide only minimal services. Additionally, some states deny benefits from Aid to Families with Dependent Children, the state welfare program, to any nonparent, even though grandparents

Not only do elderly people help in the care of their own grandchildren, but many, like this reading volunteer at the Stride Rite Intergenerational Day Care Center, play an active role in the lives of other children.

should be eligible. Over the last several years support groups like Grandparents as Parents, Grandparents Raising Grandchildren, and Grandparents United for Children's Rights have been formed to assist these families. More recently, the first public housing development in the United States designed and built exclusively for grandparents raising grandchildren opened in the Bronx. The families living in the 51 apartments all get a social worker, support groups, and parenting classes. Children receive tutoring and organized activities in the afternoon and evening (Gordon, 2006). More facilities like this are critically needed.

Great-Grandparenthood

Now that four-generation families have become more common, a few researchers are beginning to examine the meaning of the great-grandparent role in later-life families. A study of great-grandparents found that the majority expressed positive feelings about the experience (Barer, 2001). They reported a renewed zeal for life and expressed satisfaction at the continuance of their families. Despite these positive reactions, most of the respondents reported having only a remote relationship with their great-grandchildren, interacting with them on a limited and mostly ritualistic basis.

The reasons for this kind of interaction pattern are not entirely clear. A partial explanation may be that because this is a new phenomenon, few cultural norms exist to guide individual behavior in these relationships. Additionally, the geographic dispersion of family members contributes to a physical and emotional distance between the youngest and oldest generations. As some great-grandmothers reported, "I got some but I don't know the names of them. They tell me I do have some greats, I ain't never seen them. I got pictures but I haven't seen none of them" (quoted in Barer, 2001). There is some indication, however, that at least among women of color, the great-grandparenting role is much the same as the

grandparenting role—that is, it is simply a natural progression from that role (Scott, 1991). Further research is needed to study the costs and benefits of such relationships.

THE CHILD-FREE ELDERLY

Perhaps sometime in your life someone suggested to you that you should marry and have children so that you will have someone to take care of you when you get old. Although the majority of today's elderly have surviving children, a substantial minority have none. Approximately 20 percent of Americans over age 65 have no children and that number is expected to increase to about 33 percent with the aging of the baby boomer generation. A common assumption is that the childless elderly have no "natural" support system of adult children to rely on in old age. Are they, then, without potential caregivers, as folk wisdom would have us believe?

An examination of a national sample concluded that being child-free was a predictor of social isolation in later life. Compared with elderly parents, the child-free elderly had fewer social contacts. This was particularly true for those experiencing health problems (Bachrach, 1980). When marital status was controlled, however, an interesting pattern emerged. The unmarried child-free elderly interacted more frequently with friends and neighbors than did the married child-free elderly. Some researchers believe this finding reflects the tendency of married couples to rely more on each other, thus limiting other social relationships (Johnson and Catalano, 1981).

In contrast, the unmarried elderly realize that they may need help at some point in their lives and actively create a support network for themselves. For example, Robert Rubinstein and his colleagues (1991) interviewed 31 never-married child-free women 60 years of age and older and found that they consciously developed strategies to overcome the cultural emphasis on "blood ties." Not only did these women cultivate relationships with existing kin (nieces, nephews, and siblings), but they also constructed ties, often becoming fictive kin, interacting in ways traditionally associated with those related by birth. Many of our families include people we call "aunt" or "uncle" who are not formally related to us. These relationships are characterized by strong affective bonds and shared activities. Rubinstein's respondents described key friendships with other women as being "sisterlike." Although research on the role of friends in later life is just beginning, some preliminary findings show that these relationships serve as important sources of support and mental health (Wu and Hart, 2002).

Despite the fact that unmarried elderly people are resourceful and have a fairly large social network, child-free elderly women have a greater chance of becoming institutionalized than do other categories of elderly (Aykan, 2003). These women are often older and in poorer health than other elderly and thus require more care. Social programs need to take account of the fact that the child-free elderly are at greater risk of being without support than are the elderly with children. Additionally, unlike today's elderly, who preceded the period of high divorce rates, today's middle-aged population has an increasing number of stepchildren. Whether these stepchildren will be as likely as biological children to assume care for the elderly is as yet unknown, although, as we noted earlier, initial research on this population suggests that they will not (Pezzin and Schone, 1999). Because remarried men are more likely than women to live with stepchildren than with biological children, men are seen as more at risk in this regard. Hence, in the middle decades of the twenty-first century, the proportion of older people who will need to rely on institutional programs for support is likely to increase.

SIBLING RELATIONSHIPS

The social relationships of the elderly are not restricted to the younger generations. Recent research on the elderly has pointed to the importance of siblings in later-life families. Sibling relationships are particularly valuable to the elderly for two reasons. First, elderly siblings share a similar family history. Second, the relationship is potentially the longest-lasting one an individual will ever have, covering as it does the entire life course. Thus, siblings can help each other fill important needs in later life. They can reminisce about the past, be social companions, and provide emotional and other support during times of stress (Connidis and Campbell, 2001). Additionally, because of their prior experiences, older siblings can serve as role models for resolving the developmental tasks of later life (Scott, 1990).

Upward of 70 to 80 percent of all elderly adults have at least one living sibling (Cicirelli, 1995). Although much is made of sibling rivalry during childhood, it appears these conflicts are largely put aside in the desire to improve relationships in later adulthood. Researchers have consistently found that contact with siblings in later life is strongly related to feelings of social and psychological well-being. This seems particularly true of siblings who were close during childhood. During young adulthood and middle age they may have had only limited contact because of the demands of their own families. As people age, however, they often renew or increase social contacts. These contacts may be triggered by a parent's illness or other needs. This is especially true for siblings who are in geographic proximity, are without partners, and /or have experienced a decrease in contemporaries who can share life review activities (White, 2001). Sister-to-sister and sister-to-brother relationships show greater emotional closeness and more frequency of contact than brother-to-brother relationships (Connidis and Campbell, 2001).

Sibling relationships vary by race and ethnicity. African American siblings are more likely to report closer emotional ties, living in closer proximity, and a greater frequency of exchange of various types of assistance than do white siblings (Bedford, 1997). A plausible explanation offered for these differences is related to differences in cultural emphasis on family ties. Horizontal ties (i.e., siblings) are stronger among African Americans while vertical ties (i.e., parent–child, grandparent–grandchild) are stronger among Asian American, Latino, and Caucasian cultures, thus contributing to less emphasis on sibling relationships over the life span (White and Riedmann, 1992; Connidis and Campbell, 2001).

It seems evident that developing positive relationships with siblings in earlier years is a good investment for the later years; siblings are likely to be a good source of support for the elderly well into the twenty-first century. This may not be the case for the elderly who follow them, however. Over the last several decades, life expectancy has increased and birth rates have decreased. Thus, families are becoming vertical in structure in that they cut across more generational lines but have fewer siblings and other age peers within each generation.

Sibling relationships fill an important place in people's lives, especially as they age. Not only do they share family history, but the relationship is potentially the longest lasting one an individual will ever have, covering as it does the entire life course. In 1993, the Delaney sisters published their autobiography, *Having Our Say: The Delaney Sisters' First 100 Years.* Bessie lived to be 104 and Sadie lived to be 109.

HEALTH AND ILLNESS

A common fear about growing old is the loss of health and independence. Although health problems increase with age, the health status of today's elderly is varied and not as negative as is popularly portrayed. Data from the 2000-2003 National Health Interview Surveys indicate that 74 percent of older persons assessed their health as good or excellent. Only 26 percent of older persons assessed their health as fair or poor. There was little difference between women's and men's reports. However, assessments of health varied by race and ethnicity. Older African Americans (41 percent) and older Latinas/os (40 percent) were much more likely to describe their health as fair or poor than were older Asians (26 percent) or whites (24 percent). Not surprisingly, health reports varied by poverty status, with the poor reporting higher levels of fair or poor health (43 percent) compared to those not poor (20 percent) (Schoeborn, Vickerie, and Powell-Griner, 2006). Although self-ratings of health are subjective, they have been correlated with mortality. That is, older people who describe their health as poor are more likely to die within the next 5 years than are those who report their health as good (Kaplan, Barell, and Lusky, 1988). Research on Japanese elderly confirmed that self-rated health is a powerful predictor of mortality (Sugisawa, Liang, and Liu, 1994). Thus, these self-ratings reflect with some accuracy an individual's overall health status.

DEBATING SOCIAL ISSUES

SHOULD HEALTH CARE BE RATIONED ON THE BASIS OF AGE?

Proponents of age-based rationing acknowledge that age-based rationing as a solution to growing health care costs is not a pleasant one but, rather, a necessary one. They point out that the fastest growing age group is the population aged 80 and over, the part of the population that tends to require expensive and intensive medical care. An analysis of Medicare patient characteristics that influence expenditures in the 3 years prior to death found age to be the major determinant of costs during this time. Care in the last year of life represents over one-fourth of Medicare's budget (Shugarman, Campbell, and Bird, 2004). Those who favor this approach argue that rationing health care is not new and that all countries already ration health care because no one country can afford to provide all useful effective health care to everyone who wants it. They criticize existing health care systems, like the one in the United States, for discriminating against people who, through no fault of their own, cannot afford health care. They say that many of these people are young and should have years ahead of them. Yet because some people must bear the cost of rationing, it makes sense for it to be people who have lived a long life. This, they argue, would bring about the greatest good for the greatest number of people because the costs involved in keeping alive one elderly person could be more productively used to treat a larger number of younger persons whose health could be improved by less costly measures and who are still in their productive years. Finally, advocates of age-based rationing counter criticisms of ageism leveled at them by noting that everyone ages and, thus, over time, everyone will be treated equally.

Opponents of rationing health care on the basis of age argue that it is immoral to

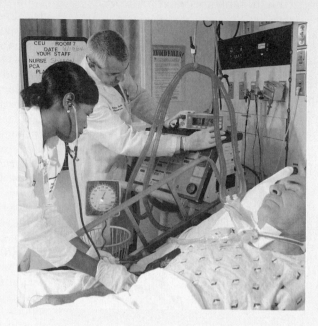

single out any one demographic group as unworthy of life-saving care. Those who take this position see it as the beginning of a slippery slope whereby other groups, such as the disabled and the mentally ill, could easily be added in attempts to further control costs. Others who oppose age-based rationing point out that older people are too diverse a group to be put in a single category, noting that people do not age at the same rates and that some older people could have many years of productive life ahead of them if they received adequate health care. Others who argue against rationing say that such a solution is premature, that it should only be considered if all other alternatives have been exhausted, for example, getting rid of waste and inefficiencies. Those who take this view point out that a single-payer system would result in considerable cost savings, noting studies that show Medicare administrative costs are only 2 percent while those of private health insurance companies are about 15 percent (Black, 2006). Similarly, others argue that

the health care system should be reformed to put more money into prevention that would eliminate the expenses involved in later treatments and to find ways to ease end-of-life situations without expensive medical treatments. Still others who oppose age-based rationing support what has been called "evidence-based medicine," asking which type of interventions work for which people and which produce results that can justify their costs (Mooney, 2003). Reducing treatments that are relatively useless, they argue, would result in significant savings

What do you think? Should the United States ration health care on the basis of age? Do you agree with Daniel Callahan that we should accept the limits of a "natural life span" of about 80 years? Explain. Is there any evidence of rationing health care in this country either age-based or other? Discuss. Who should be responsible for paying health care costs—individuals, families, employers, government, or some combination of these? Explain.

Longitudinal research that followed respondents for 60 years found that younger people can exert substantial control over their eventual physical and mental health after age 65. Those subjects who developed good health habits relatively early in life, such as regular exercise, a healthy diet, flexible coping styles, and social involvement, were healthier and happier in their later years than those subjects who had not developed such habits (Bower, 2001). Today's elderly are healthier than previous generations. Nevertheless, physical changes are a natural and inevitable part of aging and may lead to chronic conditions, long-term illnesses that are rarely cured, such as diabetes, arthritis, and heart disease. Limitations on activities because of chronic conditions increase with age. Twenty-five percent of 65- to 84-year-olds reported a limitation caused by a chronic condition compared to almost 51 percent of people 84 years and over (Kaiser Family Foundation, 2005).

Chronic conditions, illness, and injury can impact mental health and lead to depression. About 15 percent of persons aged 65 to 79 had severe symptoms of depression (deep feelings of sadness and worthlessness, loss of appetite and energy, difficulty in concentrating) compared with 21 percent of persons aged 80 to 84 and 23 percent of persons aged 85 or older. Although people of all ages forget words or appointments at times, forgetfulness is more common among the elderly. The percentage of older adults with moderate or severe memory impairment ranged from about 4 percent among persons aged 65 to 69 to about 36 percent among persons aged 85 or older ("Older Americans 2000 . . . ," 2000).

A fear that many people have about growing old is the possibility that they may get Alzheimer's disease, a progressive, degenerative disease of the brain and the most common form of dementia. Approximately 5 percent of persons over 65 and nearly half of those over 85 have Alzheimer's disease; also, a small percentage of people in their 30s and 40s develop the disease. A person with Alzheimer's lives an average of 8 to 10 years and as many as 20 years or more from the onset of symptoms (National Institute of Aging, 2006). Although there is as yet no cure for this disease, research on a number of medications and treatments offers the hope that there may be a way to prevent or at least delay its onset.

We cannot talk about health issues without paying some attention to health care costs. A study by the Office of the Actuary of the Centers for Medicare and Medicaid Services found that people 65 or older account for four times more the amount of health care spending than those under that age (Black, 2006). Given that the elderly population is growing and living longer than it the past, there is concern that the aging of the population will put even more pressure on the country's health care system. Some people, like medical ethicist Daniel Callahan (1987), author of *Setting Limits: Medical Goals in an Aging Society*, argue that such a situation is not sustainable and offer as a solution rationing health care on the basis of age that would restrict coverage of life-extending treatments, such as organ transplants, bypass surgery, and kidney dialysis (see Debating Social Issues).

FAMILY CAREGIVING

Do family members really help their needy elderly relatives, or do the government and taxpayers assume most of this responsibility? The weight of evidence in study after study indicates that families and friends, not the formal system, provide the bulk of care for the elderly across all cultural groups, providing as much as 80 percent of their long-term care at home. If the government and other health institutions delivered these services, the cost would be $257 billion dollars each year (*Care for the Family Caregiver*, 2005). In addition to providing direct care, caregivers often serve as mediators between institutional bureaucracies and the elderly, providing them with information on housing, pensions, insurance, and medical care.

A recent study by the National Alliance for Caregiving and the AARP estimates that 21 percent of the U.S. population over age 18 (45 million people) provides unpaid care to friends and family age 18 and older. According to this study, the typical caregiver is a 46-year-old female with some college experience. Seventy-nine percent of care recipients are 50 and older and the average age of care recipients 50 and older is 75. Most care recipients are female (65 percent) and many are widowed (42 percent). Caregivers of older adults report that the main problem or illness of the person they care for is old age, followed by cancer, diabetes, heart disease and Alzheimer's disease (Pandya, 2005).

In the United States, as well as around the world, women have traditionally provided the overwhelming majority of informal care for elderly relatives. Today, however, as all countries experience an increase in the number of older people, there is a growing recognition of the likelihood of a shortage of female caregivers because of demographic shifts and the increased participation of women in the labor force. Additionally, some African and Asian countries are seeing the caregiving generation being decimated by the AIDS epidemic, leaving the elderly not only to care for themselves but for the younger generation as well (Climo, 2000). Consequently, as some analysts point out (see, for example, Brewer, 2001), it is imperative that nations begin to develop strategies that enhance the ability of both women and men to share the responsibility of family caregiving. There are some positive signs that this may already be happening in the United States, at least among older men. One study found that by later middle age, more men were assuming a caregiving role, narrowing the gap somewhat between themselves and women (Marks, 1996). Estimates are that the current female/male ratio involved in caregiving is more evenly split than in the past, 61 percent female to 39 percent male (Pandya, 2005). Spouses are the first line of defense when illness strikes, followed by adult children. Compared with spouses, however, adult children provide care over a longer period of time (Chappell, 1991).

The Spouse as Caregiver

The longer a couple lives together, the more likely one of the spouses will become ill. When this happens, the healthier spouse generally assumes the caregiver role. Because men have higher rates of morbidity and mortality, wives make up the majority of spousal caregivers. The degree to which this arrangement represents a satisfactory response to a changed living condition depends on the severity of the illness or disability and on the age and health of the spousal caregiver. Although spousal caregivers may have the greatest need for assistance in fulfilling this role, they receive less assistance from family and friends than other caregivers; they are also the least likely of any group of caregivers to use formal services, regardless of the degree of frailty (C. Cox, 1993). Without outside support, spouses can be physically overwhelmed by the demands of caregiving. If there is a need to have someone in attendance at all times, caregivers

When a spouse becomes ill, the other spouse generally assumes the caregiver role, as this husband is doing for his terminally ill wife.

may find that they have little free time for themselves, with the result that they become isolated from friends. Alfred Fengler and Nancy Goodrich (1979) refer to such caregivers as "hidden patients."

Sometimes these problems can be overcome by having outside help. Nurses, physical attendants, friends, and relatives may be able to relieve the primary caregiver on a regular basis. Some senior day-care centers have been created to enable the ill spouse to participate in social activities as well as to help the primary caregiver keep going. In 1997 there were over 3000 such centers; estimates of the number of senior centers operating today range from 10,000 to 16,000 (Administration on Aging, 2004). Reactions to the caregiving role vary. Spouses who view caregiving as "reciprocity" for past affection and care experience a higher degree of gratification from their caregiving role than do spouses who view it as a matter of responsibility (Motenko, 1989). Providing care can also enhance the caregiver's sense of self-worth and well-being, especially when other family members share, at least to some degree, in caregiving tasks (Martire, Stephens, and Franks, 1997).

Former Spouses as Caretakers In Chapter 13 we pointed out that the number of older Americans who are divorced has increased dramatically in recent years. In 2004, there were approximately 2.8 million divorced persons 65 years and older compared with 1.7 million in 1994 (U.S. Census Bureau, 2006). Many of these people have not remarried. When they become ill and need help, many are without an ongoing support system. Now, however, a new source of support appears to be emerging. Medical personnel and hospice workers are reporting more cases of former spouses stepping in as caregivers, most typically a woman caring for her former husband. According to J. Donald Schumacher, chief

executive of the National Hospice and Palliative Care Organizaion, "They are acting more like a brother or sister, or cousin or extended family member, or sometimes they have the joy of being grandparents together" (quoted in Richtel, 2005:E2). This does not mean that the old emotions and conflicts disappear; rather, for most former spouses drawn together by illness and approaching death, they manage to get beyond any initial recrimination, realizing there is little to gain by rehashing the past. Divorced couples often remain in some form of contact because of their mutual children. When a serious illness strikes one parent, the former spouse is often motivated to become involved in caretaking to help their children through the process. Others are motivated by a sense of duty to complete their wedding vows. According to divorce lawyer Anita Wyzanski Robboy, author of *Aftermarriage: The Myth of Divorce* (2001), there is a special benefit to having a former spouses as a caregiver. She said, a sick or dying person "doesn't want friends to see them looking like this. Ex-spouses know each other intimately and they know each others' underbellies intimately" (quoted in Richtel, 2005: E2). Many elderly do not have a spouse or former spouse to rely on for care, however, and they turn to their children for help.

Adult Children as Caregivers

A study of the sandwich generation (those between the ages of 45 and 55) found that 54 percent cared for children, parents, or both. Twenty-two percent focused their care exclusively on a parent or in-law (American Association for Retired Persons, 2001). Adult child caregiving is especially pronounced in families of color. Adult children comprise about 75 percent of caregivers in African American and Latina/o families, compared to 40 to 60 percent in white families (Montgomery, 1996). Among the primary forms of assistance are emotional support, financial aid, help with instrumental activities (transportation, meal preparation, shopping, housework), personal care (bathing, feeding, dressing), and mediating with agencies to obtain services. All children are not equally likely to assume this role. The degree of filial responsibility is related to proximity (the child living closest to the parent frequently assumes this responsibility) and gender.

A wide range of studies has consistently shown that across all racial and ethnic groups the role of caretaker is most frequently filled by daughters. In fact, some sociologists are now speaking of a *daughter track*. Although daughters have always borne a disproportionate share of responsibility for elderly parent, in the past, the primary caregiver was generally an unmarried daughter still living at home. Today, many daughters are the leading-edge baby boomers who are lawyers, academics, media personalities, and businesswomen who choose to interrupt or give up careers to return home to care for ailing parents (Gross, 2005). Nonetheless, as we saw earlier, the gendered nature of caregiving is beginning to change. In fact, some social scientists have questioned the true extent of previously observed gender differences (Bengtson, Rosenthal, and Burton, 1996). Several factors may render men invisible in the caregiving role. First, although studies have found gender differences, they are often quite small (Miller and Cafasso, 1992).

Second, the studies of caregiving tend to focus on tasks more characteristically performed by women, such as personal care, and to discount tasks done by men, such as financial or home repair and maintenance activities (Coward, 1987). A study of adult siblings by Sarah Matthews (1995) found that brothers' actual contributions tended to be considered unimportant by both sisters and brothers. Third, demographic factors such as the longer life expectancy of women combined with a preference for personal care to be provided by a person of the same sex results in a high number of adult daughter–widowed mother caregiving relationships (Horowitz, 1992). However, a more recent study found that men were taking a more active role in performing caregiving tasks such as managing medications, changing dressings, and monitoring vital signs (National Family Caregivers Association, 2000). Another study, using qualitative interviews of paired female and male siblings, found that women's and men's contributions to the care of their parents are divided much like household responsibilities among married couples. "Helper brothers" assumed a more traditional masculine role, taking limited responsibility for tasks such as car maintenance, lawn work, household repairs, and running errands, relying on their sister to tell them what needed to be done. In contrast, "co-provider brothers" expressed a willingness and desire to share more equitably in the care of their parents and participated in a wide range of helping tasks that crossed traditional gender lines such as providing personal hygiene and health-related assistance (using the bathroom or bedpan, bathing, and inserting or removing catheters) and providing emotional support. Co-provider brothers also took more initiative. If they saw something to be done, they did it without waiting to be asked. Nevertheless, women still assumed greater responsibility in coordinating overall care (Hequembourg and Brallier, 2005). Clearly more research is needed to fully understand the role gender plays in caregiving beyond female–male dyadic sibling pairs, for example, in families with multiple siblings and with only children, especially male-only children as well as studies of other cultures. A recent study shows that adult sons in Hong Kong actively participate in the care of their elderly parents, especially in financial and emotional support, in ways similar to their female siblings (Kwok, 2006).

Additionally, the kind of help that caregivers provide is often mediated by social class. Middle-class adult children provide more emotional support and financial aid, often assuming a "care manager" role whereby they identify needed services, help obtain them, and then supervise their delivery. Children from lower socioeconomic classes are more likely to provide the direct care themselves. Providing care is often made more difficult because of the geographic mobility of the population. Nearly 7 million Americans are long-distance caregivers for an older relative who travel a distance of one or more hours to assist in some phase of caregiving (Wagner, 1997). This factor can add stress to the process of caregiving.

Children as Caregivers

Discussions of caregivers generally evoke images of adults. Yet, according to a study by the National Alliance on Caregiving and the United Hospital Fund, as many as 1.4 million children in the United States between the ages of 8 and 18 provide care for an older adult, including approximately 400,000 children between the ages of 8 and 11. Some of the key findings from this study, the first of its kind in the United States, are as follows:

- Child caregivers are pretty evenly split by gender, with girls making up 51 percent of the total, and boys 49 percent.
- Child caregivers are more likely to live in households with lower incomes than their noncaregiver peers and they are less likely than noncaregivers to live in two-parent households.
- Seven in ten child caregivers (72 percent) are caring for a parent or grandparent; one in ten (11 percent) is helping a sibling.
- Over half (58 percent) of the child caregivers help their care recipient with at least one Activity of Daily Living (ADL) such as bathing, dressing, getting in and out of bed or chair, toileting, and feeding. Nearly all young caregivers help with shopping, household chores, and preparing meals. Nearly all also spend some time just "keeping the care recipient company." Almost a third (30 percent) help with medications and 17 percent help the care recipient communicate with doctors or nurses (Hunt, Levine, and Naiditch, 2005).

In recent years considerable attention has been focused on the impact of caregiving on adults. Much less is known about the impact of caregiving on children, in large part because we see children as care recipients, not as care providers. Yet, as this initial study shows, the impact is likely to be profound in both positive and negative ways. Although child caregivers are more likely to feel appreciated for their help than noncaregivers (64 to 53 percent) and are less likely to feel people expect too much from them (12 to 19 percent), 20 percent of caregivers say their caregiving has made them miss a school activity or an afterschool activity; 15 percent say it has kept them from doing schoolwork and 8 percent say it has made them miss homework. Further, according to parents' reports of their child's behavior, child caregivers tend to show anxious or depressed behavior more than noncaregivers and a larger share of caregivers ages 12 to 18 behave more antisocially than noncaregivers of the same age.

According to researchers, the effects of caregiving on a child appear stronger when one of three factors is present: when the child performs one or more personal care tasks, when the child lives in the same household as the care recipient, and when the child lives in a minority household. This latter fact is likely explained by the finding that smaller proportions of minority caregivers report that someone else helps them with caregiving tasks (Hunt, Levine, and Naiditch, 2005).

Clearly, more research is needed to understand the full scope of child caregiving as it exists today and to distinguish it from routine tasks expected of children in most families. In this way, we can evaluate whether some responsibilities and tasks are inappropriate for children as well as to find ways to support them in a variety of caregiving situations. To this end, U.S. caregiving researchers and advocates are meeting with their counterparts in other countries, such as the United Kingdom, Australia, and New Zealand where the issue has been a matter of research and policy since the 1990s.

The Stresses and Rewards of Elderly Caregiving

Not only is caregiving physically and emotionally draining, it can be isolating and even deadly. An analysis of hospitalizations and deaths from 1993 to 2002 among 518,240 married couples, ages 65 to 98, who were enrolled in Medicare found that a spouse's hospitalization for disabling conditions such as dementia, psychiatric illness, chronic obstructive pulmonary disease, and stroke raised the partner's likelihood of dying. According to the researchers, a spouse's illness or death may hasten a partner's demise by causing severe stress and removing a primary source of emotional, financial, or practical support. These effects can undermine the body's immune system and intensify preexisting health problems. This study also found a decreasing risk for some illnesses, like terminal cancer, most likely because their course is longer, well defined, and fairly predictable, and these illnesses tend not to rob people of their lucidity until the very end (Christakis and Allison, 2006). This does not mean that these other illnesses are without consequences, however.

Caregivers are often so focused on meeting their loved one's needs that they neglect their own. Frequently, they are unaware of the resources that could help them manage their situation better. Studies show that caregivers experience high rates of sleeplessness, back pain, depression, anxiety, and stress-related problems from heart disease to gastrointestinal illnesses. This is especially the case when the illness is prolonged. According to Susan Mintz, co-founder and president of the National Family Caregivers Association, the average length of care is 8 years, with a third of caregivers providing care for a decade or more (Dang and Pitts, 2006).

For adult children, caring for an elderly parent can lead to financial hardship and can jeopardize the caregiver's own health. The most severe consequences, however, tend to be the psychological and emotional stress that comes from seeing formerly strong and independent parents become dependent as well as from the restrictions on the caregiver's time and freedom (see Strengthening Marriages and Families box). The time demands of caring for a parent compete with other responsibilities and may result in conflict, particularly with regard to employment. Many caregivers juggle work with caregiving responsibilities. Nearly six in ten (59 percent) caregivers are currently employed. Male caregivers are more likely to be employed full-time than female caregivers. Those who are not working are most likely retired or are homemakers (Pandya, 2005). Caregiving often has financial consequences for the caregiver, who may have to cut back on work hours or leave work entirely, resulting in loss of pay and reduced retirement income. According to one study, caregivers lose an average $659,130 over their lifetimes as a result of reductions in their salaries and retirement benefits. Women, on average, spend 17 years of their lives caring for children and 18 years caring for elderly parents (*Care for the Family Caregiver,* 2005). The direct caregiver is not the only one affected by the pattern of caregiving. The family's lifestyle may be disrupted. Recreational activities and vacations may have to be postponed. If the elderly person is living with the caregiver's family, lack of privacy may become a problem. If spouses and other family members are supportive, however, the intensity of these strains is lessened. If, however, the strains become too great, caretakers or their families may resort to extreme behavior, for example, elder abuse (see Chapter 11). Such behavior underscores the need for more outpatient and in-home services to help families cope with the demands of caring for an elderly relative. Expending public funds in this area is a good investment.

Despite these problems, many caregivers acknowledge that what they are doing is also rewarding. For many, it gives them a new purpose or direction. A daughter who gave up her career to help her mother take care of her father who has Alzheimer's spoke for many caregivers when she said, "Nobody asked me to do this, and it wasn't about guilt. I lived a very selfish life. I'd gotten plenty of recognition. But all I did was work, and it was getting old. I knew I could make a difference here. And it's expanded my heart and given me a chance to reclaim something I'd lost" (quoted in Gross, 2005:A1).

Certain situations arise, however, when regardless of the desires of the family, the ill spouse or parent can no longer be cared for at home. Institutionalization may be necessary in these circumstances. If this is to be done with a minimum of dislocation, both socially and psychologically, family, friends, and professionals must play a supportive role in the process.

THE EXPERIENCE OF WIDOWHOOD

In Chapter 15 we will discuss issues related to death and dying. In this chapter we examine the many adjustments required in the transition from marital to widowed status. Not only have the widowed lost their main source of support, but they often find that their entire social network is disrupted to some degree. Social life may be curtailed as in-laws and friends brought into the relationship by the deceased spouse gradually grow distant. For example, in her classic study of widowhood, Helen Lopata (1973) found that only 25 percent of the respondents saw their husbands' families on a regular basis. Additionally, both widows and widowers may feel uncomfortable in social settings dominated by couples. Widows in particular may be perceived as a potential threat to friends' marriages. The role of the widowed itself is problematic. In the United States today there are few norms to guide the newly widowed person. In the past, the role was more clearly defined. There were rules about appropriate length of time for mourning, dress, behavior, and, in some cases, guidelines for when and if remarriage could occur. Such guidelines still exist among some ethnic groups today.

STAGES OF WIDOWHOOD

Robert DiGiulio (1989), a widower himself, described four stages that widowed people experience. He emphasized the active processes of growing through widowhood (stages 1 and 2) and growing beyond widowhood (stages 3 and 4). Each stage describes in vivid terms the wide range of emotions

STRENGTHENING MARRIAGES AND FAMILIES
Talks with Family Therapist Joan Zientek

COPING WITH THE CAREGIVING ROLE

Why Is Caring for an Elderly Parent Such a Difficult Role? The number of people 85 years old and older has grown 38 percent since 1990, and is predicted to grow another 50 percent by 2010. This trend has caused a major change in the family life cycle. No longer can many in the 50 to 60 age group look forward to the fulfillment of their retirement dream of a life of travel, spending time with grandchildren, or the pursuit of a hobby or another leisure time activity; instead, it is likely that caring for an elderly parent will be central to their retirement years. This phenomenon requires a major shift in people's expectations as well as the learning of new skill sets that will be needed to meet the emotional and physical needs of aging parents. As the caregiver is confronted with this situation, she (most caregivers are women in their late 50s who work outside the home) must grieve the loss of a future that will never be; at the same time she is dealing with an aging parent who is also coping with loss—be it a home, health, friends, and/or economic independence. This can easily become an overwhelming situation. According to the National Family Caregivers Association, nearly one-half of all caregivers experience long-term depression and two-thirds feel frustrated on a regular basis.

Caring for an elderly parent places strain on the entire family system as it adjusts to this major shift in the family structure. The adult child now becomes the parent's parent and the parent slips into a childlike role of dependency. Conflict can emerge out of this role reversal concerning whose needs will be met first. Frequently, there is not enough time, energy, or resources to meet everyone's needs. There is often confusion about boundaries. What can Mom actually do for herself? With what tasks does she need assistance? When is it time for Dad to sell the house and enter an assisted-living situation? As adult children struggle to sort out the answers to these questions, the old unresolved issues rear their heads: Why do I get stuck with all the work when Mom has always favored him? Or, Dad never did like my husband or my career; and now I am expected to care for him! Once buried because these feelings were too painful to face, now they erupt as anger, shouting matches with siblings, brusqueness with parents, or fiery conversations with doctors. With all of this going on, there seems to be so precious few moments for renegotiating the bond with the most profound and influential attachments of our lives, our parents.

How Can Families Provide Care for Elderly Members without Becoming Overwhelmed? First recognize what is happening and why. In previous generations, before the birth of the wonders of modern medicine, the elderly did not linger as long, most likely a few weeks or months before succumbing quickly to cancer, heart attacks, or strokes. Today the rising numbers of dementia and Alzheimer's in the elderly confronts families with a long-term illness, fraught with the sadness of watching a parent or spouse slowly disappear. These facts, coupled with the complexities and stresses of life today, means that caregivers of the elderly burn out quite easily. In addition, because of the geographic mobility of some family members and the unwritten norms and expectations that family members have for one another, the caregiving all too frequently falls to just the spouse or to just one of the children, the one who is unmarried or who lives closer to the care recipient than other family members. To prevent burnout and resentment, it is essential that all family members communicate openly with one another, plan and cooperate in the caregiving, and provide periodic breaks for each caregiver, as well as set realistic expectations of what can and should be done. In many cases, the family by itself cannot provide all of the care needed for one of its aging members. Family members need to make themselves aware of the many elder care agencies and referral services now available. Generally, when a health care crisis arises, the medical personnel of the hospital, particularly the social worker, can be most helpful in putting the family in touch with the community resources available. Support groups can also lessen the strains and tensions involved in ongoing caregiving.

---

experienced by the widowed as they first deal with their spouse's death and then gradually reconstruct a life for themselves. The stages and their characteristics are as follows:

1. **Encounter** In this stage, which generally lasts from 3 months to 1 year, people may experience depression, shock, rage, loss of appetite, insomnia, and frequent crying. Initial reactions to the death include confusion, panic, and emotional numbness. Some widowed people become obsessed with the deceased spouse, seeking her or his presence by visiting places they frequented together or using her or his personal belongings.

2. **Respondence** Although some of the emotional reactions of the first stage continue, there is a recognition of the reality of the spouse's death. This can be a very painful time, as

the widowed now confront their unmet needs for attachment, nurturance, and reassurance. They may experience an intense loneliness that they believe can be relieved only by the deceased spouse. The widowed frequently sanctify or idealize the deceased spouse, and they frequently ask, "Why did this happen to me?" Gradually, however, the widowed begin to reach out and may join support groups or begin new relationships.

3. **Emergence** Over time, the widowed come to realize that death is a natural outcome of life and that although they have lost someone they loved, they can move on with their lives. This moving on requires them to acknowledge their new identity as single, unmarried people and to focus on the present and the future rather than reliving the past.

4. *Transformation* This stage represents a departure from and movement beyond widowhood. The grief work is over. As a result of having survived bereavement and grief, many widowed see themselves as changed people, as having grown from their experience. They have put their past in perspective and created a new life for themselves.

According to DiGiulio, the stages of widowhood are complex. Some people move through them quickly; others become stuck at one stage and never move to emergence or transformation; still others regress to an earlier stage. The reasons for these different reactions are varied. Those whose marital relationships were particularly close may feel the loss more keenly than those with a more distant relationship. Socioeconomic status also plays a role. Those with greater personal resources, such as income, education, hobbies, and membership in formal and informal organizations, typically make better long-term adjustments to widowhood. For those with fewer personal resources, the degree of integration within a group can be an important factor in adjustment. This can be seen in some ethnic groups, which provide a definitive role for the widowed in the kin and community network (Gelfand and Barresi, 1987). Because of strong kin support, African Americans, Mexican Americans, and Asian Americans seem to adjust to widowhood more easily than their white counterparts do (Pitcher and Larson, 1989).

Finally, when death is expected, the period of adjustment may pass more quickly than when death is sudden. Anticipating widowhood and discussing key issues with a spouse before death occurs can facilitate successful adjustment. Robert Hansson and Jacqueline Remondet (1987) studied 75 widows ages 60 to 90 and found that those who were more successful in resolving their grief and getting on with their lives had discussed with their spouse finances, family reactions, their own feelings, and how their lives might change as a result of the spouse's death. Although such discussions often are initiated only at the time of a terminal illness, all couples could benefit by an annual review of family finances, wills, and contingency plans in case of illness or death.

Gender Differences in Widowhood

As Figure 14.5 shows, widowhood is largely a female experience. At ages 65 and older, women are three times as likely as men to be widowed (44.3 and 14.3 percent, respectively). Although the rates vary somewhat, there are pronounced sex differences across all race and ethnic groups. Among women age 65 and over, 44 percent of whites, 51 percent of African Americans, 40 percent of Latinas, and 40 percent of Asians are widowed. In contrast, the rates for men in the same age category are 14 percent of whites, 19 percent of African Americans, 12 percent of Latinos, and 14 percent of Asians. The probability of widowhood increases with age, and although the gender gap narrows, women are still more likely to be widowed than men. At age 85 and over, 78 percent of women and 35 percent of men have lost a spouse through death. Three factors explain this sex differential in widowhood. First, men have higher mortality rates than women (with a corresponding lower life expectancy, although the gap has narrowed in recent years). Second, women tend to marry men who are older than they are.

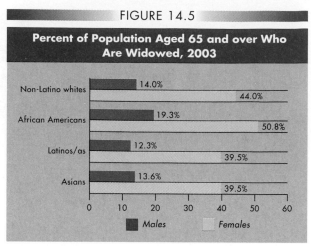

FIGURE 14.5

Percent of Population Aged 65 and over Who Are Widowed, 2003

Non-Latino whites — Males 14.0%, Females 44.0%
African Americans — Males 19.3%, Females 50.8%
Latinos/as — Males 12.3%, Females 39.5%
Asians — Males 13.6%, Females 39.5%

■ Males □ Females

Source: Adapted from W. He. et al., 2005, "65+ in the United States: 2005," *Current Population Reports,* Series P23-209 (Washington, DC: U.S. Census Bureau): Table 6-2, p. 147.

Finally, men are more likely to remarry after widowhood than are women. Although widowhood represents a major role change for both women and men, researchers have found some gender differences in how women and men experience widowhood.

Special Problems of Widows In addition to the adjustments associated with bereavement and grief, widows are likely to confront two major problems: changes in their self-identity and changes in their financial situation. For many women, especially those who are tradition-oriented, the experience of widowhood undermines the basis of their self-identity. The loss of the central role as wife may be psychologically devastating, and a widow may try to maintain her identity as "Mrs. John Smith" in her social and business interactions. Because there are few eligible men in their age category, it may be difficult for widows to recapture the wife role. Statistically, widows have less chance of remarrying than do widowers.

For other women, however, the role of wife is less central to their identity. These women place more emphasis on other roles such as mother, worker, or friend. Thus, they are less interested in preserving the wife role and more interested in being accepted in their own right. Some of these women find, however, that they must negotiate this new role with family and friends who still relate to them as "Mrs. John Smith" (Atchley, 1991).

Widows generally face a bleaker financial future than widowers do. Numerous studies contradict the popular media portrayal of the "merry widow" grown prosperous as a result of a fat insurance policy. Although the situation has improved over the past three decades, widowhood still has a significant negative financial impact on women. In the 1970s, 37 percent of new widows became poor after widowhood. By the 1990s, this rate had fallen to between 12 and 15 percent (Sevak, Weir, and Willis, 2003/2004). Although widowhood can cause financial distress for all women, women of color are particularly hard hit by loss of their husband's financial contributions as well as their own lower wages and benefits during their working years (Angel et al., 2003). Inadequate income adversely affects the quality of life of the widowed. Widows with little money cannot afford to be active socially, which in turn increases their feelings of loneliness. Even widows with adequate income may experience problems related to finances. In many marriages, husbands control the family finances, not wanting to bother their wives with these matters. Thus, some women have no knowledge of their family's financial status, nor do they acquire the necessary financial skills to cope with the routine tasks of handling insurance premiums and claims, balancing a checkbook, paying bills, and making a budget. Having to learn to deal with these matters during their time of mourning may heighten their levels of anxiety and frustration and lower their self-esteem. It is likely that some of these problems will lessen for the new generation of elderly women who are better educated and have more extensive work experiences than the current generation of elderly women.

Special Problems of Widowers Widowers, too, face several problems related to traditional gender roles. Earlier studies like those conducted by Felix Berado (1968, 1970) concluded that many older widowers are ill-prepared to deal with day-to-day domestic matters like cooking, cleaning, and laundry. One writer has referred to this as "the dialectical nature of gender relations," indicating that although men may benefit from women performing these tasks for them earlier in life, they may suffer from their lack of such skills when they are alone (Calasanti, 1999). Researchers found that men do 6.8 more hours of housework after widowhood while widows do 3.5 fewer hours compared with their continuously married counterparts (Utz et al., 2004). For younger husbands today who share more of the household tasks with their wives than did previous generations, these problems are likely to be minimized.

In the social realm, widowers often experience a double bind. Not only do they lose their major source of intimacy but they also find it more difficult than widows to move in with their children and to find a useful place there. Researchers have found that compared with widows, widowers have fewer contacts with their families and receive less social support from them following the death of their spouse (Hooyman and Kiyak, 1993; Utz et al., 2004; Ha, 2005). This may be a continuation of a pattern begun years ago. In many marriages, the wife is the primary initiator of family contacts; her death leaves a void in this area, lessening the interactions the widower is likely to have. Similarly, DiGiulio (1989) observed that women's support networks prior to and immediately following the death of their spouse were richer than men's. This pattern does not, however, appear true for African American men, who maintain contact with friends about equally as frequently as their female counterparts (Taylor, Keith, and Tucker, 1993).

Earlier research found that widowers experience higher rates of mental illness and depression than do widows (Gove, 1972) and that widowers have higher rates of death and suicide than widows during the first year following the death of their spouse (Walsh, 1980; Smith, Mercy, and Conn, 1988). More recent studies, however, suggest that there are growing similarities between the experiences of widows and widowers

on this measure (Bengtson, Rosenthal, and Burton, 1990; Lee et al., 2001). In fact, researchers Deborah Carr and Rebecca Utz (2002:67) found "a remarkable resilience of the widowed; at least 70 to 80 percent experience the widowhood transition without clinical depression."

Beyond Widowhood

Widowhood is a difficult stage for both women and men. There is increasing evidence, however, that a successful transition to widowhood depends on the variety of roles that make up a person's self-identity. People whose identities are multifaceted—who are involved in several activities and relationships—appear to cope better. They are less likely to become depressed or ill than are people with a more limited set of roles (DiGiulio, 1989). After the period of mourning and grief subsides, those who cared for an ill spouse may feel a sense of relief and freedom. For many people, widowhood may provide an opportunity for a reunion with friends or for making new friends. During marriage, family responsibilities often prevent people from participating in other activities. Many widowed people use their new time to return to school, take up a hobby, do volunteer work, travel, and in some cases remarry. Phyllis Silverman (1988) compared widows and widowers and found that in this phase both make changes in their lives, albeit in different directions. Women's changes tend to be more internal. The experience of coping with widowhood leads them to be more self-confident, assertive, independent, and willing to satisfy their own needs. Men, on the other hand, focus more externally, becoming more aware and appreciative of their friends and relationships. Nevertheless, both women and men are able to build satisfying new lives. For example, an Ohio State University study found that

The death of a spouse is a traumatic event. Yet after the period of grief and mourning passes, most widowed people are able to move on with their lives. Many people return to school, do volunteer work, learn new hobbies, and spend enjoyable time with friends. Some remarry.

women widowed an average of 12 years were as satisfied and optimistic about their lives as were married women in the same age group (Modern Maturity, 1992/93).

LESBIAN AND GAY ELDERLY

As we have seen, like the general population, considerable diversity exists among elderly persons, including differences in sexual orientation. Researchers estimate that roughly 1 to 3 million Americans 65 or older are lesbian, gay, bisexual, or transgender (LGBT) and that by 2020 their numbers will grow to approximately 4 million (Roach, 2001). Until recently, their presence, especially among the oldest-old, was largely invisible and thus their special needs ignored. Their invisibility is attributable, in large part, to generational differences. Today's LGBT elderly lived through McCarthyism and came of age before lesbian and gay rights were widely recognized. Fearing discrimination, many were reluctant to reveal their sexual orientation or to participate in LGBT organizations. Although only limited research is available on this population, what does exist suggests that older LGBT adults are satisfied with their lives and express the same kinds of concerns about aging voiced by their heterosexual peers (Cahill, South, and Spade, 2000). However, LGBT elderly confront additional problems not generally experienced by heterosexual elderly. For example, when a heterosexual spouse dies, the widow(er) receives Social Security survivor benefits, but a surviving lesbian or gay partner receives none. It is estimated that the LGBT community looses $124 million a year in survivor benefits because Social Security does not recognize same-sex unions (Friedman, 2006). As noted in Chapter 7, without careful estate planning or health directives, the death or

disability of an unmarried partner may leave the other partner without legal protection regarding property inheritance or other benefits or without power to make medical decisions for their loved one. Medicaid regulations protect the assets and homes of married spouses but not those of same-sex partners.

Although many older LGBT adults have close ties to their families, some have little or no contact or support because of their sexual orientation. LGBT seniors are more likely to live alone, be child-free, and may experience poverty at higher rates than heterosexual seniors. When ill, they may face what Patricia Dunn, public policy director of the San Francisco–based Gay and Lesbian Medical Association, called "homophobia in medicine." Thus, they may feel uncomfortable accessing the system or in raising health care concerns with their doctors and therefore not get the preventive medical care they need (Roach, 2001). Additionally, LGBT elderly sometimes encounter homophopic attitudes among staff and/or residents in retirement communities, assisted-living facilities, and nursing homes. Often when lesbian or gay life partners enter assisted living or nursing homes, they are often barred from sharing a room together. Some of these concerns are being addressed. The Palms of Manasota in Palmetto, Florida, the first retirement community solely for graying gays opened in 2003. Others soon followed in Santa Fe, New Mexico; Hollywood, California, Boston, Massachusetts; and other locations are in various stages of development in the United States, Canada, and Europe (Leff, 2006). Not everyone in the LGBT community is comfortable with the idea of voluntary self-segregation; some believe these developments undermine the efforts to force society to accept all people, regardless of sexual orientation.

WRITING YOUR OWN SCRIPT

THINKING ABOUT LATER LIFE

Have you ever looked in the mirror and wondered what it would be like to be old? For most young people this is difficult to do. Old age seems such a long way off. Most of us have a good chance of living into our 80s and 90s, and perhaps some of us will celebrate a 100th birthday. Nevertheless, many of us do not plan very well for this stage of our life. News stories consistently report that the majority of Americans do not have realistic retirement plans with savings to match. One way to begin thinking about the experi-

ence of aging is to examine our current intergenerational relationships. It may be useful to discuss some of the following questions with elderly family members.

Questions to Consider

1. How many generations are in your kinship structure? Are your parents, grandparents, great-grandparents still living? How healthy are they? How often do you see them? Do family members live in close proximity to one another? What kinds of services, if any, are exchanged by family members? In which generational direction do they flow? Are the pat-

terns in your family typical of those for most later-life families? How satisfied do you think the oldest members of your family are with the quality of their lives?

2. Are your parents or grandparents retired? How well are they managing economically? Did they have a financial plan for their retirement in place before they retired? What are the sources of their income?

3. What are your later-life goals? What age do you see as a desirable age to retire? What can you begin to do now that will contribute to your reaching your goals?

SUPPORTING FAMILIES IN LATER LIFE

As we have seen throughout this chapter, we live in a world that is rapidly aging. This development affects all social, economic, cultural, and political aspects of our lives and requires us to respond in new ways. For example, many of today's elderly became poor after family illness, widowhood, or retirement. However, many of tomorrow's elderly, especially women and children and people of color, are already poor and uninsured. Thus, to prevent an increase in the number of elderly poor in the future, we need to see aging as a life-long process. Thus, while we need policies and programs to help the current generation of elderly, we need to create new policies and programs targeting the younger generations. Specifically, we need to help younger people learn healthy lifestyles and to become life-long learners so that they can constantly upgrade their skills to be marketable regardless of economic changes. Private and public savings and pension plans need to be more widely available at all income levels.

Because the kinship structure for many families now and in the foreseeable future will contain more elderly than younger members, there is a need for support models that combine both informal caregiving (family and friends) and formal caregiving at affordable prices (for example, adult day care, visiting nurses, housekeeping services). Many caregivers do not know where to turn for help, so a program to educate the public about services that are available is critically needed. Private and governmental agencies should be encouraged to publicize their programs via the mass media, churches, places of employment, and in local communities, especially in those areas with high rates of poverty and residents of color. Caregivers need to receive recognition for what they do as well as financial help when needed. Tax incentives for elder care would be a partial solution to this problem. Many elderly have difficulties living alone. They may be lonely or need some type of assistance. Alternatives to institutional living need to be expanded—group homes, intergenerational apartment complexes, and co-housing are just a few possibilities.

Finally, social support networks need not go in one direction only, however. The elderly represent a tremendous reservoir of skills and ability. Some public schools and universities have initiated intergenerational partnership projects where the elderly serve as tutors and teachers' aides. Other elderly serve as "foster" grandparents and as business, craft, and hobby mentors. More elderly should be encouraged to use their talents for the social good either through paid employment or volunteer work, thus enhancing their sense of purpose and self-esteem.

SUMMARY

Throughout this chapter we have seen how family relationships have been altered by increased life expectancy and changing birth rates, resulting in multigenerational kinship structures. Additionally, social and demographic changes are altering the composition of elderly cohorts. In comparison with older people today, the elderly of the twenty-first century will be more heterogeneous. Future cohorts of the elderly will include a higher proportion of people of color, and more single, divorced, widowed, remarried, and child-free elderly, many of whom will be significantly older than current and past generations of elderly people.

Although most Americans fear ending their life in a nursing home, only about 5 percent of the elderly are in such institutions. The majority of older people live alone or in a household with their spouse. Elderly women are more likely to live alone, whereas elderly men are more likely to live with their spouse. Elderly of color are more likely to live with their adult children than are white elderly.

Studies of marital satisfaction in later-life families have shown diverse patterns. Some older couples experience higher levels of satisfaction than in the earlier years of their marriage, some show less, and still others show no change. Marital satisfaction is related to patterns of retirement and family income. Poverty remains a serious problem for many, especially widows and people of color. Later-life families are involved in reciprocal exchanges of services across the generations. Spouses and adult children provide the vast majority of care for elderly family members who become ill.

Later-life couples must eventually deal with bereavement and grief. The experience of widowhood requires many adjustments for both women and men.

An understanding of the strengths and the needs of later-life families is critical to social planning for the future. The multigenerational structure of families and the resulting interdependence among generations can provide a model for intergenerational cooperation and interdependence at the societal level.

KEY TERMS

sandwich generation

ageism

social gerontology

age norms

functional age

QUESTIONS FOR STUDY AND REFLECTION

1. Sharon Curtin wrote in her book, *Nobody Ever Died of Old Age*, "There is nothing to prepare you for the experience of growing old." Based on your attitudes toward aging and your experiences to date, do you agree or disagree with Curtin? How do your own ethnic and cultural experiences affect your attitudes toward aging? How would you advise today's families to approach the aging of their members?

2. Within the last decade, the world has experienced a number of severe political, economic, and social upheavals: terrorist attacks around the world, the growing AIDS epidemic in Africa and Asia, and ongoing armed conflict in the Middle East. Pick one of these problem areas and find demographic, economic, and social data to show how it is likely to affect the quality of life of the elderly and their families. Be specific.

3. Which style of grandparenting do you associate with your grandparents? If you become a grandparent, which style do you think you would adopt? What does this tell you about your view of grandparenthood? Should the role of grandparent be expanded? Why or why not? What kinds of problems do grandparents face when they assume the parenting role for their grandchildren? What kinds of resources and supports should society provide for such grandparents?

4. In Chapter 12, we asked whether the idea of a permanent marriage is a realistic option in today's society. In this chapter we noted that 6 percent of all married couples celebrated golden wedding anniversaries. Can you imagine yourself married for 50 or more years? What do you think it takes to stay married that long? The longer people stay married, the more likely they are to experience widowhood. Can or should married couples prepare for this eventuality? Would this make a difference in the way they experience widowhood? What advice and support could you give to a couple when one spouse is terminally ill? Explain your position.

ADDITIONAL RESOURCES

SOCIOLOGICAL

MARCDANTE, MARY. 2001. *My Mother, My Friend: The Ten Most Important Things to Talk about with Your Mother*. Boston: Fireside. Based on what she learned from over 400 personal interviews, Marcdante offers strategies for breaking down the barriers between mothers and daughters and talking more openly about such important matters as health, money, family secrets, and aging.

PIPHER, MARY. 2000. *Another Country: Navigating the Emotional Terrain of Our Elders*. New York: Riverhead Books. Using the analogy of a foreign country, Pipher provides a compassionate look at some of the generational differences between baby boomers and their parents and grandparents and suggests ways to build and maintain connections across generations.

SNOWDON, DAVID. 2001. *Aging with Grace: What the Nun Study Teaches Us about Leading Longer, Healthier, and More Meaningful Lives*. New York: Bantam. A deeply moving personal account of Snowdon's research on a group of elderly nuns, offering insight into dementing illnesses like Alzheimer's and providing strategies to minimize the chances of getting them.

VAILLANT, GEORGE E. 2002. *Aging Well: Surprising Guideposts to a Happier Life from the Landmark Harvard Study of Adult Development*. Boston: Little, Brown. This analysis of aging based on a Harvard Medical School study that followed 824 people from birth to old age reveals a number of factors that lead to successful physical and emotional aging.

FILM

Iris. 2001. The toll taken by Alzheimer's disease upon author Iris Murdoch and her devoted husband, novelist John Bayley, is difficult to watch, but the honest portrayal movingly reveals the power of love and intimacy in a life-span context.

Water. 2006. Deepa Mehta's film is a gentle yet impassioned depiction of the evils of India'a old Hindu widow laws on marriage. The story centers on a child bride widow sent to an ashram (widow house) and the degradation she experiences because of her loss of status in the larger community.

LITERARY

GLASS, JULIA. 2002. *Three Junes*. This debut novel draws the reader into the lives of several characters during three Junes spanning ten years—Paul McLeod, a newly widowed father of three sons; Fenno, his eldest son who is gay; and Fern, a young pregnant widow. The story alternates between joy and sorrow, exploring modern relationships and the families people both inherit and create for themselves.

TATEMY, LALITA. 2001. *Cane River*. New York: Warner. The author provides a fascinating saga of four generations of an African American family in Louisiana.

INTERNET RESOURCES

http://www.nia.nih.gov The National Institute on Aging provides links to caregiving sites as well as helpful publications on topics of aging and health.

http://www.aarp.org The American Association of Retired Persons provides information and resources on a variety of topics and activities.

http://www.seniorjournal.com The Senior Journal contains information and news on a variety of topics of interest to all ages—health, politics, finances, drugs, social security, recreation, and entertainment.

http://www.seniorlaw.com The SeniorLaw Home Page provides information for seniors and their advocates on numerous practical issues, including Medicare, Medicaid, estate planning, living wills, and the rights of the elderly and disabled.

IN THE NEWS

The United States and the World

Recently Professor Jody Heymann (2006), founder and director of the Project on Global Working Families, published the results of a groundbreaking study focusing on how globalization is affecting working families around the world. This work, *Forgotten Families: Ending the Growing Crisis Confronting Children and Working Parents in the Global Economy*, reports findings from the analysis of surveys of 55,000 people from around the globe with over 1000 in-depth interviews of families and policy-level data on over 160 countries. In this well-researched and well-documented book, Dr. Heymann (M.D., Ph.D. of Harvard and McGill Universities) vividly describes in detail many commonly shared experiences among families around the world as they struggle to earn a living in today's global economy and at the same time take care of their children. In an unprecedented number of the world's families, all parents now work in the paid labor force; an estimated 930 million children under age 15 are being raised in households where all of the adults work. Like their counterparts in industrialized countries before them, women in developing countries are following men into the paid labor force. Increasing numbers of both sexes work in nonagricultural employment and live in urban centers, with the result that fewer adults now work near their children or other family members.

Even in the countryside, the transformation of agriculture is creating separate spheres of work and home and altering patterns of caregiving for children and other family members.

Although working families in developing regions have higher caregiving burdens and far fewer resources to help them meet family needs than do their peers in more industrialized nations, Heymann found that children living in countries, like Vietnam, with progressive parental-leave policies, are less likely to be left at home alone when sick than children who live in countries without such policies. She found, for example, that 61 percent of working parents in Baltimore had left a sick child home alone or in someone else's care; in Vietnam, only 27 percent of working parents had either left a sick child home alone or had sent a child to school or day care sick. Among her other findings are the following:

- Thirty-six percent of the families interviewed had left a young child home alone; 39 percent had left a sick child home alone or had to send a child to school or day care sick; and 27 percent had left a child in the care of a paid or unpaid child. In 66 percent of the families where parents had to leave children home alone or with an unpaid child, the children suffered accidents or other emergencies. In 35 percent of the same cases, the children suffered from developmental or behavioral problems.

- Sixty-seven percent of parents with an income under $10 a day have had to choose between losing pay and leaving sick children home alone; 23 percent of parents interviewed took children to work, often under unsafe conditions.

- Working conditions that allowed parents to take leave from work—either due to paid leave or flexibility—halved the risk of parents having to leave children home alone sick; 15 percent of parents who had either flexibility or paid leave for child care had to leave children home alone sick, compared to 29 percent of parents who had neither paid leave nor flexibility. Parents who had access to formal child care were the least likely to have left a child home alone sick; 6 percent of those who used formal child care had left their child home alone sick compared to 22 percent of those who only used informal care.

WHAT WOULD YOU DO? Imagine for the moment that you are a working parent of a child under 5 who is sick and you have no paid family leave benefits. What options do you have? If you have been in this situation before, what did you do? How did you and your child feel about this solution? What are the dangers in leaving a young child, whether sick or not, at home alone while parents are working?

How do you explain the statistics above? Are the world's parents, including those in the United States, indifferent to their children's needs? Whose responsibility is it to see that children are supervised by an adult—only the parents, parents and other caregivers, schools, businesses, local, state, and federal governments? Explain.

Most people probably agree that today's world is a more colorful, complicated, and perhaps more dangerous place than the one that existed when their parents' and grandparents' generations were coming of age. Not only is today's world shrinking in time and space, but the emerging global milieu features new actors as people around the world struggle to cope with an array of global issues. Indeed, we are living in a new historical period that some have suggested is replacing the age of modernism that held sway over the last 500 years. Critical, profound, and often rapid changes have occurred in many places around the world: In 1989, communism collapsed in the former Soviet satellite countries of Eastern Europe; in 1990, East Germany and West Germany reunited; in 1994, the legally sanctioned racial stratification system of apartheid in South Africa ended and Congress passed the North American Free Trade Agreement between Canada, the United States, and Mexico; in 2001 terrorists attacked the World Trade Center and the Pentagon; in 2003 the United States invaded Iraq; in 2005 Congress passed the Central American Free Trade Agreement; and in 2006 North Korea test-fired its first missiles, to name but a few. This new age is variously referred to by scholars as postindustrialism, postmodernism, the information age, the computer age, and the global village. However, most scholars across academic disciplines use the term *globalization* to capture the diverse, and sometimes conflicting, trends occurring throughout the world today.

Joan Ferrante (1992) has defined globalization in terms of the concept **global interdependence**—a state in which the lives of people around the world are intertwined closely and in which any one nation's problems—unemployment, substance abuse, environmental pollution, disease, inequality, racism, sexism, inadequate resources, terrorism, and war, even for the noncombatants—increasingly cut across cultural and geographic boundaries. For example, as the opening discussion of *Forgotten Families* implies, families around the world are experiencing the impact of globalization as more families require multiple breadwinners and where the movement of jobs has often led to family and societal disruptions.

Globalization is not new. It began centuries ago when explorers like Christopher Columbus left their own countries in pursuit of new sources of wealth and trade. These early international contacts produced new economic and political structures that are still evident today. What is different today, however, is the depth and breadth of this process. In the past, many families, primarily those living in the dominant countries, could live out their lives largely unaware and to a marked degree unaffected by global events. Today the opposite is true. A poll conducted by the Pew Global Attitudes Project (2003) found that the 38,000 people they surveyed in 44 countries reported that globalization is now a routine fact of their everyday lives, experiencing it through trade, finance, travel, communication, and culture. Majorities in every nation surveyed said growing business and trade ties are at least somewhat good for their country and themselves. However, at the same time, people in every region are deeply concerned about a range of worsening financial and social problems in their lives—lack of good-paying jobs, deteriorating working conditions, and the growing gap between rich and poor. Many of these people also believe their traditional way of life is getting lost. A 2005 poll by the German Marshall Fund found that 46 percent of Americans had a favorable view of globalization; 36 percent of those polled had an unfavorable view and those that had a very unfavorable view (15 percent) were significantly greater than those who had a very favorable view ("Globalization," 2006). Regardless of geographic location or their country's level of development, today's families are feeling the effects of this deepening globalization as new technological developments provide easier, cheaper, and faster means of communication and transportation. But despite many positive aspects of globalization, working parents are often forced to make untenable choices between earning a living and caring for their children (Heymann, 2006).

In this final chapter we discuss some of the marriage and family trends, particularly in regard to children, that are immersed in a global context. Wherever possible and/or relevant, we make reference to both U.S. and global aspects of these trends. Our intent is to illuminate how the lives, welfare, and experiences of children and families are influenced by globalization's reach, or as C. Wright Mills (1959) encouraged us to do, to grasp history and biography and the connections between the two (see Chapter 1). By understanding the forces shaping our lives and their global significance, we can respond in ways that improve our own lives and those of the larger communities we inhabit. We begin with a brief consideration of some global economic trends and challenges.

GLOBALIZATION: ITS ECONOMIC IMPACT ON CHILDREN AND FAMILIES

For the last three decades or so, global competition for new markets has intensified. Globalization was pushed forward in the aftermath of World War II as many nations increased their efforts to strengthen international relationships. The need for rebuilding the infrastructures of the countries devastated by the war also provided new opportunities for other countries seeking expanded markets for their goods and services. Additionally, advances in telecommunications, especially computers, the Internet, and cell phones, diminished the significance of national borders. At the same time, governments removed numerous protectionist barriers to the movement of capital across international boundaries, making it easier for businesses to open branches and production facilities in other countries. These *multinational corporations* or *transnational corporations*, as they are called, are not under the control of any one nation. Operating decisions are made on the basis of corporate goals, often without consideration of how these decisions will affect the people in the countries in which the corporation does business. One consequence of this is a "new international division of labor," in which the process of production is broken down and the various tasks dispersed to different parts of the world (Ehrenreich and Fuentes, 1992). Families in wealthy and poor countries alike are told that they must adapt to this increased global competition. Yet it is increasingly clear that the benefits and burdens of globalization are not shared evenly. Consider the following:

- One-fifth of the world's population live in countries where many people think nothing of spending $2 a day on a cappuccino while another fifth survive on less than $1 a day and live in countries where children die for want of a simple antimosquito bed net (United Nations Development Programme, 2005).

- The 12 percent of the world's population living in North America and Western Europe accounts for 60 percent of private consumption spending, while the one-third living in south Asia and sub-Saharan Africa accounts for only 3.2 percent (Worldwatch Institute, 2004).

- The United States, with less than 5 percent of the global population, uses about a quarter of the world's fossil fuel resources (Worldwatch Institute, 2004). China now leads the world in the consumption of meat and steel. If China were to have three cars for every four people, as in the United States, it would have 1.1 billion cars (worldwide there are over 800 million cars) and would use 99 million barrels of oil a day; the world currently produces only 84 million barrels a day (Brown, 2006).

- One-third of the world's work force remains unemployed or underemployed (see Chapter 10 for a discussion of these concepts). Nearly 192 million people were unemployed in 2005, an increase of 2.2 million since 2004 and 34.4 million since 1995. Of the 192 million, 79 million were women and half were under 25. The Middle East and North Africa had the highest regional unemployment rate (13.2 percent) while East Asia had the lowest in the world (3.8 percent) (International Labour Office, 2006).

- An estimated 218 million children aged 5 to 17 are engaged in child labor; of those, almost three-quarters (126 million) work in hazardous situations or conditions, such as working in mines, working with chemicals and pesticides in agriculture, or working with dangerous machinery (International Labour Office, 2006).

Any one of these indicators has tremendous consequences for the well-being of the world's families. Obviously, income and wealth are related to a family's life chances. Families with a high income or substantial wealth have more control over their lives; they have greater access to the goods and services that are available in their societies. They can afford better housing, nutrition, education, and medical care. Families with limited income must devote what little resources they have to an ongoing struggle for survival. Just as in the United States, in many developing countries, married women who work are still responsible for domestic labor. However, one consequence of the long work hours for married women is the shifting of a substantial share of domestic labor to young girls, who are often forced to abandon school. Consequently, they marry and bear children at an earlier age than in the developed countries.

Increasingly, coalitions of environmentalists, antipoverty campaigners, trade unionists, and anticapitalist groups are demonstrating against globalization, alleging that industrialized countries, particularly the United States, have profited at the expense of developing countries. Other critics have linked the disparities that have developed along with globalization to growing resentment within impoverished nations where there are a lot of unemployed and angry people who have access to weapons and information technologies that give them the means to commit acts of terrorism at home and abroad. Even organizations like the World Bank and the United Nations are calling for what Nelson Mandela (2000) referred to as a globalization of responsibility—urgent global action to improve living conditions for people around the world by reducing the large inequities in income and wealth.

INEQUITIES IN INCOME AND WEALTH

As we saw in Chapter 10, recent studies have documented a widening income gap in the United States. The gap between rich and poor is growing in other industrialized countries as well, although to a lesser degree. A recent study in Australia found that between 1992 and 2002 the average annual cash payments to CEOs grew by 396 percent, from $715,566 to $3,550,000, while during the same period the average annual wages only grew by 37 percent. The study also found that the wealthiest 1 percent of Australians now took 9 percent of national income, compared with a 5 percent share in 1980 (Gordon, 2006). Other researchers have found growing inequality in the United Kingdom, Japan, Ireland, and New Zealand as well as in many developing countries including China and India and in most of the transitional postcommunist economies of the former Soviet Union and Central and Eastern Europe (see, for example, Milanovic, 2005). Although there is no consensus on why inequality is increasing in developed countries, several plausible explanations have been proposed: falling wages, tax cuts favoring the rich, the decline in union membership, and global competition.

Figure 15.1 provides insight into the income disparities that exist around the globe. The per capita gross national income (GNI) in U.S. dollars of high-income countries was $35,131 compared with only $1746 in low- and middle-income countries. Luxembourg had the highest GNI ($65,630); the United States ranked 7th, with a GNI of $43,740. Burundi had the lowest GNI at $100 (World Bank, 2006a). This disparity illuminates another trend. The poorest 40 percent of the world population—the 2.5 billion people who live on less than $2 a day—account for 5 percent of global income, while the richest 10 percent account for 54 percent (United Nations Development Programme, 2005). The number of billionaires increased from 691 in 2005

Some form of stratification exists within and across all societies. At right, train tracks separate this woman's home in a shantytown knows as Villa 31 from the homes in Recoleta, the wealthiest neighborhood in Buenos Aires. Similar disparities exist in the United States. Above, a homeless man shares the sidewalk with a well-dressed woman in front of New York's Bloomingdale's Department Store.

FIGURE 15.1

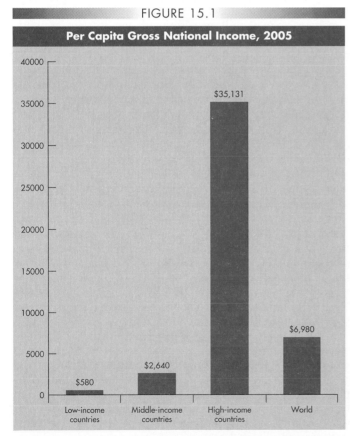

Per Capita Gross National Income, 2005

Low-income countries: $580
Middle-income countries: $2,640
High-income countries: $35,131
World: $6,980

Source: Adapted from World Bank, 2006, "GNI Per Capita, 2005, Atlas Method and PPP," World Development Indicators Database (July 1) (Accessed August 1 www.siteresources.worldbank.org/DATASTATISTICS/Resources/GNIPC.pdf).

to 793 in 2006. Their combined worth stood at $2.6 trillion, an increase of 18 percent over the previous year, and their average net worth was $3.3 billion (Kroll and Fass, 2006).

Imagine trying to feed, clothe, and shelter yourself and your family on $2 a day. Women, children, and the elderly bear the major brunt of poverty. Poor children are hit by malnutrition and illness just when their brains and bodies are developing. Over 160 million children are moderately or severely malnourished; 30,000 children under the age of 5 die each day from preventable diseases, and another 113 million do not go to school. Nearly a billion people are illiterate. Many elderly, a growing group in all regions of the world, live out their last years in deprivation and neglect (World Bank, 2001). Approximately one-half of the world's poor live in East Asia, about a third in Africa, and a substantial proportion live on the doorstep of the United States—in Mexico, and in Central and South America. The bulk of U.S. immigrants today are from these countries. The implications of this level of economic poverty for the future of the world's children are staggering. One example of this is in the area of health care.

HEALTH AND HEALTH CARE

According to the World Health Organization, **health** is a state of complete physical, mental, and social well-being rather than merely the absence of physical disease or infirmity. Table 15.1 examines three commonly used indicators of well-being—infant mortality, life expectancy, and death rates. As we can see from the table, there is a wide gap between the low infant mortality rate in Singapore (2.3) and the high rate in Angola (185.5). Although infant mortality differences

TABLE 15.1

Indicators of Well-Being in Selected Countries, 2006 Estimates

Country	Infant Mortality Rate (per 1000 Births)	Life Expectancy at Birth (Years)	Crude Death Rate (per 1000 Population)
Afghanistan	160.2	43.3	20.3
Andorra	4.0	83.5	6.3
Angola	185.4	38.6	24.2
Canada	4.7	80.0	7.8
France	4.2	79.4	9.1
India	54.6	64.0	8.2
Iran	40.3	70.3	5.5
Japan	3.2	81.0	9.2
Mozambique	129.2	40.4	21.4
Pakistan	70.4	62.6	8.2
Singapore	2.3	81.7	4.3
United States	6.4	77.3	8.3

Source: Adapted from CIA, 2006, "Rank Order Pages," *The World FactBook 2006* (Accessed August 3, www.cia.gov/cia/publications/factbook/index.html).

between developed and developing countries declined in recent years, some countries have seen their rates increase. In Afghanistan, for example, the infant mortality rate increased from 149 in 2000 to an estimated 160 in 2006. In 2000, a child born in Afghanistan had a one in seven chance of celebrating its first birthday. If that child managed to survive its first year, she or he could expect to live approximately 46 more years. Conditions have worsened in that war-torn country and a child born in 2006 can expect to live less than 44 years. That child's counterpart in Singapore is far more fortunate; not only are the odds of surviving to the age of 1 much greater, but her or his life expectancy is almost double that of an Afghan child. Improved nutrition, sanitation, and medical care as well as economic development all combined to lower infant mortality rates and to dramatically increase life expectancy in the developed countries during the past century. Life expectancy is also increasing in many developing countries due to improved economic and health conditions. Nevertheless, 29 countries still have life expectancy rates of 50 years or less; 28 of those are in Africa. Eighteen countries in Africa have experienced a decline in life expectancy since 1970 (World Health Organisation, 2006). Poverty and disease, especially AIDS, are the major culprits. And, as we have seen in the case of Afghanistan, some countries are seeing a reversal in the direction of life expectancy due to economic and political crises. Consequently, millions of children are now orphans, having lost one or both parents to disease or conflict. At the end of 2003, there were an estimate 143 million orphans under the age of 18 in 93 developing countries (Joint United Nations Programme on HIV/AIDS, 2004). Without parents or other adult caregivers, the future for these children is bleak. Their very survival is a question. Not only are they experiencing emotional suffering and grief, but they are likely to lose access to basic necessities such as shelter, food, clothing, education, and health care. Orphaned children run greater risks of being malnourished, abused, and exploited than children who have parents to look after them.

Access to Health Care

One of the critical fallouts of global and national inequity is a differential access to health care for huge numbers of people. In many areas of the world national health care systems are characterized by a lack of funds and other resources, particularly a shortage of trained health care professionals. According to a recent report by the World Health Organization (2006), at least 1.3 billion people worldwide lack access to the most basic health care, often because there is no health worker. In Afghanistan, for instance, which has one of the highest rates of maternal mortality in the world, less than 15 percent of deliveries are attended by trained health workers and less than 40 percent of Afghan children receive life-saving vaccinations (World Health Organization, 2002). The shortage is global, but the problem is greatest in countries overwhelmed by poverty and disease. A serious shortage of health workers in 57 countries is impairing provision of essential, life-saving interventions such as childhood immunization, safe pregnancy and delivery services for mothers, and access to treatment for HIV/AIDS, malaria, and tuberculosis as well as threats posed by relatively new diseases that could easily evolve into worldwide epidemics such as avian influenza. Infectious diseases and complications of pregnancy and delivery cause at least 10 million deaths each year. Better access to health workers could prevent many of those deaths. According to the report, there is clear evidence that as the ratio of health workers to population increases so, in turn, does infant, child, and maternal survival. It is estimated that more than 4 million additional doctors, nurses, midwives, managers, and public health workers are urgently needed to fill the gap in these 57 countries.

In some countries or regions of a country, health care systems have been destroyed by natural disasters such as the 2004 Indian Ocean tsunami or the 2005 Hurricane Katrina. Additionally, health care systems have been destroyed and health care workers have been driven out by warring factions in countries such as Afghanistan, Iraq, Lebanon, and the Sudan. Compared to these situations, the health care system of the United States is quite robust. Nevertheless, many people throughout the country remain largely outside its reach, largely because they are without health insurance.

The Uninsured in the United States Although the United States has among the highest per capita health expenditures of the industrialized countries, it ranks considerably lower than many of its counterparts in terms of the percentage of its population covered by public health insurance. In contrast to most other industrialized countries, where comprehensive government-run national health programs exist, access to the American health care system is primarily through private insurance, with two major exceptions—Medicare, which covers over 99 percent of the elderly, and Medicaid for the poor. Yet even with this Medicaid program, 23 million people, slightly over half of the nearly 46 million who had no health insurance in 2004, had an annual family income of less than $20,000 (Kaiser Commission, 2006). The insurance system in the United States has some serious flaws. Those who have private insurance generally obtain it as a fringe benefit of their employment. However, as insurance premiums and health care costs increased, employer-sponsored health insurance decreased. Sixty-one percent of the nonelderly population was covered by a health plan related to their employment for some or all of 2004, down from the 66 percent covered in 2000. During this same period, many employers shifted more of the insurance cost to their employees, especially the cost of insuring workers' families. Employers are not legally obligated to offer health insurance and workers can opt not to participate, as do many employees in low-paying jobs who must decide between paying for insurance or for other family needs. According to a recent study, employer-sponsored group plans cost on average $4024 per year for individual coverage and $10,880 for coverage for a family of four. The employee's share of a family premium in 2005 averaged $2713, increasing roughly $1000 since 2000 (Kaiser Commission on Medicaid and the Uninsured, 2006). Additionally, when people lose their jobs, they often lose their health insurance as well. To cope with this problem, Congress passed the 1986 Consolidated Omnibus Budget Reconciliation Act (popularly known as COBRA) to bridge the insurance gap for workers who were between jobs. Although the law has been used by millions of workers (primarily middle class), it has some serious limitations. The law does not apply to people who work for businesses with fewer than 20 workers, and it requires workers to pay the full cost of their health insurance premiums plus some administrative costs, reaching as high as $400 to $1000 a month for family coverage. Thus, many unemployed workers cannot exercise their right to continued insurance coverage because the cost is prohibitive.

In 2004, 18 percent of the nonelderly population (46 million Americans) did not have health insurance, an increase of 6 million since 2000. Those most likely to be uninsured are young adults 25 to 34 years old (22 percent), Latinas/os (34 percent), and those without a high school diploma (40 percent). In 2004, over eight in ten uninsured came from working families—almost 70 percent from families with one or more full-time workers and 13 percent from families with part-time workers. Recent efforts to enroll more children in both Medicaid and the State Children's Health Insurance Program lowered the number of uninsured children in 2004. Despite these efforts, 9 million children are still not covered by any health insurance program (Kaiser Commission, 2006). Many other Americans, both adults and children are underinsured; any serious illness quickly would exhaust their benefits. Lack of insurance coverage can be deadly. Estimates are that having insurance could reduce mortality rates for the uninsured by 10 to 15 percent. The uninsured generally receive little preventive care. They usually delay treatment until they are very sick, and then they most likely go to hospital emergency rooms, further straining an already overburdened system.

These statistics illuminate some of the problems related to the delivery of health care in the United States. Some critics have proposed establishing a national health care system modeled after the Canadian system, which guarantees all citizens equal access to health care through a national health service paid for and administered by the government. Initial attempts to reform the system during the first year of the Clinton administration failed, due in large part to the lobbying power of the insurance industry and the medical establishment. Opponents argued that such a system would be too costly and that patient–doctor relationships would be impeded by government regulation. Given the current political climate, it is unlikely that Congress will adopt the idea of a government-administered health care system any time soon. Nevertheless, polls consistently show that Americans support the extension of health insurance to more people.

Disabilities   Few people realize that the experience of disability is typical rather than rare. According to the World Bank (2006b), disability affects the lives of more than 600 million people globally, the majority living in developing countries. Of this 600 million, the United Nations Children's Fund (UNICEF) estimates that between 150 and 250 million are children. However, some studies indicate that particularly in developing countries, the proportions and numbers may be significantly higher and on the rise (Disability World, 2003). Disability can affect as much as 10 to 20 percent of a country's population, a percentage that is growing and is expected to continue to grow because of poor health care and nutrition early in life, increasing elderly populations, and violent and civil conflicts and wars throughout the world (Wolfensohn, 2002). In the United States, 51.2 million people (representing 18 percent of the population) have some level of disability, almost two-thirds (63 percent) of whom are severely disabled. Disability is a normal part of life affecting people of all ages. At the lower end of the age continuum, roughly 4 million American children between the ages of 6 and 14 have a disability; at the opposite end of the age continuum, 72 percent of people 80 years old and older have a disability, the highest of any age group. However, the majority of people with disabilities are of working age (U.S. Census Bureau, 2006).

All too often the lives of those who are disabled, especially women and children, are tied to poverty, despair, and isolation. Researchers have found a strong link between disability and poverty that goes both ways: poverty causes disability through malnutrition, poor health care, and dangerous living conditions, and disability can cause poverty by preventing the full participation of people with disabilities in the economic and social life of their communities, especially if proper supports and accommodations are not available. All over the world disabled people are among the poorest of the poor, living lives of disadvantage and deprivation. Often their disabilities are used against them to exclude them from school or the workplace or to keep them from being visible in their own neighborhoods. Consequently, many disabled persons are forced to depend on others in the family and community for physical and economic support (World Bank, 2006). In the United States, disabled people are the poorest and least educated of all citizens. However, over the last decade, there has been a significant increase in the educational attainment of disabled people, particularly higher education. Today, for instance, nearly one-half of adults with disabilities have completed some college—a proportion nearly identical to the nondisabled population (National Organization on Disability, 2001a).

Increasingly, since the emergence of the disability rights movement in the United States in the 1970s, disabled persons are asserting their right to participate fully in schools, in the workplace, in businesses, in their families, and in community affairs (Abilities 2000, 2002; National Organization on Disability, 2001a). Among its several victories, the disabled rights movement has been successful in making public facilities (buildings, bathrooms, elevators, classrooms) more accessible. This is significant, given that 2.7 million Americans 15 years of age and older use a wheelchair and another 9.1 million use an ambulatory aid such as a cane, crutches, or walker. Movement for disabled rights has occurred globally as well. For example, in Italy, the National League for the Right to Work of the Handicapped has been successful in eliminating architectural barriers to full participation in the labor force. Their efforts include making professional jobs accessible to the disabled (U.S. Census, 2006; Nuebeck and Glasberg, 1996).

Disability is not easy to define. Sociologically speaking, Joseph Shapiro (1993) defines a **disability** as a physical or health condition that stigmatizes or causes discrimination. This definition points out that disability is not purely a medical problem to be treated by nurses and doctors, but rather is also a social phenomenon best dealt with by enabling people with disabilities to lead independent lives free of prejudice and discrimination. Unfortunately, persons with disabilities continue to be targets of prejudice and discrimination; thus the impact for their families is often similar to that experienced by families who are victims of racial and ethnic discrimination. In 1989, a U.S. Senate committee documented the extent to which disabled persons face resentment, hostility, prejudice, discrimination, and the basic denial of human rights. Some of the horror stories told to senators included the following: a zookeeper would not admit children with Down syndrome because he said that these children would upset the chimpanzees; and a teacher said that a disabled student should be excluded from school because his appearance nauseated his classmates. Other stories included incidents where persons with arthritis and cancer, as well as other disabled persons, were denied or fired from jobs, not because they were unable to perform the work, but because of discrimination (cited in Nuebeck and Glasberg, 1996).

Superstitions, fear, and stigmatization of people with a disability are even more pronounced in some of the developing countries, sometimes leading parents to abandon or kill a newborn suffering from some highly visible defect. Although past negative attitudes toward disabled persons have abated some in the United States, contemporary attitudes toward the visibly disabled still tend to regard them as persons who are to be pitied, set apart, or avoided altogether. Common reactions to them continue to be condescension, ridicule, impatience, awkwardness, embarrassment, resentment, and even anger. These attitudes are not surprising, given Americans' emphasis on independence, youth, health, and attractive appearances. Thus, persons who do not fit this image are regarded with derision and hostility (Clinard and Meier, 1995). The good news, however, is that there is some evidence of changing attitudes about disabled people, at least within some segments of the population. For example, on September 11, 2001, when terrorists flew an airplane into the World Trade Center, there were people in the World Trade Center who were willing to risk or give their lives to help disabled people get out of the buildings safely. Unfortunately, most were unsuccessful. One of the things that became very apparent in

the aftermath of September 11 was that, as a country, the United States was not prepared for that kind of terrorism. And it was even less prepared to assist disabled people caught in such circumstances. In a survey conducted 3 months after the September 11 terrorist attacks, most disabled people expressed anxiety about their personal safety and said that they did not feel sufficiently prepared for future crises at work or at home (National Organization on Disability, 2001b).

Approximately one-third of American families include at least one member with a disability, and most families experience having a disabled member at some time. For those persons who are severely disabled and require prolonged care and assistance, such physical or mental requirements often severely strain family relationships. Over a long period of time, even loved ones might tire of caring for a disabled family member and begin to resent the person. On a personal level, disabled people who date or marry often face public and family attitudes similar to those faced by interracial couples: They are expected to date and marry another disabled person.

In addition to economic or class-related issues and societal attitudes toward disabled people, age and gender-related issues make contending with disability a tougher task for women and youth than for men and adults. For example, like their able-bodied counterparts, disabled women are found disproportionately among the poor. In addition to poverty, disabled women are vulnerable to a host of other personal and societal problems. As we pointed out in Chapter 11, women and children are more likely to be abused and suffer violence when they are disabled. This "feminization of vulnerability" is not unique to disabled women in the United States. Rather, it is a recurring pattern found in countries around the world. Many of these women are disabled due to violence perpetrated against them including the practice of female circumcision and infibulation. There are few educational opportunities for disabled girls. Where opportunities for education in special schools for disabled children are available, it is usually boys who receive them. In addition, the unemployment rate for disabled women in developing countries is virtually 100 percent (Disabled Women's Network Ontario, 2006).

Although disabled women are particularly vulnerable in the developing world, the quality of life for disabled women is not much better in other parts of the world. In Canada, for example, 16 percent of all women are disabled; they have an unemployment rate of 74 percent; their median income is less than half that for a disabled man ($8360 versus $19,250); and support services are often inaccessible to them and are practically nonexistent for disabled mothers. However, as we have shown repeatedly throughout this textbook, women are active agents in changing, modifying, and adapting the social worlds in which they live. Thus, like their able-bodied counterparts, disabled women globally are active agents working to tear down the barriers that prevent them from full and equal participation in society; increasingly, they are forming their own self-help groups in their countries and internationally. For example, in Kenya, disabled women are building wheelchairs, and in Uganda, women with disabilities have started MADE—Mobility Appliances by Disabled Women Entrepreneurs—to create for themselves employment and sustainable livelihoods (Snyder, 2000; Disabled Women's Network Ontario, 2006).

Like women, children are extremely vulnerable to disability. Perhaps one of the greatest contributors to child death and disability is the explosive remnants of war. According to UNICEF (2006), explosive remnants of war, including land-mines and unexploded ordnance (for example, grenades and cluster bombs that did not explode on impact but can still detonate), pose a huge threat to children and their families in more than 80 countries, most of which are no longer engaged in war. Of the 15,000 to 20,000 people who are killed or disabled each year by these deadly weapons of war, at least 20 percent are children. Indeed, children face the daily threat of explosion in every region of the world. For example, land-mines are buried in almost half of all villages in Cambodia, and in Lao PDR almost one-fourth of all villages are contaminated with explosive remnants of war. Children suffer debilitating physical injuries from mine explosions, including losing fingers, toes, and limbs; injuries to the genital area; and loss of sight and hearing. For children, the loss of a limb is especially problematic. For instance, the rapid growth of their bones means that prostheses have to be regularly refitted and new amputations may be necessary. An estimated 85 percent of child victims die before they can get medical attention. Of those who live, most of their families cannot afford life-saving or reconstructive surgery or rehabilitative care for their disabilities. Many of the problems facing mine-injured children and their families are similar to those facing all disabled children, particularly those in countries where health services are damaged, inadequate, and/or underfunded. All disabled children face the challenge of social reintegration, as well as the psychological problems that can arise from humiliation, rejection, and depression about the loss of life opportunities.

These facts notwithstanding, as a result of UNICEF and other individual and collective actions, a number of success-

ful programs have been initiated to assist disabled children, their families, and their communities (UNICEF, 2006a; Save the Children Federation USA, 2000). Today disabled people and their organizations call attention to the fact that it is economic and social barriers that stop people with disabilities from participating fully in society and not necessarily the individual characteristics of the disabled. This viewpoint is consistent with a sociological perspective of disability that focuses our attention on disabling social structures, institutions, and social environments that create, perpetuate, and maintain barriers to the equitable treatment of people with disabilities, as opposed to focusing on the individual characteristics or disabilities of the disabled.

According to some sources, 65 to 70 percent of the U.S. population will become disabled simply by living to their full life expectancy. This will certainly have important implications for marriage and family life: for example, the range of disabilities (whether severe or mild); how and if they will be covered under health insurance; who will care for aging disabled family members; and what kinds of disability-related assistance will be available to families with disabled members are but a few of the issues. Parents with disabled children are particularly vulnerable to stress, which is often produced by trying to meet the extra demands of caring for a disabled child without the necessary resources and support. Parental stress in turn can impact a disabled child's development. Thus, often it is not just disabled children that need services and support but also parents and sometimes whole families (Beresford, Rabiee, and Sloper, 2005).

Trends in Drug Use and Associated Health Problems

Drug use is another global public health issue. The trend is toward an increase in the supply and the use of both legal and illegal drugs and an earlier initiation into their use, resulting in a broad spectrum of problems, including deteriorating health, social and family disruption, and economic exploitation. Problems related to drug use have traditionally affected males. However, the rapid social and economic changes discussed throughout this textbook has contributed to a dramatic increase in use among women. Because many women drug users are of childbearing age, their use can have profound negative effects on the next generation.

Thinking about drugs is complicated by the fact that almost daily the media send out mixed messages about drugs. In the same news hour we are likely to hear about the wonders of a new drug and the devastating effects other drugs have visited on individuals or whole communities. People are often surprised to discover that they are drug users. Until relatively recently, commonly used items such as coffee, tea, and cigarettes were not viewed as drugs. There was even resistance to including alcohol on the list of commonly used drugs. Thus, it is important to clarify terms. A **drug** is any substance that alters the central nervous system and states of consciousness. Such alterations can enhance, inhibit, or distort the functioning of the body, in turn possibly affecting patterns of behavior and social functioning. The most commonly used and abused drugs are *narcotics* (opium, morphine, codeine, and heroin), *depressants* (sedatives, hypnotics, and alcohol), *stimulants* (cocaine, crack, amphetamines, caffeine,

One of the greatest contributors to children's death and disability is the explosive remnants of war. Well after particular wars are over, children in every region of the world remain at grave risk of death or debilitating physical injuries from landmines and other unexploded ordnance. The loss of limb is especially problematic. These two Cambodian amputees, with only one leg, are typical of many of the children who survive.

as in coffee or tea, and nicotine, as in tobacco), *hallucinogens* (LSD, mescaline, and peyote), *cannabis* (marijuana and hashish), and *organic solvents* (inhalants such as gasoline, airplane glue, and paint thinner, as well as certain foods, herbs, and vitamins) (Hanson and Venturelli, 1995).

Illicit drug use is common in the United States. Nearly 40 percent of the respondents in a national household survey reported using an illicit drug at some point in their lifetime, the most common being marijuana and hashish (U.S. Department of Health and Human Services, 2001b). In 2004, 19.1 million Americans (7.9 percent of the population 12 years old and older) were current illicit drug users, meaning they had used an illicit drug during the month prior to the survey (U.S. Department of Health and Human Services, 2005). Rates and patterns of drug use vary considerably by age. Children as young as 12 report using illicit drugs. Rates increase with age, peaking in the 18 to 20 age group and then generally declining after that with increasing age.

Rates of current illicit drug use varied significantly among the major racial and ethnic groups. In 2004, the rate was highest among persons reporting two or more races (13.3 percent) followed closely by Native Americans or Alaska Natives (12.3 percent), then African Americans (8.7 percent), whites (8.1 percent), and 7.2 percent for Latinas/os. Asians had the lowest rate, at 3.1 percent.

Considering the extent of drug use, we might well ask why people use drugs and when drug use becomes drug abuse. The reasons for drug use are as varied as the users themselves, but researchers have identified several common themes: to relieve pain and illness; for fun or curiosity; for pleasure; to fit in; to escape problems; and to relieve boredom, stress, and anxiety. The Food and Drug Administration defines **drug use** as the taking of a drug for its intended purpose and in an appropriate amount, frequency, strength, and manner, and **drug abuse** as the deliberate use of a substance for other than its intended purpose, in a manner that can damage health or ability to function.

Drug Abuse: An International Concern

Drug abuse is not unique to the United States. The illegal production, distribution, and use of drugs are global problems. Estimates by the United Nations Office on Drugs and Crime (2006) put the annual global rate of illicit drug consumption at 5 percent of the world population ages 15 to 64 (200 million), larger than the total population in many countries. Cannabis remains by far the most widely used drug (some 162 million people), followed by amphetamine-type stimulants, including Ecstasy (35 million people). The number of opiate abusers is estimated at some 16 million people, of which 11 million are heroin abusers. Some 13 million people are cocaine users. The estimates have remained relatively stable in recent years, with decreases in some countries offset by increases in others. Nor is this a new phenomenon. Anthropologists report that the use of mood-altering agents appears to be a common characteristic among diverse cultures. In one way or another, all societies struggle with what is appropriate use and what is abuse of these substances.

The consequences of the illegal traffic in drugs are many and varied. In the centers of production, like Colombia, it creates an economic problem, diverting money and energy that could be used for investment in legal economic activities. In the centers of consumption, like the United States, it creates a health problem, contributing annually to 3.5 percent of the total cases of diseases and millions of deaths worldwide. In both centers, where criminal organizations flourish, it is a matter that jeopardizes the very existence of the nation-state (Garcia-Pena, 1995). It is estimated that the annual revenues of the global illegal drug industry top $320 billion, a figure larger than the gross domestic product of 88 percent of the countries of the world, which can easily be used to destabilize a country's economy (United Nations Office on Drugs and Crime, 2005).

Drug Use among the World's Children

It is illegal for children in the United States to purchase alcohol or tobacco products. Nevertheless, according to the U.S. Department of Health and Human Services (2005), about 29 percent of persons aged 12 to 20 (10.8 million) reported drinking alcohol in the month prior to a survey interview in 2004. Of these, 7.4 million (19.6 percent) were binge drinkers (five or more drinks on the same occasion) and 2.4 million (6.3 percent) were heavy drinkers. Although smoking among young people was down from previous years, almost 12 percent of youths aged 12 to 17 used cigarettes. In and of themselves these patterns are cause for concern because they can lead to physical and social problems for the user. Moreover, there is evidence that the early use of alcohol and tobacco can be a gateway to the use of illicit drugs. The rate of illicit drug use, including marijuana, inhalants, and other substances, among persons 12 to 17 was 10.6 percent. These substances are also popular among the world's "street children," children made homeless because of family separations and conflicts associated with urbanization, economic crisis, political change, civil unrest, wars, epidemics, and natural disasters. Almost every country has some street children; various estimates put their number at between 10 and 150 million worldwide. Studies have found that between 25 and 98 percent of street children use substances of one kind or another. In Morocco, 98 percent of street children are thought to be dependent on glue. Cheap and easy to get, the children use glue to numb the feelings of cold, hunger, and rejection. In the process, these children become vulnerable to tuberculosis and sexually transmitted diseases because they often sell themselves to pay for their habit (Harter, 2004). Glue sniffing is also common among street children in Central and South America and in many Asian countries. The devastating consequences that follow such use include acute and chronic health and emotional problems, disruption of interpersonal relationships, school failure, social marginalization, and criminal behavior.

One of the major factors in drug use among children is the absence of a supportive family. A study by the Partnership for a Drug Free America bears this out. Researchers found that teenagers who received strong antidrug messages at home were 42 percent less likely to use drugs than teens whose parents ignored the issue. African American parents (57 percent) were more likely than Latina/o (45 percent) or white parents (44 percent) to say they discuss the risks of drugs regularly with their children. In that same study, 31 percent of African American children recalled having such conversations, compared with 29 percent of Latina/o and 19 percent of white children (Talks on Drugs, 1999). Of course, street children and children without involved parents are unlikely to have this type of support.

Alcohol Use and Abuse

Although the media pay far more attention to illegal drugs such as cocaine and heroin, alcohol abuse affects a much larger percentage of the population. The use of alcohol for recreation and social interaction has a long history. So, too, does concern with the potential for abuse. The earliest known legal code, the Hammurabi Code (circa 1758 B.C. in Babylon), contained laws regulating the operation and management of drinking establishments. The Greek philosopher Plato was concerned enough about the drinking behavior of his countrymen that he established rules for conduct at "symposia," which in reality were drinking parties (McKim, 1986, cited in Thombs, 1994). Such concerns remain with us today.

About 2 billion people worldwide consume alcoholic drinks. According to a national survey, 121 million Americans (50.3 percent) aged 12 or older reported they were current drinkers of alcohol (U.S. Department of Health and Human Services, 2005). A recent Gallup poll suggests the figure might be considerably higher. Sixty-four percent of the respondents aged 18 and older in that study said they drank alcoholic beverages, consistent with data from recent years (Jones, 2006). Consumption was highest among those making $75,000 and over (82 percent) and lowest among those making less than $30,000 (44 percent). Those who attend church weekly had lower rates of use (48 percent) compared to those who seldom or never attend church (72 percent). The majority of people drink in moderation and suffer little or any consequences from their use of alcohol; millions of others are not so fortunate.

Worldwide, some 76 million people are currently affected by alcohol-use disorders, such as alcohol dependence and abuse (World Health Organization, 2004a). According to the National Institute on Alcohol Abuse and Alcoholism (NIAAA), **alcoholism,** also known as alcohol dependency, is a disease that includes four symptoms: craving—a strong need or urge to drink; loss of control—not being able to stop drinking once drinking has begun; physical dependency—withdrawal symptoms, such as nausea, sweating, shakiness, and anxiety after stopping drinking; and tolerance—the need to drink greater amounts of alcohol to get high. Alcohol is involved in 1.8 million deaths a year, which represents 3.2 percent of all deaths worldwide. Annually across the globe, alcohol causes a loss of 58.3 million "disability-adjusted life years" (DALYs), the number of years lost due to premature deaths as well as the years spent living with disability (World Health Organization, 2004a). In the United States, excessive alcohol consumption is the third leading preventable cause of death in the United States. The Center for Disease Control (2004) estimates that there were almost 76,000 alcohol-attributable deaths (AADs) and 2.3 million years of potential life lost (YPLLs) in the United States in 2001. Seventy-two percent of AADs involved males and 6 percent involved persons under 21 years of age. According to the NIAAA (2000), the effects of alcohol, ranging from

violence to traffic crashes to lost productivity to illnesses such as heart attacks, strokes, cirrhosis of the liver, pneumonia, mental illness, sexual dysfunctions, and premature death cost the nation an estimated $185 billion per year. Problem drinking in the family is also a factor in many suicides, including adolescent suicide (Fernquist, 2000).

Other costs are social. Alcohol is often implicated in antisocial behavior; it can lower inhibitions against violence, reduce a victim's resistance, and provide an excuse for behavior. The abuse of alcohol and other drugs is often a factor in family violence (Chapter 11).

Addiction: A Family Problem

Harold Doweiko (1996) identified a number of possible combinations between marriage, family, and addiction. Many people who are or who become addicted to chemicals are married. Some marry before becoming addicted; others are already addicted, but their partners may be unaware of the addiction. Sometimes addicts marry each other in a marriage of convenience that brings with it an additional source of chemicals and money. Finally, nonaddicts may be aware of their partner's addiction but marry anyway in the hopes of "saving" the addict.

The problem of parental chemical use and abuse is a significant one. In 2001, more than 6 million children (9 percent) lived with at least one parent who abused or was dependent on alcohol or an illicit drug (Substance Abuse and Mental Health Services Administration, 2003). Most of what we know about the role addiction plays in families is based on studies involving alcohol abuse. Hence, our concentration here will be on families coping with alcohol addiction. Initially, research on and treatment of alcoholism focused on the drinking alcoholic, particularly men. In the 1950s and 1960s, the focus shifted to the "family disease" concept, recognizing that all members of the family are affected by the alcoholism of a member. Researchers now use systems theory to examine the alcoholism of a parent as a central organizing principle determining interactional patterns within the family (Brown and Yalom, 1995).

As we saw in Chapter 2, family systems theory explains how families function. It examines roles, rules, and communication processes that allow for predictable and consistent behavior. Whenever one part of the system is altered, all other parts are affected. This can readily be seen in the case of chronic alcoholism. When one member becomes chemically addicted, the remaining family members become enmeshed in the addiction process as they attempt to cope with the impact this behavior has on their lives. The spouse of an alcoholic is likely to deny the problem and cover up for her or his partner, taking on the role of an "enabler" who tries to help the alcoholic partner by engaging in behavior that allows the addiction to continue. For example, the nonaddicted spouse may report a partner as ill when in fact she or he is unable to go to work or attend a social function because of drunkenness.

Children also learn how to adapt to meet the demands of the addicted parent. In attempting to avoid a family crisis and as a means of coping with family stress, family roles and responsibilities are restructured as other family members take over the addicted parent's responsibilities. Many of these new patterns actually encourage the alcoholic to continue drinking and to become less involved in family life. For example, the oldest child often takes on the role of *hero*, looking after younger children and attempting to prevent the alcoholic parent from drinking. Conversely, a child may misbehave and in that way deflect attention away from the problems that the alcoholism creates. As a result, the child may become a *scapegoat*, receiving the anger that would otherwise be directed toward the alcoholic. Another child may react by becoming an independent loner, staying out of everyone's way. This *lost child* role is likely to lead to low self-esteem as this child receives little nurturing or attention during childhood. Finally, a child may take on the role of *mascot*, becoming entertaining and providing comic relief in an effort to distract the family's attention from its problems.

It is important to remember that there is tremendous variation in family functioning and structures. Therefore, although some chemically dependent families have members who clearly fit one of these specific roles, other families will have members who exhibit behavior characteristics of more than one role or who will shift from one role to another over time. In some families, certain roles never emerge. The longer these behaviors continue, the more difficult it is to change them. There is widespread agreement among family therapists that alcoholism is one of the most difficult family problems to treat, partly because many people who need treatment do not want it, at least not at first.

Just as the onset of alcoholism leads to changes in the stability of the family system, recovery may also disrupt family functioning. Individual members may resist change because it may alter the roles with which they have become comfortable. For example, the enabler may have taken control over the family finances and may feel resentful if the recovering spouse now wants to resume this behavior. Children, too, may resist change. During the period when a parent was drinking, a child may have assumed the role of confidant to the nonalcoholic parent. In recovery, this role may be lost. Furthermore, family members often believe all problems will be over once the alcoholic member stops drinking. When they discover that problems remain and might even be exacerbated in the early stages of recovery, they may become discouraged and resentful. Further complicating the situation is the likelihood that members may be at different stages of recovery. One child described this phase in his family's recovery:

> My parents were both immersed in their recoveries. That's all they did. They didn't speak to each other for the first two years without first calling their sponsors. They barely spoke to me. I knew someone would make dinner each night, but I never knew who, or when it would appear. I spent every afternoon and evening alone in my room with my homework and my headphones. They were busy getting sober, and I felt guilty having needs. (Quoted in Brown and Yalom, 1995:300)

Recovery is a time of great stress, and some families cannot cope; there is a high incidence of divorce within the first 3 to 5 years (Brown and Yalom, 1995). Nevertheless, with treatment many families are able to relinquish their previously unhealthy behaviors and thinking.

Children of Alcoholics　Some experts believe one out of eight children under age 18 in the United States lives with an alcoholic parent, primarily the father (Whitehouse, 2000).

For the most part, these children grow up in homes where there is considerable family stress and conflict that negatively impact the parent–child relationship. Further, children who live with an alcoholic parent are at greater risk for being physically abused and becoming abusers themselves (Widom and Hiller-Sturmhofel, 2001). Often, children of alcoholics (COAs) receive inconsistent parenting and inadequate parental support. This places these children at risk for many emotional and behavioral difficulties as they are growing up, including the probability of becoming alcoholics themselves. Another possibility is that they will marry a spouse who needs to be taken care of in the same way they took care of the addicted parent. In Chapter 3, we saw how gender identity is acquired through the process of social learning. Similarly, COAs may learn alcoholic behavior by modeling their behavior after that of an alcoholic parent, learning that drinking is an acceptable way to cope with life's problems. Researchers have established that genetic factors also play a role in the development of alcoholism, especially between fathers and sons (Wihelmsen Lab Elucidates the Genes, 2006).

Before leaving this section, it is important to note that not all COAs become maladjusted adults. Numerous studies comparing adult children of alcoholics and adults from nonalcoholic families found no clear differences in the grown children's emotional adjustment. Despite the difficulties of living in an alcoholic family, many children manage to cope and develop into happy, well-adjusted adults. This seems more likely when only one parent has a drinking problem and the other parent is able to provide support and guidance for their children (Schuckit and Smith, 2001), or when a parental surrogate such as an uncle, neighbor, or teacher is actively involved with the children (Whitehouse, 2000).

Differential Life Chances: Death and Disease

Nowhere can we so clearly see the differences in the well-being of families than by an examination of data on death and disease. A cursory glance back at Table 15.1 reveals the wide gulf between crude death rates (number of deaths during 1 year per 1000 persons based on midyear population) in the developing and developed countries. For example, a poor country like Angola has a crude death rate of 24.2 compared to a rate of 4.3 for Singapore. Another indication of well-being is access to primary health resources such as safe drinking water and sanitation facilities. Figure 15.2 reveals major disparities among regions on these two indices. On one end of the scale, large numbers of families living in the least developed regions have little or no access to safe drinking water. Although access to improved water supply and sanitation has increased since 1990, globally 1.1 billion people are without access to improved drinking water sources and a staggering 2.6 billion (42 percent of the world's population) are without access to improved sanitation. For both water supply and sanitation, the vast majority of people without access live in Eastern Asia and sub-Saharan Africa. Every year millions of people die from water-related diseases; nearly 5000 children die each day from unsafe water and lack of basic sanitation facilities (World Health Organization and UNICEF, 2005).

Additionally, women and girls in many countries suffer health burdens brought on by their efforts to carry water

FIGURE 15.2

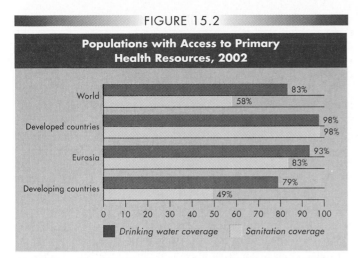

Populations with Access to Primary Health Resources, 2002

World — Drinking water coverage 83%, Sanitation coverage 58%
Developed countries — Drinking water coverage 98%, Sanitation coverage 98%
Eurasia — Drinking water coverage 93%, Sanitation coverage 83%
Developing countries — Drinking water coverage 79%, Sanitation coverage 49%

(scale: 0 10 20 30 40 50 60 70 80 90 100)

■ Drinking water coverage   □ Sanitation coverage

Source: Adapted from World Health Organization and UNICEF, 2005, *Water for Life: Making It Happen* (Geneva, Switzerland): Figures 1 and 2, p. 5.

from distant, often polluted, rivers and streams. Forty-four percent of women in rural Africa spend 30 minutes or more to fetch a single bucket of water for their family's needs. The level of water and sanitation services affect more than physical health. Children, especially girls, in countries with inadequate facilities often miss schools. Domestic chores and lack of separate school latrines force girls to stay home, thus impairing their and their family's chances to escape poverty. At the other end, families in North America and Europe have nearly universal access to basic health resources. The consequences of these differences can be seen in the different causes of death in developing and developed countries. People who live in developing countries are far more likely to die from infectious

and communicable diseases than people who live in the developed countries. Epidemics of infectious diseases are common in some parts of the world. For example, malaria affects an estimated 300 to 500 million people and kills between 1 to 2 million each year, most of them children under the age of 5. The majority of cases occur in sub-Saharan Africa, followed by parts of Asia and Latin America (World Malaria Report, 2005). This is a disease that is preventable, but because of the poverty in these regions, stocks of vaccine are too costly to maintain, and many areas are without medical services. Approximately 2 billion people still do not have access to low-cost essential medicines such as penicillin, which have been commonly available in the developed countries for decades. Fifty percent of Africa's 1-year-olds have not been immunized against diphtheria, tetanus, polio, or measles (United Nations Development Programme, 2001).

Many of the diseases in developing countries are associated with extreme poverty. In contrast, many of the diseases in developed countries are associated with affluence and unhealthful lifestyles—little physical exercise combined with a diet high in fat. Thus, diseases of the circulatory system and cancer are far more common in developed countries than in developing countries. However, as the economies of developing countries grow, many are adopting Western lifestyles and their accompanying risk factors—smoking, high-fat diets, obesity, and lack of exercise. Deaths from cardiovascular diseases are rapidly increasing in the developing world.

The world's developed countries cannot afford to ignore infectious diseases in faraway countries. If not checked, they can easily pose a threat to the developed countries. As international travel increases, so, too, does the exposure to infectious diseases. Since 1973, 20 well-known diseases, including tuberculosis and malaria, have reemerged in the United States. During this same period, 30 previously unknown diseases have been identified around the world, including HIV, Ebola, hepatitis C, avian flu, and West Nile fever. International trade provides another means for infectious diseases to cross borders. For example, in 1985, the tiger mosquito, which can transmit yellow fever, dengue, and other diseases, entered the United States inside a shipment of water-logged used tires from Asia. Within 2 years these mosquitoes were in 17 states (Heymann, 2000). It is thus in the interest of the developed countries to help eradicate infectious diseases in developing countries. Yet only 10 percent of global health research focuses on the illnesses that constitute 90 percent of the global disease burden. Besides more research dollars, efforts must be devoted to more rapid dissemination of new medical advances as well as to the training of more medical staff and the development of prevention programs in developing countries.

FAMILIES COPING WITH LOSS: DYING AND DEATH

Someone once wrote that in all of life there are only two certainties: death and taxes. We have located the topic of death in this chapter because death is a universal experience for families everywhere. Every society constructs its own rules for handling the death and mourning the loss of their members. In recent years, televised reports of national disasters, war, and deadly terrorist attacks here and abroad have brought images

Over 1 billion people, living in some of the least developed regions of the world have little or no access to safe drinking water. Here an ecologist examines a sample of underground water to assess its safety for the villagers in the area.

of death and dying into our private spaces and exposed the resultant grief and mourning to a global audience. There is no way we can adequately address the scope of this phenomenon in this limited space. Thus, our discussion will focus on some general aspects of dying, death, and mourning as experienced in the United States.

The Process of Dying

Dying is a complex process. For our purposes we will use Robert Atchley's (1991) definition of a dying person, one identified as having a condition from which no recovery can be expected. Much has been written about how people react to the news that they are terminally ill. Psychiatrist Elizabeth Kübler-Ross (1969) invited dying patients to express their thoughts, fears, and anxieties about this last phase in their lives. On the basis of 200 interviews with dying patients of different ages, she identified five stages through which she believed the dying patient moves:

- *Denial:* "No, not me. It must be a mistake" is a common reaction.
- *Anger:* "Why me?" becomes the question.
- *Bargaining:* "Please let me live to see my daughter get married." "Please let me live to make amends for what I did." The appeal may be made to God or to one's doctors.
- *Depression:* This stage is characterized by generalized feelings of loss.
- *Acceptance:* The denial, anger, bargaining, and depression are replaced by contemplation of the approaching death with a quiet readiness.

In a later work Kübler-Ross (1974) pointed out that patients may skip a stage, experience some or all of the stages simultaneously, or move through the stages in any order. Kübler-Ross's stages of dying have not received any empirical support; nevertheless, many practitioners as well as family members continue to use them in an effort to understand and respond appropriately to the behaviors of dying people. Critics of Kübler-Ross reject the notion of a progression through stages. They see the dying person as experiencing a variety of feelings and emotions and engaging in psychological defenses and maneuvers (Shneideman, 1980; Baugher et al., 1989–90). For example, Richard Kalish (1985) argues that what Kübler-Ross calls stages are simply common reactions to one's impending death. He believes that dying people also experience other reactions such as hope, relief, curiosity, and apathy. Despite such criticism, Kübler-Ross's work remains noteworthy for providing insights into the needs and tasks of the terminally ill and for initiating a much-needed discussion of these issues.

The Needs and Tasks of the Dying

One of the needs that most dying people have is to know that they are dying, yet access to this information is not always available. Although in recent years the tendency in the medical community has been to tell the patient, some doctors are still reluctant to do so. This need is strongly related to the tasks that the dying person must attend to—getting insurance and financial paperwork in order, making decisions about medical treatment, arranging for distribution of personal property, making a will, letting people know her or his wishes regarding funeral arrangements, and saying goodbye. Too often these preparations are not made until the last minute, if ever, thus leaving the grief-stricken spouse or family to cope with them during a period of enormous stress. No one likes to anticipate the loss of a loved one or to think of her or his own demise, yet doing so before the inevitable happens can make the necessary adjustments easier.

In the nineteenth century the overwhelming majority of Americans died at home, in the presence of family and friends. Information and skills for preparing the dead body were part of the common domestic knowledge of the day. The wake was held in the front parlor, and family and friends came there to pay their respects. By the twentieth century, in contrast, death had become culturally invisible (Aries, 1981). Physicians, hospitals, and nursing homes took control of the process. Today, few people ever see an untreated dead body. Instead, professional funeral directors quickly remove the body and prepare it out of sight of family members in an effort to make it appear "natural" or "sleeplike." Rather than say that someone died, we use a variety of euphemisms like *passed away, departed,* and *left us* (DeSpelder and Strickland, 1988). In the process, dying has become more depersonalized, and the rituals surrounding death have been shortened.

One of the consequences of these changes is that survivors experience greater difficulties in receiving support throughout their period of bereavement and in expressing their grief openly. **Bereavement** refers to the state of being deprived of a loved one by death; **grief** is the emotional response to this loss. Coping with a loved one's death involves a series of responses and adjustments. First is the painful process of bereavement. This typically involves a period of confusion; difficulty in concentrating; and intense feelings of loss, depression, and loneliness. There may also be physical manifestations of grief, for example, a loss of appetite, an inability to sleep, and deteriorating health. In her classic study of widows, sociologist Helen Lopata (1973) pointed out the necessity of doing "grief work," confronting and acknowledging the emotions brought about by death. Successful grief resolution involves four tasks: accepting the reality of the loss, experiencing the pain of grief, adjusting to an environment in which the deceased is missing, and withdrawing emotional energy and reinvesting it in another relationship (Worden, 1982).

Mourning refers to the outward expressions of grief, including a society's customs, rituals, and rules for coping with loss. Whatever the loss, be it an individual child, sibling, parent, spouse, or partner, or a national collective loss stemming from natural disasters like earthquakes or floods or from armed conflicts, people do not just get over it and move on with their lives. Rather, people reorganize their lives by finding ways to readjust to living in a world without the person or persons who died (Silverman, 2000). Mourning may be private or public, involving a few people or a whole country.

> Do you remember your first wake or funeral? How did you feel? Were you uncomfortable in that setting? Were you uncertain about the proper way to behave? What funeral and mourning rituals does your family or religion practice? How helpful do you think they are? Explain.

In Lebanon, people gather to mourn the loss of their relatives and friends killed during the Israel-Hezbollah conflict as a Shite Muslim Sheik prays over their coffins. Thousands of miles away, an American soldier killed in Iraq is mourned by his family and friends.

National Mourning

Following the September 11 terrorist attacks that killed over 3000 people, President Bush declared Friday, September 14, 2001, as a day of national mourning. All schools, government departments and offices, and most businesses either closed or took time off from routine matters to pause and recall the tragic events of that day. Heads of major religious denominations and public officials at all levels arranged for memorial services around the country. At noon on that day, bells were rung, and in the evening candlelight ceremonies were held in people's homes, places of worship, and public buildings to remember and honor those who died. Similar activities took place in other countries to show their sympathy for the United States. Such public expressions of grief occur whenever a nation or group of people experience a common loss, be it a political leader such as the assassination of President John F. Kennedy, or a celebrity figure who has touched the hearts of the people—for example, Princess Diana—or when many innocent people are suddenly and violently killed in natural disasters, sending shock waves through their communities. The rituals associated with national mourning help people make sense out of the loss, allow them to share their fears and insecurities, and create or reinforce people's feelings of collective solidarity. How a person dies, her or his age, and the relationship to the survivors all affect the nature of the grieving experience.

Death of a Child

In contrast to some of the developing countries with high infant mortality rates, here in the United States parents generally expect to live longer than their children. Because a child represents the past as well as future hopes and dreams, the death of a child is particularly devastating. Parents who have lost a child have consistently told researchers that they have never completely resolved their grief. The two main causes of death of children are accidents and malignant disease. The sudden, unexpected nature of an accidental death intensifies the grief experience, especially if one or the other parent was in any way involved—for instance, driving the car in which a child was killed or giving permission to go to the beach where the drowning occurred. The involved parent is likely to feel guilty. Blame from the other parent can compound such feelings.

If parents are unable to forgive each other and to help each other mourn the death in appropriate ways, over time the marriage itself may dissolve. When death follows a lengthy illness, there is the added physical, emotional, and financial stress of caregiving. However, there may also be a process of gradual adaptation to the reality of the child's impending death.

Death of a Sibling

The well sibling of terminally ill children faces many problems. The signs of sorrow, illness, and death are everywhere. A child sees the signs on a parent's face and recognizes them in the disruptions to household routines even when parents try to shield the child from what is going on. When a child is dying, the parents may be preoccupied with her or his care and the well sibling may feel excluded or deprived of parental attention. The well child may be struggling with conflicting emotions. She or he may love the ill sibling, but resent the attention the sibling is getting. When death occurs, the well child may feel guilt for the death, especially if there was any sibling rivalry in the past. Many of these feelings are kept inside because the child does not want to upset the parents any further.

A child takes its cues for coping with a sibling's death from parents. If the parents' response is dysfunctional, it can impede the surviving child's ability to cope. For example, sometimes parents resent a surviving child because she or he can be a painful reminder of the deceased child. This may compound the child's feeling of guilt. If, however, the parents listen to the surviving child, answer any questions the child has, and share their feelings of loss, giving the bereaved child opportunities to acknowledge and express grief too, chances are good that the child will cope successfully with this loss.

Death of a Parent

Reactions to the death of a parent vary depending on the age of the child. If the death occurs in childhood, the child's sense of loss may be accompanied by feelings of insecurity. The child may fear abandonment by the other parent as well. Just as we saw in the case of siblings, a child may assume responsibility for the parent's death and hence guilt:

"If I had been better, Dad would not have died." Often people assume that young children do not experience the depth of grief that adults do, or they assume that children will get over the death quickly. Yet children and adults grieve in similar ways. Both cry, get angry, blame themselves, and have problems eating and sleeping. The surviving parent or other close relatives or friends need to be sensitive to the feelings of bereaved children, providing reassurance and helping them to work through their grief.

Even for adults, the death of parents can be very traumatic. No longer do they have the people in their lives that they could always turn to for guidance and acceptance. They have, in fact, become the older generation and thus much more aware of their own mortality.

Death of a Spouse or Partner

The death of a spouse has been identified as the most stressful event that can occur in a person's life (Holmes and Rahe, 1967). Spouses and partners provide an individual with a specific role, security, and many kinds of support—physical, emotional, financial, and social. All of these losses must be dealt with and a new role must be constructed. The intensity of the grief reaction depends on a number of factors. If the spouse was ill for a long time, the grief may be coupled with relief. If the death was untimely, acceptance may be more difficult.

Suicide

According to the American Association of Suicidology, suicide is the 11th leading cause of death in the United States, with one suicide occurring on average every 17 minutes, claiming about 30,000 lives annually (Bergeron, 2006). The United States has a moderate rate of suicide (10.7 per 100,000 population) compared with other countries, for example, Lithuania (42.1), Russian Federation (38.7), Hungary (27.7), and Japan (23.8) (Wikipedia, 2006). With the exception of some parts of China, the suicide rate for males is considerably higher than for their female counterparts. Risk factors are similar from country to country and include mental illness, substance abuse, hopelessness, recent loss of loved ones, unemployment, access to lethal means, and previous suicide attempts. The groups most at risk for suicide in the United States include the unmarried, males, whites, adolescents, the elderly, and Native Americans. Although there are no official statistics compiled on attempted suicides, estimates are that about 800,000 attempts are made each year. An estimated 4.47 million Americans are survivors of the suicide of a friend, family member, or loved one (Bergeron, 2006).

Suicide is not new; it has been documented throughout recorded history. Nevertheless, it is perhaps the least understood of all human behaviors (Stillion, 1995). Cultural attitudes toward suicide vary widely. In some societies, suicide was obligatory under certain conditions. Among the Japanese, a samurai warrior's ritual suicide called *hara-kiri* often followed disgrace in battle. In premodern India the wife of a nobleman was expected to throw herself upon her husband's cremation pyre, a practice known as *suttee*. Other societies condemned suicide, viewing it as a crime or a sin.

Acceptance or condemnation depends on many factors, such as religious beliefs, level of education, and the circumstances surrounding the suicide (Ingram and Ellis, 1992). Since the 1980s one particular form of suicide has been especially devastating and the source of much political and religious debate. Suicide bombings have become a staple of the ongoing conflict in the Middle East and elsewhere, including the September 11 attacks on the United States. Although suicide is prohibited in Islam as it is in Judaism and Christianity, some Islamic fundamentalist religious leaders approve and even encourage the practice, preferring to use the term *martyrdom*, or *shahid*, instead of suicide, arguing that one who blows himself up among enemies to defend his land (until quite recently suicide bombers were almost exclusively male) is a martyr. Although the families and friends of these suicide bombers often see them as heroic figures, most cases of suicide are still met with dismay and disapproval.

All grief work is difficult, but suicide is particularly stressful for survivors. They constantly ask why and often blame themselves for not preventing the death. That someone they love has intentionally taken his or her life is difficult to accept. There is often anger and frustration. To many, a suicide conveys the ultimate rejection. Because others may also "blame" the survivors for the suicide, especially when the suicide involves children or young adults, they may not be able to provide the support needed in this situation. Suicide, like accidental death, is unexpected. The shock of sudden death may compound the grief by adding to it the burdensome feeling that the death was premature (DeSpelder and Strickland, 1996).

AIDS

Although we discussed AIDS in some detail in Chapter 6, we mention it here because the AIDS epidemic has played a leading role in heightening awareness of dying and death around the world. Just as in the case of suicide, grief work following the AIDS-related death of a loved one can be especially difficult, and survivors may not receive the support from others that is natural in times of bereavement. Several factors account for this. First of all, there is the issue of social disapproval. Some people may blame the victim for hastening her or his own death. For many, AIDS is viewed as a "dirty" disease brought on by illicit sexual behavior or intravenous drug use. Their compassion may be limited to people who are seen as "blameless," such as infants and transfusion recipients (Friedland, 1995). Second, people who die from AIDS tend to be relatively young. This makes their deaths seem untimely and out of the natural order of life. Third, despite a heavy campaign of public education, many people still worry about the possibility of contracting the disease through any kind of contact with a person with AIDS. Finally, family members may be burdened by feelings of guilt if the relationship with the deceased had been estranged because of conflicts over lifestyle.

Suicide and AIDS are not the only situation where grief work is likely to be compounded by external factors. There are a number of situations where grief is, to a large extent, disenfranchised.

Disenfranchised Grief

Gerontologists such as Kenneth Doka (1989) have called attention to **disenfranchised grief**—circumstances in which a person experiences a sense of loss but does not have a socially recognized right, role, or capacity to grieve. Societies construct norms, or "grieving rules," that tell us who can grieve, when, where, and how, and for how long and for whom. Employers reinforce those rules by establishing personnel policies that specify how much time, if any, we can take for the death of a loved one. Only some relationships, primarily familial, are socially recognized and sanctioned. When the relationship between the bereaved and deceased is not based on recognizable kin ties, the depth of the relationship may not be understood, appreciated, or acknowledged by others. Yet the roles of friends, roommates, neighbors, colleagues, in-laws, and foster parents can be intense and long-lasting. Other relationships may not be socially sanctioned, for instance, homosexual relationships, cohabitation, and extramarital affairs. In still other cases the loss itself may not be defined as significant by others. Examples may include losses due to miscarriages or abortions and even the death of a pet. In other situations a person may not be thought of as being capable of grief, such as a child or a person with a mental disability. In these cases the bereaved persons lack the supports that facilitate mourning. Although they have experienced a deep loss, they usually are not given time off from work. They may not have the opportunity to talk about their loss or to receive the expressions of sympathy and support that help people through this difficult time. Thus, their grief may be prolonged and intensified.

The Right-to-Die Movement

The discussion of death and dying would be incomplete without consideration of a major debate taking place in the United States and many other countries. With the advent of modern medical technology, it is possible to sustain life (from premature babies to the very old) under conditions that would have led to certain death in the past. People increasingly question such actions when any meaningful gain in the quality of life is unlikely. This issue is not new. For centuries people have debated the ethical issues surrounding euthanasia, or as it is popularly called, "mercy killing." The term *euthanasia* derives from Greek words meaning "good death," or dying without pain or suffering.

The 1976 landmark case involving Karen Ann Quinlan gave public impetus to the debate over the right to die with dignity. Karen, then 21, was admitted to a New Jersey hospital in a comatose state. Doctors held out no hope for her recovery. Karen's parents asked that the respirator artificially sustaining her life be disconnected. The hospital refused, and Karen's parents sued. After a lengthy legal battle, the respirator was disconnected. Karen continued in a vegetative state until her death in 1985.

Euthanasia can take two forms. In passive euthanasia, medical treatment is terminated, and nothing is done to prolong the patient's life artificially. Most states have laws that allow patients or their families to refuse treatment in the final stages of a terminal illness. This is usually done through what is called a living will, a legal document that stipulates a person's wishes in this regard. A more controversial form of euthanasia is active euthanasia, which refers to actions deliberately taken to end a person's life. The most recent debate on this issue relates to physician-assisted suicide. Proponents of physician-assisted suicide argue that it is cruel to prolong a terminally ill patient's suffering when she or he desires to die, that people are capable of making rational decisions about the quality of life they want and therefore should have the right to die in dignity with the help of a medically trained person. Opponents of physician-assisted suicide counter that this practice cheapens human life and puts society on a slippery slope that could lead to the killing of people considered a burden. They also argue that doctors are not always right and that hopeless cases have sometimes been reversed and that to assist someone in dying is contrary to the role of healer. Many health care professionals believe that increasing the availability and affordability of hospice care would eliminate the desire for physician-assisted suicide. A **hospice** is a physical environment within which supportive care is provided for terminally ill patients and their families that focuses on comfort, freedom from pain, and quality of life rather than cure. Hospice care can be provided in homes, hospitals, or nursing homes.

Thus far, Oregon is the only state to permit physician-assisted suicide. Since the 1994 passage of the Death with Dignity Act, about 200 terminally ill patients have opted to end their lives with a doctor's help. Oregon's law requires two doctors to consult and agree that the patient has a terminal illness that will lead to death within 6 months. The patient must also be 18 years of age or older, considered of sound mind, and be able to self-administer the prescribed lethal dose of medicine. A recent Gallup poll found that more than 60 percent of Respondents support "right-to-die" laws for terminally ill patients, whether that involves a doctor ending a patient's life by some painless means, or a doctor assisting a terminally ill patient to commit suicide. Senior citizens, people who frequently attend religious services, those with lower levels of education, African Americans, conservatives, and Republicans are the least likely to support euthanasia and physician-assisted suicide (Carroll, 2006).

> *What do you think? Should physician-assisted suicide be legal? If so, under what conditions? Do you support or oppose this practice? Explain. How do you think you would react if you discovered today that you had a terminal illness? How would you want those around you to react?*

THE CHALLENGE OF RACISM AND ETHNIC AND RELIGIOUS DISCRIMINATION IN FAMILY LIFE

Racism, racial discrimination, prejudice, and **xenophobia**—a fear or hatred of strangers or foreigners, or of anything foreign and/or different—are powerful forces that have stimulated migration, conflicts, wars, and subjugation throughout human history. Around the world millions of people find themselves the victims of legal, social, and political systems that crush their hopes, dreams, and aspirations, not because they have committed a crime but rather because they were born into a particular racial or ethnic group or practice a particular religion. Individuals and whole families are unable to receive quality education, health care, housing, food or clothing because they are trapped in a maze of unjust legal, social, and political practices that deny them access to the most basic human rights (Puffer and Malone, 2000). In the United States, racism, prejudice, discrimination, violence, and inequality among racial and ethnic groups are deeply interwoven into the fabric of American society. The proliferation of hate groups—groups whose ideologies include tenets of racially based hatred—in the United States was highlighted by the Southern Poverty Law Center (SPLC) (which keeps track of the actions of hate groups) in a 2001 Intelligence Report that listed 602 hate groups operating in the United States. This list included only those hate groups known to be active in 2000, whether that activity included marches, rallies, speeches, meetings, leafleting, publishing literature, or criminal acts; it did not include the numerous hate groups that operate in cyberspace.

Racism and racist actions against individuals and groups are often perpetrated by individuals either acting alone or in groups. However, wider societal and institutional racism perpetuates racist beliefs and ideologies that make it easier for individuals to commit racist acts. Research has consistently demonstrated that families, especially children, from racial and ethnic groups defined and treated as minorities suffer many forms of disadvantage because of individual and institutional racism, including poorer health, poverty, and educational underachievement.

Racism at Home and Abroad

Racism is an ideology of domination and a set of social, economic, and political practices by which one or more groups

Although violence, death and destruction because of religious intolerance are not new, in modern times, it has become almost a daily occurrence in many countries of the world. Individuals either acting alone or in groups whose primary goal is to kill those religiously different from themselves and who intend to die themselves as martyrs are particularly evident in the Middle East. Such attacks are often carried out with the help of vehicles or explosive materials such as a bomb or both. Here, victims lie on the site after a suicide attacker detonated a bomb at a mass prayer service in southern Pakistan, in 2006, killing 41 people.

define themselves as superior and other groups as inferior, then systematically deny the latter groups full access and participation in mainstream society. Racism can be both overt and covert. On the one hand, it can be manifested when individuals or groups, considering themselves superior, act against individuals whom they define as inferior. According to Stokely Carmichael and Charles Hamilton in their now classic work *Black Power: The Politics of Liberation in America* (1967), this behavior can be defined as **individual racism.** It is expressed through personal attitudes and behavior directed toward certain racial or ethnic groups by individual people. It can range from individual acts such as derogatory name-calling, biased treatment during face-to-face contact, and avoidance, to overt acts by individuals that cause death, injury, or the violent destruction of property. This type of racism can be reached by television cameras and videocassette recorders; it can often be observed while it is taking place, such as the infamous Rodney King beating by five white Los Angeles policemen; or the brutal beating of Mexican immigrants in Los Angeles; or the brutality against an African American female motorist by a highway patrolman, videotaped by his own police camera. This kind of racism receives the most media attention and it focuses our attention on the individual perpetrator and the individual victim. Thus, we seldom realize that these actions extend far beyond the individuals involved.

On the other hand, racism can be manifested when a total community or whole society acts against another entire community. This behavior can be defined as institutional racism. Institutional racism is less overt, far more subtle, and far less easy to identify in terms of specific individuals committing the acts than is individual racism. However, it is no less destructive to human life. This kind of racism has its origins in the operation of established and respected forces in the society and thus receives far less public attention, scrutiny, and condemnation than do individual acts of racism. **Institutional racism** consists of established laws, customs, and practices that systematically reflect and produce racial inequalities in a society, whether or not the individuals maintaining these practices have racist intentions (Newman, 1995).

When a group of white students at the University of Connecticut spit at and taunt a small group of Asian American students who are on their way to a dance; when white terrorists burn down African American churches; when a white female author co-opts Native American culture and artifacts for publication and profit; and when a Latina/o student is belittled by a teacher for not speaking "proper" English, it is an individual act of racism and condemned by many people. Although the impact of these acts extends beyond the individuals involved, they are nonetheless individual actions from which "respectable" members of society can divorce themselves. However, when in cities all across this country a highly disproportionate number of African American children are born into poverty or die because of a lack of adequate food, shelter, and medical facilities; when a disproportionate percentage of Latina/o students drop out of school; when the federal government evacuates over 100,000 persons of Japanese ancestry into concentration camps, two-thirds of whom are American citizens; when a group of people are made wards of the government and forced to live on reservations and to assimilate; and when law enforcement agencies around the country (police, state troopers, and airport immigration officials) routinely use racial profiling against specific racial and ethnic groups—using race and or suspected religion as a basis to stop and search an individual—it is an example of institutional racism. Although both types of racism are insidious and damaging to marriages and families, our primary concern in this section is with the impact of institutional racism for various families in the United States and globally. It is worth noting, however, that individual racism does not operate in a vacuum. Wider societal and institutional norms, values, and practices maintain, perpetuate, and reinforce racist beliefs and ideologies that make it easier for individuals to commit and even justify their racist acts.

Racism at Home   Historically, various groups of color in the United States have often been routinely victimized by the powerful force of institutional and individual acts of racism. Although the focus here is on institutional racism, keep in mind that race does not operate in a vacuum and is intricately interwoven with class, gender, sexual orientation, and other important social axes of experience to shape marriage and family life.

Discrimination is no longer legal, but informal practices persist. A variety of studies (for example, ABC News, 1991; U.S. Department of Housing and Urban Development, 1991; Ahmad, 1993; Harris, 2003) shows that African Americans and whites are often treated differently when they shop, apply for jobs, attempt to rent or buy housing, and apply for mortgages. In addition, racist epithets, slurs, and actions have been increasingly, perpetrated against blacks as well as Middle Easterners on college campuses, and intolerance and racism are increasingly expressed by whites on local and national talk radio, television, and the Internet. Likewise, the ongoing racism and hostility faced by Asian Americans such as the Chinese are said to be important factors that help explain Chinese poverty. Chicanos, whose families have lived in the United States for generations, find themselves blamed, along with new Latina/o immigrants, for many of the economic problems of this country. And the rights of Native American families continue to be subordinated to the rights of white Americans.

The increasing immigration of peoples into the United States has had and continues to have a significant impact on race and ethnic relations in this country; and racial and ethnic prejudice, discrimination, and violence have often been influenced by international relationships. A classic example occurred during the 1940s, when over 100,000 Japanese Americans, many of whom were U.S. citizens, were interned for over 2 years in concentration camps. In addition to the racially inspired imprisonment of Japanese women, men, and children, many of these individuals and families lost most or all of their possessions, property, and businesses. When the war was over, many of these families were left homeless and destitute. Another example occurred during the 1991 Persian Gulf War; hate crimes against Arab Americans tripled over the previous year. In 2001, the September terrorist attacks triggered a violent outbreak of American racism and religious intolerance against people identified as or thought to be of Middle Eastern descent and Muslim. Just 4 days after the attacks on the World Trade Center and the Pentagon, for example, shopkeepers were shot to death in California, Texas, and Arizona as a racist and anti-Muslim backlash broke out around the country. Moreover, the targets of hate were not limited to people of Middle Eastern descent. Next to natives of the Middle East, the American Sikh community was the hardest hit by hate crimes, and Native Americans, Asian Americans, Latinas/os, and natives of Israel were also targets of the racism of American "patriots," acting both individually and in groups (SPLC Intelligence Report, 2001b). And after a terrorist scare in the United Kingdom in 2006, racial profiling and other acts of racism against those identified or perceived to be Arabs and Muslims increased.

Many forces impinge on family life in the United States; however, racism continues to be one of the major challenges to the well-being of many families, particularly families of color and immigrant families. It is commonly believed that many, if not all, of the problems that these families experience are a function of either a lack of or decline in family values or their unauthorized (illegal) status. Nevertheless, because of the persistent racism and discrimination in major societal institutions such as education and the work force, these families are forced, structurally, to bear a disproportionately higher percentage of poverty, unemployment and underemployment, welfare dependency, dropping out of schools, infant mortality, illness, and early death.

Although families of color continually make serious efforts to defend the integrity of their cultures and their families and to advance their social position in the face of such persistent racism, prejudice, and discrimination from the wider society, many whites continue to think of individuals and families of color in stereotypic terms. They believe, for example, that many people of color prefer welfare to jobs, and that they are lazy, violent, less intelligent, and less patriotic than whites. In addition, many whites believe that there is little or no racial inequality present in American society today. They generally believe that the American system is a fair one and that other groups have just as many if not more opportunities for success in American society. Thus, if these groups are disadvantaged they are themselves responsible for that disadvantage (Kluegel, 1990; Duke, 1991; Polling Report, 2001). However, even a cursory examination of statistics descriptive of the general quality of life of families of color contradicts this point of view.

Middle-class families of color have made some gains; nevertheless, among most of these groups a number of their members are part of a growing underclass. This impoverished underclass, which outnumbers the middle class among all four major groups of color, is trapped in poverty and unable to move up. These families remain disadvantaged by racial and ethnic inequality on almost every measure of status and well-being in U.S. society. Numerous discriminatory processes exist that make it harder for many of these families to get ahead in American society than it is for white families. For many families of color, this means that life is a day-to-day struggle for survival. For all families of color, it means facing socially imposed disadvantages that they would not face if they were white. For instance, poor education, concentrated poverty, and rising unemployment in the country's predominantly African American and Latina/o inner cities are making it increasingly difficult for individuals and families that live there to develop the skills needed in today's high-tech economic environment. The effects of growing up in poverty are alone enough to greatly reduce the opportunities one has in life. Various research studies provide ample evidence of a link between race, racism, and poverty. For example, institutional racism and discrimination often lock a group into a cycle of poverty, illiteracy, hopelessness, and violence.

Moreover, this research shows that widespread economic inequality and marginality are perhaps the greatest threats today to the vitality and long-term survival of marriages and families of color. It has devastating effects, particularly on children of color. In the United States, for example, institutional racism and the pressure on immigrant cultures to assimilate have a particularly negative effect on children. And in Africa, children still suffer from the aftermath of the apartheid and colonialism. The seriousness of the impact of racism on children is reflected in the fact that in 2002, the U.N. General Assembly hosted an international conference on children. This special session on children was the first such session devoted exclusively to children and the first to include them as official delegates.

Some social scientists (such as Wilson, 1980) have argued that race has declined as a significant factor in the discriminatory treatment and unequal socioeconomic status of some racial groups, especially African Americans. If this is the case, then we would expect that middle- and upper-class members of these groups would face little, if any, discrimination. However, research shows that, in fact, middle- and upper-class members of various racial groups face discrimination and prejudice, from a lack of respect to outright exclusion. In her study of the effects of race in the lives of African American elites, for example, researcher Lois Benjamin (1991) debunked the myth that racism affects only poor people of color. Benjamin found that racism continues to shape the lives of people of color no matter how far they move up the socioeconomic ladder, that individual effort and personal achievement do not free people of color from the experience of hostility based on skin color nor the general burden of racism, and that there is a race-based "glass ceiling" that limits mobility into the highest social and political positions in this society. Other research such as that conducted by Joe Feagin (1991) is consistent with Benjamin's findings.

Not only are the quality of life and the well-being of individuals and families in the United States challenged by racism and prejudice, but so is their physical well-being. This is especially true for people of color and Jews. For example, in 1999, Benjamin Smith, a 22-year-old white youth who was a member of a midwestern-based racist hate group went on a two-state killing spree, killing an African American and an Asian American and injuring nine others, all members of minority groups, before killing himself. And, as we have noted, the health and well-being of people of Middle Eastern descent and those who embrace the Muslim religion are increasingly threatened by those who blame them for the terrorist attacks against the United States on September 11 as well as other ongoing acts of terrorism.

According to Daniel Goleman (1990), two-thirds of hate crimes in the United States involve attacks made on families of color moving into a neighborhood where they are not welcome. Most such crimes are committed by young white males in their teens to 20s. These crimes should not be mistaken for youthful folly, however. These young perpetrators of hate and violence are acting out attitudes and values, opinions, and beliefs shared by their families, friends, and/or communities (Gelles and Levine, 1995). W. E. B. DuBois (1967) suggested at the dawn of the twentieth century that the problem of the twentieth century would be the problem of the color line. It is perhaps safe to say that the problem of the twenty-first century continues to be the problem of the color line. Unless the attitudes and institutional arrangements that serve to benefit some groups while disadvantaging others change, the well-being of families such as those described here will remain at risk.

Racism in a Global Context   Racism, prejudice, and discrimination are not limited to the United States. They are common throughout the world. Racial and ethnic pride and solidarity among some groups are on the rise, and racial and ethnic conflict around the world is increasing. Wherever racial and ethnic conflicts are played out, the consequences for marriages and families have been devastation and despair. In Western European countries, for example, the rise of neo-Nazism suggests that far from being a fringe activity, racism, violence, and neonationalism have become normal in many countries (Shah, 1998). In many of these countries, growing immigrant populations have been accompanied by high levels of prejudice and discrimination, sometimes mild and covert but increasingly overt and extremely violent. The United Kingdom, in this regard, has one of the highest rates of racial violence in Western Europe. For example, in 1999, neo-Nazi groups bombed several predominantly ethnic minority areas in London within 1 week, and the summer of 2001 was characterized by a high number of race-related riots in various parts of northern England. In Germany, hatred and violent attacks against "foreigners" escalated throughout the 1990s. Members of various right-wing white supremacist groups such as the neo-Nazis and the skinheads openly sported swastikas, dressed in a manner reminiscent of Nazi storm troopers, and called for "kicking the foreigners out" of Germany. These foreigners—Africans, Turks, Gypsies, and other immigrant groups identifiable by skin color—have suffered increasing violence, including death, at the hands of these groups. Violent attacks against these groups have resulted in scores of injuries, and arson attacks on their homes have left many families homeless. In France, extremist groups push for the ouster of North African immigrants (about 8 percent of the population) and claim that France must be made "racially pure"; in Italy, there is an increasing racist reaction to the rise in undocumented immigrants from Tunisia. Spain is also experiencing an increase in racial violence. The growing Spanish economy invites immigrants from North African countries such as Morocco but the poor conditions that immigrants have to endure in an already racially charged region have led to friction and racial confrontations. And in the Middle East, the most visible racism and violence occur between Palestinians and Israelis. Extreme views and religious intolerance within both groups have resulted in ongoing hostilities, racism, and violence perpetrated by people from both groups (Shah, 1998).

This glut of global racial and ethnic hatred and violence and its impact on marriages and families is perhaps nowhere more blatantly exemplified than in countries that have in the past or continue today to practice so-called **ethnic cleansing,** by which one category of people tries to rid the region of others who are different in some significant way. This policy has included the massive murder of thousands of Bosnians, Serbs, Croats, and Kosovars and their families. As in Europe, the collapse of totalitarian states in Africa and Asia has been accompanied by a resurgence of sometimes long-standing racial and ethnic hatred and conflict. The consequences of these conflicts have been devastating for individuals and families. For example, although apartheid has been dismantled in South Africa, deep racial tensions continue; in Zimbabwe, there has been increasing racism directed toward white farmers, due to poverty and a lack of landownership by Africans; and in India and other Asian nations, differences in color and culture frequently lead to prejudice, discrimination, violence, and death. In far too many instances, racial or ethnic groups have been enslaved, impoverished, disenfranchised, and even exterminated in the name of power and ethnic purity. For instance, in just 100 days in 1994, up to a million men, women, and children were slaughtered and millions more were uprooted in the African nations of Burundi and Rwanda as the result of an ethnic war between the Hutus and the Tutsi (two groups who consider themselves distinct races) (Amnesty International, 2001a). And in what has been described as the world's worst humanitarian crisis, in Darfur, Western Sudan, Arab-Muslim militia have targeted and murdered an untold thousands (or millions) of non-Muslim Black Sudanese in a systematic practice of ethnic cleansing.

It is generally cases such as these (some of the worst violations of human rights based on racism) that we hear about, but abuses based partially or entirely on racism take place every day around the world. For example, have you ever heard of the Roma? Probably not. However, Roma, more commonly known as Gypsies, have been viewed as outsiders since shortly after their arrival in Europe. Like Jews during the Nazi regime, Roma were subjected to interment, forced labor, and massacre. Thought of as "racially inferior," the Roma continue to face widespread discrimination in Europe today (Amnesty International, 2001a; U.S. Holocaust Memorial Museum, 2002). And finally, in the wake of the terrorism committed in the United States on September 11, 2001, not only has there been an outpouring of violent racial hatred against people of Middle Eastern descent in this country but with the American-led attacks in Afghanistan and the Iraqi War (launched by the United States in 2003 and called the "War Against Terrorism") in retaliation for those terrorist attacks, from Egypt to Pakistan there also have been violent street protests as well as racist acts against anyone and anything that appears to be Western, especially American (Shah, 2001). Moreover, in this contemporary age of advanced technology, a discussion of global racism would not be complete without at least mentioning that ideas of racial superiority have spread to new media like the World Wide Web (the Internet), fueling the prejudice and hatred of peoples around the world.

So, then, individuals and families move in and out of countries fleeing prejudice, discrimination, racism, poverty, and political oppression only to face new prejudice, discrimination, and racism. The resulting injury, humiliation, and destructiveness affect not only individual lives but also whole families and whole societies. For example, what of the mothers, fathers, siblings, and marital partners of the thousands of women, men, and children who have been slaughtered in Bosnia-Herzegovina? In Kosovo? In Burundi? In Rwanda? In Darfur? What impact must the constant strife, violence, and ethnic wars have for family life and well-being? How do families cope with the reality of soldiers burning down their homes? Raping and/or murdering their loved ones, simply because of the racial or ethnic group they happen to be born into? These are compelling and challenging questions for the future well-being of individuals and groups and of marriages and families around the world. Racism, racial discrimination, xenophobia, and related intolerance attack the most basic notion of human rights—that everyone is equal in dignity and worth (Amnesty International, 2001b). As racial discrimination and ethnic violence grow in complexity and spiral in intensity, they become more and more a challenge for the global community.

In its quest to meet the global challenge not only of making the world aware of global racism but also to create a new world vision to combat racism and other human rights violations in the twenty-first century, in 2001 the U.N. General Assembly held a World Conference against Racism in Durban, South Africa. Although the conference was fraught with disputes ranging from reparations for slavery to Zionism as racism against Palestinians and from castes to individual, according to Amnesty International (2001b), it did achieve some important successes. For example, for the first time, the plight of groups such as Dalits, Roma, Tibetans, indigenous people, those who face multiple forms of racism and discrimination such as refugees, women, and gays and lesbians, and those living under political occupation was put forcefully on the world agenda. Conference attendees and the world heard from the victims of racism themselves, and despite disagreements and walkouts, governments were still bound by their international obligations to take effective action against racism (Amnesty International, 2001b:1). A spokesperson for Amnesty International said that the level and extent of racism around the world were made clear at the conference and, if nothing else, the conference succeeded in establishing the beginnings of a global alliance against racism. How successful this alliance against racism will be remains to be seen.

> *Is life very different for poor, working-class, and families of color in the United States who are often caught in a web of violence, violence both directly and indirectly related to deep-rooted racism, bigotry, and discrimination? How do these families cope with such violence? What impact does it have on the structure and stability of family life?*

The Domestic and Global Challenge: Immigration, Migration, and Mass Displacement

The international migration of people is largely driven by individuals and families who leave real or perceived poverty and poor living conditions in their own country in hope of acquiring a job and better living conditions in a new country. America has long been known as a land of immigrants. Known as the land of opportunity, millions of people throughout this country's long history, have migrated to the United States looking for relief from poverty, misery, and oppression. Although the U.S. government has welcomed many new immigrants, that welcome has been highly selective. Historically, for instance, the majority of immigrants to the United States came from Europe. Because of immigration restrictions and racial and ethnic quotas, only a small number came from Asia, Africa, and Central and South America. However, since 1965, with a revision in the immigration act, this trend has been reversed; the majority of immigrants presently come primarily from Asian, Latin American, and Caribbean countries.

Today, more than one-third (37 percent) of the new immigrants to the United States are from Mexico (Scott and Schwartz, 2006). At least in the past, because Mexicans could easily cross the border into the United States, the population of both documented and undocumented Mexican immigrants have grown steadily, especially since the 1990s. Lacking the ability or resources to come into the United States legally, many of these immigrants are willing to risk their lives to get into the United States. Attempting to stay one step ahead of the border police, undocumented migrants have often found creative ways to cross the border, albeit most often unsuccessful. Recently, for example, U.S. Customs and Border Protection officers arrested a man who they said tried to smuggle three Mexican migrants into the country by sewing them in the upholstery of a GMC Ventura conversion van (NBC11.com, 2006).

In 2000, the U.S. Census Bureau estimated that the unauthorized immigrant population in the United States was 8 million, more than double the 3.5 million estimated in 1990 (Center for Immigration Studies, 2006). One-half or more of these unauthorized immigrants live in five states: California, Texas, New York, Illinois, and Florida. Mexico is the leading source of unauthorized immigration, accounting for roughly 69 percent of the total unauthorized resident population in 2000. Sometimes, racial and ethnic prejudice and violence accompany surges in immigration into the United States. Most often the targets of this discrimination and violence have been non-European immigrants of color. In the wake of the surge of Mexican immigrants, both documented and undocumented, there is a reported increase in violence and other hate crimes against Mexicans as well as an increasing public debate and concern about immigration, especially unauthorized immigration. Researchers at the Southern Poverty Law Center, for instance, report that the raging debate in the United States over immigration has fueled racist extremism and violent, anti-Hispanic hate crimes, regardless of their immigration status. Such crimes appear to be on the rise and include being beaten, burned, and even sodomized. For example, in 2006, a 17-year-old Hispanic high school football player was dragged from a suburban house party in Texas and savagely attacked by two white assailants, one of them a neo-Nazi skinhead. Police said the attackers were apparently enraged because the victim tried to kiss a young girl they believed to be Caucasian.

After forcing the Hispanic youth into a backyard, they burned his neck with cigarettes, stomped his head with steel-toed boots, and slashed his chest with a knife, all while shouting racial slurs. They then stripped him naked and sodomized him with a patio umbrella pole (Buchanan and Holthouse, 2006).

A growing number of Americans, whose ancestors themselves were immigrants, oppose immigration and are increasingly intolerant of immigrants. For example, national polls reveal that although three-fifths of Americans believe immigration was a good thing in the past, they think it is a bad thing today. Furthermore, among those polled, there is considerably more opposition to immigration from Latin America, Africa, Asia, and the Caribbean than to immigration from Eastern Europe. Fully one-half, or one of every two people, polled believe immigration should be limited and people immigrating illegally should be vigorously prosecuted while one in five believe immigration should be stopped immediately (Morganthau, 1993; Zogby National Poll, 2000).

Likewise, Americans are divided in their views about the overall effect of immigration. For instance, 52 percent of Americans believe immigrants are a burden to the country, taking jobs and housing and creating strains on the already overworked health care system, while 41 percent believe immigrants strengthen the United States with their hard work and talents. However, the public is divided in its views about what should be done about the increasing migration, especially unauthorized migration, into the United States. Fifty-three percent of Americans, for instance, believe that unauthorized migrants should be required to go home while 40 percent of those polled believe that they should be allowed to stay (Pew Research Center, 2006a). Even high school students, when asked to identify their greatest concerns for the future of the United States from a list of ten issues, identified concern about immigration fourth most often. Over one-half (52 percent) of the students indicated that the solution to immigration would be to accept fewer immigrants into the country and crack down on illegal immigration (Forum on America's Future, 2000). And since September 11, 2001, a majority of Americans say they favor having Arabs, even those who are U.S. citizens, being subjected to separate, more intensive security procedures at airports, and about half favor requiring Arabs, including those who are U.S. citizens, to carry special identification (Gallup Tuesday Briefing, 2001a).

Americans' racial and ethnic opposition and intolerance of Latina/o immigrants and their families are increasingly manifest not only in violent actions and activities but also in local and national legislation. For example, the growth of the Latina/o population has sparked the passage of English as the "official language" legislation; in 1993, the governor of California proposed restrictive legislation aimed at controlling so-called illegal immigration. Among the goals of the legislation was the elimination of social service benefits to which even children of illegal immigrants had previously been legally entitled (Farley, 1995); in 1996, Proposition 209—legislation that eliminated state and local government affirmative action programs in public employment, public education, and public contracting—won in the state of California by a 54 percent to 46 percent vote; in 2005, President Bush outlined plans to create new jails to make deportation a quicker process for illegal immigrants and to have a "temporary worker program" that would allow immigrants to stay in the country and work at jobs "that Americans will not do" (Lamothe, 2006).

These actions, along with recent polls and surveys of American attitudes about immigration, reflect America's continuing and indeed growing quandary about immigration, particularly unauthorized immigration. Like most public debates today, the ongoing debate about unauthorized immigration reflects the American political divide. In 2006, the legislative debate over unauthorized immigration not only pit Republicans against Democrats but also pit Republicans against Republicans. The debate ranges from proposals to deny state-funded health care, unemployment and welfare benefits to unauthorized immigrants to legalizing driver's licenses for unauthorized immigrants to enforcing the laws we have today and sending unauthorized immigrants home (see Debating Social Issues box). The heated debate (both in Congress and the public) has also sparked a massive "illegal" immigration movement in this country. Throughout 2006, for instance, throngs of immigrants and their families as well as their advocates took to the streets in cities across the United States to protest proposed negative immigration laws (for example, tighter restrictions on immigration). Children skipped school, women and men walked off their jobs, and others did not even bother going to work. Businesses shut down for lack of patrons and/or employees. One such day of protest was dubbed "A Day Without Immigrants." Despite the massive protests, however, some who typically support immigrants questioned the effectiveness of the walkouts. Others, such as a coalition of Hispanic-American groups, held a news conference to stress that the protesters did not represent all Hispanics (CNN, 2006). What this all means for Mexican immigrants and their families, both documented and undocumented, already in this country remains to be resolved.

Not unlike the United States, France is also dealing with the issue of illegal immigrants. Because French schools are obliged to take in children regardless of whether they are in the country legally, the issue of illegal immigration is particularly pronounced in the country's school system. It is estimated that between 50,000 to 100,000 children of illegal immigrant families are enrolled in French schools, which prompted French officials to legislate new immigration laws. In 2006, however, in response to a nationwide protest movement that sprung up over plans to expel thousands of illegal immigrant families whose children are in French schools, the French government began reconsidering deportation on the basis of criteria such as whether a child has "strong ties" to France, showing that the immigrant children were born in France or arrived before the age of 13, the child has been at school in France for two years, or has no link with the country of her or his parents (Caleidoscop, 2006).

A World of Refugees: Mass Migration and Dislocation

One of the most significant global demographic trends of the twentieth century was the massive immigration of people from one country to another all over the world. Exacerbated by ongoing and new wars and conflicts as well as international and domestic terrorism at the end of the twentieth century and the beginning of the twenty-first, this trend continues today. Sometimes this immigration is voluntary, in that people leave their homelands seeking economic opportunities in other lands. All too often, however, the massive movement of people from one land to another has been and continues to be the result of communal violence and war. According to some sources, 22 million, or 1 out of every 275 persons on earth, have been forced into flight. These **refugees**—people who leave their country because of a "well-founded fear" of persecution for reasons of race, religion, nationality, social group, or political opinion (United Nations High Commissioner for Refugees [UNHCR], 2001)—are sometimes welcomed in the host countries; at other times they are met with resentment, hostility, and violence.

According to the United Nations High Commissioner for Refugees (UNHCR, 2006) annual global count, at the end of 2005 there were 8.4 million refugees worldwide and 21 million uprooted or internally displaced people—persons living in refugeelike situations within their own countries. The mass movement of millions of refugees has transformed or is currently transforming the way of life in many countries throughout the world, the majority of which are in developing nations often already struggling to meet the needs of their own citizens. For example, the terrorism of September 11 catapulted Afghanistan into the epicenter of fear and war, and millions of Afghan civilians, half a world away, became unintentional victims in the fallout, following history's worst single act of terrorism in the United States. In a 10-day period in February 2002 alone, more than 20,000 Afghan refugees crossed the border into Pakistan. According to the UNHCR, Afghans constitute the largest single refugee population in the world (1.9 million in 72 asylum countries). Civilians from the Central African state of Burundi constitute the second largest group, with 568,000 refugees living mainly in Tanzania, and Iraqis comprise the third largest population, with 512,800 refugees living mainly in Iran. In 2005, 78 percent of all refugees came from 10 areas: Afghanistan, Angola, Burma, Burundi, Congo-Kinshasa, Eritrea, Iraq, the Palestinian territories, Somalia, and Sudan.

The global refugee crisis affects every continent and almost every country. Civil war and revolutions in Central American countries such as Nicaragua, El Salvador, and Guatemala have contributed significantly to the migrant population of the United States. To escape ethnic cleansing carried out by Serb forces, over 1 million people from the former Yugoslavia have fled to other European countries, most notably Germany. And some 2.4 million Rwandans have left their central African homeland primarily for Zaire and Tanzania in an effort to escape the genocidal war that pitted Hutus and Tutsis against each other (Alliance for a Global Community, 1996; Soroka and Bryjak, 1999).

Gender and age are important factors in communal war and violence. Women and children, for example, make up more than 80 percent of the world's refugees. An estimated 45 percent of refugees are below the age of 18, and 14 percent are below the age of 5. Ten percent of refugees are 60 years or older, over one-half of whom are females. The massive number of displaced children is of immense concern as they are particularly vulnerable to threats to their safety and well-being. These include separation from families, sexual exploitation, HIV/AIDS infection, forced labor or slavery, abuse and

DEBATING SOCIAL ISSUES

AMERICA'S IMMIGRATION QUANDARY: SHOULD UNAUTHORIZED MIGRANTS BE REQUIRED TO GO HOME OR SHOULD THEY BE GRANTED LEGAL STATUS AND ALLOWED TO STAY IN THE UNITED STATES?

One of the latest culture wars in American society centers on unauthorized immigrants and immigration reform. In 2006, the debate over immigration reform took center stage in the nation's capital and portends to be a hot-button issue for the 2008 election year. A debate though it is, it is not altogether easy to come up with two clear opposing sides of the issue based on political party affiliation. For example, legislators (Republicans and Democrats) have introduced as many as 25 immigration reform bills, some with only minor differences, while others have significant differences. Although there is a range of proposals for immigration reform floating about the legislative arena, the issue divides people very clearly, with little room for a middle ground (Weisman and Vandehei, 2006). Clearly on one side of the debate are those who take the posi-

tion that if people are in this country illegally, they need to be sent home. According to this viewpoint, there is no need for new or reformed laws. Rather we need to enforce the laws that we already have. On the other side are those who propose reforming the immigration laws to provide a guest-worker plan that would allow millions of unauthorized immigrants to continue working in the United States, meeting the demand for unskilled labor and to address the 12 million unauthorized immigrants already living in the United States.

Looking at the controversy through political glasses, the issues sometimes get muddled. Not all Republicans, for instance, agree on what immigration reform should look like or even if there should be immigration reform at all. Republican President George W. Bush has called for tighter border security but would like to secure

On May 1, 2006, as the United States Congress grappled with immigration legislation, protestors rallied on Wilshire Boulevard in Los Angeles while thousands of other immigrants and their supporters likewise gathered in cities across the country for demonstrations and an economic boycott intended to show the impact that immigrant workers, both documented and undocumented, have on the nation's economy
Source: Monica Almeida/The New York Times.

lawful employment opportunities for unauthorized immigrants with a guest-worker

---

violence, forcible recruitment into armed groups, trafficking, lack of access to education and basic assistance, detention, and denial of access to asylum or family-reunification procedures. Unaccompanied refugee children are at greatest risk because they lack the protection, physical care, and emotional support provided by the family (Betts et al., 2006). For several years after the genocide in Rwanda ended, thousands of abandoned or displaced children roamed the streets of Kigali, the capital city of Rwanda. Girls were not seen or talked about much because they were used for sex or housework; the fate of these girls is a taboo subject. Another 100,000 "unaccompanied" Rwandan children (refugee children without an accompanying parent or other family) went to Zaire; many were seriously injured. In Sudan, during more than 20 years of civil war, killing, and the displacement of millions, approximately 20,000 Sudanese children, mostly boys between 7 and 17 years of age, referred to as the "lost boys of the Sudan," have been separated from their families and have sought refuge in Ethiopia, Kenya, and Uganda (Church World Service, 2005; UNHCR, 2001). After a

decade in a Kenyan refugee camp, nearly 4000 "lost boys" came to the United States. Unfortunately, the "lost girls" of the Sudan have been grossly overlooked by UNHCR and the United States. Like their male counterparts, they were chased from their homes, and separated from and/or witnessed the murder of their families. Their original numbers were estimated at between 17,000 and 25,000; however, fewer than 11,000 reached the Kakuma refugee camp in Kenya. Of note, while the United States has received almost 4000 "lost boys" it has received only 89 "lost girls" (Refugees International, 2002). And as of 2006, as a result of the ongoing conflict in Darfur, Sudan, almost 2 million people, the majority of whom were children, had been forced to flee their homes and relocate to displacement camps. Nearly a quarter million Sudanese had fled across the border into eastern Chad, too afraid to return home (UNICEF, 2006b).

Although the majority of refugees prefer to and do return home as soon as circumstances permit (generally, when a war or conflict has ended and a degree of stability has been restored), at any given time only about 6 percent of refugees

plan that would allow millions of unauthorized immigrants to continue working in the United States. In contrast, Senate Majority Leader Bill Frist (R-Tenn) is for tightening control of the nation's borders without creating a guest-worker program. Some Republicans have come out with a very strong anti-immigration position (Weisman and VandeHei, 2006). Other Republications have introduced bills ranging from one that would deny state-funded health care, unemployment, and welfare benefits to unauthorized immigrants to another that would require unauthorized immigrant students to pay higher college tuition fees (CNN.com, 2006). According to a 2005 Manhattan Institute poll, over three-fourths (78 percent) of Republicans support penalizing employers of unauthorized immigrants but allowing unauthorized immigrants to come forward and register for a temporary work program with a path towards citizenship (Fachner, 2006). Then there are conservative Republicans, some of whom have taken a hard line and want to clamp down on unauthorized immigration; they propose much tougher border enforcement, a crackdown on asylum seekers, and state driver's license requirements for unauthorized immigrants. Essentially, law and order conservatives are pitted against business interests that rely on immigrant labor, one wanting to deport people and the other wanting to acknowledge unauthorized immigrants' growing economic importance (Murray, 2006).

Although all leading bills call for tighter border enforcement with more police on the borders and more technology tracking illegal crossings, on the other side, Democratic lawmakers have reintroduced legislation that would legalize driver's licenses for undocumented immigrants. However, Democrats have not been nearly as vocal on the issue as Republicans. Exceptions include Senator Hillary Clinton and New Mexico Governor Bill Richardson, the nation's only Latino governor. Both embrace high-tech measures to control the border with Mexico and fines for employers who hire unauthorized immigrants. Senator Clinton proposed a new bill that would guarantee in-state college tuition rates for the children of illegal immigrants as well as amnesty to some 65,000 undocumented immigrant students who graduate from U.S. high schools each year.

It should be noted, to further muddy the debate, some Republicans and Democrats share the same point of view on the issue or have worked together for a compromise. For example, Senators John McCain (R/Ariz) and Ted Kennedy (D/Ma) have cosponsored a bill that offers an easier road to citizenship for unauthorized immi-

grants already in the country (Richardson, 2006).

Finally, in December 2005 the House of Representatives passed HR 4437. This bill would make "unlawful presence" in the United States punishable by a year in jail; would erect a 700-mile fence along the U.S.–Mexico border; and would mandate detention of immigrants (except Cubans) caught illegally entering the United States along the border of any point of entry. Various bills add such items as criminalizing organizations or individuals who offer illegal immigrants humanitarian assistance. Those found guilty of helping illegal immigrants could face up to 5 years in prison (Johnson, 2006).

What do you think? *Is immigration generally and unauthorized immigration specifically a serious issue that calls for legislative reform? What is your position on the issue of unauthorized Mexican immigrants? Do you believe they take jobs, housing, and social services from American citizens? Should the government wall off much of the U.S.–Mexican border? Should the United States commit the National Guard to monitor the Mexican border? Do you think that Americans have the same feeling about unauthorized immigrants from other countries? Explain.*

return home. In any event, the magnitude of the mass movement of people can be fraught with challenges—both for the refugees and for the host country. There must be an adjustment on the part of the host society as well as at the individual level. For instance, on a societal level, large numbers of refugees into a society can impact its stability, particularly if the society is poor and already overcrowded. Newcomers to societies often intensify the competition for scarce resources—for jobs, education, housing, recreational activities, and sources of supplemental financial assistance. Because of diverse cultural practices, language barriers, and few or no personal resources, they also create a need for increasing numbers of professionals and service providers, such as social workers, lawyers, judges, child and family therapists and workers.

On an individual and familial level, the first order of business for refugees is often the task of trying to piece together their families, who were shattered and separated by war, violence, and the exodus from their homelands. In addition, not only do refugees have to deal with the trauma of war and

being separated from their cultural base, but they must also adjust and adapt to a new way of life. As we have indicated, their existence in foreign lands is sometimes complicated by racism, discrimination, and/or intolerance. Some people believe that some of the cultural practices that refugees bring with them test the limits of tolerance on the part of the host society. People within host societies are often willing to accept cultural practices that seem to reinforce their own cultural values. However, those that differ are often met with intolerance, rejection, ridicule, and sometimes legal ramifications. For example, in Maine, a refugee from Afghanistan was observed kissing the penis of his baby son, a traditional expression of love by this father. However, to his American neighbors, social service agencies, and the police, this behavior was seen as child abuse and the man's son was taken away from him (the child was later returned to the father by a state supreme court ruling). Some sociologists and other social scientists argue that American laws and welfare services have often left immigrants terrified of the intrusive power of the government (Crossette, 1999).

Does being tolerant mean accepting cultural practices such as "female genital mutilation," "immolation of widows," and "coining"?[1] Many Americans confront the issue of whether the government should have the power to intervene in the most intimate details of family life (Crossette, 1999) and/or if being nonethnocentric or tolerant means accepting cultural practices that are harmful to the health and well-being of fellow human beings. Does it mean accepting cultural practices that repel Western ideals, such as the disciplinary techniques of shaming and physical punishment, parent–child cosleeping arrangements, rituals of group identity and ceremonies of initiation involving scarification and body piercing, arranged marriage and child marriage, polygamy, the segregation of gender roles, and bilingualism? As this discussion should make clear, war, terrorism, violence, and the often resulting mass migration of people seeking asylum in a host country have an impact on all of us. Refugees have to adapt to the cultural and legal norms of a host society, and the host society must confront large-scale economic and political issues as well as the social issues of tolerance and cultural relativism.

SAFETY AND SECURITY: GANGS, STREET VIOLENCE, AND VIOLENCE IN AMERICA'S SCHOOLS

The term *gang* strikes fear into the hearts of some people; disgust, resentment, and hatred in others. Still others use the term as a code word to describe inner-city neighborhoods and their residents as well as to rationalize the widening gap between rich and poor, people of color and whites, and the alarming increase in police brutality and murder of people of color. Gangs are not new in the United States. Major cities across the country have long been the home of gangs, some of which have been around for 50 or more years. For example, in Chicago, the first street gangs appeared at the turn of the twentieth century, mostly in Irish communities. However, when most people think about gangs today, they picture African American and Latino/a youths. But white street gangs continue to exist (Macko, 1996). Gangs are usually composed of people of the same race or ethnicity. In Los Angeles, for instance, there are street gangs representing almost every racial and ethnic group living in the city.

Gangs

Gangs and gang violence is a serious problem, particularly in large urban cities. But gangs are not limited to cities. Gangs can also be found in rural areas across the United States. Often rural areas contain chapters of major gangs found in cities. Some experts estimate that gangs account for as much as 40 percent of crime and violence in this country. Over the last 2 decades, gang violence has escalated in many cities across the country, and the attendant loss of life is staggering.

According to Louis Sullivan, former secretary of the Department of Health and Human Services, every 100 hours more young men are killed on the streets of America than were killed in a 100 hours of ground war in the Persian Gulf (cited in Soroka and Bryjak, 1995). Gang-related killings have become so common that police departments now use the term *gang homicide* to denote it as a separate and unique category of criminal behavior (Senna and Siegel, 1999).

The economic, physical, and psychological costs of gangs and their activities to individuals and their families are extremely high. Especially devastating to families and the community are the ongoing illegal activities and violence that often accompany gangs (Senna and Siegel, 1999). These activities can be lucrative for gang members but can have a debilitating effect on family and community life. With substantial sums of money at stake, gang members often fight over dominance and control of these illegal activities. The results of these battles are deaths and injuries that equal those of a small war (Howell, 1998). Not only do gang members kill each other, but as in contemporary war, innocent bystanders (civilians) are increasingly the victims of gang violence. A growing number of these victims are children, murdered by stray bullets from drive-by shootings or the cross fire from open gang warfare on city streets.

Most parents and family members have not had to wonder if their children would be safe playing in front of their homes, sitting on the porch, or, for that matter, sitting in their living rooms. One of the consequences of living with this kind of fear for individuals and families is the separation of family members. For example, some parents, fearing gang recruitment and other activities, send their children to live with relatives in other cities. Others who can afford it send their children to private or parochial schools or to boarding schools outside of the city. Parents worry about daughters as well as sons. Although seldom focused upon, a large number of female gangs operate around the country, and their members are sometimes equally as violent as their male counterparts. It is estimated that somewhere between 10 and 25 percent of gang members nationwide are female (Thornberry and Burch, 1997; Adler, Mueller, and Laufer, 1998).

Gangs are not only a serious problem in the United States. Countries such as Canada and even Japan are experiencing problems with gangs. The Japanese term *bosozoku* (translated to mean "violent running tribes") refers to Japanese street gangs whose membership includes women as well as men between the ages of 16 and the mid-20s. These gangs often roam the streets in packs of over one 100 members, harassing, intimidating, and physically attacking innocent victims (Yates, 1990; Sakurai, 2001). Moreover, we can increasingly see the global connection to gangs and gang activities in the United States. For instance, once they are in the United States, many immigrant youths form or join gangs, contributing to the proliferation of gangs and gang-related problems in many major U.S. cities. The reverse is often true, as well. That is, immigrants who were gang members in the United States sometimes take their gang affiliations and criminal behavior back to their homelands (Wilkinson, 1994). Many of the more powerful gangs in the United States have expanded their area of operations far beyond the local community; many have ties to drug-producing countries around the

---

[1]Female genital mutilation, at minimum, usually involves removing the clitoris; immolation of widows involves sacrificing women's lives upon the death of their husbands; and coining involves pressing hot objects on a child's forehead or back as cures for various maladies.

world, from whom they secure their supplies, thus closing the circle of global connection.

Street Violence

Although the activities of street gangs constitute a high proportion of crime and violence in communities around the country, gangs are not the only source of violence. More and more, individuals worry about how to protect themselves and family members in an increasingly criminal and violent atmosphere, where crime and violence are often random and pointless. Although street violence and crimes in the United States have continuously declined over the past decade, there is still considerable violence in the United States (U.S. Department of Justice, 2006). The rates of murder, robbery, rape, and aggravated assault in this country far exceed those in other industrialized countries. For example, the murder rate in the United States is 2 times that of Northern Ireland, where there is ongoing civil strife; 4 times that of Italy; 9 times higher than in England; and 11 times higher than Japan.

Any discussion of crime and violence in the United States almost always raises the issue of race, because many people link crime with certain racial or ethnic groups of color. In addition, most white Americans express fear of being victimized by African American strangers. In reality, however, two-thirds of the arrests police make for serious crimes involve white people. Furthermore, violent crime in the United States is primarily *intraracial*. That is, about 80 percent of single-offender violent crimes committed by African Americans are against African American victims. Similarly, 75 percent of such crimes committed by whites involve white victims. In addition, a little more than one-half (53 percent) of all victims know their offender (U.S. Department of Justice, 2006). Nonetheless, the link between race and criminal victimization and its differential impact across marriages and families in the United States is clear. Families living in big cities are especially affected by crime and random violence. Although the amount of crime varies throughout urban and rural areas, the greatest concentration of offenses occurs in poverty-stricken, inner-city communities of color. The poorest U.S. families, with incomes under $7500, are 60 percent more likely to be victimized by crime or violence than are affluent families with incomes over $75,000. The problems generated by crime are worst in overwhelmingly African American urban neighborhoods. Despite some progress in the nation's fight against violent crime over the past decade, African American youths across all age groups are more likely to be victims of violent crime than their white counterparts (Davis and Mulhausen, 2000; Children's Defense Fund, 2001b). The burden of crime and violence is not only a human tragedy for individuals and communities across the country, stifling economic and social development by scaring off businesses, particularly in the inner city, but it is also extremely tragic and disruptive of social and family life (Davis and Mulhausen, 2000).

Crime and urban violence are on the rise everywhere. For example, in Lagos, Nigeria, one of Africa's most economically and technologically advanced countries, violent crime is a constant risk, and many streets have become so dangerous that few people go out at night (Macionis and Parrillo, 1998).

And in Japan, commuter trains, once a symbol of Japan's safety and efficiency, have become increasingly dangerous as violent crimes in Japan's trains and stations nearly doubled from 1996 to 2000 (Sakurai, 2001).

Youth Violence

The amount of violence among young people in the United States today is startling. With the proliferation of handguns, families are losing members to handgun violence at a phenomenal rate, both as victims and as offenders. Children are particularly vulnerable to handgun violence and likely to be victims. The Children's Defense Fund reports that every 2 hours a child is killed by a gun. Although the rate of violent crime among adult offenders has declined some in recent years, violent crime rates among young people have been rising alarmingly, especially among 18- to 20-year-olds. They make up only about 4 percent of the population, but 18- to 20-year-olds commit 24 percent of America's gun murders. In fact, 18-year-olds are the most violent: They commit 35 percent more gun murders than 21-year-olds; double the gun murders of 24-year-olds; triple the gun murders of 28-year-olds; and four times the murders of 30-year-olds (U.S. Newswire, 1999).

Youthful violence is not confined to the United States. For example, in Japan, when a 43-year-old man growled at a group of Japanese youths after one of them stepped on his foot during his train commute home, the youths growled back. When the man disembarked the train, the youths followed and beat him senseless on the platform and ran away. The man, who never awakened from his coma, died a week later. Japanese sociologists suggest that the basis for the increasing youth violence in Japan may be the growing alienation among Japanese youth who are feeling increasingly disenfranchised by society. Japan, a country with one-half the population of the United States, has only approximately 700 killings a year. That compares to over 20,000 in the United States (Sakurai, 2001).

A large number of American families have handguns or other types of firearms in the home for self-protection or for sport, such as hunting. In fact, two of every five adults live in households where one or more guns are owned and one in every six live in households with a rifle, shotgun, and pistol present (Harris Poll, 2001). Moreover, recent polls indicate that 40 percent of American households with children present have guns (Gallup Tuesday Briefing, 2001a). Put another way, 34 percent of children in the United States (representing more than 2 million children in 11 million homes) live in homes with at least one firearm, and in over two-thirds (69 percent) of these homes more than one firearm is present (RAND Corporation, 2001). Increasingly, we read about children who have found a handgun in the home and accidentally shot themselves, siblings, or neighbors. In addition, handguns owned by parents are often used by children to commit suicide. According to some experts, every 7 hours a child or teenager is killed in a firearm-related accident or suicide. From 1994 to 1999, an average of 5 children died everyday in nonhomicide firearm incidents. The overall firearm-related death rate among U.S. children 14 years or younger is nearly 12 times higher than among children in 25 other industrialized countries combined. Indeed, more American children die from gunfire than from cancer, pneumonia, influenza, asthma, and HIV/AIDS combined (Centers for Disease Control and Prevention, 1997; Children's Defense Fund, 2001a; Common Sense about Kids and Guns, 2001; Hoyert et al., 2001). Children as young as 6 years old take their parents' handguns to school, sometimes to protect themselves from gangs and other violators and other times to punish those who they perceive to have wronged them in some way. One consequence of this has been the proliferation of violence and death in the nation's schools.

Violence in Schools

During the 1990s, there was an incredible rise in the use of handguns to commit acts of violence, very often murder, in American schools. Despite a decrease in the percentage of students carrying weapons to school and a decrease in reports of fights, stolen property, and marijuana use on school property, school violence remains a public concern. Before white kids began killing white kids on school grounds, school violence was not an issue of national concern. However, over a period of time from the mid-1990s through the first two years of this century, of 19 violent incidents in U.S. schools reported in the media, 16 involved white male shooters, several of which resulted in multiple deaths. Perhaps the most violent and dramatic of these incidents, certainly the one with the greatest number of casualties to date, was the 1999 mass murders at Columbine High School in Littleton, Colorado (a suburb of Denver), where two male students initiated a gun and bomb assault that killed 15 people—14 students and a teacher. The two gunmen, seniors Eric Harris and Dylan Klebold, began their attack in the parking lot and proceeded to a ground-floor cafeteria, school hallways, and a second-floor library before killing themselves.

TERRORISM AND WAR

Gangs, crime, violence, terrorism, and war are different faces of the same coin. In the not-to-distant past, when Americans thought of terrorism, they generally thought about faraway lands where governments practiced terrorism to sustain their power, and where individuals and groups within these countries practiced it in retaliation for oppressive governmental rule. Today, however, we are far more aware of terrorism in this country and recognize that it does not just occur in "foreign" or developing countries. Increasingly since the early 1990s and especially after the September 11, 2001, terrorist attacks on New York's World Trade Center and the Pentagon, Americans are not only more aware of terrorism but also have experienced firsthand its consequences for individuals, marriages, and families, as well as the terror that people in other countries around the world have, in the past and continue today, to experience on a daily basis. Technology (for example, jet travel, satellite communications, plastic bombs, compact automatic weapons) has enabled terrorists to invade political arenas around the world and to make known their ideological view and goals; the end of

Contemporary terrorism knows no boundaries; today it can be felt in almost every arena of human life and no one is exempt. In 2004, for example, women and schoolchildren were the targets of terrorism when heavily armed militants, some strapped with explosives, seized a school in southern Russia near the separatist republic of Chechnya, a traditionally Sunni Muslim region, taking scores of parents, teachers and children hostage. Reports of at least 2 hostage deaths circulated as a group of about 30 women and children broke out of the school into the waiting protection of Russian soldiers.

colonial rule has been accelerated by terrorist actions carried out in the name of various oppressed racial and ethnic groups seeking self-rule.

Terrorism can be defined as the calculated use of unlawful violence or the threat of unlawful violence by individuals or groups intended to inculcate fear or to intimidate and/or coerce governments or societies as a political or revolutionary strategy to achieve political, religious, or ideological goals (Center for Defense Information, 2001a). According to Michael Soroka and George Bryjak (1999), political terrorism is a form of warfare without any humanitarian constraints or rules. In general, the goal of such actions is to initiate a significant change in or outright overthrow of existing governments. Often the goal is simply to intimidate. The Palestine Liberation Organization (PLO), the Irish Republican Army (IRA), the Red Brigades in Italy, and the Basque separatists in Spain have all come to be household names in the vocabulary of political terrorism. Regional or domestic terrorism has existed throughout human history. However, terrorism as an international concern only emerged during the 1960s after a series of airplane hijackings became international news. And when the 1972 Munich Olympic Games were disrupted by a Palestinian group's attempt to take Israeli athletes hostage, terrorism as an international concern was put on the U.N. General Assembly's agenda.

In the past, the majority of terrorist attacks fell under the heading of state-sponsored terrorism—governments that support international terrorism either by engaging in terrorist activity themselves or by providing arms, training, safe haven, diplomatic facilities, financial backing, and material, logistic, or other support to terrorists. Increasingly, each year, almost one-half of the terrorist attacks worldwide have been labeled anti-United States. Although there has been a slight increase in the number of terrorist attacks worldwide, state-sponsored terrorism has declined. This decline is attributed, at least in part, to the declining willingness of national governments to take part directly in terrorist attacks and the United States' vigorous campaign of sanctions and other punitive measures against terrorist-supporting countries (Snowden and Hayes, 2001).

There is no doubt that September 11 changed the world. Although the 9/11 terrorists were not the first to use an airplane as a weapon of terror, their actions ushered in a new phase of terrorism: terror in the skies. Contemporary terrorism can be felt most keenly at airports and not just through the interminable delays and difficulties in getting into and out of various cities or countries. Today's terrorism centers around plots to destroy human lives through the use of commercial airliners. In 2006, for example, British officials arrested 25 suspects in an alleged plot to blow up U.S.-bound jetliners. Authorities reported finding bomb-making equipment and martyrdom videos (MSNBC, 2006). As a consequence of the newest scheme of airline terror—using liquid bombs—airport security became even more restrictive such that passengers, at least for a time, were not allowed to bring any liquids (including water and baby formula), gels or creams onboard an airliner.

To date, terrorists have been overwhelmingly male. However, there are women who have joined their ranks. Some observers (for instance, Laquer, 1987) claim that women terrorists are actually more effective because they are tougher, more fanatical, more loyal, and have a greater capacity for suffering than their male counterparts. For example, it is alleged that among those who plotted to blow up U.S.-bound airliners departing from Britain in 2006, were women who planned to hide their liquid bombs in baby formula. Regardless of gender, terrorists and their leaders nevertheless always profess that they seek to redress some political, social, or religious injustice and are fueled by a hatred that knows no bounds. For example, according to the Center for Defense Information (2001a), at the heart of Osama bin Laden's al-Qaeda terrorism is a fierce duel hatred of the present rulers of his native Saudi Arabia, whom he considers to be apostates to Islam (secularists) and thus unworthy to rule, and of the United States, whose presence in Saudi Arabia he believes defiles the holy land of Mecca and Medina. This new terrorism springs from an unswerving conviction that to destroy America is to do God's work. As the various terrorist acts, including the September 11 attacks on New York and Washington, DC, perpetrated by Osama bin Laden and his followers indicate, their hatred is so deep that they rationalize and justify the use of unlimited violence, unencumbered by pity or compassion, in the name of religious rage.

Terrorism in the United States

In the past, American citizens were most vulnerable to terrorism and violence when traveling in foreign lands, particularly those openly hostile toward the American government. Although American citizens continue to be prime targets of terrorism worldwide (targets in one in four terrorist acts), over the last decade not only individual citizens but also entire families have become increasingly vulnerable to and

victims of terrorist actions at home. The worst terrorist attack on American soil, to date, has been the September 11, 2001, attacks on the World Trade Center and the Pentagon, where an estimated 3000 to 5000 American and foreign-born women, men, and children were killed. Most people still cannot fathom the full extent of the carnage, horror, grieving, and loss of this act.

Terrorists in the United States are not always imported from other countries. Many are homegrown. For example, U.S. citizen Timothy McVeigh was convicted of perpetrating perhaps the single-most destructive terrorist act ever committed on U.S. soil: the bombing of a federal building in 1995, in Oklahoma. One hundred sixty-eight people died and another 467 were injured as a result of the blast. The loss of life and the devastation of this terrorist act for individuals and families will last a lifetime and beyond. Even so, the September 11 attacks struck at the very heart and soul of the American people and have been described as the worst acts of terrorism in modern history, leaving Americans feeling stunned and extremely vulnerable. For example, in a December 2001 Fox News poll, 37 percent of those polled said that they were either somewhat or very worried that terrorist attacks might take place where they live or work. And in a January 2002 Gallup poll, 47 percent of those polled said they were somewhat or very dissatisfied with the nation's security from terrorism; only 10 percent said that they were very satisfied (Polling Report, 2002). By 2006, with increasing terrorists threats and plots uncovered, Americans' concern about terrorism had not risen significantly. For example, in a 2006 Pew Research Center poll, 54 percent of Americans said they closely followed the news that British officials had stopped a terrorist plot to blow up planes flying to the United States, higher public attention than most other terror-related news stories since the September 11, 2001, attacks. However, there was only a small increase in the percentage of people who expressed concern about the latest terrorism plot. For instance, only 25 percent said they were "very concerned" that there would soon be another terrorist attack on the United States. By comparison, slightly fewer (17 percent) respondents interviewed prior to the announcement of the British plot reported that level of concern (Pew Research Center, 2006b). For more facts and figures about terrorism in the United States, see Table 15.3.

War

Most experts on war agree that the intensity and frequency of wars increased in the twentieth century. For example, as the twentieth century came to a close, there had been 250 wars and 109,746,000 war-related deaths, a number somewhat larger than the total current population of France, Belgium, Netherlands, and the four Scandinavian countries Denmark, Finland, Norway, and Sweden. Since mid twentieth century, wars have become more frequent and much more deadly. There have been six times as many deaths per war in the twentieth century as in the nineteenth. Since the mid-1940s alone, more than 23 million people have died as a result of war and another 20 million have died as a result of war-related factors. A major characteristic of contemporary war is that civilians are the primary victims. In the 1980s, for example, 74 percent of wartime casualties were civilians. By

---

TABLE 15.3

Facts and Figures about Terrorism in the United States

- February 23, 1993: The truck bombing of the World Trade Center.

- October 3 and 4, 1993: Al-Qaeda-trained fighters claimed responsibility for bringing down two U.S. helicopters in Somalia and killing 18 U.S. rangers.

- June 25, 1996: A truck bomb kills 19 U.S. servicemen in the Air Force's Khobar Towers housing complex in Dhahran, Saudi Arabia, wounding over 500 people.

- August 7, 1998: Truck bombs destroy U.S. embassies in Nairobi, Kenya, and Dar es Salaam, Tanzania, killing 234, including 12 Americans, and injuring more than 5000.

- October 12, 2000: Two suicide bombers in a boat detonated explosives that blew a 40-foot hole in the side of the USS *Cole* (a 505-foot U.S. Navy guided missile destroyer) as the ship took on fuel in Aden, Yemen, killing 17 crew members and wounding 39.

- September 11, 2001: Al-Qaeda operatives hijacked U.S. aircrafts, using them as bombs to destroy the twin towers and other buildings in the World Trade Center complex, and to severely damaged the Pentagon with an estimated loss of life between 3000 and 5000 people.

Source: Center for Defense Information, 2001b, "The International Islamic Terrorist Network," Terrorism Project (September 14): www.cdi.org/terrorism/terrorist-network-pr.cfm (Accessed: January 18, 2002); CNN.com, 2001, "USS Cole Relaunched with Little Fanfare" (September 16), www.cnn.com/2001/US/09/16/gen.cole.repairs/ (Accessed: February 16, 2001).

1990, civilians constituted 90 percent of such casualties (Sivard, et al., 1996). By the beginning of 2006, an estimated 40,000 to 45,000 Iraqi civilians had been killed in the United States' ongoing war against Iraq (Iraq Body Count Press Release 13, 2006). And after nearly 5 weeks of war between

A major characteristic of contemporary war is that civilians are the primary victims. For instance, after nearly five weeks of war between Israel and Lebanon in 2006, an estimated 5,000 Lebanese civilians were killed or wounded and 1 million Lebanese were displaced. Typical of those who survived the civilian attacks, the Lebanese family in this photo tries to salvage some of their life belongings as a bulldozer removes rubble that was once their house in the southern Lebanese town of Siddiqine.

Israel and Lebanon in 2006, an estimated 5000 Lebanese civilians were killed or wounded and 1 million Lebanese were displaced. By comparison, 157 Israelis died, the majority of whom were soldiers. In a published report, Amnesty International (2006) presented facts suggesting that Israel deliberately attacked the civilian population and government of Lebanon in a conscious effort to turn them against Hezbollah. However, in several reports during the summer of 2006, Human Rights Watch documented indiscriminate use of force against civilians by both the Israel Defense Forces and Hezbollah (Human Rights Watch, 2006).

Today, wars are fought not on some distant battlefield but deep within the homeland of the warring factions. Even when civilians are not purposefully targeted, they end up the major casualties. For example, as horrific as the terrorist attacks on the United States were, their consequences for individuals, marriages, and families extended far beyond the American borders. For instance, the United States' intense campaign of aerial bombardment of various targets in Afghanistan immediately after September 11 killed an untold number of Afghan civilians and prompted a humanitarian disaster, with 20,000 civilians pushed up against closed borders and hundreds of thousands more on the move. Although there are no official statistics available on the civilian death toll in Afghanistan as a result of the U.S. "war on terrorism," there have been reports of civilian casualties arising from U.S.-led attacks on civilian objectives, including an air attack on the village of Khorum, where a number of civilians were reportedly killed, an attack on an International Red Cross warehouse in Kabul, and an air attack on an Afghan radio station. And eyewitnesses have described seeing bodies of Afghan civilians buried in the rubble of houses or those of people killed while riding in civilian vehicles. U.S. officials have admitted that a number of civilian targets were hit as a result of error (Amnesty International, 2001c, 2001d). It is accepted that war causes many dire consequences for the civilian population even if they are not directly killed or injured in military strikes. They may suffer long-term injury or illness (as a result, for instance, of radiation, postconflict contact with unexploded munitions, pollution from spillage of toxic materials). People may suffer deep psychological trauma, miscarriage, bereavement, dislocation, and loss of home and property. Destruction of civil infrastructure and economic systems can have effects that last for generations (Amnesty International, 2006).

Terrorism as a weapon of war is not new. It has been used historically in domestic, regional, and international disputes. It sometimes has been linked to specific conflicts such as in Northern Ireland and the Basque separatist movement in Spain. And, as we have indicated, the United States has dealt with different manifestations of terrorism for years. However, as Americans have found since September 11, the weapons of war are no longer just the traditional bombs and warheads of the past but increasingly include chemical and biological weapons as well.

The weapons of war often have an impact on individuals and families well after the war is officially over. For example, America's use of cluster bombs in Afghanistan has a similar consequence as land mines. According to experts on the subject, at least 5 percent of such bombs do not explode upon impact, becoming de facto land mines and remaining a threat to people, including civilians, who come into contact with them (Amnesty International, 2001c). Moreover, during the Persian Gulf War, U.S. soldiers (women and men) were exposed to chemical warfare that has affected not only their own health but also that of their partners and children. Testifying before a Senate committee about the symptoms they suffer as a result of chemical attacks in the Persian Gulf, hundreds of soldiers reported that their spouses and children displayed the same symptoms as they do, raising the possibility that exposure to debilitating chemicals can be passed on (Soroka and Bryjak, 1999).

Most often, the majority of civilian casualties of war are women and children. In addition to deaths resulting from air strikes and bombing, huge numbers of civilians have died as a result of the collapse of their country's public health system, destroyed during bombings. Consequently, water purification and sewage systems are destroyed, creating the conditions for the development of water-transported diseases that are especially fatal for children and older people (Soroka and Bryjak, 1999). Perhaps the most heinous war-related behavior, to date, is the mass rape of women and girls. For example, the Serbs not only brutalized and murdered thousands of Muslim men but they conducted mass rapes of Muslim women and girls. Some eyewitness accounts of these atrocities as well as first-person accounts by survivors tell how women and girls were often assaulted in their own homes in front of their families, while others were taken to hotels or camps where they were locked up and raped repeatedly by soldiers. Sometimes girls as young as 6 years of age were raped in front of their parents and other family members. Entire villages became "rape camps," where women were raped and sodomized by as many as 20 men per night, every night. The attacks were so violent and vicious that many of the victims died. Added to this horror is that many of the women and girls who survived this assault to their humanity were held captive until impregnated by their rapists (*Ms.* magazine, 1993; Post, 1993; Bryjak and Soroka, 1994; Gelles and Levine, 1995).

Mass rape as a tool of men's wars is not unique to Bosnia. Women fleeing Kosovo also reported stories of systematic rape by Serb forces. The pattern was the same and echoed the rape horror stories that emerged from the Bosnian war: Young Albanian girls and women were separated from their families and brutally sexually assaulted (ABC News, 1999). Historically, the sexual assault of women has been an integral part of war and conquest. What better way to conquer an enemy than to destroy families, and what better way to destroy families than to attack its most vulnerable members—women and girls. When a girl or woman is raped, she, her family, and her community are all victims (Peterson, Wunder, and Mueller, 1999). Table 15.4 presents a brief snapshot of some of the documented cases of war and mass rape in recent human history. The damage done to families as a result of the rape and impregnation of thousands of women is manifold. Women and girls who survive the physical assault of rape often are so psychologically traumatized that they never completely recover. Many of these women never marry or reproduce, because of the lingering psychological damage or because they are considered damaged goods (no matter that they were raped) and are ostracized when the war is over.

Children, Terrorism, and War

Children around the world bear a disproportionately high cost of war; they are

---

TABLE 15.4

- From 1937 to 1938, during the infamous "Rape of Nanking," Japanese soldiers slaughtered more than a quarter of a million people and raped 20,000 or more Chinese women, many of whom died after repeated sexual assaults.

- During World War I, German soldiers raped thousands of Belgian women.

- During World War II, 3 million Polish Jews and an untold number of Russian women were raped and murdered by Nazi soldiers.

- During World War II, as many as 250,000 Korean, Chinese, Manchurian, and Filipino girls and women (age 13 and up) were forcibly abducted and raped for extended periods of time by Japanese soldiers.

- In the waning days of World War II, Soviet soldiers brutalized and raped 2 million German women.

- During the 1971 civil war between Bangladesh and Pakistan, Pakistani soldiers raped more than 280,000 Bangali girls and women.

- During the U.S. and Vietnamese War, American soldiers gang-raped Vietnamese women and girls.

Source: George J. Bryjak and Michael P. Soroka, 1994, *Sociology: Cultural Diversity in a Changing World* (Needham Heights, MA: Allyn and Bacon): 300–301; Michael P. Soroka and George J. Bryjak, 1999, *Social Problems: A World at Risk* (Needham Heights, MA: Allyn and Bacon).

---

displaced, disabled, and psychologically traumatized by war. In the last decade alone, wars in countries such as Rwanda, Bosnia-Herzegovina, Kosovo, Mozambique, Angola, Somalia, Sudan, Afghanistan, Cambodia, and Haiti claimed the lives of and injured far more children than soldiers. For example, more than 2 million children died in wars, 4 to 5 million were physically disabled, another 1 million were orphaned, 12 million were left homeless, and some 10 million suffer psychological trauma (OneWorld, 2002; UNICEF, 2002). Children are the victims of war in many ways. Thousands are killed in the indiscriminate bombing and shelling of their homes, schools, or playing fields; thousands are or have been subject to deliberate and arbitrary killings at the hands of armed political groups. And as we reported earlier, many children have been killed or maimed by the millions of land mines (one for every twenty children around the world) that litter their countries. Decades of war, for instance, have devastated the lives of millions of Afghan children. Families have been torn apart; many of these children have been separated from or have lost parents or siblings and are psychologically scarred from their exposure to violence, death, and illness. Others have been forced to flee their homes, and all have suffered from disrupted schooling and economic hardship (Amnesty International, 1999; UNICEF, 2002). The psychological trauma experienced by Afghan and other children under conditions of war is unprecedented. For example, a UNICEF survey of 3000 Rwandan children in 1995 found that during the genocidal massacres in their country in 1994, 95 percent of these children had witnessed massacres, over one-third had seen the murders of family members, almost all of the children believed they would die, almost two-thirds were threatened with death, and over 80 percent of them said they had had to hide to protect themselves, sometimes up to 8 weeks or longer (UNICEF, 2002). In the United States, the terrorist attacks of September 11 have left many children with questions about things that many

STRENGTHENING MARRIAGES AND FAMILIES
Talks with Family Therapist Joan Zientek

TALKING ABOUT TERRORISM AND THE WAR

Why is it important to talk about the events of 9/11 and their aftermath? Since September 11, 2001, America began a new era. The security that we took for granted vanished. We lost our sense of personal safety and we lost the image of America as untouchable. Images of suicide bombers in faraway places with names previously unknown to us are now in our living rooms in graphic detail. Then the bombings in England in 2005 and earlier in Spain and France brought these tragedies closer to home. We are now dealing with new realities that leave us with intense emotions of anger, fear, worry, anxiety, and sadness.

As we struggle to make sense of these events, we try to protect our children and help them cope. On TV they see the events of war recounted over and over; they see troops being deployed and others returned; they see the worried looks of children as they say goodbye to their moms and dads; they see government leaders debating the best course of action; and they see people protesting. Even if the younger child

does not understand the meaning of all the words spoken, that child picks up on the emotions that accompany those words and carries those feelings inside. As a result, children are confused; they worry if their parents will leave or whether their friend's parents will return; they worry every time a parent goes on a business trip and wonder if their city and home are safe or will they too be bombed. While children are dealing with the complexities of these realities, post-9/11 research has shown that almost 25 percent of parents reported that they never talked to their children about terrorism and war. If we, as adults, do not deal with our feelings about these events or if we do not help our children cope with their feelings, these feelings will get expressed in indirect ways.

Do adults and children react the same way to disasters? Common responses to any disaster include disbelief and shock, fear and anxiety about the future, disorientation (difficulty making decisions or concentrating), emotional numbing, irritable and angry behavior, somatic complaints, difficulty sleeping, nightmares, sadness, and depression. Children may develop regressive behaviors: bed-wetting,

thumb sucking, and separation anxiety. Adolescents may cover their fears with an attitude of false bravado or by engaging in reckless behaviors. However, most of these reactions will diminish with time and with the resumption of a normal routine. Each person will have her or his own time line of recovery, so it is important not to compare oneself to others or to judge others' reactions and responses.

Although we as adults struggle to make sense of all these events, young children especially struggle because they do not have the experience of the verbal or cognitive ability to understand what is happening. Children take their cues from the adults around them and pattern their own reactions on the behaviors they observe. Children's reactions will vary according to their age. Young children worry most about the safety of their parents and fear that they will be separated from them. School-age children worry that the acts of terrorism that they see on TV will be repeated and that something worse will happen to their city or neighborhood. Because young children confuse fact with fantasy and mix reality with movie scripts, they may come to mistaken conclusions. Although adolescents may mask their feelings, the trauma they

---

small children in this country typically have not had to face in the past. Buildings on fire, buildings falling down, daddy or mommy or both suddenly yanked from their lives—either missing or dead.

Parents around the country have found ways to talk to their children about the terror, horror, and fear of September 11 and to help them understand what happened. Teachers, family therapists, and a host of other professionals and laypersons have developed curricula and methods by which adults can work collectively to ease the trauma of terrorist threats for children (see the Strengthening Marriages and Families box). With the increased high security screening at airports and other public facilities, parents again have to talk to their children about terrorism.

Sometimes children are deliberately used or targeted in war. In 2006, for example, Hezbollah militia were accused of using children (and women) as human shields in the war with Israel. In many conflict situations children are used as soldiers to supplement adult armies and militias. Those who do not die and live to see peace are usually left with the

legacy of a violent past. In recent years, in more than 40 countries, including in Latin America, the Middle East, Asia, and Africa, thousands of children under the age of 18, some as young as 7 years old, have been routinely used in this way. According to a published report on child soldiers produced by a coalition of groups against the use of children as soldiers, more than 500,000 children, girls and boys, under the age of 18 are in government armies or guerrilla groups around the world; at any one time, more than one-half (300,000) of them are in actual combat. These children—small, agile, and relatively powerless—are recruited, captured, demobilized, wounded, or even killed everyday. Children are considered a cheap and expendable commodity, and the lighter weight of today's weapons makes it easier to arm them. The dangers these children face are not only on the frontlines of war but also in myriad other situations. For example, children are routinely used as spies, messengers, sentries, porters, servants, and sexual slaves; they are often used to lay and clear land mines or are conditioned to commit atrocities even against their own

have experienced prompts them to reflect on the meaning of life and moves them to desire to take some action.

How can parents help themselves and their children cope with these events? There are several things we all can do to cope:

■ *Talk about it.* Let your child know that it is okay to talk about it and to ask questions. Ask children what they have heard from friends or on TV. Use their response as a starting point. Give appropriate information relative to the age and emotional maturity of the child. Do not minimize your child's feelings or try to talk them out of what they are feeling. Avoid intense, extreme expressions. Share your own feelings without putting your anxiety on the child or using your child for emotional support.

■ *Take care of yourself.* Take time to think about and deal with your own feelings. If you do not, children will sense your anxiety and model themselves after you. Get extra rest and exercise. Eat healthy foods. Do things that you enjoy and that are soothing and relaxing.

■ *Limit exposure.* Too much TV viewing can be overwhelming and confusing, especially to your children. They may think that each replay of an event is a new happening. A child's stress level is directly related to the amount of TV viewing and parental stress.

■ *Be reassuring.* Stress that these events, while they do happen, are rare. Tell children what the government is doing to keep America safe, and tell them that you are voting for government leaders who make sound decisions. Let them know that you will do everything you can to keep them safe. Say "I love you" often.

■ *Help children use creative outlets.* Because young children cannot adequately express themselves verbally, they work out their feelings through play and creative outlets, such as drawing.

■ *Make a family plan.* Keep emergency supplies at the ready. Have a designated place to meet or one contact person to call in case of an emergency.

■ *Maintain a sense of balance.* Keep up-to-date about the facts of the war; remember, however, that there are other aspects of your life and the lives of your children that need attention. Pay attention to your feelings so you will know when to take a break.

■ *Stay connected to family and friends.* Plan family nights and family outings. Do fun things together. Play games and plan family meals. Keep in touch with those out of town by phone or e-mail. Send care packages to college students.

■ *Take some action.* Get involved in positive activities that your church or community sponsors. Donate food or clothing. Write letters of appreciation.

■ *Gain a sense of control.* Do something that gives a sense of completion like baking cookies, cleaning closets, doing a hobby, or painting a room.

Most of all we need to give our children a signal that we are available to talk by discussing the war and terrorism in a calm, loving manner. By admitting our fears and worries and showing that we can handle them, we teach our children how to cope and give them the confidence that intense emotions can be managed. Some children, as well as adults, may need help in their efforts to cope with their fears and worries. If a person is preoccupied with the traumatic events and is unable to get involved in the daily tasks of life, the need for professional help may be indicated. Persons who have been subjected to past traumas or experience current traumas in their lives may be most affected.

In spite of the turmoil of the new age of terrorism, people are able to make changes to improve the quality of their lives. Many have come to a new appreciation of friends and family, recommitted to relationships with a willingness to work out problems, pursued interests otherwise neglected, and rekindled their love of and loyalty to America.

---

families and communities. Moreover, most child soldiers suffer physical and other abuses within the armed forces; in extreme cases, they commit suicide or murder when the mistreatment becomes unbearable (Coalition to Stop the Use of Child Soldiers, 2001).

The good news (if there can be good news about children in armed conflict and the abuse of children) is that, due in part to the work of UNICEF and human rights organizations and groups around the world, 73 countries to date have adopted legislation that prohibits the recruitment of children under the age of 18. In addition, 80 countries, including the United States, have signed an international agreement barring children in armed conflict, although only five of these countries—Andorra, Bangladesh, Canada, Congo, and Sri Lanka—have ratified the treaty. On the other side of this coin, however, thousands of children are still being recruited or forced to fight in armies in various African countries. In Colombia, at least 14,000 children are fighting with both guerrilla groups and antirebel paramilitaries, and in Sri Lanka, a guerrilla army is still recruiting or drafting girls and boys into the army, some of whom are drafted specifically to undertake suicide missions (Crossette, 2001).

This discussion of the well-being of children has focused on the impact of war, violence, and terrorism, but they are not the only threats to children. Although there are vast cultural differences around the world, cross-culturally it is generally assumed that families have the primary responsibility for protecting and caring for their children. However, as the Internet Resources: Applying the Sociological Imagination box shows, reality is often quite different. As this chapter makes clear, around the world natural disasters, economic disruptions, diseases, substance abuse, racism, terrorism, and armed conflict are disrupting the lives of millions of children every day. In many places in the world, children have been orphaned or find themselves in environments made dangerous as a result of these events. Additionally, some children are at risk because their parents are unwilling or unable to care for them properly, often due to of problems with drugs and alcohol. Creating policies and structures that ensure that orphans and children at risk have a

APPLYING THE SOCIOLOGICAL IMAGINATION
The Vulnerability or Children Around the World

- Every second a public school student is suspended.
- Every 20 seconds a child is arrested.
- Every 35 seconds a child is confirmed as abused or neglected.
- Every 35 seconds a baby is born into poverty.

For more of these moments, go to www.childrensdefense.org/site/pageserver?pagename=Research_National_Data_Moments

Facts on Children Across the World

- More than 1 billion children suffer from a lack of proper nutrition, safe drinking water, decent sanitation facilities, health care services, shelter, education, and information.
- The exact number of street children is impossible to count, but estimates are that tens of millions exist across the world.
- It is estimated that trafficking affects about 1.2 million children each year.

For more facts on the world's children, go to www.unicef.org/voy/explore/sowc06/explore_2463.html

As you visit these sites and reflect on the status of millions of children in the United States and across the world, what is your reaction? How is it that so many children are uncared for and unprotected? What are the consequences for the children and for their societies, if these trends continue? Are these inevitable problems, or can the situations for these children be improved? To help you answer this last question, visit the United Nations Web site (www.mdgs.un.org/unsd/mdg/Default.aspx) to assess to what degree millennium development goals are being reached and to find out what various countries, including the United States, are doing to meet these goals.

---

safe and permanent home is an issue that challenges government officials everywhere. Foster care and adoption are two common responses to this need.

MEETING THE NEEDS OF CHILDREN: FOSTER CARE AND ADOPTION

The idea behind foster care is that substitute families will provide short-term care until the children can be adopted or returned to their biological parents. Foster care is practiced in many different ways throughout the world, depending on the culture and the structures in place. Although kinship or informal fostering by family or friends occurs to some degree in all societies, it is especially normative in developing countries. Additionally, many countries have developed or are in the process of developing a formal legal system of foster care with explicit procedures and regulations.

Here in the United States, in 2004, some 517,000 children were without permanent homes and living in foster care, 47 percent female and 53 percent male, drawn from major racial and ethnic groups: African Americans (34 percent), white (40 percent), Latina/o (18 percent), Native American/Alaskan Native (2 percent), Asian (1 percent), multiple races, unknown/unable to determine (5 percent) (Administration for Children and Families, 2006). Many of these children were removed from their homes as a result of being neglected, abused, or abandoned. Many children remain in foster care for extended periods of time; others move in and out of the system several times over. This is especially true for older children, those with behavioral or emotional problems, and children of color. In 2004, the median length of stay in foster care was 16.5 months; the average length of stay was 30 months. Children move out of foster care in a variety of ways. In 2004, 54 percent were reunited with their parents, 18 percent were adopted, 12 percent were living with other relatives, and 8 percent were emancipated (Administration for Children and Families, 2006).

Problems Confronting Foster Care

Whether it is the United States or some other country, the foster care system is plagued by similar problems. The needs of children in care are becoming increasingly complex and specialized at a time when there are limited resources available to meet their needs. Welfare workers continue to turn over at a high rate, and many are underpaid, poorly trained, overworked, and demoralized. The pool of foster families is inadequate, especially the kind qualified to care for children with multiple problems. Permanent adoptive homes for older, handicapped, and healthy children of color are in short supply. For example, there is a shortage of at least 10,000 foster parents across the United Kingdom (Tapsfield and Collier, 2005). And, in sub-Sahara Africa the number of available adult caregivers has been drastically reduced through illness and disease. Additionally, in war-torn countries few resources are available to try to reunite children with parents or other relatives.

Numerous studies show a variety of outcomes for children in foster care. On the positive side, many children benefit by being placed in a safe environment where they receive the medical and mental health services they need. Many find adults they can trust and who are good role models for later life (Whiting and Lee, 2003). On the negative side, however, studies have found poor school outcomes among foster children compared to the general population (Christian, 2003) and higher levels of mental impairment (Landsverk and Garland, 2000). Additionally, the prospects for many children who remain in foster care are not good. After aging out of foster care, 10 percent of females and 27 percent of males were incarcerated within 12 to 18 months;

37 percent had not finished high school; 50 percent were unemployed; and 33 percent received public assistance (National Adoption Information Clearing house, 2006). A major problem in studying the effect of foster care on well-being in later life is the difficulty in distinguishing what is attributable to foster care per se and what is due to the circumstances that have preceded it. Living in an intact or foster care setting characterized by emotional warmth and support is likely to produce positive outcomes whereas living in an abusive setting is likely to damage the child.

Prior to 1975, agencies discouraged foster parents from adopting the children in their care but reversed themselves later as they recognized the benefits of continuity for children who could not be returned to their birth parents. Foster parent adoptions have increased dramatically over the last decade. In 2004, 30,884 (or 59 percent) of the 52,000 children adopted from foster care that year were adopted by their foster parents (Administration for Children and Families, 2006).

Becoming Parents through Adoption

There are several important differences between foster care and adoption. In adoption, parents assume full legal, financial, and decision-making responsibility for a child and incorporate the child as a permanent member of their own family. Adoption has a long history. The early Greeks, Romans, Egyptians, and Babylonians had adoption systems. Informal adoptions whereby orphaned children were taken into the homes of others existed in early America as well. However, it was not until the mid-nineteenth century that it became enshrined in our legal system. Adoption is highly regarded in the United States. In a 2002 survey, 94 percent of Americans had very or somewhat favorable opinions regarding adoption, up from 90 percent in 1997. Thirty-nine percent had very or somewhat seriously considered adopting a child, up from 36 percent in 1997, and 64 percent said that a family member or close friend was adopted, had adopted, or put a child up for adoption, up from 57 percent 5 years earlier. Perhaps even more significant is the finding that between 1997 and 2002, there was an 11 percent increase (46 to 57 percent) of respondents who believe adoptive parents derive the same satisfaction from raising adopted and biological children (National Adoption Attitudes Survey, 2002).

The 2000 Census was the first time that the Census Bureau systematically collected data on adopted children and found that an estimated 2.1 million children (8 percent of all children) live with adoptive parents; 18,000 of these children were foreign-born (Kreider, 2003).

Individuals and couples wishing to adopt have several options. In *public adoptions* children in the public child welfare system are placed in permanent homes by government-operated agencies. *Private adoptions* involve the placement of children in nonrelatives' homes through the services of a licensed nonprofit or for-profit agency. In *independent adoptions* children are placed in the homes of either relatives or nonrelatives directly by the birth parents or through services of a medical doctor, a member of the clergy, an attorney, or a licensed or unlicensed facilitator. Independent adoptions are illegal in some states. In *kinship* adoptions children are placed in relatives' homes with or without the services of a public agency. In *stepparent adoptions*, children are adopted by the spouse of one birth parent. Today adoptions can be open or closed. In a *closed adoption*, the adoptive parents and the birth parents do not meet. In *open adoptions*, however, the two parties meet and together work out the process of adoption. The birth mother may even take an active role in selecting the adoptive parents. In some cases the adoptive parents will invite the birth mother to live with them during her pregnancy. Some open adoptions are characterized by ongoing contact with the birth mother. The extent of the contact may vary from periodic reports of the child's progress to the birth mother's integration into the family as a friend or **fictive kin,** in which kinship terms are attributed to nonrelatives.

Who Can Adopt? Characteristics and Current Controversies

In the past, adoption agencies considered only married couples as suitable candidates to adopt children. Around 1978, however, single-parent adoptions became possible. Since then there has been a steady increase in such adoptions, especially of children with special needs. All 50 states currently allow single people to adopt. In 2004, 27 percent of adoptions of children in foster care were single women; 3 percent were single men; 68 percent were married couples; and 2 percent were unmarried couples (Administration for Children and Families, 2006).

Although single heterosexuals have been accepted as adoptive parents for the past two decades, it is only recently that lesbians and gays have been allowed that same right. Sixty percent of adoption agencies now work with gays and lesbians, and the number of such families is growing steadily (Rubin, 2006). Public attitudes seem to be moving in the direction of greater acceptance as well. In 1999, most Americans (57 percent) opposed allowing lesbians and gays to adopt children while just 38 percent were in favor. By 2006, respondents were about equally divided, with 46 percent in favor and 48 percent opposed (Pew Research Center, 2006c). Although attitudes are more approving, efforts to ban lesbians and gays from adopting, children are gaining traction reminiscent of the struggle over same-sex marriage that intensified during the 2004 elections. In 2006, sixteen states were considering initiatives to ban lesbian and gay adoptions. Florida has long had a law banning lesbians and gays from adopting, although the state permits homosexuals to be foster parents. Thus, men like Dough Houghton, a nurse practitioner, who became the legal guardian of a 3-year-old boy with health problems and learning disabilities, and Steve Lofton, a pediatric nurse who raised a 10-year-old boy from infancy and who with his longtime partner did such a fine job as caregivers that the Children's Home Society honored them with the first Foster Parents of the Year award, were denied the right to adopt the children in their care (Crary, 2001; Bell, 2001). Unlike their heterosexual counterparts, Houghton and Lofton were judged unsuitable not in terms of their ability to rear and nurture children but in terms of their sexual orientation (see Chapter 9 for a discussion of the issues surrounding lesbian and gay parenting).

International Adoptions

Because of a shortage of available healthy babies in the United States (see Chapter 9) many people have turned to international adoptions. Over 80 countries allow their children to be adopted by U.S. citizens, primarily countries in Asia, Latin America, and Eastern Europe. The majority of international adoptions involve infants of color from economically disadvantaged countries. In 1980, there were approximately 5000 international adoptions; in 2005, U.S. parents adopted 22,728 children from other countries. Nearly 80 percent of these children came from four countries: China, Russia, Guatemala, and South Korea (International Adoption Trends, 2006). In the case of China, where there is an intense preference for male heirs, it is estimated that as many as 150,000 female infants are abandoned each year. The Chinese government has allowed foreign adoptions as one means of dealing with this problem; the vast majority of children adopted from China are girls while for the remaining nations of origin there is little gender disparity. Although not widely publicized or tracked, a number of U.S. children are placed for adoption with non-U.S. citizens each year. Statistics from the Canadian immigration bureau indicate that 786 children have been adopted by Canadian citizens from 1993 to 2002 (Child Welfare Information Gateway, 2004). Other countries receiving U.S. infants, mostly African Americans, are Germany, France, Belgium, the Netherlands, and England, where most of the adopting parents are Caucasian (Davenport, 2004).

Although the vast majority of international adoptions are successfully completed and bring great joy to the adopting parents and children (see Family Profile box), they can be risky. There have been allegations of baby selling in a number of countries, so prospective adopting parents are advised to be well informed about the agency and/or individuals they are dealing with and to seek appropriate legal guidance throughout the process. In general, there are many bureaucratic regulations (both in the United States and abroad) that must be met before the proceedings are finalized and the child is allowed to leave the country. These adoption proceedings are costly, ranging from $15,000 to $35,000, depending on the country. The cost includes legal fees in both countries and sometimes the payment of "contributions" or bribes to various agencies and officials, putting international adoptions beyond the reach of many people. Some agencies are not up front in revealing important information about the children being placed for adoption. For example, in the past some of the international children available for adoption have been institutionalized for extensive periods of time and, as a result, their emotional development has been stunted, making it difficult for them to bond with their new parents; others may have acute illnesses that are not disclosed to the adoptive parents. Some adoptive parents find that they are unable to cope with a child with so many needs and they seek to terminate the adoption.

Adoptions are terminated either through *disruption*, an adoption process that ends after the child is placed in an adoptive home but before the adoption is legally finalized, or *dissolution*, an adoption that ends after it is legally finalized. In both cases the child is returned to (or enters into) foster care or placement with new adoptive parents. Parents who make this decision do not do so lightly and they suffer pain, guilt, embarrassment, grief, and a sense of failure. Children suffer, too. They may become even more emotionally withdrawn and, as a result, become more difficult to place with another family. Although figures are not available for disruptions or dissolutions involving international adoptions, social workers do report seeing an increase. They attribute this pattern to the increased number of children coming from institutionalized settings after being abused, neglected, or abandoned, as well as an increase in the number of older children placed for adoption. Domestic adoptions also run into similar problems. Studies indicate domestic disruption rates ranging from 10 to 25 percent. Between 1 and 10 percent of adoptions are dissolved (Festinger, 2002). However, adoptions of children of any age with special needs are more likely to be disrupted than children without special needs. Often a major contributing factor to the difficulties parents face is their lack of information about where to go for services and/or inadequate resources to pay for them when available. The older the child and the more emotional and physical problems the child has, the higher the disruption rate. The growing public recognition of disruptions led Congress to include a provision in the 1997 Adoption and Safe Families Act that provides federal assistance for children who, their adoptions disrupted, must return to foster care.

Transracial (Interracial) Adoptions

Race is also a factor in the politics and policies of the adoption process. With the exception of Native American children, transracial adoption was largely unheard until the 1950s. The prevailing policy and practice of adoption agencies was race-matching in the belief that this was in the best interest of the child and the community. However, this began to change in the 1960s with the civil rights movement. Increased attention began to focus on children of color who were placed in foster care. During the 1960s and early 1970s there was a rapid growth in transracial adoptions. Between 1969 and 1974 more than 80 percent of the Native American children adopted were placed with white families. During the same time, many Native Americans were rejected as adoptive parents because they did not meet agency criteria. By 1972, approximately 10,000 African American children had been adopted by white couples (cited in McRoy, 1989). Alarmed by this trend, the National Association of Black Social Workers and some Native American organizations came out against transracial adoptions, raising concerns about the possible adjustment problems these children might have and the loss of these children to their original communities—what they saw as "cultural genocide." This controversy led many agencies to revert to race matching for adoption placements; in the 1980s only about 8 percent of adoptions were interracial (Bachrach et al., 1990).

In the 1990s, however, the controversy took another turn. Some public officials, believing that race-matching practices deny thousands of children of color a stable and permanent home, pushed for legislation to limit the practice and to reduce the length of time children wait to be adopted

FAMILY PROFILE

THE WILLIS FAMILY

Length of Relationship: 13.5 years

Challenges of Having Two Children 21 Years Apart: When Orna and I married, my biggest challenge was trying to figure out my role as a new parent to a 13-year-old stepdaughter. I accomplished this mostly by trial and error. I decided that my best chance of success with Shiri was not to try to insinuate myself into her life but rather to make myself worthy of her trust. One of the first things I asked of Shiri is that she give me permission to refer to her as my daughter, not stepdaughter, although I did not expect that she refer to me as her dad. I also hit on the idea of never referring to Orna as "your mom"; I always used *Mom*. In kind, Shiri naturally started saying *Mom*, not *my* mom. If these distinctions sound minor, they are not. They were little things that had a huge impact on our relationship, which was rocky for a year or two before we found a way to trust each other. Through patience and persistence we grew to appreciate each other and to build a loving relationship, which had a predictably positive impact on the marriage.

When Shiri was 21 years old, a time when most middle-aged couples are feeling a little guilty about enjoying their freedom from their children, Orna and I decided to adopt a baby. Because of our age and the small number of available infants in the United States, we decided to look into international adoptions. After considerable searching, Orna discovered an orphanage in Cambodia founded by a wonderful pediatrician who believed that each orphan should be cared for by one nanny. The process was arduous, but it was just as well. We could have dropped out at any time but the more that was asked of us (including having to secure letters of recommendation from two U.S. senators), the greater was our resolve. Patience and persistence again served us well. A few months into the adoption process we got the call informing us of the arrival of a baby girl that was ours if we wanted her. We said "yes" and when we received her picture the following week, we fell in love with her on the

Shiri, Reid, Orna, and Nina Willis

spot. From that moment, Nina was our second daughter.

At age 44, I bravely faced the challenge of having to change diapers for the first time while Orna marveled at the obsolescence of diaper pins. When people asked me what it is like to raise a baby at my age, I would say I don't know—I never did it before. There are challenges to having infants at an advanced age, but we don't feel unusual. We live in a neighborhood where Nina attends a preschool with a wonderful mix of kids. Many of her playmates are products of international adoptions and some of the parents are our age or older. We do wonder whether Nina will face taunting by other kids because of her color or ancestry. If that happens, we will help her to deal with it. We want Nina to know who she is and be proud of where she came from. Her room is filled with pictures, books, and mementos from Cambodia. She already knows she lives in Philadelphia but comes from Cambodia.

While in law school, sister Shiri did her public service internship in Cambodia

and visited the orphanage where Nina lived; Shiri also met the nanny who took care of her during her entire stay in the orphanage. As Nina gets older, she and Shiri will have that to share. And, when Nina is old enough to appreciate being there, we will all go back to Cambodia together.

Having postponed the empty nest, we have had to reconsider our plans for retirement. We will be working longer than we initially expected but we do not regret that for a second.

Relationship Philosophy: We recognize that our children are different; consequently, we do not love them the same, we love them differently. We have learned to be flexible in setting rules, choosing our "no's" carefully and being open to negotiations on most issues. We want to learn who our children are and what motivates them, encouraging them to be open to learning many things. Finally, we believe in finding reasons to celebrate each day.

or placed in foster care. In response to these pressures, Congress passed the Multiethnic Placement Act of 1994. The law prohibits any agency that receives federal funds from denying a foster care or adoption placement solely on the basis of race, color, or national origin. Since the passage of that legislation, the rates of transracial adoptions began to move upward. By 1998, approximately 14 percent of black children adopted from foster care (about 2200) were adopted transracially, nearly all by whites. By 2004, the percentage had increased to 26 percent, 4200 adoptions (Clemetson and Nixon, 2006). Besides this legislation, several other factors contributed to this increase. Attitudes became more accepting of multicultural families as the number of international adoptions grew. Between 1990 and 2005, Americans adopted more than 227,000 children from overseas, half of them from Asia. The high costs of international adoptions combined with changes in the foster care system, making adoptions easier, also played a part. The foster care system instituted a more aggressive recruiting campaign among prospective families and provided more support for would-be adopters. Finally, the need for transracial adoption remains. Over half of the children waiting in foster care are children of color: 38 percent African American, 14 percent Latina/o, 2 percent Native American, 38 percent white, and the remaining 7 percent are of more than one race or unknown/unable to determine (Administration for Children and Families, 2006).

Most of the objections to transracial adoptions center on the possible adjustment these children might have as well as issues of identity. The first concern has not materialized. Research shows that adopted children raised in interracial homes generally adjust quite well (Morrison, 2004). However, research findings on identity issues are more mixed. A study of transracially and intraracially adopted young adults found no statistical difference in problem behaviors between the two groups. However, transracial adoptees living in mostly white neighborhoods were more likely to feel discomfort about their appearance than transracial adoptees who lived in more racially mixed neighborhoods, and those young adults who felt discomfort and experienced discrimination were more likely to have behavioral problems (Feigelman, 2000). Similarly, other researchers have found that when adoptive families encourage the adoptive child's participation in multicultural and multiracial activities, identify issues are not a significant problem (Simon and Altstein, 2000). Yet anecdotal evidence suggests it may be more complicated than that. For example, Rodney Williams, aged 29, was adopted by a white couple when he was 3 days old. He is still searching for where he belongs. He said, "Black people think I'm arrogant, because I talk 'proper.' White people? You're not like most black people. That's what I get" (quoted in Gammage, 2006).

As we saw earlier, racism is still a major problem in the United States and there is concern that transracial adoptees may not be as fully prepared to cope with it as children of color raised in same-race homes. Until more progress is made in improving race relations, transracial adoptions are likely to remain controversial and one-sided. With rare exception have people of color been able to adopt white children.

Regina Bush hugs her two adopted daughters after Stacey's adoption became final in Flint, Michigan, in 1998. Bush's adoption of 9-year-old Stacey (right) followed months of legal struggle. Stacey's adoption attracted media attention because it is one of the relatively rare cases involving the adoption of a white child by an African American parent.

With an increasing number of children living in biracial or multiracial families, either as a result of adoption or birth, racial identity is fast becoming one of the most urgent and controversial issues facing marriages, families, schools, the work force, and society at large today. Given the nature of U.S. race relations and the demographic changes that ushered in the twenty-first century, it is imperative that we reexamine the manner in which people are categorized racially and ethnically and then treated on the basis of these categories.

SUPPORTING CHILDREN AND FAMILIES HERE AND ABROAD

Finally, as we have seen, families everywhere are experiencing the challenges of living in a global world. After reading this chapter you may be tempted to think that the world is out of control, that the challenges humans face are so complex and overwhelming that positive change is not only improbable but next to impossible. This kind of thinking can give rise to feelings of depression and hopelessness. However, history teaches us that problems can be solved; that concerned people can and do meet a wide variety of human challenges. An example from the past comes quickly to mind. Legalized discrimination—for instance, the apartheid system in South Africa or the "Jim Crow" system of racial segregation in the southern United States—has been abolished. Clearly this has not eliminated racism, but it is a major step forward and an example of people working individually and collectively to find solutions. Although we

WRITING YOUR OWN SCRIPT

THINKING GLOBALLY

At the end of one century and into a new one, we find ourselves living in a world filled with contradictions. On the one hand, there are deep conflicts, tensions, and forms of extreme inequality. On the other hand, technological innovations provide us with amazing power to improve our lives for the better. One thing is certain, however. Human beings everywhere are, for better or worse, part of a common future. The choices we make as individuals and in groups will shape the quality of life we all experience.

Questions to Consider

1. Given the rate of change taking place around the world, what are you doing and can you do in the future to prepare yourself for living in a global society? Do you think any new political structures are warranted in terms of global interdependence? If so, what kind of structures can you envision?

2. What do you think the advantages and disadvantages of the worldwide migration currently taking place are? Would you consider migrating to another country? Why or why not? If you did migrate to another country, what problems do you think you and your family might encounter as "outsiders?" How do you think you would feel in such a situation?

3. Have you or any one in your family ever been discriminated against? What do you think the basis of that discrimination was? What was your reaction? Did you ever, consciously or unconsciously, discriminate against someone else? Why or why not? Can you as an individual or can your family do anything to eliminate discrimination here in the United States or in the larger society? If yes, what can you do? If no, why can't you? Do societies have a moral responsibility to end all forms of discrimination?

4. What do you think of the movement to allow transracial adoptions? Would you consider adopting a child from another racial or ethnic group? If so, why or why not? Do you think transracial adoptions are good for the adopted child? If you were raising a child from another race or ethnic group, how would you prepare her or him to live in a society that frequently undervalues her or his group?

5. If you could change anything about the society (or the world) in which we live today, what would it be? How would you want things changed? Why? Do you think any other people share your view? What could you begin to do now to help bring this change about?

---

have pointed out some horrific problems that exist locally, nationally, and globally, there are movements to alleviate many of them. These problems are complex and multifaceted; thus, resolutions will not be easy or quick. Many of the factors contributing to these problems are structural in nature and therefore will require structural changes to solve them. Space permits only a few examples of what the international community can do to provide a friendlier environment for families. A report by the United Nations Development Programme (2005) found that developing countries lose about $24 billion a year because wealthy countries insist on agriculture protectionism and subsidies for their own agricultural industry. A fair trade policy could play a central role in poverty reduction in many countries, thus improving the life chances of children and their families around the globe. Similarly, an estimated $11.3 billion a year could bring improved drinking water and sanitation services to much of the world currently lacking these resources. Not only would millions of lives be saved, but more children would go to and remain in school, fewer workdays would be lost to disease, and productivity would increase. Altogether, the World Health Organization estimates the return on this investment would be $84 billion (World Health Organization, 2004). Additionally, all governments need to involve both professional and laypeople alike in meaningful dialogue and action to confront racism, violence, war, terrorism and to encourage more of their citizens to become caregivers for orphaned and abandoned children.

SUMMARY

Increasingly, the lives of people around the world are intertwined. Any one nation's problems—unemployment, substance abuse, disease, inequality, racism, sexism, inadequate resources, terrorism, war, and displacement—cut across cultural and geographic boundaries. The process of globalization is not new. What is different today is the depth and breadth of the process. For the past three decades or so, global competition for new markets has intensified. Families in wealthy and poor countries alike are hearing that they must adapt to this increased competition, yet the benefits and the burdens of adapting are not shared evenly.

These inequities are apparent in the health of a population as well as in its access to health care. Infant mortality rates tend to be higher and life expectancy rates tend to be lower in developing countries than they are in developed countries. Even today billions of people are without clean water or adequate sanitation services, leaving them vulnerable to diseases and early death. Even in the United States, where per capita health expenditures are the highest of any of the industrialized countries, over 18 percent of the population, nearly 46 million people, do not have health insurance.

Few people realize that the experience of disability is typical rather than rare. Disability is a normal part of life affecting people of all ages. More than 600 million people globally are disabled, almost one-third of whom are children. In the United States, 51.2 million people (representing 18 percent of the population) have some level of disability, almost two-thirds (63 percent) of whom are severely disabled.

Another challenge that many families face is coping with members who are addicted to alcohol or other drugs. The abuse of alcohol and other drugs creates numerous economic and health problems and often causes major restructuring of family roles, in some cases leading to the death of a family member or to the dissolution of the family.

All families must cope with the loss of loved ones. People need to be able to express their sorrow and to receive social support as they do their grief work. Because some social relationships are either unrecognized or socially disapproved, many individuals experience disenfranchised grief.

Although many forces impinge on family life in the United States, racism continues to be one of the major challenges to the well-being of many families, particularly families of color. Despite improvements in the life conditions of some families of color, the majority remain disadvantaged by racism and discrimination. Because of the persistence of racism and discrimination in major U.S. institutions such as education and the work force, families of color are forced to bear a disproportionately higher amount of poverty, unemployment and underemployment, welfare dependency, dropping out of school, infant mortality, illness, and death.

Racism, prejudice, ethnic discrimination racism, xenophobia, hate, and violence are not limited to the United States but can be found in a number of countries around the world. Wherever racial and ethnic conflicts are played out, the consequences for marriages and families have been devastation and despair.

Although America is known as a land of immigrants, the increasing number of unauthorized immigrants into the country, especially unauthorized Mexican immigrants, have spawn both a spirited public and legislative debate about unauthorized immigrants as well as a growing "illegal immigrant" movement to keep unauthorized immigrants in the country.

One of the most significant global demographic trends of the twentieth century was the massive immigration of people from one country to another all over the world. Sometimes this immigration is voluntary, in that people leave their homelands seeking economic opportunities in other lands. All too often, however, the massive movement of people from one land to another has been and continues to be the result of communal violence and war. One out of every 275 persons on earth has been forced into flight.

In addition to the challenge of racism and discrimination, families around the world are confronted with gangs and gang violence. Although street violence and crime decreased in the United States in the mid-1990s, the rate of juvenile or youth violence and criminal behavior has increased at an alarming rate. In addition, of increasing concern to parents is the violence that occurs inside the nation's schools. Over the last decade, there have been a number of highly publicized violent crimes committed on American school grounds, the overwhelming majority of which involved white male student shooters.

Terrorism, war, and displacement also take a tremendous toll on family life. The terrorist events of September 11, 2001, dramatically demonstrated Americans' increasing vulnerability to terrorist acts at home.

Over 500,000 children are currently without permanent homes in this country alone. Many of these children were removed from their homes as a result of being neglected or abused as a result of parental addiction and escalating poverty. Only a small percentage of children currently in foster care are eligible for adoption. There are many controversies surrounding adoption today. Adoption costs are high, thus prohibiting many poor and working-class families, especially those of color, from being able to adopt.

Although these challenges sometimes seem insurmountable, history teaches us that problems can be solved and that concerned people can and do meet a variety of challenges.

KEY TERMS

global interdependence	drug abuse	disenfranchised grief	institutional racism
health	alcoholism	hospice	ethnic cleansing
disability	bereavement	xenophobia	terrorism
drug	grief	racism	refugees
drug use	mourning	individual racism	fictive kin

QUESTIONS FOR STUDY AND REFLECTION

1. Throughout this chapter we have examined a number of international issues (globalization, worldwide inequalities, health issues, substance abuse, death and dying, racism, street violence, terrorism, war, foster care, and adoption). How appropriate is it to consider these issues in a marriages and families text? Would you add to this list or eliminate any issues? Explain. Does the United States, and by extension its citizens, have a responsibility to be involved in what happens to families in other parts of the world? Explain.

2. Search the Internet for sites pertaining to either disabilities or the status and welfare of children. What do these sites tell us about disabilities? The status of children? Compare the information of different countries around the globe. Write an essay on either topic that includes a comparative analysis of data you find and that ends with a policy statement on the subject.

3. It is often said that the United States is a death-denying society, that we remove the dying to hospitals and nursing homes and use euphemisms for death—she has "passed on," he has "gone to a better place"—and that, consequently, Americans are not well prepared for this last stage of life. Do you agree or disagree? Explain. Do you think that televised reports of death in the Middle East and elsewhere are changing attitudes toward death and dying? Explain. How much experience have you had with death or dying? Should there be death education in the schools? What should people do to prepare for their own death or that of a loved one? Explain.

4. Hypothetically, you and a number of college students from across the country are asked to develop and implement a youth summit on the health and well-being of the world's children. What are some of the issues or themes you would suggest for the summit? Who would you suggest should be involved? Are there people who should not be involved? Explain.

ADDITIONAL RESOURCES

SOCIOLOGICAL

BONILLA-SILVA, EDUARDO. 2003. *Racism Without Racists: Color-Blind Racism and the Persistence of Racial Inequality in the United States.* Lanham, MD: Rowman and Littlefield. A probing analysis of white racial attitudes that challenges the persistent individualistic interpretations of race and racism by leading survey researchers. The author presents compelling evidence of persistent prejudice and discrimination in American society and the often subtle, but no less compelling, everyday racism faced by various groups of color.

LAUFMAN, NATALIE HEVENER. 2002. *Globalization and Children.* New York: Springer-Verlag. Experts from a variety of disciplines examine how global changes are affecting the everyday lives of children and the kinds of strategies that would advance their well-being.

MICKELSON, ROSLYN, ED. 2000. *Children on the Streets of the Americas: Globalization, Homelessness and Education in the United States, Brazil, and Cuba.* New York: Routledge. The contributors to this volume provide insight into why the number of street children is increasing in the midst of prosperity, give glimpses into the devastating lives they lead, and suggest the kinds of programs most likely to serve their needs.

STEINBERG, GAIL, AND BETH HALL. 2000. *Inside Transracial Adoption.* Indianapolis, IN: Perspective Press. The authors, both adoptive moms, tackle the challenges, emotions, responsibilities, and joys of transracial adoptions and insist that adoptive parents face the realities of racism in the United States.

FILM

Tsotsi. 2006. Orphaned at a young age, Tsotsi, whose nickname means "thug," struggles to survive in a bleak world of crime and poverty in South Africa. One night he steals a car and discovers an infant in the back seat, eventually finding a chance for redemption.

War Tapes. 2006. Through the eyes and cameras of several members of the New Hampshire National Guard, we learn their stories, what it is like to be deployed in a war zone, and the impact their service has on their intimate relationships.

LITERARY

HOLTHE, TESS URIZA. 2002. *When the Elephants Dance.* New York: Crown. An interesting war story about the experience of the Japanese occupation of the Philippines during World War II from a variety of civilian perspectives. The novel centers on a small, mismatched group of families and neighbors who huddle in a cellar while Japanese occupiers terrorize and pillage above. Grounded in Philippine myth and culture, the novel conveys the terrifying experience of war, including the torture of civilians, especially children, and the equally horrendous experience of waiting for loved ones to return from war.

TERKEL, STUDS. 2001. *Will the Circle Be Unbroken? Reflections on Death, Rebirth and Hunger for a Faith.* New York: New Press. In the latest oral history by a Pulitzer Prize winner, 63 people share their feelings about faith and death in a readable and moving way.

INTERNET

www.who.int/en   The World Health Organization site contains excellent information on environmental, health, and human rights issues around the world and offers links to many governmental and nongovernmental sites that also deal with these issues.

www.globalissues.org   This Web site looks into global issues that affect everyone and attempts to show how most of them are interrelated. It provides links to news articles and Web sites on a variety of social issues, such as human rights, geopolitics, poverty and globalization, the economy, and the environment.

www.hsph.harvard.edu/globalworkingfamilies.index.html The Project on Global Working Families studies and documents how globalization of the economy affects parental working conditions and social supports, their impact on children's health and development, and the public and private policy solutions available.

www.worldfamilyorganization.org   The World Family Organization's goal is to promote policies to bring about better life conditions for all families. It is now part of the United Nations; it provides resources and links to other international organizations.

Appendix A

SEXUAL DYSFUNCTIONS

Sexual dysfunction is a broad term that includes a number of specific problems. We describe the most common sexual dysfunctions found among women and men, distinguishing them as much as possible along gender lines.

Sexual Dysfunctions in Women

The most common sexual dysfunctions found among women are related to penetration and orgasm.

Inhibited sexual excitement refers to a lack of erotic response or feeling during sexual activity. A woman who experiences inhibited sexual excitement does not show any of the physiological manifestations of arousal such as expansion of the vagina, nipple erection, or vaginal lubrication. Consequently, sexual intercourse might be uncomfortable or even painful. In some cases a woman may never have experienced arousal (a *primary* dysfunction). In other cases a woman may have experienced arousal in the past but is not currently experiencing it (a *secondary* dysfunction).

Anorgasmia refers to the inability of a woman to reach orgasm. Prior to 1970, this dysfunction along with several others was lumped under the term *frigidity*. There are many forms of anorgasmia. In *primary anorgasmia*, no matter what type of stimulation has been tried, a woman has never experienced orgasm. In *secondary anorgasmia*, a woman has been regularly orgasmic in the past but is not currently orgasmic. A third category, *situational anorgasmia*, describes a woman who experiences orgasm only under certain specific circumstances, such as in a hotel room but not in her own bedroom. Finally, *random anorgasmia* refers to a woman who has experienced orgasm in a variety of sexual activities but only on an infrequent basis.

The immediate cause of anorgasmia is an involuntary inhibition of the natural orgasmic reflex, but other factors can contribute to this condition, such as severe chronic illness, drug and alcohol abuse, hormonal deficiencies, diabetes, and various medications such as tranquilizers and blood pressure medications. In addition, social factors such as the double standard regarding the acceptability of sexual feelings in women and men can also contribute to anorgasmia. Some anorgasmic women find sexual activities pleasurable and satisfying even though they do not experience orgasm; others experience depression, a lack of self-esteem, or a sense of futility.

About 2 to 3 percent of adult women experience pain during penetration. *Vaginismus* is a condition in which the muscles around the outer part of the vagina contract involuntarily during penetration, closing the vagina almost totally. In most cases, vaginismus is specific to vaginal penetration and does not necessarily affect other aspects of a woman's sexual responsiveness. In some women, however, the same involuntary muscle spasms may occur in response to any attempt to enter the vagina. Therefore, foreplay, such as the insertion of a finger, or even gynecological exams will produce the involuntary spasms and vaginal closure.

Vaginismus may be caused by factors such as poor vaginal lubrication, the use of various drugs, some illnesses, vaginal infections, and pelvic disorders. Most often, however, it seems to be a result of psychological factors, for example, a strict religious upbringing, having been taught that sex is unpleasant and painful, fear of or hostility toward men, and psychological reactions to rape. Reactions by partners of a woman with vaginismus range from self-blame or passivity about sex to impatience, resentment, and open hostility. Sometimes vaginismus can be treated with simple relaxation exercises.

Another sexual dysfunction of women is *dyspareunia*, or painful intercourse, which can occur at any point during or immediately following intercourse. The pain of dyspareunia can range from burning sensations to sharp, searing pain or cramps and can occur in the vagina or in the pelvic region or abdomen. Although the exact incidence of dyspareunia is not known, it is estimated that approximately 15 percent of adult women experience painful intercourse a few times each year, and 1 to 2 percent experience it on a regular basis. The anxiety about the pain associated with intercourse can make a woman tense and decrease her sexual enjoyment or cause her to abstain altogether either from sexual intercourse or from all forms of sexual activity.

Finally, a very small number of women experience *rapid orgasm*, a condition in which a woman reaches orgasm too quickly. A minority of women who experience rapid orgasm lose interest in further sexual activity and may even find further activity to be physically uncomfortable. Most of these women, however, remain sexually aroused and interested, sometimes going on to have multiple orgasms. These women frequently view this condition as an asset rather than a liability. Sometimes the woman's partner will view this condition in personal terms, taking it to be symbolic of her or his unique lovemaking ability.

Sexual Dysfunctions in Men

The most common sexual dysfunctions among males are related to erection and ejaculation.

Erectile dysfunction refers to the condition in which a male cannot have or maintain an erection that is firm enough for coitus. Erectile dysfunction is sometimes referred to as *impotence* and can be classified as either *primary*, in which case a male has never experienced an erection that has been adequate enough to have sexual intercourse, or *secondary*, in which case a male has previously experienced one or more erections. Of the two, secondary erectile dysfunction is more common. Erectile dysfunction can occur at any age, and it takes many forms. In only a few cases is the man totally unable to have an erection. Usually the man has partial erections, but they are not firm enough for vaginal or anal insertion. In some cases, a man may be able to have an erection but only under certain conditions, such as during masturbation. Because losing or not having erections is so common among men, isolated incidents do *not* constitute a sexual dysfunction. Only when such incidents occur in at least 25 percent of a man's sexual activities is the man said to be experiencing secondary impotence.

Although some physical conditions can cause primary erectile dysfunction, most cases are caused by psychological conditions such as a high level of anxiety or stress, a highly religious upbringing, early homosexual experiences that led to feelings of guilt and confusion, or a single traumatic sexual intercourse experience. Secondary erectile dysfunction is also caused by a number of factors. In most cases it is brought on by some precipitating event such as fatigue, work pressure, financial problems, drug or alcohol abuse, depression, or arguments. Men react to erectile dysfunction in a number of ways, the most common of which is a feeling of dismay. The partner of a male with erectile dysfunction may blame herself or himself, thinking that she or he is not skilled enough to arouse the man's passion.

Premature ejaculation, or *rapid ejaculation*, is a common dysfunction in which a male reaches orgasm too quickly. In most cases, the male ejaculates just before or immediately after entering his partner. Because ejaculation is so rapid, stimulation of his partner does not occur. As a result, both partners are often dissatisfied. Some men are not bothered by ejaculating quickly, whereas others become embarrassed or frustrated, develop low self-esteem, or question their masculinity.

Premature ejaculation is believed to be the most common male sexual dysfunction, affecting an estimated 15 to 20 percent of men on a regular basis. Less than 20 percent of these men consider this condition to be problematic enough to seek therapy. The primary causes of premature ejaculation are psychological factors such as anxiety or early experiences with rushing through intercourse or other sexual activity for fear of being caught (for example, having sex in the backseat of a car).

Another sexual dysfunction for men is *inhibited male orgasm*, sometimes referred to as *retarded ejaculation*, in which a man is unable to ejaculate during sexual intercourse despite a firm erection. Although the muscle contractions of orgasm do not occur, fluid containing sperm may leave the penis and enter the vagina; thus, pregnancy is possible. As with erectile dysfunction, inhibited orgasm can be *primary*, in which a man has never ejaculated during coitus, or *secondary*, in which a man who has experienced ejaculation and orgasm in the past suddenly develops a problem. In both instances, ejaculation is often possible by masturbation or some other noncoital stimulation. Drug and alcohol use accounts for about 10 percent of cases of inhibited male orgasm. Inhibited male orgasm should be distinguished from *retrograde ejaculation*, a condition in which the bladder neck does not close off properly during orgasm, causing the semen to spurt backward into the bladder.

Another male dysfunction, *priapism*, is a condition in which the penis remains erect for prolonged periods of time. Priapism results from damage to valves that are supposed to regulate penile blood flow. Under this condition, erection can last for days, but it is generally not accompanied by a desire for sex. Prolonged erection can be painful as well as embarrassing for most men.

Finally, men, like women, can suffer from *painful intercourse*, or *dyspareunia*. Typically, the pain is felt in the penis. Some men, however, experience the pain in the testes or even internally, where it might be related to a problem with the prostate or seminal vesicles. Both physical and psychological factors can contribute to dyspareunia. Physical factors include inflammation or infection of the penis, testes, urethra, foreskin, or prostate. A few men experience pain if the tip of the penis is irritated by vaginal contraceptive foams or creams.

Sexually Transmitted Diseases

Sexually transmitted diseases (STDs) is a broad term used to describe a variety of bacterial, viral, yeast, and protozoan infections that are almost always transmitted by sexual contact and to refer to various other infections that are sometimes transmitted in nonsexual ways. In the past, many of these diseases were referred to as *venereal diseases*. Most STDs are transmitted through genital–genital, oral–genital, and anal–genital contact. Some STDs, such as AIDS and hepatitis B, however, can be transmitted through blood transfusions or the use of infected needles. In addition, as we pointed out in Chapter 9, some STDs can also be passed from the mother to the fetus through the placenta and from the mother to the newborn as it passes through the birth canal.

STDs vary greatly in terms of their symptoms, progressions, treatments, seriousness, and outcomes. Most STDs can be prevented with proper care and can be cured with drugs. Being cured does not mean that a person cannot contract the same STD again at a later time. In addition, it is possible for a person to contract more than one STD at a time. In this appendix we present some of the most common STDs: chlamydia, gonorrhea, syphilis, genital herpes, papilloma, hepatitis B, trichomoniasis, moniliasis, lymphogranuloma venereum, and chancroid. A full discussion of AIDS appears in Chapter 6.

Chlamydia is probably the most common sexually transmitted disease in this country. It affects between 3 million and 4 million people every year. Chlamydial infections are caused by a bacterium (*Chlamydia trachomatis*) that attacks the reproductive system. The majority of infected females and about one-third of infected males experience no symptoms. In the other two-thirds of males, symptoms include a whitish discharge from the penis. Sometimes infected females or males experience a mild irritation of the genitals and an itching or burning sensation during urination. Because chlamydia has symptoms similar to gonorrhea, it sometimes goes undetected. Untreated, it can result in sterility in both females and males, pelvic inflammatory disease (PID), infection of the uterus and tubes, infections in newborns, miscarriages, and stillbirths (Allgeier and Allgeier, 1988). Chlamydia can be cured with antibiotics such as tetracycline.

Gonorrhea is a highly infectious disease that can affect the genitourinary tract, tissues of the genitals, fallopian tubes, rectum, and cervix. It can also occur in other areas of the body such as the mouth, throat, and eyes. Gonorrhea is caused by the bacterium *Neisseria gonorrhoeae*. It can be transmitted by any form of sexual contact ranging from sexual intercourse to fellatio, anal intercourse, and, in rare cases, cunnilingus and kissing. It is almost always transmitted through sexual intercourse, however, because the bacterium cannot live more than a few seconds outside the human body. It generally takes from 2 to 7 days after contact with an infected person for symptoms to appear. A woman who has intercourse once with an infected male runs a 50 percent risk of contracting gonorrhea, whereas a man who has intercourse once with an infected female runs only about a 20 to 25 percent risk of contracting the disease.

Symptoms in women include a yellowish green vaginal discharge, pain in the abdominal area, burning during urination, fever, abnormal menstrual bleeding, and pain in the stomach. In males, symptoms include a thick yellowish green discharge from the penis, inflammation of the tip of the penis, burning during urination, and the appearance of pus or blood in the urine. As with chlamydia, many males and the majority of females show no symptoms during the early stages of the disease. When left untreated, gonorrhea can cause considerable damage to a person's reproductive capabilities, possibly causing sterility. It can also cause PID, heart disease, arthritis, and blindness. Gonorrhea can be cured with antibiotics, the most effective of which is penicillin G.

Syphilis is a chronic infectious disease caused by a type of bacterium known as a spirochete. Because the bacterium generally dies within seconds outside the body, it is usually transmitted through sexual intercourse, but it can also be contracted from a blood transfusion, or it can be transmitted from a mother to the fetus. Syphilis progresses through three stages of increasing severity: the primary, secondary, and tertiary stages. If allowed to run its full course, syphilis can cause paralysis, blindness, heart disease, nervous disorders, insanity, and even death. The incubation period for syphilis is 10 to 90 days.

Primary stage. Between 2 and 4 weeks after infection a hard, crusty, painless oval sore called a *chancre* appears on the vaginal wall, cervix, penis, scrotum, anus, tongue, lips, or throat. It begins as a dull red spot that develops first into a pimple and then into the chancre. If immediate attention is not given to these symptoms they may disappear, but this does not mean that the syphilis has cured itself. The syphilis remains, and after several months the symptoms of the secondary stage appear.

Secondary stage. The secondary stage begins anywhere from 1 week to 6 months after the chancre heals if it has been untreated. In this phase, a person may experience reddish patches in the mouth and around the genitals that emit a clear liquid and are highly infectious. Other symptoms include a nonitching rash, sore throat, fever, headaches, and weight and hair loss. These symptoms can last from 3 to 6 months, but, as in the primary stage, they may disappear if they are not treated. For some people, these symptoms will appear and disappear many times if untreated. Between 50 and 70 percent of people with untreated syphilis remain in this stage for the rest of their lives. In the remaining cases, syphilis resurfaces after a latency period that can last for many years.

Tertiary stage. In this stage a number of more serious symptoms appear. Some people develop ulcers in the eyes, liver, lungs, or digestive tract. A few people suffer damage to the brain and spinal cord, which can result in paralysis, dementia, or fatal heart damage. Pregnant women with syphilis almost always pass it on to their offspring, who may be born blind, deaf, or deformed, or may die soon after birth.

Penicillin is the best treatment for syphilis and is effective at all stages of the disease. Although existing damage cannot be reversed, penicillin can prevent further damage.

The term *herpes* refers to any one of several viral diseases characterized by the eruption of blisters of the skin or mucous membrane. One type, *genital herpes*, received widespread attention in the 1980s as a result of its epidemic spread. Genital herpes is caused by the herpes simplex virus types 1 and 2. Genital herpes is usually transmitted by sexual contact but can also be transmitted by kissing or by touching your genitals after putting your fingers in your mouth. The incubation period for genital herpes is 2 to 6 days after being infected. Symptoms of the infection are similar for women and men. The first signs are itching, irritation, and a rash at the site of the infection. Other fairly common symptoms include pain or burning during urination, discharge from the urethra or vagina, soreness and swelling of lymph nodes in the groin, fever, weakness, and fatigue. Symptomatic blisters usually occur on the penis, scrotum, anus, vulva, clitoris, cervix, or mouth. These blisters are extremely painful and, over time, will rupture and eventually heal themselves even without treatment.

As with syphilis, the disappearance of the blisters does not mean that the virus is no longer in the body. Instead, the virus is still present, and blistering can recur at any time. Untreated, genital herpes can increase the risk of cervical cancer in women and can spread to women's and men's eyes from the hands. Women, more often than men, also develop aseptic meningitis, an inflammation of the covering of the brain. Pregnant women with herpes are likely to pass it on to their offspring, who might suffer blindness, brain damage, or even death. There is no cure for genital herpes, nor is there a single effective treatment. A drug called acyclovir is useful in lessening the severity of the symptoms. People with herpes should avoid having sexual contact during periods when the blisters are apparent.

Papilloma, or venereal warts, is one of the fastest-growing STDs. Venereal warts are dry, often painless, grayish white warts with a cauliflowerlike surface that grow on, inside, or near the genitals or anus. These warts are caused by a sexually transmitted virus and are not always visible. There may be one or a cluster of warts, and they may coexist with other STDs. Venereal warts may cause pain during sex and may multiply during pregnancy. If untreated, venereal warts increase the risk of cervical cancer in women and penile cancer in men. There is no known cure for venereal warts. They can, however, be treated with liquid nitrogen or podophyllin ointment, or they can be burned off surgically.

Hepatitis B is one of three main types of viral hepatitis (the other two are hepatitis A, and non-A, non-B hepatitis). It is a viral infection of the liver and varies in terms of seriousness from mild symptoms such as poor appetite or indigestion, to diarrhea, vomiting, fever, and fatigue; to more serious medical problems such as jaundiced skin and eyes. Although hepatitis B is generally transmitted through blood or blood products, many Americans contract the disease through sexual contact. Hepatitis B can also be spread by saliva, vaginal secretions, seminal fluid, and other body fluids. Many people with hepatitis B remain in a carrier state for years or even a lifetime. Hepatitis B increases the risk of liver cancer and other liver diseases.

Trichomoniasis is caused by a one-celled protozoan, *Trichomonas vaginalis*, that thrives and grows rapidly in moist, warm tissues such as the vagina and the urethra. The disease is most common among women. As many as 25 percent of women will probably contract trichomoniasis at some point. Trichomoniasis has probably received the least attention of all STDs. In fact, because it can be transmitted in many different ways besides sexual contact, some experts in the field do not consider it an STD.

Among women symptoms are generally a foul-smelling, foamy, yellowish green vaginal discharge accompanied by vaginal itching and irritation. In addition, sexual intercourse may be painful. Men experience itching, pain in the urethra, and a slight discharge similar to that caused by gonorrhea. Most infected people do not exhibit symptoms, however. Although lack of treatment does not carry any serious consequences, it does make control of the spread of trichomoniasis difficult. Trichomoniasis is commonly treated with the drug metronidazole, which is about 80 percent effective in both women and men.

Moniliasis, like trichomoniasis, is an infection that can be contracted through both sexual and nonsexual contact. Sometimes referred to as a *yeast infection*, moniliasis is caused by the fungus *Candida albicans*. Women and men seldom exhibit symptoms of this infection. When it invades the vaginal area of women, however, it sometimes produces a lumpy, white discharge that resembles cottage cheese. There is also itching and inflammation of the vaginal area, and intercourse becomes extremely painful. If untreated, moniliasis does not produce any serious complications, but it is extremely uncomfortable and severely limits sexual activity. It is generally treated with vaginal creams or suppositories that contain the drug nyastatin, but the infection can and does recur repeatedly with some women.

Lymphogranuloma venereum (LGV) is a bacterial infection caused by *Chlamydia trachomatis*, which invades the lymph system, a network of vessels in close contact with blood vessels. Of Asian origin, this disease was almost nonexistent in the United States before the Vietnam War. The first symptom of LGV is a small blister that usually appears on the external genitals between 5 and 21 days after contact. Sometimes, however, the blister appears inside the vagina or the urethra. The blister usually heals itself within a few days, but the disease moves on and settles in the lymph glands nearest the infected site. The glands swell and form a painful sausage-shaped mass that settles within the fold of the groin. Other symptoms are similar to those of the flu, including chills, fever, headache, pain in the joints, and upset stomach. If untreated, LGV can produce serious effects, including swelling of the inguinal (groin) lymph nodes, penis, labia or clitoris, and closure of the rectum. Although the disease is curable, treatment is often difficult because the infection responds very slowly to antibiotics. The most effective forms of treatment seem to be tetracycline and sulfa drugs.

Chancroid, like LGV, is a tropical bacterial infection that is usually transmitted by sexual intercourse, although it also can be contracted through less intimate contact. Chancroid is caused by the bacterium *Haemophilus ducreyi* and is particularly contagious if there are breaks or cuts in the skin. The primary symptom of chancroid is one or more ulcerated sores that appear on the genitals 3 to 7 days after exposure. In the beginning the sores appear as pimplelike bumps, that eventually burst into very painful and open sores that bleed easily. The lymph glands in the groin area may also become swollen, and in some cases the sores may spread over the entire genital area. If the disease is left untreated, chancroid gangrene can occur. Chancroid can be cured within a short period of time with tetracycline or sulfa drugs.

Appendix B

FEMALE INTERNAL ANATOMY AND PHYSIOLOGY

The parts of a woman's anatomy that are critical to reproduction are internal and include the vagina, ovaries, paired fallopian tubes, uterus, and cervix. Figure B.1 shows the female reproductive system and the major structures of the uterus.

Leading from the vaginal opening to inside the woman's body is the *vagina*, a thin-walled elastic structure 3 to 4 inches long. The vagina functions in a number of ways: It receives the penis during heterosexual intercourse and serves as a depository for sperm during intercourse, as a passageway for menstrual flow, and as the birth canal.

The female body contains two *ovaries*, almond-shaped structures that lie on each side of the uterus. The ovaries produce ova (eggs) and the hormones estrogen and progesterone. Ova are embedded in follicles near the surfaces of ovaries; each follicle contains one ovum. A female is born with about 400,000 immature eggs. Only about 400 of these eggs mature and are released over the course of a woman's fertile years, however. More specifically, each month during a woman's reproductive years one or the other ovary releases one (or infrequently more than one) egg on a day approximately midway between the menstrual periods into the abdominal cavity, a process known as *ovulation*.

Following ovulation the egg begins to migrate toward the *fallopian tubes*, small structures extending 4 inches laterally from each side of the uterus to the ovaries. Hairlike projections called *fimbria* at the end of the fallopian tubes create currents with lashing movements that draw eggs into and down through the tube. Fertilization generally occurs inside the fallopian tubes at the end closest to the ovaries.

Once fertilized, the egg continues its journey through the fallopian tube and into the *uterus*, or *womb*. The uterus is a hollow, pear-shaped organ, approximately 3 inches long and 3 inches wide, composed of three alternating layers of muscle: endometrium, myometrium, and perimetrium. The endometrium—the innermost layer—is rich in blood vessels after ovulation. If fertilization does not occur, the endometrium sloughs off and is discharged from the body during menstruation. If the egg is fertilized, it implants in the endometrium, where it develops, is nourished, and grows for approximately 9 months.

At the lower end of the uterus is the *cervix*, a narrow opening leading into the vagina. At birth, the baby forces itself through the cervix and the vagina to the outside world.

MALE INTERNAL ANATOMY AND PHYSIOLOGY

Male reproductive organs can be found both within and outside the body (see Figure B.2). The external organs (testes, scrotum, penis) are important in both sexual arousal and gratification as well as reproduction. The internal reproductive system includes the seminal vesicles, prostate gland, vas deferens, seminiferous tubules, Cowper's glands, urethra, epididymis, and interstitial cells.

The *testes* (*testicles*), the primary reproductive organs in males, produce both the spermatozoa necessary for reproduction and male hormones, primarily testosterone. Each testicle consists of three sets of tissue that come together to form a tube: seminiferous tubules, where sperm are produced; epididymis, where sperm are stored; and interstitial cells, where the male sex hormones are produced. From the testes the sperm travel through a duct system (epididymis, vas deferens, ejaculatory duct, and urethra) until they are expelled from the penis during ejaculation.

If ejaculation occurs, sperm leave the testes through the second part of the duct, two small tubes called the *vas deferens*, which lead from the testes to the prostate gland, where they form the urethra. Contractions during ejaculation send the sperm into the two *ejaculatory ducts* that run through the prostate gland. After mixing with seminal fluid to form semen, sperm are propelled through the *urethra*, the tube through which males urinate and through which sperm leave the body.

Three male organs play key roles in helping the sperm move through the reproductive system to the penis and outside the body: the seminal vesicles, the prostate gland, and the Cowper's glands. The *seminal vesicles*, two small organs located behind the bladder, secrete fluids, many of which come from the prostate gland. These fluids add volume to the semen. The *prostate gland*, located under the bladder, where the vas deferens meet, adds an alkaline fluid to semen that protects the sperm. During orgasm it contracts, helping the semen to move out of the urethra. Located just below the prostate gland are two glands called *Cowper's glands*, or *bulbourethral glands*. These tiny glands produce an alkaline fluid that prolongs the life of sperm.

532

FIGURE B.1

FEMALE REPRODUCTIVE SYSTEM (ABOVE) AND MAJOR STRUCTURES OF THE UTERUS (RIGHT)

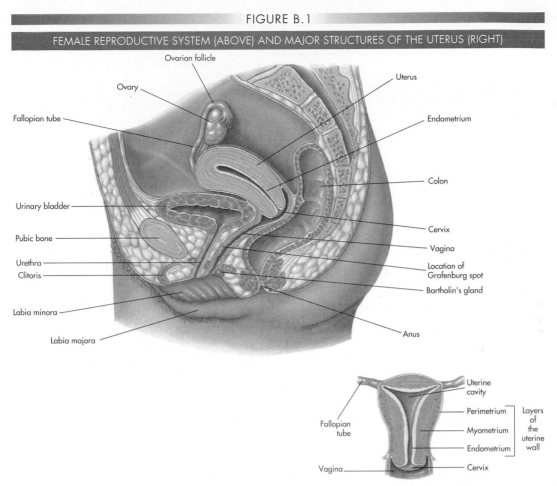

Source: Adapted from Frederic Martini, *Fundamentals of Anatomy and Physiology,* 2nd ed. Englewood Cliffs, NJ: Prentice Hall, 1992. Drawings by William C. Ober, M.D., and Claire W. Garrison, R.N.

FIGURE B.2

MALE REPRODUCTIVE SYSTEM AND STRUCTURES OF THE SCROTUM(RIGHT)

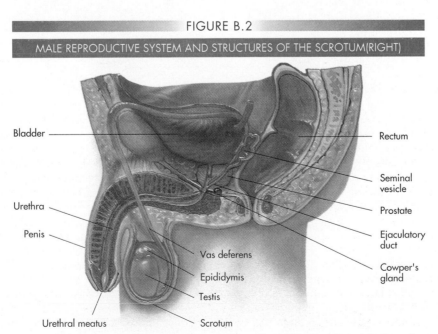

Source: Adapted from Frederic Martini, *Fundamentals of Anatomy and Physiology,* 2nd ed. Englewood Cliffs, NJ: Prentice Hall, 1992. Drawing by Craig Luce.

CONCEPTION, PREGNANCY, AND CHILDBIRTH

Conception, pregnancy, and childbirth are profound events. When female ovum and male sperm unite, conception occurs, marking the beginning of pregnancy. During the course of a pregnancy a woman's body experiences a number of internal and external changes as she carries a developing embryo and later fetus within her uterus. By the end of the fourth month of pregnancy, most women begin to "show" (their stomach swells as the fetus develops and grows) and can feel the fetus moving. Once the fetus is ready for birth it will turn its body so that its head is downward toward the cervix. Figure B.3 illustrates the various stages of labor and delivery. In most cases, the fetus is expelled from the uterus without complications.

FIGURE B.3

LABOR AND DELIVERY

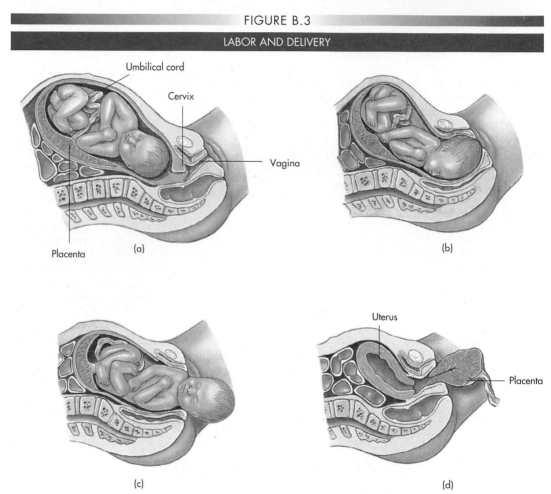

Source: Adapted from Frederic Martini, *Fundamentals of Anatomy and Physiology,* 2nd ed. Englewood Cliffs, NJ: Prentice Hall, 1992, p. 977, Figure 29–14.

Appendix C

Approximately one-third of all reported abortions are spontaneous (miscarriages), whereby the developing embryo or fetus is expelled from the uterus naturally. Spontaneous abortions are triggered by many factors: emotional shock, abnormal development of the fetus, wearing an intrauterine (IUD) while pregnant, and other problems that prevent further development of the fetus. Abortions can also be induced through medication or surgery.

MEDICATION-INDUCED ABORTIONS

Medication abortion (also called medical abortion, pharmacological abortion, RU-486, and the abortion pill) uses pharmacological agents, such as mifepristone and misoprostol, usually during the first 9 weeks of pregnancy. Used in combination, these medications stimulate uterine contractions and cause expulsion of the pregnancy. RU-486, developed in France, has been used successfully by millions of women worldwide. Protests against the drug by antiabortion groups delayed its testing in the United States until 1993. Although approved by the Food and Drug Administration in 2000, the drug remains controversial and its use has been greatly restricted. Most women undergoing medication abortion experience some amount of abdominal cramping and bleeding. Other possible side effects, depending on dosage and route of administration, include vomiting, nausea, diarrhea, chills, and fever.

SURGERY-INDUCED ABORTION

Abortion in the early stages of pregnancy is a relatively simple and safe procedure, although any surgical procedure runs some risk and can have varying degrees of discomfort. The most common surgical methods of abortion in the first trimester are dilation and curettage and vacuum aspiration. Dilation and evacuation and hysterotomy are the methods used in second-trimester abortions.

Vacuum Aspiration Used early in a pregnancy, this procedure, also known as suction curettage, is performed under local anesthesia, often in a doctor's office. The cervix is dilated (made larger) with a series of instruments. A tube is inserted into the uterus connected to a strong vacuum. The embryo is removed by suction. Over the next few days the woman may experience some cramping and bleeding. She is advised not to use tampons or have sexual intercourse for a week or two after the procedure.

Dilation and Curettage (D&C) This procedure is used later in the first trimester; it is the same technique used after miscarriages. The cervix is dilated, after which a curette (a spoon-shaped surgical instrument) is used to scrape the uterine wall. This procedure is usually done in a hospital, with the woman under local or general anesthesia. Some women experience pain and bleeding after this procedure, but full recovery occurs within 10 to 14 days; women are advised to abstain from sexual intercourse for several weeks.

Dilation and Evacuation (D&E) Similar to a D&C, this procedure is performed later in the pregnancy, usually between the thirteenth and sixteenth weeks. Local or general anesthesia is used. Because the pregnancy is more advanced and the fetus is larger, the cervix requires more dilation, and the uterine contents are removed through a combination of suction equipment, special forceps, and scraping with a curette. Women may experience cramping and blood loss after undergoing a D&E.

Hysterotomy Performed in the second trimester, this procedure is similar to a Cesarean section; an incision is made into the woman's abdomen and the fetus is removed. Hospitalization is required. Hysterotomy carries the most risk and therefore is rarely used.

Intact Dialation and Extraction (D&X) The most controversial method of abortion, usually performed in the fifth or sixth month, involves removing the fetus intact by dilating a pregnant woman's cervix, then pulling the entire body out through the birth canal. The National Right to Life Committee coined the term "partial-birth" abortion and lobbied Congress to pass legislation outlawing the procedure, which it did in 2003. President Bush signed the bill, which was immediately appealed. Proponents argue the procedure may be necessary to safeguard the health of the mother; opponents argue that it amounts to killing the fetus. There is currently no statistical information available on why D&X abortions are performed or on how many actually take place. Three different appeals courts at the federal level have ruled the prohibition unconstitutional. The Supreme Court has agreed to hear arguments and is expected to issue an opinion in the case in the summer of 2007.

Appendix D

Avoiding sexual intercourse is the surest, safest, and most cost-effective way to prevent pregnancy. Many sex education programs aimed at adolescents stress abstinence as a way to avoid both pregnancy and sexually transmitted diseases, including AIDS. However, abstinence is not a popular choice with people who desire a mutually satisfying sexual relationship but do not want children. The following section examines the birth control techniques that are legally available to couples living in the United States.

Sterilization

Surgical sterilization runs a close second to abstinence in both reliability and, if a long-term view is taken, cost-effectiveness. This is now the most popular form of birth control among married couples in the United States. Traditional female sterilization, called *tubal ligation*, is the procedure by which a woman's fallopian tubes are cut and tied, thus preventing passage of the egg, which disintegrates and is discharged during menstruation. The procedure is performed by laparoscopy, whereby a laparoscope (a thin instrument with a viewing lens) is inserted through a small incision in the abdomen. Using this incision or a tiny second one, the surgeon inserts another small instrument that cauterizes the interior of the fallopian tubes. A new procedure, *Essure*, provides an alternative to tubal ligation and surgery. Approved by the Federal Drug Administration in 2002, after being used successfully in other countries, Essure is made of a flexible device called a micro-insert that is inserted into the fallopian tubes, where body tissue will then grow into it, causing blockage in the fallopian tubes. This prevents fertilization by blocking the sperm from reaching an egg. Most women can return to normal activities within 24 to 48 hours after undergoing the procedure. It has been found to be more than 99 percent effective in preventing pregnancy in the first 3 years of use. The most common side effects are light bleeding, mild cramping, nausea, and vomiting following the insertion procedure. It is not reversible.

Male sterilization is called a *vasectomy*. During the procedure small incisions are made on each side of the scrotum, and then the vas deferens is tied off and cut, preventing passage of sperm through the male's reproductive tract. This procedure does not prevent sperm production.

Rather, when sperm are produced, instead of being ejaculated they are absorbed in the man's body. Discomfort is minimal. However, live sperm remain in parts of the reproductive system for several weeks after the vasectomy, so to be safe a couple should use an additional form of contraception. This other form of contraception can be eliminated once the semen is examined and found to be sperm free. Many insurance policies cover both female and male sterilization. Sterilization has several clear advantages. Once it is done, no further thought need be given to the task of prevention. It is 100 percent effective, except in rare instances when the procedures have not been performed properly. Most women and men who have undergone sterilization report little or no decrease in sexual desire or sexual pleasure. Some even report more enjoyment after the fear of pregnancy is removed. Sterilization has the added advantage of not interfering with sexual spontaneity. Sterilization has certain drawbacks, however. A small percentage of women and men experience some psychological problems after sterilization, equating their loss of fertility with diminished feelings of femininity and masculinity.

Oral Contraceptives ("The Pill")

The birth control pill, available since the early 1960s, is the most popular type of contraceptive. Pills come in packs of 21 or 28 pills. There are two basic types—combination pills (synthetic estrogen and progestin) and progestin-only pills. Combination pills work by preventing a woman's ovaries from releasing eggs and by thickening the cervical mucus, which inhibits sperm from joining with an egg. Progestin-only pills work by thickening the cervical mucus. Taking the pill daily maintains the level of hormone needed to prevent pregnancy. The advantages of the pill are its convenience, its noninterference with spontaneity during intercourse, and its high rate of effectiveness (95 to 98 percent) when used correctly. Additionally, many women report reduced premenstrual tension and cramps and lighter blood flows during menstruation. Birth control pills are available only with a doctor's prescription. A woman's medical history may rule out use of the Pill. Women suffering from hypertension, poor blood circulation, and other risk factors should not take the Pill because of the danger of blood clots and high blood pressure. Side effects may include nausea, breast tenderness, weight gains due to water retention, migraine headaches, mood changes, and an increased tendency to develop yeast infections.

Morning-After Pill (See the Debating Social Policy box in Chapter 7).

Hormonal Methods: Implants, Patches, and Injections

Implanon is a matchstick-size device that health care providers inject into the underside of a woman's arm, where it releases a continuous dosage of the synthetic hormone progestin over a 3-year period. It stops ovaries from releasing eggs and thickens cervical mucus, preventing sperm from fertilizing any released egg. It is 99 percent effective. Its major side effect is irregular menstrual cycles. Implanon does not affect long-term fertility. When the implant is removed, pregnancy can result within a month. Used successfully in Europe since 1998, Implanon was approved for use in the United States in 2006 and will be available by 2007. It replaces Norplant, which was removed from the U.S. market in 2002 after numerous lawsuits were filed against the manufacturer. The *Ortho Evra Contraceptive Patch* is a new hormonal alternative to the birth control pill. This thin patch is placed on the body once a week for 3 weeks and then removed for 1 week to allow for a menstrual period. Hormones are continuously released through the skin into the bloodstream, thereby preventing pregnancy. It has a 99 percent effective rate but requires a prescription. The side effects are similar to the birth control pill.

Depo-Provera injection, popularly known as "the Shot," contains synthetic progesterone that blocks ovulation. It is injected into the buttocks every 3 months and it is 99 percent effective. Although some women experience irregular bleeding during the first year of use, most women stop menstruating entirely after a year. Depo-Provera has a number of beneficial effects: it relieves some of the discomfort associated with premenstrual syndrome and decreases the risk of inflammatory disease and yeast infections. Side effects include menstrual irregularities, fatigue, dizziness, and headaches. A similar injection, *Lunelle*, is given once a month, every 28 to 30 days. The shot must be given in a physician's office. Like Depo-Provera, Lunelle is 99 percent effective. It may cause spotting and bleeding.

Intrauterine Device

An IUD is a T-shaped device made of flexible plastic that is inserted into the uterus through the cervical opening. If inserted improperly, it can pierce the uterine wall and cause serious injury. For this reason, an IUD should be inserted only by a medical practitioner. Two types of IUDs are currently available in the United States. *Para Gard* contains copper and can be left in place for 12 years. *Mirena* releases a low dose of progesterone into the uterus, causing the lining to thin, and is effective for up to five years. Both work by preventing sperm from joining with an egg. This process is seen by some critics as equivalent to abortion and therefore morally objectionable. Small strings are left in the vagina to allow women to check to see if the IUD is still in place. Spontaneous expulsions occur in about 10 percent of users, primarily during menstruation, so periodic checking is important. The IUD is 99 percent effective, requires little care, is reversible, and does not interfere with sexual spontaneity. Side effects include spotting, backaches, and infection.

Barrier Devices

Male condoms have been around since the early Romans used a condom made of animal intestine and bladder. The condoms used today consist of a thin cover of latex rubber (recommended) or processed sheep's intestine (not recommended because they are porous and can be penetrated by HIV and other viruses) that is placed over the erect penis by either partner to prevent the sperm from entering the vagina. Condoms come in different sizes and colors. They are convenient (can be carried in a wallet or purse) and can be purchased over the counter in drugstores and supermarkets. Condoms are about 90 to 98 percent effective, depending on use. Latex condoms protect against various sexually transmitted diseases, including AIDS. The drawback to the condom is that it is put on after the man is aroused but before he enters his partner. Because sexual activity must be interrupted to do this, some couples neglect or forget to put it on. Some men complain that condoms interfere with sensation and spontaneity. Also, condoms can tear or slip off when in use and must be carefully removed after intercourse to avoid spilling the ejaculate.

The *female condom* is a 7-inch-long lubricated, thin, polyurethane pouch with an inner and outer ring. The inner ring fits over the cervix, like a diaphragm; the outer ring covers part of the vulva. The female condom has several advantages over the male condom. It tears less, and there is less chance of exposure to semen. Like the latex male condom, it can prevent the spread of sexually transmitted diseases, including AIDS. However, some couples find the pouch less spontaneous and somewhat comical. It is 85 to 95 percent effective. It may cause vaginal irritation.

Another barrier device, the *diaphragm*, originated in Western Europe as early as 1600 when women used scooped-out halves of lemons and pomegranates to prevent pregnancy. The modern diaphragm is a flexible, dome-shaped rubber cup inserted into the vagina to cover the mouth of the cervix. A *cervical cap* is a thimble-shaped device, similar to a diaphragm in appearance and function but considerably smaller. Either method can be inserted up to 6 hours before intercourse and must not be removed until at least 6 hours after ejaculation. It is recommended that both of these methods be used with contraceptive creams and jellies. Both methods block sperm from entering the uterus and fertilizing the egg. Both methods require a prescription after an internal pelvic examination. To be effective both must be properly fitted to conform to a woman's vaginal opening, and to ensure proper fit they should be checked every 2 years or after childbirth, an abortion, or significant weight changes. A woman (or her partner) inserts the diaphragm or cervical cap before having sex. The diaphragm is about 81 to 95 percent effective and the cervical cap is 82 to 94 percent effective. Both are reversible methods and neither interferes with a woman's hormonal system. Although there are few side effects, some women develop bladder infections or experience

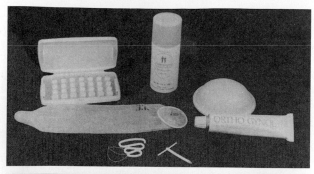

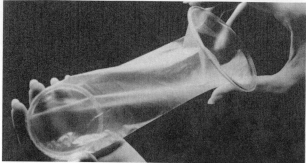

Birth control devices include IUDs, male and female condoms, oral contraceptives, and diaphragms.

a mild allergic reaction to the rubber, cream, or jelly. Some women see these methods as messy, and some feel that the required preparation takes away from spontaneity.

The newest entry to barrier methods is the *Lea Shield*, which is similar to the diaphragm and cervical cap. This dome-shaped, reusable, silicone device covers the cervix, and prevents the sperm and egg from joining. It can be inserted hours before intercourse and is to be left in place for at least 8 hours after ejaculation. When used with spermicide, it is 79 to 92 percent effective. Women do not need to have the Lea's contraceptive fitted by a doctor as one size fits all and it can be bought over the counter at most pharmacies. Some women have found it uncomfortable to insert and some men complain they can feel it during intercourse.

A *contraceptive sponge* is a small disposable polyurethane device, containing spermicide. The sponge fits over the cervix, blocking and killing sperm. It can be inserted hours before intercourse and needs to be left in at least 6 hours after intercourse (for a maximum of up to 12 hours after being inserted). It is 72 to 82 percent effective, easily available (no prescription is needed), and convenient. The sponge cannot be used during menstruation. If left in for more than 12 hours, women can develop toxic shock syndrome; some women are allergic to the spermicide contained in the sponge.

Spermicides

A variety of chemical sperm-killing agents called spermicides (foams, creams, jellies, suppositories, tablets, and contraceptive film) can be purchased over the counter. They are more effective when used with a barrier method, but they can be used alone. They are inserted into the vagina and when used alone have an effectiveness of 79 percent. They are safe,

simple to use, and reversible. However, some users complain of irritation and burning sensations, and some find them messy. Because they must be used shortly before intercourse, couples sometimes feel they interrupt the sexual mood.

Fertility Awareness

Fertility awareness, also called natural family planning because it uses no mechanical or hormonal barriers to conception, makes use of the recurring pattern of fertile and infertile phases of a woman's body during the menstrual cycle. The goal of fertility awareness methods is to predict these phases so that couples can abstain from sexual activity during the fertile period. To determine the "safe" days, it is necessary to determine the time of ovulation. This can be done in several ways: (1) The rhythm method uses a calendar calculation of unsafe days based on the length of a woman's menstrual cycle. (2) The basal body temperature (BBT) method calculates temperature change. A woman's temperature dips slightly just before ovulation and increases after ovulation. (3) The cervical mucus method, also called the Billings or ovulation method, examines the change in appearance and consistency of cervical mucus. The general pattern moves from no visible mucus for several days after menstruation to whitish, sticky mucus, then to clear and slippery mucus during ovulation, and then back to a cloudy discharge when ovulation ends. (4) The symptothermal method is a combination of the BBT and mucus methods. This method is the most successful because it uses two indicators of fertility rather than one.

All of these methods are designed to help women check changing body signs so that they will know when ovulation occurs. The effectiveness of these methods thus depends on a woman's knowledge of her reproductive cycle as well as the couple's self-control (abstinence) during fertile periods. Although it is difficult to ascertain exactly when ovulation occurs, when these methods are used diligently they have a high effectiveness rate. However, risk taking during the fertile phase contributes to a fairly high failure rate. These methods are acceptable to most religious groups. There are no side effects. However, couples may experience frustration during periods of abstinence, which can last from 7 to 14 days.

Withdrawal (Coitus Interruptus)

The withdrawal of the penis from the vagina prior to ejaculation can be an attractive form of contraception because it is simple, it does not require any devices, and it is free. Unfortunately, it also does not work very well. Withdrawal requires great control by the man, and it may limit sexual gratification for one or both partners. In addition, leakage of semen can occur prior to ejaculation.

Douching

Douching, or washing out the vagina, is another old but unreliable method of birth control. Douching after intercourse may actually push some sperm toward the cervix. In addition, douching can lead to pelvic inflammatory disease.

Future Contraceptive Strategies

Research to find safer, more effective, and less expensive methods of birth control is underway in many countries. For example, doctors in India are developing a birth control vaccine for women that would be effective for a year. Preliminary testing is encouraging, but the vaccine will not be available for several years. Most contraceptive research remains centered on the woman's reproductive system. However, some researchers are now investigating a male contraceptive pill that would inhibit sperm production.

CAUTION: Most of these contraceptive devices, when used alone, do not protect against sexually transmitted infections. Therefore, it is a good idea to use a latex condom in conjunction with these other devices.

Glossary

ABORTION The termination of a pregnancy before the fetus can survive on its own. This can occur either spontaneously (miscarriage) or be induced through a variety of external methods.

ACHIEVED STATUS A position we hold in society by virtue of our own efforts, for example, that of teacher or mother.

ACQUAINTANCE RAPE Sexual assault by a person with whom the victim is familiar.

ACQUIRED IMMUNE DEFICIENCY SYNDROME (AIDS) A viral syndrome that destroys the body's immune system.

ADULTERY Extramarital sexual intercourse.

AFFINAL RELATIVES People related by marriage and not by blood, for example, a brother- or sister-in-law.

AGAPE (pronounced "ah GAH pay") A style of loving that combiness eros and storge, is selfless and giving, expecting nothing in return.

AGEISM The application of negative stereotypes and discriminatory treatment to elderly people.

AGE NORMS The expectations of how one is to behave at specific ages in the life cycle.

AGENTS OF SOCIALIZATION Individuals, groups, and institutions that help form an individual's attitudes, behaviors, and self-concepts.

ALCOHOLISM A chronic behavioral disorder manifested by repeated drinking of alcoholic beverages in excess of the dietary and social uses of the community and to the extent that it interferes with the drinker's health or social and economic functioning.

ALIMONY Court-ordered financial support paid to a former spouse following a divorce.

AMNIOCENTESIS A prenatal test in which a needle is inserted into the mother's uterus to collect cells cast off by the fetus for the purpose of testing for genetic diseases or defects in the fetus.

ANDROGYNOUS Expressing a wide range of attitudes and behaviors with no gender role differentiation. Androgyny is the combination of both culturally defined feminine and masculine traits in an individual.

ANNULMENT A legal declaration that a marriage never existed, leaving both parties free to marry.

ANTICIPATORY SOCIALIZATION Socialization directed toward learning future roles.

ANTINATALIST FORCES Policies or practices that discourage people from having children.

ARTIFICIAL INSEMINATION The injection of sperm into the vagina or uterus of an ovulating woman.

ASCRIBED STATUS A position we hold in society because we were born into it, for example, that of being female or male.

ASSISTED REPRODUCTIVE TECHNOLOGY (ART) A general term that includes all treatments or procedures involving the handling of human eggs and sperm to establish a pregnancy.

AUTOEROTICISM Sexual activities involving only the self, for example, masturbation, sexual fantasy, and erotic dreams.

BATTERED-CHILD SYNDROME A group of symptoms that collectively describe a clinical condition in children who have received severe physical abuse.

BATTERED-WOMAN SYNDROME A group of symptoms that collectively describe a general pattern of physical battering experienced by women. It is defined in terms of frequency, severity, deliberateness, and ability to demonstrate injury.

BEREAVEMENT The state of being deprived of a loved one by death.

BIGAMY The act of marrying one person while still being legally married to another person.

BISEXUALITY A person who has partners of both sexes either simultaneously or at different times.

BOUNDARY AMBIGUITY Who is in and who is out of the family system.

CASE STUDY A detailed and in-depth examination of a single unit or instance of some phenomenon.

CENOGAMY (GROUP MARRIAGE) A situation in which the women and men in a group are simultaneously married to one another.

COGNITIVE-DEVELOPMENT THEORY A theory that asserts that children take an active role in organizing their world, including learning gender identity.

COITUS Penile–vaginal intercourse.

COLLABORATIVE LAW A way of practicing law in which the attorneys for both parties to a family dispute agree to assist in resolving the conflict by using cooperative techniques rather than adversarial strategies and litigation, with the goal of reaching an efficient, fair, and comprehensive out-of-court settlement of all issues.

COMMON-LAW MARRIAGE A cohabitive relationship that is based on the mutual consent of the persons involved, is not solemnized by a ceremony, and is recognized as valid by the state.

COMMUNE A group of people (single or married, with or without children) who live together, sharing many aspects of their lives.

COMMUNITY DIVORCE The changes in social relationships that often accompany a divorce—the loss of relatives and friends who were previously shared with a spouse and their replacement with new friends.

COMMUNITY REMARRIAGE The changes in social relationships that often accompany a remarriage—the integration of new in-laws and "couple-oriented" relationships, and sometimes the loss of unmarried friends.

COMMUTER MARRIAGE A marriage in which each partner works in a different geographic location and therefore maintains a separate place of residence.

CONCEPTION The process by which a female ovum (egg) is penetrated by a male sperm cell, creating a fertilized egg.

CONCILIATION COUNSELING Counseling intended to determine whether marital problems can be resolved and the couple reconciled. Some states require conciliation counseling before the courts will consider granting a divorce.

CONFLICT THEORY   A theoretical perspective that focuses on conflicting interests among various groups and institutions in society.

CONGENITAL   Existing at birth but not hereditary.

CONJUGAL RIGHTS   A set of rights pertaining to the marriage relationship.

CONTENT ANALYSIS   A research technique used to examine the content of books, documents, and programs.

CONTRACEPTION   Mechanisms for preventing fertilization.

COPARENTAL DIVORCE   The arrangements divorcing couples work out concerning child custody, visitation rights, and the financial and legal responsibilities of each parent.

COURTSHIP   The process of selecting a mate and developing an intimate relationship.

COUVADE   Sympathetic pregnancy; a condition in which some men experience many of the symptoms of pregnancy.

COVERTURE   The traditional belief that a wife is under the protection and influence of her husband.

CRUDE DIVORCE RATE (CDR)   The number of divorces per 1000 people in the population.

CRUISING   An activity in which several teenagers (usually male) pack into a car and drive around the neighborhood looking for females to pick up.

CUNNILINGUS   Oral stimulation of the female genitals.

DATE RAPE   Sexual assault by a person with whom the victim had gone on a date.

DATING   A process of pairing off that involves the open choice of mates and engagement in activities that allow people to get to know one another and progress toward mate selection.

DATING VIOLENCE   The perpetration or threat of an act of violence by at least one member of an unmarried couple on the other member within the context of dating or courtship, encompassing any form of sexual assault, physical violence, and verbal or emotional abuse.

DESERTION   The abandonment of a spouse or family.

DEVELOPMENTAL FAMILY LIFE CYCLE THEORY   A theory that explains family life in terms of a process that unfolds over the life course of families.

DISABILITY   A physical or mental condition that often stigmatizes or causes discrimination.

DISENFRANCHISED GRIEF   Circumstances in which a person experiences a sense of loss but does not have a socially recognized right, role, or capacity to grieve.

DIVORCE COUNSELING   Counseling intended to help couples replace the adversarial and often destructive aspects that frequently accompany divorce with a more cooperative spirit and to help them distance themselves from the relationship so that acceptance of the loss and subsequent healing can take place.

DIVORCE MEDIATION   A procedure in which trained professionals help divorcing couples negotiate a fair and mutually agreed-upon resolution of such issues as marital property distribution, child custody, visitation rights, and financial support.

DOMESTIC PARTNERSHIP   A category of relationships consisting of unmarried couples who live together and share housing and financial responsibilities. Some communities and businesses allow unmarried couples who register as domestic partners to receive certain legal rights similar to those of married couples.

DOWRIES   A sum of money or property brought by the female to a marriage.

DRUG   Any substance that alters the central nervous system and states of consciousness.

DRUG ABUSE   The deliberate use of a substance for other than its intended purpose, in a manner that can damage health or ability to function.

DRUG USE   The taking of a drug for its intended purpose and in an appropriate amount, frequency, strength, and manner.

DYSFUNCTIONAL   Having a negative consequence or performing a negative service by hampering the achievement of group goals or disrupting the balance of the system.

ECONOMIC DIVORCE   The division of marital property and assets between the two former partners.

ECONOMIC REMARRIAGE   The establishment of a new marital household as an economically productive unit.

EJACULATION   Expulsion of semen from the penis.

ELDER ABUSE   Physical, psychological, or material maltreatment and neglect of older people.

EMBRYO TRANSPLANT   A procedure whereby a fertilized egg from a donor is implanted into an infertile woman.

EMOTIONAL DIVORCE   A period during which one or both partners withdraw emotionally from a marriage.

EMOTIONAL REMARRIAGE   The process of reestablishing a bond of attraction, love, commitment, and trust with another person.

EMPIRICAL EVIDENCE   Data or evidence that can be confirmed by the use of one or more of the human senses.

ENCULTURATED LENS THEORY   A theory of gender role acquisition that argues that hidden cultural assumptions about how societal members should look, behave, and feel are so deeply embedded in social institutions and cultural discourse, and hence individual psyches, that these behaviors and ways of thinking are systematically reproduced from one generation to the next.

ENDOGAMY   The practice of requiring people to marry within a particular social group.

ENVY   Unhappiness or discontent that arises from the belief that something about oneself does not measure up to the level of someone else.

EROS   A style of loving characterized by an immediate, powerful attraction to the physical appearance of another.

ETHNIC CLEANSING   A term euphemistically applied to the process whereby one group of people tries to rid the region of others who are different in some significant way.

ETHNOGRAPHY   A research technique of describing a social group from the group's point of view.

EXOGAMY   The practice of requiring people to marry outside particular groups.

EXPRESSIVE TRAITS   Personality traits that encourage nurturing, emotionality, sensitivity, and warmth.

EXTENDED OR MULTIGENERATIONAL FAMILY   A family consisting of one or both parents, siblings, if any, and other relatives, such as grandparents, aunts, uncles, or cousins.

FAMILY   Any relatively stable group of people who are related to one another through blood, marriage, or adoption, or who simply live together, and who provide one another with economic and emotional support.

FAMILY ABDUCTION   The taking or keeping of a child by a family member in violation of a custody order, a decree, or other legitimate custodial rights, where the taking or keeping involved some element of concealment, flight, or intent to deprive a lawful custodian indefinitely of custodial privileges.

FAMILY AND MEDICAL LEAVE ACT A law that allows either parent to take up to 3 months of unpaid leave for births, adoptions, and family emergencies.

FAMILY OF ORIENTATION The family into which a person is born and raised.

FAMILY OF PROCREATION A family that is created when two people marry or enter into an intimate relationship and have or adopt children of their own.

FELLATIO Oral stimulation of the male genitals.

FEMINIZATION OF POVERTY The increase in the proportion of poor people who are women or children.

FERTILITY The actual number of live births in a population.

FERTILITY RATE The number of births per 1000 women in their childbearing years (ages 15 to 44).

FETAL ALCOHOL SYNDROME A condition caused by a mother's consumption of alcohol during pregnancy and characterized by physical deformities in the fetus.

FICTIVE KIN The attribution of kinship terms to nonrelatives.

FLEXTIME An arrangement that allows employees to choose within specified time limits when they arrive at and leave work.

FORNICATION Sexual intercourse outside legal marriage.

FUNCTIONAL Having a positive consequence or performing a positive service by promoting the achievement of group goals or helping maintain a system in a balanced state.

FUNCTIONAL AGE The use of an individual's physical, intellectual, and social capacities and accomplishments as a measurement of age rather than the number of years lived.

GENDER The socially learned behaviors, attitudes, and expectations associated with being female or male; what we call femininity and masculinity.

GENDER IDENTITY A person's awareness of being female or male.

GENDER ROLE SOCIALIZATION The process whereby people learn and adopt the gender roles that their culture deems appropriate for them.

GENDER ROLE STEREOTYPES The oversimplified expectations of what it means to be a woman or a man.

GENERALIZED OTHERS The viewpoints of society at large—widespread cultural norms and values that individuals use as a reference when evaluating themselves.

GETTING TOGETHER A pattern of dating that involves women and men meeting in groups, playing similar roles in initiating dates, and sharing equally in the cost of activities.

GLOBAL INTERDEPENDENCE A state in which the lives of people around the world are intertwined closely and in which any one nation's problems increasingly cut across cultural and geographic boundaries.

GOING STEADY An exclusive dating relationship with one partner.

GRIEF The emotional response to the loss of a loved one.

GROUP MARRIAGE A marriage of at least four people, two female and two male, in which each partner is married to all partners of the opposite sex.

HAWTHORNE EFFECT The distortion of research results that occurs when people modify their behaviors, either deliberately or subconsciously, because they are aware they are being studied.

HEALTH A state of complete physical, mental, and social well-being, not merely the absence of physical disease or infirmity.

HETEROGAMOUS MARRIAGE Marriage in which the partners are unlike each other in terms of various social and demographic characteristics, such as race, age, religious background, social class, and education.

HETEROSEXISM The notion that heterosexuality is the only right, natural, and acceptable sexual orientation.

HETEROSEXUALITY Both identity and behavior; includes a preference for sexual activities with a person of the other sex.

HIV EMBRYOPATHY Used by some researchers to describe specific facial malformations (for example, small heads, slanted eyes that sit far apart from each other, a square forehead, a wide and flat nose, loosely shaped lips, and a growth deficiency).

HOMOGAMY The attraction of people who are alike in terms of various social and demographic characteristics such as race, age, religious background, social class, and education.

HOMOPHOBIA An extreme and irrational fear or hatred of homosexuals.

HOMOSEXUALITY Both identity and behavior; includes preference for sexual activities with a person of the same sex.

HOSPICE A physical environment within which supportive care is provided for terminally ill patients and their families that focuses on comfort, freedom from pain, and quality of life rather than cure.

HOUSEHOLDS All persons who occupy a housing unit, such as a house, apartment, single room, or other space intended to be living quarters.

HUMAN SEXUALITY The feelings, thoughts, and behaviors of humans who have learned a set of cues that evoke a sexual or an erotic response.

HYPERGAMY Marrying upward in social status.

HYPOGAMY Marrying downward in social status.

HYPOTHESIS Statement of a relationship between two or more variables.

IDEOLOGY A set of ideas and beliefs that support the interests of a group in society.

INCEST Sexual abuse by a blood relative or someone who is thought of as a part of a person's family.

INDIVIDUAL RACISM Behavior by individuals or groups who define themselves as superior toward individuals whom they define as inferior.

INFANT MORTALITY RATE The rate at which babies die before their first birthday.

INFANTICIDE Killing of infants and young children.

INFATUATION A strong attraction to another person based on an idealized picture of that person.

INFERTILITY The inability to conceive after 12 months of unprotected intercourse or the inability to carry a pregnancy to live birth.

INSTITUTION Patterns of ideas, beliefs, values, and behavior that are built around the basic needs of individuals and society and that persist over time.

INSTITUTIONAL RACISM Established laws, customs, and practices that systematically reflect and produce racial inequalities in a society, whether or not the individuals maintaining these practices have racist intentions.

INSTRUMENTAL TRAITS Personality traits that encourage self-confidence, rationality, competition, and coolness;

for example, an orientation to action, achievement, and leadership.

INTERSEXUALITY Condition where an infant's genitalia are ambiguous in appearance and whose sexual anatomy cannot clearly be differentiated at birth.

INTERVIEW A method of collecting data in which a researcher asks subjects a series of questions and records the answers.

IN VITRO FERTILIZATION A reproductive technique that involves surgically removing a woman's eggs, fertilizing them in a petri dish with the partner's or donor's sperm, and then implanting one or more of the fertilized eggs in the woman's uterus.

JEALOUSY Thoughts and feelings of envy, resentment, and insecurity directed toward someone a person is fearful of losing.

JOB SHARING An employment pattern in which two workers split a single full-time job.

JOINT CUSTODY A situation in which both divorced parents are given legal responsibility for raising their children.

KINSHIP Relationships resulting from blood, marriage, or adoption, or among people who consider one another family.

LABOR FORCE PARTICIPATION RATE The percentage of workers in a particular group who are employed or who are actively seeking employment.

LATENT FUNCTIONS Unintended, unrecognized consequences or effects of any part of a social system or the system as a whole for the maintenance and stability of that system.

LEGAL DIVORCE The official dissolution of a marriage by the state, leaving both former partners legally free to remarry.

LEGAL MARRIAGE A legally binding agreement or contractual relationship between two people that is defined and regulated by the state.

LEGAL REMARRIAGE The establishment of a new legally recognized relationship.

LIKING A positive feeling toward someone that is less intense than love—a feeling typical of friendship in its most simple terms.

LIMERENCE A style of love characterized by a complete absorption or obsessive preoccupation with and attachment to another person. It is accompanied by extreme emotional highs when the love is reciprocated and lows when it is not.

LOVE MAP A group of physical, psychological, and behavioral traits that one finds attractive in a mate.

LUDUS A style of loving that is playful, non possessive—a challenging love, without a deep commitment or lasting emotional involvement.

MANIC A style of loving that combines eros and ludus, is characterized by obsession and possessiveness. It is a jealous and stressful love that demands constant displays of attention, caring, and affection from the partner.

MANIFEST FUNCTIONS Intended, overt consequences or effects of any part of a social system or the system as a whole for the maintenance and stability of that system.

MARITAL ADJUSTMENT The process by which marital partners change or adapt their behavior, attitudes, and interactions to develop a good working relationship and to satisfy each other's needs over the marital life course.

MARRIAGE A union between people that unites them sexually, socially, and economically, that is relatively consistent over time, and that accords each person certain agreed-upon rights.

MARRIAGE GRADIENT Phenomenon by which women marry upward in social status and men marry downward in social status. As a result, women at the top and men at the bottom of the social class ladder have a smaller pool of eligible mates to choose from than do members of the other classes.

MARRIAGE MARKET Analogy of the commercial marketplace to explain how individuals choose the people they date, mate, live with, and marry by "comparison shopping" and "bargaining for" the mate with the most desirable characteristics.

MARRIAGE SQUEEZE A condition in which one sex has a more limited pool of eligibles from which to choose than the other does. Sociologists use the concept to describe the phenomenon of an excess of baby boom women who had reached marriageable age during the 1960s compared with marriage-aged men.

MASTER (KEY) STATUS A position we hold that affects all aspects of our lives, for example, being female or male.

MASTURBATION Erotic stimulation of self through caressing or otherwise stimulating the genitals for the purpose of sexual pleasure.

MATE SELECTION The wide range of behaviors and social relationships individuals engage in prior to marriage and that lead to long- or short-term pairing or coupling.

MATRILINEAL Kinship or family lineage (descent) and inheritance come through the mother and her blood relatives.

MENOPAUSE A period in the female life cycle (typically between ages 45 and 50) characterized by the cessation of ovulation, the menstrual cycle, and fertility.

MIDWIFE Most often a woman who is trained either to deliver a baby or to assist a woman in childbirth. Most midwives today are professionals who practice in birth centers or who deliver babies at home.

MODELING A process of learning through imitation of others.

MODIFIED EXTENDED FAMILY Family in which a variety of relatives live, not necessarily in the same household, but in very close proximity to one another, interact on a frequent basis, and provide emotional and economic support to each other.

MONOGAMY Exclusivity in an intimate relationship. In marriage, it means marriage to only one person at a time.

MORBIDITY The rate of occurrence of illness or disease in a population.

MORTALITY The rate of occurrence of death in a population.

MOTHERHOOD MYSTIQUE The traditional belief that the ultimate achievement and fulfillment of womanhood is through motherhood.

MOURNING The outward expression of grief, including a society's customs, rituals, and rules for coping with loss.

MYTH A false, fictitious, imaginary, or exaggerated belief about someone or something.

NOCTURNAL EMISSIONS (WET DREAMS) Erotic dreams that lead to orgasm during sleep.

NO-FAULT DIVORCE The dissolution of a marriage on the basis of irreconcilable differences; neither party is judged at fault for the divorce.

NORMS Cultural guidelines or rules of conduct that direct people to behave in particular ways.

NUCLEAR FAMILY A family consisting of a mother and father and their natural or adopted offspring.

OCCUPATIONAL DISTRIBUTION The location of workers in different occupations; for example, women are more heavily concentrated in lower-paying clerical or service jobs, whereas men are concentrated in the higher-paying jobs of craft workers and operators.

ORGASM   A human sexual response that occurs at the height of sexual arousal. It is characterized by the involuntary release of sexual tension through rhythmic contractions in the genitals and is accompanied in most males by ejaculation.

OVERLAPPING HOUSEHOLDS   The dual membership of children in the separate households of their divorced (and frequently remarried) parents.

OVULATION   The release of the mature egg.

PALIMONY   A payment similar to alimony made to a former unmarried live-in partner and based on the existence of a contract (written or implied) between the partners regarding aspects of their relationship.

PARENTAL REMARRIAGE   A process that involves the establishment of relationships with the children of the new spouse.

PARRICIDE   The killing of one's parents.

PATRIARCHAL FAMILY   A family organized around the principle of male dominance, wherein the male (husband or father) is head of the family and exercises authority and decision-making power over other family members, especially his wife and children.

PATRILINEAL   Kinship or family lineage (descent) and inheritance come through the father and his blood relatives.

PAY EQUITY   Equal pay for work of equal value.

PERSONAL MARRIAGE AGREEMENT   A written agreement between a married couple in which issues of role responsibility, obligation, and sharing are addressed in a manner tailored to their own personal preferences, desires, and expectations.

PETTING   Various types of physical contact and activities for the purpose of sexual arousal and pleasure without engaging in penile–vaginal intercourse. It is common among adolescent girls and boys.

PLEASURING   Engaging in activities during a sexual encounter that feel good; giving and receiving pleasurable feelings without the necessity of intercourse.

POLYANDRY   A form of marriage in which one female is married to two or more males.

POLYGAMY   A broad category applied to forms of marriage that involve multiple partners. In heterosexual marriage, polygamy involves a person of one sex being married to two or more people of the other sex (either polyandry or polygyny).

POLYGYNY   A form of marriage in which one male is married to two or more females.

POOL OF ELIGIBLES   People who are potential mates by virtue of birth and societal definition as appropriate or acceptable partners.

POSTNATAL DEPRESSION   A condition experienced after the birth of a child and characterized by mood shifts, irritability, and fatigue.

PREGNANCY DISCRIMINATION ACT OF 1978   Requires that pregnant employees be treated the same as employees with any temporary disability.

PREIMPLANTATION GENETIC DIAGNOSIS   Allows physicians to identify abnormalities such as Down Syndrome or genetic diseases such as muscular dystrophy in the embryo before implantation.

PRENUPTIAL AGREEMENT   An agreement developed and worked out in consultation with an attorney and filed as a legal document prior to marriage.

PRINCIPLE OF LEGITIMACY   The notion that all children ought to have a socially and legally recognized father.

PRONATALIST ATTITUDE   A cultural attitude that encourages childbearing.

PROPINQUITY   Proximity, or closeness in time, place, and space; an important factor in mate selection.

PSYCHIC DIVORCE   A redefinition of self away from the mutuality of couplehood and back to a sense of singularity and autonomy.

PSYCHIC REMARRIAGE   A process in which a remarried individual moves from the recently acquired identity of a single person to a couple identity.

PSYCHOANALYTIC/IDENTIFICATION THEORY   A theory developed by Sigmund Freud that asserts that children learn gender-appropriate behaviors by unconsciously identifying with their same-sex parent and that they pass through a series of stages in their psychosexual development.

PUSH/PULL FACTORS   Negative and positive factors in a current situation that influence our decision making.

QUALITATIVE ANALYSIS   Focuses on specific or distinct qualities within the data that show patterns of similarity or differences among the research subjects.

QUANTITATIVE ANALYSIS   A processs in which data can be analyzed using numerical categories and statistical techniques (for example, determining the percentage who report certain attitudes or behaviors numerically).

QUESTIONNAIRE   A research method of collecting data in which research subjects read and respond to a set of printed questions.

RACISM   An ideology of domination and a set of social, economic, and political practices by which one or more groups define themselves as superior and other groups as inferior, and then systematically deny these groups full access to and participation in mainstream society.

RAPE   Sexual intercourse forced by one person upon another against the person's will; usually perpetrated by a male against a female.

RAPE SYNDROME   Men's proclivity to rape—the group of factors that collectively characterize men's likelihood to rape.

REFINED DIVORCE RATE   The number of divorces per 1000 married women age 15 and over.

REFUGEE   A person who leaves his country because of a fear of persecution for reason of race, religion, nationality, social group, or political opinion.

RELIABILITY   The degree to which scientific research measures or instruments yield the same results when repeated by the same researcher or other researchers, or when applied to the same individuals over time or different individuals at one time; consistency in measurement.

REMARRIED FAMILY   A two-parent, two-generation unit that comes into being on the legal remarriage of a widowed or divorced person who is regularly involved with biological or adopted children from a prior union. The children may or may not live with the remarried couple, but in either case, they have ongoing and significant psychological, social, and legal ties with them.

ROLE   A set of socially prescribed behaviors associated with a particular status or position in society.

ROLE CONFLICT   A situation in which a person occupies two different roles that involve contradictory expectations of what should be done at a given time.

ROLE OVERLOAD   A situation in which a person's various roles carry more responsibilities than that person can reasonably manage.

ROMANTIC LOVE   A deeply tender or highly intense set of feelings, emotions, and thoughts coupled with sexual passion and erotic expression directed by one person toward another.

SACRAMENT   A sacred union or rite.

SAFE SEX   Protection from AIDS and other sexually transmitted diseases through abstinence or use of protective methods such as condoms.

SANDWICH GENERATION   The middle-aged adults who find themselves pressured by responsibilities for both their children and their elderly parents.

SCIENTIFIC METHOD   A set of procedures intended to ensure accuracy and honesty throughout the research process.

SCIENTIFIC RESEARCH   Research that provides empirical evidence as a basis for knowledge or theories.

SELF-ESTEEM   The overall feelings, positive and negative, that a person has about her- or himself.

SEPARATION   The termination of marital cohabitation; the couple remains legally married, and neither party is free to remarry.

SERIAL MONOGAMY   A system in which an individual marries several times but only after each prior marriage is ended by death or divorce.

SEX   The physiological characteristics that differentiate females from males. These include external genitalia (vulva and penis), gonads (ovaries and testes), sex chromosomes, and hormones.

SEXISM   An ideology or set of beliefs about the inferiority of women and the superiority of men that is used to justify prejudice and discrimination against women.

SEX RATIO   The number of men to every 100 women in a society or group.

SEXUAL ASSAULT   Violence in the form of forced sexual acts that include vaginal, oral, or anal penetration; bondage; beating; mutilation; beastiality; and group or gang rape.

SEXUAL DOUBLE STANDARD   Differing sets of norms based on gender.

SEXUAL DYSFUNCTION   A psychological or physical condition in which a person is unable to engage in or enjoy sexual activities.

SEXUAL HARASSMENT   Unwanted leers, comments, suggestions, or physical contact of a sexual nature, as well as unwelcome requests for sexual favors.

SEXUAL IDENTITY   Refers to how a person describes her or his sexuality and how that person expressed that self to others.

SEXUAL ORIENTATION   The ways in which people understand and identify themselves sexually.

SEXUAL SCRIPT   Societal or cultural guidelines for defining and engaging in sexual behaviors.

SEXUALLY TRANSMITTED DISEASES (STDs)   Contagious diseases transmitted or acquired primarily through sexual contact or that can be, but are not always, spread through sexual contact.

SIGNIFICANT OTHERS   People who play an important role in a person's life, such as parents, friends, relatives, and religious figures.

SOCIAL CONSTRUCTIONISM   A perspective that focuses on the processes by which human beings give meaning to their own behavior and the behavior of others.

SOCIAL CONSTRUCTION OF REALITY   The process by which individuals shape or determine reality as they interact with other human beings.

SOCIAL-EXCHANGE THEORY   A theoretical perspective that adopts an economic model of human behavior based on cost, benefit, and the expectation of reciprocity and that focuses on how people bargain and exchange one thing for another in social relationships.

SOCIAL GERONTOLOGY   The study of the impact of sociocultural conditions on the process and consequences of aging.

SOCIALIZATION   The lifelong process of social interaction through which people learn knowledge, skills, patterns of thinking and behaving, and other elements of a culture that are essential for effective participation in social life.

SOCIAL-LEARNING THEORY   A theory that asserts that gender roles and gender identity are learned directly through a system of positive reinforcement (rewards) and negative reinforcement (punishments).

SOCIAL MARRIAGE   A relationship between people who cohabit and engage in behavior that is essentially the same as that within legal marriages except that the couple has not engaged in a marriage ceremony that is validated or defined as legally binding by the state.

SOCIAL STRUCTURE   Recurrent, stable, and patterned ways that people relate to one another in a society or group.

SOCIOLOGICAL IMAGINATION   A way of looking at the world whereby one sees the relations between history and biography within society.

SOLE CUSTODY   A situation in which one divorced parent is given legal responsibility for raising children.

SONOGRAM   A visual image made of a fetus and generated and printed out on a screen during ultrasound.

SPLIT CUSTODY   A situation whereby siblings are split up between their two biological parents following a divorce. A typical pattern is for mothers to have custody of daughters and fathers to have custody of sons.

STATIONS OF DIVORCE   The multiple types of divorces that couples experience in dissolving their marital relationship: emotional, legal, economic, coparental, community, and psychic.

STATUS   A social position that a person occupies within a group or society.

STORGE (pronounced "stor gay")   A style of loving that is said to be unexciting and uneventful; an affectionate style of love with an emphasis on companionship.

STRUCTURAL FUNCTIONALISM   A theoretical perspective that views society as an organized system, analogous to the human system, that is made up of a variety of interrelated parts or structures that work together to generate social stability and maintain society.

SURROGACY   The process whereby a woman agrees to be artificially inseminated with a man's sperm, carry the fetus to term, and relinquish all rights to the child after it is born.

SURVEY   A research method in which researchers collect data by asking people questions, for example, using questionnaires or face-to-face interviews.

SYMBOLIC INTERACTIONISM   A theoretical perspective that focuses on micropatterns (small-scale) of face-to-face interactions among people in specific settings, such as in marriages and families.

SYMBOLS   Objects, words, sounds, or events that are given particular meaning and are recognized by members of a culture.

TERRORISM   The employment or threat of violence, fear, or intimidation by individuals or groups as a political or revolutionary strategy to achieve political goals.

THEORY A set of interrelated statements or propositions constructed to explain some phenomenon.

THEORY MODEL A minitheory; a set of propositions intended to account for a limited set of facts.

TOTAL FERTILITY RATE The average number of children women have over their lifetime if current birth rates were to remain constant.

TRANSGENDERED Refers to living life as the opposite sex.

TRANSMISSION OF VICTIMIZATION Abuse carried from one generation to the next.

TRANSSEXUALS Persons who believe they were born with the body of the wrong sex.

TRUST Feelings of confidence and belief in another person; reliance upon another person to provide for or meet one's needs.

ULTRASOUND A prenatal test that allows a physician to observe the developing fetus directly by viewing electronically the echoes of sound waves pulsating through the pregnant woman's body.

UNDEREMPLOYMENT A concept that refers to several patterns of employment: part-time workers who want to work full-time, full-time workers who make very low wages, and workers with skills higher than those required by their current job.

VALIDITY The degree to which scientific research or instruments measure exactly what they are supposed to measure.

VARIABLES A factor or concept whose value changes from one case or observation to another.

VICTIM BLAMING Justifying the unequal or negative treatment of individuals or groups by finding defects in the victims rather than examining the social and economic factors or conditions that create and contribute to their condition.

WET DREAMS Erotic dreams that lead to orgasm during sleep.

WHEEL THEORY OF LOVE A perspective of love developed by social scientist Ira Reiss in which love is viewed in terms of a four-stage, circular progression from rapport through self-revelation, mutual dependence, and personality need-fulfillment as a couple interacts over time.

WOMAN BATTERING A range of behaviors that includes hitting, kicking, choking, and the use or threatened use of weapons, such as guns and knives.

WORKING POOR Underemployed individuals who work full time but make very low wages.

XENOPHOBIA A fear or hatred of strangers or foreigners or of anything foreign or different.

ZYGOTE A single-celled fertilized ovum (egg) that contains the complete genetic code for a human being.

References

AARP. 2004. *The Divorce Experience: A Study of Divorce at Midlife and Beyond.* Washington, DC: The American Association of Retired Persons.

Abbott, J., R. Johnson, J. Koziol-McLain, and S. Lowenstein. 1995. "Domestic Violence against Women: Incidence and Prevalence in an Emergency Department Population." *JAMA, The Journal of the American Medical Association* 273:1763–68.

ABC News. 1991. "True Colors." *Prime Time Live* (September 26).

———. 1999. "Accusations of Rape: Women Say They Were Attacked by Serb Forces" (April 13). http://abcnews.go.com/sections/world/DailyNews/Kosovo990413-refugees.html (June 10).

———. 2000. "Pre-Nup Woes: Douglas, Zeta-Jones Deny Pre-Nup Spat." http://more.abcnews.go.com/sections/entertainment/DailyNews/zetadouglas000627.html (2001, November 10).

abelard. 2001. "Children and Television Violence." http://www.abelard.org/tv/tv.htm (2002, January 8).

Abelson, R. 2001. "Men, Increasingly, Are the Ones Claiming Sex Harassment by Men." *New York Times* (June 10):1, 29.

Abilities 2000. 2002. "Myths and Facts about People with Disabilities." http://www.abilities2000.com/myths.html (2002, January 30).

Abma, J., A. Chandra, W. Mosher, L. Peterson, and L. Piccino. 1997. *Fertility, Family Planning, and Women's Health: New Data from the 1995 National Survey of Family Growth.* Washington, DC: National Center for Health Statistics, Vital Health Stat 23, 19.

Abrahamy, M., E. B. Finkelson, C. Lydon, and K. Murray. 2003. "Caregivers' Socialization of Gender Roles in a Children's Museum." *Perspectives in Psychology* (Spring):19–25.

"Abstinence Groups Sponsor 'National Week of Chasity'". 2000. *Maranatha Christian Journal.* http://www.mcjonline.com/news/00/20000214e.htm (2001, February 4).

ACADV. 2006. "Barriers to Leaving." http://www.acadv.org/barriers.html (2006, July 14).

ACLU. 1998. "Protecting Teen Health: Comprehensive Sexuality Education and Condom Availability Programs in the Public Schools." (April 9).

Adams, S., J. Kuebli, P.A. Boyle, and R. Fivush. 1995. "Gender Differences in Parent–Child Conversations about Past Emotions: A Longitudinal Investigation." *Sex Roles* 33:309–23.

Adams, V. 1982. "Getting at the Heart of Jealous Love." *Psychology Today* (May):38–47.

Aday, R. H., C. Rice, and E. Evans. 1991. "Intergenerational Partners Project: A Model Linking Elementary Students with Senior Center Volunteers." *Gerontologist* 31, 2:263–66.

Ade-Ridder, L. 1990. "Sexuality and Marital Quality among Older Married Couples." In T. H. Brubaker, ed., *Family Relationships in Later Life,* 48–67. Newbury Park, CA: Sage.

———, and T. H. Brubaker. 1983. "The Quality of Long-Term Marriages." In T. H. Brubaker, ed., *Family Relationships in Later Life,* 19–30. Beverly Hills, CA: Sage.

Adler-Baeder, F., L. Taylor, and K. Pasley. 2005. *Marital Transitions in Military Families: Their Relevance for Adaption to Military Life.* Final Report. (March). Lafayette, IN: The Military Family Research Institute.

Adler, F., G. Mueller, and W. Laufer. 1998. *Criminology.* Boston: McGraw-Hill.

Adler, J. 1996. "Building a Better Dad." *Newsweek* (June 17): 58–64.

———. 1997. "A Matter of Faith." *Newsweek* (December 15): 49–54.

———. 2005. "Granparents Raising Another Generation Struggle to Find Adequate Housing." Chicago Tribune (November 27): Sec. 16, p. 1.

Adler, N. L., S. S. Hendrick, and C. Hendrick. 1987. "Male Sexual Preference and Attitudes toward Love and Sexuality." *Journal of Sex Education and Therapy* 12, 2:27–30.

Administration for Children and Families, 2006. " The AFCARS Report." (June). http://www.acf.dhhs.gov/programs/cb/stats_research?afcars/tar/report11.htm.

———. 2001. "A Profile of Older Americans." http://www.aoa.dhhs.gov/aoa/STATS/profile/2001/highlights.html (2001, December 28).

Administration on Aging. 2004. "Aging Internet Information Notes." (September 9). http://www.aoa.gov.prof/notes/notes_senior_centers.asp (2006, June 27).

Administration for Children and Families. 2000. "How Many Children Were in Foster Care on March 31, 1999?" Washington, DC: U.S. Department of Health and Human Services. http://www.aacf.dhhs.gov/programs/cb/publications/afcars/rpt0100/ar0100c.htm (2002, January 15).

ADPSR. 2004. "Prison Design Boycott Campaign: Racism and Poverty." Berkeley, CA: ADPSR National Forum. http://www.adpsr.org/prisons/racism.htm (2006, February 10).

Agosto, D. 2004 "Girls and Gaming: A Summary of the Research with Implications for Practice." Teacher Librarian 31,3:8–14.

Aguirre, A., and J. Turner. 2001. *American Ethnicity: The Dynamics and Consequences of Discrimination.* Boston: McGraw-Hill.

Ahlburg, D. A., and C. J. DeVita. 1992. "New Realities of the American Family." *Population Bulletin* 47, 2 (August):1–44. Washington, DC: Population Reference Bureau.

Ahmad, I. L. 1993. "Redliners Better Beware: Discrimination in Housing Hits Pocketbooks." *St. Louis American* (July 1–7):1A, 7A.

Ahrons, C. 1980. "Crises in Family Transitions." *Family Relations* 29:533–40.

———. 1994. *The Good Divorce: Keeping Your Family Together When Your Marriage Comes Apart.* New York: HarperCollins.

———. 2004. *We're Still Family: What Grown Children Have to Say About Their Parents' Divorce.* New York: Harper Collins.

———, and L. Wallish. 1986. "The Close Relationships between Former Spouses." In S. Duck and D. Perlman, eds., *Close Relationships: Development, Dynamics, and Deterioration,* 269–96. Beverly Hills, CA: Sage.

"AIDS around the World." 2001. http://www.unaids.org (2001, December 13).

"AIDS in Africa." 2001. *Avert.* http://www.avert.org/aafrica.htm (2001, December 14).

Akin, D. 2003. "Girls Less Confident on Computer Study." Globeandmail.com. (June 24). www.globetechnology.com/servlet/story/ RTGAM.2003624/BNPrint/tec (2004, April 5).

Alan Guttmacher Institute. 2002a. "Sexual and Reproductive Health: Women and Men." http://www.guttmacher.org/pubs/fb_10–02.html (2006, March 17).

———. 2002b. "In Their Own Right: Addressing the Sexual and Reproductive Health Needs of American Men." New York: AGI.

———. 2005. "Facts in Brief: Contraceptive Use." http://www.guttmacher.org/pubs/fb_contr_use.html (2006, March 27).

Alba, R. D. 1985. "Marriage across Ethnic Lines." *Marriage and Divorce Today* 10:3.

Albas, D., and C. M. Albas. 1989a. "Love and Marriage." In K. Ishwaran, ed., *Family and Marriage: Cross-Cultural Perspectives,* 125–42. Toronto: Wall and Thompson.

———. 1989b. "Sexuality and Marriage." In K. Ishwaran, ed., *Family and Marriage: Cross-Cultural Perspectives,* 145–62. Toronto: Wall and Thompson.

———. 1987. "The Pulley Alternative for the Wheel Theory of the Development of Love." *International Journal of Comparative Sociology* 28 (3–4):223–27.

Albert, B. 2004. *With One Voice: America's Adults and Teens Sound Off About Teen Pregnancy.* Washington, DC: National Campaign to Prevent Teen Pregnancy.

Aldous, J. 1987. "New Views of the Family Life of the Elderly." *Journal of Marriage and the Family* 49:227–34.

———, E. Klaus, and D. Klein. 1985. "The Understanding Heart: Aging Parents and Their Favorite Children." *Child Development* 56:303–16.

Alexander, B. 2005. "Sex Ed on the Web: The Birds and the Bees at the Click of a Mouse." MSNBC.com (January 27). http://www.msnbc.msn.com/id/6860487/pring/displaymode/1098/ (2006, March 22).

Alford, S., and A. Feijoo. 2001 (Updated Edition). *Adolescent Sexual Health in Europe and the U.S.—Why the Difference?* Advocates for Youth.

Allan, C. A., and D. J. Cooke. 1985. "Stressful Life Events and Alcohol Misuse in Women: A Critical Review." *Journal of Studies on Alcohol* 46:147–52.

Allan, G. 1989. *Friendship: Developing a Sociological Perspective.* Boulder, CO: Westview Press.

Allen, K. 1989. *Single Women/Family Ties.* Newbury Park, CA: Sage.

Allen, K. S., and G. F. Moorman. 1997. "Leaving Home: The Emigration of Home-Office Workers." *American Demographics* 19 (October):57–61.

Allgeier, E., and Wiederman, M. 1991. "Love and Mate Selection in the 1990s." *Free Inquiry* 11, 25–27.

Alliance for a Global Community. 1996. "Flight: Global Refugee Protection." *Connections* 2, 5 (Summer).

Alpert-Gillis, L. J., and J. P. Connell. 1989. "Gender and Sex-Role Influences on Children's Self-Esteem." *Journal of Personality* 57:97–114.

Alstein, H., and R. J. Simon. 1992. *Adoption, Race, and Identity: From Infancy through Adolescence.* New York: Praeger.

Althaus, F. 1991. "Young Adults Choose Alternatives to Marriage, Remain Single Longer." *Family Planning Perspectives* 23:45–46.

Altschuler, C. L. 2000. "Help from Afar: How to Care for a Parent When You Can't Be There." *Chicago Tribune* (May 31):sec. 8, 1.

Alzheimer's Association. 2000. "General Statistics/Demographics." http://www.alz.org/research/current/stats.htm (2002, January 7).

Amato, P. R. 2000. "The Consequences of Divorce for Adults and Children." *Journal of Marriage and the Family* 62, 4:1269–87.

———. 2003. "Reconciling Divergent Perspectives: Judith Wallerstein, Quantitative Family Research, and Children of Divorce." *Family Relations* 52, 4(October):332–339.

———, and A. Booth. 1996. "A Prospective Study of Divorce and Parent–Child Relationships." *Journal of Marriage and the Family* 58 (May):356–65.

———. 1997. *A Generation at Risk.* Cambridge, MA: Harvard University Press.

———. and D. D. DeBoer. 2001. "The Transmission of Marital Instability Across Generations: Relationship Skills or Commitment to Marriage?" *Journal of Marriage and Family* 63:1038–1051.

———. and D. Previti. 2003. "People's Reasons for Divorcing: Gender, Social Class, the Life Course, and Adjustment." *Journal of Family Issues* 24:602–626.

———. D. R. Johnson, A. Booth, and S. J. Rogers. 2003. "Continuity and Change in Marital Quality Between 1980 and 2000." *Journal of Marriage and Family* 65:1–22.

———. and J. Cheadle. 2005. "The Long Reach of Divorce: Divorce and Child Well-Being Across Three Generations." *Journal of Marriage and Family* 67, 1(February):191–206.

———. and S. J. Rezac. 1994. "Contact with Nonresident Parents, Interparental Conflict, and Children's Behavior." *Journal of Family Issues* 15 (June):191–207.

———. and S. J. Rogers. 1997. "A Longitudinal Study of Marital Problems and Subsequent Divorce." *Journal of Marriage and the Family* 59 (August):612–24.

Ambert, A. 1986. "Being a Stepparent: Live-in and Visiting Children." *Journal of Marriage and the Family* 48:795–804.

———. 1988. "Relationships with Former In-Laws after Divorce: A Research Note." *Journal of Marriage and the Family* 50:679–86.

———. 2001. *Families in the New Millennium.* Boston: Allyn & Bacon.

Ameen, J. 2006. "Divorce in Malta." *The Malta Independent Online* (February 19). http://2117.145.4.56/ind/news2.asp?artid=28483 (2006, March 21).

American Academy of Family Physicians. 2002, 2003. "Children's Health. http://www.aafp.org/x16320.xml?printxml (2006, April 28).

American Academy of Pediatrics. Committee on Adolescence. 1994. "Sexual Assault and the Adolescent." 94, 5 (November):761–65.

American Association for Retired Persons. 2001. "In the Middle: A Report on Multicultural Boomers Coping with Family and Aging Issues." http://research.aarp.org/il/in_the_middle_1.html (2002, January 7).

———. 2002. *The Grandparent Study 2002 Report.* Washington, DC: AARP.

———. 2003. *Lean on Me: Support and Minority Outreach for Grandparents Raising Grandchildren.* Washington, DC: AARP.

American Association of Suicidology. 2001. "U.S.A. Suicide: 1999 Official Final Data." Washington, DC. http://www.suicidology.org (2002, January 27).

American Association of University Women (AAUW). 1991. *Shortchanging Girls, Shortchanging America.* Washington, DC: Greenberg-Lake Analysis Group.

———. 1995. *How Schools Shortchange Girls.* New York: Marlowe.

American Bar Association. 1999. "The Commission on Domestic Violence: Statistics." Chicago. http://www.abanet.org/somviol/stats.html (1999, June 4).

American College of Nurse–Midwives. 2004. "Domestic Violence." http://www.mymidwife.org/momstobe/dv.cfm (2006, July 11).

American Humane Fact Sheets. 2004. "America's Children: How Are They Doing? Child Fact Sheets." http://www.americanhumane.org/site/PageServe (2006, July 19).

American Psychological Association. 1996. "Violence and the Family: Report of the American Psychological Association Presidential Task Force on Violence and the Family," 11, 80.

———. 2001. "Understanding Child Sexual Abuse: Education, Prevention, and Recovery." Office of Public Communications, Washington, DC. PsycNET. http://www.apa.org/ releases/sexabuse/homepage.html (2002, January 19).

———. 2006. "Elder Abuse and Neglect: In Search of Solutions." *APA Online.*http://www.apa.org/pi/aging/eldabuse.htm (2006, July 20).

"Americans and the Wealth Gap."1999. *Chicago Tribune* (September 27):14.

Amnesty International. 1999. "Children Devastated by War" (January 11). http://web.amnest.org/ai.nsf/Index/ASA110131999?OpenDocument&of=THEMES\CHIL...(2002, February 3).

———. 2001a. "Racism and the Administration of Justice." http:// www.Amnesty.org/ai.nsf/Index/ACT400202001?OpenDocument&of=THEMES\ RACIS...(2002, February 3).

———. 2001b. "World Conference against Racism Ends: Successes Must Not Be Overshadowed by Disputes." http://www.amnesty.org (2002, February 5).

———. 2001c. "Afghanistan: Accountability for Civilian Deaths" (October 26). http://web.amnesty.org/ai.nsf/Index/ASA110222001?OpenDocument&of=COUNTRIES\A... (2002, February 3).

———. 2001d. "Afghanistan: The Hidden Human Face of the War" (December 20). http://web.amnesty.org/ai.nsf/Index/ASA110502001?OpenDocument&of=COUNTRIES\A...(2002, February 3).

Amnesty International. 2004. "Making Violence Against Women Count: Facts and Figures." Media Briefing. (March 5). http://web.amnesty.org/library/index/ENGACT770362004 (2006, July 7).

———. 2006. "Israel/Lebanon: Deliberate Destruction or 'Collateral Damage'? Israel Attacks on Civilian Infrastructure." (August 23). http://web.amnesty.org/library/index/ENGMDE/180072006 (2006, August 24).

Amott, T. 1993. *Caught in the Crisis: Women and the U.S. Economy Today.* New York: Monthly Review Press.

———, and J. A. Matthaei. 1991. *Race, Gender, and Work: A Multicultural History of Women in the United States.* Boston: South End Press.

Anders, G. 1994. "The Search for Love Goes on." *Washington Post* (September 19):D5.

Andersen, M. 1988. *Thinking about Women: Sociological Perspectives on Sex and Gender,* 2d ed. New York: Macmillan.

———. 1993. *Thinking about Women: Sociological Perspectives on Sex and Gender,* 3d ed. New York: Macmillan.

———. 2000. *Thinking about Women: Sociological Perspectives on Sex and Gender,* 5th ed. Boston: Allyn & Bacon.

———. 2003. *Thinking About Women: Sociological Perspectives on Sex and Gender,* 6th ed. Boston: Allyn & Bacon.

———. 2005. *Thinking About Women: Sociological Perspectives in Sex and Gender.* 7th ed. Boston: Allyn & Bacon.

———, and P. H. Collins. 1992. *Race, Class, and Gender: An Anthology.* Belmont, CA: Wadsworth.

Anderson, B. "Commentary: "'Safer Sex' Approach Isn't Really Very Safe." *The Minnesota Family Council/Institute* 5, 3. June. http://www.mfc.org/pfn/99-6/index.htm (2006, April 5).

Anderson, K. G., H. Kaplan, and J. B. Lancester. 2001. *Men's Financial Expenditures on Genetic Children and Stepchildren from Current and Former Relationships.* PSC Research Report No. 01–484. Population Studies Center, Institute for Social Research, University of Michigan.

Anderson, S. A., C. S. Russell, and W. R. Schumm. 1983. "Perceived Marital Quality and Family Life-Cycle Categories: A Further Analysis." *Journal of Marriage and the Family* 45:127–39.

Anderson, S., J. Cavanagh, C. Hartman, S. Klinger, and S. Chan. *Executive Excess 2004: Campaign Contributions, Outsourcing, Unexpensed Stock Options and Rising CEO Pay.* Boston: United for a Fair Economy and the Institute for Policy Studies.

Angermeier, W. F. 1994. "Operant Learning." In V. S. Ramachandran, ed., *Encyclopedia of Human Behavior* 23, 351–66. New York: Academic Press.

Annenberg Public Policy Center of the University of Pennsylvania. 2000. *Media in the Home* 2000. Philadelphia: APPCUP.

Annie E. Casey Foundation. *2003. Kids Count Data Book.* Baltimore: Annie E. Casey Foundation.

Annie E. Casey Foundation. *2005. Kids Count Data Book: 38.* Baltimore: Annie E. Casey Foundation.

Administrational for Children and Families, 2006. "The AFCARS Reports." (June). http://www.acf.dhhs.gov/programs/cb/states-research?afears/fears/tar/report 11.htm

Apfel, N. H., and V. Seitz. 1991. "Four Models of Adolescent Mother–Grandmother Relationships in Black Inner-City Families." *Family Relations* 40:421–29.

Aquilino, W. S. 1991. "Predicting Parents' Experiences with Coresident Adult Children." *Journal of Family Issues* 12:323–42.

———, and K. R. Supple. 1991. "Parent–Child Relations and Parental Satisfaction with Living Arrangements When Adult Children Live at Home." *Journal of Marriage and the Family* 53:13–27.

Arber, S. 2004. "Gender, Marital Status, and Ageing." Linking Material, Health, and Social Resources." *Journal of Aging Studies* 18, 1(February):91–108.

Arber, S., K. Perren, and K. Davidson. 2002. "Involvement in Social Organizations in Later Life: Variations by Gender and Class." In L. Anderson, ed., *Cultural Gerontology,* 77–93. Wetport, CT: Greenwood.

Archbold, P. G. 1983. "The Impact of Parent-Caring on Women." *Family Relations* 32:39–45.

Arendell, T. 1986. *Mothers and Divorce: Legal, Economic, and Social Dilemmas.* Berkeley: University of California Press.

———. 1995. *Fathers and Divorce.* Thousand Oaks, CA: Sage.

Aries, P. 1981. *The Hour of Our Death.* New York: Knopf.

Arkes, H. 1991. "Principled Playfulness: Case Study 1." *National Review* 43 (June 24):26–27.

Arliss, L. 1991. *Gender Communication.* Upper Saddle River, NJ: Prentice Hall.

Armour, S. 2004. "Some Moms Quit as Offices Scrap Family-Friendliness." *USA Today* http://usatoday.printthis.clicability.com/pt/cpt?action=cpt&title=USATODAY.com+-+So). (2006, February 19).

Arndt, B. 1985. "The Great Male Shortage." *World Press Review* 32 (July):58.

Arnett, J. 2003. *Adolescence and Emerging Adulthood: A Cultural Approach,* revised, 2nd ed. Upper Saddle River, NJ: Prentice Hall.

Arnold, Chandler. 1998. "Children and Stepfamilies: A Snapshot." http://www.clasp.org/pubs/familyformation/stepfamiliesfinal.BK!.htm.

Arp, C., and D. Arp. 2001. "The Magic of Older Love: Stoking Your Marital Fires Through the Years." In J. R. Levine and H. J. Markman, eds., *Why Do Fools Fall in Love? Experiencing the Magic, Mystery, and Meaning of Successful Relationships,* 117–122. San Francisco, CA: Jossey-Bass.

Artazcoz, L. 2004. "Unemployment and Mental Health: Understanding the Interactions Among Gender, Family Roles, and Social Class." *American Journal of Public Health* 94, 1(January); 82–88.

AsherMeadow. 2001. "The Many Faces of MSP." *MSP Magazine.* http://www.ashermeadow.com/amm/notes2.htm (2002, January 24).

"Asia." 2006. *New York Times* (July 1):A6.

Associated Press. 1997a. "28,000 Couples at Moon's Marriage Pledge." *Chicago Tribune* (November 30):15.

———. 1997b. "UN: Women Still Hold Few Top Jobs; Pay Also Lagging." *Chicago Tribune* (December 11):8.

———. 1999. "Alabama Moves to End Biracial Marriage Ban." *Chicago Tribune* (April 18):14.

———. 2000. "Americans Vote No to Gay Marriage, Yes to Partner Rights." *Daily Reflector* (June 1):A3.

———. 2001. "U.S. Male Population Nears That of Women." *Chicago Tribune* (September 10):6.

———. 2003. "Asian-American Divorce Rate Up, Census Shows." *Starbulletin.com* (May 29). http://starbulletin.com/2003/05/29/new/story5.html (2006, March 9).

———. 2005. "You Couldn't Ask for a More Perfect Union." *Chicago Tribune* (June 30).

Atchley, R. 1991. *Social Forces and Aging,* 6th ed. Belmont, CA: Wadsworth.

Athealth. 2006. "Domestic Violence Fact Sheet." http://www.athealth.com/consumer/Disorders/DomViolFacts.html (2006, July 13).

"At Least 100 Children a Year Leave U.S. to Be Adopted." 1997. *Baltimore Sun* (August 28):10A.

Atoh, M. 2001. "Very Low Fertility in Japan and Value Change Hypotheses." *Review of Population and Social Policy* 10:1–21.

Attanasio, O., and V. Lechene. 2002. "Tests of Income Pooling in Household Decisions." *Review of Economic Dynamics* 5, 4:720–748.

Atwater, L. 1982. *The Extramarital Connection: Sex, Intimacy, Identity.* New York: Irvington.

Avon Foundation. 2006. "Speak Out Against Domestic Violence." http://www.avoncompany.com/women/speakout/informational_materials/pa (2006, July 16).

Axinn, W. G., and A. Thornton. 1992. "The Relationship between Cohabitation and Divorce: Selectivity or Causal Influence?" *Demography* 29:357–74.

Aykan, H. 2003. "Effect of Childlessness on Nursing Home and Home Health Care Use." *Journal of Aging and Social Policy* 15, 1:33–53.

Baars, J., and F. Thomese. 1994. "Communes of Elderly People: Between Independence and Colonization." *Journal of Aging Studies* 8 (Winter):341–56.

Baca Zinn, M. 1994. "Adaptation and Continuity in Mexican-Origin Families." In R. L. Taylor, ed., *Minority Families in the United States: A Multicultural Perspective,* 64–71. Englewood Cliffs, NJ: Prentice Hall.

Bachman, R. 1994. *Violence against Women: A National Crime Victimization Survey Report.* U.S. Department of Justice, Office of Justice Programs, Bureau of Justice Statistics (Fall).

Bachrach, C. A. 1980. "Childlessness and Social Isolation among the Elderly." *Journal of Marriage and the Family* 42:627–37.

———. 1986. "Adoption Plans, Adopted Children, and Adoptive Mothers." *Journal of Marriage and the Family* 48:243–53.

———, P. F. Adams, S. Sambrano, and K. A. London. 1990. *Adoption in the 1980s.* U.S. National Center for Health Statistics, Advance Data no. 181 (January 5).

Bachu, A., and M. O'Connell. 2001. *Fertility of American Women: June 2000.* Current Population Reports, P20–543RV. Washington, DC: U.S. Census Bureau.

Baig, E. C. 1994. "Love at First Byte." *Business Week* (May 18):128.

Bailey, R. 2005. "Abort Plan B! The FDA's War on Promiscuity." *Reason* (January 12). (Accessed October 15, http://www.rppi.org/phprint.php.

Bailey, R. H. 1978. *The Home Front: U.S.A.* Alexandria, VA: Time-Life Books.

Baker, M. 2000. "Adolphus Gets Married; Soon He'll Meet His Wife." *Christian Science Monitor.* (February):15, 7.

Balaguer, A., and H. Markman. 1994. "Mate Selection." In V. S. Ramachandran, ed., *Encyclopedia of Human Behavior*, vol. 3, 127–35. New York: Academic Press.

Bales, K. 1999. *Disposable People: New Slavery in the Global Economy.* Berkeley: University of California Press.

Ball, E. 1998/1999. *Slaves in the Family.* New York: Ballantine.

Banis, R., ed. 2006. *Sexually Transmitted Diseases: Symptoms, Diagnosis, Treatment*, Prevention.

Banker, B. S., and S. L. Gaertner. 1998. "Achieving Stepfamily Harmony: An Intergroup-Relations Approach." *Journal of Family Psychology* 12, 3 (September):310–25.

———. 2001. *Intergroup Relations in Stepfamilies: In Search of Processes Involved in the Attainment of Stepfamily Harmony.* Paper presented at the annual meeting of the Society for the Study of Social Problems, Anaheim, CA.

Bannister, S. A. 1991. "The Criminalization of Women Fighting Back against Male Abuse: Imprisoned Battered Women as Political Prisoners." *Humanity and Society* 15, 4:400–16.

Barber, C.E. and K. R. Tremblay, Jr. 2004. "Grandparents: Styles and Satisfactions." (Oct. 7). http://www.ext.colostate.edu/pubs/consumer/10239.html(2006, June 15).

Barcus, E. F. 1983. *Images of Life on Children's Television: Sex Roles, Minorities and Families.* New York: Praeger.

Bardas, E., and M. Taylor. 2005. "Marriages and Wages." Working Papers of the Institute for Social and Economic Research. Paper 2005–1. Colchester: University of Essex.

Barer, B. M. 2001. "The 'Grands and Greats' of Very Old Black Grandmothers." *Journal of Aging Studies* 15, 1 (March):1–11.

Barker, O. "Never-Married Singles Face Negative Reaction." *USA Today* (February 22):E1.

Barlett, D. L., and J. B. Steele. 1992. *America: What Went Wrong?* Kansas City, MO: Andrews and McMeel.

Barling, J. 1991. "Father's Employment: A Neglected Influence on Children." In J. V. Lerner and N. L. Galambos, eds., *Employed Mothers and Their Children*, 181–209. New York: Garland.

Barnard, K E., and J. E. Solchany, 2002. "Mothering." In M. H. Borstein, ed., *Handbook of Parenting: Being and Becoming a Parent*, 2nd ed., Vol. 2, 3–25. Hillsdale, NJ. Erlbaum.

Barnes, S. 1998. "Keeping It Together." *Chicago Tribune* (August 2):sec. 13, 1.

Barnett, O. W., C. L. Miller-Perrin, and R. D. Perrin. 1997. *Family Violence across the Lifespan.* Thousand Oaks, CA: Sage.

Barnett, R. and C. Rivers. 2004. *Same Difference: How Gender Myths Are Hurting Our Relationships, Our Children, and Our Jobs.* New York: Basic Books.

Barr, M. 2005. "Shaken Baby Syndrome Is Real and Based on Medical Evidence." National Center on Shaken Baby Syndrome. www.dontshake.com (2006, July 19).

Barranti, C. R. 1985. "The Grandparent–Grandchild Relationship: Family Resources in an Era of Voluntary Bonds." *Family Relations* 34:343–52.

Barth, R. P., and M. Berry. 1988. *Adoption and Disruption Rates, Risks, and Responses.* Hawthorne, NY: Aldine de Gruyter.

———. D. Brooks, and S. Iyer. 1995. *Adoptions in California: Current Demographic Profiles and Projections through the End of the Century.* Berkeley: Child Welfare Research Center.

Bartkowski, J. 1999. "One Step Forward, One Step Back: Progressive Traditionalism and the Negotiation of Domestic Labor in Evangelical Families." *Gender Issues* 17, 4 (Fall):37–61.

Baruch, G., R. Barnett, and C. Rivers. 1983. *Lifeprints: New Patterns of Love and Work for Today's Women.* New York: McGraw-Hill.

Basow, S. 1986. *Gender Stereotypes: Traditions and Alternatives.* Monterey, CA: Brooks/Cole.

———. 1992. *Gender: Stereotypes and Roles*, 3d ed. Belmont, CA: Brooks/Cole.

Batalova, J. A., and P. N. Cohen. 2002. "Premarital Cohabitation and Housework: Couples in Cross-National Perspective." *Journal of Marriage and the Family* 64:743–755.

Battle, J., C. Cohen, D. Warren, G. Fergerson, and S. Audam. 2002. *Say It Loud, I'm Black and I'm Proud: Black Pride Survey* 2000. New York: The National Gay and Lesbian Task Force Policy Institute.

Baugher, R. J., C. Burger, R. Smith, and K. Wallstron. 1989–90. "A Comparison of Terminally Ill Persons at Various Time Periods to Death." *Omega* 20:103–15.

Baumrind, D. 1968. "Authoritarian versus Authoritative Parental Control." *Adolescence* 3:255–72.

———. 1979. "Current Patterns of Parental Authority." *Developmental Psychology Monographs* 41:255.

———. 1991. "Effective Parenting during the Early Adolescent Transition." In P. Cowan and E. M. Hetherington, eds., *Advances in Family Research*: vol. 2, Family Transition, 111–63. Hillsdale, NJ: Erlbaum.

Bauserman, R. 2002. "Child Adjustment in Joint-Custody Versus Sole-Custody Arrangements: A Meta-Analytic Review." *Journal of Family Psychology* 16, 1:91–162.

BBC News. 2000. "Globalisation: What on Earth Is It All About?" (September 14). http://news.bbc.co.uk/hi/english/special_report/1999/02/99/e-cyclopedia/newsid_711000/71... (2002, January 18).

Bean, F., R. Curtis, Jr., and J. Marcum. 1977. "Familism and Marital Satisfaction among Mexican Americans: The Effects of Family Size, Wife's Labor Force Participation, and Conjugal Power." *Journal of Marriage and the Family* 39 (November):759–67.

Bearman, P., and H. Bruckner. 2001. "Promising the Future: Virginity Pledges and First Intercourse." *American Journal of Sociology*, vol. 106, no. 4.

Bedford, V. H.1997. "Sibling Relationships in Middle Adulthood and Old Age." In R. M. Blieszner and V. H. Bedford, eds., *Handbook on Aging and The Family*, 201–222, Westport, CT: Greenwood.

Becerra, R. M. 1998. "The Mexican-American Family." In Charles H. Mindel, R. W. Habenstein, and R. Wright, Jr. *Ethnic Families in America: Patterns and Variations*, 153–71. Upper Saddle River, NJ: Prentice Hall.

———, and D. Shaw. 1984. *The Hispanic Elderly.* Lanham, MD: University Press of America.

Beck, M. 1988. "Willing Families, Waiting Kids." *Newsweek* (September 12):64.

Becker, H. 1977. "Whose Side Are We On?"

Bedard, J. 1992. *Breaking with Tradition: Diversity, Conflict, and Change in Contemporary American Families.* Dix Hills, NY: General Hall.

Bedard, K., and O. Deschenes. 2005. "Sex Preferences, Marital Dissolution, and the Economic Status of Women." *The Journal of Human Resources* 40, 2 (Spring):411–434.

Beer, W. R., 1983. *Househusbands: Men and Housework in American Families.* South Hadley, MA: Bergen and Garvey.

———. 1989. *Strangers in the House: The World of Stepsiblings and Half-Siblings.* New Brunswick, NJ: Transaction.

Behrens, L. 1990. "Study Shows Men's Capacity for Care." *Chicago Tribune* (October 28):sec. 6, 2.

Belcastro, P. A. 1985. "Sexual Behavior Differences between Black and White Students." *Journal of Sex Research* 21:56–57.

Belkin, L. 2003. "The Opt-Out Revolution." *The New York Times Magazine* (October 26):42.

Bell, A. P., and M. Weinberg. 1978. *Homosexualities: A Study of Diversities among Men.* New York: Simon & Schuster.

———, and S. Hammersmith. 1981. *Sexual Preference: Its Development in Men and Women.* Bloomington: Indiana University Press.

Bell, M. 2001. "Gay Adoption Ban Upheld by U.S. Judge." *Chicago Tribune* (August 31):1, 2.

Bell, R. 1971. *Marriage and Family Interaction*, 3d ed. Homewood, IL: Dorsey.

Bem, S. L. 1983. "Gender Schema Theory and Its Implications for Child Development: Raising Gender-Schematic Children in a Gender-Schematic Society." *Signs* 8:598–616.

———. 1993. *The Lenses of Gender: Transforming the Debate on Social Inequality*. New Haven, CT: Yale University Press.

Bengtson, V., and D. Dannefer. 1987. "Families, Work and Aging: Implications of Disordered Cohort Flow for the 21st Century." In R. Ward and S. Tobin, eds., *Health in Aging: Sociological Issues and Policy Directions*, 256–89. New York: Springer.

———. and R. Harootyan, eds. 1994. *Hidden Connections: Intergenerational Linkages in American Society*. New York: Springer.

———. C. Rosenthal, and L. Burton. 1990. "Families and Aging: Diversity and Heterogeneity." In R. H. Binstock and L. K. George, eds., *Handbook of Aging and the Social Sciences*, 3d ed., 263–87. New York: Academic Press.

———. 1996. "Paradoxes of Families and Aging." In R. H. Binstock and L. K. George, eds., *Handbook of Aging and the Social Sciences*, 3d ed., 253–82. New York: Academic Press.

Benjamin, L. 1991. *The Black Elite: Facing the Color Line in the Twilight of the Twentieth Century*. Chicago: Nelson-Hall.

Benjamin, O., and O. Sullivan. 1996. "The Importance of Difference." *Sociological Review* 44, 2:225–51.

Bennett, J. 1989. "The Data Game." *New Republic* 200 (February 13):20–22.

Benokraitis, N. V., and J. R. Feagin. 1986. *Modern Sexism*. Englewood Cliffs, NJ: Prentice Hall.

Berado, F. M. 1968. "Widowhood Status in the U.S.: Perspectives on a Neglected Aspect of the Family Life Cycle." *Family Coordinator* 17:191–203.

———. 1970. "Survivorship and Social Isolation: The Case of the Aged Widower." *Family Coordinator* 19:11–15.

Beresford, B., P. Rabiee, and T. Sloper. 2005. "Priorities and Perceptions of Disabled Children and Young People and their Families Regarding Outcomes of Social Care." *The University of York, Social Policy Research Center*. http://www.york.ac.uk/inst/spru/research/summs/priorpercep. htm (2006, August 17).

Berger, R. 1982. *Gay and Gray: The Older Homosexual Man*. Chicago: University of Illinois Press.

———. 1998. *Stepfamilies: A Multi-Dimensional Perspective*. New York: Haworth Press.

———. 2001. "Gay Stepfamilies: A Triple-Stigmatized Group." In J. M. Lehmann, ed., *The Gay and Lesbian Marriage and Family Reader*, 171–194. Lincoln: University of Nebraska Press.

Bergeron, K. E. 2006. *Science and Practice in Suicidology: Promoting Collaboration, Integration and Understanding*. Washington, DC: American Association of Suicidology.

Berkofsky, J. 2001. "By Numbers, NJPS Paints Portrait of American Jewry." *Jewish Community Federation* (September 10).http://www. sfjcf.org/news/archive/story.asp?ArticleID=84299 (2006, February 10).

Berlin, I. 1974. *Slaves without Masters: The Free Negro in the Antebellum South*. New York: Pantheon.

Bernard, J. 1972. *The Future of Marriage*. New York: World.

———. 1982. *The Future of Marriage*, 2d ed. New Haven, CT: Yale University Press.

———. 1984. "The Good-Provider Role: Its Rise and Fall." In P. Voydanoff, ed., *Work and Family: Changing Roles of Men and Women*, 43–60. Palo Alto, CA: Mayfield.

Besharov, D. J. 1987. "Suffer the Little Children: How Child Abuse Programs Hurt Poor Families." *Policy Review* 39 (Winter):52–55.

Best, J., ed. 1995. *Images of Issues: Typifying Contemporary Social Problems*. New York: Aldine de Gruyter.

Better Homes and Gardens. 1988. "What's Happening to American Families? Report from the Editors." Meredith Corporation.

Bhanot, R., and J. Jovanovic. 2005. "Do Parental Academic Stereotypes Influence Whether They Intrude on Their Children's Homework?" *Sex Roles* 52, 9/10(May):597–607.

Bhopal, K. 1997. "South Asian Women Within Households: Dowries, Degradation and Despair." *Women's Studies International Forum* 20(4):489–492.

Bianchi, S. 2000. "Maternal Employment and Time with Children: Dramatic Change or Surprising Continuity?" Presidential address to the Population Association of America, Los Angeles, March 24.

———, and D. Spain. 1986. *American Women in Transition*. New York: Russell Sage Foundation.

Bibby, R. W. 2005. "Child Care Aspirations." *The Vanier Institute of the Family* (February 10). http://www.vifamily.ca/newsroom/press_feb_ 10_05_c.html (2006, January 18).

Bilefsky, D. 2006. "How to Avoid Honor Killing in Turkey? Honor Suicide." *New York Times* (July 16):3.

Billingsley, A. 1968. *Black Families in White America*. Englewood Cliffs, NJ: Prentice Hall.

Bingham, S. G. 1996. "Sexual Harassment on the Job, on the Campus." In J. T. Wood, ed., *Gendered Relationships*, 233–51. Belmont, CA: Wadsworth.

Binnie, J. 1997. "Invisible Europeans: Sexual Citizenship in the New Europe." *Environment and Planning* A. 29 (February):237–48.

Black, D., G. Gates, S. Sanders, and L. Taylor. 2000. "Demographics of the Gay and Lesbian Population in the United States: Evidence from Available Systematic Data Sources." *Demography* 37:139–54.

Black, H. 2006. "Weighing Age, Care: Elderly Are Target of Calls for Ration of Health Care." *Milwaukee Journal Sentinel*. (April 9). http://www. jsonline.com/story/index.aspx?id=414101 (2006, June 26).

Blackless, M., A. Charuvastra, A. Derryck, A. Fausto-Sterling, K. Lauzanne, and E. Lee. 2000. "How Sexually Dimorphic Are We? Review and Synthesis." *American Journal of Human Biology* 12:151–166.

Blackwell, J. E. 1985. *The Black Community: Diversity and Unity*. New York: Harper & Row.

Blake, W. M., and C. A. Darling. 2000. "Quality of Life: Perceptions of African Americans." *Journal of Black Studies* 30(January):411–427.

Blanchard, R., B. W. Steiner, and L. H. Clemmensen. 1985. "Gender Dysphoria, Gender Reorientation, and the Management of Trans-sexualism." *Journal of Consulting and Clinical Psychology* 53, 3:295–304.

Blank, R. 1988. "Making Babies: The State of the Art." In J. Gipson Wells, ed., *Current Issues in Marriage and the Family*, 171–77. New York: Macmillan.

Blankenhorn, D. 1998. "The Diminishment of American Fatherhood." In S. J. Ferguson, ed., *Shifting the Center: Understanding Contemporary Families*, 337–35. Mountain View, CA: Mayfield.

Blassingame, J. 1979. *The Slave Community*, 2d ed. New York: Oxford University Press.

Blau, P. 1964. *Exchange and Power in Social Life*. New York: Wiley.

———, and O. Duncan. 1967. *The American Occupational Structure*. New York: Wiley.

Blieszner, R., and R. C. Adams. 1992. *Adult Friendships*. Newbury Park, CA: Sage.

———. and V. H. Bedford, eds. 1995. *Handbook of Aging and the Family*. Westport, CT: Greenwood.

Block, J. 1981. "Your Marriage Survival Kit." *Parents* (April):61+.

Blood, R. O., Jr., and D. M. Wolfe. 1960. *Husbands and Wives*. New York: Macmillan.

Bluestone, B. 1987. "Deindustrialization and Unemployment in America." In P. D. Staudohar and H. E. Brown, eds., *Deindustrialization and Plant Closure*, 6–7. Lexington, MA: D. C. Heath.

Blum, D. 1997. *Sex on the Brain*. New York: Viking.

Blumstein, P., and P. Schwartz. 1983. *American Couples: Money, Work, Sex*. New York: Morrow.

Boeringer, S. B., C. L. Shehan, and R. L. Akers. 1991. "Social Contests and Social Learning in Sexual Coercion and Aggression: Assessing the Contribution of Fraternity Membership." *Family Relations* 40:58–64.

Bohannan, P. 1970. *Divorce and After*. New York: Doubleday.

———. 1985. *All the Happy Families*. New York: McGraw-Hill.

Bojorquez, J. 1997. "Line by Line, Their Marriage Is Working." *Sacramento Bee* (February 10). http://www.sacbee.com/static/archive/ news/projects/lessons/linebyline.html (2001, November 11).

Bolig, R., P. J. Stein, and P. C. McHenry. 1984. "The Self-Advertisement Approach to Dating: Male–Female Differences." *Family Relations* 33:587–92.

Bond, J. T., C. Thompson, E. Galinsky, and D. Prottas. 2003. *2002 National Study of the Changing Workforce*. Families and Work Institute.

———. E. Galinsky, S. S. Kim, and E. Brownfield. 2005. *2005 National Study of Employers*. Families and Work Institute.

Booth, A., and P. R. Amato. 1994. "Parental Marital Quality, Parental Divorce, and Relations with Parents." *Journal of Marriage and the Family* 56:21–34.

———. and J. N. Edwards. 1992. "Starting Over: Why Remarriages Are More Unstable." *Journal of Family Issues* 13, 2 (June):179–94.

———. D. Johnson, L. K. White, and J. N. Edwards. 1986. "Divorce and Marital Instability over the Life Course." *Journal of Family Issues* 7:421–42.

Borden, S. 1999. "Teen Dating Violence." http://www.infolane.com/save/teen.html.

Borland, D. M. 1975. "An Alternative Model of the Wheel Theory." *Family Coordinator* 24 (July):289–92.

Bossard, J. 1932. "Residential Propinquity as a Factor in Mate Selection." *American Journal of Sociology* 38:219–24.

Boston Women's Health Book Collective. 1992. *The New Our Bodies, Ourselves*, rev. ed. New York: Simon & Schuster.

———. 2005. *Our Bodies, Ourselves: A New Eddition for a New Era*. New York: Touchstone Books.

Boswell, T. D., and J. R. Curtis. 1983. *The Cuban-American Experience: Culture, Images and Perspectives*. Totowa, NJ: Rowman and Allanheld.

Botta, R. A. 1999. "Television Images and Adolescent Girls' Body Image Disturbance." *Journal of Communication* 49, 2 (Spring):22–41.

Bound, J., G. Duncan, D. Laren, and L. Oleinick. 1991. "Poverty Dynamics in Widowhood." *Journal of Gerontology* 46, 3 (May): S115–24.

Bowcott, O. 2001. "Counting Costs of Illegal Drug Trade." *The Guardian* (July 4). http://www.guardian.co.uk/drugs/Story/o,2763,516481,00.html (2002, January 23).

Bower, B. 2001. "Healthy Aging May Depend on Past Habits." *Science News* 159, 24 (June 16):373.

Bowman, P. J. 1993. "The Impact of Economic Marginality among African American Husbands and Fathers." In H. P. McAdoo, ed., *Family Ethnicity: Strength in Diversity*, 120–37, Thousand Oaks, CA: Sage.

Boyer, D., and Fineman, F. "Sexual Abuse as a Factor in Adolescent Pregnancy and Child Maltreatment." *Family Planning Perspectives* 14, 1 (January/February):4–12.

Boyer, L. 2004. "Grandparents Parenting." Colorado State University Cooperative Extension Family and Consumer Science, Morgan County.http://www.ext.colostate.edu/PUBS/columnha/ha9804.html (2005, May 6).

Boyle, M. 1995. "Abuse Victims Trapped in Violent Cycle." Standard-Times [online].

Bozett, F. W. 1987. *Gay and Lesbian Parents*. New York: Praeger.

———. 1990. *Homosexuality and Family Relations*. New York: Haworth Press.

Bradsher, K. 1989. "Employers Urge Men to Wed for Success." *News and Observer* (December 23):3D.

Braithwaite, D. O., L. N. Olson, T. D. Golish, C. Soukup, and P. Turnman. 2001. "Becoming a Family: Developmental Processes Represented in Blended Family Discourse." *Journal of Applied Communication Research* 29:221–247.

Bramlett, M. D., and W. D. Mosher. 2002. Cohabitation, Marriage, Divorce, and Remarriage in the United States. Hyattsville, MD: National Center for Health Statistics.

———. 2001. *First Marriage Dissolution, Divorce, and Remarriage: United States*. Advance Data from Vital and Health Statistics, no. 323 (May 31). Hyattsville, MD: National Center for Health Statistics, 2001.

Brandon, J. 2000. "Raising the World's Standard of Living." *Christian Science Monitor* (January 3). http://www.igc.org/globalpolicy/socecon/global/livstand.htm (2002, January 18).

Brandon, K. 1996. "Emerging Fertility Clinic Scandal Has Californians Rapt." *Chicago Tribune* (March 24):6.

———. 1999. "Teen Girls Wising up on Having Children: Peers, Parents and Contraception Bring Drop in Pregnancies." *Chicago Tribune* (May 3):1.

Braver, S. L. 1998. *Divorced Dads: Shattering the Myths*. New York: Tarcher/Putnam.

Bray, J., and J. Kelly. 1998. *Stepfamilies: Love, Marriage and Parenting in the First Decade*. New York: Broadway Books.

Brayton-Purcell. 2003. "Family Members Responsible for Most Instances of Elder Abuse, Legislative Committee Says." http://www.elder-abuse-information.com/news/news_111403_family_abuse (2006, July 11).

Brecher, E. 1984. *Love, Sex, and Aging*. Boston: Little, Brown.

Brehm, S., R. Miller, D. Perlman, and S. Campbell. 2001. *Intimate Relationships*. New York: McGraw Hill.

Brehm, S. S. 1992. *Intimate Relationships*. New York: McGraw-Hill.

Brewer, L. 2001. "Gender Socialization and the Cultural Construction of Elder Caregivers." *Journal of Aging Studies* 15, 3 (September):217–35.

Brewer, R. 1999. "Marriage Vows Revisited." Interview, Chicago.

Brewster, K., J. Billy, and W. R. Grady. 1993. "Social Context and Adolescent Behavior: The Impact of Community on the Transition to Sexual Activity." *Social Forces* 71:713–40.

Brines, J., and K. Joyner. 1999. "The Ties That Bind: Principles of Cohesion in Cohabitation and Marriage." *American Sociological Review* 64 (June):333–55.

"Britain's New Minority." 1999. *Chicago Tribune* (January 31):sec. 13, 3.

Brod, H., ed. 1987. *The Making of Masculinities: The New Men's Studies*. Boston: Allen & Unwin.

Brodbar-Nemzer, J. Y. 1986. "Divorce and Group Commitment: The Case of Jews." *Journal of Marriage and the Family* 48:329–40.

Brody, J. 2006. "Children, Media and Sex: A Big Book of Blank Pages." *New York Times* (January 31): Sec. F, p. 7.

Brody, J. E. 1999. "Earlier Work with Children Steers Them from Crime." *New York Times* (March 15):A16.

Brooks, D. 2002. "Making It: Love and Success at America's Finest Universities." *The Weekly Standard*, 15 December 23.

Bronstein, P. 1988. "Father–Child Interaction: Implications for Gender Role Socialization." In P. Bronstein and C. P. Cowan, eds., *Fatherhood Today: Men's Changing Role in the Family*, 107–24. New York: Wiley.

Bronte-Tinkew, J., K. A. Moore, R. C. Capps, and J. Zaff. 2006. "The Influence of Father Involvement on Youth Risk Behaviors Among Adolescents: A Comparison of Native-Born and Immigrant Families." *Social Science Research* 35:181–209.

Brosnahan, T. 2006. "Women in Turkish Society." http://www.turkeytravel-lplanner.com/TravelDetails/WomenTravelers/WomenInTkSociety.html (2006, January 16).

Brotman, B. 1992. "A Shaker Cares." *Chicago Tribune* (February 19):sec. 5, 1, 5.

Broverman, I., D. M. Broverman, F. E. Clarkson, P. S. Rosenkrantz, and S. R. Vogel. 1970. "Sex-Role Stereotypes and Clinical Judgments of Mental Health." *Journal of Consulting and Clinical Psychology* 34:1–7.

Brown, G., and B. Anderson. 1991. "Psychiatric Morbidity in Adult Inpatients with Childhood Histories of Sexual and Physical Abuse." *American Journal of Psychiatry* 148:55–61.

Brown, J. 2002. "Mass Media Influences on Sexuality." *The Journal of Sex Research*, 39, 1:42–45.

———. and S. Keller. 2000. "Can the Mass Media Be Healthy Sex Educators?" *Family Planning Perspectives*. 32, 5 (September/October): 255–56.

Brown, L. R. 2006. "A New World Order." *The Guardian* (January 25). http://www.guardian.co.uk/China/story/0,,1694346,00.html (2006, August 6).

Brown, M. R. 2001. "African Americans in the Middle." *Black Enterprise* 32, 2 (September):26.

Brown, P. L. 2006. "Growing Old Together, in New Kind of Commune." *The New York Times* (February 27):A1, A16.

Brown, S., and I. D. Yalom. *Treating Alcoholism*. San Francisco: Jossey-Bass.

Browne, A. 1993. "Family Violence and Homelessness: The Relevance of Trauma Histories in the Lives of Homeless Women." *American Journal of Orthopsychiatry* 63, 3 (July):370–84.

Brownsworth, V. 1996. "Tying the Knot or the Hangman's Noose: The Case against Marriage." *Journal of Gay, Lesbian, and Bisexual Identity* 1 (January):91–98.

Brubaker, T. H. 1985. *Later Life Families*. Beverly Hills, CA: Sage.

———. 1990. *Family Relationships in Later Life*, 2d ed. Newbury Park, CA: Sage.

Bruno, B. 2001. "A New National Holiday: Stepparents Day." http://www/selfgrowth.com/articles/Bruno.html (2001, December 3).

Bryjak, G. J., and M. P. Soroka. 1994. *Sociology: Cultural Diversity in a Changing World*. Needham Heights, MA: Allyn & Bacon.

Bryson, K., and L. M. Casper. 1999. "Coresident Grandparents and Grandchildren." *Current Population Reports*, P23–198. Washington, DC: U.S. Census Bureau.

Buchler, C. A. Krishnakuman, G. Stone, C. Anthony, S. Pemerton, and J. Gerard. 1998. "Interparental Conflict Styles and Youth Problem Behaviors: A Two-Sample Replication Study." *Journal of Marriage and the Family* 60:119–32.

———. and M. Langenbrunner. 1987. "Divorce-Related Stressors: Occurrence, Disruptiveness, and Area of Life Change." *Journal of Divorce* 11:25–50.

Bulcroft, K., and M. O'Connor-Roden. 1986. "Never Too Late." *Psychology Today* (June): 66–69.

Bulcroft, R. A., and K. A. Bulcroft. 1993. "Race Differences in Attitudinal and Motivational Factors in the Decision to Marry." *Journal of Marriage and the Family* (May):55:338–55.

Bumiller, E. 1996. "Enter Smiling, the Stylish Carolyn Bessette." *New York Times* (September 29):sec. 1, 39.

Bumpass, L. L., and H. Lu. 2000. "Trends in Cohabitation and Implications for Children's Family Contexts in the United States." *Population Studies* 54:29–41.

Bumpass, L. L., R. K. Raley, and J. A. Sweet. 1995. "The Changing Character of Stepfamilies: Implications of Cohabitation and Nonmarital Childbearing." *Demography* 32, 3 (August):425–35.

Bumpass, L. L., J. A. Sweet, and A. Cherlin. 1991. "The Role of Cohabitation in Declining Rates of Marriage." *Journal of Marriage and the Family* 53:913–27.

Bumpass, L. L., J. A. Sweet, and T. Castro-Martin. 1990. "Changing Patterns of Remarriage." *Journal of Marriage and the Family* 52:747–56.

Bunch, C. 1979. "Learning from Lesbian Separatism." In Sheila Ruth, ed., *Issues in Feminism*, 551–56. Boston: Houghton Mifflin.

Bunker, B. B., J. M. Zubek, V. J. Vanderslice, and R. W. Rice. 1992. "Quality of Life in Dual-Career Families: Commuting versus Single-Residence Couples." *Journal of Marriage and the Family* 54:399–407.

Bureau of Justice Statistics Crime Data Brief. 2003.

Bureau of Labor Statistics, 2004. "Displaced Workers Summary." (July 30). http://www.bls.gov/news.release/disp.nr0.htm (2006, January 2).

———. 2005. *American Time Use Survey* Washington, DC: U.S. Department of Labor.

———. 2006. "Median Weekly Earnings of Full-time Wage and Salary Workers by Union Affiliation and Selected Characteristics (January 20). www.bls.gov/news.release/union2.to2.htm (2006, January 20).

Burger, J. M., and L. Burns. 1988. "The Illusion of Unique Invulnerability and the Use of Effective Contraception." *Personality and Social Psychology Bulletin* 14:264–70.

Burgess, E. W. 1926. "The Family as a Unity of Interacting Personalities." *Family* 7:3–9.

Burman, P. 1988. *Killing Time, Losing Ground: Experiences of Unemployment*. Toronto: Wall and Thompson.

Burns, A. L., G. Mitchell, and S. Obradovich. 1989. "Of Sex Roles and Strollers: Female and Male Attention to Toddlers at the Zoo." *Sex Roles* 20:309–15.

Burns, J. F. 1998. "Though Illegal, Child Marriage Is Popular in Part of India." *New York Times* (May 11):A1.

Burwell, M. 2006. "Celebrity Weddings—Flowers, Favors, Details." *About, Inc.*: A part of *the New York Times Company*. http:// weddings.about.com/cs/bridesandgrooms/a/celebritywed_2.htm(2006, April 24).

BushGreenwatch. 2005. "Bush Administration Manipulates Science in Grazing Report." (June 28). http://www.bushgreenwatch.org (2005, June 28).

Buss, D., R. Larsen, D. Westen, and J. Semmelroth. 1992. "Sex Differences in Jealousy: Evolution, Physiology, and Psychology." *Psychological Science* 3:251–255.

Bussey, K., and A. Bandura. 1984. "Influence of Gender Constancy and Social Power on Sex-Linked Modeling." *Journal of Personality and Social Psychology* 47:1292–1302.

Butler, D. 1999. "Healthy Ideas: Pregnant and Prosecuted." http://healthyideas.com/poll/980825/html (1999, May 19).

Butler, R. 1975. *Why Survive? Being Old in America*. New York: Harper & Row.

Butrica, B. A., and H. M. Iams. 2000. "Divorced Women at Retirement: Projections of Economic Well-Being in the Near Future." *Social Security Bulletin* 63, 3:3–12.

Buunk, B. B., and B. van Driel. 1989. *Variant Lifestyles and Relationships*. Newbury Park, CA: Sage.

Byer, C., and L. Shainberg. 1994. *Dimensions of Human Sexuality*. Madison, WI: Brown and Benchmark.

Cahill, S., K. South, and J. Spade. 2000. *Outing Age: Public Policy Issues Affecting Gay, Lesbian, Bisexual and Transgender Elders*. Washington, DC: National Gay and Lesbian Task Force.

Calasanti, T. 1999. "Feminism and Gerontology: Not Just for Women." *Hallym International Journal of Aging* 1, 1:44–55.

Calhoun, A. W. 1917. *A Social History of the American Family: from Colonial Times to the Present*, vol. 1. Cleveland: Arthur H. Clark.

Caleidoscop. 2006. "Amnesty for Thousands of Illegal Immigrants." http://www.caleidoscop.org.ro/Members/Marius. (2006, August 23).

California State Parent Teacher Association. 1998. "Teen Dating Violence." *Newsletter* 60, 3 (Winter). http://www.capta.org/I...o.3winter/7dating.html (1999, March 19).

Call, V., S. Sprecher, and P. Schwartz. 1995. "The Incidence and Frequency of Marital Sex in a National Sample." *Journal of Marriage and the Family* 57:639–52.

Camarota, S. A. 2002. "Immigrants in the United States—2002." Center for Immigration Studies (November). http:///www.cis.org/articles/2002/back1302.html (2006, April 17).

Campbell, S. 2001. "Moving On: Parental Breakups May Not Always Be Bad for Kids." *Psychology Today* 34, 4 (July/August):16.

Campo-Flores, B., and Y. Rosenberg. 2000. "A Return to Wilding." *Newsweek* (June 26):28.

Canada, G. 1998. *Reaching Up for Manhood: Transforming the Lives of Boys in America*. Boston: Beacon Press.

Cancian, F. M. 1991. "The Feminization of Love." In M. Hutter, ed., *The Family Experience*, 367–82. New York: Macmillan.

———. 1993. "Gender Politics: Love and Power in the Private and Public Spheres." In B. J. Fox, ed., *Family Patterns, Gender Relations*, 204–12. Toronto: Oxford University Press.

Cano, A., and K. O'Leary. 1997. "Romantic Jealousy and Affairs: Research and Implications for Couple Therapy." *Journal of Sex and Marital Therapy* 23, (4): 249–275.

Cantor, M. H., and V. Little. 1985. "Aging and Social Care." In R. H. Binstock and E. Shanas, eds., *Handbook of Aging*, 745–81. New York: Van Nostrand Reinhold.

Capell, K., L. Cohn, R. Tiplady, and J. Ewing. 2004. "Sex-Bias Suits: The Fight Gets Ugly." *Business Week* 64–65.

Cardell, M., S. Finn, and J. Marecek. 1981. "Sex-Role Identity, Sex-Role Behavior, and Satisfaction in Heterosexual, Lesbian, and Gay Male Couples." *Psychology of Women Quarterly* 5:488–94.

Care for the Family Caregiver: A Place to Start 2005. Washington, DC: National Alliance for Caregivers and the Health Plan of New York.

Carlier, A. 1972. *Marriage in the United States*. New York: Arno Press.

Carlson, D. 2001. "Over Half of Americans Believe in Love at First Sight." *Gallup News Service* (February 14). http://www.gallup.com/poll/releases/pr010214d.asp (2001, September 28).

Carlson, D. K. 2005. "Do Americans Give Women A Fighting Chance?" The Gallup Organization (June 14). www.gallup.com/poll/content/print.aspx?ci=16810 (2005, June 14).

Carmichael, S., and C. V. Hamilton. 1967. *Black Power: The Politics of Liberation in America*. New York: Vintage Books/Random House.

Caron, S. L., and M. Ulin. 1997. "Closeting and the Quality of Lesbian Relationships." *Families in Society* 78 (July/August):413–19.

Carr, D., and R. Utz. 2002. "Later-Life Widowhood in the United States: New Directions in Research and Theory." *Aging International* 27, 1:65–88.

Carr, L. G., and L. S. Walsh. 1983. "The Planter's Wife: The Experience of White Women in 17th Century Maryland." In M. Gordon, ed., *The American Family in Social-Historical Perspective*, 263–88. New York: St. Martin's Press.

Carrere, S., and J. Gottman. 1999. "Predicting Divorce among Newlyweds from the First Three Minutes of a Marital Conflict Discussion." *Family Process* 38 (Fall):293–302.

Carrigan, T., B. Connell, and J. Lee. 1987. "Toward a New Sociology of Masculinity." In H. Brod, ed., *The Making of Masculinities*, 63–100. Boston: Allen & Unwin.

Carroll, J. 2005a. "Who's Worried About Their Weight?" The Gallup Organization (August 9). www.gallup.com/poll/content/print.aspx?ci= 17752 (2005, August 16).

———. 2005b "Six in 10 Americans Have Attempted to Lose Weight." The Gallup Organization (August 16) www.gallup.com/poll/content/ print.aspx?ci=17890.

———. 2006 "Public Continues to Support Right-to-Die for Terminally Ill Patients." *The Gallup Poll* (June 19). http://poll.gallup. com/content/ default.aspx?ci=23356 & VERSION=p (2006, June 26).

———. 2005c. "Americans' Financial Woes." The Gallup Poll. (December 6). http://poll.gallup.com/content/default.aspx?ci=10618 & VERSION=p (2006, January 5).

———. 2005d. "American's Personal Satisfaction." The Gallup Poll http://poll.gallup.com/content/default.aspx?ci=14506 & pg=2#pageTop (2005, January 10).

Carter, B. 1991. "Children's TV, Where Boys Are King." *New York Times* (May 1):A1, C18.

Carter, H., and P. Glick. 1976. *Marriage and Divorce: A Social and Economic Study*, 2d ed. Cambridge, MA: Harvard University Press.

Casper, L. M., and S. M. Bianchi. 2002. *Continuity and Change in the American Family*. Thousand Oaks, CA: Sage.

"Catalyst Census Finds Few Women Corporate Officers." 2000. *Catalyst* (February 8). http://www.catalystwomen.org/press/releases/ release020800.html (2001, October 17).

"Catalyst Fact Sheet: 2000 Catalyst Census of Women Corporate Officers and Top Earners of the Fortune 500." 2000. *Catalyst*. http://www. catalystwomen.org/press/factsheets/factscote00.html (2001, October 17).

Catalyst. 2003. "Women in the Fortune 500." www.catalyst.org/presswom/ press_releases/2–10-05%20catalyst%20Female%20CEOs%20Fact% 20sheet.pdf (2006, January 12).

Cattell, M. 1996. "Gender, Aging, and Health: A Comparative Approach." In E. Sargent and C. Bretell, eds., *Gender and Health: An International Perspective*, 87–111. Upper Saddle River, NJ: Prentice Hall.

Caulfield, M. D. 1985. "Sexuality in Human Evolution: What Is Natural in Sex?" *Feminist Studies* 11 (Summer):343–64.

Cavanaugh, J. 1993. *Adult Development and Aging*, 2d ed. Pacific Grove, CA: Brooks/Cole.

CBS News. 2004. "Staying at Home." (October 10). http://www. cbsnews.com/stories/2004/10/08/60minutes/printable648240.shtml (2006, January 4).

———. 2005. "Celeb Prenups Rule Hollywood." (December 14), http://www.palmbeachpost.com/accent/content/accent/epaper/2005/ 01/21/a1e_new_TRUMP_PRENUP_0121.html (2006, April 24).

"CDC Report Shows That Age Continues to be a Major Factor in Determining Success of Assisted Reproductive Technology." 2006. *Press Release* (December 21). http://www.cdc.gov/od/oc/media/ pressrel/r051221.htm (2006, April 24).

CDC. 1994. "1992 National Health Interview Survey [NHIS]," *Morbidity and Mortality Weekly Report* 43, 13 (April 8):231–33.

———. 1997. "Rates of Homicide, Suicide, and Firearm-Related Death among Children—26 Industrialized Countries." *Morbidity and Mortality Weekly Report* 46(05):101–5 (February 7).

———. 1998. "Joint HHS and DOJ Survey Shows Extent of Violence against Women." CDC, National Center for Injury Prevention and Control. http://waisgate.hhs.go...+O&WAISaction+retrieve (1999, June 2).

———. 1999. *Assisted Reproductive Technology Success Rates: National Summary and Fertility Clinic Reports*. Atlanta: Division of Reproductive Health. http://www.cdc.gov/nccdphp/drh/art.htm.

———. 2000. *HIV/AIDS Surveillance Report, Year-End Edition*, vol. 12, no. 2.

CDC. 2000a. "HIV/AIDS among U.S. Women: Minority and Young Women at Continuing Risk." Centers for Disease Control and Prevention (September).

———. 2000b. "HIV/AIDS among Hispanics in the United States." Centers for Disease Control and Prevention (September).

Celio, A. A., M. F. Zabinski, and D. E. Wilfley. 2002. "African American Body Images." In T. F. Cash & T. Pruzinsky, eds., *Body Image*, 234–242. New York: Guilford Press.

Center on Budget and Policies Priorities. 2001. "Poverty Trends for Families Headed by Working Single Mothers, 1993 to 1999." http://www.cbpp.org/8-16-01.wel.htm (2001, October 24).

Center for Defense Information. 2001a. "On Terror and Terrorism." *Terrorism* Project (December 3). http://www.cdi.org/terrorism/ onterror-pr/cfm (2002, January 18).

———. 2001b. "The International Islamic Terrorist Network." *Terrorism Project* (September 14). http://www.cdi.org/terrorism/terrorist-network- pr.cfm (2002, January 18).

Center for Defense and International Security Studies. 1999. "Terrorism." http://www.cdiss.org/terror.htm (2002, February 16).

Center for Media Literacy. 2003. "Media's New Mood: Sexual Violence, an Interview with UCLA Media Researcher Neil Malamuth." http://www.medialit.org/reading_room/article443 (2006, July 22).

———. 2002. Fact Sheet, "Young People at Risk: HIV/AIDS Among America's Youth." *National Center for HIV, STD and TB Prevention* (March).

———. 2003. *Costs of Intimate Partner Violence Against Women in the United States*. Department of Health and Human Services, National Center for Injury Prevention and Control, Atlanta, GA.

———. 2004. *Sexually Transmitted Disease Surveillance*. Atlanta, GA: U.S. Department of Health and Human Services, Centers for Disease Control and Prevention. www.CDC.gov/STD/stats (2006, April 3).

———. 2004. "Alcohol-Attributable Deaths and Years of Potential Life Lost—United States, 2001." (September 24). http://www.cdc.gov/ mmwr/preview/mmwrhtml/mm5337a2.htm (2006, August 9).

———. 2005. "Prevention of Specific Infectious Diseases." *Travelers' Health: Yellow Book, Health Information for International Travel, 2005–2006*. Washington, DC.

———. 2006a. *Child Maltreatment: Fact Sheet*.Washington, DC: National Center for Injury Prevention and Control.http://www.cdc.gov/ncipc/ factsheets/cmfacts.htm (2006, July 14).

———. 2006b. *Sexual Violence: Fact Sheet*. Washington, DC: National Center for Injury Prevention and Control.http://www.cdc.gov/ncipc/factsheets/ svfacts.htm (2006, July 14).

"Census Shows Trend to Bachelor Villages." 2001. *Chicago Tribune* (May 30):6.

Chafetz, J. S. 1988. *Feminist Sociology: An Overview of Contemporary Theories*. Itasca, IL: Peacock.

Chamberlain, P., S. Moreland, and K. Reid. 1992. "Enhanced Services and Stipends for Foster Parents: Effects on Retention Rates and Outcomes for Children." *Child Welfare* 71, 5 (September/October):387–402.

Chambers-Schiller, L. V. 1984. *Liberty, a Better Husband: Single Women in America, the Generations of 1780–1840*. New Haven, CT: Yale University Press.

Chan, F. 1988. "To Be Old and Asian: An Unsettling Life in America." *Aging* 358:14–15.

Chandy, J., R. Blum, and M. Resnick. 1996. "History of Sexual Abuse and Parental Alcohol Misuse: Risk, Outcomes and Protective Factors in Adolescents." *Child and Adolescent Social Work Journal* 13:411–34.

Chang, J., Berg, C., Saltzman, L., and Herndon, J. 2005. "Homocide: A Leading Cause of Injury Deaths Among Pregnant and Postpartum Women in the United States, 1991–1999." *American Journal of Public Health* 95, 3:471–477.

Chappell, N. 1991. "Living Arrangements and Sources of Caring." *Journal of Gerontology* 46, 1 (January):51–58.

Charles, M., and K. Bradley. 2005. "A Matter of Degrees: Female Underrepresentation in Computer Science Programs Cross-Nationally." In J. McGrath Cohoon & W. C. Aspray, eds., *Women and Information Technology: Reasons for Underrepresentation.* Cambridge: MIT Press. (forthcoming)

Chase-Lansdale, P. L., and E. M. Hetherington. 1990. "The Impact of Divorce on Life-Span Development: Short and Long Term Effects." In P. B. Bates, D. L. Featherman, and R. M. Lerner, eds., *Life-Span Development and Behavior,* 10, 105–50. Hillsdale, NJ: Erlbaum.

Chassler, S. 1997. "Teenage Girls Talk about Pregnancy." *Parade* (February 2).

Chasteen, A. L. 1994. "The World around Me: The Environment and Single Women." *Sex Roles* 31, 5/6:309–28.

Cheal, D. 1989. "The Meanings of Family Life: Theoretical Approaches and Theory Models." In K. Ishwaran, ed., *Family and Marriage: Cross-Cultural Perspectives,* 33–42. Toronto: Wall and Thompson.

Cheal, D. J. 2003. "Children's Home Responsibilities: Factors Predicting Children's Household Work." *Social Behavior and Personality* 31, 8:789–794.

Cherlin, A. 1978. "Remarriage as an Incomplete Institution." *American Journal of Sociology* 84, 3:634–50.

———. 1981. *Marriage, Divorce, Remarriage.* Cambridge, MA: Harvard University Press.

———. 1992. *Marriage, Divorce, Remarriage,* rev. ed. Cambridge, MA: Harvard University Press.

———, and F. F. Furstenberg, Jr. 1983. "The American Family in the Year 2000." *Futurist* (June):7–14.

———. 1986a. "Styles and Strategies of Grandparenting." In Vern L. Bengston and Joan Robertson, eds., *Grandparenthood,* 97–116. Beverly Hills, CA: Sage.

———. 1986b. *The New American Grandparent: A Place in the Family, a Life Apart.* New York: Basic Books.

———. 1988. "The Changing European Family." *Journal of Family Issues* 9:291–97.

———. 2000a. "Toward a New Home Socioeconomics of Union Formation." In L. J. Waite, C. Bachrach, M. Hindin, E. Thomson, and A. Thornton, eds., *Ties That Bind: Perspectives on Marriage and Cohabitation,* 126–44. Hawthorne, NY: Aldine de Gruyter.

———. 2000b. "The Unexpected Legacy of Divorce" (book review). *The Nation* 271, 19 (December 11):62–68.

Cherry, K. 1987. *Womansword: What Japanese Words Say about Women.* Tokyo/New York: Kodansha International.

Cherry, R. 2001. *Who Gets the Good Jobs? Combating Race and Gender Disparities.* New Brunswick, NJ: Rutgers University Press.

Chicago Tribune. 1991. "Chinese Find Perfect Solution for Those Who Put Off Marriage." (May 14):sec. 1, 8.

Childabuse.com. 2000. "The Relationship between Domestic Violence and Child Abuse." Study Number: 20. http://www.childabuse.com/fs20.htm (2002, January 6).

Childhelp. 2005. "National Child Abuse Statistics." http://www.childhelpusa.org/resources/learning_center/statistics (2006, July 15).

"Child Marriages and the Impact on Girls." 2001. http://3rdworld.about.com/library/weekly/aa031501.htm?PM=59_0103_T (2001, July 13).

Children Now. 2004. *Fall Colors 2003-04: Prime Time Diversity Report.* Oakland, CA.

Children's Defense Fund. 1997. *The State of America's Children Yearbook: 1997.* Washington, DC.

———. 2001a. "Overall Child Poverty Rate Dropped in 2000 but Poverty Rose for Children in Full-Time Working Families." http://www.childrensdefense.org/release010925.htm (2001, October 24).

———. 2001b. "Moments in America for Children." http://www.childrensdefense.org/factsfiguresmoments.htm (2002, January 5).

———. 2001c. "Protect Children Instead of Guns." (December). http://www.childrensdefense.org/gunsfacts,htm (2002, February 10).

———. 2001d. "In America...Facts on Black Youth, Violence, & Crime." http://www.childrensdefense.org/ssviolence_youthdev_factsbl.htm (2002, February 9).

———. 2005. *State of America's Children, 2005.*

Child Welfare Information Gateway. 2004. "U. S. Children Placed for Adoption with Non-U.S. Citizens." http://www.childwelfare.gov/pubs/four.cfm (2006, August 14).

"China's Elderly Population to Reach 400 Million by 2040." *China Knowledge* (October 11). http://www.chinaknowledge.com/news_print.asp?ID=292&cat=economy (2006, April 10).

Chiriboga, D. A., and M. Thurnher. 1980. "Marital Lifestyles and Adjustments to Separation." *Journal of Divorce* 3:379–90.

Chodorow, N. 1978. *The Reproduction of Mothering: Psychoanalysis and the Sociology of Gender.* Berkeley: University of California Press.

———. 1990. *Feminism and Psychoanalytic Theory.* New Haven, CT: Yale University Press.

Choo, K. 1999. "Mothers Are Paying Children's Expenses at the Expense of the Children." *Chicago Tribune* (January 10):sec. 13, 1.

Christakis, N. A., and P. D. Allison. 2006. "Mortality After the Hospitalization of a Spouse." *New England Journal of Medicine* 354(February 16):719–730.

Christian, S. 2003. *Educating Children in Foster Care.* Washington, DC: National Conference of State Legislatures.

Christopher, S., and S. Sprecher. 2000. "Sexuality in Marriage, Dating, and Other Relationships: A Decade Review." *Journal of Marriage and the Family* 62, 4 (November):999–1018.

Church World Service. 2005. "The War in the Sudan." http://www.churchworldservice.org/betterworld2/lost-boys2.html (2006, August 23).

Chun, H., and I. Lee. 2001. "Why Do Married Men Earn More? Productivity or Marriage Selection." *Economic Inquiry* 39, 2:307–319.

CIA. 2006. "The World Factbook." (March 29). http://www.cia.gov/cia/publications/factbook/rankorder/2127rank.html (2006, April 17).

Cicirelli, V. G. 1995. *Sibling Relationships Across the Life Span.* New York: Plenum Press.

Clallam County Courts. 2006. "Domestic Violence." http://www.clallam.net/Courts/html/court_domesticviolence.htm (2006, July 12).

Clanton, G., and L. G. Smith, eds. 1986. *Jealousy.* Lanham, MD: University Press of America.

Clark, A. L., and P. Wallin. 1965. "Women's Sexual Responsiveness and the Duration and Quality of Their Marriage." *American Journal of Sociology* 71:187–96.

Clark, C., P. Shaver, and M. Abrahams. 1999. "Strategic Behaviors in Romantic Relationship Initiation." *Personality and Social Psychology Bulletin* 25, 6:707–720.

Clark, H. 1988. *The Law of Domestic Relations in the United States,* 2d ed. Minneapolis: West.

Clark, J. 1999. *Doing the Work of Love: Men and Commitment in Same-Sex Couples.* Harriman, TN: Men's Studies Press.

Clark, R. A. 1994. "Children's and Adolescents' Gender Preferences." *Journal of Social and Personal Relationships* 11:313–19.

Clark, S. C., and B. F. Wilson. 1994. "The Relative Stability of Remarriages: A Cohort Approach Using Vital Statistics." *Family Relations* 43, 3 (July):305–10.

Clark County Prosecuting Attorney. 1999. "Myths and Facts about Domestic Violence." http://www.clarkprosec...html/domviol/myths.htm (1999, June 1).

Clements, M. 1994. "Sex in America Today." *Chicago Tribune Parade* magazine (August 7):4–7.

Clemetson, L. 2006. "For U.S. Muslims, an Aversion to Nursing Homes." *New York Times* (June 13):A1, A18.

———. and R. Nixon. 2006. "Breaking Through Adoption's Racial Barriers." *The New York Times* (August 17):A1, A18.

Climo, J. 2000. "Eldercare as Woman's Work in Poor Countries." In N. Johnson and J. Climo, eds., *Special Issue: Aging and Elder Care in Lesser Developed Countries,* 692–713. Thousand Oaks, CA: Sage.

Clinard, M. B., and R. F. Meier. 1995. *Sociology of Deviant Behavior,* 9th ed. New York: Harcourt Brace.

Clingempeel, W. G., and E. Brand. 1985. "Quasi-Kin Relationships, Structural Complexity, and Marital Quality in Stepfamilies: A Replication, Extension, and Clinical Implications." *Family Relations* 34:401–9.

Clingempeel, W. G., and S. Segal. 1986. "Stepparent–Stepchild Relationships and the Psychological Adjustment of Children in Stepmother and Stepfather Families." *Child Development* 57:474–84.

Clothesline Project, The. 1995. "Bearing Witness to Violence against Women" (August 26). http://home.cybergrrl.com/dv/orgs/cp.html (1999, June 4).

Cloward, R., and F. F. Piven. 1993. "The Fraud of Workfare." *Nation* (May 24):693–96.

CNN. 2000. "Bob Jones University Ends Ban on Interracial Dating." (March 4, 2000). http://www.cnn.com/2000/US/03/04/bob.jones/index.html (2001, September 3).

———. 2006. "Thousands March for Immigrant Rights." (May 1). http://www.cnn.com/2006/US/05/01/immigrant (2006, August 21).

CNN.com. 2001. "USS Cole Relaunched with Little Fanfare." (September 16). http://www.cnn.com/2001/US/09/16/gen.cole.repairs/ (2001, February 16).

CNN.com/World. 2001. "Wife Accepts Archbishop's Decision." http://www.cnn.com/2001/WORLD/europe/08/30/bishop,wife/index.html (2001, September 8).

CNNmoney. 2000. "Pragmatism and Prenups." http://money.cnn.com/2000/05/06/home_auto/sat_prenup/ (2001, November 9).

CNNMoney.com. 2006. "Wedding $eason: Bridal Spending Has Increased 100% Over Last 15 Years, the Average Cost of a Wedding Now Tops $27,000." (February 10). http://money.cnn.com/2006/02/10/pf/weddings_costs/index.htm (2006, April 24).

CNN News. 1999. "The 'Fishing' Promises to Be Good at Lake Lovemaking." http://cnn.com/WORLD/e...OlderSex.ap/index.html (January 16), (1999, March 24).

Coalition for Asian American Children and Families. 1999.http://www.cacf.org/ (2002, January 5).

Coalition to End Family Violence. 2006. "Myths and Reality." http://www.thecoalition.org/education/myths.html (2006, July 11).

Coalition to Stop the Use of Child Soldiers. 2001. "Child Soldiers: Global Report." http://www.child-soldiers.org/report2001/global_report_contents.html (2002, February 3).

Coates, J. 1986. *Women, Men and Language.* New York: Longman.

Coats, P. P., and S. J. Overman. 1992. "Childhood Play Experiences of Women in Traditional and Nontraditional Professions." *Sex Roles* 26:261–71.

Cocco, M. 1998. "Viagra Is Sign of Double Standard." *Baltimore Sun* (May 24):41.

Cockerham, W. C. 1991. *This Aging Society.* Englewood Cliffs, NJ: Prentice Hall.

Cockrum, J., and P. White. 1985. "Influences on the Life Satisfaction of Never-Married Men and Women." *Family Relations* 34:551–56.

Cohan, C. I., and S. Kleinbaum. 2002. "Toward a Greater Understanding of the Cohabitation Effect: Premarital Cohabitation and Marital Communication." *Journal of Marriage and the Family* 64(February):180–192.

Cohen, O. 2003. "Reasons for Divorce Among Muslim Arabs in Israel: An Exploratory Study." *European Societies* 5, 3:303–326.

Cohn, L. 2005. "Remarriage After Retirement." *Christian Science Monitor* (June 9):11.

———. and W. Merkel. 2004. *One Family, Two Family, New Family: Stories and Advice for Stepfamilies.* Edmonton, Alberta: RiverWood Books.

Cohoon, J. M. 2001. "Toward Improving Female Retention in the Computer Science Major." *Communications of the ACM* 44, 5:108–114.

Coke, M. M., and J. A. Twaite. 1995. *The Black Elderly: Satisfaction and Quality of Later Life.* New York: Haworth Press.

Coker, D. R. 1984. "The Relationship among Concepts and Cognitive Maturity in Preschool Children." *Sex Roles* 10:19–31.

Colapinto, J. 2000. *As Nature Made Him: The Boy Who Was Raised as a Girl.* New York: HarperCollins.

———. 2004. "What Were the Real Reasons Behind David Reimer"s Suicide?" (June 3). http://slate.msn.com/id2101678 (2005, May 16).

Colasanto, D., and J. Shriver. 1989. "Middle-Aged Face Marital Crises." *Gallup Report* 284 (May):34–38.

Coleman, J. 2003. *Imperfect Harmony: How to Stay Married for the Sake of the Children and Still Be Happy.* New York: St. Martin's Press.

Coleman, M. M. A. Fine, L. H. Ganong, K. Downs, and N. Pauk. 2001. "When You're Not the Brady Bunch: Identifying Perceived Conflicts and Resolution Strategies in Stepfamilies." *Personal Relationships* 8:55–73.

Coleman, M., L. H. Ganong, and M. Fine. 2002. "Reinvestigating Remarriage: Another Decade of Progress." In. R. M. Milardo, ed., *Understanding Families Into the New Milennium: A Decade in Review,* 507–526. Minneapolis: National Council on Family Relations.

Coleman, M., and L. H. Ganong. 1991. "Remarriage and Stepfamily Research in the 1980s." In A. Booth, ed., *Contemporary Families: Looking Forward, Looking Back,* 192–207. Minneapolis: National Council on Family Relations.

———, and M. Fine. 2000. "Reinvestigating Remarriage: Another Decade of Progress." *Journal of Marriage and the Family* 62, 4:1288–1307.

Coles, R., and G. Stokes. 1985. *Sex and the American Teenager.* New York: Harper & Row, Colophon Books.

CollegeGrad.com. 2004. "Underemployment Affects 18% of Entry Level Job Seekers." (September 9). www.collegegrad.com/ press/underemployed.shtml (2006, January 10).

Collins, N. L., and S. J. Read. 1994. "Cognitive Representations of Attachment: The Structure and Function of Working Models." In K. Bartholomew and D. Perlman, eds., *Advances in Personal Relationships. Vol. 5: Attachment Processes in Adulthood,* pp. 53–90. London: Jessica Kingsley.

Collins, W. A., and L. A. Sroufe. 1999. "Capacity for Intimate Relationships: A Developmental Construction." In W. Furman, B. Bradford Brown, and C. Fiering, eds., *The Development of Romantic Relationships in Adolescence,* pp. 125–147. Cambridge, UK: Cambridge University Press.

Collins, P. H. 1989. "The Social Construction of Black Feminist Thought," *Signs: Journal of Women in Culture and Society* 14, 4:745–73.

———. 1991. "The Meaning of Motherhood in Black Culture." In R. Staples, ed., *The Black Family: Essays and Studies,* 4th ed., 169–78. Belmont, CA: Wadsworth.

Collins, R. 1986. "Courtly Politics and the Status of Women." In R. Collins, ed., *Weberian Sociological Theory.* New York: Cambridge University Press.

Collins, S. 1991. "The Transition from Lone Parent Family to Stepfamily." In M. Hardey and G. Crow, eds., *Lone Parenthood: Coping with Constraints and Making Opportunities in Single-Parent Families,* 156–74. Toronto: University of Toronto Press.

Coltrane, S. 1996. *Family Man: Fatherhood, Housework, and Gender Equality.* New York: Oxford University Press.

———. 1998. *Gender and Families.* Thousands Oaks, CA: Pine Forge Press.

———, and R. Collins. 2001. *Sociology of Marriage and the Family.* Belmont, CA: Wadsworth/Thompson Learning.

———, and M. Messineo. 2000. "The Perpetuation of Subtle Prejudice: Race and Gender Imagery in 1990s Television Advertising." *Sex Roles* 42, 5/6 (March):363–80.

"Common Sense about Kids and Guns." 2001. Centers for Disease Control and Prevention's National Center for Health Statistics, 1994–1999. http://www.kidsandguns.org/study/fact_file.asp (2002, February 10).

Condry, J. 1989. *The Psychology of Television.* Hillsdale, NJ: Erlbaum.

Connelly, R., D. DeGraff, and R. Willis. 2004. *Kids at Work: The Value of Employer-Sponsored On-Site Child Care Centers.* Kalamazoo, MI: Upjohn Institute for Employment Research.

Conner, K. 1992. *Aging America: Issues Facing an Aging Society.* Englewood Cliffs, NJ: Prentice Hall.

Connidis, I. A. 1994. "Sibling Support in Older Age." *Journal of Gerontology* 49, 6 (November):309–17.

———, and L. D. Campbell. 2001. "Closeness, Confiding, and Contact Among Siblings in Middle and Late Adulthood." In A. J. Walker, M. Manoogian-O'Dell, L. A. McGraw, and D. L. G. White, eds., *Families in Later Life: Connections and Transitions,* 149–155. Thousand Oaks, CA: Pine Forge Press.

Constantine, L., and J. Constantine. 1972. "The Group Marriage." In M. Gordon, ed., *The Nuclear Family in Crisis: The Search for an Alternative,* 204–22. New York: Harper & Row.

———. 1973. *Group Marriage.* New York: Collier.

"Consumer Views of the Economy." 2006. *The Gallup Poll* (January 10). http://poll.gallup.com/content/defaultaspx?ci=1609 (2006, January 10).

"Contraceptive Use." 1998. New York: The Alan Guttmacher Institute. http://www.agi-usa.org (2001, December 17).

Cool Nurse. 2005. "Teen Dating Violence." http://www.coolnurse.com/dating_violence.htm (2006, February 20).

Cooney, T. 1994. "Young Adults' Relations with Parents: The Influence of Recent Parental Divorce." *Journal of Marriage and the Family* 56:45–56.

Cooney, T., M. K. Hutchinson, and D. M. Leather. 1995. "Surviving the Breakup: Predictors of Parent–Adult Child Relations after Parental Divorce." *Family Relations* 44:153–61.

Cooney, T., and L. A. Smith. 1996. "Young Adults' Relations with Grandparents Following Recent Parental Divorce." *Journal of Gerontology: Social Sciences* 51B, 2:591–95.

Cooney, T., and P. Uhlenberg. 1989. "Family-Building Patterns of Professional Women: A Comparison of Lawyers, Physicians, and Postsecondary Teachers." *Journal of Marriage and the Family* 51:749–58.

———. 1990. "The Role of Divorce in Men's Relations with Their Adult Children after Mid-Life." *Journal of Marriage and the Family* 52:677–88.

Coontz, S. 1988. *The Social Origins of Private Life.* New York: Verso.

———. 1992. *The Way We Never Were: American Families and the Nostalgia Trap.* New York: Basic Books.

———. 1997. *The Way We Really Are: Coming to Terms with America's Changing Families.* New York: Basic Books.

———. 2000. "Marriage: Then and Now." *Phi Kappa Phi Journal* 80:16–20.

———. 2005. *Marriage, A History.* New York: Viking.

———. 2006. "A Pop Quiz on Marriage." *New York Times* (February 19): Sec. 4, p. 12.

Cornell, D. 2001. "School Violence: Fear versus Facts." Charlottesville: University of Virginia, Youth Violence Project. http://cox.house.gov/scott/youth_violence_briefing_cornell_remarks.htm (2002, February 10).

Cornfield, N. 1983. "The Success of Urban Communes." *Journal of Marriage and the Family* 45, 1:115–26.

Cose, E. 1995. *A Man's World.* New York: HarperCollins.

Costa, Jr., P. T., A. Terracciano, and R. R. McCrae. 2001. "Gender Differences in Personality Traits Across Cultures: Robust and Surprising Findings." *Journal of Personality and Social Psychology* 81, 2 (August): 322–331.

Couric, E. 1989. "An NLJ/West Survey, Women in the Law: Awaiting Their Turn." *National Law Journal* 11 (December):S1, S12.

Court TV's Legal Café. 1997. "Frequently Asked Questions about Prenuptial Agreements." http://www.courttv.com/legalcafé/family/prenup/prenup_background.html. (2001, November 10).

"Court Upholds Right to Bar Embryo Use." 2001. *New York Times* (August 15):A21.

Covel, S. 2003a. "The Heart Never Forgets." *American Demographics* 25(June):15.

———. 2003b. "Cheating Hearts." *American Demographics* 25 (July/August):16.

———. 2003c. "Cheating Hearts." *American Demographics* 25(June):16.

Coward, R. T. 1987. "Factors Associated with the Configuration of the Helping Networks of Noninstitutionalized Elders." *Gerontological Social Work* 10:113–32.

Cox, C. 1993. *The Frail Elderly: Problems, Needs, and Community Responses.* Westport, CT: Auburn House.

Cox, H. 1993. *Later Life: The Realities of Aging*, 3d ed. Englewood Cliffs, NJ: Prentice Hall.

Crane, D. R., J. N. Soderquist, and M. D. Gardner. 1995. "Gender Differences in Cognitive and Behavioral Steps toward Divorce." *American Journal of Family Therapy* 23, 2:99–105.

Crary, D. 2001. "Florida Gay-Adoption Ban to Face Federal Challenge." *Chicago Tribune* (June 4):13.

Crawford, L. 1995. "Whittling Down Your Wedding Cost." *San Francisco Examiner* (June 25) [online].

Creager, E. 1995. "So Old So Soon." *Chicago Tribune* (November 12): sec. 13, 10.

Cromer, K. 2005. "Building Blocks for Gender Equity." *Chicago Tribune* (May 25): Sec. 8, p. 3.

Crompton, R. 1999. *Restructuring Gender Relations and Employment: The Decline of the Male Breadwinner.* Cambridge: Oxford University Press.

Crowder, K., and J. Teachman. 2004. "Do Residential Conditions Explain the Relationship Between Living Arrangements and Adolescent Behavior?" *Journal of Marriage and Family* 68:721–738.

Crowley, K. 2000. "Parent Differences During Museum Visits: Gender Differences in How Children Hear Informal Science." *Visitor Studies Today* 3, 3:21–28.

Crosbie-Burnett, M. 1984. "The Centrality of the Step Relationship: A Challenge to Family Theory and Practice." *Family Relations* 33:459–64.

———. 1994/1995. "The Interface between Stepparent Families and Schools: Research Theory, Policy and Practice." In K. Pasley and M. Ihinger-Tallman, eds., *Stepparenting: Issues in Theory, Research, and Practice*, 199–216. Westport, CT: Greenwood.

———. Ada Skyles, and June Becker-Haven. 1988. "Exploring Stepfamilies from a Feminist Perspective." In Sanford M. Dornbush and Myra H. Strober, eds., *Feminism, Children, and the New Families*, 297–326. New York: Guilford Press.

Crossen, C. 1991. "Is TV Too Sexy?" *McCalls* 119 (October):100.

Crossette, B. 1999. "Testing the Limits of Tolerance as Cultures Mix." *New York Times* (March 6):A15,17.

———. 2001. "War Endangers Legions of World's Young, U.N. Report Says." *New York Times* (June 14):A10.

Cubbins, L. A., and D. Vannoy. 2004. "Division of Household Labor as a Source of Contention for Married and Cohabiting Couples in Metropolitan Moscow." *Journal of Family Issues* 25, 2:182–215.

Cuda, A. 2005. "Gift of Life—Surrogates Help Couples Become Parents." (September 28). http://www.reproductivelawyer.com/news/giftoflife.asp (2006, April 24).

Cuber, J. F., and P. B. Harroff. 1966. *The Significant Americans.* New York: Random House. (Published also as "Five Types of Marriage." In A. S. Skolnick and J. H. Skolnick, eds., *Family in Transition*, 7th ed., 177–88. New York: HarperCollins, 1992.)

Cudina, M., and J. Obradovic. 2001. "A Child's Emotional Well-Being and Parental Marriage Stability in Croatia." *Journal of Comparative Family Studies* 32, 2 (Spring):247–61.

Cunningham, J. D., and J. K. Antill. 1995. "Current Trends in Nonmarital Cohabitation: In Search of the POSSLQ." In J. T. Wood and S. Duck, eds., *Under-Studied Relationships: Off the Beaten Track*, 148–72. Thousand Oaks, CA: Sage.

Cunningham-Burley, S. 1987. "The Experience of Grandfatherhood." In C. Lewis and M. O'Brien, eds., *Reassessing Fatherhood: New Observations on Fathers and the Modern Family*, 91–105. Beverly Hills, CA: Sage.

Curry, G. E. 1992. "New York State May Bar Mothers for Hire." *Chicago Tribune* (May 31):17, 22.

Curtis, C. M. 1996. "The Adoption of African American Children by Whites: A Renewed Conflict." *Families in Society: The Journal of Contemporary Human Services* (March):156–64.

Cutler, B. 1988. "Band of Gold: The Earnings of Married versus Unmarried Males." *American Demographics* 10 (November):14.

Cyranowski, J. M., E. Frank, E. Young, and M. K. Shear. 2000. "Adolescent Onset of the Gender Difference in Lifetime Rates of Major Depression." *Archives General Psychiatry* 57:21–27.

Cytrynbaum, P. 1995. "Today's Singles Are Looking for Match Made in Cyberspace." *Chicago Tribune* (October 25):sec. 1, 1,15.

"Dad of the Month." 2006. *iParenting* (January 4). http://iparenting.com/dad/1000.php (2006, January 4).

"Dade County Jury Awards $1.5 Million to Sexual Harassment Plaintiff." 2005. Jackson/Lewis (January 12). http://www.jacksonlewis.com/legalupdates/article.cfm?aid=698 (2006, January 12).

Dahir, M. 1998. "Gay Marriage Looking Up." http://www.suba.com/~outlines/dahir1298.html (1999, April 23).

Dahl, G. B., and E. Moretti. 2004. "The Demand for Sons: Evidence from Divorce, Fertility, and Shotgun Marriage." *NBER Web site* http://www.nber.org/papers/w10281 (2006, March 13).

Dahlberg, T. 2002. "Violence Plagues Youth Sports." http://www.davie. net/ayflmain/pages/violence.htm (2002, February 10).

Dailard, C. 2000. "Abortion in Context: United States and Worldwide." New York: The Alan Guttmacher Institute. http://www. guttmacher. org/pubs/ib_0599.html (2001, December 17).

Dainton, M. 1993. "The Myth and Misconceptions of the Stepmother Identity." *Family Relations* 42:93–98.

Dalakar, J. 2001. *Poverty in the United States: 2000.* Current Population Reports, P60–214. Washington, DC: U.S. Census Bureau.

Dalton, A. 2006. "Couple Take Their Vows After 13-Mile Run to Arrive at Ceremony." *The scotsman.* (April 24). http://news.scotsman.com/ uk.cfm?id=612072006 (2006, April 24).

Daly, E. 2005. "DNA Test Gives Students Ethnic Shocks." *The New York Times* (April 13):A18.

Daly, K. J. 1999. "Crisis of Genealogy: Facing the Challenges of Infertility." In H. I. McCubbin et al., eds., *The Dynamics of Resilient Families,* 1–40. Thousand Oaks, CA: Sage.

Daly, M., 1978. *Gyn/Ecology: The Metaethics of Radical Feminism.* Boston: Beacon Press.

———. and M. Wilson. 1994. "Some Differential Attributes of Lethal Assaults on Small Children by Stepfathers vs. Genetic Fathers." *Ethology and Sociobiology* 15:207–17.

Daniels, R. 1990. *Coming to America: A History of Immigration and Ethnicity in American Life.* New York: HarperCollins.

Dang, A., and S. Frazer. 2005. *Black Same-Sex Households in the United States: A Report From the 2000 Census.* New York: National Gay and Lesbian Task Force Policy Institute.

Dang, D. T., and J. Pitts. 2006. "Caregivers Feel Love's Anguish." *Chicago Tribune* (March 8):1, 6.

Darling, C., D. J. Kallen, and J. E. VanDusen. 1989. "Sex in Transition: 1900–1980." In A. S. Skolnick and J. H. Skolnick, eds., *Family in Transition,* 6th ed., 236–78. New York: Scott, Foresman.

Darrett, B., and A. H. Rutman. 1979. "New Wives and Sons-in-Law: Parental Death in Seventeenth-Century Virginia Country." In T. W. Tote and D. L. Ammerman, eds., *The Chesapeake in the Seventeenth Century.* Chapel Hill: University of North Carolina Press.

D'Augelli, A. R., S. L. Hershberger, and N. W. Pilkington. 1998. "Lesbian, Gay, and Bisexual Youth and Their Families: Disclosure of Sexual Orientation and Its Consequences." *American Journal of Orthopsychiatry* 68, 3:361–71.

Davenport, D. 2004. "Born in America, Adopted Abroad." *The Christian Science Monitor* (October 27):11.

Davidson, D. 2001. "Issue Facing Elderly Gay Men and Lesbians." May www.neln.org/bibs/davidson.html (2005, December 7).

Davis, G., and Mulhausen, D. 2000. "Young African American Males: Continuing Victims of High Homicide Rates in Urban Communities." http://www.heritage.org/library/cda/cda00-05.html (2001, February 9).

Davis, K. 1940. "Extreme Social Isolation of a Child." *American Journal of Sociology* 45, 4 (January):554–65.

———. 1947. "Final Note on a Case of Extreme Isolation." *American Journal of Sociology* 52, 5 (March):432–37.

Davis, K. E. 1985. "Near and Dear: Friendship and Love Compared." *Psychology Today* (February 24):22–28, 30.

———, and M. Todd. 1985. "Assessing Friendship: Prototypes, Paradigm Cases and Relationship Description." In S. Duck and D. Perlman, eds., *Understanding Personal Relationships: An Interdisciplinary Approach,* 17–38. London: Sage.

Davis, K. 2004. *Love's Many Faces Apprehended.* Washington, DC: American Psychological Association.

Davis, R. F. 1998. "Life with Father: A Solo Dad Documents the Ties That Thrive." *Chicago Tribune* (November 29):sec. 2, 5.

———. 1996. "Adoptive Parents Not Going It Alone." *Chicago Tribune* (April 15):1.

Davis, S. 1990. "Men as Success Objects and Women as Sex Objects: A Study of Personal Advertisements." *Sex Roles* 23, 1/2:43–50.

Davis, S. N., and T. N. Greenstein. 2004. "Cross-National Variations in the Division of Household Labor." *Journal of Marriage and Family* 66(December):1260–1271.

Davidson, D. 2001. "Issues Facing Elderly Gay Men and Lesbians." (May) www.neln.org/bibs/davidson.html (2005, December 7).

Dawson, D. 1991. "Family Structure and Children's Health and Well-Being: Data from the 1988 National Health Survey on Child Health." *Journal of Marriage and the Family* 53:573–84.

Day, R. D., and S. J. Bahr. 1986. "Income Changes Following Divorce and Remarriage." *Journal of Divorce* 9:75–88.

Deane, C., et al. 2000. "Leaving Tradition Behind: Latinos in the Great American Melting Pot." *Public Perspective* 11 (May/June):5–7, 10.

Degler, C. 1980. *At Odds: Women and the Family in America from the Revolution to the Present.* New York: Oxford University Press.

DeLamaster, J. 1987. "Gender Differences in Sexual Scenarios." In K. Kelly, ed., *Females, Males, and Sexuality,* 127–39. Albany: State University of New York Press.

DeLisi, R., and L. Soundranayagam. 1990. "The Conceptual Structure of Sex-Role Stereotypes in College Students." *Sex Roles* 23, 11/12: 593–611.

del Pinal, J., and A. Singer. 1997. "Generations of Diversity: Latinos in the United States." *Population Bulletin* 52 (October). Washington, DC: Population Reference Bureau.

DeMaris, A., and W. MacDonald. 1993. "Premarital Cohabitation and Marital Instability: A Test of the Unconventionality Hypothesis." *Journal of Marriage and the Family* 50 (August):619–48.

Demaris, O. 1991. "Political Terrorism." In J. Stimson, A. Stimson, and V. N. Parrillo, eds., *Social Problems: Contemporary Readings,* 2d ed., 123–31. Itasca, IL: Peacock.

De Mente, B. 1989. *Everything Japanese.* Lincolnwood, IL: Passport Books.

D'Emilio, J., and E. B. Freedman. 1988. *Intimate Matters: A History of Sexuality in America.* New York: Harper & Row.

DeMillo, A. 2001. "Home Violence Study Reveals Police Findings." *Washington Post* (August 25):B01.

Demo, D. H., and A. C. Acock. 1988. "The Impact of Divorce on Children." *Journal of Marriage and the Family* 50:619–48.

DeMont, J. 2000. "I Am Single." *Maclean's* 113, 9 (May 8):36–40.

Demos, J. 1970. *A Little Commonwealth: Family Life in Plymouth Colony.* New York: Oxford University Press.

———. 1974. "The American Family in Past Time." *American Scholar* 43:422–46.

DeNavas-Walt, C., B. Proctor, and C. Lee. 2005. *Income, Poverty, and Health Insurance* Coverage in the United States: 2004. U.S. Census Bureau, Current Populations Reports,

De Navas-Walt, C., R. W. Cleveland, and M. I. Roemer. 2001. *Money Income in the United States: 2000.* Current Population Reports, P60–213, Washington, DC: U. S. Census Bureau.

Dermer, M., and T. A. Pyszczynski. 1978. "Effects of Erotica upon Men's Loving and Liking Responses for Women They Love." *Journal of Personality and Social Psychology* 24:1–10.

DeSpelder, L. A., and A. L. Strickland. 1988. *The Last Dance.* Mountain View, CA: Mayfield.

———. 1996. *The Last Dance: Encountering Death and Dying,* 4th ed. Mountain View, CA: Mayfield.

Dessoff, A. 2001. "Caregiving Burdens Hit Low-Income and Minority Boomers the Hardest." *AARP Bulletin* (September):6.

Deutsch, F. M. 1999. *Halving It All: How Equally Shared Parenting Works.* Cambridge, MA: Harvard University Press.

DeVault, M. L. 1990. "What Counts as Feminist Ethnography?" Paper presented at Exploring New Frontiers: Qualitative Research Conference, York University, Toronto.

De Vaus, D., L. Qu, and R. Weston. 2003. "Premarital Cohabitation and Subsequent Marital Stability." *Family Matters* 65(Winter):34–39.

DeVita, C. 1996. "The United States at Mid-Decade." *Population Bulletin* 50:4. Washington, DC: Population Reference Bureau.

De Voss, S. 2000. "Kinship Ties and Solitary Living among Unmarried Elderly Women in Chile and Mexico." *Research on Aging* 22, 3 (May): 262–90. http://www.aoa.gov/may2001/factsheets/family-caregiving.html (2001, December 29).

DHHS. 2000. "Domestic Violence." U.S. Department of Health and Human Services, Administration for Children and Families. http://www.acf.dhhs.gov/programs/opa/facts/domsvio.htm (2002, January 8).

———. 2005. *Child Maltreatment 2003.* U.S. Department of Health and Human Services, Administration on Children, Youth, and Families Washington, DC: U.S. Government Printing Office, Online Summary. http://www.acf.hhs.gov/programs/cb/publications/ (2006, July 11).

Diamond, M., and H. K. Sigmundson. 1997. "Sex Reassignment at Birth: Long-Term Review and Clinical Implication." *Archives of Pediatric and Adolescent Medicine* 151:298–304.

DiCaro, V. "NFI Releases Report on National Marriage Survey." *Fatherhood Today* 10, 3(Summer):4–5.

Dicky, C., and D. McGinn. 2001. "Meet the bin Ladens." Newsweek (October 15):55–56.

Diesenhouse, S. 2001. "His and Hers: A House Divided, Lovingly." *New York Times* (August 23):B1, B9.

Dieter, P. 1989. "Shooting Her with Video, Drugs, Bullets, and Promises." Paper presented at the meeting of the Association of Women in Psychology, Newport, RI.

DiGiulio, R. C. 1989. *Beyond Widowhood: From Bereavement to Emergence and Hope.* New York: Free Press.

Dingfelder, S. F. 2005. "The Kids Are All Right." *Monitor* 36, 11 (December):66.

Dinkmeyer, D., and J. Carlson. 1984. *Time for a Better Marriage.* Circle Pines, MN: American Guidance Service.

Dion, K. K., and K. L. Dion. 1998. "Individualistic and Collectivistic Perspectives on Gender and the Cultural Context of Love and Intimacy." In D. L. Anselmi and A. L. Law, eds., *Questions of Gender: Perspectives and Paradoxes,* 520–31. New York: McGraw-Hill.

Dionne, E. J. Jr. 2001. "Day Care Culture War." *Washington Post* (April 26).

Disability Rights. 1999. "Statistics Page." http://www.comsource.net/~awiggins/statistics.html (June 11).

Disabled Women's Network Ontario. 2002. "Fact Sheet." http://www.servl.thot.net/~dawn/fact.html (2002, February 2).

———. 2006. "Factsheets on Women with Disabilities." http://www.dawn.thot.net/main.html (2006, August 16).

Disability World. 2003. "UNICEF and Disabled Children and Youths." *Disability World.* no. 19 (June–August). http://www.disabilityworld.org/06–08_03/children/unicef.shtml (2006, August 16).

Do, D. 1999. *The Vietnamese Americans.* Westport, CT: Greenwood.

Dobash, R. E., and R. P. Dobash. 1979. *Violence against Wives: A Case against Patriarchy.* New York: Free Press.

Dobson, C. 1983. "Sex-Role and Marital-Role Expectations." In T. H. Brubaker, ed., *Family Relationships in Later Life,* 109–26. Beverly Hills, CA: Sage.

Doka, K., ed. 1989. *Disenfranchised Grief: Recognizing Hidden Sorrow.* Lexington, MA: Lexington Books.

Doll, L., L. Petersen, C. White, E. Johnson, J. Ward, and the Blood Donor Study Group. 1992. "Homosexual and Nonhomosexual Identified Men: A Behavioral Comparison." *Journal of Sex Research* 29:1–14.

Dorfman, R., K. Walters, P. Burke, L. Hardin, T. Karanki, and E. Silverstein. 1995. "Old, Sad, and Alone: The Myth of the Aging Homosexual." *Journal of Gerontological Social Work* 24 (1/2):29–44.

Donovan, P. 1998. "School-Based Sexuality Education: The Issues and Challenges." *Family Planning Perspectives* 20, 4. (July/August).

Dortch, S. 1995. "The Future of Kinship." *American Demographics* (September):4, 6.

Dover, K. 1978. *Greek Homosexuality.* Cambridge, MA: Harvard University Press.

Dow, B. J. 1996. *Prime-Time Feminism.* Philadelphia: University of Pennsylvania Press.

Doweiko, H. E. 1996. *Concepts of Chemical Dependency.* Boston: Brooks/Cole.

Downs, A. C. 1983. "Letters to Santa Claus: Elementary School-Age Children's Sex-Typed Toy Preferences in a Natural Setting." *Sex Roles* 9:159–63.

Doyle, J., and M. Paludi. 1997. *Sex and Gender: The Human Experience,* 4th ed. Blacklick, OH: McGraw-Hill.

Doyle, J. A., and M. A. Paludi. 1995. *Sex and Gender: The Human Experience.* Dubuque, IA: William C. Brown.

Draughon, M. 1975. "Stepmother's Model of Identification in Relation to Mourning in the Child." *Psychological Reports* 36:183–89.

Dreger, A. D. 1998. 'Ambiguous Sex'—Or Ambivalent Medicine? Ethical Issues in the Treatment of Intersexuality." *The Hastings Center Report* 28, 3:23–36.

Drell, A. 1999. "Parents of Teenage Killer in Contempt." *Chicago Sun-Times* (May 7):24.

Dressel, P. L., and B. B. Hess. 1983. "Alternatives for the Elderly." In E. D. Macklin and R. Rubin, eds., *Contemporary Families and Alternative Lifestyles: Handbook on Research and Theory.* Beverly Hills, CA: Sage.

"Drug Abuse and Pregnancy." 1999. http://medceu.com/test...buse_and_pregnancy.html (May 19).

Duberman, L. 1973. "Stepkin Relationships." *Journal of Marriage and the Family* 35:283–92.

DuBois, W. E. B. 1967. *The Philadelphia Negro: A Social Study.* New York: Schocken. (Originally published 1899.)

Dugger, C. W. 1996. "Immigrant Cultures Raising Issues of Child Punishment." *New York Times* (February 29):A1.

———. 2001. "Abortions in India Spurred by Sex Test Skew the Ratio against Girls." *New York Times International* (April 22):10.

Duke, I. 1991. "Whites' Racial Stereotypes Persist: Most Retain Negative Beliefs about Minorities, Survey Finds." *Washington Post* (January 1): A1, A4.

DuLong, J. 2004. "Challenging Masculinity: A Rise in Male-on-Male Sexual Harassment in the Workplace Is More About Homophobia Than Sexual Favors." (October 26). www.findarticles.com/p/articles/mi_m1589/os_2004_Oct_26/ai_n8591946/print (2006, January 12).

Duncan, G., and S. Hoffman. 1985. "A Reconsideration of the Economic Consequences of Marital Dissolution." *Demography* 22:485–97.

Duncan, S. F. 2001. "Relationships with Extended Family Members." http://www.montana.edu/wwwhd/family/comchal.html (2001, December 3).

Dunkin, A. 2000. "Adopting? You Deserve Benefits, Too." *Business Week* (February 21):160.

Dunn, K., P. Croft, and G. Hackett. 2000. "Satisfaction in the Sex Life of a General Population Sample." *Journal of Sex and Marital Therapy* 26:141–51.

Dunwald, S. 2005. "15 Year Old Weds 37 Year-Old." *WGRZ Channel 2 News.* File://C:\MyFiles/woman weds 15 year old_files\redir.htm (Accessed: December, 18, 2005).

Dupree, A., and W. Primus. 2001. "Declining Share of Children Lived with Single Mothers in the Late 1990s." Washington, DC: Center on Budget and Policy Priorities. http://www.cbpp.org (2002, January 5).

Durex. 2005. "Global Sex Survey, 2005." http://www.durex.com/uk/globalsexsurvey/index.asp (2005, March 17).

Durkheim, E. 1951/1897. *Suicide, A Study in Sociology.* New York: Free Press.

Dush, C., C. L. Cohan, and P. R. Amato. 2003. "The Relationship Between Cohabitation and Marital Quality and Stability: Change Across Cohorts?" *Journal of Marriage and Family* 65:539–549.

"Dutch Have Lowest Teen Pregnancy." 1994. *Chicago Tribune* (February 28):1.

Dutton, D. G. 1988. *The Domestic Assault of Women.* Boston: Allyn & Bacon.

Duvall, E. M. 1977. *Marriage and Family Development,* 5th ed. Philadelphia: Lippincott.

Dworkin, A. 1987. *Intercourse.* New York: Free Press.

Dwyer, J., and R. T. Coward. 1991. "A Multivariate Comparison of the Involvement of Adult Sons versus Daughters in the Care of Impaired Parents." *Journal of Gerontology* 46, 5 (September):5259–69.

Dye, J. L. 2005. Fertility of American Women: June 2004. *Current Population Reports,* P20-555. Washington, DC: U.S. Census Bureau.

Earle, A. M. 1893. *Customs and Fashions in Old New England.* New York: Scribner's.

Earls, A. 2003. "Men Still Worry About Taking Time to be Dads." *Boston Globe* (November 23). http://bostonworks.boston.com/globe/articles/112303-dads.html (2006, February 8).

Eckland, B. 1968. "Theories of Mate Selection." *Eugenics Quarterly* 15:79.

Edelhart, C. 1995. "Male Rape Survivors Also Deal with Myths." *Chicago Tribune* (June 1):4.

Edelman, R. 1996. "Prenuptial Agreements—True Love or True Greed?" http://www.ricedelman.com/planning/weddingtips/prenuptial.asp (2001, November 10).

Edelmann, R. J. 2004. "Surrogacy: the Psychological Issues." *Journal of Reproductive and Infant Psychology* 22, 2(May):123–136.

Edin, K., and L. Lein. 1997. *Making Ends Meet: How Single Mothers Survive Welfare and Low-Wage Work*. New York: Russell Sage Foundation.

Edmark, K. 2005. "The Effects of Unemployment in Property Crime: Evidence from a Period of Unusually Large Swings in the Business Cycle." *Scandinavian Journal of Economics* 353–373.

Edwards, J. N. 1969. "Familial Behavior as Social Exchange." *Journal of Marriage and the Family* 31:518–26.

Edwards, T. M. 2000. "Flying Solo." *Time* (28 August):47–53.

Ehrenreich, B., and A. Fuentes. 1992. "Life on the Global Assembly Line." In H. F. Lena, W. B. Helmreich, and W. McCord, eds. *Contemporary Issues in Society*, 104–11. New York: McGraw-Hill.

Ehrenreich, B., E. Hess, and G. Jacobs. 1986. *Re-Making Love: The Feminization of Sex*. Garden City, NY: Anchor Press.

Einstein, E. 1985. *The Stepfamily: Living, Loving, and Learning*. Boston: Shambhala.

"Elderly Abandoned at Hospitals: Granny Dumping Is a Variation of Baby-on-Doorstep." 1991. *Chicago Tribune* (November 29):sec. 1, 27.

Elles, L. 1993. *Social Stratification and Socioeconomic Inequality*. Westport, CT: Praeger.

Ellis, B. J., J. E. Bates, K. A. Dodge, D. M. Fergusson, L. J. Horwood, S. G. Petit, and L. Woodward. 2003. "Does Father Absence Place Daughters at Special Risk for Early Sexual Activity and Teenage Pregnancy?" *Child Development* 74, 3 (May):P60–229. Washington, DC: U.S. Government Printing Office.

Elmer-Dewitt, P. 1994. "Now for the Truth about Americans and SEX." *Time* (October 17):62–70.

El Nasser, H. 2004. "For More Parents, 3 Kids Are a Charm." *USA Today* (March 10):1, 2.

Emery, R. E. 1994. *Renegotiating Family Relationships: Divorce, Child Custody, and Mediation*. New York: Guilford Press.

———. 1995. "Divorce Mediation: Negotiating Agreements and Renegotiating Relationships." *Family Relations* 44:377–83.

Emory Health Sciences Press Release. 2004.

Eng, H. 2005. "Grads Coming Home and Staying: 'Boomerang Generation Moving Back.'" *Boston Herald*. www.findarticles.com/p/articles/me_qn4154/is_20050823/ai_n14914229/print (2005, October 15).

Enge, M. 2000. "Ad Seeks Donor Eggs for $100,000, Possible New High." *Chicago Tribune* (February 10):3.

Engley, H. L. 1999. "A Nuclear Family Reaction." *Chicago Sun-Times* (March 21):35A.

Enright, E. 2004. "A House Divided." *AARP Magazine* (July/August). Assessed March 2, 2006. http://www.aarpmagazine.org/family/Articles/a2004-05–26-mag-divorce.html/?print.

Equal Employment Opportunity Commission. 2005. "Sexual Harassment." http://www.eeoc.gov/types/sexual_harassment.html (2006, January 11).

———. 2006. "Pregnancy Discrimination Charges. (January 27). http://www.eeoc.gov/stats/pregnac.html (2006, February 20).

"Equal Pay for Working Families: National and State Data." 1999. AFL-CIO. http://www.aflcio.org/women/exec99.htm (2001, October 20).

Erickson, R. J. 1993. "Reconceptualizing Family Work: The Effect of Emotion Work on Perceptions of Marital Quality." *Journal of Marriage and the Family* 55 (November):888–900.

Erikson, E. 1968. *Identity: Youth and Crisis*. New York: W. W. Norton.

Eschbach, K. 1995. "Enduring and Vanishing American Indian: American Indian Population Growth and Intermarriage in 1990." *Ethnic and Racial Studies*, 18 (1):89–108.

Escobar-Chaves, S., S. Tortolero, C. Markhan, and B. Low. 2004. "Impact of the Media on Adolescent Sexual Attitudes and Behaviors." Atlanta, GA: Centers for Disease Control and Prevention. Grant #H75/CCH623007-01-1.

Eshleman, J. R. 1991. *The Family: An Introduction*. Boston: Allyn & Bacon.

———, and R. Bulcroft. 2005. *The Family*, 11th ed. Boston: Allyn & Bacon.

Estes, C. L., J. H. Swan, and Associates. 1993. *The Long-Term Care Crisis: Elderly Trapped in the No-Care Zone*. Newbury Park, CA: Sage.

Estioko-Griffin, A. 1986. "Daughters of the Forest." *Natural History* 95 (May):5.

Etaugh, C., and J. Malstrom. 1981. "The Effect of Marital Status on Person Perception." *Journal of Marriage and the Family* 43:801–5.

Etzioni, A. 1997. "HIV Testing for Infants and Pregnant Women: A Case Study in Privacy and Public Health." *The Communication Network*. http://www.gwu.edu/~ccps/hivtest.html (2001, December 21).

Evans, L. 2000. "No Sissy Boys Here: A Content Analysis of the Representation of Masculinity in Elementary School Reading Textbooks." *Sex Roles* 42, 3/4:255–70.

Fachner, G. 2006. "Making Sense of the Debate Over Illegal Immigration." *Associated Content*: http://www.associatedcontent.com/article/31430/making_sense_of_the_d (2006, August 24).

"Facts and Figures About Our TV Habit." 2005. *TV-Turnoff Network*. www.tvturnoff.org/images/facts&figs/factsheets/FactsFigs.pdf (2005, August 24).

Facts for Features. 2006. (June 18). http://www.census.gov/Press-Release/www/releases/archives/facts_for_features_special_editions/006794.html (2006, September 10).

"Fact Sheet: How Equal Pay Helps Men." 2006. AFL-CIO. www.aflcio.org/issues/jobseconomy/women/equalpay/FactSheetHowEqual PayHelp. (2006, January 20).

"Fact Sheet: In Vitro Fertilization (IVF)." 2000–2001. American Society for Reproductive Medicine. http://www.asrm.com/Patients/Fact Sheets/invitro.html (2001, December 17).

"Facts about Media Violence and Effects on the American Family." 1997. Baby Bag Online. http://www.babybag.com/articles/amaviol.htm. (2002, January 8).

Faderman, L. 1989. "A History of Romantic Friendship and Lesbian Love." In B. Risman and P. Schwartz, eds., *Gender and Intimate Relationships*, 26–31. Belmont, CA: Wadsworth.

Fahim, K., A. Farmer, and C. Moynihan. 2006. "Mother Is Charged in Killing of 3-Year-Old Brooklyn Girl." *New York Times* (June 29): Sec. B, p. 4.

Fain, T. C., and D. L. Anderson. 1987. "Sexual Harassment: Organizational Context and Diffuse Status." *Sex Roles* 5/6:291–311.

Faison, S. 1995. "In China, Rapid Social Changes Bring a Surge in the Divorce Rate." *New York Times* (August 22):A1.

Falk, C. 1984. *Love, Anarchy, and Emma Goldman*. New York: Holt, Rinehart & Winston.

"Family Caregiving–Fact Sheet." 2001. Administration on Aging. http://www.aoa.dhhs.gov/may2001/factsheets/family%2Dcaregiving.html (2001, December 29).

Family First. 1999. "Marriage Survey Summary." http://flfamily.org/marrig.html (1999, April 17).

Family Violence Prevention Fund. 2006a. "The Facts on Domestic Violence." http://www.endabuse.org/resources/facts/ (2006, June 30).

———. 2006b. "Celebrity Watch: Hall of Shame." http://www.endabuse.org/celebritywatch/index.php?Fame=N (2006, July 11).

———. 1999. "General Statistics." http://www.fvpf.org/the_facts/stats.html (1999, June 2).

Fan, C. S., and H. Lui, 2004. "Extramarital Affairs, Marital Satisfaction, and Divorce: Evidence from Hong Kong." *Contemporary Economic Policy* 22, 4(October):442–452.

Farley, J. E. 1995. *Majority–Minority Relations*, 3d ed. Englewood Cliffs, NJ: Prentice Hall.

Farrell, D. 1997. "Jealousy and Desire." In Roger E. Lamb, ed., *Love Analyzed*, 165–188. Boulder, CO: Westview.

Fass, S., and N. K. Cauthen. 2005. "Who Are America's Poor Children?" National Center for Children in Poverty. www.nccp.org (2006, January 6).

Fausto-Sterling, A. 1985. *Myths of Gender*. New York: Basic Books.

———. 2000. "The Five Sexes, Revisited." *Sciences* 40, 4 (July/August). http://ehostvgw19.epnet.com/get_xml.asp?booleanTerm=The+Five+Sexes&fuzzyTerm=&l…(2001, July, 25).

Faux, M. 1984. *Childless by Choice: Choosing Childlessness in the 80s.* Garden City, NY: Anchor Press/Doubleday.

Fayette County Government. 2004. "Domestic Violence." www.admin.co. fayette.ga.us/courts/solicitor/domestic_violence.htm (2006, June 30).

FBI Uniform Crime Report, 1999. http://www.fbi.gov/ucr/99hate.pdf (2001, September 20).

Feagin, J. R. 1991. "The Continuing Significance of Race: Antiblack Discrimination in Public Places." *American Sociological Review* 56:101–16.

———, and C. B. Feagin. 1996. *Racial and Ethnic Relations*, 5th ed. Upper Saddle River, NJ: Prentice Hall.

Federal Bureau of Investigation (FBI). 1996. *Crime in the United States, 1995.* Washington, DC: U.S. Government Printing Office.

Feeney, J. A. 1999a. "Issues of Closeness and Distance in Dating Relationships: Effects of Sex and Attachment Style." *Journal of Social and Personal Relationships.* 16, 5:571–590.

———. 1999b. "Romantic Bonds in Young Adulthood: Links with Family Experiences." *Journal of Family Studies* 5, 1:25–46.

———., and P. Noller. 1996. *Adult Attachment.* Thousand Oaks, CA: Sage.

Feigelman, W. 2000. "Adjustments of Transracially and Inracially Adopted Young Adults." *Child and Adolescent Social Work Journal* 17, 3(June):165–184.

Feldman, M. 2001. "Parenthood Betrayed: The Dilemma of Munchausen Syndrome by Proxy." http://www.shpm.com/articles/parenting/hsmun.html (2002, January 24).

"Female on Male Sexual Harassment." 2004. http://www.fightsexualharassment.com/facts/female_on_male_sexual_harassment.htm (2006, January 12).

Feng, W. 2005. "Can China Afford to Continue Its One-Child Policy?" *Asia Pacific Issues* No. 77 (March):1–12.

Feng, D., R. Giarruso, V. L. Bengston, and N. Frye. 1999. "Intergenerational Transmission of Marital Quality and Marital Instability." *Journal of Marriage and the Family* 61 (May):451–63.

Fengler, A., and N. Goodrich. 1979. "Wives of Elderly Men: The Hidden Patients." *Gerontologist* 19 (April):175–83.

Ferber, M. A. 1982. "Women and Work: A Review Essay." *Signs* 8 (Winter):273–95.

Ferdinand, P. 2001. "Shaken but Unharmed, Mass. School Says, 'The System Worked.'" *Washington Post* (December 27):A03.

Ferguson, C. 1998. "Dating Violence as a Social Phenomenon." In N. A. Jackson and G. C. Oates, eds., *Violence in Intimate Relationships: Examining Sociological and Psychological Issues*, 83–118. Boston, MA: Butterworth-Heinemann.

Ferguson, S. 1995. "Marriage Timing of Chinese American and Japanese American Women." *Journal of Family Issues* 16:314–43.

———, ed. 2001. *Shifting the Center: Understanding Contemporary Families*, 2d ed., 129–39. Mountain View, CA: Mayfield.

Ferk, D. J. 2005. "Organizational Commitment Among Married Dual-Career Employees: Traveling Commuter Versus Single Residence." *SAM Advanced Management Journal* (Spring):21–26, 35.

Fernea, E. 1965. *Guests of the Sheik.* Garden City, NY: Doubleday.

Fernquist, R. M. 2000. "Problem Drinking in the Family and Youth Suicide." *Adolescence* 35, 139 (Fall):551–58.

Ferrante, J. 1992. *Sociology: A Global Perspective.* Belmont, CA: Wadsworth.

Ferri, E., and K. Smith. 2003. "Partnerships and Parenthood." In E. Ferri, J. Bynner, and M. Wadsworth, eds., *Changing Britain, Changing Lives.* London, England: Institute of Education.

Festinger, T. 2002. "After Adoption: Dissolution or Permanence?" *Child Welfare* 81, 3:515–533.

Fetal Alcohol Fact Sheet. 1999. http://weber.u.washing...oMoreLabels/fetal.html (1999, May 13).

Field, A., C. Camargo, C. Barr Taylor, C. Berkey, and G. Colditz. 2001. "Peer, Parent, and Media Influences on the Development of Weight Concerns and Frequent Dieting Among Preadolescent and Adolescent Girls and Boys." *Pediatrics* 107, 1:54–60.

Field, A. E., et al. 1999. "Exposure to the Mass Media and Weight Concerns among Girls." *Pediatrics* 103, 3 (March):36. http://www.pediatrics.org/cgi/content/full/103/3/e36 (2001, August 3, 2001).

Fields, J. 2003. "America's Families and Living Arrangements: 2003." *Current Population Reports*, P20–553. U.S. Census Bureau, Washington, DC.

———. 2003. *Children's Living Arrangements and Characteristics: March 2002.* Current Population Reports, P20-547. Washington, DC: U.S. Census Bureau.

———. 2004. "America's Families and Living Arrangements: 2003." U.S. Census Bureau, *Current Population Reports*, Series P-20-537 (Washington, DC: U.S. Government Printing Office):4, Figure 2.

———., and L. M. Casper. 2001. *America's Families and Living Arrangements: March 2000.* Current Population Reports, P20–537. Washington, DC: U.S. Census Bureau.

Fiese, B. H., T. Tomcho, M. Douglas, K. Josephs, S. Poltrock, and T. Baker. 2002. "A Review of 50 Years of Research on Naturally Occurring Family Routines and Rituals: Cause for Celebration?" *Journal of Family Psychology* 16, 4:381–390.

Fillenbaum, G. G., L. K. George, and E. B. Palmore. 1985. "Determinants and Consequences of Retirement among Men of Different Races and Economic Levels." *Journal of Gerontology* 40:85–94.

Fine, M., and D. Fine. 1992. "Recent Changes in Laws Affecting Stepfamilies: Suggestions for Legal Reform." *Family Relations* 41:334–40.

Fine, M. A., P.C. McKenry, B.W. Donnelly, and P. Voydanoff. 1992. "Perceived Adjustment of Parents and Children: Variations by Family Structure, Race, and Gender." *Journal of Marriage and the Family* 54:118–127.

Finkelhor, D., G. Hotaling, and A. Sedlak. 1990. "Abducted, Runaway, and Throwaway Children in America." *First Report: Numbers and Characteristics, National Incidence Studies, Executive Summary.* Washington, DC: U.S. Department of Justice, Office of Juvenile Justice and Delinquency Prevention.

Finkelhor, D., and K. Yllo. 1995. "Types of Marital Rape." In Patricia Searles and Ronald Berger, eds., *Rape and Society: Readings on the Problem of Sexual Assault*, 152–59. Boulder, CO: Westview Press.

Finkelman, P., ed. 1989. *Women and the Family in a Slave Society.* New York: Garland.

Firebaugh, G. and L. Tach. 2005. "Relative Income and Happiness: Are Americans on a Hedonistic Treadmill?" Paper presented at the American Sociological Association Centennial Annual Meeting, Philadelphia, August 14.

Fischer, J., and M. Heesacker. 1995. "Men's and Women's Preferences Regarding Sex-Related and Nurturing Traits in Dating Partners." *Journal of College Student Development* 36, 3:258–68.

Fischer, T. F., P. M. de Graaf, and M. Kalmijn. 2005. "Friendly and Antagonistic Contact Between Former Spouses After Divorce." *Journal of Family Issues* 26, 8:1131–1163.

Fisher, H. 1999. "The Origin of Romantic Love and Human Family Life." In L. H. Stone, ed., *Selected Readings in Marriage and Family*, 65–68. San Diego, CA: Greenhaven Press.

Fishman, B. 1983. "The Economic Behavior of Stepfamilies." *Family Relations* 32:359–66.

———, and B. Hamel. 1991. "From Nuclear to Stepfamily Ideology: A Stressful Change." In J. N. Edwards and D. H. Demo, eds., *Marriage and Families in Transition*, 436–52. Boston: Allyn & Bacon.

Flaherty, Sr., M. J., L. Facteau, and P. Garver. 1991. "Grandmother Functions in Multigenerational Families: An Exploratory Study of Black Adolescent Mothers and Their Infants." In R. Staples, ed., *The Black Family: Essays and Studies*, 4th ed., 192–200. Belmont, CA: Wadsworth.

Flanigan, C., R. Huffman, and J. Smith. 2005. "Teens Attitudes Toward Marriage, Cohabitation, and Divorce, 2002." *Science Says*, 14. Washington, DC: The National Campaign to Prevent Teen Pregnancy.

Florence, B. 2000. "A Different Divorce—Collaborative Lawyering." *Utah Bar Journal* 13, 10 (December):18–19.

Flowers, B. J. 1991. "His and Her Marriage: A Multivariate Study of Gender and Marital Satisfaction." *Sex Roles* 24:209–21.

Floyd, F. J., S. N. Hanes, E. R. Doll, D. Winemiller, C. Lemsky, T. M. Burgy, M. Werle, and N. Heilman. 1992. "Assessing Retirement Satisfaction and Perceptions of Retirement Experiences." *Psychology and Aging* 7:609–21.

Folk, K. F., J. W. Graham, and A. H. Beller. 1992. "Child Support and Remarriage: Implications for the Economic Well-Being of Children." *Journal of Family Issues* 13:142–47.

Foner, N. 1993. "When the Contract Fails: Care for the Elderly in Nonindustrial Cultures." In V. L. Bengtson and A. Achenbaum, eds., *The Changing Contract across Generations*. New York: Aldine de Gruyter.

Food and Agriculture Organization of the United Nations. 1997. "Pioneer Project on Mushroom-Growing for Disabled People in Thailand—A First for FAO" (July 4). http://www.fao.org/News/1997/970701-e.html (1997, June 11).

Foreign Press Center Japan. 2005. "Concern Deepens Over Continuing Slide of Birth Rate in Japan; No Halt in Sight." http://www.fpcj.jp/e/mres/japanbrief/jb_534.html (2006, April 7).

FORGE. 2006. "LGBT Elders: Domestic Violence/Sexual Assault Resource Sheet." http://www.forge-forward.org/handouts/LGBTEld (2006, July 21).

Forging Connections: *Challenges and Opportunities of Older Caregivers Raising Children*. 2004. New York: New York: Council on Adoptable Children, Inc.

Fornek, S. 2001. "Elder Abuse Ranges from Scams to Murder." *Chicago Sun-Times*, News Special Edition (December 16):16.

"Forum on America's Future." 2000. *Chicago Tribune* (July 23).

Fossett, M. A., and K. J. Kiecolt. 1993. "Mate Availability and Family Structure among African Americans in U.S. Metropolitan Areas." *Journal of Marriage and the Family* 55 (May):288–302.

Fountain, J. 2001. "Fear Is No Stranger in Chicago Ghetto." *New York Times* (October 21), Premium Archive. http://nytimes.qpass.com (2002, January 10).

Fox, G. L. 1980. "Love Match and Arranged Marriage in a Modernizing Nation: Mate Selection in Ankara, Turkey." *Journal of Marriage and the Family* 42, 4 (November):180–93.

———, and R. F. Kelly. 1995. "Determinants of Child Custody Arrangements at Divorce." *Journal of Marriage and the Family* 57 (August):693–708.

FOX News. 2005. "Fox News/Opinion Dynamics Poll." (February 5). http://www.foxnews.com/projects/pdf/poll_021105.pdf (2005, February 5).

FOX News/Opinion Dynamics Poll. 2006. Law and Civil Rights, PollingReport.com (April 4–5): http://www.pollingreport.com/civil.htm (2006, April 19).

Fox, V. C., and M. H. Quitt. 1980. "Stage VI: Spouse Loss." In V. C. Fox and M. H. Quitt, eds., *Loving, Parenting and Dying: The Family Cycle in England and America, Past and Present*, 49–61. New York: Psychohistory Press.

Frank, R. 1998. "Dads Find Contentment Tending to Home Alone." *Chicago Tribune* (March 15):sec. 13, 9.

Franklin, C. W. 1988. *Men and Society*. Chicago: Nelson-Hall.

———. 1992. "Friendship among Black Men." In P. Nardi, ed., *Men's Friendships*, 201–14. Newbury Park, CA: Sage.

Franklin, M. 1999. "Till a Long-Distance Job Do Us Part." *Kiplinger's* 56, 1 (January):56.

Frazer, J. 1995. "Community Justice Course." http://www.tafe.lib.rmit.edu.au/judy/overview.html (1995, December 12).

Frazier, E. F. 1939. *The Negro Family in the United States*. Chicago: University of Chicago Press.

Freeman, R., and P. Klaus. 1984. "Blessed or Not: The New Spinster in England and the United States in the Late Nineteenth and Early Twentieth Centuries." *Journal of Family History* 9:394–414.

Freiberg, P. 1991. "Parental-Notification Laws Termed Harmful." *APA Monitor* (March):28.

French, H. W. 1998. "In Africa's Back-Street Clinics, Illicit Abortions Take Heavy Toll." *New York Times* (June 3):A1.

———. 2001a. "Royal Path: Late Births Lose Stigma in Japan." *New York Times* (December 9):A25.

———. 2001b. "Fighting Sex Harassment, and Stigma, in Japan." *New York Times* (July 15):1, 10.

Frieden, T. 2001. "Four Charged with Enslaving Russian Women" (February 22). http://www5.cnn.com/2001/LAW/02/22/slavery.indictment/ (2001, September 26).

Friedland, G. H. 1995. "Clinical Care in the AIDS Epidemic." In J. B. Williamson and E. S. Shneidman, eds., *Death: Current Perspectives*, 4th ed., 105–17. Mountain View, CA: Mayfield.

Friedman, B. 1999. "Prenuptial Agreements: Not Just for the Rich and Famous." http://www.barnsl.org/stlawyer/archive/99/Oct99/bruce-_friedman.htm. (2001, November 8).

Friedman, S. 2006. "Time to Recognize Gay Seniors." (June 3). http://www.newsday.com/news/columnists/nybzsaul4766895jun03,0,7094119.column?coll-ny-rightrail-columnist (2006, June 28).

Friend, R. A. 1990. "Older Lesbian and Gay People: A Theory of Successful Aging." *Journal of Homosexuality* 20 (3/4):99–118.

Frisco, M., and K. Williams. 2003. "Perceived Housework, Equity, Marital Happiness, and Divorce in Dual-Earner Households." *Journal of Family Issues* 24, 1(January):51–73.

Fromm, E. 1956. *The Art of Loving*. New York: Bantam.

Frye, M. 1995. "Lesbian Sex." In A. Kesselman, L. D. McNair, and N. Schniedewind. eds., *Women: Images and Reality*, 122–24. Mountain View, CA: Mayfield.

Fulcher, J. 2002. "Domestic Violence and the Rights of Women in Japan and the United States." *Human Rights Magazine, International Women's Rights*, 29, 3(Summer). Section of Individual Rights and Responsibilities, American Bar Association, Washington, DC. www.abanet.org/irr/jr/si,,er02/summer02.html (2006, July 11).

Furman, E. 2005. *Boomerang Nation: How to Survive Living with Your Parents*. New York: Fireside.

Furnham, A. 1999. "Sex-Role Stereotyping in Television Commercials: A Review and Comparison of Fourteen Studies Done on Five Continents over 25 Years." *Sex Roles* 41, 5/6 (September):413–38.

Furstenberg, F., Jr., and A. Cherlin. 1991. *Divided Families: What Happens to Children When Parents Part?* Cambridge, MA: Harvard University Press.

———., S. D. Hoffman, and L. Shrestha. 1995. "The Effect of Divorce on Intergenerational Transfers: New Evidence." *Demography* 32, 3 (August):319–33.

———., and G. B. Spanier. 1984. *Recycling the Family: Remarriage after Divorce*. Beverly Hills, CA: Sage.

———. 1987. *Recycling the Family: Remarriage after Divorce*. Newbury Park, CA: Sage.

Furukawa, S. 1994. "The Diverse Living Arrangements of Children: Summer 1991." U.S. Census Bureau, *Current Population Reports*, Series P–70, no. 38. Washington, DC: U.S. Government Printing Office.

Fuwa, M. 2004. "Macro-Level Gender Inequality and the Division of Household Labor in 22 Countries." *American Sociological Review* 69(December):751–767.

Gagnon, J. H., and W. Simon. 1973. *Sexual Conduct: The Social Sources of Human Sexuality*. Chicago: Aldine.

———. 1987. "Sexual Scripting of Oral Genital Contacts." *Archives of Sexual Behavior* 16(1):1–25.

Gale Group. 2001. "Restaurant Adds Latest Version of 'Dating Game' to Menu." *Restaurant News*, 1.

Galinsky, E. 2004. "Testimony: Subcommittee on Children and Families." http://familiesandwork.org/3w/testimony.html (2006, January 17).

Gallup Poll. 1996. *Gender and Society: Status and Stereotypes*. Princeton, NJ: Gallup Organization.

———. 1997. "Global Study of Family Values." http://www.gallup.com/poll/reports/family.asp (2001, November 6).

———. 2006. "Moral Issues." http://poll.gallup.com/content/default.aspx?ci=1681 (2006, March 21).

Gallup Tuesday Briefing. 2001a. Special Edition. "Attack on America: Public Opinion" (September 18). http://www.gallup.com/tuesdaybriefing.asp (2001, September 18).

———. 2001b. *Gallup Poll Vault* (December 4). http://www.gallup.com/tuesdaybriefing.asp (2001, December 4).

Gammage, J. 2006. "For Adoptees, Racial Divide Still Wide." (May 8) http://www.philly.com/mld/inquirer/new/local/14525508.htm (2006, August 17).

Ganahl, J. 2005. "Single-Minded: The New Unmarried Mommy Is of a Certain Age." *San Francisco Chronicle* (November 13):D2.

———. 1989. "Preparing for Remarriage: Anticipating the Issues, Seeking Solutions." *Family Relations* 38:28–33.

———. 1994. *Remarried Family Relationships.* Thousand Oaks, CA: Sage.

———. 1997. "How Society Views Stepfamilies." *Marriage & Family Review* 26, 1/2:85–106.

Ganong, L. H., and M. Coleman. 1987. "Sex, Sex Roles, and Familial Love." *Journal of Genetic Psychology* 148:45–52.

———. 2006. "Obligations to Stepparents Acquired in Later Life: Relationship Quality and Acuity of Needs." *The Journals of Gerontology Series B: Psychological Sciences and Social Sciences* 61:S80–S88.

Garcia-Pena, R. P. 1995. "The Issue of Drug Traffic in Colombian–U.S. Relations: Cooperation as an Imperative." *Journal of Interamerican Studies and World Affairs* 37, 1 (Spring):101–11.

Gardmer, A. 2005. "CDC Survey: Oral Sex Substitutes for Intercourse with Many Teenagers." *HealthDay Reporter* (December 21). http://kcc-tvhealth.ip2m.com/index.cfm?pt=itemDetail & Item_ID=119822 & Site_Cat_

Gardner, J. 1995. "Worker Displacement: A Decade of Change." *Monthly Labor Review* (April):45–57.

Garfinkel, I., S. S. McLanahan, and P. K. Robins, eds. 1994. *Child Support and Child Well-Being.* Washington, DC: Urban Institute Press.

Garner, A. 2002. "Don't 'Protect' Me; Give Me Your Respect." *Newsweek* (February 11).

Garza, M. M. 1995. "Unemployed Find the Pressure's On." *Chicago Tribune* (December 19):sec. 3, 1.

Gately, S., and A. I. Schwebel. 1992. "Favorable Outcomes in Children after Parental Divorce." In E. Everett, ed., *Effects on Young Adults' Patterns of Intimacy and Expectations for Marriage,* 57–78. New York: Haworth Press.

Gaudin, J., N. Polansky, A. Kilpatrick, and P. Shilton. 1996. "Family Functioning in Neglectful Families." *Child Abuse and Neglect* 20 (April):363–77.

"Gay Britons Prepare to Tie the Knot." 2005. *Chicago Tribune* (December 6): 2.

Gecas, V., and M. L. Schwalbe. 1983. "Beyond the Looking-Glass Self: Social Structure and Efficacy-Based Self-Esteem." *Social Psychology Quarterly* 46:77–88.

Geiss, S. K., and K. D. O'Leary. 1981. "Therapists' Ratings of Frequency and Severity of Marital Problems: Implications for Research." *Journal of Marital and Family Therapy* 7:515–20.

Gelfand, D. E., and C. M. Barresi, eds. 1987. *Ethnic Dimensions of Aging.* New York: Springer.

Gelles, R. 1997. *Intimate Violence in Families,* (3rd ed. Newbury Park, CA: Sage.

Gelles, R. J. 1995. *Contemporary Families: A Sociological View.* Thousand Oaks, CA: Sage.

———. 1997. *Intimate Violence in Families,* 3d ed. Thousand Oaks, CA: Sage.

———, and C. P. Cornell. 1990. *Intimate Violence in Families,* 2d ed. Newbury Park, CA: Sage.

———., and E. F. Hargreaves. 1987. "Maternal Employment and Violence toward Children." In R. J. Gelles, ed., *Family Violence,* 108–25. Newbury Park, CA: Sage.

———., and A. Levine. 1995. *Sociology,* 5th ed. New York: McGraw-Hill.

———., and M. Straus. 1987. "Is Violence toward Children Increasing? A Comparison of 1975 and 1985 National Survey Rates." *Journal of Interpersonal Violence* 2:212–22.

———. 1988. *Intimate Violence: The Definitive Study of Cases and Consequences of Abuse in the American Family.* New York: Simon & Schuster.

"General Facts about Domestic Violence." 1999. http://www.newcountryc... n/statistics/facts.html (1999, June 4).

Genuis, S., and S. Genuis. 2006. "Parental Guidance: Talking to Your Teens About Sex." http://www.christianwomentoday.com/parenting/teensex.html (2006, March 23).

Genovese, E. D. 1974. *Roll, Jordan, Roll.* New York: Pantheon.

Gerstel, N. 1990. "Divorce and Stigma." In Christopher Carlson, ed., *Perspectives on the Family: History, Class, and Feminism,* 460–78. Belmont, CA: Wadsworth.

Gentleman, A. 2006. "Millions of Abortions of Female Fetuses Reported in India." *The New York Times* (January 10):A10.

Ghista, G. 2005. "Marital Rape." World Prout Assembly. http://www.world-proutassembly.org/archives/2005/05/marital_rape.html (2006, July 17).

Giarrusso, R., P. Johnson, J. Goodchilds, and G. Zellman. 1979. "Adolescents' Cues and Signals: Sex and Assault." Paper presented at the annual meeting of the Western Psychological Association, San Diego, CA, April.

Gibbs, N. 1993a. "How Should We Teach Our Children about SEX?" *Time* (May 24):60–66.

———. 1993b. "Bringing Up Father." *Time* (June 28):53–56.

Gibson, J. T. 1991. "Disciplining Toddlers." *Parents* (May):190.

Gibson, R. 1986. "Blacks in an Aging Society." *Daedalus* 115:349–71.

———. 1991. "Retirement in Black America." In J. S. Jackson, ed., *Life in Black America,* 179–98. Newbury Park, CA: Sage.

———. 1996. "The Black American Retirement Experience." In J. Quadagno and D. Street, eds., *Aging for the Twenty-First Century: Readings in Social Gerontology,* 309–26. New York: St. Martin's Press.

Giddens, A. 1996. *Introduction to Sociology.* New York: W. W. Norton.

Gilbert, E. 1994. "Pregnancy Discrimination Alert." *Working Mother* (June):34–35.

Gilbert, L. A., and M. Scher. 1999. *Gender and Sex in Counseling and Psychotherapy.* Boston: Allyn & Bacon.

Giles-Sims, J. 1984. "The Stepparent Role: Expectations, Behavior, and Sanctions." *Journal of Family Issues* 5, 1:116–30.

Gilford, R. 1984. "Contrasts in Marital Satisfaction throughout Old Age: An Exchange Theory Analysis." *Journal of Gerontology* 39:325–33.

Gill, R. T., N. Glazer, and S. A. Thernstrom. 1992. *Our Changing Population.* Englewood Cliffs, NJ: Prentice Hall.

Gillespie, M. 2001. "Americans Consider Infidelity Wrong, but Acknowledge Its Prevalence in Society." *The Gallup Organization.* http://www.gallup.com/poll/releases/pr010709b.asp (2001, November 4).

Gilligan, C. 1990. "Teaching Shakespeare's Sister: Notes from the Underground of Female Adolescence." In C. Gilligan, N. P. Lyons, and T. J. Hammer, eds., *Making Connections,* 6–29. Cambridge, MA: Harvard University Press.

Gillis, J. 1999. "Myths of Family Past." In A. Skolnick and J. Skolnick, eds., *Family in Transition,* 10th ed., 21–34. New York: Longman.

Gillis, J. R. 1985. *For Better, For Worse: British Marriages: 1600 to the Present.* New York: Oxford University Press.

Gilmore, D. 1990. *Masculinity in the Making: Cultural Concepts of Masculinity.* New Haven, CT: Yale University Press.

Giuliano, T. A., and K. E. Popp. 2000. "Footballs versus Barbies: Childhood Play Activities as Predictors of Sports Participation by Women." *Sex Roles* 42, 3 (February):159–82.

Giunta, C. T., and B. E. Compas. 1994. "Adult Daughters of Alcoholics: Are They Unique?" *Journal of Studies on Alcohol* 55:600–606.

Gjerdingen, D. 2004. "The Effects of Domestic Work Responsibilities On Parents' Marital Satisfaction and Mental Health." A paper presented at a Conference and Signature Study of the Hubert H. Humphrey Institute of Public Affairs Conducted in Collaboration with the School of Public Health, University of Minnesota (October 1).

Glaberson, W. 1999. "What Did Parents Know, and Are They to Blame?" *New York Times* (April 27):A20.

Glader, P., and K. Maher. 2005. "Mining, Metals Unions Seek International Allies." *Wall Street Journal* (March 15).

Gladwell, M. 1988. "Surrogate Parenting: Legal Labor Pains." In J. G. Wells, ed., *Current Issues in Marriage and the Family,* 179–84. New York: Macmillan.

Glasmeier, A. 2005. *An Atlas of Poverty in America: One Nation Pulling Apart, 1960–2003.* Routledge.

Glendon, M. A. 1987. *Abortion and Divorce in Western Law.* Cambridge, MA: Harvard University Press.

Glenn, E. N. 1983. "Split Household, Small Producer and Dual Wage Earner: An Analysis of Chinese American Family Strategies." *Journal of Marriage and the Family* 45 (February):35–46.

———. 1994. "Social Constructions of Mothering: A Thematic Overview." In E. N. Glenn, G. Chang, and L. R. Forcey, eds., *Mothering: Ideology, Experience, and Agency*, 1–29. New York: Routledge.

Glenn, N. 2005. "With This Ring . . . National Survey on Marriage in America." *National Fatherhood Initiative.* http://www.fatherhood.org/doclibrary/nms.pdf (2006, April 14).

Glenn, N. D. 1982. "Interreligious Marriage in the United States: Patterns and Recent Trends." *Journal of Marriage and the Family* 44 (August):555–66.

———. 1990. "Quantitative Research on Marital Quality in the 1980s: A Critical Review." *Journal of Marriage and the Family* 52:818–31.

———. 1991. "Quantitative Research on Marital Quality in the 1980s." In A. Booth, ed., *Contemporary Families: Looking Forward, Looking Back*, 28–41. Minneapolis: National Council on Family Relations.

———. 1997a. *Closed Hearts, Closed Minds, A Report from the Council on Families.* New York: Institute for American Values.

———. 1997b. "A Critique of Twenty Family and Marriage Textbooks." *Family Relations* 46 (July):197–208.

———. 1999. "Values, Attitudes, and the State of American Marriage." In C. Albers, ed., *Sociology of Families Reader*, 58–67. Thousand Oaks, CA: Pine Forge Press.

———, and M. Supancic. 1984. "The Social and Demographic Correlates of Divorce and Separation in the United States: An Update and Reconsideration." *Journal of Marriage and the Family* 46:563–75.

———, and C. N. Weaver. 1988. "The Changing Relationship of Marital Status to Reported Happiness." *Journal of Marriage and the Family* 50:317–24.

Glick, P. 1980. "Remarriage: Some Recent Changes and Variations." *Journal of Family Issues* 1, 4:455–78.

———. 1984. "Marriage, Divorce, and Living Arrangements: Prospective Changes." *Journal of Family Issues* 5:7–26.

———, and S. Lin. 1986. "Recent Changes in Divorce and Remarriage." *Journal of Marriage and the Family* 48:737–47.

———, and A. Norton. 1977. "Marrying, Divorcing, and Living Together in the U.S. Today." *Population Bulletin* 32:2–39.

Glick, P., and R. Parke. 1965. "New Approaches in Studying the Life Cycle of the Family." *Demography* 2:187–202.

"Globalization." 2006. http://www.americans-world.org/digest/ global_issues/globalization/general.cfm (2006, July 18).

"Global Statistical Information." 2001. http://www.unaids.org (2001, December 13).

Godwin, D. D., and J. Scanzoni. 1989. "Couple Consensus during Marital Joint Decision-Making: A Context, Process, Outcome Model." *Journal of Marriage and the Family* 51:943–56.

Goetting, A. 1979. "Some Societal-Level Explanations for the Rising Divorce Rate." *Family Therapy* 6, 2:83–87.

———. 1982. "The Six Stations of Remarriage: Developmental Task of Remarriage after Divorce." *Family Relations* 31:213–22.

Golant, S. M., and A. J. LaGreca. 1994. "Differences in the Housing Quality of White, Black, and Hispanic U.S. Elderly Households." *Journal of Applied Gerontology* 13:413–37.

———. 1995. "The Relative Deprivation of U.S. Elderly Households as Judged by Their Housing Problems." *Journal of Gerontology*, Series B, 50B:513–23.

Goldberg, C. 2001. "Quiet Anniversary for Civil Unions." *New York Times* (July 31):A14.

———, with J. Elder. 1998. "Public Backs Abortion, but Wants Limits, Poll Says." *New York Times* (January 16):A1.

Golding, J. M. 1990. "Division of Household Labor, Strain, and Depressive Symptoms among Mexican American and Non-Hispanic Whites." *Psychology of Women Quarterly* 14:103–17.

Goldscheider, F. K., and C. Goldscheider. 1993. *Leaving Home before Marriage: Ethnicity, Familism, and Generational Relationships.* Madison: University of Wisconsin Press.

Goldstein, S. 2006. "We Are Family." Broadsheet (March 23). http://www.letters.salon.com/mwt/broadsheet/2006/03/23/shelltrack/view?order=asc (2006, April 3).

Goleman, D. 1987. "Two Views of Marriage Explored: His and Hers." In O. Pocs, ed., *Marriage and Family 87/88: Annual Editions*, 58–59. Sluice Dock, Guilford, CT: Dushkin.

———. 1990. "As Bias Crimes Seem to Rise, Scientists Study Roots of Racism." *New York Times* (March 29):C1.

———. 1995. "Eating Disorder Rates Surprise the Experts." *New York Times* (October 4):B7.

———. 1996. *Emotional Intelligence.* New York: Bantam Books.

Golin, J. 2004. *Gender Representations in Television and Video Programs for Children Ages 0–6: A Literature Review.* Boston, MA: Media Center of the Judge Baker Children's Center.

Goode, E. 1994. "Till Death Do Them Part?" *U.S. News and World Report* (July 4):24–28.

———. 1999. "New Study Finds Middle Age Is Prime of Life." *New York Times* (February 16):D6.

———. 2001. "Findings Give Some Support to Advocates of Spanking." *New York Times* (August 25):A6.

———. 2001b. "A Rainbow of Differences in Gays' Children." *New York Times* (July 17):F1.

Goode, W. 1959. "The Theoretical Importance of Love." *American Sociological Review* 24, 1 (February):38–47.

———. 1993. *World Changes in Divorce Patterns.* New Haven, CT: Yale University Press.

Goodman, D. 2000. "A More Civil Union." *Mother Jones* (July/August):48–53, 78.

Goodman, E. 2006. "Redefining Marital Happiness." Boston Globe (March 17). http://www.boston.com/news/globe/editorial_opinion/oped/articles/2006/03/17/redefining_marital_happiness/ (2006, April 14).

Gordon, P. 2006. "Grandparents Raising Grandchildren." *Gotham Gazette* (April 12). http://www.gothamgazette.com/print/1816 (2006, June 20).

Gordon, S. M., and S. Thompson. 1995. "The Changing Epidemiology of Human Immunodeficiency Virus Infection in Older Persons." *Journal of the American Geriatrics Society* 43 (January):7–9.

Gorner, P. 1994a. "Sex Study Shatters Kinky Assumptions." *Chicago Tribune* (October 6):1, 28.

———. 1994b. "What Is Normal?" *Chicago Tribune* (October 9):1, 4.

Gornick, J. C. 2002. "Reconcilable Differences." *The American Prospect* 13, 7 (April 8). www.prospect.org/print-friendly/print/V13/7/gornick-j.html (2006, February 8).

Gottman, J. 1990. "Children of Gay and Lesbian Parents." In F. W. Bozett and M. B. Sussman, eds., *Homosexuality and Family Relations.* New York: Harrington Park Press.

———. 1994a. "What Makes Marriage Work?" *Psychology Today* (March/April):38–43, 68.

———. 1994b. *What Predicts Divorce? The Relationship between Marital Processes and Marital Outcomes.* Hillsdale, NJ: Erlbaum.

Gottman, J. M., R. W. Levenson, C. Swanson, K. Swanson, R. Tyson, and D. Yoshimoto. 2003. "Observing Gay, Lesbian and Heterosexual Couples' Relationships: Mathematical Modeling of Conflict Interaction." Journal of *Homosexuality* 45, 1:65–91.

Gove, W. 1972. "The Relationship between Sex Roles, Marital Status, and Mental Illness." *Social Forces* 51:34–44.

Govan, F. 2005. "More Couples Getting Married But Trend Is to Wait Until Older." (May 2). http://www.telegraph.co.uk/core/Content/displayPrintable.jhtml?xml=/news/2005/02/05/nmarry05.xml & site=5 (2006, March 26).

Goyer, A. 2005. "Intergenerational Relationships: Grandparents Raising Grandchildren." (November). http://www.aarp.org/research/international/perspectives/nov_05_grandparents.html (2006, June 16).

Graber, J. L. 1999. "Words Can Hurt Divorced Parents' Best Intentions." *Chicago Tribune* (March 14):sec. 13, 1.

Graham, J. 2006. "Unwilling Father Tests Men's Rights." *Chicago Tribune* (March 10): Sec 1, p. 3.

Graham, S. 2001. "German Gays Embrace Union Law." *Chicago Tribune* (August 2):8.

Grall, T. S. 1993. "Our Nation's Housing in 1991." In U.S. Census Bureau, *Current Housing Reports*, Series H121/93–2. Washington, DC: U.S. Government Printing Office.

———. 2000. *Child Support for Custodial Mothers and Fathers*. Current Population Reports, P60–212 (October). U.S. Census Bureau. Washington, DC: U.S. Government Printing Office.

Granat, D. 1997. "She's Having Our Baby." *Washingtonian* 32 (July):54–57.

Grant, L., L. Simpson, and L. R. Xue. 1990. "Gender, Parenthood, and Work Hours of Physicians." *Journal of Marriage and the Family* 52:39–49.

Gray, J. S. 1997. "The Fall in Men's Return to Marriage: Declining Productivity Effects or Changing Selection?" *Journal of Human Resources* 32 (Summer):481–504.

Grebe, S. C. 1986. "Mediation in Separation and Divorce." *Journal of Counseling and Development* 64:377–82.

Green, B., and N. Boyd-Franklin. 1996. "African American Lesbians: Issues in Couple Therapy." In J. Laird and R. Green, eds., *Lesbians and Gays in Couples and Families*, 251–71. San Francisco: Jossey-Bass.

Greenhouse, S. 2001. "Americans' International Lead In Hours Worked Grew in 90's, Report Shows." *New York Times* (September 1):A6.

Greenstein, B., K. Porter, W. Primus, and I. Shapiro. 2001. "Poverty Rates Fell in 2000 as Unemployment Reached 31-Year Low." *Center on Budget and Policy Priorities*. http://www/cbpp.org/9-25-01pov.htm (2001, October 24).

Greenstein, T. N. 1990. "Marital Disruption and the Employment of Married Women." *Journal of Marriage and the Family* 52:657–76.

———. 1995. "Gender Ideology, Marital Disruption and the Employment of Married Women." *Journal of Marriage and the Family* 57 (February):31–32.

Greider, L. 2001. "Hard Times Drive Adult Kids Home." *AARP Bulletin* (December):3, 14.

Greif, G. L. 1985. *Single Fathers*. Lexington, MA: Lexington Books.

———, and M. S. Pabst. 1988. *Mothers without Custody*. Lexington, MA: D. C. Heath.

Greil, A. L. 1991. *Not Yet Pregnant: Infertile Couples in Contemporary America*. New Brunswick, NJ: Rutgers University Press.

Greven, P. 1970. *Four Generations: Population, Land and Family in Colonial Andover, Mass.* Ithaca, NY: Cornell University Press.

Griffin, J. L. 1992. "Most Take Middle Ground on Abortion." *Chicago Tribune* (July 2):1.

Griffin, S. 1979. *Rape: The Power of Consciousness*. San Francisco: Harper & Row.

Griffith, K. 2005. "Brainwashed No More." *Advocate* (August 30):40–42.

Grimm, T. K., and M. Perry-Jenkins. 1994. "All in a Day's Work: Job Experience, Self-Esteem, and Fathering in Working-Class Families." *Family Relations* 43, 2 (April):174–81.

Griswold del Castillo, R. 1984. *La Familia*. Notre Dame, IN: University of Notre Dame Press.

Gross, H. E. 1980. "Dual Career Couples Who Live Apart: Two Types." *Journal of Marriage and the Family* 42:567–76.

Gross, J. 2005. "Forget the Career: My Parents Need Me at Home." *The New York Times* (November 24):A1, A20.

Gross, P. 1987. "Defining Post-divorce Remarriage Families: A Typology Based on the Subjective Perceptions of Children." *Journal of Divorce* 10, 1/2:205–17.

Grossman, C., and I. Yoo. 2003. "Civil Marriage on the Rise Across USA." *USA Today* (October 7):A, 01.

Grossman, H., and S. H. Grossman. 1994. *Gender Issues in Education*. Boston: Allyn & Bacon.

Groza, V., and K. Rosenberg. 1998. *Clinical and Practice Issues in Adoption: Bridging the Gap between Adoptees Placed as Infants and as Older Children*. Westport, CT: Praeger.

Gruber, J. E., and P. Morgan, eds. 2004. *In the Company of Men: Male Dominance and Sexual Harassment*. Boston: Northeastern University Press.

Grunbaum, J., et al. 2002. "Youth Risk Behavior Surveillance (YRBS)—United States, 2001." In Surveillance Summaries, *Morbidity and Mortality Weekly Report* 51, no. SS-4 (June 28):1–64.

Guang, X. 1996. "A Comment on Interracial Marriage" (March 18):1 [online].

Gubrium, J. F. 1975. "Being Single in Old Age." *Aging and Human Development* 6:29–41.

———. 1976. *Time, Roles, and Self in Old Age*. New York: Human Science Press.

Guinness Book of World Records. 1990. New York: Sterling.

———. 2001. Tim Footman, ed. New York: Bantam.

Guisinger, S., P. A. Cowan, and D. Schuldberg. 1989. "Changing Parent and Spouse Relations in the First Years of Remarriage of Divorced Fathers." *Journal of Marriage and the Family* 51:445–56.

Gunn, C. 2003. "Dominant or Different? Gender Issues in Computer Supported Learning." *Journal of Asynchronous Learning Networks* 7, 1:14–30.

Gura, T. 1994a. "New Factor Found in Fixing Sex." *Chicago Tribune* (August 1):4.

———. 1994b. "Generation X Is Not Generation Sex." *Chicago Tribune* (October 9):1, 6.

Gutman, H. G. 1976. *The Black Family in Slavery and Freedom: 1750–1925*. New York: Vintage Books.

Gwartney-Gibbs, P. A. 1986. "The Institutionalization of Premarital Cohabitation: Estimates from Marriage License Applications, 1970 and 1980." *Journal of Marriage and the Family* 48:423–34.

Ha, J. 2005. "Gender Difference in Social Contact after Spousal Loss." http://paa2005.princeton.edu/download.aspx?submissionId=51340 (2006, June 28).

Haddock, S. A., T. S. Zimmerman, S. J. Ziemba, and L. R. Current. 2001. "Ten Adaptive Strategies for Work and Family Balance: Advice From Successful Families." *Journal of Marital and Family Therapy* 27:445–458.

Haddock, S., T. S. Zimmerman, L. R. Current, and A. Harvey. 2002. "The Parenting Practice of Dual-Earner Couples Who Successfully Balance Family and Work." *Journal of Feminist Family Therapy* 14, 3/4:37–55.

Haddocks, R. 1995. "Live-in Relationships More Prone to Violence." *Standard-Times* [online], 3.

Haffner, D. 1999. "Facing Facts: Sexual Healing for American Adolescents." *Human Development and Family Life Bulletin* 4 (Winter):1–3.

Hagestad, G. 1986. "The Family: Women and Grandparents as Kinkeepers." In A. Pifer and L. Bronte, eds., *Our Aging Society*, 141–60. New York: W. W. Norton.

Hahn, B. A. 1993. "Marital Status in Women's Health: The Effect of Economic and Marital Acquisitions." *Journal of Marriage and the Family* 55:495–504.

Hahn, L. 2006. "Couples Remarrying Their Ex-spouses: What Are they Thinking?" *Chicago Tribune* (January 24): Sec. 5, 1, 7.

Hahn, R. A., and D. M. Kleist. 2000. "Divorce Mediation: Research and Implications for Family and Couples Counseling." *Family Journal* 9(April):165–171.

Hailparn, R. 2005. In Tim Warstall "Cosmetic Gynecology." http://timworstall.typepad.com/timworstall/2005/05/cosmetic_gyneco.html (2006, March 21).

Halberstadt, A. G., and M. B. Saitta. 1987. "Gender, Nonverbal Behavior, and Perceived Dominance: A Test of the Theory." *Journal of Personality and Social Psychology* 53:257–72.

Hale, D. 1999. "The Joy of Midlife SEX." In S. J. Bunting, ed., *Human Sexuality 99/00*, 164–67. Sluice Dock, Guilford, CT: Dushkin/McGraw-Hill.

Hale-Benson, J. 1986. *Black Children: Their Roots, Culture, and Learning Styles*, rev. ed. Provo, UT: Brigham Young University Press.

"Half-Full or Half-Empty? Health Care, Child Care, and Youth Programs for Asian American Children in New York City." 1999. *Executive Summary* (April). New York: Coalition for Asian American Children and Families.

Hall, D. R., and J. Zhao. 1995. "Cohabitation and Divorce in Canada: Testing the Selectivity Hypothesis." *Journal of Marriage and the Family* 57 (May):421–27.

Hall, R. M., and B. R. Sandler. 1985. "A Chilly Climate in the Classroom." In A. Sargent, ed., *Beyond Sex Roles*, 503–10. New York: West.

Halpern-Felsher, B., J. Cornell, R. Kropp, and J. Tschann. 2005. "Oral Versus Vaginal Sex." Journal/Vol/pp?

Hamburg, D. A. 1992. *Today's Children: Creating a Future for a Generation in Crisis.* New York: Time Books.

Hammer, H., D. Finkelhor, and A. J. Sedlak. 2002. "Children Abducted by Family Members: National Estimates and Characteristics." *National Incidence Studies of Missing, Abducted, Runaway, and Throwaway Children* (October): 2.

Hamilton, B, S. Ventura, J. Martin, and P. Sutton. 2006. *Preliminary Births for 2004.* Centers for Disease Control and Prevention, National Center for Health Statistics, Hyattsville, MD.

Hanna, J. 1996. "Divorce Law: A Debate about to Happen, Again." *Chicago Tribune* (January 7):sec. 2, 1.

Hansen, G. L. 1985. "Perceived Threats and Marital Jealousy." *Social Psychology Quarterly* 48:262–68.

Hansen, J. E., and W. J. Schuldt. 1984. "Marital Self-Disclosure and Marital Satisfaction." *Journal of Marriage and the Family* 46:923–32.

Hansen, K. 1992. "Our Eyes Behold Each Other: Masculinity and Intimate Friendship in Antebellum New England." In P. Nardi, ed., *Men's Friendships*, 35–58. Newbury Park, CA: Sage.

Hanson, G., and P. Venturelli. 1995. *Drugs and Society.* Boston: Jones and Bartlett.

Hanson, S. M. 1988. "Divorced Fathers with Custody." In P. Bronstein and C. P. Cowan, eds., *Fatherhood Today: Men's Changing Role in the Family*, 166–94. New York: Wiley.

Hansson, R. O., M. F. Knopf, E. A. Downs, P. R. Monroe, S. E. Stegman, and D. S. Wadley. 1984. "Femininity, Masculinity, and Adjustment of Divorce among Women." *Psychology of Women Quarterly* 8, 3:248–49.

Hansson, R. O., and J. H. Remondet. 1987. "Relationships and Aging Family: A Social Psychological Analysis." In S. Oskamp, ed., *Family Processes and Problems: Social Psychological Aspects.* Beverly Hills, CA: Sage.

Harden, B. 2001. "Bible Belt Couples 'Put Assunder' More, Despite New Efforts." *New York Times* (May 21):A1, A14.

Haring-Hidore, M., W. A. Stock, M. A. Okum, and R. A. Witter. 1985. "Marital Status and Subjective Well-Being: A Research Synthesis." *Journal of Marriage and the Family* 47 (November):947–53.

Harmatz, M. G., and M. A. Novak. 1983. *Human Sexuality.* New York: Harper & Row.

Harmon, A. 2005. "Ask Them (All 8 of Them) About Their Grandson." *The New York Times* (March 20):1; 18.

Harris, A. 2003. "Shopping While Black: Applying 42 U.S.C. § 1981 to Cases of Consumer Racial Profiling." *Boston College Third World Law Journal* (Winter, 2003):1–55.

Harris Poll. 2001. "Gun Ownership: Two in Five Americans Live in Gun-Owning Households." Harris Poll #25 (May 30).

Harrison, P. M., and J. C. Karberg. 2003. *Prison and Jail Inmates at Midyear 2002.* Washington, DC: U.S. Department of Justice.

Harrow, B. S., S. L. Tennestedt, and J. B. McKinlay. 1995. "How Costly Is It to Care for Disabled Elders in a Community Setting?" *The Gerontologist* 35, 6:803–13.

Harry, J. 1982. "Decision Making and Age Differences among Gay Couples." *Journal of Homosexuality* 2:9–21.

———. 1983. "Gay Male and Lesbian Relationships." In E. D. Macklin and R. H. Rubin, eds., *Contemporary Families and Alternative Lifestyles: Handbook on Research and Theory*, 216–54. Newbury Park, CA: Sage.

———. 1984. *Gay Couples.* New York: Praeger.

———. 1988. "Some Problems of Gay/Lesbian Families." In C. Chilman, E. W. Nunally, and F. M. Cox, eds., *Variant Family Forms*, 96–113. Newbury Park, CA: Sage.

———, and W. DeVall. 1978. *The Social Organization of Gay Males.* New York: Praeger.

Hartinger, B. 1994. "A Case for Gay Marriage: In Support of Loving and Monogamous Relationships." In Robert T. Francoeur, ed., *Taking Sides: Clashing Views on Controversial Issue in Human Sexuality*, 236–41. Guilford, CN: Dushkin.

Hartman, S. 1988. "Arranged Marriages Live On." *New York Times* (August 10): C12.

Harter, P. 2004. "Child Glue Sniffing Rises in Morocco." *BBC News* (December 21). http://news.bbc.co.uk/2/hi/africa/4113441.stm (2006, August 8).

Hartsoe, S. 2005. "ACLU Challenges N.C. Cohabitation Law." *Washington Post* (May 10):A6.

Harvard Law Review. 1993. "Notes." 106:1905–25.

Harvard University, Joint Center for Housing Studies. 1993. *The State of the Nation's Housing* 1993. Cambridge, MA.

Harvey, D. 1992. "The Psychologists Who Changed Our Minds." *San Francisco Chronicle*, Datebook (June 14):31–32.

Harvey, D. L. 1993. *Potter Addition: Poverty, Family, and Kinship in a Heartland Community.* New York: Aldine de Gruyter.

Harvey, E. 1999. "Short-Term and Long-Term Effects of Early Parental Employment on Children of the National Longitudinal Survey of Youth." *Developmental Psychology* 35, 21:445–59.

Hatfield, E. 1983. "What Do Women and Men Want from Love and Sex?" In E. R. Allgeier and N. B. McCormick, eds., *Changing Boundaries: Gender Roles and Sexual Behavior*, 106–34. Mountain View, CA: Mayfield.

———, and G. W. Walster. 1978. *A New Look at Love.* Reading, MA: Addison-Wesley.

Hauser, D. 2004. "Five Years of Abstinence-Only-Until-Marriage Education: Assessing the Impact." *Advocates for Youth* (September).

Hauser, E. L. 2006. "Maybe You Just Don't Know." *Chicago Tribune* (March 16):25.

Hawkins, D. N. 2005. "Unhappily Ever After: Effects of Long-Term, Low-Quality Marriages on Well-Being." *Social Forces* 84, 1(September): 451–471.

Hayghe, H. V., and S. M. Bianchi. 1994. "Married Mother's Work Patterns: The Job–Family Compromise." *Monthly Labor Review* (June):24–30.

Hayslip, B., and R. Goldberg-Glen, eds. 2000. Grandparents Raising Grandchildren. *Theoretical, empirical, and Clinical Perspectives.* New York: Springer.

Hazan, C., and P. Shaver. 1987. "Conceptualizing Romantic Love as an Attachment Process." *Journal of Personality and Social Psychology* 52:511–24.

Hazler, R. J. 2004. "The Developmental Origins and Treatment Needs of Female Adolescent with Depression." *Journal of Counseling and Development* 82, 1(Winter):18–24.

He, W., M. Sengupta, V. A. Velkoff, and K. A. DeBarros. 2005. *65+ in the United States: 2005.* Current Population Reports, Series P23-209. Washington, DC: U.S. Census Bureau.

Healthwise. 2001. "AIDS Dysmorphic Syndrome." http://health.yahoo.com/topic/hiv/symptoms/article/healthwise/nord519 (2006, May 17).

Heaton, T. B. 1990. "Marital Stability throughout the Childrearing Years." *Demography* 27, 1 (February):55–63.

———., and E. L. Pratt. 1990. "The Effects of Religious Homogamy on Marital Satisfaction and Stability." *Journal of Family Issues* 11:191–207.

Hedges, W. 1994. "Sexual Dysfunction." http://h-devil-www.mc....h-devil/sex/dysfun.html (1999, April 4).

Hendrick, C., and S. Hendrick. 1989. "Research on Love: Does It Measure Up?" *Journal of Personality and Social Psychology* 56:784–94.

Hendrick, S., and C. Hendrick. 1983. *Liking, Loving, and Relating.* Monterey, CA: Brooks Cole.

———. 1987. "Love and Sexual Attitudes, Self-Disclosure and Sensation Seeking." *Journal of Social and Personal Relationships* 4:281–97.

———. 1992. *Liking, Loving, and Relating.* Pacific Grove, CA: Brooks/Cole.

———. 1993. "Lovers as Friends." *Journal of Social and Personal Relationships* 10:459–66.

———. 1995. "Gender Differences and Similarities in Sex and Love." *Personal Relationships* 2:55–65.

———. 1996. "Gender and the Experience of Heterosexual Love." In Julia T. Wood, ed., *Gendered Relationships*, 131–48. Mountain View, CA: Mayfield.

———, and N. L. Adler. 1988. "Romantic Relationships: Love, Satisfaction, and Staying Together." *Journal of Personality and Social Psychology* 34, 6:980–88.

Henkens, K., and H. Van Dalen. 2003. "Early Retirement Systems and Behavior in an International Perspective." In G. A. Adams and T. A. Beehr, eds., *Retirement: Reasons, Processes and Results*, 242–263. New York: Springer.

Henry, C. S., and S. G. Lovelace. 1995. "Family Resources and Adolescent Family Life Satisfaction in Remarried Family Households." *Journal of Family Issues* 16, 6 (November):765–86.

Hepp, R. 2001. "Mom Dies, Daughter Accused of Neglect." *Chicago Tribune* (December 31).

Herbert, B. 2001a. "A Black AIDS Epidemic." *New York Times* (June 4):A21.

———. 2001b. "In America: Protecting Children." *New York Times* (October 11):A23.

Herek, G. 1990. "Gay People in Government Security Clearances: A Social Science Perspective." *American Psychologist* 45, 9:1035–40.

Herek, G. M. 2000. "Homosexuality." www.psychology.ucdavis.edu/ rainbow/html/eop_2000.pdf (2005, December 6).

Herman, D. F. 1989. "The Rape Culture." In J. Freeman, ed., *Women: A Feminist Perspective*, 4th ed., 20–44. Mountain View, CA: Mayfield.

Herrerias, C. 1995. "Noncustodial Mothers Following Divorce." *Marriage and Family Review* 20, 1/2:233–55.

Hertz, R. 1986. *More Equal Than Others: Women and Men in Dual-Couples.* Berkeley: University of California Press.

Hessellund, H. 1976. "Masturbation and Sexual Fantasy in Married Couples." *Archives of Sexual Behavior* 5:133–47.

Hetherington, E. M. 1989. "Coping with Family Transitions: Winners, Losers, and Survivors." *Child Development* 60:1–18.

———, ed. 1999. *Coping with Divorce, Single Parenting, and Remarriage: A Risk and Resiliency Perspective.* Mahwah, NJ: Erlbaum.

———. 2002. "Marriage and Divorce American Style." *American Prospect* 13, 7(April 8):62–63.

———, and W. C. Clingempeel. 1992. "Coping with Marital Transitions: A Family Systems Perspective." *Monographs of the Society for Research in Child Development* 57, 2/3, serial no. 227.

———, and S. H. Henderson. 1997. "Fathers in Stepfamilies: In M. E. Lamb, ed., *The Role of the Father in Child Development*, 212–26. New York: Wiley.

———, and K. M. Jodl. 1994. "Stepfamilies as Settings for Child Development." In A. Booth and J. Dunn, eds., *Stepfamilies: Who Benefits? Who Does Not?* 55–79. Hillsdale, NJ: Erlbaum.

———, and J. Kelly. 2002. *For Better or Worse: Divorce Reconsidered.* New York: W. W. Norton.

———, T. C. Law, and T. G. O'Connor. 1993. "Divorce: Challenges, Changes, and New Chances." In F. Walsh, ed., *Normal Family Processes*, 2d ed., 208–34. New York: Guilford Press.

Heymann, D. L. 2000. "The Urgency of a Massive Effort against Infectious Diseases." Statement presented to the Committee on International Relations of the U.S. House of Representatives, June 29. Washington, DC.

Heymann, J., A. Earle, S. Simmons, S. M. Breslow, and A. Kuehnhoff. 2004. *The Work, Family, and Equity Index: Where Does the United States Stand Globally?* Cambridge, MA: The Project on Global Working Families, Harvard School of Public Health.

HHS Press Release. 1998. "Smoking among Teen Mothers Is on the Rise: Overall Smoking during Pregnancy Drops Steadily." http://www.hhs. gov/new...s/1998pres/981119.html. (November 19).

Hiedemann, B., O. Suholinova, and A. M. O'Rand. 1998. "Economic Independence, Economic Status, and Empty Nest in Midlife Marital Disruption." *Journal of Marriage and the Family* 60 (February):219–31.

Higginbotham, E., and L. Weber. 1995. "Moving Up with Kin and Community: Upward Social Mobility for Black and White Women." In M. L. Andersen and P. H. Collins, eds., *Race, Class and Gender: An Anthology*, 2d ed., 134–47. Belmont, CA: Wadsworth.

Higginbotham, R. 1991. "Friendship as an Ethical Paradigm for Same-Sex Couples." Unpublished paper, Seabury-Western Theological Seminary, Evanston, IL.

Higgins, C., L. Duxbury, and C. Lee. 1994. "Impact of Life-Cycle Stage and Gender on the Ability to Balance Work and Family Responsibilities." *Family Relations* 43, 2 (April):144–50.

Hill, A. 2000. "Divorce: He's Richer, She's Poorer." *The Observer* (October 22). http://www.observer.co.uk/Print/ 0,3858,4079957,00. html (2001, November 8).

Hill, C., Z. Rubin, and L. Peplau. 1976. "Breakups before Marriage: The End of 103 Affairs." *Journal of Social Issues* 32, 1 (Winter): 147–68.

Hill, C.T. 1989. "Attitudes to Love." In A. Campbell, ed., *The Opposite Sex*, 152–57. Topsfield, MA: Salem House.

Hill, N. 1995. "The Relationship between Family Environment and Parenting Style: A Preliminary Study of African American Families." *Journal of Black Psychology* 31, 4 (November):408–23.

Hill, R. 1958. "Generic Features of Families under Stress." *Social Casework* 39 (February/March):139–50.

———. 1972. *The Strengths of Black Families.* New York: Emerson Hall.

———. 1997. *The Strengths of African American Families: Twenty-Five Years Later.* Washington, DC: R & B Publishers.

———. 1998. "Understanding Black Family Functioning: A Holistic Perspective." *Journal of Comparative Family Studies* 29 (Spring):15–25.

Hill, S. 2005. *Black Intimacies: A Gender Perspective on Families and Relationships.* (The Gender Lens Series). Walnut Creek, CA: Altamira Press.

Himes, C. L. 1992. "Future Caregivers: Projected Family Structures of Older People." *Journals of Gerontology* 47, 1:23.

Hirsch, M. B., and W. D. Mosher. 1987. "Characteristics of Infertile Women in the United States and Their Use of Fertility Services." *Fertility and Sterility* 47:618–25.

Hirshman, L. 2005. "America's Stay-at-Home Feminists." *The American Prospect (November 24).* http://www.alternet.org/module/ printversion/ 28621 (2006, November 25).

Hite, S. 1976. *The Hite Report: A Nationwide Study of Female Sexuality.* New York: Macmillan.

———. 1981. *The Hite Report on Male Sexuality.* New York: Knopf.

Hobson, M. 2001. "Divorce's Financial Toll." New York: ABCNews.com (June 28) (2001, November 10).

Hochschild, A. R. 1989. *The Second Shift: Working Parents and the Revolution at Home.* New York: Viking.

———. 1997. *The Time Bind: When Work Becomes Home and Home Becomes Work.* New York: Metropolitan Books.

———. 1999. "Understanding the Future of Fatherhood: The 'Daddy Hierarchy' and Beyond." In C. C. Albers, ed., *Sociology of Families: Readings*, 195–207. Thousand Oaks, CA: Pine Forge.

Hodson, D. S., and P. Skeen. 1994. "Sexuality and Aging: The Hammerlock of Myths." *Journal of Applied Gerontology* 13 (September): 219–35.

Hodson, R., and T. Sullivan. 1995. *The Social Organization of Work.* Belmont, CA: Wadsworth.

Hoff, L. A. 1990. *Battered Women as Survivors.* New York: Routledge.

Hofferth, S. L. 1985. "Updating Children's Life Course." *Journal of Marriage and the Family* 47:93–115.

———, and K. Anderson. 2003. "Are All Dads Equal? Biology vs. Marriage as Basis for Parental Investiment." *Journal of Marriagae and Family* 65:213–232.

Hoffnung, M. 1998. "Motherhood: Contemporary Conflict for Women." In S. J. Ferguson, ed., *Shifting the Center: Understanding Contemporary Families*, 277–91. Mountain View, CA: Mayfield.

Hogan, D. P., and J. I. Farkas. 1995. "The Demography of Changing Intergenerational Relationships." In V. L. Bengtson and K. W. Schaie, eds., *Adult Intergenerational Relations: Effects of Societal Change*, 1–18. New York: Springer.

Hoge, H. 2002. *Women's Stories of Divorce at Childbirth: When the Baby Rocks the Cradle.* Binghamton, NY: Haworth Press.

Holland, D. C., and M. A. Eisenhart. 1990. *Educated in Romance: Women, Achievement, and College Culture.* Chicago: University of Chicago Press.

Holmes, T., and R. Rahe. 1967. "The Social Readjustment Rating Scale." *Journal of Psychosomatic Research* 11:213–18.

Holmes, W., and G. Slap. 1998. "Sexual Abuse of Boys: Definition, Prevalence, Correlates, Sequelae, and Management." *JAMA.* 280:1855–62.

Homans, G. 1961. *Social Behavior in Elementary Forms*. New York: Harcourt, Brace and World.

"Homosexuality." 1997. *The Public Perspective* 8 (October/November):22.

Hondagneu-Sotelo, P., and E. Avila. 1997. "I'm Here, but I'm There: The Meanings of Latina Transnational Motherhood." *Gender and Society* 11 (October):548–71.

"Hooking Up, Hanging Out, and Hoping for Mr. Right: College Women on Dating and Mating Today." 2001. Independent Women's Forum. http://www.iwf.org/news/010727.shtml (2001, October 20).

hooks, b. 1984. *Feminist Theory: From Margin to Center*. Boston: South End Press.

———. 1994. "Sexism, Misogyny: Who Takes the Rap? Misogyny, Gangsta Rap, and the Piano." Race and Ethnicity. http://www.race.eserver.org/misogyny.html (2006, July 22).

Hooyman, N., and H. A. Kiyak. 1993. *Social Gerontology: A Multi-disciplinary Perspective*, 3d ed. Boston: Allyn & Bacon.

Horin, A. "Why Mothers Need Work Insurance against Divorce. 2000." *News Review* (May 27). http://www.smh.com.au/news/0005/27/review/review13.html (2000, November 8).

Horney, K. 1967. *Feminine Psychology*. New York: W. W. Norton.

Hornike, D. 2001. "Can the Church Get in Step with Stepfamilies?" *U.S. Catholic* 66, 7 (July):33–34.

Horowitz, A. 1992. "Methodological Issues in the Study of Gender within Family Caregiving Relationships." In J. Dwyer and R. Coward, eds., *Gender, Families, and Elder Care*, 132–50. Newbury Park, CA: Sage.

Hort, B. E., B. I. Fagot, and M. D. Leinbach. 1990. "Are People's Notions of Maleness More Stereotypically Framed Than Their Notions of Femaleness?" *Sex Roles* 23, 3/4:197–212.

"Househusbands on the Increase." 2004. Korea Update 15 (August 19). www.koreaemb.org/archive/2004/8_2culture/culture2_print.asp (2006, January 3).

Houseknecht, S. K., and G. B. Spanier. 1980. "Marital Disruption and Higher Education among Women in the United States." *Sociological Quarterly* 21:375–89.

Houston Area Women's Center. 1999. "The Facts." http://www.hawc.org/teen/facts.html (1999, March 19).

Hout, M. 2000. "Angry and Alienated: Divorced and Remarried Catholics in the United States." *America* 183, 20 (December 16):10–12.

Hovell, M. F., C. Sipan, and E. Blumberg. 1994. *Journal of Marriage and the Family* 56 (November):73–86.

Howell, J. 1998. "Youth Gangs: An Overview." *Juvenile Justice Bulletin*. U.S. Department of Justice, Office of Juvenile Justice and Delinquency Prevention (August).

Hoyenga, K. B., and K. T. Hoyenga. 1993. *Gender-Related Differences*. Boston: Allyn & Bacon.

Hoyert, D., E. Arias, B. Smith, S. Murphy, and K. Kochanek. 2001. "Deaths: Final Data for 1999." Centers for Disease Control and Prevention, National Center for Health Statistics. NVSR 49(8) (September 21).

Huang, A. 1999. "More Women in Taiwan Choose Divorce." *Chicago Tribune* (January 10):sec. 13, 8.

Hubbard, R. 1990. *The Politics of Women's Biology*. New Brunswick, NJ: Rutgers University Press.

Huber, B. R., and J. W. Schofield. 1998. "I Like Computers, But Many Girls Don't: Gender and the Sociocultural Context of Computing." In H. Bromley and M. W. Apple, eds., *Education/Technology/Power: Educational Computing as a Social Practice*, 103–131. Albany: State University of New York Press.

Huber, J. 1980. "Will U.S. Fertility Decline toward Zero?" *Sociological Quarterly* 21:481–92.

Hudnall, C. E. 2001. "Grandparents Get Help." *AARP Bulletin* (November):9, 12.

Hughes, Z. 2001. "How to Get What You Want from the Man in Your Life." *Ebony* (March):124–28.

Human Rights Watch. 2006. "U.N.: Open Independent Inquiry into Civilian Deaths." http://hrw.org/english/docs/2006/08/08/lebano13939.htm (2006, August 24).

Humes, K., and J. McKinnon. 2000. *The Asian and Pacific Islander Population in the United States: March 1999*. U.S. Census Bureau, Current Population Reports, Series P20–529. Washington, DC: U.S. Government Printing Office.

Humphrys, J. 2001. "We're Tricking the Poorer Nations Out of Their Money." *Sunday Times* (November 4). http://www.igc.apc.org/globalpolicy/socecon/inequal/2001/1/1104trade.htm (2002, January 18).

Hundley, C. 2005. "Camilla Gets Her Prince." *Chicago Tribune* (February 11):1, 6.

———. 2004. "U.S. Led a Resurgence Last Year Among Millionaires World-Wide" (June 15). www.globalpolicy.org/socecon/inequal/2004/0615millonaires.htm (2006, January 20).

Hunt, J. G., and L. L. Hunt. 1986. "The Dualities of Careers and Families: New Integrations or New Polarizations?" In A. S. Skolnick and J. H. Skolnick, eds., *Family in Transition: Rethinking Marriage, Sexuality, Child Rearing and Family Organization*, 275–89. Boston: Little, Brown.

Hunt, L. L., and J. G. Hunt. 1975. "Race and the Father–Son Connection: The Conditional Relevance of Father Absence for the Orientations and Identities of Adolescent Boys." *Social Problems* 23:35–52.

Hunt, M. 1959. *The Natural History of Love*. New York: Knopf.

———. 1974. *Sexual Behavior in the 1970s*. Chicago: Playboy Press.

Hupka, R. 1981. "Cultural Determinants of Jealousy." *Alternative Lifestyles* 4:310–56.

———. 1985. "Romantic Jealousy and Romantic Envy: A Seven-Nation Study." *Journal of Cross-Cultural Psychology*, 16:423–46.

———. 1991. "The Motive for the Arousal of Romantic Jealousy: Its Cultural Origin. In P. Salovey, ed., *The Psychology of Jealousy and Envy*. New York: Guilford.

Huppertz, N. 2002. "Importance of Language." (March 13). www.womenssportsfoundation.org/cgi-bin/iowa/issues/disc/article.htm?record=872 (2005, August 23).

Husted, J., and A. Edwards. 1976. "Personality Correlates of Male Sexual Arousal and Behavior." *Archives of Sexual Behavior* (March).

Huston, M., and P. Schwartz. 1996. "Gendered Dynamics in the Romantic Relationships of Lesbians and Gay Men." In J. T. Wood, ed., *Gendered Relationships*, 163–76. Mountain View, CA: Mayfield.

Huyck, M. H. 2001. "Returning a Mother's Kindness." *Chicago Tribune* (May 13):sec. 2, 1.

Hyde, J. S. 1984. "Children's Understanding of Sexist Language." *Developmental Psychology* 20, 4:697–706.

Hyman, S. E. 2000. Statement before the Senate Appropriations Committee, Hearing on Suicide Awareness and Prevention, Washington, DC (February 8). http://www.nimh.nih.gov/about/000208.cfm (2002, January 26).

Hymowitz, K. S. 2003. "The Cohabitation Blues." *Commentary* 116 (March):66–69.

Iazetto, D. 1989. "When the Body Is Not an Easy Place to Be." Ph.D. diss., Union Institute, Cincinnati, OH.

Idaho Council on Domestic Violence. 1998. "Rape Is a Crime Principally Committed against Young People." National Institute of Justice "Fax" Sheet.

Ihinger-Tallman, M. 1987. "Sibling and Stepfamily Bonding in Stepfamilies." In K. Pasley and M. Ihinger-Tallman, eds., *Remarriage and Stepparenting: Current Research and Theory*, 164–82. New York: Guilford Press.

———, and K. Pasley. 1987. "Divorce and Remarriage in the American Family: A Historical Review." In K. Pasley and M. Ihinger-Tallman, eds., *Remarriage and Stepparenting: Current Research and Theory*, 3–18. New York: Guilford Press.

———. 1991. "Children in Stepfamilies." In J. N. Edwards and D. H. Demo, eds., *Marriage and Family in Transition*, 453–69. Boston: Allyn & Bacon.

Illinois Coalition against Sexual Assault. 1994. "Sexual Violence: Facts and Statistics."

"Induced Abortion." 2000. New York: Alan Guttmacher Institute. http://www.guttmacher.org/pubs/fb_induced_abortion.html (2001, December 17).

"Induced Abortion in the United States." 2005. *Facts in Brief* (May 5). New York: The Alan Guttmacher Institute.

Inglehart, R., and P. Norris. 2003. *Rising Tide—Gender Equality and Cultural Change Around the World*. Cambridge: Cambridge University Press.

Ingram, E., and J. B. Ellis. 1992. "Attitudes toward Suicidal Behavior: A Review of the Literature." *Death Studies* 16:31–43.

Inman, C. 1996. "Friendships among Men: Closeness in the Doing." In J. T. Wood, ed., *Gendered Relationships*, 95–110. Mountain View, CA: Mayfield.

"Insurer Law for Fertility Treatments." 2001. *New York Times* (September 1):A10.

"Interracial Marriage." 2006. Wikipedia (April 25). http://en.wikipedia. org/wiki/Interracial_marriage (2006, May 1).

International Labour Conference. 2006. *The End of Child Labour: Within Reach*. Geneva, Switzerland: International Labour Office.

International Labour Office. 2006. *Global Employment Trends Brief, January 2006*. Geneva, Switzerland.

International Labor Organization. 2001. *World Employment Report* 2001. Geneva, Switzerland.

IPPF. 1999. "15-Year-Old Girl Jailed for Abortion in Nepal Released from Prison This Week" (October 4). http://www.ippf.org/newsinfo/ pressreleases/nepal9910.htm (2002, January 21).

Iraq Body Count Press Release 13. 2006. "Iraq Death Toll in Third Year of Occupation Is Highest Yet." http://www.iraqbodycount.net (2006, August 24).

"It's Time for Working Women to Earn Equal Pay." 2001. American Federation of Labor-Congress of Industrial Organizations. http://www. aflcio.org/women/equalpay.htm (2001, October 20).

Jaccard, J., P. Dittus, and V. Gordon. 2000. "Parent-Teen Communication about Premarital Sex: Factors Associated with the Extent of Communication." *Journal of Adolescent Research* 15:187–208.

Jackson, A. P., R. P. Brown, and K. E. Patterson-Stewart. 2000. "African Americans in Dual-Career Commuter Marriages: An Investigation of Their Experiences." *Family Journal: Counseling and Therapy for Couples and Families* 8:22–36.

Jacob, H. 1988. *Silent Revolution: The Transformation of Divorce Law in the United States*. Chicago: University of Chicago Press.

Jacob, T. 1992. "Family Studies of Alcoholism." *Journal of Psychology* 5:319–38.

Jadva, V., C. Murray, E. Lycett, F. MacCallum, and S. Golombok. 2003. "Surrogacy: The Experiences of Surrogate Mothers." Human Reproduction 18, 10(October):2196–2204.

James, J. 2004. "And What About the Dads?" Time Europe 163, 19 (May 10). http://www.time.com/time/europe/magazine/printout/0,13- 155,901040510-631996m00.html (2006, February 8).

James, R. 1997. "Campus Interracial Couple." *Eclipse* (October 14). http://www.inform.umd.edu/News/Eclipse/eclipse/10-14-97/ 10-14-97-campusinterracial.html (2001, November 12).

Jankowiak, W. R., and E. F. Fischer. 1992. "A Cross-Cultural Perspective on Romantic Love." *Ethnology* 31, 2 (April):149–55.

Janofsky, M. 2001. "Polygamy Case Raises Thorny Issues." *Chicago Tribune* (May 15):sec. 1, 9.

"Japanese Teenager Charged in Second Murder." *New York Times* (July 16):7.

Jarman, N., and A. Tennant. 2003. *An Unacceptable Prejudice: Homophobic Violence and Harassment in Northern Ireland*. Belfast: Institute for Conflict Research.

Jarrett, R. L. 1992. "A Family Case Study: An Examination of the Underclass Debate." In J. F. Gilgun, K. Daly, and G. Handel, eds., *Qualitative Methods in Family Research*, 173–96. Newbury Park, CA: Sage.

———. 1995. "Growing up Poor: The Family Experiences of Socially Mobile Youth in Low-Income African American Neighborhoods." *Journal of Adolescent Research* 10 (January):111–35.

Jay, K., and A. Young. 1977. *The Gay Report*. New York: Summit.

Jaynes, G. D., and R. M. Williams, Jr., eds. 1989. *A Common Destiny: Blacks and American Society*. Washington, DC: National Academy Press.

Jayson, S. 2005a. "Dating Game Changes After 40." *USA Today* (December 1): D4.

Jayson, S. 2005b. "Teens Define Sex in New Ways." USA Today (October 19). http://www.usatoday.com/news/health/2005-10-18-teens-sex_x. htm (2006, March 3).

Jendrek, M. P. 1996. "Grandparents Who Parent Their Grandchildren: Effects on Lifestyle." In J. Quadagno and D. Street, eds., *Aging for the Twenty-First Century*, 286–305. New York: St. Martin's Press.

Jenny, C., K. Hymel, A. Ritzen, S. Reinert, and T. Hay. 1999. "Analysis of Missed Cases of Abusive Head Trauma," *JAMA* 281 (February): 621–26.

Jerome, R., J. Fowler, D. Stuart, J. Blonka, P. Grout, and J. Bane. 2004. "The Cyberporn Generation." People 61(16):72, 5p, 8c.

Jhally, S. 1995. *Dreamworlds II: Gender/Sex/Power in Music Video*. (55 Minute Video Documentary). Northhampton, MA: Media Education Foundation.

Joint United Nations Programme on HIV/AIDS, United Nations Children's Fund and the United States Agency for International Development. 2004. *Children on the Brink 2004: A Joint Report of New Orphan Estimates and a Framework for Action*. Washington, DC: Population, Health and Nutrition Information Project for USAID.

John, D., and B. Shelton. 1997. "The Production of Gender among Black and White Women and Men: The Case of Household Labor." *Sex Roles* 36 (February):171–93.

John, R. 1998. "Native American Families." In C. H. Mindel, R. W. Habenstein, and R. Wright, Jr., eds., *Ethnic Families in America: Patterns and Variations*, 382–421. Upper Saddle River, NJ: Prentice Hall.

Johnson, A. G. 1980. "On the Prevalence of Rape in the United States." *Signs* 6:136–46.

Johnson, C. 2006. "Legislative Debate Over Illegal Immigration Heats Up." News10/KXTV. http://www.news10.net/storyfull2.aspx?storyID= 16768 (2006, August 24).

Johnson, C. L. 1988. *Exfamilia*. New Brunswick, NJ: Rutgers University Press.

———, and D. J. Catalano. 1981. "Childless Elderly and Their Family Supports." *Gerontologist* 21:610–18.

Johnson, F. L. 1996. "Friendships among Women: Closeness in Dialogue." In J. T. Wood, ed., *Gendered Relationships*, 79–93. Mountain View, CA: Mayfield.

Johnson, J. O. 2005. *Whose Minding the Kids: Child Care Arrangements: Winter 2002*. Current Population Reports, P70-101. Washington, DC: U.S. Census Bureau.

Johnson, L. A. "Experts: Girls Using Steroids for 'Weight Control." *Chicago Tribune* April 26): 10.

Johnson, S. M. 2003. "The Revolution in Couple Therapy: A Practitioner-Scientist Perspective." *Journal of Marital and Family Therapy* 29:365–384.

———., and E. O"Conner. 2002. *The Gay Baby Boom*. New York: New York University Press.

Johnston, J. R. 1995. "Research Update: Children's Adjustment in Sole Custody Compared to Joint Custody Families and Principles for Custody Decision Making." *Family Conciliation Courts Review* 33:415–25.

Johnston, L. D., J. G. Bachman, and P. M. O'Malley. 1997. *Monitoring the Future: Questionnaire Responses from the Nation's High School Seniors, 1995*. Ann Arbor, MI: Institute for Social Research.

Johnston, W. R. 2005. "Worldwide Abortion Legislation." (August 12). (http://www.johnstonsarchive.net/policy/abortion/wrjp334al.html (2006, April 19).

Jones, A. 1995. "For Better or Worse for a Little While Longer." *Chicago Tribune* (September 21):1.

Jones, J. 2006. "Marriage is for White People." *Washington Post* (March 26):BO1.

Jones, J. M. 2005a. "Gender Differences in Views of Job Opportunity." *The Gallup Organization* (August 2). www.gallup.com/poll/content/ print.aspx?ci+17614P (2005, August 2).

———. 2005b. "Shift in Public Perceptions About Union, Strength, Influence." 2005. *The Gallup Organization* (August 23). www.gallup. com/poll/content/print.aspx?ci=18040 (2005, September 23).

———. 2006. "Public Solidly Supports Increase in Minimum Wage." *The Gallup Poll* (January 4). http://poll.galup.com/content/default. aspx?ci=20710 (2006, January 30).

Jones, P. 2005. "TV Terror." *Chicago Tribune* (October 18): Sec. 5, p. 1, 5.

Juby, H. 2003/2004. "Yours, Mine, and Ours: New Boundaries for the Modern Stepfamily." *Transition Magazine* 33, 4(Winter):2–6.

Kahle, J. 1990. "Why Girls Don't Know." In M. Rowe, ed., *What Research Says to the Science Teacher: The Process of Knowing*, 655–67. Washington, DC: National Science Teachers Association.

Kahn, J., C. Brindis, and D. Glei. 1999. "Pregnancies Averted among U.S. Teenagers by the Use of Contraceptives." *Family Planning Perspectives* (January/February): 31, 1.

Kain, E. 1990. *The Myth of Family Decline: Understanding Families in a World of Rapid Social Change*. Lexington, MA: D. C. Heath.

Kaiser Commission on Medicaid and the Uninsured. 2006. *The Uninsured: A Primer*. Washington, DC: Kaiser Family Foundation.

Kaiser Family Foundation. 2005. *Medicare Chart Book 2005*. http://www.kff.org/medicare/7284.cfm (2006, June 27).

———. and TM Magazine. 1998. *National Survey of Teens: Teens Talk About Dating, Intimacy, and Their Sexual Experiences*. Menlo Park, CA: The Foundation.

Kalajian, B. 2006. "Making Love Last: Communication, Commitment and Giving More Than 50 Percent Among Secrets to Marital Longevity." *The Record Eagle* (February 12). http://www.record-eagle.com/2006/feb/12marr.htm (2006, April 14).

Kalil, A. 2005. "Unemployment and Job Displacement: The Impact on Families and Children." *Ivey Business Journal* (July/August):1–5.

Kalish, R. A. 1985. *Death, Grief, and Caring Relationships*, 2d ed. Monterey, CA: Brooks/Cole.

Kalmijn, M. 1998. "Intermarriage and Homogamy: Causes, Patterns, Trends." *Annual Review of Sociology* 24:395–421.

———. 1999. "Father Involvement in Childrearing and the Perceived Stability of Marriage." *Journal of Marriage and the Family* 61 (May): 409–21.

Kamerman, S. B. 1996. "Child and Family Policies: An International Overview." In E. F. Zigler; S. L. Kagan, and N. W. Hall, eds., *Children, Families, and Government: Preparing for the Twenty-First Century*, 31–48. New York: Cambridge University Press.

Kaminer, W. 2001. "Virtual Rape." *The New York Times Magazine*. (November 25): 70–73.

Kanabus, A. 2005. "HIV, Pregnancy, Mothers and Babies." http://www.avert.org/pregnancy.htm (2006, May 17).

Kanin, E. J., K. B. Davidson, and S. R. Scheck. 1970. "A Research Note on Male-Female Differentials in the Experience of Heterosexual Love." *Journal of Sex Research* 6, 1 (February):64–72.

Kann, L., S. Kinchen, B. Williams, J. Ross, R. Lowry, J. Grunbaum, and L. Kolbe. 2000. "Youth Risk Behavior Surveillance—United States, 1999." CDC Surveillance Summaries, June. *Morbidity and Mortality Weekly Report*. 49:1–96.

Kanter, R. M. 1977. *Work and Family in the United States*. New York: Russell Sage Foundation.

Kantor, 2005. *Commitment and Community: Communes and Utopias in Sociological Perspective*. Cambridge, MA: Harvard University Press.

Kapos, S. 2005. "Bloom Falls Off the Rose for Internet Matchups." *Chicago Tribune* (February 14): Sec. 4, pp. 1,7.

Kao, H., and A. Stuifbergen. 1999. "Family Experiences Related to the Decision to Institutionalize an Elderly Member in Taiwan: An Exploratory Study." *Social Science and Medicine* 49:1115–23.

Kaplan, G., V. Barell, and A. Lusky. 1988. "Subjective State of Health and Survival among Elderly Adults." *Journal of Gerontology* 43: S114–120.

Karen, R. 1987. "Giving and Getting in Love and Marriage." *Cosmopolitan* (March):228–31, 236–37, 293.

Karp, D. A., and W. Yoels. 1993. *Sociology in Everyday Life*. Itasca, IL: Peacock.

Karp, S., D. Silber, R. Holmstrom, and L. Stock. 1995. "Personality of Rape Survivors as a Group and by Relation of Survivor to Perpetrator." *Journal of Clinical Psychology* 51:587–92.

Karp, David, William Yoels, and Barbara Vann. 2003. *Sociology in Everyday Life*. Long Grove, IL: Waveland Press.

Katzev, A. R., R. L. Warner, and A. C. Acock. 1994. "Girls or Boys? Relationship of Child Gender to Marital Instability." *Journal of Marriage and the Family* 56 (February):89–100.

Kaufman, M. 2005. "FDA Official Quits Over Delay on Plan B." *Washington Post* (September 1):A8.

Kauffold, M. P. 1990. "Seeds of Doubt: Bill Takes Aim at 'Test Tube' Baby Industry." *Chicago Tribune* (October 14):4.

Keating, N. C., and P. Cole. 1980. "What Do I Do with Him 24 Hours a Day? Changes in the Housewife Role after Retirement." *Gerontologist* 20:84–89.

Kehoe, M. 1989. *Lesbians over 60 Speak for Themselves*. New York: Haworth Press.

Keith, P. 1986. "Isolation of the Unmarried in Later Life." *Family Relations* 35:389–96.

Keith, V. M., and B. Finlay. 1988. "The Impact of Parental Divorce on Children's Educational Attainment, Marital Timing, and Likelihood of Divorce." *Journal of Marriage and the Family* 50:797–809.

Kelley, P. 1995. *Developing Healthy Stepfamilies: Twenty Families Tell Their Stories*. New York: Haworth Press.

Kelly, G. F. 1995. *Sexuality Today*. Dubuque, IA: Brown and Benchmark.

Kelly, J. 1977. "The Aging Male Homosexual: Myth and Reality?" *Gerontologist* 17:328–32.

Kelly, J. B. 2000. "Children's Adjustment in Conflicted Marriage and Divorce: A Decade Review of Research." *Journal of the American Academy of Child and Adolescent Psychiatry* 39, 8 (August):963–73.

———., and R. E. Emery. 2003. "Children's Adjustment Following Divorce: Risk and Resilience Perspectives." *Family Relations* 52:352–362.

Kempe, C. H., F. N. Silverman, B. Steele, W. Droegemueller, and H. K. Silver. 1962. "The Battered Child Syndrome." *Journal of the American Medical Association* 181:17–24.

Kennedy-Bergen, R. 1999. "In Brief: Marital Rape." National Electronic Network on Violence Against Women: Applied Research Forum. VAWnet, a Project of the National Resource Center on Domestic Violence. http://www.vawnet.org/DomesticViolence/Research/VAWnetDocs/AR_mrape.php (2006, April 22).

Kennen, R. 1997. "Midlife Pregnancy." http://www.midlifemomm.../midlifepregnancy.html (May 13).

Kephart, W. 1967. "Some Correlates of Romantic Love." *Journal of Marriage and the Family* 29:470–74.

Kephart, W. M. 1988. "The Oneida Community." In N. D. Glenn and M. Tolbert, eds., *Family Relations: A Reader*, 17–24. Belmont, CA: Wadsworth.

Kepner, A. 2005. "Stay at Home Fathers Bond With Kids and One Another." *The News Journal*(December 29). www.delawareonlinecom/apps/pbcs.dll/article?AID=20051229/NEWS/512290336/1006 (2006, January 3).

Kerckhoff, A. C. 1976. "Patterns of Marriage and Family Formation and Dissolution." *Journal of Consumer Research* 2:262.

Kessler, S. J. 1996. "The Medical Construction of Gender: Case Management of Intersexed Infants." In B. Laslett, S. G. Kohlstedt, H. Longino, and E. Hammonds, eds., *Gender and Scientific Authority*, 340–63. Chicago: University of Chicago Press.

Kessler-Harris, A. 1981. *Women Have Always Worked: A Historical Overview*. New York: Feminist Press.

———. 1982. *Out to Work: A History of Wage-Earning Women in the United States*. New York: Oxford University Press.

Kheshgi-Genovese, S., and T. A. Genovese. 1997. "Developing the Spousal Relationship within Stepfamilies." *Families in Society: The Journal of Contemporary Human Services* 78 (May–June):255–64.

Kidder, R. M. 1988. "Marriage in America: Why Marry?" In O. Pocs, ed., *Marriage and Family. 88/89: Annual Editions*, 44–47. Sluice Dock, Guilford, CT: Dushkin.

Kiefer, H. 2004. "Teens: Sometimes Love Just Ain't Enough." (September 28). *The Gallup Organization!* www.gallup.com (2006, April 14).

Kiernan, K. 1990. "Ringing Changes." *New Statesman and Society* 3 (February 16):25.

———. 1992. "The Impact of Family Disruption in Childhood on Transitions Made in Young Adult Life." *Population Studies* 46:213–34.

———. 2002. "Cohabitation in Western Europe: Trends, Issues, and Implications." In A. Booth and A. Crouter, eds., *Just Living Together: Implications of Cohabitation on Families, Children, and Social Policy*, 3–32. Mahway, NJ: Erlbaum.

Kilborn, P. 2004. "Alive, Well and on the Prowl, It's the Geriatric Mating Game." *New York Times* (March 7):.

Kim, E. K. 2006. "Black Jack's Rule on Unwed Parents is Unusual Here." *STLtoday.com*, (February 23). http://www.stltoday.com/stltoday/news/special/srlinks.nsf/0/F9FCE3731F7C4BD38625712300801F1B?OpenDocument (2006, April 3).

Kimmel, M. 2000. *The Gendered Society*. New York: Oxford University Press.

———. 2001. "Manhood and Violence: The Deadliest Equation." *Newsday* (March 8):A-41.

———, and M. Messner. 2001. Men's Lives, 5th ed. Needham Heights, MA: Allyn & Bacon.

Kinder, D. R., and D. O. Sears. 1981. "Symbolic Racism versus Racial Threats to the Good Life." *Journal of Personality and Social Psychology* 40:414–31.

King, D. K. 1990. "Multiple Jeopardy, Multiple Consciousness." In M. R. Malson, E. Mudimbe-Boyi, J. F. O'Barr, and M. Wyer, eds., *Black Women in America*, 265–95. Chicago: University of Chicago Press.

King, V., K. M. Harris, and H. E. Heard. 2004. "Racial and Ethnic Diversity in Nonresident Father Involvement." *Journal of Marriage and Family* 66:1–21.

Kinnon, J. 2003. "The Shocking State of Black Marriage." *Ebony* no. 1 (November):59.

Kinsey, A., W. B. Pomeroy, and C. E. Martin. 1948. *Sexual Behavior in the Human Male*. Philadelphia: Saunders.

———, and P. H. Gebhard. 1953. *Sexual Behavior in the Human Female*. Philadelphia: Saunders.

Kiser, L., L. Bennett, J. Heston, and M. Paavola. 2005. "Family Ritual and Routine: Comparison of Clinical and Non-clinical Families." *Journal of Child and Family Studies* 14, 3(September):357–372.

Kitano, H. L. 1988. "The Japanese American Family." In C. H. Mindel, R. W. Habenstein, and R. Wright, Jr., eds., *Ethnic Families in America: Patterns and Variations*, 258–75. New York: Elsevier.

Kitano, K., and H. Kitano. 1998. "The Japanese American Family." In C. Mindel, R. Habenstein, and R. Wright, Jr., eds. *Ethnic Families in America: Patterns and Variations*, 311–30. Upper Saddle River, NJ: Prentice Hall.

Kivett, V. R. 1991. "Centrality of the Grandfather Role among Older Rural Black and White Men." *Journal of Gerontology* 46, 5 (September):250–58.

Kleiman, C. 1995. "Men Clean Up in Wages as Women Keep House." *Chicago Tribune* (September 18):4, 5.

———. 1996. "Odd Hours: Moving to and around the Clock Economy." *Chicago Tribune* (January 28):sec. 6.

———. 1999. "Corporations Find On-site Day Care a Two-Way Perk." *Chicago Tribune* (February 2):sec. 3, 1.

Kleiman, K. 2001. "Can Men Get the Postpartum Blues?" http://www.babycenter.com/expert/3870.html (2001, December 21).

Klerman, G. L., and M. M. Weissman. 1980. "Depressions among Women: Their Nature and Causes." In M. Guttentak, S. Salasin, and D. Belle, eds., *The Mental Health of Women*, 57–92. New York: Academic Press.

Klimek, D. 1979. *Beneath Mate Selection in Marriage: The Unconscious Motives in Human Pairing*. New York: Van Nostrand Reinhold.

Kloehn, S. 1998. "Southern Baptists Approve Submissive Wives Doctrine." *Chicago Tribune* (June 10):1, 11.

Kluegel, J. R. 1990. "Trends in Whites' Explanation of the Black-White Gap in Socioeconomic Status, 1977–1989." *American Sociological Review* 55:512–25.

Kluwer, E. S., J. A. M. Heesink, and E. Van De Vliert. 1996. "Marital Conflict about the Division of Household Labor and Paid Work." *Journal of Marriage and the Family* 58 (November):958–69.

Knaub, P., S. L. Hanna, and N. Stinnett. 1984. "Strengths of Remarried Families." *Journal of Divorce* 7, 3:41–55.

Knowles, J., and D. Dimitrov. 2002. "Human Sexuality: What Children Need to Know and When They Need to Know It." Planned *Parenthood*. http://www.plannedparenthood.org/PARENTS/human sexuality1.html (2006, March 22).

Knox, D., C. Schacht, and M. Zusman. 1999. "Love Relationships among College Students." *College Student Journal* 33, 1 (March):149–51.

Knox, D., and M. Zusman. 2001. "Marrying a Man with 'Baggage': Implications for Second Wives." *Journal of Divorce and Remarriage* 35, 3/4:67–79.

———, M. Kaluzny, and C. Cooper. 2000. "College Student Recovery from a Broken Heart" 34, 3 (September):322–324.

Knox, N. 2004. "Nordic Family Ties Don't Mean Tying the Knot." *USA Today* (December 16):15A, 16A.

Knudson-Martin, C., and A. R. Mahoney. 2005. "Moving Beyond Gender: Processes That Create Relationship Equality." *Journal of Marital and Family Therapy* 31, 2(April):235–246.

Kogan, T. S. 2004. "Transsexuals, Intersexuals, and Same-Sex Marriages." *BYU Journal of Public Law* 18, 2:371–418.

Kohlberg, L. 1966. "A Cognitive-Developmental Analysis of Children's Sex-Role Concepts and Attitudes." In E. Maccoby, ed., *The Development of Sex Differences*, 82–173. Stanford, CA: Stanford University Press.

Kohn, M. 1977. *Class and Conformity*. Chicago: University of Chicago Press.

Koivula, N. 1999. "Gender Stereotyping in Televised Media Sport Coverage." *Sex Roles* 41, 7/8 (October):589–605.

Kom, D. J. 2001. "B.E. Guide to Family Finances: Yours, Mine, and Ours." *Black Enterprise* 32, 2(October):123–128.

Kong, C. 1998. "Sometimes Love Hurts: When Romance Turns Rocky." *Summer Romance*: special issue. http://enterprise.sjme...talhigh/love/abuse.html (March 19).

Kong, D. 2002. "Home for Asian Elderly Defies Past." *Chicago Tribune* (January 2):9.

Konrad, R. 2002. "From High=Tech to Blue Collar." *NEWS.COM* (February 8). http://news.com.com/2102–1017_3–832553.html?tag=st.util.print (2006, January 10).

Korenman, S., and D. Neumark. 1991. "Does Marriage Really Make Men More Productive?" *The Journal of Human Resources* 26, 2(Spring): 248–268.

Kosmin, B., E. Mayer, and A. Keysar. 2001. American Religious Identification Survey. New York: City University of New York, Graduate Center. http://www.gc.cuny.edu/studies/arisindex.htm (2006, April 10).

Kovacs, J. 2005. "U.S. Teacher Sexpidemic Spreading Across Planet." WorldNetDaily. www.worldnetdaily.com (2005, December 18).

Koss, M. P., K. E. Leonard, D. A. Beezley, and C. J. Oros. 1985. "Non-Stranger Sexual Aggression: A Discriminant Analysis of the Psychological Characteristics of Undetected Offenders." *Sex Roles* 12:981–92.

Kotulak, R. 1999. "Study Finds Midlife 'Best Time, Best Place to Be'." *Chicago Tribune* (February 16):1.

Kposowa, A. 2000. "Marital Status and Suicide in the National Longitudinal Mortality Study." Journal of Epidemiology and Community Health 54:254–261.

Kreider, R. M. 2003. *Adopted Children and Stepchildren: 2000*. Washington, DC: U. S. Census Bureau.

———. 2005. *Number, Timing, and Duration of Marriages and Divorces, 2001*. Current Population Reports, P70-97. Washington, DC: U.S. Census Bureau.

———., and Jason Fields. 2005. *Living Arrangements of Children: 2001*. Current Population Reports, P70-104. Washington, DC: U.S. Census Bureau.

Kroll, L., and L. Fass. 2006. The World's Billionaires." (March 19). http://www.forbes.com/billionaires (2006, August 1).

Kristof, N. 1996. "Who Needs Love? In Japan Many Couples Don't." *New York Times* (February 11):A6.

———. 2005. "Blacks, Whites and Love in America." *New York Times* (April 24): Sec. 4, p. 13.

Kübler-Ross, E. 1969. *On Death and Dying*. New York: Macmillan.

———. 1974. *Questions and Answers on Death and Dying*. New York: Macmillan.

Kuebli, J., S. A. Butler, and R. Fivush. 1995. "Mother-Child Talk about Past Emotions: Relations of Maternal Language and Child Gender over Time." *Cognition and Emotion* 9:265–83.

Kunkel, D., K. Eyal, K. Finnerty, E. Biely, and E. Donnerstein. 2005. *Sex on TV4*. Menlo Park, CA: The Henry Kaiser Family Foundation.

Kulik, L. 2002. "The Impact of Social Background on Gender-Role Ideology." *Journal of Family Issues* 23, 1:53–73.

Kurdek, L. 2004. "Are Gay and Lesbian Cohabiting Couples Really Different from Heterosexual Married Couples?" *Journal of Marriage and Family* 66, 4:880–900.

Kurdek, L. A. 1993. "Predicting Marital Dissolution: A 5-Year Prospective Longitudinal Study of Newlywed Couples." *Journal of Personality and Social Psychology* 64, 2:221–42.

———. 1998. "Relationship Outcomes and Their Predictors: Longitudinal Evidence From Heteroseexual, Married, Gay, Cohabiting, and Lesbian Cohabiting Couples." *Journal of Marriage and the Family* 60:553–568.

———. 1994. "Areas of Conflict for Gay, Lesbian, and Heterosexual Couples: What Couples Argue about Influences Relationship Satisfaction." *Journal of Marriage and the Family* 56, 4 (November):923–24.

———, and M. A. Fine. 1993. "The Relation between Family Structure and Young Adolescents' Appraisals of Family Climate and Parenting Behavior." *Journal of Family Issues* 14:279–90.

———, and J. P. Schmitt. 1986. "Relationship Quality of Partners in Heterosexual Married, Heterosexual Cohabiting, and Gay and Lesbian Relationships." *Journal of Personality and Social Psychology* 51 (October):711–20.

Kuriki, C. 1994. "Japanese Law Does Little to Reach Workplace Equality." *Chicago Tribune* (October 9):sec. 6, 9.

Kuzma, C. 2005. "The Kids Are Alright." *AlterNet* (June 9). http://www.alternet.org/module/printversion/22199 (2006, April 25).

Kwok, H. 2006. "The Son Also Acts as Major Caregiver to Elderly Parents." *Current Sociology* 54, 2:257–272.

Lacey, N. A. 1999. "Love + Loving + Better Health." *Conscious Choice: The Journal of Ecology and Natural Living* (February). http://www.consciouschoice.com/issues/cc1202.healthoflove.html (2001, September 8).

La Ferla, R. 2000. "The Once and Future Virgins." *New York Times* (July 23). http://www.nytimes.qpass.com/qpass-archives (2001, December 4).

Lai, T. 1992. "Asian American Women: Not for Sale." In M. Anderson and P. H. Collins, eds., *Race, Class, and Gender*, 163–71. Belmont, CA: Wadsworth.

———. 2005. "The New Dad." www.carleton.ca/ottawainsight/ s12.html (2006, January 3).

Laird, J. 1993. "Lesbian and Gay Families." In F. Walsh, ed., *Normal Family Process*, 2d ed., 282–330. New York: Guilford Press.

Lakoff, R. 1975. *Language and Woman's Place*. New York: Colophon.

Lamb, M. 1987. *The Father's Role: Cross-Cultural Perspectives*. Hillsdale, NJ: Erlbaum.

Lamothe, R. 2006. "Commentary: Immigration Policy Amnesty Irrational." *The Northeastern News* (August 16). http://www.nu-news.com/media/storage/paper6 (2006, August 21).

Lance, L. M. 1998. "Gender Differences in Heterosexual Dating: A Content Analysis of Personal Ads." *Journal of Men's Studies* 6, 3 (Spring):297–305.

Landale, N. S., and R. Forste. 1991. "Pattern of Entry into Cohabitation and Marriage among Mainland Puerto Rican Women." *Demography* 28:587–607.

———, and S. E. Tolnay. 1991. "Group Differences in Economic Opportunity and the Timing of Marriage." *American Sociological Review* 56, 1 (February):33–45.

Landhaus, E. 2004. "Pre-implantation Genetic Diagnosis Offers Hope But Prompts Ethical Concerns." *Stanford Report* (March 3). http://new-service.stanford.edu/news/2004/march3/invitro-33.html (2004, April 24).

Landler, M. 2002. "Sharing Grief to Find Understanding." *New York Times* (January 17):A14.

Landrine, H. 1985. "Race and Class Stereotypes of Women." *Sex Roles* 13:65–75.

———, and E.A. Klonoff. 1997. *Discrimination against Women: Prevalence, Consequences, Remedies*. Thousand Oaks, CA: Sage.

Landry-Meyer, L., and K. Fournier. 1997. "Grandparents Raising Grandchildren." Columbus: The Ohio State University, Cooperative Extension Service.

Landsverk, J., and A. F. Garland. 2000. "Foster Care and Pathways to Mental Health Services." In P. A. Curtis et al., eds., *The Foster Care Crisis: Translating Research into Policy and Practice*, 193–210. Lincoln: the University of Nebraska Press.

Langer, G., C. Arndt, and D. Sussman. 2004. "Primetime Live Poll: American Sex Survey." A Peek Beneath the Sheets. *ABC News*. http://abcnews. go. com/Primetime/News/story?id=174461 & page=1 (2006, March 20).

Lanzendorfer, J. 2002. "It's 10pm, Do You Know? Kids Aren't Having Casual Sex, They're Having Oral Sex." *North Bay Bohemian* (October 17–23). Santa Rosa, CA: Metro Publishing, Inc. http://www.metroactive. com/papers/sonoma/10.17.02/sex-0242.html (2006, March 3).

Laquer, W. 1987. *The Age of Terrorism*. Boston: Little, Brown.

Lareau, A. 2003. *Unequal Childhoods: Class, Race, and Family Life*. Berkeley, CA: University of California Press.

Larson, J. H., S. M. Wilson, and R. Beley. 1994. "The Impact of Job Insecurity on Marital and Family Relationships." *Family Relations* 43, 2 (April):138–43.

Larsson, C., G. Hensing, and P. Allebeck. 2003. "Sexual and Gender-Related Harassment in Medical Education and Research Training: Results from a Swedish Survey." *Medical Education* 37, 1 (January) :39–50.

Lasch, C. 1977. *Haven in a Heartless World: The Family Besieged*. New York: Basic Books.

———. 1978. *The Culture of Narcissism*. New York: W. W. Norton.

Laslett, P. 1971. *The World We Have Lost*, 2d ed. New York: Scribner's.

Lasswell, M. E., and N. M. Lobsenz. 1981. *Styles of Loving: Why You Love the Way You Do*. New York: Ballantine.

Latham, L. M. 2000. "Southern Governors Declare War on Divorce." *Salon* (January 24). www.salon.com/mwt/featire/2000/01/24/divorce/ (2001, October 30).

Lauer, J., and R. Lauer. 1985. "Marriages Made to Last." *Psychology Today* (June):22–26.

Lauer, N. 2001. "Campaign Begins to Urge Pregnant Smokers to Quit." *LIWomen.Com*. http://www.liwomen.com/campaign.htm (2006, May 12).

Lauer, R., and J. Lauer. 1988. *Watersheds: Mastering Life's Unpredictable Crises*. New York: Little, Brown.

———. 1991. *The Quest for Intimacy*. Dubuque, IA: Brown.

Lauer, R. H. 1992. *Social Problems and the Quality of Life*, 5th ed. Dubuque, IA: William C. Brown.

Laumann, E. O., J. H. Gagnon, R. T. Michael, and S. Michaels. 1994. *The Social Organization of Sexuality: Sexual Practices in the United States* Chicago: University of Chicago Press.

LaVee, Y., and D. H. Olson. 1993. "Seven Types of Marriage: Empirical Typology Based on Research." *Journal of Marital and Family Therapy* 19 (October):325–40.

Lavin, C. 1991. "What's Best, and Worst, about Being Single." *Chicago Tribune* (July 21):sec. 5, 3.

Lawler, E., and J. Yoon. 1996. "Commitment in Exchange Relations: Test of a Theory of Relational Cohesion. *American Sociological Review* 61:89–108.

Lawrence, A. A. 2003. "Factors Associated with Satisfaction or Regret Following Male-to-Female Sex Reassignment Surgery." *Archives of Sexual Behavior* 32, 4:299–315.

Lawson, G., S. Peterson, and A. Lawson. 1983. *Alcoholism and the Family: A Guide to Treatment and Prevention*. Rockville, MD: Aspen.

Lino, M. 2006. *Expenditures on Children by Families*, 2005. U.S. Department of Agriculture. Center for Nutrition Policy and Promotion.

Le, C. N. 2006b. "Interracial Dating and Marriage." *Asian-Nation: the Landscape of Asian America*. http://www.asian-nation.org/multiracial. shtml (2006, April 24).

Leach, P. 1994. *Children First: What Society Must Do (and Is Not Doing) for Our Children Today*. New York: Knopf.

Leaper, C. 2002. "Parenting Girls and Boys. In M. H. Bornstein, ed., *Handbook of Parenting*, 2nd ed., 189–215. Mahwah, NJ. Erlbaum.

Leas, 2003. "Stay-at-Home Mothers Grow in Number; Mocha Moms Fill a Void." *Columbia News Service* (June 22). http://www. jrn.columbia. edu/studentwork/cns/2003–06-22/316.asp (2006, January 4).

Lee, G. R. 1988. "Marital Intimacy among Older Persons." *Journal of Family Issues* 9:273–84.

————, A. DeMaris, S. Bavin, and R. Sullivan. 2001. "Gendered Differences in the Depression Effect of Widowhood in Later Life." *Journal of Gerontology B: Psychological Sciences and Social Sciences* 56B, 1:S56–S61.

————, K. Seccombe, and C. L. Shehan. 1991. "Marital Status and Personal Happiness: An Analysis of Trends and Data." *Journal of Marriage and the Family* 53:839–44.

————, and C. L. Shehan. 1991. "Retirement and Marital Satisfaction." *Journal of Gerontology* 44, 6:226–30.

————, K. Seccombe, and C. L. Shehan. 1991. "Marital Status and Personal

————, and L. H. Stone. 1980. "Mate-Selection Systems and Criteria: Variation According to Family Structure." *Journal of Marriage and the Family* 42:319–26.

Lee, J. A. 1974. "The Styles of Loving." *Psychology Today* 8, 5 (October): 46–51.

Lee, S., and B. Edmonston. 2005. "New Marriages, New Families: U.S. Racial and Hispanic Intermarriage." *Population Bulletin* 60(2). Washington, DC: Population Reference Bureau.

Lee, S. M. 1998. "Asian Americans: Diverse and Growing." *Population Bulletin* 53, 2 (June). Washington, DC: Population Reference Bureau.

Leeder, Elaine. 2004. *The Family in Global Perspective: A Gendered Journey.* Thousand Oaks, CA: Sage.

Leff, L. 2006. "Aging Gays Fuel Specialized Market. (June 10). http://www.bistib.cin/news/nation/articles/2006/06/10/aging_gays_fuel_specialized_housing_market/?page=1 (2006, June 26).

Lehman College Art Gallery. 1998. "Myths vs. Reality." http://math240.lehman...rt/Hernandez/myths.html (1999, June 4).

Lehr, R., and P. MacMillan. 2001. "The Psychological and Emotional Impact of Divorce: The Noncustodial Fathers' Perspective." *Families in Society* 82, 4 (July/August):273–382.

Lehren, A., and J. Leland. 2006. "Scant Drop Seen in Abortions if Parents Are Told." *The New York Times* (March 6):A1, A19.

Lehrer, E. L., and C. U. Chiswick. 1993. "Religion as a Determinant of Marital Stability." *Demography* 30, 3 (August):385–404.

Leicester, J. 2005. "France Eyes More Aid to Foster Baby Boom." *Chicago Tribune* (September 22):3.

Leland, J. "Gays Seeking Asylum Find Familiar Prejudices in U.S." *New York Times* (August 1):A10.

————, and M. Miller. 1998. "Can Gays Convert?" *Newsweek* (August 17):47.

LeMasters, E. 1957. *Modern Courtship and Marriage.* New York: Macmillan.

Lempert, L. B. 1999. "Other Fathers: An Alternative Perspective on African American Community Caring." In R. Staples, ed., *The Black Family: Essays and Studies*, 6th ed., 189–201. Belmont, CA: Wadsworth.

Lengermann, P. M., and J. N. Brantley. 1988. "Feminist Theory." In G. Ritzer, ed., *Sociological Theory*, 400–443. New York: Knopf.

Lepowsky, M. 1993. *Fruit of the Motherland: Gender in an Egalitarian Society.* New York: Columbia University Press.

Lerman, R. I., and T. J. Ooms, eds. 1993. *Young Unwed Fathers: Changing Roles and Emerging Policies.* Philadelphia: Temple University Press.

Lerner, J. V. 1994. *Working Women and Their Families.* Thousand Oaks, CA: Sage.

"Lesbians, Gays Gaining Acceptance." 2005. *China Daily* (October 10). www.chinadaily.com.cn/english/doc/2005–10/10/content_483531.htm (2005, October 10).

Lessinger, J. 2002. "Asian Indian Marriages—Arranged, Semi-Arranged, or Based on Love?" In Nijole Benokraitis, ed., *Contemporary Ethnic Families in the United States*, 101–4, Upper Saddle River, NJ: Prentice Hall.

Lester, D. 1996. "The Impact of Unemployment on Marriage and Divorce." *Journal of Divorce and Remarriage* 25, 3/4:151–53.

Lev, M. A. 1998. "Japan Worries as Women Turn from Marriage." *Chicago Tribune* (March 30):1.

————. "In China, It's a Boy-Boy-Boy-Girl World." *Chicago Tribune* (January 30):1, 8.

Lever, J. 1978. "Sex Differences in the Complexity of Children's Play and Games." *American Sociological Review* 43:471–83.

————, D. Kanouse, W. Rogers, S. Carson, and R. Hertz. 1992. "Behavior Patterns and Sexual Identity of Bisexual Males." *Journal of Sex Research* 29:141–67.

Levine, A., and J. Cureton, eds. 1998. *When Hope and Fear Collide: A Portrait of Today's College Students.* San Francisco: Jossey-Bass.

Levine, B. 2005. "Back to the Nest." *Chicago Tribune* (October 8): Sec. 5, 1, 8, and 9.

Levine, M. P. and L. Smolak. 2002. "Body Image Development in Adolescence." In T. F. Cash & T. Pruzinsky, eds., *Body Image*, 74–82. New York: Guilford Press.

Levinger, G. 1965. "Marital Cohesiveness and Dissolution: An Integrative Review." *Journal of Marriage and the Family* 27:19–28.

————. 1979. "A Social Psychological Perspective on Marital Dissolution." In G. Levinger and O. Moles, eds., *Divorce and Separation*, 37–60. New York: Basic Books.

Levinson, C. 2005. "Egyptian women See Divorce as a Religious Right." *Womense News* (January 9). http://www.womensenews.org/article.cfm/dyn/aid/2139/context/archieve (2006, March 21).

Levinson, D. 1981. "Physical Punishment of Children and Wife Beating in Cross-Cultural Perspective." *Child Abuse and Neglect* 5, 4:193–96.

Levy, B., ed. 1991. *Dating Violence: Young Women in Danger.* Seattle, WA: Seal Press.

————. 1992. "A Closer Look." NBC.

Lewin, T. 1994a. "Sex in America: Faithfulness in Marriage Thrives after All." *New York Times* (October 7):A1, A11.

————. 1994b. "So, Now We Know What Americans Do in Bed. So?" *New York Times* (October 9):E3.

————. 1995. "Parents Poll Finds Child Abuse to Be More Common." *New York Times* (December 7).

————. 1998a. "Men Assuming Bigger Share at Home, New Study Shows." *New York Times* (April 15):A16.

————. 1998b. "New Families Redraw Racial Boundaries." *New York Times* (October 27):A1.

————. 1999. "Father Awarded $375,000 in a Parental Leave Case." (February 3):A11.

————. 2006. "Unwed Fathers Fight for Babies Placed for Adoption by Mothers." *New York Times* (March 19):1, 23.

Lichter, D. T., and Z. C. Qian. 2004. *Marriaage and Family in a Multiracial Society.* Washington, DC: Russell Sage Foundation and the Population Reference Bureau.

Lieberman, B. 1985. "Extra-Premarital Intercourse." Unpublished manuscript, University of Pittsburgh, Department of Sociology, Pittsburgh.

Liem, R. 1985. "Unemployment: A Family as Well as a Personal Crisis." In J. Boulet, A. M. Debritto, and S. A. Ray, eds., *Understanding the Economic Crisis*, 112–18. Ann Arbor: University of Michigan Press.

Light, D., S. Keller, and C. Calhoun. 1989. *Sociology*, 5th ed. New York: Knopf.

Lin, G., and P. A. Rogerson. 1995. "Elderly Parents and the Geographic Availability of Their Adult Children." *Research on Aging* 17, 3:303–31.

Lindberg L., et al. 1997. "Age Differences Between Minors Who Give Birth and Their Adult Partners." *Family Planning Perspectives*, 29(2):61–66.

Lindsay, J. W. 1995. *Teen-Age Couples: Caring, Commitment, and Change.* Buena Park, CA: Morning Glory Press.

Lindsey, L. 1990. *Gender Roles: A Sociological Perspective.* Englewood Cliffs, NJ: Prentice Hall.

————. 1994. *Gender Roles: A Sociological Perspective*, 2d ed. Englewood Cliffs, NJ: Prentice Hall.

————. 2005. *Gender Roles: A Sociological Perspective*, 4th ed. Upper Saddle River, NJ: Prentice Hall.

Link, B., et al. 1995. "Life-Time and Five-Year Prevalence of Homelessness in the United States: New Evidence on an Old Debate." *American Journal of Orthopsychiatry* 65, 3 (July):347–54.

Lino, M. 2006. *Expenditures on Children by Families, 2005.* U.S. Department of Agriculture. Center for Nutrition Policy and Promotion.

Lips, H. 1993. *Sex and Gender: An Introduction.* Mountain View, CA: Mayfield.

————. 1995. "Gender-Role Socialization: Lessons in Femininity." In J. Freeman, ed., *Women: A Feminist Perspective, 5th ed.*, 128–148. Mountain View, CA: Mayfield.

Liptak, A. 2005. "Same-Sex Parents' Rights Expanded." *Chicago Tribune* (August 23):1.

Liss, M. B. 1992. "Home, School, and Playroom: Training Grounds for Adult Gender Roles." *Sex Roles* 26, 3/4:129–47.

Little, H. 1995. "Out of Retirement: Parenting the Second Time Around Isn't Always So Grand." *Chicago Tribune* (September 10):1.

Littman, M. 2001. "She Can Bring Home the Bacon. . . ." *Chicago Tribune* (March 7):sec. 8, 1, 7.

Liu, P., and C. S. Chan. 1996. "Bisexual Asian Americans and Their Families." In J. Laird and R. Green, eds., *Lesbians and Gays in Couples and Families*, 137–52. San Francisco: Jossey-Bass.

Liu, X., C. Guo, and M. Okawa. 2000. "Behavioral and Emotional Problems in Chinese Children of Divorced Parents." *Journal of the American Academy of Child Adolescent Psychiatry* 39, 7:896–903.

Lloyd, P. C. 1968. "Divorce among the Yoruba." *American Anthropologist* 70:67–81.

Lloyd, S. A., and R. M. Cote. 1984. "Predicting Premarital Relationship Stability: A Methodological Refinement." *Journal of Marriage and the Family* 46:71–76.

Locke, R. 2001. "No Fences Make Good Neighbors at Co-housing Complex." *Berkeley Daily Planet* (January 29). www.berkeleydaily. org/article.cfm?storyID=3205. (13 December 2001).

Locin, M. 1991. "Study: Parental-Leave Laws Work Well." *Chicago Tribune* (May 22):sec. 1, 3.

Logue, B. J. 1991. "Women at Risk: Predictions of Financial Stress for Retired Women Workers." *Gerontologist* 31, 5:657–65.

Loh, E. S. 1996. "Productivity Differences and the Marriage Wage Premium for White Males." *Journal of Human Resources* 31, 3:566–589.

London, K. A. 1990. *Cohabitation, Marriage, Marital Dissolution, and Remarriage: United States, 1988*. Vital and Health Statistics, Advance Data no. 194. Hyattsville, MD: National Center for Health Statistics.

Long, B. C. 1989. "Sex-Role Orientation, Coping Strategies, and Self-Efficacy of Women in Traditional and Nontraditional Occupations." *Psychology of Women Quarterly* 13:307–24.

Longino, C. F., Jr. 1988. "A Population Profile of Very Old Men and Women in the United States." *Sociological Quarterly* 29:559–64.

Loomis, L. S., and N. Landale. 1994. "Nonmarital Cohabitation and Childbearing among Black and White American Women." *Journal of Marriage and the Family* 56 (November):949–62.

Lopata, H. Z. 1973. *Widowhood in an American City*. Cambridge, MA: Schenkman.

Lorber, J. 1994. *Paradoxes of Gender*. New Haven, CT: Yale University Press.

"Loss of High-Paying Jobs Forces Tough Decisions." 2005. *The Idaho Statesman* (July 25). http://www.idahostatesman.com/apps/pbcs.dll/article?AID=/20050725/NEWS02/40725034 (2006, January 2).

Lott, B. 1994. *Women's Lives: Themes and Variations in Gender Learning*, 2d ed. Pacific Grove, CA: Brooks/Cole.

"Love Is Colorblind . . . Or Is It?" 2000. *American Demographics* 22, 6 (June):11.

Lowe, E. T. 2005. *Hunger and Homelessness Survey 2005*. Washington, DC: U.S. Conference of Mayors and Sodexho, Inc.

Lowenstein, L. F. 2005. "Causes and Associated Features of Divorce As Seen by Recent Research." *Journal of Divorce and Remarriage* 42, 3/4:153–171.

Lowenstein, S. F. 1985. "On the Diversity of Love Object Orientations among Women." *Journal of Social Work and Human Sexuality* 3, 2/3 (Winter/Spring, 1984/85):7–24.

Lu, Z., D. J. Maume, and M. L. Bellas. 2000. "Chinese Husbands' Participation in Household Labor." *Journal of Comparative Family Studies* 31, 2 (Spring):191–215.

Ludwig, J. 2004. "Acceptance of Interracial Marriage at Record High." Gallup Poll (June 1). www.gallup.com/poll (2006, April 24).

Luhman, R. 1996. *The Sociological Outlook: A Text with Readings*. San Diego, CA: Collegiate Press.

Lund, K. 1990. "A Feminist Perspective and Divorce Therapy for Women." *Journal of Divorce* 13, 3:57–67.

Lyall, S. 2005. *The New York Times* (December 22): A4.

Lynch, J. M. 2000a. "Considerations of Family Structure and Gender Composition: The Lesbian and Gay Stepfamily." *Journal of Homosexuality* 40, 2:81–95.

Lynch, S. 2000b. "Let's Sing About Sex, Baby." *Sex, Etc.* www.sexetc.org (2006, March 24).

Lynn, D. 1966. "The Process of Learning Parental and Sex-Role Identification." *Journal of Marriage and the Family* 28:466–70.

Lyon, J. 1992. "Keeping Score." *Chicago Tribune* magazine (November 29):14–16, 28–32, 34–35.

MacCallum, F. E., C. Murray Lycett, V. Jadva, and S. Golombok. 2003. "Surrogacy: The Experience of Commissioning Couples." *Human Reproduction* 18, 6(June): 1334–1342.

Maccoby, E., and C. Jacklin. 1987. "Gender Segregation in Childhood." *Advances in Child Development and Behavior* 20:239–87.

Maccoby, E., and R. Mnookin. 1992. *Dividing the Child: Social and Legal Dilemmas of Custody*. Cambridge, MA: Harvard University Press.

MacDonald, K., and R. D. Parke. 1986. "Parent-Child Physical Play: The Effects of Sex and Age on Children and Parents." *Sex Roles* 15:367–78.

MacDonald, W. L., and A. DeMaris. 1996. "Parenting Stepchildren and Biological Children: The Effects of Stepparent's Gender and New Biological Children." *Journal of Family Issues* 17, 1 (January):5–25.

MacFarquhar, N. 2001. "Egypt Tries 52 Men Suspected of Being Gay." *New York Times* (July 19):A10.

Macionis, J. 1991. *Sociology*, 3rd ed. Englewood Cliffs, NJ: Prentice Hall.

———. 1995. *Sociology*, 5th ed. Englewood Cliffs, NJ: Prentice Hall.

———, and V. Parrillo. 1998. *Cities and Urban Life*. Upper Saddle River, NJ: Prentice Hall.

Macklin, E. D. 1972. "Heterosexual Cohabitation among Unmarried Students." *Family Coordinator* 21:463–72.

Macko, S. 1996. "Street Gangs Come to a Quiet Chicago Neighborhood." *EmergencyNet News Service*, vol. 2, no. 30. http://www.emergency.com/swcjgng.htm (2002, February 5),

MacRae, H. 1992. "Fictive Kin as a Component of the Social Networks of Older People." *Research on Aging* 14:226–47.

Madigan, C. M. 1999. "Marriage 101: Skip the Trial Run." *Chicago Tribune* (January 31):sec. 2, 1.

Madsen, W. 1964. *The Mexican American of South Texas*. New York: Holt, Rinehart & Winston.

Magdol, L., T. E. Moffitt, and A. Caspi. 1998. "Hitting without a License: Testing Explanations for Differences in Partner Abuse between Young Adult Daters and Cohabitants." *Journal of Marriage and the Family* 60, 1 (February):41–55.

Maginnis, R.L. 1995. "Marriage Protects Women from Violence." *Insight*. Washington, DC: Family Research Council, 1–3.

Mahoney, D. 2000. "Pastor Shuts Door on Interracial Couple." *Columbus Dispatch* (July 8). http://www.dispatch.com/news/newsfea00/jul00/341709.html (2001, November 15).

Maier, R. 1984. *Sexuality in Perspective*. Chicago: Nelson-Hall.

Maines, J. 1993. "Long-Distance Romances." *American Demographics* (May): 47.

Majors, R. 1995. "Cool Pose: The Proud Signature of Black Survival." In M. S. Kimmel and M. A. Messner, eds., *Men's Lives*, 82–85. Boston: Allyn & Bacon.

Maldonado, S. 2005. "Beyond Economic Fatherhood: Encouraging Divorced Fathers to Parent." *University of Pennsylvania Law Review* 153:1–84.

Malinowski, B. 1929. *The Sexual Life of Savages in North Western Melanesia*. New York: Harcourt Brace.

Malia, S. E. 2004. "Stepparent Policy Reforms." *Policy Brief*. (September): Columbia, MO: Center for Family Policy and Research.

Maloof, P. S. 2003. Muslim Refugees in the United States: A Guide for Service Providers. Center for Applied Linguistics. *Cultural Orientation Resource Center*. www.culturalorientation.net (2005, August 4).

Mammen, K. 2003. "The Effect of Children's Gender on Divorce and Child Support." (June). http://www.columbia.edu/~/kmm13/Mammen _Divorce_C5_6_03.pdf (2006, March 15).

"Managing the Miles in Long-distance Relationships." 2004. *Optum* (May). www.healthforums.com/print/articlePrint?brand=HealthForums %Ecom pkg-hf2 (2006, January 4).

Mandate the Future. 2002. "13-Year-Old Rape Victim Sentenced to 21 Years in Prison!!" (February 5). http://www.ctrkaktesc,irg/abortion/01/02/02/0656200.shtml (2002, January 21).

Mandela, N. 2000. "Globalizing Responsibility." *Boston Globe* (January 4). http://www.igc.apc.org/globalpolicy/socecon/inequal/nelson.htm (2002, January 18).

Manier, J., and O. Obejas. 2001. "AIDS Roars Back; Blacks Hit Hardest." *Chicago Tribune* (June 1):1, 24.

Manis, R., ed. 2001. *The Marriage and Family Workbook: An Interactive Reader, Text, and Workbook*. Boston: Allyn & Bacon.

Mann, D. 2000. "Fatal Beating Calls Attention to Problem at Youth Sporting Events." WebMD Medical News. http://webmd.lycos.com/content/article/1728.59319 (2002, February 10).

Mann, J. 1995. "Girls and TV: A Dearth of Role Models." *Washington Post* (September 29):E3.

Manning, W. D., and P. J. Smock. 2005. "Measuring and Modeling Cohabitation: New Perspectives From Qualitative Data." *Journal of Marriage and Family* 67(November):989–1002.

Manlove, J., E. Terry, L. Gitelson, A. Papillo, and S. Russell. 2000. "Explaining Demographic Trends in Teenage Fertility, 1980-1995." *Family Planning Perspectives* 32, (July–August): 166–175.

March of Dimes. 2002. "HIV and AIDS in Pregnancy."

———. 2006a. "U.S. Mortality Rate Fails to Improve." (May 8). http://www.marchofdimes.com/15796_19840.asp (2006, May 12).

———. 2006b. "Illicit Drug Use During Pregnancy." (2006, May 12).

———, PeriStats. 2006. "Singleton and Multiple Birth Rates." www.marchofdimes.com/peristats/calculations.aspx?reg=&top= &id=19 (2006, May 12).

Marelich, W., S. Gaines, and M. Banzet. 2003. "Commitment, Insecurity, and Arousability: Testing a Transactional Model of Jealousy." *Representative Research in Social Psychology*, 27, 23–31.

Marino, V. 1995. "When Children Flock Back to the Family Roost." *Chicago Tribune* (November 7):sec. 6.

Marion, R., A. A. Wiznia, G. Hutcheon, and A. Rubinstein. 1986. "Human T-Cell Lymphotrophic Virus Type III (Htlv–III) Embryopathy." *American Journal of Diseases of Children* 140:638–40.

Markides, K. S. 1978. "Reasons for Retirement and Adaptation to Retirement by Elderly Mexican Americans." In E. P. Stanford, ed., *Retirement: Concepts and Realities of Minority Elders*, 83–90. San Diego, CA: San Diego State University.

———, and C. H. Mindel. 1987. *Aging and Ethnicity*. Newbury Park, CA: Sage.

Marks, N. F. 1996. "Caregiving across the Lifespan: National Prevalence and Predictors." *Family Relations* 45:27–36.

Marquardt, E. 2005. "My Daddy's Name Is Donor." (May 15). http://www.americanvalues.org/html/donor.html (2006, April 14).

Marquis, C. 2001. "Military's Ouster of Gays Rose 17 Percent Last Year." *New York Times* (June 2):A9.

Marriage License Bureau and Cook County Clerk's Office. 1993. "Marriage License Requirements for the State of Illinois." Telephone interview, Chicago.

"Marriage on the Rocks in Britain." 2005 (September 30). http://news.yahoo.com/s/afp/20050930/ts_afp/afplifestylebritain_050-930140708 printer. (2005, October 19).

Marriott, N. 2001. "What's Love Got to Do with It?" In Robert Manis, ed., *Marriage and Family: An Interactive Reader, Text, and Workbook*, 79–81. Boston: Allyn & Bacon.

Marriott, S. S. 1994. "Violence and Its Impact on Women." *Vital Sign* 10, 2:6.

Marshall, J. 1999. "A Wealth of Information Tells Dads How to Parent." *Chicago Tribune* (November 7):sec. 13, 8.

Marshall, S., and C. Markstrom-Adams. 1995. "Attitudes on Interfaith Dating Among Jewish Adolescents." *Journal of Family Issues*. 16:787–811.

Marsiglio, W. 2004. *Stepdads: Stories of Love, Hope and Repair*. Lanham, MD: Rowman and Littlefield.

Martin, C. L. 1990. "Attitudes and Expectations about Children with Nontraditional and Traditional Gender Roles." *Sex Roles* 22:151–65.

———, and R. A. Fabes. 2001. "The Stability and Consequences of Young Children's Same-Sex Peer Interaction. *Developmental Psychology* 37(May):431–466.

Martin, J., B. Hamilton, and S. Ventura. 2001. *Preliminary Data for 2000*. National Vital Statistics Reports 49, 5:4. Hyattsville, MD: National Center for Health Statistics: 4.

Martin, P., and R. Hummer. 1993. "Fraternities and Rape on Campus." In P. Bart and E. Moran, eds., *Violence against Women*, 114–31. Thousand Oaks, CA: Sage.

Martin, T. C., and L. L. Bumpass. 1989. "Recent Trends in Marital Disruption." *Demography* 26:37–52.

Martire, L. M., M. P. Stephens, and M. M. Franks. 1997. "Multiple Roles of Women Caregivers: Feelings of Mastery and Self-Esteem as Predictors of Psychosocial Well-Being." *Journal of Women & Aging* 9, 1/2:117–31.

Mason, M. A. 1999. *The Custody Wars*. New York: Basic Books.

Mason, P. 1996. *Joblessness and Unemployment: A Review of the Literature* (LR-JU-96–03). Philadelphia: National Center on Fathers and Families.

"Mass Media and Teen Health." 2003. *Family Life Forum*. University of Tennessee Family Life Project 2, 2 (November). http://web.utk.edu/~famlife/FLPNewsletter.pdf (2006, March 22).

Mastekaasa, A. 1992. "Marriage and Psychological Well-Being: Some Evidence on Selection into Marriage." *Journal of Marriage and the Family* 54:901–11.

Masters, W., and V. Johnson. 1966. *Human Sexual Response*. Boston: Little, Brown.

———, and R. C. Kolodny. 1985. *Human Sexual Response*, 2d ed. Boston: Little, Brown.

———. 1986. *On Sex and Human Loving*. Boston: Little, Brown.

———. 1992. *Human Sexual Response*, 4th ed. Boston: Little, Brown.

Mather, M. K. Rivers, and L. Jacobsen. 2005. "The American Community Survey." *Population Bulletin* 60, 3 (September). Washington, DC: Population Reference Bureau.

Mathews, L. 1996. "Who Pays?" *Chicago Tribune* (January 21):sec. 3.

Mathur, I. 2006. "First Comes Marriage, Then Comes Love." http://www.geocities.com/Wellesley/3321/win4a.htm (2006, January 16).

Matthews, S. H. 1995. "Gender and the Division of Filial Responsibility between Lone Sisters and Their Brothers." *Journal of Gerontology: Social Sciences* 50B:S312–S320.

———, and J. Sprey. 1985. "Adolescents' Relationships with Grandparents: An Empirical Contribution to Conceptual Clarification." *Journal of Gerontology* 40:621–26.

Matthews, T., and M. MacDorman. 2006. "Infant Mortality Statistics From the 2003 Period Linked Birth/Infant Death Data Set." *National Vital Statistics Reports* 54, 16 (May 3). Washington, DC: U.S. Department of Health and Human Services, Centers for Disease Control and Prevention National Center for Health Statistics.

Maugh, T. H. H. 1990. "Sex: American Style Trend to the Traditional." *Los Angeles Times* (February 18):sec. A1, A22.

Mauldin, T. A. 1990. "Women Who Remain above the Poverty Level in Divorce: Implications for Family Policy." *Family Relations* 39:141–46.

———, and C. B. Meeks. 1990. "Sex Differences in Children's Time Use." *Sex Roles* 22, 9/10:537–54.

Max, E. 1985. "Custody Criteria, Visitation and Child Support." *Women's Advocate* (September):1–4.

Max, W., P. Webber., and P. Fox. 1995. "Alzheimer's Disease: The Unpaid Burden of Caring." *Journal of Aging of Health* 7, 2:179–99.

Maxwell, J. 1997. "Oh Baby, Mom Delivers 7." Channel 4000. http://www.wcco.com/news/stories/news971119–130925.html (1999, May 6).

Mays, V. M., and S. D. Cochran. 1991. "The Black Women's Relationships Project: A National Survey of Black Lesbians." In R. Staples, ed., *The Black Family: Essays and Studies*, 4th ed., 92–100. Belmont, CA: Wadsworth.

———. 2001. "Mental Health Correlates of Perceived Discrimination Among Lesbian, Gay, and Bisexual Adults in the United States." *American Journal of Public Health* 91:1869–1876.

Maza, P., and J. A. Hall. 1988. *Homeless Children and Their Families: A Preliminary Study*. Washington, DC: Child Welfare League of America.

Mazur, F. 1989. "Predicting Gender Differences in Same-Sex Friendships from Affiliation Motive and Value." *Psychology of Women Quarterly* 13:277–91.

———. 1993. "Decision Making and Marital Satisfaction in African American Families." In H. P. McAdoo, ed., *Family Ethnicity: Strength in Diversity*, 109–19. Thousand Oaks, CA: Sage.

McAdoo, J. L., and J. B. McAdoo. 1995. "The African-American Father's Roles within the Family." In M. S. Kimmel and M. A. Messner, eds., *Men's Lives*, 3d ed. Boston: Allyn & Bacon.

McAllister-Williams, H. 2005. "Postnatal Depression." (May 1). http://www.netdoctor.co.uk/health_advice/facts/depressionpostnatal.htm (2006, May 17).

McCabe, M. P., and L. A. Ricciardelli. 2003. "Sociocultural Influences on Body Image and Body Changes Among Adolescent Boys and Girls." *Journal of Social Psychology* 14:5–26.

McCary, J. L. 1978. *Human Sexuality: Instructor's Guide*. New York: Van Nostrand.

McClelland, K., and C. Auster. 1990. "Public Platitudes and Hidden Tensions: Racial Climates at Predominantly White Liberal Arts Colleges." *Journal of Higher Education* 61:607–42.

McCloskey, L., A. Figueredo, and M. Koss. 1995. "The Effects of Systemic Family Violence on Children's Mental Health." *Child Development* 66:1239–61.

McCoy, L. P., and T. L. Heafner. 2004. "Effect of Gender on Computer Use and Attitudes of College Seniors." *Journal of Women and Minorities in Science and Engineering* 10, 1:55–66.

McCurry, J. "Japan's Virgin Wives Turn to Sex Volunteers." *Gaurdian Unlimited* (April 4). http://www.guardian.co.uk/print/0,,5162349 -108018,00.html (2006, April 7).

———, J., and R. Allison. 2004. "40m Bachelors and No Women." *The Gaurdian*. (March 9). http://www.guardian.co.uk/china/story/0,7369, 1165129,00.html (2006, January 16).

McElroy, W. 2004. "A Feminist Version of 'Joe Millionaire'? Enter Stage Right." http://www.enterstageright.com/archive/articles/0504/0504 femjoemil.htm (2006, February 10).

McGhee, J. L. 1985. "The Effects of Siblings on the Life Satisfaction of the Rural Elderly." *Journal of Marriage and the Family* 47:85–91.

McGrath, E. 2002. "The Power of Love." *Psychology Today Magazine* (December 1).

———, G. B. Keita, B. R. Strickland, and N. F. Russo, eds. 1990. *Women and Depression: Risk Factors and Treatment Issues*. Hyattsville, MD: American Psychological Association.

McKelvey, C. A., and J. Stevens. 1994. *Adoption Crisis: The Truth behind Adoption and Foster Care*. Golden, CO: Fulcrum.

McKeough, K. 2001. "A Date or Not a Date?" *Chicago Tribune* (May 2):sec 8, 2.

McKim, W. A. 1986. *Drugs and Behavior: An Introduction to Behavioral Pharmacology*. Englewood Cliffs, NJ: Prentice Hall.

McLanahan, S. 2002. "Life Without Father: What Happens to the Children? *Context* 1(Spring):35–44.

———, and L. Casper, 1995. "Growing Diversity and Inequality in the American Family." In R. Farley, ed., *State of the Union: America in the 1990s*, vol. 2, 1–46. New York: Russell Sage Foundation.

McLanahan, S. S. 1999. "Father Absence and Children's Welfare." In E. M. Hetherington, ed., *Coping with Divorce, Single Parenting, and Remarriage: A Risk and Resiliency Perspective*. Mahwah, NJ: Erlbaum.

———, and L. Bumpass. 1988. "Intergenerational Consequences of Family Disruption." *American Journal of Sociology* 94:130–52.

McMullin, J. A., and J. Cairney. 2004. "Self-Esteem and the Interaction of Age, Class, and Gender." *Journal of Aging Studies* 18, 1 (February):75–90.

McMurray, C. 2004. "The Fit-Fat Struggle in U.S., Canada, Britain." The Gallup Organization (January 20). www.gallup.com/poll/content/ print.aspx?ci=10342 (2005, August 2005).

McNeal, C., and P. Amato. 1998. "Parents' Marital Violence: Long-Term Consequences for Children." *Journal of Family Issues* 19:123–40.

McNeil, D., Jr. 2001. "Rare Condoms, Deadly Odds for Truck-Stop Prostitutes." *New York Times* (November 29):A14.

McRoy, R. G. 1989. "An Organizational Dilemma: The Case of Transracial Adoptions." *Journal of Applied Behavioral Science* 25, 2:145–60.

———, H. Grotevant, and L. A. Zurcher, Jr. 1988. *Emotional Disturbances in Adopted Adolescents: Origins and Development*. New York: Praeger.

McTaggart L. 1980. *The Baby Brokers: The Marketing of White Babies in America* New York: Dial Press.

Mead, M. 1935. *Sex and Temperament in Three Primitive Societies* New York: Morrow.

——— 1970. "Communes: A Challenge to All of Us." *Redbook* 35 (August): 51–52.

Mederer, H. J. 1993 "Division of Labor in Two-Earner Homes: Task Accomplishment versus Household Management as Critical Variables in Perceptions about Family Work." *Journal of Marriage and the Family* 55:133–45.

Media Awareness Network. 2005. "Ethnic and Visible Minorities in Entertainment Media". www.media-awarness.ca/english/issues/ stereotyping/ethnics_and_minorities/minori... (2005, August 27).

———. 2006. "Media Violence Debates." http://www.media-awareness.ca/ english/issues/ (2006, July 22).

"Median Weekly Earnings of Full-Time Wage and Salary Workers by Union Affiliation and Selected Characteristics." 2001. U.S. Department of Labor. http://www.bls.gov/news.release/union2.t02.htm (2001, October 25).

MedLawPlus.com. 2006. "Premarital Agreement: State Law." http://www. medlawplus.com/legalforms/instruct/statelaw.tpl (2006, April 24).

Medved, M. 1992. *Hollywood vs. America: Popular Culture and the War on Traditional Values*. New York: HarperCollins.

Meezan, W., and J. Rauch. 2005. "Gay Marriage, Same-Sex Parenting, and America's Children." *The Future of Children* 15, 2(Fall:97–115.

Mehta, M. 2005. "Unsentimental Education. "*AlterNet (June 21)*. http://www.alternet.org/story/22273/ (2005, December, 12).

Meier, B. 1996. "Bias Complaints against Wall St. Firms." *New York Times* (November 21):D4.

Melton, W., and L. Lindsey. 1987. "Instrumental and Expressive Values in Mate Selection among College Students Revisited: Feminism, Love and Economic Necessity." Paper presented at the annual meeting of the Midwest Sociological Society, Chicago.

Mendel, M. 1995. *The Male Survivor: The Impact of Sexual Abuse*. Thousand Oaks, CA: Sage.

"Men Won't Budge for Wives' Careers." 1997. *Chicago Tribune* (July 13): sec. 13, 3.

Meredith, D. 1985. "Mom, Dad, and the Kids." *Psychology Today* (June): 62–67.

Merighi, J. R., and M. D. Grimes 2000. "Coming Out to Families in a Multicultural Context." *Families in Society* 81, 1 (January/February): 32–41.

Metropolitan Life Insurance Company. 1997. *The Met Life Study of Employer Costs for Working Caregivers*. Westport, CT: MetLife Mature Market Group.

Meyer, A. 2004. "Bringing Science Back to the People." *Catalyst*. 3,1 (Spring):

Meyer, I. H. 2003. "Prejudice, Social Stress, and Mental Health in Lesbian, Gay, and Bisexual Populations: Conceptual Issues and Research Evidence." *Psychological Bulletin* 129:674–697.

Michael, R., J. Gagnon, E. O. Laumann, and G. Kolata. 1994. *Sex in America: The Definitive Survey*. Boston: Little, Brown.

Middlebrook, P. N. 1974. *Social Psychology and Modern Life*. New York: Knopf.

Mignon, S., C. Larson, and W. Holmes. 2002. *Family Abuse: Consequences, Theories, and Responses*. Boston: Allyn & Bacon.

Milanovic, B. 2005. "Half a World: Regional Inequality in Five Great Federations." World Bank Policy Research Working Paper 3699. Washington, DC: World Bank.

Miller, B. 2001. "Life-Styles of Gay Husbands and Fathers." In M. Kimmel and M. Messner,, eds., *Men's Lives*, 443–50. Needham Heights, MA: Allyn & Bacon.

———, and L. Cafasso. 1992. "Gender Differences in Caregiving: Fact or Artifact?" *Gerontologist* 32, 4:498–507.

Miller, B. C., and S. L. Bowen. 1982. "Father-to-Newborn Attachment Behavior in Relation to Prenatal Classes and Presence at Delivery." *Family Relations* 31:71–78.

Miller, B. C., and K. A. Moore. 1990. "Adolescent Sexual Behavior, Pregnancy, and Parenting: Research through the 1980s." *Journal of Marriage and the Family* 52 (November):1025–44.

Miller, L. 1993. "Spurning Isolation to Forge a New Generation of Communities." *USA Today* (December 14):8D.

Miller, N. 1992. *Out in the World.* New York: Random House.

Miller, P. G. 2005. "How Female Homeownership Drives the Economy." (October 25). http://www.privatemi.com/survey/Peter_Miller_article.cfm. (2005, October 25).

Miller, S. 1994. "Conference Proceedings: The Role of Men in Children's Lives." Nashville, TN (July 10–11). St. Paul: Minnesota Children, Youth and Families Consortium Electronic Clearinghouse.

Miller, T. 1998. *The Quest for Utopia in Twentieth Century America, Vol. 1:1900–1960* Syracuse, NY: Syracuse University Press.

Mills, C., and B. Granoff. 1992. "Date and Acquaintance Rape among a Sample of College Students." *Social Work* 37:504–9.

Mills, C. W. 1959. *The Sociological Imagination.* New York: Oxford University Press.

Min, P. G. 1988. "The Korean American Family." In C. H. Mindel, R. W. Habenstein, and R. Wright, Jr., eds., *Ethnic Families in America*, 199–229. New York: Elsevier.

———. 1993. "Korean Immigrants in Los Angeles." In Ivan Light and Parminder Bhachu, eds., *Immigration and Entrepreneurship*, 185–204. New York: Transaction.

———. 1998. "The Korean-American Family." In C. H. Mindel, R. W. Habenstein, and R. Wright, Jr., eds., *Ethnic Families in America: Patterns and Variations*, 223–53. Upper Saddle River, NJ: Prentice Hall.

Mindel, C. H. 1983. "The Elderly in Minority Families." In T. H. Brubaker, ed., *Family Relationships in Later Life*, 193–208. Beverly Hills, CA: Sage.

———, R. W. Habenstein, and R. Wright. 1998. *Ethnic Families in America: Patterns and Variations.* Upper Saddle River, NJ: Prentice Hall.

Minino, A., and B. Smith. 2001. "Deaths: Preliminary Data for 2000." *National Vital Statistics Report.* Department of Health and Human Services, Centers for Disease Control and Prevention, National Center for Health Statistics (October 9), vol. 49, no. 12.

Mintz, S., and S. Kellog. 1988. *Domestic Revolution: A Social History of American Family Life* New York: Free Press.

Miranda-Maniquis, E. 1993. "The Silence about Women." *World Press Review* 40 (February):26.

Mirande, A. 1985. *The Chicano Experience: An Alternative Perspective.* Notre Dame, IN: University of Notre Dame Press.

———. 1988. "Chicano Fathers: Traditional Perceptions and Current Realities." In P. Bronstein and C. Cowan, eds., *Fatherhood Today*, 93–106. New York: Wiley.

———. 1991. "Ethnicity and Fatherhood." In F. W. Bozett and S. M. H. Hanson, eds., *Fatherhood and Families in Cultural Context*, 33–82. New York: Springer.

Mirchandi, V. K. 1973. "Attitudes toward Love among Blacks." Master's thesis, East Carolina University, Greenville, NC.

Mistiaen, V. 1994. "New-Baby Blues? Here's the News: Dad's Got 'Em Too." *Chicago Tribune* (October 2):1.

Mitchell, J. 1998. "Happy Stepfamilies Don't Happen Overnight." http://seattletimes.com/news/lifestyles/html98/altstep081398.html.

———, and J. C. Register. 1984. "An Exploration of Family Interaction with the Elderly by Race, Socioeconomic Status and Residence." *Gerontologist* 24:48–54.

Modern Maturity. 1992/1993. "Time Improves Lives of Older Widows" (December/January):8.

Moen, P., J. E. Kim, and H. Hofmeister. 2001. "Couple's Work/Retirement Transitions, Gender, and Marital Quality." *Social Psychology Quarterly* 64:55–71.

Moline, A. 2002." European Union Tells Members to Bar Sexual Harassment."Women's E News (July 22). www.womensenews.org/articlecfm/dyn/aid/980/ (2006, January 12).

Money, J., and A. Ehrhardt. 1972. *Man and Woman, Boy and Girl.* Baltimore, MD: Johns Hopkins University Press.

Monkerud, D. 2006. "Covenant Marriage on the Rocks: Few Want More Difficult Divorce." *OpEDNews.com* (February 6). www.opednews.com/maxwrite/print-friendly.php?p=genera_don_monk_060206_cov (2006, February 6).

Montgomery, P. 1996. "The Influence of Social Context on the Caregiving Experience." In Z. S. Khachaturian and T. S. Radenbaugh, eds., *Alzheimer's Disease: Causes, Diagnosis, Treatment and Care*, 313–21. New York: CRC Press.

Mooney, C. 2003. "Rational Choice?" *SageCrossroads* (July 14). http://www.sagecrossroads.org?Default.aspx?tabid=28 & newsType=ArticleView & articleId=20 (2006, June 26).

Moore, D. W. 2005. "Gender Stereotypes Prevail on Working Outside Home." *The Gallup Poll* (August 17). http://poll.gallup.com/content/default.aspx?ci=17896 (2006, January 18).

———, and L. Saad. 1995. "Most Americans Worried about Retirement." *Gallup Poll Monthly* (May):17–21.

Moore, F. 1995. "Girls Shortchanged by TV, Seek More Diverse Shows." *Chicago Tribune* (October 1):sec. 13.

Moore, J., and H. Pachon. 1985. *Hispanics in the United States.* Englewood Cliffs, NJ: Prentice Hall.

Moore, K. A., and I. V. Sawhill. 1984. "Implication of Women's Employment for Home and Family Life." In P. Voydanoff, ed., *Work and Family: Changing Roles of Men and Women*, 153–71. Palo Alto, CA: Mayfield.

Moore, P., with C. P. Conn. 1985. *Disguised.* Waco, TX: Word Books.

Moore, S., and C. Leung. 2002. "Young People's Romantic Attachment Styles and Their Association with Well-Being." *Journal of Adolescence* 25:243–255.

Moore, W. E. 1978. "Functionalism." In T. Bottommore and R. Nisbet, eds., *A History of Sociological Analyses*, 321–61. New York: Basic Books.

Morales, E. 1996. "Gender Roles among Latino Gay and Bisexual Men: Implications for Family and Couple Relationships." In J. Laird and R. Green, eds., *Lesbians and Gays in Couples and Families*, 272–97. San Francisco: Jossey-Bass.

Morell, C. 1994. *Unwomanly Conduct: The Challenges of Intentional Childlessness.* New York: Routledge.

Morgan, S. P., D. Lye, and G. Condran. 1988. "Sons, Daughters, and the Risk of Marital Disruption." *American Journal of Sociology* 94:110–29.

Morganthau, T. 1993. "America: Still a Melting Pot?" *Newsweek* (August 9):16–23.

Morin, R., and M. Rosenfeld. 1998. "With More Equity, More Sweat." *Washington Post* (March 22):A1.

Morris, J. 1974. *Conundrum.* New York: Harcourt Brace Jovanovich.

Morrison, A. 2004. "Transracial Adoption: The Pros and Cons and the Parents' Perspective." *Harvard BlackLetter Law Journal* 20:163–202.

Mortimer, J. T., and J. London. 1984. "The Varying Linkages of Work and Family." In P. Voydanoff, ed., *Work and Family: Changing Roles of Men and Women*, 20–35. Palo Alto, CA: Mayfield.

Moseley, R. 1995. "Ireland Narrowly Lifts Divorce Ban." *Chicago Tribune* (November 26):1.

Mosher, W. D. 1990. "Contraceptive Practice in the United States, 1982–1988." *Family Planning Perspectives* 22:198–205.

———. G. M. Martinez, A. Chandra, J. C. Abma, and S. J. Wilson. 2004. Use of Contraception and Use of Family Planning Services in the United States: 1982–2002. Advanced Data From Vital and Health Statistics, No. 350. Hyattsville, MD: National Center for Health Statistics.

Moskowitz, M., and C. Townsend. 1995. "100 Best Companies for Working Mothers." *Working Mother* (October):18+.

Moss, B. F., and A. I. Schwebel. 1993. "Marriage and Romantic Relationships, Defining Intimacy in Romantic Relationships." *Family Relations* 42:31–37.

Motenko, A. K. 1989. "The Frustrations, Gratifications and Well-Being of Dementia Caregivers." *Gerontologist* 29, 2:166–72.

"Mother Accused of Killing Her 3 Children Found Guilty." 2001. *USATODAY.com.* http://www.usatoday.com/news/nation/2001/12/19/killer-mom.htm (2002, January 13).

Mowery, J. 1978. "Systemic Requisites of Communal Groups." *Alternative Lifestyles* 2:235–61.

Moyle, E. 1999. "Catch of Day: Single Dads" (March 18). http://www.canoe.com:8...3/19_singlefather.html.

Moynihan, D. P. 1965. *The Negro Family: The Case for National Action.* U.S. Department of Labor, Office of Policy Planning and Research. Washington, DC: U.S. Government Printing Office.

Ms. magazine. 1993. "Action Alert: International News." (January/February):12–13.

MSNBC. 2006. "Few Poor Pregnant Women Getting AIDS Drugs." MSNBC.com (March 27). http://www.msnbc.msn.com/id/12042764 (2006, May 17).

———. 2006. "11 of 23 Held in UK Plot Charged." http://www.msnbc.msn.com/id/14287289/ (2006, August 23).

MSNBC.com. 2005. "Nearly 3 in 10 Young Teens 'Sexually Active:'" NBC News/People Magazine Commission Landmark National Poll. http://www.msnbc.msn.com/id/6839072 (2006, March 3).

Muller, R., and K. Lemieux. 2000. "Social Support, Attachment, and Psychopathology in High Risk Formerly Maltreated Adults." *Child Abuse and Neglect* 24:883–900.

Mullins, L. C., K. P. Brackett, D. W. Bogie, and D. Pruett. "The Impact of Religious Homogeneity on the Rate of Divorce in the United States." *Sociological Inquiry* 74, 3:338–354.

Mullis, I., and L. Jenkins. 1988. *The Science Report Card*, Report no. 17–S–01. Princeton, NJ: Educational Testing Service.

"Multigenerational Community Recreates Family." 1997. *Journal of Property Management* 62 (July/August):30.

Murphy, D. 2002. "Need a Mate? In Singapore, Ask the Government." *Christian Science* Monitor (July 16):1, 10.

Murphy, M., et al. 1991. "Substance Abuse and Serious Child Mistreatment, Child Abuse and Neglect." *International Journal* 15, 3:197–211.

Murray, B., and B. Duffy. 1998. "Jefferson's Secret Life." *U.S. News & World Report* (November 9).

Murray, S. 2006. "Conservatives Split in Debate on Curbing Illegal Immigration." *Washington Post* (March 25):A02.

Murstein, B. I. 1971. "A Theory of Marital Choice." In B. I. Murstein, ed., *Theories of Attraction and Love*, 100–51. New York: Springer.

———. 1974. *Love, Sex, and Marriage through the Ages.* New York: Springer.

———. 1980. "Mate Selection in the 1970's." *Journal of Marriage and the Family* 42:777–92.

———. 1986. *Paths to Marriage.* Beverly Hills, CA: Sage.

———. 1987. "A Classification and Extension of the SVR Theory of Dyadic Pairing." *Journal of Marriage and the Family* 42:777–92.

Mutran, E. 1985. "Intergenerational Family Support among Blacks and Whites." *Journal of Gerontology* 40 (May):382–89.

Muwakkil, S. 2001. "AIDS and the State of Denial." *Chicago Tribune* (June18):11.

Mydans, S. 1995. "Hispanic Gang Members Keep Strong Family Ties." *New York Times* (September 11):1.

———. 2001. "U.S. Interrupts Cambodian Adoptions." *New York Times* (November 5):A7.

Myers, D. J., and K. B. Dugan. 1996. "Sexism in Graduate School Classrooms: Consequences for Students and Faculty." *Gender & Society* 10:330–50.

Naifeh, M. L. 1993. "Housing of the Elderly: 1991." *Current Housing Reports*, Series H123/93–1. Washington, DC: U.S. Government Printing Office.

Najman, J. M., B. C. Behrens, M. Anderson, W. Bor, M. O'Callaghan, and G. M. Williams. 1997. "Impact of Family Type and Family Quality on Child Behavior Problems: A Longitudinal Study." *Journal of the American Academy of Child and Adolescent Psychiatry* 36:1357–65.

Nakonezny, P. A., R. D. Shull, and J. L. Rodgers. 1995. "The Effect of No-Fault Divorce Laws on the Divorce Rate across the 50 States and Its Relation to Income, Education and Religiosity." *Journal of Marriage and the Family* (May):477–88.

Nanda, S. 1994. *Cultural Anthropology.* Belmont, CA: Wadsworth.

Nardi, P. 2001. "The Politics of Gay Men's Friendships." In M. Kimmel and M. Messner. *Men's Lives*, 5th ed., 380–83. Needham Heights, MA: Allyn & Bacon.

———, and Sherrod, D. 1994. "Friendship in the Lives of Gay Men and Lesbians." *Journal of Social and Personal Relationships* 11 (May):185–99.

National Adoption Attitudes Survey. 2002. (June). http://www.adoptioninstitute.org/survey/Adoption_Attitudes_Survey.pdf (2006, August 13).

National Adoption Information Clearinghouse, 2000a. "Intercountry Adoption." http://www;calib.com/naic/pubs/s_inter.htm (2002, January 15).

———. 2000b. "Adoptions from Foster Care." http://calib.com/naic/pubs/s_foster.htm (2002, January 15).

———. 2000c. "Transracial Adoptions." http://www.calib.com/naic/pubs/s_trans.htm (2002, January 15).

National Association for Girls and Women in Sport. 2005. "Fact Sheet: Title IX in Athletics." www.aahperd.org/advocacy/fact_titleix.pdf (2005, August 23).

National Association of Anorexia Nervosa and Associated Disorders. 2001. "Facts about Eating Disorders." http://www.anad.org/facts.htm (2001, August 26).

National Association of Non-Custodial Moms, Inc. 2006. www.nancm.com/?page=company-profile (2006, March 23).

National CASA Association. 2000. "Statistics on Child Abuse and Neglect, Foster Care, Adoption and CASA Programs." http://www.casanet.org/library/abuse/abuse-stats98.htm (2002, January 26).

National Center for Health Statistics. 1993. *Morbidity and Mortality Weekly Report* 23, 20. Washington, DC: U.S. Government Printing Office.

———. 1996. "Advance Report of Mortality Statistics." *Monthly Vital Statistic Report* 45, 3 (supplement):63.

———. 2001. "New Series of Reports to Monitor Health of Older Americans." http://www.cdc.gov/nchs/releases/01/olderame.htm (2001, December 4).

———. 2004. Health, United States, 2004. Washington, DC: U.S. Department of Health and Human Services, Centers for Disease Control and Prevention, National Center for Health Statistics (September), DHHS Publication No. 2004–1232.

———. 2006. "Births, Marriages, Divorces, and Deaths: Provisional Data for July 2005." *National Vital Statistics Reports* 54, 11 (February 7), Hyattsville, MD.

National Center for Injury Prevention and Control Division of Violence. 1999. Centers for Disease Control and Prevention, Atlanta, GA. http://www.cdc.gov/ncipc/dvp/datviol.html (March 19).

National Center on Elder Abuse. 2005. "Domestic Violence: Older Women Can Be Victims Too." Fact Sheet. Washington, DC: National Center on Elder Abuse. http://www.elderabusecenter.org/pdf/publications (2006, July 21).

———. 2006. "Abuse of Adults Aged 60+ 2004 Survey of Adult Protective Services." Washington, DC: National Center on Elder Abuse (February). http://www.elderabusecenter.org/ pdf/2-14-06% (2006, July 21).

National Center for Lesbian Rights. 2002. "Fact Sheet: Custody Cases." http://www.nclrights.org/publications/pubs_custody.html (2002, January 31).

National Center for Policy Analysis. 2001. "Single Father Households on the Rise." http://www.ncpa.org/pd/social/pd051801d.html (2001, December 19).

National Center for Prosecution of Child Abuse. 2000. *Child Fatalities Fact Sheet.* Washington, DC: National Clearinghouse on Child Abuse and Neglect Information (June).

National Clearinghouse on Marital and Date Rape. 2005. http://members.aol.com/ncmdr/state_law_chart.htm (2006, April 19).

National Coalition against Domestic Violence. 1996. (April 22) [online].

———. 1998. "Research & Statistics on Domestic Violence." http://www.healthtouch.com (1999, June 2).

———. 2006b. "Abuse in Later Life." http://www.ncadv.org/files/AbuseinLaterLife (2006, July 11).

National Coalition of Anti-Violence Programs. 2005. "Annual Report on Anti-LGBT Hate Violence Released." (April 26). (Accessed December 7 www.ncavp.org/media/MediaReleaseDEtail.aspx?p=1420 & d=1492

National Congress of American Indians. 2002. "Testimony of the National Congress of American Indians on FY2003 Appropriations for the Bureau of Indian Affairs." (April 5) http://www.ncai.org/ncai/advocacy/otherissue/docs/BIA03.pdf (2006, May 16).

National Council of Jewish Women. 1999. "Myths and Facts about Domestic Violence." http://www.ncjw.org/programs/myths.htm (1999, June 4).

National Family Caregivers Association. 2000. *Caregiver Survey—2000*. Kensington, MD.

———. 2000. "Random Sample Survey of Family Caretakers." (Summer). Unpublished.

National Institute of Aging. 2006. "General Information." (May 26). http://wwwlh8alh8ylg9v/Alsheimers/AlzheimersInformation/General Info/ (2006, June 27).

National Institute on Alcohol Abuse and Alcoholism. 2000. *10th Special Report to the U.S. Congress on Alcohol and Health*. Bethesda, MD.

National Institute on Drug Abuse. 1994. "Substance Abuse among Women and Parents" (July) [online].

National Institute of Justice. 1997. "Guns in America: National Survey on Private Ownership and Use of Firearms." U.S. Department of Justice, Office of Justice Programs (May).

National Law Center on Homelessness and Poverty. 2005. "Housing." www.nlchp.org/FA%5FHousing (2005, December 30).

National Opinion Research Center (NORC). 1992. "The National Health and Social Life Survey." http://www.norc.uchicago.edu/split/fags/sex.htm.

National Organization on Disability. 2001a. "People with Disabilities Unprepared for Terrorist, Other Crises at Home or at Work, New Poll Finds" (December 11). http://www.nod.org/cont/dsp_cont_item_view.cfm?viewTypeitemView&contentld (2002, January 30).

———. 2001b. "Education Levels of People with Disabilities" (July 25). http://www.nod.org/cont/dsp_cont_item_view.cfm?viewType-itemView&contentld (2002, January 30).

———. 2001c. "Employment Rates of People with Disabilities" (July 24). http://www.nod.org/cont/dsp_cont_item_view.cfm?viewType-itemView&contentld (2002, January 30).

"National Survey Results Reveal Startling Lack of Awareness of Infertility Even as Numbers Climb to 7.3 Million." 2005. (October 27). http://www.resolve.org/site/PageServer?pagename=fmed_mcpr200510 27 (2006, April 24).

National Woman Abuse Action Project. 1991. *Understanding Domestic Violence*. Washington, DC: National Woman Abuse Action Project.

National Women's Health Information Center. 1999. "Substance Use during Pregnancy." http://www.4woman.gov/x/owh/Pub/woc/figure24.html (May 19).

———. 2005. "Sexually Transmitted Diseases: Overview." U.S. Department of Health and Human Services, Office on Women's Health. http://www.4woman.gov/ faq/stdsgen.htm (2006, April 3).

Nature. 1998. "Scientific Correspondence." 36, 5 (November):27–28.

Navarro, M. 1996. "Teen-Age Mothers Viewed as Abused Prey of Older Men." *New York Times* (May 19):1.

———. 2004. "The Most Private of Makeovers." *The New York Times* (November 28): Section 9, pp.1–2.

NBC11.com. 2006. "3 Mexican Immigrants Found Sewn in Car Upholstery." (August 8). http://www.nbc11.com/news/9649540/detail.html (2006, August 21).

NCAVP. 2005. "Domestic Violence." National Coalition of Anti-Violence Programs. http://www.ncavp.org/issues/domesticviolence. aspx (2006, July 12).

NCHS (National Center for Health Statistics). 2001. "Life Expectancy Hits New High in 2000; Mortality Declines for Several Leading Causes of Death" (news release). Hyattsville, MD: U.S. Department of Health and Human Services, Centers for Disease Control and Prevention.

Neal, A. G., H. T. Groat, and J. W. Wicks. 1989. "Attitudes about Having Children: A Study of 600 Couples in the Early Years of Marriage." *Journal of Marriage and the Family* 59:313–28.

Needle, R. H., S. S. Su, and W. J. Doherty. 1990. "Divorce, Remarriage and Adolescent Substance Use." *Journal of Marriage and the Family* 52:157–70.

Neft, N., and A. D. Levine. 1997. *Where Women Stand: An International Report on the Status of Women in over 140 Countries, 1997–1998*. New York: Random House.

Neher, L. S., and J. L. Short. 1998. "Risk and Protective Factors for Children's Substance Use and Antisocial Behavior Following Parental Divorce." *American Journal of Orthopsychiatry* 68:154–61.

Neikirk, W. 1996. "Clinton Adds Endorsement to Tax Break for Adoption." *Chicago Tribune* (May 7):1.

Nelson, N. 1999. "The Crime of Rape, Statistics." http://www.nancynelson.com/makedif/crime2.htm (2002, January 18).

Nelson, S. 1992. "It's Not Black and White." *Seventeen* 51(January):80–83.

Neugarten, B., and D. Neugarten. 1992. "Age in the Aging Society." In H. Lena, W. Helmreich, and W. McCord, eds., *Contemporary Issues in Society*, 208–19. New York: McGraw-Hill.

Neugarten, B., and K. Weinstein. 1964. "The Changing American Grandparent." *Journal of Marriage and the Family* 26:199–204.

Neumark, D., and Washer, W. 2003. "Minimum Wages, Labor Market Institutions, Youth Employment: A Cross-National Analysis." (March). www.federalreserve.gov/pubs/feds/2003/200323/200323pap.pdf (2006, January 30).

Neumark-Sztainer, and P. J. Hannan. 2000. "Weight-Related Behaviors among Adolescent Girls and Boys." *Archives Pediatrics & Adolescent Medicine* 154:569–77.

Newcomb, P. R. 1979. "Cohabitation in America: An Assessment of Consequences." *Journal of Marriage and the Family* 41:597–602.

Newman, B. S., and P. G. Muzzonigro. 1993. "The Effects of Traditional Family Values on the Coming Out Process of Gay Male Adolescents." *Adolescence* 28,109:213–26.

Newman, D. M. 1995. *Sociology: Exploring the Architecture of Everyday Life*. Thousand Oaks, CA: Pine Forge Press.

Newman, J. 2000. "Dad Has His Day: Fathers' Growing Involvement with the Family Makes Them Increasingly a Media Target." *Ladies Home Journal*.

New Mexico Governor's Task Force on HIV/AIDS. 1999. "Position Statement: HIV Counseling and Testing of Pregnant Women." *Infonet*. http://www.aidsinfonet.org/gatf/gatf-[regmamt-women.html (2001, December 21).

Newport, F. 1996. "Americans Generally Happy with Their Marriages." Gallup Poll Monthly (September):18–22.

———. 1999. "Americans Agree That Being Attractive Is a Plus in American Society." *Gallup News Service, Poll Analyses* (September 15):1-5. http://www.gallup.com/poll/releases/pr990915.asp (2001, September 8).

———. 2001. "Americans See Women as Emotional and Affectionate, Men as More Aggressive." http://www.gallup.com/poll/release/pr010221.asp (2001, July 12).

———, and L. Saad. 2006. "Religion, Politics Inform Americans' Views on Abortion." *The Gallup Poll* (April 3). http://poll.gallup.com/content/default.aspx?ci=22222 & VERSION=p (2006, April 12).

"New Problems Seen as World's Young and Old Increase Rapidly." 1998. *Chicago Tribune* (September 2):9.

"New Report Explodes Myths on Nonmarital Pregnancy." 1995. *Footnotes* 23, 8 (November):1.

"New Study Finds One in Five Girls Suffer Dating Violence." 2001. Brown University Child and Adolescent Behavior Letter. http://www.findarticles.com/cf_0/m0537/9_17/77841748/print.jhtml (2001, October 24).

"New Survey Shows Attitudes More Open toward Interracial Relationships." 1995. *Jet* 88 (October 2):22.

Newsweek Magazine. 2006. "Sex and the Single Boomer." *Newsweek* (February 20).

"New Zealand Attracting Young Female Immigrants." 2005. Workpermit.com (July 27). http://www.workpermit.com/news/2005_07_27/australia/nz_attracts_females.htm (2006, February 10).

Nezu, A. M., and C. M. Nezu. 1987. "Psychological Distress, Problem-Solving, and Coping Reactions: Sex Role Differences." *Sex Roles* 16:205–14.

Nicholas, M., and K. Milewski. 1999. "Downloading Love: A Content Analysis of Internet Personal Advertisements Placed by College Students." *College Student Journal*. (March). http://www.findarticles.

com/cf_0/mOFCR/1_33/62894065/p1/article.jhtml?term=Research (2001, October 26).

Niebuhr, G. 1996. "An Interfaith-Marriage Vote Has Reform Judaism Divided." *New York Times* (December 14):11.

———. 1998. "Southern Baptists Declare Wife Should 'Submit' to Her Husband." *New York Times* (June 10):A1, A20.

Nielsen, L. 1999. "College Aged Students with Divorced Parents: Facts and Fiction." *College Student Journal* 33, 4 (December):543–72.

———. 1999. "Stepmothers: Why So Much Stress: A Review of the Literature." *Journal of Divorce and Remarriage* 30:115–148.

———. 2000. "Black Undergraduate and White Undergraduate Eating Disorders and Related Attitudes." *College Student Journal* 34, 3 (September):353–70.

Nieves, E., and A. S. Tyson. 2005. "Fewer Gays Being Discharged Since 9/11." *Washington Post* (February 12):A1.

Nock, S. L. 1979. "The Family Life Cycle." *Journal of Marriage and the Family* 41 (February):15–26.

———, and P. W. Kingston. 1990. *The Sociology of Public Issues*. Belmont, CA: Wadsworth.

Nord, C. W., D. Brimhall, and J. West. 1997. *Fathers' Involvement in Their Children's Schools*. Washington, DC: National Center for Education Statistics.

Norment, L. 1994. "Black Men/White Women: What's Behind the Furor?" *Ebony* 50 (November):44–47.

North Carolina Coalition against Domestic Violence. 2002. "A Fact Sheet on Sexual Assault." http://www.nccadv.org/Handouts/Sexual_Assault. htm (2002, January 8).

Norton, A. J., and L. F. Miller. 1992. "Marriage, Divorce, and Remarriage in the 1990's." In U.S. Census Bureau, Current Population Reports, P23–180. Washington, DC: U.S. Government Printing Office.

Norwitz, E. R., et al., 2001. "Implantation and the Survival of Early Pregnancy," *New England Journal of Medicine* 345, 19:1400–1408.

Nowinski, J. 1980. *Becoming Satisfied: A Man's Guide to Sexual Fulfillment*. Englewood Cliffs, NJ: Prentice Hall.

Nuebeck, K. J., and D. S. Glasberg. 1996. *Sociology: A Critical Approach*. New York: McGraw-Hill.

NWHIC. 2000. "Factors Affecting the Health of Women of Color: Asian Americans." *The National Women's Health Information Center*. Washington, DC: Department of Health and Human Services. http://www.4woman.gov/owh/pub/woc/asian.htm (2002, January 2).

Oakley, A. 1974. *The Sociology of Housework*. New York: Pantheon.

O'Brien, M. 1991. "Taking Sibling Incest Seriously." In M. Q. Patton, ed., *Family Sexual Abuse*, 75–92. Newbury Park, CA: Sage.

O'Connor, J. 2004. "Healthy Babies: Efforts to Improve Birth Outcomes and Reduce High Risk Births." *NGA Center for Best Practices, Health Division*. Washington, DC.

Office of Technology Assessment. 1988. *Infertility: Medical and Social Choices*. Washington, DC: U.S. Government Printing Office.

O'Flaherty, K. M., and L. W. Eells. 1988. "Courtship Behavior of the Remarried." *Journal of Marriage and the Family* 50:499–506.

Ogintz, E. 1991. "Goodbye to the Myth of Unmarried Women." *Chicago Tribune* (October 22):sec. 5, 1, 2.

Ogletree, S., S. Williams, P. Raffeld, B. Mason, and K. Fricke. 1990. "Female Attractiveness and Eating Disorders: Do Children's Television Commercials Play a Role?" *Sex Roles* 22, 11/12:791–97.

O'Grady-LeShane, R. 1993. "Changes in the Lives of Women and Their Families: Have Old Age Pensions Kept Pace?" *Generations* 17, 4 (Winter):27–33.

Ogunwole, S. 2006. *We the People: American Indians and Alaska Natives in the United States*. Census 2000 Special Reports, CENSR-28, (February). Washington, DC: Department of Commerce, Economics and Statistics Administration, U.S. Census Bureau.

O'Hare, W. P., and J. C. Felt. 1991. "Asian Americans: America's Fastest-Growing Minority Group." *Population Trends and Public Policy* 19 (February). Washington, DC: Population Reference Bureau.

Ohio Department of Health. 1999. "Alcohol and Tobacco Use during Pregnancy." http://www.odh.state.o.../book2/statssmoke.html (1999, May 13).

O'Kelly, C. G., and L. Carney. 1986. *Women and Men in Society: Cross-Cultural Perspectives on Gender Stratification*. Belmont, CA: Wadsworth.

"Older Americans 2000: Key Indicators of Well-Being." 2000. Federal Interagency Forum on Aging-Related Statistics. http://www.agingstats. gov/chartbook2000/OlderAmericans2000.pdf (2002, January 7).

O'Loughlin, T. 2000. "Gap between Rich and Poor Grows" (November 15). http://www.smh.com.au/news/0011/15/pageone/pageone14.html (2001, October 19).

Olson, D., and Olson, A. 2000. *Empowering Couples: Building on Your Strengths*. Minneapolis, MN: Life Innovations.

Olson, D. H. 1986. "What Makes Families Work?" In S. VanZandt, *Family Strengths Seven: Vital Connections*, 1–12. Lincoln: University of Nebraska Press.

Olson, E. 2006. "Wedding Lore and Traditions." Pearson Education: Fact Monster.

O'Neil, J. M. 1981. "Patterns of Gender-Role Conflict and Strain: The Fear of Femininity in Men's Lives." *Personnel and Guidance Journal* 60:203–10.

OneWorld. 2002. "Children and War." http://www.oneworld.org/ childrights/chwar.htm (2002, February 18).

Oppenheimer, V. K. 1988. "A Theory of Marriage Timing." *Journal of Marriage and the Family* 42:777–92.

———. 1997. "Women's Employment and the Gain to Marriage: The Specialization and Trading Model." *Annual Review of Sociology* 23:431–53.

Oregon Department of Human Services. 2002. *Oregon's Death with Dignity Act, Annual Report*, Table 1. Portland. http://www.Ohd.hr.state. or.us/chs/pas/ar-tbl-1.htm (2002, January 29).

Orenstein, P. 1994. *School Girls: Young Women, Self-Esteem, and the Confidence Gap*. New York: Anchor Press.

Ornish, D. 1998. *Love and Survival, The Scientific Basis for the Healing Power of Intimacy*. New York: HarperCollins.

Oropesa, R. S., D. T. Lichter, and R. N. Anderson. 1994. "Marriage Markets and the Paradox of Mexican American Nuptiality." *Journal of Marriage and the Family* 56 (November):889–907.

Osnos, E. 2005. "Chinese Peasants Jailed to Enforce 1-Child Rule." *Chicago Tribune* (October 2): 1, 9.

Pace, L. 1986. "Interfaith Marriage Barrier Proves Not Insurmountable." *Norwich Bulletin* (February 12).

Pack, W. 2005. "Discouraged Workers Don't Show Up in Bureau of Labor Stats: They're Not Counted as Part of Monthly Unemployment Rates." *San Antonio Express News* (February 18).

Packer, A. J. 1997. "Everything Your Kids Want to Know about Sex and Aren't Afraid to Ask." In S. J. Bunting, ed., *Human Sexuality: Annual Editions*, 163–65. Sluice Dock, Guilford, CT: Dushkin/McGraw-Hill.

Page, C. 2001. "2-Parent Homes Are Disappearing." *Chicago Tribune* (June 3):37.

Page, M. E., and A. H. Stevens. 2004. "The Economic Consequences of Absent Parents." *The Journal of Human Resources 39*, 1(Winter):80–107.

Pagelow, M. D. 1984. *Family Violence*. New York: Praeger.

———. 1988. "Marital Rape." In V. B. Van Hasselt, R. L. Morrison, A. S. Bellack, and M. Hersen, eds., *Handbook of Family Violence*, 207–32. New York: Plenum.

Palmer, M. 1995. "The Re-Emergence of Family Law in Post-Mao China: Marriage, Divorce, and Reproduction." *China Quarterly* (March): 110–34.

Palmore, E. 1980. "The Facts on Aging Quiz: A Review of Findings." *Gerontologist* 20:669–72.

Pew Research Center. "The 2004 Political Landscape: Evenly Divided and Increasingly Polarized." (November 5). Washington, DC: The Pew Research Center for the People and the Press. www.pewresearch.org.

Pan-American Health Organization. 2006. "Domestic violence During Pregnancy." http://www.paho.org/English/AD/GE/VAWPregnancy. pdf (2006, July 13).

Pandey, G. 2004. "Muslim Women Fight Instant Divorce." BBC News (August 4). http://newsvote.bbc.co.uk/mpapps/pagetools/print/news.bbc. co.uk/2/hi/south_asia/3530608.stm (2006, March 21).

Pandya, S. M. 2005. "Caregiving in the United States." (April). Washington, DC: AARP Public Policy Institute.

Papalia, D., and S. Olds. 1989. *Human Development*. New York: McGraw-Hill.

Papanek, H. 1973. "Men, Women, and Work: Reflections on the Two-Person Career." *American Journal of Sociology* 78, 4 (January):852–72.

Papernow, P. 2001."What Works (and What Doesn't) in Building Healthy Stepfamilies." Paper presented at the First Annual Ohio State University Extension Family Live Electonic In-Service: A Systemic Examination of Stepfamily Relationships. Columbus, OH, May 8–10.

Papernow, P. L. 1993. *Becoming a Stepfamily: Patterns of Development in Remarried Families*. San Francisco: Jossey-Bass.

———. 1998. *Becoming a Stepfamily: Patterns of Development in Remarried Families*. Hillsdale, NJ: Analytic Press.

Parenting. 1999. "Single Mothers as Good as Dads." *Chicago Tribune* (January 17):sec. 13, 3.

Parents Forever. 2001. "Gender Differences in Parenting." The University of Minnesota Extension Service. http://www.extension.umn.edu/parentsforever/unit1/unit1=3a.asp (2001, December 30).

Parke, R. D. 1996. *Fatherhood*. Cambridge, MA: Harvard University Press.

———. 2002. "Fathers and Families." In M. H. Bornstein, ed., *Handbook of Parenting: Being and Becoming a Parent*, Vol. 3, 27–73. Hillsdale, NJ: Erlbaum.

Parker, G. B., E. A. Barrett, and I. B. Hickie. 1992. "From Nurture to Network: Examining Links between Perceptions of Parenting Received in Childhood and Social Bonds in Adulthood." *American Journal of Psychiatry* 149:877–85.

Parker, L. 2002. "Mom's Sanity Focus of Drowning Trial; Texas Woman Faces Death in 5 Kids' Slayings." *USA Today* (January 4).

Parnell, T., and D. Day, eds. 1998. *Munchausen by Proxy Syndrome*. Thousand Oaks, CA: Sage.

Parron, E. M. 1982. "Golden Wedding Couples: Lessons in Marital Longevity." *Generations* 7, 2:14–16.

Parrot, A., and M. J. Ellis. 1985. "Homosexuals Should Be Allowed to Marry and Adopt and Rear Children." In H. Feldman and M. Feldman, eds., *Current Controversies in Marriage and Family*. Beverly Hills, CA: Sage.

Parrot, W. G., and R. H. Smith. 1987. "Differentiating the Experiences of Envy and Jealousy." Paper presented at the annual meeting of the American Psychological Association, New York, August.

Parsons, T. 1955. "The American Family." In T. Parsons and R. Bales, eds., *Family, Socialization and Interaction Process*, 3–34. Glencoe, IL: Free Press.

———. 1964. *The Social System*. New York: Free Press.

Pasley, K., D. C. Dollahite, and M. Ihinger-Tallman. 1993. "Clinical Applications of Research Findings on the Spouse and Stepparent Roles in Remarriage." *Family Relations* 42:315–22.

Pasley, K., and M. Ihinger-Tallman. 1987. "The Evolution of a Field of Investigation: Issues and Concerns." In K. Pasley and M. Ihinger-Tallman, eds., *Remarriage and Stepparenting: Current Research and Theory*, 303–13. New York: Guilford Press.

Patel, P. 2000. "Pakistan: Killing in the Name of Honor." *The Asia Pacific Advocate* (Summer). http://www,apcjp.org/pakistan.htm (2001, May 15).

———. 2001. "Immigrants Bring Gender Bias to U.S." *Chicago Sun-Times* (September 3):7.

Patterson, C. J. 1992. "Children of Lesbian and Gay Parents." *Child Development* 63 (October):1025–42.

———. 1995. *Lesbian and Gay Parenting: A Resource for Psychologists*. Washington, DC: American Psychological Association.

———. 2002. "Lesbian and Gay Parenthood." In M. H. Bornstein, ed., *Handbook of Parenting*. Vol. 3, 317–338. Mahwah, NJ: Erlbaum.

Patterson, J., and P. Kim. 1991. *The Day America Told the Truth: What People Really Believe about Everything That Really Matters*. Englewood Cliffs, NJ: Prentice Hall.

Patterson, S. 2005. "Rare Ruling: Felon Can Raise Teen." *Chicago Sun Times* (October 9):15A.

Patzer, G. L. 1985. *The Physical Attractiveness Phenomenon*. New York: Plenum.

Paul, A. M. 1998. "Not Married—And Not Interested." *Psychology Today* 31 (March/April):19.

Pauly, B. 1992. "The Number of Happily Never-Marrieds Is on the Rise." *Chicago Tribune* (October 4):sec. 6, 5.

"Paying Out for Sexual Taunts." 2004. www.smh.com.au/articles/2004/07/18/1090089036551.html?from+storylhs (2006, January 12).

Pear, R. 1996. "Many States Fail to Meet Mandates on Child Welfare." *New York Times* (March 17):A1.

Pearson, J. 1989. *Communication in the Family*. New York: Harper & Row.

Pennsylvania Coalition against Domestic Violence. 2001. "Are You as Outraged as We Are?" Harrisburg. www.pcadv.org. (2002, January 7).

Peplau, L., A. Fingerhut, and K. Beals. 2004. "Sexuality in the Relationships of Lesbians and Gay Men." In J. Harvey, A. Wenzel, and S. Sprecher, eds., *Handbook of Sexuality in Close Relationships*, 349–369. Mahwah, NJ: Erlbaum.

Peplau, L. A. 1981. "What Do Homosexuals Want?" *Psychology Today* (March):28–38.

———. 1986. "What Homosexuals Want." In L. Simkins, ed., *Alternative Sexual Lifestyles*, 118–23. Acton, MA: Copley Publishing Group.

———. 1991. "Lesbian and Gay Relationships." In J. C. Gonsiorek and J. D. Weinrich, eds., *Homosexuality: Research Implications for Public Policy*. Newbury Park, CA: Sage.

———. 1994. "Men and Women in Love." In D. L. Sollie and L. A. Leslie, eds. *Gender, Families, and Close Relationships: Feminist Research Journeys.*" Thousand Oaks, CA: Sage.

———, and S. D. Cochran. 1981. "Value Orientations in the Intimate Relationships of Gay Men." *Journal of Homosexuality* 6:1–29.

Peplau, L. A., and S. L. Gordon. 1983. "The Intimate Relationships of Lesbians and Gay Men." In E. R. Allgeier and N. McCormick, eds., *Changing Boundaries: Gender Roles and Sexual Behavior*, 1–14. Mountain View, CA: Mayfield.

Peres, J. 1996. "Adoptees Say Love, Not Race, Matters." *Chicago Tribune* (May 12):21.

Perkins, H. W., and A. D. Berkowitz. 1991. "Collegiate COAs and Alcohol Abuse: Problem Drinking in Relation to Assessments of Parent and Grandparent Alcoholism." *Journal of Counseling and Development* 69:237–40.

Perkins, K. P. 2000. "Cultural Victims Die in 'Crimes of Honor.'" *Seattle Post-Intelligencer* (February 28). http://seatlep-i.nwsource.com/printer/ (2001, May 15).

Perozynski, L., and L. Kramer. 1999. "Parental Beliefs about Managing Sibling Conflict." *Developmental Psychology* 35:489–99.

Perrin, E. C., and the Committee on Psychosocial Aspects of Child and Family Health. 2002. "Technical Report: Co-Parent or Second-Parent Adoption by Same-Sex Parents." *Pediatrics* 109, 2:341–344.

Perry, I. 1995. "It's My Thang and I'll Swing It the Way That I Feel." In Gail Dines and Jean Humez, eds., *Gender, Race and Class in Media*, 524–30. Thousand Oaks, CA: Sage.

Perry, T., C. Steele, and A. Hilliard III. 2003. *Young, Gifted and Black: Promoting High Achievement Among African American Students*. New York: Beacon.

Perry-Jenkins, M., and A. C. Crouter. 1990. "Men's Provider Role Attitudes: Implications for Household Work and Marital Satisfaction." *Journal of Family Issues* 11:136–56.

Perry-Jenkins, M., and K. Folk. 1994. "Class, Couples, and Conflict: Effects of the Division of Labor on Assessments of Marriage in Dual-Earner Families." *Journal of Marriage and the Family* 56 (February):165–80.

Pert, C. 1997. *Molecules of Emotion, Why You Feel the Way You Do*. New York: Scribner's.

Pesek, W. 2006. "Durex Offers Japan a Population Wake-Up Call." Bloomberg.com. http://www.bloomberg.com/apps/news?pid=71000001 refer=columnis (2006, April 7).

Peter Hart Research Associates. 1999. "Americans' Attitudes on Children's Access to Guns: A National Poll for Common Sense about Kids and Guns" (June 16).

Peterman, L. M., and C. G. Dixon. 2003. "Domestic Violence Between Same Sex Partners: Implications for Counseling." *Journal of Counseling and Development* 81, 1(Winter):40–47.

Petersen, J., A. Kretchner, B. Nellis, J. Lever, and R. Hertz. 1983. "The Playboy Reader's Sex Survey, Parts I and II." *Playboy* (February/March):108, 241–50.

Peterson, C., and J. Peterson. 1988. "Old Men's and Women's Relationships with Adult Kin: How Equitable Are They?" *International Journal of Aging and Human Development* 27, 3:221–31.

Peterson, C. C. 1999. "Grandfatherss' and Grandmothers' Satisfaction with the Grandparenting Role: Seeking New Answers to Old Questions." *International Journal of Aging and Human Development* 49, 1:61–78.

Peterson, J. L., and N. Zill. 1986. "Marital Disruption, Parent-Child Relationships, and Behavior Problems in Children." *Journal of Marriage and the Family* 48:295–307.

Peterson, K. 2000. "Younger Kids Trying It Now, Often Ignorant of Disease Risks." *USA Today* (November 16). http://pqasb.pqarchiver.com/USAToday/main/doc (2001, November 29).

———. 1997. "Teen-age Dating Shows Racial Barriers Falling" (November 3). http://www.detnews.com...n/9711/03/11030094.html (March 5).

———. 2001. "College Women Can't Find Mr. Right." *Chicago Sun-Times* (July 27):1, 2.

Peterson, R. D., D. F. Wunder, and H. L. Mueller. 1999. *Social Problems: Globalization in the Twenty-First Century.* Upper Saddle River, NJ: Prentice Hall.

Peterson, R. R. 1996. "A Re-Evaluation of the Economic Consequences of Divorce." *American Sociological Review* 61:528–36.

Pettigrew, T. F. 1985. "New Black-White Patterns: How Best to Conceptualize Them." In R. H. Turner and J. F. Short, eds., *Annual Review of Sociology* 2:329–46. Palo Alto, CA: Annual Reviews.

Pew Research Center. 2003. "Globalization with Few Discontents?" (June 3). http://yaleglobal.yale.edu/display.article?id=1764 (2006, July 27).

———. 2006a. "No Consensus on Immigration Problem or Proposed Fixes: America's Immigration Quandary." *The Pew Research Center for the People and the Press and Pew Hispanic Center (March 30).* http://www.pewhispanic.org/files/reports/63.pdf (2006, August 21).

———. 2006b. "American Attitudes Hold Steady in Face of Foreign Crises." http://www.people-press.org/reports/display.php3? Report (2006, August 24).

———. 2006c. "Less Opposition to Gay Marriage, Adoption and Military Service." (March 22). http://people_press.org/reports/display.php3?ReportID=273 (2006, August 16).

———. 2006d. "Guess Whose Coming to Dinner." Pew Research Center Social Trends Report. Washington, DC. http://pewresearch.org (2006, April 26).

———. 2006e. *Families Drawn Together By Communication Revolution.* Washington, DC.

Pezzin, L. E., and B. S. Schone. 1999. "Parental Marital Disruption and Intergenerational Transfers: An Analysis of Lone Elderly Parents and Their Children." *Demography* 36, 3 (August):287–97.

Phillips, R. 1988. *Putting Asunder: A History of Divorce in Western Society.* Cambridge, MA: Cambridge University Press.

Pichierri, M., and C. Corcoran. 2005. "Respect for Individuals that Engage in Premarital Sexual Intercourse: The Influence of Gender and Family Structure." *FSC Journal of Behavioral Sciences*, Vol. 9.

Pike, R. 1999. "Multiple Births Add Up." ABCNews Health and Living. http://more.abcnews.go.com/sections/living/septuplets_numbers/index.html (May 6).

Pill, C. J. 1990. "Stepfamilies: Redefining the Family." *Family Relations* 39:186–93.

Pillemer, K. A., and David Finkelhor. 1988. "The Prevalence of Elder Abuse: A Random-Sample Survey." *Gerontologist* 28, 1:51–57.

Pines, A. 1998. *Romantic Jealousy: Causes, Symptoms, Cures.* New York: Routledge.

———. and E. Aronson. 1983. "Antecedents, Correlates, Consequences of Secret Jealousy." *Journal of Personality* 51:108–9.

Pinkerton, S., L. Bogart, H. Cecil, and P. Abramson. 2002. "Factors Associated with Masturbation in a Collegiate Sample." *Journal of Psychology and Human Sexuality* 14(2/3): 103–121.

Pipher, M. 1994. *Reviving Ophelia: Saving the Selves of Adolescent Girls.* New York: Ballantine.

Pitcher, B. L., and D. C. Larson. 1989. "Early Widowhood." In S. J. Bahr and E. T. Peterson, eds., *Aging and the Family*, 59–81. Lexington, MA: Lexington Books.

Pitts, L. 2001. "Deadbeat Dad's Punishment Is Troubling." *Chicago Tribune* (July 17):17.

Pitzer, R. 1992. "Research on Father Involvement." Specialist Research Report. Minnesota Extension Service. St. Paul: Minnesota Children, Youth and Families Consortium Electronic Clearinghouse (March).

Pizzey, E. 1974. *Scream Quietly or the Neighbors Will Hear.* Harmondsworth, England: Penguin.

Platner, J. 2004. "Politics and Science: A Conversation with U.S. Rep. Henry Waxman." *Planned Parenthood Federation of America, Inc.* (June 15). http://www.plannedparenthood.org/pp2/portal/files/portal/webzine/newspoliticsactivism/fean-040615-waxman-interview.xml (2005, August 22).

Pleck, E. 1989. "Criminal Approaches to Family Violence." In L. Ohlin and M. Tonry, eds., *Family Violence*, 19–58. Chicago: University of Chicago Press.

Pleck, J. H. 1988. "Fathers and Infant Care Leave." In E. F. Zigler and M. Franks, eds., *The Parental Leave Crisis*, 177–94. New Haven, CT: Yale University Press.

Pollack, W.S. 1998. *Real Boys: Rescuing Our Sons from the Myths of Boyhood.* New York: Random House.

Pollard, K., and W. O'Hare. 1999. "America's Racial and Ethnic Minorities." *Population Bulletin*, 54, 3 (September):50.

Polling Report. 2001. "Race and Ethnicity." http://www.pollingreport.com/race.htm (2002, February 3).

———. 2002. "War on Terrorism." http://www.pollingreport.com/terror.htm (2002, February 3).

Pomerleau, A., D. Bolduc, G. Makuit, and L. Cossette. 1990. "Pink or Blue: Environmental Stereotypes in the First Two Years of Life." *Sex Roles* 22, 5/6:359–67.

Pomeroy, S. 1975. *Goddesses, Whores, Wives, and Slaves: Women in Classical Antiquity.* New York: Schocken.

Ponzetti, J., Jr., and R. M. Cate. 1986. "The Development Course of Conflict in the Marital Dissolution Process." *Journal of Divorce* 10:1–15.

Popenoe, D. 1999. "Parental Androgyny." In C. Albers, ed., *Sociology of Families: Readings*, 187–94. Thousand Oaks, CA: Pine Forge.

———, and B. Whitehead. 2002. *Sex Without Strings: Relationships Without Rings.* Piscataway, NJ: The National Marriage Project, Rutgers.

Population Reference Bureau. 2003. "Traditional Families Account for Only 7 Percent of U.S. Households." www.prb.org (2006, January 3).

Porter, E. 2006. "Stretched to Limit, Women Stall March to Work." *The New York Times* (March 2):A1, C2.

Portes, A. 2002. "Immigration's Aftermath." *The American Prospect* (April 8). http://www.prospect.org/pring-friendly/print/V13/7/portes-a.html (2002, February 8).

Potier, B. 2003. "For Many, Prenups Seem to Predict Doom." *Harvard University Gazette.* (October 16). http://www.news.harvard.edu/gazette/2003/10.16/01-prenup.html (2006, April 24).

Post, T. 1993. "A Pattern of Rape." *Newsweek* (January 4):32–36.

"Postnatal Depression." 2001. http://health.iafrica.com/psychonline/articles/postnatal.htm (2001, December 21).

Potok, M. 1995. "Out-of-Wedlock Childbirth Rising." *USA Today* (November 8):2.

Pound, P., C. Sabin, and S. Ebrahim. 1999. "Observing the Process of Care: A Stroke Unit, Elderly Care Unit and General Medical Ward Compared." *Age and Ageing* 28, 5 (September):433–40.

Poussaint, A. F., and J. P. Comer. 1993. *Raising Black Children.* New York: Plume.

Powdthavee, N. 2005. "Life Satisfaction, Income, and Friendship: Evidence From Panel Data." (July). http://www2.warwick.ac.uk/fac/ soc/economics/research/phds/n.powdthavee/friends2005.pdf (2005, October 25).

Powell, K. A., and L. Abels. 2002. "Sex-Role Stereotypes in TV Programs Aimed at the Preschool Audience: An Analysis of Teletubbies and Barney & Friends." *Urbana* 25, 1:14–27.

Powers, E. 1966. *Crime and Punishment in Early Massachusetts, 1620–1692: A Documentary History*. Boston: Beacon Press.

Preece, M. 2003/2004. "When Lone Parents Marry: The Challenge of Stepfamily Relationships." *Transition Magazine* 33, 4(Winter):7–15.

Pregnancy Discrimination Charges. 2001. U.S. Equal Opportunity Commission. www/eepc/gpv/stats/pregnanc.html (2001, October 26).

"Pregnant Student Defies Graduation Ban." 2005. CNN.com (May 30 http://cnnfyi.printthis.clickability.com/pt/cpt?action=cpt&title+CMM/cp,_+Pregnant+stu.).

President's Council on Physical Fitness and Sports. 1997. *Physical Activity and Sport in the Lives of Girls*. Minneapolis: Center for Research on Girls and Women in Sport, University of Minnesota.

Pressley, S. 2001. "S.C. Verdict Fuels Debate Over Rights of the Unborn: Jury Finds Mother Guilty of Homicide in Stillbirth." *Washington Post* (May 27):A03.

Presser, H. B. 2003. *Working in a 24/7 Economy: Challenges for American Families*. New York: Russell Sage Foundation.

Prevalence and Incidence of Fetal Alcohol Syndrome. 2006. (March 15). http://www.wrongdiagnosis.com. (2006, May 12).

"Prevalence of Sexual Harassment." 2003. Stop Violence Against Women. www.stopvaw.org/Prevalence_of_Sexual_Harassment. html (2006, January 12).

Previti, D., and P. R. Amato. 2003. "Why Stay Married? Rewards, Barriers, and Marital Stability. *Journal of Marriage and Family* 65(August): 561–563.

Prime, J. 2005. "Women 'Take Care,' Men 'Take Charge:' Stereotyping of U.S. Business Leaders Exposed." *Catalyst*. www.catalyst.org (2006, January 12).

PRNetwire. 2002. "Multiple Births Skyrocket." Send2Press.com http://www.send2press.com/PRnetwire/pr_02_0814-allbaby.shtml (2006, May 12).

Price-Bonham, S., and J. O. Balswick. 1980. "The Noninstitutions: Divorce, Desertion, and Remarriage." *Journal of Marriage and the Family* 42, 4:959–72.

"Probe Interracial Dating Policy at Bible College." 1987. *Jet* 71 (February 23): 21.

Pruett, M. K., and K. Hoganbruen. 1998. "Joint Custody and Shared Parenting: Research and Interventions." *Child Adolescent Psychiatric Clinic North America* 7:273–94.

Pryor, J., and B. Rodgers. 2001. *Children in Changing Families: Life After Parental Separation*. Maulden, MA: Blackwell.

Public Agenda. 2002. "Terrorism. Overview: The Issue at a Glance." http://www.publicagenda.org/specials/terrorism/terror_overview.htm (2002, February 3).

Public Opinion Polls on Same-Sex Marriages. 2001. http://www.religioustolerance.org/hom_marp.html (2001, November 8).

Punke, H. H. 1940. "Marriage Rate among Women Teachers." *American Sociological Review* 5, 4:505–11.

Purcell, P., and L. Stewart. 1990. "Dick and Jane in 1989." *Sex Roles* 22:177–85.

Pyke, K. D. 1994. "Women's Employment as Gift or Burden?" *Gender and Society* 8:73–91.

Qamruzzaman, M. 2006. "Conference Explores Indian Divorce Stigmas." *Michigan Daily* (February 6). www.michigandaily.com/news/2006/02/06/ (2006, March 2).

qian, zhenchao. 2005. "Breaking the Last Taboo: Interracial Marriage in America." *Contexts* 4, 4:33–37.

Qu, L., and R. Weston. 2001. "Starting Out Together Through Cohabitation or Marriage: *Family Matters* 60(Spring/Summer):76–79.

Queen, S. A., R. W. Habenstein, and J. S. Quadagno. 1985. *The Family in Various Cultures*. New York: Harper & Row.

RAINN. 2006. "Statistics." http://www.rainn.org. (2006, July 15).

RAINN Statistics. 2002. http://www.rainn.org/statistics.html (2002, January 20).

Raley, R. K., and E. Wildsmith. 2004. "Cohabitation and Children's Family Instability." *Journal of Marriage and Family* 66:210–219.

Ramos, J. 2002. "'For Adults Only' Maybe Not, as Marketing of Sexy Products Reaches Kids." ABCNEWS Internet Ventures. www.abcnews.go.com/setions/business/DailyNews/Ramos_adultproduct_020612.hmtl (2004, May 28).

Ramsey, S. 1995. "Stepparents and the Law: a Nebulous Status and a Need for Reform." In K. Pasley and M. Ihinger-Tallman, eds., *Stepparenting: Issues in Theory, Research, and Practice*, 217–37. Westport, CT: Praeger.

Ramu, G. N. 1989. "Patterns of Mate Selection." In K. Ishwaran, ed., *Family and Marriage: Cross-Cultural Perspectives*, 165–78. Toronto: Wall and Thompson.

RAND Corporation. 2001. "Guns in the Family: Firearm Storage Patterns in U.S. Homes with Children" (March). http://www.rand.org/publications/RB/RB4535/.

Rank, M. R. 1989. "Fertility among Women on Welfare: Incidence and Determinants." *American Sociological Review* 54:296–304.

Rape Statistics. 1999. http://www.cs.utk.edu/~bartley/sa/stats.html (1999, March 19).

Rasmussen, P. K., and K. J. Ferraro. 1991. "The Divorce Process." In J. N. Edwards and D. H. Demo, eds., *Marriage and Family in Transition*, 376–88. Boston: Allyn & Bacon.

Rathus, S. A., J. S. Nevid, and L. Fichner-Rathus. 1997. *Human Sexuality in a World of Diversity*, 3d ed. Boston: Allyn & Bacon.

Ravo, N. 1991. "Forget the Dress, the Flowers, Mendelssohn. Just Run Away." *New York Times* (October 2):C1.

Rawlings, S. 1978. "Perspectives on American Husbands and Wives." *Current Population Reports*, Series P–23, no. 77. Washington, DC: U.S. Census Bureau.

Rawlins, W. K. 1993. "Communication in Cross-Sex Friendships." In L. Arliss and D. Borisoff, eds., *Women and Men Communicating*. Fort Worth, TX: Harcourt Brace Jovanovich.

Ray, O., and C. Ksir. 1999. *Drugs, Society and Human Behavior*, 8th ed. Boston: WCB/McGraw-Hill.

Raybeck, D., S. Dorenbosch, M. Sarapata, and D. Herrman. 2000. "The Quest for Love and Meaning in the Personals." Unpublished paper.

Rayman, P. 2000. *Life's Work: Generational Attitudes Toward Work and Life Integration*. Cambridge, MA: Radcliff Public Policy Center.

Raymond, J. 2001. "The Ex-Files." *American Demographics* 23, 2 (February): 60–64.

"Real People." 1996. NBC (April 25).

Real, T. 1997. *I Don't Want to Talk about It*. New York: Scribner's.

Reardon, P. T. 1992. "More Dads Trying Single-Parenting." *Chicago Tribune* (August 9):1, 8.

Recler, N. K. 2001. "The Wicked Stepmother Myth." *Family Taperstries*. The Ohio State University Extension.

Red Horse, J. 1980. "Family Structure and Value Orientation in American Indians." *Social Casework* 61(8):462–67.

Reeve, C. 1991. "Corporate Wives." *Chicago Tribune* (March 17):sec. 6, 1, 7.

Reeves, T. J., and C. E. Bennett. 2004. *We the People: Asians in the United States*. Washington, DC: U.S. Census Bureau.

Refugees International. 2002. "Do Not Forget the Lost Girls of Sudan." http://www.refugeesinternational.org/content/article/detail/1073 (2006, August 23).

Regan, T. 2005. "Communities Shunning FEMA Trailers." *CBS NEWS* (December 29).

Reid, G.M. 1994. "Maternal Stereotyping of Newborns." *Psychological Reports* 75:1443–50.

Reik, T. A. 1946. *A Psychologist Looks at Love*. New York: Lancer.

Reingold, J. 2000. "Executive Pay." *Business Week*. http://www.businessweek.com:/2000/00_16/b3677014.htm?scriptFramed (2001, October 24).

Reinisch, J. M. 1990. *The Kinsey Institute New Report on Sex*. New York: St. Martin's Press.

Reisman, J. 1998. "Images of Children, Crime and Violence in Playboy, Penthouse, and Hustler." Abstract of final report for OJJDP Grant 84–JN–AX–K007. http://www.iglou.com/first-principles/abstract.html (2001, January 27).

Reisman, J. M. 1990. "Intimacy in Same-Sex Friendships." *Sex Roles* 23: 65–82.

Reiss, I. L. 1960. "Toward a Sociology of Heterosexual Love Relationship." *Marriage and Family Living* 22, 2 (May):139–45.

———. 1971. *The Family System in America*. New York: Holt, Rinehart & Winston.

———. 1980. *Family Systems in America*, 3d ed. New York: Holt, Rinehart & Winston.

"Remarriage Can Strain Family Ties." 1998. *Chicago Tribune* (July 12): sec. 13, 3.

ReligiousTolerance.org. 2003. "Longitudinal U.S. Public Opinion Polls: Same-Sex Marriage and Civil Unions." www.religioustolerance.org/hom_poll5.html (2005, December 13).

"Remarriage Industry Sees Rapid Growth." 2006. *Digital Chosunilb.* (March 20). http://english.chosun.com/cgi-bin/printNews?id=200603 200024 (2006, March 26).

Remez, L. 1998. In Turkey, Women's Fertility Is Linked to Education, Employment, and Freedom to Choose a Husband." *International Family Planning Perspectives* 24, 2:97–98.

———. 2000. "Oral Sex among Adolescents: Is It Sex or Is It Abstinence?" *Family Planning Perspectives* 32 (November/December):6.

Rempel, J., and J. Holmes. 1986. "How Do I Love Thee?" *Psychology Today* (February):30–31.

Renzetti, C., and D. Curran. 2002. *Women, Men, and Society*, 5th ed. Boston: Allyn Bacon.

Renzetti, C. M., and D. J. Curran. 1992. *Women, Men, and Society: The Sociology of Gender*, 2d ed. Boston: Allyn & Bacon.

———. 1995. *Women, Men, and Society*, 3d ed. Boston: Allyn & Bacon.

———. 1999. *Women, Men, and Society*, 4th ed. Boston: Allyn & Bacon.

Report from the Urban Institute. 1999. "A General Profile of the Welfare Population." http://www.doleta.gov/ohrw2w/recruit/urban.html (February 2).

Research America. 2006. "Health and Longevity." http://www.researchamerica.org/polldata/2006/Longevity_fullresults.pdf (2006, June 26).

Reskin, B. F., and I. Padavic. 1994. *Women and Men at Work*. Thousand Oaks, CA: Pine Forge Press.

Rheingold, H. L., and K. V. Cook. 1975. "The Content of Boys' and Girls' Rooms as an Index of Parents' Behavior." *Child Development* 46:459–63.

Rich, A. 1980. "Compulsory Heterosexuality and Lesbin Existence." *Signs* 5:631–60.

Richardson, B. 2006. ""Run for the Border: Democrats try to Outflank the GOP on Immigration." *Wall Street Journal, Opinion Journal, Editorial Page* http://www.opinionjournal.com/forms/printThis.html (2006, August 24).

Richardson, J. P., and A. Lazar. 1995. "Sexuality in the Nursing Home Patient." *American Family Physician* 51 (January):121–24.

Richman, J. A., and K. M. Rospenda. 2005. "Sexual Harassment and Alcohol Use." *Psychiatric Times* 22, 2 (February). www.psychiatrictimes.com/showArticle.jhtml?articleId=60403927 (2006, January 12).

Richmond-Abbott, M. 1983. *Masculine and Feminine*. New York: Random House.

Richtel, M. 2005. "Past Divorce, Compassion at the End." The New *York Times* (May 19):E1, E2.

Rideout, V., D. F. Roberts, and U. G. Foehr. 2005. *Generation M: Media in theLives of 8-18 Year-Olds*. Menlo Park, CA: The Kaiser Family Foundation.

Rideout, V., E. A. Vandewater, and E. Wartella. 2003. *Electronic Media in the Lives of Infants, Toddlers, and Preschoolers*. Menlo Park, CA: The Kaiser Family Foundation.

Riessman, C. K. 1990. *Divorce Talk: Women and Men Make Sense of Personal Relationships*. New Brunswick, NJ: Rutgers University Press.

Riley, G. 1987. *Investing the American Woman: A Perspective on Women's History*. Arlington Heights, IL: Harlan Davidson.

———. 1991. *Divorce: An American Tradition*. New York: Oxford University Press.

Rimer, S. 1998. "Rural Elderly Create Vital Communities as Young Leave Void." *New York Times* (February 1):A18.

Risman, B., and P. Schwartz. 2002. "After the Sexual Revolution: Gender Politics in Teen Dating." *Contexts* 1, 1, (Spring): 16–24.

Ritter, J. 2001a. "AIDS 20 Years Later: Hope, but No Cure." *Chicago Sun-Times* (June 1):6–7.

———. 2001b. "AIDS Experts Say U.S. Ignores Africa." *Chicago Sun-Times* (February 5):8.

———. 2004. "Chicago Lab Helps Couples Create Made-to-Order Babies." *Chicago Sun-Times* (May 5):8.

Rivers, C., and Barnett, R. 2006. "Happy Homemakers." Alternet (March 30). http://www.alternet.org/story/34003/ (2006, April 14).

Roach, M. 2001. "New Challenges Ahead as Gay Population Ages." *Chicago Tribune* (October 24):7.

Robbins, R. H. 1993. *Cultural Anthropology: A Problem-Based Approach.* Itasca, IL: Peacock.

Roberto, K. A., 1990. "Grandparent and Grandchild Relationships." In T. H. Brubaker, ed., *Family Relationships in Later Life*, 100–12. Newbury Park, CA: Sage.

Roberts, K. A., and J. Stroes. 1992. "Grandchildren and Grandparents: Roles, Influences, and Relationships." *Journal of Aging and Human Development* 34:227–39.

Roberts, M. 2005. "Surrogate Starts Off Family in a Big Way." *Chicago Tribune* (April 27):15.

Roberts, S. 1994. "Black Women Graduates Outpace Male Counterparts." *New York Times* (October 31):A8.

Roberts, W. L. 1979/1980. "Significant Elements in the Relationship of Long-Married Couples." *International Journal of Aging and Human Development* 10:265–72.

Robertson, J., and L. F. Fitzgerald. 1990. "The (Mis)treatment of Men: Effects of Client Gender Role and Life-Style on Diagnosis and Attribution of Pathology." *Journal of Counseling Psychology* 37:3–9.

Robinson, B. 2000a. "Employee Benefits and Municipal Registration for Same-Sex Couples: Same-Sex Benefits in the Workplace." *Religious Tolerance.org* (October 5). http://www.religioustolerance.org/hom_sseb.htm (2006, April 19).

———. 2000b. "U. S. Divorce Rates: For Various Faith Groups, Age Groups, and Geographic Areas." *Religious Tolerance.org* (April 27). http://www.religioustolerance.org/chr_dira.htm (2006, April 26).

———. 2005. "Governments Which Have Recognized Same Sex Relationships." Religious Tolerance.org (December 2). http://www.religioustolerance.org/hom_sseb.htm (2006, April 19).

Robinson, I., K. Ziss, B. Ganza, and S. Katz. 1991. "Twenty Years of the Sexual Revolution, 1965–1985: An Update." *Journal of Marriage and the Family* 53 (February):216–20.

Robinson, J. P. 1977. *How Americans Use Time*. New York: Praeger.

———, and G. Bodbey. 1997. *Time for Life: The Surprising Ways Americans Use Their Time*. University Park: Pennsylvania State University Press.

Robinson, L. G., and P. W. Blanton. 1993. "Marital Strengths in Enduring Marriages." *Family Relations* 42:38–45.

Robison, J. 2002a. "The Future of Marriage: Part III." *The Gallup Poll* (August 13). http://poll.gallup.com/content/default.aspx?ci=6592 &VERSION=p (2006, August 13).

Robson, P. 1994. *Forbidden Drugs: Understanding Drugs and Why People Take Them*. New York: Oxford University Press.

Rochlin, M. 1992. "The Heterosexual Questionnaire." In M. Kimmel and M. A. Messner, *Men's Lives*, 2d ed., 482–83. New York: Macmillan.

Rodgers, W. L., and A. Thornton. 1985. "Changing Patterns of First Marriage in the United States." *Demography* 22:265–79.

Rodriguez, N. 2006. "What to Expect When You Find Out Your Teen is Having Sex." *The Desert Sun* www.thedesertsun.com/apps/pbcs. dll/article?AID=/20060221/LIFESTYLES12/602210308/ (2006, March 22). (February 21).

Rogers, S. J. "Spillover Between Marital Quality and Job Satisfacction: Long-Term Patterns and Gender Differences." *Journal of Marriage and Family* 65 (May):482–495.

———, and P. R. Amato. 2000. "Have Changes in Gender Relations Affected Marital Quality?" *Social Forces* 79, 2:731–53.

Rokach, R., O. Cohen, and S. Dreman. 2004. "Triggers and Fuses in Late Divorce: The Role of Short Term Crises vs Ongoing Frustration on Marital Break-Up." *Journal of Divorce and Remarriage* 40, 3/4:41–61.

Rollins, J. 1986. "Single Men and Women: Differences and Similarities." *Family Perspectives* 20:117–25.

"Romance on the Web." 2003. *Newsweek* (May 12):E20.

Romano, L. 2006. "Multiple Single Mums, One Nameless Donor." *Washington Post* (February 27):A02.

Roosa, M. W., J. Tein, N. Croppenbacher, N. Michaels, and L. Dumea. 1993. "Mother's Parenting Behavior and Child Mental Health in Families with a Problem-Drinking Parent." *Journal of Marriage and the Family* 55:107–18.

Roper Organization. 1990. *The Virginia Slims Opinion Poll: A 20-Year Perspective of Women's Issues.* Storrs: University of Connecticut.

Rosenblatt, P., Karis, T., and Powell, R. 1995. *Multiracial Couples.* Thousand Oaks, CA: Sage.

Rosenblum, K. E., and T. C. Travis. 1996. *The Meaning of Difference.* New York: McGraw-Hill.

Rosenfeld, M. 1998. "Little Boys Blue: Reexamining the Plight of Young Males." *Washington Post* (March 26):A1.

Rosenthal, C. J. 1986. "Family Supports in Later Life: Does Ethnicity Make a Difference?" *Gerontologist* 26:19–24.

Rosenthal, C. S., J. Jones, and J. A. Rosenthal. 2003. "Gendered Discourse in the Political Behavior of Adolescents." *Political Research Quarterly* 56, 1(March):97–104.

Rosier, K. B., and L. S. Feld. 2000. "Covenant Marriage: A New Alternative for Traditional Families." *Journal of Comparative Family Studies* 31, 3 (Summer):385–94.

Ross, C. E., J. Mirowsky, and J. Huber. 1983. "Dividing Work, Sharing Work and In Between: Marriage Patterns and Depression." *American Sociological Review* 48:809–23.

Ross, E. 2001. "British Put Limits on Embryo Transfers." *Chicago Tribune* (August 15):sec. 8, 5.

Ross, J. 2004. "Chilean Women Celebrate Gaining Right to Divorce." *WomenseNews* (December 3). http://www.womensenews.org/article. cfm/dyn/aid/2095/context/archieve (2006, March 20).

Ross, L. E., and A. C. Davis. 1996. "Black-White College Student Attitudes and Expectations in Paying for Dates." *Sex Roles: A Journal of Research* (July) 35, 1–2:43–56.

Rossi, P. H. 1989. *Down and Out in America.* Chicago: University of Chicago Press.

Rothman, B. K. 1989. *Recreating Motherhood: Ideology and Technology in a Patriarchal Society.* New York: W. W. Norton.

Roulet, M. 2003. "Technical Assistance Series—Fatherhood Programs and Domestic Violence." Madison, WI: Center for Family Policy and Practice. http://www.cffpp.org/publications/fatherhood_programs.html (2006, July 12).

Ruane, J. M., and K. A. Cerulo. 1997. *Second Thoughts: Seeing Conventional Wisdom through the Sociological Eye.* Thousand Oaks, CA: Pine Forge Press.

Rubin, B. 2000. "More Dads Are Earning the Title of Father." *Chicago Tribune* (June18):1, 8.

———. 2001. "The Thirty-Year Itch." *Chicago Tribune Magazine* (April 15): 4–20, 32.

Rubin, B. M. 2006. "Are Gay Adoptions Shaping Up as Nation's Next Culture Clash?" *Chicago Tribune* (March 20):1, 2.

———, and J. Anderson. 1997. "What Is an Exec's Wife Worth? Plenty, If You Ask Court." *Chicago Tribune* (December 14):sec. 4, 1.

Rubin, J. Z., F. J. Provenzano, and Z. Luria. 1974. "The Eye of the Beholder: Parents' Views on Sex of Newborns." *American Journal of Orthopsychiatry* 44:512–19.

Rubin, L. B. 1985. *Just Friends: The Role of Friendship in Our Lives.* New York: Harper & Row.

———. 1990. *Erotic Wars: What Happened to the Sexual Revolution?* New York: HarperCollins.

———. 1994. *Families on the Fault Line: America's Working Class Speaks about the Family, the Economy, Race, and Ethnicity.* New York: HarperCollins.

Rubin, R. H. 2002. "Alternative Lifestyles Revisited, or Whatever Happened to Swingers, Group Marriages, and Communes?" *Journal of Family Issues* 22, 6(September):711–727.

Rubin, Z. 1973. *Liking and Loving: An Invitation to Social Psychology.* New York: Holt, Rinehart & Winston.

———. 1974. "Lovers and Other Strangers: The Development of Intimacy in Encounters and Relationships." *American Scientist* 62:182–90.

———, L. A. Peplau, and C. T. Hill. 1981. "Loving and Learning: Sex Differences in Romantic Attachments." *Sex Roles* 7:821–35.

Rubinstein, R. L. 1986. *Singular Paths: Old Men Living Alone.* New York: Columbia University Press.

———. B. B. Alexander, M. Goodman, and M. Luborsky. 1991. "Key Relationships of Never-Married Childless Older Women: A Cultural Analysis." *Journal of Gerontology* 46, 5 (September):270–77.

Ruggles, S. 1994. "The Origins of African-American Family Structure." *American Sociological Review* 59:136–51.

Rusbult, C. E. 1983. "A Longitudinal Test of the Investment Model: The Development (and Deterioration) of Satisfaction and Commitment in Heterosexual Involvements." *Journal of Personality and Social Psychology* 45:101–17.

Russel, D., and N. VandeVen. 1976. *International Crimes against Women.* Conference publication. Proceedings les Femmes.

Russell, C. 1995. "Why Teen Births Boom." *American Demographics* (September):8.

Russell, D. 1982. *Rape in Marriage.* New York: Macmillan.

———. 1990. *Rape in Marriage,* 2d ed. Bloomington: Indiana University Press.

Saad, L. 2001. "Majority Considers Sex before Marriage Morally Okay." *Gallup News Service* (May 24). http://www.gallup.com/poll/ releases/pr010524.asp (2000, July 24).

———. 2006. "Future 'Retirees' Planning to Keep Busy on the Job." The *Gallup Poll* (June 27). http://poll.gallup.com/content/default.aspx? ci=23497 VERSION=p (2006, June 28).

Sack, K. 2001. "Epidemic Takes Toll on Black Women." *New York Times* (July 3):A1, A12.

Sadker, M., and D. Sadker. 1994. *Failing at Fairness: How America's Schools Cheat Girls.* New York: Scribner's.

Saenz, R., W. J. Goudy, and L. Frederick. 1989. "The Effects of Employment and Marital Relations on Depression among Mexican American Women." *Journal of Marriage and the Family* 51:239–51.

Safire, W. 1995. "News about Jews." *New York Times* (July 17).

Sahadi, J. 2003. "When She Makes More Than He." *CNNMoney* http://money.cnn.com/2003/02/28/commentary/everyday/sahadi (2006, January 17).

Said, L. 2005. "Pessimissim About Crime is Up Despite Declining Crime Rate." The Gallup Poll (October 23). http://poll.gallup.com/ content/default.aspx?ci=9559 (2005, October 25).

Sailer, Steve. 2003 (June 27). Black Illegitimacy Rates Declines, Others' Rise." http://www.isteve.com/2003_Black_Illegitimacy_Rate_Declines. htm (2005, July 21).

Sakurai, J. 2001. "Train Violence Shocks Japan." *Chicago Sun-Times* (October 22):26.

Saline, C. 1984. "Bleeding in the Suburbs." *Philadelphia* magazine (August): 81–85, 144–51.

Salovey, P., and J. Rodin. 1989. "Envy and Jealousy in Close Relationships." In C. Hendrick, ed., *Close Relationships,* 221–46. Newbury Park, CA: Sage.

Saluter, A. F. 1994. "Marital Status and Living Arrangements: March 1993." U.S. Census Bureau, Current Population Reports, Series P20–478. Washington, DC: U.S. Government Printing Office.

Saltzman, A. 1999. "From Diapers to High Heels." *U.S. News & World Report.* (July 26):57–58.

Salzman, J. 1996. "Why Ordinary Americans Like Daytime Talk Shows." *USA Today* (November):63.

Sanchez, L., S. L. Nock, J. L. Wilson, and J. D. Wright. 2002. "Is Covenant Marriage a Policy that Preaches to the Choir? A Comparison of Covenant and Standard Married Newlywed Couples in Louisiana." Working Paper Series 02–06. *Center for Family and Demographic Research,* Bowling Green State University.

Sanders, G. F., and R. L. Mullis. 1988. "Family Influences on Sexual Attitudes and Knowledge as Reported by College Students." *Adolescence* 92 (Winter):837–46.

Sanders, G. F., and D. W. Trygstad. 1989. "Stepgrandparents and Grandparents: The View from Young Adults." *Family Relations* 38:71–75.

Sanders, J. 2005. "Gender and Technology in Education: A Research Review (June). www.josanders.com/pdf/gendertech0705.pdf (2005, August 21).

Sandin, E. A., D. H. Baucom, C. K. Burnett, N. Epstein, and L. A. Rankin-Esquer. 2001. "Decision-Making Power, Autonomy, and Communication in Remarried Spouses Compared with First-Married Spouses." *Family Relations.* 50, 4(October):326–336.

Sandnabba, N. K., and C. Ahlberg. 1999. "Parents' Attitudes and Expectations about Children's Cross-Gender Behavior." *Sex Roles* 40, 3/4 (February):249–64.

Sandroff, R. 1989. "Why Pro-Family Policies Are Good for Business and America." *Working Women* (November):126.

Santrock, J . W., and K. A. Sitterle. 1987. "Parent-Child Relationships in Stepmother Families." In K. Pasley and M. Ihinger-Tallman, eds., *Remarriage and Stepparenting: Current Research and Theory*, 273–299. New York: Guilford Press.

Sapiro, V. 1986. *Women in American Society.* Mountain View, CA: Mayfield.

———. 1990. *Women in American Society*, 2d ed. Mountain View, CA: Mayfield.

———. 1999. *Women in American Society: An Introduction to Women's Studies*, 4th ed. Mountain View, CA: Mayfield.

Sarler, C. 2000. "Divorce Your Husband and Watch Him Get Rich." *New Statesman* 129 (October 30):8–9.

Schoeni, R. F. 1995. "Marital Status and Earnings in Developed Countries." *Journal of Population Economics* 8:557–586.

Saunders, D. G. 1988. "What Do You Know about Abuser Recidivism? A Critique of Recidivism in Abuser Programs." *Victimology: An International Journal.*

Savaagae, H. A. 1999. *Who Could Afford to Buy a House in 1995?* Current Housing Reports. Washington, DC: Government Printing Office.

Stewart, 2005. "Boundary Ambiguity in Stepfamilies." *Journal of Family Issues* 26, 7:1002–1029.

Save the Children Federation, USA. 2000. "Child Landmine Survivors: An Inclusive Approach to Policy and Practice." Working Paper No. 2. London W6 9LZ, United Kingdom: International Save the Children Alliance. ISBN 1-888-393-02-5.

Sax, L. J.; A. W. Astin; W. S. Korn; and K. M. Mahoney. 2001. *The American Freshman: National Norms for Fall 2000:* Los Angeles: UCLA.

Scanzoni, J. 1980. "Contemporary Marriage Types." *Journal of Family Issues* 1:125–40.

Schemo, D. J. 1996. "Adoptions in Paraguay: Mothers Cry Theft." *New York Times* (March 19):A1.

———. 2001a. "Virginity Pledges by Teenagers Can Be Highly Effective, Federal Study Finds." *New York Times* (January 4). http://www.nytimes.qpass.com/qpass-archives (2001, December 4).

———. 2001b. "Word for Word/Saving Themselves: What Teenagers Talk about When They Talk about Chastity." *New York Times* (January 28). http://www.nytimes.qpass.com/qpass-archives (2001, December 4).

Schenck-Yglesias, C. G. 1995. "A Frail Mom Is a Full-Time Job." *American Demographics* (September):14–15.

Scher, A., and R. Sharabany. 2005. "Parenting Anxiety and Stress: Does Gender Play a Part at 3 Months of Age? *The Journal of Genetic Psychology* 166, 2:203–213.

Schmeeckle, M., R. Giarrusso, and V. L. Bengtson. 1994. "Siblings: The Role of a Lifetime." Paper presented at the annual meeting of the Gerontological Society of America, Atlanta, GA.

Schmetzer, U. 1992. "Puritan China Faces Gay Question." *Chicago Tribune* (September 27):sec. 1.

———. 1999a. "In Bangladesh, Acid Ruins Women's Faces and Their Dreams." *Chicago Tribune* (January 31):15.

———. 1999b. "Thinking Small." *Chicago Tribune* (February 3):6.

Schneir, M., ed. 1972. *Feminism: The Essential Historical Writing*, 104–5. New York: Vintage Books/Random House.

———. ed. 1994. *Feminism: The Essential Historical Writing*, 104–5. New York: Vintage Books/Random House.

Schoen, C., K. Davis, K. Collins, L. Greenberg, C. DesRoches and M. Abrams. 1997. "The Commonwealth Fund Survey of the Health of Adolescent Girls." http://www.cmwf.org/programs/women/adoleshl.asp (2002, January 19).

Schoen, C., K. Davis, C. DesRoches, and A. Shekhdar. 1997. "The Health of Adolescent Boys: Commonwealth Fund Survey Findings. http://www.cmwf.org/programs/women/boysv27.asp (2002, January 19).

Schnieders, K., and E. Schnieders. 2005. *"You're Not My Mom: Confessions of a Formerly "Wicked" Stepmom.* Harrisburg, PA: NavPress Publishing Group.

Schoen, R. 2002. "Women's Employment, Marital Happiness, and Divorce." *Social Forces 81*, 2(December):643–662.

———, and R. M. Weinick. 1993. "Partner Choice in Marriages and Cohabitation." *Journal of Marriage and the Family* 55:408–14.

Schoenborn, C. A., J. L. Vickerie, and E. Powell-Griner. 2006. *Health Characteristics of Adults 55 Years of Age and Over: United States, 2000–2003.* Advance Data from Vital and Health Statistics, No. 370 (April 11). Hyattsville, MD: National Center for Health Statistics.

Schoeni, R. F. 1995. "Marital Status and Earnings in Developed Countries." Journal of Population Economics 8:557–586.

Schuckit, M. A., and T. L. Smith. 2001. "Correlates of Unpredicted Outcomes in Sons of Alcoholics and Controls." *Journal of Studies on Alcohol* 62, 4 (July):477–85.

Schuman, H., and C. Steeh. 1992. "Young White Adults: Did Racial Attitudes Change in the 1980s?" *American Journal of Sociology* 98 (September):340–67.

Schumm, W. R. 1986. "Marital Quality over the Marital Career: Alternative Explanations." *Journal of Marriage and the Family* 48:165–68.

Schvaneveldt, P. L., M. H. Young, and J. D. Schvaneveldt. 2001. "Dual-Resident Marriages in Thailand: A Comparison of Two Cultural Groups of Women." *Journal of Comparative Family Studies* 32, 3 (Summer):347–60.

Schwartz, F. N. 1989. "Management Women and the New Facts of Life." *Harvard Business Review* (January/February):65–76.

Schwartz, M. A. 1976. "Career Strategies of the Never-Married." Paper presented at the 71st annual meeting of the American Sociological Association, New York, August.

———, and P. Wolf. 1976. "Singlehood and the American Experience: Prospectives for a Changing Status." *Humboldt Journal of Social Relations* 4, 1 (Fall/Winter):17–24.

Schwartz, P. 1999. "Peer Marriage: What Does It Take to Create a Truly Egalitarian Relationship?" In A. S. Skolnick and J. H. Skolnick, *Family in Transition*, 154–63. New York: Addison Wesley Longman.

———, and V. Rutter. 1998. *The Gender of Sexuality.* Thousand Oaks, CA: Pine Forge Press.

Sciara, F. J. 1975. "Effects of Fathers' Absence on the Educational Achievement of Urban Black Children." *Child Study Journal* 5:45–55.

Science Daily. 2002. "Closeness to Mother Can Delay First Instance of Sexual Intercourse Among Younger Teens." http://www.sciencedaily.com/releases/2002/09/020911073512.htm (2006, March 22).

Scott, B., and M. A. Schwartz. 2006. *Sociology: Making Sense of the Social World.* Boston: Pearson/Allyn Bacon.

Scott, B. M. 1988. "The Making of a Middle-Class Black Woman: A Socialization for Success." Ph.D. diss., Northwestern University, Evanston, IL.

———. 1991. Unpublished interviews with African American women.

———, and M. A. Schwartz. 2000. *Sociology: Making Sense of the Social World.* Boston: Allyn & Bacon.

Scott, D., and B. Wishy, eds., 1982. *America's Families: A Documentary History.* New York: Harper & Row.

Scott, J. 1980. "Black Polygamous Family Formulation." *Alternative Scott,Lifestyles* 3:41–64.

———. 1994. "Social and Cultural Issues Related to Violence." *Vital Signs* 10, 2 (April/May/June):8.

J. P. 1990. "Sibling Interaction in Later Life." In T. H. Brubaker, ed., *Family Relationships in Later Life*, 86–99. Newbury Park, CA: Sage.

Scott, S. M. 2003. "What Really is the Divorce Rate?" *PREP.* http://www.prepinc.com/main/docs/what_really_div_rate.html (2006, March 3).

Seager, J. 1997. *The State of Women in the World Atlas*, 2d ed. London: Penguin Reference.

Sealey, G. 2002. "No More Big Man on Campus? College Gender Gap Could Men Women Lose Mating Game." (July 18). ABCNews.com (2006, February 10).

Sears, H. A., and N. L. Galambos. 1992. "Women's Work Condition and Marital Adjustment in Two-Career Couples: A Structural Model." *Journal of Marriage and the Family* 54:789–97.

Seccombe, K., and M. Ishir-Kuntz. 1994. "Gender and Social Relationships among the Never-Married." *Sex Roles* 30, 7/8:585–603.

Seff, M. A. 1995. "Cohabitation and the Law." *Marriage and Family Review* 21, 3/4:141–65.

Segura, D. A. 1994. "Working at Motherhood: Chicana and Mexicana Immigrant Mothers and Employment," In Evelyn Nakano Glenn, Grace Chang, and Linda Rennie Forcey, eds., *Mothering: Ideology, Experience, and Agency*. New York: Routledge.

———, and J. L. Pierce. 1993. "Chicana/o Family Structure and Gender Personality: Chodorow, Familism and Psychoanalytic Sociology Revisited." *Sign* 19:62–91.

Seidman, S. 1992. *Embattled Eros*. New York: Routledge, Chapman and Hall.

Seilhamer, R. A., T. Jacob, and N. J. Dunn. 1993. "The Impact of Alcohol Consumption on Parent-Child Relationships in Families of Alcoholics." *Journal of Studies of Alcohol* 54, 2:189–98.

Seltzer, J. 1998. "Father by Law: Effects of Joint Legal Custody on Nonresident Fathers' Involvement with Children." *Demography* 35:135–46.

———. 2000. "Families Formed Outside of Marriage." *Journal of Marriage and the Family* 62, 4:1247–69.

———, and I. Garfinkel. 1990. "Inequality in Divorce Settlements: An Investigation of Property Settlements and Child Support Awards." *Social Science Research* 19:82–111.

Senior Journal. 2005. "Primetime Live Sex Survey Has Interesting Findings About Senior Citizens." *Senior Journal* (October 31). http://www.seniorjournal.com/NEWS/Sex/4–10–22SexSurvey.htm (2006, March 21).

Seltzer, J. A. 2000. "Families Formed Outside of Marriage." *Journal of Marriage and the Family* 62:1247–1268.

Selvaraj, R. 2005. "The Challenges of Being Different: The Perspective of an Asian Immigrant On Cultural Diversity in the Workplace." Ramond. Selvaraj@WaitemataDHB.govt.nz.

Senna, J., and L. Siegel. 1999. *Introduction to Criminal Justice*. Belmont, CA: West/Wadsworth.

Seraph. 2005. "Interracial Marriages Decrease Among Asian Americans." Fighting 44s.com (November 24). http://www.thefighting44s.com/article.php?id_art=43 (2006, April 26).

Sevak, P., D. R. Weir, and R. J. Willis. 2003/2004. "The Economic Consequences of a Husband's Death: Evidence from the HRS and AHEAD." *Social Security Bulletin* 65, 3:31–44.

Sexualityandu.ca. 2004. "The Development of Sexuality From Infancy to Puberty: Development Outcomes, Common Behaviours, Concerns, and Learning Objectives." *Parents*. www.sexualityandu.ca/eng/parents/SCD/ (2006, March 22).

Shah, A. 2001. "Global Issues: Racism" (July 20). http://www.globalissues.org/HumanRights/Racism.asp (2002, February 1).

Shanas, E. 1979. "The Family as a Social Support System in Old Age." *Gerontologist* 19:169–74.

———. 1980. "Older People and Their Families: The New Pioneers." *Journal of Marriage and the Family* 42, 1:9–15.

Shane, B. 1997. "Family Planning Saves Lives, Prevents Abortion." *Population Today* 25, 3 (March):1–2.

Shapiro, J. 1993. *No Pity: People with Disabilities Forging a New Civil Rights Movement*. New York: Time Books.

Shapiro, J. L. 1987. "The Expectant Father." *Psychology Today* (January): 36–9, 42.

Shapiro, J. P. 1997. "The Un-Nursing Home." *U. S. News & World Report* (June 2):72.

Sharma, A. R., M. K. McGue, and P. I. Benson. 1996. "The Emotional and Behavioral Adjustment of United States Adopted Adolescents: Part I. An Overview." *Children & Youth Services Review* 18:83–100.

Shaver, P., and C. Hazan. 1988. "A Biased Overview of the Study of Love." *Journal of Social and Personal Relationships* 5:473–501.

———, and D. Bradshaw. 1988. "Love as Attachment: The Integration of Three Behavioral Systems." In R. J. Sternberg and M. L. Barnes, eds., *The Psychology of Love*, 68–99. New Haven, CT: Yale University Press.

Sheehy, S. 2000. *Connecting the Enduring Power of Female Friendship*. New York: HarperCollins.

Shehan, C. L., E. W. Bock, and G. R. Lee. 1990. "Religious Heterogamy, Religiosity, and Marital Happiness: The Case of Catholicism." *Journal of Marriage and the Family* 52:73–79.

Shelton, B. A., and D. John. 1990. "The Division of Household Labor: A Comparison of Cohabiting and Married Couples." Paper presented at the 85th annual meeting of the American Sociological Association, Washington, DC, August.

———. 1993. "Does Marital Status Make a Difference? Housework among Married and Cohabiting Men and Women." *Journal of Family Issues* 14:401–20.

Shenon, P. 1994. "Wanted: A Wife." *Chicago Tribune* (September 11):sec. 6, 5.

Shettel-Neuber, J., J. Bryson, and I. E. Young. 1978. "Physical Attractiveness of the 'Other' Person." *Personality and Social Psychology Bulletin* 4:612–15.

Shinn, M. 1978. "Father Absence and Children's Cognitive Development." *Psychological Bulletin* 85:295–324.

Shneidman, E. 1980. *Voices of Death*. New York: Harper & Row.

Shoop, R. J., and D. L. Edwards. 1994. *How to Stop Sexual Harassment in Our Schools*. Boston: Allyn & Bacon.

Shope, D. F. 1975. *Interpersonal Sexuality*. Philadelphia: Saunders.

Shostak, A. 1987. "Singlehood." In M. Sussman and S. Steinmetz, eds., *Handbook of Marriage and the Family*, 355–66. New York: Plenum.

Shriver, S., C. Byer, L. Shanberg, and G. Galliano. 2002. *Dimensions of Human Sexuality*, 6th ed. New York: McGraw-Hill.

Shucksmith, J. L., B. Hendry, and A. Glendinning. 1995. "Models of Parenting: Implications for Adolescent Well-Being within Different Types of Family Contexts." *Journal of Adolescence* 18:253–70.

Shugarman, L. R., D. E. Campbell, and C. E. Bird. 2004. "Differences in Medicare Expenditures During the Last Three Years of Life." *Journal of General Internal Medicine* 19:127–135.

SIECUS Fact Sheet. 2004. "Public Support for Comprehensive Sexuality Education." http://www.siecus.org/pubs/fact/index.html (2006, March 21).

Sigler, E. 2005. "Latinos & Love." *Hispanic* 18, 1/2 (Jan/Feb):44–46.

Sigler, R. T. 1989. *Domestic Violence in Context*. Lexington, MA: D. C. Heath.

Signorielli, N. 1997. *A Content Analysis: Reflections of Girls in the Media*. Menlo Park, CA: Children Now and the Kaiser Family Foundation.

———. 2001. "Television's Gender Role Images and Contribution to Sterotyping: Past, Present, Future. In D. G. Singer and J. L. Singer, eds., *Handbook of Children and the Media*, 341–358. Thousand Oaks, CA: Sage.

———, and A. Bacue. 1999. "Recognition and Respect: A Content Analysis of Prime-Time Television Characters across Three Decades." *Sex Roles* 40, 7/8 (April):527–45.

Silverman, P. 1988. "Research as a Process: Exploring the Meaning of Widowhood." In S. Reinharz and G. Rowles, eds., *Qualitative Gerontology*, 217–40. New York: Springer.

———. 2000. *Never Too Young to Know: Death in Children's Lives*. New York: Oxford University Press.

Silverstein, M., and L. J. Waite. 1993. "Are Blacks More Likely Than Whites to Receive and Provide Social Support in Middle and Old Age? Yes, No, and Maybe So." *Journal of Gerontology: Social Sciences* 48:S212–22.

Simenauer, J., and D. Carroll. 1982. *Singles: The New Americans*. New York: Simon & Schuster.

Simmons, C. 2002. "Multiple Births Skyrocket." *Send2Press* Newswire. http://www.send2press.com/PRnetwire/pr_02_0814-allbaby.shtml (2006, May 10).

Simmons, T., and M. O'Connell. 2003. "Married-Couple and Unmarried-Partner Households: 2000. *Census 2000 Special Reports* (February).

Simmons, W. 2000. "When It Comes to Having Children, Americans Still Prefer Boys." *Gallup News Service* (December 26).

Simon, B. L. 1987. *Never-Married Women*. Philadelphia: Temple University Press.

Simon, R. J., and H. Altstein. 2000. *Adoption Across Borders: Serving the Children in Transracial and Intercountry Adoptions*. Lanham, MD: Rowman and Littlefield.

Simpson, B. 1994. "Bringing the Unclear Family into Focus: Divorce and Remarriage in Contemporary Britain." *Man* 29 (December):831–51.

Simpson, V. 1991. "Europe's Liberal Laws Debated." *Milwaukee Journal* (May 12):J3.

Sims, S. 1989. "Violent." *Chicago Tribune* (June 11):sec. 6, 1, 6.

Situmorang, A. 2005. "Staying Single in a Married World: The Life of Never Married Women in Yogyakarta and Medan,. Working Paper, No. 38 (April). www.ari.nus.edu.sg/pub/wps.htm (2005, October 20).

Sivard, R., Brauer, A., Lumpe, L., and Walker, P. 1996. World Military and Social Expenditures 1996. Washington, DC: World Priorities. ISBN 0–918281-09–1.

Sivard, R. L. 1991. *World Military and Social Expenditures: 1991*. Washington, DC: World Priorities.

Skipper, J. K., Jr., and G. Nass. 1966. "Dating Behavior: A Framework for Analysis and an Illustration." *Journal of Marriage and the Family* 28:412–20.

Skolnick, A. S., and J. H. Skolnick, eds. 1987. *The Family in Transition*, 6th ed. Glenview, IL: Scott, Foresman.

———. 1999. *Family in Transition*, 10th ed. New York: Longman.

Skolnick, A.S., and S. Rosencrantz. 1994. "The New Crusade for the Old Family." *The American Prospect* (Summer):59–65.

Slovan, M. 1997. "Some Go to Great Lengths to Avoid Having a Baby Girl." *Chicago Tribune* (August 3):sec. 13, 1.

Smallwood, D. 1995. "Domestic Violence: How to Get Help." *N'DIGO* 86 (June 15–28):6–9.

Smith, A. D., and W. J. Reid. 1986. *Role-Sharing Marriage*. New York: Columbia University Press.

Smith, C. 2001. "Quandary in U.S. over Use of Organs of Chinese Inmates." *New York Times* (November 11):A1, A10.

Smith, D. 1990. *Stepmothering*. New York: St. Martin's Press.

———, and M. Hindus. 1975. "Premarital Pregnancy in America: 1640–1971." *Journal of Interdisciplinary History* 4 (Spring):537–70.

Smith, E. A., J. R. Udry, and N. M. Morris. 1985. "Pubertal Development and Friends: A Biosocial Explanation of Adolescent Sexual Behavior." *Journal of Health and Social Behavior* 26:183–92.

Smith, H., and E. Israel. 1997. "Sibling Incest: A Study of the Dynamics of 25 Cases." *Child Abuse and Neglect* 11:101–8.

Smith, H. W. 1981. *Strategies of Social Research: The Methodological Imagination*. Englewood Cliffs, NJ: Prentice Hall.

Smith, J., J. Mercy, and J. Conn. 1988. "Marital Status and the Risk of Suicide." *American Journal of Public Health* 78, 1:78–80.

Smith, J., V. Waldorf, and D. Trembath. 1990. "Single White Male Looking for Thin, Very Attractive. . . ." *Sex Roles* 23:675–85.

Smith, J. A., and R. G. Adler. 1991. "Children Hospitalized with Child Abuse and Neglect: A Case-Control Study." *International Journal* 5, 4:437–45.

Smith, K. 2000. *Who's Minding the Kids? Child Care Arrangements, Fall 1995*. Current Population Reports, P70–7. Washington, DC: U.S. Census Bureau..

Smith, L. G., and G. Clanton. 1977. *Jealousy*. Englewood Cliffs, NJ: Prentice Hall.

Smith, M. 1996. "Aboriginal Street Gangs in Winnipeg." Canada's National Aboriginal News Service. http://www.ayn.ca/[ages/gangs.htm (2002, February 5).

———. 2004. "Relationships of Children in Stepfamilies with Their Non-resident Fathers." *Family Matters* 67:28–35.

Smith, S. 1996. "Dating-Partner Preferences among a Group of Inner-City African American High School Students." *Adolescence* 31 (Spring): 79–90.

Smith, T. W. 1999. "Teenage Sexuality and Contraceptive Use: An Update." http://www.welfareref.../papers/smith_talk.html (April 4).

———. 1999. "The Emerging 21st Century American Family." *GSS Social Change Report Number 42*. Chicago: National Opinion Research Center, University of Chicago.

Smock, P. J. 1993. "The Economic Costs of Marital Disruption for Young Women over the Past Two Decades." *Demography* 30 (August): 353–71.

———, and W. Manning. 1997. "Cohabiting Partners' Economic Circumstances and Marriage." *Demography* 34, 3:331–41.

Smock, P. J., and S. Gupta. 2002. "Cohabitiation in Contemporary North American." In A. Booth and A. C. Crouter, eds. *Just Living Together*, 53–84. Mahwah, NJ: Erlbaum.

Smock, P. J., and W. D. Manning. 2004. "Living Together Unmarried in the United States: Demographic Perspectives and Implications for Family Policy. *Law and Policy* 26, 1:87–114.

Smolowe, J. 1993. "Giving the Cold Shoulder." *Time* (December 6):28–31.

Snowden, B., and L. Hayes. 2001. "International Terrorism Trends." Learning Network. http://www.infoplease.com/spot/terrorism1.html (2002, January 17).

Snyder, M. 2000. "Issues in Gender-Sensitive and Disability-Responsive Policy Research, Training and Action." http://www.un.org/esa/socdev/enable/disrppeg.htm (2002, January 30).

Sobey, A. R. 1997. "Alert: All Pregnant Women Avoid South Carolina." http://kubby.com/pr/971031.html (1999, October 31).

Soldo, B. J., and M. C. Hill. 1994. *Intergenerational Transfers and Family Structure in the Health and Retirement Survey*. Health and Retirement Working Paper no. 94–1004. Ann Arbor, MI: University of Michigan, Institute for Social Research.

Solomon, R. C. 1981. *Love, Emotion, Myth, and Metaphor*. Garden City, NY: Anchor/Doubleday.

Solomon, S. 2005. "Money, Housework, Sex, and Conflict: Same-Sex Couples in Civil Unions, Those Not in Civil Unions, and Heterosexual Married Siblings." *Sex Roles* (May).

Some Statistics on Bi-Racial Families. 1999. http://www.geocities.com/Athens/Oracle/1103/stats.htm.

Sommers, C. H. 2000. *The War Against Boys*. New York. Simon & Schuster.

Sonenstein, F., J. Pleck, and L. Ku. 1989. "Sexual Activity, Condom Use and AIDS Awareness among Adolescent Males." *Family Planning Perspective* 21, 4:152–58.

———. 1991. "Levels of Sexual Activity among Adolescent Males in the United States." *Family Planning Perspectives* 23:162–67.

Song, I. Y. 1991. "Single Asian American Women as a Result of Divorce: Depressive Affect and Changes in Social Support." In S. S. Volgy, ed., *Women, Men, and Divorce: Gender Differences in Separation, Divorce, and Remarriage*, 219–30. New York: Haworth Press.

Soroka, M. P., and G. J. Bryjak. 1995. *Social Problems: A World at Risk*. Boston: Allyn & Bacon.

———. 1999. *Social Problems: A World at Risk*, 2d ed. Boston: Allyn & Bacon.

Southern Poverty Law Center. 2001a. "Active Hate Groups in the U.S. in 2000." http://www.splcenter.org/intelligenceproject/ip-2.html (2002, February 2).

———. 2001b. Intelligence Report. "Raging against the Other." http://www.splcenter.org/intelligenceproject/ip-4t6.html (2002, February 2).

Spade, J. 1989. "Bringing Home the Bacon: A Sex-Integrated Approach to the Impact of Work on the Family." In B. Risman and P. Schwartz, eds., *Gender in Intimate Relationships*, 184–92. Belmont, CA: Wadsworth.

Spain, D. 1999. *America's Diversity: On the Edge of Two Centuries*. Washington, DC: Population Reference Bureau.

———, and S. M. Bianchi. 1996. *Balancing Act*. New York: Russell Sage Foundation.

Spanier, G. B., and P. C. Glick. 1981. "Marital Instability in the United States: Some Correlates and Recent Changes." *Family Relations* 31 (July):329–38.

Spanier, G. B., R. A. Lewis, and C. L. Cole. 1975. "Marital Adjustment over the Family Life Cycle: The Issue of Curvilinearity." *Journal of Marriage and the Family* 37 (May):263–75.

Spanier, G. B., and L. Thompson. 1988. "Moving toward Separation." In N. D. Glenn and M. T. Coleman, eds., *Family Relations: A Reader,* 326–41. Belmont, CA: Wadsworth.

Spar, D. L. 2006. *The Baby Business: How Money, Science, and Politics Drive the Commerce of Conception.* Cambridge, MA: Harvard Business School Press.

Spitze, G. 1988. "Women's Employment and Family Relations: A Review." *Journal of Marriage and the Family* 50:585–618.

———, and J. Logan. 1992. "Helping as a Component of Parent-Adult Child Relations." *Research on Aging* 14, 3:291–312.

Spearin, C. E. 2006. "Rorming a Union Plus Kids: The Role of Children in Stepfamily Formation." http://paa2006.princeton.edu/download.aspx?submissionld=60477 (2006, March 31).

Sprecher, S. 1989. "Pre-Marital Sexual Standards for Different Categories of Individuals." *Journal of Sex Research* 26, 2 (May):232–48.

———, and S. Metts. 1989. "Development of the 'Romantic Beliefs Scale' and Examination of the Effects of Gender and Gender-Role Orientation." *Journal of Social and Personal Relationships* 6:387–411.

Sprey, J. 1979. "Conflict Theory and the Study of Marriage and the Family." In W. Burr, R. Hill, F. I. Nye, and I. L. Reiss, eds., *Contemporary Theories about the Family,* 20–22. New York: Free Press.

Spring, S. 2006. "The Trade in Fertility." *Newsweek* (April 12). http://www.msnbc.msn.com/id/12289078/site/newsweek/print/1/displaymode/1098/ (2006, April 24).

Springs, H. H. 1989. *New Age Community Guidebook.* Available from Community Bookshelf, Rte. l, Box 155–F, Rutledge, MO 63563.

Spruill, J. C. 1938. *Women's Life and Work in the Southern Colonies.* New York: Russell and Russell.

Stacey, J. 1996. *In the Name of the Family: Rethinking Family Values in the Postmodern Age.* Boston: Beacon Press.

———. 2003. "Gay and Lesbian Families: Queer Like Us." In M. A. Mason, A. Skolnik, and D. Sugarman, eds., *All Our Families: New Policies for a New Century,* pp. 144–169, New York: Oxford University Press.

———, and T. Biblarz. 2001. "(How) Does the Sexual Orientation of the Parent Matter?" *American Sociological Review* 66, 2:164.

Stack, C., and L. Burton. 1994. "Kinscripts: Reflections on Family, Generation and Culture." In E. N. Glenn, G. Chang, and L. R. Forcey, eds., *Mothering: Ideology, Experience, and Agency,* 33–44. New York: Routledge.

Stafford, D. 2000. "Disparity between Pay for Average Worker, CEO Draws Fire." *Kansas City Star* (September 15). http://www/lcstar/cp,/item/pages/business.pat,business/3774c332.915,.html (2001, October 24).

Stainton, M. C. 1985. "The Fetus: A Growing Member of the Family." *Family Relations* 34:321–26.

Stanley, S. 2005. *The Power of Commitment: A Guide to Active, Lifelong Love.* Jossey-Bass.

Staples, R. 1981b. *The World of Black Singles: Changing Patterns of Male/Female Relations.* Westport, CT: Greenwood Press.

———. 1988. "The Black American Family." In C. H. Mindel, R. Habenstein, and R. Wright, Jr., eds., *Ethnic Families in America: Patterns and Variations,* 303–24. New York: Elsevier.

———, ed. 1991. *The Black Family: Essays and Studies,* 4th ed. Belmont, CA: Wadsworth.

———, ed. 1994. *The Black Family: Essays and Studies,* 5th ed. Belmont, CA: Wadsworth.

———. 1999. *The Black Family: Essays and Studies,* 6th ed. Belmont, CA: Wadsworth.

———, and T. Jones. 1985. "Culture, Ideology, and Black Television Images." *Black Scholar* 16:10–20.

Stark, E., and A. Flitcraft. 1988. "Violence among Intimates: An Epidemiological Review." In V. Van Hasselt, R. Morrison, A. Bellack, and M. Hersen, eds., *Handbook of Family Violence,* 293–318. New York: Plenum.

Starr, B. D., and M. B. Weiner. 1981. *Sex and Sexuality in the Mature Years.* New York: Stein and Day.

"Statement from NCAA President Myles Brand Regarding Department of Education Title IX Clarification." 2005. (March 22). www.2.ncaa.org/media_and_events/march/20050322_brand_stmt.titleix_survey.html (2005, March 22).

State of the World Population 1997 Report. 1997. "Rights for Sexual Reproductive Health." In *The Right to Choose: Reproductive Rights and Reproductive Health.* Online (November 11):1–17.

Stayton, W. R. 1984. "Lifestyle Spectrum 1984." Sex Information and Educational Council of the U.S. Reports (SIECUS) 12, 3:1–4.

Steck, L., D. Levitan, D. McLane, and H. H. Kelley. 1982. "Care, Need, and Conceptions of Love." *Journal of Personality and Social Psychology* 43:481–91.

Stein, P. 1976. *Single.* Englewood Cliffs, NJ: Prentice Hall.

———, ed. 1981. *Single Life: Unmarried Adults in Social Context.* New York: St. Martin's Press.

———, and M. Fingrutd. 1985. "The Single Life Has More Potential for Happiness Than Marriage and Parenthood for Both Men and Women." In H. Feldman and M. Feldman, eds., *Current Controversies in Marriage and the Family,* 81–89. Beverly Hills, CA: Sage.

Steinfirst, S., and B. B. Moran. 1989. "The New Mating Game: Matchmaking via the Personal Columns in the 1980's." *Journal of Popular Culture* 22, 4:129–40.

Steinhauer, J. 1995. "Living Together without Marriage or Apologies." *New York Times* (July 6):A9.

Steinmetz, S. 1977. "The Battered Husband Syndrome." *Victimology: An International Journal* 2, 3/4:499–509.

Stephen, E. H., and A. Chandra. 2006. "Infertility Service Utilization Among Women Aged 15–44 in the United States: 2002." A poster paper presented at the 2006 annual meeting of the Population Association of America, March 30–April 1, Los Angeles, CA.

Stepp, L. 2005. "Study: Half of All Teens Have Had Oral Sex." *Washington Post* (September 16):A07.

Sternberg, R. J. 1986. "A Triangular Theory of Love." *Psychological Review* 93, 2:119–35.

———. 1988. *The Triangle of Love: Intimacy, Passion, and Commitment.* New York: Basic Books.

——— 1998. *Love Is a Story.* London: Oxford University Press.

———. 2001. *What's Your Love Story?* In Kathleen R. Gilbert, ed., Annual Editions: *The Family.* Guilford, CT: McGraw-Hill/Duskin.

Stets, J. E. 1991. "Cohabiting and Marital Aggression in Marriage: The Role of Social Isolation." *Journal of Marriage and Family* 53:669–80.

Stevens, D., G. Kiger, and P. J. Riley. 2002. "Coming Unglued? Workplace Characteristics, Work Satisfaction, and Family Cohesion." *Social Behavior and Personality.*

Stewart, 2005. "Boundary Ambiguity in Stepfamilies." *Journal of Family Issues* 26, 7:1002–1029.

Stewart, A. J., A. P. Copeland, N. L. Chester, J. E. Malley, and N. B. Barenbaum. 1997. *Separating Together: How Divorce Transforms Families.* New York: Guilford Press.

Stewart, J. K. 1999. "Long-Distance Marriages Not Such a Long Shot." *Chicago Tribune* (October 6):sec. 8, 1, 8.

Stewat, S. D. 2003. "Nonresident Parenting and Adolescent Adjustment." *Journal of Family Issues* 24(March):217–244.

St. George, D. 2004. "Pregnant Women Murdered at an Alarming Rate." *The Washington Post* (December 19).

Stillion, J. M. 1995. "Premature Exits: Understanding Suicide." In L. A. DeSpelder and A. L. Strickland, eds., *The Paths Ahead: Readings in Death and Dying,* 182–97. Mountain View, CA: Mayfield.

Stinnet, N., and C. Birdsong. 1978. *The Family and Alternative Life Styles.* Chicago: Nelson-Hall.

St. Jean, Y., and Feagin, J. 1998. *Double Burden: Black Women and Everyday Racism.* New York: M. E. Sharpe.

Stodghill, R. 1999. "Where'd You Learn That?" In S. J. Bunting, ed., *Human Sexuality 99/00,* 140–44. Sluice Dock, Guilford, CT: Dushkin/McGraw-Hill.

Stokes, J. P., and J. S. Peyton. 1986. "Attitudinal Differences between Full-Time Homemakers and Women Who Work Outside the Home." *Sex Roles* 15:299–310.

Stolberg, S. 1998. "U.S. Awakes to Epidemic of Sexual Diseases." *New York Times* (March 9):A1, A14.

———. 1999. "U.S. Birth Rate at New Low as Teen-Age Pregnancy Falls." *New York Times* (April 29):A22.

———. 2001. "Study Paints Daycare as Hothouse for Aggression." *National Post* (April 20).

Stone, L. 1997. *Kinship and Marriage*. Boulder, CO: Westview Press.

Stone, L. H., ed. 1999. *Selected Readings in Marriage and Family*. San Diego, CA: Greenhaven Press.

Stone, R., G. L. Cafferata, and J. Sangl. 1987. "Caregivers of the Frail Elderly: A National Profile." *Gerontologist* 27:616–26.

Stoneman, Z., G.H. Brody, and C.E. MacKinnon. 1986. "Same-Sex and Cross-Sex Siblings: Activity Choices, Roles, Behavior, and Gender Stereotypes." *Sex Roles* 15:495–511.

Strada, M. J. 1999. *Through the Global Lens: An Introduction to the Social Sciences*. Upper Saddle River, NJ: Prentice Hall.

Straus, M. 1994. *Beating the Devil Out of Them: Corporal Punishment in American Families and Its Effect on Children*. New York: Lexington Books.

———, and D. Donnelly. 2001. *Beating the Devil Out of Them: Corporal Punishment in American Families and Its Effects on Children*. New Brunswick, NJ: Transaction.

Straus, M., R. Gelles, and S. Steinmetz. 1980. *Behind Closed Doors*. Garden City, NY: Anchor Books.

Straus, M. A. 1999. "Is It Time to Ban Corporal Punishment?" *Canadian Medical Association Journal* 161, 7(October 5): 821.

———. 2001. *Beating the Devil Out of Them: Corporal Punishment in American Families and Its effects on Children*, 2nd ed. Somerset, NJ: Transaction Publishers.

———, and J. H. Stewart. 1999. "Corporal Punishment by American Parents: National Data on Prevalence, Chronicity, Severity, and Duration, in Relation to Child and Family Characteristics." *Clinical Child and Family Psychology Review* 2 (June):55–70.

Streetwise. 1995. "Special Report: Life in the Streets." 4, 1 (September 16–30):2–14.

Stroebe, W., C. A. Insko, V. D. Thompson, and B. D. Layton. 1971. "Effects of Physical Attractiveness, Attitude Similarity, and Sex on Various Aspects of Interpersonal Attraction." *Journal of Personality and Social Psychology* 18:79–91.

Strong, B., C. DeVault, B. Sayad, and W. Yarber. 2004. *Human Sexuality: Diversity in Contemporary America*. New York: McGraw-Hill.

Strong, B., S. Wilson, L. M. Clarke, and T. Johns. 1978. *Human Sexuality*. New York: West.

"Study." 1998. *Chicago Tribune* (July 12):sec. 13, 3.

Stutzer, A., and B. S. Frey. 2003. "Does Marriage Make People Happy or Do Happy People Get Married?" Working Paper Series, Paper 143, Institute for Empirical Research in Economics, University of Zurich.

Suarez, Z. E. 1998. "Cuban-American Families." In C H. Mindel, R. W. Habenstein, and R. Wright, Jr. *Ethnic Families in America: Patterns and Variations*, 172–98. Upper Saddle River, NJ: Prentice Hall.

Substance Abuse and Mental Health Services Administration. 2003. "Children Living with Substance-Abusing or Substance-Dependent Parents." *The National Household Survey on Drug Abuse Report* (June):1–3.

Sudarkasa, N. 1993. "Female-Headed African American Households: Some Neglected Dimensions." In H. P. McAdoo, ed., *Family Ethnicity: Strength in Diversity*. Newbury Park, CA: Sage.

Sugisawa, H., J. Liang, and X. Liu. 1994. "Social Networks, Social Support, and Mortality among Older People in Japan." *Journal of Gerontology* 49:S3–S13.

Suhr, J. 2006. "Illinois Doctor who Killed Sons, Self Accused Wife of Cheating." WBBMNews Radio 780 Chicago, *Associated Press News:* (June 26)

Sung-Jin, K. 2006. "Divorce Falls, Remarriage Rises." *The Korea Times* (January 6). http://times.hankooki.com/lpage/200601/ kt2006010617132810440.htm (2006, March 26).

Supporting Family Values. 2005. http://www.ronrolheiser.com/arc052905.html (2005, July 21).

Surgeon General. 2001. "The Surgeon General's Call to Action to Promote Sexual Health and Responsible Sexual Behavior." Rockville,

MD: U.S. Department of Health and Human Services, Office of the Surgeon General. News Release (July 9). http://www.surgeongeneral.gov/news/pressreleases/pr_sexualhealth.html (2005, August 25).

Suro, roberto. 2001. "Mixed Doubles." *American Demographics*. http://www.inside.com/product/product_print.asp?pf_id (2001, November 14).

Surra, C. A. 1991. "Research and Theory on Mate Selection and Premarital Relationships in the 1980s." In A. Booth, ed., *Contemporary Families: Looking Forward, Looking Back*. Minneapolis: National Council on Family Relations.

Sussman, M. 1985. "The Family Life of Old People." In R. Binstock and E. Shanas, eds., *Handbook of Aging and the Social Sciences*, 415–49. New York: Van Nostrand Reinhold.

Sutton-Smith, B. 1971. "The Expressive Profile." In A. Paredes and R. Bauman, eds., *Toward New Perspectives in Folklore*, 80–92. Austin: University of Texas Press.

Swanbrow, D. 1989. "The Paradox of Happiness." *Psychology Today* (July/August):37–39.

———. 2003. "Childhood Viewing of TV Violence Affects Women as Well as Men." (March 10). http://www.umich.edu/news/releases/2003/mar03/r031003a.html (2006, July 22).

Sweemeu. 1995. "Remarriage of Men and Women: The Role of Socioeconomic Prospects." CDE Working Paper No. 95–08. Centre for Demography and Ecology, University of Madison-Wisoconsin, USA.

Sweeney, J. F. 2001. "Jay Belsky Doesn't Play Well with Others." http://www.salon.com/mwt/feature/2001/04/26/belsky/index.html (2001, July 20).

Sweeney, M. M. 2002. "Remarriage and the Nature of Divorce: Does It Matter Which Spouse Chooses to Leave?" *Journal of Family Issues* 23:410–440.

Sweet, J. A., and L. L. Bumpass. 1987. *American Families and Households*. New York: Russell Sage Foundation.

Swoboda, F. 2000. "Big 3 Extend Benefits to Domestic Partners." *Washington Post* (June 6):A1, A22.

Szapocznik, J., and R. Hernandez. 1988. "The Cuban American Family." In C. H. Mindel, R. W. Habenstein, and R. H. Wright, Jr., eds., *Ethnic Families in America: Patterns and Variations*, 160–72. New York: Elsevier.

Tafoya, S., H. Johnson, and L. Hill. 2004. "Who Chooses to Choose Two? Multiracial Identification and Census 2000." *The American People Series*. www/[rb/prg/AmericanPeople (2006, April 24).

Tagprda. R. 2005. "Trends in Interracial Dating." *Outside the Beltway* (June 25).

Takagi, D. Y. 1998. "Japanese American Families." In R. L. Taylor, ed., *Minority Families in the United States: A Multicultural Perspective*, 2d ed., 159–75. Upper Saddle River, NJ: Prentice Hall.

———. 1994. "Japanese American Families." In R. L. Taylor, ed., *Minority Families in the United States: A Multicultural Perspective*, 146–63. Upper Saddle River, NJ: Prentice Hall.

Talbott, M. M. 1998. "Older Widows' Attitudes toward Men and Remarriage." *Journal of Aging Studies* 12, 4 (Winter):429–49.

"Talks on Drugs Linked to Use." 1999. *Chicago Tribune* (April 26):4.

Tallichet, S. E. 1995. "Gendered Relations in the Mines and the Division of Labor Underground." *Gender & Society* 9:697–711.

Tanfer, K. 1987. "Patterns of Premarital Cohabitation among Never-Married Women in the United States." *Journal of Marriage and the Family* 49:483–97.

Taniguchi, H. 1999. "The Timing of Childbearing and Women's Wages." *Journal of Marriage and the Family* 61 (November):1008–19.

Tannen, D. 1990. *You Just Don't Understand: Women and Men in Conversation*. New York: Ballantine.

———. 1994. *Talking from 9 to 5. Women and Men in the Workplace: Language, Sex and Power*. New York: Avon Books.

———. 2002. *I Only Say This Because I Love You: Talking to Your Parents, Partner, Sibs, and Kids When You're All Adults*. New York: Ballantine Books.

Tanner, Gerald, and Sandra. Tanner. 2001. "Polygamist Sentenced to Five Years in Prison." *Salt Lake City Messenger* (October): No. 97.

Tapsfield, R., and F. Collier. 2005. "The Cost of Foster Car: Investing in our Children's Future." http://www.crin.org/bcn/details.asp?id=9769 themeID=1002 topicID=1013 (2006, August 15).

Task Force on Aging Research. 1995. *The Threshold of Discovery: Future Directions for Research on Aging.* Washington, DC: U.S. Government Printing Office.

Tatara, T. 1998. "The National Elder Abuse Incidence Study." The National Center on Elder Abuse and the American Public Humane Services Association. http://www.aoa.gov/abuse/report/main-pdf.htm (2001, December 18).

Tavris, C. 2000. "Women as Love's Experts and Love's Victims." In N. Benokraitis, ed., *Feuds about Families,* 123–30. Upper Saddle River, NJ: Prentice Hall.

Taylor, J., J. Jackson, and L. Chatters, eds., 1997. *Family Life in Black America.* Thousand Oaks, CA: Sage.

Taylor, L. C., I. D. Hinton, and M. Wilson. 1995. "Parental Influences on Academic Performance in African-American Students." *Journal of Child and Family Studies* 4:293–302.

Taylor, R. J. 1990. "Need for Support and Family Involvement among Black Americans." *Journal of Marriage and the Family* 52:114–25.

———, M. B. Tucker, and E. Lewis. 1990. "Development in Research on Black Families: A Decade Review." *Journal of Marriage and the Family* 52 (November):993–1014.

———, V. M. Keith, and M. B. Tucker. 1993. "Gender, Marital, Familial, and Friendship Roles." In J. S. Jackson, L. M. Chatters, and R. J. Taylor, eds., *Aging in Black America,* 49–68. Newbury Park, CA: Sage.

Taylor, R. L. 1998. *Minority Families in the United States: A Multicultural Perspective.* Upper Saddle River, NJ: Prentice Hall.

Teachman, J. 2002. "Stability Across Cohorts in Divorce Risk Factors." *Demography* 39:331–351.

———. 2003. "Premarital Cohabitation Among Never-Married Women in the United States." *Journal of Marriage and the Family* 65(May):444–455.

Teachman, J. D., L. M. Tedrow, and K. D. Crowder. 2000. "The Changing Demography of America's Families." *Journal of Marriage and the Family* 62, 4:1234–46.

Teenpregnancy.org, 2004. "Teen Pregnancy—So What?" http://www.teenpregnancy.org/whycare/sowhat.asp (2006, March 27).

Telecomworldwire. 2001. "Both Men and Women Turn to SMS to Find New Partners—Study" (September 19). http://www.findarticles.com/cf_0/m0ECZ/2001_Sept_19/78408573/p1/article.jhtml?term=... (2001, October 24).

Temple, A. 1998. "Dating Rituals May Be a Matter of Keeping the Faith." *Chicago Tribune* (August 9):sec. 13, 1, 8.

Tenenbaum, H. R., and C. Leper. 2003. "Parent-Child Conversations About Science: The Socialization of Gender Inequities?" *Developmental Psychology* 39 (January):34-47.

Tennis, C. 2005. "I Wish My Stepchildren Would Go Away." (Dec. 1). http://dir.salon.com/story/mwt/col/tenn/2005/12/01/stepmom/index.html (2006, March 27).

Tennov, D. 1979. *Love and Limerence: The Experience of Being in Love.* Briarcliff Manor, NY: Stein and Day.

Thackeray, A. 2000. "Interracial Acceptance: Is America Ready?" *One Magazine* (Spring). http://www.onemagazine.net/race.htm (2001, November 12).

The AFCARS Report. 2005 (May). U.S. Department of Health and Human Services, Administration for Children and Families, Administration on Children, Youth and Families, Children's Bureau, Preliminary Estimates for FY 2003 as of April 2005. www.acf.hhs.gov/programs/cb (2005, July 23).

The 8 Minute Matchmaker. 2002. Tufts e-News (June 13). http://www.8minutedating.com/press/pdfs/Tufts.htm (2006, February 17).

The Irish Presidency of the European Union in Association with FGS Consulting and A. McGolgan, 2004. *Report on Sexual Harassment in the Workplace in European Member States* (June). www.justice. ie/80256EO10039C5AF/vWeb/pcJUSQ63QLTx-en (2006, January 12).

"The Gender Gap: Work Outside the Home or Stay at Home." *Poll Insights.* The Gallup Organization (August 23). www.gallup.com/poll/pollinsigts/?pw=8/23/2005%205:00 (24 August).

"The Role of Media in Childhood Obesity." 2004. *Issues Brief* (February). Washington, DC: The Kaiser Family Foundation.

The White House Project. 2001. *Who's Talking? An Analysis of Sunday Morning Talk Shows* (December). New York.

"The World Communal Scene." 2005. www.communa.org.il/world.htm (2005, December 7).

Thompson, T. L., and E. Zerbinos. 1997. "Television Cartoons: Do Children Notice It's a Boy's World?" *Sex Roles* 37, 5/6:415–433.

Thomsen, S. R., M. M. Weber, and L. B. Brown. 2001. "The Relationship Between Health Magazine Reading and Eating-Disordered Weight-Loss Methods Among High School Girls. *American Journal of Health Education* 32: 133–138.

Thrupkaew, N. 2002. "The Myth of the Model Minority." *The American Prospect* (April 8). http://www.prospect.org/print-friendly/print/V13/7/thrupkaew-n.html (2006, February 8).

Thies, C. F. 2000. "The Success of American Communes." *Southern Economic Journal* 67, 1 (July):186–99.

Thomas, J. L. 1986. "Gender Differences in Satisfaction with Grandparenting." *Psychology and Aging* 1:215–19.

Thomas, V. G. 1990. "Determinants of Global Life Happiness and Marital Happiness in Dual-Career Black Couples." *Family Relations* 39:174–78.

Thombs, D. 1994. *Introduction to Addictive Behaviors.* New York: Guilford Press.

Thompson, B. W. 1994. *A Hunger So Wide and So Deep: American Women Speak Out on Eating Problems.* Minneapolis: University of Minnesota Press.

Thompson, G. 1999. "Smugglers Made False Promises to Poor Mexican Mothers." *Chicago Tribune* (October 20).

Thompson, L., and A. J. Walker. 1991. "Gender in Families." In A. Booth, ed., *Contemporary Families: Looking Forward, Looking Back,* 76–102. Minneapolis: National Council on Family Relations.

Thomsen, D., and I. Chang. 2000. "Predictors of Satisfaction with First Intercourse: A New Perspective for Sexuality Education." Poster Presentation at 62nd Annual Conference of the National Council on Family Relations, Minneapolis (November).

Thornberry, T., and J. Burch. 1997. "Gang Members and Delinquent Behavior." Washington, DC: Office of Juvenile Justice and Delinquency Prevention.

Thornton, A. 1990. "The Courtship Process and Adolescent Sexuality." *Journal of Family Issues* 11, 3:239–73.

Thornton, E. 1994. "Video Dating in Japan." *Fortune* (January 24):12.

Tierney, J. 2006. "The Happiest Wives." *New York Times* (February 28): Sec. A, p. 19.

Tilly, L., and J. W. Scott. 1978. *Women, Work and Family.* New York: Holt.

Tilson, D., and U. Larsen. 2000. "Divorce in Ethiopia: The Impact of Early Marriage and Childlessness." *Journal of Biosocial Science* 32, 3(July):355–372.

Timberlake, J. M., and F. F. Furstenberg, Jr. 2003. "Shifting Childrearing to Single Mothers: Results from 17 Western Countries." *Population and Development Review* 29, 1:47–71.

Tolbert, K. 2001. "Premier's Family Reflects Japan's Painful Divorce Custom." *Chicago Tribune* (May 20):4.

Totenberg, N. 1985. "How to Write a Marriage Contract." In O. Pocs and R. Walsh, eds., *Marriage and Family: Annual Editions,* 46–47. Sluice Dock, Guilford, CT: Dushkin.

Toth, J., and X. Xu. 1999. "Ethnic and Cultural Diversity in Fathers' Involvement: A Racial/Ethnic Comparison of African American, Hispanic, and White Fathers." *Youth and Society* 31 (September):76–99.

Tower, C. 2002. *Understanding Child Abuse and Neglect,* 5th ed. Boston: Allyn & Bacon.

———. 2004. *Understanding Child Abuse and Neglect,* 6th ed. Boston: Allyn Bacon.

Townsend, B., and K. O'Neil. 1990. "American Women Get Mad." *American Demographics* (August):26–29, 32.

Tracy, L. 1990. "The Television Image in Children's Lives." *New York Times* (May 13):sec. M.

"Transgendered Economist Publishes First Book as a Woman." 1997. *Chronicle of Higher Education* (May 2):A15.

Trauma Intervention Program. 2006. "Facts About Domestic Violence." http://www.tipnational.org/node/262 (2006, July 13).

Treas, J. 1995. "Older Americans in the 1990s and Beyond." *Population Bulletin* 50:2. Washington, DC: Population Reference Bureau.

———, and D. Giesen. 2000. "Sexual Infidelity Among Married and Cohabiting Americans." *Journal of Marriage and the Family* 62(February):48–60.

———, and V. L. Bengtson. 1987. "The Family in Later Years." In M. B. Sussman and S. K. Steinmetz, eds., *Handbook of Marriage and the Family*, 625–48. New York: Plenum.

Tribe, L. H. 1990. *Abortion: The Clash of Absolutes*. New York: W. W. Norton.

Troll, L. 1988. "New Thoughts on Old Families." *Gerontologist* 28, 5:586–91.

Tubman, J. G. 1993. "Family Risk Factors, Parental Alcohol Use, and Problem Behaviors among School-Age Children." *Family Relations* 42:81–86.

Tucker, M., and C. Mitchell-Kernan. 1990. "New Trends in Black American Interracial Marriage: The Social Structural Context." *Journal of Marriage and the Family*, 26:279–90.

———, eds. 1995. *The Decline in Marriage among African Americans*. New York: Russell Sage Foundation.

———. 1999. "Marital Behavior and Expectations: Ethnic Comparisons of Attitudinal and Structural Correlates." In Cheryl Albers, *Sociology of Families Readings*, 90–100. Thousand Oaks, CA: Pine Forge Press.

Tucker, M. B., and R. J. Taylor. 1989. "Demographic Correlates of Relationship Status among Black Americans." *Journal of Marriage and the Family* 51:655–66.

Turner, D. 2003. "Japan's Mating Culture Extends Baby Drought." *The Financial Times* (December 9). http://yaleglobal.yale.edu/ article. print?id=3686 (2006, April 15).

Turner, J., and A. Z. Maryanski. 1979. *Functionalism*. Menlo Park, CA: Benjamin/Cummings.

"TV Soaps Focus on Role of Sex." 1994. *Chicago Tribune* (October 23):8.

Tweed, S. H., and C. D. Ryff. 1991. "Profiles of Wellness amidst Distress." *Journal of Studies on Alcohol* 52:133–41.

Twenge, J. M., W. K. Campbell, and C. A. Foster. 2003. "Parenthood and Marital Satisfaction: A Meta-Analytic Review. *Journal of Marriage and Family* 65, 3(August):574–583.

———. 2003. "Parenthood and Marital Satisfaction: A Meta-Analytic Review." *Journal of Marriage and Family* 65, 3 (August): 574–583.

Tyson, A. S. 1997. "Young Love Bridges Race Divide" (December 3). http://www.csmonitor.c...997/12/03/us/us.4.html (1999, March 5).

Uhlenberg, P. 1980. "Death and the Family." *Journal of Family History* (Fall):313–21.

UNHCR. 2006. "UNHCR Global Refugee Tally at 26-Year Low While Internally Displaced Increase." Press Release. (June 9). http://www.unhcr.org/cgi-bin/texis/Vtx/news/opendoc.htm (2006, August 23).

UNAIDS. 2001. "Report on the Global HIV/AIDS Epidemic: Global Summary of the HIV/AIDS Epidemic, End 1999." http://www. unaids.org/epidemic_update/report/Epi_report_chap_glo_estim.htm (2001, December 13).

UNAIDS/WHO. 2005. "AIDS Epidemic Update: December 2005." http://www.unaids.org/epi/2005/doc/report_pdf.asp (2006, April 3).

UNICEF. 1996. "The State of the World's Children." http://www.unicef. org/sowc96/16relief.html (1998, April 8).

———. 2002. "Children and War." Voices of Youth. http://www/ imocef/prg/voy/meeting/war-exp2.hmtl (2002, February 18).

———. 2003 "Every Day, 1,400 Women Die Giving Birth." (March 7). http://www.unicef.org/media/media_7594.html (2006, May 12).

———. 2006a. "Saving Children From the Tragedy of Landmines." Press Release. http://www.unicef.org/media/media_32034.html (2006, August 16).

———. 2006b. "For the Children of Darfur, Western Sudan, the Conflict Feels Like it Will Never End." http://www.unicef.com. au/documents/Darfur (2006, August 23).

University of Michigan Health System. 2005. "Sibling Abuse." http://www.med.umich.edu/libr/yourchild/sibabuse.html (2006, July 21).

United Nations. 2000. "The Aging of the World's Population." http://www. un.org/esa/socdev/ageing/agewpop.htm (2001, December 28).

———. 2005. *Demographic Yearbook, 2002*. New York: United Nations. http://unstats.un.org/unsd/demographic/products/dyb/ dybpub 2002. htm (2006, March 27).

United Nations Development Programme. 1999. *Human Development Report, 1999*. New York: Oxford University Press.

———. 2001. *Human Development Report, 2001*. New York: Oxford University Press.

United Nations Development Programme. 2005. *Hunan Development Report 2005*. New York: Oxford University Press.

United Nations High Commissioner for Refugees. 2001. "Refugees by Numbers 2001 Edition (July 1). http://www.unhcr.ch/cgi-bin/texis/vtx/[romt?tbl=VISITORS&id=3b028097c (2002, January 14).

United Nations Office of Drug Control and Crime Prevention. 2001. "Terrorism." The Terrorism Prevention Branch. http://www.undcp. org/terrorism.html (2002, February 16).

United Nations Office on Drugs and Crime. 2005. *World Drug Report* 2005. New York.

———. 2006. *World Drug Report* 2006. New York.

United Nations Population Division. 2005. *World Population Prospects: The 2004 Revision*. New York: United Nations.

United Nations Population Fund. 2004. "Safe Motherhood in Africa: Social and Economic Impact of Maternal Deaths." (August 31). http://cst.addisababa.unfpa.org/412_1607.asp) (2006, May 12).

United Press International. 1990. "Men Love Looks, Women Love Money: U.M. Study." *Chicago Tribune*.

USA Today. 2004. "USA TODAY Snapshots." (May 19): p. 1.

USA Today/Gallup Poll. 1007. "Interracial Teen Dating." (October 13–20).

U.S. Census Bureau. 1987. "Money Income and Poverty Status of Families and Persons in the United States: 1986 (Advance Data from the March 1987 Current Population Survey)." *Current Population Reports*, Series P–60, no. 157. Washington, DC: U.S. Government Printing Office.

———. 1991. "Marital Status and Living Arrangements: March 1990." *Current Population Reports*, Series P–20, no. 450. Washington, DC: U.S. Government Printing Office.

———. 1992. "Who's Minding the Kids?" *Current Population Reports*, Series P–70, no. 30. Washington, DC: U.S. Government Printing Office.

———. 1993. *Statistical Abstract of the United States*, 113th ed. Washington, DC: U.S. Government Printing Office.

———. 1995. *Statistical Abstract of the United States*, 115th ed. Washington, DC: U.S. Government Printing Office.

———. 1997. *Statistical Abstract of the United States, 1997*, 117th ed. Washington, DC: U.S. Government Printing Office.

———. 1998. *Statistical Abstract of the United States, 1998*, 118th ed. Washington, DC: U.S. Government Printing Office.

———. 1999. "Poverty Rate Down, Household Income Up." Press Release. http://www.census.gov/Press-Release/cb98–175.html.

———. 2000a. *Statistical Abstract of the United States, 2000*, 120th ed. Washington, DC: U.S. Government Printing Office.

———. 2000b. "Current Population Survey, March 2000. Racial Statistics Population Division. Washington, DC: U.S. Department of Commerce (2001, February 22).

———. 2000c. "Fertility of American Women: June 2000." Current Population Reports, P20–543RV. Washington, DC: U.S. Department of Commerce, Economics and Statistics Administration.

———. 2001a. "Multigenerational Households Number 4 Million." http://www.census.gov/Press-Release/www/2001/cb01cn182.html (2001, December 3).

———. 2001b. "More People Have Health Insurance, Census Bureau Reports." http://www.census.gov/ftp/pub/Press-Release/www/2001/ cb01-162.html (2001, September 28).

———. 2001c. "Health Insurance Coverage: 2000." Table A (September 28). http://www.census.gov/ftp/pub/hhes/hlthins/hlthin00/hi00ta.html (2001, September 28).

———. 2002. *American Housing Survey for the United States, 2001*. Government Housing Reports, H150/01. Washington, DC: Government Printing Office.

———. 2002. *Statistical Abstract of the United States: 2002.*Washington, DC: Government Printing Office.

———. 2003. *Current Population Survey/Housing Vacancy Survey 2003.Washington*, DC: Government Printing Office.

———. *2003 March Current Population Survey: 1994 to 2003*. Washington, DC: Government Printing Office.

———. 2003. *Statistical Abstract of the United States* (123rd ed.). Washington, DC: U.S. Government Printing Office.

———. 2004–2005. *Statistical Abstract of the United States, 2004–2005*. Washington, DC: U.S. Government Printing Office.

———. 2005. "Child Custody Statistics 2004." *America's Families and Living Arrangements, 2004*. Current Population Survey, March 2005. Table FG-6. www.gocrc.com/research/custody-stats.html (2006, March 23).

———. 2006. "Facts for Features: Americans with Disabilities Act: July 26." (July 19): CB06-FF, 10–2. http://www.census.gov/ PressRelease/www/releases/archives/facts_for_. . . (2006, August 16).

———. 2006. *Statistical Abstract of the United States, 2006*. Washington, DC: Government Printing Office.

U.S. Conference of Mayors. 2000. *A Status Report on Hunger and Homelessness in America's Cities, 2000*. Washington, DC.

———. 2004. *A Status Report on Hunger and Homelessness in America's Cities*. Washington, DC.

U.S. Department of Agriculture. 2001. "USDA Estimates Child Rearing Costs." News Release (June 11). http://www.usda.gov/news/releases/ 2001/06/0097.htm (2001, December 17).

U.S. Department of Commerce. 1993. *Social and Economic Characteristics: United States*. Washington, DC: U.S. Government Printing Office.

U.S. Department of Education. 1997. *1994 Elementary and Secondary School Civil Rights Compliance Report*. Washington, DC.

———. 1998. *Digest of Education Statistics*. Washington, DC: National Center for Education Statistics.

U.S. Department of Health and Human Services, National Center on Child Abuse and Neglect. 1996. *Third National Incidence Study of Child Abuse and Neglect: Final Report* (NIS–3). Washington, DC: U.S. Government Printing Office.

———. 1998. *The National Elder Abuse Incidence Study* (September). Washington, DC.

———. 2001a. *Child Maltreatment 1999: Reports from the States to the National Child Abuse and Neglect Data System*. Washington, DC: U.S. Government Printing Office.

———. 2001b. "Closing the Health Gap: Reducing Health Disparities Affecting African Americans." http://www.aoa.dhhs.gov/pressroom/ Pr2001/healthgap-FS.html (2001, December 26).

———. 2001c. *Summary of Findings from the 2000 National Household Survey on Drug Use*. Washington, DC: U.S. Government Printing Office.

———. 2004. *Child Maltreatment, 2004*. Administration for Children and Families. www.acf.hhs. gov/programs/cb/pubs/cm04/chapterone.htm (2006, July 19).

———. 2005. *Overview of Findings from the 2004 National Survey on Drug Use and Health*. Washington, DC.

U.S. Department of Housing and Urban Development. 1991. *1989 Housing Discrimination Study*. Washington, DC: U.S. Government Printing Office.

U.S. Department of Justice. 1996a. Bureau of Justice Statistics. *Sourcebook of Criminal Justice Statistics, 1996*. Washington, DC.

———. 1996b. Bureau of Justice Statistics. *Statistics about Crime and Victims*. Bureau of Justice Crime and Victims Publication. BJS Home Page (April 22) [online].

———. 1997. Bureau of Justice Statistics. *Criminal Offenders Statistics*. http://www.ojp.usdoj.gov/bjs/crimoff/htm#summary (1999, May 29).

———. 1998. "Joint Justice Department/Education Department Study Shows Little Increase in School Crime between 1989 and 1995" (April 12). http://www.ojp.usdoj.gov/bjs/pub/press/srsc.pr (1999, June 15).

———. 1998. "Sex Offenses and Offenders." Bureau of Justice Statistics. http://www.ojp.usdoj.gov/bjs (2002, January 19).

———. 2000a. "People 65 Years Old and Older Are Less Likely to Be Victims of Violent Crime Than Younger U.S. Residents." Bureau of Justice Statistics. http://www.ojp.usdoj.gov/bjs/ (2002, January 7).

———. 2000b. "Sexual Assault of Young Children as Reported to Law Enforcement: Victim, Incident, and Offender Characteristics." Bureau of Justice Statistics. http://www.ojp.usdoj.gov/bjs/abstract/saycrle.htm (2002, January 7).

———. 2001a. "Victim Characteristics." Bureau of Justice Statistics. http://www.ojp.usdoj.gov/bjs/cvict_v.html (2002, January 7).

———. 2001b. "Criminal Victimization 2000: Changes 1999–2000 with Trends 1993–2000." Bureau of Justice Statistics. http://www.ojp. usdoj.gov/bjs/cvict_v.html (2002, January 18).

———. 2001c. "Criminal Victimization in United States, 1999 Statistical Tables." National Crime Victimization Survery. Washington, DC: Office of Justice Programs, Bureau of Justice Statistics.

———. 2004. "Criminal Victimization in the United States." Office of Justice Programs, Bureau of Justice Statistics. http://www.ojp.usdoj.gov/bjs/cvict.htm (2006, July 15).

———. 2006a. "Criminal Victimization: Summary Findings." Office of Justice Programs, Bureau of Justice Statistics. http://www.ojp.usdoj.gov/bjs/pubalp2.htm (2006, July 8).

———. 2006b. "About Domestic Violence." Office on Violence Against Women. http://www.ojp.usdoj.gov/vawo/ (2006, July 11).

U.S. Department of Labor. 2000. *balancing the Needs of Families and Employers: The Family and Medical Leave Surveys 2000 Update*. Washington, DC.

———. 2001. *Highlights of Women's Earnings in 2000*. Washington, DC: U.S. Government Printing Office.

———. 2002. "The Employment Situation: December 2001" (January 4). Washington, DC: Bureau of Labor Statistics. ftp://ftp.bls.gov/pub/ news.release/empsit.txt (2002, January 11).

———. 2005. "Usual Weekly Earnings of Wage and Salary Workers: Third Quarter 2005." www.bls.gov/news.release/ wkyeng.nr0.htm (2006, January 16).

U.S. Department of Veteran Affairs. 2006. "Child Sexual Abuse." http://www.ncptsd.va.gov/facts/specific/fs_child_sexual_abuse.html (2006, July 19).

U.S. Holocaust Memorial Museum. 2002. "Genocide of European Roma." http://www.ushmm.org/wle/article.jsp?ModuleId=10005219 (2002, March 21).

U.S. Newswire. 1999. "Gore Releases New Study Showing High Rate of Gun Violence among Teenagers" (June 14). http://www. usnewswire..._Releases/0614-136.html (1999, June 15).

Utech, M. R. 1994. *Violence, Abuse, and Neglect: The American Home*. Dix Hills, NY: General Hall.

Utz, R. L., E. B. Reidy, D. H. Carr, R. Nesse, and C. Wortman. 2004. "The Daily Consequences of Widowhood: The Role of Gender and Intergenerational Transfers on Subsequent Housework Performance." *Journal of Family Issues* 25, 5(July):683–712.

Vaillant, C. O., and G. E. Vaillant. 1993. "Is the V-Curve of Marital Satisfaction an Illusion? A 40-Year Study of Marriage." *Journal of Marriage and the Family* 55, 1:230–39.

Vallianatos, C. 2002. "Gay Parents' Rights Backed: Parents' Sexual Orientation "Appears to be Irrelevant." *NASW News*. Washington, DC: Natioan Association of Social Workers.

Van Dam, M. A. 2004. "Mothers in Two Types of Lesbian Families: Stigma Experiences, Supports, and Burdens." *Journal of Family Nursing* 10, 4:450–484.

Vandell, D. L., K. McCartney, M. T. Owen, C. Booth, and A. Clarke-Stewart. 2003. "Variations in Child Care by Grandparents During the First Three Years." *Journal of Marriage and Family* 65(May):375–381.

VanGoethem, J. 2005. *Living Together: A Guide to Counseling Unmarried Couples*. Kregel Publications.

Van Solinge, H., and K. Henkens. 2005. "Couples' Adjustment to Retirement: A Multi-Actor Panel Study." *The Journals of Gerontology Series B: Psychological Sciences and Social Sciences* 60:S11–S20.

Vandewater, E., and J. Lansford. 1998. "Influences of Family Structure and Parental Conflict on Children's Well-Being." *Family Relations* 47: 323–30.

Vazquez-Nuttall, E., I. Romero-Garcia, and B. DeLeon. 1987. "Sex Roles and Perceptions of Femininity and Masculinity of Hispanic Women: A Review of the Literature." *Psychology of Women Quarterly* 11:409–25.

Vedantam, S. 2001. "Child Aggressiveness Study Cites Day Care." *Washington Post* (April 19).

Vega, W. 1995. "The Study of Latino Families." In R. Zambrana, ed., *Understanding Latino Families*. Thousand Oaks, CA: Sage.

Veith, G. E. 1999. "Bible Belt Breakups." *World* (November 27). www.worldmag.com/world/issue/11-27-99/cultural_2.asp (2001, October 30).

Ventura, S., T. Matthews, and B. Hamilton. 2001. "Births to Teenagers in the United States, 1940–2000." *Centers for Disease Control and Prevention, National Vital Statistics Reports* (September 25):49, 10.

Verhovek, S. H. 1999. "Oregon Reporting 15 Deaths in Year under Suicide Law." *New York Times* (February 18):A1.

Violence against Women. 1992. *The National Women's Health Report*. The National Women's Health Resource Center (September/October) [online].

———. 1994. *A National Crime Victimization Survey Report*. U.S. Department of Justice, Washington, DC (January) [online].

"Violence Kills More U.S. Kids." 1997. *San Francisco Chronicle* (February 7):A1.

Visher, E. 1994. "Lessons from Remarried Families." *American Journal of Family Therapy* 22, 4:327–36.

———, and J. Visher. 1982. *How to Win as a Stepfamily*. New York: Dembner Books.

———. 1993. "Remarriage, Families, and Stepparenting." In F. Walsh, ed., *Normal Family Processes*, 2d ed., 235–53. New York: Guilford Press.

Visher, E. B. 2001. "Strengthening the Couple Relationship in Stepfamilies." Paper presented at the First Annual Ohio State University Extension Family Life Electronic In-Service: A Systemic Examination of Stepfamily Relationships. Columbus, OH, May 8–10.

Vitagliano, E. 2001. "Majority of Unwed Moms Are Not Teens." http://www.thruthcast.com/agape/010625unwedmoms.htm (2002, January 5).

Vital and Health Statistics from the Centers for Disease Control and Prevention. 1995. "Fertility, Family Planning, and Women's Health: New Data from the 1995 National Survey of Family Growth." Washington, DC: National Center for Health Statistics, Series 23, No. 19.

Vobejda, B. 1998. "Multiple Births in Dramatic Increase." *Seattle Times*. http://kyle.seattletimes.com/news/nation-world/html98/altbirt_070198.html (1999, May 6).

"Voice of Mom Report 2005". 2005. ClubMom. http://www.clubmom.com/display/202659 (2006, January 4).

"Voters Remove State Interracial Marriage Ban." 2000. *Birmingham News* (November 8):1.

Voydanoff, P. 1983. "Unemployment and Family Stress." In H. Z. Lopata and J. H. Pleck, eds., *Research in the Interweave of Social Roles: Families and Jobs*, 239–50. Greenwich, CT: JAI Press.

———. 1987. *Work and Family*. Beverly Hills, CA: Sage.

Vuchinich, S., E. M. Hetherington, R. Vuchinich, and W. G. Clingempeel. 1991. "Parent-Child Interaction and Gender Differences in Early Adolescents' Adaptation to Stepfamilies." *Developmental Psychology* 27, 4:618–26.

Wade, C., and S. Cirese. 1991. *Human Sexuality*, 2d ed. New York: Harcourt Brace Jovanovich.

Wagemaar, T., and R. Coates. 1999. "Race and Children: The Dynamics of Early Socialization." *Education* 120 (Winter):220–36.

Wagner, D. L. 1997. *Healthcare and Aging*. Washington, DC: National Council on the Aging.

Wainwright, J. L., S. T. Russell, and C. J. Patterson. Psychosocial Adjustment, School Outcomes, and Romantic Relationships of Adolescents with Same-Sex Parents." *Child Development* 75, 6 (December):186–1898.

Waite, L., and F. K. Goldscheider. 1992. "Work in the Home: The Productive Context of Family Relationships." In S. J. South and S. E. Tolnay, eds., *The Changing American Family*, 267–69. Boulder, CO: Westview Press.

Waite, L., and K. Joyner. 2001. "Emotional Satisfaction and Physical Pleasure in Sexual Unions: Time Horizon, Sexual Behavior, and Sexual Exclusivity." *Journal of Marriage and Family* 63(Feb):247–264.

Waite, L., and M. Gallagher. 2000. *The Case for Marriage: Why Married People are Happier, Healthier and Better Off Financially*. New York: Doubleday.

Waite, L. J., and K. Joyner. 1996. "Men's and Women's General Happiness and Sexual Satisfaction in Marriage, Cohabitation and Single Living." Unpublished manuscript. Chicago: Population Research Center, University of Chicago.

Wald, E. 1981. *The Remarried Family: Challenge and Promise*. New York: Family Service Association of America.

Walker, K. 1994. "Men, Women, and Friendship: What They Say, What They Do." *Gender and Society* 8:246–65.

———. 1995. "Always There for Me: Friendship Patterns and Expectations among Middle and Working Class Men and Women." *Sociological Forum* 10 (2):273–96.

———. 2001. "I'm Not Friends the Way She's Friends: Ideological and Behavioral Constructions of Masculinity in Men's Friendships." In M. Kimmel and M. Messner, *Men's Lives*, 5th ed., 367–79. Needham Heights, MA: Allyn & Bacon.

———. F. Dickson, and P. Hughes. 2005. " An Exploratory Investigation into Dating Among Later-Life Women." (January 1). *Western Journal of Communication*.

Walker, K. E., and M. Woods. 1976. *Time Use: A Measure of Household Production of Goods and Services*. Washington, DC: American Home Economics Association.

Walker, L. 1978. "Treatment Alternatives for Battered Women." In J. R. Chapman and M. Gates, eds., *The Victimization of Women*, 143–74. Beverly Hills, CA: Sage.

———. 1984. *The Battered Woman Syndrome*. New York: Springer.

Wallace, C. P. 1992. "For Sale: The Poor's Body Parts." *Los Angeles Times* (April 27):A1.

Wallace, H. 1996. *Family Violence: Legal, Medical, and Social Perspectives*. Needham Heights, MA: Allyn & Bacon.

———, 2002. *Family Violence: Legal, Medical, and Social Perspective*, 3d ed. Boston: Allyn & Bacon.

———. 2004. *Family Violence: Legal, Medical, and Social Perspectives*, 4th ed. Boston: Allyn Bacon.

Wallace, R. A., and A. Wolf. 1991. *Contemporary Sociological Theory*. Englewood Cliffs, NJ: Prentice Hall.

Waller, W. 1937. "The Rating and Dating Complex." *American Sociological Review* 2:727–35.

———, and R. Hill. 1951. *The Family: A Dynamic Interpretation*. New York: Dryden Press.

Wallerstein, J. S. 1986. "Women after Divorce: Preliminary Report from a Ten-Year Follow-Up." *American Journal of Orthopsychiatry* 56:65–77.

———. 1992. *Second Chances: Men, Women, and Children a Decade after Divorce*, 3d ed. Boston: Houghton Mifflin.

———. 1995. *The Good Marriage: How and Why Love Lasts*. Boston: Houghton Mifflin.

———. 1996. *Second Chances: Men, Women, and Children a Decade After Divorce*, 4th ed. Boston: Houghton Mifflin.

———, and J. Kelly. 1980. *Surviving the Break-up. How Children Actually Cope with Divorce*. New York: Basic Books.

———, J. M. Lewis, and S. Blakeslee. 2000. *The Unexpected Legacy of Divorce: A 25 Year Landmark Study*. New York: Hyperion.

———, and S. Blakeslee. 1989. *Second Chances: Men, Women, and Children a Decade after Divorce*. New York: Ticknor and Fields.

Walsh, A. 1991. *The Science of Love: Understanding Love and Its Effects on Mind and Body*. Buffalo, NY: Prometheus Books.

Walsh, F. 1980. "The Family in Later Life." In E. A. Carter and M. McGoldrick, eds., *The Family Life Cycle: A Framework for Family Therapy*. New York: Gardner Press.

Walster, E., W. Walster, and J. Traupmann. 1978. "Equity and Premarital Sex." *Journal of Personality and Social Psychology* 36:82–92.

Ward, M. C. 1999. *A World Full of Women*, 2d ed. Boston: Allyn & Bacon.

Warda, J. 2000. "Stepping Up to Protect a Son's Feelings." *Chicago Tribune* (July 30):sec. 13, 2.

Washington Post-ABC News Poll. 2003. "Washington Post-ABC News Poll: The Pope and the Catholic Church." (October 15). http://www.washingtonpost.com (2005, September 30).

Waters, L. E., and K. A. Moore. 2002. "Predicting Self-Esteem During Unemployment: The Effect of Gender, Financial Deprivation, Alternate Roles, and Social Support." *Journal of Employment Counseling* 39, 4(December):171–189.

Warmack, L. F. 2004. "Women in Taiwan Find Marriage is No Fairy Tale." *The Mercury News* (February 22). www.internationa-divorce.com/d-taiwan.htm (2006, March 20).

Watkins, B., and A. Bentovim. 1992. "Male Children and Adolescents as Victims: A Review of Current Knowledge." In . G. Mezey and M. King, eds., *Male Victims of Sexual Assault*, 27–66. Oxford: Oxford University Press.

Watson, R., and P. DeMeo. 1987. "Premarital Cohabitation vs. Traditional Courtship: Their Effects on Subsequent Marital Adjustment: A Replication and Follow Up." *Family Relations* 36:193–97.

Watts, J. 1977. "The End of Work and the End of Welfare." *Contemporary Sociology* 26 (July):409–12.

Wayne, J. H., and B. L. Cordeiro. 2003. "Who is a Good Organizational Citizen? Social Perception of Male and Female Employees Who Use Family Leave." *Vocational Behavior* 49, 5/6:233–247.

Weaver, S. W., and M. Coleman. 2005. "A Mothering But Not a Mother Role: A Grounded Theory Study of the Nonresidential Stepmother Role." *Journal of Social and Personal Relationships* 22, 4:477–497.

Webber, R., U. Ritterfeld, and K. Mathiak. 2006. "Does Playing Violent Video Games Induce Aggression? Empirical Evidence of a Functional Magnetic Resonance Imaging Study." *Media Psychology* 8, 1:39–60.

Weerth, C., and A. Kalma. 1995. "Gender Differences in Awareness of Courtship Initiation Tactics." *Sex Roles* (June):32, 717–34.

Wei, T. 2005. "Another Chance at Love." (May 12). http:// www.bjreview.com.cn?En-2005/05–12-e/12-china-3.htm (2006, April 9).

"Wedding Traditions Date Back for Centuries." 1988. *Chicago Sun-Times* (January 17):special advertising sec., 2.

Weibel-Orlando, J. 1990. "Grandparenting Styles: Native American Perspectives." In J. Sokolovsky, ed., *The Cultural Context of Aging*, 109–25. New York: Bergin and Garvey.

———. 2000. "Grandparenting Styles: Native American Perspectives." In E. P. Stoller and R. C. Gibson, eds., *Worlds of Difference*, 249–251. Thousand Oaks, CA: Pine Forge Press.

Weiser, C. 1996. "Legal Gay Marriage on Hawaii's Horizon." *USA Today* (January 2):6A.

Weihua, C. 2006. "Divorce Rate Surges Across China." *China Daily* (February 15). http://www.chinadaily.com.cn/english/doc/2006–02/15/content_520204.htm (2006, February 15).

Weisman, J., and VandeHei, J. 2006. "Immigration Debate is Shaped by '08 Election." *Washington Post* (March 24):A01.

Weiss, R. 2003. "Bush Misuses Science, Report Says." *Washington Post* (August 8):A15.

Weissbourd, R. 1994. "Divided Families, Whole Children." *The American Prospect* 18 (Summer):66–72.

Weitzman, L. 1977. "To Love, Honor, and Obey: Traditional Legal Marriage and Alternative Family Forms." In A. S. Skolnick and J. H. Skolnick, eds., *Family in Transition*, 2d ed., 288–313. Boston: Little, Brown.

———. 1985. *The Divorce Revolution: The Unexpected Social and Economic Consequences for Women and Children in America*. New York: Free Press.

Weitzman, N., B. Birns, and R. Friend. 1985. "Traditional and Nontraditional Mothers' Communication with Their Daughters and Sons." *Child Development* 56:894–96.

Weitzman, S. 2001. *"Not People Like Us": Hidden Abuse in Upscale Marriages*. New York: Basic Books.

Wellesley Centers for Women. 1998. "The Wife Rape Information Page." http://www.wellesley.edu/wcw/projects/mrape.html (2006, July 17).

Wellman, B. 1992. "Men in Networks: Private Communities, Domestic Friendships." In P. Nardi, ed., *Men's Friendships*, 74–114. Newbury Park, CA: Sage.

Wellner, A. S. 2005. (June). "U.S. Attitudes Toward Interracial Dating Are Liberalizing." Washington, DC: *Population Reference Bureau*. www.prb.org.

Wells, R. 1978. "Family History and Demographic Transition." In M. Gordon, ed., *The American Family in Social-Historical Perspective*, 516–32. New York: St. Martin's Press.

Welter, B. 1978. "The Cult of True Womanhood: 1820–1860." In M. Gordon, ed., *The American Family in Social-Historical Perspective*, 313–33. New York: St. Martin's Press.

Werking, K. J. 1994. "Hidden Assumptions: A Critique of Cross-Sex Friendship." *Research Issues* 2:8–11.

Werland, R. 1999. "A Kinder, Gentler Divorce." *Chicago Tribune* (September 26):sec. 13, 1, 5.

Werner, E. E. 1989. "Children of the Garden Island." *Scientific American* 260, 4:106–11.

Westoff, C. F., and N. Goldman. 1988. "Figuring the Odds in the Marriage Market." In J. G. Wells, ed., *Current Issues in Marriage and the Family*, 39–46. New York: Macmillan.

Weston, K. 1991. *Families We Choose: Lesbians, Gays, Kinship*. New York: Columbia University Press.

Westside Pregnancy Resource Center. 2006. "Teen Sex and Pregnancy: Facts and Figures." http://www.wprc.org/9.28.0.0.1.0.phtml (2006, April 3).

"Where Rape Is a Proposal of Marriage." 1999 (June 18). http://www.sn.apc.org/wmail/issues/990618/NEWS47.HTML (2002, January 21).

Whisman, M. A., and N. S. Jacobson. 1988. "Depression, Marital Satisfaction, and Marital and Personality Measures of Sex Roles." *Journal of Marital and Family Therapy* 15:177-86.

White, G. L. 1980a. "Including Jealousy: A Power Perspective." *Personality and Social Psychology Bulletin* 6:222-27.

———. 1980b. "Physical Attractiveness and Courtship Progress." *Journal of Personality and Social Psychology* 39:660–68.

White, J. 1987. "Premarital Cohabitation and Marital Stability in Canada." *Journal of Marriage and the Family* 49:641–47.

White, L. K. 1981. "A Note on Racial Differences in the Effect of Female Opportunity on Marriage Rates." *Demography* 18:349–54.

———. 1990. "Determinants of Divorce: A Review of Research in the Eighties." *Journal of Marriage and the Family* 52:904–12.

———. 1991. "Determinants of Divorce." In A. Booth, ed., *Contemporary Families: Looking Forward, Looking Back*, 150–61. Minneapolis: National Council on Family Relations.

———. 1994. "Growing Up with Single Parents and Stepparents: Long-Term Effects on Family Solidarity." *Journal of Marriage and the Family* 56 (November):935–48.

———, and A. Riedman. 1992. "When the Brady Bunch Grows Up: Step-/ Half- and Full-Sibling Relationships in Adulthood." *Journal of Marriage and the Family* 54:197–208.

———. 2001. "Sibling Relationships Over the Life Course: A Panel Analysis. *Journal of Marriage and the Family* 63: 555–568.

———, and A. Riedmann. 1992. "Ties Among Adult Siblings." *Social Forces* 71:85–102.

White, N. 1995. "Batterers Seldom Stop after the First Time." *New Standard*, pp. 1–7 [online].

Whiteford, L. M., and L. Gonzalez. 1995. "Stigma: The Hidden Burden of Infertility." *Social Science and Medicine* 40 (January):27–36.

Whitehead, B. 1993. "Dan Quayle Was Right." *Atlantic Monthly* 271 (April):47–84.

Whitehead, B., and D. Popenoe. 2004. "The State of Our Unions: The Social Health of Marriage in America." *The National Marriage Project Report*. Piscataway, NJ: Rutgers, The State University of New Jersey (June). http://marriage.rutgers.edu/Publications/SOOU/TEXTSOOU2004.htm (2006, April 14).

Whitehead, B. D. 1997. *The Divorce Culture*. New York: Knopf.

Whitehouse, B. 2000. "Alcohol and the Family." *Parenting* 14, 5 (June/July):154–62.

Whiting, B., and C. P. Edwards. 1988. *Children of Different Worlds: The Formation of Social Behavior*. Cambridge, MA: Harvard University Press.

Whiting, J. B., and R. E. Lee III. 2003. "Voices from the System: A Qualitative Study of Foster Children's Stories." *Family Relations* 52(July):288–295.

Whitsett, D., and H. Land. 1992. "The Development of a Role Strain Index for Stepparents." *Families in Society: The Journal of Contemporary Human Services* 73, 1:14–22.

Whyte, M. K. 1990. *Dating, Mating, and Marriage.* New York: Aldine de Gruyter.

———. 2001. "Choosing Mates—The American Way." In S. Ferguson, ed., *Shifting the Center: Understanding Contemporary Families,* 2d ed., 129–39. Mountain View, CA: Mayfield.

Widom, C. S. 1992. *The Cycle of Violence, Research in Brief.* Washington, DC: U.S. Department of Justice, National Institute of Justice (September), NCJ 136607.

———, and S. Hiller-Sturmhofel. 2001. "Alcohol Abuse as a Risk Factor for and Consequence of Child Abuse." *Alcohol Research and Health* 25, 1:52–57.

Wieche, V. R. 1990. *Sibling Abuse: Hidden Physical, Emotional, and Sexual Trauma.* Lexington, MA: Lexington Books.

Wiese, D., and D. Daro. 1995. *Current Trends in Child Abuse Reporting and Fatalities: The Results of the 1994 Annual Fifty States Survey.* Chicago: National Committee to Prevent Child Abuse.

Wiggins, G. 1994. "Children's TV Needs Fine-Tuning Says APA." *APA Monitor* (September):6.

Wikipedia. 2005. "Polyandry." http://www.en.wikipedia.org/wiki/Polyandry (2005, July 21).

———. 2006. "List of Countries by Suicide Rates." http://en.wikipedia.org/wiki/List_of_Countries_by_Suicide_rate (2006, August 10).

Wilcox, B., and S. Nock. 2006. "What's Love Got to do With It?: Equality, Equity, Commitment, and Women's Marital Quality." *Social Forces* 84, 3(March):1321–1345.

"Wilhelmsen Lab Elucidates the Genes that Underlie Hereditary Aspects of Alcoholism." 2006. *Center Line,* Bowles Center for Alcohol Studies 17, 3(March):1–2.

Wilgoren, J. 2005. "Rape Charge Follows Marriage to a 14-Year-Old." *New York Times.* (August 30):A1, A16.

Wilkinson, T. 1994. "Gangs Find Fresh Turf in Salvador." *Los Angeles Times* (June 16):A1.

Williams, C. 1992. "The Glass Escalator: Hidden Advantages for Men in the 'Female' Professions." *Social Problems* 39, 3 (August):253–67.

Williams, G. 1998. "Toxic Dads." *Parental Magazine.* Online Collection: parenting.com. (October).

Williams, J. 1993. "Sexuality in Marriage." In B. Wolman and J. Money, eds., *Handbook of Human Sexuality,* 93–122. Northvale, NJ: Jason Aronson.

Williams, J. E., and D. L. Best. 1990. *Measuring Sex Stereotypes: A Multinational Study,* rev. ed. Newbury Park, CA: Sage.

Williamson, M. 1994. *Thoughts, Prayer, Rites of Passage.* New York: Random House.

Willie, C. V. 1981. *A New Look at the Black Family.* Bayside, NY: General Hall.

Wilsnak, S., N. Vogeltanz, A. Klassen, and T. Harris. 1997. "Childhood Sexual Abuse and Women's Substance Abuse: National Survey Findings." *Journal of Studies on Alcohol* 58:264–72.

Wilson, E., and S. H. Ng. 1988. "Sex Bias in Visual Images Evoked by Generics: A New Zealand Study." *Sex Roles* 18:159–68.

Wilson, E. D. 1975. *Sociology: The New Synthesis.* Cambridge, MA: Harvard University Press.

Wilson, K. 2005. "Women in RP Face Uphill Fight for Right to Divorce." *The Manila Times* (March 19). http://www.manilatimes.net/national/2005/mar/19/yehey/top_stories/20050319top9.html (2006, March 20).

Wilson, J. Q. 2002. *The Marriage Problem: How Our Culture Has Weakened Families.* New York: HarperCollins.

Wilson, W. J. 1980. *The Declining Significance of Race.* Chicago: University of Chicago Press.

———. 1987. *The Truly Disadvantaged: The Inner City, the Underclass, and Public Policy.* Chicago: University of Chicago Press.

Wilton, V., and J. A. Davey. 2006. *Grandfathers-Their Changing Family Roles and Contributions.* Wellington, New Zealand: New Zealand Institute for Research on Aging.

Winch, R. R., T. Ktsanes, and V. Ktsanes. 1954. "The Theory of Complementary Needs in Mate Selection: An Analytic and Descriptive Study." *American Sociological Review* 19:241–49.

Wineberg, H. 1988. "Duration between Marriage and First Birth and Marital Stability." *Social Biology* 35:91–102.

———. 1990. "Childbearing in Remarriage." *Journal of Marriage and the Family* 52:31–38.

———. 1994. "Marital Reconciliation in the United States: Which Couples Are Successful?" *Journal of Marriage and the Family* 56 (February):80–88.

———. 1996. "The Prevalence and Characteristics of Blacks Having a Successful Marital Reconciliation." *Journal of Divorce and Remarriage* 25, 1/2:75–86.

———, and J. McCarthy. 1993. "Separation and Reconciliation in American Marriages." *Journal of Divorce and Remarriage* 20:21–42.

Wiscott, R., and K. Kopera-Frye. 2000. "Sharing of Culture: Adult Grandchildren's Perceptions of Intergenerational Relations." *International Journal of Aging and Human Development* 51, 3:199–215.

Wisdom, S., and J. Green. 2002. *Stepcoupling: Creating and Sustaining a Strong Marriage in Today's Blended Family.* Three Rivers, MI: Three Rivers Press.

Wiseman, P. 2004. "No Sex Please—We're Japanese." *USA Today* (June 2). http://www.usatoday.com/news/world/2004–06-02-japan-women-usat_x.htm (2006, April 3).

Wolcott, J. 2004. "Is Dating Dated on College Campuses?" *Christian Science Monitor* (March 2, 2004). http://www.csmonitor.com/2004/0302/p11s01-legn.html (2006, January 18).

Wolfe, A. 1998. *One Nation, After All.* New York: Viking.

Wolfensohn, J. 2002. "Poor, Disabled and Shut Out." *Washington Post* (December 3):A, 25.

Wolfinger, N. H. 2000. " Beyond the Intergenerational Transmission of Divorce: Do People Replicate the Pattern of Marital Instability They Grew Up With?" *Journal of Family Issues* 21:1061–1086.

Wolfinger, N. H. 2001. "The Effects of Family Structure of Origin on Offspring Cohabitation Duration." *Sociological Inquiry* 71:293–313.

———. 2003. "Parental Divorce and Offspring Marriage: Early or Late?" *Social Forces* 82, 1(September):337–353.

———. 2005. *Understanding the Divorce Cycle.* New York: Cambridge.

Wolfson, E. 1996. "Why We Should Fight for the Freedom to Marry: The Challenges and Opportunities That Will Follow a Win in Hawaii." *Journal of Gay, Lesbian, and Bisexual Identity* 1 (1):79–89.

W.O.M.A.N., Inc. 1996. "Myths and Facts about Violence." http://www.norcov.com/womaninc/myths.html (1999, June 4).

Women against Abuse. 1996. "Statistics on Domestic Violence." Philadelphia: Women against Abuse.

Wong, M. G. 1988. "The Chinese American Family." In C. Mindel, R. W. Habenstein, and R. Wright, Jr., eds., *Ethnic Families in America: Patterns and Variations,* 230–57. New York: Elsevier.

"Women and the Board—Times Are Not a Changing." 2006. *EXPATICA* (January 16). www.expatica.com/source/site_article.asp?subchannel_id=75 story_id=8945 nam (2006, January 16).

Women's Health Care House. 2002. "Fact Sheet: Domestic Violence." http://www.members.iinet.net.au/~wwwhch/womanhealth/dvl.html (2002, January 8).

Women's Sports Foundation. 1998. *Women's Sports Facts.* East Meadow, NY: Women's Sports Foundation.

———. 2004. "Athlete's Earnings Gap Index." www.womenssports foundation.org/cgibin/iowa/issues/business/article.html?record=866) (2005, August 22).

Wong, M. G. 1998. "The Chinese-American Family." In C. H. Mindel, R. W. Habenstein, and R. Wright, Jr. *Ethnic Families in America: Patterns and Variations,* 284–310. Upper Saddle River, NJ: Prentice Hall.

Wood, J. T. 1994. *Gendered Lives: Communication, Gender, and Culture.* Belmont, CA: Wadsworth.

———, ed. 1996. *Gendered Relationships.* Mountain View, CA: Mayfield.

———. 2004. *Gendered Livers: Communication, Gender, and Culture.* Belmont, CA: Wadsworth.

Woodard, A. 1998. "Father-Child Relationships." *Gale Encyclopedia of Childhood and Adolescence.* Detroit: Gale.

Woodman, S. 1995. "How Teen Pregnancy Has Become a Political Football." *Ms.* (January/February):90–91.

Woods, R. D. 1996. "Grandmother Roles: A Cross Cultural View." *Journal of Instructional Psychology* 23 (December):286–92.

Worden, J. W. 1982. *Grief Counseling and Grief Therapy: A Handbook for the Mental Health Practitioner.* New York: Springer.

"Working Women Say . . . 2000. AFL-CIO. http://www.aflcio.org/women/survey1.htm (2001, October 17).

World Almanac Book of Facts, 1991. 1990. New York: Pharos Books.

World Almanac. 2000. *World Almanac and Book of Facts* 2000, Millennium Edition. New York: St. Martin's Press.

World Bank. 2001. *World Development Indicators, 2001.* Washington, DC.

———. 2006a. "GNI Per Capita, 2005, Atlas Method and PPP." World Development Indicators Database (July 1). http://siteresources.worldbank.org/DATASTATISTICS/Resources/GNIPC.pdf (2006, August 1).

———. 2006b."Disability and Development." http://web.worldbank.org/WBSITE/EXTERNAL/TOPICS/EXTSOCIALPROTEC-TION/. . . (2006, August 16).

World Health Organization. 1997. "Substance Use among Street Children and Other Children and Youth in Especially Difficult Circumstances" (March):Fact Sheet N151. http://www.who.org/inf-fs/en/fact151.html.

———. 1998. "Fifty Facts from the World Health Report 1998." http://www.who.int/whr/1998/factse.htm.

———. 2000a. *Global Water Supply and Sanitation Assessment 2000 Report.* Geneva, Switzerland. http://www.who.int/water_sanitation_health/Globassesment/Global2.1.htm (2002, January 22).

———. 2000b. "Substance Dependence." http://www.who.int/substance_abuse/More.html (2002, January 22).

———. 2002. "Special Report: Health in Afghanistan Situation Analysis" (January 21). http://www.who.int/disasters/emergency.cfm?emergencyID=2&doctypeID=2 (2002, January 22).

———. 2004a. *Global Status Report on Alcohol 2004.* Geneva, Switzerland.

———. 2004b. *Evaluation of the Costs and Benefits of Water and Sanitation Improvements at the Global Level.* Geneva, Switzerland.

———. 2006. *The World Health Report 2006: Working Together for Health.* Geneva, Switzerland.

World Health Report. 1998. "Executive Summary: Life in the 21st Century—A Vision for All" (March 5). http://www.who.int/whr/1998/exsum98e.html.

World Malaria Report 2005. Geneva, Switzerland: Roll Back Malaria, World Health Organization and UNICEF.

Worldwatch Institute. 2004. *State of the World 2004: Special Focus: The Consumer Society.* Washington, DC.

Worling, J. R. 1995. "Adolescent Sibling-Incest Offenders: Differences in Family and Individual Functioning When Compared to Adolescent Nonsibling Sex Offenders." *Child Abuse & Neglect* 19:633–643.

Worthington, R. 1994. "Adding Father to Family: Paternity Law Takes Aim at Poor." *Chicago Tribune* (February 14):1, 8.

Wright, J. D. 1989. *Address Unknown: The Homeless in America.* New York: Aldine de Gruyter.

Wright, J. M. 1998. *Lesbian Step Families: An Ethnography of Love.* New York: Haworth Press.

Wu, Z. 1994. "Remarriage in Canada: Exchange Perspective." *Journal of Divorce and Remarriage* 21, 3/4:191–224.

———. 1995. "The Stability of Cohabitation Relationships: The Role of Children." *Journal of Marriage and the Family* 57 (February):231–36.

———. 2000. *Cohabitation: An Alternative Form of Family Living.* Toronto: Oxford University Press.

———. and R. Hart. 2002. "The Mental Health of the Childless Elderly." *Sociological Inquiry* 72, 1:21–42.

———, and M. J. Penning. 1997. "Marital Instability after Midlife." *Journal of Family Issues* 18 (September):459–78.

WuDunn, S. 1996. "In Single Motherhood, Japan Trails the World." *New York Times* (March 13):sec. A.

———. 1997. "Korean Women Still Feel Demands to Bear a Son." *New York Times* (January 14):3.

Wurtele, S., A. Melzer, and L. Kast. 1992. "Preschoolers Knowledge of and Ability to Learn Genital Terminology." *Journal of Sex Education and Therapy* 18, 2:115–22.

Xu, X., C. Hudspeth, and S. Estes. 1997. "The Effects of H.usbands' Involvement in Child Rearing Activities and Participation in Household Labor on Marital Quality: A Racial Comparison." *Journal of Gender, Culture, and Health* 2 (3):171–93.

Yalom, M., and L. Carstensen, eds. 2002. *Inside the American Couple: New Thinking, New Challenges.* Berkeley, CA: University of California Press.

Yardley, J. 1999a. "Investigators Say Embryologist Knew He Erred in Egg Mix-Up." *New York Times* (April 17):A13.

———. 1999b. "After Embryo Mix-Up, Couple Say They Will Give Up One Baby." *New York Times* (March 30).

Yates, R. E. 1990. "Japan's Violent Young Rebels Fight Back." *San Diego Union* (April 8).

Yednak, C. 2001. "Wilmette Principal Has Gender Changed." *Chicago Tribune* (August 22):5.

Yellowbird, M., and C. M. Snipp. 1994. "American Indian Families." In R. L. Taylor, ed., *Minority Families in the United States: A Multicultural Perspective,* 179–201. Upper Saddle River, NJ: Prentice Hall.

Yllo, K. "Wife Rape: A Social Problem for the 21st Century." *Violence Against Women* 5, 9. (September).

Young, M. 1998. *Guinness Book of World Records 1998.*

Yuen, M. 1998a. "Same-Sex Marriage Strongly Rejected" (November 4). http://starbulletin.co...11/04/news/story3.html.

———. 1998b. "Same-Sex Marriage Debate Rages On, Now over Domestic Partnership Bill" (November 6). http://starbulletin.co...11/06/news/story9.html.

Zablocki, B. 1980. *Alienation and Charisma: A Study of Contemporary Communes.* New York: Free Press.

Zach, T., and Parmanik, A. 2006. "Multiple Births." *eMedicine.com.* http://www.emedicine.com/PED/topic2599.htm (2006, May 12).

Zambrano, M. 1995. "Social and Cultural Reasons for Abuse." In A. Kesselman, L. McNair, and N. Schniedewind, eds., *Women: Images and Realities,* 316–18. Mountain View, CA: Mayfield.

Zavella, P. 1987. *Women's Work and Chicano Families: Cannery Workers of the Santa Clara Valley.* Ithaca, NY: Cornell University Press.

Zebroski, S. 1997. "Findings for Research on Interracial Marriages." *Interrace:* SoftLine Information, Inc. http://www.sistahspace.com/nommo/ir13.html (2001, November 14).

Zedeck, S., and K. Mosier. 1990. "Work in the Family and Employing Organizations." *American Psychologist* 45, 2:240–51.

Zernike, K. 1998. "Feminism Has Created Progress, but Man, oh, Man, Look What Else." *Chicago Tribune* (June 21):1, 8.

Zimmerman, J., and G. Reavill. 1998. *Raising Our Athletic Daughters: How Sports Can Build Self-Esteem and Save Girls' Lives.* New York: Doubleday.

Zogby National Poll. 2000. *Zogby International* (February). http://www.zogby.com (2002, February 3).

Zuckerman, D. M., and D. H. Sayre. 1982. "Cultural Sex-Role Expectations and Children's Sex-Role Concepts." *Sex Roles* 8:853–62.

Zuckerman, M. B. 1993. "The Victims of Violence." *U.S. News & World Report* (August 2):64.

Zuger, A. 1998. "Girls and Women Are as Aggressive as Males, Studies Show." *Chicago Tribune* (December 27):sec. 13, 2.

Zuravin, S., and F. DiBlasio. 1996. "The Correlates of Child Physical Abuse and Neglect by Adolescent Mothers." *Journal of Family Violence,* 11 (June):149–66.

Photo Credits

CHAPTER 1: Getty Images, Inc. - Taxi, 1; Corbis/Stock Market, 6; Getty Images, Inc., 8; Joan Zientek, 10; Rick Friedman / CORBIS- NY, 13; AP Wide World Photos, 20; Omni-Photo Communications, Inc. , 21; Corbis/Bettmann, 24; AP Wide World Photos, 26

CHAPTER 2: Pearson Education/PH College, 33; Getty Images, Inc., 38; SuperStock, Inc., 46; Wamucii Njogu, 48; The Granger Collection, New York, 51 (top left and center); (c) Bettmann/CORBIS, 51 (top right); The Granger Collection, New York, 51 (middle left); Culver Pictures, Inc., 51 (middle center); The Granger Collection, New York, 51 (middle right); Patricia Hill Collins, McMicken College of Arts and Sciences, 51 (bottom left); American Sociological Association, 51 (bottom center); Courtesy of Prof. Chela Sandoval , 51 (bottom right); AP Wide World Photos, 58.

CHAPTER 3: (c) Stephanie Sinclair / CORBIS All Rights Reserved, 66; Boston Public Library/Rare Books Department. Courtesy of the Trustees., 69 (left and right); David Burgess / Blink Portraits, 71 (Left and Right); Pearson Education/PH College, 75; (c) (Paul Mounce) / CORBIS All Rights Reserved., 79; Newscom, 83; Corbis/SABA Press Photos, Inc., 85; PhotoEdit Inc., 86; Getty Images, Inc. - Taxi, 87;

CHAPTER 4: Pearson Education/PH College, 91; Photo Researchers, Inc., 101; Anthony Neste, 103; Time & Life Pictures / Getty Images, 108; Photofest, 113; (c) 2005 Kathy Hutchins / Hutchins Photo / NewsCom, 114;

CHAPTER 5: Stock Boston, 128; Photo Researchers, Inc., 132; Douglas Mason/Woodfin Camp & Associates, 134 (top left); Photo Researchers, Inc., 134 (top right and bottom left); Getty Images/Digital Vision, 136; PhotoEdit Inc., 153; Brian Smith, Photographer, 156; The Image Works, 160;

CHAPTER 6: Pearson Education/PH College, 166; Corbis/Bettmann, 171; PhotoEdit Inc., 174; Getty Images, Inc. - Taxi, 182; Slick.com, 184; Corbis/Bettmann, 189; Joel Gordon Photography, 198; PhotoEdit Inc., 200; Photo Researchers, Inc., 203, Getty Images, Inc., 210; eStock Photography LLC, 211

CHAPTER 7: Corbis/Bettmann, 218; Getty Images, Inc., 222; Bachman/Lonely Planet Images/ Photo 20-20, 225; Vicki Byard, 226; Frank Siteman, 231; Splash News and Pictures / NewsCom, 233; [Luke Frazza]/Agence France Presse/Getty Images, 235; ASAP/Sarit Uzieli / Photo Researchers, Inc., 237; ASAP/Sarit Uzieli/Photo Researchers, Inc., 222.

CHAPTER 8: The Terry Wild Studio, Inc., 258; Universal Pictures / Photofest, 260; Getty Images, Inc., 262 (top); African American Root, Inc., 262 (bottom); Dr. Christopher Schroeder, 271; Corbis/Bettmann, 275; © Knight Ridder/Tribune Media Information Services. All Rights Reserved. Reprinted by permission, 276; PhotoEdit Inc., 279; J. B. Forbes/ST. LOUIS POST-DISPATCH, 280.

CHAPTER 9: Merrill Education, 285; The Image Works, 290; Universal Press Syndicate, 291; AP Wide World Photos, 293; AP Wide World Photos, 294; Dave Cruz/INFGoff.com Ref, 301; Ina May Gaskin, The Safe Motherhood Quilt Project, 304; Joel Gordon Photography/Design Conceptios, 307; Getty Images, Inc., 309; Steinberg/Svitojus/INFGoff.com, 322; PhotoEdit Inc., 325.

CHAPTER 10: Getty Images, Inc. - PhotoDisc, 329; Getty Images, Inc., 331;PhotoEdit Inc., 335; Craig Parkinson, 340; PhotoEdit Inc., 343 (left and right); (c) Jennifer Berman, 347; Robert Harbison, 350; Getty Images, Inc. , 351; Getty Images, Inc. , 354;

CHAPTER 11: NewsCom, 364; REUTERS/Brett Coomer/Houston Chronicle/NewsCom, 366; CBS/Landov LLC, 370; Family Violence Prevention Fund/Ad Council. (c) date 1994., 376; (c) Lynsey Addario / CORBIS All Rights Reserved, 382; © Lynsey Addario / CORBIS All Rights Reserved, 385; Getty Images, Inc., 386; Getty Images, Inc., 387; NewsCom, 388; National Association of State Units on Aging, 390; Armando Arorizo/ZUMA Press/NewsCom, 391; National Association of State Units on Aging, 393.

CHAPTER 12: Getty Images, Inc., 401; Getty Images, Inc. - Taxi, 404; Stock Boston, 406; Getty Images, Inc. - PhotoDisc, 411; Photofest, 415; Getty Images, Inc.- Photodisc., 420, PhotoEdit Inc., 422, Stock Boston, 426,

CHAPTER 13: Kayte Deioma / Photo Edit, 431; AP Wide World Photos, 434; Private Collection/The Bridgeman Art Library, 436; Getty Images, Inc. - PhotoDisc, 440; Photo Researchers, Inc., 442; WENN/NewsCom, 443 (top); Chapel Bride, 443 (bottom); Lori Waselchuk/The New York Times, 445; The Image Works, 447; Mimi Forsyth, 450; WireImage.com, 452.

CHAPTER 14: Reuters Limited, 461; Lawrence Migdale/Pix, 466; Joseph Nettis/Photo Researchers, Inc., 467; Mr. And Mrs. Harry Gottlieb, 469; Ken Huang/Getty Images, Inc., 471; © Rick Friedman Photography, 474; Jacques M. Chenet-NWK/Getty Images, Inc - Liaison, 475; Yoav Levy/Phototake NYC, 476;Janice Fullman/Index Stock Imagery, Inc., 44; EyeWire Collection/Getty Images - Photodisc, 483.

CHAPTER 15: © Richard T. Nowitz / CORBIS All Rights Reserved, 487; (a) Andrew Holbrooke / CORBIS All Rights Reserved, 491 (right); (b) Enrique Marcarian/Corbis/Reuters America LLC, 491 (left); Peter Arnold, Inc., 495; Creative Eye/MIRA.com, 499; Sergey Ponomarev/AP Wide World Photos, 501 (left); The Saginaw News, Melanie/AP Wide World Photos, 501 (right); AP Wide World Photos, 504; Monica Almeida/The New York Times, 510; AP/Wide World Photos, 514; Karel Prinsloo/AP Wide World Photos, 516; Reid Willis, 523; AP Wide World Photos, 524.

APPENDIXES: Materials courtesy Planned Parenthood, NYC/Teri Stratford/S&S PH College, 538 (top); The Female Health Company, 538 (bottom).

Name Index

Subject Index